AFTER THE RAPTURE

AFTER THE RAPTURE

By Jerry L. Dart

Y'SHUA PUBLISHING
Greeley, Colorado

PUBLISHED BY Y'SHUA PUBLISHING
P.O. Box 337551
Greeley, Colorado 80633

AFTER THE RAPTURE

Copyright © 2003 by Y'shua Enterprises. All rights reserved. Printed in the United States of America. No part of this book may be used or reproduced in any form without permission in writing from the publisher except in the case of brief quotations in critical articles and reviews.

Scripture quotations in this publication are from:

Scripture taken from the HOLY BIBLE: NEW INTERNATIONAL VERSION ®. NIV ®. Copyright © 1973, 1978, 1984 by International Bible Society. Used by permission of Zondervan. The "NIV" and "New International Version" trademarks are registered in the United States Patent and Trademark Office by International Bible Society.

The Bible text designated (KJV) are taken from the KING JAMES VERSION.

The Bible text designated (NKJ) are taken from THE NEW KING JAMES VERSION, Copyright © 1982, Thomas Nelson, Inc. All rights reserved.

Scripture taken from the NEW AMERICAN STANDARD BIBLE, © Copyright The Lockman Foundation 1960, 1962, 1963, 1968, 1971, 1972, 1973, 1975, 1977, 1988. Used by permission. When used the Bible text is designated as (NAS).

The Bible text designated (NJB) are taken from THE NEW JERUSALEM BIBLE, Copyright © 1985 by Darton, Longman & Todd Ltd and Doubleday, a division of Bantam Doubleday Dell Publishing Group, Inc.

Artwork titled "The First Four Seals; Four Horsemen" has been used by permission. It is from a series of 35 illustrations by Pat Marvenko Smith © 1982, 1992, on the Book of Revelation called "Revelation Illustrated", available as art prints and teaching aids. A free brochure about the art is available from: Revelation Productions, 1740 Ridgeview Drive, North Huntingdon, PA 15642 USA. 1-800-327-7330.
Website: www.revelationillustrated.com

ISBN: 0-9725837-0-X

THIS BOOK IS DEDICATED TO
DEBBIE VIEROW AND CLAUDIA (SCHECK) DART

Both died of a tragic death before their time.
I hope to see them in heaven – SOON!

I would also like to dedicate this book to Paul Odenbaugh
who is my uncle and mentor.

CONTENTS

Dedications		v
Acknowledgments		xi
List of Charts & Illustrations		13
Preface		14
From the Author		15
Introduction		21
Chapter One	Day of the Lord	27
Chapter Two	In the Beginning	34
	Plan	34
Chapter Three	What Day Is It?	38
	10-26-96	38
	Day	39
	Last Days	41
	Last Day	46
	Day of Christ	49
	Kingdom Age	54
	After Two Days	57
	Latter Days	60
	End of the Age	62
Chapter Four	**Laodicean Church 1900-1948**	**64**
	Church at Philadelphia	65
	Start of Apostasy	67
	Signs of the Times	69
	War	75
Chapter Five	**Israel—May 14, 1948—Can a Nation Be Born in a Day?**	**78**
	Blessings for Obedience	79
	Curses for Disobedience	80
	Jewish History—2165 B.C. to 135 A.D.	85
	Jewish History—483 Years to Christ in Daniel's Eyes	97
	Jewish History—135 A.D. to 1870 A.D.	102
	Jewish History—1870 A.D. to May 8, 1945 (VE Day)	105
	Anti-Semitism	107
	Adolf Hitler and the Occult	109
	Holocaust	113
	Jewish History—1945 to Rapture	121
Chapter Six	**Yom Ha-Din—Days of Awe—A Jewish Wedding**	**126**
	Yom ha-Din—Day of Judgment	126
	Ten Days of Repentance—Aseret Yemei Teshuvah	133
	Month of Elul	134
	Blow the Shofar	138
	Three Books	139
	Rosh Hashanah—Judgment Day	140
	7 Intermediate Days	145
	Fast of Gedaliah	146

	Sabbath of Return	146
	Thirteen Qualities	147
	Eve of Yom Kippur	148
	Yom Kippur—Day of Atonement	148
	The Jewish Festivals in Prophecy	152
	Jewish Wedding	158
Chapter Seven	**1948 to the Rapture**	**168**
	Apostasy	168
	Primary Signs of the Times	169
	Secondary Signs of the Times	173
	Anti-Christ Revealed	175
	Why a Tribulation Period	177
	End of the Age	181
	End of Indignation	183
	Second Coming	184
Chapter Eight	**After the Rapture and Before the Tribulation Period**	**195**
	The Kingdom Age	206
	Rapture	214
	The Voice of God	217
	The Last Trumpet	221
	Trumpet Blasts	226
	Gates of Heaven	230
	Heavenly Scene	232
	Jesus Crowned King	233
	Judgment Seat of Christ	236
	The Books are Opened	237
	A Marriage Made in Heaven	242
	Anti-Christ Released	245
	False Prophet	249
	Revived Roman Empire	251
	Earthly Scene	264
Chapter Nine	**The Tribulation Period—The First 3 ½ Years**	**271**
	A Wedding Feast	271
	7 Seals	272
	Russian Invasion	275
	War in Heaven	297
Chapter Ten		**308**
Chapter Eleven	**The Tribulation Period—The Time of Jacob's Trouble**	**309**
	Great Day of the Lord	311
	Preaching the Gospel	318
	144,000 Servants	319
	Two Witnesses	320
	Three Angelic Messengers	322
	Two Jewish Idioms	324
	Birth Pains	325
	Cup of Wrath	327

	The Time of Jacob's Trouble	328
	Second Holocaust	336
	Abomination of Desolation	339
	Jewish People Flee	341
	Mark of the Beast	357
	Trumpet Judgments	358
	Judgment of the Nations	368
	Jerusalem And The Towns Of Judah	390
	Egypt and Her Allies	396
	Cush and Put	404
	Assyria and Ninevah	406
	Elam	407
	Meshech and Tubal	408
	Edom	408
	Sidon and Tyre	411
	Philistines	412
	Moab	413
	Ammon	415
	Damascus	417
	Arabian Tribes — Kedar and Hazor	418
	Bowl Judgments	422
	Babylon	426
	Marriage Supper of the Lamb	436
Chapter Twelve	**The Day of Vengeance—The Year of the Lord's Favor**	**440**
	30 Days	444
	45 Days	444
	Glorious Return of Christ	445
	Great Trumpet	449
	Gather the Elect	450
	Gather the Nations	463
	Harvest of the Earth	463
	Battle of Armageddon	468
	Great Supper of God	487
	Defeat of the Anti-Christ	488
	Satan Bound	493
	Earth Destroyed By Fire	494
	Resurrection of the Tribulation Saints	495
	The Year of the Lord's Favor	498
	A Feast For All Peoples	508
Chapter Thirteen	**The Rest of the Millennium**	**511**
	New Heavens and New Earth	513
	JESUS	522
	As King	522
	As Judge	524
	As Redeemer	525
	As the Branch	526

	As a Rock	527
	As High Priest	529
	Israel – God's People	531
	Jerusalem	545
	The Heavenly Jerusalem	546
	Salem	553
	City of David	557
	City of Peace	559
	Rebuild the Temple	566
	Reestablish the Feasts	573
	The Nations	576
Chapter Fourteen	**Learning From History**	**583**
	Learning From Old Testament History	583
	Angel of the Lord	586
	Glory of the Lord	594
	Dwell Among His People	616
	Shekinah Glory	631
	Learning From New Testament History	632
	The Throne of the Lord—The Lord is There	647
	Visions of God and Jesus	669
	God is Light	679
	Fire from God	682
Chapter Fifteen	**The End and the Beginning**	**687**
	Satan's Doom	688
	Great White Throne Judgment	688
	Last Enemy—Death	690
	Lake of Fire	693
	The Beginning of Forever	701
	The Kingdom of God	702
	The Day of God—Eternity	707
	New Heaven and New Earth	709
	The New Jerusalem	709
Chapter Sixteen	**What Should We Do As Christians?**	**717**
	False Messiah's, Prophets, Teachers & Believers	719
	Date Setters	723
	Do Not Be Fearful	726
	Misguided Perceptions	731
	Live Our Lives Like Christ	733
	Sons of the Light	737
	Watch!	738
Notes		**741**
Index of Selected Scripture		**745**
Maps and Charts		**756**

ACKNOWLEDGMENTS

The first person I want to thank for helping make this book a reality is Don Shaffer. He is a good Christian friend who helped Sarah and me through some difficult times when I was working seven days a week on this book. Don is a fellow truck driver and can appreciate what it took to write this book.

I would like to thank Sarah's daughter Nancy Jo Jacobs for helping Sarah with the typing of a portion of the manuscript.

I want to thank Gary Stearman from *Prophecy in the News* for taking the time to look at my book. Just before Thanksgiving in 1999, right out of the clear blue sky, Sarah and I dropped by his office in Oklahoma City and handed him a copy of the book and ask him to sort of review it.

I cannot even express enough gratitude for my Uncle Paul and Aunt Irene Odenbaugh. Their continual prayer for me and Sarah is appreciated. Uncle Paul and Aunt Irene have had a love in their hearts for Jesus for a long time. Uncle Paul knows as much about Bible prophecy as anybody I know and he gave me the best critical reading of this book. After reading chapter three he pointed out that the phrases *"the day"* and *"that day"* have as much significance in the New Testament as they do in the Old Testament and because of his input I made some critical additions to chapter three. Uncle Paul has also been my ardent and faithful supporter.

Eliezer Urbach—whom I quoted in this book—and his wife Sara have become good friends of me and Sarah as we have stopped by their home in Denver to ask Eliezer various questions about the Jewish portions of this book. It has been a joy to listen to Eliezer and his wife speak conversational Hebrew while we were visiting them. I once had the opportunity to hear Eliezer blow a shofar (Rams horn) and it made the hair stand up on the back of my neck. Eliezer and Sara patiently await the return of their beloved Messiah.

Once again I need to acknowledge Mr. Stearman from *Prophecy in the News*. Just as I was about to complete this book I called Gary concerning a question I did not have answered in my book. Through his knowledge of Greek, Gary was able to answer my question concerning the voice of the Archangel. With a few corrections, after learning the meaning of this subject, I was able to finish this book. Thanks again Mr. Stearman. I might add here that it took another three years after contacting Mr. Stearman at that time to complete this book.

We would like to thank these members of my family: My mother Luella Reese; my brother's Jim Dart and Mike Dart; my sister's Chris Betz, Glenda Boyce and Vicki Tobel; my son Jerry Jr. and his wife Angie and my two grandson's Jacob and Levi Dart.

We would like to thank these members of Sarah's family: Her father and mother, Lester and Josie Royce (gone to be with Jesus); her brother's Raymond Royce, Luke Royce and Walter Royce; her sister's Marci Croschere, Marie Golden and Sharon (gone home to glory); her son's Brian Jacobs and Adam Weigant; and her daughter's Stephanie Norton and Nancy Jacobs. Marci gave us the most spiritual support in the first few years of writing this book. Marci has a deep love in her heart for Jesus and is a blessing to us. Thank you Walt for working on Sarah's big truck (Peterbilt).

Finally, this book would never have been completed had it not been for Sarah. Not only did she support both of us by working, but she also typed most of the manuscript, did a super job on the maps and charts and also named the book. She never once complained to me about working while I stayed home and completed this book. She would work during the day and type at night and on the weekends. We both love Jesus dearly and we dedicated the last 7 years of our lives to what we felt Jesus wanted us to do. Again, without Sarah, this book would not have been completed. Also I received nothing but enthusiasm, encouragement and excitement from Sarah. It is truly our book. Sarah has wanted a new truck for quite a while now, but she said that the book comes first. Thanks Sarah, I love you.

Thank you David Lynn for the extra effort of working with us when our computer went down.

LIST OF CHARTS AND ILLUSTRATIONS

TIME-LINE	36
Crowning the King	214
7-Year Peace Treaty	270
Russian Invasion	757
Judgment of the Nations	758
Harvest of the Earth	759
Battle of Armageddon	760
What Day Is It?	761
Tribulation Period-Days of Awe-Jewish Wedding	762
The Tribulation Period (Book of Revelation)	763
Days of Awe	764
Jewish Wedding	765
Activities of the Triune God (Trinity) – Jerusalem	766
7 World Empires	767
The Plagues of Revelation (Birth Pains)	768

PREFACE

On a personal note it has been a pleasure to have been able to have taken on the project of writing this book. It was a dual effort on the part of me and my wife. I hope it blesses you as much as it has us.

I have found that someone, somewhere, agrees with most of what I have portrayed in this book, but because there are so many differing views on unfilled Bible prophecy, nobody agrees on the totality of what lies ahead for mankind. The common practice of Bible prophecy writers is to quote someone who agrees with their opinion, but most say nothing about those who disagree with them. As a result of that I have quoted very few people on the subject of Bible prophecy in this book.

Not long after I started writing this book I began to feel that I could not disagree with the teachings and opinions of big-name prophecy teachers. I felt uncomfortable about disagreeing with certain people, but the more research that I did the more I realized that these teachers also disagree a great deal with each other. I found myself unable to agree with any one person and at the same time disappointing everyone because I did not totally agree with their opinion. After struggling with it for a while I finally decided to follow the Bible and try to determine what it had to say. After completing this book I have peace in my heart about what I have written. Any errors that have occurred in this writing will be cleared up when these events take place in the near future.

The primary purpose for writing this book has been to reveal the total plan of God. I hope this book will help people get excited about the return of Jesus. Hopefully you will read the entire Bible with a renewed excitement as you see Jesus in His pre-incarnate ministry in the Old Testament.

Most of the Bible prophecy ministries that are in existence today are very good ministries. They are credible and follow along the lines of scripture and what it has to reveal to us, even though they may disagree on the smaller details. As always there are a few prophecy ministries who distort the truth and have more of a sensational approach to their thoughts. Beware of them and prove their predictions from what the entire Bible presents to us and not just what the local newspapers are reporting at the moment.

My wife Sarah and I sincerely hope you will enjoy reading this book.

God Bless You,
Jerry and Sarah Dart

FROM THE AUTHOR

Before you read this book I would like to review the topic of Bible translation. Most Christians today are unaware of the fact that the original manuscripts of both the Old Testament and the New Testament are not known to exist today. The original transcripts of the Old Testament were written in Hebrew—the language of ancient Israel—with a few portions written in Aramaic. The Aramaic passages occur in Genesis 31:47, Jeremiah 10:11, the Aramaic sections of Daniel 2:4-7:28 and Ezra 4:8; 6:18; 7:12-26. The New Testament was originally written in Greek and is saturated with Hebrew scripture references and quotations. The books of the Old Testament were written over a period of 1000 years and ended with the book of Malachi approximately 400 years before Christ was born. The New Testament was written over a period of approximately 50 to 60 years beginning somewhere around 50 AD.

Translating the Bible into different languages is a complex process and has been going on for thousands of years. It is a fascinating subject, but time and space will only allow me to give you a general overview. The primary purpose of translating the Bible into other languages is to allow people to worship and study the Bible in the common language they understand to meet their religious needs. It can become a tedious and thought-provoking endeavor as all languages do not translate across the board as far as word meaning. Trying to match Bible text or the exact word or meaning of words from one language into another can be difficult and not all language interpreters agree on the final translation. One must keep in mind as he or she reads the Bible is the fact that the translation that is being read is exactly that—a translation.

Before writing existed the word of God was passed on orally. Eventually God, beginning with Moses, instructed the prophets to compile His word into written form.

Exod 34:27 *Then the LORD said to Moses, "<u>Write down these words</u>, for in accordance with these words I have made a covenant with you and with Israel." (NIV)*

Jer 36:1-2 *In the fourth year of Jehoiakim son of Josiah king of Judah, this word came to Jeremiah from the LORD: "Take a scroll and <u>write on it all the words I have spoken to you</u> concerning Israel, Judah and all the other nations from the time I began speaking to you in the reign of Josiah till now.* (NIV)

The entire Bible, consisting of both the Old and New Testaments, was inspired by God and was originally written by men chosen of God. Throughout the centuries languages slowly changed from their original format. Words were added, changed or even deleted at times. As people expanded around the world foreign words entered their own language. Even the Hebrew of today is a far cry from the Hebrew that Moses spoke in his time. The meanings of some Hebrew words and some of the rules of grammar are lost. This presents problems for Bible translators, but that does not mean that the overall meaning of scripture is wrong. It simply means that the textual transmission is not exact. This leaves room for different translations of the earliest manuscripts and why today we have so many different translations of the Bible. Most people today have their favorite translation of the Bible that they read and study and very seldom consult the other translations to know that they may differ slightly at times. They will all have the correct salvation message interpreted, which is the most important factor of the gospel. What they may differ in are smaller details concerning doctrine and that could even effect Bible prophecy to some degree. One of the most fascinating parts of studying Bible prophecy is to compare the various translations of the Bible with the original language in which they were written—Hebrew and Greek.

The biblical books of the Old Testament were first written in the ancient Hebrew script that is known as Paleo-Hebrew. Paleo-Hebrew originally had no vowels and early scribes probably used dots to separate their words as the Phoenicians did, but later this script minimally employed vowel letters (*yud, heh, vav*). When the Old Testament writers finished writing their scrolls, they needed scribes to reproduce the old and worn out original scrolls. At all stages of its transmission the biblical text was considered holy by the early scribes, but in early times the concept of holiness did not prevent scribes from changing the text and adding or omitting details. Though there may have been an original or first edition of each biblical book, the copies that circulated in ancient times were not uniform.

An important change in the Hebrew language occurred around 500 BC, when the scribes began using a square Aramaic script that they learned during their exile in Babylon. By 500 BC Aramaic had become the common language of commerce and education in the Near East. This is when the Israelites adopted the Aramaic writing system. The Dead Sea Scrolls cover this period of transition. Some of them are written in the rounded Paleo-Hebrew script, but most are in the square Aramaic. The Hebrew scribes did not begin using the Aramaic language, they simply borrowed its scripts and used it to express their own Hebrew words. They were allowed to accomplish this because both were Semitic languages, nations that had descended from Noah's son Shem.

The desire to achieve a single standard text arose in rabbinic times in which laws and teachings were derived from textual details, thus requiring that all Jews have identical texts of the Bible. Somewhere around 500 AD the scribes developed a system of showing the vowel sounds. A small Jewish sect in Babylon known as the Qaraites developed the system of vowel marks. A Masoretic family known as ben Asher produced a better system of vowel markings in the ninth and tenth centuries. The exact wording from the Old Testament Hebrew from ancient scrolls and medieval manuscripts handed down for centuries as the central text of Judaism comes from the Masoretic Text and is the best known. In 1524, Jacob ben Hayyim published a printed text of the Hebrew Old Testament using manuscripts that had been copied from the ben Asher manuscripts and became the first printed edition of the Hebrew Old Testament and also became a standard for printed Bibles. Gerhard Kittel's *Biblica Hebraica,* perhaps the best-known Hebrew Old Testament of the twentieth century, listed the variations of the ben Hayyim text in its footnotes, but did not include them in the text.

The Old Testament has come down to us from other languages besides Hebrew. Around 300 BC, a community of Jewish scholars in Alexandria, Egypt compiled a Greek version and called it the Septuagint, the Greek word for seventy. In print, scholars usually refer to it by LXX (70 in Roman numerals). After AD 200, Jewish scholars began compiling Aramaic paraphrases of the Old Testament called *targums*. The targums were made from Hebrew manuscripts written in the time of Jesus or later.

The New Testament was written in an age when literature flourished. It was copied constantly from the start and has survived the centuries well. We have approximately 15,000 complete manuscripts and quotations of the New Testament today. God moved writers of the New Testament faithfully to record His word as He had the Old Testament writers. Paul and the gospel writers often showed themselves conscious of what the Holy Spirit was doing through them.

We have many fragments of the New Testament text that were written in the second century AD. More important are the papyrus manuscripts written on an early form of paper made from matted papyrus reeds. Most of these manuscripts were written on vellum (parchment) *uncials* and nearly 275 have been found. Scribes used the uncial style of writing on vellum and papyrus until about the ninth century, when they began copying the manuscripts in a small cursive Greek script. These later manuscripts are called *minuscules*. We have over 2,700 New Testament manuscripts written in this style.

When there came to be many Latin-speaking Christians, the Bible was translated into Latin. It is believed that this was done around AD 200, although no Latin manuscripts survive from that time. Christian scribes copied this Old Latin version many times and eventually their copies picked up some striking differences. Pope Damascus I commissioned the scholar *Jerome* (AD 340-420) to produce a standard text of the Latin Bible which he completed around AD 400. His version is called the Vulgate.

Pope Leo X was the greatest scholar and manuscript collector among the Renaissance popes. He suggested a scholarly edition of the Bible be edited by Cardinal Ximines of Spain. In 1517, a printer in Alcala, Spain, completed this printed Bible with the Vulgate and the Greek arranged in parallel columns. It became known as the Complutensian Polyglot. The editors of this edition said they used "very ancient and correct" Greek manuscripts that Pope Leo X provided for their work.

Joannes Froben, a printer in Brazil, Switzerland, persuaded the noted biblical scholar Erasmus of Rotterdam to come to Basel to prepare a printed Greek New Testament. Using manuscripts from the library of Basel University, Erasmus and Froben produced their Greek text in March 1516. Erasmus' text became the *textus receptus* (Latin, "received text") of the New Testament and served as a basic guide for the translators of the King James Version.

Two hundred years later, scholars began to replace Erasmus' text with printed texts based on earlier Greek manuscripts, which they assumed to be better than the textus receptus. In 1831, Charles Lachmann published such a text.

Later, Constantine von Tischendorf zealously collected ancient manuscripts and issued several editions of the Greek text, with notations of variant readings in the margins. From 1856 to 1879, Samuel Prideaux Tregelles tried to develop an improved text, seeking the best reading at each point where selected manuscripts diverged. Tregelles sought to evaluate the Greek manuscripts by the age of the various readings, not the age of the manuscripts themselves.

Two of the great names in the history of textual studies were Brooke Foss Westcott (1825-1901) and Fenton John Anthony Hort (1828-1892). After classifying the Greek texts according to the age of the various readings, they concluded that there were four basic text types: Syrian, Western, Alexandrian, and Neutral. In 1881, after 30 years' work, they published their own Greek text of the New Testament, entitled the *New Testament in the Original Greek*. It soon replaced Erasmus' text as the textus receptus of the New Testament.

Textual study has made some notable advances since the days of Westcott and Hort. Now scholars agree that the early textual history of the Greek New Testament was more complicated than Westcott and Hort supposed. Scholars still basically follow the Westcott and Hort principles and conclusions. Many scholars now believe that internal evidence (i.e., content) should carry more weight than the text types in determining which readings are the most reliable.

Bishop Aldhelm of Sherborne (d. AD 709) translated the Psalms into Anglo-Saxon, an early form of the English language. A tenth-century priest named Aldred wrote an English translation of the gospels between the lines of a Latin text he was copying. This manuscript is our earliest evidence of an English translation of the New Testament. Around AD 1000, Alfric of Bath produced an English translation of the Gospels.

John Wycliffe published the first complete Bible in English in 1382. Wycliffe used primarily the Latin Vulgate, and his translation was weak in some respects. But the common people of England gladly received the book, and Wycliffe organized a group of ministers known as the Lollards, because they used the lollardy (common) speech to travel throughout the country and preach from his translation. The Roman Catholic Church condemned Wycliffe's work and burned many of the handwritten copies. Nevertheless, about 150 copies of Wycliffe's Version have survived, but only one is complete.

Another Englishman, William Tyndale, began printing the next important English translation of the New Testament at Cologne, Germany, in 1525. Because Tyndale was a close friend of Martin Luther, Roman Catholic authorities attempted to halt the project. Yet Tyndale succeeded in finishing the book and smuggled his printed New Testaments into England. In 1536, after he had completed translations of the Pentateuch and Jonah, British agents captured him in Belgium, strangled him, and burned his body at the stake.

In 1535, an Englishman named Miles Coverdale published an English translation of the whole Bible in the city of Zurich. This edition had the support of King Henry VIII because Coverdale translated many passages in a way that supported Anglican Catholic doctrine and undermined the use of the Latin Vulgate. Coverdale then began work on another English Bible that would incorporate the best of Tyndale and other English translators, as well as new insights from the Greek and Hebrew manuscripts. He prepared huge 9" by 15" pages for this volume, earning it the name of the Great Bible. He completed it in 1539, and the British government ordered the clergy to display the book prominently in churches throughout the land. This stirred popular interest in the Scriptures.

In 1553, Mary Tudor came to the throne in England and enforced strict Catholic policies upon the people. She banned the use of all English Bibles, in favor of the Latin versions. Coverdale and other Bible translators fled to Geneva, Switzerland, where John Calvin had established a Protestant stronghold.

William Whittingham of Geneva organized several of these scholars to begin work on a new English Bible, which they published in 1650. It was the first Bible to divide the Scriptures into verses. This was the work of Robert Estienne, a Parisian printer of Greek New Testaments. Booksellers called this book the Geneva Bible or the Breeches Bible. Whittingham and his colleagues dedicated this translation to Queen Elizabeth I, who had

From the Author

taken the throne of England in 1558. The people of England used the Geneva Bible very widely for the next two generations. In 1604, James VI of Scotland became King James I of England and began a program of peacemaking between the hostile religious factions of Great Britain. That same year he convened a meeting of religious leaders at Hampton Court. Dr. John Reynolds, the Puritan spokesman, proposed that a New English translation of the Bible be issued in honor of the king. The King James Version (KJV) was to become an important watershed in the history of English Bible translations.

King James appointed 54 scholars to the task of making a new translation. For the Old Testament, they relied primarily upon ben Hayyim's edition of the ben Asher text. For the New Testament, they relied upon the Greek text of Erasmus and a bilingual Greek-and-Latin text of the sixth century found by Theodore Beza. The translators followed chapter divisions made by Archbishop Stephan Langton in 1551 and verse divisions of Robert Estienne. Because King James had authorized this project, the new Bible became known as the Authorized Version. It was first published in 1611 and revised in 1615, 1629, 1638, and 1762.

An edition of the KJV published by bishop William Lloyd in 1701 was the first Bible to contain marginal notes dating biblical events in relation to the birth of Christ. (B.C. and A.D.). Lloyd's edition also contained the chronology laid out by Archbishop James Ussher (1581-1656) that dated creation at 4004 BC. This chronology was first used in an Oxford edition of the KJV published in 1679. Many subsequent editions of the KJV have reprinted this chronology. The 1762 revision is what most people know as the KJV. [1]

Most of the material used in this section concerning Bible translations came from the *Dictionary of Biblical Literacy*, compiled by Cecil B. Murphy, Historic Texts and Their Translations, pp 52-69, Nashville, TN: Oliver Nelson Books, ©1989.

In the twentieth century, there was an explosion of Bible translations into many languages. Translators who are making an effort to translate the Bible into the meaning of the oldest and most correct manuscripts. As you can probably surmise, there does not exist a perfect translation of the Bible. This might surprise some people, but Christians today, with the help of the English translation, can approach the Bible with great confidence. In their Greek New Testament not one word in a thousand is seriously uncertain and no established doctrine is called in question by any of the continuing doubts about the correct reading.

There are those people out there that believe that the King James Version is the only translation of the English Bible that is correct and that it should be the only translation to read and study. However, I do not think that is a fair statement to make. I love my King James Version copy of the Bible, but one thing I learned when I was researching this book is that several translations of the Bible need to be consulted and also compared with the original Hebrew and Greek manuscripts in order to study the meaning of Bible Prophecy. I quoted from several translations in this book and tried to use the translation that best explained what was being discussed and also followed the Hebrew and Greek.

In preparing for the writing of this book, over the last seven years, I personally prefer the New International Version of the Bible. It is the most readable in English and is better suited for the people who are just beginning to study Bible Prophecy. In the Old Testament I found that the King James Version translated many of the Bible Prophecy passages in a far better light in some instances.

AFTER THE RAPTURE

God also reveals things to mankind at the time He desires. In the Old Testament, God revealed to the Israelites what would happen to them in advance, according to their obedience or disobedience. God revealed dreams and visions to Daniel and then told him to seal up their meaning, for the meaning will be revealed in the distant future (toward the end of the age). In the New Testament, God revealed more of His plan through His disciples by showing them mysteries that were hidden from man previously, new revelations that are relevant for the people during the Dispensation of Grace. One new mystery (revelation) was the Rapture of the living saints, unknown in the Old Testament.

> 1 Cor 15:51-52   ***Behold, I shew you a mystery;*** *We shall not all sleep, but we shall all be changed, In a moment, in the twinkling of an eye, at the last trump: for the trumpet shall sound, and the dead shall be raised incorruptible, and we shall be changed.* (KJV)

> 1 Thes 4:16-18   *For the Lord himself will come down from heaven, with a loud command, with the voice of the archangel and with the trumpet call of God, and the dead in Christ will rise first.* ***After that, we who are still alive and are left will be caught up together with them in the clouds to meet the Lord in the air.*** *And so we will be with the Lord forever. Therefore encourage each other with these words.* (NIV)

Basically, God will reveal to mankind what He wants to reveal at the time He wants it to be revealed. God reveals details and events through men such as; Daniel and Ezekiel in the Old Testament; Peter, Paul and John in the New Testament; and men at the end of the age to unseal the meaning of Daniel. Not just one man, but a multitude of men, men of God who have a love in their hearts for studying Bible Prophecy. These men will work together for the advancement of the Gospel and will prepare the believers for the Rapture, the most important event to take place in the lives of the believers.

Throughout this book the scripture references are printed in italics. All of the bold and underlined portions of scripture were placed there by the author to highlight the portions that pertain to the subject matter that is being discussed. The scripture references are followed by the abbreviation of the translation of the Bible that was referenced in each instance. The different translations used in this book are:

    NIV — New International Version
    KJV — King James Version
    NKJ — New King James
    NAS — New American Standard
    NJB — New Jerusalem Bible

INTRODUCTION

This book is about Bible Prophecy taken from an Old Testament Biblical perspective. Today there are many books and varying views concerning unfilled Bible Prophecy. My perspective will be presented from what is laid out in the Bible, instead of what the newspapers are reporting around the globe. Although it is exciting to watch the final days of this dispensation come to a close, we need to refer to what God's word has to say about Bible Prophecy and rely less on what the news media is reporting. One thing that should be remembered, when studying prophecy, is that the foundation of Bible Prophecy is found in the Old Testament with the New Testament building on that foundation.

Too many prophecy ministries today are so interested in sensationalizing the events that are transpiring in the world today that they are making many people fear the events of the end time. That is contrary to what the New Testament teaches as you will see as you continue to read this book. Many prophecy books have very little to say about the Old Testament and contain a lot of quotations from newspapers. God did not write the newspapers (man did), but He did write the Bible. We appreciate being able to view what is taking place on the world scene so readily these days. With the technological advances available, we are even allowed to see the events as they are actually being played out. It is not theologically correct to scour the newspapers to try to place an event, such as the tragedy of the World Trade Center in New York City, into Bible prophecy. Picking events from the recent past out of newspapers and placing them in the prophecies of the Book of Revelation does not gain support from the Old Testament.

When studying Bible Prophecy one must remember that conflicts between nations (wars) have been going on for thousands of years. When people try to place the current conflicts of the nations from around the world into Bible Prophecy they are eventually proven wrong as time progresses. As new conflicts begin to develop on the scene, the people who have been proven wrong usually restructure their prophetic views to fit the same scenario with the new conflicts. Take two aspirins and call me in the morning if that does not work. The best perspective to take concerning the study of Bible Prophecy is to first consult the Bible itself, then watch the events occurring on the world scene today and follow along as we draw closer to the return of Jesus Christ. Most of the conflicts concerning Bible Prophecy will not take place during the Christian Dispensation. Scripture clearly teaches us that the condition of the world will be in a state of apostasy just prior to God's judgment of mankind. Along with that the people of the world will be in a state of apathy toward the end of the age and unaware of what is about to take place, unexpectedly like a trap.

Always remember that God is in control of the universe and His plan for mankind will play out by His timing. God's word says that at a set time (Hebrew - *moed*) by Him certain events are prescribed to take place, and you better believe that they will take place. It is God's intention to allow mankind to comprehend His total plan progressively. The people who lived during Old Testament times, before Christ, were not provided with the details of the time after the rejection of the Messiah (the rest of the story). The New Testament provides us with new revelations (mysteries) for our generation (the times after Christ). Just prior to the second coming of Jesus Christ, God will unseal the meaning of the prophecies from the Book of Daniel. God will allow mankind to understand certain things at certain times for the benefit of the people living at the time He gives them the understanding.

AFTER THE RAPTURE

Deut 29:4 *But to this day the LORD has not given you a mind that understands or eyes that see or ears that hear.* (NIV)

For your convenience, me and my wife (her suggestion) have inserted the scripture verses that apply to this study in the text so you do not have to stop reading the study to look them up. There are over 7400 verses. Along with the subject of Bible Prophecy, I have discussed many topics that can be controversial. Some of the topics in this book include:

- The prophetic implications of the ancient Jewish Festivals and how they reflect as a shadow of the things to come.

- An account of Bible Prophecy that clearly ties the Old Testament in with the New Testament.

- A detailed chronological step-by-step order of the Rapture as Jesus calls for His saints to come home.

- A chronological order of the events that transpire *After The Rapture*, including what will be going on in heaven and on the earth at this time.

- A detailed account of the Antichrist as he attempts to conquer the entire world.

- The most detailed account of the Battle of Armageddon ever written.

- What heaven and hell are like.

- What our resurrected bodies are going to be like.

- An account of what it will be like living on earth during the Millennium and beyond that in eternity.

Some of the non prophetic topics in this book include:

- A view of the past history of the Jewish people.

- Some of the past history of both the Old Testament and the New Testament as it applies to Bible Prophecy.

- Some of the eschatological views of Orthodox Judaism.

- The corporeality of God.

- Some of the names and duties of Jesus Christ in the Old Testament as He performed His pre-incarnate ministry.

Introduction

When I first began writing *After the Rapture*, I wanted to write this for those people who were left on earth *After the Rapture*. Me and my wife Sarah both agreed on that. We wanted this book to be readable for people who have never read the Bible, to be for people who have a little knowledge about the Bible and to be food for thought for those serious teachers and students of eschatology (the study of end time events).

I never intended on writing a commentary so diverse from current thoughts and teachings on the interpretation of Bible Prophecy. I have felt for a long time now that the Tribulation Period could not start at the Rapture of the church. It did not seem to tie in with the prophetic scripture I was studying, but it is not my intention to inform Bible scholars, preachers, teachers of eschatology, students of eschatology or anybody else that they are wrong in their interpretation of the Bible. On the contrary, I hope they read this book with an open mind and heart, perhaps I might just be right on some of my interpretation. My preference would be that all of God's children live their lives in harmony and agreement and as a part of one body. We should be able to agree to disagree on Bible Prophecy and not change the unity of the body of Christ. God will not reveal all the meaning of end time prophecy to any one man. He will reveal certain things to certain people at certain times. We as people, who study prophecy, are to read and study all we can about the future history that is about to break out on the face of the earth. Collectively, we can put our thoughts together to teach the people on earth what will happen just before and *After the Rapture*. Scripture clearly teaches that the book of Daniel is sealed up to the end of the age, to be revealed to God's people at the right time. What is revealed to us should bring peace of mind to us individually, while urging us to share the message revealed with others so they might turn from their wicked ways and follow the Lord. This message is not intended to scare anyone to salvation, but to inform them of the consequences of what is about to take place on the earth to a sinful and unregenerate people. If God did not want people to know about these things, then why did He put them in His word and tell us He would reveal their meaning at a designated time?

Before I ever started this book I had a yearning to seek the meaning of the Jewish festivals and also a Jewish wedding. Never in my wildest dreams did I perceive of writing a book like the one that I hope you will read from cover to cover. To be honest with you, when I wrote one of the earlier chapters, I said that I would only have minor changes to current Bible teachings and interpretations of the end times. Later I had to rewrite that chapter to say that I have some major changes I would like you to look at.

I would like to add that I did not write this book to try to impress anyone, or as far as that goes, to disagree with anyone. I wrote this book from my heart and I felt led by a wonderful and awesome God. I am not worried by anything that any man might say about me concerning anything I have written in this book. I already know that this book will be controversial. It is really hard to please everyone at the same time. My thought is that if you are not getting criticism from someone, you are not working hard enough for the Lord.

Jesus, Sarah and I want to tell you how much we love you with all our hearts and hopefully this book will show you that!!!!

1 Thes 2:4 ...***We are not trying to please men but God, who tests our hearts.*** (NIV)

AFTER THE RAPTURE

WHAT? Another book on prophecy and the doom and gloom of the evil times ahead! I will have to admit that the earth will go through the most horrible time of its existence since God created it and there will never be a time like it again. It will literally be the **ugliest** time of human history.

- Matt 24:21 *"**For then there will be great tribulation,** such as has not been since the beginning of the world until this time, no, nor ever shall be.* (NKJ)

- Dan 12:1 *...**There will be a time of distress** such as has not happened from the beginning of nations until then. But at that time your people—everyone whose name is found written in the book—will be delivered.* (NIV)

- Jer 30:7 *Alas! For that day is great, so that none is like it; and it is **the time of Jacob's trouble,** but he shall be saved out of it.* (NKJ)

Nevertheless, God informed us of these future events in His word for a reason and we need to remember that God Himself writes every word in the Bible.

- 2 Tim 3:16 ***All** Scripture is inspired by God and profitable for teaching, for reproof, for correction, for training in righteousness;* (NAS)

It was given to men to write down, but He gave them the words to write. One of the reasons God is showing us this terrible future period of events is to give us peace of mind. He loves us enough to tell us about it and then assures us that He is in control and watching over us.

- Col 3:15 ***Let the peace of Christ rule in your hearts,** since as members of one body you were called to peace. And be thankful.* (NIV)

- Phil 4:7 *And the **peace of God, which surpasses all comprehension,** shall guard your hearts and your minds in Christ Jesus.* (NAS)

He does not want us to be fearful or get paranoid about it. God's timing is perfect.

- 1 Thes 4:18 *Wherefore **comfort one another** with these words.* (KJV)

- 1 Thes 5:11 ***Therefore comfort each other and edify one another,** just as you also are doing.* (NKJ)

- 2 Thes 2:1-2 *Concerning the coming of our Lord Jesus Christ and our being gathered to him, we ask you, brothers, **not to become easily unsettled or alarmed by some prophecy,** report or letter supposed*

Introduction

to have come from us, saying that the day of the Lord has already come. (NIV)

God wants us to live this life here on earth at the time He put us here. God wants us to do the job He put us here to do to the best of our ability. Each of us has been given a degree of talents and God expects from us according to the abilities He has given us.

Matt 25:14-15 *For the kingdom of heaven is as a man travelling into a far country, who called his own servants, and delivered unto them his goods.* ***And unto one he gave five talents, to another two, and to another one;*** *<u>to every man according to his several ability;</u> and straightway took his journey.* (KJV)

At the Judgment Seat of Christ, which is the saints (believers) appearing before Jesus Christ, all the saints will receive rewards for what they have done for God in this life.

1 Cor 3:10-15 *According to the grace of God which is given unto me, as a wise masterbuilder, I have laid the foundation, and another buildeth thereon. But let every man take heed how he buildeth thereupon. For other foundation can no man lay than that is laid, which is Jesus Christ. Now if any man build upon this foundation gold, silver, precious stones, wood, hay, stubble;* **Every man's work shall be made manifest:** *for the day shall declare it, because it shall be revealed by fire; and the fire shall try every man's work of what sort it is. If any man's work abide which he hath built thereupon,* ***<u>he shall receive a reward.</u>*** *If any man's work shall be burned, he shall suffer loss: but he himself shall be saved; yet so as by fire.* (KJV)

I count it all joy to have had the honor to author this book. Oh yes, I have had doubts and Satan has given me and my wife all kinds of reasons and excuses not to finish this work, but by God's grace we finished it. If it brings but one soul to salvation or gives but one believer peace of mind, concerning the time at the end of the age, it will all have been worth it. That is not even counting what peace of mind it has brought to me and my wife Sarah, who has supported me wholeheartedly the entire time it took to complete the manuscript. By the way as I mentioned before she named the book and what a great title it is.

There have been many books published concerning the Rapture, the Tribulation Period, Armageddon, the Millennium, and the New Heaven and the New Earth, but very little has been published about the time period between the Rapture of the church and the beginning of the 7-Year Peace Treaty. In fact, I have only come across one source that has even suggested that there might be a time period between the Rapture and the Tribulation Period, and it is *Prophecy in the News*. This is probably because God's word does not have a lot to say about it. I personally do not believe it will be a very long period of time and the events on the earth will be happening at a rapid pace. I can think of three reasons why it is possible to write a book like this called *After the Rapture* at this time in history. They are:

1. The unsealing of the book of Daniel.
2. Prophecy that has already been fulfilled.
3. The events that are occurring in the Middle East.

As you read this book, keep an open mind, pray about it and check out all the scripture that is quoted. God's word is the key to anyone's teaching. The more I study prophecy, the more it amazes me how much and how minutely God reveals to us (believers) in advance what will happen in the future. I do not profess to have all the sequences in order in this book. Only God knows everything for sure. I will have events that have never been presented like I see them happening. I agree with most of the Bible scholars and teachers that form the pre-tribulation Rapture view of the church. The main differences in this book are an added short period of time that I believe will happen *After the Rapture* and before the 7-Year Peace Treaty is signed, and a new thought that the Tribulation Period will occur after the church age (Dispensation of Grace) is over, during the first few years of the Millennium. I also believe that these events mentioned will occur during the Day of the Lord.

GOD BLESS YOU ALL!

CHAPTER ONE

DAY OF THE LORD

I believe that the term or phrase, "the Day of the Lord" is probably the most misunderstood of all the subjects in the study of eschatology. Correctly interpreting this phrase will determine the correct chronological order of the end times. To me the scripture verses from both the Old and New Testaments, the Jewish Feasts and Festivals, an Ancient Jewish Wedding Ceremony and the Coronation of a Jewish King all synchronize to bring together the correct understanding of "the Day of the Lord."

Without the Jewish perspective it would be very difficult to pinpoint the time frame for the Day of the Lord. I had accepted the traditional viewpoint of Bible scholars and teachers of eschatology that the Tribulation Period would occur at the end of the Dispensation of Grace, which would be before the Millennium, but I could not get the pieces of the eschatological puzzle to fit by using this scenario. I ended up being confused. Only when I placed the location of the Tribulation Period within the Day of the Lord did all the scriptures fit. By the way, if you have not figured it out yet, I believe that the Day of the Lord is what is referred to primarily today as the Millennium. Please remember that in this book I will be referring to both the Day of the Lord and the Millennium and they will always be referring to the last period of the creation week of 1000 years. They are one and the same. In the Old Testament it will always be referred to as the Day of the Lord or by such phrases as *"the day"* or *"that day."* There are only five times and possibly six that the Day of the Lord is mentioned in the New Testament. Once in the book of Acts, written by Luke, who is quoting Peter, who is quoting the Day of the Lord from the Old Testament book of Joel (Acts 2:20). Paul refers to it in 1 Corinthians 5:5, and he mentions it twice in his letters to the Thessalonians; once in his first letter in 1 Thessalonians 5:2 and again in his second letter in 2 Thessalonians 2:2. Peter again mentions the Day of the Lord in his second letter in 2 Peter 3:10. Almost everybody today refers to this period of one thousand years as the Millennium.

In 1 Corinthians 5:5, the translators of the King James Version (KJV), the New King James (NKJ), the American Standard Version (ASV) and the New American Standard (NAS), have all added the name *"Jesus"* at the end of the Day of the Lord. Only the New International Version (NIV) is correct in not putting it into their translation. In the Greek manuscripts they do not show it. The Greek word that they added was *iesous* (pronounced ee-ay-sooce') and is of Hebrew origin. Taken in context the Day of the Lord in 1 Corinthians chapter five is talking about the judgment of sexually immoral people. Sexually immoral people will be judged during the Day of the Lord, not the Day of the Lord Jesus which will include the Rapture for the believers.

In 2 Thessalonians 2:2, we also have translation problems. The King James Version and the New King James translations have mistranslated *"the day of the Lord"* to read *"the day of Christ."* In the Greek the word used is *kur'ios* which is the word for "Lord." The Greek for Christ is *Christos*. Actually in verse one, it is referring to the Day of Christ when it talks about the coming of our Lord and the saints being gathered to meet Him in the air, but in verse two it is referring to the Day of the Lord when the people on earth will suffer extreme persecution. The Christians in Thessalonica, at that time (54 AD), were going through sufferings so severe that someone sent them a letter purporting it to be from Paul and his entourage, saying that the Day of the Lord had already come. Their concern was that they had missed the Rapture and were suffering the effects of the beginning portion of the Day of the Lord. Paul wrote them this letter, 2 Thessalonians, to tell them not to worry about some prophecy or letter supposedly from them, saying that the Day of the Lord had arrived because they were going through such extreme sufferings. Paul warns them not to be deceived by anyone in any way for the Day of the Lord will not come until two things happen. They are: the apostasy occurs and then the Antichrist will be revealed. Then he told them to remember the things he had told them at the time he was with them when he was in Thessalonica (2 Thessalonians 1:4-5; 2 Thessalonians 2:1-5).

> 2 Thes 2:2 *not to become easily unsettled or alarmed by some prophecy, report or letter supposed to have come from us,* **saying that <u>the day of the Lord</u> has already come.** (NIV)

I believe that the apostle John is also referring to the Day of the Lord in the book of Revelation, but here it is mentioned as *"the Lord's Day."*

> Rev 1:10 ***I was in the Spirit on <u>the Lord's day</u>**, and heard behind me a great voice, as of a trumpet*, (KJV)

John was literally transported to the future time period of the Day of the Lord to see the view of the seven churches in Revelation chapters two and three. In chapter four, when Jesus called John up to heaven to receive the revelation of the Day of the Lord, his physical body probably remained in Patmos during that time. From heaven John is given a vision of the scene in heaven at the beginning of the Kingdom Age. That scene in heaven, in Revelation chapters four and five, is Jesus setting on His throne crowned as King. The scene on earth during the Tribulation Period is picked up in Revelation chapters six through sixteen. Revelation chapters seventeen and eighteen are a reflection of the final destruction of Babylon. Revelation chapter nineteen reveals the return of Jesus at the Battle of Armageddon. Revelation chapter twenty deals with the defeat of Satan and the judgment of unsaved mankind. The revelation culminates with what it will be like living in eternity, in Revelation chapters twenty-one and twenty-two.

Although the New Testament book of Revelation gives us a good order of events, it lacks a full understanding without the help of the study of the Old Testament and what God taught and promised the chosen (Jewish) people. The book of Revelation furnishes us with a view from a Christian mind set, but at the end of the Christian era God will graft the Jewish people back and fulfill the promises He made to them. This will all occur during the period of the Day of the Lord, more commonly known as the Millennium.

The biggest stumbling block for me, and will probably be for many people who read this book, is the fact that the Millennium is taught to be 1000 years of peace. No where in scripture could I find that to be true. If that is true, then my theory will be incorrect, because you cannot have 1000 years of peace and have it include a short period of seven years, known as the Tribulation Period, which will be the most treacherous period of human history. Jesus will reign as King of Kings and Lord of Lords for 1000 years, but He will not set up His kingdom on earth until after the Battle of Armageddon is completed. He will rule on His throne from heaven for the first nine years of the Day of the Lord. After that He will rebuild the Temple and rule the world from Jerusalem. Details of how this will happen are contained in the pages of this book. As we look at the Day of the Lord it will show that Jesus will fulfill the prophecy of Daniel 9:24 during the beginning of the Millennium and not as the last act of the church age. It will take the full account of the Old Testament to support this view.

> Dan 9:24 *"Seventy 'sevens' are decreed for your people and your holy city to finish transgression, to put an end to sin, to atone for wickedness, to bring in everlasting righteousness, to seal up vision and prophecy and to anoint the most holy.* (NIV)

If the concept that the Tribulation Period will take place at the beginning of the Day of the Lord is correct, it will be a small change in the present interpretation of the end time chronological order of things. I still basically agree with most of the current teachings of eschatology. I am just moving the Tribulation Period from the end of the present age, that we are currently living, to the new age just ahead of us called the Millennium. I first read about this similar viewpoint from Avi Ben Mordechai in his book, *Signs in the Heavens, A Jewish Messianic Perspective of the Last Days & Coming Millennium.*

The Day of the Lord for some reason is not given the emphasis it needs to have when studying end time prophecy. It is clear from studying past history that the terrible events described by the prophets in the Old Testament, concerning the Day of the Lord, have not yet transpired. Please notice in Isaiah chapter thirteen that the Day of the Lord will come as a destruction from God. He will lay the land desolate and will destroy the sinners out of it. God will punish the wicked for their sin. He will cause the arrogance of the proud to cease and as a result of that God will shake the heavens and the earth will remove out of her place. As far as I know, God has never removed all the sinners from the earth anytime in the past. Ever since the fall of man, both saved and unsaved people have been living on earth, even counting the time when Noah was the only righteous man left on earth.

> Isa 13:6-13 ***Wail, for the day of the LORD is near; it will come like destruction from the Almighty.*** *Because of this, all hands will go limp, every man's heart will melt. Terror will seize them, pain and anguish will grip them; they will writhe like a woman in labor. They will look aghast at each other, their faces aflame.* ***See, the day of the LORD is coming a cruel day, with wrath and fierce anger—to make the land desolate and destroy the sinners within it.*** *The stars of heaven and their constellations will not show their light. The rising sun will be darkened and the moon will not give its light.* ***I will punish the world for its evil, the wicked for their sins.*** *I will put an end to the arrogance of the haughty and will humble the pride of the ruthless.*

AFTER THE RAPTURE

I will make man scarcer than pure gold, more rare than the gold of Ophir. ***Therefore I will make the heavens tremble; and the earth will shake from its place at the wrath of the LORD Almighty, in the day of his burning anger.*** (NIV)

Joel 2:1-2 ***Blow the trumpet in Zion; sound the alarm on my holy hill. Let all who live in the land tremble, for the day of the LORD is coming. It is close at hand—a day of darkness and gloom, a day of clouds and blackness.*** *Like dawn spreading across the mountains a large and mighty army comes, such as never was of old nor ever will be in ages to come.* (NIV)

History clearly teaches us that the world has never experienced this terrible time of righteous judgment from the Almighty and *"woe"* to those that will be here on earth during this horrendous period of time. But as sure as there is a God, His word tells us that it will happen and it could very well happen in our lifetime. The order of the events concerning the beginning of the Day of the Lord will go something like this:

"For the Lord Himself will descend from heaven with a shout, with the voice of the archangel, and with the trump of God: and the dead in Christ shall rise first: Then we which are alive and remain shall be caught up together with them in the clouds, to meet the Lord in the air: and so shall we ever be with the Lord." (1 Thessalonians 4:14-16) This event, of course, is the Rapture and it is the end of the two thousand year period of the Dispensation of Grace or the church age.

The Day of Christ is the beginning of the Kingdom Age in heaven for all the people of faith from Adam up to and including the Rapture. After they are gathered in the air, the resurrected saints (the dead in Christ along with those who are alive and remain) will be escorted to heaven to participate in the Judgment Seat of Christ. The saints from the Old Testament period will also accompany the church age saints, after their meeting in the air, on this journey to heaven to be in the Presence of God. The Day of Christ will correspond and run concurrent with the Day of the Lord. It will also last for a thousand years and will pertain to the resurrected saints *After the Rapture,* who will dwell in heaven for the duration of the thousand years. They will be allowed to visit the earth after the Glorious Return of the King (Jesus), to worship and serve God, but they will abide in heaven. The Day of the Lord and the Day of Christ relate to different groups of people in different locations. Some of the scripture verses that pertain to the Day of Christ are:

Phil 1:9-10 *And this is my prayer: That your love may abound more and more in knowledge and depth of insight, so that you may be able to discern what is best and may be pure and blameless until **the day of Christ**,* (NIV)

Phil 2:16 *Holding forth the word of life; that I may rejoice in **the day of Christ**, that I have not run in vain, neither laboured in vain.* (KJV)

Day of the Lord

It is known as the Day of Christ Jesus:

> Phil 1:6 *being confident of this, that he who began a good work in you will carry it on to completion until **the day of Christ Jesus.*** (NIV)

It is known as the Day of our Lord Jesus Christ:

> 1 Cor 1:7-8 *Therefore you do not lack any spiritual gift as you eagerly wait for our Lord Jesus Christ to be revealed. He will keep you strong to the end, so that you will be blameless on **the day of our Lord Jesus Christ.*** (NIV)

And also the Day of the Lord Jesus:

> 2 Cor 1:13-14 *For we do not write you anything you cannot read or understand. And I hope that, as you have understood us in part, you will come to understand fully that you can boast of us just as we will boast of you in **the day of the Lord Jesus.*** (NIV)

Dr. David Webber and Rev. N.W. Hutchings, in their commentary on *Joel in the Day of the Lord,* are correct when they say, "The 'Day of Jesus Christ' is not a day of wrath, judgment and destruction. Paul wrote that it was a day for Christians to look forward to; a day for rejoicing; a day that will end the testimony and service of Christians here on earth. For it will be a day when Christians go to be with Jesus and receive their rewards." [1]

The Day of the Lord also begins at the Rapture, but pertains to the unregenerate population that will remain on earth *After the Rapture.* They will go through the Tribulation Period. After the judgment of sinful mankind, during the Tribulation Period, followed by the Battle of Armageddon where the unsaved will be purged from the earth, the remainder of the Day of the Lord will be fixed on earth. It will pertain to the saved portion of mankind who survived the onslaught and will then be living on earth in their fleshly bodies. They will spend the remaining portion of the Day of the Lord on earth with the King (Jesus), to worship and serve Him. These are the people who will repopulate the earth during the Millennium. The shout from Jesus will be the command to call the saints up to meet Him in the air at the Rapture. This command signals the end of the age. When the apostle John was taken up to heaven in 96 AD, to see a vision of the events of the Tribulation Period, it was a type of the Rapture.

> Rev 4:1 *After this I looked, and there before me was a door standing open in heaven. **And the voice I had first heard speaking to me like a trumpet said, "Come up here, and I will show you what must take place after this."*** (NIV)

The voice sounding like a trumpet is Jesus calling John to come up to heaven to show him the vision. That is exactly how Jesus will call up the saints at the Rapture, commanding them to *"come up here"* to meet Him in the air.

The voice of Jesus calling the saints up to meet Him at the Day of Christ is also the trumpet that starts the Day of the Lord and that trumpet sound will be the same trumpet sound to start the Jewish festival of Rosh Hashanah, also known as the Feast of Trumpets. At the beginning of the Day of the Lord, on Rosh Hashanah, Jesus will be crowned as King of Kings and Lord of Lords and will be seated on His throne. John sees a second vision of Jesus (the first vision was on the island of Patmos in Revelation 1:12), only this time He is in heaven on a throne. This is the scene we just mentioned above. What a beautiful sight this vision must have been when John beheld the newly crowned King.

> Rev 4:2-3 *At once I was in the Spirit, <u>and there before me was a throne in heaven with someone sitting on it</u>. And the one who sat there had the appearance of jasper and carnelian. A rainbow, resembling an emerald, encircled the throne.* (NIV)

What a wonderful picture of Jesus setting on the throne with a rainbow round about it.

> Zech 14:9 *<u>And the LORD shall be king over all the earth</u>: in that day shall there be one LORD, and his name one.* (KJV)

During the last two thousand years, following His death on the cross and His resurrection, Jesus has been at the right hand of God waiting to be coronated as King of His kingdom. *"Your kingdom come. Your will be done on earth as it is in heaven,"* will finally come to be realized.

As a King, it will be up to Jesus to judge and by His righteous judgment He will cleanse the earth during a period known as the Tribulation Period. While the King is getting ready to cleanse the earth He will be preparing for a wedding in heaven. Jesus will be the bridegroom and the church will be the bride. What a glorious time it will be in heaven and what a horrible time it will be on earth. The wedding will take place in heaven just before the Tribulation Period begins and Jesus with His new wife will take part in the Marriage Feast in heaven.

After that Jesus will bring His kingdom to the earth to attend the Great Supper of God. This of course will take place after the Battle of Armageddon. Armageddon and the Great Supper of God will take place on Yom Kippur. Yom Kippur is the Jewish festival for the Day of Atonement. It will be atonement for those Jews who are saved and still alive at the end of the Tribulation Period. The righteous or those who believe in Jesus Christ *After the Rapture* will be allowed to continue living on earth throughout the remainder of the Day of the Lord (Millennium). The wicked or unsaved people will be purged from the earth and their souls will be sent to Hades (Hell) to await the judgment of all the unsaved people throughout history. This will occur after the Millennium is over. It is known in the Bible as the Great White Throne Judgment. For the people who have accepted Jesus Christ as their personal Savior, during their time on earth, it will be forever with the Lord throughout eternity. For those who knew Him not, it will be separation from God and everlasting torment for eternity.

Day of the Lord

The standard definition for the Day of the Lord among most Bible historians and prophecy teachers today is:

> A phrase used in the Bible to emphasize special interventions of God in human history. Times when God will intervene in the affairs of mankind; to judge the nations, discipline Israel and establish His rule in the Messianic Kingdom. This could include times in the past as well as times in the future.

The point at which I differ from this definition is that the Day of the Lord has played a part in past history. I believe that the Day of the Lord is only a single time period referred to in the entire Bible and is in fact the Messianic Kingdom. All the references to the Day of the Lord, including both the Old Testament and the New Testament, are going to be played out in the future during the Millennium.

Another common thought among some prophecy teachers today is that the Day of the Lord will be a separate time period that will exist between the church age (Dispensation of Grace) and the Millennium. Some believe that this period will last for seven years and will include the Tribulation Period or the last period of Daniel's Seventy Weeks. My belief is that this seven-year period will take place at the beginning of the Millennium.

In this first chapter I have presented an overview of what this book is all about. As I have been studying Bible prophecy over the years, I could never put a chronological order of events together that would make the scriptures synchronize or all come together in agreement and still I do not claim to have all the answers. I only ask that you read the book with an open mind and certainly look at the scripture references. As all of us draw near to the second coming of our Lord and Savior, Jesus Christ, God will reveal, more and more, the meaning of His total plan through men of God. Now we will continue with a more concise and detailed study of the things contained in this first chapter.

CHAPTER TWO

IN THE BEGINNING

PLAN

Did you know that God has a plan? He had it even before He created any of the heavens, earth or anything in heaven or earth. It is called the <u>plan of salvation</u>.

2 Tim 1:9   *who has saved us and called us with a holy calling, not according to our works, but according to His own purpose and grace which was given to us in Christ Jesus <u>**before time began,**</u>* (NKJ)

Eph 1:9-10   ***And he made known to us the mystery of his will according to his good pleasure, which he purposed in Christ, <u>to be put into effect when the times will have reached their fulfillment</u>***—*to bring all things in heaven and on earth together under one head, even Christ.* (NIV)

1 Pet 1:18-20   *knowing that you were not redeemed with perishable things like silver or gold from your futile way of life inherited from your forefathers, but with precious blood, as of a lamb unblemished and spotless, {the blood} of Christ.* ***For He was foreknown before the foundation of the world, but has appeared in these last times for the sake of you...*** (NAS)

Although God did not have a beginning, nor does He have an ending, time as we know it today had its beginning when God created the sun and the moon.

Gen 1:14-19   *Then God said,* <u>***"Let there be lights in the firmament of the heavens to divide the day from the night; and let them be for signs and seasons, and for days and years;***</u> *"and let them be for lights in the firmament of the heavens to give light on the earth"; and it was so.* ***Then God made two great lights: the greater light to rule the day, and the lesser light to rule the night. He made the stars also. God set them in the firmament of the heavens to give light on the earth, and to rule over the day and over the night, and to divide the light from the darkness. And God saw that it was good.*** *So the evening and the morning were the fourth day.* (NKJ)

Now we have seconds, minutes, hours, days, weeks, months, and years. That is how we measure time. Time also has an ending. It will end after the period known as the Millennium when we no longer need the sun and moon for light.

In the Beginning

Rev 21:23 *<u>The city does not need the sun or the moon to shine on it, for the glory of God gives it light, and the Lamb is its lamp.</u>* (NIV)

Eternity existed before we had time and will continue to exist after time, as we know it, no longer exists. Therefore, God was and always will be in eternity.

This period of time, of which the plan of salvation plays out, will be the period that the created beings, including the celestial (heavenly) and terrestrial (human) beings, decide where they will spend eternity. The two choices they have are either heaven (with God) or hell (without God) forever in eternity.

Theologians, or for that matter scientists, are not sure, nor do they all agree on, when God's six days of creation occurred. Many Bible scholars and teachers of eschatology (the study of end-time events) believe that the fall of mankind happened about six thousand years ago, approximately four thousand years before Christ was crucified. Starting with eternity, here are a few major personalities and events from the Bible on a time-line to bring you up to the twentieth century (1900 AD) where our study begins.

(See time-line on the next page!!!)

The dates used for this time-line are not exact as nobody but God knows the exact dates that all these events occurred. I took them from various study guides to show you how history proceeded down through the centuries. This time-line covers almost six thousand years after the fall of man. The time period we are going to study in this book was referred to when the disciples had asked Jesus about it just a few days before He was crucified—the sign of His coming and the end of the age.

Matt 24:1-3 *Jesus left the temple and was walking away when his disciples came up to him to call his attention to its buildings. "Do you see all these things?" he asked. "I tell you the truth, not one stone here will be left on another; every one will be thrown down." As Jesus was sitting on the Mount of Olives, the disciples came to him privately. "<u>Tell us</u>," they said, "<u>when will this happen, and what will be the sign of your coming and of the end of the age</u>?"* (NIV)

This scene pictured here is in Jerusalem as Jesus was leaving the Temple. It was just days before the Passover Feast. The disciples were pointing out how beautiful the Temple buildings were. King Herod the Great was appointed King by the Romans over Judea, which included Jerusalem, starting in 37 BC and ending in 4 BC. In 20 BC, Herod, determined to please the Jewish people, started rebuilding their place of worship. He surrounded the whole enclosure with magnificent porches, particularly the royal portico along the southern wall. Even though our scene is in 30 AD, work on the Temple was not completed until 64 AD. The prophecy of, *"there shall not be left here one stone upon another that shall not be thrown down,"* in Matthew 24:2, was given to the disciples directly by Jesus Himself. That prophecy was literally fulfilled just six years after the rebuilding of the Temple was completed. In 70 AD, the Roman General Titus destroyed Jerusalem and the Temple. Since

AFTER THE RAPTURE

TIME-LINE

4000 BC	3378	2944	2344	?
FALL OF MANKIND				

CREATION? ADAM & EVE ENOCH NOAH NIMROD
ETERNITY
GARDEN OF EDEN TREE OF KNOWLEDGE FLOOD TOWER OF BABEL

2165	2065	2005	1915	1525	1445	1237	1191	1067

ABRAHAM ISAAC JACOB **EGYPTIANS** RAMSES II MOSES DEBORAH GIDEON SAMSON
12 TRIBES

FATHER OF ISRAEL AND MANY NATIONS   430 YEARS IN EXILE IN EGYPT (JOSEPH)   40 YEARS OF WANDERING IN WILDERNESS   PERIOD OF JUDGES

1043 1011 971	931	845	722	606 / 586	539

SAUL DAVID SOLOMON DIVIDED MONARCHY **ASSYRIANS** **BABYLONIANS** **MEDO-PERSIANS**
TEMPLE BUILT REHOBOAM (JUDAH) SENNACHERIB NEBUCHADNEZZAR CYRUS
          JEROBOAM (ISRAEL)   TEMPLE DESTROYED TEMPLE REBUILT

PERIOD OF KINGS   DIVIDED KINGDOM
                              MAJOR & MINOR PROPHETS
                  OBADIAH ISAIAH JEREMIAH DANIEL EZEKIEL ZACHARIAH

433	322	63	20	5	4 BC	30 AD	35	44	60	60?

                                    BIRTH OF
GREEK **ROMAN**   JOHN **JESUS**   JESUS   PAUL'S   JAMES
ALEXANDER CAESAR THE BAPTIST   CONVERSION PETER
THE GREAT   HEROD   PAUL
MALACHI   TEMPLE REDONE   CRUCIFIED   MARTYRED
...PERIOD OF SILENCE FROM HEAVEN...   & RESURRECTED   APOSTLES
.........NO PROPHET FROM GOD.........   NEW TESTAMENT WRITTEN

70	96	313	1096-1312	1492	1776	1812	1900

TITUS APOSTLE CONSTANTINE THE CRUSADES COLUMBUS AMERICA NAPOLEON
       JOHN AT THE GREAT   DISCOVERS IS
       PATMOS   AMERICA   BORN

TEMPLE   DECLARED
DESTROYED   CHRISTIANITY
                TO BE ROMAN
                STATE RELIGION

............................DISPENSATION OF GRACE............................
(PERIOD BETWEEN 1ST & 2ND COMING OF CHRIST)

then Jerusalem has been rebuilt as a city, but to this day the Jewish people have not been allowed to rebuild the Temple. The next time the Temple will be rebuilt will be discussed later on in another chapter.

At this time I might add that God's time piece is the tiny nation of Israel. The chosen people (the Jewish people) and the area known as the Middle East is where the history of mankind will end its phase of dominance and God will begin the Kingdom Age, before history plays out its final resolution a thousands years later. It is also the place where the final war, after the Tribulation Period is over, will culminate. At that time **ALL** the nations of the world will come together in the nation of Israel against God Himself—at the Battle of **Armageddon**.

> Rev 19:19 *And I saw the beast, and the kings of the earth, and their armies, gathered together to make war against him that sat on the horse, and against his army.* (KJV)

CHAPTER THREE

WHAT DAY IS IT ?

10-26-96

Why it is Saturday, October 26, 1996. Well that was easy! It is not quite that simple in the scriptures. To try to understand what Jesus meant when He was revealing prophetic events, it is really imperative that the time sequence He is referring to is in the correct order. The Holy Scriptures are not organized and written in chronological order. In both the Old Testament and the New Testament, the time frame of an event being discussed can catapult forward thousands of years into the future and just as suddenly return to the present time. The time can jump ahead or fall behind from just a few years to hundreds or even thousands of years. A good example of this can be found in Daniel 9:24-27. In these few short verses it covers the time period of 483 years before Christ was crucified to the end of the Tribulation Period and includes a hidden period of 2000 years called the Dispensation of Grace. There are two prerequisites for teaching from the Bible. They are:

1. The in-filling of the Holy Spirit.
2. A thorough understanding of the Scriptures.

Something else that needs to be followed when studying God's word is to know who He is speaking to or about in the particular scriptures you are studying. When the apostle Paul was instructing Timothy and ultimately pastors and teachers throughout the church age, in 2 Timothy 2:15, he said, *"Study to show thyself approved unto God, a workman that needeth not to be ashamed, rightly dividing the word of truth."* In other words, do your best to present yourself to God as one approved, do not be ashamed about it and correctly handle the word of God. Make sure what time frame He is referring to; that is past, present or future. Many Bible scholars have erred with their interpretations or predictions because they were referring to either the wrong person, place, nation, event or even the wrong time frame.

This is an excellent time to add that God does not reveal all the meaning of scripture to any one person at any one time. One of the first signs of a cult is when the leader of the group proclaims that he or she knows the whole meaning of the Bible and that God revealed everything to him or her, including new revelations adding to the existing Bible. My advice to you if you are in a situation like this is to get out of it and into a real Bible believing congregation. God actually uses thousands of people throughout history to teach people the way back to Him, which is the theme of the Bible and this book. In Old Testament times, God used prophets with the aid of the Holy Spirit to teach the people. In the New Testament, He uses disciples, apostles, evangelists, pastors, scholars, you and me to know what the meaning of the Bible has to say to us, but on this side of heaven we are not allowed to know everything, even as born again believers. We are presently still living in a sinful world. Paul in the "love" chapter to the Corinthians tells us that at the present time mankind in his finite mind can only comprehend everything in part, but God will reveal everything to us fully at His second coming.

What Day Is It?

1 Cor 13:9-12 *For we know in part, and we prophesy in part. But when that which is perfect is come, then that which is in part shall be done away. When I was a child, I spake as a child, I understood as a child, I thought as a child: but when I became a man, I put away childish things.* **For now we see through a glass, darkly; but then face to face: now I know in part; but then shall I know even as also I am known.** (KJV)

I would like to remind Bible scholars and especially students of eschatology that they should not be too dogmatic about their predictions of unfulfilled prophetic events. The only thing I want to be dogmatic about is that everyone **must** accept Jesus Christ as their personal Savior and believe that He died on the cross for them. He took their place on the cross and His shed blood washed their sins away.

Rom 10:8-10 *But what does it say? "The word is near you; it is in your mouth and in your heart," that is, the word of faith we are proclaiming:* **That if you confess with your mouth, "Jesus is Lord," and believe in your heart that God raised him from the dead, you will be saved.** *For it is with your heart that you believe and are justified, and it is with your mouth that you confess and are saved.* (NIV)

I have been involved with Bible prophecy for more than 20 years. I remember back many years ago when my business accountant Rich Bartels made the comment after a mens Bible study we were in that I should write a book about Bible prophecy. I laughed about it at the time, but in the last few years the Lord has laid it on my heart to write that book that Rich was talking about. I want to thank you Rich and list a few of the Bible teachers whose materials I have been studying throughout the years. They include: Tim LaHaye, Clarence Larkin, J. R. Church, Gary Stearman, David Webber, Noah Hutchings, J. Dwight Pentecost, H.A. Ironside, E.W. Bullinger, Alva J. McClain, Zola Levitt, Charles Swindol, John G. Walvoord, Henry M. Morris, M. R. DeHaan, Gary G. Cohen, Salem Kirban, Dave Hunt, Mike Russ, F. Kenton Beshore, F. F. Bruce, C. S. Lewis, David Reagan, Hal Lindsey, Dennis Fountain, Jack Van Impe, Spiros Zodheates, Avi Ben Mordechai, Dave Breese, Paul N. Benware and probably a few names I have missed mentioning. Special thanks goes to assistant Pastor Bill Berg from Congregation Roeh Israel, in Denver, Colorado, for taking time out of his busy schedule to read the manuscript and for working with me on the Jewish transliteration on the charts in this book.

DAY

Now it is time to resume our study on "day." In the Scriptures, a day can be the time period of 24 hours of one period of light and one period of darkness. It can mean from sunrise to sunset or from one sunset to the next. It can also mean a space of time defined by an associated term, as in age. The term "Day of the Lord" is not a 24 hour day, but a period lasting one thousand years. We will do our study on the "last day," which is "the Day of the

Lord," starting with chapter eight of this book.

In Ezekiel, God is symbolizing the siege of Jerusalem that will take place. The story concerns the divided Kingdoms of Israel and Judah and is about the transgression of the Jewish people against God. Israel's sin is for 390 days and Judah's is for 40 days, for a total of 430 days. Then note in verse six that each day that Ezekiel lies on his side will actually represent one year, so that the transgression will actually be for 430 years instead of 430 days. The one day for one year theory is also used in Daniel's seventy weeks. Anybody who knows anything about Bible prophecy should be familiar with the seventy-weeks of Daniel. In it, the seventy weeks equal 490 days (years) of which the last week of seven days equals seven years, this of course being the Tribulation Period. So we often see judgment on the Israelites symbolized in days, but in actuality their punishment equates into years.

> Ezek 4:1-8 "*Now, son of man, take a clay tablet, put it in front of you and draw the city of Jerusalem on it. Then lay siege to it: Erect siege works against it, build a ramp up to it, set up camps against it and put battering rams around it. Then take an iron pan, place it as an iron wall between you and the city and turn your face toward it. It will be under siege, and you shall besiege it. **This will be a sign to the house of Israel.** "Then lie on your left side and put the sin of the house of Israel upon yourself. You are to bear their sin for the number of days you lie on your side. **I have assigned you the same number of days as the years of their sin.** So for 390 days you will bear the sin of the house of Israel. "After you have finished this, lie down again, this time on your right side, and bear the sin of the house of Judah. **I have assigned you 40 days, a day for each year.** Turn your face toward the siege of Jerusalem and with bared arm prophesy against her. I will tie you up with ropes so that you cannot turn from one side to the other until you have finished the days of your siege.* (NIV)

Also note Numbers 14:26-35, for an example, as we see the punishment of the Israelites as they suffer for their sins—forty years of punishment for forty days of sin. So every time "day" is used in scripture, it needs to be noted that it is not always a day as we know it in the English language. Rev. Clarence Larkin has a chart that explains the "day" or "days" theory. It is titled, *The Prophetic Days of Scripture.* [1] In it, he explains the different days of time periods in the Bible. Listed below are the different days mentioned in his chart.

SCRIPTURE	**DAY**	**PERTAINS TO-LOCATION**		**TIME SPAN**
John 8:56	Days of His flesh	Jesus Christ	Physical Life on Earth	33 ½ Years
Hebrews 5:7	Day of Jesus	Jesus Christ	Earthly Ministry	3 ½ Years
2 Cor 6:2	Day of Salvation	Church	Earth between 1st & 2nd coming of Christ	2000 years ?

What Day Is It?

SCRIPTURE	DAY	PERTAINS TO	LOCATION	TIME SPAN
1 Cor 4:3	Day of Man	Man	Earth	2000 years
Acts 13:33 Hebrews 5:5	Day of the Son	Jesus Christ	Heaven-Right Hand of God	2000 years
Phil 1:6,10	Day of Christ	Resurrected Saints	Heaven City of God	1000 years
Joel 2:1-11	Day of the Lord	Jesus Jesus & Man	Heaven Earth	10 years 990 years
2 Thes 2:1-12	Day of Antichrist	Satan	Earth after Rapture to Armageddon	9 years plus 30 days
James 5:5 Isaiah 30:25	Day of Slaughter *	Man	Armageddon	10th year of the Day of the Lord
Joel 2:31	Great & Terrible Day of the Lord *	Jesus	Earth at 2nd Half of the Tribulation Period	3 ½ years
2 Peter 3:7	Day of Judgment	Israel Nations	Days of Awe* Armageddon	10 years - Day of the Lord
1 Cor 15:24-28	Day of God	God & Jesus (Saved)	New Heaven & New Earth in Eternity	Eternity (forever)
Rev 20:10-15	Day of God	Satan (Unsaved)	Lake of Fire & Brimstone	Eternity (forever)

* added by the author

LAST DAYS

I do not know whether you know it or not, but we are living in the last days right now. The "last days" had their beginning at the first advent of Jesus Christ and will end at the completion of the Millennium. It is a three thousand-year period. At times in scripture the term "last days" refers to a two thousand year period and at other times it refers to a period of three thousand years. This depends on the context of the period to which it is relating. The first four thousand years, after the fall of man, represent the first four days of the creation week of 1000 years each. After the first advent of Jesus Christ, the last 3000 years of human history are referred to as the last days. When the period is for two thousand years, it is referring to the Dispensation of Grace. Occasionally, it refers to a three thousand year period which would include the Dispensation of Grace and the Day of the Lord. The apostle Peter made an interesting comment in 2 Peter 3:8, he said, *"But, beloved, be not ignorant of this one thing, that one day is with the Lord as a thousand years and a thousand years as one day."* What does that mean? This is a reference to show us that God can count a period of 1000 years as a day, thus creating the 1000 year creation week theory.

The Jewish people have a concept known as the 7000-year week. This theory teaches that the plan of salvation will play out in a 7000-year period. The Jews take the seven days of creation and equate each day of creation with a thousand years. This teaching has existed for thousands of years and is referenced from the book of Psalms.

> Ps 90:4 *<u>For a thousand years in your sight are like a day that has just gone by</u>, or like a watch in the night.* (NIV)

The Jews perceive that mankind has precisely 6000 years to complete his days on earth. After that the people on earth will live under the Divine rule of God for the last 1000 years. They equate this period of 1000 years as a Sabbatical Rest just like the seventh day is the Sabbath of Rest for the Jews. The Jews believe that after the 7000 years are completed, the heavens and earth will be renewed to their original state at creation. It is my belief that this Jewish concept of the 7000 year-week theory is correct and can be substantiated in the New Testament, but please remember as we continue this study that the Bible does not state this concept in so many words.

In chapter three of second Peter, the apostle is warning the Christians that there will be scoffers walking after their own lusts in the last days, questioning the second coming of Jesus Christ. This reference to the "last days," refers mainly to the 2000 years of the Dispensation of Grace. In verse nine, Peter reminds us that the Lord is not slack concerning His promise about His coming back again.

In 2 Peter 3 we have another example of how the different time periods in the Bible can jump around. Also look at how many time periods are used with "day" or "days."

> 2 Pet 3:3-12 *First of all, you must understand that in <u>the last days</u> scoffers will come, scoffing and following their own evil desires. They will say, "<u>Where is this 'coming' he promised</u>? Ever since our fathers died, everything goes on as it has since the beginning of creation." But they deliberately forget that long ago by God's word the heavens existed and the earth was formed out of water and by water. By these waters also the world of that time was deluged and destroyed. By the same word the present heavens and earth are reserved for fire, being kept for <u>the day of judgment and destruction of unGodly men</u>. But do not forget this one thing, dear friends: <u>With the Lord a day is like a thousand years, and a thousand years are like a day</u>. The Lord is not slow in keeping his promise, as some understand slowness. He is patient with you, not wanting anyone to perish, but everyone to come to repentance. But <u>the day of the Lord</u> will come like a thief. The heavens will disappear with a roar; the elements will be destroyed by fire, and the earth and everything in it will be laid bare. Since everything will be destroyed in this way, what kind of people ought you to be? You ought to live holy and Godly lives as you look forward to <u>the day of God</u> and speed its coming. That day will bring about the destruction of the heavens by fire, and the elements will melt in the heat.* (NIV)

What Day Is It?

VERSE	REFERENCE	TIME PERIOD COVERED
3 & 4	Last days	Between 1st & 2nd coming of Christ-probably two thousand years (if Jesus comes back in our lifetime)
7	Day of judgment	Armageddon - fire on the day of judgment
8	One day	A thousand years
10	Day of the Lord	Starts at the end of the Dispensation of Grace and covers all the Millennium - 1000 Years
12	Day of God	Forever (eternity with God)

What a great chapter, Peter talks about the beginning of creation in verse four and ends in eternity with God in verse twelve. He covers the entire period of what we know of as "time." Here God is telling us, through Peter, that at times a day is referred to as a thousand-year period of time. A great example of this is the Millennium. It lasts a thousand years and is the period referred to in scripture as the Day of the Lord and at times the Day of Christ.

> Rev 20:2-7 *He seized the dragon, that ancient serpent, who is the devil, or Satan, and bound him for **a thousand years**. He threw him into the Abyss, and locked and sealed it over him, to keep him from deceiving the nations anymore until **the thousand years** were ended. After that, he must be set free for a short time. I saw thrones on which were seated those who had been given authority to judge. And I saw the souls of those who had been beheaded because of their testimony for Jesus and because of the word of God. They had not worshiped the beast or his image and had not received his mark on their foreheads or their hands. They came to life and reigned with Christ **a thousand years**. (The rest of the dead did not come to life until **the thousand years** were ended.) This is the first resurrection. Blessed and holy are those who have part in the first resurrection. The second death has no power over them, but they will be priests of God and of Christ and will reign with him for **a thousand years**. When **the thousand years** are over, Satan will be released from his prison* (NIV)

In the verses above, in 2 Peter 3, we find the parallel verse to the Old Testament concept of the ancient Jewish teaching of the creation week. With God, a day can be a thousand years and a thousand years can be a day. This is one method God uses to teach the total plan He has for mankind. It separates the ages or dispensations into distinct periods.

How can we be sure we are living in the last days? In the first chapter of Hebrews, in verse one, it says that God spoke to the people at various times and in different ways and in the past by prophets. "In the past," it is referring to the time before Jesus Christ came to earth in a fleshly body like man. It is referring to Old Testament times. In the next verse, it refers to "these last days," as God speaking to us by His Son Jesus Christ. So it is crystal clear that "the last days" begin after Christ's first advent.

> Heb 1:1-2   ***In the past** God spoke to our forefathers through the prophets at many times and in various ways, **but in these last days he has spoken to us by his Son**, whom he appointed heir of all things, and through whom he made the universe.* (NIV)

> Heb 9:26   *Then Christ would have had to suffer many times since the creation of the world. **But now he has appeared once for all at the end of the ages** to do away with sin by the sacrifice of himself.* (NIV)

> 1 Pet 1:19-20   *but with the precious blood of Christ, a lamb without blemish or defect. **He was chosen before the creation of the world, but was revealed in these last times** for your sake.* (NIV)

Let us look at a couple of references to the last 1000 year period of the "last days." This day is the last day and is called the Day of the Lord and at times the Day of Christ.

> Isa 2:2   *And it shall come to pass in **the last days**, that the mountain of the LORD's house shall be established in the top of the mountains, and shall be exalted above the hills; and all nations shall flow unto it.* (KJV)

> Micah 4:1   *But in **the last days** it shall come to pass, that the mountain of the house of the LORD shall be established in the top of the mountains, and it shall be exalted above the hills; and people shall flow unto it.* (KJV)

Now look at 2 Timothy 3, to see what the New Testament tells us *"the last days"* have in store for us. Not a pretty picture, is it? It is referring to the times after Christ.

> 2 Tim 3:1-5   ***But mark this: There will be terrible times in the last days.*** *People will be lovers of themselves, lovers of money, boastful, proud, abusive, disobedient to their parents, ungrateful, unholy, without love, unforgiving, slanderous, without self-control, brutal, not lovers of the good, treacherous, rash, conceited, lovers of pleasure rather than lovers of God—**having a form of Godliness but denying its power.** Have nothing to do with them.* (NIV)

This portion of the last days will include the Dispensation of Grace and the first nine years of the Day of the Lord. Look at the world today! Sound familiar? Do not forget that this description of the "last days" will be far worse at the close of the age when the world is in a state of apostasy just prior to the Lord's second coming. The very worst time of this description of mankind will play out during the Tribulation Period.

Throughout history, no matter how bad mankind becomes, it is God's will that no one should perish. God is patient with man and wants everyone to come to repentance.

> 2 Pet 3:9 *<u>**The Lord is not slow in keeping his promise,**</u> as some understand slowness. <u>**He is patient with you, not wanting anyone to perish, but everyone to come to repentance.**</u>* (NIV)

To the age-old question of whether mankind can and does learn from the past, Alva J. McClain makes this comment in his book, *The Greatness of the Kingdom*.

What then can we learn from past history that we may be able to infer something reliable about what to expect in the future? Well, if there is anything crystal-clear in Biblical history, it is that the existence of our sinful race falls into periods of time (call them *eras, ages, dispensations*, or whatever you will), and that each age represents an advance over the preceding age, when looked at from the standpoint of what God is giving and doing for man. It is true that sinful man is always failing; but where sin abounded, grace did much more abound. Thus to the old question, "Is the world getting better or worse?" from one standpoint we might answer, "The *age* is getting worse, but the course of history by the grace of God is moving forward." [2]

Four more New Testament verses, where some list *"time"* or *"times,"* instead of *"last days,"* are all referring to the time after the first appearing of Jesus. They are:

> 1 Pet 1:20 *He was chosen before the creation of the world, but was revealed in **these last times** for your sake.* (NIV)

> 2 Pet 3:3-4 *First of all, you must understand that in **the last days** scoffers will come, scoffing and following their own evil desires. They will say, "Where is this 'coming' he promised? Ever since our fathers died, everything goes on as it has since the beginning of creation."* (NIV)

> 1 John 2:18 *Little children, it is **the last time:** and as ye have heard that antichrist shall come, even now are there many antichrists; whereby we know that it is **the last time.*** (KJV)

> Jude 1:18 *They said to you, "In **the last times** there will be scoffers who will follow their own unGodly desires."* (NIV)

Prophecy teachers today usually refer to the last days as the days just prior to the second coming of Christ. The concept of the last days paints a much broader picture than that for this time period. After establishing the last days as a three thousand-year period, the chronological order of future history begins to fall into place. In a sense no harm can come

AFTER THE RAPTURE

from saying that we are living in the last days, meaning that the last days are the days just prior to the return of Christ. The reason for that is no matter how you refer to the last days, we are living in the final days just prior to Christ's return!

LAST DAY

This is the last day of 1000 years that fulfills the 7000 year period of the creation week. It is the third and final day of the last days. It is the Sabbatical Rest spoken of by the Old Testament prophets. It is the Kingdom Age. It is the Day of the Lord. It is the Day of Christ. It is the finale! The last dispensation or age before the age of eternity (Day of God).

As the Day of Christ, it will be 1000 years of peace for the resurrected saints who will dwell in heaven during this time. As the Kingdom Age, Jesus will reign for 1000 years, beginning in heaven for a short time and then establishing His throne on earth. As the Day of the Lord, it will begin with a short period of doom and gloom and end in peace. An old Jewish belief likens this period with a literal twenty-four-hour day. The Jews begin their days at sunset and because of this their day begins in darkness and ends in light. So they believe that the Sabbatical Rest of 1000 years will begin with darkness and end in light. It will start out in turmoil and end in peace. Oh how right they are!

After Jesus becomes King in heaven at the beginning of this last day, He will have some duties to perform in order to get the earth ready for peace. He will begin His judgeship in heaven with the Judgment Seat of Christ, where the saints will receive their rewards. Then Jesus will get married, which will also take place in heaven. After that His focus will turn to the task here on earth. Over the next seven years Jesus will once more shake the earth and this time it will include the heavens.

Heb 12:25-29 *See to it that you do not refuse him who speaks. If they did not escape when they refused him who warned them on earth, how much less will we, if we turn away from him who warns us from heaven? At that time his voice shook the earth, but now he has promised, **"Once more I will shake not only the earth but also the heavens."** The words "once more" indicate the removing of what can be shaken—that is, created things—so that what cannot be shaken may remain. Therefore, since we are receiving a kingdom that cannot be shaken, let us be thankful, and so worship God acceptably with reverence and awe, for our **"God is a consuming fire."** (NIV)*

Amos 5:18-20 ***Woe to you who long for the day of the LORD! Why do you long for the day of the LORD?*** *That day will be darkness, not light. It will be as though a man fled from a lion only to meet a bear, as though he entered his house and rested his hand on the wall only to have a snake bite him.* ***Will not the day of the LORD be darkness, not light—pitch-dark, without a ray of brightness?*** *(NIV)*

It will be time for the day of judgment and the destruction of ungodly men. It will be

What Day Is It?

time to make the land desolate and to destroy the sinners within it.

2 Pet 3:7-10 — *By the same word the present heavens and earth are reserved for fire, <u>being kept for the day of judgment and destruction of unGodly men</u>. But do not forget this one thing, dear friends: With the Lord a day is like a thousand years, and a thousand years are like a day. The Lord is not slow in keeping his promise, as some understand slowness. He is patient with you, not wanting anyone to perish, but everyone to come to repentance. <u>But the day of the Lord will come like a thief</u>. The heavens will disappear with a roar; the elements will be destroyed by fire, and the earth and everything in it will be laid bare.* (NIV)

Isa 13:6-13 — *<u>Wail, for the day of the LORD is near; it will come like destruction from the Almighty</u>. Because of this, all hands will go limp, every man's heart will melt. Terror will seize them, pain and anguish will grip them; they will writhe like a woman in labor. They will look aghast at each other, their faces aflame. See, the day of the LORD is coming a cruel day, with wrath and fierce anger—<u>to make the land desolate and destroy the sinners within it</u>. The stars of heaven and their constellations will not show their light. The rising sun will be darkened and the moon will not give its light. <u>I will punish the world for its evil, the wicked for their sins</u>. I will put an end to the arrogance of the haughty and will humble the pride of the ruthless. I will make man scarcer than pure gold, more rare than the gold of Ophir. Therefore I will make the heavens tremble; and the earth will shake from its place at the wrath of the LORD Almighty, in the day of his burning anger.* (NIV)

Ps 104:35 — *<u>May sinners be consumed from the earth, and the wicked be no more</u>. Bless the LORD, O my soul! Praise the LORD!* (NKJ)

Prov 2:22 — *But the wicked will be cut off from the earth, and the unfaithful will be uprooted from it.* (NKJ)

Isa 24:1 — *<u>See, the LORD is going to lay waste the earth and devastate it</u>; he will ruin its face and scatter its inhabitants—* (NIV)

Zeph 1:2-3 — *"<u>I will sweep away everything from the face of the earth</u>," declares the LORD. "I will sweep away both men and animals; I will sweep away the birds of the air and the fish of the sea. <u>The wicked will have only heaps of rubble when I cut off man from the face of the earth</u>," declares the LORD.* (NIV)

AFTER THE RAPTURE

The transgressions weigh so heavy upon the people of the earth that it falls never to rise again in this state. Punishment will be for those in heaven, along with those on earth.

Isa 24:19-23　*__The earth is broken up, the earth is split asunder, the earth is thoroughly shaken__. The earth reels like a drunkard, it sways like a hut in the wind; __so heavy upon it is the guilt of its rebellion that it falls—never to rise again__. In that day the LORD will punish the powers in the heavens above and the kings on the earth below. They will be herded together like prisoners bound in a dungeon; they will be shut up in prison and be punished after many days. The moon will be abashed, the sun ashamed; for the LORD Almighty will reign on Mount Zion and in Jerusalem, and before its elders, gloriously.* (NIV)

It is a day of wrath and it will come like destruction from the Almighty.

Zeph 1:14-18　*"__The great day of the LORD is near—near and coming quickly__. Listen! The cry on the day of the LORD will be bitter, the shouting of the warrior there. That day will be a day of wrath, a day of distress and anguish, a day of trouble and ruin, a day of darkness and gloom, a day of clouds and blackness, a day of trumpet and battle cry against the fortified cities and against the corner towers. I will bring distress on the people and they will walk like blind men, because they have sinned against the LORD. Their blood will be poured out like dust and their entrails like filth. Neither their silver nor their gold will be able to save them on the day of the LORD's wrath. __In the fire of his jealousy the whole world will be consumed, for he will make a sudden end of all who live in the earth__."* (NIV)

Joel 1:15　*Alas for that day! For the day of the LORD is near; it will come like destruction from the Almighty.* (NIV)

All this will take place after Jesus appears at the Rapture and begins His kingdom reign. Notice that His kingdom will begin at His appearing.

2 Tim 4:1-2　*I charge you therefore before God and __the Lord Jesus Christ, who will judge the living and the dead at His appearing and His kingdom__: Preach the word! Be ready in season and out of season. Convince, rebuke, exhort, with all longsuffering and teaching.* (NKJ)

It is the hour of trial that is coming upon the whole world to test the people living on earth, of which you do not have to be a part, if your heart is right with Jesus.

Rev 3:10　*Since you have kept my command to endure patiently, __I will also*__

keep you from the hour of trial that is going to come upon the whole world to test those who live on the earth. (NIV)

DAY OF CHRIST

The Day of Christ is probably as misunderstood as the Day of the Lord, but once the Day of the Lord is properly positioned in chronological order, the Day of Christ comes into focus. The Kingdom Age, the Day of the Lord and the Day of Christ are all synonymous and represent the 1000 year reign of Jesus Christ as King, with each one having a different significance. The chart *What Day Is It?* on page 761 will show this application of days.

THE KINGDOM AGE represents the 1000 years as they apply to Jesus as King. His kingdom begins in heaven where He begins to judge. After the fierce anger of His judgment is completed Jesus will establish His rule on earth in Jerusalem.

THE DAY OF THE LORD represents a view from a Jewish perspective and is found primarily in the Old Testament, with a few references in the New Testament. This 1000 year period will apply to the scene on earth. *After the Rapture,* the scene on earth will begin with all unbelievers. True believers in Jesus will be removed from the earth at the Rapture. The first few years of the Day of the Lord will be doom and gloom, caused by the fierce anger of the Lord (Jesus), followed by a period of peace for all the nations. After the Battle of Armageddon, the earth will be restored for those people who survive the Battle of Armageddon. They will live in fleshly bodies and repopulate the earth for the remainder of the Day of the Lord.

THE DAY OF CHRIST represents a view from a Christian or church age perspective and is only found in the New Testament, although it will also effect the Old Testament saints. All believers in Jesus as their Savior should look forward—with joy—to the Day of Christ. The Day of Christ begins at the Rapture and lasts for 1000 years. The main focus of the Day of Christ is for those people who are saved and have received their resurrected bodies for eternity. At the Rapture, those who receive their glorious bodies will go to heaven to the place prepared for them by God and live there during the Day of Christ. They will participate in the Judgment Seat of Christ and a wedding, followed by a wedding feast and a wedding banquet (Marriage Supper of the Lamb). During the 1000 year period of the Day of Christ the resurrected saints will abide in the heavenly city of Jerusalem. They will rule and reign with Christ and make periodic visits to earth to worship Jesus and receive instructions from Him in the earthly city of Jerusalem.

After the 1000 year period of the Kingdom Age is over, which is also the Day of the Lord and the Day of Christ, the Day of God will be ushered in. In that period—also known as eternity—God the Father and God the Son will rule forever.

To give you a more detailed picture of the Day of Christ, we begin with it as it applies to us today as church age believers. We look forward to it as a day of joyful anticipation. Notice that the church age ends when the Day of Christ arrives. The Day is approaching!

AFTER THE RAPTURE

Phil 1:3-11 — *I thank my God every time I remember you. In all my prayers for all of you, I always pray with joy because of your partnership in the gospel from the first day until now, being confident of this, that he who began a good work in you will carry it on to completion until **the day of Christ Jesus**. It is right for me to feel this way about all of you, since I have you in my heart; for whether I am in chains or defending and confirming the gospel, all of you share in God's grace with me. God can testify how I long for all of you with the affection of Christ Jesus.* **And this is my prayer: that your love may abound more and more in knowledge and depth of insight, so that you may be able to discern what is best and may be pure and blameless until the day of Christ, filled with the fruit of righteousness that comes through Jesus Christ—to the glory and praise of God.** (NIV)

1 Cor 1:7-9 — *Therefore you do not lack any spiritual gift as you eagerly wait for our Lord Jesus Christ to be revealed.* **He will keep you strong to the end***, so that you will be blameless on* **the day of our Lord Jesus Christ.** *God, who has called you into fellowship with his Son Jesus Christ our Lord, is faithful.* (NIV)

Phil 2:14-16 — *Do everything without complaining or arguing, so that you may become blameless and pure, children of God without fault in a crooked and depraved generation, in which you shine like stars in the universe as you hold out the word of life—in order that I may boast on* **the day of Christ** *that I did not run or labor for nothing.* (NIV)

Heb 10:25 — **Let us not give up meeting together, as some are in the habit of doing, but let us encourage one another—and all the more as you see the Day approaching.** (NIV)

Even as Christians our time of grief is in this life. When Jesus comes back at the Rapture, no one will be able to take our joy from us.

John 16:22-23 — **So with you: Now is your time of grief, but I will see you again and you will rejoice, and no one will take away your joy. In that day you will no longer ask me anything. I tell you the truth, my Father will give you whatever you ask in my name.** (NIV)

John 14:15-21 — *"If you love me, you will obey what I command. And I will ask the Father, and he will give you another Counselor to be with you forever—the Spirit of truth. The world cannot accept him, because it neither sees him nor knows him. But you know him, for he lives with you and will be in you. I will not leave you as orphans; I will come to you. Before long, the world will not see me anymore, but you will* *see me. Because I live, you also will live. **On that day you will realize that I am in my Father, and you are in me, and I am in you.** Whoever has my commands and obeys them, he is the one who loves me. He who loves me will be loved by my Father, and I too will love him and show myself to him."* (NIV)

We should not let the Day of Christ (Rapture) catch us unprepared. By accepting Christ, as our personal Savior, we will be able to escape the Tribulation Period and we will be participants at the Judgment Seat of Christ as we stand before the Son of Man.

Luke 21:34-36 ***"Be careful, or your hearts will be weighed down with dissipation, drunkenness and the anxieties of life, and that day will close on you unexpectedly like a trap. For it will come upon all those who live on the face of the whole earth. Be always on the watch, and pray that you may be able to escape all that is about to happen, and that you may be able to stand before the Son of Man."*** (NIV)

The verses that pertain to the Judgment Seat of Christ mention *"the day"* or *"that day"* referring to the Day of Christ.

Rom 2:16 *This will take place on **the day** when God will judge men's secrets through Jesus Christ, as my gospel declares.* (NIV)

1 Cor 3:13 *his work will be shown for what it is, because **the Day** will bring it to light. It will be revealed with fire, and the fire will test the quality of each man's work.* (NIV)

2 Tim 4:8 ***Now there is in store for me the crown of righteousness, which the Lord, the righteous Judge, will award to me on that day**—and not only to me, but also to all who have longed for his appearing.* (NIV)

Paul, in the last chapter of the last letter he wrote, referred to the safety of God's heavenly kingdom, where his spirit will go at the time of his death.

2 Tim 4:18 ***The Lord will rescue me from every evil attack and will bring me safely to his heavenly kingdom.** To him be glory for ever and ever. Amen.* (NIV)

Jesus referred to the Day of Christ as the kingdom of God.

Luke 6:20-23 ***Looking at his disciples, he said: "Blessed are you who are poor, for yours is the kingdom of God.** Blessed are you who hunger now, for you will be satisfied. Blessed are you who weep now, for you will laugh. Blessed are you when men hate you, when they exclude you*

> *and insult you and reject your name as evil, because of the Son of Man. "Rejoice in <u>that day</u> and leap for joy, <u>because great is your reward in heaven</u>. For that is how their fathers treated the prophets.* (NIV)

Paul again talks about the Day of Christ at the time of the Rapture, when Jesus will be glorified and extolled among believers.

> 2 Thes 1:10 *when He comes, <u>in that Day</u>, to be glorified in His saints and to be admired among all those who believe, because our testimony among you was believed.* (NKJ)

In Paul's second letter to the Thessalonians, we find an instance where Paul mentions both the Day of Christ and the Day of the Lord in the same sentence.

> 2 Thes 2:1-3 <u>*Concerning the coming of our Lord Jesus Christ and our being gathered to him*</u>*, we ask you, brothers, not to become easily <u>unsettled or alarmed</u> by some prophecy, report or letter supposed to have come from us, saying that <u>the day of the Lord</u> has already come. Don't let anyone deceive you in any way, for <u>that day</u> will not come until <u>the rebellion</u> occurs and <u>the man of lawlessness is revealed</u>, the man doomed to destruction.* (NIV)

In the first verse Paul is referring to the Day of Christ, when he mentions the gathering of the believers to meet Jesus in the air at the Rapture. In the second and third verses Paul is talking about the Day of the Lord, which refers to the people who will be left behind at the Rapture, those people will go through the Tribulation Period. At the time Paul wrote this letter to the Thessalonians, they were going through a period of extreme persecution. Because of this persecution someone sent a letter to the Thessalonians purporting it to be from Paul saying that the Day of the Lord was in progress. Nevertheless, Paul warned them not to be deceived by the false letter and informed them that the apostasy must occur and the Antichrist has to be revealed before the Day of the Lord begins.

I believe that the early church, which was made up of a majority of Jewish converts, had a thorough understanding of the concept of the Day of the Lord as it ties in with the Old Testament. These early Christians were taught by Paul that the Day of the Lord was exactly what the Old Testament said it would be—a day of doom and gloom, a day of persecution. A letter came to the people of Thessalonica telling them that they were living in the Day of the Lord, which frightened them. If that were true then they would have missed the Rapture. They were disturbed by this letter. The New Testament did not exist when Paul wrote this second epistle to the Thessalonians. Eventually this letter became part of the New Testament.

In Paul's mild rebuke to the Thessalonians, it is clear that he was a little perturbed by the people who lived in Thessalonica. He was not happy because they were deceived by the false letter they had received. Paul's comment to the Thessalonians in verse five was, *"don't you remember that when I was with you I used to tell you these things?"* (NIV)

What Day Is It?

The true meaning of the Day of the Lord started to become distorted about three hundred years after Jesus left to be at the right hand of God. At that time the leaders of the church began to spiritualize the meaning of scripture. The Jewish teachings of the Old Testament were cast aside for the next sixteen to seventeen hundred years.

Most of the mysteries (new revelations from God) were given to Paul to teach to the church. These new revelations that appear in the New Testament were not allowed to be known to the people before Christ was crucified, because they did not apply to them. Only after the crucifixion did God want people to know the continuing plan of salvation. Paul was given a special task of making these things known to the church. Even Peter made the comment that some of the things that Paul wrote about in his letters were hard to understand. He further comments that those people who were ignorant (untaught) and unstable, twist and distort the scriptures to their own destruction. In other words they were teaching falsely and were headed for hell. This also applies to ignorant and unstable people who are living today.

> 2 Pet 3:15-18   *Bear in mind that our Lord's patience means salvation, just as our dear brother Paul also wrote you with the wisdom that God gave him. He writes the same way in all his letters, speaking in them of these matters. <u>His letters contain some things that are hard to understand, which ignorant and unstable people distort, as they do the other Scriptures, to their own destruction.</u> Therefore, dear friends, since you already know this, be on your guard so that you may not be carried away by the error of lawless men and fall from your secure position. But grow in the grace and knowledge of our Lord and Savior Jesus Christ. To him be glory both now and forever! Amen.* (NIV)

After Jesus sets up His throne on earth and rules from Jerusalem the resurrected saints will abide in heaven for the remainder of the Day of Christ. They are going home to the place God prepared for them a long time ago. The place prepared for the saints in heaven, by God, is actually a city where they will dwell during the Kingdom Age. After the Millennium they will come down to earth with the New Jerusalem. When the New Jerusalem comes down from heaven, after the Kingdom Age is over, the resurrected saints will dwell on the new earth. This will be their dwelling place for eternity. It is a far better place to be than on this present earth. Abel, Enoch, Noah, Abraham and many people from the Old Testament;

> Heb 11:13-16   *All these people were still living by faith when they died. They did not receive the things promised; they only saw them and welcomed them from a distance. And they admitted that they were aliens and strangers on earth. People who say such things show that they are looking for a country of their own. If they had been thinking of the country they had left, they would have had opportunity to return. <u>Instead, they were longing for a better country—a heavenly one. Therefore God is not ashamed to be called their God, for he has prepared a city for them.</u>* (NIV)

KINGDOM AGE

For those of you who are just beginning to study the Bible, the phrase, " Kingdom Age," is a reference to the period when Jesus will be set up as the King of the world. He will reign as King for a thousand years. Actually, Jesus appeared on the scene two thousand years ago to usher in the Kingdom Age, but was rejected by the people of that day.

Mark 1:14-15   *After John was put in prison, Jesus went into Galilee, proclaiming the good news of God.* ***"The time has come,"*** *he said.* ***"The kingdom of God is near.*** *Repent and believe the good news!"* (NIV)

Luke 10:1-11   *After this the Lord appointed seventy-two others and sent them two by two ahead of him to every town and place where he was about to go. He told them, "The harvest is plentiful, but the workers are few. Ask the Lord of the harvest, therefore, to send out workers into his harvest field. Go! I am sending you out like lambs among wolves. Do not take a purse or bag or sandals; and do not greet anyone on the road. "When you enter a house, first say, 'Peace to this house.' If a man of peace is there, your peace will rest on him; if not, it will return to you. Stay in that house, eating and drinking whatever they give you, for the worker deserves his wages. Do not move around from house to house. "When you enter a town and are welcomed, eat what is set before you. Heal the sick who are there and tell them,* ***'The kingdom of God is near you.'*** *But when you enter a town and are not welcomed, go into its streets and say, 'Even the dust of your town that sticks to our feet we wipe off against you. Yet be sure of this:* ***The kingdom of God is near.'*** (NIV)

Because of the rejection Jesus was crucified and went to heaven to be at the right hand of God. The Kingdom Age was postponed for two thousand years. This period is known as the Dispensation of Grace and is the period of time in which we are presently living. This age or period of time will end at the Rapture. Some people confuse this time with the end of the world, but that is not the case. The world as we know it—populated with human beings with fleshly bodies—will not end until shortly after the Kingdom Age comes to a close.

After the present age of the Dispensation of Grace is over, God will crown His Son King and seat Jesus on the throne to rule for a thousand years. It will be the final age or dispensation of time to end the plan of salvation. After the Kingdom Age is completed, Jesus, along with God the Father, will rule the new heavens and new earth. Once Jesus is crowned King, His kingdom will last for a thousand years and after that He will rule jointly with God the Father throughout all eternity.

Luke 1:30-33   *But the angel said to her, "Do not be afraid, Mary, you have found favor with God. You will be with child and give birth to a son, and you are to give him the name Jesus. He will be great and will be* *called the Son of the Most High. **The Lord God will give him the throne of his father David, and he will reign over the house of Jacob forever; his kingdom will never end.**"* (NIV)

Below, I have created a time line to show you how the periods of time are completed in God's plan. It will take 7000 years to come to completion. It is called the Creation Week theory and follows the ancient Jewish theory of one day equals a thousand years and a thousand years equal one day.

We are currently living somewhere toward the end of the first six thousand years. After the fall of Adam and Eve God allowed a period of six thousand years for mankind to return to Him. During the last 6000 years, with most of it in our past, mankind as a whole has basically not come back to God. It will literally take Divine intervention to separate saved people from unsaved people, *After the Rapture*. In order for the Kingdom Age to become peaceful Jesus will have to take drastic measures to accomplish His purpose. Those drastic measures will unfold during the Tribulation Period. After the Tribulation Period is over Jesus will return to earth from heaven—where He was crowned King—to begin His reign on earth during the Kingdom Age.

CREATION WEEK (7 DAYS OR 7000 YEARS)

	FORMER DAYS 4 DAYS OLD TESTAMENT				LAST DAYS 2 DAYS NEW TESTAMENT		1 DAY	DAY OF GOD
	FALL		**CHRIST**				2ND COMING	
							* **DAY OF CHRIST**	
ETERNITY (FOREVER)	1000	2000	3000	4000	5000	6000	7000	ETERNITY (FOREVER)
					CHURCH AGE DISPENSATION OF GRACE		**KINGDOM AGE** **DAY OF THE LORD**	
	DAYS OF MAN 6 DAYS OR 6000 YEARS						1 DAY OR 1000 YEARS OLAM HA-BA	

* We are here

To the Jewish people Rosh Hashanah is a microcosm of world history. It represents the entire Jewish calendar year in miniature and by extension, all world history. Jewish sages, not long after Christ, taught through the Talmud that world history trisects into three periods of two thousand years each. Talmud Tractate Sanhedrin 97a, circa 200 BC, the Tanna rebe (Rabbi) Eliyyahu teaches:

> The world is to exist six thousand years. In the first two
> thousand there is desolation; two thousand years the
> Torah flourished; and the next two thousand years is
> the Messianic era... ³

In this quotation the concept of a week of millenniums can be seen—six days/six thousand years and the seventh day/a one thousand year period of rest is established. The seventh day or the seventh year (a thousand years) being equivalent to the Sabbatical rest.

This concept follows the CREATION WEEK time-line I presented on the previous page and breaks down like this:

YEARS
2000   1– 2000 Adam to Abraham (two thousand years of desolation)
2000   2001– 4000 Abraham to Christ (Period of the Law)
2000   4001– 6000 Christ (1st Advent to 2nd Advent – Dispensation of Grace)
1000   6001– 7000 Kingdom Age/Day of Christ/Day of the Lord (The Last Day)

Based on the principles taught by ancient Jewish teachings and also what is presented in the Bible, concerning the Week of Days and the Week of Millenniums, it strongly suggests that there could very well be 7000 years between the fall of mankind and the last day of redemption. This theory holds a substantial amount of credibility when the correct understanding of the Day of the Lord comes into play. It allows future Bible prophecy to fall into place and also presents a better chronological order.

I cannot express to you how important it is that you distinguish between the times before and after Jesus came to earth in the flesh almost two thousand years ago. The chronological order of events throughout the entire Bible cannot fall into place until the former days (before Christ) and the latter days (after Christ) are understood in their proper perspective. Before Christ the people who were on the earth looked forward to Christ (the Messiah) and after Christ came the people living on the earth are to look back at His first coming and forward to His second coming. The first appearing of Jesus is a real turning point in history as far as a dividing line for understanding Bible prophecy. The correct chronological order of future events need to be analyzed from this pivotal point in history.

Peter speaks of *"the last days"* as *"the last times"* beginning with Jesus. Jesus was chosen to be the Sacrificial Lamb before creation, but was not revealed to the world until after the first four thousand years of human history, as part of God's plan.

> 1 Pet 1:18-20   *For you know that it was not with perishable things such as silver or gold that you were redeemed from the empty way of life handed down to you from your forefathers, but with the precious blood of Christ, a lamb without blemish or defect.* **He was chosen before the creation of the world, <u>but was revealed in these last times for your sake.</u>** *Through him you believe in God, who raised him from the dead and glorified him, and so your faith and hope are in God.* (NIV)

After four thousand years Jesus came to the earth in human form to set up His kingdom, but was rejected by mankind. The Holy Spirit came to live in the hearts of men during the church age period of two thousand years. At the end of the church age Jesus will come down from the right hand of God to meet the saints in the air. A loud command will end the church age and start the Kingdom Age. The voice of Jesus (shout) will be the signal at the Rapture when Jesus will transform all the believers who have died in the past, along with those who remain alive on earth at that time, to be with Him in heaven. Jesus as King during the

What Day Is It?

Kingdom Age will judge the living and the dead. *After the Rapture,* Jesus will judge those people who are alive and remain on earth and also the saints who have been transformed into their resurrected bodies in heaven.

> 2 Tim 4:1   ***In the presence of God and of Christ Jesus, <u>who will judge the living and the dead</u>, <u>and in view of his appearing and his kingdom</u>, I give you this charge:*** (NIV)

AFTER TWO DAYS

In the Old Testament the prophet Hosea makes a very interesting comment that deserves our attention and applies to our study.

> Hosea 5:14-15   *For I will be like a lion to Ephraim, like a great lion to Judah. I will tear them to pieces and go away; I will carry them off, with no one to rescue them. Then I will go back to my place until they admit their guilt. And they will seek my face; in their misery they will earnestly seek me."* (NIV)

> Hosea 6:1-2   *"Come, let us return to the LORD. He has torn us to pieces but he will heal us; he has injured us but he will bind up our wounds. **<u>After two days</u>** he will revive us; **<u>on the third day</u>** he will restore us, that we may live in his presence.* (NIV)

These verses come as a rebuke to the Jewish people, including the divided kingdoms of Israel and Judah. In a few short verses Hosea covers a time span from the time God allows Gentile nations to conquer these two kingdoms to the end of the Millennium. Let us refresh our memory about what Peter said concerning his statement, *"that one day is with the Lord as a thousand years, and a thousand years as one day."* As we apply this to Hosea's scripture we make a very exciting discovery. Now let us break these verses down in Hosea verse by verse.

VERSE	INTERPRETATION
Hosea 5:	
14 *For I will be like a lion to Ephraim, like a great lion to Judah. I will tear them to pieces and go away; I will carry them off,*	In these verses, we have in view the times that God allows the divided kingdoms of Israel (the Assyrians in 722 BC) and Judah (the Babylonians in 606 BC) to be captured, with the Jewish people being led into exile. Notice that the Assyrians are like a lion, while the Babylonians are referred to as a great lion. The significance is that Babylon will be a more powerful nation than Assyria.
with no one to rescue them.	No nation will be allowed to come to the aid of these two kingdoms.

VERSE	INTERPRETATION
15 *Then I will go back to my place until they admit their guilt.*	At first glance this appears to be Jesus who came years after the destruction of Jerusalem in 586 BC, but a closer examination of this text probably points to the glory of the Lord (Shekinah Glory) when God returned to heaven (left the Temple) in 593 BC.
And they will seek my face; in their misery they will earnestly seek me.	During the Tribulation Period the Jewish people will earnestly be looking for God and in the end all Israel will be saved. When Jesus rebuilds the Temple in Jerusalem, after the Battle of Armageddon, the Shekinah Glory will return to dwell among His people (chapter 14 has a detailed account of this).
Hosea 6:	
1 *"Come, let us return to the Lord. He has torn us to pieces but he will heal us; he has injured us but he will bind up our wounds.*	During the Time of Jacob's Trouble the Jewish people will be torn to pieces and injured worse than anytime in their history. Finally, when the persecution is finished, they will say, *"Come, let us return to the Lord"* and be healed. They will finally recognize Jesus as their Messiah. God will dwell in their midst.
2 *After two days he will revive us:*	This is a reference to two days or prophetically speaking, 2000 years of the Dispensation of Grace. Notice that this verse says *"after two days"* meaning after the Dispensation of Grace has ended and the Day of the Lord has begun.
on the third day he will restore us,	The third day is also a reference to the Day of the Lord. After the Time of Jacob's Trouble is completed and Jesus has separated the believers from the unbelievers, the remnant of believers who remain will have accepted the Messiah. Then God will restore the nation of Israel as the head of the nations during the remainder of the Day of the Lord.
that we may live in his presence.	After the nation of Israel is restored, the Jewish people will live in God's Presence in Jerusalem in the land of Israel.

God allowed the Assyrians to defeat the kingdom of Israel and more than a hundred years later Babylon defeated the kingdom of Judah. God did not allow anyone to rescue Israel. Even today, they have not been rescued. In a later chapter we will discuss in more detail just how and when they will finally be rescued.

Although Jesus came to earth almost two thousand years ago, to rescue the Jewish people, they did not accept Him as the Messiah and therefore it delayed their being rescued. At that time Jesus returned to heaven to be at the right hand of God where He exists in His resurrected body. This is where Jesus is at the present time. Jesus will remain in heaven until the Jewish people acknowledge their offense—which is rejecting the Messiah—and seek God's face. *"In their misery,"* is not the persecution that the Jewish people have suffered for the last 2500 years, including the Holocaust of World War II, but the persecution they will suffer *After the Rapture* of the church. In the Time of Jacob's Trouble this prophecy will be fulfilled. After that, they will seek the Lord.

> Zech 12:10 *"And I will pour out on the house of David and the inhabitants of Jerusalem a spirit of grace and supplication. **They will look on me, the one they have pierced**, and they will mourn for him as one mourns for an only child, and grieve bitterly for him as one grieves for a firstborn son.* (NIV)
>
> Rom 11:26 ***And so all Israel will be saved**, as it is written: "The deliverer will come from Zion; he will turn Godlessness away from Jacob.* (NIV)
>
> Hosea 6:1 *"**Come, let us return to the LORD**. He has torn us to pieces but he will heal us; he has injured us but he will bind up our wounds.* (NIV)

Here the Jewish people are acknowledging the Lord. At this time, they know it was God who allowed a people who had turned away from Him to suffer and it will be that same God who will take them back and allow them to live in His Presence. It will take a long time, over 2000 years, but the Jews will finally realize that Jesus was the true Messiah they had been seeking all those years. This prophecy is so important that we need to look at it again.

> Hosea 6:2 ***After two days he will revive us; on the third day he will restore us**, that we may live in his presence.* (NIV)

This is exciting stuff! Bible scholars pretty well agree that the Jewish nation will be set up as the head nation during the Millennium. This period will last 1000 years and since Jesus will rule as King of Kings and Lord of Lords on earth, during most of this time, the Jewish people will live in God's sight with the return of the Divine Presence. Now if we back up to the beginning of this sentence, we can understand that after two days or two thousand years the church age will end and the Day of the Lord will begin. God will revive or allow all the chosen people to return to their homeland and live in peace and security. This prophetic event will be fulfilled during the first half of the Tribulation Period. This was not fulfilled in the 20th Century, as some Bible interpreters suggest. It clearly states that this event will take place after two days or after the Dispensation of Grace is over. *"After two days"* and *"in the third day,"* both refer to the Kingdom Age or the Day of the Lord, but they are two distinct events that take place during this period. The Jewish people will be raised up as the head of the nations after they have suffered through the second half of the Tribulation Period and have acknowledged their Messiah. Here is the chronological order of the events listed in Hosea 5:14 – 6:2.

1. Israel was defeated in 722 BC and Judah was defeated in 606 BC.

AFTER THE RAPTURE

2. In 593 BC, the Divine Presence (Shekinah Glory) returned to His place in heaven.
3. After two days (2000 years), after the end of the Dispensation of Grace and during the first 3½ years of the Tribulation Period, under the false Messiah (the Antichrist), the Jewish nation will be revived. At that time all Israel will return to their homeland.
4. On the third day (Day of the Lord), after Jesus has finished His dealings with the chosen people during the second 3 ½ years of the Tribulation Period (the Time of Jacob' Trouble), the Jewish nation will be restored as head of the nations. The Shekinah Glory will return and the Jewish people will live in God's Presence.

These verses are some of the many verses that lead me to believe that the Rapture of the church is right at our door step. It has been almost two thousand years or two days since the Messiah was cut off (crucified). I truly believe in my heart that Jesus will come back sometime in our generation.

LATTER DAYS

When the prophets were referring to latter days, day, years or time they were making reference to future history for them—after the first four thousand years of human history had transpired. The break point between former days and latter days is the first advent of Jesus Christ. Latter Days should be taken into account as far as the Creation Week theory is concerned. Latter days are the same as last days. Latter and last are both derived from the same Hebrew word - *achariyth*. Former days make up the first four thousand years of human history, while the latter or last days conclude the last three thousand years of human history. We see both periods mentioned in Hebrews.

> Heb 1:1-2   ***In the past*** *God spoke to our forefathers through the prophets at many times and in various ways, but **in these last days** he has spoken to us by his Son, whom he appointed heir of all things, and through whom he made the universe.* (NIV)

All of the verses listed below, pertaining to *"latter,"* are yet future for us today. Their prophetic implication will take place at the time of the second advent of Jesus Christ.

LATTER	SCRIPTURE	TIME PERIOD	DESCRIPTION
Day	Job 19:25-29 *For I know that **my redeemer** liveth, and that he shall stand at **the latter day** upon the earth: And though after my skin worms destroy this body, yet in my flesh shall I see God: Whom I shall see for myself, and mine eyes shall behold, and not another; though my reins be consumed within me. But ye should say, Why persecute*	Day of the Lord	Glorious Return of Jesus

What Day Is It?

LATTER	SCRIPTURE	TIME PERIOD	DESCRIPTION
	we him, seeing the root of the matter is found in me? Be ye afraid of the sword: for wrath bringeth the punishments of the sword, that ye may know there is a judgment. (KJV)		Tribulation Period
Days	Jer 23:19-20 *Behold, a whirlwind of the Lord has gone forth in fury—a violent whirlwind! It will fall violently on the head of the wicked. The anger of the LORD will not turn back until He has executed and performed the thoughts of His heart. In **the latter days** you will understand it perfectly.* (NKJ)	Day of the Lord Dispensation of Grace	Tribulation Period We will understand the Lord's wrath
Years	Ezek 38:8 *After many days thou shalt be visited: **in latter years** thou shalt come into the land that is brought back from the sword, and is gathered out of many people, against the mountains of Israel, which have been always waste: but it is brought forth out of the nations, and they shall dwell safely all of them.* (KJV)	First half of the Tribulation Period	Russian Invasion
Days	Ezek 38:16 *and thou shalt come up against my people of Israel, as a cloud to cover the land; it shall be in **the latter days,** and I will bring thee against my land, that the heathen may know me, when I shall be sanctified in thee, O Gog, before their eyes.* (KJV)	First half of the Tribulation Period	Russian Invasion
Days	Dan 2:28-29 *But there is a God in heaven that revealeth secrets, and maketh known to the king Nebuchadnezzar what shall be in **the latter days.** Thy dream, and the visions of thy head upon thy bed, are these; As for thee, O king, thy thoughts came into thy mind upon thy bed, what should come to pass hereafter: and he that revealeth secrets maketh known to thee what shall come to pass.* (KJV)	Day of the Lord	Vision of end times made known
Time	Dan 8:23-24 *And in **the latter time** of their kingdom when the transgressors are come to the full, a king of fierce*	Revived Roman Empire	Antichrist

AFTER THE RAPTURE

LATTER	**SCRIPTURE**	**TIME PERIOD**	**DESCRIPTION**
	countenance, and understanding dark sentences, shall stand up. And his power shall be mighty, but not by his own power: and he shall destroy wonderfully, and shall prosper, and practise, and shall destroy the mighty and the holy people. (KJV)	Time of Jacob's Trouble	Great Tribulation
Days	<u>Dan 10:14</u> *Now I am come to make thee understand what shall befall thy people in **the latter days**: for yet the vision is for many days.* (KJV)	Day of the Lord	Jewish People
Days	<u>Hosea 3:4-5</u> *For the children of Israel shall abide many days without a king, and without a prince, and without a sacrifice, and without an image, and without an ephod, and without teraphim: Afterward shall the children of Israel return, and seek the LORD their God, and David their king; and shall fear the LORD and his goodness in **the latter days**.* (KJV)	593 BC to the Day of the Lord Day of the Lord	Without a king Jews accept Christ

These verses associated with *"latter,"* will all take place during the Tribulation Period, so I think it would be safe to say that they refer to the Day of the Lord or time when God will deal with the nation of Israel and unrepentant mankind. It is comforting to know that God really is in control and watches over His own! He writes history in advance for us. We truly do have a God who watches over us.

END OF THE AGE

Before we conclude this chapter we need to look at another event spoken of in the Bible. We will need to return to the Olivet Discourse where Jesus was conversing with His disciples. After Jesus told the disciples that the beautiful Temple they had just departed from was going to be destroyed, the disciples asked Jesus three questions.

> Matt 24:1-3 *Jesus left the temple and was walking away when his disciples came up to him to call his attention to its buildings. "Do you see all these things?" he asked. "I tell you the truth, not one stone here will be left on another; every one will be thrown down." **As Jesus was sitting on the Mount of Olives, the disciples came to him privately. "Tell us,"** they said, "**when will this happen, and what will be the sign of your coming and of the end of the age?**"* (NIV)

What Day Is It?

All three of these questions were prophetic in nature. The first question was, *"tell us, when will this happen?"* Here the disciples were referring back to the statement Jesus made about the Temple being destroyed. Jesus does not answer this question in Matthew, but in Luke 21:20 He does answer this question.

Luke 21:20 *"But when you see Jerusalem surrounded by armies, then recognize that her desolation is at hand.* (NAS)

This prophetic event came to fulfillment in 70 AD, when the Roman General Titus destroyed the Temple. We will discuss more about this event in the next chapter. Then the disciples asked Jesus two more questions.

1. *...and what will be the sign of your coming?*
2. *...and of the end of the age?*

Jesus answers both of these questions in the remaining verses of Matthew 24 and 25. I really do like the poetic style and language of the King James Version of the Holy Bible, but if you are reading this translation of the Bible there are several words in this translation that might have had a better word translated in a few instances. One of the more important instances is the word they used at the end of the third question that the disciples asked Jesus. Instead of the word, "world," I think a better translation would have been "age." Both the New International and the Revised Standard translations of the Bible use the word, "age" in place of "world." As we examine the time frame for this question, we will find out that the world does not come to an end at this time. The world will not come to an end until at least 1000 years later at the end of the Millennium, when it is dissolved by fire and replaced by the New Heaven and the New Earth.

The end of the age, which is the end of the Dispensation of Grace, is what the disciples were asking Jesus about. When Jesus comes back again it will be at the end of the age we are living in now. After the Dispensation of Grace is completed, a new age, the Millennium or the Day of the Lord will begin. Look back at the second question and see how the two questions tie together.

We have a very comforting statement in Matthew chapter twenty-eight. After the resurrection of Jesus the eleven disciples went to Galilee as they were instructed to do. The very last sentence in the book of Matthew is a promise from Jesus that He will be with Christians until the very end of the age, which is the end of the Dispensation of Grace or sometimes called the church age.

Matt 28:20 *<u>And surely I am with you always, to the very end of the age.</u>* (NIV)

CHAPTER FOUR

THE LAODICEAN CHURCH 1900—1948

Below, I will break down our study into periods starting at 1900 AD to the end of time and then on into eternity. The time line below will show you how we will break out the periods into chapters.

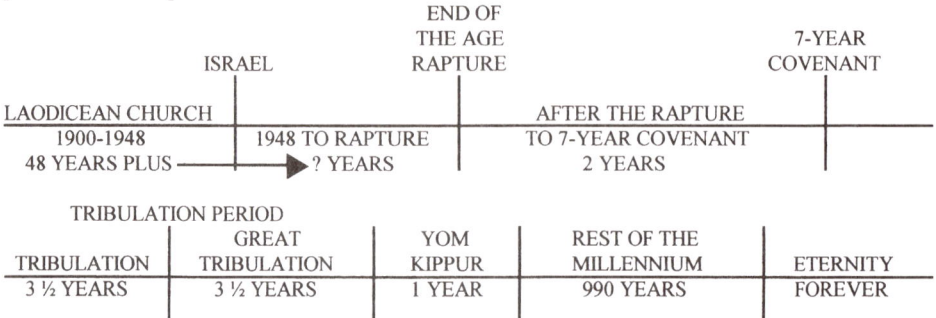

LAODICEAN CHURCH	ISRAEL	END OF THE AGE RAPTURE		7-YEAR COVENANT
1900-1948	1948 TO RAPTURE		AFTER THE RAPTURE TO 7-YEAR COVENANT	
48 YEARS PLUS →	→ ? YEARS		2 YEARS	

TRIBULATION PERIOD				
TRIBULATION	GREAT TRIBULATION	YOM KIPPUR	REST OF THE MILLENNIUM	ETERNITY
3 ½ YEARS	3 ½ YEARS	1 YEAR	990 YEARS	FOREVER

The book of Revelation was written by the apostle John probably around 96 AD as he was exiled on the Island called Patmos located in the Aegean Sea. The reason for his exile was because he was a Christian and for his witness of Jesus Christ. The death of all the other apostles had preceded him. Most of them were martyrs for their faith. John was an elderly man at the time he wrote the book of Revelation. He was given the task of revealing Jesus Christ to His servants. His servants are all born again believers throughout the church age or Dispensation of Grace. Chapters two and three of Revelation are messages to seven churches throughout what was then Asia Minor. Since these messages are to the church, keep in mind that the Lord is speaking to people who profess to be born-again believers.

The Laodicean Church period probably had a good foot hold around the beginning of the 20th Century and will continue up to the Rapture of the church, which is the end of the church age. In this chapter we will only cover the time period from 1900 to 1948 when the nation of Israel was once again reestablished, but keep in mind that the apostasy of the Laodicean Church continues until the church age is ended and believers are caught up to meet the LORD in the air.

There are at least four lessons to be learned from the seven churches that existed in Asia Minor around 96 AD, when the apostle John wrote about them in the second and third chapters of the book of Revelation. The present day location of where these churches existed is in the country of Turkey. The Lord was speaking to each of these seven churches by way of a commendation, a condemnation, council and a challenge. Jesus also has a beautiful description of Himself to each church in a way most appropriate to each church. Some Bible prophecy teachers today, teach that these messages to these seven churches can have these four applications.

1. The seven churches that existed in John's day.
2. The seven types of churches that exist today.
3. The seven characteristics that can exist in any church or individual Christian

throughout the church age.
4. The seven basic divisions of church history.

A list of the seven churches and the times of their dominance throughout the church age are as follows:

1. EPHESUS   AD 30-100
2. SMYRNA   AD 100-312
3. PERGAMUM   AD 312-606
4. THYATIRA   AD 606-1520
5. SARDIS   AD 1520-1750
6. PHILADELPHIA   AD 1750-1900
7. LAODICEA   AD 1900-End of the age

Since we are not going to study these seven churches in detail, we need to look at the last two churches that apply to church history which will apply to our study. A study of history reveals that it is possible that the church has gone through seven basic periods. This type of study would not have been possible at the beginning of the church age, but now that we are well into the period of the Laodicean Church and close to the second coming of the Lord it is easier to see this application. History is easy to figure out after it happens. Let us look at the message to the church of Laodicea.

Rev 3:14-22   *"**To the angel of the church in Laodicea write:** These are the words of the Amen, the faithful and true witness, the ruler of God's creation. **I know your deeds, that you are neither cold nor hot. I wish you were either one or the other! So, because you are lukewarm— neither hot nor cold—I am about to spit you out of my mouth.** You say, 'I am rich; I have acquired wealth and do not need a thing.' But you do not realize that you are wretched, pitiful, poor, blind and naked. I counsel you to buy from me gold refined in the fire, so you can become rich; and white clothes to wear, so you can cover your shameful nakedness; and salve to put on your eyes, so you can see. Those whom I love I rebuke and discipline. So be earnest, and repent. Here I am! I stand at the door and knock. If anyone hears my voice and opens the door, I will come in and eat with him, and he with me. To him who overcomes, I will give the right to sit with me on my throne, just as I overcame and sat down with my Father on his throne. **He who has an ear, let him hear what the Spirit says to the churches.**"* (NIV)

CHURCH AT PHILADELPHIA

One interesting point I would like to make before we look at the church in Laodicea, is to briefly take a glance at the church that preceded it. It was the church in Philadelphia and

AFTER THE RAPTURE

covered the period in chronological order starting around 1750 AD.

Rev 3:7-13 *"**To the angel of the church in Philadelphia write:** These are the words of him who is holy and true, who holds the key of David. What he opens no one can shut, and what he shuts no one can open. **I know your deeds. See, I have placed before you an open door that no one can shut. I know that you have little strength, yet you have kept my word and have not denied my name.** I will make those who are of the synagogue of Satan, who claim to be Jews though they are not, but are liars—I will make them come and fall down at your feet and acknowledge that I have loved you. Since you have kept my command to endure patiently, I will also keep you from the hour of trial that is going to come upon the whole world to test those who live on the earth. I am coming soon. Hold on to what you have, so that no one will take your crown. Him who overcomes I will make a pillar in the temple of my God. Never again will he leave it. I will write on him the name of my God and the name of the city of my God, the new Jerusalem, which is coming down out of heaven from my God; and I will also write on him my new name. **He who has an ear, let him hear what the Spirit says to the churches.*** (NIV)

The Protestant Reformation was a big part of this church and after studying the three churches before this church, it was a rather depressing time for the church as a whole. A great revival was born and mankind had made a giant step back to God. Revivals in Europe spread to America and the creation of the United States, probably the most God fearing country that has existed throughout the church age. Nevertheless, even it has slipped into that period of the Laodicean Church. I believe that the United States has two main reasons for the blessings we have received from God since becoming a nation.

1. We founded our nation on God's word and principles.
2. We have treated the Jewish people favorably.

Unfortunately, we are moving further and further away from these two principles and will suffer the consequences for our actions, more on this later in our book. I would like to compare the commendation, condemnation, and council of these two churches.

	PHILADELPHIA (1750 TO 1900 AD)	**LAODICEA** (1900 AD TO RAPTURE)
COMMENDATION	1. GOOD WORKS (MISSIONS) 2. KEPT MY WORD 3. HAVE NOT DENIED MY NAME	1. NONE
CONDEMNATION	1. NONE	1. THOU ARE LUKEWARM WRETCHED, MISERABLE POOR, BLIND AND NAKED

The Laodicean Church 1900-1948

	PHILADELPHIA	**LAODICEA**
COUNCIL	1. HOLD THAT FAST WHICH THOU HAST	1. BUY GOLD TRIED BY FIRE AND WHITE RAIMENT 2. ANOINT THINE EYES 3. BE ZEALOUS AND REPENT

As we compare these two churches, notice that the church in Laodicea has no commendation, while the church in Philadelphia has no condemnation. Philadelphia is told to *"Hold on to what you have,"* while Laodicea is told to *"be earnest and repent."* It is no wonder that if you ask a pastor to pick a church of the seven listed to describe his church, he will invariably pick the church in Philadelphia (a question I asked Roy Pedersen).

START OF APOSTASY

The church takes a step backward and gradually it starts turning its back toward God, until it becomes lukewarm. After God reveals to the Laodicean Church that they are lukewarm, their response to Him in verse seventeen is, *"You say, 'I am rich; I have acquired wealth and do not need a thing.'"* The church fits this scenario more today than it has throughout its history and will continue to prosper right up to the Rapture of the saints. It will still be saying, *"I need nothing."* Do not forget that Jesus is talking to the Christian church. Since they are lukewarm, He says that He will spue them out of His mouth.

Many church members in churches today are religious, but if the Rapture of the saints were to occur during the Sunday morning service, how many people (including many pastors) would be left behind to face the Tribulation Period, which would be just ahead for them. You will not be included in the Rapture by being religious, but by having a born again experience with Jesus Christ.

> John 3:1-7   *Now there was a man of the Pharisees named Nicodemus, a member of the Jewish ruling council. He came to Jesus at night and said, "Rabbi, we know you are a teacher who has come from God. For no one could perform the miraculous signs you are doing if God were not with him." **In reply Jesus declared, "I tell you the truth, no one can see the kingdom of God unless he is born again."** "How can a man be born when he is old?" Nicodemus asked. "Surely he cannot enter a second time into his mother's womb to be born!" Jesus answered, "I tell you the truth, no one can enter the kingdom of God unless he is born of water and the Spirit. **Flesh gives birth to flesh, but the Spirit gives birth to spirit. You should not be surprised at my saying, 'You must be born again.'*** (NIV)

The prerequisite to becoming a faithful member of the true church of Jesus Christ (nondenominational) is to have a personal relationship with the Son of God.

Let me add here that all people who are born again believers are saints (Romans 16:2; Ephesians 5:3 NKJ). This includes all the Old Testament people of faith (Psalms 106:16;

1 Samuel 2:9). Believers are called saints because they belong to God who provides for their sanctification. They are consecrated as being set apart for His own and in the New Testament they are members of the Body of Christ. The idea of a person being appointed to a saintly position is incorrect. Being a saint has nothing to do with a persons' character. The idea that is so common today, that the degrees of the progress of a persons character can make them eligible to a position of sainthood is a false teaching. Throughout this book the mention of saint or saints will always refer to the people who have come back to God through a personal relationship with Him by faith—a child of God.

In 1900 AD, as we move into the 20th Century and the beginning of the modernization of the world, near the beginning of the Laodicean church period, it is no coincidence that when they say, *"I am rich; I have acquired wealth and do not need a thing,"* that it is also the beginning of the world turning away from God and starting to become lukewarm. Three of Daniel's prophecies in chapter twelve had their beginning starting around this time.

> Dan 12:4 ***But thou, O Daniel, shut up the words, and seal the book, even to the time of the end: many shall run to and fro, and knowledge shall be increased.*** (KJV)

1. Unsealing of the book of Daniel
2. Many shall run to and fro
3. Knowledge shall be increased

Just before the Rapture of the church, when travel and knowledge starts to increase, I believe that God will start to unseal the prophecies in the book of Daniel. During the 20th Century travel has abounded. It is nothing to hop on a plane and fly anywhere in the world. A knowledge explosion is occurring like no other hundred-year period of time in history. If you could wake up someone who died a hundred years ago, he would be startled at what the world is like today. Even I can remember my grandparents "out house," a toilet outside the house. A hole dug in the ground with a little shack built over it with a two-seater stool to sit on. On the floor a pile of yesterdays newspapers and magazines used in place of toilet paper. Scriptural knowledge will also increase for the true believers as Daniel's message is unsealed.

I was not aware of just how far the Christian church has slipped away from God until I, my wife Sarah, Uncle Paul and Aunt Irene, attended a short prophecy seminar at The First Baptist Church in Ft. Lupton, Colorado in the Fall of 2000. Dr. David Reagan, from Lamb & Lion Ministries, presented a shocking account of his experiences in various churches where he has spoken. One particular church did not even allow Bibles to be brought to church services. The pastor did not even have a copy of the Bible. At another church, Dr. Reagan was not allowed to talk about the Holy Spirit. I think it would be safe to say that Satan is using the Christian Church today as a tool to keep people away from God. That would be hard to believe if it were not confirmed in the Bible. God's plan and foreknowledge are superb and allow us to know about the future. No other god can do that! Just like the signs the Jewish people were given almost two thousand years ago, concerning the coming of the Messiah, we are today in the midst of the signs of His second return.

SIGNS OF THE TIMES

There appears to be three separate times in the New Testament where signs will appear to announce events that will take place in the future. The first set of events of the three will take place early in the Dispensation of Grace, while the second set of events will take place toward the end of the Dispensation of Grace. The third set of signs will take place during the Tribulation Period in the Day of the Lord. Please remember that the Glorious Return of Jesus is not the Rapture and will take place after the Tribulation Period is over, when Jesus returns from heaven to the earth coming on the clouds.

The three times that the Signs of the Times appear to people are:

1. Signs for the early church to warn them of the impending destruction of Jerusalem and the Temple. This event took place in 70 AD and the account is found in Luke.
2. Signs for the church, to warn them that the church age is about to come to an end and the Rapture is about to take place. These signs are in our midst today, with the Rapture occurring in the near future. These signs are found in the New Testament.
3. Signs for the Jewish people, during the Tribulation Period. These signs will appear to the Jews in Jerusalem while they are under the protection of the Antichrist during the first 3 ½ years of the Tribulation Period. These signs are mentioned in Matthew, Mark and Luke.

Of the three accounts of the Olivet Discourse, in the synoptic Gospels, only Luke answers the question concerning the destruction of the Temple, although the question appears in all three of the Gospels. Matthew and Mark skip over the answer, while Luke gives us a detailed account of this tragic event. In fact, in Luke's account, it gives us a detailed look at what the early Christians went through at that time. The viewpoint of the Olivet Discourse from the account in Luke points to a church age perspective, while the account in Matthew takes on a Messianic or a Jewish perspective, as we will see later. Let us begin with Luke, since the destruction of Jerusalem and the Temple took place more than 1900 years ago. The scene below took place the week before Jesus was crucified in 30 AD, while Jesus was with some of His disciples at the Temple site in Jerusalem.

> Luke 21:5-7 *Some of his disciples were remarking about how the temple was adorned with beautiful stones and with gifts dedicated to God.* **But Jesus said, "As for what you see here, the time will come when not one stone will be left on another; every one of them will be thrown down." "Teacher," they asked, "when will these things happen? And what will be the sign that they are about to take place?"** (NIV)

The first thing Jesus did before He answered the question of when the Temple would be destroyed, was to warn them about false Messiah's or people who claimed to be the Messiah. They would also be claiming that the time for the arrival of the Kingdom Age (Millennium) would be near. Between 30 AD and 135 AD, there were numerous people who claimed to be the Messiah. Several of them who had large followings caused serious consequences to befall Jerusalem, the Temple, the Jewish people and also their nation. Messianic emotionalism became intense shortly before 70 AD. At that time several false Messiah's appeared in New Testament times and vividly reflected the Messianic ferment of the time. The Jewish people have had many false Messiahs throughout their history which resulted in disasters for the Jewish people as a whole.

> Luke 21:8   He replied: *"Watch out that you are not deceived. **For many will come in my name, claiming, 'I am he,' and, 'The time is near.' Do not follow them.*** (NIV)

Throughout the entire two thousand year period of the Christian dispensation it has been cluttered with false Messiah's. I would probably venture to guess that there could possibly be as many as 50 to 100 people living today all over the world who profess to be and believe that they are Jesus Christ the Messiah. Jesus warns us repeatedly in the Bible to watch out for and not to follow these false Messiahs. A few of the more familiar names that come to mind during our lifetime are Adolf Hitler, Charles Manson (Helter Skelter), Jim Jones (Guiana), David Koresh (Waco, Texas), and Marshall Herff Applewhite (Hale-Bopp Comet/Heavens Gate Cult). Most cult leaders eventually evolve into believing that they are the Christ or even Christ like. They find some hidden meaning behind scripture that reveals them to be Christ and so they teach their followers that they are the Messiah.

The false Messiah's or religious zealots who sprang up after Jesus was crucified, riled up the Jews so much during that time that they caused the Jewish people to revolt against their Roman protectorate and caused the Great Revolt which started in 66 AD. This revolt eventually caused the destruction of Jerusalem and the sacred Temple. Jesus even warned the early Christians that there would be wars and revolutions. They were not to be frightened by them. These wars and revolutions pertain to the Christians from 30 to 70 AD.

> Luke 21:9-11   *__When you hear of wars and revolutions, do not be frightened.__ These things must happen first, but the end will not come right away." Then he said to them: "Nation will rise against nation, and kingdom against kingdom. There will be great earthquakes, famines and pestilences in various places, and fearful events and great signs from heaven.* (NIV)

After warning the early Christians about wars and revolutions that would take place in their time, Jesus continues by telling Christians that wars, earthquakes, famine, pestilence and great signs from heaven will appear. These signs are for the end of the church age. He tells them that the end (of the age) will not come right away. In other words, at the time of the destruction of the Temple in 70 AD the end of the age and the setting up of the kingdom would not come for awhile, in fact, for quite awhile. Here we are close to two thousand years later and the end has still not arrived. You must remember that at this early time the Christian Church was made up almost entirely of Jews. The disciples, who were also Jews (with the possible exception of Luke), had been taught by Jesus and had a thorough understanding of the Kingdom Age and that the Jewish nation would someday be set up as the head of the

The Laodicean Church 1900-1948

nations with Jesus as the King. The persecution listed below returns to the early Christians who suffered from the Orthodox Jews and the Romans before the Jewish Temple and Jerusalem were destroyed in 70 AD. At the time of the early church it was not a very popular time to become a Christian.

Luke 21:12-19   ***"But before all this, they will lay hands on you and persecute you. They will deliver you to synagogues and prisons, and you will be brought before kings and governors, and all on account of my name. This will result in your being witnesses to them. But make up your mind not to worry beforehand how you will defend yourselves. For I will give you words and wisdom that none of your adversaries will be able to resist or contradict. You will be betrayed even by parents, brothers, relatives and friends, and they will put some of you to death. All men will hate you because of me. But not a hair of your head will perish. By standing firm you will gain life.*** (NIV)

In this account in Luke, we see the early Christians as they pay the price for following Christ. Would you defend your faith if you were under such circumstances?

1. They will seize you and persecute you. This was done by both the Orthodox Jews and the leaders of the Roman Empire.
2. They will take you to synagogues and prisons. Again, the Orthodox Jews took the Christians to synagogues and the Romans took them to prison as part of the persecution.
3. You will be brought before kings and governors. Because the nation was under the protection of Rome, the Orthodox Jews would take the Christian Jews before the Roman authority and bring accusations against them and have them thrown in prison, where they would suffer persecution.
4. Because the Christians were witnessing for their God, all their sufferings were brought about because of their faith in Jesus.
5. Nevertheless, Jesus told them ahead of time not to worry about defending themselves. He said that He—and this through the Holy Spirit—would give them wisdom and the words to speak to their adversaries.
6. The Christians would be betrayed, even by their own parents, brothers, relatives and friends.
7. Some of the Christians would be martyred.
8. All men (unsaved) would hate the Christians because of Jesus.
9. Still, though they would suffer, even to the point of death, none of the Christians would perish as long as they believed in Jesus. They would gain eternal life.

During the early years of the Christian Church the followers of Jesus suffered enormously for their belief in the one true God. These verses above in Luke, along with the book of Acts and the epistles (letters) of the New Testament, are filled with accounts of the religious persecution that the early church sustained. In the beginning the Christian Church was made up of a big majority of Jewish people and they were accused of being a cult by the Orthodox Jews and the Roman population. Even the great apostle Paul, who started out as an Orthodox Jew with a vengeance against the Christian Jews, suffered extreme persecution as he was spreading the gospel message outside Jerusalem to the Gentiles. He even went to prison several times for his faith in Jesus Christ.

Acts 14:1 **At Iconium Paul and Barnabas went as usual into the Jewish synagogue. There they spoke so effectively that a great number of Jews and Gentiles believed.** (NIV)

2 Cor 11:23-28 *Are they servants of Christ? (I am out of my mind to talk like this.) I am more. I have worked much harder, been in prison more frequently, been flogged more severely, and been exposed to death again and again. Five times I received from the Jews the forty lashes minus one. Three times I was beaten with rods, once I was stoned, three times I was shipwrecked, I spent a night and a day in the open sea, I have been constantly on the move. I have been in danger from rivers, in danger from bandits, in danger from my own countrymen, in danger from Gentiles, in danger in the city, in danger in the country, in danger at sea; and in danger from false brothers. I have labored and toiled and have often gone without sleep; I have known hunger and thirst and have often gone without food; I have been cold and naked.* **Besides everything else, I face daily the pressure of my concern for all the churches.** (NIV)

Phil 1:12-14 <u>**Now I want you to know, brothers, that what has happened to me has really served to advance the gospel.**</u> **As a result, it has become clear throughout the whole palace guard and to everyone else that <u>I am in chains for Christ.</u>** *Because of my chains, most of the brothers in the Lord have been encouraged to speak the word of God more courageously and fearlessly.* (NIV)

As Paul penned his epistles to the Christians in Thessalonica, somewhere around 54 AD, they were going through a period of such extreme persecution that they truly believed that "the Day of the Lord" was near, which they believed would usher in the return of Christ.

2 Thes 2:3-4 <u>**Don't let anyone deceive you in any way, for that day will not come until the rebellion occurs and the man of lawlessness is revealed, the man doomed to destruction.**</u> *He will oppose and will exalt himself over everything that is called God or is worshiped, so that he sets himself up in God's temple, proclaiming himself to be God.* (NIV)

After supplying us with the picture of the persecution of the early Christians in Luke

The Laodicean Church 1900-1948

21:12-19, Jesus finally answers the original question of the disciples, *"When will these things happen? And what will be the sign that they are about to take place?"* When will the Temple be thrown down? The sign is:

Luke 21:20-22   *"<u>When you see Jerusalem being surrounded by armies, you will know that its desolation is near.</u> Then let those who are in Judea flee to the mountains, let those in the city get out, and let those in the country not enter the city. For this is the time of punishment in fulfillment of all that has been written.* (NIV)

The revolt that took place between 66-73 AD is known as the Great Revolt. Jerusalem was besieged by the Romans under Titus, who destroyed the city and the Temple in 70 AD. The last remaining rebels fled the city to the remote mountains of Masada. This group consisted of approximately 1000 men, women and children. Masada in Hebrew means fortress. Under the leadership of Eleazer Ben Jair, they withstood a two-year siege by the Roman Tenth Legion. As the Roman Army under Silva made the final assault on Masada, the remaining Jews, with the exception of seven Jews, killed themselves rather than surrender. [1]

A large portion of the Jewish people were exiled as a result of the Great Revolt. The destruction of the Temple fulfilled the prophetic utterance of Jesus only 40 years earlier. We also see Jesus making a reference to the destruction of Jerusalem and the Temple just days before He had the conversation with the disciples on Mount Olivet, at which time, He made the prophecy known. As Jesus made His triumphal entry into Jerusalem, seven days before His death, He wept as soon as He saw the city and made this statement.

Luke 19:41-44   *<u>As he approached Jerusalem and saw the city, he wept over it</u> and said, "If you, even you, had only known on this day what would bring you peace—but now it is hidden from your eyes. The days will come upon you when your enemies will build an embankment against you and encircle you and hem you in on every side. They will dash you to the ground, you and the children within your walls. <u>They will not leave one stone on another, because you did not recognize the time of God's coming to you.</u>"* (NIV)

Jesus went on in Luke 21 of His prophecy by informing us that the punishment of the Christian Jewish people would be severe in the early church. There would be a time of judgment against the land of Israel and the unsaved Jewish people and many would be killed. It is estimated that as many as one million Jews might have died in the Great Revolt against Rome. They would be taken as prisoners and scattered throughout all the nations. This punishment would continue until the Times of the Gentiles are fulfilled.

Luke 21:23-24   *<u>How dreadful it will be in those days for pregnant women and nursing mothers!</u> There will be great distress in the land and wrath against this people. They will fall by the sword and will be taken as*

> *prisoners to all the nations. <u>Jerusalem will be trampled on by the Gentiles until the times of the Gentiles are fulfilled</u>.* (NIV)

If that was not enough misery to be inflicted on the Jewish people, as a result of their own rebellion, another uprising would spring up only a short time later from the people who were left in the land after the Great Revolt. Around 60 years after the Great Revolt, a man by the name of Simon bar-Kokhba appeared on the scene and claimed to be the Messiah. With the religious stigma of the Old Testament prophecy that the Jewish captivity would last for 70 years, Simon bar-Kokhba—joined by tens of thousands of his followers—once again revolted against Rome. This time, this false Messiah led the Jewish people in a revolt from 132-135 AD that left 585,000 Jews slaughtered in battles and skirmishes. Countless more died of starvation, fire and sword. Nearly the entire land of Judea lay waste. By the time the Romans finished putting down the rebellion, 50 percent of Judea's population was dead. Tens of thousands of Jewish men and women were sold into slavery, while other women were forced to become prostitutes. Jews were forbidden to visit Jerusalem. Even the name of the city was changed to Aelia Capitolina. The area became known as Palestine.

In fact, Jerusalem will not be given back to the Jewish people by Jesus until the Times of the Gentiles are fulfilled. The Times of the Gentiles had its beginning when the Babylonians captured Judah and Jerusalem in 606 BC. In 593 BC, the glory of the Lord departed from the Temple to allow the Babylonians to completely destroy Jerusalem and the Temple in 586 BC. Since that time the world has been living in the Times of the Gentiles. The Times of the Gentiles will not come to an end until the Dispensation of Grace has ended and Jesus is crowned King. Jesus, after the Battle of Armageddon is completed, will rebuild the Temple, at which time the glory of the Lord will return to dwell among His people. Even during the Day of the Lord there will be a short period of time when the Gentiles will be given control of the Temple area. It will be during the second half of the Tribulation Period.

Rev 11:1-2   *I was given a reed like a measuring rod and was told, "Go and measure the temple of God and the altar, and count the worshipers there. **But exclude the outer court; do not measure it, <u>because it has been given to the Gentiles. They will trample on the holy city for 42 months</u>**.* (NIV)

The apostle Paul adds to the story when he reveals that because of the rejection of their Messiah (Jesus Christ), the Jews during the Dispensation of Grace would experience a partial hardening until the dominance of the Gentiles has been completed. In other words, a portion of the Jewish people will not be saved during this time because they do not accept Christ as their Savior. If you travel back through almost two thousand years of Jewish history, you will find out that this has been the case. Gentile nations have dominated Jerusalem and the Temple Mount and the Jewish people have been scattered throughout the world and to a large degree they have rejected Jesus.

Rom. 11:25   *I do not want you to be ignorant of this mystery, brothers, so that you may not be conceited: <u>Israel has experienced a hardening in</u>*

The Laodicean Church 1900-1948

part until the full number of the Gentiles has come in. (NIV)

We will take a detailed look at the Signs of the Times as they appear to the church just prior to the Rapture in chapter seven and the signs for the Jewish people will be covered in chapter eleven under the subtitle of Birth Pains.

WAR

No study of the Tribulation Period would be complete without taking a look at war and the effects it has had on mankind ever since the fall of Adam and Eve. How horrible it is and how Satan uses it as a tool to exploit people for evil.

Ps 140:1-3   *Deliver me, O LORD, from **the evil man:** preserve me from **the violent man;** Which imagine mischiefs in their heart; **continually are they gathered together for war.** They have sharpened their tongues like a serpent; adders' poison is under their lips. Selah.* (KJV)

What is the direct cause of war? This verse in Psalms tells us that evil violent men are devising evil plans. Men like Hitler and Stalin in the past and the Antichrist coming up in the near future.

Rom 1:28-32   *And even as they did not like to retain God in their knowledge, **God gave them over to a reprobate mind, to do those things which are not convenient;** Being filled with all unrighteousness, fornication, wickedness, covetousness, maliciousness; full of envy, murder, debate, deceit, malignity; whisperers, Backbiters, haters of God, despiteful, proud, boasters, inventors of evil things, disobedient to parents, Without understanding, covenant breakers, without natural affection, implacable, unmerciful: **Who knowing the judgment of God, that they which commit such things are worthy of death, not only do the same, but have pleasure in them that do them.*** (KJV)

Eph 4:19   *Who being past feeling have given themselves over unto lasciviousness, to work all uncleanness with greediness.* (KJV)

War is a horrible thing! Millions of lives have been lost because of senseless wars throughout the centuries, not to mention the plight of innocent women, children, the aged, accidental victims of battles and air raids. Rape, suicide, famine and pestilence are indirect results of wars. Power and greed are the driving force behind evil men and do not forget the influence of Satan himself.

Even in the Old Testament God commanded the Israelites to invade the land of Canaan (promised land) and to destroy all the inhabitants in the land when they entered it.

Josh 9:24   *And they answered Joshua, and said, Because it was certainly told* *thy servants, how that the LORD thy God commanded his servant Moses to give you all the land, **and to destroy all the inhabitants of the land from before you,** therefore we were sore afraid of our lives because of you, and have done this thing.* (KJV)

The inhabitants living in Canaan at that time were not following God. War in the Old Testament needs to be viewed from a different perspective than we perceive it today. The wars commissioned by God in the Old Testament were a Divine enterprise in which human instruments were employed and were entirely subordinate to the Divine will.

No discussion of war would be complete without mentioning the two greatest wars of human history. Both took place during the first half of the 20th Century. World War I, which took place in Europe between 1914 and 1918, is referred to in history as The Great War. This war became global and eventually involved thirty-two nations. The fundamental causes of the conflict were rooted deeply in the European history of the previous century, particularly in the political and economic policies that prevailed on the Continent after 1871. This was the year that marked the emergence of Germany as a great power. With a total of 8,538,315 killed from deaths caused by military sources, 21,219,452 people wounded and 7,750,919 prisoners and missing, World War I was the worst war in human history up to that time. New weapons such as the airplane and tank were introduced, along with sea warfare being revolutionized by the submarine. The aggregate direct cost of the war of all the nations involved in the conflict amounted to about 186 billion dollars.

That war was small in comparison to what happened next. A little more than twenty years later World War II exploded on the scene. This global military conflict began in 1939 as a European dispute between Germany and an Anglo-French coalition, but eventually expanded to include most of the nations of the world. It ended in 1945, with a new world order dominated by the United States and the USSR. More than any previous war, World War II involved the commitment of a nation's entire human and economic resources, the blurring of the distinction between combatant and noncombatant, and the expansion of the battle field to include all of the enemy's territory. Toward the end of the war, two radically new weapons were introduced—the long range rocket and the atomic bomb. In terms of lives lost and material destruction, World War II was the most devastating war in human history up to the present time.

Most statistics on World War II are only estimates. A rough consensus has been reached on the total cost of the war. In terms of money spent the cost has been put at more than 1 trillion dollars, which makes it more costly than all the other previous wars combined in history. The human cost, not including more than 6 million Jews killed in the Holocaust, who were intended victims of the war, is 55 million dead (25 million of those were military casualties and 30 million were civilian casualties). It is a sad day when we have to report that because of the greed of one man, Adolf Hitler, over 60 million people lost their lives because of a foolish war. In Germany alone, bombing and the effects of war produced 4 billion cubic meters (5 billion cubic yards) of rubble. [2]

Even World War II will not compare to the destruction that will be meted out by the Antichrist during the Tribulation Period. There will not be a nation on earth that will not take part in the worst time of human history. Matthew has this to say about this very time!

The Laodicean Church 1900-1948

Matt 24:21 ***For then there will be great distress, unequaled from the beginning of the world until now—and never to be equaled again.*** (NIV)

I know that this is not a very consoling bit of information, but the answers to the final solution are found in the Bible. A big problem today, and has been in the past, seems to be a few prophecy ministries who are more than a little bit sensational. These ministries usually draw large groups of people who become afraid of the current events of the day. These people become frightened, which is contrary to what the Bible teaches. These ministries limit their study of Prophecy to only a small amount of scripture, which distorts the total panorama of the future. They are more concerned with what the daily newspapers are reporting than with what the Bible is predicting. They continue to try to place the conflicts of today into scripture and when they do not come to pass, these ministries change their predictions to correspond to a more current world event. That in turn gives a bad name to the rest of the prophecy ministries who are on the scene today who are doing an excellent job of reporting what the Bible really says.

A final thought I would like you to think about before you continue reading this book, is what the Bible says about the condition of the world just prior to the Rapture. Anyone interested in Bible Prophecy should know the Bible predicts that the world will be in a general state of peace just prior to the Rapture. In the near future, look for the larger nations of the world to come together to set the stage for world peace. The Arab/Israeli conflict, the United States aggression against Afghanistan (war on terrorism), the Iraq situation with Saddam Hussein, the Afghanistan/Pakistan disagreement over Cashmere, the China/Taiwan hot spot, the flare-up in North Korea, along with the past world conflicts of World War I and World War II, will bring the largest nations from around the world against the countries who will be threatening world peace. As the world situation begins to settle down, as the current world conflicts are being dealt with from a world wide perspective, the scene will develop into a peace that will lull the world into a quite sleep. That does not mean that there will not be some skirmishes going on somewhere in the world. Scripture clearly teaches that the Day of the Lord will come like a thief in the night and when the people around the world are saying, *"Peace and safety,"* then suddenly destruction will come upon them.

1 Thes 5:1-3 *Now, brothers, about times and dates we do not need to write to you, for you know very well that the day of the Lord will come like a thief in the night.* ***While people are saying, "Peace and safety,"*** *destruction will come on them suddenly, as labor pains on a pregnant woman, and they will not escape.* (NIV)

Do not let the prophecy ministries who are reporting such things as one-third of the world population (2 billion people) will be killed (Revelation 9:13-19), by the Chinese army (later changed to possibly being Islam, after 911), before the Rapture takes place. My wife heard, on September 19, 2002, from one of her co-worker's that he heard a prophecy teacher say that the destruction of Babylon was going to take place when America attacks Iraq. My advice to you is to stay tuned to current events, but stay abreast to what the Bible is teaching. You will have a better chance of understanding what the future has in store for us.

CHAPTER FIVE

ISRAEL, MAY 14, 1948
CAN A NATION BE BORN IN A DAY?

A miracle of religious sorts occurred on May 14, 1948 when Israel became a nation. This occurred after November 29, 1947 when the United Nations passed a resolution on the partition of Palestine calling for the establishment of the Jewish state. Never in history has a nation existed, been destroyed and its people scattered all over the world for more than 2500 years, and become a self-governed nation again. Some Bible prophecy teachers insist that this was a fulfillment of a prophecy in Isaiah.

> Isa 66:8 *"Who has heard such a thing? Who has seen such things? <u>Can a land be born in one day? Can a nation be brought forth all at once?</u> As soon as Zion travailed, she also brought forth her sons.* (NAS)

It might be a type of that fulfillment, but what God was actually referring to here will be fulfilled during the Day of the Lord when Israel is set up as head of the nations.

> Deut 28:13 *<u>The LORD will make you the head, not the tail.</u> If you pay attention to the commands of the LORD your God that I give you this day and carefully follow them, <u>you will always be at the top</u>, never at the bottom.* (NIV)

Taken in context in Isaiah 66, after God has finished His last 3 ½ years of dealing with the Jews (Time of Jacob's Trouble), He *"will extend peace to her like a river."* This has not happened in Israel over the last fifty years.

> Isa 66:12 *For this is what the LORD says: "<u>I will extend peace to her like a river</u>, and the wealth of nations like a flooding stream; you will nurse and be carried on her arm and dandled on her knees.* (NIV)

Instead of fulfilling this prophecy in Isaiah, I believe that Israel becoming a nation on May 14, 1948 is fulfilling the prophecy in Matthew twenty-four, where it speaks of the lesson of the fig tree. It is a sign of the times for the church to let them know that from the time that the Jews return to Israel and the time that the Son of Man will appear in the sky (Glorious Return of Jesus), a generation of the people living at that time will not pass away. Please take note that the events of the Tribulation Period will be included in the events that are to take place before the Glorious Return of Jesus. The Jewish people returning in 1948 also signals the second coming of the Lord at the Rapture.

> Matt 24:32-35 *"Now learn this lesson from the fig tree: As soon as its twigs get tender and its leaves come out, you know that summer is near. Even*

Israel, May 14, 1948 — Can a Nation be Born in a Day?

> *so, when you see all these things, you know that it is near, right at the door. **I tell you the truth, <u>this generation will certainly not pass away until all these things have happened</u>.** Heaven and earth will pass away, but my words will never pass away.* (NIV)

The fig tree is the answer to the second and third parts of the question the disciples ask Jesus in verse three of Matthew twenty-four.

Matt 24:3   *As Jesus was sitting on the Mount of Olives, the disciples came to him privately. "Tell us," they said, "when will this happen, **and what will be the sign of your coming and of the end of the age?"*** (NIV)

It would be impossible to understand or come up with some sort of chronological order of the sequence of events of the end times without a thorough screening of the Old Testament, including its history, religious order and even Jewish tradition. In order to make our study complete and to understand the position of the Jews throughout history, I would like to supply you with a brief history of the Jewish people and nation since its inception. Adam and Eve were not Jewish. In fact, it was 2000 years after the fall of mankind before the birth of the chosen people was to take place. Mankind during the first 2000 years of human existence was doing evil continually, so God decided to call out a nation from among all the nations of the world. They were given His ordinances so that they could teach them to all the nations of the world. They were to be a holy nation by which the rest of the nations could find God.

Deut 7:6   ***For thou art an holy people unto the LORD thy God: <u>the LORD thy God hath chosen thee to be a special people unto himself, above all people that are upon the face of the earth</u>.*** (KJV)

Even though they are a chosen people, that does not make them a better people. For we are all part of God's creation and He shows no favoritism. However, since they were a chosen people and accepted that "chosen" status, God said that their punishment would be harsh if they did not follow His commandments. In fact, God warned the Israelites (Jews) beforehand what their fate would be for obedience and also for disobedience.

BLESSINGS FOR OBEDIENCE

Deut 28:1-14   ***<u>If you fully obey the LORD your God</u> and carefully follow all his commands I give you today, the LORD your God will set you high above all the nations on earth. All these blessings will come upon you and accompany you if you obey the LORD your God:*** *You will be blessed in the city and blessed in the country. The fruit of your womb will be blessed, and the crops of your land and the young of your livestock—the calves of your herds and the lambs of your flocks. Your basket and your kneading trough will be blessed. You will be* *blessed when you come in and blessed when you go out. The LORD will grant that the enemies who rise up against you will be defeated before you. They will come at you from one direction but flee from you in seven. The LORD will send a blessing on your barns and on everything you put your hand to. The LORD your God will bless you in the land he is giving you.* ***The LORD will establish you as his holy people, as he promised you on oath, if you keep the commands of the LORD your God and walk in his ways.*** *Then all the peoples on earth will see that you are called by the name of the LORD, and they will fear you. The LORD will grant you abundant prosperity—in the fruit of your womb, the young of your livestock and the crops of your ground—in the land he swore to your forefathers to give you. The LORD will open the heavens, the storehouse of his bounty, to send rain on your land in season and to bless all the work of your hands. You will lend to many nations but will borrow from none. The LORD will make you the head, not the tail. If you pay attention to the commands of the LORD your God that I give you this day and carefully follow them, you will always be at the top, never at the bottom. Do not turn aside from any of the commands I give you today, to the right or to the left, following other Gods and serving them.* (NIV)

CURSES FOR DISOBEDIENCE

Deut 28:15-68 ***However, if you do not obey the LORD your God*** *and do not carefully follow all his commands and decrees I am giving you today, all these curses will come upon you and overtake you: You will be cursed in the city and cursed in the country. Your basket and your kneading trough will be cursed. The fruit of your womb will be cursed, and the crops of your land, and the calves of your herds and the lambs of your flocks. You will be cursed when you come in and cursed when you go out. The LORD will send on you curses, confusion and rebuke in everything you put your hand to, until you are destroyed and come to sudden ruin because of the evil you have done in forsaking him. The LORD will plague you with diseases until he has destroyed you from the land you are entering to possess. The LORD will strike you with wasting disease, with fever and inflammation, with scorching heat and drought, with blight and mildew, which will plague you until you perish. The sky over your head will be bronze, the ground beneath you iron. The LORD will turn the rain of your country into dust and powder; it will come down from the skies until you are destroyed. The LORD will cause you to be defeated before your enemies. You will come at them from one direction but flee from them in seven, and you will become a thing of* *horror to all the kingdoms on earth. Your carcasses will be food for all the birds of the air and the beasts of the earth, and there will be no one to frighten them away. The LORD will afflict you with the boils of Egypt and with tumors, festering sores and the itch, from which you cannot be cured. The LORD will afflict you with madness, blindness and confusion of mind. At midday you will grope about like a blind man in the dark. You will be unsuccessful in everything you do; day after day you will be oppressed and robbed, with no one to rescue you. You will be pledged to be married to a woman, but another will take her and ravish her. You will build a house, but you will not live in it. You will plant a vineyard, but you will not even begin to enjoy its fruit. Your ox will be slaughtered before your eyes, but you will eat none of it. Your donkey will be forcibly taken from you and will not be returned. Your sheep will be given to your enemies, and no one will rescue them. Your sons and daughters will be given to another nation, and you will wear out your eyes watching for them day after day, powerless to lift a hand. A people that you do not know will eat what your land and labor produce, and you will have nothing but cruel oppression all your days. The sights you see will drive you mad. The LORD will afflict your knees and legs with painful boils that cannot be cured, spreading from the soles of your feet to the top of your head. The LORD will drive you and the king you set over you to a nation unknown to you or your fathers. There you will worship other Gods, Gods of wood and stone. You will become a thing of horror and an object of scorn and ridicule to all the nations where the LORD will drive you. You will sow much seed in the field but you will harvest little, because locusts will devour it. You will plant vineyards and cultivate them but you will not drink the wine or gather the grapes, because worms will eat them. You will have olive trees throughout your country but you will not use the oil, because the olives will drop off. You will have sons and daughters but you will not keep them, because they will go into captivity. Swarms of locusts will take over all your trees and the crops of your land. The alien who lives among you will rise above you higher and higher, but you will sink lower and lower. He will lend to you, but you will not lend to him. He will be the head, but you will be the tail. All these curses will come upon you. They will pursue you and overtake you until you are destroyed, because you did not obey the LORD your God and observe the commands and decrees he gave you. They will be a sign and a wonder to you and your descendants forever. Because you did not serve the LORD your God joyfully and gladly in the time of prosperity, therefore in hunger and thirst, in nakedness and dire poverty, you will serve the enemies the LORD sends against you. He will put an iron yoke on your neck until he has destroyed you. The LORD will bring a nation against you from far away, from the ends of the earth, like an eagle swooping down, a nation whose language you will not understand, a fierce-looking nation without respect for the old or pity for the young. They will devour the young of your livestock and the crops of your land until you are destroyed. They will leave you no grain, new wine or oil, nor any calves of your herds or lambs of your flocks until you are ruined. They will lay siege to all the cities throughout your land until the high fortified walls in which you trust fall down. They will besiege all the cities throughout the land the LORD your God is giving you. Because of the suffering that your enemy will inflict on you during the siege, you will eat the fruit of the womb, the flesh of the sons and daughters the LORD your God has given you. Even the most gentle and sensitive man among you will have no compassion on his own brother or the wife he loves or his surviving children, and he will not give to one of them any of the flesh of his children that he is eating. It will be all he has left because of the suffering your enemy will inflict on you during the siege of all your cities. The most gentle and sensitive woman among you—so sensitive and gentle that she would not venture to touch the ground with the sole of her foot—will begrudge the husband she loves and her own son or daughter the afterbirth from her womb and the children she bears. For she intends to eat them secretly during the siege and in the distress that your enemy will inflict on you in your cities. If you do not carefully follow all the words of this law, which are written in this book, and do not revere this glorious and awesome name—the LORD your God—the LORD will send fearful plagues on you and your descendants, harsh and prolonged disasters, and severe and lingering illnesses. He will bring upon you all the diseases of Egypt that you dreaded, and they will cling to you. The LORD will also bring on you every kind of sickness and disaster not recorded in this Book of the Law, until you are destroyed. You who were as numerous as the stars in the sky will be left but few in number, because you did not obey the LORD your God. Just as it pleased the LORD to make you prosper and increase in number, so it will please him to ruin and destroy you. You will be uprooted from the land you are entering to possess. Then the LORD will scatter you among all nations, from one end of the earth to the other. There you will worship other Gods—Gods of wood and stone, which neither you nor your fathers have known. Among those nations you will find no repose, no resting place for the sole of your foot. There the LORD will give you an anxious mind, eyes weary with longing, and a despairing heart. You will live in constant suspense, filled with dread both night and day, never sure of your life. In the morning you will say, "If only it were evening!" and in the evening,*

Israel, May 14, 1948 — Can a Nation be Born in a Day?

> *"If only it were morning!"— because of the terror that will fill your hearts and the sights that your eyes will see. The LORD will send you back in ships to Egypt on a journey I said you should never make again. There you will offer yourselves for sale to your enemies as male and female slaves, but no one will buy you.* (NIV)

After you read the history of the Jewish people it is plain to see that the Jews, for the most part, followed the path of disobedience throughout their existence. The Jews failed miserably in their promise to *"do everything the Lord has said; we will obey."*

Exod 24:7   *Then he took the Book of the Covenant and read it to the people. They responded, "<u>We will do everything the LORD has said; we will obey.</u>"* (NIV)

With the exception of a few periods of prosperity over the last 4000 years, the Jews have paid for their <u>DISOBEDIENCE</u>! Nevertheless, God still loves His chosen ones and even with their disobedience He will fulfill His unconditional covenant He made with them, but as you will see in this book God is not finished with the Jews as of yet. Here is what God has to say about His feelings for this great people chosen by Him.

Exod 19:1-6   *In the third month after the Israelites left Egypt—on the very day—they came to the Desert of Sinai. After they set out from Rephidim, they entered the Desert of Sinai, and Israel camped there in the desert in front of the mountain. Then Moses went up to God, and the LORD called to him from the mountain and said, "This is what you are to say to the house of Jacob and what you are to tell the people of Israel: 'You yourselves have seen what I did to Egypt, and how I carried you on eagles' wings and brought you to myself. <u>Now if you obey me fully and keep my covenant, then out of all nations you will be my treasured possession.</u> Although the whole earth is mine, you will be for me a kingdom of priests and a holy nation.' These are the words you are to speak to the Israelites."* (NIV)

Deut 14:2   *"For you are a holy people to the LORD your God, <u>and the LORD has chosen you to be a people for Himself, a special treasure above all the peoples who are on the face of the earth.</u>* (NKJ)

Deut 26:19   *He has declared that he will set you in praise, fame and honor high above all the nations he has made and that you will be a people holy to the LORD your God, as he promised.* (NIV)

Ps 148:13-14   *Let them praise the name of the LORD, for his name alone is exalted; his splendor is above the earth and the heavens. <u>He has raised up for his people a horn, the praise of all his saints, of Israel, the</u>*

AFTER THE RAPTURE

people close to his heart. Praise the LORD. (NIV)

Isa 41:8-9 *"But you, O Israel, my servant, Jacob, whom I have chosen, you descendants of Abraham my friend, I took you from the ends of the earth, from its farthest corners I called you. I said, 'You are my servant'; I have chosen you and have not rejected you.* (NIV)

Isa 62:12 *They will be called the Holy People, the Redeemed of the LORD; and you will be called Sought After, the City No Longer Deserted.* (NIV)

Isa 65:9 *I will bring forth descendants from Jacob, and from Judah those who will possess my mountains; my chosen people will inherit them, and there will my servants live.* (NIV)

Jer 31:35-36 *This is what the LORD says, he who appoints the sun to shine by day, who decrees the moon and stars to shine by night, who stirs up the sea so that its waves roar—the LORD Almighty is his name: "Only if these decrees vanish from my sight," declares the LORD, "will the descendants of Israel ever cease to be a nation before me."* (NIV)

We will now look at a brief history of the Jewish people. In ancient history they were known as the Israelites and later became known as Jews. From the time of the fall of Adam and Eve a time period of roughly two thousand years transpired before the nation of Israel was born. The flood was the major event that took place before they became a nation.

God appeared to Abram and commanded him to leave his country and go to a land to be shown to him. He will be made into a great nation and be blessed. His name will be changed to Abraham and many nations will come from him. Among those nations was Israel.

Gen 12:1-3 *The LORD had said to Abram, "Leave your country, your people and your father's household and go to the land I will show you. "I will make you into a great nation and I will bless you; I will make your name great, and you will be a blessing. I will bless those who bless you, and whoever curses you I will curse; and all peoples on earth will be blessed through you."* (NIV)

Gen 17:5-8 *No longer will you be called Abram; your name will be Abraham, for I have made you a father of many nations. I will make you very fruitful; I will make nations of you, and kings will come from you. I will establish my covenant as an everlasting covenant between me and you and your descendants after you for the generations to come, to be your God and the God of your descendants after you. The whole land of Canaan, where you are now an alien, I will give*

84

Israel, May 14, 1948 – Can a Nation Be Born In a Day?

as an everlasting possession to you and your descendants after you; and I will be their God." (NIV)

Gen 18:18-19   ***Abraham will surely become a great and powerful nation, and all nations on earth will be blessed through him.*** *For I have chosen him, so that he will direct his children and his household after him to keep the way of the LORD by doing what is right and just, so that the LORD will bring about for Abraham what he has promised him."* (NIV)

The patriarchs or founders of the Jewish nation are:

1. Abraham
2. Isaac his son
3. Jacob, Isaac's son

JEWISH HISTORY — 2165 BC TO 135 AD

DATE	EVENT
2165-1990 BC	Abraham lived to be 175 years old.
2065-1885 BC	Isaac lived to be 180 years old.
2005-1858 BC	Jacob lived to be 147 years old and his name was changed to Israel. Jacob had twelve sons and they came to be known as the twelve tribes of Israel.
1921 BC	Birth of Jacob's firstborn — Reuben.
1897 BC	Jacob's son Joseph — his brothers sell him into Egyptian slavery.
1875-1445 BC	Israelites lived in Egypt for 430 years.

    Exod 12:40-41   *Now the length of time the Israelite people lived in Egypt was 430 years. **At the end of the 430 years, to the very day, all the LORD's divisions left Egypt.*** (NIV)

    Gal 3:16-18   *The promises were spoken to Abraham and to his seed. The Scripture does not say "and to seeds," meaning many people, but "and to your seed," meaning one person, who is Christ. What I mean is this: **The law, introduced 430 years later, does not set aside the covenant previously established by God and thus do away with the promise. For if the inheritance depends on the law, then it no longer depends on a promise; but God in his grace gave it to Abraham through a promise.*** (NIV)

    Exod 7:16   *Then say to him, 'The LORD, the God of the Hebrews, has sent me to say to you: **Let my people go, so that they may worship me in the desert.** But until now you have not listened.* (NIV)

1445 BC   Moses leads the Israelites out of Egyptian bondage.

AFTER THE RAPTURE

1445 BC	Jubilee — Moses receives "Ten Commandments" on Mount Sinai.
1445 BC	Israelites chose to follow God.

> Exod 24:7 *Then he took the Book of the Covenant and read it to the people. They responded, "We will do everything the LORD has said; we will obey."* (NIV)

1445 BC Sin of the golden calf.

> Deut 9:7-8 *Remember this and never forget how you provoked the LORD your God to anger in the desert. From the day you left Egypt until you arrived here, you have been rebellious against the LORD. At Horeb you aroused the LORD's wrath so that he was angry enough to destroy you.* (NIV)

1445 BC The third 40-day period Moses was on Mount Sinai was the first penitential period for the Israelites. It was from Elul 1 to Tishri 10 and included the first period of the Ten Days of Awe (Tishri 1 to Tishri 10).

1445-1405 BC The Israelites wander in the wilderness for forty years.

> Num 32:13 *The LORD's anger burned against Israel and he made them wander in the desert forty years, until the whole generation of those who had done evil in his sight was gone.* (NIV)

1410 BC Moses — God foretells the unfaithfulness of the nation of Israel to Moses after they enter the promised land.

> Deut 31:15-18 *Then the LORD appeared at the Tent in a pillar of cloud, and the cloud stood over the entrance to the Tent. And the LORD said to Moses: "You are going to rest with your fathers, and these people will soon prostitute themselves to the foreign Gods of the land they are entering.* **They will forsake me and break the covenant I made with them. On that day I will become angry with them and forsake them; I will hide my face from them, and they will be destroyed.** *Many disasters and difficulties will come upon them, and on that day they will ask, 'Have not these disasters come upon us because our God is not with us?' And I will certainly hide my face on that day because of all their wickedness in turning to other Gods.* (NIV)

1405 BC Joshua leads Israelites into the land of Canaan (the promised land). In the book of Psalms we see the history of these times—from Abraham to Joshua entering Canaan.

> Ps 105:1-45 *Give thanks to the LORD, call on his name; make known among the nations what he has done. Sing to him, sing praise to him; tell of all his wonderful acts. Glory in his holy name; let the hearts of those who seek the LORD rejoice. Look to the LORD and his strength; seek his face always. Remember the wonders he has done, his miracles, and the judgments he*

Israel, May 14, 1948 – Can a Nation Be Born In a Day?

pronounced, O descendants of Abraham his servant, O sons of Jacob, his chosen ones. He is the LORD our God; his judgments are in all the earth. He remembers his covenant forever, the word he commanded, for a thousand generations, the covenant he made with Abraham, the oath he swore to Isaac. He confirmed it to Jacob as a decree, to Israel as an everlasting covenant: "To you I will give the land of Canaan as the portion you will inherit." When they were but few in number, few indeed, and strangers in it, they wandered from nation to nation, from one kingdom to another. He allowed no one to oppress them; for their sake he rebuked kings: "Do not touch my anointed ones; do my prophets no harm." He called down famine on the land and destroyed all their supplies of food; and he sent a man before them—Joseph, sold as a slave. They bruised his feet with shackles, his neck was put in irons, till what he foretold came to pass, till the word of the LORD proved him true. The king sent and released him, the ruler of peoples set him free. He made him master of his household, ruler over all he possessed, to instruct his princes as he pleased and teach his elders wisdom. Then Israel entered Egypt; Jacob lived as an alien in the land of Ham. The LORD made his people very fruitful; he made them too numerous for their foes, whose hearts he turned to hate his people, to conspire against his servants. He sent Moses his servant, and Aaron, whom he had chosen. They performed his miraculous signs among them, his wonders in the land of Ham. He sent darkness and made the land dark—for had they not rebelled against his words? He turned their waters into blood, causing their fish to die. Their land teemed with frogs, which went up into the bedrooms of their rulers. He spoke, and there came swarms of flies, and gnats throughout their country. He turned their rain into hail, with lightning throughout their land; he struck down their vines and fig trees and shattered the trees of their country. He spoke, and the locusts came, grasshoppers without number; they ate up every green thing in their land, ate up the produce of their soil. Then he struck down all the firstborn in their land, the firstfruits of all their manhood. He brought out Israel, laden with silver and gold, and from among their tribes no one faltered. Egypt was glad when they left, because dread of Israel had fallen on them. He spread out a cloud as a covering, and a fire to give light at night. They asked, and he brought them quail and satisfied them with the bread of heaven. He opened the rock, and water gushed out; like a river it flowed in the desert. **For he remembered his holy promise given to his servant Abraham. He brought out his people with** *rejoicing, his chosen ones with shouts of joy; he gave them the lands of the nations, and they fell heir to what others had toiled for—that they might keep his precepts and observe his laws. Praise the LORD.* (NIV)

1237-1043 BC	Period of the Judges (Deborah, Gideon, Samson, Samuel, ect.).
1043 BC	Period of the Kings begins.
1043-1011 BC	Saul — Israel's first King.
1011-971 BC	David — "The golden age" of Jewish history. David ruled for forty years.
971-931 BC	Solomon (David's son as King). Solomon ruled for forty years.
966 BC	Solomon begins building the first Temple (It is called Solomon's Temple).

> 1 Kings 6:1   *In the four hundred and eightieth year after the Israelites had come out of Egypt, in the fourth year of Solomon's reign over Israel, in the month of Ziv, the second month,* **he began to build the temple of the LORD.** (NIV)
>
> 1 Kings 8:41-43   *"As for the foreigner who does not belong to your people Israel but has come from a distant land because of your name—for men will hear of your great name and your mighty hand and your outstretched arm—when he comes and prays toward this temple, then hear from heaven, your dwelling place, and do whatever the foreigner asks of you, so that all the peoples of the earth may know your name and fear you, as do your own people Israel,* **and may know that this house I have built bears your Name.** (NIV)

931 BC	Divided kingdom — Israel (Northern 10 tribes), Judah (Southern 2 tribes).
860-795 BC	Time of the prophets Elijah and Elisha.
845-722 BC	Pre-exilic prophets — Obadiah, Joel, Jonah, Amos, Hosea, Isaiah, Micah.
775-750 BC	Amos — to the chosen people, *"I will punish you for all your sins."* Prophecy of the coming destruction of the kingdom of Israel.

> Amos 3:2   **"You only have I chosen of all the families of the earth; therefore I will punish you for all your sins."** (NIV)
>
> Amos 3:11   **Therefore this is what the Sovereign LORD says: "An enemy will overrun the land; he will pull down your strongholds and plunder your fortresses."** (NIV)
>
> Amos 7:9   **"The high places of Isaac will be destroyed and the sanctuaries of Israel will be ruined; with my sword I will rise against the house of Jeroboam."** (NIV)

750-725 BC	Hosea — Prophecy of Israel being without a king for many days.

> Hosea 3:4-5   **For the Israelites will live many days without king or prince,** *without sacrifice or sacred stones, without ephod or idol. Afterward the Israelites will return and seek the*

Israel, May 14, 1948 – Can a Nation Be Born In a Day?

LORD their God and David their king. They will come trembling to the LORD and to his blessings in the last days. (NIV)
Hosea 4:1 *Hear the word of the LORD, you Israelites, because the LORD has a charge to bring against you who live in the land:* **"There is no faithfulness, no love, no acknowledgment of God in the land.** (NIV)

739-690 BC Isaiah — JESUS (Servant) a light for the Gentiles.
Isa 49:6 *he says: "It is too small a thing for you to be my servant to restore the tribes of Jacob and bring back those of Israel I have kept.* **I will also make you a light for the Gentiles,** *that you may bring my salvation to the ends of the earth."* (NIV)

722 BC Kingdom of Israel defeated and destroyed by Assyria. 1st part of 1st scattering of the Jews in exile. These ten tribes are referred to today as the 10 lost tribes of Israel.
2 Kings 17:5-23 ***The king of Assyria invaded the entire land, marched against Samaria and laid siege to it for three years.*** *In the ninth year of Hoshea, the king of Assyria captured Samaria and deported the Israelites to Assyria. He settled them in Halah, in Gozan on the Habor River and in the towns of the Medes.* **All this took place because the Israelites had sinned against the LORD their God,** *who had brought them up out of Egypt from under the power of Pharaoh king of Egypt. They worshiped other Gods and followed the practices of the nations the LORD had driven out before them, as well as the practices that the kings of Israel had introduced.* **The Israelites secretly did things against the LORD their God that were not right.** *From watchtower to fortified city they built themselves high places in all their towns. They set up sacred stones and Asherah poles on every high hill and under every spreading tree. At every high place they burned incense, as the nations whom the LORD had driven out before them had done.* **They did wicked things that provoked the LORD to anger.** *They worshiped idols, though the LORD had said, "You shall not do this." The LORD warned Israel and Judah through all his prophets and seers: "Turn from your evil ways. Observe my commands and decrees, in accordance with the entire Law that I commanded your fathers to obey and that I delivered to you through my servants the prophets." But they would not listen and were as stiff-necked as their fathers, who did not trust in the LORD their God. They rejected his decrees and the covenant he had made with their fathers and the warnings he had given them.* **They followed worthless idols and themselves became worthless.** *They imitated the nations around them although the LORD had ordered them, "Do not do as they do," and they did the things*

the LORD had forbidden them to do. They forsook all the commands of the LORD their God and made for themselves two idols cast in the shape of calves, and an Asherah pole. They bowed down to all the starry hosts, and they worshiped Baal. They sacrificed their sons and daughters in the fire. They practiced divination and sorcery and sold themselves to do evil in the eyes of the LORD, provoking him to anger. So the LORD was very angry with Israel and removed them from his presence. Only the tribe of Judah was left, and even Judah did not keep the commands of the LORD their God. They followed the practices Israel had introduced. Therefore the LORD rejected all the people of Israel; he afflicted them and gave them into the hands of plunderers, until he thrust them from his presence. When he tore Israel away from the house of David, they made Jeroboam son of Nebat their king. Jeroboam enticed Israel away from following the LORD and caused them to commit a great sin. The Israelites persisted in all the sins of Jeroboam and did not turn away from them until the LORD removed them from his presence, as he had warned through all his servants the prophets. **So the people of Israel were taken from their homeland into exile in Assyria, and they are still there.** (NIV)

650-400 BC	Post-exilic prophets — Nahum, Zephaniah, Jeremiah, Habakkuk, Daniel, Ezekiel, Haggai, Zechariah, Malachi.
650-620 BC	Jeremiah — predicting the Babylonian destruction. God's favor is withdrawn from Judah.

Jer 16:3-7 *For this is what the LORD says about the sons and daughters born in this land and about the women who are their mothers and the men who are their fathers:* "*They will die of deadly diseases. They will not be mourned or buried but will be like refuse lying on the ground. They will perish by sword and famine, and their dead bodies will become food for the birds of the air and the beasts of the earth.*" *For this is what the LORD says:* "*Do not enter a house where there is a funeral meal; do not go to mourn or show sympathy, because I have withdrawn my blessing, my love and my pity from this people,*" *declares the LORD.* "*Both high and low will die in this land.* ***They will not be buried or mourned, and no one will cut himself or shave his head for them. No one will offer food to comfort those who mourn for the dead—not even for a father or a mother—nor will anyone give them a drink to console them.*** (NIV)

609 BC	Habakkuk — the just shall live by his faith.

Hab 2:4 *Behold, his soul which is lifted up is not upright in him:* ***but the just shall live by his faith.*** (KJV)

606 BC	Babylonian Empire — King Nebuchadnezzar conquers Judah in 606

BC. The height of the neo-Babylonian Empire came at this time.

Dan 1:1-2 *In the third year of the reign of Jehoiakim king of Judah, Nebuchadnezzar king of Babylon came to Jerusalem and besieged it. And the Lord delivered Jehoiakim king of Judah into his hand, along with some of the articles from the temple of God. These he carried off to the temple of his God in Babylonia and put in the treasure house of his God.* (NIV)

606-536 BC Judah's 70 year exile in Babylon, 2nd part of the 1st scattering of Jews in exile.

Ps 44:9-16 *But now you have rejected and humbled us; you no longer go out with our armies. You made us retreat before the enemy, and our adversaries have plundered us. You gave us up to be devoured like sheep and have scattered us among the nations. You sold your people for a pittance, gaining nothing from their sale. You have made us a reproach to our neighbors, the scorn and derision of those around us. You have made us a byword among the nations; the peoples shake their heads at us. My disgrace is before me all day long, and my face is covered with shame at the taunts of those who reproach and revile me, because of the enemy, who is bent on revenge.* (NIV)

Ps 137:1-6 *By the rivers of Babylon we sat and wept when we remembered Zion. There on the poplars we hung our harps, for there our captors asked us for songs, our tormentors demanded songs of joy; they said, "Sing us one of the songs of Zion!" How can we sing the songs of the LORD while in a foreign land? If I forget you, O Jerusalem, may my right hand forget [its skill]. May my tongue cling to the roof of my mouth if I do not remember you, if I do not consider Jerusalem my highest joy.* (NIV)

A short synopsis of the failure of the chosen people during their early history can be found in the book of Psalms.

Ps 106:1-48 *Praise ye the LORD. O give thanks unto the LORD; for he is good: for his mercy endureth for ever. Who can utter the mighty acts of the LORD? who can shew forth all his praise? Blessed are they that keep judgment, and he that doeth righteousness at all times. Remember me, O LORD, with the favour that thou bearest unto thy people: O visit me with thy salvation; That I may see the good of thy chosen, that I may rejoice in the gladness of thy nation, that I may glory with thine inheritance. We have sinned with our fathers, we have committed iniquity, we have done wickedly. Our fathers understood not thy wonders in Egypt; they remembered not the multitude of thy mercies; but provoked him at the sea, even at the Red sea. Nevertheless he saved them for his name's sake, that he might make his mighty power to be known. He rebuked the Red sea also, and it was dried up: so he led them through the depths, as through the wilderness. And he saved them from the hand of him that hated them, and redeemed them from the hand of the enemy. And the waters covered their enemies: there was not one of them left. Then believed they his words; they sang his praise.* **They soon forgat his works; they waited not for his counsel: <u>But lusted exceedingly in the wilderness, and tempted God in the desert.</u>** *And he gave them their request; but sent leanness into their soul. They envied Moses also in the camp, and Aaron the saint of the LORD. The earth opened and swallowed up Dathan, and covered the company of Abiram. And a fire was kindled in their company; the flame burned up the wicked.* **<u>They made a calf in Horeb</u>, and worshipped the molten image.** *Thus they changed their glory into the similitude of an ox that eateth grass.* **<u>They forgat God their saviour</u>, which had done great things in Egypt;** *Wondrous works in the land of Ham, and terrible things by the Red sea. Therefore he said that he would destroy them, had not Moses his chosen stood before him in the breach, to turn away his wrath, lest he should destroy them.* **<u>Yea, they despised the pleasant land, they believed not his word: But murmured in their tents, and hearkened not unto the voice of the LORD</u>.** *Therefore he lifted up his hand against them, to overthrow them in the wilderness: To overthrow their seed also among the nations, and to scatter them in the lands.* **They joined themselves also unto Baalpeor, <u>and ate the sacrifices of the dead</u>.** *Thus they provoked him to anger with their inventions: and the plague brake in upon them. Then stood up Phinehas, and executed judgment: and so the plague was stayed. And that was counted unto him for righteousness unto all generations for evermore.* **<u>They angered him also at the waters of strife</u>, so that it went ill with Moses for their sakes: <u>Because they provoked his spirit</u>, so that he spake unadvisedly with his lips. <u>They did not destroy the nations</u>, concerning whom the LORD commanded them: But were mingled among the heathen, and learned their works. <u>And they served their idols</u>: which were a snare unto them. Yea, they sacrificed their sons and their daughters unto devils, And shed innocent blood, even the blood of their sons and of their daughters, whom they sacrificed unto the idols of Canaan: and the land was polluted with blood. <u>Thus were they defiled with their own works, and went a whoring with their own inventions</u>.** *Therefore was the wrath of the LORD kindled against his people, insomuch that he abhorred his own inheritance. And he gave them into the* *hand of the heathen; and they that hated them ruled over them. Their enemies also oppressed them, and they were brought into subjection under their hand. Many times did he deliver them; <u>but they provoked him with their counsel, and were brought low for their iniquity.</u> Nevertheless he regarded their affliction, when he heard their cry: And he remembered for them his covenant, and repented according to the multitude of his mercies. **He made them also to be pitied of all those that carried them captives.** Save us, O LORD our God, and gather us from among the heathen, to give thanks unto thy holy name, and to triumph in thy praise. Blessed be the LORD God of Israel from everlasting to everlasting: and let all the people say, Amen. Praise ye the LORD.* (KJV)

593 BC   SHEKINAH GLORY leaves the Temple in Jerusalem.

Ezek 11:22-23   *Then the cherubim, with the wheels beside them, spread their wings, and the glory of the God of Israel was above them. <u>The glory of the LORD went up from within the city and stopped above the mountain east of it.</u>* (NIV)

586 BC   Babylonian destruction of Solomon's Temple and Jerusalem on the 9th of Av.

Jer 19:11   *and say to them, 'This is what the LORD Almighty says: <u>I will smash this nation and this city just as this potter's jar is smashed and cannot be repaired.</u> They will bury the dead in Topheth until there is no more room.* (NIV)

Lam 1:1   *<u>How deserted lies the city</u>, once so full of people! How like a widow is she, who once was great among the nations! She who was queen among the provinces has now become a slave.* (NIV)

2 Kings 25:1-26   *And it came to pass in the ninth year of his reign, in the tenth month, in the tenth day of the month, <u>that Nebuchadnezzar king of Babylon came, he, and all his host, against Jerusalem, and pitched against it; and they built forts against it round about.</u> And the city was besieged unto the eleventh year of king Zedekiah. And on the ninth day of the fourth month the famine prevailed in the city, and there was no bread for the people of the land. And the city was broken up, and all the men of war fled by night by the way of the gate between two walls, which is by the king's garden: (now the Chaldees were against the city round about:) and the king went the way toward the plain. And the army of the Chaldees pursued after the king, and overtook him in the plains of Jericho: and all his army were scattered from him. So they took the king, and brought him up to the king of Babylon to Riblah; and they gave judgment upon him. And they slew the sons of Zedekiah before*

his eyes, and put out the eyes of Zedekiah, and bound him with fetters of brass, and carried him to Babylon. And in the fifth month, on the seventh day of the month, which is the nineteenth year of king Nebuchadnezzar king of Babylon, came Nebuzaradan, captain of the guard, a servant of the king of Babylon, unto Jerusalem: **And he burnt the house of the LORD, and the king's house, and all the houses of Jerusalem, and every great man's house burnt he with fire.** And all the army of the Chaldees, that were with the captain of the guard, brake down the walls of Jerusalem round about. Now the rest of the people that were left in the city, and the fugitives that fell away to the king of Babylon, with the remnant of the multitude, did Nebuzaradan the captain of the guard carry away. But the captain of the guard left of the poor of the land to be vinedressers and husbandmen. And the pillars of brass that were in the house of the LORD, and the bases, and the brasen sea that was in the house of the LORD, did the Chaldees break in pieces, and carried the brass of them to Babylon. And the pots, and the shovels, and the snuffers, and the spoons, and all the vessels of brass wherewith they ministered, took they away. And the firepans, and the bowls, and such things as were of gold, in gold, and of silver, in silver, the captain of the guard took away. The two pillars, one sea, and the bases which Solomon had made for the house of the LORD; the brass of all these vessels was without weight. The height of the one pillar was eighteen cubits, and the chapiter upon it was brass: and the height of the chapiter three cubits; and the wreathen work, and pomegranates upon the chapiter round about, all of brass: and like unto these had the second pillar with wreathen work. And the captain of the guard took Seraiah the chief priest, and Zephaniah the second priest, and the three keepers of the door: And out of the city he took an officer that was set over the men of war, and five men of them that were in the king's presence, which were found in the city, and the principal scribe of the host, which mustered the people of the land, and threescore men of the people of the land that were found in the city: And Nebuzaradan captain of the guard took these, and brought them to the king of Babylon to Riblah: And the king of Babylon smote them, and slew them at Riblah in the land of Hamath. So Judah was carried away out of their land. And as for the people that remained in the land of Judah, whom Nebuchadnezzar king of Babylon had left, even over them he made Gedaliah the son of Ahikam, the son of Shaphan, ruler. And when all the captains of the armies, they and their men, heard that the king of Babylon had made

Israel, May 14, 1948 – Can a Nation Be Born In a Day?

Gedaliah governor, there came to Gedaliah to Mizpah, even Ishmael the son of Nethaniah, and Johanan the son of Careah, and Seraiah the son of Tanhumeth the Netophathite, and Jaazaniah the son of a Maachathite, they and their men. And Gedaliah sware to them, and to their men, and said unto them, Fear not to be the servants of the Chaldees: dwell in the land, and serve the king of Babylon; and it shall be well with you. But it came to pass in the seventh month, that Ishmael the son of Nethaniah, the son of Elishama, of the seed royal, came, and ten men with him, and smote Gedaliah, that he died, and the Jews and the Chaldees that were with him at Mizpah. And all the people, both small and great, and the captains of the armies, arose, and came to Egypt: for they were afraid of the Chaldees. (KJV)

Lam 2:6 ***He has laid waste his dwelling like a garden; he has destroyed his place of meeting**. The LORD has made Zion forget her appointed feasts and her Sabbaths; in his fierce anger he has spurned both king and priest.* (NIV)

Jer 52:27-30 ***And the king of Babylon smote them, and put them to death in Riblah in the land of Hamath. Thus Judah was carried away captive out of his own land**. This is the people whom Nebuchadrezzar carried away captive: in the seventh year three thousand Jews and three and twenty: In the eighteenth year of Nebuchadrezzar he carried away captive from Jerusalem eight hundred thirty and two persons: In the three and twentieth year of Nebuchadrezzar Nebuzaradan the captain of the guard carried away captive of the Jews seven hundred forty and five persons: **all the persons were four thousand and six hundred**.* (KJV)

539-331 BC   Medo-Persian Empire — Cyrus the Great defeats Babylon.

Isa 45:1-5 *"**This is what the LORD says to his anointed, to Cyrus, whose right hand I take hold of to subdue nations before him and to strip kings of their armor, to open doors before him so that gates will not be shut: I will go before you and will level the mountains; I will break down gates of bronze and cut through bars of iron. I will give you the treasures of darkness, riches stored in secret places, so that you may know that I am the LORD, the God of Israel, who summons you by name.** For the sake of Jacob my servant, of Israel my chosen, I summon you by name and bestow on you a title of honor, though you do not acknowledge me. I am the LORD, and there is no other; apart from me there is no God. I will strengthen you, though you have not acknowledged me,* (NIV)

Jer 29:10 *This is what the LORD says: "**When seventy years***

	*are completed for Babylon, **I will come to you and fulfill my gracious promise to bring you back to this place**.* (NIV)
536-516 BC	The Jews are allowed to return to Judah and rebuild the Temple that was destroyed by the Babylonians in 586 BC. It is the second Temple to be built in Jerusalem and is known as Zerubbabel's Temple. The glory of the Lord does not return to dwell in this Temple.
500 BC ?	Zechariah — the lesson from history.
	Zech 7:4-14 *Then the word of the LORD Almighty came to me: "Ask all the people of the land and the priests, 'When you fasted and mourned in the fifth and seventh months for the past seventy years, was it really for me that you fasted? And when you were eating and drinking, were you not just feasting for yourselves? Are these not the words the LORD proclaimed through the earlier prophets when Jerusalem and its surrounding towns were at rest and prosperous, and the Negev and the western foothills were settled?'" And the word of the LORD came again to Zechariah: "This is what the LORD Almighty says: 'Administer true justice; show mercy and compassion to one another. Do not oppress the widow or the fatherless, the alien or the poor. In your hearts do not think evil of each other.' "But they refused to pay attention; stubbornly they turned their backs and stopped up their ears.* ***They made their hearts as hard as flint and would not listen to the law or to the words that the LORD Almighty had sent by his Spirit through the earlier prophets. So the LORD Almighty was very angry.*** *"'When I called, they did not listen; so when they called, I would not listen,' says the LORD Almighty. 'I scattered them with a whirlwind among all the nations, where they were strangers. The land was left so desolate behind them that no one could come or go. This is how they made the pleasant land desolate.'"* (NIV)
438-415 BC ?	Malachi — last of the writing prophets who wrote the last book in the Old Testament. This begins a period of more than 400 years of silence from God. The next prophet from God will be John the Baptist. The division of the religious sects of the Pharisees and the Sadducees developed during the period between these two prophets.
331-63 BC	Greek Empire – under Alexander the Great defeats the Medo-Persian Empire. Israel falls under Greek authority.
168 BC (Dec.)	The Syrian king Antiochus Epiphanes, Greek for "God-manifest," desecrated the Temple in Jerusalem (a province under his rule). By penalty of death he outlawed circumcision, Sabbath observance and even possession of a Bible. He ordered his soldiers to sacrifice pigs at the Temple and then compelled Jews to do the same. A statue of the Greek God Jupiter was set up in the Temple's Holy of Holies. [1]

Israel, May 14, 1948 – Can a Nation Be Born In a Day?

63 BC- AD 500	Roman Empire – occupies Jerusalem in 63 BC. Pompey encountered resistance only at the Temple Mount. After a three-month siege the Romans succeeded in entering the Temple after killing several thousand of its priests and defenders. [2]
20 BC-AD 64	Herod the Great undertook the task of rebuilding Zerubbabel's Temple on a grander scale. He wanted to impress the Jewish people who lived there. His intent was to enlarge and further beautify the existing Temple. The job is completed in 64 AD, after King Herod's death in 6 AD. He was succeeded by his son Herod Archelaus.
4 BC	Jesus is born.
AD 26	John the Baptist's first public appearance.
AD 27	Jesus begins His public ministry. It will last for 3 ½ years.
AD 30	Jesus is crucified on Passover.

JEWISH HISTORY – 483 YEARS TO CHRIST IN DANIEL'S EYES

Dan 9:24-27   *"__Seventy 'sevens' are decreed for your people and your holy city__ to finish transgression, to put an end to sin, to atone for wickedness, to bring in everlasting righteousness, to seal up vision and prophecy and to anoint the most holy. "Know and understand this: From the issuing of the decree to restore and rebuild Jerusalem until the Anointed One, the ruler, comes, there will be seven 'sevens,' and sixty-two 'sevens.' It will be rebuilt with streets and a trench, but in times of trouble. After the sixty-two 'sevens,' the Anointed One will be cut off and will have nothing. The people of the ruler who will come will destroy the city and the sanctuary. The end will come like a flood: War will continue until the end, and desolations have been decreed. __He will confirm a covenant with many for one 'seven.'__ In the middle of the 'seven' he will put an end to sacrifice and offering. And on a wing [of the temple] he will set up an abomination that causes desolation, until the end that is decreed is poured out on him."* (NIV)

What an amazing story that is presented in these four verses. It is the last 490-year period that God will deal with His chosen people and the holy city of Jerusalem and what a fantastic story it is. After this 490-year period is completed—all Israel will be saved.

God has foreordained this time to comply with His plan of salvation. He will not wait forever for mankind to come back to Him, not even for the chosen people (Jews). Since Daniel wrote this as a prophetic event, it was yet a future period of time for the Jewish people, a period of time to be fulfilled in the distant future. Daniel wrote these passages around the middle of the sixth century BC.

It will take 490 years to settle the decrees set by God against His people (the Jews) and upon the holy city (Jerusalem). You need to remember that this account is strictly dealing with the Jewish people and when this period is over the Jews will realize what has been promised to them for thousands of years. The Jewish people were correct thousands of years ago when they believed that the fulfillment of these verses in Daniel were to be fulfilled in the distant future. Verse twenty-four reveals what will be accomplished during the 490-year period. Daniel starts by telling us that it will take 490 years to accomplish the following:

1. ***to finish transgression*** — The Hebrew word for "to finish," is *kala* and has a deeper meaning. The only time this word is translated to mean, "to finish," is in Daniel 9:24. It is usually translated; to restrict, to restrain, to withhold, to shut up, to keep back, to refrain or to forbid. A better translation here would be to restrict or refrain. Likewise the word for transgression, *pesha`*, also means a rebellion or a revolt. At the end of this 490-year period it will bring an end or restrict the rebellion of the Jewish people against God that has existed for thousands of years.
2. ***to put an end to sin*** — Translations here again are misleading. The Hebrew word, *chatham,* is better rendered; to seal up or to fasten up by sealing. Again the only time this word is translated to mean, *"to make an end of,"* is in Daniel 9:24. There are three Hebrew words that are used for sin in the Old Testament. The word used for sin in Daniel 9:24 is *chatta'ah*. In the *Strong's Hebrew Definition,* this word can mean, "an offence" (sometimes habitual sinfulness). At the end of this 490-year period the habitual sinfulness of the Jewish people will be sealed up. We all know that sin will still exist during the Millennium, but it will be reduced because of the result of Satan's absence and God's appearance.
3. ***to atone for wickedness*** — At the end of the 490-year period Jesus will have intervened at this time in history to judge every person who has existed from Adam. The saved will receive their just rewards and the unsaved will have been purged from the earth. This includes those who were alive at this time, along with those who have already died. Those left on earth in the flesh after this 490-year period will replenish the earth and will **all** be saved as individual people.
4. ***to bring in everlasting righteousness*** — The Hebrew word used here for righteousness, *tsedeq*, can also be translated to mean; justice, prosperity, deliverance or victory. With Jesus as our King and Judge, living on the earth after the 490-year period is over, He will bring in everlasting justice and also victory.
5. ***to seal up vision and prophecy*** — This is pretty self explanatory in the English. With Jesus in our midst there will no longer be a need for visions like Daniel received or prophecy from prophets to teach the people who will be living on the earth, including their offspring. These teachings will come from the throne of Jesus in Jerusalem.
6. ***to anoint the most holy*** —This is more than likely a reference to the reestablishing of the Holy of Holies when Jesus rebuilds the Temple after the Tribulation Period is over. The Hebrew word for, "most" and "holy," is *qodesh* and usually refers to a sacred place or thing. Occasionally, it is used in the abstract as, "Holiness unto the Lord." In this sense, it could refer to Jesus. Actually, either interpretation would be correct as the Holy of Holies and Jesus will both be anointed during the Kingdom Age.

Israel, May 14, 1948 – Can a Nation Be Born In a Day?

For translation references in Hebrew for this book I consulted the *Brown-Driver-Briggs Hebrew Definition*, along with *Strong's Hebrew Definition*, to look at the words that are translated into English from Hebrew and to conform to what the entire Bible teaches on the destiny of the Jewish people during the Kingdom Age (Day of the Lord). I believe these six events translate better as: Seventy-sevens (490 years) are decreed for your (Daniel's) people (the Jews) and your holy city (Jerusalem):

1. to restrict the rebellion of the Jewish people against God
2. to fasten up by sealing the habitual sinfulness of the Jewish people
3. to make atonement for sin (judge)
4. to bring in everlasting justice (victory)
5. to bring an end to visions and prophecies
6. and to anoint the Holy of Holies

The best translation available can be found in the *New Jerusalem Bible*.

> Dan 9:24   *Seventy weeks are decreed for your people and your holy city, for putting an end to transgression, for placing the seal on sin, for expiating crime, for introducing everlasting uprightness for setting the seal on vision and on prophecy, for anointing the holy of holies.* (NJB)

This will usher in the most remarkable period of history, a period of peace and prosperity. Daniel states it best in chapter twelve.

> Dan 12:7b   ***When the power of the holy people has been finally broken, all these things will be completed.*** " (NIV)

In Daniel 9:25, he tells us to know and understand something. To fully understand the meaning of what Daniel was talking about in verse twenty-four, history would have had to have taken place. Since some of the prophetic events that Daniel is speaking about have already come to fulfillment, it makes it easier to figure out what has not been fulfilled. As we look back at history we know that King Nebuchadnezzar destroyed Jerusalem in 586 BC. It was in 539 BC when the Medo-Persian empire conquered the Babylonians and set up their empire. They had a king by the name of Cyrus. He made a decree to allow the Jewish people to leave their exiled Babylonian captivity to return to Jerusalem and to restore the city and rebuild their holy Temple. This happened around 538 BC. Daniel even predicts that it will be rebuilt in times of trouble and that was exactly how it happened. We have to remember that one seven, spoken of here, is equal to seven years. So seventy times seven is meant to be a period of 490 years. Using this same formula, Daniel now gives us two periods of time to let us know how long it will be before the Anointed One (Jesus) is crucified. To the Jews it is the Messiah or literally their Deliverer or Savior. These two periods of time are seven 'sevens'(49 years) and sixty-two 'sevens' (434 years). When you add the two together, you come up with 483 years. So we now know that the 490-year period that Daniel is referring

AFTER THE RAPTURE

to had its beginning 483 years before Jesus Christ was crucified.

Then we are told that after the sixty-two 'sevens' or the 434-year period the Anointed One (Jesus) *"will be cut off and will have nothing."* This is a reference to the crucifixion of our Lord and Savior Jesus. It is at this point that there is a big gap in history that does not appear in print. The *"ruler who will come,"* in verse twenty-six, is speaking of the Antichrist who will appear almost two thousand years later at the end of the age. We know that the Antichrist is spoken of here because of the reference to the Abomination of Desolation in verse twenty-seven. This gap or time period is the time we are currently living in today. It is referred to as the Dispensation of Grace on all the charts listed in this book. It is the time between the first and second comings of Jesus.

The rest of verse twenty-six and all of verse twenty-seven are consumed in the last period of one 'seven' or 7 years that complete the entire period of 490 years. This 7-year period is known in Bible prophecy as the Tribulation Period. We have a short synopsis of the Tribulation Period in these verses. The people of the ruler who will come are the wicked unsaved people who will be living on the earth during that 7-year period. They will once again conquer Jerusalem and desecrate the Temple at the midpoint of the Tribulation Period. The end will come in a short period of time (3 ½ years). War and devastation are purposed by God. The Antichrist will make a peace treaty with Israel and many other countries (Arab) for one 'seven' or 7 years. Half way through the seven years the Antichrist will break the peace treaty by going to Jerusalem, claim himself to be God and start his pursuit to destroy all the Jews living on the face of the earth. The last 3 ½ year period talked about here is also known as the Time of Jacob's Trouble.

Jer 30:7   *Alas! for that day is great, so that none is like it: it is even <u>the time of Jacob's trouble</u>; but he shall be saved out of it.* (KJV)

During the time period of 483 years to the time of Christ's crucifixion the Jews were basically turned away from God. However, remember that God always has a remnant who comes to Him by faith. The religious idolatry of the Jews before this time finally brought silence from God in heaven. The last prophet from the Old Testament, Malachi, will be the last prophet sent by God to instruct His people until the forerunner (John the Baptist) is sent to usher in the Messiah (Jesus). Malachi's ministry ended somewhere around 415 BC, so you can see this period of silence from God lasted somewhere around four hundred years.

Can you imagine how perverse the Jewish religious leaders became during those 400 years? They were so bad by the time Jesus appeared on the scene that He called them a brood of snakes.

Matt 23:33   *"<u>You snakes! You brood of vipers!</u> How will you escape being condemned to hell?* (NIV)

The nation of Israel was eagerly expecting the Messiah when Christ appeared on the scene. It is too bad that they did not accept Him instead of rejecting Him. Their comment was, *"Let his blood be on us and on our children."*

Israel, May 14, 1948 – Can a Nation Be Born In a Day?

Matt 27:25 *All the people answered, "<u>Let his blood be on us and on our children!</u>"* (NIV)

We again resume our story and pick up the scene at the Mount of Olives where Jesus is conversing with some of His disciples during the week just before He was crucified. Jesus is predicting the destruction of the Temple forty years later.

AD 30   Jesus prophecy of the destruction of the Temple.
> Luke 21:6-7   *As for these things which ye behold, <u>the days will come, in the which there shall not be left one stone upon another, that shall not be thrown down.</u> And they asked him, saying, Master, but when shall these things be? and what sign will there be when these things shall come to pass?* (KJV)

AD 66-70   The Great Revolt — About the time Christ was a small boy, a new group of Jews arose known as Zealots. They were anti-Roman rebels who were active for more than six decades. They later instigated the Great Revolt. The Romans vanquished the Galilee and an estimated 100,000 Jews were killed or sold into slavery. It is estimated that as many as one million Jews died in the Great Revolt against Rome. [3]

AD 70   This is the fulfillment of the prophecy by Jesus in 30 AD. Roman soldiers destroy Jerusalem and the second Temple on the 9th of Av.
> Luke 21:20-24   *"<u>When you see Jerusalem being surrounded by armies, you will know that its desolation is near.</u> Then let those who are in Judea flee to the mountains, let those in the city get out, and let those in the country not enter the city. **For this is the time of punishment in fulfillment of all that has been written.** How dreadful it will be in those days for pregnant women and nursing mothers! There will be great distress in the land and wrath against this people. They will fall by the sword and will be taken as prisoners to all the nations. <u>Jerusalem will be trampled on by the Gentiles until the times of the Gentiles are fulfilled</u>.* (NIV)

AD 73   Masada — After Rome destroyed Jerusalem and the second Temple in 70 AD, the Great Revolt ended—except for the surviving Zealots who fled Jerusalem to the fortress of Masada, near the Dead Sea. There, they held out for three years. At the end of the siege, 960 Jews committed suicide rather than be captured. Only two women and five children managed to hide themselves during the mass suicide. [4]

AD 132-135   Bar-Kokhba Rebellion — Simon bar-Kokhba proclaimed himself to be the Messiah. Bar-Kokhba himself must have been a charismatic figure, because tens of thousands of Jews flocked to join his army. The Great Revolt of 66-70 AD, followed some sixty years later by the Bar-Kokhba revolt, were the greatest calamities in Jewish history prior to the Holocaust. [5]

This brings an end to the first portion of Jewish history that we will be discussing. In 135 AD, after the Bar-Kokhba revolt, the Roman general Vespasian left the landscape desolate. The second scattering of the Jews came about as the result of the two rebellions— The Great Revolt in 66-70 AD and the Bar-Kokhba revolt in 132-135 AD. In the next section of Jewish history we will follow the second scattering of the Jewish people. How they were pushed, shoved, pulled and tugged around until a large number of Jews ended up in Eastern Europe and became involved in the Holocaust almost two thousand years later.

JEWISH HISTORY—135 AD TO 1870 AD

During this section of Jewish history we will talk about a people who were literally scattered to almost every nation of the then known world. Starting with the defeat of the ten northern tribes of Israel by the Assyrians in 722 BC and including the defeat of the two tribes of Israel in the Kingdom of Judah, the Jewish people have been fulfilling the disobedience portion of their prophecy from the book of Deuteronomy. They will not become a self-governing nation again for more than 2500 years.

After Pompey occupied Jerusalem in 63 BC and declared the territory a Roman province, Palestine was subject to Roman rule for the next seven hundred years. After the Bar-Kokhba rebellion was over in 135 AD, the ancient kingdom was devastated. Towns and villages were razed, thousands of Jews were sold into slavery and all Jews were forbidden to enter Jerusalem, now rebuilt and named Aelia Capitolina. It was also the bitter end of Judaism in Palestine.

The situation for the Jews settled down after 135 AD, until the Roman Emperor Constantine adopted Christianity as the official religion of the empire in 313 AD. At this time the Jews were quickly placed under various legal restrictions. Jews who converted their Christian wives to Judaism were liable to the death penalty. A marriage between a Christian and a Jew was declared to be adulterous. A hundred years later in the 5th Century, Jews were not allowed positions in the civil service or the army; Jewish courts could only try cases between Jewish people; and synagogues could only be repaired with special permission. Almost from the beginning of institutionalized Christianity, preachers publicly incited the common people to attack Jewish people, their districts and their synagogues.

In the 4th Century a fierce exponent of the Jews, John Chrysostom, wrote the most virulent kind of literary attack against the Jews. From his pulpit in Antioch, Chrysostom delivered eight sermons attributing all manner of perversions to the Jews. He even compared the Jews to the Devil. John Chrysostom's preaching paved the way for the Anti-Semitism of the Middle Ages.

The Western Roman Empire came to its political end in 455 AD, when Rome was defeated by the Vandals. At that time the papacy became the dominant force in Rome, the old capital of the empire. The moral authority of the papacy was acknowledged by all western Christendom at this time and as a result of that the history of the Jews of Christian Europe was a reflection of papal policy for the next 1400 years.

In the 7th Century, the progress of Islam was astonishing. By 644 AD, they had conquered Israel, Syria, Egypt, Iraq and Persia, and became a part of the New Islamic Empire. As a whole the Jews were treated well under Muslim rule with both Christians and

Israel, May 14, 1948 – Can a Nation Be Born In a Day?

Jews being recognized as "People of the Book." As long as the Jews living there accepted the supremacy of the Muslim state they were guaranteed exemption from serving in the military and also granted religious autonomy and toleration.

The time period from the 8th to the late 11th Century was an unusual time of peace and prosperity for the Jewish people of the West and lasted up to the time of the Crusades. The favorable times in Central Europe came to an end with the Crusades. This was a major turning point in Jewish history. The Crusades severely affected relations between Christians and Jews up to modern times.

Proclaiming to free Jerusalem, the Holy City of the Bible, from Muslim control, Pope Urban II launched the First Crusade in 1096. When the people began to realize just how many "heathens" were living among them, they began killing with almost no opposition, all Jews who refused to be baptized into the Christian faith. Entire Jewish communities were annihilated and an estimated 12,000 Jewish people were killed within twelve months.

The Second Crusade, in 1146-1147 and the Third Crusade in 1189-1193, were no less devastating. Relations between Jews and Christians in Europe underwent a drastic change after the Crusades. They laid the foundation of the irrational hatred the Jews faced in the Middle Ages. The hatred often found in the imagery and paintings of Christian Churches and Cathedrals. Paintings depicting the Jews as a symbol of evil and the synagogue as a decrepit old woman wearing a lopsided crown with her eyes blindfolded, her scepter cracked, bearing broken Tables of the Law, sitting astride a pig and portrayed with other equally denigrating features. The Jews were also derided and mocked in the Christian mystery plays. After the invention of the printing press, Jews became the subject of offensive engravings which appear to have originated in Germany.

Such portrayals made such a deep impression on the common people that false accusations began to be made against the Jews. Notorious among these accusations was one of ritual murder, whereby the Jews were accused of sacrificing Christian children during the Passover in a travesty of the Passion of Christ and used the blood in their rituals. These rumors spread across all of Continental Europe.

Of all the false accusations made against the Jews, the one of poisoning wells and rivers became extremely fatal. During the period from 1348 to 1350, when the plague of the Black Death swept across Europe, this accusation was made. The Jews were held responsible and tens of thousands of Jews were slaughtered.

At the Fourth Lateran Council in 1215, the Church decreed that all Jews living in Christian lands were to wear a distinctive badge, generally a solid yellow circle sewn on an upper garment. The Fourth Lateran Council was convened by the deeply Anti-Semitic pope, Pope Innocent III.

The Spanish Inquisition from 1480-1834 was a perverse attempt to save the souls of people by torturing their bodies. The Inquisitors reasoned that since only Christians of pure faith could go to heaven, all others would be sentenced to the eternal torment in hell. It made sense to them to temporarily torture people of impure faith until they accepted Christ to thereby save their souls from the never-ending tortures of the next world.

Contrary to a popular misconception, the Spanish Inquisition was not directed only toward the Jews. It was directed toward all supposed heretics, but it paid particular attention to former Jews who had converted to Christianity.

AFTER THE RAPTURE

On July 20, 1492, the entire Jewish community was expelled from Spain. It was made up of some 200,000 people. Thousands of Jewish refugees died while trying to reach safety. This Jewish expulsion was the pet project of the Spanish Inquisition and was headed up by Father Tomas de Torquemada. These Jews known as Sephardim, ended up mainly in Turkey, North Africa and Italy with some of them spread out throughout Europe and the Arab world.

Medieval Jews were forcibly confined into overcrowded neighborhoods known as ghettos. This institution originated in Italy, where the ghettos were under the rule of the popes. In the papal bull, *Cum Nimis absurdum* (1555), Pope Paul IV formalized the institution. Pope Paul IV was extremely Anti-Semitic. In the papal bull, it stated that it was absurd for Christians to act lovingly to the very people who had been condemned by God for their sins. Pope Paul IV, therefore legislated that the Jews who were residing in areas under papal rule were to be segregated into ghettos.

Europe finally emerged from the Middle Ages to enter modern history at the end of the 15th Century. The transition is marked by the Renaissance and also humanism. From its cradle in Italy, humanism spread across Germany and western Europe. The new ideas brought restoration of culture, the development of national sentiment and freedom of worship. These ideas caused a conflict within the Catholic Church, who from Rome controlled the destinies of the Christian kingdoms. When the Jews were expelled from a country, they would be welcomed into another. This caused them to be spread all over Western and Eastern Europe, Asia, Africa and eventually the Americas.

The Protestant Reformation had its beginning in 1517, when Martin Luther nailed his ninety-five thesis to the door of a Catholic Church. In the early years, after Martin Luther broke from the Catholic Church, he showed favor to the Jewish people. After a failed attempt to bring large numbers of Jews to Christianity, Martin Luther became a fanatical Anti-Semite. He produced the most Anti-Semitic writings in Germany up to the time of Adolf Hitler. Luther was so incensed that the Jews had not followed his brand of Christianity that he outlined eight actions to be taken against them. They were:

1. Burn all synagogues
2. Destroy all Jewish homes
3. Confiscate all Jewish Holy Books
4. Forbid rabbis to teach, on pain of death
5. Forbid Jews to travel
6. Confiscate Jewish property
7. Force Jews to do physical labor
8. Expel all the Jews (In case the above measures failed)

On one occasion, Martin Luther who was an earlier exponent of Christian love said, "I would threaten to cut their tongues out from their throats, if they refuse to acknowledge the truth that God is a trinity and not a plain unity."

In 1665, Shabbetai Zevi, who was a Turkish Jew, proclaimed himself to be "the Messiah." Possibly more than half the Jews in the world at that time believed in him. They believed that he would liberate Palestine from Turkish rule and restore it as an independent Jewish state. As Shabbetai confronted the Turkish Sultan with a demand for Palestine, he was confronted with a threat from the monarch—either convert to Islam or be tortured to death.

Not long after that confrontation, Shabbetai entered the Sultan's palace wearing a turban and taking the Muslim name Mehemet Effendi. The shock was overwhelming to the Jewish community. Once again, the Jewish people suffered a major failure with a "Messiah." Jesus had become the father of Christianity, Bar-Kokhba had led the Jews into a disastrous revolt against the Romans and now Shabbetai had become a Muslim.

France was the first European country to give the Jewish people equal rights in 1791 in the aftermath of the French Revolution. When Napoleon became the Emperor of France, in 1804, he established the right for every French citizen to follow any trade. Gradually emancipation of the Jews in western Europe began a slow and laborious process. As the control over most of western Europe expanded, at the time of Napoleon's Empire, emancipation in the form of laws followed. When Napoleon fell, the Jewish people of Europe lost most of their newly won rights. The exceptions were France and Holland.

JEWISH HISTORY 1870 AD TO MAY 9, 1945 (VE DAY)

It was not long after the progress of emancipated Jewry started before it began to wane. After the Franco-Prussian War of 1870-1871, a period of political upheaval arose in Germany that caused an economic crisis, social turmoil followed by the collapse of the stock exchange in 1873. This served as a setting for the re-emergence of organized anti-Jewish activity. At this time a new movement known as Anti-Semitism was founded by Wilhelm Marr, a convert whose father had been Jewish. There is a fundamental difference between the anti-Jewish attitude of the Medieval Church and Marr's, "Anti-Semitism." The aim of the former was to convert the Jewish people to Christianity, while the latter sought to eliminate the Jewish people altogether.

The movement became organized in 1879 within the German Christian Social Party founded by Adolf Stocker, a chaplain at the imperial court. He attracted the most reactionary elements of the Reichstag, who in turn demanded that the Jews be disenfranchised. A pseudoscientific basis for the movement was supplied by Houston Stewart Chamberlain. Chamberlain, among other writers, compared the "Noble Aryan race" to the "depraved Semites." The question was no longer one of the age-old religious based arguments (which now impressed no one), but rather of secular arguments with a pseudo biological basis. In other words the Jews were a threat to modern civilization because of their "impure" racial characteristics. These theories were echoed in hundreds of publications and although refuted by many liberal social-democratic thinkers, led to outbreaks of violence in Germany and were taken up in other countries. Austria became another stronghold for hatred of the Jews along with France. The Anti-Semitic mottoes, notions and slogans that sprang up in western Europe, just before the end of the 19th Century, were later adopted and reshaped within the racist policies of Adolf Hitler and those responsible for the Holocaust.

Practically nothing of the emancipation process that took place in western Europe affected the Jewish people in eastern Europe. This was due to the successive partitioning of Poland in the late 18th Century that left the vast majority of the population belonging to the Russian Empire. To keep the Jews out of the interior of Russia, the czar mapped out a region

AFTER THE RAPTURE

where all Jews were forced to live, called the Pale of Settlement. Hundreds of anti-Jewish laws and regulations were passed against the Jews and applied mercilessly. It did not matter which czar sat on the throne, persecution of the Jews continued. Anti-Semitism was just like an official faith that was observed and respected everywhere in the Russian Empire.

The assassination of Alexander II in 1881, led to a wave of brutal massacres known as pogroms. They were organized riots accompanied by murder, rape and pillage of the Jewish communities. Three main waves of pogroms occurred against the Jews in Russia (1881-1884, 1903-1906, 1918-1920). The most serious of the pogroms occurred from 1918-1920. They took place after World War I when Russia had been plunged into a civil war. The Jews were being targeted by both the Ukrainian units of the Red Army and the counter revolutionaries of the White Army. Pogroms took place in every region from the Ukraine to Siberia, where an estimated 150,000 Jews died in the onslaught.

For most of the Jews at the end of the 19th Century, a safe haven turned out to be in the United States. In 1880 the Jewish population of the United States stood at approximately 250,000. Between 1881 and 1914, approximately another two million Jews emigrated to the United States.

The founder of the Zionist movement at the end of the 19th Century, is generally agreed by the Jews to be Theodor Herzl (1860-1904). In 1897, he convened the First Zionist Conference in Basel, Switzerland. By the 19th Century, there were thirty farming colonies in Palestine and a Jewish population of almost 6,000 people. Between 1904 and 1914, a new wave of immigrants arrived, mainly from Russia, to bring the number of new colonists in Palestine to 12,000.

After World War I, there remained a large population of Jews in eastern Europe. Poland had 3 to 3 ½ million Jews, in the Soviet Union there were over 2 ½ million, Rumania had 750,000 and in Hungary there were approximately 500,000.

Between World War I and World War II, the Jews in western and central Europe were in the process of assimilating into the population of the countries where they were living. By and large emancipation for these Jews was headed in the right direction, even though they had the usual slang jokes and sporadic incidents of violence that goes along with a minority nationality living in another country. Nevertheless, there was also an Anti-Semitic movement in place at that time.

In eastern Europe, it was a different story. Of the 11 million Jews in Europe, more than 7 million were in the eastern section. In Russia, most of the Jews were positioned in the Pale of Settlement.

During World War II, seven million Jews were subject to German domination or fell under the rule of a German satellite state. Nine million were outside this sphere with fewer than 20,000 in neutral Switzerland, a little more than 2 million in territories of the Soviet Union (not overrun by the Germans), Britain and Palestine each with a few hundred thousand and almost 5 million in the United States (with nearly 2 million Jews living in New York City).

The largest concentration of Christian Jews was probably in Greater Hungary, where in 1941, it is estimated that about 62,000 lived. In 1933, in Germany, there were around 40,000, while in Austria at the time of its annexation into the Third Reich in March of 1938, up to 25,000 Christian Jews were living there. Bohemia-Moravia in 1939 had up to 10,000, truncated Romania in 1942 close to 4,000, the Netherlands in 1942 had more than 2,500 and Slovakia in 1939 had more than 2,000 Christian Jews. Italy had several thousand Christian Jews and in Poland the figure was at least in the thousands.

ANTI-SEMITISM

Before we can understand some sort of reasoning behind the Holocaust, we need to look at the Anti-Semitic movement starting around 1870, to see what the atmosphere of Europe was like in the last half of the 19th Century.

Anti-Semitism is hatred of and hostility toward the Jew. The term was coined by the anti-Jewish writer Wilhelm Marr, but it has entered into general usage to apply to all forms of hatred of the Jewish people throughout the ages. As such, it has a long history.

It was within Christianity that Anti-Semitism assumed the most tragic consequences. Although Christianity has denied all other religions, Christianity had found itself in an extremely hostile position toward the Jewish religion. The spread and ultimate political success of Christianity led to conclusions that the Jews were hated by God, because they had rejected the Messiah. Jews were gradually forced out of every aspect of political influence and deprived of civil and political rights.

The Christian church's attempt to erect barriers, between Jew and non-Jew, were propagated into legislation affecting all aspects of Jewish life. Conversion to Judaism became an offense punishable by death. From the fifth century on, a movement for the destruction of synagogues and forced conversions of the Jewish people was powerful. Exclusion of Jews from economic life was the next objective followed in the later Middle Ages by frequent expulsions. Hatred of the Jews was fed by liturgical and other dramatic commemorations of the crucifixion of Christ. A particular volatile time for violence and organized attacks on the Jewish people occurred during Easter Season.

Religious Anti-Semitism reached its first climax in the period of the Crusades, followed by the plague of the Black Death and then the Spanish Inquisition. These early Anti-Semite reactions only effected the Jews who did not convert to Christianity. Baptism automatically removed all disabilities from a Jew. In fact, the discrimination and persecution were solely for the purpose of producing conversion to the Christian religion. There is no record of church discrimination against converted Jews before the 16th Century, when such discrimination occurred in Spain. The doctrine of the Medieval Church that the Jewish crime of deicide and the Jewish refusal to accept the divinity of Jesus meant that the Jews become the "spawn of the devil" and the enemies of God. This reasoning was largely responsible for the concept that Jews, as a group, were inherently wicked and depraved and had to be treated accordingly.

In the Muslim world, Anti-Semitic treatment was far less overt, except in times of religious extremism. There was little specific Anti-Semitism and Jews were treated or mistreated like other infidels.

The end of the Middle Ages did not bring much change to Anti-Semitism. The Counter-Reformation in the Catholic world renewed and increased anti-Jewish legislation and enforced the introduction of the ghetto system. Protestants in general followed the Medieval pattern and Luther advocated an extreme anti-Jewish policy in his later years, but it was in the Protestant countries that anti-Jewish barriers were first removed. In the 19th Century, the religious foundations of Christian Europe were weakened and with them religious prejudices. The exceptions were Czarist Russia, which followed the Eastern rite of Christianity and wherever the Catholic Church continued to press an Anti-Semitic policy.

In the 19th Century, scientific Anti-Semitism gradually replaced religious Anti-Semitism. The Jews were represented as living among the Nordic or Aryan people as a distinct Semitic ethnic group inferior to those around them. So their integration and assimilation into their environment would corrupt society and bring about the decline of the prevailing standards. Modern Anti-Semitism was built on racial, not religious, foundations therefore adoption to the prevailing faith no longer provided an escape route for persecuted Jews. Modern racial Anti-Semitism reached its tragic extreme with the rise of Adolf Hitler and his infamous Final Solution of the Jewish Problem. [6]

The theory of modern Anti-Semitism was ultimately based on the distinction between Aryan and Semitic language groups. It was first realized at the close of the 18th Century, partly through the advocacy of Ernest Renan and gave rise to the unsound theory of Aryan and Semitic races. Later, different characteristics to Aryans and Semites developed with the former being identified especially with the Teutonic peoples. They were depicted as the elite of humanity, while the Semites were regarded as the antithesis.

Wide popularity was achieved by the term Anti-Semitism to designate the anti-Jewish movement. This movement had been spreading rapidly in Germany since 1873, when the wave of speculation, after the Franco-Prussian war, had resulted in the inevitable crash of the stock exchange. This crash was blamed on Jewish financiers. A number of agitators, such as Eugen Diehring, now seized the opportunity to publish works against Jewish supremacy in German life and clamoring for corrective measures.

It has been suggested that in 1879, the movement received a sudden impetus through the secret support of the German chancellor Bismark. He hoped to discredit the Liberal opposition to his regime. Jews played active rolls of leadership in this opposition group.

The historian, Treitschke, lent the prestige of his name to the cause and a court chaplain, Adolph Stocker, organized the Christian Social Union as an instrument. Later, a demagogue named Hermann Ahlwardt took over as the leader of the movement and for a time received the support of the Conservative party. The "Judenrein" (clear of Jews) program was adopted in a political conference of German Conservatives and Christian Socialists on July 30, 1878, therefore, it is accepted as a natal act of Anti-Semitism.

An Anti-Semitic League had been organized and in 1881 a petition that bore no fewer than 255,000 signatures was presented. This petition demanded the disenfranchisement of the Jews. Anti-Jewish rioting broke out in some parts of Germany. At Zanten and other places ritual murder charges in the Medieval style were leveled. In 1893, the Anti-Semitic party gained fifteen seats in the Reichstag.

The movement spread from Germany to other countries in Europe. In Russia, the German example was partly responsible for the renewal in 1881 of religious persecutions. These persecutions were conceived from Medieval form prompting a wave of Russian refugees to sweep through Europe providing a powerful impetus for reaction in other countries. In Austria, an Anti-Semitic party was organized in parliament in 1882 by Georg von Schonerer. From 1895, there was a declared Anti-Semitic administration in Vienna headed by Karl Lueger. The Austrians were perhaps the most Anti-Semitic people on earth at the time of Adolf Hitler. Hitler was born in Austria and went to school in Vienna, one of the most Anti-Semitic cities in Europe at the time.

In Hungary in 1882, the agitation was responsible for the ritual murder charge in Tiszaeszlar. Even in France, the pioneer of Jewish emancipation in Europe, there was a virulent outburst of propaganda. This public outburst was largely due to Paul Bontoux, a ruined speculator, and Edouard Drumont, author of *La France Juive*. In 1886, this newspaper had a vast circulation. This culminated in the Dreyfus case that convulsed French daily life between 1894 and 1899.

Even countries such as England, Italy and the United States did not remain completely unaffected. In 1882, at Dresden, the first of a series of international Anti-Semitic conferences took place that demanded unbelievable restrictions to be placed on the Jewish people.

The calmer conditions of the first decade of the 20th Century resulted in considerably less tension in the world. However, Houston Stewart Chamberlain, English by birth, now provided a philosophical basis for new racial concepts by placing the Germans at the summit of humanity and the Jews at the lowest. Hitler went a step beyond that and placed the Jews below the level of humanity and called them "vermin."

After World War I, with the reactionary identification of Judaism with Bolshevism and the publication of the preposterous *Protocols of the Learned Elders of Zion*, it led to revival of Anti-Semitic propaganda in a new style in many countries. This publication purported to prove that an international Jewish conspiracy was out to control the world. Among the consequences of this new propaganda was the outbreak of violence against the Jews in Hungary on the suppression of the Bolshevik administration in 1920 and the assassination of Walter Rathenau in 1922, who was Jewish and the German foreign minister.

New Anti-Semitic groups sprang up in some countries. In the United States the automobile manufacturer Henry Ford, at least for a time, would lend both his name and financial support to the movement.

In the course of the following decade, the strength of the old prejudices, resentment at defeat in the field and the craving to find a scapegoat, stimulated by the widespread economic distress and the resentment of the reactionaries against liberal ideas and policies played into the hands of Adolf Hitler. Hitler made Anti-Semitism one of the principle planks of the program of his National Socialist Party (NAZI), officially organized in 1920. After Hitler's advent to power in 1933, he exploited the more or less latent Anti-Semitism to be found in other countries. He also pushed forward the German expansionists aims and ultimately, after 1939, weakened the resistance of other nations. [7]

ADOLF HITLER AND THE OCCULT

Most people today do not know that Hitler was deeply steeped in the occult. People like Hitler cannot begin to cause the destruction they bring about without the aid of the devil.

"Follow Hitler! He will dance, but it is I who have called the tune! I have initiated him into the 'Secret Doctrine', opened his centers in vision and given him the means to communicate with the Powers. Do not mourn for me: I shall have influenced history more than any other German."

So spoke Deitrich Echart as he lay dying in 1923. Echart was one of seven founders of the Nazi party and a dedicated Satanist, a man immersed in black magic and the Thule group of occultists. Echart had been looking for a pupil, someone whom he could introduce to the spiritual forces, someone to catapult Germany to the dizzying heights of world conquest. In a series of seances, he claims that he had a "Satan annunciation," that he was destined to prepare the vessel for the Antichrist, the man who would inspire the world and lead the Aryan race to world conquest. When he met Hitler he said, "Here is the one for whom I was but the prophet and forerunner."

After Echart's death, Karl Haushofer became Hitler's spiritual mentor, taking him through the deepest levels of occult transformation until he became a throughly demonized being. Hitler was even transformed sexually; he became a sadomasochist practicing various forms of sexual perversion. He was stimulated sexually by violence, brutality, and blood. Hermann Rauschning, a friend of Hitler who later defected to the Allies, said of him, "Hatred is like wine to him, it intoxicates him…he had the instincts of a sadist finding sexual excitement in torturing others."

Haushofer had made several trips to India and was well versed in Eastern occultism. He also lived in Japan for a time where he was initiated into an esoteric Buddhist society called the Green Dragon. Through these contacts a colony of Tibetan lamas settled in Berlin, and when the Russians took the city in 1945, they found a thousand Tibetan corpses in German uniforms. Haushofer, more than any other, challenged Hitler with the vision of world conquest.

Thus, a new religion with a new cross was begun; an ancient broken cross was used to rally the masses. Hitler stated openly that it was his intention to begin a new religion, a religion that would accomplish what Christianity had failed to bring about. Christianity, by honoring mercy and forgiveness, had weakened the German nation. In contrast, Hitler's religion would be "a joyous message that liberated men from the things that burdened their life. We should no longer have any fear of death and a bad conscience." This new religion would restore the greatness of Germany, avenge the failures of the past, and map out the blueprint for a grand future. Men "would be able to trust their instincts, would no longer be citizens of two worlds, but would be rooted in the single eternal life of this world."

Hitler offered himself as a Messiah with a divine mission to save Germany. On one occasion he displayed the whip he often carried to demonstrate that "in driving out the Jews I remind myself of Jesus in the temple." He declared, "Just like Christ, I have a duty to my own people." He even boasted that just as Christ's birth had changed the calendar, so his victory over the Jews would be the beginning of a new age. "What Christ began," he said, "I will complete." In a speech just days after becoming chancellor, he parodied the Lord's Prayer promising that under him a new kingdom would come on earth and that his would be "the power and the glory, Amen." He added that if he did not fulfill his mission, "you should then crucify me."

Hitler made other claims reminiscent of Christ. If Christ had His "elect," Hitler had his too. He promised, "Whoever proclaims his allegiance to me is by this very proclamation and the manner in which it is made, one of the chosen." Just as Jesus suffered at the hands of the Jews, so the Nazis believed they also were suffering, crucified by the betrayal of the Jews in World War I and now a new Germany was resurrected with vigor and hope.

Israel, May 14, 1948 – Can a Nation Be Born In a Day?

In the Hofberg Library in Vienna, there is a spear believed by many to be the one used to pierce the side of Christ. One day when Adolf Hitler was in his early twenties, he overheard a tour guide point the spear out to a group of visitors and say, "This spear is shrouded in mystery; whoever unlocks its secrets will rule the world." Later Hitler said that those words changed his life.

Hitler soon discovered that many spears vied for the dubious honor of being the one used to smite Christ's side. Nevertheless, he became convinced that the one in the Hofberg Library did have awesome powers for good or evil. He noted that when kings or emperors had it in their possession, they were victorious; when it fell from their possession, they lost the battle. Standing before the spear, Hitler made an irreversible vow to follow Satan.

Hitler stared at this object for hours, inviting its hidden powers to invade his soul. He believed that this ancient weapon was a bridge between the world of sense and the world of spirit. He felt as if he had held it in his hands in an earlier century.

Walter Stein, who befriended Hitler in those days, said that Hitler stood before the spear like a man in a trance, a man over whom some dreadful spell had been cast...The very space around him seemed enlivened with some subtle irradiation, a kind of ghostly ecto plasmic light. [He] appeared transformed as if some mighty Spirit now inhabited his very soul, creating within and around him a kind of evil transformation of its own nature and power.

Standing there in the Hofberg, Dr. Stein said, Hitler experienced a kind of "eclipse of consciousness." When Hitler marched into Vienna, he was convinced that Fate had decreed that he should personally become the possessor of the magical spear that he had gazed upon years before. According to Trevor Ravenscroft, Hitler took the spear from behind the glass and it became for him a spear of revelation. "It was," Hitler said, "as if I were holding the whole world in my hand."

If this story seems to be unbelievable, we must remember that any object given over to Satan can become the means of entry into the spirit world. Though that particular spear most probably was not the spear used to pierce Christ's side, it was a bridge that kings and emperors used to make contact with Satan. For Hitler it not only symbolized the Roman antagonism toward Christ, but also was a path to Luciferic transformation.

The doctrine of the transformation of consciousness, which is as old as paganism, teaches that we can be in touch with nonhuman intelligences from whom we gain wisdom and power. These beings, often referred to today as "masters of wisdom," are available to those who wish to pay the price of initiation. The details vary from culture to culture, but the message is the same: Altered states of consciousness are possible if we are willing to expand our mental horizons and get in touch with "the powers." Quite literally, this is a "new birth," an esoteric experience of enlightenment. To have the experience is to belong to an elite group of initiated ones.

Although mesmerized by Eastern occultism, Hitler was impatient with transcendental meditation and preferred the speedier route of drugs to connect with the spiritual powers. He befriended a used book dealer, Earnest Pretzsche, who introduced him to a psychedelic drug that produced clairvoyant visions and heightened spiritual perceptions. In this way he was empowered to perform the deeds that he believed Fate had decreed.

Even those who knew Hitler from his early days were well aware of his occult powers. August Kubizek, a friend, said, "It was as if another being spoke out of his body...It was not a case of a speaker carried away by his own words...I felt as though he himself listened with astonishment and emotion to what broke forth from him."

After Hitler joined the group that became known as the Nazi party, he was initiated into deeper levels of occult transformation. Through rituals and pacts with demonic forces, he was changed into a man of such awesome power that skeptics regularly became fanatics just by listening to his speeches. And when he finished his harangue, he often would collapse in exhaustion, just like a medium who had been in touch with the netherworld. He needed time to rest and be revived.

Hitler also believed in the Eastern doctrine of reincarnation, a conviction that would serve him well in his attempt to exterminate the Jews. Hitler believed he was the reincarnation of many ancient kings, including Tiberius of Rome.

But even if we grant, as Erwin W. Lutzer believes (and I might add that I believe it also) that Hitler was indwelt by an evil spirit(s), we are faced with a question: what about his millions of followers? What made them fanatically committed to the dictates of "Der Führer?"

Let us remember that a demonic leader is able to unleash spiritual forces that influence others. As Houston Chamberlain, who was the occult adviser to Kaiser Wilhelm II said "Hitler is an awakener of souls, the vehicle of Messianic powers." Serving as a Satanic channel was especially possible in a country that was already steeped in occultism.

This national obsession with occultism prepared the way for Hitler's meteoric rise to world prominence. Heinrich Himmler's masseur said that the nation was caught up in "the mysticism of a political movement" and in "no country were so many miracles performed, so many ghosts conjured, so many illnesses cured by magnetism, so many horoscopes read." There were telepathy, seances, and spiritual experiences of every sort, which camouflaged Hitler's deceptions. Just as the New Age movement today might well be preparing the world to accept the miracles of the Antichrist, so the occultism of Germany made mass deception much more difficult to detect.

Hitler's closest associates were occultists in their own right. Himmler was a dedicated occultist; so were Rosenberg and Göebbels. As the Nazi party grew, it attracted those who belonged to numerous Satanic organizations. The inner Nazi circle drew power directly from these hidden forces. But in a nation that was already steeped in occult doctrines, millions of others came under Hitler's magic spell.

We must remember that those who submit themselves to someone who is demonized, risk the possibility of personal deception and a bonding influence to their leader. Interestingly, even some who disagreed with Hitler, nevertheless came under his aura and supported him anyway. Powerful deceivers can deceive others who then come under varying degrees of demonic control. Given Germany's spiritual vacuum, the nation was almost eager to be deceived.

Of course, Hitler had to pay for his power. No one can be in league with Satan "on the cheap." Rauschning describes a recurring scenario: "He yells for help...seized with power that makes him tremble so violently his bed shakes...in his bedroom he is muttering...'It is he! It is he! He's here!' His lips turn blue...He was dripping with sweat...He was given a massage and something to drink...then all of a sudden he screamed, 'There! Over there in the corner!'"

Many who despise Hitler today, many who pride themselves in condemning Nazism, are actually embracing the same doctrines that made Nazism the powerful force it was in the world. Astute readers will realize that what is popularly called the New Age movement is ancient occultism, or we could call it the spiritual doctrines of Nazism with a friendly American face.

Obviously, not everyone who embraces the doctrines of personal transformation becomes as evil as Hitler. Indeed, a person might experience personal improvement, be more fulfilled, more in touch with himself or herself and more confident of the future. Satan does different things to different people. If you are seeking peace, he will try to give it to you; if you are in need of advice, he will do his best to predict the future and give you secret information through the stars or a fortune-teller. If you are in need of self-confidence or even a miracle, he will try to do that too. In Hitler's case, he needed power to rule and Satan made that available.

The Bible forbids any contact with the spirit world for one good reason: Demons masquerade as angels of light seeking to deceive as many as they can. Of course, there are "masters," or nonhuman intelligences waiting for an opportunity to get in touch with human beings. To bring about such a transformation of consciousness is exactly what the Evil One desires. [8] This sub-chapter is entirely from *Hitler's Cross,* by Erwin W. Lutzer. Thank you Mr. Lutzer for your interesting insight. Adolf Hitler would ultimately become the person who would become responsible for the deaths of over 60 million people, including 6 million Jews, in a period of six years, from 1939 to 1945 during World War II.

HOLOCAUST

As you can see from the above history of the late 1800's and early 1900's, the time was ripe for the picking. Hitler was set in the wrong time for the wrong reason. He just followed through and completed what the Anti-Semitic movement was teaching for more than fifty years. Hitler had a lot of help developing the ideas and hatred from his very youth. He took the plan of the movement and implemented it.

A quotation from *A Mosaic of Victims, Non-Jews Persecuted and Murdered by the Nazis,* Edited by Michael Berenbaum, is a composite of the Holocaust. I highly recommend the reading of this book for an excellent portrayal of the persecution of non-Jews during World War II.

> "The Holocaust was the planned, systematic attempt by Hitler and the Nazis to annihilate the Jews of Europe and to eradicate every vestige of Jewish life and culture from the European continent. Others, before and after the German Third Reich, have left their bloody fingerprints on history, but the Holocaust was something more than just the central event of the twentieth century. The Holocaust was the hinge of modern history, the definitive refutation of the grand illusion that human beings become better as they become more educated.
>
> For centuries civilized society has targeted certain people, Jews in particular but also Gypsies, as "outsiders," people who "did not belong," people beyond the moral universe of concern for their well-being. Cruelty to Jews and other

vulnerable people is nothing new, but the Nazi assault constituted an unprecedented mobilization of the resources of the state to single out a people for extinction. As the Ukrainian-American scholar Bohdan Wytwychy writes: Jews were slated for total annihilation as a people, and Hitler in fact managed to kill and estimated 65 to 70 % of all European Jewry, including virtually all of the German and East European Jews. The circle neighboring that of the Jews was reserved for the Gypsies, who also were designated for complete extinction. However, the German mania for exterminating the Gypsies did not quite achieve the same pitch of madness as that directed toward the Jews." [9]

The Holocaust, which is also known as the "Catastrophe " to the Jews, was the most tragic period in all of Jewish history. It began in Germany on January 30, 1933, and ended on May 8, 1945. The Holocaust was 12 years of threats, persecutions, agonizing torture, and death for the Jews living in Nazi controlled Europe. When it was finally over, six million Jews had been brutally murdered. Their wealth had been confiscated and had amounted to more than twelve billion dollars. Who can measure the loss to the Jewish communities of central, eastern, and southern Europe? These large Jewish communities, along with their great centers of learning, came to an abrupt end. They virtually disappeared from the scene of history.

Systematically, the Holocaust can be divided into two six-year periods. The first period spanned from 1933 to 1939. This period marked the beginning of the rise of Nazi power and German military expansion. On January 30, 1933, the president of Germany, Paul von Hindenburg, appointed Adolf Hitler, leader of the National Socialist (Nazi) German Workers Party (the NSDAP), to be chancellor of the Reich. Hitler's book *Mein Kampf* (1925), became the guide for his program and power. This book overflows with hatred and contempt for the Jews. With it, Hitler was able to forge a program of governmental control that proclaimed racial identity as the criteria for citizenship. He instituted racial Anti-Semitism as an official government program.

Hitler stated, in 1920, that "It is our duty to arouse, to whip up and to incite in our people the intensive repugnance of the Jews." [10] In Germany, there were approximately 525,000 Jews living there when Hitler became Chancellor (that was less than one percent of the population). It appears that Hitler had two main goals that he wanted to fulfill during his lifetime. He wanted his people the Germans to live in a country that had more living space (lebensraum) and he wanted that country to be free of all Jews (Judenfrei). From his early political mistakes he learned that in order to meet these objectives he needed to follow a slow and systematic course. Hitler's fanatic obsession with the expulsion of the Jews finally turned to the extermination of the Jews and that obsession followed him to the grave.

Before the war began, right after Hitler became chancellor, Nazi propaganda prepared the way for separating the Jews from the rest of the population. Minister of Propaganda, Joseph Göebbels, began to barrage the public every day with complaints and threats against the Jews. The next step came in the form of open terror. During a whole week in March of 1933, *Jude verrecke* (Jews perish) rang through the streets while Storm Troopers beat, robbed and murdered the Jewish people at will. The police stood by and watched on orders from the Nazis.

Israel, May 14, 1948 – Can a Nation Be Born In a Day?

On April 1, 1933, the Nazis sprang a boycott against the Jews as the first official governmental act against them. SS and SA men picketed the Jewish owned stores, factories and shops trying to keep people from entering them. Written across the windows was smeared the word *Jude*. The Nazi intent was to cut off Jewish enterprises from customers and suppliers with the idea of forcing the owners to sell their businesses to non-Jews for a minimal amount of money. This tactic was known as Aryanization (*Arisierung*). At first from 1933 to November 1938 it was voluntary, but after that it became mandatory.

Concentration camps were created almost immediately after the Hitler regime came into power as places to hold people in protective custody. They ended up becoming the killing centers for millions of people—Jews and non-Jews alike. After it was all over, we know that at least 18 million Europeans passed through this system. At least 11 million died in concentration camps, with 4 million at Auschwitz/Birkenau alone. The Nazis murdered more than six million Jews and not all of them were in the concentration camp system. The Nazis also purposefully and systematically murdered more than 5 million non-Jews. More than one million children were murdered, with many of them being small children and newborn or unborn babies. Every person who took part in the concentration camp system went through brutal treatment, starvation, torture, overwork and disease at the very least. [11]

In 1935, Hitler made Anti-Semitism a part of Germany's basic legal code. On September 15, the Nuremberg Laws were introduced. They were concerned with Citizenship and the Protection of German Blood and German Honor. Under these laws, the Jewish people were deprived of their political rights. They were no longer citizens, but were reduced to subjects. Mixed marriages and extramarital sexual relations between Jews and Aryans (the Master race) became criminal offenses. The Nazis simply legalized the terror against the Jews that had preceded the laws to build a structure of new decrees to rob the Jews of their last remaining rights.

By the end of 1937, in Germany, the Jews had no civil rights. They were not citizens. They could not vote or attend a political meeting. They had not freedom of speech, nor could they defend themselves in print. They were not allowed to be employed as civil servants, writers, artists, musicians or actors before the Aryan public. They could not be a teacher, work in a public hospital or belong to any professional organization. If they owned a business, their livelihood had either vanished or was in danger of evaporating. They were denied food and drugs from certain stores. Along with all of this, they had to face day-by-day ostracism of their neighbors and friends.

By this time emigration was the only answer for the Jews. During 1937, only 23,000 Jews left Germany. That brought the total number of Jews who had emigrated since 1933 to 129,000 (a little over ¼ of the Jewish population of Germany in 1933). In the following year of 1938, conditions worsened for the Jews and the urgency for them to leave Germany became even more apparent, but by then their opportunities had greatly diminished. By 1938, German Jewish life was weakened by economic blows, physical threats and physical depletion. Fear and defeatism were apparent among those who could not emigrate. The events of 1938 mark the great divide between Jewish emigration and the Nazi policy that was to follow—annihilation.

The infamous riots and pogroms of Kristallnacht, the Night of Broken Glass, occurred on November 9, 1938. In this orgy of arson, property destruction and murder, over 800 shops had their windows broken. Over 170 homes and 76 synagogues were destroyed. Thirty-six Jews were killed, thirty-six were seriously wounded and 191 synagogues throughout Germany were set on fire. Thousands of Jews were arrested and sent to concentration camps, mainly Buchenwald. With this destruction, Hitler made a giant step toward the annihilation policy that shortly came to be implemented.

As Hitler moved closer to war, the fate of the Jewish people moved from expulsion to extermination. Hitler, speaking to the Reichstag on January 30, 1939 (the sixth anniversary of becoming chancellor of Germany), made a prophetic statement:

> "Today I will once more be a prophet! If the international Jewish financiers inside and outside Europe should again succeed in plunging the nations into a world war, the result will be not the bolshevization of the earth and thus the victory of Jewry, but the annihilation of the Jewish race throughout Europe." [12]

Germany declared war on Poland on September 1, 1939. Poland at that time had the largest concentration of Jewish people of any country in Europe. Of the estimated 3,300,000 Jews in Poland, 3,200,000 were killed by the Nazis before the war was over. Poland, the historic center of European Jewry, was to become the site for the attempted annihilation of the Jews in Europe.

The German soldiers who invaded Poland saw themselves as heroes of the Master race. Their victims, the Poles, were *Untermenchen* (subhuman). The Jews among them were considered to be even a lower category—bacilli. A group of Nazis known as the *Einsatzgruppen* searched out and systematically murdered thousands of Jews in Poland.

By late 1939, the official policy and primary action of the Nazi government regarding Jews was their expulsion into eastern Poland. By the thousands the Jews were herded into trains for the trip without food or water. These were open railroad cars traveling in winter conditions. When the sealed cars were opened hundreds of people (including children) were found frozen to death.

The next stage of the Holocaust was enclosure, when the Medieval system of the ghetto was re-instituted. In Warsaw, Poland, the largest ghetto in Europe was created. Nearly 500,000 Jews (30 % of Warsaw's population) were crowded into a one hundred block section of housing. Walls were constructed with twenty-two gates to keep the Jews enclosed. The gates were covered with barbed wire and guarded by Germans with guns. The top of the eleven-mile length of the wall was studded with broken glass. By the winter of 1943, only 60,000 of the nearly 500,000 Jews were left in the ghetto. More than 400,000 had died or been deported to concentration camps, where most of them were murdered within days of their arrival.

The mass extermination of the Jews began on June 22, 1941, when the Germans invaded Russia, dubbed Operation Barbarossa. The *Einsatzgruppen* were instructed to murder the Jewish people at will. This execution was made possible by the early success and expansion of the fighting in Russia. During the first year of the Russian war, more than 1,000,000 Jews in the occupied Soviet Union were slaughtered, many with a single shot in the back of the neck with the victim tumbling down an embankment into a massive grave below. The largest single-most massacre recorded took place on September 29-30, 1941, when the men of

Israel, May 14, 1948 – Can a Nation Be Born In a Day?

Einsatzgruppen C murdered 33,771 people (mostly Jews) at Babi Yar in Kiev.

On January 20, 1942, the Wannsee Conference took place. At this meeting, headed by Reinhard Heydrich and with Adolf Eichmann in attendance, plans for the implementation of the "Final Solution" were put into place. A plan for the extermination of the 11 million Jews in Europe.

The gas chamber proved to be an ideal instrument for large-scale murder. It was relatively quick and did not leave a mess like shooting. It made no sound that would prematurely alert the victims of their fate. A few men could dispose of many people at once. Gas chambers were constructed. Some of them with crematoriums to dispose of those killed by burning the bodies. Zyklon B was the gas used in most of these operations. All of the concentration camps that had installed gas chambers were located in the German occupied country of Poland.

The massacres of the Jewish people began in Russia in 1941. That year the Germans killed approximately 1.1 million Jews. In 1942, they murdered another 2.7 million Jews (of which 200,000 died in Auschwitz). In 1943, the year the crematoria in Auschwitz began operation, the number of Jewish victims dropped to 500,000 (half of whom were killed at Auschwitz). All the Jews that the Germans had access to and who could be caught were trapped. By the end of 1943, the Germans closed down the death camps built specifically to exterminate the Jews: Chelmno (360,000 victims), Kulmhof (150,000 Jews), Sobibor (200,000-250,000 Jews), Belzec (600,000 victims/500,000 Jews) and Treblinka (900,000 victims/750,000 Jews). Only Auschwitz remained operational.

In 1944, the Hungarian Jews were the only remaining Jewish community left in Europe. The Germans occupied Hungary in March and because of the labor shortage, 100,000 Jewish slave workers were taken from Hungary to Auschwitz. Of the total 438,000 incoming Jews from Hungary, toward the end of the war, between 10 and 30 percent were found fit for labor exercises. The rest were doomed to the gas chambers. At no other time was Auschwitz more efficient as a killing center. In May and June, the number of victims murdered exceeded the official incineration capacity of 132,000 corpses per month. The onslaught continued through July. Of the 600,000 Jews that were killed in 1944, one-half to two-thirds were killed at Auschwitz. In the 32 months that Auschwitz operated as a designated extermination center (from March 1942 until November 1944), between one million and 1.1 million Jewish people were killed. That is an average of 32,000 to 34,000 per month. During the Hungarian action that average increased by five to sixfold.

If all of this was not enough for the Jewish people, as the Soviet army was pushing the Germans back to their homeland toward the end of the war, the Germans evacuated the death camps. On August 6, 1944, the SS began to drive the concentration camp inmates (Jews and non-Jews) back into the interior of Germany. On October 26, Heinrich Himmler ordered the destruction of the Auschwitz crematoriums as the Nazis tried to get rid of the evidence of the death camps.

These death marches, as they became known, killed thousands of people (a large portion of them Jewish). These long distance marches were excruciation for the death camp inmates who were already in terrible physical condition from their captivity. Various estimates of the death rate from the death marches during the final months of the war are from between 250,000 and 375,000 people. After surviving the perils of the concentration camps these

AFTER THE RAPTURE

victims were faced with the treachery of these horrible death marches.

As the ravages of war swept across nearly every country of Europe, it had a devastating effect on millions of civilian people. Of the 11 million civilians, 500,000 were Gypsies, 500,000 were French, Italian and British, 4 million Poles, Russians, Ukrainians, and other Slavs who were forced into slave labor and 6 million were Jews. Approximately one million Jews perished as victims of the *Einsatzgruppen* or other firing squads. Two million died in camps and ghettos from starvation, disease, overwork and extreme cruelty. At least three million marched to the furnaces of the death camps.

Elie Wiesel said it best in his book, *The Oath*, as an old wanderer, Azriel, implores:

> "There is no beautiful death. Nor is there a just death. Every death is absurd. Useless. And ugly…All you get in return is a corpse. And corpses stink." [13]

After I completed this chapter of the book I ran into Dave Strong, an old school acquaintance who had access to some unpublished photos from World War II and he gave me permission to use them in this book. The photos are from a man who was in Buchenwald when the Americans liberated the camp in April 1945 and wishes to remain anonymous. Early in April of 1945, orders were given to a special mechanized infantry unit under General George Patton. This unit was primarily used to take care of hot spots. These orders were to take and secure Camp Buchenwald, more accurately called Death Camp Buchenwald. On April 11, 1945, this task was completed. Patton's special mechanized infantry stayed for only a few days and then another unit was assigned the rest of the cleanup of the camp. The pictures shown on the following pages were taken with two German cameras found in the camp when it was secured. Only one prisoner could speak a little English. This was a Polish man who weighed only sixty pounds, who was sitting by a fence.

Conditions in the camp were extremely harsh and little food was available.

118

Israel, May 14, 1948 – Can a Nation Be Born In a Day?

Here we see a concentration camp inmate in his prison uniform.

Below, you will see the four methods the Germans used for executing prisoners at Buchenwald. They were; beatings to the point of death, crucifixion on a pole, hanging, and by shooting. The Polish man and a few other concentration camp victims assembled a dummy to show the liberators the methods that the prisoners were executed. The photos below depict these scenes.

The sign above the prisoner roughly reads:

MODEL
The original sign was destroyed by the SS assassins before their retreat.
The so-called BOCK! (Sawhorse) is a monument of the Nazi culture in all concentration camps.
25 or more blows for the most futile motive on the bare buttocks.
If the prisoner becomes unconscious, he was sprinkled with cold water until he recovered and thereafter he was further beaten.

AFTER THE RAPTURE

The photo to the right shows the four foot high pile of human bones after cremation. This is the same pile of bones that would have been in view of those prisoners being hung in the photo on the top right.

Death Camp Buchenwald could cremate 80 to 100 corpses in a day. This is what the liberators found at Buchenwald on the day they arrived to free the prisoners.

Israel, May 14, 1948 – Can a Nation Be Born In a Day?

JEWISH HISTORY - 1945 TO THE RAPTURE

Perhaps this would be a good time to clarify something that is probably confusing to a lot of people—Palestine. *Webster's Dictionary* calls Palestine the Holy Land and the Biblical name, Canaan, as an ancient country in southwest Asia on the east coast of the Mediterranean Sea. Palestine has been the geographical term for the Holy Land, from 135 AD (when the Romans put down the final revolt of the Jewish people during the Bar-Kokhba rebellion), up to 1948 when the region was divided into three sections: Israel, Jordan and Egypt (the Gaza Strip). The Arabs today claim to be Palestinians, descendants from the ancient inhabitants of Palestine. They advocate the establishment of an Arab homeland in Israel, thus the reason for the continuing hostility in that region of the world.

At the end of World War II, it was mass confusion and a hardship for everyone involved in the war in Europe. It was especially difficult for the exiled Jews returning to their original homes before the war had started and also for those Jews who survived the concentration camps and death marches. I have known Eliezer Urbach and his wife Sara for quite sometime and I consider them friends in Jesus. Eliezer Urbach is a Polish Jew who lost his entire family to the Nazis during World War II. Years ago I contacted him, in Denver, Colorado, and ask him to come to the Sunday School class I was teaching and to talk about anything God laid on his heart. I can still remember the hair standing up on the back of my neck as he blew the ram's horn (shofar). His lesson was on the Rapture. Eliezer and Sara are hard working Messianic Jews who love Jesus dearly. Eliezer wrote a book about his life, *Out of the Fury—The Incredible Odyssey of Eliezer Urbach,* and it describes the condition of Palestine just after World War II. The area of Israel was known as Palestine before it became the nation of Israel in 1948.

By 1946, the atmosphere in Palestine was crackling with tension. The embryo nation of Jews had been sweating and toiling to reclaim the promised homeland since the turn of the century. In 1897, at the First Zionist Congress in Basil, Switzerland, Theodor Herzl, spiritual father of the Jewish State, proclaimed the right of Jewish people to reestablish a national homeland. This right was recognized in the Balfour Declaration of 1917. However, the British, anxious to placate the Arab world, refused to carry out the Balfour Declaration. The mandate for Palestine decreed by the League of Nations gave international sanctions to the biblical and historic connection between Jews and Eretz-Israel (the Land of Israel).

The legitimate sanctions notwithstanding, in 1946, the British government implemented plans to crush Jewish resistance. By a concentrated "purge" of the settlements, mass arrests, disarming of the Haganah, the detention of Jewish Agency executives, and widespread military operations, Britain hoped to shake the Israelis from their national aspirations. Strict curfews were imposed, and armored cars cruised along deserted thoroughfares. Riots and bombings were everyday occurrences. Hundreds of young men were arrested and taken to concentration camps by the British. [14]

On November 29, 1947, the United Nations passed a resolution on the partition of Palestine, calling for the establishment of the Jewish state. All Tel Aviv danced in the streets. Old men, young men, women, girls and children shouted and sang, "A Jewish Land." Even some of the British soldiers joined in the celebration.

The celebration was short-lived. From surrounding countries, Arab soldiers stirred up the Arab villages and blockaded Jerusalem, attempting to thwart the U.N. resolution with terrorism. Bombs exploded under railway bridges, grenades were thrown at buses while passing through Arab towns. All Palestine could feel the preparation for a bitter eye-for-eye and tooth-for-tooth war. The Arabs attacked the settlements, burned homes, and disrupted communications lines.

Every man in the settlements who was able was called to guard duty. The men bought their own shotguns and patrolled the settlement borders. Only two villages separated Givat Shmuel from the Arab border. People were killed on guard duty. A Romanian Jew, with whom I worked at the factory, was cut to pieces by the Arabs. …The Jews were desperately short of weapons. Preparing for withdrawal, the British gave their weapons to the Arabs. On May 14, 1948, the last of the British staff left Palestine, and the Mandate era ended. In a short ceremony at a gathering of all Jewish leaders in Tel Aviv, David Ben-Gurion read the Proclamation of Independence of the State of Israel. Within eight hours, after the public announcement came over the radio that Israel was an independent State, the Arab armies began to invade Israel. Egyptian planes bombed the Tel Aviv area. On May 15, every able-bodied Israeli was drafted into the Army.

…The prospects of an Arab victory was frightening to contemplate. Everyone knew the odds. A nation of 650,000 Jews was contending in battle with nations totaling over 40 million. The Arab armies drew forces from Egypt, Jordan, Syria, Iraq, and Saudi Arabia [15]

Miraculously, Israel ended up defeating the Arabs and the tiny nation of Israel was off and running. Jewish people from all over the world began returning to a country that they could call their own homeland.

The population in Israel in 1948 was around 660,000 people, but with the establishment of the new nation that was about to change. Immigration has played a vital role in Israel over the last fifty years, with millions of Jewish people returning to their ancient homeland. By 1964, Israel's population grew to 2 ½ million. These vast numbers of people coming into the country have brought both joy and hardship to this tiny country. Since becoming a nation in 1948, the Soviet Union was reluctant to allow mass immigration of Jewish people, but finally from 1989 through 1990, with the collapse of the Soviet empire, more than 200,000 Jews settled in Israel. By 1994, nearly 500,000 Jews had arrived from the Soviet Union. Today the population of Israel is a little over 6,000,000 people, almost ten times what it was when it became a nation in 1948.

Throughout the years, Israel has suffered through birth pains and evolved into an international country with a thriving agricultural base. Through much help from the United States it has modernized its infrastructure and cities. It has also become a leading military stronghold in the Middle East.

Although Israel defeated the Arabs in the 1948 conflict, it has not stopped the fighting in Israel. It has been fraught with Arab uprisings and war. Attempts to convert the 1949 Arab-Israeli armistice agreements into peace treaties were unsuccessful. There were skirmishes between the two, until finally Egypt refused to permit Israeli ships to use the Suez Canal. Israel perceived this to be an act of war and the second Arab-Israeli war took place in the fall of 1956.

The third major conflict happened in 1967 and became known as the Six-Day War. Israel attacked Egypt, Jordan and Syria simultaneously on June 5th of that year. The war

Israel, May 14, 1948 – Can a Nation Be Born In a Day?

ended six days later with a decisive victory for Israel. The Six-Day War left Israel in control of the Gaza Strip and the Sinai Peninsula, which it conquered from Egypt; East Jerusalem and the West Bank, which it conquered from Jordan; and the Golan Heights, which it conquered from Syria. The size of Israel expanded four times its size with these wartime acquisitions. It also left Israel with an Arab population of about 1.5 million.

In October of 1973, Egypt joined Syria in a war against Israel in an effort to regain the territories they lost in the 1967 conflict. The two Arab nations made a surprise attack on Israel on Yom Kippur, the holiest day of the year. After a bloody three-week struggle, Israel once again managed to defeat their aggressors, but suffered heavy casualties. Israel emerged from the war demoralized.

A strong showing from the Arabs during this war won support from the Soviet Union and most of the developing countries around the world. Saudi Arabia and Kuwait financed the Arab military, making it possible for Egypt and Syria to purchase the most sophisticated Soviet weapons. Along with that, the Arab oil-producing nations cut off petroleum exports to the United States and other western nations in retaliation for their aid to Israel.

The oil crisis led European leaders to adopt a more humble attitude toward the Middle East oil-producing nations. This led to a shift in policy regarding the Arab-Israeli conflict. In a joint statement, issued by the foreign ministers of the European Community on November 6, 1973, they stressed the need for Israel to end the territorial occupation that it had maintained since the conflict of 1967. It also referred to the legitimate rights of the Palestinians for the first time.

The ensuing international energy crisis threw the industrialized world into a state of panic and began a period of recession. In Europe, this eventually transformed the Middle Eastern oil-producing nations into the arbiters of world events. In 1975, the United Nations General Assembly adopted a resolution asserting that Zionism was "a form of racism and racial discrimination."

This caused a dramatic change in the perception of Israel in the world. After 1967, Israel was a proud nation and was reflecting success. Suddenly they faced a new and disturbing situation. Israel was transformed from an object of pride into a state of insecurity.

In 1982, the Israeli forces invaded Lebanon. Their objective was to destroy the bases of the Palestinian Liberation Organization (PLO). This act destabilized the whole area. This invasion swayed world public opinion. The Jewish people were no longer seen as the outnumbered victims of hostile Arabs, but instead, they had become the aggressor.

In the late 1980's, the relations between Israel and the Palestinians entered a new phase. A series of uprisings in the occupied Israeli territories, including demonstrations, strikes and rock throwing attacks on Israeli soldiers and civilians, is known as *intifada*. The harsh response by the Israeli government drew criticism from the United Nations and also the United States. As the intifada drew attention to conditions in the West Bank, it came to be felt as if the Israelis were guilty of brutality and that they were meeting sticks and stones with tear gas and bullets. Among some Israeli citizens, many started to believe that the only solution would be an autonomous state.

Even today, the intifada is still a part of everyday life in Israel. As the world entered the year 2001 there was renewed violence in Israel between the Arabs and the Israelis in the occupied areas. Hundreds of lives were lost in the fighting.

AFTER THE RAPTURE

In 1992, peace talks were renewed and in 1995, a pact was signed between Yasir Arafat, the leader of the Palestinian Liberation Organization, and Yitzak Rabin, the prime minister of Israel. The "land for peace" process had its beginning as large tracts of land were handed back to Palestinian Self-rule. Many people in Israel were very upset at this idea, particularly the Orthodox settlers in the West Bank. As a result, a fanatical Israeli student assassinated Yitzak Rabin. This senseless act did not stop the peace negotiations that are supposable going on today.

What is it like to be Jewish and living in Israel today? Although the religious establishment in Israel is Orthodox, the vast majority of Israelis do not follow Orthodox-Jewish practices. In fact, the majority of Jews today living in Israel are secular and must be seen as a threat to the Jewish religion. Most non-Orthodox Jews do not accept the Divine authorship of the law and many do not even believe in God. A large portion of the Diaspora Jews have no religious affiliation at all. There is a fairly large movement of Messianic Jews (those who believe in Jesus as the Messiah) and that movement is growing at this time. Judaism is no longer a unified structure.

In the second half of the 20th Century, the Jewish community has had two main focuses—the Holocaust and the nation of Israel. The Holocaust was a tragedy of such magnitude that few Jews today can come to terms with it. It convinced many people that the Jewish people can never be completely safe living as a minority group among other nations. It is commonplace for Jews around the world to declare, "We are not religious, but we do support Israel!" For many Jews today, God and the law have been replaced in a very real sense by the Holocaust and the state of Israel. Most religious commentators believe that these two focuses will not be enough to sustain the Jewish people in the future. More than 55 years have passed since the dreadful days of Hitler's Germany. In the next ten to twenty years there will be no survivors left to give eyewitness accounts of the Holocaust.

Today, Israel has become increasingly more self supporting and less willing to bow to outside opinion. The "land for peace" process is still ongoing. The Jewish people are evermore under the umbrella of the threat of Arabs living within the occupied areas and also of the surrounding Arab nations. Will there ever be peace in Israel?

Both the Orthodox and Reform religious authorities are convinced that religious renewal is essential for the survival of Jewish civilization. They have accepted the fact that their task is to present the beliefs of Abraham, Isaac and Jacob in a way that speaks to the Jewish people today. The Jewish people have maintained their special identity for over 4000 years. The argument runs: they must return to their religious roots in order to keep from disappearing from history. Only then can the Pillar of Cloud, the Divine Presence, return to dwell among His people. [16]A fitting quote from my Messianic Jewish friend, Eliezer Urbach.

> "The Gospel message of salvation was fully told in the Old Testament. It awaited only the coming into the world of God's Servant Messiah to become flesh and blood fact. God always meant to redeem his beloved fallen creatures, and the plan for our salvation begins to unfold in the first chapter of Genesis. After the call of our father Abraham, God patiently pursued the Children of Israel through centuries of our repeated rebellion, disobedience, apostasy, and idolatrous wanderings away from his revealed will. Although given all the help we could imagine, the Law, the

Israel, May 14, 1948 – Can a Nation Be Born In a Day?

Prophets, and elaborate sacrificial system, human sin prevailed in our nature and kept us separated from real communion with our holy God. We could not perfectly keep even the first commandment, much less 613 Mosaic expansions of the Decalogue. Worse than this, our forefathers lost sight of the purpose for which the Jewish people were called into existence—to be a light to the Gentiles and to all the nations of the world."

Again I quote, from page 217 of his book, *Out of the Fury—The Incredible Odyssey of Eliezer Urbach*;

"The rejection of Yeshua as the Messiah by the leadership of Israel resulted in the extension of the 'unsearchable riches of Christ' to the Gentiles." [17]

Before we move to chapter six, I thought that you might be interested in what the basic idea of the Messiah is in Orthodox Judaism. The belief in the eventual coming of the Messiah is a basic and fundamental part of traditional Judaism. In the Shemoneh Esrei prayer, recited three times every day, the Jewish people pray for all the elements of the coming of the Messiah; ingathering of the exiles; restoration of the religious courts of justice; an end of wickedness, sin and heresy; reward to the righteous; rebuilding of Jerusalem; restoration of the line of King David; and restoration of Temple service.

Modern Jewish scholars suggest that the messianic concept was introduced later in the history of Judaism, during the age of the prophets. They note that the messianic concept is not mentioned in the Torah (the first five books of the Bible). However, traditional Judaism maintains that the messianic idea has always been a part of Judaism. The Messiah is not mentioned explicitly in the Torah, because the Torah was written in terms that all people could understand, and the abstract concept of a distant, spiritual, future reward was beyond the comprehension of some people. However, the Torah contains several references to "the End of Days" (Acharit Hayamim), which is the time of the Messiah; thus, the concept of Messiah was known in the most ancient times. The Messiah is the one who will be anointed as king in the End of Days.

Orthodox Judaism believes that the Messiah will be a great political leader descended from King David (Jeremiah 23:5). The Messiah is often referred to as "Messiah, son of David." He will be well-versed in Jewish law, and observant of its commandments (Isaiah 11:2-5). He will be a charismatic leader, inspiring others to follow his example. He will be a great military leader, who will win battles for Israel. He will be a great judge, who will make righteous decisions (Jeremiah 33:15). But above all, he will be a human being, not a god, demigod or other supernatural being.

Before the time of the Messiah there will be war and suffering (Ezekiel 38:16). The Messiah will bring about the political and spiritual redemption of the Jewish people by bringing them back to Israel and restoring Jerusalem (Isaiah 11:11-12; Jeremiah 23:8; Hosea 3:4-5). He will establish a government in Israel that will be the center of all world government (Isaiah 2:2-4). He will rebuild the Temple and reestablish its worship and He will restore the religious court system of Israel and establish Jewish law as the law of the land (Jeremiah 33:15, 18). The Orthodox Jews do not believe that Jesus was the Messiah.

CHAPTER SIX

YOM HA-DIN
DAYS OF AWE
A JEWISH WEDDING

This is the crux of this book from the Jewish perspective. The chronological order of the events of the end times were calculated from thousands of years of Jewish beliefs and teachings concerning their belief in a coming "Messiah."

YOM HA-DIN — DAY OF JUDGMENT

I would like to begin this section of the chapter with several quotations from two sources. They are:

1. *The New Standard Jewish Encyclopedia*, edited by Dr. Cecil Roth and Dr. Geoffrey Wigoder.
2. *The Oxford Dictionary of the Jewish Religion*, edited by R. J. Zwi Werblowsky and Geoffrey Wigoder.

You will find some very interesting reading that reflects Jewish thinking that goes back in time thousands of years. Please keep in mind that these are quotes from Orthodox Jewish sources with little Christian influence. I hope you also realize how precisely they tie in with the New Testament eschatological plan (study of end-time events). All of the bold and underlined manuscript passages are for emphasis from me, not from the references.

Our first quotation is from *The Oxford Dictionary of the Jewish Religion*:

"YOM HA-DIN (יוֹם הַדִּין), **day on which mankind will be judged by God (or one of his appointed) at the end of days** (*aharit ha-yamim*). The biblical idea of *reward and punishment in this world was paralleled by the concept of the *__Day of the Lord, the day upon which Israel would be exalted and her foes delivered up to divine justice.__ This predominantly nationalistic idea was transformed by the prophets (particularly *Amos), who proclaimed that on Yom ha-Din all evildoers would be judged, including those among the people of Israel, whose punishment would be exile. Once the nation was purged of its sinful dross, the *remnant of Israel, the upright and righteous, would return to the land (ingathering of the *exiles) and enjoy a long and prosperous life. These hopes of return are emphatically expressed by the post-exilic prophets, particularly Haggai and Zechariah, who believed that the reestablishment of the Jewish community in Jerusalem and the rebuilding of the Temple heralded the dawn of the messianic era. When this hope was not fulfilled, the notion of the final Yom ha-Din was transformed—it had not yet occurred but would happen only at the end of days.

Yom ha-Din became a major feature of apocalyptic literature. Not only would it witness the judgment of Israel, but the judgment of mankind and the cosmos as

Yom Ha-Din — Days of Awe — A Jewish Wedding

a whole; even the wicked angels would be called to account. Later apocalyptic literature assumed that the *resurrection of the dead would occur before Yom ha-Din, so that the dead might also be judged. There is a wide divergence of views regarding Yom ha-Din in pseudepigraphous and tannaitic literature. On that great and terrible day, either God himself or his anointed *Messiah will judge the entire world and declare its fate. **In earlier apocalyptic literature, the eschatological Yom ha-Din was identified with "messianic woes," the period of trial and tribulation preceding the advent of Messiah.** In later apocalyptic works (Syriac *Apocalypse of Baruch*, the *Fourth Book of Esdras*), the view is expressed that the messianic age is merely a transitional period between this world and a new era, described as the "world to come" (see 'OLAM HA-ZEH AND 'OLAM HA-BA'). The distinction between the messianic age and the world to come is also made in tannaitic and later rabbinic literature (see ESCHATOLOGY).

Yom ha-Din is also a name for *Ro'sh ha-Shanah, the day on which, according to tradition (R. Ha-Sh. 1.2;T., R. ha-Sh. 1.13) all humankind is judged by God. The decisions about each person's fate are sealed on Yom Kippur." [1]

The next quotation is from *The New Standard Jewish Encyclopedia*:

"**ESCHATOLOGY:** Doctrine of the end of days, referring to the fundamental changing of the present world by Divine plan at a period determined by God. The eschatological world is not necessarily one that has never previously existed; **the view is sometimes advanced that on the last day the world, which was entirely good at creation and only corrupted by human deviations, will be restored to its pristine condition**...A general line is nevertheless discernible in Jewish eschatology from its very beginnings in the early sections of the Bible. Originally, eschatological theory was an expression of popular faith in the glorious future anticipated for the nation after a period of suffering. In its full development, it possessed a religious and moral content, and was introduced by the great Hebrew prophets into their teachings, albeit with their own moral coloring which transformed the naive folk beliefs. The popular conception of the eschatological era was of a period when the renewed people of Israel would wreak vengeance on their foes and set up a great, powerful kingdom; this victorious period was called **"the Day of the Lord."** The prophets, however, added moral content and threatened catastrophe in the absence of genuine repentance; thus, **the Day of the Lord became a day of doom.** This transition is patently clear in Amos and recurs in various forms and degrees in the writings of the other great prophets. **But disaster was not the only element in prophetic eschatology; the final day was also envisioned as the great day when God would reform the world and reign over all peoples in justice. A new heaven and earth will be created, while God will renew his covenant with Israel and establish his throne in Zion.** This trend is particularly apparent in the latter chapters of Isaiah. However, no distinction between the present world and the world to come is known to prophetic eschatology which recognizes only this world. The resuscitation of the Jewish people and the land of Israel and the appearance of the king-messiah are described as events which will occur in the real world. But as reality became ever more remote from the expected glory, so the accounts of the Day of the Lord became more glowing, exaggerated and imaginative. Eschatology was thus transformed into apocalyptic beliefs (see APOCALYPSE) as can be seen in the Book of Ezekiel and the visions of Zechariah. A new element is thought by many scholars to have been introduced into Jewish eschatology by the Book of Daniel, which they date in the Maccabean Period. The persecutions of Antiochus Epiphanes depressed the nation's religious groups, and the messianic kingdom, receding from this world, took on the aspect of a kingdom beyond human reality. The change is symbolized by the figure of the "son of man" who descends from the heavens and proclaims the proximity of the kingdom of God. At the threshold of the new epoch stand the resurrection of the dead and Judgment Day when evil will be outlawed and the wise will receive their due reward. The APOCRYPHA (including pseudepigraphic literature) and aggadah provide an unfailing source of information on eschatological outlooks during and after Second Temple times, reflecting all shades of religious opinion. The development of the apocalyptic aspect of the eschatological beliefs, adumbrated under Antiochus Epiphanes, eventually encompassed the nation as a whole, in addition to its individuals, and this proved of particular importance in the early stages of Christianity. The eschatological thinker comprehends the entire world, knowing the period of its duration and the events of its latter days. **The "end" will be an era of suffering and catastrophes under the rule of the ANTI-CHRIST.** The apocalyptic sources, from the Book of Daniel onward, regard the "end" as a sign of the advent of the MESSIAH. They speak of "the agonies of the Messiah," a terrible last war—the war of GOG AND MAGOG—ranging over Jerusalem. According to one view, the Messiah Son of Joseph, the forerunner of the Messiah Son of David, will fall in this war. But the forces of evil will be defeated whereupon Elijah will appear and announce the advent of the Messiah and this will be the signal for the ingathering of the Diaspora and the freedom of Israel from subjection to gentile kingdoms. A new Jerusalem will arise, and Israel's glory will be manifest to the world. The duration of the messianic kingdom is, however, restricted; it will be succeeded by the Kingdom of God and Judgment Day when the just and wise (generally meaning Israel) will receive their reward, and the wicked (generally the gentiles who have oppressed Israel) will descend to Gehinnom "to everlasting abhorrence." [2]

The last two quotations are from *The Oxford Dictionary of the Jewish Religion*:

"**MESSIAH**. The verb *m sh ḥ* (anoint [with oil]) is used in Biblical Hebrew in connection with material objects as well as persons. The noun *mashiaḥ* (anointed), which is the source of the English word *messiah*, in due course came to mean a consecrated person charged with a special mission from God (kings, prophets, priests; in one case even the gentile king Cyrus, founder of the Persian empire, is given this title [see *Is.* 45.1]). More specifically, the term signified the kings of the Davidic dynasty ("David and his seed"), and in particular the future "Son of David," who would deliver Israel from foreign bondage, restore the glories of a former golden age, and inaugurate the ingathering of Israel and God's kingdom of righteousness and peace...**The prophets described a vision of a severe judgment, which would be followed by a glorious future, at least for a righteous remnant**...Thus, the rebuilding of the Temple became a central feature of the "messianic complex" after its destruction...Various eschatological ideas (the messianic age, the *kingdom of heaven, the last judgment, the *resurrection of the dead, etc.) were held by different groups in different combinations and with varying emphases already in Second Temple times...the *"Son of Man" who will descend from heaven to save the elect...The heterogeneity of the material also suggested a distinction between two different dispensations: a more this-worldly messianic age (ingathering of the dispersed, restoration of the Davidic kingdom, delivery from bondage, rebuilding of the Temple) and the eschatological "end of days" (day of judgment, resurrection of the dead).

To what extent revolts and uprisings, such as the Bar-Kokhba' Revolt, were "messianic" in character has to be examined in detail in every case. The disastrous failure of uprisings had two significant consequences. It strengthened the element of "apocalyptic" catastrophe in the eschatological scheme: the final consummation would be preceded by great suffering (the messianic woes, *hevlei mashiah*); moral degeneracy; wars and cosmic upheavals (Armageddon, *Gog and Magog); and a messianic "Son of Joseph" (possibly an indirect reference to the ten tribes), who would heroically fall in battle against the forces of evil before the ultimate triumph of the victorious Son of David. Another result was an increasingly quietistic emphasis, accompanied by warnings against attempts "to force the end." Messianic faith came to mean patient waiting, and "calculating the end: by means of interpreting certain biblical numbers (e.g., in the *Book of Daniel*) was discouraged by the rabbis, though the prohibition was not always obeyed. *Redemption, the rabbis asserted, will be brought about by God in his own time and not by human activity, though its advent could be hastened by ascetic piety, strict observance of the law, penitence and mystical mediation...

The faith in an ultimately redeemed world of peace and justice, and in a messianic future for mankind (as distinct from faith in a personal Messiah), is shared by most trends in modern Jewry. Classical Reform rejected the concept of a personal Messiah, substituting the conviction that humankind was moving toward a messianic era of perfect peace and justice. Similarly, Conservative thinkers have adopted the concept of a messianic period to be achieved without supernatural intervention. Post-Enlightenment secularism identified messianism with either the social and political goals of tolerance, liberalism and full emancipation or, alternatively, socialism, and rejected Zionist nationalism in favor of universalist ideas. Contemporary attitudes toward nationalism and messianism are changing. While secularists might support a Jewish national identity without messianic expectations, Religious Zionism has undergone an ideological messianization. **The**

prayer sanctioned by the chief rabbinate of Israel, and recited also in synagogues in the Diaspora, defines the State of Israel as "the beginning of the sprouting of our redemption," wording which implies that the messianic era has begun and that the State of Israel constitutes the beginning of the messianic process." [3]

"ESCHATOLOGY...Amos, the first of the classical prophets (mid-eighth cent. BCE), provides the earliest biblical evidence for the expectation of a coming Day of Judgment (see YOM HA-DIN), a "*Day of the Lord" (*Am.* 5.18-20). The prophet rejects what was apparently the popular view of that day as the moment when the Lord would take vengeance on Israel's enemies and grant his people the peace and prosperity they lacked. Rather he insists that the Day of the Lord is a day of judgment for the people of Israel as well.

Later prophets follow Amos in claiming that God's judgment would not spare the people of Israel, but they emphasized the subsequent restoration. **Isaiah of Jerusalem, a younger contemporary active in Judah, the southern kingdom, from the middle of the eighth through the beginning of the seventh century BCE, suggests that a righteous remnant of the people of Israel will survive the judgment and enjoy the new age.** Other prophets also pictured a future reconciliation between God and the whole people or a pious and holy remnant.

The sack of Jerusalem by the Babylonians in 586 BCE overturned the basic assumptions of the southern kingdom: the divine inviolability of the house of David, of the house of the Lord, the Temple, and the City of the Lord, which was also the City of David. The prophet known as Deutero-Isaiah interpreted the conquest of Babylonia by the Persian king Cyrus in 538 BCE as an event fraught with eschatological significance. His prophetic interpretation seemed confirmed when Cyrus issued his decree permitting the exiles to return to their land and rebuild the Temple. But reality failed to measure up to the prophet's high hopes. The new Temple was a sad sight for those who remembered the first, and it stood in the midst of a divided community ruled by a Persian governor rather than a descendant of David.

The hope for the restoration of national sovereignty made eschatology a central concern of the Second Temple period as Hellenistic and Roman rulers followed the Persians, with only a century of independence under the Hasmoneans. Other subjects of the Hellenistic empire, particularly the Egyptians, produced prophecies about a new era in which a native king would be restored to the throne and proper order again established. Nevertheless, the content of Jewish eschatology was unique, because it was embedded in biblical traditions and prophetic utterance.

According to the eschatology of the Second Temple period, the course of history represented the unfolding of a plan determined by God. The *Book of Daniel*, for example, says that Israel had to be subjugated to four foreign kingdoms in succession before the establishment of "the kingdom of the holy ones of the Most High." Antiochus IV Epiphanes, the enemy at the time of the book's composition, is the last of the kings of the last kingdom. In the *Fourth Book of Ezra*, written

Yom Ha-Din — Days of Awe — A Jewish Wedding

several centuries later, after the destruction of the Second Temple by the Romans in 70 CE, a vision identifies the Roman empire as the last of the four kingdoms.

Responses to the belief in the imminent end of history were varied. The *Qumran community practiced an intensified version of the purity rules of the Bible. The earliest Christians introduced new practices in keeping with their belief that the Messiah had already appeared and inaugurated the end time. For others, the knowledge that the end was near inspired political and military action. According to Josephus, a number of messianic pretenders who led small groups of followers against the Romans toward the end of the Second Temple period and the Jewish revolt against the Romans from 66 to 70, which led to the destruction of the Second Temple, had eschatological components. The timing of the Bar-Kokhba' Revolt between 132 and 135 seems also to reflect eschatological expectation; since the Second Temple was rebuilt roughly seventy years after the First Temple was destroyed, some Jews believed that the time was ripe for the establishment of the third and final temple as the seventy-year mark from the destruction of the Second Temple approached.

The belief in a future era of redemption is central to rabbinic thought, and it is expressed clearly in the liturgy of the synagogue as well as in rabbinic literature. The new era is always presided over by the *Messiah, who was not a constant feature of the eschatological scenarios of the prophets and the authors of the Second Temple period. Still, the rabbis remained cautious, which is not surprising in light of the unhappy outcome of the revolts against Rome. **While the end was certain to come, its coming could not be forced by human beings.**

No unified picture of the end of time emerges from the literature. Indeed, Gershom Scholem has suggested that there is a fundamental split in Jewish eschatology between "restorative" and "utopian" strands. The restorative strand comprises visions of an end that is possible in the world as we know it: Israel is established in its own land under a new Davidic king. The utopian strand on the other hand, is not limited by the world as it is; the lion lies down with the lamb and death is abolished.

The third-century Babylonian rabbi Shemu'el insisted that the only difference between his age and the messianic era was that Israel would no longer be subjugated to the nations. He cites *Deuteronomy* 15.11, "The poor shall never cease from the midst of the land," as proof of his anti-utopian position. Such a position is less of an incitement to messianic activity than a more utopian one. Maimonides' picture of the messianic era in his legal code, the *Mishneh Torah*, comes from Shemu'el: the Messiah will be recognized as such because he will succeed in restoring the Jews to their homeland and rebuilding the Temple; there will be nothing supernatural about what he accomplishes; anyone who fails to restore Israel to its biblical state is not the Messiah." [4]

After reading these quotations from a Jewish eschatological perspective, you can see the amazing proximity to Christian eschatological thinking. As we continue, you will also see how the ancient Jewish festivals bear on the end time scenario that is about to play out in the near future. It is exciting to look at the Jewish perspective on Bible prophecy.

As I have mentioned throughout this book, concerning the phrase "the Day of the Lord", I believe it is the most misunderstood subject of the study of the end times. With the proper understanding of the chronological order of the Day of the Lord, it is easier to figure out the order of events that take place just ahead of us. It also separates God's dealings with the Jews, the Gentiles and the Church. It creates a clean break between the end of this age and the beginning of the next. As far as I am concerned, it brings the Old and New Testaments together cohesively. It harmonizes the understanding and makes all scripture concerning future events realistic. It allows time for all the events mentioned in the Bible to take place.

Separating the Tribulation Period from the Millennium has created some misunderstandings. The Millennium is not a thousand years of peace for those on earth. The Day of the Lord is a time for the righteousness of God to come to fruition. At the beginning of the Day of the Lord, for a period of ten years, Jesus as King of Kings and Lord of Lords will judge the saints in heaven and also wicked (unsaved) mankind who will be living on the earth at the same time. This will allow time for God to finish His dealings with His chosen people (the Jews). In the first two-year period there will be activity both in heaven and on the earth. In heaven, Jesus will be dealing with the believers from Adam to the Rapture.

> 2 Cor 5:10 ***For we must all appear before the judgment seat of Christ,*** *that each one may receive what is due him for the things done while in the body, whether good or bad.* (NIV)

On earth it will be the beginning of the dealings with unregenerate mankind.

> Matt 24:21 *"**For then there will be great tribulation,** such as has not been since the beginning of the world until this time, no, nor ever shall be.* (NKJ)

An ancient Jewish wedding can also play a part in determining the end-time chronological order of events. It can warrant a two-year period for a ritual cleansing (Mikveh) before the seven-day wedding feast, a time for the bride (church) and the wedding guests (Old Testament Saints) to put on their white garments.

Another reason why I believe that there will be a two-year period *After the Rapture* and before the Tribulation Period is found in the chronological order of the book of Revelation. There is a time period between chapter three and chapter six. Time for the church to be preparing for a wedding that will take place in heaven, followed by a marriage feast for seven years, while the earth is experiencing turmoil. I do not believe, as some Bible scholars believe, that the Judgment Seat of Christ will be going on in heaven at the same time the Tribulation Period is being played out on the earth. The Judgment Seat of Christ will take place in heaven before the Tribulation Period begins. A two-year period will exist *After the Rapture* and before the Tribulation Period begins, which means that the chronological order of Revelation is continuous and not simultaneous in chapters four and five. If that is true, the Judgment Seat of Christ will take place in heaven before the Tribulation Period begins on earth. The charts at end of the book show the chronological order of these events.

During the Day of the Lord, it will be a thousand-year period with Jesus on the throne. Jesus will begin His rule in heaven as a King by finishing His dealings with His chosen people and wicked mankind for ten years before He restores the earth to finish the final nine hundred and ninety years of the Millennium—where the world will live in a time of peace and safety. We continue our study from a Jewish perspective by looking at the festivals of the High Holy Days.

TEN DAYS OF REPENTANCE — ASERET YEMEI TESHUVAH

"Aseret Yemei Teshuvah (עֲשֶׂרֶת יְמֵי תְשׁוּבָה ; Ten Days of Repentance)—quoting from *The Oxford Dictionary of the Jewish Religion,* "penitential period commencing with *Ro'sh ha-Shanah and concluding with *Yom Kippur. According to the Mishnah (R. ha-Sh. 1.2), 1 Tishrei (New Year) is the Day of Judgment. The Talmud, however, explains (R. ha-Sh. 16b) that on Ro'sh ha-Shanah final judgment is passed only on the "perfectly righteous" and the "utterly wicked"; judgment of all others is suspended until Yom Kippur on the tenth of the month. As a result, the entire ten-day period became one of penitence, in anticipation of that final judgment." [5]

First, let me start by telling you that not very many Christians, including true believers, know very much about these Jewish feasts that take place once every year and have been in practice ever since Moses was instructed by God to put them in place somewhere around 1445 BC.

Num 29:1-11   *"'On the first day of the seventh month hold a sacred assembly and do no regular work. <u>It is a day for you to sound the trumpets.</u> As an aroma pleasing to the LORD, prepare a burnt offering of one young bull, one ram and seven male lambs a year old, all without defect. With the bull prepare a grain offering of three-tenths of an ephah of fine flour mixed with oil; with the ram, two-tenths; and with each of the seven lambs, one-tenth. Include one male goat as a sin offering to make atonement for you. These are in addition to the monthly and daily burnt offerings with their grain offerings and drink offerings as specified. They are offerings made to the LORD by fire—a pleasing aroma. "'<u>On the tenth day of this seventh month hold a sacred assembly.</u> You must deny yourselves and do no work. Present as an aroma pleasing to the LORD a burnt offering of one young bull, one ram and seven male lambs a year old, all without defect. With the bull prepare a grain offering of three-tenths of an ephah of fine flour mixed with oil; with the ram, two-tenths; and with each of the seven lambs, one-tenth. Include one male goat as a sin offering, in addition to the sin offering for atonement and the regular burnt offering with its grain offering, and their drink offerings.* (NIV)

I had been drawn by the Holy Spirit for several years to study the Jewish feasts and festivals of the Old Testament. I do not believe that a full understanding of the Bible can be obtained without the knowledge of the teachings God has for the "chosen people." They are God's "time piece" and the Holy land is God's "time place."

Let us take a more concise look at the forty days of introspection and repentance the Jewish people observe every year that culminates with the Ten Days of Awe. The Jewish month that precedes the month of Tishri is Elul. The thirty days of Elul are a preparatory period for the Jewish people to prepare for the first ten days of Tishri, which make up a time known to the Jewish people as the High Holy Days.

To come to a full understanding of the meaning of the Days of Awe, which are the High Holy Days for the Jewish people, we must travel back in time to when Moses was leading the Jews out of the bondage of the Egyptians more than 3400 years ago. This section of this chapter will be Jewish to the core, but as we study it, you will be amazed at how precisely it ties in with the New Testament. Before I started writing this book, I knew that the Old and New Testaments were one book. After researching the Jewish Feasts and the concept of an ancient Jewish wedding, I am astounded at just how exact both sections of God's Holy Word are one complete book. The Jews have it right on (with the exception of rejecting the Messiah) and the Christians almost have the same exact message. How tragic it has been for thousands of years that the two sides have been alienated from one another and even more sad when you realize that the chosen people as a whole have rejected Jesus as the true Messiah. Add to that the supposed believers in Jesus as the Savior (Christians), who persecuted the Jews throughout the last two thousand years. Let us now join forces as we await the return of our Messiah, Savior, King, Husband, High Priest, and Prophet.

His name is **Y'SHUA HAMASHIACH—JESUS CHRIST(MESSIAH)**.

Acts 4:10-12   ***then know this, you and all the people of Israel: It is by the name of Jesus Christ of Nazareth, whom you crucified but whom God raised from the dead, that this man stands before you healed. He is "'the stone you builders rejected, which has become the capstone.' Salvation is found in no one else, for there is no other name under heaven given to men by which we must be saved."***
(NIV)

MONTH OF ELUL

Although we are following a Jewish perspective, everything we are studying applies to Christianity in a prophetic sense. I sincerely hope that this chapter will add to your knowledge of the Bible and God's plan for events yet future for all of us.

The month of Elul for the Jewish people is a period of Divine grace and is a preparation period for the Jewish New Year, observed as a religious holiday in September or October. It is the thirty days before Rosh Hashanah, the great Judgment Day. The month of Elul is commonly thought of as a time of Divine goodwill and contributes to the special grace these days have for people who repent. The special quality of these days of Divine Grace are to prepare the Jews to return to God. It has its roots in the first Elul Israel experienced as a nation, when the Jewish people were going through an intense repentance over the sin of the golden calf. The people were restored to Hashem's (a Jewish name for God—it actually means "The Name") good graces on Rosh Chodesh (month) Elul, when Moses ascended Mount Sinai for the third forty-day period. God sealed His relationship with the Jewish people by forming a covenant with them.

> Exod 34:9-10   *"O Lord, if I have found favor in your eyes," he said, "then let the Lord go with us. Although this is a stiff-necked people, forgive our wickedness and our sin, and take us as your inheritance." **Then the LORD said: "I am making a covenant with you.** Before all your people I will do wonders never before done in any nation in all the world. The people you live among will see how awesome is the work that I, the LORD, will do for you.* (NIV)

Let us follow this general description with a more precise account of the story. As Moses was leading the Israelites out of bondage from the Egyptians toward the promised land, they stopped at Mount Sinai to receive special instructions from God that included the Ten Commandments. This was the first forty-day/forty-night period Moses spent on Mount Sinai.

> Exod 24:12-18   ***The LORD said to Moses, "Come up to me on the mountain and stay here, and I will give you the tablets of stone, with the law and commands I have written for their instruction."*** *Then Moses set out with Joshua his aide, and Moses went up on the mountain of God. He said to the elders, "Wait here for us until we come back to you. Aaron and Hur are with you, and anyone involved in a dispute can go to them." When Moses went up on the mountain, the cloud covered it, and the glory of the LORD settled on Mount Sinai. For six days the cloud covered the mountain, and on the seventh day the LORD called to Moses from within the cloud.* ***To the Israelites the glory of the LORD looked like a consuming fire on top of the mountain. Then Moses entered the cloud as he went on up the mountain. And he stayed on the mountain forty days and forty nights.*** (NIV)

The Jewish thought is that Moses spent forty days on Mount Sinai reading the Written Law by day and reviewing the Oral Law by night (their belief). While Moses was up on Mount Sinai, the Israelites became worried that Moses would not return to them, possibly assuming he was consumed by the fire. The people ask Aaron, Moses brother, to make them Gods who would go before them.

> Exod 32:1   ***When the people saw that Moses was so long in coming down from the mountain, they gathered around Aaron and said, "Come, make us Gods who will go before us.*** *As for this fellow Moses who brought us up out of Egypt, we don't know what has happened to him."* (NIV)

Aaron fashioned a golden calf made out of the jewelry from the Israelites and they bowed down and sacrificed to the idol. By this dreadful act they committed a great sin.

When Moses finally came down, he took the tablets and descended Mount Sinai into the camp on the seventeenth day of Tammuz. He broke the tablets in a fit of rage. Moses then proceeded to grind the golden calf to powder and burn it, slaying all the people who had kissed the idol, and destroyed idol worship from Israel. God was so angry with this abomination that He wanted to destroy the Israelites and make a great nation out of Moses.

Exod 32:9-12   *"<u>I have seen these people</u>," the LORD said to Moses, "<u>and they are a stiff-necked people. Now leave me alone so that my anger may burn against them and that I may destroy them.</u> Then I will make you into a great nation."* But Moses sought the favor of the LORD his God. *"O LORD,"* he said, *"why should your anger burn against your people, whom you brought out of Egypt with great power and a mighty hand? Why should the Egyptians say, 'It was with evil intent that he brought them out, to kill them in the mountains and to wipe them off the face of the earth'? Turn from your fierce anger; relent and do not bring disaster on your people.* (NIV)

Exod 32:30   *The next day Moses said to the people, "<u>You have committed a great sin</u>. But now I will go up to the LORD; perhaps I can make atonement for your sin."* (NIV)

Moses spent a second forty-day/forty-night period on Mount Sinai that lasted from the eighteenth of Tammuz until the twenty-ninth of Av, at which time he was pleading with God to forgive the Israelites. Moses asked God not to destroy them. The pleadings of Moses must have been successful because God relented from destroying them.

Exod 32:14   *Then the LORD relented and did not bring on his people the disaster he had threatened.* (NIV)

Moses made a final trip up to the top of Mount Sinai for forty days and forty nights. It was to make atonement for the great sin of idol worship that the Israelites were performing while Moses was on Mount Sinai for the first forty-day period. Moses took a second set of stone tablets to God, as instructed, to replace the first set he threw to the ground and broke into pieces. This third period of forty days started on the first day of the month of Elul and ended on the tenth day of the month of Tishri. The month of Elul is the last month of the year and Tishri is the first month of the next year. This is the very first time that the Jewish people partook of the "Season of our Repentance" and it has been an annual event every year since then, as it was commanded by God for the Jewish people—for almost 3500 years. Before we move on, I should explain to you that the Jewish people celebrate several New Years throughout the year and two of them are main New Years.

In the spring of the year they celebrate the new religious year with the month of Nisan and end with the month of Adar. It follows our present calendar like this:

Yom Ha-Din — Days of Awe — A Jewish Wedding

1. Nisan   (Mar-Apr)
2. Iyar   (Apr-May)
3. Sivan   (May-June)
4. Tammuz   (June-July)
5. Av   (July-Aug)
6. Elul   (Aug-Sept)
7. Tishri   (Sept-Oct)
8. Heshvan   (Oct-Nov)
9. Chislev   (Nov-Dec)
10. Tevet   (Dec-Jan)
11. Shevat   (Jan-Feb)
12. Adar   (Feb-Mar)

This religious New Year, which counts the month of Nisan as the first month, is celebrated a few weeks ahead of the Jewish Feast of Passover, which includes the Feast of Unleavened Bread and the Feast of First Fruits. It falls in the spring of the year. In the fall of the year a New Year is celebrated in the month of Tishri. It is considered a civil calendar. The sage's of old inform us that the world was created in the month of Tishri. It is the time of judgment for all things. The Jewish calendar year from this perspective looks like this:

7. Tishri   (Sept-Oct)
8. Heshvan   (Oct-Nov)
9. Chislev   (Nov-Dec)
10. Tevet   (Dec-Jan)
11. Shevat   (Jan-Feb)
12. Adar   (Feb-Mar)
1. Nisan   (Mar-Apr)
2. Iyar   (Apr-May)
3. Sivan   (May-June)
4. Tammuz   (June-July)
5. Av   (July-Aug)
6. Elul   (Aug-Sept)

Please take note that the numbers of the months on this calendar are numbered the same as the calendar for the New Year religious calendar. The first month of this civil calendar is Tishri, but it is numbered as the seventh month. This is important to remember as we continue with the Days of Awe study and also how these months are listed in the Old Testament. When the seventh month is mentioned it is always referring to Tishri.

The third forty-day period, when Moses made atonement for the Jewish peoples sin of idol worship and his receiving the second set of stone tablets, was from the first day of Elul and ended on the tenth day of Tishri. This was the first "Season of our Repentance" that the Jewish people commemorated. It is celebrated annually and it ends with the Day of Atonement on the tenth of Tishri. The tenth day of Tishri is known as Yom Kippur and put a covering over the sins of the past year for all the Jewish people who truly repented.

Of this forty-day period, the first thirty days or the entire month of Elul is a preparatory period known as a period of Divine grace of goodwill. The last ten days are referred to as the Days of Awe and are the first ten days of Tishri, also known as the High Holy Days. The first day of Tishri (New Years Day) is the Feast of Trumpets, also known as Rosh Hashanah, and lasts for two days. The seven days between Rosh Hashanah and Yom Kippur are known as the Seven Intermediate Days. The tenth day of Tishri is the Day of Atonement and its Jewish name is Yom Kippur. This annual forty-day celebration by the Jewish people all over the world is a period of their inner feeling and repentance. In the book of Leviticus, God commanded the Jewish people to make a lasting ordinance for the atonement, once a year, for all the sins of the Israelites.

Lev 16:34 *"This is to be a lasting ordinance for you: <u>Atonement is to be made once a year for all the sins of the Israelites</u>." And it was done, as the LORD commanded Moses.* (NIV)

My personal belief is that if you use the theory of counting one year for every day of the forty days of the "Season of Our Repentance," we will probably have a Messianic Jewish movement of great proportion the last thirty years before the trumpet sound at the Rapture! Look for it! It is in our midst today as a full Messianic Jewish movement is under way.

BLOW THE SHOFAR

"I have installed my King on Zion, my holy hill." I will proclaim the decree of the LORD: He said to me, "You are my Son; today I have become your Father. Ask of me, and I will make the nations your inheritance, the ends of the earth your possession. (Psalms 2:6-8 NIV)

This scene is in heaven at the coronation of a King, not just any king, but the King of Kings and Lord of Lords, Jesus Christ. The thirty-year period of Elul will have transpired at the end of the Dispensation of Grace or the church age. The sound of a ram's horn will signal the end of the church age that will last for two thousand years. This sound is known as the *"last trumpet"* in 1 Corinthians 15:52, and it is referred to as the *"trumpet call of God"* in 1 Thessalonians 4:16-17. Today, it is commonly referred to us as the Rapture, the second coming of our Lord and Savior, Jesus Christ.

1 Cor 15:52 *In a moment, in the twinkling of an eye, <u>at the last trump</u>: for the trumpet shall sound, and the dead shall be raised incorruptible, and we shall be changed.* (KJV)

1 Thes 4:16-17 *For the Lord himself shall descend from heaven with a shout, with the voice of the archangel, <u>and with the trump of God</u>: and the dead in Christ shall rise first: Then we which are alive and remain shall be caught up together with them in the clouds, to meet the Lord in the air: and so shall we ever be with the Lord.* (KJV)

Yom Ha-Din — Days of Awe — A Jewish Wedding

This sound of a trumpet in the New Testament is the same sound of the ram's horn (shofar) from a Jewish perspective in the Old Testament. It is also a signal for the Jewish New Year (civil) that begins on the Feast of Rosh Hashanah in the Jewish month of Tishri. Since this sound of the ram's horn will come from Jesus Himself, it will be the long awaited time for the beginning of the seventh creation day of one thousand years known in the Bible as the Day of the Lord.

> Joel 2:1   *Blow the trumpet in Zion; sound the alarm on my holy hill. Let all who live in the land tremble, <u>for the day of the LORD is coming</u>. It is close at hand—* (NIV)

> Joel 3:18   *'<u>In that day</u> the mountains will drip new wine, and the hills will flow with milk; all the ravines of Judah will run with water. A fountain will flow out of the LORD's house and will water the valley of acacias.* (NIV)

The Jews who believe in Jesus by faith as the Messiah during the Dispensation of Grace will belong to the church age believers. They will be a part of the bride of Christ. For the unsaved Jews left on earth the Day of the Lord will begin with a short period of the fierce anger of the Lord and will culminate with peace. They will take part in the purging process of God when He removes the unsaved Jews from the earth. This will take place before Jesus sets up His Kingdom on earth in Jerusalem.

THREE BOOKS

Before we move on, I would like to show you an interesting teaching from some ancient rabbis. In a book titled, *"Days of Awe,"* by Shmuel Yosef Agnon, I would like to quote from page 14, "Said Rabbi Kruspedai, in the name of Rabbi Yohanan: Three books are opened on Rosh ha-Shanah: one for the wholly righteous, one for the wholly wicked, and one for the intermediates. The wholly righteous are at once inscribed and sealed in the book of life; the wholly wicked are at once inscribed and sealed in the book of death; and the intermediates are held suspended from Rosh ha-Shanah until Yom Kippur. If they are found worthy, they are inscribed for life; if found unworthy, they are inscribed for death. (Rosh ha-Shanah 166, version of En Yaakov)." [6] We can decipher from the above quote that from the Jewish point of view, spoken of here, there will be three books to be opened at the sounding of the ram's horn on Rosh Hashanah. This ancient Jewish teaching can apply to the Days of Awe theory in this book. They are:

1. **A book for the wholly righteous** — On Rosh Hashanah, their names are immediately inscribed in the book of life and sealed. This book will contain the names of the saints who are already in heaven (dead in Christ) and also the saints who are alive and remain on earth at the time of the Rapture.

2. **A book for the wholly wicked** — On Rosh Hashanah, the names of the wicked

AFTER THE RAPTURE

are at once blotted out of the book of life and placed in the book of death and sealed. This book will contain the names of all the lost souls who have rejected God for all time up to the Rapture. This group will include all of the unsaved people who will have died physically up to this time.

3. **A book for the intermediates** — This book will contain the names of those who remain alive all over the world *After the Rapture*. They are all unsaved at this time. They are allowed nine days (9 years) until the Day of Atonement (Yom Kippur) to repent and become righteous. These people will go through the period of judgment on earth that will include the fierce anger of God. It will include Jews and Gentiles. They will go through the Tribulation Period. During the period of the Days of Awe, they will make their individual decisions of accepting or rejecting Jesus Christ. If they decide for Christ, their names will be written in the book of life. If they reject Christ, their names will be written in the book of death.

In other words, the people living on earth *After the Rapture* will make their decision concerning how they believe in the Lord while they are in this life. Just like we do now on this side of the Day of the Lord. The only difference for them is that they will have to go through the worst time of human history while they are making their decision.

ROSH HASHANAH — JUDGMENT DAY

With the sound of the shofar or ram's horn (trumpet) on Rosh Hashanah, it will mark the beginning of three periods of time for the Jewish people who missed the Rapture. They are:

1. **Day of the Lord** — The seventh day of the creation week that will last for 1000 years.
2. **Days of Awe** — A ten day (10 years as I count them in this study) period of Jewish repentance that will be marked with wrath and redemption.
3. **Rosh Hashanah** — A two-day Jewish holiday that is celebrated annually by the Jewish people. The first two days (2 years) of the Days of Awe.

Rosh Hashanah is packed full of meaning. It will start the "new age" that most religions of the world are looking for today, a new Millennium or era. With this trumpet sound the world will never be the same again. The themes for Rosh Hashanah are numerous and are listed below. They are also listed on the chart—Days of Awe—on page 764.

1. **FEAST OF TRUMPETS** — The sound like a trumpet made by Jesus as He comes down from heaven, from the right hand of God with the dead in Christ (including Old Testament saints), to call up those who remain alive (church age believers on earth at the time of the Rapture), so they can be led into the presence of God.
   1 Thes 4:16-18 *For the Lord Himself will descend from heaven with a shout, with the voice of an archangel, **and with the trumpet of God**. And the dead in Christ*

will rise first. Then we who are alive and remain shall be caught up together with them in the clouds to meet the Lord in the air. And thus we shall always be with the Lord. Therefore comfort one another with these words. (NKJ)

Ps 81:3-5 **Blow the trumpet** *at the time of the New Moon, at the full moon, on our solemn feast day. For this is a statute for Israel, a law of the God of Jacob. This He established in Joseph as a testimony, when He went throughout the land of Egypt, where I heard a language I did not understand.* (NKJ)

2. **DAY OF THE AWAKENING BLAST** — This is a reference to the time when the saints will receive their resurrected bodies. It will take place when the sound of the trumpet is heard. This is not to be confused with soul sleep.

   Isa 26:19 *But your dead will live; their bodies will rise.* ***You who dwell in the dust, wake up and shout for joy.*** *Your dew is like the dew of the morning; the earth will give birth to her dead.* (NIV)

   Rom 13:11 *And do this, understanding the present time.* ***The hour has come for you to wake up from your slumber****, because our salvation is nearer now than when we first believed.* (NIV)

   Eph 5:13-14 *But everything exposed by the light becomes visible, for it is light that makes everything visible. This is why it is said: "Wake up, O sleeper,* ***rise from the dead, and Christ will shine on you.****"* (NIV)

3. **CORONATION OF THE KING** — The long awaited crowning of Jesus by His Father has arrived at last. There will be a literal Kingly coronation that will take place in heaven. He will be crowned King of Kings and Lord of Lords. We discussed it earlier in this chapter. There are to many Bible passages concerning Jesus when He receives His Kingship, so we will only mention a few of them.

   Ps 2:6-9 ***"Yet I have set My King on My holy hill of Zion."*** *"I will declare the decree: the LORD has said to Me, '****You are My Son, today I have begotten You.*** *Ask of Me, and I will give You the nations for Your inheritance, and the ends of the earth for Your possession. You shall break them with a rod of iron; you shall dash them to pieces like a potter's vessel.'"* (NKJ)

   Ps 24:7-10 *Lift up your heads, O you gates; be lifted up, you ancient doors, that the King of glory may come in.* ***Who is this King of glory?*** *The LORD strong and mighty, the LORD mighty in battle. Lift up your heads, O you gates; lift them up, you ancient doors, that the King of glory may come in. Who is he, this King of glory?* ***The LORD Almighty—he is the King of glory.*** *Selah* (NIV)

   Ps 99:1-5 *The LORD reigns, let the nations tremble; he sits enthroned between the cherubim, let the earth shake. Great is the LORD in Zion; he is exalted over all the nations. Let them praise your great and awesome name—he is holy.* ***The King is mighty****, he loves justice—you have established equity; in Jacob you have done what is just and right. Exalt the LORD our God and worship at his footstool; he is holy.* (NIV)

   Dan 7:13-14 *"In my vision at night I looked, and there before me was one like* ***a son of man****, coming with the clouds of heaven. He approached the Ancient of*

*Days and was led into his presence. **He was given authority, glory and sovereign power**; all peoples, nations and men of every language worshiped him. His dominion is an everlasting dominion that will not pass away, and his kingdom is one that will never be destroyed.* (NIV)

4. **DAY OF JUDGMENT** — As a King it will be the ultimate responsibility of Jesus to be a righteous Judge.

    Ps 94:1-3 *O LORD, the God who avenges, O God who avenges, shine forth. Rise up, **O Judge of the earth**; pay back to the proud what they deserve. How long will the wicked, O LORD, how long will the wicked be jubilant?* (NIV)

    Ps 94:15 ***Judgment will again be founded on righteousness**, and all the upright in heart will follow it.* (NIV)

    Ps 98:9 *let them sing before the LORD, for he comes to judge the earth. **He will judge the world in righteousness and the peoples with equity**.* (NIV)

    James 5:7-9 *Be patient, then, brothers, until the Lord's coming. See how the farmer waits for the land to yield its valuable crop and how patient he is for the autumn and spring rains. You too, be patient and stand firm, because the Lord's coming is near. Don't grumble against each other, brothers, or you will be judged. **The Judge is standing at the door!*** (NIV)

During the Days of Awe, judgment will take place in heaven and on earth. Let us now look at both the scene in heaven and the scene on earth during this period of time. At this time we will only look at a shortened scenario. In the chapters to follow we will look at a more detailed version. The reign of Jesus will extend from heaven to the earth. He will be on His throne in heavenly splendor.

SCENE IN HEAVEN

In heaven, during the two-year period of Rosh Hashanah, the Judgment Seat of Christ will be in session. The saints will be appearing before the Judge to receive their rewards.

> 2 Cor 5:10 ***For we must all appear before the judgment seat of Christ***, *that each one may receive what is due him for the things done while in the body, whether good or bad.* (NIV)

> Rom 14:10-11 *But why dost thou judge thy brother? or why dost thou set at nought thy brother? **for we shall all stand before the judgment seat of Christ**. For it is written, As I live, saith the Lord, every knee shall bow to me, and every tongue shall confess to God.* (KJV)

> Dan 7:10 *A river of fire was flowing, coming out from before him. Thousands upon thousands attended him; ten thousand times ten thousand stood before him. **The court was seated, and the books were opened**.* (NIV)

Yom Ha-Din — Days of Awe — A Jewish Wedding

This court, that will be set up, will be for believers only. Those who will stand face-to-face before their righteous judge, Jesus, at this time, will have no sins to answer for. As Jesus opens the Lamb's Book of Life, to the page that has their name written on it, their sins will be missing. They have been washed by the blood of the Lamb and have been cleansed of their sins. They will be redeemed! Instead of punishment, they are here before Jesus to receive the rewards for what they have accomplished for the up-building of the Kingdom of God. What have you done for Jesus in this lifetime? Did you witness for him? Were you kind to people? Did you visit people while they were in the hospital or in jail? Are you applying the special gifts God has appointed for you for His service? Whatever a saint has done for Jesus in this life, they will receive their rewards for those acts at this time in heaven, while they are in their resurrected bodies standing before their righteous Judge. What a comfort to know that they do not need to answer for the sins of this life.

1 Cor 3:8-9 *The man who plants and the man who waters have one purpose, and each will be rewarded according to his own labor. For we are God's fellow workers; you are God's field, God's building.* (NIV)

1 Cor 3:10-15 *By the grace God has given me, I laid a foundation as an expert builder, and someone else is building on it. But each one should be careful how he builds. For no one can lay any foundation other than the one already laid, which is Jesus Christ. If any man builds on this foundation using gold, silver, costly stones, wood, hay or straw, his work will be shown for what it is, because the Day will bring it to light. It will be revealed with fire, and the fire will test the quality of each man's work. **If what he has built survives, he will receive his reward.** If it is burned up, he will suffer loss; he himself will be saved, but only as one escaping through the flames.* (NIV)

It will take two years to complete the Judgment Seat of Christ, the receiving of the rewards of the believers in heaven. It will be the same two-year period in the Jewish wedding known as the Mikveh (ritual bath). This will be a two year period before the seven-year wedding feast begins in heaven.

SCENE ON EARTH

On the earth, Rosh Hashanah, will be a two-year period of what I refer to in this book as, *After the Rapture* and before the Tribulation Period. It will be a 2-year preparatory period before the 7-year period of God's fierce anger is unleashed. The Antichrist will be released at the beginning of this period to begin his quest to take over the world. It will be a two-year preparatory time to begin the fulfillment of Daniel, when God will finish His dealings with the Jewish people and the city of Jerusalem; to put an end to sin, to atone for wickedness, to bring in everlasting righteousness and to anoint the most holy.

It will be the beginning of the end as it leads up to the worst time in human history. This portion of God's judgment will take place here on the earth. The Antichrist will have very little power at this time, but his influence will gain momentum with the encouragement of the False Prophet. This two-year period will be a period of chaos all over the world. The Tribulation Period, when God will send forth His fierce anger in the form of the plagues mentioned in the book of Revelation, will not start until after this two-year period is over. It will still not be a very pretty site on earth for this first two-year period. As you continue reading this book, you will see just how horrible it will be on earth during this time.

5. **DAY OF OUR CONCEALMENT** — God never brings the wrath of His fierce anger upon man without warning him beforehand. In the passage quoted in Psalms 27, below, we are told, almost 3000 years ago by David, that the saints will be sheltered from the coming period of destruction, hidden in the shelter of God's tabernacle in heaven. The Old Testament saints will enter their dwellings.
Ps 27:5-6 *For in the day of trouble he will keep me safe in his dwelling; **he will hide me in the shelter of his tabernacle and set me high upon a rock**. Then my head will be exalted above the enemies who surround me; at his tabernacle will I sacrifice with shouts of joy; I will sing and make music to the LORD.* (NIV)
Isa 26:20-21 *Go, my people, enter your rooms and shut the doors behind you; **hide yourselves for a little while until his wrath has passed by**. See, the LORD is coming out of his dwelling to punish the people of the earth for their sins. The earth will disclose the blood shed upon her; she will conceal her slain no longer.* (NIV)
Luke 21:34-36 *"But take heed to yourselves, lest your hearts be weighed down with carousing, drunkenness, and cares of this life, and **that Day** come on you unexpectedly. "For it will come as a snare on all those who dwell on the face of the whole earth. "**Watch therefore, and pray always that you may be counted worthy to escape all these things that will come to pass**, and to stand before the Son of Man."* (NKJ)

The prerequisite for missing the judgment on earth is to have a personal relationship with Jesus Christ. In Isaiah 26, the Old Testament saints are seen entering their rooms prepared for them that exist in heaven. These chambers await the arrival of the saints. The saints will have to pass through the gates of heaven to get to the chambers. In Isaiah 26 above, it also shows the Old Testament saints safe inside God's dwelling place in heaven during the time of God's righteous judgment on sinful mankind living on earth.

6. **DAY OF REMEMBRANCE** — Rabbi Yosef Stern, in his book titled, *Days of Awe, Ideas and insights of the Sfas Emes on the High Holy Days,* as quoted from page 52— "...the designation of Rosh Hashanah as a day of remembrance...— in which all men are remembered and judged by Hashem...." [7] This leads me to believe that all the saved of mankind up to the Rapture, whether they are Jew or Gentile, will stand before Jesus to have the books opened and account for what they have done in their lifetime.

7. **DAYS OF TESHUVAH (REPENTANCE)** — Rosh Hashanah is the first day of

Yom Ha-Din — Days of Awe — A Jewish Wedding

the ten days (years) of Teshuvah. Those who missed the Rapture will have to endure this period of the wrath of God's anger that will befall those on the earth. In a sense you can say that they will have a second chance. Not a good choice! Quoting from Avi Ben Mordechai in *Signs in the Heavens,* he writes on page 265, "The sounding of the Shofar or ram's horn on the first day of the seventh month was indeed a day to bow down to the King of Israel and heed an awakening blast that effectively would say, 'If you wish to, wake up, repent and obtain G-d's mercy now; if not don't complain on Yom Kippur when judgment is meted out.'" [8] His quotation is from the *Midrash Rabbah, Song of Songs,* Vol 9.1.12, p 79. The judgment meted out on Yom Kippur would be the destruction of the unsaved at the Battle of Armageddon, following the return of Jesus riding on a white horse.

8. **NEW CALENDAR YEAR** — The first day of the seventh month commemorates the anniversary of creation. A quotation from *Rosh Hashanah—Its Significance, Laws, and Prayers* edited by Rabbis Nosson Scherman and Meir Zlotowitz reads as follows, "By calling the day Rosh Hashanah, the Jew testifies that God is the Creator and we crown him as our king on the anniversary of the Creation (R'Yaakov Zicherman in Nachalas Yaakov)." [9]

9. **MARRIAGE** — And last, but certainly not least, the theme of Rosh Hashanah is marriage. In the Old Testament the wife of God was Israel, but she became unfaithful (worshiped idols) and God divorced her. In the New Testament, there will be another marriage. God's son Jesus will be the groom and the church will be the bride. God's wife (from Old Testament times), after He takes Israel back, will be the guests at the wedding that will take place in heaven.
Eph 5:31-32 *"For this reason a man will leave his father and mother and be united to his wife, and the two will become one flesh." This is a profound mystery—but I am talking about Christ and the church.* (NIV)

7 INTERMEDIATE DAYS

After the 2-year period of Rosh Hashanah is completed it will be time for a seven-year period known as the intermediate days that fall between Rosh Hashanah and Yom Kippur. They are composed of days (years) three through nine. These seven days (years) represent the Tribulation Period. This seven-year period will be the same seven-year period that shows up on each of the following charts:

CHART	Page	EVENT TRANSPIRING
Comparison Chart	762	Daniel's (One Seven)
The Tribulation Period	763	Tribulation Period
Days Of Awe	764	Intermediate Days
Jewish Wedding	765	Chupah (Wedding Feast)

These charts can be found at the back of this book. Each of these seven year periods are referring to the exact same time frame, only told from a different perspective. In this section we will only discuss the Jewish holidays as they pertain to our study. This seven-year period has two separate scenes transpiring at the same time. One in heaven, which we will discuss in more detail when we look at the Jewish Wedding, and the scene on earth that is extensively covered in the book of Revelation will be throughly dissected in several of the upcoming chapters.

In the three books that we discussed earlier, the third book that was opened on Rosh Hashanah was for those people who did not make it through the gates when they were opened for the saints at the Rapture. The people who are alive on earth, *After the Rapture*, will be the people who will go through this intermediate period. On page 110 of *Days of Awe,* by Shmuel Yosef Agnon, I quote, "the ten days between Rosh ha-Shanah and Yom Kippur were set aside for prayer and supplication, because all earthly life is judged on Rosh ha-Shanah, and he who returns to God is forgiven on Yom Kippur…" [10] This is a reference to those saved souls who turn to God during this intermediate period.

FAST OF GEDALIAH

The third day of the Days of Awe will begin this intermediate period. It will be a fast day and is called the Fast of Gedaliah. This fast commemorates the assassination of Gedaliah ben Ahikam, a member of the Shaphan family, which had supported the prophet Jeremiah. The time frame was 600 years before Christ when Daniel, Ezekiel and the Jewish people were taken to Babylon in exile. Gedaliah was appointed governor of the Kingdom of Judah, by Nebuchadnezzar, after the destruction of the first Temple in 586 BC. The assassins were led by Ishmael, son of Nethaniah, a member of the royal family. This political conspiracy was the last straw for the Babylonians and caused the ultimate exile. It was the end of self-government in Judah.

> 2 Kings 25:25   *In the seventh month, however, Ishmael son of Nethaniah, the son of Elishama, who was of royal blood, came with ten men and assassinated Gedaliah and also the men of Judah and the Babylonians who were with him at Mizpah.* (NIV)

I do not want to be dogmatic about this, but do not be surprised if history repeats itself at the beginning of the third year of the Day of the Lord. Possibly a leader of Israel might just be assassinated at this time. Another political conspiracy? We will fill in the details of this event coming up in another chapter.

SABBATH OF RETURN

The name in Hebrew is *Shabbat Shuvah*. It is the name given to the Sabbath that falls during the Ten Days of Awe, between Rosh Hashanah and Yom Kippur. It is customary for the Rabbi to deliver a sermon on the theme of repentance on this Sabbath. The congregation reads from the prophets Hosea and Joel. Let us first look at the reading in Hosea.

Yom Ha-Din — Days of Awe — A Jewish Wedding

Hosea 14:2 *__Take words with you and return to the LORD__. Say to him: "__Forgive all our sins and receive us graciously__, that we may offer __the fruit of our lips__.* (NIV)

Then let us look at the reading in the book of Joel. In Hosea, it admonishes Israel to return to the Lord their God and the verses in Joel speak about the time when the Jews are back in their land enjoying abundant living, after they have suffered through the effects of the Tribulation Period. These events will take place in the future during the Day of the Lord.

Joel 2:15-27 *Blow the trumpet in Zion, declare a holy fast, call a sacred assembly. Gather the people, consecrate the assembly; bring together the elders, gather the children, those nursing at the breast. Let the bridegroom leave his room and the bride her chamber. Let the priests, who minister before the LORD, weep between the temple porch and the altar. Let them say, 'Spare your people, O LORD. Do not make your inheritance an object of scorn, a byword among the nations. Why should they say among the peoples, 'Where is their God?" Then the LORD will be jealous for his land and take pity on his people. The LORD will reply to them: 'I am sending you grain, new wine and oil, enough to satisfy you fully; never again will I make you an object of scorn to the nations. 'I will drive the northern army far from you, pushing it into a parched and barren land, with its front columns going into the eastern sea and those in the rear into the western sea. And its stench will go up; its smell will rise.' Surely he has done great things. Be not afraid, O land; be glad and rejoice.* **Surely the LORD has done great things.** *Be not afraid, O wild animals, for the open pastures are becoming green. The trees are bearing their fruit; the fig tree and the vine yield their riches.* **Be glad, O people of Zion, rejoice in the LORD your God, for he has given you the autumn rains in righteousness.** *He sends you abundant showers, both autumn and spring rains, as before. The threshing floors will be filled with grain; the vats will overflow with new wine and oil. 'I will repay you for the years the locusts have eaten—the great locust and the young locust, the other locusts and the locust swarm—my great army that I sent among you. You will have plenty to eat, until you are full, and you will praise the name of the LORD your God, who has worked wonders for you; never again will my people be shamed.* __Then you will know that I am in Israel, that I am the LORD your God, and that there is no other;__ __never again will my people be shamed__. (NIV)

THIRTEEN QUALITIES

The eighth day of Tishri is called the "Thirteen Qualities." These are the *Thirteen*

Principles of Faith composed by Moses Maimonides, in 1172 AD, and are included in Jewish doctrine today. They are recited on the eighth of Tishri and have a Messianic connotation. From *The Oxford Dictionary of the Jewish Religion* we read: "THIRTEEN PRINCIPLES OF FAITH, customary designation for Moses Maimonides' formulation of the basic principles underlying Judaism. The first *Mishnah* of the tenth chapter of tractate *Sanhedrin* reads, "All Israelites have a share in the world to come..." Maimonides took the last clause to mean that those denying the beliefs enumerated there were heretics. In his otherwise succinct commentary to the Mishnah, he expands his explanation of this particular statement into a long and detailed examination of the principles of Judaism: "The existence of God, creator of all things. His absolute unity; his incorporeality; his eternity; the obligation to serve and worship him alone; the authenticity of prophecy; the superiority of Moses above all other prophets; the Torah as God's revelation to Moses; the immutability of the Torah; God's omniscience and foreknowledge; Divine retribution; the advent of the Messiah; and the resurrection of the dead." [11] With the exception of a few of these qualities, it sounds like this came out of the New Testament, does it not?

EVE OF YOM KIPPUR

Whoever eats and drinks on the ninth of Tishri, the eve of Yom Kippur, tradition considers as if he fasted on both the ninth and the tenth. In *Days of Awe* we quote, "It is an established tradition that by eating on *Erev* Yom Kippur we rectify any sin that may have arisen as a result of eating improperly all year long (e.g., eating without a *berachah*, eating non-kosher food, etc.). This statement is based on the realization that food and drink can often involve inordinate excess and many times are the root cause of sin...Just as the World to Come is so sacred that it cannot be approached without the preparatory phase of this world (cf. *Avos* 4:16 comparing this world to a corridor that opens into the palace), so too the most hallowed of days, Yom Kippur—which itself is compared to the World to Come—can only be approached through the intermediary of *Erev* Yom Kippur. By eating on *Erev* Yom Kippur with the intention of performing a *mitzvah* (not to satisfy physical cravings), we prepare ourselves on this earth for the microcosm of the World to Come—that totally spiritual occasion, Yom Kippur. By extension, we may argue that all the pleasures of this world are merely a prelude to—and a means of attaining—the true bliss of the World to Come." [12]

Prophetically speaking, this banquet will be fulfilled in heaven at the Marriage Supper of the Lamb. The location in heaven for this banquet will be in the hidden chamber where the seven-year wedding feast will take place. It will take place toward the end of this seven-year wedding feast on the eve (day before) of Yom Kippur. It will be the last event in heaven prior to Jesus exiting this chamber to descend to earth at His Glorious Return.

YOM KIPPUR — Day of Atonement

A good description of this day is found in *The Oxford Dictionary of the Jewish Religion:* "Yom Kippur (יוֹם כִּפּוּר Day of Atonement), the most solemn occasion of the Jewish calendar, falling on 10 Tishrei; the only fast day never postponed, even if it

Yom Ha-Din — Days of Awe — A Jewish Wedding

falls on a Sabbath. Although strictly observed from sunset as a twenty-five-hour fast (see FASTS) in accordance with the biblical injunction "and you shall afflict yourselves," it formally belongs to the category of festivals (see Haggim). The biblical commandment regulating its observance (Lv. 23:26:32) indicates no link with the holiday observed a few days earlier on 1 Tishrei (Rosh ha-Shanah), but at an early period the two were linked in the framework of the 'Aseret Yemei Teshuvah. **The concept was that on Ro'sh ha-Shanah the fate of every individual for the coming year is decreed, and on Yom Kippur it is sealed.** An unfavorable decree can be averted by repentance, prayer, and charity. The rabbis insist that a worshiper's contrite behavior on Yom Kippur itself will not effect forgiveness unless it is accompanied by sincere repentance (Yoma' 8.8-9; tractate Yoma' is entirely devoted to Yom Kippur). During Temple times, Yom Kippur was the occasion for an elaborate sacrificial ceremony based on *Leviticus* 16. This consisted of two parts, the first was the sacrificial service in the Temple, at which the high priest pronounced the threefold confession of sins on behalf of himself, the priests, and all Israel. The climax came when, clothed in white linen, he entered the Holy of Holies (the one occasion during the year when this was permitted) to sprinkle the blood of the sacrifice there and to offer incense. The second part of the ceremony consisted of hurling the scapegoat that "shall bear upon him all their iniquities—that is, to which the sins of the community had been symbolically transferred—to its death in the wilderness (see Azazel). ...The festival prayer is divided into five services, the first of which is the evening service (Ma'ariv), preceded in most rites by the recitation of Kol Nidrei; hence, Yom Kippur eve has come to be known as Kol Nidrei. The services on the day itself include the morning (Shaharit), the additional (Musaf), the afternoon (Minhah), and the concluding service (Ne'ilah). Five mortifications are prescribed for the day; abstention from food, drink, marital intercourse, anointing with oil, and wearing leather shoes. All Sabbath work prohibitions are in effect on Yom Kippur. The prayers of the day stress confession of sins and supplications for forgiveness. Like all congregational prayers, they are couched in the plural, confession and forgiveness being sought on behalf of "the whole congregation of Israel (Nm.25.26)."...The dominating theme of the Ne'ilah concludes with the declaration of God's unity, the sounding of the shofar, and the prayer La-Shanah ha-Ba'ah bi-Yerushalayim (in Israel, Jerusalem Rebuilt)...The greeting on Yom Kippur is *gemar hatimah tovah*, "A propitious final sealing (of Divine judgment).'" [13]

Because of the sin of the golden calf, Israel had been commanded to annually atone for their sins on Yom Kippur through the blood sacrifice of animals.

Lev 23:26-32 *The LORD said to Moses, "The tenth day of this seventh month is the Day of Atonement. Hold a sacred assembly and deny yourselves, and present an offering made to the LORD by fire. Do no work on that day, because it is the Day of Atonement, when atonement is made for you before the LORD your God. Anyone who does not deny himself on that day must be cut off from his people. I will destroy from among his people anyone who does any work on that day. You shall do no work at all. This is to be a lasting ordinance for the generations to come, wherever you live. It is a sabbath of rest for you, and you must deny yourselves. From the evening of the ninth day of the month until the following evening you are to observe your sabbath."* (NIV).

The Hebrew word for "everlasting," in Leviticus 16:34, can mean for a long duration.

Lev 16:34   ***And this shall be an everlasting statute unto you, to make an atonement for the children of Israel for all their sins once a year. And he did as the LORD commanded Moses.*** (KJV)

In the Old Testament, it was a temporary (substitute) atonement (covering of sin) until the real sacrificial Lamb would come to replace it. The permanent atonement came in the name and person of Jesus, but was rejected by the chosen people. After the real atonement for sin appeared, there was no need for the temporary. After Jesus was crucified the Jewish people continued to atone for their sins with the temporary system, but God put an end to it in the Temple forty years after His death, when in 70 AD, He allowed the Romans to destroy Jerusalem and the Temple. They in turn exiled the Jews and for the last two thousand years they have literally been scattered all over the earth, at times suffering extreme periods of persecution and death. The synopsis below includes the one day for one year theory.

"Season of Our Repentance"

Month of Elul (30 days or 30 years) Last 30 years of the Dispensation of Grace
    Heaven — God is preparing to coronate Jesus as King
    Earth — Messianic Jewish movement (which is now taking place)

Sounding of the Shofar (Day of the Trumpet Blast) is the beginning of the Day of the Lord on earth and the Day of Christ in heaven. It will be the Kingdom Age in heaven and on the earth at this time
    Heaven — After the saints meet Jesus in the air, the gates of heaven will be opened for an instant to allow the saints to enter heaven. The gates are closed immediately after the saints enter heaven to prevent the wicked (unsaved) from entering heaven.
    Earth — At this time the earth will be full of the unsaved people left behind.

Days of Awe (10 days or 10 years)
    Rosh Hashanah (2 days or 2 years)
        Heaven — Coronation of Jesus as King – Angels will lead Jesus into the presence of the Ancient of Days (God)
            Judgment Seat of Christ
            Wedding will take place
        Earth — Antichrist released

Intermediate Days (7 days or 7 years)

Yom Ha-Din — Days of Awe — A Jewish Wedding

- Heaven — Days of our concealment (in their chambers)
- Heaven — Wedding Feast
- Heaven — Marriage Supper of the Lamb (Eve of Yom Kippur)
- Earth — Tribulation Period

Yom Kippur (1 day or 1 year)
- Heaven — Day of Atonement (sound of a great trumpet to gather the elect/exiles)
- Earth — Battle of Armageddon
- Earth — Great Supper of God
- Neilah — Jesus sounds the trumpet and the gates of heaven are closed

Although the Old Testament religious festivals do not need to be practiced by non-Jews, after the crucifixion of Jesus, it does not mean that we should ignore their significance and the meaning that they have in God's word. Paul in his letter to the Colossians tells us not to worry about anyone who criticizes us for not observing these Jewish holidays. He goes on to say that these festivals are only an outline (shadow) of things to come. Prophetically speaking, their fulfillment is found at the first and second advent of Jesus Christ.

Col 2:16-17   *Therefore do not let anyone judge you by what you eat or drink, or with regard to a religious festival, a New Moon celebration or a Sabbath day.* ***These are a shadow of the things that were to come; the reality, however, is found in Christ.*** (NIV)

The third to the last verse in the Old Testament also exhorts the Jews to remember the statutes and ordinances that God gave to Moses on Mount Horeb (Sinai). The Jews who believe in Jesus as the true Messiah and non-Jews alike, are to acknowledge the feasts as holidays of remembrance for what they represent.

Mal 4:4   ***Remember ye the law of Moses my servant, which I commanded unto him in Horeb for all Israel,*** *with the statutes and judgments.* (KJV)

God allowed the Roman soldiers, on the ninth of Av, to destroy the Temple in Jerusalem in 70 AD. This has kept the Jews from performing the sacrificial atonement of their sins once a year by the shed blood of animals. That was only a temporary atonement until the real atonement would arrive. The real sacrifice was the shed blood of Jesus Christ on the cross. The atonement of Jesus is not to be performed every year, but was initiated once, almost two thousand years ago, for all the sins of mankind (past, present and future).

Heb 10:10   *And by that will,* ***we have been made holy through the sacrifice of the body of Jesus Christ once for all.*** (NIV)

There is a multitude of information that can be gleaned from studying the Old Testament feasts. These feasts paint a miraculous picture of prophecy.

THE JEWISH FESTIVALS IN PROPHECY

The feasts that God commanded the Israelites to follow every year were given to Moses to give to the people after they were let out of bondage from the Egyptians and on their way to the promised land. They were prophetic and a shadow of things to come. For us today, we can perceive a special meaning from these eight feasts. Prophetically, we can look at them as being divided into two parts. The first four were fulfilled at the first advent of Christ and the last four will be fulfilled at the second advent of Christ. The festivals here are listed in the order of their annual fulfillment and also how they will play out prophetically.

1. **The Passover Feast** — (Pesach - Nisan 14) This festival commemorates the liberation of the Israelites from Egypt. The sacrifice of a lamb slaughtered and the blood from it was sprinkled on the door posts of their houses, so that when the Lord passed through Egypt on the night of Nisan 14, and saw the blood on the doorposts, He would spare the first born that were in the houses. This Paschal Lamb was a type of Jesus, the Lamb of God, and is celebrated by Christians on Good Friday. Exod 12:1-14 *The LORD said to Moses and Aaron in Egypt, "This month is to be for you the first month, the first month of your year. Tell the whole community of Israel that on the tenth day of this month each man is to take a lamb for his family, one for each household. If any household is too small for a whole lamb, they must share one with their nearest neighbor, having taken into account the number of people there are. You are to determine the amount of lamb needed in accordance with what each person will eat. The animals you choose must be year-old males without defect, and you may take them from the sheep or the goats. Take care of them until the fourteenth day of the month, when all the people of the community of Israel must slaughter them at twilight.* **Then they are to take some of the blood and put it on the sides and tops of the doorframes of the houses where they eat the lambs.** *That same night they are to eat the meat roasted over the fire, along with bitter herbs, and bread made without yeast. Do not eat the meat raw or cooked in water, but roast it over the fire—head, legs and inner parts. Do not leave any of it till morning; if some is left till morning, you must burn it. This is how you are to eat it: with your cloak tucked into your belt, your sandals on your feet and your staff in your hand.* **Eat it in haste; *it is the LORD's Passover.*** *"On that same night I will pass through Egypt and strike down every firstborn—both men and animals—and I will bring judgment on all the Gods of Egypt. I am the LORD. The blood will be a sign for you on the houses where you are; and when I see the blood, I will pass over you. No destructive plague will touch you when I strike Egypt.* **"This is a day you are to commemorate; for the generations to come you shall celebrate it as a festival to the LORD—a lasting ordinance.** (NIV) 1 Cor 5:7 ...***For Christ, our Passover lamb, has been sacrificed.*** (NIV)

2. **Feast of Unleavened Bread** — (Pesach - Nisan 15-22) This festival began on the day after Passover and lasted for seven days. It is a type of the walk of the believers. The seven days look forward to the life of the believer after their

Yom Ha-Din — Days of Awe — A Jewish Wedding

conversion. The symbolic meaning of leaven in the Bible is evil. Since we have been saved by the shed blood of Jesus Christ, which is our Passover, we are to walk according to a new life through Christ.

Exod 12:15-20 *For seven days you are to eat bread made without yeast. On the first day remove the yeast from your houses, for whoever eats anything with yeast in it from the first day through the seventh must be cut off from Israel. On the first day hold a sacred assembly, and another one on the seventh day. Do no work at all on these days, except to prepare food for everyone to eat—that is all you may do.* **"Celebrate the Feast of Unleavened Bread, because it was on this very day that I brought your divisions out of Egypt. Celebrate this day as a lasting ordinance for the generations to come.** *In the first month you are to eat bread made without yeast, from the evening of the fourteenth day until the evening of the twenty-first day. For seven days no yeast is to be found in your houses. And whoever eats anything with yeast in it must be cut off from the community of Israel, whether he is an alien or native-born.* **Eat nothing made with yeast.** <u>**Wherever you live, you must eat unleavened bread.**</u> *"* (NIV)

2 Cor 5:17-21 **Therefore,** <u>**if anyone is in Christ, he is a new creation; the old has gone, the new has come!**</u> *All this is from God, who reconciled us to himself through Christ and gave us the ministry of reconciliation: that God was reconciling the world to himself in Christ, not counting men's sins against them. And he has committed to us the message of reconciliation. We are therefore Christ's ambassadors, as though God were making his appeal through us. We implore you on Christ's behalf: Be reconciled to God. God made him who had no sin to be sin for us, so that in him we might become the righteousness of God.* (NIV)

3. **Feast of First Fruits** — (Pesach - Nisan 16) Passover took place on Nisan 14, the Feast of Unleavened Bread on the next day, which was Nisan 15 (a Sabbath), and following that on Nisan 16, is celebrated the Feast of First Fruits, and are all a part of Passover. This celebration could not be celebrated until after the Israelites entered the promised land. This festival is a type of Christ's resurrection. He arose on the third day to become the first person to receive a resurrected body. Christians today celebrate the resurrection of Jesus, the firstfruits, on Easter every year.

Lev 23:9-14 *The LORD said to Moses, "Speak to the Israelites and say to them:* <u>**'When you enter the land I am going to give you and you reap its harvest, bring to the priest a sheaf of the first grain you harvest.**</u> *He is to wave the sheaf before the LORD so it will be accepted on your behalf; the priest is to wave it on the day after the Sabbath.* **On the day you wave the sheaf, you must sacrifice as a burnt offering to the LORD a lamb a year old without defect,** *together with its grain offering of two-tenths of an ephah of fine flour mixed with oil—an offering made to the LORD by fire, a pleasing aroma—and its drink offering of a quarter of a hin of wine. You must not eat any bread, or roasted or new grain, until the very day you bring this offering to your God.* **This is to be a lasting ordinance for the generations to come, wherever you live.** (NIV)

AFTER THE RAPTURE

1 Cor 15:22-23 For as in Adam all die, so in Christ all will be made alive. But each in his own turn: <u>Christ, the firstfruits</u>; then, when he comes, those who belong to him. (NIV)

4. **Feast of Pentecost** — (Shavu'ot - Sivan 7) The Feast of Pentecost is observed fifty days after the Feast of First Fruits. The time between these two feasts include seven Sabbath's and is called the Feast of Weeks. On Pentecost, a new grain offering was to be offered to the Lord. It was to be made of grain from the new harvest. The sacrifice of the flesh of the body was fulfilled by Jesus and is to be replaced by grain. Christ was resurrected on the Feast of First Fruits and fifty days later, on the Feast of Pentecost, the comforter (Holy Spirit) came to the earth to be with true believers throughout the Christian Dispensation. This is considered to be the beginning (birthday) of the Church.

    Lev 23:15-16 *"'From the day after the Sabbath, the day you brought the sheaf of the wave offering, count off seven full weeks. **Count off fifty days up to the day after the seventh Sabbath, <u>and then present an offering of new grain to the LORD</u>.*** (NIV)

    Acts 2:1-2 ***When the day of Pentecost came**, they were all together in one place. Suddenly a sound like the blowing of a violent wind came from heaven and filled the whole house where they were sitting.* (NIV)

Prophetically speaking, these four festivals were fulfilled at the first advent of Jesus. The last four festivals are to be fulfilled when Jesus comes at His second coming. Since this whole chapter has been about the next two festivals, they should be a little familiar. There is a four-month interval between the Feast of Pentecost and the Feast of Trumpets. This represents the interval between the two advents of Jesus Christ, known as the Dispensation of Grace. During this time the Gentiles will be grafted in the olive tree and the Jews will be set aside and scattered among all the nations of the world. If they accept Christ, they will become a member of the body of Christ. This will continue until the end of the church age. The Jews will be grafted back into the olive tree in the age to follow (the Day of the Lord).

> Rom 11:25 *I do not want you to be ignorant of this mystery, brothers, so that you may not be conceited: <u>Israel has experienced a hardening in part until the full number of the Gentiles has come in</u>.* (NIV)

5. **Feast of Trumpets** — (Rosh Hashanah - Tishri 1) At the end of the long period of time after the Feast of Pentecost (four months), it will harken the trumpet sound. This will be the end of the Church Age for the saints and will be the Day of Christ. Rapture! That same trumpet sound will be the beginning of the new age, known as the Day of the Lord. God will then finish His dealings with His chosen people (Jews). Rosh Hashanah is the beginning of the Days of Awe. During the ten-year period of the Days of Awe, Jesus, coronated as King, will judge both the saved people in heaven and unsaved people on earth. The Judgment Seat of Christ will take place in heaven and the Tribulation Period will take place on the earth.

Yom Ha-Din — Days of Awe — A Jewish Wedding

Lev 23:23-25 *The LORD said to Moses, "Say to the Israelites: 'On the first day of the seventh month you are to have a day of rest, a sacred assembly commemorated with trumpet blasts. Do no regular work, but present an offering made to the LORD by fire.'"* (NIV)

1 Cor 15:51-52 *Behold, I shew you a mystery; We shall not all sleep, but we shall all be changed, In a moment, in the twinkling of an eye, at the last trump: for the trumpet shall sound, and the dead shall be raised incorruptible, and we shall be changed.* (KJV)

6. **Feast of the Day of Atonement** — (Yom Kippur - Tishri 10) The Glorious Return of Jesus will transpire as He sets up His Kingdom on earth with Himself reigning as King of Kings and Lord of Lords. He will reign in Jerusalem in a rebuilt Temple. This will be the time that all the Jews will finally recognize Jesus as the true Messiah and fulfill the prophecy in Romans 11:26, which states, *"And so all Israel will be saved,..."* (NIV) The Battle of Armageddon will be fought and the wicked will be purged from the earth so Jesus can begin to rebuild the earth. The nation of Israel will be set up as the head of the nations, as God promised them thousands of years ago. Yom Kippur is important in Jewish eschatology because of its role as the Day of Atonement for the righteous and the day of final judgment for the wicked (unsaved) people living on the earth after the Tribulation Period. Concerning judgment, Yom Kippur is the day set aside by God to remove the wicked.

Lev 23:26-32 *The LORD said to Moses, "The tenth day of this seventh month is the Day of Atonement. Hold a sacred assembly and deny yourselves, and present an offering made to the LORD by fire. Do no work on that day, because it is the Day of Atonement, when atonement is made for you before the LORD your God. Anyone who does not deny himself on that day must be cut off from his people. I will destroy from among his people anyone who does any work on that day. You shall do no work at all. This is to be a lasting ordinance for the generations to come, wherever you live. It is a sabbath of rest for you, and you must deny yourselves. From the evening of the ninth day of the month until the following evening you are to observe your sabbath."* (NIV)

7. **The Feast of Tabernacles** — (Sukkot - Tishri 15-21) The last two feasts in Leviticus 23, given to Moses, to present to the Israelites, cover an eight-day period. Sukkot is a celebration to be observed at the end of the harvest and was to be for a duration of seven days. It represents the period of the Sabbatical rest and will last for 1000 years, the seventh year of the seven-year creation week (1000 years for a day). It is also known as the Day of the Lord or the Millennium.

Lev 23:33-44 *The LORD said to Moses, "Say to the Israelites: 'On the fifteenth day of the seventh month the LORD's Feast of Tabernacles begins, and it lasts for seven days. The first day is a sacred assembly; do no regular work. For seven days present offerings made to the LORD by fire, and on the eighth day hold a sacred assembly and present an offering made to the LORD by fire. It is the closing assembly; do no regular work. ('"These are the LORD's appointed feasts, which you are to proclaim as sacred assemblies for bringing offerings made to the LORD by fire—the burnt offerings and grain offerings, sacrifices and drink offerings required for each day. These offerings are in addition to those for the LORD's Sabbaths and in addition to your gifts and whatever you have vowed and all the freewill offerings you give to the LORD.) "'So beginning with the fifteenth day of the seventh month, after you have gathered the crops of the land, celebrate the festival to the LORD for seven days; the first day is a day of rest, and the eighth day also is a day of rest. On the first day you are to take choice fruit from the trees, and palm fronds, leafy branches and poplars, and rejoice before the LORD your God for seven days.* **Celebrate this as a festival to the LORD for seven days each year. This is to be a lasting ordinance for the generations to come; celebrate it in the seventh month. Live in booths for seven days: All native-born Israelites are to live in booths so your descendants will know that I had the Israelites live in booths when I brought them out of Egypt.** *I am the LORD your God.'" So Moses announced to the Israelites the appointed feasts of the LORD.* (NIV)

Amos 9:13-15 *"The days are coming," declares the LORD, "when the reaper will be overtaken by the plowman and the planter by the one treading grapes. New wine will drip from the mountains and flow from all the hills. I will bring back my exiled people Israel; they will rebuild the ruined cities and live in them. They will plant vineyards and drink their wine; they will make gardens and eat their fruit.* **I will plant Israel in their own land, never again to be uprooted from the land I have given them,"** *says the LORD your God.* (NIV)

Zech 14:16-21 **Then the survivors from all the nations that have attacked Jerusalem will go up year after year to worship the King, the LORD Almighty, and to celebrate the Feast of Tabernacles.** *If any of the peoples of the earth do not go up to Jerusalem to worship the King, the LORD Almighty, they will have no rain. If the Egyptian people do not go up and take part, they will have no rain. The LORD will bring on them the plague he inflicts on the nations that do not go up to celebrate the Feast of Tabernacles. This will be the punishment of Egypt and the punishment of all the nations that do not go up to celebrate the Feast of Tabernacles. On that day HOLY TO THE LORD will be inscribed on the bells of the horses, and the cooking pots in the LORD's house will be like the sacred bowls in front of the altar. Every pot in Jerusalem and Judah will be holy to the LORD Almighty, and all who come to sacrifice will take some of the pots and cook in them.* **And on that day there will no longer be a Canaanite in the house of the LORD Almighty.** (NIV)

8. **The Assembly of the Eighth (day)** — (Shemini Atzeret - Tishri 22) The day after the seventh day of Sukkot is the feast (holiday) of Shemini Atzeret. Sukkot and Shemini Atzeret are commonly thought of as part of Sukkot, but that is technically incorrect. Shemini Atzeret is a holiday in its own right and does not involve the special observances of Sukkot. The term, "until all is accomplished," refers to the all-important Jewish eight-day festival of Shemini Atzeret at the end of the 1000-year (millennial) reign of Jesus Christ. In the study of numerology, the number

Yom Ha-Din — Days of Awe — A Jewish Wedding

eight has the significance of a new beginning. During the Sabbatical rest of the Day of the Lord, the plan of God will come to completion (until all is accomplished). After that on Shemini Atzeret (the assembly of the eighth day) all things will return to their original state of perfection as in the Garden of Eden. It will literally be a new beginning and the final day of rest for eternity (the Day of God).

Lev 23:36 *For seven days present offerings made to the LORD by fire, <u>and on the eighth day hold a sacred assembly and present an offering made to the LORD by fire</u>. It is the closing assembly; do no regular work.* (NIV)

Lev 23:39 *"'So beginning with the fifteenth day of the seventh month, after you have gathered the crops of the land, celebrate the festival to the LORD for seven days; the first day is a day of rest, <u>and the eighth day also is a day of rest</u>.* (NIV)

I am gratefully indebted to Clarence Larkin and his book, *"The Greatest Book on Dispensational Truth in the World."* [14] It was a great help in my understanding the prophetic implications of the Jewish festivals. I have added the feast of Shemini Atzeret to Reverend Larkin's list. I am looking forward to seeing him at the shout from Jesus.

Of the eight Jewish Festivals listed above, three of them are said to be a memorial to commemorate an event effecting the Jewish people from the past. They are:

1. **The Feast of Passover** — This holiday is to remind the Jewish people that God brought them out of the bondage of the Egyptians (Exodus 13:3-10).
2. **The Feast of Trumpets** (Rosh Hashanah) — This holiday is to remind the Jewish people that God spoke to them on Mount Sinai (Leviticus 23:24). The voice of God sounded like a very loud trumpet. For the true believers of Jesus, today, this holiday should remind us that on Rosh Hashanah, the voice of Jesus (with a loud shout) is about to sound in the near future.
3. **The Feast of Tabernacles** — This holiday is to remind the Jewish people that God had them live in tents when He brought them out of Egypt (Leviticus 23:43).

No one but God knows the exact date of Rosh Hashanah. The Jews have attempted to reestablish their ancient calendar, but their dates have many flaws. The Rapture will occur on Rosh Hashanah, but it is doubtful that it will be the date on the current Jewish calendar.

Before we move on to study the Jewish wedding, we need to look at one more Jewish term, Olam Ha-Ba—the world to come. The spiritual afterlife is referred to in Hebrew as Olam Ha-Ba. Although this term is referred to as the Messianic Age, it is also referred to as a higher state of being. The resurrection of the dead will occur in the Messianic Age, but the term is also used to refer to the spiritual afterlife. When the Messiah comes to initiate the perfect world of peace and prosperity, the righteous dead will be brought back to life. In the Mishnah, a rabbi says, "This world is like a lobby before the Olam Ha-Ba. Prepare yourself in the lobby so that you may enter the banquet hall." Similarly, the Talmud says, "This world is like the eve of Shabbat, and the Olam Ha-Ba is like Shabbat. He who prepares on the eve of Shabbat will have food to eat on Shabbat." The Olam Ha-Ba will include the feast of Sukkot (the Millennium) and also the feast of Shemini Atzeret (throughout eternity). These Jewish feasts are all listed on the Days of Awe chart on page 764.

JEWISH WEDDING

An ancient Jewish Wedding was unique and I believe that God can use it as a means to teach us about an upcoming wedding that is about take place in heaven. To coin an old expression, "A marriage made in heaven." We can enlighten our understanding of the end-time events by following this ancient practice in place at the time Christ was on earth. Not every book I read on this subject is in total agreement, but over all the structure is quite clear as to the chronological order of the ceremony. The diaspora or scattering of the Jews to almost all the nations of the world, has over thousands of years, caused some changes in their traditional or local practices, resulting in the various parts of the ceremony having different names.

To get an overall view I quote from *The New Standard Jewish Encyclopedia:*

> "**MARRIAGE**: Judaism makes obligatory the requirement to reproduce and continue the human race...the first commandment in the Bible is "be fruitful and multiply" (Gen 1:22). Men are therefore obligated to marry in order to fulfill this commandment. ...According to Jewish practice since early times there are two stages in the marriage ceremony: betrothal and marriage. Betrothal (*erusin* or *kiddushin*) is the ceremony whereby a woman becomes the wife of the betrother so that she may be married to no one else (unless her husband die or divorce her). ...Betrothal is performed by the man, but has no validity unless the woman gives her consent. The second stage of the marriage ceremony is *nissuin*, which is the act of availing oneself of the rights obtained in the act of betrothal, i.e., bringing the woman into the home in order to live a marital life with her. ...In early times, long periods often intervened between *erusin* and *nissuin*; it later became customary for *nissuin* to follow the betrothal ceremony immediately. The accepted ceremony of marriage—including both *erusin* and *nissuin*—is as follows: the bride and groom stand under a canopy (*huppah*). Ten people are normally required to be present. ...The Ketubah is then read, generally by the rabbi. ...The bride and groom usually fast until after the ceremony and immediately after the ceremony go into a separate room where they eat together. It was formerly customary (and is still observed by the Orthodox) to prepare a marriage feast for each day of the following week (the "seven days of feasting") during which the "seven benedictions" are repeated at the table." [15]

Using this as a background, let us now look at that wedding made in heaven. In ancient times, a man would go to the home of a girl and seek permission to marry her. She would also have to give her consent to marry him. Please follow the chart called, "Jewish Wedding" at the end of this book on page 765 as we describe an ancient Jewish wedding. It is a time line following the wedding process between the Bridegroom (Jesus) and the Bride (Church).

MOHAR (Bride Price) Quoting from *Signs in the Heavens* by Avi Ben Mordechai we read, "If a man desired to marry a woman, he arrived at the prospective bride's home to talk with the parents and the bride. Discussion included prenuptial conditions, the bride price or *Mohar*, and the setting of a wedding date. The bride would be asked if she desired marriage to the young man. If she accepted, all said a special Hebrew blessing and then partook of a cup of wine and a festive meal. This sealed the contract. What followed was betrothal, a legal status of marriage without consummation." [16]

ERUSIN (Betrothal) From *The Oxford Dictionary of the Jewish Religion* we read, "BETROTHAL (Heb. *Shiddukhin*), an agreement to marry at some future date. *Shiddukhin* (also *erusin* or *giddushin*) is a legal term, in contrast to the current, popular terms of *betrothal* or *engagement*. In Talmudic times, marriage without preliminary betrothal was frowned upon in Jewish practice; the prescribed punishment was flogging (Qid.12b). Betrothal is accompanied by a festive celebration, but does not create any conjugal relationship; both parties are free to retract their promise of marriage without having compromised their marital eligibility. Because of the time lag between the betrothal and the wedding (*hatunnah*), the Talmud (Qid.50b) discusses the question of whether gifts received by the bride (*kallah*) from the groom (*hatan*) are an indication that formal *giddushin* has taken place. [17]

T'NAIM (Legal document of Betrothal) Avi Ben Mordechai says, "A *T'naim* is a legal document of betrothal unique to Judaism and a precursor to the *ketubah*. It sets forth the conditions of marriage between two parties, their obligation and commitment to the marriage, the financial resources or possessions each person brings to the relationship, the responsibilities of each family to the other and finally the penalties to be paid should either side break off the engagement." [18] And in *The Oxford Dictionary of the Jewish Religion*, "A document called *tena'im* is drawn up with the terms of *shiddukhim* and includes the time, place, and size of the wedding, as well as any other obligations such as the dowry or other financial matters." [19]

QINYAN (Acquisition) In *The Oxford Dictionary of the Jewish Religion* it says, "Betrothal, as part of the marriage ceremony, requires an act of *qinyan* (*acquisition) of the bride by the groom. In accepting something of value from the groom and giving her consent, the new relationship is effected." [20] That something of value that the groom (Jesus) gave to the bride (Church) was his life.

Again from Mr. Mordechai, "After the betrothal (Hebrew: *Erusin*) ceremony the young man returned to his father's house and prepared a bridal chamber or *chupah*. After one or two years, he came back for his bride amid trumpets and celebration taking her away (Hebrew: *Nissuin*) for seven days, to the *chupah* (the bridal chamber especially prepared in his father's home)." In the book of John, we see Jesus returning to his father's house to prepare the *chupah* (Bridal Chamber)." [21]

John 14:1-3   *"<u>Do not let your hearts be troubled. Trust in God; trust also in me.</u> In my Father's house are many rooms; if it were not so, I would have told you. <u>I am going there to prepare a place for you.</u> And if I go and prepare a place for you, I will come back and take you to be with me that you also may be where I am.* (NIV)

Continuing on, "The bride is responsible for learning and obeying the groom's customs while he is away preparing their bridal chamber." [22]

Matt 11:29-30   *Take my yoke upon you, and learn of me; for I am meek and lowly in heart: and ye shall find rest unto your souls. For my yoke is easy, and my burden is light.* (KJV)

There will be a two thousand-year period of Betrothal for this wedding. It will be the Dispensation of Grace and will be a period of time to allow the bride (Church) to complete her full number. All the people on earth who accept Jesus as their Savior, during this period between the wedding betrothal (*erusin*) and the wedding (*nissuin*), will become members of the Bride of Christ.

Every time a person takes the step of faith and accepts Jesus into their heart, they immediately become betrothed. They then become part of the Bride of Christ and will eventually become His wife at the time the wedding ceremony takes place in heaven. In an ancient Jewish wedding a trumpet was blown before the groom to announce the marriage.

MINYAN (Ten Attendants) From *Signs in the Heavens* we read, "As the groom came for his bride, ten attendants (Hebrew. *Minyan*) blew the shofar ahead of him, amid pomp and celebration, thus announcing that the groom was coming to take his bride away." [23] The only difference I see here is that the trumpet sound will come from Jesus.

1 Thes 4:16-17   *For the Lord Himself will descend from heaven with a shout, with the voice of an archangel, and with the trumpet of God. And the dead in Christ will rise first. Then we who are alive and remain shall be caught up together with them in the clouds to meet the Lord in the air. And thus we shall always be with the Lord.* (NKJ)

The ten attendants could be the friends of the bridegroom. Since this verse below, is spoken by John the Baptist, we know that he could be one of the ten friends of the bridegroom at His coming for the bride.

John 3:29   *The bride belongs to the bridegroom. The friend who attends the bridegroom waits and listens for him, and is full of joy when he hears the bridegroom's voice. That joy is mine, and it is now complete.* (NIV)

At the sound of the trumpet (Rapture) the groom (Jesus) will come down from the right hand of God to meet the bride (Church) in the clouds (in the air). This will happen on Rosh Hashanah and will begin a two-year period to prepare the bride (Church) and the wedding guests (Old Testament Saints) for a wedding (*nissuin*).

MIKVEH (Ritual Bath) This two-year period will be the time when the participants of the wedding take a ritual bath and put on the white garments to prepare for the wedding ceremony. This process is completed at the Judgment Seat of Christ when the believers receive their just rewards.

> Rev 19:7-8 *Let us rejoice and be glad and give him glory! For the wedding of the Lamb has come, and his bride has made herself ready.* <u>*Fine linen, bright and clean, was given her to wear.*</u>*" (Fine linen stands for the righteous acts of the saints.)* (NIV)

NISSUIN (Wedding) After the last saint has stood before Jesus (face-to-face) at the Judgment Seat of Christ, it will be time for the wedding ceremony to take place, which is brief and simple.

CHUPAH (Bridal Chamber) Again a quotation from Avi Ben Mordechai, "A Jewish marriage ceremony must take place in a bridal chamber or *chupah*. The *chupah* represents holiness and sanctification under G-d. Usually after a one-year preparation period the bride was taken to the groom's wedding chamber for seven days." [24] In this case it will be a two-year preparation period.

KETUBAH (Wedding Contract) Quoting from *Jewish Literacy* by Rabbi Joseph Telushkin concerning the *ketubah*, "The wedding ceremony itself is brief and simple...The rabbi then reads aloud the Aramaic marriage contract known as the ketubah, which lists the groom's obligations to the bride." [25] He continues, "For the week after the wedding it is traditional for relatives and friends of the newly married couple to make a party for them each day. ...The ketubah is the marriage contract that all grooms are required to give their brides at a Jewish wedding. It spells out the husband's obligations to the wife, ...In the ketubah the man undertakes to provide his wife with "food, clothing, and necessities, and live with you as a husband according to universal custom." [26]

CHUPAH (Wedding Chamber) From *Signs in the Heavens*, "The groom and his bride were taken to the wedding chamber—the *chupah*—specially prepared in the home of the groom's father. There, the bride and groom were served and every need met. For seven days they celebrated a feast with their invited guests." [27] They were concealed in the wedding chamber alone for seven days. Mr. Mordechai goes on by saying, "The seven days of feasting and celebration with their invited guests was a special time. The new bride and groom were treated as a king and queen. Neither groom nor bride would emerge from the home for seven days." [28]

After the wedding ceremony is completed, the young wife (Church age saints) will enter the wedding chamber (chupah). This is the place of Divine protection for the wife for the next seven years during the wedding feast. The husband (Jesus) will reside in an innermost room (dwelling) during the same seven-year period, where He will leave occasionally to inflict punishment on the earth, where the people are suffering through the effects of the Tribulation Period.

> Isa 26:21 <u>*See, the LORD is coming out of his dwelling to punish the people*</u>

of the earth for their sins. The earth will disclose the blood shed upon her; she will conceal her slain no longer. (NIV)

In the book of Joel, we find both the husband (Jesus) and the young wife (Church age saints) as they exit their respective locations where they spent the previous seven years.

Joel 2:16 *Gather the people, consecrate the assembly; bring together the elders, gather the children, those nursing at the breast. Let the bridegroom leave his room and the bride her chamber.* (NIV)

The wedding guests (Old Testament saints) will leave the wedding ceremony and go to the abode or dwelling place prepared for them by God in the heavenly Jerusalem. This will be their place of Divine protection for the next seven years and also their home for eternity.

Ps 122:3-5 *Jerusalem is built like a city that is closely compacted together. That is where the tribes go up, the tribes of the LORD, to praise the name of the LORD according to the statute given to Israel. There the thrones for judgment stand, the thrones of the house of David.* (NIV)

Heb 11:16 *Instead, they were longing for a better country—a heavenly one. Therefore God is not ashamed to be called their God, for he has prepared a city for them.* (NIV)

The wedding chamber is in heaven and everyone who attended the wedding seven years earlier will attend one more supper before the husband and wife exit the wedding chamber. It is known in scripture as the Marriage Supper of the Lamb. It will take place on the eve of Yom Kippur.

Rev 19:9 *Then he said to me, "Write: 'Blessed are those who are called to the marriage supper of the Lamb!'" And he said to me, "These are the true sayings of God."* (NKJ)

Everyone who is in attendance at this supper will be believers (saints). Are you going to be in attendance??? God wants all of us to be there, but by our own free will choice. Each one of us individually will decide if we will be at this wedding supper, but few decide to be there. How sad! Nothing in this life is worth enough to miss this banquet in heaven.

In the Old Testament, God was the husband and Israel (Jewish people) was His wife. Israel was probably wed to God at Mount Sinai in 1445 BC. The bride was assembled at the foot of that mountain to meet God as He came down from heaven. The marriage contract (ketubah) was the Ten Commandments. God also made a covenant with the Israelites at that time. The Israelites who wandered through the wilderness for forty years broke that covenant. God then renewed His covenant with the descendants of the Israelites who entered the promised land (Deuteronomy 4-6). These chapters command the Israelites to be obedient to God. God tells them to *"Hear, O Israel."* The Hebrew word for "hear" is *shama`*, often

Yom Ha-Din — Days of Awe — A Jewish Wedding

spelled *shema*, and many Messianic Jewish congregations obey the command to *"Love the LORD your God with all your heart and with all your soul and with all your strength."*

Deut 6:4-9   ***Hear, O Israel: The LORD our God, the LORD is one. Love the LORD your God with all your heart and with all your soul and with all your strength.*** *These commandments that I give you today are to be upon your hearts. Impress them on your children. Talk about them when you sit at home and when you walk along the road, when you lie down and when you get up. Tie them as symbols on your hands and bind them on your foreheads. Write them on the doorframes of your houses and on your gates.* (NIV)

The Israelites who entered the promised land were not much better at obeying God's commands and also fell into the practice of worshiping false idols (gods). Because of their transgressions, God finally divorced Israel. This probably took place in 593 BC when God (Shekinah Glory) returned to heaven. When Israel repents and returns to God, He will take Israel back as His wife. This will take place during the beginning years of the Day of the Lord, after they go through their period of cleansing and come back to God. In the New Testament, God's Son Jesus will be the groom and the bride will be the church. Please plan to be a part of the Bride of Christ, along with me and Sarah. The time is getting closer and closer. Below, I have made a little illustration that explains who I think might possibly be attending the Marriage Supper of the Lamb.

<u>Honored</u>
    Husband — Jesus
    Young Wife — Church

<u>Guests</u>
    Old Testament Saints

<u>Special Guests from the Tribulation Period</u>
    Tribulation Saints

Upon exiting the wedding chamber, after the seven-year wedding feast is completed, the Church age saints will be allowed to enter their permanent dwellings that were prepared for them by God. All of the resurrected saints, who received their resurrected bodies at the Rapture, will spend the remainder of the Day of Christ in their dwelling places in the heavenly city of Jerusalem and will probably be allowed to make periodic visits to earth.

I am gratefully indebted to Avi Ben Mordechai and his book, *Signs in the Heavens*. This book provided me with the general information for an ancient Jewish wedding. Without his Messianic Jewish perspective on an ancient Jewish wedding it would have been very difficult to come to the understanding of the prophetic viewpoint of a Jewish wedding. Thanks again Mr. Mordechai!

As we summarize the last two chapters, which are totally Jewish in thought, we see some very interesting prophetic time tables fall into place. A good foundation for the chronological order of future events develop through the teachings of men chosen by God. We begin with the prophet Daniel from the Old Testament. According to current Judaic thought, Daniel is not one of the fifty-five prophets of the Old Testament. His writings include visions of the future, which they believe to be true, however they believe his mission was not that of a prophet. They believe his visions of the future were never intended to be proclaimed to the people. They were designed to be written down for future generations, therefore, they are classified with the books of the Writings and not of the Prophets. In fact, in times past, Jews were even discouraged from interpreting certain Biblical numbers from the writings of Daniel. The prohibition was not always obeyed. By not including the writings of Daniel in their prophetic teachings, the Jews leave a big gap in their understanding of Bible prophecy.

Ironically, in the fourth century, the rabbinic leaders placed the book of Daniel among the "Writings," the third division of their canon. Yet in the older arrangement of their canon, attested to by Josephus, a Jewish historian at the time of Christ, Daniel was included among the section of the "Prophets." The section of the "Prophets," followed the section known as the "Law" and preceded the section known as the "Poets." However, notice that even Jesus Christ considered Daniel to be a prophet.

> Matt 24:15 *"So when you see standing in the holy place <u>'the abomination that causes desolation,' spoken of through the prophet Daniel</u>—let the reader understand—* (NIV)

Daniel's teachings are paramount to understanding the chronological order of the events of the Tribulation Period, the period that effects God's stern dealings with His people (the Jews) and His holy city (Jerusalem). The Seventy Weeks of Daniel are almost universally agreed, by prophecy teachers today, to be a period of 490 years (Daniel 9:24-27). They are calculating one day to equal one year for the seventy-week period (70 weeks = 490 days). In the book of Ezekiel, another great Old Testament prophet, the same principle of one day equaling one year of punishment for the Jewish people can be found (Ezekiel 4:4-8). As we move to the New Testament, Peter reveals to us that at times God counts a day as a thousand years and a thousand years as a day (2 Peter 3:8). This revelation gives some credence to the ancient Jewish thought of the Creation Week Theory. This theory is that one day equals a thousand years of time to complete God's plan of redemption for mankind. For six thousand years mankind will rule the earth, while the last thousand-year period will be ruled by God. The Jews consider this to be a thousand year Sabbatical Rest.

In both the Old Testament and the New Testament, the Day of the Lord is mentioned numerous times. This day (1000 years) is the Sabbatical Rest mentioned above. It will begin at the Rapture, which closes the six thousand-year period of the days of man and also begins the one thousand-year period of the Day of the Lord. Hosea makes an incredible prophetic statement concerning this time. Two days (2000 years) after Jesus returns to heaven (this 2000 year period is the Dispensation of Grace), God will revive the Jewish people (bring all of them back to their land). Remember that this will take place after the 2000 years of the Dispensation of Grace has ended, which is also the third day referred to in Hosea. On the third day, after He has dealt with His people, God will restore the Jews to a position as head of the nations during the Day of the Lord.

Before we end this chapter, I would like to discuss the first four verses of Daniel chapter twelve. Many prophecy teachers today believe that these verses reveal that the Old Testament saints will be resurrected after the Tribulation Period is over. We know that these verses are referring to the Jewish people because we know that Daniel's visions and revelations always concern *"your people."*

> Dan 12:1-4 *"At that time Michael, the great prince who protects <u>**your people,**</u> will arise. There will be a time of distress such as has not happened from the beginning of nations until then. **But at that time your people—everyone whose name is found written in the book—will be delivered. <u>Multitudes who sleep in the dust of the earth will awake</u>: some to everlasting life, others to shame and everlasting contempt.** Those who are wise will shine like the brightness of the heavens, and those who lead many to righteousness, like the stars for ever and ever. **But you, Daniel, close up and seal the words of the scroll until the time of the end.** Many will go here and there to increase knowledge."* (NIV)

Some prophecy teachers believe that since this passage is following the events of the Tribulation Period, discussed in chapter eleven, the Old Testament saints will not be a part of the resurrection at the time of the Rapture. They place the resurrection of the Old Testament saints after the Tribulation Period has taken place. They believe that only the church age saints are resurrected at the Rapture. If that was the only time where this subject was mentioned in the Old Testament, that premise could possibly be surmised, but Isaiah adds a better perspective to the account.

There are two reasons why I believe that the Old Testament saints will be resurrected at the Rapture. A more concise Old Testament resurrection passage can be found in the book of Isaiah.

> Isa 26:19-21 *<u>**But your dead will live; their bodies will rise. You who dwell in the dust, wake up and shout for joy.**</u> Your dew is like the dew of the morning; the earth will give birth to her dead. **Go, my people, enter your rooms and shut the doors behind you; hide yourselves for a little while until his wrath has passed by.** See, the LORD is coming out of his dwelling to punish the people of the earth for their sins. The earth will disclose the blood shed upon her; she will conceal her slain no longer.* (NIV)

In these verses we find the Old Testament saints resurrected and in heaven. They are told to enter their rooms of Divine protection and to hide themselves for a little while (7 years), until the Lord passes judgment on the world. In these verses it is perfectly clear that the Old Testament saints are in their rooms of Divine protection after their resurrection, during the Tribulation Period.

The second reason I believe that the Old Testament saints will be resurrected at the Rapture is that they will be the guests at the wedding that will take place in heaven two years *After the Rapture*. During that first two-year period (Mikveh) they will be preparing for the wedding by putting on white garments. The wedding will take place in heaven followed by a seven year wedding feast. The Old Testament saints will be in their respective rooms of Divine protection in heaven at the same time the Tribulation Period is taking place on earth.

As we return to Daniel we do see a resurrection of the Jewish people and it does take place after the Tribulation Period is completed. It appears that the first four verses of Daniel twelve are a continuation of the discourse of the Tribulation Period; the worst time of human history that was expounded on in the last part of chapter eleven. At that time, during the Tribulation Period, Michael and his army of holy angels will rise up and defeat Satan and his army of fallen angels in heaven. During the war in heaven Michael and his angels will be the victors and cast Satan and his angels to the earth. At the time Satan is cast down to the earth the deadliest period of human history will take place. Chapter twelve then continues to give us details concerning the last 3 ½ year period of the worst time of human history. This, of course, being the Time of Jacob's Trouble.

> Jer 30:7 *How awful that day will be! None will be like it. <u>It will be a time of trouble for Jacob</u>, but he will be saved out of it.* (NIV)

At that time—the Time of Jacob's Trouble—your (Daniel's) people (the Jews) will be delivered. A portion of the Jewish people will even be protected from the Antichrist during this time. Notice here that only those people who have believed in the Messiah (whose names are found in the book of life) will be delivered. After the Tribulation Period is completed, multitudes of Jewish believers who died, the majority of them possibly being martyred, will receive their resurrected bodies. This will take place during the forty-five-day period between the 1290 days and the 1335 days mentioned later in Daniel chapter twelve, and is for the saved Jews who died *After the Rapture*.

The best explanation I was able to come across concerning the Jewish resurrection of Daniel chapter twelve is in, *THE GREATNESS OF THE KINGDOM*, by Alva J. McClain.

> First, this is a *physical* resurrection. The people involved are those "that sleep in the dust of the earth" (vs.2). These words could only refer to the physical body.
>
> Second, it is a resurrection of *Israelites*. As the angelic messenger clearly indicated to Daniel, the primary subject of the passage is "thy people" (vs. 1). It is Daniel's historic people who will suffer the terrible time of trouble, and the same people are to be subjects of this resurrection.
>
> Third, even among the Israelites it will be a *selective* resurrection. Not all, but only "many" of them that sleep in the dust of the earth shall awake. By no reasonable device of interpretation can "*many*" be turned into *all*. Furthermore, the resurrection does not include both good and bad, as the King James version seems to indicate. Verse 2 may be rendered as follows: "Many *from among* the sleepers... *these* shall be unto everlasting life: but *those* [the rest of the sleepers

Yom Ha-Din — Days of Awe — A Jewish Wedding

who do not awake at this time] shall be unto shame." Thus, just as there is a selective deliverance among the *living* Israelites, restricted to those "found written in the book" (vs. 1); even so there is a selective resurrection among the *dead*, restricted to those who shall be awakened to everlasting life. Scripture knows nothing of a general resurrection, either of Israelites or of all men, both good and bad, simultaneously. [29]

It is reported that Tregelles reads the passage in this way and the Jewish commentators support this rendering of Daniel 12:1-3. In verse four, Daniel is then told to close the scroll and seal it. The total meaning will not be revealed until the time of the end. At that time, travel will be greatly enhanced around the world and there will be a knowledge explosion like no other time in history.

I believe that a comprehensive study of the Jewish Festivals, ordained by God on Mount Sinai in 1445 BC, can reveal some prophetic utterances. Using the same theory of one day equaling one year and applying it to the High Holy Days of the Jewish people, by placing the Days of Awe at the beginning of the Day of the Lord, can reveal a chronological order of the events that effect the Jewish people on earth at that time. The Seven Intermediate Days correspond to the last seven days of Daniel's Seventy Weeks. Both of them prophetically equal seven years, but the Days of Awe are a ten-day period. After looking at the theme of the entire ten day period, you can see that the entire festival also has prophetic implications (See Days of Awe chart on page 764).

A step beyond that reveals that an ancient Jewish Wedding can also have prophetic implications for both the Old Testament saints (guests) and the New Testament saints (Bride). Since this wedding will take place in heaven, the wedding feast will also take place in heaven. An ancient Jewish wedding feast would last for seven days. Again, as we apply the theory of one day for one year, we can see that the wedding celebration that will take place after the marriage will last for seven years (Follow the entire wedding ceremony in the chart on page 765).

A third chart is provided for the Apostle John, who was shown a detailed vision of the future seven-year Tribulation Period in Revelation chapters 6-16 (This chart is on page 763).

As you follow the chronological order of the time-line of each of these charts, you will need to keep in mind that each chart has a significance of its own. The first chart, Tribulation Period – Days of Awe – Jewish Wedding, is a composite of the remaining three charts and can be found on page 762. It shows that they are all following the same time-line. The second chart, The Tribulation Period (Book of Revelation), is an outline of the book of Revelation and follows the order of the activity mainly on earth as mankind suffers the blow of the fierce anger of God and is found on page 763. The third chart, Days of Awe, has a Jewish perspective and focuses in on God's final dealings with His chosen people and the city of Jerusalem and can be found on page 764. This will be the worst time of Jewish history followed by the best time of Jewish history. The fourth chart, Jewish Wedding, deals with the scene in heaven as it follows the promises made to the Bride of Christ and can be found on page 765. These people will not be concerned with the activity taking place on the earth at this time. As you continue on, in this study, please refer to these charts as often as needed to get a clear picture of the order of events that are about to transpire.

CHAPTER SEVEN

1948 TO THE RAPTURE

APOSTASY

As we pick up where we left off in chapter four we see a world after World War II on a steady decline away from God. Even the Christian church is filled with people who have a form of Godliness, but who do not have a true or saving relationship with Jesus. Many Christian's are religious, but not saved. They are playing church on Sunday, but are becoming progressively more lukewarm. The scriptures indicate that this will be the general condition of the people around the world toward the end of the Dispensation of Grace. That is not saying that there are not any saved people living at this time, on the contrary, there are millions of people who truly are saved, but there are billions who are not saved. In fact, the church today is the salt of the earth and is responsible for most of what morality is left in the world, but I am afraid that the salt is losing its saltiness.

> Matt 5:11-13 *"Blessed are you when people insult you, persecute you and falsely say all kinds of evil against you because of me. Rejoice and be glad, because great is your reward in heaven, for in the same way they persecuted the prophets who were before you. **"You are the salt of the earth.** But if the salt loses its saltiness, how can it be made salty again? It is no longer good for anything, except to be thrown out and trampled by men.* (NIV)

Paul is perfectly clear in his second letter to the Thessalonians that the Day of the Lord and the return of Jesus at the Rapture will not come about until two things happen; a rebellion against God (apostasy) and the revealing of the man of lawlessness (the Antichrist). Although Adolf Hitler took advantage of the Laodicean period and prematurely tried to do the same things the Antichrist will try to accomplish, Hitler does not even come close to the disaster the world will face during the Tribulation Period.

> 2 Thes 2:1-3 **Concerning the coming of our Lord Jesus Christ and our being gathered to him,** *we ask you, brothers, not to become easily unsettled or alarmed by some prophecy, report or letter supposed to have come from us, saying that* **the day of the Lord** *has already come. Don't let anyone deceive you in any way,* **for that day will not come until the rebellion occurs and the man of lawlessness is revealed,** *the man doomed to destruction.* (NIV)

First, the apostasy will take place which will last right up to the time of the Rapture and carry over to the start of the Millennium, where it will be a force to be reckoned with. Sometime during the latter part of the apostasy toward the end of the age, the Antichrist will be revealed, but with restraint. The correct understanding of the Day of the Lord will allow

PRIMARY SIGNS OF THE TIMES

There are signs that the true Church can be looking for to give them the general time frame of the second coming of Christ. I will break them down into two categories—primary and secondary. Because the Church of the Laodicean period is lukewarm, most of the Christian Church will miss these signs. It is sad to say, but many pastors and priests in our churches today do not know enough about Bible prophecy to be teaching the members of their congregations the signs that are taking place at this very hour. It is even more sad to say that many of them are not even saved. The Church needs to be teaching these signs to believers in order for them to be ready for the Rapture, but the responsibility does not rest solely with the pastors, priests and Sunday School teachers. Christians are supposed to be responsible enough to read—not only read but study—the word of God and pray for understanding from the Holy Spirit. You control your own destiny.

It was Luke who provided us with the signs for the destruction of the Temple and he will also provide us with some of the signs for the Rapture. In Luke's account of the Olivet Discourse, his is the only account of the three gospels that actually lists the three separate times that signs appear for an event. If you follow his account chronologically in chapter 21; in verses 8-9 it lists the signs for the destruction of the Temple in 70 AD, verses 10-11 are signs for the end of the church age and verses 12-23 revert back to the signs in 70 AD. Verse 24 contains the Diaspora (dispersion) of the Jews during the Dispensation of Grace. The third set of signs that take place during the Tribulation Period are listed in verses 25-27.

Luke 21:25-27 *"**There will be signs in the sun, moon and stars**. On the earth, nations will be in anguish and perplexity at the roaring and tossing of the sea. **Men will faint from terror, apprehensive of what is coming on the world, for the heavenly bodies will be shaken**. At that time they will see the Son of Man coming in a cloud with power and great glory.*" (NIV)

These are the same signs that are listed for the Jewish people in the Olivet Discourse in both Matthew and Mark. We know that these are signs for the Tribulation Period because we see the Glorious Return of Jesus in verse twenty-seven. These verses also mention other events that will take place during the Tribulation Period, such as signs in the sun, moon and stars, along with the anguish and perplexity of the people around the world. The heavenly bodies (stars) are not shaken out of their place until the time of the Tribulation Period. If you will notice in verse twenty-eight, Luke uses these future signs as a beginning point of the signs for the redemption of the saints at the Rapture. When these things begin to take place:

Luke 21:28 ***When these things begin to take place**, stand up and lift up your heads, **because your redemption is drawing near**.*" (NIV)

When these things begin to take place:

AFTER THE RAPTURE

1. Signs in the sun, moon and stars—astrological alignment of the stars designed by God. (J. R. Church from *Prophecy in the News* has some excellent teachings on this subject).

2. Nations will be in anguish and perplexity—a reference to the two great wars of the twentieth century. Terrorism also seems to be playing a part of this prophecy.

These are some of the signs to let us know that the time of the redemption of those living at that time is drawing near. As Luke continues, he then proceeds to tell us about what Jesus had to say concerning the parable of the fig tree. We are again looking at signs for the end of the church age. We see this same account in Matthew and Mark, where only the fig tree is mentioned, but in this account by Luke another element is added.

Luke 21: 29-31 *He told them this parable: "Look at the fig tree and all the trees. When they sprout leaves, you can see for yourselves and know that summer is near. Even so, when you see these things happening, you know that the kingdom of God is near.* (NIV)

Trees spoken of symbolically always represent kingdoms (nations). In this account, not only is the fig tree (nation of Israel) mentioned, but Jesus added all the trees (Gentile nations). Jesus is telling us in this parable that when Israel becomes a nation and a group of nations known as the Revived Roman Empire materializes, the Kingdom Age is near. The Kingdom of God—when Jesus will rule during the Millennium—is right at our door step. Look for the Rapture! When the world exists with Israel as an independent nation—which is happening today—a generation will not pass away until the Tribulation Period is completed. In this case a generation could be referring to seventy or eighty years.

Luke 21:32-33 *"I tell you the truth, this generation will certainly not pass away until all these things have happened. Heaven and earth will pass away, but my words will never pass away.* (NIV)

Ps 90:10 *The length of our days is seventy years—or eighty, if we have the strength; yet their span is but trouble and sorrow, for they quickly pass, and we fly away.* (NIV)

Jesus then consoles us by telling us not to be taken over by the anxieties of this life. Be watchful and pray that you will be able to escape the horror of the Tribulation Period and that you will be a participant at the Judgment Seat of Christ.

Luke 21:34-36 *"Be careful, or your hearts will be weighed down with dissipation, drunkenness and the anxieties of life, and that day will close on you unexpectedly like a trap. For it will come upon all those who live on the face of the whole earth. Be always on the watch, and pray that you may be able to escape all that is about to happen, and that you may be able to stand before the Son of Man."* (NIV)

This account in Luke is intended for church age believers. The terrible events of the Tribulation Period have their earliest beginnings at the end of the church age and will carry over *After the Rapture* and take place during the Tribulation Period. Jesus clearly reveals that we can escape the fierce anger of God, but to do that we have to know Jesus and WATCH!!!

1 Thes 5:6   *Therefore let us not sleep, as others do, **but let us watch** and be sober.* (NKJ)

Rev 3:3   ***Remember, therefore, what you have received and heard; obey it, and repent.*** *But if you do not wake up, I will come like a thief, and you will not know at what time I will come to you.* (NIV)

A sign that will make itself known at the end of the age is the condition of the church. We have already mentioned it, but because it is so important it needs to be mentioned again, especially the part about the church becoming rich.

Rev 3:14-18   ***And unto the angel of the church of the Laodiceans write;*** *These things saith the Amen, the faithful and true witness, the beginning of the creation of God; I know thy works, that thou art neither cold nor hot: I would thou wert cold or hot.* ***So then because thou art lukewarm, and neither cold nor hot, I will spue thee out of my mouth. Because thou sayest, I am rich, and increased with goods, and have need of nothing; and knowest not that thou art wretched, and miserable, and poor, and blind, and naked:*** *I counsel thee to buy of me gold tried in the fire, that thou mayest be rich; and white raiment, that thou mayest be clothed, and that the shame of thy nakedness do not appear; and anoint thine eyes with eyesalve, that thou mayest see.* (KJV)

It does not take long after looking at religious institutions of today to see that many of them are not lacking in material goods; such as majestic buildings, fancy worldly gadgets, good salaries for the clergy and plenty of tithe money to go around. Big fancy churches with a lot of money and celebrity status do not guarantee a future spot in heaven. The message of prosperity is being taught in many churches today. Because of the prosperous condition of the world, at the end of the age, the prosperity will spill over into the Church.

In the message to the church of Laodicea, we have a description of the last stage of the professing church on earth. It is described as neither hot nor cold, but nauseatingly lukewarm, so that Christ says that He will *"spue thee out of my mouth."* Playing church will not be sufficient enough to be saved. It boastfully claims to be *"rich"* and *"increased with goods,"* having *"need of nothing."* Money, material possessions and worldly ambitions will all be a part of the end-time church. They will have everything but happiness and salvation. Even Jesus will be missing in their lives, for He will be outside the door. The church will be ignorant of its true condition; that it is wretched, and miserable, and poor, and blind and naked. Unspeakably sad, it is the condition, to a large extent, of the so-called professing church of today. That is not to say that there are not good churches out there today.

Daniel makes a most remarkable revelation in the final chapter of his awesome book after he had been shown the outline of future events—which upon receiving he became direly ill. Daniel is talking about a time when the earth will go through an extremely dire period. At that time, God will finish His dealings with Daniel's beloved people. Daniel was then given the reassuring words that his soul would rest until *"the end of the days,"* referring to the end of the Dispensation of Grace, at which time he will be resurrected and be given his allotted inheritance. *"At that time,"* is the time Daniel will take his place before the Judgment Seat of Christ to receive his rewards and position of authority that he will hold during the Day of Christ, followed by the eternal state. Daniel's final instructions from God were to go about his daily affairs until he died.

> Dan 12:13 *"As for you, go your way till the end. **You will rest, and then at the end of the days you will rise to receive your allotted inheritance.**"* (NIV)

Just before Daniel heard these words, he was told what would happen at the *"time of the end,"* which is another reference to the end of the Dispensation of Grace. In these verses, these things will happen or be happening at the end of the age.

> Dan 12:4 *"But you, **Daniel, shut up the words, and seal the book until the time of the end**; many shall run to and fro, and knowledge shall increase."* (NKJ)

Here Daniel is instructed that the meaning of the prophecies, he recorded in his writings, are not to be revealed until *"the time of the end."* The Hebrew word used for "shut up" or "close up" is *catham* and can be translated, "to keep secret" or "hidden." So in a sense the meanings of the visions of Daniel are to be kept secret until the end of the church age, at which time God will reveal their meaning to the people living at that time. Then Daniel is given a picture of what it will be like at *"the time of the end." "Many shall run to and fro,"* means, "to travel" or "to rove about" and is referring to the advanced condition of the means of transportation that are a part of the world at the time of the end, a time when people will be traveling around the world in ships, planes, trains and automobiles. Today, we can literally hop on an airplane and fly halfway around the globe in a matter of hours. Planes, especially, have shortened the borders of every nation on the face of the earth. The second thing Daniel revealed was that *"knowledge shall increase,"* which basically is referring to the knowledge explosion that has occurred in the twentieth century and is carrying over to the twenty-first century. The world one hundred years ago was primitive compared to what it is like today.

One added comment made to Daniel, at that time, also reveals the condition of the saved and the unsaved during the time that elapses between the time in which Daniel was living and the end of the age. A time span of some 2600 years.

1948 to the Rapture

Dan 12:9-10 *He replied, "<u>Go your way, Daniel, because the words are closed up and sealed until the time of the end.</u> Many will be purified, made spotless and refined, but the wicked will continue to be wicked. <u>None of the wicked will understand, but those who are wise will understand.</u>* (NIV)

Many, referring to some people, will find the way to salvation while others will not. In other words, life will not change during this time. It will still depend on each person to decide his own fate for eternity, to accept God or reject Him. The wicked (unsaved) will continue being wicked (unsaved). A great point closes these verses; none of the unsaved will understand. Satan's goal is to convince mankind that there is not a God or even that a loving God would not allow terrible things to happen. He wants everyone to believe what is false. He wants people to believe the big lie, but those who are wise (believers) will understand and have salvation. The message is in the Bible if you want to take advantage of it.

Along with revealing the fact that Daniel's visions would be made known at the end of the present age, the one we are now living in, he revealed two signs of the times that we need to be looking for. My guess is that these two prophecies of Daniel are being fulfilled at this very hour – travel will abound and knowledge will explode! What do you think?

SECONDARY SIGNS OF THE TIMES

Some Bible prophecy teachers believe that certain scriptures referring to the *"last days"* in the New Testament are making reference to the end of the age. Basically the last days in scripture had their beginning two thousand years ago when Christ came the first time. So these so-called end-time signs have really been a part of the Dispensation of Grace. Before we look at them let me add that because of the end-time apostasy these conditions will be more severe during the time just prior to the return of Christ. They will also carry over into the Tribulation Period. As a result of these conditions being a part of the Dispensation of Grace and significantly more prominent toward the end of the age, I will list them only as secondary Signs of the Times.

1. **Departing from the faith** — People who have known Jesus as their personal Savior will abandon the Christian faith and will follow false teachings.
   1 Tim 4:1-5 *Now the Spirit speaketh expressly, that in the latter times some shall depart from the faith, giving heed to seducing spirits, and doctrines of devils; Speaking lies in hypocrisy; having their conscience seared with a hot iron; Forbidding to marry, and commanding to abstain from meats, which God hath created to be received with thanksgiving of them which believe and know the truth. For every creature of God is good, and nothing to be refused, if it be received with thanksgiving: For it is sanctified by the word of God and prayer.* (KJV)

2. **False Teachers** — Many of the denominations today, that claim to be Christians, are not true believers of Jesus. They teach a different Jesus. You do not have to work your way to heaven or belong to a certain denomination that is the exclusive

AFTER THE RAPTURE

Christian religion. The true church is made up of any person who confesses Jesus Christ and truly believes that He died on the cross for their sins. The sad part about these false Christian churches of today is that they have been assimilated into the Orthodox Christian Church and have been accepted by them as true believers.

2 Tim 4:3-4 *For the time will come when they will not endure sound doctrine; but after their own lusts shall they heap to themselves teachers, having itching ears; And they shall turn away their ears from the truth, and shall be turned unto fables.* (KJV)

3. **Rich men** — In the last days there shall be a class of rich men who shall have heaped treasure together and that by fraud and who shall use their ill-gotten gain in the pursuit of pleasure and wantonness. God will hear the cry of those who have been cheated of their just share of the profits, and will send a sore judgment upon the guilty. What a description we have here of the unprincipled, speculative and profiteering spirit of the days in which we live, when men become millionaires or even multimillionaires in just a few years and where millions of dollars are being stolen by Corporate executives. Truly we are living in the last days of this age.

   James 5:1-5 *Now listen, you rich people, weep and wail because of the misery that is coming upon you. Your wealth has rotted, and moths have eaten your clothes. Your gold and silver are corroded. Their corrosion will testify against you and eat your flesh like fire. You have hoarded wealth in the last days. Look! The wages you failed to pay the workmen who mowed your fields are crying out against you. The cries of the harvesters have reached the ears of the Lord Almighty. You have lived on earth in luxury and self-indulgence. You have fattened yourselves in the day of slaughter.* (NIV)

4. **Scoffers** — With the world in a state of apostasy, there are many people today who refute the doctrine of the second coming of the Lord. On a radio show several years ago, where the host was interviewing Dave Hunt, I heard the host criticize Dave Hunt and complain that people have been saying for two thousand years that Jesus was going to come back. The host then made the comment, "But where is He?" At that point the host ended the interview and would not allow Dave Hunt to respond to his statement. The interviewer did not know it, but he was fulfilling prophecy. A sad state of affairs today is that some of the opposition concerning the second coming of Christ is coming from many prominent Christian religious leaders.

   2 Pet 3:3-4 *First of all, you must understand that in the last days scoffers will come, scoffing and following their own evil desires. They will say, "<u>Where is this 'coming' he promised</u>? Ever since our fathers died, everything goes on as it has since the beginning of creation."* (NIV)

5. **Perilous Times** — Because of the apostasy, this description of the condition of mankind will be extremely bad just prior to the time of the Rapture. Compare these verses with the condition of the world today. The only point I want to expound on is that people *"having a form of Godliness but denying its power,"* is referring to

people acting religious, but not having a personal relationship with Jesus. **Religion does not save you, Jesus does!**

2 Tim 3:1-5 *This know also, that in the last days perilous times shall come. For men shall be lovers of their own selves, covetous, boasters, proud, blasphemers, disobedient to parents, unthankful, unholy, Without natural affection, trucebreakers, false accusers, incontinent, fierce, despisers of those that are good, Traitors, heady, highminded, lovers of pleasures more than lovers of God; Having a form of Godliness, but denying the power thereof: from such turn away.* (KJV)

You have just read about the world in its extreme condition just prior to the return of Jesus at the Rapture. The beginning sign we need to be looking for is an apostasy or falling away from God. There will be wars of great magnitude with nations fighting other nations (World War I and World War II). The nation of Israel (fig tree) will once more come into existence. A group of nations (all the trees) will begin to unify (Revived Roman Empire). A knowledge explosion like no other time will occur, which will spur inventions to greatly enhance the travel capabilities and the living conditions of those people living on the earth at that time. To the true believers of the church, God will unseal the visions of Daniel and reveal their meaning. Not long before the Rapture the Antichrist will enter the world scene. At that time, not many people will recognize him as the future one-world leader.

Although we do not know the exact time of when Jesus will return for us at the Rapture, we are provided with signs to make us aware of the season of this impending event. Do not be like the religious leaders during the time of Jesus who did not recognize the signs of their time, the signs of His first appearance.

Matt 16:1-3 *The Pharisees and Sadducees came to Jesus and tested him by asking him to show them a sign from heaven. He replied, "When evening comes, you say, 'It will be fair weather, for the sky is red,' and in the morning, 'Today it will be stormy, for the sky is red and overcast.'* ***You know how to interpret the appearance of the sky, but you cannot interpret the signs of the times.*** (NIV)

ANTICHRIST REVEALED

This event has to be expounded on before we depart on our journey to meet Jesus in the air at the Rapture. It is not a sign as far as the Signs of the Times are concerned, but Paul informs us in his second letter to the Thessalonians that two events precede the Rapture of the Church. The scripture verse can be found in 2 Thessalonians 2:3.

1. The falling away (apostasy)
2. The man of sin is revealed (Antichrist)

Notice that the apostasy comes first and then the Antichrist is revealed. We mentioned earlier that the apostasy of the end times probably had its beginning more than a hundred years ago. If the Antichrist were to be born at the start of the apostasy, it would make him too old to be the world dictator *After the Rapture*. So we know that the apostasy will precede the birth of the Antichrist and will probably have a good foothold on the world when the Antichrist is born. I picture the Antichrist as a young charismatic political figure, probably between 40 and 50 years old when the Rapture takes place. If the Rapture occurs sometime before the year 2028, which is eighty years after Israel (fig tree) became a nation (sprouts leaves), that would present the possibility that the Antichrist could possibly be alive today. If the Lord would happen to tarry until 2028, then the Antichrist could possibly be between 15 and 25 years old at the present time. I personally believe that the Antichrist is alive and living somewhere in the world today. Who knows where?

It must be remembered that the Antichrist will only be revealed before the Rapture. At that time he will probably have very little worldwide notoriety. He could possibly be a young upcoming political figure on a national level. The chaos of the times following the Rapture will catapult him to worldwide recognition as a person who can pull the world together after the financial collapse of the world monetary system.

Before the Rapture the Antichrist will be restrained by the Holy Spirit. The Antichrist will not be allowed to come to great power until *After the Rapture* of the Church has taken place.

> 2 Thes 2:6-7 — *And now you know what is holding him back, so that he may be revealed at the proper time. For the secret power of lawlessness is already at work; but the one who now holds it back will continue to do so till he is taken out of the way.* (NIV)

Throughout the Dispensation of Grace people have tried to figure out who the person of the Antichrist is. There have been all kinds of names thrown out. As I have already mentioned before, I think Adolf Hitler ran a close second. In the book of Revelation it tells us that the number of his name can be calculated to the number 666. If you have wisdom and insight, you can figure out who he is when he comes on the world scene.

> Rev 13:18 — *This calls for wisdom. If anyone has insight, let him calculate the number of the beast, for it is man's number. His number is 666.* (NIV)

Today, it is all right to try to figure out who the Antichrist is, but I would not hesitate to tell you not to be to dogmatic about your predictions. There will be people on the earth before the Rapture who will correctly pick the identity of the Antichrist. Are you that wise person with insight? Please use caution and discretion in this matter, as it would be rather repulsive to be accused of being the Antichrist—especially if they turned out not to be the Antichrist.

There are some people today who are correctly placing the revealing of the Antichrist before the Rapture, but this is contrary to the teaching of many Bible prophecy teachers. In fact, most Bible prophecy teachers follow this older teaching. Those prophecy teachers are highly critical of people today, including me, who are saying that the Antichrist will be revealed before the Rapture of the church. They are saying that those people who have this opinion are replacing the revealing of Jesus, at the Rapture, with the Antichrist. That we are looking for the Antichrist instead of Jesus. That is not so! What I am saying is that before the Day of the Lord begins, which includes the Tribulation Period, the Antichrist will be revealed, but he will not be allowed to begin his drive to a position of a world dictator until *After the Rapture*. The presence of the Holy Spirit will hinder his activity in the early part of his life. As I have mentioned before, not everyone will recognize the Antichrist when he is revealed, this includes true believers in Jesus. Whether a certain believer does or does not recognize the Antichrist, after he comes on the world scene, does not effect that persons salvation or the timing of the Rapture.

I might add here that I personally do not think there will be much time between the revealing of the Antichrist and the Rapture. The clear teaching of 2 Thessalonians 2 is that day (the day of the Lord) will not come until the apostasy takes place first and then the Antichrist is revealed. As a matter of fact, I do not even consider the revealing of the Antichrist as a sign of the times before Christ comes back, but an event that will take place.

WHY A TRIBULATION PERIOD?

Why is there going to be a Tribulation Period? Why does God allow things like this to happen? It is not unreasonable, even as a Christian, to question why God will allow such an event to take place. It is above our understanding. Many people today will have a hard time believing what is printed in this book concerning the coming time of God's fierce anger. "How can a loving God...?" is a common phrase spoken today even among Christians. My answer to them is, "How can such a sinful people reject such a loving God?" God is slow to anger, but eventually His righteous judgment will prevail.

Even at that, it is hard to comprehend why the world will go through such a dreadful period. All we can do on this side of heaven is believe in Jesus Christ and know that He is in control. We cannot answer for God or know why certain things are allowed to happen. God is so powerful that He knows time from the end to the beginning. By His foreknowledge God knows everything before it happens. It is not ours to question God!

> Acts 2:22-23 *"Men of Israel, listen to this: Jesus of Nazareth was a man accredited by God to you by miracles, wonders and signs, which God did among you through him, as you yourselves know. **This man was handed over to you by God's set purpose and foreknowledge; and you, with the help of wicked men, put him to death by nailing him to the cross.*** (NIV)
>
> 1 Pet 1:2 *who have been chosen according to **the foreknowledge of God the Father**, through the sanctifying work of the Spirit, for obedience to Jesus Christ and sprinkling by his blood: Grace and peace be yours in abundance.* (NIV)

The answer to those who wonder why God will allow the Tribulation Period to take place is found in the three letter word: SIN—which produces evil.

Col 3:5-6   *Put to death, therefore, whatever belongs to your earthly nature: sexual immorality, impurity, lust, evil desires and greed, which is idolatry. <u>Because of these, the wrath of God is coming.</u>* (NIV)

God will finish His dealings with His chosen people (Israel) and sinful mankind (nations) during the same ten-year period. He will judge the whole world for their wickedness. The whole world will truly have to go through the worst time of human history.

Dan 9:24   *"<u>Seventy 'sevens' are decreed for your people and your holy city</u> to finish transgression, to put an end to sin, to atone for wickedness, to bring in everlasting righteousness, to seal up vision and prophecy and to anoint the most holy.* (NIV)

Obad 1:15   *"<u>The day of the LORD is near for all nations.</u> As you have done, it will be done to you; your deeds will return upon your own head.* (NIV)

Isa 2:6-22   *You have abandoned your people, the house of Jacob. They are full of superstitions from the East; they practice divination like the Philistines and clasp hands with pagans. Their land is full of silver and gold; there is no end to their treasures. Their land is full of horses; there is no end to their chariots. Their land is full of idols; they bow down to the work of their hands, to what their fingers have made.* **<u>So man will be brought low and mankind humbled—do not forgive them.</u>** *Go into the rocks, hide in the ground from dread of the LORD and the splendor of his majesty!* **<u>The eyes of the arrogant man will be humbled</u>** *and the pride of men brought low; the LORD alone will be exalted in that day.* **<u>The LORD Almighty has a day in store for all the proud and lofty, for all that is exalted (and they will be humbled)</u>**, *for all the cedars of Lebanon, tall and lofty, and all the oaks of Bashan, for all the towering mountains and all the high hills, for every lofty tower and every fortified wall, for every trading ship and every stately vessel.* **The arrogance of man will be brought low and the pride of men humbled; the LORD alone will be exalted in that day, and the idols will totally** *disappear. Men will flee to caves in the rocks and to holes in the ground from dread of the LORD and the splendor of his majesty,* **<u>when he rises to shake the earth.</u>** *In that day men will throw away to the rodents and bats their idols of silver and idols of gold, which they made to worship. They will flee to caverns in the rocks and to the overhanging crags from dread of the LORD and the splendor of his majesty,* **when he rises to shake the earth. <u>Stop trusting in man, who has but a breath in his nostrils. Of</u>**

what account is he? (NIV)

Ps 110:5-7   *The Lord is at your right hand; <u>he will crush kings on the day of his wrath</u>. He will judge the nations, heaping up the dead and crushing the rulers of the whole earth. He will drink from a brook beside the way; therefore he will lift up his head.* (NIV)

Isa 13:6-13   *Wail, for the day of the LORD is near; it will come like destruction from the Almighty. Because of this, all hands will go limp, every man's heart will melt. Terror will seize them, pain and anguish will grip them; they will writhe like a woman in labor. They will look aghast at each other, their faces aflame. <u>See, the day of the LORD is coming a cruel day, with wrath and fierce anger—to make the land desolate and destroy the sinners within it.</u> The stars of heaven and their constellations will not show their light. The rising sun will be darkened and the moon will not give its light. <u>I will punish the world for its evil, the wicked for their sins.</u> I will put an end to the arrogance of the haughty and will humble the pride of the ruthless. I will make man scarcer than pure gold, more rare than the gold of Ophir. Therefore I will make the heavens tremble; and the earth will shake from its place at the wrath of the LORD Almighty, <u>in the day of his burning anger.</u>* (NIV)

Rev 3:10   *Since you have kept my command to endure patiently, I will also keep you from <u>the hour of trial</u> that is going to come upon the whole world to test those who live on the earth.* (NIV)

It is at this point (the Rapture) that we can answer the question poised by the writer in Psalms 94, *"Lord, how long shall the wicked triumph?"* The wicked will be able to triumph a little more than nine years at this point, until after the Tribulation Period is over and the Battle of Armageddon is fought.

Ps 13:2   *How long must I wrestle with my thoughts and every day have sorrow in my heart? <u>How long will my enemy triumph over me</u>?* (NIV)

Ps 74:10   *<u>How long will the enemy mock you, O God</u>? Will the foe revile your name forever?* (NIV)

Ps 94:1-23   *O LORD, the God who avenges, O God who avenges, shine forth. Rise up, O Judge of the earth; pay back to the proud what they deserve. <u>How long will the wicked, O LORD, how long will the wicked be jubilant</u>? They pour out arrogant words; all the evildoers are full of boasting. They crush your people, O LORD; they oppress* *your inheritance. They slay the widow and the alien; they murder the fatherless. They say, "The LORD does not see; the God of Jacob pays no heed." Take heed, you senseless ones among the people; you fools, when will you become wise? Does he who implanted the ear not hear? Does he who formed the eye not see?* **Does he who disciplines nations not punish? Does he who teaches man lack knowledge? <u>The LORD knows the thoughts of man; he knows that they are futile.</u>** *Blessed is the man you discipline, O LORD, the man you teach from your law; you grant him relief from days of trouble, till a pit is dug for the wicked. For the LORD will not reject his people; he will never forsake his inheritance.* **<u>Judgment will again be founded on righteousness, and all the upright in heart will follow it.</u>** *Who will rise up for me against the wicked? Who will take a stand for me against evildoers? Unless the LORD had given me help, I would soon have dwelt in the silence of death. When I said, "My foot is slipping," your love, O LORD, supported me. When anxiety was great within me, your consolation brought joy to my soul. Can a corrupt throne be allied with you—one that brings on misery by its decrees? They band together against the righteous and condemn the innocent to death.* **But the LORD has become my fortress, and my God the rock in whom I take refuge. <u>He will repay them for their sins and destroy them for their wickedness; the LORD our God will destroy them.</u>** (NIV)

God has set a day, a time when He will judge the world.

Acts 17:24-31   *"The God who made the world and everything in it is the Lord of heaven and earth and does not live in temples built by hands. And he is not served by human hands, as if he needed anything, because he himself gives all men life and breath and everything else.* **<u>From one man he made every nation of men, that they should inhabit the whole earth; and he determined the times set for them and the exact places where they should live.</u>** *God did this so that men would seek him and perhaps reach out for him and find him, though he is not far from each one of us. 'For in him we live and move and have our being.' As some of your own poets have said, 'We are his offspring.' "Therefore since we are God's offspring, we should not think that the divine being is like gold or silver or stone—an image made by man's design and skill. In the past God overlooked such ignorance, but now he commands all people everywhere to repent.* **<u>For he has set a day when he will judge the world with justice by the man he has appointed.</u>** *He has given proof of this to all men by raising him from the dead."* (NIV)

The good news is that God is gracious enough to rescue His own from the future devastation. It is so clear in scripture, that God will take His own out of the world before He delivers His judgment, that it is hard to believe that there are those today that are teaching otherwise. God is a loving God!

1 Thes 1:10	*And to wait for his Son from heaven, whom he raised from the dead, **even Jesus, which delivered us from the wrath to come.*** (KJV)
Rev 3:10	*Since you have kept my command to endure patiently, **I will also keep you from the hour of trial that is going to come upon the whole world to test those who live on the earth.*** (NIV)
Rom 5:9	*Much more then, being now justified by his blood, **we shall be saved from wrath through him.*** (KJV)
1 Thes 5:9	***For God hath not appointed us to wrath**, but to obtain salvation by our Lord Jesus Christ,* (KJV)
Isa 26:20	*Go, my people, enter your rooms and shut the doors behind you; **hide yourselves for a little while until his wrath has passed by.*** (NIV)
Ps 27:5	*For in the day of trouble he will keep me safe in his dwelling; **he will hide me in the shelter of his tabernacle and set me high upon a rock.*** (NIV)

END OF THE AGE

What does Jesus mean when he says in Matthew 28:20, *"... And surely I am with you always, to the very end of the age?"* What is the end of the age? Jesus is referring to the end of the Christian age, also known as the Dispensation of Grace. If the Lord returns during our lifetime, as I firmly believe He will, it will have been 2000 years since He came in the flesh. According to 2 Peter 3:8, *"...With the Lord a day is like a thousand years, and a thousand years are like a day,"* this would mean two days or two thousand years. Two thousand years since Christ was crucified is fast approaching.

The Orthodox, Reform and Reconstructionist Jews, even today, do not believe that Jesus was the Messiah that they have been expecting for thousands of years. In Hosea 6:1-2, Hosea is making reference to unrepentant Israel. Because of unbelief, God has allowed the Jewish people to suffer terrible persecution for literally thousands of years; from their bondage in Egypt, through exile by the Assyrians and the Babylonians, from domination by the Greeks, through destruction of Jerusalem and their Temple by the Romans, and let us not forget the anti-Jewish and the Anti-Semitism the Jews have gone through during the Christian Dispensation. During the past two thousand-year period of time the Jews have suffered through the Crusades, the Black Death, the Inquisitions, and please do not forget the Holocaust of World War II. For some excellent reading concerning Israel's unbelief please read Romans chapter eleven.

In Hosea 6:1, he is referring to the punishment the Jewish people will suffer during the Time of Jacob's Trouble, because of their unbelief. He says, *"He has torn us to pieces...he has injured us."* Then look at verse two, where it says that the Lord will revive Israel after two days. I believe that these two days represent the two thousand years of the Dispensation of Grace. Then Hosea says that on the third day (last day of the last days) He will restore Israel so that they may live in His Presence. That is exactly what will happen during the Day of the Lord or the Millennium. Israel will be given the promised land and be set up as the head of all the nations of the world after their period of testing has been completed.

Because of the failure of the Jewish nation (people) to take God's precepts to the rest of the world, His Son was sent as a suffering servant and to be a light to the Gentiles. As a result of that, it is now time for the Church to take God's word to the world. Looking back on the history of the last two thousand years of the Christian Church, as a whole, reveals that the Church has not done a very good job of the task set before them. Notice below, that Jesus will also be the One who will bring the Jewish people back to God.

Isa 49:5-6 *And now the LORD says—he who formed me in the womb to be his servant to bring Jacob back to him and gather Israel to himself, for I am honored in the eyes of the LORD and my God has been my strength—he says: "It is too small a thing for you to be my servant to restore the tribes of Jacob and bring back those of Israel I have kept. I will also make you a light for the Gentiles, that you may bring my salvation to the ends of the earth."* (NIV)

Also notice that this is in agreement with Romans 11:19, where it speaks about the non-Jews being grafted into the olive tree. Please do not take this to mean that the church is to replace the Jews as far as what has been promised to the chosen people. This is only a temporary change until the Jews are grafted back into the olive tree. Only God is able to graft them back into the olive tree.

Rom 11:23 *And if they do not persist in unbelief, they will be grafted in, for God is able to graft them in again.* (NIV)

Now let us look at the New Testament perspective of why I think the end of the church age will be at the Rapture. As we take a look at Matthew 28:16-20, please notice that this is the great commission that Jesus gave to the eleven disciples on a mountain in Galilee. His command to them was, *"Therefore go and make disciples of all nations, baptizing them in the name of the Father and of the Son and of the Holy Spirit. And teaching them to obey everything I have commanded you. And surely I am with you always, to the very end of the age."*

The church age will end and Christ will have been with all believers until that age comes to an end. When it does end, Jesus will remove the true believers. It will then be time to complete an unfinished period mentioned by Daniel as a period of *"one seven"* or the last seven years of the 490-year period that will deal with His chosen people, Israel, and their city, Jerusalem. God will finish transgression, put an end to sin, atone for wickedness, bring in everlasting righteousness, seal up vision and prophecy and anoint the most holy. All of these events occur during the last day of one thousand years also known as the Day of the Lord or the Millennium. So Matthew 28:20 is a promise from God that He will be with the true believers during the times we are living in now. With the Holy Spirit as our *"Comforter,"* the Holy Spirit living in our hearts, He is fulfilling His promise and will do so until He takes His church out of the way. At the Rapture it will truly be the *"end of the age."* If you are a true believer in Jesus, please comfort yourselves with these words.

END OF INDIGNATION

Please do not confuse the end of the age with the end of indignation. The end of the age will close the church age or Dispensation of Grace and the end of indignation will end nine years later after the Tribulation Period is over. *Webster's Dictionary* has this to say about indignation: strong displeasure at something deemed unworthy, unjust, or base; righteous anger. Distinguishing between "the end of the age" and "the end of indignation" will help the flow of the chronological order of the times yet to come. To show the perspective of each, here are some verses concerning each of them.

END OF THE AGE

End of the age — Matt 24:3 *As Jesus was sitting on the Mount of Olives, the disciples came to him privately. "Tell us," they said, "when will this happen, and what will be the sign of your coming and of **the end of the age**?"* (NIV)

Matt 28:20 *"and teaching them to obey everything I have commanded you. And surely I am with you always, **to the very end of the age.**"* (NIV)

Time of the end — Dan 12:4 *But thou, O Daniel, shut up the words, and seal the book even to **the time of the end**: many shall run to and fro, and knowledge shall be increased.* (KJV)

End of days — Dan 12:13 *"As for you, go your way till the end. You will rest, and then at **the end of the days** you will rise to receive your allotted inheritance."* (NIV)

In Matthew 24:3, the disciples are asking Jesus about His coming at the end of the church age. This happens at the Rapture. In Matthew 28:20, Jesus is telling us that during the church age, He will be with us to the very end of this age. Daniel 12:4 and Daniel 12:13 are both referring to the end of the Dispensation of Grace when the message of Daniel will be unsealed and he will receive his resurrected body and his just reward. This end is the end of the days of man (6000 years). This ties in perfectly with the seven thousand year creation week theory of the Jewish sages from the past. If they are correct in their interpretation, we should be getting close to the end of the first six thousand years of the days of man.

AFTER THE RAPTURE

END OF INDIGNATION

Time of the End — <u>Dan 8:17</u> *As he came near the place where I was standing, I was terrified and fell prostrate. "Son of man," he said to me, "understand that the vision concerns **<u>the time of the end.</u>**"* (NIV)

The End — Daniel 12:7 furnishes us with a view of the last half of the Tribulation Period and reveals its length as 3 ½ years.
<u>Dan 12:7</u> *The man clothed in linen, who was above the waters of the river, lifted his right hand and his left hand toward heaven, and I heard him swear by him who lives forever, saying,* ***"It will be for a time, times and half a time. When the power of the holy people has been finally broken, all these things will be completed."*** (NIV)
<u>Matt 24:13-14</u> ***But he that shall endure unto <u>the end</u>, the same shall be saved. And this gospel of the kingdom shall be preached in all the world for a witness unto all nations; <u>and then shall the end come</u>.*** (KJV)

Daniel 8:17, is referring to the entire seven-year Tribulation Period, while Daniel 12:7 is referring to the last half of the Tribulation Period. In Matthew 24:13-14, it is speaking to those people who will go through the Tribulation Period. These activities will take place *After the Rapture*. This end spoken of here is the end of the Tribulation Period.

Scripture is speaking about two different events separated by a nine-year period. After the end of indignation, Jesus will set up His Kingdom on earth. So think of the *"end of the age"* as referring to the church when the time of the Dispensation of Grace ends and the *"end of indignation"* as the end of the time when God will judge all mankind with His fierce anger—the Tribulation Period. This end, is the end of the fierce anger of God upon sinful mankind. Only Armageddon, the final purging of sinful mankind, will remain after this.

SECOND COMING

I agree with the common thought of pre-tribulation prophecy teachers that the return of Jesus will take place in two stages. A secret return at the Rapture (in the air), as the first stage, and a Glorious Return after the Tribulation Period is completed (to the earth), as the second stage. The Rapture will occur when Jesus comes down from heaven to meet the resurrected saints in the air to take them home. This begins the Day of the Lord and the Day of Christ. At the end of the Tribulation Period Jesus will return to earth. That will be the Glorious Return and it will be the time when Jesus will be establishing His kingdom on earth, the one God established in heaven nine years earlier. What a glorious time it will be.

To end the Dispensation of Grace and begin the Kingdom Age, which includes both the Day of Christ in heaven and the Day of the Lord on the earth, there will come a shout from Jesus as He comes down from heaven. This shout will be a command for the saints to come up to heaven to meet Him in the clouds. Only the saints will hear this shout. The unbelievers could possibly hear a loud rumble from heaven. It will frighten those people who are left behind at the Rapture. The rumbling noise from heaven will resemble a loud trumpet. This scene will be something like Paul experienced when he was confronted by Jesus from heaven. Paul understood the voice from Jesus, but those around him did not understand.

Acts 22:6-11 *"About noon as I came near Damascus, suddenly a bright light from heaven flashed around me. <u>I fell to the ground and heard a voice say to me, 'Saul! Saul! Why do you persecute me?'</u> "'Who are you, Lord?' I asked. "'I am Jesus of Nazareth, whom you are persecuting,' he replied. <u>My companions saw the light, but they did not understand the voice of him who was speaking to me.</u> "'What shall I do, Lord?' I asked. "'Get up,' the Lord said, 'and go into Damascus. There you will be told all that you have been assigned to do.' My companions led me by the hand into Damascus, because the brilliance of the light had blinded me.* (NIV)

At the Rapture the people left on earth will be confused because of the amount of people who have died, which will cause chaos and mass confusion all around the world. In a sense, you can say this is the secret stage of the second coming of Jesus. Jesus will be fulfilling the promise that He made to the saints; that He would return to heaven, prepare a place for them and then return again for them. Jesus said that He would keep them from the hour of trial that is coming on the entire world. Only God knows when this event will transpire. It says repeatedly in scripture that nobody knows the day or the hour of the exact time of the Rapture. When the Signs of the Times begin to appear, we will know the general time of the Rapture. When these conditions begin to happen, we know that the return of our Savior is close at hand. We as believers in Jesus are of the light and are admonished to *"watch"* and be ready for His return. If we are ready—know Jesus as our personal Savior—we will be able to escape the horrible events that are about to happen and we will be able to stand before Jesus at the Judgment Seat of Christ. The season to sprout leaves is at hand, but

Mark 13:32 *"<u>No one knows about that day or hour</u>, not even the angels in heaven, nor the Son, but only the Father.* (NIV)

Luke 21:29-31 *He told them this parable: "<u>Look at the fig tree and all the trees</u>. <u>When they sprout leaves, you can see for yourselves and know that summer is near</u>. Even so, when you see these things happening, you know that the kingdom of God is near.* (NIV)

Matt 24:42 *"Therefore keep watch, <u>because you do not know on what day your Lord will come</u>.* (NIV)

Mark 13:33-37 *Be on guard! Be alert! <u>You do not know when that time will come</u>. It's like a man going away: He leaves his house and puts his servants in charge, each with his assigned task, and tells the one at the door*

AFTER THE RAPTURE

to keep watch. **"*Therefore keep watch** because you do not know when the owner of the house will come back—whether in the evening, or at midnight, or when the rooster crows, or at dawn. If he comes suddenly, do not let him find you sleeping.* *What I say to you, I say to everyone: '**Watch**!'"* (NIV)

1 Thes 5:4-6 ***But you, brothers, are not in darkness so that this day should surprise you like a thief.*** *You are all sons of the light and sons of the day. We do not belong to the night or to the darkness. So then, let us not be like others, who are asleep, but let us be alert and self-controlled.* (NIV)

Luke 21:36 ***Be always on the watch***, *and pray that you may be able to escape all that is about to happen, and that you may be able to stand before the Son of Man."* (NIV)

The best way to separate the two stages of the return of Jesus is to look at the two different Greek words used for each stage. Keep in mind that the word "Rapture" does not appear anywhere in the Bible. We get the word from the Latin word *raptus*. The primary word we are concerned with is *"coming"* and there are many Greek words that can be translated into this word. We will look at two of these words that apply to the second coming of Christ. First, we will look at the Greek word *parousia* (par-oo-see'-ah). This is the primary word used when referring to the first stage of the second coming of Christ. *Thayer's* incorrectly makes the statement that this is a visible return.

<u>Thayer's Greek Definition</u>
3952 parousia-
1) presence
2) a coming, an arrival, an advent;
   the future visible return from heaven of Jesus, to raise the dead, to hold the last judgment and set up formally and gloriously the kingdom of God

Parousia, is always translated as "coming" or "presence." At the Rapture, the people left behind on the earth will not see the coming of Jesus or the ascending of the saints as they rendezvous in the air. Contrary to teaching today, our present earthly bodies will not be caught up to heaven. These bodies (natural) will be left behind on earth as the saints receive their glorious (spiritual) bodies. Let us look at some verses that use the word *parousia*.

Matt 24:3 *As Jesus was sitting on the Mount of Olives, the disciples came to him privately. "Tell us," they said, "when will this happen, and what will be the sign of your **coming** and of the end of the age?"* (NIV)

Matt 24:37-42 *As it was in the days of Noah, so it will be at the **coming** of the Son of Man. For in the days before the flood, people were eating and*

186

*drinking, marrying and giving in marriage, up to the day Noah entered the ark; and they knew nothing about what would happen until the flood came and took them all away. That is how it will be at the **coming** of the Son of Man. Two men will be in the field; one will be taken and the other left. Two women will be grinding with a hand mill; one will be taken and the other left. "Therefore keep watch, because you do not know on what day your Lord will come.* (NIV)

From the verses in Matthew 24:37-42, we see that some of the people on earth at the time of the Rapture will be taken to meet Jesus and some of them will be left on the earth. Do not be left behind! Paul assured the people in Thessalonica that if anyone died (fell asleep) before Christ returned for His own, they would be with Jesus at the time of the Rapture, when He returns from heaven to gather those who remain alive at His coming.

1 Thes 4:13-18   ***Brothers, we do not want you to be ignorant about those who fall asleep, or to grieve like the rest of men, who have no hope. We believe that Jesus died and rose again and so we believe that God will bring with Jesus those who have fallen asleep in him.*** *According to the Lord's own word, we tell you that we who are still alive, who are left till the **coming** of the Lord, **will certainly not precede those who have fallen asleep.** For the Lord himself will come down from heaven, with a loud command, with the voice of the archangel and with the trumpet call of God, **and the dead in Christ will rise first.** After that, we who are still alive and are left will be caught up together with them in the clouds to meet the Lord in the air.* ***And so we will be with the Lord forever.*** *Therefore encourage each other with these words.* (NIV)

Be patient and stand firm in your faith, because Jesus is coming soon.

James 5:7-8   *Be patient, then, brothers, until the Lord's **coming**. See how the farmer waits for the land to yield its valuable crop and how patient he is for the autumn and spring rains. You too, be patient and stand firm, because the Lord's **coming** is near.* (NIV)

Peter made it a point to remind us to be sure we are truly saved, so we can receive a rich welcome into the eternal kingdom of God in heaven, where Jesus will take the saints *After the Rapture*. Please take note here that Jesus made it clear to Peter that when he died, he would leave his natural body behind as his soul and spirit returns to heaven to await the time for a resurrected (spiritual) body.

2 Pet 1:10-16   ***Therefore, my brothers, be all the more eager to make your calling and election sure. For if you do these things, you will never fall, and you will receive a rich welcome into the eternal kingdom of our***

Lord and Savior Jesus Christ. So I will always remind you of these things, even though you know them and are firmly established in the truth you now have. I think it is right to refresh your memory as long as I live in the tent of this body, because I know that I will soon put it aside, as our Lord Jesus Christ has made clear to me. And I will make every effort to see that after my departure you will always be able to remember these things. We did not follow cleverly invented stories when we told you about the power and **_coming_** of our Lord Jesus Christ, but we were eyewitnesses of his majesty. (NIV)

Peter also lets us know that there will be scoffers who will mock us about the promised coming of Jesus. Remember that all of these verses have the Greek word *parousia* in them.

2 Pet 3:3-4 *First of all, you must understand that in the last days scoffers will come, scoffing and following their own evil desires. They will say, "Where is this **'coming'** he promised? Ever since our fathers died, everything goes on as it has since the beginning of creation."* (NIV)

Paul is clearly making a reference to the Rapture in these verses.

2 Thes 2:1 *Concerning the **_coming_** of our Lord Jesus Christ and our being gathered to him, we ask you, brothers,* (NIV)

1 Thes 3:13 *May he strengthen your hearts so that you will be blameless and holy in the presence of our God and Father when our Lord Jesus **_comes_** with all his holy ones.* (NIV)

In 1 Thessalonians 3:13, we see Jesus as He leads the saints into the presence of God the Father, after their rendezvous in the air where Jesus gathers them. Our hope and joy are in Jesus when He comes for us.

1 Thes 2:19 *For what is our hope, our joy, or the crown in which we will glory in the presence of our Lord Jesus when he **_comes_**? Is it not you?* (NIV)

As we live out our lives here on earth, we need to live them in such a way that we will be blameless when Jesus comes back to earth. That includes both those who have died before He comes and those who remain alive at His coming.

1 Thes 5:23 *May God himself, the God of peace, sanctify you through and through. May your whole spirit, soul and body be kept blameless at the **_coming_** of our Lord Jesus Christ.* (NIV)

1 John 2:28 *And now, dear children, continue in him, so that when he appears we*

*may be confident and unashamed before him at his **coming**.* (NIV)

A point of interest can be found in 1 Thessalonians 4:17, where we find the phrase *"shall be caught up,"* the Greek word *harpazo* means; to seize, catch (away, up), to carry off by force, to claim for oneself eagerly, to snatch away. Compare this with the parallel Hebrew word `alah which can mean; to ascend, to be taken away, to bring up or arise. All of the above verses translate the word *parousia* as "coming" or "comes" and they all refer to the first stage of the second coming of Christ, also known as the Rapture.

The Greek word that is usually used when referring to the second stage of the second coming of Jesus is *erchomai* (er'-khom-ahee). This second stage of the return of Jesus is commonly referred to as "the Glorious Return."

Thayer's Greek Definition
2064 erchomai-
1) to come; used of persons:
1) to come from one place to another, and used both of persons arriving
2) to appear, make one's appearance, to come before the public
2) metaphorically:
   a) to come into being, to arise, to come forth, to show itself, to find place or influence
   b) to be established, to become known, to come (fall) into or unto
3) to go, to follow one

The most common translation for *erchomai* is "to come" and then "came." Occasionally it is translated as "coming," especially when it is speaking about the Glorious appearing of Jesus. Unlike the Rapture, where the people left on the earth do not see Jesus when He comes for the saints, at the Glorious Return, every person who is remaining on earth (after the wrath of God has run its course) will see Jesus coming on the clouds. He is literally coming to appear before the public (mankind).

Matt 24:30   *"At that time the sign of the Son of Man will appear in the sky, and all the nations of the earth will mourn. They will see the Son of Man **coming** on the clouds of the sky, with power and great glory.* (NIV)

Rev 1:7   *Look, he is **coming** with the clouds, and every eye will see him, even those who pierced him; and all the peoples of the earth will mourn because of him. So shall it be! Amen.* (NIV)

Matt 16:27   *For the Son of Man is going **to come** in his Father's glory with his angels, and then he will reward each person according to what he has done.* (NIV)

Matt 25:31   *"When the Son of Man **comes** in his glory, and all the angels with him, he will sit on his throne in heavenly glory.* (NIV)

AFTER THE RAPTURE

Matt 26:64 *"Yes, it is as you say," Jesus replied. "But I say to all of you: In the future you will see the Son of Man sitting at the right hand of the Mighty One and **coming** on the clouds of heaven." (NIV)*

Luke 21:27 *At that time they will see the Son of Man **coming** in a cloud with power and great glory. (NIV)*

This set of verses, above, all have the Greek word *erchomai*, where it refers to the second coming of Jesus, which is referring to His Glorious Return. Notice here that Jesus is referred to as the Son of Man. Some of the differences that separate the Rapture from the Glorious Return of Jesus are:

1. Rapture – **No one knows the exact time** when Jesus will come
   Glorious Return – Jesus is coming **immediately following the Tribulation Period**

2. Rapture – The saints wait in **joyful anticipation** for Jesus to appear
   Glorious Return – The people on earth **wail** because of His glorious appearance

3. Rapture – Jesus is coming **before** He is crowned King
   Glorious Return – Jesus is coming **after** He has been crowned King

4. Rapture – Jesus is coming **as the Lamb** of God (meekly)
   Glorious Return – Jesus is coming **as the Lion** from the tribe of Judah (at Armageddon)

5. Rapture – Jesus is coming **for** those living church age saints (in Christ)
   Glorious Return – Jesus is coming **with** the Tribulation saints (at Armageddon)

In the Old Testament, there is no mention of the Rapture. It was hidden and was not supposed to be revealed until after Christ was rejected, but there are many references to a resurrection. What can be found in the Old Testament are numerous references to Jesus as He comes back to earth to judge and to the final judgment of the unsaved people who are left after the Tribulation Period is completed. The Hebrew word for "coming," that we are concerned with, is *bow'* (bo) and is a correlation to the Greek word *erchomai* found in the New Testament. Most of the references to the return of the Lord (Jesus) in the Old Testament are in reference to the Battle of Armageddon, when the final judgment of the nations will take place. This being the final act of purging the wicked from the earth.

Zech 14:5 *Then you shall flee through My mountain valley, for the mountain valley shall reach to Azal. Yes, you shall flee as you fled from the earthquake in the days of Uzziah king of Judah. Thus the LORD my God will **come,** and all the saints with You. (NKJ)*

Isa 66:15-16 *See, the LORD is **coming** with fire, and his chariots are like a*

1948 to the Rapture

whirlwind; he will bring down his anger with fury, and his rebuke with flames of fire. For with fire and with his sword the LORD will execute judgment upon all men, and many will be those slain by the LORD. (NIV)

Ps 98:9 *let them sing before the LORD, for he **comes** to judge the earth. He will judge the world in righteousness and the peoples with equity.* (NIV)

Ps 97:1-6 *The LORD reigns, let the earth be glad; let the distant shores rejoice. Clouds and thick darkness surround him; righteousness and justice are the foundation of his throne. Fire goes before him and consumes his foes on every side.* **His lightning lights up the world; the earth sees and trembles.** *The mountains melt like wax before the LORD, before the Lord of all the earth.* **The heavens proclaim his righteousness, and all the peoples see his glory.** (NIV)

Isa 40:10 *See, the Sovereign LORD **comes** with power, and his arm rules for him. See, his reward is with him, and his recompense accompanies him.* (NIV)

Isa 62:11 *The LORD has made proclamation to the ends of the earth: "Say to the Daughter of Zion, 'See, your Savior **comes**! See, his reward is with him, and his recompense accompanies him.'"* (NIV)

An interesting point needs to be made here: Israel as a nation will finally recognize Jesus (Yeshua) as their Messiah (the anointed one) after the Tribulation Period is over. When Jesus appears in heaven in all of His Glory, the Jewish people (those who are saved) will finally recognize the one whom they pierced.

Rev 1:7 **Look, he is _coming_ with the clouds, and every eye will see him, _even those who pierced him_; and all the peoples of the earth will mourn because of him. So shall it be! Amen.** (NIV)

After the Battle of Armageddon, all the Jewish people who remain on earth will know Jesus as the Messiah, thus, all Israel will be saved. Jesus is their salvation (deliverer). It is no accident that the Hebrew word for "Jesus" is *yeshuw`ah* (yesh-oo' aw), it can be spelled Jeshua, Y'shua, Yeshua or Yahshua. Yeshua comes from the Hebrew word *yesha`*, which comes from the root word *yasha* (which means; to save, to be saved, to be delivered, to be victorious) and it is translated as:

Brown-Driver-Brigg's Hebrew Definition
3468 yesha` or yesha`-
deliverance, salvation, rescue, safety, welfare

AFTER THE RAPTURE

a) safety, welfare, prosperity
b) salvation
c) victory

Often times translators could have used the word "deliver" instead of "save" when translating this word. Salvation and deliverance will come from the one who is the deliverer (Jesus). I believe that this says it all, need I add more? Jesus is truly **_salvation_**!

> Ps 18:2   *The LORD is my rock, my fortress and **my deliverer;** my God is my rock, in whom I take refuge. He is my shield and the horn of my **salvation**, my stronghold.* (NIV)

> Rom 11:26   ***And so all Israel will be saved**, as it is written: "**The deliverer will come from Zion**; he will turn Godlessness away from Jacob.*** (NIV)

Although the world will be getting farther and farther from God, what will everyday life be like just prior to the end of the age? It will be business as usual. Jesus likens the time to the days of Noah. People were mocking Noah about his prediction of the coming flood. They did this right up to the time of the flood. Then it was too late. The flood came and destroyed them all. This is what it will be like at the end of the age. People will be living out their lives in a normal day-by-day fashion. There will be a small number of saved people living on earth at this time, but the majority will be unsaved, even among members of the churches. Some will even mock the Christians about the coming of the Lord, with most of the supposed Christians teaching a false gospel. It will be exactly like it is today in the world right up to the time of the Rapture. Then things will turn progressively worse.

> Luke 17:26-27   ***"Just as it was in the days of Noah, so also will it be in the days of the Son of Man**. People were eating, drinking, marrying and being given in marriage up to the day Noah entered the ark. **Then the flood came and destroyed them all**.*** (NIV)

This brings us up to the next prophetic event to occur at the end of the age and I believe it could very well happen in our lifetime. The Rapture! The Rapture should not catch the true church by surprise. With the signs that are being revealed to us today, we should know that the imminent return of our Lord is at hand. Even though there will be various skirmishes and wars, including the Israeli/Arab conflict in progress, the rest of the world will be living fairly peacefully. After two major World Wars in the last century, the world today is living in a state of relative peace and safety. This includes the current war on terrorism which is being fought by the United States and the rest of the world.

> 1 Thes 5:1-11   *Now, brothers, about times and dates we do not need to write to you, for you know very well that **the day of the Lord** will come like a thief in the night. While people are saying, "**Peace and safety**," destruction will come on them suddenly, as labor pains on a*

*pregnant woman, and they will not escape. But you, brothers, are not in darkness so that <u>this day</u> should surprise you like a thief. You are all sons of the light and sons of the day. We do not belong to the night or to the darkness. So then, let us not be like others, who are asleep, but let us be alert and self-controlled. For those who sleep, sleep at night, and those who get drunk, get drunk at night. But since we belong to the day, let us be self-controlled, putting on faith and love as a breastplate, and the hope of salvation as a helmet. <u>**For God did not appoint us to suffer wrath but to receive salvation through our Lord Jesus Christ.**</u> **He died for us so that, whether we are awake or asleep, we may live together with him. <u>Therefore encourage one another and build each other up, just as in fact you are doing.</u>*** (NIV)

In 2 Thessalonians, we are told that two events must occur before the gathering of the saints will take place. These verses reveal that the Rapture—the coming of Jesus to meet the saints in the air—signals the start of the Day of the Lord. Just because we might be going through periods of extreme persecution, it warns us not to be deceived by people saying that the Day of the Lord has already come. Two things have to happen before the Rapture takes place and the Day of the Lord begins. The apostasy or religious falling away from God and the revealing of the Antichrist will have to happen before the saints are gathered together to meet Jesus in the air. We do not need to let what is taking place on the world scene today alarm us, although we may become concerned. In God's time Jesus will come for His own.

2 Thes 2:1-3   *Concerning the coming of our Lord Jesus Christ and our being gathered to him, we ask you, brothers, not to become easily unsettled or alarmed by some prophecy, report or letter supposed to have come from us, saying that the day of the Lord has already come. Don't let anyone deceive you in any way, <u>for that day will not come until the rebellion occurs and the man of lawlessness is revealed</u>, the man doomed to destruction.* (NIV)

If the world is currently in a state of extreme apostasy, which it is, that means that the Antichrist is probably living somewhere in the world today. I think it is plain to see that even the Christian Church is so lukewarm today that what the apostasy Paul was speaking about is probably taking place before our very eyes. Even though the Antichrist is revealed before the Rapture, he is restrained by the Holy Spirit. A lot of people today are accused of being the Antichrist. People will continue to try to figure out who he is, but most will probably be wrong. As I said before, some people will actually figure out who he is. All the Signs of the Time are in place for the return of Jesus Christ.

2 Thes 2:5-6   *Don't you remember that when I was with you I used to tell you these things? <u>And now you know what is holding him back, so that he may be revealed at the proper time.</u>* (NIV)

AFTER THE RAPTURE

As sure as Jesus came the first time, He will return a second time to take His own out of the way, so He can begin His judgment. He will remain in heaven at the right hand of God until He comes back at the Rapture. Notice that when a person accepts Jesus, as their Savior, it becomes times of refreshing for them from the Lord. Jesus is about to appear a second time to bring salvation (deliverance) to those who are waiting for Him.

WHERE DO YOU STAND?

Acts 3:17-26 — *"Now, brothers, I know that you acted in ignorance, as did your leaders. But this is how God fulfilled what he had foretold through all the prophets, saying that his Christ would suffer.* **Repent, then, and turn to God, so that your sins may be wiped out, <u>that times of refreshing may come from the Lord</u>, and that he may send the Christ, who has been appointed for you—even Jesus. He must remain in heaven until the time comes for God to restore everything, as he promised long ago through his holy prophets.** *For Moses said, 'The Lord your God will raise up for you a prophet like me from among your own people; you must listen to everything he tells you. Anyone who does not listen to him will be completely cut off from among his people.'* **"<u>Indeed, all the prophets from Samuel on, as many as have spoken, have foretold these days</u>.** *And you are heirs of the prophets and of the covenant God made with your fathers. He said to Abraham, 'Through your offspring all peoples on earth will be blessed.'* **<u>When God raised up his servant, he sent him first to you to bless you by turning each of you from your wicked ways</u>."** (NIV)

1 Sam 2:9-10 — *<u>He will guard the feet of his saints, but the wicked will be silenced in darkness.</u> "It is not by strength that one prevails; those who oppose the LORD will be shattered. <u>He will thunder against them from heaven; the LORD will judge the ends of the earth.</u> "He will give strength to his king and exalt the horn of his anointed."* (NIV)

Heb 9:28 — *so Christ was sacrificed once to take away the sins of many people; <u>and he will appear a second time, not to bear sin, but to bring salvation to those who are waiting for him</u>.* (NIV)

John 14:1-3 — *Let not your heart be troubled: ye believe in God, believe also in me. In my Father's house are many mansions: if it were not so, I would have told you.* ***I go to prepare a place for you. And if I go and prepare a place for you, <u>I will come again, and receive you unto myself; that where I am, there ye may be also</u>.*** (KJV)

CHAPTER EIGHT

AFTER THE RAPTURE
AND
BEFORE THE TRIBULATION PERIOD

This is the chapter that prompted me to write this book. Several things were very puzzling for me, starting several years after I started studying Bible prophecy. Most of the books that concern the study of the end times usually begin the Tribulation Period at the Rapture of the church and before the Millennium, and is known as Premillennialism. I could not put a chronological order of events together that would apply to scripture and conform to current eschatological teachings by using this theory.

My biggest problem was I could never understand how the Tribulation Period could start right *After the Rapture.* How can the Antichrist be revealed (2 Thessalonians 2:3), make a 7-Year Peace Treaty (Daniel 9:27), and start his conquest to take over the whole earth all on the same day (Revelation 6:1-2)?

2 Thes 2:3 *Don't let anyone deceive you in any way, **for that day will not come until the rebellion occurs and the man of lawlessness is revealed**, the man doomed to destruction.* (NIV)

Dan 9:27 ***He will confirm a covenant with many for one 'seven.'*** *In the middle of the 'seven' he will put an end to sacrifice and offering. And on a wing [of the temple] he will set up an abomination that causes desolation, until the end that is decreed is poured out on him."* (NIV)

Rev 6:1-2 *I watched as the Lamb opened the first of the seven seals. Then I heard one of the four living creatures say in a voice like thunder, **"Come!" I looked, and there before me was a white horse! Its rider held a bow, and he was given a crown, and he rode out as a conqueror bent on conquest.*** (NIV)

Along with all that, I could not understand how Russia could attack Israel while they were living in "peace and safety," especially with times like we are living in today! Although the Jewish people are back in their land, they are not living in a land of unwalled villages (without protection). In these days turmoil seems to be Israel's middle name.

Ezek 38:8 *After many days you will be called to arms. In future years you will invade a land that has recovered from war, whose people were gathered from many nations to the mountains of Israel, which had long been desolate.* ***They had been brought out from the nations, and now all of them live in safety.*** (NIV

Ezek 38:11 *You will say, "**I will invade a land of unwalled villages; I will***

AFTER THE RAPTURE

attack a peaceful and unsuspecting people—all of them living without walls and without gates and bars. (NIV)

Ezek 38:14   *"Therefore, son of man, prophesy and say to Gog: 'This is what the Sovereign LORD says: In that day, when my people Israel are living in safety, will you not take notice of it?* (NIV)

There has to be some events occurring between the Rapture and the beginning of the Tribulation Period for the Jewish people to be living in safety in their land. There has to be some time after the Antichrist has his restraint removed before he can negotiate a 7-Year Peace Treaty. There has to be some time for the Antichrist to gain enough power and authority to start his one-world conquest.

The best and most complete picture of the beginning of the Day of the Lord (the first ten years) is found in chapter twenty-four of Isaiah. It covers the period of time from the Rapture on through to the time when Jesus sets up His kingdom on earth. Most devastating will be the last 3 ½ years of the Tribulation Period followed by the Battle of Armageddon.

Isa 24:1-23   *See, the LORD is going to lay waste the earth and devastate it; he will ruin its face and scatter its inhabitants; it will be the same for priest as for people, for master as for servant, for mistress as for maid, for seller as for buyer, for borrower as for lender, for debtor as for creditor. The earth will be completely laid waste and totally plundered. The LORD has spoken this word. The earth dries up and withers, the world languishes and withers, the exalted of the earth languish. The earth is defiled by its people; they have disobeyed the laws, violated the statutes and broken the everlasting covenant. Therefore a curse consumes the earth; its people must bear their guilt. Therefore earth's inhabitants are burned up, and very few are left. The new wine dries up and the vine withers; all the merrymakers groan. The gaiety of the tambourines is stilled, the noise of the revelers has stopped, the joyful harp is silent. No longer do they drink wine with a song; the beer is bitter to its drinkers. The ruined city lies desolate; the entrance to every house is barred. In the streets they cry out for wine; all joy turns to gloom, all gaiety is banished from the earth. The city is left in ruins, its gate is battered to pieces. So will it be on the earth and among the nations, as when an olive tree is beaten, or as when gleanings are left after the grape harvest. They raise their voices, they shout for joy; from the west they acclaim the LORD's majesty. Therefore in the east give glory to the LORD; exalt the name of the LORD, the God of Israel, in the islands of the sea. From the ends of the earth we hear singing: "Glory to the Righteous One." But I said, "I waste away, I waste away! Woe to me! The treacherous betray! With treachery the treacherous betray!" Terror and pit and snare await you, O people of the earth. Whoever*

After the Rapture and Before the Tribulation Period

> *flees at the sound of terror will fall into a pit; whoever climbs out of the pit will be caught in a snare. The floodgates of the heavens are opened, the foundations of the earth shake.* ***The earth is broken up, the earth is split asunder, the earth is thoroughly shaken.*** *The earth reels like a drunkard, it sways like a hut in the wind; so heavy upon it is the guilt of its rebellion that it falls—never to rise again.* ***<u>In that day the LORD will punish the powers in the heavens above and the kings on the earth below.</u>*** *They will be herded together like prisoners bound in a dungeon; they will be shut up in prison and be punished after many days.* ***The moon will be abashed, the sun ashamed; <u>for the LORD Almighty will reign on Mount Zion and in Jerusalem</u>, and before its elders, gloriously.*** (NIV)

Some Bible historians believe that this was fulfilled in Jerusalem in 586 BC, but these verses explain what will happen on earth during the doom and gloom portion of the Day of the Lord. Its destruction will take a little more than nine years to complete. It will include:

1. the face of the earth will be ruined (verse 1)
2. all the people on the earth will be effected (verse 2)
3. very few people are left on the earth at the end of this period (verse 6)
4. music and happiness are banished during this period (verse 6, 11)
5. Jerusalem is destroyed for the last time (verse 12)
6. the earth is thoroughly shaken (verse 19)
7. the Lord will punish: (verse 21)
    a. Satan and the fallen angels in heaven
    b. leaders of the nations on earth
8. the sun and moon will be turned to darkness (verse 23)
9. Jesus (the LORD Almighty-NIV and the LORD of hosts-KJV) will be reigning from His throne in heaven on Mount Zion at this time (verse 23)

No where in scripture have I found a more concise and complete description of the entire hour of trial that is coming upon the whole earth. God has been telling people about it for a long time, but the complete understanding of the meaning of it is reserved until the end of the age. At the proper time, when mankind needs to understand it, the meaning will be unsealed and given to His own. As far back in time as when Adam was living on earth, one of God's prophets predicted (before the flood) the events that will culminate when God judges during the future period of time we are studying in this book. A judgment for man and even the angels.

> Jude 1:14-15 *Enoch, the seventh from Adam, prophesied about these men: "<u>See, the Lord is coming with thousands upon thousands of his holy ones to judge everyone</u>, and to convict all the ungodly of all the ungodly acts they have done in the ungodly way, and of all the harsh words ungodly sinners have spoken against him."* (NIV)

Once again, God warned the Israelites about the last days. At the time, just before Jacob died (around 1885 BC), he called his twelve sons together and gave a discourse to them on what would collectively happen to their succeeding or future generations in the last days. This is a description of what would befall the people of Israel (the twelve tribes of Israel) after Jesus comes to earth during the last day of the last days (the Day of the Lord).

> Gen 49:1-2 — **And Jacob called unto his sons, and said, Gather yourselves together, <u>that I may tell you that which shall befall you in the last days</u>. Gather yourselves together, and hear, ye sons of Jacob; and hearken unto Israel your father.** (KJV)

It is worth repeating the message given to his son Judah. The lineage of the Messiah will flow through Judah. Shiloh is Jesus Christ and the Jews will be obedient to Him (this will happen after the Tribulation Period). The first advent of Jesus is pictured by revealing the tying of a donkey to a vine and then Jesus is pictured at the Battle of Armageddon. From these verses, Jesus picks up the title—the Lion from the tribe of Judah.

> Gen. 49:8-12 — *"Judah, you are he whom your brothers shall praise; your hand shall be on the neck of your enemies; your father's children shall bow down before you. <u>Judah is a lion's whelp; from the prey, my son, you have gone up. He bows down, he lies down as a lion; and as a lion, who shall rouse him?</u> <u>The scepter shall not depart from Judah</u>, <u>nor a lawgiver from between his feet</u>, <u>until Shiloh comes</u>; and to Him shall be the obedience of the people. Binding his donkey to the vine, and his donkey's colt to the choice vine, <u>he washed his garments in wine</u>, <u>and his clothes in the blood of grapes</u>. His eyes are darker than wine, and his teeth whiter than milk.* (NKJ)

Next, we move forward to the time when the Israelites are about to enter the promised land (1405 BC). Moses is near death and will pass the leadership of the people to Joshua. Moses calls all the people together to tell them that God is renewing the covenant He made with Abraham, Isaac and Jacob. This discourse covers the period from 1405 BC (their time) on through to the Battle of Armageddon, which will be the last time God shows His furious anger and pours down His great wrath. Notice the complete devastation of the land of Israel.

> Deut 29:1-29 — *These are the terms of the covenant the LORD commanded Moses to make with the Israelites in Moab, in addition to the covenant he had made with them at Horeb. Moses summoned all the Israelites and said to them: Your eyes have seen all that the LORD did in Egypt to Pharaoh, to all his officials and to all his land. With your own eyes you saw those great trials, those miraculous signs and great wonders. But to this day the LORD has not given you a mind that understands or eyes that see or ears that hear. During the forty years that I led you through the desert, your clothes did not wear out, nor*

After the Rapture and Before the Tribulation Period

*did the sandals on your feet. You ate no bread and drank no wine or other fermented drink. I did this so that you might know that I am the LORD your God. When you reached this place, Sihon king of Heshbon and Og king of Bashan came out to fight against us, but we defeated them. We took their land and gave it as an inheritance to the Reubenites, the Gadites and the half-tribe of Manasseh. Carefully follow the terms of this covenant, so that you may prosper in everything you do. All of you are standing today in the presence of the LORD your God—your leaders and chief men, your elders and officials, and all the other men of Israel, together with your children and your wives, and the aliens living in your camps who chop your wood and carry your water. You are standing here in order to enter into a covenant with the LORD your God, a covenant the LORD is making with you this day and sealing with an oath, to confirm you this day as his people, that he may be your God as he promised you and as he swore to your fathers, **Abraham, Isaac and Jacob. I am making this covenant, with its oath, not only with you who are standing here with us today in the presence of the LORD our God <u>but also with those who are not here today.</u>** You yourselves know how we lived in Egypt and how we passed through the countries on the way here. You saw among them their detestable images and idols of wood and stone, of silver and gold. Make sure there is no man or woman, clan or tribe among you today whose heart turns away from the LORD our God to go and worship the gods of those nations; make sure there is no root among you that produces such bitter poison. When such a person hears the words of this oath, he invokes a blessing on himself and therefore thinks, "I will be safe, even though I persist in going my own way." This will bring disaster on the watered land as well as the dry. The LORD will never be willing to forgive him; his wrath and zeal will burn against that man. All the curses written in this book will fall upon him, and the LORD will blot out his name from under heaven. The LORD will single him out from all the tribes of Israel for disaster, according to all the curses of the covenant written in this Book of the Law. <u>**Your children who follow you in later generations and foreigners who come from distant lands**</u> **will see the calamities that have fallen on the land and the diseases with which the LORD has afflicted it. <u>The whole land will be a burning waste of salt and sulfur—nothing planted, nothing sprouting, no vegetation growing on it. It will be like the destruction of Sodom and Gomorrah,</u> Admah and Zeboiim, which the LORD overthrew in fierce anger. All the nations will ask: "<u>Why has the LORD done this to this land? Why this fierce, burning anger?</u>" And the answer will be: "<u>It is because this people abandoned the covenant of the LORD, the God of their fathers, the</u>***

covenant he made with them when he brought them out of Egypt. They went off and worshiped other gods and bowed down to them, gods they did not know, gods he had not given them. Therefore the LORD's anger burned against this land, so that he brought on it all the curses written in this book. In furious anger and in great wrath the LORD uprooted them from their land and thrust them into another land, as it is now." The secret things belong to the LORD our God, but the things revealed belong to us and to our children forever, that we may follow all the words of this law. (NIV)

Continuing in chapter thirty, the story is a picture of the chosen people after the Battle of Armageddon has taken place and they have accepted Jesus as their Messiah.

Deut 30:1-10 *When all these blessings and curses I have set before you come upon you and you take them to heart wherever the LORD your God disperses you among the nations, <u>and when you and your children return to the LORD your God and obey him with all your heart and with all your soul according to everything I command you today, then the LORD your God will restore your fortunes and have compassion on you and gather you again from all the nations where he scattered you.</u> Even if you have been banished to the most distant land under the heavens, from there the LORD your God will gather you and bring you back. He will bring you to the land that belonged to your fathers, and you will take possession of it. He will make you more prosperous and numerous than your fathers. The LORD your God will circumcise your hearts and the hearts of your descendants, so that you may love him with all your heart and with all your soul, and live. The LORD your God will put all these curses on your enemies who hate and persecute you. <u>You will again obey the LORD and follow all his commands I am giving you today.</u> Then the LORD your God will make you most prosperous in all the work of your hands and in the fruit of your womb, the young of your livestock and the crops of your land. The LORD will again delight in you and make you prosperous, just as he delighted in your fathers, if you obey the LORD your God and keep his commands and decrees that are written in this Book of the Law and turn to the LORD your God with all your heart and with all your soul.* (NIV)

A thousand years before Christ, we see the king of Israel, David, mention the Day of the Lord's wrath in Psalms 110. Jesus (the Lord at thy right hand) will judge the nations.

Ps 110:5-6 <u>*The Lord at thy right hand shall strike through kings in the day of his wrath.*</u> *He shall judge among the heathen, he shall fill the*

> *places with the dead bodies; he shall wound the heads over many countries.* (KJV)

The bulk of the teachings, concerning the Day of the Lord, are interspersed in the writings of the classical prophets. The major and minor prophets cover a time period from the middle of the eighth century to the beginning of the fifth century (760 BC to 400 BC). Listen to their teachings about the beginning of the Day of the Lord.

> Isa 2:12-17 — **_The LORD Almighty has a day in store for all the proud and lofty, for all that is exalted (and they will be humbled),_** *for all the cedars of Lebanon, tall and lofty, and all the oaks of Bashan, for all the towering mountains and all the high hills, for every lofty tower and every fortified wall, for every trading ship and every stately vessel.* **_The arrogance of man will be brought low and the pride of men humbled;_** *the LORD alone will be exalted in that day,* (NIV)

> Isa 13:6-9 — **_Wail, for the day of the LORD is near; it will come like destruction from the Almighty._** *Because of this, all hands will go limp, every man's heart will melt. Terror will seize them, pain and anguish will grip them; they will writhe like a woman in labor. They will look aghast at each other, their faces aflame. See, the day of the LORD is coming a cruel day, with wrath and fierce anger—to make the land desolate and destroy the sinners within it.* (NIV)

Isaiah even makes the comment that God foretold what was to happen long before his time. Isaiah probably made this statement around 690 BC.

> Isa 44:6-8 — *"This is what the LORD says—Israel's King and Redeemer, the LORD Almighty: I am the first and I am the last; apart from me there is no God. Who then is like me? Let him proclaim it. Let him declare and lay out before me what has happened since I established my ancient people, and what is yet to come—yes, let him foretell what will come. Do not tremble, do not be afraid.* **_Did I not proclaim this and foretell it long ago? You are my witnesses. Is there any God besides me? No, there is no other Rock; I know not one._** *"* (NIV)

Some of the other prophets had this to say:

> Ezek 30:3 — *For the day is near, the day of the LORD is near—a day of clouds, a time of doom for the nations.* (NIV)

> Jer 10:10 — *But the LORD is the true God; he is the living God, the eternal King.* **_When he is angry, the earth trembles; the nations cannot endure his wrath._** (NIV)

AFTER THE RAPTURE

Joel 1:15 — *Alas for the day! for the day of the LORD is at hand, and as a destruction from the Almighty shall it come.* (KJV)

Amos 5:18-20 — *Woe to you who long for the day of the LORD! Why do you long for the day of the LORD? That day will be darkness, not light. It will be as though a man fled from a lion only to meet a bear, as though he entered his house and rested his hand on the wall only to have a snake bite him.* **Will not the day of the LORD be darkness, not light—pitch-dark, without a ray of brightness?** (NIV)

Obad 1:15-16 — "**The day of the LORD is near for all nations.** *As you have done, it will be done to you; your deeds will return upon your own head. Just as you drank on my holy hill, so all the nations will drink continually; they will drink and drink and be as if they had never been.* (NIV)

Zeph 1:2-3 — "**I will sweep away everything from the face of the earth,**" **declares the LORD.** "*I will sweep away both men and animals; I will sweep away the birds of the air and the fish of the sea.* **The wicked will have only heaps of rubble when I cut off man from the face of the earth,**" *declares the LORD.* (NIV)

Mal 4:5 — "*See, I will send you the prophet Elijah before that great and dreadful day of the LORD comes.* (NIV)

Four hundred years after Malachi, the last prophet in the Old Testament, the New Testament writers continued the teachings on the Day of the Lord. The Day of the Lord is the set time when God will judge the world with justice by the man He has appointed. That man is Jesus Christ.

Luke 21:34-36 — "*Be careful, or your hearts will be weighed down with dissipation, drunkenness and the anxieties of life, and that day will close on you unexpectedly like a trap.* **For it will come upon all those who live on the face of the whole earth.** *Be always on the watch, and pray that you may be able to escape all that is about to happen, and that you may be able to stand before the Son of Man.*" (NIV)

Acts 17:31 — **For he has set a day when he will judge the world with justice by the man he has appointed.** *He has given proof of this to all men by raising him from the dead."* (NIV)

2 Thes 2:1-3 — *Concerning the coming of our Lord Jesus Christ and our being gathered to him, we ask you, brothers, not to become easily unsettled or alarmed by some prophecy, report or letter supposed to have*

> *come from us, saying that **the day of the Lord** has already come. Don't let anyone deceive you in any way, for that day will not come until the rebellion occurs and the man of lawlessness is revealed, the man doomed to destruction.* (NIV)

2 Pet 3:10-11 — *But the day of the Lord will come like a thief. **The heavens will disappear with a roar; the elements will be destroyed by fire, and the earth and everything in it will be laid bare.** Since everything will be destroyed in this way, what kind of people ought you to be? You ought to live holy and godly lives* (NIV)

Rev 3:10 — ***Since you have kept my command to endure patiently, I will also keep you from the hour of trial that is going to come upon the whole world to test those who live on the earth.*** (NIV)

God has been teaching the second coming of Christ to all generations from the time of the fall of Adam and Eve up to the present time, but God will not give mankind a mind to understand the devastation coming upon the earth until the end of the age.

How can things be so horrible and so wonderful in the same age? How can the worst time of human history (10 years - Days of Awe), and the best time of human history (990 years of peace) exist in the same 1000 year period? It is because of the righteousness of God. Only God knows the timing of His plan and when He has appointed certain things to take place. I believe God will reveal the hidden meaning of Daniel's prophecies when the time is right. The right time will be toward the end of the age. God will not allow sin to dominate mankind forever. He has a time allotted to deal with it.

Rom 2:5 — *But because of your stubbornness and your unrepentant heart, you are storing up wrath against yourself for **the day of God's wrath, when his righteous judgment will be revealed.*** (NIV)

In Luke chapter seventeen, it lets us know the condition of the world just prior to the Rapture. It seems to be business as usual. People will be going about their everyday business quite unaware that Jesus is about to come back for His own. Boy, are they in for a surprise! Just like the times of Noah, when the people were warned for 120 years to turn from their evil ways, it will be too late for the people of our day *After the Rapture*.

Luke 17:26-30 — *"Just as it was in the days of Noah, so also will it be in the days of the Son of Man. People were eating, drinking, marrying and being given in marriage up to the day Noah entered the ark. Then the flood came and destroyed them all. "It was the same in the days of Lot. People were eating and drinking, buying and selling, planting and building. But the day Lot left Sodom, fire and sulfur rained down from heaven and destroyed them all. "**It will be just like this on the day the Son of Man is revealed**.* (NIV)

AFTER THE RAPTURE

Overall, the world economy will be in a state of prosperity and relative peace at the time of the Rapture. It will probably have gone through the most prosperous period of its history, starting after World War II. Coinciding with the knowledge explosion predicted in the book of Daniel, the world today has more and advanced technology to make the world an easier place to live. The world economy makes it easier to purchase the houses (with their modern appliances), vehicles, electronic devices (including computers) and the many other inventions needed to make our lives easier. There is more wealth in the world today than there has ever been and the war on terrorism will bring the world closer to globalism.

The condition of world prosperity will filter into the church. Again we take a look at the message to the Laodicean church and find them saying that they are rich with lots of material goods and do not need anything.

Rev 3:14-17 *"To the angel of the church in Laodicea write: These are the words of the Amen, the faithful and true witness, the ruler of God's creation. I know your deeds, that you are neither cold nor hot. I wish you were either one or the other! So, because you are lukewarm—neither hot nor cold—I am about to spit you out of my mouth.* **You say, '<u>I am rich</u>; I have acquired wealth and do not need a thing.' But you do not realize that you are wretched, pitiful, poor, blind and naked.** (NIV)

The problem with wealth and human knowledge is that they are not the answer to happiness. People might think that money cures all ills, but the answer is much deeper than that. The answer lies in spiritual knowledge and understanding. People today are looking for peace in their lives, but cannot find it. It can only be found in Jesus Christ.

Phil 4:6-9 <u>*Do not be anxious about anything, but in everything, by prayer and petition, with thanksgiving, present your requests to God. And the peace of God, which transcends all understanding, will guard your*</u> **hearts and your minds in Christ Jesus.** *Finally, brothers, whatever is true, whatever is noble, whatever is right, whatever is pure, whatever is lovely, whatever is admirable—if anything is excellent or praiseworthy—think about such things. Whatever you have learned or received or heard from me, or seen in me—put it into practice.* **<u>And the God of peace will be with you.</u>** (NIV)

In the book of Revelation it tells us how miserable this wealth is, but the people do not even realize their condition. Haven't most of us acknowledged how blessed we are because of the material gains we have today over people even fifty years ago? We want our children to have what we did not have as kids, yet our real problem is explained in verse seventeen.

Rev 3:17 *You say, '<u>I am rich</u>; I have acquired wealth and do not need a thing.' But <u>you do not realize</u> that you are wretched, pitiful, poor, blind and naked.* (NIV)

After the Rapture and Before the Tribulation Period

> Prov 13:7   *One man pretends to be rich, yet has nothing; another pretends to be poor, yet has great wealth.* (NIV)

> Luke 6:24   *"<u>But woe to you who are rich</u>, for you have already received your comfort.*" (NIV)

Even though the world will go through a financial crisis *After the Rapture*, there will still be people with great wealth on the earth. James talks about them in his book and tells of their demise.

> James 5:1-6   *<u>Now listen, you rich people</u>, weep and wail because of the misery that is coming upon you. Your wealth has rotted, and moths have eaten your clothes. Your gold and silver are corroded. Their corrosion will testify against you and eat your flesh like fire. <u>You have hoarded wealth in the last days</u>. Look! The wages you failed to pay the workmen who mowed your fields are crying out against you. The cries of the harvesters have reached the ears of the Lord Almighty. You have lived on earth in luxury and self-indulgence. You have fattened yourselves in <u>the day of slaughter</u>. You have condemned and murdered innocent men, who were not opposing you.* (NIV)

Please note that they have gathered their wealth through deceit, fraud and murder. They have lived in luxury, but their destruction will culminate when they perish in the day of slaughter, which is the Battle of Armageddon.

The scriptures inform us that it is very difficult for rich people to go to heaven, but it does not say it is impossible. The problem with most rich people is that most of them end up worshiping money instead of God.

> Matt 6:24   *"No one can serve two masters. Either he will hate the one and love the other, or he will be devoted to the one and despise the other. <u>You cannot serve both God and Money</u>.* (NIV)

> Matt 19:23-24   *Then Jesus said to his disciples, "<u>I tell you the truth, it is hard for a rich man to enter the kingdom of heaven</u>. Again I tell you, it is easier for a camel to go through the eye of a needle than for a rich man to enter the kingdom of God."* (NIV)

> Prov 11:4   *<u>Wealth is worthless in the day of wrath</u>, but righteousness delivers from death.* (NIV)

> Prov 11:28   *<u>He that trusteth in his riches shall fall</u>: but the righteous shall flourish as a branch.* (KJV)

James 1:11   *For the sun rises with scorching heat and withers the plant; its blossom falls and its beauty is destroyed. <u>In the same way, the rich man will fade away even while he goes about his business</u>.* (NIV)

1 Tim 6:6-10   *<u>But godliness with contentment is great gain</u>. For we brought nothing into this world, and it is certain we can carry nothing out. And having food and raiment let us be therewith content. <u>But they that will be rich fall into temptation and a snare</u>, and into many foolish and hurtful lusts, which drown men in destruction and perdition. <u>For the love of money is the root of all evil</u>: which while some coveted after, they have erred from the faith, and pierced themselves through with many sorrows.* (KJV)

Please notice, in 1 Timothy above, that it does not say that money or even having money is evil. It says that the love of money is the root of all evil. If you covet money, you will probably have wandered from the faith. Do not put money ahead of God.

As the world is believing more and more that peace can be achieved by becoming a one world unity and followed close behind by the religious establishment, suddenly the Rapture will occur and the world will be thrown into a tailspin.

1 Thes 5:1-3   *Now, brothers, about times and dates we do not need to write to you, for you know very well that the day of the Lord will come like a thief in the night. <u>While people are saying, "Peace and safety,"</u> destruction will come on them <u>suddenly</u>, as labor pains on a pregnant woman, and they will not escape.* (NIV)

THE KINGDOM AGE

Whether you know it or not, the Rapture should be the exact moment that you should be looking for. This is the moment that Jesus will return to take all the people living on the earth, those who have a personal relationship with Him, to heaven where He dwells. It will be the end of the Dispensation of Grace, the Times of the Gentiles and the six thousand year period of the creation week, which is the end of the days of man and the beginning of the Day of Christ, the Day of the Lord and the Kingdom Age. Just like the prophets from the Old Testament, the apostle Paul and anyone who has suffered persecution in this life, our reward is in the future. Mankind was subject to frustration because of sin. We live in a world that is not perfect. We live in a body that is not perfect. Humanity, from Adam forward, has been waiting for this moment that is about to take place. Any sufferings in this lifetime are not worth comparing to our future glory. Amen!

Rom 8:18-25   *<u>I consider that our present sufferings are not worth comparing with the glory that will be revealed in us. The creation waits in eager expectation for the sons of God to be revealed.</u> For the creation was subjected to frustration, not by its own choice, but by*

After the Rapture and Before the Tribulation Period

> *the will of the one who subjected it, in hope that the creation itself will be liberated from its bondage to decay and brought into the glorious freedom of the children of God. We know that the whole creation has been groaning as in the pains of childbirth right up to the present time. Not only so, but we ourselves, who have the firstfruits of the Spirit, groan inwardly as we wait eagerly for our adoption as sons, the redemption of our bodies. For in this hope we were saved. But hope that is seen is no hope at all. Who hopes for what he already has? <u>But if we hope for what we do not yet have, we wait for it patiently.</u>* (NIV)

Jesus is coming to take us to His dwelling place in heaven. It is known as the Kingdom of God. It is above the clouds and above the sun, moon and the stars. There are actually three levels of heaven. The primary meaning of heaven is: that which is above. The three levels of heaven are:

1. **The Atmospheric Heavens** — This level of heaven contains the clouds and the air that we breath.
2. **The Celestial Heavens** — This level of heaven is above the Atmospheric Heavens and is the home of the sun, moon and the stars.
3. **The Dwelling of God** — This level of heaven is above the Celestial Heavens and is the eternal dwelling of God.

I highly recommend the book, *The Biblical Doctrine of Heaven*, by Wilbur M. Smith, published by Moody Press, Chicago, Illinois, for a concise account of the different levels of heaven. I might add here that the Jewish people believe that there are seven levels of heaven. No matter how many levels there are, the highest level is reserved for the Kingdom of God. This universal and natural kingdom or dominion of God embraces all objects, persons, events, the lives of every individual, the matters of every nation and all operations and changes of nature and history. Look toward the end of this book, at the chart on page 766, to get a better picture of the levels of heaven.

The kingdom that Jesus will rule, as King of Kings and Lord of Lords, is prophetic and is yet to be established. Sometime in the future God will crown His Son King in heaven.

> Ps 103:19   *<u>The LORD has established his throne in heaven</u>, and his kingdom rules over all.* (NIV)

The first event that will take place in the third level of heaven *After the Rapture* will be the coronation ceremony. After Jesus is crowned King, His kingdom is perpetual and will never cease to exist. In Psalms 145, we have a view of this future kingdom. Notice that the saints are there praising their King in the glorious splendor of His kingdom.

> Ps 145:1-21   *<u>I will exalt you, my God the King</u>; I will praise your name for ever and ever. Every day I will praise you and extol your name for ever*

and ever. Great is the LORD and most worthy of praise; his greatness no one can fathom. One generation will commend your works to another; they will tell of your mighty acts. They will speak of the glorious splendor of your majesty, and I will meditate on your wonderful works. They will tell of the power of your awesome works, and I will proclaim your great deeds. They will celebrate your abundant goodness and joyfully sing of your righteousness. The LORD is gracious and compassionate, slow to anger and rich in love. The LORD is good to all; he has compassion on all he has made. ***All you have made will praise you, O LORD; your saints will extol you. They will tell of the glory of your kingdom and speak of your might, so that all men may know of your mighty acts and the glorious splendor of your kingdom. Your kingdom is an everlasting kingdom, and your dominion endures through all generations.*** *The LORD is faithful to all his promises and loving toward all he has made. The LORD upholds all those who fall and lifts up all who are bowed down. The eyes of all look to you, and you give them their food at the proper time. You open your hand and satisfy the desires of every living thing. The LORD is righteous in all his ways and loving toward all he has made. The LORD is near to all who call on him, to all who call on him in truth. He fulfills the desires of those who fear him; he hears their cry and saves them.* ***<u>The LORD watches over all who love him</u>, but all the wicked he will destroy. My mouth will speak in praise of the LORD. Let every creature praise his holy name for ever and ever.*** (NIV)

Ps 102:12-22   ***But you, <u>O LORD</u>, <u>sit enthroned forever</u>; your renown endures through all generations. You will arise and have compassion on Zion, for it is time to show favor to her; <u>the appointed time has come</u>.*** *For her stones are dear to your servants; her very dust moves them to pity. The nations will fear the name of the LORD, all the kings of the earth will revere your glory.* ***For the LORD will rebuild Zion and appear in his glory.*** *He will respond to the prayer of the destitute; he will not despise their plea. Let this be written for a future generation, that a people not yet created may praise the LORD: "The LORD looked down from his sanctuary on high, from heaven he viewed the earth, to hear the groans of the prisoners and release those condemned to death."* ***<u>So the name of the LORD will be declared in Zion and his praise in Jerusalem when the peoples and the kingdoms assemble to worship the LORD</u>.*** (NIV)

In Psalms 102, it provides even more details concerning the everlasting Kingdom of Jesus. These events will take place after the portion of God's fiery wrath is completed. After Jesus establishes His Kingdom on earth, it will be time for:

After the Rapture and Before the Tribulation Period

1. compassion on Zion (Jewish people), it will be time to show favor to her.
2. the nations (people), to revere the name of the Lord (Jesus).
3. all of the kings (leaders of the nations), to stand in awe of Jesus.
4. Jesus to rebuild Zion (the Temple), and sit on His throne.
5. the name of Jesus to be declared in Zion (the Temple), which will be standing in the midst of Jerusalem.
6. all the people and kingdoms (nations), to assemble to worship Jesus.

The angel Gabriel informed Mary, almost 2000 years ago, that her son would become a king and reign over the Jewish people forever.

Luke 1:26-33   *In the sixth month, God sent the angel Gabriel to Nazareth, a town in Galilee, to a virgin pledged to be married to a man named Joseph, a descendant of David. The virgin's name was Mary. The angel went to her and said, "Greetings, you who are highly favored! The Lord is with you." Mary was greatly troubled at his words and wondered what kind of greeting this might be. But the angel said to her, "<u>Do not be afraid, Mary, you have found favor with God. You will be with child and give birth to a son, and you are to give him the name Jesus.</u> He will be great and will be called the Son of the Most High. The Lord God will give him the throne of his father David, and he will reign over the house of Jacob forever; <u>his kingdom will never end.</u>"* (NIV)

Scripture reveals that the saints will be ushered into the kingdom of God. Jesus will escort the saints into this kingdom. Only those who accept Him will be honored enough to participate in this glorious event.

2 Pet 1:10-11   *Therefore, my brothers, be all the more eager to make your calling and election sure. <u>For if you do these things, you will never fall, and you will receive a rich welcome into the eternal kingdom of our Lord and Savior Jesus Christ.</u>* (NIV)

As a matter of fact, you must be born again!

John 3:1-8   *<u>Now there was a man of the Pharisees named Nicodemus, a member of the Jewish ruling council.</u> He came to Jesus at night and said, "Rabbi, we know you are a teacher who has come from God. For no one could perform the miraculous signs you are doing if God were not with him." In reply Jesus declared, "<u>I tell you the truth, no one can see the kingdom of God unless he is born again.</u>" How can a man be born when he is old?" Nicodemus asked. "Surely he cannot enter a second time into his mother's womb to be born!" Jesus answered, "I tell you the truth, no one can enter the kingdom of*

God unless he is born of water and the Spirit. Flesh gives birth to flesh, but the Spirit gives birth to spirit. You should not be surprised at my saying, '<u>You must be born again.</u>' The wind blows wherever it pleases. You hear its sound, but you cannot tell where it comes from or where it is going. So it is with everyone born of the Spirit." (NIV)

1 Pet 1:3-23   ***Praise be to the God and Father of our Lord Jesus Christ! In his great mercy he has given us new birth into a living hope through the resurrection of Jesus Christ from the dead, and into an inheritance that can never perish, spoil or fade—kept in heaven for you, who through faith are shielded by God's power until <u>the coming of the salvation that is ready to be revealed in the last time.</u>*** *In this you greatly rejoice, though now for a little while you may have had to suffer grief in all kinds of trials. These have come so that your faith—of greater worth than gold, which perishes even though refined by fire—may be proved genuine and may result in praise, glory and honor when Jesus Christ is revealed. Though you have not seen him, you love him; and even though you do not see him now, you believe in him and are filled with an inexpressible and glorious joy, for you are receiving the goal of your faith, the salvation of your souls. Concerning this salvation, the prophets, who spoke of the grace that was to come to you, searched intently and with the greatest care, trying to find out the time and circumstances to which the Spirit of Christ in them was pointing when he predicted the sufferings of Christ and the glories that would follow. It was revealed to them that they were not serving themselves but you, when they spoke of the things that have now been told you by those who have preached the gospel to you by the Holy Spirit sent from heaven. Even angels long to look into these things.* ***Therefore, prepare your minds for action; be self-controlled; <u>set your hope fully on the grace to be given you when Jesus Christ is revealed.</u>*** *As obedient children, do not conform to the evil desires you had when you lived in ignorance. But just as he who called you is holy, so be holy in all you do; for it is written: "Be holy, because I am holy." Since you call on a Father who judges each man's work impartially, live your lives as strangers here in reverent fear. For you know that it was not with perishable things such as silver or gold that you were redeemed from the empty way of life handed down to you from your forefathers, but with the precious blood of Christ, a lamb without blemish or defect. He was chosen before the creation of the world, but was revealed in these last times for your sake. Through him you believe in God, who raised him from the dead and glorified him, and so your faith and hope are in God. Now that you have purified yourselves by obeying the truth*

> *so that you have sincere love for your brothers, love one another deeply, from the heart. **For you have been born again**, not of perishable seed, but of imperishable, through the living and enduring word of God.* (NIV)

In the passage above, the coming of the salvation that is ready to be revealed in the last times is referring to Jesus at the Rapture. When exactly will the Kingdom Age be ushered in? We all know that we will not know the exact moment when it begins, but we have mentioned some generalities in chapter seven. We can also look to Daniel for some clues.

Dan 2:42-45 *As the toes were partly iron and partly clay, so this kingdom will be partly strong and partly brittle. And just as you saw the iron mixed with baked clay, so the people will be a mixture and will not remain united, any more than iron mixes with clay. "**In the time of those kings, the God of heaven will set up a kingdom that will never be destroyed**, nor will it be left to another people. It will crush all those kingdoms and bring them to an end, but it will itself endure forever. This is the meaning of the vision of the rock cut out of a mountain, but not by human hands—a rock that broke the iron, the bronze, the clay, the silver and the gold to pieces. "The great God has shown the king what will take place in the future. The dream is true and the interpretation is trustworthy."* (NIV)

Coming up in this chapter, we will discover that the ten toes, spoken of in these verses above, represent the Revived Roman Empire that appears on the earth just prior to the Rapture. In these verses, we can ascertain that at the time the Revived Roman Empire is on the scene, God will set up the everlasting kingdom with His Son, Jesus, as King.

We as believers in Jesus Christ look for the very moment that the shout from Jesus in heaven calls us up out of this world, to be in His Presence and rescues us from the coming wrath that will be poured out on the earth. We wait in joyful anticipation for that very moment.

1 Thes 2:19 *For what is our hope, our joy, or the crown in which we will glory in the presence of our Lord Jesus when he comes? **Is it not you**?* (NIV)

1 Cor 1:7 *Therefore you do not lack any spiritual gift as you eagerly wait for our Lord Jesus Christ to be revealed.* (NIV)

2 Tim 4:8 *__Now there is in store for me the crown of righteousness__, __which the Lord, the righteous Judge__, will award to me on that day—and not only to me, but also to all who have longed for his appearing.* (NIV)

Titus 2:11-13 *For the grace of God that brings salvation has appeared to all men.*

It teaches us to say "No" to ungodliness and worldly passions, and to live self-controlled, upright and godly lives in this present age, while we wait for the blessed hope—the glorious appearing of our great God and Savior, Jesus Christ, (NIV)

Heb 9:28 *so Christ was sacrificed once to take away the sins of many people; and <u>he will appear a second time</u>, not to bear sin, but to bring salvation to those who are waiting for him.* (NIV)

Phil 3:20-21 *<u>But our citizenship is in heaven. And we eagerly await a Savior from there, the Lord Jesus Christ</u>, who, by the power that enables him to bring everything under his control, will transform our lowly bodies so that they will be like his glorious body.* (NIV)

We will be entering a kingdom that cannot be shaken.

Heb 12:28 *<u>Therefore, since we are receiving a kingdom that cannot be shaken, let us be thankful, and so</u> worship God acceptably with reverence and awe,* (NIV)

We are to fix our eyes on heaven, which is our eternal glory. In this life we have momentary troubles, which we can see, but they are only a temporary situation. What is unseen is heaven and it is eternal. We will attain eternal glory when we are raised up to meet Jesus in the air. We need to fix our eyes on what is unseen!

2 Cor 4:13-18 *It is written: "I believed; therefore I have spoken." With that same spirit of faith we also believe and therefore speak, <u>because we know that the one who raised the Lord Jesus from the dead will also raise us with Jesus and present us with you in his presence</u>. All this is for your benefit, so that the grace that is reaching more and more people may cause thanksgiving to overflow to the glory of God. Therefore we do not lose heart. Though outwardly we are wasting away, yet inwardly we are being renewed day by day. **For our light and momentary troubles are achieving for us an eternal glory that far outweighs them all. So we fix our eyes not on what is seen, but on what is unseen. For what is seen is temporary, but what is unseen is eternal.** (NIV)*

We will not attain eternal glory in this age (Dispensation of Grace), but in the age to come (the Day of Christ). Whatever we do for Jesus in this life is building a foundation for the next life, which is eternal.

1 Tim 6:17-19 *<u>Command those who are rich in this present world not to be arrogant nor to put their hope in wealth, which is so uncertain</u>, but*

to put their hope in God, who richly provides us with everything for our enjoyment. Command them to do good, to be rich in good deeds, and to be generous and willing to share. <u>In this way they will lay up treasure for themselves as a firm foundation for the coming age, so that they may take hold of the life that is truly life</u>. (NIV)

Mark 10:29-31 *"I tell you the truth," Jesus replied, "no one who has left home or brothers or sisters or mother or father or children or fields for me and the gospel will fail to receive a hundred times as much in this present age (homes, brothers, sisters, mothers, children and fields—and with them, persecutions) <u>and in the age to come, eternal life</u>. But many who are first will be last, and the last first."* (NIV)

We receive eternal life through our precious Savior, Jesus Christ.

1 John 5:11-13 *And this is the testimony: <u>God has given us eternal life, and this life is in his Son</u>. He who has the Son has life; he who does not have the Son of God does not have life. I write these things to you who believe in the name of the Son of God so that you may know that you have eternal life.* (NIV)

1 John 5:20 *We know also that the Son of God has come and has given us understanding, so that we may know him who is true. And we are in him who is true—even in his Son Jesus Christ. <u>He is the true God and eternal life</u>.* (NIV)

Rom 6:23 *For the wages of sin is death, <u>but the gift of God is eternal life in Christ Jesus our Lord</u>.* (NIV)

John 3:14-21 *Just as Moses lifted up the snake in the desert, so the Son of Man must be lifted up, <u>that everyone who believes in him may have eternal life</u>. "For God so loved the world that he gave his one and only Son, <u>that whoever believes in him shall not perish but have eternal life</u>. For God did not send his Son into the world to condemn the world, but to save the world through him. <u>Whoever believes in him is not condemned, but whoever does not believe stands condemned already because he has not believed in the name of God's one and only Son</u>. This is the verdict: Light has come into the world, but men loved darkness instead of light because their deeds were evil. Everyone who does evil hates the light, and will not come into the light for fear that his deeds will be exposed. But whoever lives by the truth comes into the light, so that it may be seen plainly that what he has done has been done through God."* (NIV)

AFTER THE RAPTURE

The unsaved will not inherit the Kingdom of God.

1 Cor 6:9-10 *Do you not know that the wicked will not inherit the kingdom of God? Do not be deceived: Neither the sexually immoral nor idolaters nor adulterers nor male prostitutes nor homosexual offenders nor thieves nor the greedy nor drunkards nor slanderers nor swindlers will inherit the kingdom of God.* (NIV)

RAPTURE

CROWNING THE KING

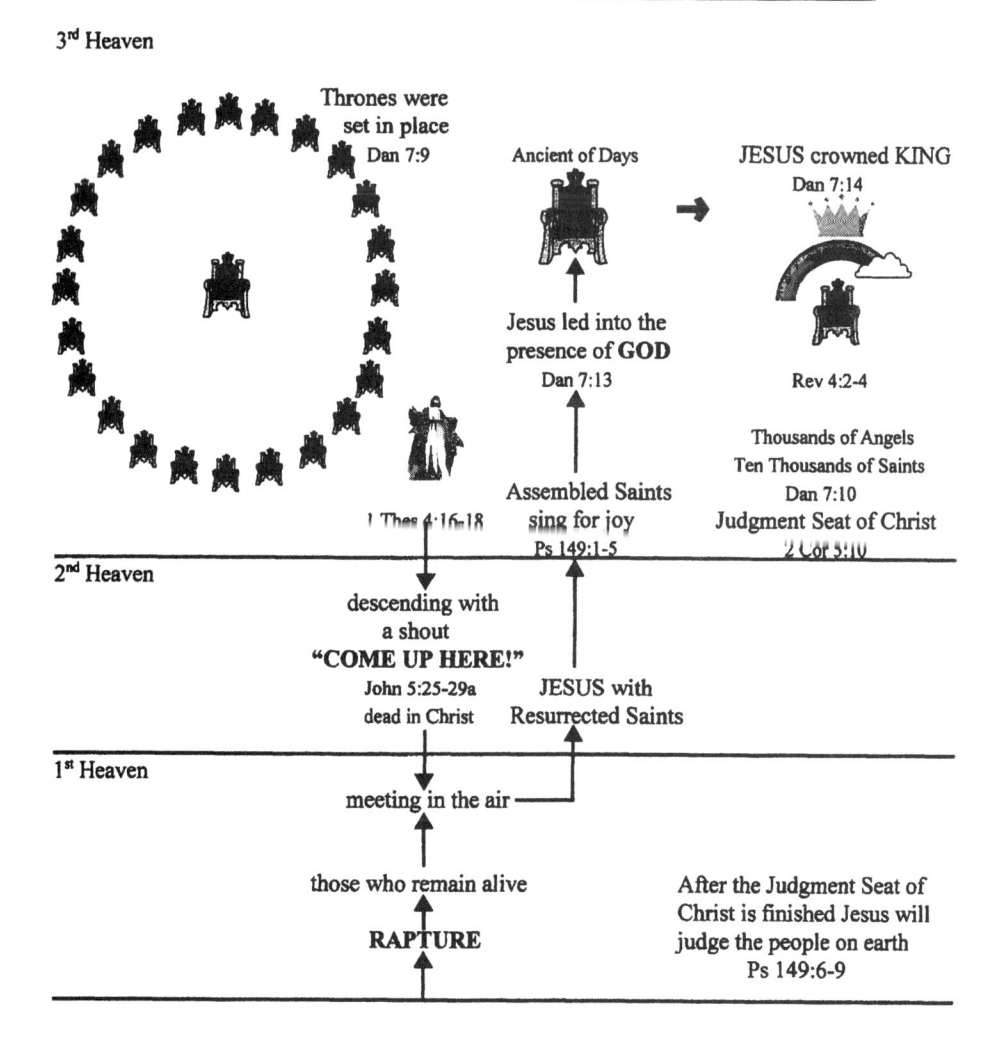

3rd Heaven

Thrones were set in place
Dan 7:9

Ancient of Days

JESUS crowned KING
Dan 7:14

Jesus led into the presence of **GOD**
Dan 7:13

Rev 4:2-4

Thousands of Angels
Ten Thousands of Saints
Dan 7:10

Assembled Saints sing for joy
Ps 149:1-5

Judgment Seat of Christ
2 Cor 5:10

1 Thes 4:16-18

2nd Heaven

descending with a shout
"COME UP HERE!"
John 5:25-29a
dead in Christ

JESUS with Resurrected Saints

1st Heaven

meeting in the air

those who remain alive

RAPTURE

After the Judgment Seat of Christ is finished Jesus will judge the people on earth
Ps 149:6-9

After the Rapture and Before the Tribulation Period

With all this as a backdrop, let us now take a more detailed journey into the future. Throughout the remainder of this book, you will find a detailed account of what it will be like for the saved and unsaved people after Jesus comes back, what it will be like in heaven, on earth and in hell (the Lake of Fire) for eternity. Follow the detailed events of the Rapture shown on the diagram on the preceding page.

The scene in heaven, just prior to the time Jesus leaves to meet the saints in the air, will find heaven bustling with activity and excitement. The angels are making preparations for a kingly coronation by putting the thrones in place. God (the Ancient of Days) will take His seat and wait for Jesus to return with the saints in their resurrected bodies.

Dan 7:9 — *"As I looked, "thrones were set in place, and the Ancient of Days took his seat. His clothing was as white as snow; the hair of his head was white like wool. His throne was flaming with fire, and its wheels were all ablaze.* (NIV)

At the proper time Jesus will leave heaven and head toward the earth. Jesus will bring the souls and spirits of the saints who are in Paradise awaiting this very moment with Him. As Jesus is descending He will shout the command to draw the living saints on earth to Him.

COME UP HERE!

1 Thes 4:13-18 — *Brothers, we do not want you to be ignorant about those who fall asleep, or to grieve like the rest of men, who have no hope. We believe that Jesus died and rose again and so we believe that God will bring with Jesus those who have fallen asleep in him. According to the Lord's own word, we tell you that we who are still alive, who are left till the coming of the Lord, will certainly not precede those who have fallen asleep.* **For the Lord himself will come down from heaven, with a loud command, *with the voice of the archangel and with the trumpet call of God, and the dead in Christ will rise first. After that, we who are still alive and are left will be caught up together with them in the clouds to meet the Lord in the air.*** *And so we will be with the Lord forever. Therefore encourage each other with these words.* (NIV)

1 Cor 15:51-52 — *Listen, I tell you a mystery: We will not all sleep, but we will all be changed—in a flash, in the twinkling of an eye, at the last trumpet.* **For the trumpet will sound, the dead will be raised imperishable, and we will be changed.** (NIV)

After all the saints are gathered with Jesus in the air, in their resurrected bodies, Jesus will escort them into the third level of heaven into the presence of God and the holy angels. The patient waiting of the saints has finally reached fruition as they receive their glorified (spiritual) bodies.

AFTER THE RAPTURE

> 2 Cor 4:14   *because we know that the one who raised the Lord Jesus from the dead will also raise us with Jesus and present us with you in his presence.* (NIV)

> 1 Thes 3:13   *May he strengthen your hearts so that you will be blameless and holy in the presence of our God and Father when our Lord Jesus comes with all his holy ones.* (NIV)

Can you imagine the awesome sight in heaven as Jesus leads all the saints into the presence of God the Father sitting on His throne? After the saints are assembled in heaven they will sing a new song to Jesus. It is almost hard to fathom the joy and excitement at this moment in time. I get excited just thinking about it!

> Ps 149:1   *Praise the LORD. Sing to the LORD a new song, <u>his praise in the assembly of the saints</u>.* (NIV)

Then it will be time for Jesus to be led into the presence of God to be crowned King of Kings and Lord of Lords. It does not state who will lead Jesus into God's Presence. It could possibly be the angels or maybe even the glorious saints. More than likely it will be the angels.

> Dan 7:13-14   *"In my vision at night I looked, and there before me was one like a son of man, coming with the clouds of heaven. <u>He approached the Ancient of Days and was led into his presence</u>. He was given authority, glory and sovereign power; all peoples, nations and men of every language worshiped him. His dominion is an everlasting dominion that will not pass away, and his kingdom is one that will never be destroyed.* (NIV)

After the coronation ceremony is completed the scene in heaven will be full of joy and excitement with shouting and cries of joy. The King is on His throne amid all His majesty and glory, the King of the Jews and of the Gentiles.

> Ps 149:2-5   *Let Israel rejoice in their Maker; let the people of Zion be glad in their King. Let them praise his name with dancing and make music to him with tambourine and harp. For the LORD takes delight in his people; he crowns the humble with salvation. Let the saints rejoice in this honor and sing for joy on their beds.* (NIV)

As we focus in on the scene in heaven, where we see God sitting on His throne, we notice two enormous groups.

> Dan 7:10   *A river of fire was flowing, coming out from before him. <u>Thousands upon thousands attended him; ten thousand times ten</u>*

After the Rapture and Before the Tribulation Period

> *thousand stood before him. The court was seated, and the books were opened.* (NIV)

The first group mentioned, as thousands upon thousands, are the holy angels whose sole purpose of existence is to minister to and serve God. The second group, which is much larger—ten thousand times ten thousand, is standing before God. This innumerable group is the saints that were resurrected and escorted to heaven by Jesus. We can surmise this from the fact that in the next verse we see the court being seated (Jesus on His throne) and the Lamb's Book of Life being opened to start the Judgment Seat of Christ.

The scene in Psalms then reverts to the judgment that will take place on the earth.

> Ps 149:6-9   *May the praise of God be in their mouths and a double-edged sword in their hands, **to inflict vengeance on the nations and punishment on the peoples**, to bind their kings with fetters, their nobles with shackles of iron, **to carry out the sentence written against them**. This is the glory of all his saints. Praise the LORD.* (NIV)

As you contemplate this fabulous event, can you imagine the honor and excitement it will be for the saints who will be taking part in these activities as they meet Jesus in the air! They are then escorted into the presence of God and the angels, sing a new song, watch Jesus being crowned King and then receive their own rewards at the Judgment Seat of Christ. **THINK ABOUT IT!!!** Please make it a point to be there. It kind of makes you ready for this eternal vacation!

After you have settled down and have come back down to earth I would like to take a more detailed look at the events that we just talked about.

THE VOICE OF GOD

As we back up to the time of the Rapture, when Jesus calls for the saints to be caught up to meet Him in the air in their resurrected bodies, we notice that there appears to be three events that take place. This can be found in 1 Thessalonians 4:16.

1. Jesus with a shout (a loud command)
2. the voice of the archangel
3. the trumpet call of God

The original Greek text seems to indicate that these three events are three descriptions of the same event. The trumpet call of God will not be an actual trumpet blowing, but the voice of Jesus sounding like a trumpet. Let us see what scripture has to say to support this theory.

The phrase, "with the voice of the archangel" should be translated as *"with the voice of the commander of the hosts"* (Israelites). In Joshua 5:14, we see Jesus as commander of the Lord's host (army), referring to the Israelites. In the Old Testament the title *"the Lord of hosts"* is most often a title for Jesus. I discovered this error in translation when I was researching the idea of what exactly the archangel might be saying. The same is true of the trumpet call of God. These three events are a copulative force and not a cumulative force.

The significance of the voice of God throughout past, present or future history is probably not understood by people today, including those who attend church services regularly. Although it is not taught in the church today God has in the past played an active role in the affairs of man on earth. From the beginning of mankind God has interacted with man and He speaks to him from all aspects of the Trinity. God Himself even interacted with the people of Israel in a redemptive role at the exodus from Egypt. A detailed account of this interaction from God will be coming up in chapter fourteen. God's voice has been heard by the people who have lived on earth since the time of Adam and Eve.

GOD
1. audibly from heaven — God's Presence (glory of the Lord) from Mount Sinai
2. in heaven to Jesus, the Holy Spirit, and the angels along with Satan (Job 1:6-7)
3. in the midst of a cloud as when He uttered, *"This is my Son, whom I love, with him I am well pleased. Listen to him!"* (Matthew 17:5)

JESUS
1. in the form of a man walking and talking to Adam and Eve in the Garden of Eden
2. in the form of a man as when He visited Abraham with two angels
3. as a messenger such as the angel of the Lord in a burning bush
4. in a vision to people like Ezekiel, Daniel and John
5. in the form of a man as when, *"the word of the Lord that came to Hosea"*
6. in the flesh when the Word became man
7. in His resurrected body after His crucifixion
8. through His word (the Bible)
9. audibly from heaven with Paul (Acts 9:3-4), with John (Revelation 4:1), in the future with the sound like a trumpet at the Rapture (1 Thessalonians 4:16; 1 Corinthians 15:52)

HOLY SPIRIT (in your conscience)
1. the spirit of the Lord came upon them (Old Testament)
2. indwelling the believers (New Testament), a still small voice (Hebrews 3)

The activities of the Triune God can be seen on the chart on page 766. On this chart you can observe; God from the third level of heaven and also as He interacts with the chosen people on earth; Jesus as God's messenger in His pre-incarnate state, along with the time He came to earth in the flesh and finally as He becomes King; and the activities of the Holy Spirit. In Old Testament times the Holy Spirit would enter (came upon) a particular person for a particular reason and then leave. In the New Testament the Holy Spirit enters a person at the time of accepting Jesus (born-again) as their personal Savior. During the Dispensation of Grace the saints represent the Temple of God on earth and the Holy Spirit enters their bodies and dwells within them during this age. The Dispensation of Grace could also be called the Dispensation of the Holy Spirit. This chart contains a very small selected portion of the activities of the Triune God. Search the scriptures for a more concise study. As you can see from this chart, God in the form of the Trinity has always been active on earth, starting at creation.

With our focus on the voice of God, which in a sense includes any person of the Trinity, we are particularly concerned with the time that the Lord (God) was speaking to the Israelites as they came upon Mount Sinai. They had just come there after fleeing Egypt during the exodus somewhere around 1445 BC. As we study this important event from Jewish history, we discover just how important God's voice is when He interacts with mankind. At that time God spoke to the Israelites from heaven. At the Rapture Jesus will be the One speaking as He calls His own out of this world. He does not want them to suffer through what is about to take place during the Tribulation Period.

There are two places in the book of Revelation that give us the clearest indication that the voice at the Rapture sounds like a trumpet and is in fact the voice of Jesus. In Revelation 1:9-18, John was on the island of Patmos when he heard a loud voice that sounded like a trumpet. The voice told John to write down the vision he was about to be shown concerning the seven churches and send it to them. John then turned around to see who was speaking to him and discovered that it was someone that resembled the Son of Man. It was Jesus who was speaking to him with a voice sounding like a trumpet. This activity took place on the island of Patmos somewhere around 96 AD.

Rev 1:9-18 *__I, John, your brother and companion in the suffering and kingdom and patient endurance that are ours in Jesus,__ was on the island of Patmos because of the word of God and the testimony of Jesus. On the Lord's Day I was in the Spirit, and I heard behind me a loud voice like a trumpet, which said: "Write on a scroll what you see and send it to the seven churches: to Ephesus, Smyrna, Pergamum, Thyatira, Sardis, Philadelphia and Laodicea." __I turned around to see the voice that was speaking to me.__ And when I turned I saw seven golden lampstands, and among the lampstands was someone __"like a son of man,"__ dressed in a robe reaching down to his feet and with a golden sash around his chest. His head and hair were white like wool, as white as snow, and his eyes were like blazing fire. __His feet were like bronze glowing in a furnace, and his voice was like the sound of rushing waters.__ In his right hand he held seven stars, and out of his mouth came a sharp double-edged sword. His face was like the sun shining in all its brilliance. When I saw him, I fell at his feet as though dead. Then he placed his right hand on me and said: "Do not be afraid. I am the First and the Last. I am the Living One; I was dead, and behold I am alive for ever and ever! And I hold the keys of death and Hades.* (NIV)

In the next episode we see John after his vision of the seven churches is finished. After the church age is over a door to heaven will be opened and the saints will hear a voice sounding like a trumpet and it will say, *"Come up here."* Please take note at this time that

AFTER THE RAPTURE

John was transported to heaven where he was in the presence of Jesus on a throne with twenty-four other thrones. At this point John was transported to the future period of the Day of the Lord to view the events that transpire in heaven at the beginning of this period of time. John being called to heaven is a type of the Rapture. Chapters four and five are the scenes in heaven *After the Rapture* when the saints enter the Kingdom of God on the Day of Christ and chapters six through sixteen are a view of the Tribulation Period on earth that are a part of the Day of the Lord.

Rev 4:1-11 *After this I looked, and there before me was a door standing open in heaven. And the voice I had first heard speaking to me like a trumpet said, "Come up here, and I will show you what must take place after this." At once I was in the Spirit, and there before me was a throne in heaven with someone sitting on it. And the one who sat there had the appearance of jasper and carnelian. A rainbow, resembling an emerald, encircled the throne. Surrounding the throne were twenty-four other thrones, and seated on them were twenty-four elders. They were dressed in white and had crowns of gold on their heads. From the throne came flashes of lightning, rumblings and peals of thunder. Before the throne, seven lamps were blazing. These are the seven spirits of God. Also before the throne there was what looked like a sea of glass, clear as crystal. In the center, around the throne, were four living creatures, and they were covered with eyes, in front and in back. The first living creature was like a lion, the second was like an ox, the third had a face like a man, the fourth was like a flying eagle. Each of the four living creatures had six wings and was covered with eyes all around, even under his wings. Day and night they never stop saying: "Holy, holy, holy is the Lord God Almighty, who was, and is, and is to come." Whenever the living creatures give glory, honor and thanks to him who sits on the throne and who lives for ever and ever, the twenty-four elders fall down before him who sits on the throne, and worship him who lives for ever and ever. They lay their crowns before the throne and say: "You are worthy, our Lord and God, to receive glory and honor and power, for you created all things, and by your will they were created and have their being."* (NIV)

With joyful anticipation we await the loud shout from Jesus that sounds like a trumpet. Then we are out of here. Do not forget that the voice of Jesus when He shouts will sound like a loud trumpet. This is very important to remember.

Rev 4:1-2 *After this I looked, and there before me was a door standing open in heaven. **And the voice I had first heard speaking to me like a trumpet said, "Come up here, and I will show you what must take place after this."** At once I was in the Spirit, and there before me* *was a throne in heaven with someone sitting on it.* (NIV)

In the scripture verses below we see two more events where the loud command from Jesus is significant. First, we see Jesus as He raised Lazarus from the dead (in the past) and then we see Him call the two special witnesses to heaven during the Tribulation Period (in the future).

John 11:43-44 *When he had said this, Jesus called in a loud voice, "**Lazarus, come out**!" The dead man came out, his hands and feet wrapped with strips of linen, and a cloth around his face. Jesus said to them, "Take off the grave clothes and let him go."* (NIV)

Rev 11:11-12 *But after the three and a half days a breath of life from God entered them, and they stood on their feet, and terror struck those who saw them.* **Then they heard a loud voice from heaven saying to them, "Come up here."** *And they went up to heaven in a cloud, while their enemies looked on.* (NIV)

THE LAST TRUMPET

If that is not enough we can take a look at 1 Corinthians 15 where the meaning of a mystery hidden in times past is revealed to us. In the Old Testament it teaches us that some day there is going to be a bodily resurrection of the dead (Isaiah 26:19). At the time of Christ the religious sects of the Pharisees and the Sadducees had different views concerning the resurrection, with the Pharisees agreeing that there would be a resurrection someday. After Jesus departed, Paul came along and added a new dimension to the teaching of the resurrection.

1 Cor 15:50-58 *I declare to you, brothers, that flesh and blood cannot inherit the kingdom of God, nor does the perishable inherit the imperishable.* **Listen, I tell you a mystery: We will not all sleep, but we will all be changed—in a flash, in the twinkling of an eye, at the last trumpet.** *For the trumpet will sound, the dead will be raised imperishable, and we will be changed. For the perishable must clothe itself with the imperishable, and the mortal with immortality. When the perishable has been clothed with the imperishable, and the mortal with immortality, then the saying that is written will come true: "Death has been swallowed up in victory." "Where, O death, is your victory? Where, O death, is your sting?" The sting of death is sin, and the power of sin is the law. But thanks be to God! He gives us the victory through our Lord Jesus Christ. Therefore, my dear brothers, stand firm. Let nothing move you. Always give yourselves fully to the work of the Lord, because you know that your labor in the Lord is not in vain.* (NIV)

AFTER THE RAPTURE

Paul reveals to us today that not only is there going to be a resurrection of the dead, but that at the time of the resurrection the people who are alive on earth and believe in Jesus will also receive a resurrected body. Paul also reveals the time when the resurrection will take place and how long it will take for the saints to be changed into their resurrected bodies. At the Rapture, when Jesus shouts the command to *"Come up here,"* in a moment (in the twinkling of an eye) all the saints (those with Jesus and those on earth) will receive their glorious bodies. At the voice of Jesus the believers on earth will have their souls and spirits clothed (changed) into their resurrected bodies to be ready for the trip to heaven to meet the resurrected saints who are already with Jesus in the air. Women never dressed so fast.

1 Thes 4:15-18   *<u>According to the Lord's own word, we tell you that we who are still alive, who are left till the coming of the Lord, will certainly not precede those who have fallen asleep.</u> For the Lord himself will come down from heaven, with a loud command, with the voice of the archangel and with the trumpet call of God, <u>and the dead in Christ will rise first.</u> After that, we who are still alive and are left will be caught up together with them in the clouds to meet the Lord in the air. And so we will be with the Lord forever. Therefore encourage each other with these words.* (NIV)

In the statement above, *"...and the dead in Christ will rise first,"* some people understand this to mean that the spirits in heaven will return to earth for their resurrected bodies to precede those who are alive and remain on earth at the time of the Rapture. What will actually happen is when Jesus shouts His command, the saints (dead in Christ) who will come with Him when He leaves heaven will receive their resurrected bodies in heaven at the exact same time that the saints on earth receive their resurrected bodies—in the twinkling of an eye. Then the saints from earth will join Jesus and the saints in heaven in the air. The confusion comes from the Greek word *anistemi*, that is translated as "rise." It can also be translated as "to bring" or "to cause to appear." The saints that Jesus brings with Him from heaven will appear with Him in their resurrected bodies before those on earth are immediately caught up to meet both Jesus and the saints with Him. It is clear in the book of John that the voice of Jesus is the command that is sounded to resurrect the dead. Notice below that Jesus is referred to as the Son of God and the Son of Man.

John 5:16-30   *So, because Jesus was doing these things on the Sabbath, the Jews persecuted him. Jesus said to them, "<u>My Father is always at his work to this very day</u>, and I, too, am working." For this reason the Jews tried all the harder to kill him; not only was he breaking the Sabbath, but he was even calling God his own Father, making himself equal with God. Jesus gave them this answer: "I tell you the truth, the Son can do nothing by himself; he can do only what he sees his Father doing, because whatever the Father does the Son also does. For the Father loves the Son and shows him all he does. Yes, to your amazement he will show him even greater things than these.*

After the Rapture and Before the Tribulation Period

> *For just as the Father raises the dead and gives them life, even so the Son gives life to whom he is pleased to give it. Moreover, the Father judges no one, but has entrusted all judgment to the Son, that all may honor the Son just as they honor the Father. He who does not honor the Son does not honor the Father, who sent him. "I tell you the truth, whoever hears my word and believes him who sent me has eternal life and will not be condemned; he has crossed over from death to life. I tell you the truth, <u>**a time is coming and has now come when the dead will hear the voice of the Son of God and those who hear will live.**</u> For as the Father has life in himself, so he has granted the Son to have life in himself. **And he has given him authority to judge because he is <u>the Son of Man.</u>** "Do not be amazed at this, <u>**for a time is coming when all who are in their graves will hear his voice and come out**</u>—those who have done good will rise to live, and those who have done evil will rise to be condemned. By myself I can do nothing; I judge only as I hear, and my judgment is just, for I seek not to please myself but him who sent me.* (NIV)

In these verses we get an excellent picture of God as He runs the affairs of the universe. He is always working. We also see that Jesus has duties and responsibilities separate from God. To honor God we must honor Jesus the Son whom God sent to us. It is not mentioned here, but the Holy Spirit (the third person of the Trinity) also has separate duties and responsibilities.

Does anybody really know what our resurrected bodies will consist of or look like? Well we are not really sure. We do know that they will not be like the fleshly bodies we currently have now while we live here on earth.

1 Cor 15:50   *I declare to you, brothers, <u>**that flesh and blood cannot inherit the kingdom of God,**</u> **nor does the perishable inherit the imperishable.** (NIV)*

Eccl 3:20   *All go to the same place; all come from dust, <u>**and to dust all return.**</u>*(NIV)

Eccl 12:7   <u>***and the dust returns to the ground it came from,***</u> ***and the spirit returns to God who gave it.*** (NIV)

Earlier in the resurrection chapter it explains that there is a difference between our natural (earthly/flesh) bodies we have now and the spiritual (heavenly/glorious/pure) bodies the saints will receive at the Resurrection/Rapture.

1 Cor 15:35-44   *But someone may ask, "<u>**How are the dead raised? With what kind of body will they come**</u>?" How foolish! What you sow does not come to life unless it dies. When you sow, you do not plant the body that*

will be, but just a seed, perhaps of wheat or of something else. But God gives it a body as he has determined, and to each kind of seed he gives its own body. All flesh is not the same: Men have one kind of flesh, animals have another, birds another and fish another. ***There are also heavenly bodies and there are earthly bodies; but the splendor of the heavenly bodies is one kind, and the splendor of the earthly bodies is another.*** *The sun has one kind of splendor, the moon another and the stars another; and star differs from star in splendor.* <u>***So will it be with the resurrection of the dead.***</u> ***The body that is sown is perishable, it is raised imperishable; it is sown in dishonor, it is raised in glory; it is sown in weakness, it is raised in power;*** <u>***it is sown a natural body, it is raised a spiritual body.***</u> <u>***If there is a natural body, there is also a spiritual body.***</u> (NIV)

At the exact moment Jesus commands the saints to come up to meet Him in the air, their bodies will be changed (transformed) into their beautiful glorious spiritual bodies.

Col 3:1-4 — *Since, then, you have been raised with Christ, set your hearts on things above, where Christ is seated at the right hand of God. Set your minds on things above, not on earthly things. For you died, and your life is now hidden with Christ in God.* ***When Christ, who is your life, appears, then you also will appear with him in glory.*** (NIV)

Phil 3:20-21 — ***But our citizenship is in heaven. And we eagerly await a Savior from there, the Lord Jesus Christ, who, by the power that enables him to bring everything under his control,*** <u>***will transform our lowly bodies so that they will be like his glorious body.***</u> (NIV)

1 John 2:28-3:3 — ***And now, dear children, continue in him, so that when he appears we may be confident and unashamed before him at his coming.*** *If you know that he is righteous, you know that everyone who does what is right has been born of him. How great is the love the Father has lavished on us, that we should be called children of God! And that is what we are! The reason the world does not know us is that it did not know him.* ***Dear friends, now we are children of God, and what we will be has not yet been made known.*** <u>***But we know that when he appears, we shall be like him, for we shall see him as he is.***</u> *Everyone who has this hope in him purifies himself, just as he is pure.* (NIV)

We still need to establish why this trumpet call is referred to as the last trumpet. There are many opinions and theories concerning this last trumpet and when it will take place. I remember once reading a book that mentioned that the Rapture would occur at the blowing of the seventh trumpet in the book of Revelation, just because it was the last trumpet mentioned in the Bible. A more concise study of the last trumpet should disprove this theory. The trumpets mentioned in the last half of the Tribulation Period are designed for judgment of mankind on earth. If the Rapture does not take place until the seventh trumpet, that would place the church age saints passing through most of the Tribulation Period. This would be a direct contradiction to the verses in scripture that clearly teach that the church age saints will not have to participate in the fierce anger of God's wrath.

The only mention of the last trumpet sound in the entire Bible is found in 1 Corinthians chapter fifteen. Almost all Bible scholars agree that this is a Rapture passage, but there is some disagreement as to when the trumpet sound will take place. Some people place it at the beginning of the Tribulation Period and are referred to as pre-tribulation Rapture believers. Others place the trumpet blast in the middle of the Tribulation Period and are known as mid-tribulation Rapture believers. Still others are known as post-tribulation Rapture believers because they believe that the Rapture will take place at the end of the Tribulation Period, just prior to the Glorious Return of Jesus. In my opinion scripture clearly distinguishes that a pre-tribulation Rapture is applicable.

The Greek word for "last" in 1 Corinthians 15:52 is *eschatos* and *Thayer's* definition is:

1. extreme
   a. last in time or in place
   b. last in a series of places
   c. last in a temporal succession
2. the last
   a. last, referring to time
   b. used of place, the uttermost part, the end (used of earth)
   c. used of rank, grade of worth, last, that is, lowest

We can discover from the Greek meaning of the word "last" that we are dealing with the last trumpet sound as a series in a certain time frame. Last in a temporal succession is of particular interest. By defining the word temporal it will give us some sort of parameter to look for in our understanding for the search of when this last trumpet sound will take place. *Webster* defines temporal as such:

1. of or pertaining to time
2. pertaining to or concerned with the present life or this world; worldly
3. enduring for a time only; temporary; transitory (opposed to eternal)
4. secular, lay, or civil, as opposed to ecclesiastical

It appears that the last trumpet sound that we are studying will take place during this present life time or world we are living in now. The Dispensation of Grace is the final period of two thousand years that will end the Days of Man. For six days or six thousand years we have been fulfilling the Days of Man, to be followed by the last day or the Day of the Lord. The last trumpet sound, referred to in 1 Corinthians, will signal the end of the Dispensation of Grace and at the same time usher in the Day of the Lord (Sabbatical rest). This last trumpet sound will end the six thousand year period of this temporal succession of years. There will be numerous trumpet sounds that follow this last trumpet sound in the first part of the Day of the Lord. The Tribulation Period is packed full of trumpet sounds.

If the last trumpet is sounded at the Rapture and it is a succession of trumpet sounds, then what preceded this trumpet sound? The first trumpet or voice of God sounded in 1445 BC, when God spoke to the Israelites at Mount Sinai. At that time it was a call from God to assemble the Israelites to the base of the mountain to converse with them. This was the first trumpet sound. An extensive account of this event in history will be studied in chapter fourteen, where we will take a look at some of the history of the Israelites.

TRUMPET BLASTS

The trumpet sound from heaven has a great deal of significance, especially for the Jewish people. If, when Jesus shouts from heaven you do not hear His command, you will be left behind. Only those who hear His voice will be taken out of the way. The voice of Jesus will only be for the saints (dead in Christ) in heaven and the saved people who are alive on earth at the time of the shout. For them it will begin the Day of Christ. For those people who are left behind, it will be a loud thunder sound as if it were the loud blast from a trumpet. Its significance will be a battle cry or the alarm of war. It will be a warning for the people left behind on the earth that the time has arrived for Jesus to start the process of purging all the unsaved people from the earth. For those people it will be the beginning of the Day of the Lord.

After the Israelites received the Ten Commandments, at Mount Sinai, they remained there for almost a year as they waited to continue their journey to the promised land. At that time they were commanded by God to construct two silver trumpets. These trumpets had a threefold purpose at that time. First, they were used as a signal to assemble the Israelites and also to direct their movement as they wandered through the Sinai Desert. Second, they were blown as an alarm or battle cry of war against their enemies. Third, they were used for some of their appointed feasts, such as the New Moon, the Feast of Trumpets (Rosh Hashanah) and on the Day of Atonement (Yom Kippur – during the year of the Jubilee).

> Num 10:1-10 *The LORD said to Moses: "Make two trumpets of hammered silver, and use them for calling the community together and for having the camps set out. When both are sounded, the whole community is to assemble before you at the entrance to the Tent of Meeting. If only one is sounded, the leaders—the heads of the clans of Israel—are to assemble before you. When a trumpet blast is sounded, the tribes camping on the east are to set out. At the sounding of a second blast, the camps on the south are to set out. The blast will be the signal for setting out. To gather the assembly, blow the trumpets, but not with the same signal."* The sons of Aaron, the priests, are to blow the trumpets. This is to be a lasting ordinance for you and the generations to come. *When you go into*

> *battle in your own land against an enemy who is oppressing you, sound a blast on the trumpets.* *Then you will be remembered by the LORD your God and rescued from your enemies.* <u>*Also at your times of rejoicing—your appointed feasts and New Moon festivals—you are to sound the trumpets over your burnt offerings and fellowship offerings, and they will be a memorial for you before your God.*</u> *I am the LORD your God."* (NIV)

From the time the Israelites were commanded to construct these two trumpets, their blast has played a central part of Jewish life. Even today, the sound of the shofar can be heard on Jewish festivals. Most Christians today are not all that familiar with the significance of the trumpet blast, but in all actuality the sound as if it were a trumpet will be the event that will end the Dispensation of Grace and begin the Kingdom Age. During the church age the trumpet blast does not have any significance for non-Jews. It literally does not play a part during the Dispensation of Grace other than the last trumpet (the voice of Jesus that sounds like a trumpet) at the Rapture. During the Kingdom Age the blowing of the trumpet will again be reestablished during the celebration of the annual Jewish feasts and festivals.

As we have mentioned previously the last trumpet sound we are studying will take place during the present time or age that we are currently living in. The Dispensation of Grace is the final period of two thousand years that will end the Days of Man. For six days or six thousand years we have been fulfilling the Days of Man, to be followed by the last day. The last trumpet sound referred to in 1 Corinthians will signal the end of the Dispensation of Grace and at the same time usher in the Day of Christ, the Day of the Lord and the Kingdom Age that will last for one thousand years. Trumpets play a significant role during the Tribulation Period as can be seen in the seven trumpet judgments of Revelation chapters eight and nine. You do not want to be around when these trumpet judgments are pouring out their plaques on the earth.

The trumpet sound at the last trumpet (Rapture) has great significance for the Jewish people. It will come on Rosh Hashanah, the Feast of Trumpets, and will begin the penitential period of the Days of Awe, which will come at the beginning of the Day of the Lord. This final period of testing for the Jewish people will precede their return to the status as head of the nations.

Lev 23:24   *"Say to the Israelites: 'On the first day of the seventh month you are to have a day of rest, <u>a sacred assembly commemorated with trumpet blasts</u>.* (NIV)

Ps 81:3   *Blow up the trumpet in the new moon, in the time appointed, on our solemn feast day.* (KJV)

Ps 47:5   *God has gone up with a shout, the LORD with the sound of a trumpet.* (NKJ)

As we take a closer look at the Hebrew word for "shout," in Psalms 47:5, we discover that it can apply to both the saved and the unsaved at the time it is sounded. The Hebrew word is *teruw`ah-* (ter-oo-aw`) and the *Brown-Driver-Briggs Hebrew Definition* lists the meaning as:

an alarm, a signal, a sound of tempest, a shout, a shout or blast of war or alarm or joy
  a) an alarm of war, a war-cry, a battle-cry
  b) a blast (for marching)
  c) a shout of joy (with religious impulse)
  d) a shout of joy (in general)

As a shout of joy, the saints will be called to heaven to witness the coronation of their King, appear before the court, take part in a wedding followed by a wedding feast. The Day of Christ has begun. For those who remain on earth, it will be a shout for the alarm of war, which includes passing through the judgment of mankind on earth. Some people will pass through the Tribulation Period and will also take part in the Battle of Armageddon. This trumpet sound will be the beginning of the Day of the Lord.

> Phil 2:16 — *holding fast the word of life, so that I may rejoice in **the day of Christ** that I have not run in vain or labored in vain.* (NKJ)

> 1 Cor 1:7-8 — *Therefore you do not lack any spiritual gift as you eagerly wait for our Lord Jesus Christ to be revealed. He will keep you strong to the end, so that you will be blameless on **the day of our Lord Jesus Christ**.* (NIV)

> Zeph 1:14-18 — *"**The great day of the LORD is near**—near and coming quickly. Listen! The cry on **the day of the LORD** will be bitter, the shouting of the warrior there. **That day** will be **a day** of wrath, **a day** of distress and anguish, **a day** of trouble and ruin, **a day** of darkness and gloom, **a day** of clouds and blackness, **a day of trumpet and battle cry** against the fortified cities and against the corner towers. I will bring distress on the people and they will walk like blind men, because they have sinned against the LORD. Their blood will be poured out like dust and their entrails like filth. Neither their silver nor their gold will be able to save them on **the day of the LORD's wrath**. In the fire of his jealousy the whole world will be consumed, for he will make a sudden end of all who live in the earth."* (NIV)

> Joel 2:1-2 — *Blow the trumpet in Zion; sound the alarm on my holy hill. Let all who live in the land tremble, **for the day of the LORD is coming**. It is close at hand—**a day** of darkness and gloom, **a day** of clouds and blackness. Like dawn spreading across the mountains a large and mighty army comes, such as never was of old nor ever will be in ages to come.* (NIV)

After the Rapture and Before the Tribulation Period

To give you some sort of order of the trumpet blasts and the voice of God throughout history as they appear in scripture, I have created a time line for each of them. The time line can be found on the next page. Every time the trumpet sounds and every time the voice of God or Jesus sounds will take place in the time frame of each column. Everything past the first column will take place in the future. The first trumpet sound (voice of God) took place above Mount Sinai in heaven. The loud sound from God was the command for the Israelites to assemble at the foot of the mountain. God then descended to the top of Mount Sinai in a dark cloud to speak to the people. The last trumpet sound (voice of Jesus) will come from heaven, possible from within the midst of a cloud, at the Rapture. This command from Jesus will be the signal for the resurrected saints on earth to meet Jesus in the air, so that He can escort them to the heavenly Mount Zion to be in the presence of God. Again, I remind you that a more concise understanding of the event that took place on Mount Sinai, in 1445 BC, is coming up in chapter fourteen. The Rapture will be a type of the scene that took place at Mt. Sinai in Exodus chapter nineteen.

> Exod 19:13   *'Not a hand shall touch him, but he shall surely be stoned or shot with an arrow; whether man or beast, he shall not live.' <u>When the trumpet sounds long, they shall come near the mountain.</u>"* (NKJ)

To the Israelites this was at Mount Sinai in the past. Today, it is like the Rapture, in a sense that it applies to us when the voice of the Lord (Jesus) sounds loud, when we (saints) will go up to Mount Zion, which is in heaven (the heavenly Jerusalem). We as true Christians patiently and with joyful anticipation wait for the sweet sound of the voice of Jesus to call us to heaven, where the angels will be assembled and singing with joy.

> Heb 12:22   *But you have come to Mount Zion, to the heavenly Jerusalem, the city of the living God. <u>You have come to thousands upon thousands of angels in joyful assembly,</u>* (NIV)

Never underestimate the power of the voice of God!

> Ps 29:4   *The voice of the LORD is powerful; the voice of the LORD is full of majesty.* (KJV)

> Job 37:5   *God's voice thunders in marvelous ways; he does great things beyond our understanding.* (NIV)

Below, is the time line that shows the trumpet blasts and the voice of God, whether it be God or Jesus doing the speaking. No matter which person of the trinity is speaking it can be a reference to the voice of God!

The most important message you can glean from this chapter is that you need to hear the voice of Jesus at the Rapture. Those who hear a loud rumbling noise (thunder) from heaven will be facing the worst time of human history. Everyone living at that time will probably hear one sound or the other.

AFTER THE RAPTURE

TRUMPET BLASTS

	ROSH HASHANAH	TRIBULATION PERIOD	YOM KIPPUR	ARMAGEDDON
Lev 23:24	Ps 47:5	Isa 18:3	Joel 2:15	
Lev 25:8-15	Ps 81:3	Jer 4:5-6, 19-21		
Num 10:4	Joel 2:1	Jer 6:1		
Joshua 6:5	Zeph 1:16	Jer 49:2		
Judges 3:27		Jer 51:27		
1 Sam 13:3		Hosea 5:8		
Neh 4:20		Rev 8:6		
		Rev 10:7		
PAST	**FUTURE**			

VOICE OF GOD

	RAPTURE LAST TRUMPET		GREAT TRUMPET	TRUMPET
Gen 3:8-9 (Jesus)	1 Cor 15:52	Isa 66:5-6	Isa 27:13	Zech 9:14
FIRST TRUMPET	1 Thes 4:16	Rev 10:4, 8	Matt 24:31	Isa 42:13
Ex 19:13 (God)	Ps 47:5	Rev 11:12		Ps 18:13
Heb 12:18-20 (God)	Heb 12:22-24	Rev 16:17		Isa 30:30-31
Ex 19:16-19 (God)				Jer 25:30
Isa 6:8 (Jesus)				Joel 3:16
Matt 17:5 (God)				Amos 1:2
Luke 3:22 (God)				
John 11:43 (Jesus)				
Rev 1:10 (Jesus)				
Rev 4:1 (Jesus)				

GATES OF HEAVEN

At the very moment the saints on earth are commanded to *"Come up here,"* to join the heavenly saints and Jesus in the air, the gates of heaven will be prepared to open to allow the saints to ascend toward heaven to be in the presence of God. The gates will only be open for an instant and will only be accessible for the believers. This door will be closed to the unbelievers. The Jewish word for "closed door" or "gate" is *Neilah*. There will be a closed door (Neilah) at the beginning of the Days of Awe on Rosh Hashanah and another one at the end of the Days of Awe on Yom Kippur. These open gates appear to us in the book of Psalms. Notice in these verses that only the righteous may enter through the gates.

> Ps 100:1-5   *Make a joyful noise unto the LORD, all ye lands. Serve the LORD with gladness: come before his presence with singing. Know ye that the LORD he is God: it is he that hath made us, and not we ourselves; we are his people, and the sheep of his pasture.* ***Enter into his gates with thanksgiving, and into his courts with praise: be thankful unto him, and bless his name.*** *For the LORD is good; his mercy is everlasting; and his truth endureth to all generations.* (KJV)

> Ps 118:19-21   ***Open for me the gates of righteousness; I will enter and give***

*thanks to the LORD. **This is the gate of the LORD through which the righteous may enter.** I will give you thanks, for you answered me; you have become my salvation.* (NIV)

Here the resurrected saints enter through the gates or door to be taken to heaven to appear before the courts to be judged. The passages below are from the New Testament showing the saints who will be traveling through those gates to heaven in their resurrected bodies. In some of the New Testament passages it is referred to as the resurrection at the last day. These references to the last day are referring to the Day of Christ, because it is referring to the saved who are taken out of the world and transported to heaven.

John 6:44	*"No one can come to me unless the Father who sent me draws him, **and I will raise him up at the last day.*** (NIV)
John 11:21-24	*"Lord," Martha said to Jesus, "if you had been here, my brother would not have died. But I know that even now God will give you whatever you ask." Jesus said to her, **"Your brother will rise again."** Martha answered, **"I know he will rise again in the resurrection at the last day."*** (NIV)
Eph 5:14	*Wherefore he saith, Awake thou that sleepest, **and arise from the dead,** and Christ shall give thee light.* (KJV)
1 Cor 15:20-23	*But Christ has indeed been raised from the dead, the firstfruits of those who have fallen asleep. For since death came through a man, **the resurrection of the dead comes also through a man.** For as in Adam all die, so in Christ all will be made alive. But each in his own turn: Christ, the firstfruits; then, **when he comes,** **those who belong to him.*** (NIV)

When we see Jesus standing at the door, in His message to the Laodicean church, it applies to Christians during the Dispensation of Grace.

Rev 3:20-22	***Here I am!** I stand at the door and knock. If anyone hears my voice and opens the door, I will come in and eat with him, and he with me. To him who overcomes, I will give the right to sit with me on my throne, just as I overcame and sat down with my Father on his throne. He who has an ear, let him hear what the Spirit says to the churches."* (NIV)

Here we see Jesus standing on the outside of a door knocking on your heart. If you hear His message and believe it, you will actually open the door so Jesus can come in and share an intimate relationship with you. Jesus is not the one who opens this door. This door has to be opened by you by believing that He died on the cross for you. Notice the reward of those who do open the door—Jesus will give you the right to sit with Him on His throne. *"He who has an ear, let him hear what the Spirit says to the churches."* If you open this door for Jesus in this lifetime, He will open the door for you in heaven at the Rapture. Let us now see what the scene in heaven will be like during the first two years *After the Rapture*. After that we will look at the scene on earth during this same two-year period.

HEAVENLY SCENE

After the saints enter heaven through the gates in their resurrected bodies, we see them assembled in heaven singing a new song. Remember that these saints are the saved people from the earth, whether they are Jew or Gentile. They are the accumulated believers from Adam to the end of the days of man (Dispensation of Grace). Jesus has gathered them in the air and has escorted them to the heavenly Jerusalem, the city of the living God. He is taking them to the place God has prepared for them a long time ago. The heavenly Jerusalem has many rooms awaiting the glorious saints.

Ps 149:1-5   ***Praise the LORD. Sing to the LORD a new song, his praise <u>in the assembly of the saints</u>.*** *Let Israel rejoice in their Maker; let the people of Zion be glad in their King. Let them praise his name with dancing and make music to him with tambourine and harp. For the LORD takes delight in his people; he crowns the humble with salvation. Let the saints rejoice in this honor and sing for joy on their beds.* (NIV)

Isa 42:8-10   *"I am the LORD; that is my name! I will not give my glory to another or my praise to idols. **<u>See</u>, <u>the former things have taken place</u>, <u>and new things I declare</u>;** before they spring into being I announce them to you." Sing to the LORD a new song, his praise from the ends of the earth, you who go down to the sea, and all that is in it, you islands, and all who live in them.* (NIV)

Ps 89:7   ***God is greatly to be feared <u>in the assembly of the saints</u>, and to be held in reverence by all those around Him.*** (NKJ)

Ps 107:32   ***Let them exalt him <u>in the assembly of the people</u> and praise him in the council of the elders.*** (NIV)

Ps 111:1-9   ***Praise the LORD. I will extol the LORD with all my heart in the council of the upright and <u>in the assembly</u>.*** *Great are the works of the LORD; they are pondered by all who delight in them. Glorious and majestic are his deeds, and his righteousness endures forever. He has caused his wonders to be remembered; the LORD is gracious and compassionate. He provides food for those who fear him; he remembers his covenant forever. He has shown his people the power*

After the Rapture and Before the Tribulation Period

of his works, giving them the lands of other nations. The works of his hands are faithful and just; all his precepts are trustworthy. They are steadfast for ever and ever, done in faithfulness and uprightness. ***He provided redemption for his people; he ordained his covenant forever—holy and awesome is his name.*** (NIV)

At this time in heaven there will be nothing but happiness, joy, singing and praising God. The first event to take place in heaven *After the Rapture* will be the coronation of our King (Jesus) in the sanctuary on Mount Zion, the heavenly Jerusalem, the city of the living God.

JESUS CROWNED KING

It has been a long time in coming (6000 years), but the appointed time has come. God is preparing for a kingly coronation. He will crown His Son King and His kingdom will last forever. Thrones will be placed in heaven where the coronation ceremony will take place. God the Father as the *"Ancient of Days"* will take a seat on His throne that is flaming with fire. After the angels have finished preparing the thrones in heaven, we see Jesus coming with the clouds of heaven. Jesus is approaching His Father and will be led into His Presence.

Dan 7:13 *"In my vision at night I looked, and there before me was one like a son of man, coming with the clouds of heaven. <u>He approached the Ancient of Days and was led into his presence.</u>* (NIV)

At this time Jesus will be crowned King of Kings and Lord of Lords by God as He anoints Jesus with the *"oil of joy."* As King, He is given authority to rule. His Kingdom will last forever and will never be destroyed. Before the King sets up His kingdom on earth, He will cleanse it by purging sinful mankind from the earth.

Ps 45:6-8 *<u>Your throne, O God, will last for ever and ever; a scepter of justice will be the scepter of your kingdom.</u> You love righteousness and hate wickedness; therefore God, your God, <u>has set you above your companions by anointing you with the oil of joy.</u> All your robes are fragrant with myrrh and aloes and cassia; from palaces adorned with ivory the music of the strings makes you glad.* (NIV)

Heb 1:8-9 *<u>But about the Son he says,</u> "<u>Your throne, O God, will last for ever and ever, and righteousness will be the scepter of your kingdom.</u> You have loved righteousness and hated wickedness; therefore God, your God, <u>has set you above your companions by anointing you with the oil of joy.</u>"* (NIV)

Dan 7:14 *He was given authority, glory and sovereign power; all peoples, nations and men of every language worshiped him. His dominion is an everlasting dominion that will not pass away, and his kingdom is one that will never be destroyed.* (NIV)

The King has arrived! He comes to judge the saints in heaven and the people on earth. He will judge the people of the nations with equity and righteousness.

Ps 93:1-2 ***The LORD reigns, he is robed in majesty; the LORD is robed in majesty and is armed with strength. The world is firmly established; it cannot be moved. Your throne was established long ago; you are from all eternity.*** (NIV)

Ps 96:10-13 *Say among the nations, "**The LORD reigns.**" The world is firmly established, it cannot be moved; he will judge the peoples with equity. Let the heavens rejoice, let the earth be glad; let the sea resound, and all that is in it; let the fields be jubilant, and everything in them. **Then all the trees of the forest will sing for joy; they will sing before the LORD, for he comes, he comes to judge the earth. He will judge the world in righteousness and the peoples in his truth.*** (NIV)

In these verses, Jesus is setting on His throne in heaven judging righteously. Let us now turn to the book of Revelation where it appears that Jesus is sitting on His throne at this very moment getting ready to preside over the Judgment Seat of Christ.

Rev 4:1-3 *After this I looked, and there before me was a door standing open in heaven. And the voice I had first heard speaking to me like a trumpet said, "Come up here, and I will show you what must take place after this." **At once I was in the Spirit, and there before me was a throne in heaven with someone sitting on it**. And the one who sat there had the appearance of jasper and carnelian. A rainbow, resembling an emerald, encircled the throne.* (NIV)

Notice that this scene is after the church age has ended. *"After this,"* refers to what follows in the previous verse, which ends the teachings on the churches (or church age).

Following this will be the scene in heaven immediately *After the Rapture*. It will be a period of two years. After we are through discussing this scene in heaven, we will look at what will be happening on the earth while the Judgment Seat of Christ is taking place in heaven. Instantly, the Apostle John was in heaven and he sees before him a throne with someone sitting on it. That someone is none other than Jesus Christ. John gives us a description of Jesus and notices a rainbow around the throne.

There were twenty-four thrones surrounding the throne that Jesus was sitting on. On these thrones were twenty-four elders. The twenty-four elders are made up of the heads of the twelve tribes of Israel and the twelve apostles. During the time they were living out their lives here on earth they went through trials and tribulations. Their just reward was yet future

After the Rapture and Before the Tribulation Period

for them. Here they are in heaven where God has a throne for each of them and they are surrounding the throne of Jesus. Spectacular! We know that they are actually personages because in Revelation 7:13-15, we see one of them conversing with John. John even refers to the elder as *"Sir."*

> Rev 7:13-15 *Then one of the elders answered, saying to me, "Who are these arrayed in white robes, and where did they come from?" And I said to him, "<u>Sir</u>, you know." So he said to me, "These are the ones who come out of the great tribulation, and washed their robes and made them white in the blood of the Lamb. "Therefore they are before the throne of God, and serve Him day and night in His temple. And He who sits on the throne will dwell among them.* (NKJ)

The twenty-four elders could also represent all of the people who have been saved from Adam up to the end of the church age. The Old Testament saints are represented by the twelve tribes of Israel and the New Testament saints are represented by the twelve Apostles. The white garments they are dressed in, along with the gold crowns on their heads, reveal to us that they are part of the redeemed saints from the resurrection at the time of the Rapture.

> Rev 4:4 *Surrounding the throne were twenty-four other thrones, and seated on them were twenty-four elders. <u>They were dressed in white and had crowns of gold on their heads</u>.* (NIV)

Jesus tells the twelve disciples that they will set on these thrones as their future reward and will judge the Jewish people from these thrones during the Millennium. The remaining twelve thrones will be filled by the twelve sons of Jacob.

> Matt 19:27-28 *Peter answered him, "<u>We have left everything to follow you! What then will there be for us</u>?" Jesus said to them, "I tell you the truth, at the renewal of all things, when the Son of Man sits on his glorious throne, <u>you who have followed me will also sit on twelve thrones, judging the twelve tribes of Israel</u>.* (NIV)

In Psalms 122, we can see both the resurrected Jews of the Old Testament period and these thrones of judgment. By the way this scene is in the heavenly Jerusalem.

> Ps 122:1-5 *I rejoiced with those who said to me, "Let us go to the house of the LORD." Our feet are standing in your gates, O Jerusalem. Jerusalem is built like a city that is closely compacted together. <u>That is where the tribes go up</u>, <u>the tribes of the LORD</u>, to praise the name of the LORD according to the statute given to Israel. <u>There the thrones for judgment stand</u>, <u>the thrones of the house of David</u>.* (NIV)

Lightning and thunder came from the throne. In front of the throne were seven lamps (menorahs) with fire, which represent the seven spirits of God. In Isaiah 11:2, the seven spirits are explained for us.

> Rev 4:5 *From the throne came flashes of lightning, rumblings and peals of thunder. Before the throne, seven lamps were blazing.* **These are the seven spirits of God.** (NIV)

> Isa 11:2 **The Spirit of the LORD will rest on him—the Spirit of wisdom and of understanding, the Spirit of counsel and of power, the Spirit of knowledge and of the fear of the LORD—** (NIV)

JUDGMENT SEAT OF CHRIST

What looked like a sea of glass, clear as crystal, before the throne are all of the redeemed saints awaiting their turn to appear face-to-face before Jesus to receive their just rewards. The sea of glass is symbolism for the redeemed saints. The sea is representing the glorious saints who were led into God's Presence. The glass as clear as crystal is representing the condition of the saints as being free from sin. The four living creatures in these verses are celestial beings. The Judgment (Bema) Seat of Christ is present—let the judgment begin! Do not forget that this event is only for the **true believers**.

> Rev 4:6 *Also before the throne there was what looked like <u>a sea of glass, clear as crystal</u>. In the center, around the throne, were four living creatures, and they were covered with eyes, in front and in back.* (NIV)

> 2 Cor 5:10 *For we must all appear before the judgment seat of Christ, that each one may receive what is due him, for the things done while in the body, whether good or bad.* (NIV)

> Rom 14:10-12 *You, then, why do you judge your brother? Or why do you look down on your brother? For we will all stand before God's judgment seat. It is written: "'As surely as I live,' says the Lord, 'every knee will bow before me; every tongue will confess to God.'" <u>So then, each of us will give an account of himself to God</u>.* (NIV)

> 1 Cor 3:10-15 *By the grace God has given me, I laid a foundation as an expert builder, and someone else is building on it. But each one should be careful how he builds. For no one can lay any foundation other than the one already laid, which is Jesus Christ. If any man builds on this foundation using gold, silver, costly stones, wood, hay or straw, his work will be shown for what it is,* **because <u>the Day</u> will bring it to light.** *It will be revealed with fire, and the fire will test the quality of*

After the Rapture and Before the Tribulation Period

*each man's work. **If what he has built survives, he will receive his reward. If it is burned up, he will suffer loss;** he himself will be saved, but only as one escaping through the flames.* (NIV)

1 Cor 4:1-5 *So then, men ought to regard us as servants of Christ and as those entrusted with the secret things of God. Now it is required that those who have been given a trust must prove faithful. I care very little if I am judged by you or by any human court; indeed, I do not even judge myself. My conscience is clear, but that does not make me innocent. **It is the Lord who judges me. Therefore judge nothing before the appointed time; wait till the Lord comes.** He will bring to light what is hidden in darkness and will expose the motives of men's hearts. **At that time each will receive his praise from God.*** (NIV)

Rom 4:4-8 *Now when a man works, his wages are not credited to him as a gift, but as an obligation. However, to the man who does not work but trusts God who justifies the wicked, his faith is credited as righteousness. David says the same thing when he speaks of the blessedness of the man to whom God credits righteousness apart from works: **"Blessed are they whose transgressions are forgiven, whose sins are covered. Blessed is the man whose sin the Lord will never count against him."*** (NIV)

Dan 7:10 *A river of fire was flowing, coming out from before him. Thousands upon thousands attended him; **ten thousand times ten thousand stood before him. The court was seated, and the books were opened.*** (NIV)

THE BOOKS ARE OPENED

God has a set of books in heaven! One book is the book of life, while the other is the book of death. Every soul that has ever existed will have their name inscribed in one of these books. Every soul will be given a body and allowed to come to earth to live during the time God has appointed each of us to live. At the time each person dies, his name will be in one of these two books. During mankind's time on earth, it will be the time for him to make his free-will choice to recognize and accept God by faith. That recognition of God is through His Son Jesus. At the time a person accepts Jesus as his personal Savior, his name is placed in the Lamb's Book of Life. Whether your name is in the Lamb's Book of Life or the book of death, your lifetime activities will be recorded in the book that has your name in it. The exciting fact is that when your name is written in the Lamb's Book of Life, your sins are blotted out and will be forgiven and forgotten forever by God. They have been washed away by the blood of the Lamb (Jesus).

Scripture teaches us that there will be judgment for the saved and the unsaved and the judgment will be at different times.

AFTER THE RAPTURE

John 5:28-29 *"Do not be amazed at this, for a time is coming when all who are in their graves will hear his voice and come out—<u>those who have done good will rise to live</u>, <u>and those who have done evil will rise to be condemned.</u>* (NIV)

Judgment of the:

1. **Saved**—Judgment Seat of Christ—This judgment is for believers who receive rewards for the works they have performed for Jesus and will take place at three different times. They are at the Rapture, at the end of the Tribulation Period (Tribulation saints) and the third time is after the Day of the Lord is completed.

2. **Unsaved**—Great White Throne Judgment—This judgment is for all the unbelievers throughout history. They only have one judgment and it will take place after the Day of the Lord is completed (more on this later).

Every soul that has ever existed will appear <u>face-to-face</u> before the Judge (Jesus Christ) at the proper time. At the Judgment Seat of Christ the saints will receive rewards for the works they have performed while they were here on earth for the up-building of God's kingdom. At the Great White Throne Judgment the sinners (unbelievers) will be judged for the sins they committed while they lived their lives here on earth.

We as true believers should not fear physical death. At the time of our salvation we go from life to life, whereas the unbelievers go from life to death (for eternity) even though their judgment is in the future. In Psalms 69, below, it appears that those human beings who have not accepted Jesus, by the time of their physical death, will have their names blotted out of the book of life. After the unsaved are blotted out of the book of life, their name and a list of their sins will appear before them in the books that are opened at the Great White Throne Judgment, where they will stand before Jesus to receive the degree of punishment meted out to them according to their sins. We will all reap what we sow. That includes the saved and the unsaved. God is no respecter of men and shows no favoritism toward men or angels. He is a fair Judge and before Him will be a record of their lifetime activities. The main difference between the two books is that those who appear in the Lamb's Book of Life will not be judged for sin. Those names found written in the Lamb's Book of Life will spend eternity in heaven, while those whose names are found in the book of death will spend eternity in the Lake of Fire. Please remember that God makes allowances for people who die before the age of accountability; those who are mentally incapable; aborted babies; and anyone who is unable to make a free-will decision for Christ. They will be in heaven because of the righteousness of God. There is no judge on earth who will be as fair as Jesus will be as our Judge. Praise God! Moses even mentions the book of life in Exodus 32:31-33.

Ps 69:24-28 *__Pour out your wrath on them; let your fierce anger overtake them.__ May their place be deserted; let there be no one to dwell in their tents. For they persecute those you wound and talk about the pain of those you hurt. Charge them with crime upon crime; do not let them*

After the Rapture and Before the Tribulation Period

*share in your salvation. **May they be blotted out of the book of life and not be listed with the righteous.*** (NIV)

Phil 4:1-7   *Therefore, my brothers, you whom I love and long for, my joy and crown, that is how you should stand firm in the Lord, dear friends! I plead with Euodia and I plead with Syntyche to agree with each other in the Lord.* **Yes, and I ask you, loyal yokefellow, help these women who have contended at my side in the cause of the gospel, along with Clement and the rest of my fellow workers, whose names are in the book of life.** *Rejoice in the Lord always. I will say it again: Rejoice! Let your gentleness be evident to all. The Lord is near. Do not be anxious about anything, but in everything, by prayer and petition, with thanksgiving, present your requests to God. And the peace of God, which transcends all understanding, will guard your hearts and your minds in Christ Jesus.* (NIV)

Rev 3:5   ***He who overcomes** will, like them, be dressed in white. **I will never blot out his name from the book of life**, but will acknowledge his name before my Father and his angels.* (NIV)

Rev 20:12-15   *And I saw the dead, great and small, standing before the throne, and books were opened. Another book was opened, which is the book of life. The dead were judged according to what they had done as recorded in the books. The sea gave up the dead that were in it, and death and Hades gave up the dead that were in them, and each person was judged according to what he had done. Then death and Hades were thrown into the lake of fire. The lake of fire is the second death.* ***If anyone's name was not found written in the book of life, he was thrown into the lake of fire.*** (NIV)

Rev 21:27   *Nothing impure will ever enter it, nor will anyone who does what is shameful or deceitful, **but only those whose names are written in the Lamb's book of life.*** (NIV)

Heb 12:22-23   *But you have come to Mount Zion, to the heavenly Jerusalem, the city of the living God.* **You have come to thousands upon thousands of angels in joyful assembly, to the church of the firstborn, whose names are written in heaven.** *You have come to God, the judge of all men, to the spirits of righteous men made perfect,* (NIV)

Isa 43:25   ***"I, even I, am he who blots out your transgressions, for my own sake, and remembers your sins no more.*** (NIV)

WHICH BOOK WILL HAVE **YOUR NAME** IN IT?

In the center, around the throne, we see four members of the celestial order that never stop (day or night) saying: *"Holy, holy, holy is the Lord God Almighty, who was, and is, and is to come."* In Ezekiel, we also see these celestial beings with a form like a man.

> Ezek 1:4-5 *I looked, and I saw a windstorm coming out of the north—an immense cloud with flashing lightning and surrounded by brilliant light. **The center of the fire looked like glowing metal, and in the fire was what looked like four living creatures. <u>In appearance their form was that of a man</u>***, (NIV)

How beautiful it is to see the celestial beings and the twenty-four elders giving the honor and glory to Jesus our God who deserves it.

> Rev 4:7-11 *The first living creature was like a lion, the second was like an ox, the third had a face like a man, the fourth was like a flying eagle. Each of the four living creatures had six wings and was covered with eyes all around, even under his wings. **Day and night they never stop saying: "<u>Holy, holy, holy is the Lord God Almighty, who was, and is, and is to come.</u>"** Whenever the living creatures give glory, honor and thanks to him who sits on the throne and who lives for ever and ever, the twenty-four elders fall down before him who sits on the throne, and worship him who lives for ever and ever. They lay their crowns before the throne and say: **"You are worthy, our Lord and God, to receive glory and honor and power, for you created all things, and by your will they were created and have their being."** (NIV)*

Judgment Day will not happen all at once. In fact, the Day of Judgment, at the beginning of the Day of the Lord, will take place during a period of ten years. It will take place in four different time periods and will involve different groups of people. When it is over a long period of peace will envelope the world for 990 years. The first part of the Day of Judgment will last for two years and will take place in heaven. It involves the Old Testament saints and the church age saints. Following that judgment will be the start of the Tribulation Period, when the plagues listed in the book of Revelation begin to fall on the earth. The Jewish people will be protected by the Antichrist during the first 3 ½ years of the Tribulation Period. Their judgment will primarily take place during the last 3 ½ years of the Tribulation Period and is known as the Time of Jacob's Trouble. The nations will also be judged at this time. During the seven years of the Tribulation Period, the plagues in the book of Revelation will fall on all the people living on the earth. The wrath of God will effect both the saved (those people on earth who accept Jesus as their personal Savior *After the Rapture*) and the unsaved, both the Jew and the Gentile. After the Tribulation Period is over it will be time for God's final judgment to fall on the remaining Jews and the people from the Nations (Gentiles) who are still left on the earth after the Tribulation Period is over.

After God shields the righteous (saved) people who are still alive on the earth, He will destroy the wicked (unsaved) people at the Battle of Armageddon. The final act of the Day of Judgment will be for those saved people who believed in Jesus *After the Rapture*, including a multitude of martyrs. They are generally referred to as the Tribulation Saints and will receive their just rewards and positions to be filled for the remaining portion of the Day of the Lord and they will reign and reside on earth with Jesus during the remaining portion of the Millennium (Revelation 5:10; 7:15). After that they will reside in the New Heaven and the New Earth that replaces our current heaven and earth, where they will live for eternity.

Judgment Day will begin in heaven after the crowning ceremony is finished. Two events listed in Revelation will take place in heaven before the judgments begin to be poured out on earth. First, the judgment of the saints (Judgment Seat of Christ) will take place and after that is over Jesus will open the scroll to start the judgment that will be poured out on the earth during the Tribulation Period. The Judgment Seat of Christ will take up most of the two-year period. That scene is pictured in Revelation chapter four. Jesus preparing to break the seal on the scroll is pictured in Revelation chapter five. Even though the plagues of the judgments will not begin on earth, during this first two years, does not mean that things will be going well. The chaos on earth *After the Rapture* will be devastating, only to become increasingly unbearable as time progresses to the end of the Tribulation Period.

> 2 Pet 2:9-10 *if this is so, then the Lord knows how to rescue godly men from trials and to hold the unrighteous for <u>the day of judgment</u>, while continuing their punishment. This is especially true of those who follow the corrupt desire of the sinful nature and despise authority.* (NIV)

> 2 Pet 3:7-11 *By the same word the present heavens and earth are reserved for fire, being kept for <u>the day of judgment</u> and destruction of ungodly men. But do not forget this one thing, dear friends: With the Lord a day is like a thousand years, and a thousand years are like a day. The Lord is not slow in keeping his promise, as some understand slowness. He is patient with you, not wanting anyone to perish, but everyone to come to repentance. But the day of the Lord will come like a thief. The heavens will disappear with a roar; the elements will be destroyed by fire, and the earth and everything in it will be laid bare. Since everything will be destroyed in this way, what kind of people ought you to be? You ought to live holy and godly lives* (NIV)

> Jude 1:6 *And the angels who did not keep their proper domain, but left their own abode, He has reserved in everlasting chains under darkness for <u>the judgment of the great day</u>;* (NKJ)

The judgments during the Day of the Lord will follow the order of events listed on the diagram on the next page. They begin in heaven and end on the earth. The destruction of the earth is reserved for fire by God and includes the complete removal of the unsaved people living on earth at that time.

AFTER THE RAPTURE

DAY OF JUDGMENT

HEAVEN SAINTS Judgment Seat of Christ Wedding				
		ISRAEL Jews Time of Jacob's Trouble Nations	NATIONS Jews & Gentiles **Armageddon** Tribulation Saints	
	Beginning of birth pains			
EARTH				**Peace**
2 Years	3 ½ Years	3 ½ Years	1 Year	990 Years
	Hour of Trial Tribulation Period			
Day of the Lord (1000 Years)				

A MARRIAGE MADE IN HEAVEN

After the Judgment Seat of Christ has reached completion and all of the Old Testament saints, along with the church age saints, have received their rewards, it will be time for a wedding. It will take place toward the end of this two-year period and will be consummated in the wedding chamber (Chupah) in heaven. The bride (church) and the wedding guests (Old Testament saints) are all dressed in white (clean and pure). The Groom (Christ) is present in all of His splendor. What a joyous occasion! It will take the Bride (church) two thousand years to come to completion on earth and another two years in heaven to put on her white garments. The wedding guests (Old Testament saints) will also put on white garments for the occasion (Mikveh-Ritual Bath). It is time for the wedding (NISSUIN). Refer to the end of the book, to the chart on page 765, for a detailed description of a Jewish Wedding. The King is getting married!

Below, in Psalms 45, we see Jesus on His Throne (adorned in His robe) in His heavenly palace. At His right side is His royal bride. The royal wedding ceremony is taking place.

> Ps 45:6-9 *Your throne, O God, will last for ever and ever; a scepter of justice will be the scepter of your kingdom. You love righteousness and hate wickedness; therefore God, your God, has set you above your companions by anointing you with the oil of joy. All your robes are fragrant with myrrh and aloes and cassia; from palaces adorned with ivory the music of the strings makes you glad. Daughters of kings are among your honored women; <u>at your right hand is the royal bride in gold of Ophir.</u>*

Following this we have the bride in view, here referred to as a princess in her chamber.

After the Rapture and Before the Tribulation Period

As she is led into the King's palace, she will be followed by her virgin companions (probably the Old Testament saints cleansed of their sins).

> Ps 45:13-15 *__All glorious is the princess__ within (her chamber); her gown is interwoven with gold. In embroidered garments she is led to the king; her virgin companions follow her and are brought to you. They are led in with joy and gladness; they enter the palace of the king.* (NIV)

If you think Prince Charles and Princess Diana had a beautiful wedding, wait till you see the royal wedding that will take place in heaven!

In Revelation chapter five, John notices a scroll in the right hand of God as He was setting on His throne in heaven. The scroll is sealed with seven seals and contains the judgment that is about to be thrown down from heaven onto a sinful world. This judgment will take place during the first half of the Tribulation Period and will last 3 ½ years. We will look at it in the next chapter. The One who is sitting on the throne here is God.

> Rev 5:1 *Then I saw in the right hand of him who sat on the throne __a scroll with writing on both sides and sealed with seven seals.__* (NIV)

This event will take place in heaven after the wedding is over. John starts to weep when he thinks that no one is able to open the scroll or even look inside it.

> Rev 5:2-4 *And I saw a mighty angel proclaiming in a loud voice, "Who is worthy to break the seals and open the scroll?" But no one in heaven or on earth or under the earth could open the scroll or even look inside it. __I wept and wept because no one was found who was worthy to open the scroll or look inside.__* (NIV)

Then one of the elders, probably an elder from one of the twelve tribes, told John, *"Do not weep!"* Jesus triumphed. Jesus is referred to as the Lion from the tribe of Judah, which signifies righteous judgment. The Root of David makes reference to Jesus, who has followed the lineage of King David through the tribe of Judah, the tribe designated for this purpose. Jesus is an heir to the throne of king David from the Old Testament.

> Rev 5:5 *Then one of the elders said to me, "__Do not weep__! __See, the Lion of the tribe of Judah, the Root of David, has triumphed. He is able to open the scroll and its seven seals.__"* (NIV)

John then sees a lamb, looking as if it had been slain, standing in the center of the throne. He had seven horns and seven eyes.

> Rev 5:6 *Then I saw __a Lamb__, __looking as if it had been slain__, standing in the center of the throne, encircled by the four living creatures and the*

elders. He had seven horns and seven eyes, which are the seven spirits of God sent out into all the earth. (NIV)

This lamb that looks as if it had been slain is a symbolic representation of Jesus Christ. "The Lamb of God" is a phrase typically used of Christ as the sin-bearer of the world.

Isa 53:7 *He was oppressed and afflicted, yet he did not open his mouth; <u>he was led like a lamb to the slaughter, and as a sheep before her shearers is silent, so he did not open his mouth</u>.* (NIV)

Christ is likened to a Paschal lamb, because of His death; innocently and patiently endured to make an atonement for the sin of all mankind. Because of the redemptive work of Christ, no one other than the Savior of the world is worthy to open the seal judgments that are about to be poured out on the earth. No one in heaven or on earth or under the earth could open the scroll. Nobody except the person who drank the cup filled with sin, in the garden of Gethsemane, is deserving enough to break the seal on this scroll.

Acts 8:32-35 *The eunuch was reading this passage of Scripture: "<u>He was led like a sheep to the slaughter, and as a lamb before the shearer is silent, so he did not open his mouth</u>. In his humiliation he was deprived of justice. Who can speak of his descendants? For his life was taken from the earth." The eunuch asked Philip, "Tell me, please, who is the prophet talking about, himself or someone else?" <u>Then Philip began with that very passage of Scripture and told him the good news about Jesus</u>.* (NIV)

John 1:29-36 *The next day John saw Jesus coming toward him and said, "<u>Look, the Lamb of God, who takes away the sin of the world</u>! This is the one I meant when I said, 'A man who comes after me has surpassed me because he was before me.' I myself did not know him, but the reason I came baptizing with water was that he might be revealed to Israel." Then John gave this testimony: "I saw the Spirit come down from heaven as a dove and remain on him. I would not have known him, except that the one who sent me to baptize with water told me, 'The man on whom you see the Spirit come down and remain is he who will baptize with the Holy Spirit.' I have seen and I testify that this is the Son of God." The next day John was there again with two of his disciples. When he saw Jesus passing by, he said, "<u>Look, the Lamb of God!</u>"* (NIV)

1 Pet 1:18-19 *For you know that it was not with perishable things such as silver or gold that you were redeemed from the empty way of life handed down to you from your forefathers, but with the precious blood of <u>Christ, a lamb without blemish or defect</u>.* (NIV)

After the Rapture and Before the Tribulation Period

Matt 26:42   *He went away a second time and prayed, "<u>My Father, if it is not possible for this cup to be taken away unless I drink it, may your will be done.</u>"* (NIV)

The remaining scripture verses in chapter five are a wonderful scene in heaven after Jesus takes the scroll from the right hand of God. The four living creatures, the twenty-four elders, thousands upon thousands of angels and every creature in heaven, on earth and under the earth are singing songs and worshiping our precious Lord, Jesus.

Rev 5:7-14   *He came and took the scroll from the right hand of him who sat on the throne. And when he had taken it, the four living creatures and the twenty-four elders fell down before the Lamb. Each one had a harp and they were holding golden bowls full of incense, which are the prayers of the saints. And they sang a new song: "<u>You are worthy to take the scroll and to open its seals, because you were slain, and with your blood you purchased men for God from every tribe and language and people and nation</u>. You have made them to be a kingdom and priests to serve our God, and they will reign on the earth." Then I looked and heard the voice of many angels, numbering thousands upon thousands, and ten thousand times ten thousand. They encircled the throne and the living creatures and the elders. In a loud voice they sang: "<u>Worthy is the Lamb</u>, <u>who was slain</u>, to receive power and wealth and wisdom and strength and honor and glory and praise!" Then I heard every creature in heaven and on earth and under the earth and on the sea, and all that is in them, singing: "To him who sits on the throne and to the Lamb be praise and honor and glory and power, for ever and ever!" The four living creatures said, "Amen," and the elders fell down and worshiped.* (NIV)

Before we look at the scene on the earth during this two-year period, we need to have a little background information in order to comprehend the meaning of the symbolism found in the books of Daniel and Revelation. It will help us to better understand the hour of trial that is coming on the whole world.

ANTICHRIST RELEASED

The event that will stand out the most, during this two-year period on earth, will be the restraint that has been removed that was holding back the Antichrist. *After the Rapture* he will be allowed to begin his move to become a one-world dictator. To better understand all the symbolic figures coming up in the next part of our study, I have created a chart to make it easier to try to understand this horrible phase of history. Follow along on the chart on page 767 as we cover this section of our study. There is far more information in the Bible concerning the Antichrist than is currently being reported by most prophecy teachers today.

> 2 Thes 2:5-7 *Do you not remember that when I was still with you I told you these things? <u>And now you know what is restraining, that he may be revealed in his own time.</u> For the mystery of lawlessness is already at work; <u>only He who now restrains will do so until He is taken out of the way.</u>* (NKJ)

To better understand this supposed Messiah, we find a detailed account of him and his predicted conquest to dominate a one world government in the Old Testament book of Daniel. The prophecies in Daniel cover the period of time in which he was living (606 BC), until just after the Tribulation Period is completed. In Daniel chapter seven, at the time Belshazzar was King of Babylon, Daniel had a dream about a little horn that had eyes like a man and was very boastful. This is the Antichrist *After the Rapture*, but before he becomes the head of the Revived Roman Empire.

> Dan 7:8 *"While I was thinking about the horns, there before me was <u>another horn, a little one</u>, which came up among them; and three of the first horns were uprooted before it. <u>This horn had eyes like the eyes of a man and a mouth that spoke boastfully.</u>* (NIV)

A very interesting point needs to be made here. The verses following this revelation of the Antichrist are describing the scene of Jesus being crowned King. Thus strengthening my position that Jesus will be crowned King in heaven, while on earth the Antichrist will be starting his quest for world dominance.

> Dan 7:9-10 *"As I looked, "thrones were set in place, and the Ancient of Days took his seat. His clothing was as white as snow; the hair of his head was white like wool. His throne was flaming with fire, and its wheels were all ablaze. A river of fire was flowing, coming out from before him. Thousands upon thousands attended him; ten thousand times ten thousand stood before him. The court was seated, and the books were opened.* (NIV)

Daniel then continues to watch the Antichrist as he brags about himself. Daniel kept watching until the Antichrist was defeated at the Battle of Armageddon.

> Dan 7:11-12 *"Then I continued to watch because of the boastful words the horn was speaking. **I kept looking until <u>the beast</u> was slain and its body destroyed and thrown into the blazing fire.** (The other beasts had been stripped of their authority, but were allowed to live for a period of time.)* (NIV)

Once more, the scene reverts back to Jesus as His Kingdom is being set up to last forever. One like the son of man is Jesus as He approaches God (the Ancient of Days) to be led into His Presence to be crowned King.

After the Rapture and Before the Tribulation Period

Dan 7:13-15 *"In my vision at night I looked, and there before me was one like a son of man, coming with the clouds of heaven. He approached the Ancient of Days and was led into his presence. He was given authority, glory and sovereign power; all peoples, nations and men of every language worshiped him. His dominion is an everlasting dominion that will not pass away, and his kingdom is one that will never be destroyed. "I, Daniel, was troubled in spirit, and the visions that passed through my mind disturbed me.* (NIV)

I do not believe that God randomly picked this time to show us the coronation of Jesus as King of His everlasting Kingdom. It fits perfectly with the chronological order of the Day of the Lord theory shown in the charts of this book. Although the Antichrist is allowed by God to become a worldwide ruler at the appointed time, he will receive his power from Satan. He will perform counterfeit miracles, signs and wonders to deceive the people of the earth. He will perform these miracles in the last 3 ½ years of his world dominance.

2 Thes 2:9-10 *The coming of the lawless one will be in accordance with the work of Satan displayed in all kinds of counterfeit miracles, signs and wonders, and in every sort of evil that deceives those who are perishing. They perish because they refused to love the truth and so be saved.* (NIV)

Another description of the Antichrist can be found in the book of Revelation, where John refers to him as a beast who will rise up out of the sea. The symbolism for sea spoken of here is referring to people. So we can ascertain here that the Antichrist will rise up from among the people of the world. Notice that he speaks against God and that Satan gives him power and great authority.

Rev 13:1-2 *And the dragon stood on the shore of the sea. And I saw a beast coming out of the sea. He had ten horns and seven heads, with ten crowns on his horns, and on each head a blasphemous name. The beast I saw resembled a leopard, but had feet like those of a bear and a mouth like that of a lion. The dragon gave the beast his power and his throne and great authority.* (NIV)

The majority of the people living on earth at this time (somewhere around 6 billion) will perish because they did not believe the truth. Instead, they believe a lie and subsequently follow the Antichrist. Jesus came in His Father's name and people do not accept Him, but the Antichrist will come in his own name and a big majority of the people, who are left on earth *After the Rapture,* will accept him.

2 Thes 2:11-12 *For this reason God sends them a powerful delusion so that they will believe the lie and so that all will be condemned who have not believed the truth but have delighted in wickedness.* (NIV)

AFTER THE RAPTURE

Rom 1:25 *__They exchanged the truth of God for a lie__, and worshiped and served created things rather than the Creator—who is forever praised. Amen.* (NIV)

John 5:43 *I have come in my Father's name, and you do not accept me; __but if someone else comes in his own name, you will accept him__.* (NIV)

Isa 28:14-15 *Therefore hear the word of the LORD, you scoffers who rule this people in Jerusalem. You boast, "We have entered into a covenant with death, with the grave we have made an agreement.* ***When an overwhelming scourge sweeps by, it cannot touch us,*** *__for we have made a lie our refuge and falsehood our hiding place.__"* (NIV)

Hitler made the comment that a big lie is more easily believed than a small one. From the book, *Hitler's Cross*, by Erwin W. Lutzer:

"Hitler believed in lies. He said that 'the magnitude of a lie always contains a certain factor of credibility since the great masses of people…more easily fall victim to a big lie than to a little one.' He shaped the culture and religion of Germany with lies that were soon reflected in laws.

After he was sworn in as chancellor, he paid tribute to Christianity as 'an essential element for safeguarding the soul of the German people' and promised to respect the rights of the churches. He declared his ambition to have 'a peaceful accord between church and state.' He expressed intentions to improve his relationship with Pope Pius XII.

He was willing to give the churches freedom, he said, 'as long as they did not do anything subversive to the state.' Of course behind that promise lay his own definition of what might be subversive. But his guarded promise, as well as a concordat with the Vatican that guaranteed freedom to the Catholic church, was welcomed.

Article 24 of the party platform demanded 'liberty for all religious denominations in the State so far as they are not a danger…to the moral feelings of the German race.' Hitler spoke approvingly of his 'positive Christianity,' which would contribute to the German struggle. He won some goodwill by appearing to be conciliatory; the churches liked his use of the word 'freedom'. Apparently he hoped that the people would feel good about him in the beginning, even if they didn't feel so good about him later on.

Privately, however Hitler revealed his true intentions. Herman Rauschning records that shortly after his ascent to power Hitler remarked that there was no future for either Catholic or Protestant denominations. Making peace with the church, he said, 'won't stop me from stamping out Christianity in Germany, root and branch. One is either a Christian or a German. You can't be both." [1]

The Antichrist will be a bigger liar than even Hitler was more than fifty years ago. His career will be full of lies and deceitfulness. The Antichrist will have some advantages over Hitler. For one thing the true church, having been removed at the Rapture, will not be in the way of the Antichrist. The lukewarm church that remains will, by and large, become engrossed in the false system about to be thrust upon them in full force.

FALSE PROPHET

Another advantage the Antichrist will have will be a prominent religious figure who will help him catapult to power. He is mentioned in scripture as the false prophet. He is also mentioned as a beast who comes up out of the earth, which can also be translated as world. He is pictured as a lamb with two horns and as speaking like a dragon. He will appear godlike or seem to be highly religious in the eyes of the public. Appearing as a lamb could possibly mean that people might, in the beginning, even think of him as Jesus and put their trust in him and believe in his teachings. He will appear as a god in times of confusion *After the Rapture*. The two horns symbolize that he will speak with great and powerful authority, but as time progresses, it will reveal that his speaking is from Satan (dragon) instead of God.

> Rev 13:11 *Then I saw another beast, coming out of the earth. He had two horns like a lamb, but he spoke like a dragon.* (NIV)

Scripture clearly warns us concerning false teachers. With the church out of the way it will make his job of convincing the people of the world to follow the Antichrist a lot easier.

> Matt 7:15 *Beware of false prophets, which come to you in sheep's clothing, but inwardly they are ravening wolves.* (KJV)

> 2 Cor 11:13-15 *For such men are false apostles, deceitful workmen, masquerading as apostles of Christ. And no wonder, for Satan himself masquerades as an angel of light. It is not surprising, then, if his servants masquerade as servants of righteousness. Their end will be what their actions deserve.* (NIV)

> 2 Pet 2:1 *But there were also false prophets among the people, just as there will be false teachers among you. They will secretly introduce destructive heresies, even denying the sovereign Lord who bought them—bringing swift destruction on themselves.* (NIV)

The Antichrist, the false prophet and false teachers have all been deceived by Satan.

> 2 Tim 3:13 *while evil men and impostors will go from bad to worse, deceiving and being deceived.* (NIV)

The platform the false prophet will use to entice the world to eventually follow the Antichrist will be the entire world religious system left on earth *After the Rapture*. He will unite them into a single unit or one-world ecclesiastical system. Today it is known as globalism. Erwin W. Lutzer has this to say about it in *Hitler's Cross*.

"Globalism has always been the long-term goal of occult religions. At the Parliament of the World's Religions in Chicago in 1993, six thousand delegates came from all over the world to discuss the need to unite the religions of the world. The assumption was that world hunger, war, and injustice are so staggering that only a unified religion and government can solve these problems. A global ethic was adopted, in which the word *God* does not appear, but the word *Earth* is capitalized throughout. The document says that there cannot be a transformation of earth unless there is a transformation of consciousness.

> 'In conclusion we appeal to all inhabitants of this planet. Earth cannot be changed for the better unless the consciousness of individuals is changed. We pledge to work for such transformation in individual and collective consciousness, of the wakening of our spiritual powers…Together we can move mountains.'

When people are desperate, they usually seek to unite under the banner of men rather than under the banner of God. Whether in Nazi Germany or in our own day, the Cross is pushed aside in deference to some other flag. To dominate the world is an ambition that does not die easily within the human breast." [2]

As you can see from the above quotation the worldwide religious order of today is well on its way—looking for a leader to unite them into one unit. It is just around the corner.

As I was completing one of the final proof readings of this book a United Nations Millennium Summit was taking place in New York City. The Millennium World Peace Summit took place from September 6-8, 2000, with 150 world leaders in attendance to chart the course of the United Nations in the 21st century, particularly its efforts to forge peace. The largest such gathering in recorded history. The world's presidents, prime ministers and kings pledged Friday (Sept. 8) to solve humankind's problems, ending a historic three-day summit with a New Millennium resolution vowing to send every child to school and deliver millions from destitution by 2015. An eight page Millennium Declaration, negotiated for weeks and adopted by acclamation, is a catalog of the world's troubles—poverty, war, AIDS, pollution, human rights violations and much more—and a promise to deal with them.

As part of this summit, world religious leaders gathered together for a four-day summit previous to the meeting of these world leaders. From August 28 through 31 swamis, rabbis, monks, and ministers gathered at the United Nations for the Millennium World Peace Summit to discuss how to resolve the conflicts that divide countries. More than 1,000 religious leaders gathered for the summit. In the lobby of The Waldorf-Astoria Hotel, where most summit participants were staying, barefoot monks mingled with white-robed swamis on Sunday (Aug. 27). Inca Indians in wool tunics and tasseled hats looked in wonder at the processions of veils, caps and turbans. Participants said they hoped the summit would result in resolutions on peace, poverty and the environment, as well as the formation of a permanent council of religious leaders to advise the United Nations on preventing and settling disputes. Among the leaders on the program were: Cardinal Francis Arinze, president of the Vatican's Pontifical Council for Interreligious Dialogue; Cambodian Buddhist leader Samdech Preah Maha Ghosananda; the Grand Mufti of Bosnia, Mustafa

Ceric; Israeli Chief Rabbi Meir Lau; the Rev. Jesse Jackson; Evangelist Anne Graham Lotz, the Rev. Billy Graham's daughter; and numerous indigenous leaders including Chief Oren Lyons, faithkeeper of the Onondaga Nation in upstate New York.

September 11, 2001, changed the course of current history. This onslaught of innocent victims by radical religious terrorists on the World Trade Center in New York City and the Pentagon in Washington, D.C. will leave the entire world in a different state than it was before this tragedy took place. This single event will be a big boost to globalism as most of the nations of the world unite to fight the war on terrorism. Even people living in America will feel the change as they seek protection from a global perspective. America's homeland security will take away many rights of its citizens. The future goal of the Antichrist, as the leader of a global economy, had a big shot in the arm because of this tragedy.

REVIVED ROMAN EMPIRE

Satan is now preparing, and God is allowing, an empire to come on the scene at the end of the age that will take up the slack when all this is taking place. It is the Revived Roman Empire in scripture and today will probably emerge from what is known as the European Union. This confederated union of nations will accept the person who will come on the scene to solve all the problems the chaos of the world has afflicted *After the Rapture*. This person just happens to be the Antichrist. At first ten leaders, probably the most prominent, will look favorably toward the Antichrist, but three of those leaders will come to oppose him and he will eventually subdue them. God revealed all the particulars of this scene to Daniel more than 2500 years ago, around 604 BC, in a dream that King Nebuchadnezzar of Babylon had one night. God revealed the meaning of the dream through Daniel. In the dream it told about a colossal statue of a man. Please follow along on the chart on page 767.

Dan 2:26-35   *The king asked Daniel (also called Belteshazzar), "Are you able to tell me what I saw in my dream and interpret it?" Daniel replied, "No wise man, enchanter, magician or diviner can explain to the king the mystery he has asked about, <u>but there is a God in heaven who reveals mysteries</u>.* He has shown King Nebuchadnezzar what will happen in days to come. Your dream and the visions that passed through your mind as you lay on your bed are these: "As you were lying there, O king, your mind turned to things to come, and the revealer of mysteries showed you what is going to happen. As for me, this mystery has been revealed to me, not because I have greater wisdom than other living men, but so that you, O king, may know the interpretation and that you may understand what went through your mind. *"You looked, O king, and there before you stood a large statue—an enormous, dazzling statue, awesome in appearance.* The head of the statue was made of pure gold, its chest and arms of silver, its belly and thighs of bronze, its legs of iron, its feet partly of iron and partly of baked clay. While you were watching, a rock was cut out, but not by human hands. It struck the statue on its feet of iron *and clay and smashed them. Then the iron, the clay, the bronze, the silver and the gold were broken to pieces at the same time and became like chaff on a threshing floor in the summer. The wind swept them away without leaving a trace. But the rock that struck the statue became a huge mountain and filled the whole earth.* (NIV)

Daniel then gave the interpretation of the dream to King Nebuchadnezzar.

Dan 2:36-45 *"**This was the dream, and now we will interpret it to the king.** You, O king, are the king of kings. The God of heaven has given you dominion and power and might and glory; in your hands he has placed mankind and the beasts of the field and the birds of the air. Wherever they live, he has made you ruler over them all. You are that head of gold. "After you, another kingdom will rise, inferior to yours. Next, a third kingdom, one of bronze, will rule over the whole earth. Finally, there will be a fourth kingdom, strong as iron—for iron breaks and smashes everything—and as iron breaks things to pieces, so it will crush and break all the others. Just as you saw that the feet and toes were partly of baked clay and partly of iron, so this will be a divided kingdom; yet it will have some of the strength of iron in it, even as you saw iron mixed with clay. As the toes were partly iron and partly clay, so this kingdom will be partly strong and partly brittle. And just as you saw the iron mixed with baked clay, so the people will be a mixture and will not remain united, any more than iron mixes with clay. **"In the time of those kings, the God of heaven will set up a kingdom that will never be destroyed, nor will it be left to another people.** It will crush all those kingdoms and bring them to an end, but it will itself endure forever. This is the meaning of the vision of the rock cut out of a mountain, but not by human hands—a rock that broke the iron, the bronze, the clay, the silver and the gold to pieces. **"The great God has shown the king what will take place in the future.** The dream is true and the interpretation is trustworthy."* (NIV)

Daniel revealed that the statue represented four kingdoms (empires) and that King Nebuchadnezzar was the king of the first kingdom. History reveals to us today that the Medo-Persian empire followed the Babylonian Empire. Next, came the Greek Empire followed by the Roman Empire, which was in existence at the time Christ appeared on the world scene. The fourth kingdom (Roman) will be a divided kingdom. In other words, it will split and exist at two different times. The latter part is represented by the ten toes of the statue and will be partly strong and partly weak. The people will be of mixed nationalities and will be divided. In other words, the Revived Roman Empire will be made up of a combination of all the people of the previous kingdoms that preceded it, with mixed nationalities. Because of this there will be some division among the member nations that make up this empire. There will be contention among some of the member nations. They did not know it then but from the time of Daniel to the time of Christ was a period of 600 years, at which time the Roman Empire was in place. However, the story does not end there.

In the time of the ten toe portion of the kingdom, God will set up a kingdom that will never be destroyed. That kingdom is none other than Jesus in the Kingdom Age, which is the Day of the Lord. This kingdom that crushes these four kingdoms will endure forever. The rock is figurative of Jesus Christ who will be the one who defeats the nations of the world at Armageddon. Daniel will add more details to this story as he proceeds throughout his book and then John the Apostle adds still more revelations to the story in the book of Revelation. Let us see what they tell us. In 545 BC, around 60 years after Daniel interpreted the dream of King Nebuchadnezzar, when Belshazzar was king of Babylon, Daniel had a dream. This time the dream was about four great beasts, each one different, coming up out of the sea. The sea here, again, being symbolic for people.

Dan 7:1-14   ***In the first year of Belshazzar king of Babylon, Daniel had a dream, and visions passed through his mind as he was lying on his bed.*** *He wrote down the substance of his dream. Daniel said: "In my vision at night I looked, and there before me were the four winds of heaven churning up the great sea.* ***Four great beasts, each different from the others, came up out of the sea.*** *"The first was like a lion, and it had the wings of an eagle. I watched until its wings were torn off and it was lifted from the ground so that it stood on two feet like a man, and the heart of a man was given to it. "And there before me was a second beast, which looked like a bear. It was raised up on one of its sides, and it had three ribs in its mouth between its teeth. It was told, 'Get up and eat your fill of flesh!' "After that, I looked, and there before me was another beast, one that looked like a leopard. And on its back it had four wings like those of a bird. This beast had four heads, and it was given authority to rule. "After that, in my vision at night I looked, and there before me was a fourth beast—terrifying and frightening and very powerful. It had large iron teeth; it crushed and devoured its victims and trampled underfoot whatever was left. It was different from all the former beasts, and it had ten horns. "While I was thinking about the horns, there before me was another horn, a little one, which came up among them; and three of the first horns were uprooted before it. This horn had eyes like the eyes of a man and a mouth that spoke boastfully. "As I looked, "thrones were set in place, and the Ancient of Days took his seat. His clothing was as white as snow; the hair of his head was white like wool. His throne was flaming with fire, and its wheels were all ablaze. A river of fire was flowing, coming out from before him. Thousands upon thousands attended him; ten thousand times ten thousand stood before him. The court was seated, and the books were opened. "Then I continued to watch because of the boastful* *words the horn was speaking. I kept looking until the beast was slain and its body destroyed and thrown into the blazing fire. (The other beasts had been stripped of their authority, but were allowed to live for a period of time.) "In my vision at night I looked, and there before me was one like a son of man, coming with the clouds of heaven. He approached the Ancient of Days and was led into his presence. He was given authority, glory and sovereign power; all peoples, nations and men of every language worshiped him. His dominion is an everlasting dominion that will not pass away, and his kingdom is one that will never be destroyed.* (NIV)

After Daniel had this dream, the meaning was not revealed to him right away and it troubled him. Then he was given the interpretation of the dream.

Dan 7:15-28   ***"I, Daniel, was troubled in spirit, and the visions that passed through my mind disturbed me. I approached one of those standing there and asked him the true meaning of all this. "So he told me and gave me the interpretation of these things: 'The four great beasts are four kingdoms that will rise from the earth.*** *But the saints of the Most High will receive the kingdom and will possess it forever—yes, for ever and ever.' "Then I wanted to know the true meaning of the fourth beast, which was different from all the others and most terrifying, with its iron teeth and bronze claws—the beast that crushed and devoured its victims and trampled underfoot whatever was left. I also wanted to know about the ten horns on its head and about the other horn that came up, before which three of them fell—the horn that looked more imposing than the others and that had eyes and a mouth that spoke boastfully. As I watched, this horn was waging war against the saints and defeating them, until the Ancient of Days came and pronounced judgment in favor of the saints of the Most High, and the time came when they possessed the kingdom. "He gave me this explanation: 'The fourth beast is a fourth kingdom that will appear on earth. It will be different from all the other kingdoms and will devour the whole earth, trampling it down and crushing it. The ten horns are ten kings who will come from this kingdom. After them another king will arise, different from the earlier ones; he will subdue three kings. He will speak against the Most High and oppress his saints and try to change the set times and the laws. The saints will be handed over to him for a time, times and half a time. "'But the court will sit, and his power will be taken away and completely destroyed forever. Then the sovereignty, power and greatness of the kingdoms under the whole heaven will be handed over to the saints, the people of the Most High. His kingdom will be an everlasting kingdom, and all rulers will worship and obey him.'*

After the Rapture and Before the Tribulation Period

> *"This is the end of the matter. I, Daniel, was deeply troubled by my thoughts, and my face turned pale, but I kept the matter to myself."*(NIV)

This dream concerned the same four kingdoms that the earlier dream King Nebuchadnezzar had, but this time they appear as four beasts and contain even more detail. Notice that this dream contained the vision of the Kingly coronation of Jesus as King. After Daniel learned that these four beasts represented the same four kingdoms, that the dream sixty years earlier had represented, he was curious about the fourth beast that represents the Roman Empire. He then wanted to know about the ten horns that were on the head of this beast. It does not indicate it here, but there is a gap in time between the fourth kingdom (Roman) and the ten horns (kings) who will come from this Roman Empire. History reveals that the Roman Empire that dominated the earth at the time of Christ was a powerful empire for the next four hundred years, but it was never defeated by a world dominating empire. It just faded out of existence as far as a world power. This took place between 400 and 500 AD. After that time and until today there has not been a world empire that has ruled the world. There have been several attempts to do it, but in the end they failed. Two of the attempts in modern times were by the French in the early 1800's, lead by their famous General and leader Napoleon, and the Germans in the middle of the 20th century, lead by Adolf Hitler. Scripture clearly teaches us that the Roman Empire will come back to life.

The ten horns represent ten kings or leaders of nations that come together to represent the Revived Roman Empire that will exist at the time God sets up His everlasting kingdom (Day of the Lord). After these leaders form a union, another king (leader) will appear on the scene. This king or leader (little horn) represents the Antichrist who will wrest control of this Revived Roman Empire. Three of the ten leaders of the Revived Roman Empire will oppose the Antichrist as he attempts to become their leader and he will subdue them. The Antichrist will speak against the Most High (God) and put-down or crush the saints (believers in Jesus). He will change the calenders and laws (Jewish Festivals). The saints will be handed over to the Antichrist for 3 ½ years. This is a reference to the last 3 ½ years of the Tribulation Period when the mark of the beast will be set up. This vision given to Daniel in a dream ends with the defeat of the Antichrist and the victory of Jesus and the saints. His kingdom will last forever and all rulers will worship Him. Even after Daniel learned the interpretation of this dream, he was worried and turned pale, but he kept all this to himself.

Continuing the story, while adding still more details, is John in the book of Revelation. John penned this writing probably around 96 AD, while he was exiled on the island of Patmos. Another point that is rather interesting here is that we are still referring to Babylon. In chapter seventeen we see a woman sitting on a beast.

Rev 17:1-8   *One of the seven angels who had the seven bowls came and said to me, "Come, __I will show you the punishment of the great prostitute, who sits on many waters.__ With her the kings of the earth committed adultery and the inhabitants of the earth were intoxicated with the wine of her adulteries." Then the angel carried me away in the Spirit into a desert.* ***There I saw a woman sitting on a scarlet beast that*** *was covered with blasphemous names and had seven heads and ten horns. The woman was dressed in purple and scarlet, and was glittering with gold, precious stones and pearls. She held a golden cup in her hand, filled with abominable things and the filth of her adulteries. This title was written on her forehead: MYSTERY BABYLON THE GREAT THE MOTHER OF PROSTITUTES AND OF THE ABOMINATIONS OF THE EARTH. I saw that the woman was drunk with the blood of the saints, the blood of those who bore testimony to Jesus. When I saw her, I was greatly astonished. Then the angel said to me: "Why are you astonished?* **I will explain to you the mystery of the woman and of the beast she rides, which has the seven heads and ten horns.** *The beast, which you saw, once was, now is not, and will come up out of the Abyss and go to his destruction. The inhabitants of the earth whose names have not been written in the book of life from the creation of the world will be astonished when they see the beast, because he once was, now is not, and yet will come.* (NIV)

What a horrible picture! What could all this mean?

Rev 17:9-11 **"This calls for a mind with wisdom. The seven heads are seven hills on which the woman sits.** *They are also seven kings. Five have fallen, one is, the other has not yet come; but when he does come, he must remain for a little while. The beast who once was, and now is not, is an eighth king. He belongs to the seven and is going to his destruction.* (NIV)

The riddle cannot be solved until John, in the last book of the Bible, tells us the rest of the story, kind of like Paul Harvey, Again, I remind you to follow along on the chart on page 767 as we try to solve the riddle. In Revelation chapter twelve we see a symbolic figure called a red dragon and that red dragon is Satan. This is the time that the war in heaven will take place and Satan and his cohorts will be expelled from the heavenly realm.

Rev 12:3 *Then another sign appeared in heaven:* **an enormous red dragon with seven heads and ten horns and seven crowns on his heads.** (NIV)

Rev 12:9 **The great dragon was hurled down—that ancient serpent called the devil, or <u>Satan, who leads the whole world astray.</u>** *He was hurled to the earth, and his angels with him.* (NIV)

The red dragon is mentioned as having seven heads and ten horns and seven crowns on his heads. It is also revealed that his job is to lead the whole world astray. To understand who the seven heads are, turn back to Revelation chapter seventeen for the answer.

After the Rapture and Before the Tribulation Period

Rev 17:9-10 *"This calls for a mind with wisdom. <u>The seven heads are seven hills on which the woman sits. They are also seven kings.</u> Five have fallen, one is, the other has not yet come; but when he does come, he must remain for a little while.* (NIV)

Here we discover that the seven heads are seven mountains. Mountains when used as symbolism refer to kingdoms (empires). In the original Greek the word is *"oros"* and means mountains. The King James Version has the correct translation. In verse ten it goes on to reveal that the seven heads are symbolic for kings. Kings always have kingdoms and kingdoms always have kings, there are no leaderless societies. Continuing, it says that five of these kings have fallen, one is, and the other is yet to come. It is my belief that the seven heads are referring to seven world wide empires that will exist on earth throughout all of history. In verse eleven the beast is the eighth king who represents the Antichrist after his wound and healing, but he belongs to the seventh kingdom (Revived Roman Empire). At the end of the seventh empire Jesus will set up His Kingdom on earth.

Daniel only mentioned four world empires in the Old Testament, while John in the New Testament, listed seven kingdoms. As John looks at the bigger picture, he adds three kingdoms to his revelation. His seven kingdoms list two kingdoms that existed before the Babylonian Empire and one that will exist after the Roman Empire, the one that existed in the time of Jesus. I might add here that Daniel does list the Revived Roman Empire as a separate empire, but he shows it as the last half of the divided Roman Empire, whereas, John counts it as kingdom number seven. See the list below.

SEVEN KINGDOMS (EMPIRES)

1. Egypt — 2920 BC to 1100 BC (start to decline as a world empire)
2. Assyria — 1100 BC to 606 BC
3. Babylon — 606 BC to 538 BC (Daniel and Ezekiel in exile in Babylon)
4. Medo-Persian — 538 BC to 330 BC
5. Greek — 330 BC to 146 BC (start of the rise of the Roman Empire)
6. Roman — 146 BC to 500 AD ? (John on the island of Patmos in 96AD)
7. Revived Roman Empire — starts to materialize at the end of the age, but is fully realized *After the Rapture.*

John tells us that five of the world empires have fallen, one is, and the other is yet to come. Since John was living in 96 AD, when the Roman Empire was in existence, it makes sense to say that the first five world empires were not around anymore, that the Roman Empire he was living in was the empire that he referred to as the *"one is,"* and that one empire was still to come in the future. When the future kingdom arrives it will only last for a short time. That will be the Revived Roman Empire.

Now that we have established that the seven heads are the seven world empires that will exist on the earth throughout most of its history, we need to look at another detail before we move on. We need to establish who the first beast of Revelation thirteen is symbolically. Back in Revelation 12:3, it mentions that the seven heads had crowns. Crowns used as a symbol, always represent sovereignty, power and authority. This follows the New Testament teaching that Satan is literally the ruler (leader) of this world. In fact, Satan has been the prince (ruler) of this world ever since the fall of mankind, for almost 6000 years. The following verses are all references to Satan, the great deceiver.

> 2 Cor 4:4 *In whom <u>the God of this world</u> hath blinded the minds of them which believe not, lest the light of the glorious gospel of Christ, who is the image of God, should shine unto them.* (KJV)
>
> Eph 2:1-2 *And you hath he quickened, who were dead in trespasses and sins; Wherein in time past ye walked according to the course of this world, according to <u>the prince of the power of the air</u>, the spirit that now worketh in the children of disobedience:* (KJV)
>
> John 12:31 *Now is the judgment of this world: now shall <u>the prince of this world</u> be cast out.* (KJV)

We will now look at the first beast in Revelation thirteen, which we earlier revealed to be the Antichrist. The Antichrist has many names and we will take an in depth look at them in chapter eleven. These various names have confused Bible scholars for centuries.

> Rev 13:1-4 *And the dragon stood on the shore of the sea. <u>And I saw a beast coming out of the sea.</u> He had ten horns and seven heads, with ten crowns on his horns, and on each head a blasphemous name. The beast I saw resembled a leopard, but had feet like those of a bear and a mouth like that of a lion. The dragon gave the beast his power and his throne and great authority. One of the heads of the beast seemed to have had a fatal wound, but the fatal wound had been healed. The whole world was astonished and followed the beast. Men worshiped the dragon because he had given authority to the beast, and they also worshiped the beast and asked, "Who is like the beast? Who can make war against him?"* (NIV)

For me, this was the hardest part of the riddle to understand. After I surmised that this beast must have two meanings that can represent the same conclusion, it started to make more sense to me. At times the beast represents the Antichrist and at times it represents his kingdom, the Revived Roman Empire (10 horns), which is the seventh head (empire) in the list of seven world empires and at times it even represents both. Follow along closely as we break down these first four verses to see when the beast is represented as the Antichrist, when it is referring to his kingdom or both of them together. Figuring out the identities of all the symbolic figures in Daniel and Revelation is paramount to understanding the chronological order of all the events that are yet to take place in the near future. Once the parameters of the Antichrist are established, it clears the way for us to follow his path of destruction of the entire world. A breakdown of Revelation 13:1-4 goes something like this:

VERSE	**INTERPRETATION**
1. *And I saw a beast coming out of the sea. He had ten horns and seven heads, with ten crowns on his horns,*	This beast represents the Antichrist, because it refers to it as *"his"* ten horns and *"his"* seven heads in the same verse, but it also represents his kingdom (10 horns) as part of the seven world empires (7 heads). The Antichrist and his kingdom both rise up out of the people in the world.
and on each head a blasphemous name.	Each head had a blasphemous name, which indicates that all of the seven world empires were basically anti-God, including the one that is now in view (Revived Roman Empire).
2. *The beast I saw resembled a leopard, but had feet like those of a bear and a mouth like that of a lion.*	This represents the kingdom portion as we see that its people are a mixture of the previous world empires. As each empire was conquered by the previous empire, the remaining people would assimilate into the new empire. So by the time of the Revived Roman Empire, they will be a people of mixed nationalities from the Greek, Medo-Persian and Babylonian empires.
The dragon gave the beast his power and his throne and great authority.	Here we see the Antichrist. In order we see the sequence of his rise to be a world dictator—first he receives his power, not long after that he will become a leader of his empire and finally during the last 3 ½ years he will be given great authority. Take note—it all comes from Satan.
3. *One of the heads of the beast seemed to have had a fatal wound, but the fatal wound had been healed. The whole world was astonished and followed the beast.*	Here again, the Antichrist is in view as we see him when he receives what looks like a fatal wound, but he will be healed. This event takes place near the middle of the Tribulation Period. Because of the healing of the Antichrist, the whole world will be amazed and follow him.
4. *Men worshiped the dragon because he had given authority to the beast, and they also worshiped the beast and asked, "Who is like the beast? Who can make war against him?"*	This verse shows a scene during the last 3½ years of the Tribulation Period, after Satan has taken the body of the Antichrist and also given him great authority. By this time the people will worship the Antichrist and Satan, finally realizing that the Antichrist is the one who receives his power from Satan. God even quotes men during this time. In awe they look upon him and marvel, "Is anybody like this man

AFTER THE RAPTURE

VERSE	**INTERPRETATION**
	the Antichrist," and "Is anyone strong enough to try to defeat him?"

Who are the ten horns that keep popping up? The ten horns in the book of Revelation coincide perfectly with the scripture we just looked at in Daniel chapters two (10 toes) and seven (10 horns). John describes them in chapter seventeen in the book of Revelation where they show up in verses three, seven and twelve.

Rev 17:12-13 *"**The ten horns you saw are ten kings who have not yet received a kingdom, but who for one hour will receive authority as kings along with the beast. They have one purpose and will give their power and authority to the beast.*** (NIV)

The ten horns are ten kings, who, up to the time of John (96 AD), had not yet existed. Yet in the future for one hour, referring to a short period of time (mentioned in Revelation 3:10), they will receive their authority along with the Antichrist. Notice next that their sole purpose for existing is to give their power and authority to the Antichrist.

Rev 3:10 *Since you have kept my command to endure patiently, I will also keep you from **the hour of trial** that is going to come upon the whole world to test those who live on the earth.* (NIV)

Here, in the book of Revelation, the ten horns are revealed to be ten nations who have yet to come to power. Back in Daniel chapter two we were told that this kingdom (legs of iron) would be divided, meaning that it would be a world empire at two different times in history (verse 41). In Daniel chapter seven we were told that the ten horns are ten kings who will come from the Roman Empire (verse 24). More than six hundred years later, in 96 AD, John is telling us that the ten horns are ten kings (leaders) who have not yet received a kingdom (empire). We have to catapult back to Daniel two to find out that these ten kings (leaders) will be in existence at the time God sets up the Kingdom Age (verse 44). Now we all know that we are not living in the Kingdom Age today. Bingo, we have just traveled through the maze to discover that this is the Revived Roman Empire, ten nations who have not yet received their power under a great leader. Can you see why I call this portion of this chapter a riddle? However, we are not finished yet.

A point of interest here needs to be noted. In verse one of chapter thirteen it shows the Antichrist and his kingdom (10 horns) with ten crowns. That reveals to us that the Antichrist is the king of this kingdom that will rule the world (Revived Roman Empire). Now look back at Satan in chapter twelve where we see the seven world empires (7 heads) with crowns. That denotes that Satan is king over the seven world empires, including the seventh kingdom. Satan is the big boss!

The last symbolic figure we need to look at before we move on is a mysterious woman sitting on a scarlet beast. Her name is:

After the Rapture and Before the Tribulation Period

MYSTERY
BABYLON THE GREAT
THE MOTHER OF HARLOTS
AND ABOMINATIONS OF THE EARTH

What and awful name! In the King James translation, she is referred to as a *"great whore"* and a *"great prostitute"* in the New International Version. The first eight verses of Revelation chapter seventeen give us a symbolic picture of her.

> Rev 17:1-8 *One of the seven angels who had the seven bowls came and said to me, "Come, I will show you the punishment of the great prostitute, who sits on many waters. With her the kings of the earth committed adultery and the inhabitants of the earth were intoxicated with the wine of her adulteries." Then the angel carried me away in the Spirit into a desert.* **There I saw a woman sitting on a scarlet beast that was covered with blasphemous names and had seven heads and ten horns.** *The woman was dressed in purple and scarlet, and was glittering with gold, precious stones and pearls. She held a golden cup in her hand, filled with abominable things and the filth of her adulteries. This title was written on her forehead: MYSTERY BABYLON THE GREAT THE MOTHER OF PROSTITUTES AND OF THE ABOMINATIONS OF THE EARTH. I saw that the woman was drunk with the blood of the saints, the blood of those who bore testimony to Jesus. When I saw her, I was greatly astonished. Then the angel said to me: "Why are you astonished? I will explain to you the mystery of the woman and of the beast she rides, which has the seven heads and ten horns. The beast, which you saw, once was, now is not, and will come up out of the Abyss and go to his destruction. The inhabitants of the earth whose names have not been written in the book of life from the creation of the world will be astonished when they see the beast, because he once was, now is not, and yet will come.* (NIV)

The woman who is portrayed as unfaithful and adulterous is the false religious system that will exist on earth during the period *After the Rapture* and will last until the time it is destroyed, but we have a bigger picture here. The woman was sitting on a scarlet beast with seven heads and ten horns. From this we can surmise that the beast represents the seven world empires that we discussed in detail earlier in this chapter—including the last world empire to exist. The idea of the woman riding on these seven empires leads me to believe that she had substantial influence over them and dominated them throughout their existence.

This false religious system, used by Satan, had its beginning when Nimrod, the great apostate, defied God and built a city and named it Babylon. This occurred shortly after the flood (2344 BC). Within the city, Nimrod had the Tower of Babel constructed. At that time it was probably the first great organized apostate system to enter the then known world. This false religious system that was set up in the city of Babylon has since existed throughout history and has invaded all of the seven world empires and their kings. Thus, the name Babylon followed this false religious system throughout history.

Satan used this as a tool to separate mankind from God and called it religion. It is kind of ironic that Satan's most successful effort was in the form of false religious systems. Even today, in the lukewarm Christian Church, there are multitudes of unsaved people who believe in religion and that there is a God. They are good people and not half as bad as a lot of the people in their church. Surely "a loving God"…!!! People who act out religion will be on the wrong side of eternity someday, being deceived by this false religious system. Not everyone who says *"Lord, Lord, will enter the kingdom of heaven."* Only those who have a personal relationship with Jesus will have the right to enter through the gates of heaven.

> Matt 7:21-23 *"<u>Not everyone who says to me, 'Lord, Lord,' will enter the kingdom of heaven</u>, but only he who does the will of my Father who is in heaven. Many will say to me on that day, 'Lord, Lord, did we not prophesy in your name, and in your name drive out demons and perform many miracles?' Then I will tell them plainly, 'I never knew you. Away from me, you evildoers!'* (NIV)

During the first nine years *After the Rapture,* the woman in the form of a prostitute will sit on many waters, which is symbolic of the peoples of the world.

> Rev 17:15 *Then the angel said to me, "The waters you saw, where the prostitute sits, are peoples, multitudes, nations and languages.* (NIV)

With the prostitute, the leaders of the world, having been deceived by this false religious system, will lead the rest of the people of the world into believing this false doctrine.

> Rev 17:2 *<u>With her the kings of the earth committed adultery</u> and the inhabitants of the earth were intoxicated with the wine of her adulteries."* (NIV)

The amount of blood that will be spilled during this period is reflected in verse six where we see the martyrs who lose their lives for their faith in Jesus. Also, the color of the beast that she was riding was scarlet, which probably denotes the blood shed during this worst time of human history. This is the only time we see a beast as dressed in the color red.

> Rev 17:3 *Then the angel carried me away in the Spirit into a desert. There I saw a woman sitting on <u>a scarlet beast</u> that was covered with blasphemous names and had seven heads and ten horns.* (NIV)

> Rev 17:6 *<u>I saw that the woman was drunk with the blood of the saints</u>, <u>the blood of those who bore testimony to Jesus</u>. When I saw her, I was*

After the Rapture and Before the Tribulation Period

greatly astonished. (NIV)

The woman (false religious system) is revealed to be the great city that ruled over the leaders of the earth. At her destruction, in Revelation chapter sixteen, it identifies the city as Babylon the Great. We will discuss the destruction of Babylon in chapter eleven.

Rev 17:18   *The woman you saw is the great city that rules over the kings of the earth."* (NIV)

Rev 16:19   *The great city split into three parts, and the cities of the nations collapsed. God remembered Babylon the Great and gave her the cup filled with the wine of the fury of his wrath.* (NIV)

During the first years *After the Rapture* the false prophet and his false religious system (prostitute) will have substantial influence over both the Antichrist (beast) and the Revived Roman Empire (10 horns). Enough influence to make the Antichrist and the Revived Roman Empire hate the false religious system and in the end it will be the Antichrist as head of the Revived Roman Empire who will destroy this false religious system.

Rev 17:16-17   *The beast and the ten horns you saw will hate the prostitute. They will bring her to ruin and leave her naked; they will eat her flesh and burn her with fire. For God has put it into their hearts to accomplish his purpose by agreeing to give the beast their power to rule, until God's words are fulfilled.* (NIV)

With these thoughts imbedded in your mind—two systems with two individual leaders gaining prominence *After the Rapture*—we can move on. Below is a description of the goals of these two erroneous figures that show up *After the Rapture*, during the Tribulation Period. It is hard to imagine the destruction that these two people will bring upon the whole world.

SYSTEM	**LEADER**	**GOAL**
Religious	false prophet	To form a one-world religious system to deceive the people of the earth and make them worship the Antichrist.
Political	Antichrist	To form a one-world government and become its leader. To proclaim himself to be god and have the people worship him.

By all accounts, the Bible has a lot to say about the political system that will receive the Antichrist and provide him with a power base to launch his attack on the world and to become a one-world leader. As I mentioned before, it is known today as the European Union (EU). In the late 1940's, the idea of European Unification had its beginnings. At that time ten Western European countries established the Council of Europe. Then it was more commonly known as the Common Market. It was originally formed as a block of nations to strengthen their economic stature around the world. In 1957, the European Economic Community (EEC) was established. European Unification is the predecessor to the Revived Roman Empire, which will come to completion *After the Rapture*. With this as a backdrop we can now look at the scene that will take place on the earth during the two years *After the Rapture* and before the Tribulation Period begins.

EARTHLY SCENE

Below, I am going to give you a scenario of how I believe the first two years of the Day of the Lord could possibly play out. These are strictly my thoughts and express my view of how I think things might take place during this future time. The Bible has little to say about what is taking place on earth during this first two-year period of the Millennium. It reveals a lot more about the same two-year period as it applies to the scene in heaven, which we covered extensively earlier in this chapter.

The period of God's new Millennium on earth begins with the strangest event of human history. An extremely loud sound like thunder will come from heaven! What is strange about this, is there are no clouds in the sky in some areas and everyone all over the world will hear this sound. The sound will be so loud that it will sound like an extremely loud trumpet blast. Millions upon millions of people will die instantly, without any explanation. People who will be flying planes, driving vehicles, at work, at home, walking their dog, reading the paper, some will be sleeping, some will be eating and doing everything imaginable. Some of the people will be sick, but most of them are perfectly healthy. Some of the people, who will die in this multitude of deaths, will be pastors of church's, but strangely enough many of them will remain alive. What does all this mean? Most of the people around the world will have no idea, but as God's appointed time it will be the beginning of the end for God to deal with a sinful world.

As the scene opens, because of the Rapture, we see terrible disasters all around the globe. Plane crashes, train crashes, car wrecks, and accidents at work all cause more people to lose their lives. The chaos will turn the world into a tailspin. As a result of being the country who will have the most Christians raptured, the United States will suffer the worst devastation of all. Even though the United States is in the apostate state of the lukewarm Laodicean church, it will still be the most God-fearing nation on earth at the time of the Rapture. Percentage wise and probably numerically it will have the most people raptured of all the nations of the world. A vast number of people who hold leadership rolls in our country will die. Believe it or not a large number of government officials, military leaders, businessmen, religious leaders and people that make up the moral fiber of our nation today will have died. It will cripple our economy and probably cause the stock market to crash. Because of that, the dollar and its status among the international monetary system will be wiped away immediately. These activities will leave the United States in a position of protecting itself, instead of being the world dominating power that it is today. It will not even have a leader who can step in and take control of the situation. *"Big brother"* will change continents and move to Western Europe, the strongest area remaining *After the Rapture*.

After the Rapture and Before the Tribulation Period

As the dust begins to settle around the globe the European Union will emerge as the strongest world order, both monetarily and militarily. The Euro, the new currency that is currently being introduced in Europe, will replace the dollar as the standard for the international monetary system. The NATO forces will emerge as the most powerful military command around the world. As the leaders of the European Union hold emergency meetings, to try to come up with a plan to bring order, not only on their continent but around the world, ten of the most prominent leaders of the European Union will be at the forefront of these meetings. All of a sudden a young charismatic leader appears on the scene. He could possibly be a leader of one of the smaller nations of the European Union, but not have as much notoriety as the leaders of the bigger nations. He could possibly be the leader of the nation of Greece, but somehow he has some Jewish lineage. All of this will probably start to take effect only days *After the Rapture*. Of course, this young leader is the Antichrist.

> Dan 7:7b-8 *...It was different from all the former beasts, and it had ten horns. "While I was thinking about the horns, there before me was <u>another horn, a little one</u>, which came up among them; and three of the first horns were uprooted before it. <u>This horn</u> had eyes like the eyes of a man and a mouth that spoke boastfully.* (NIV)
>
> Dan 7:20 *I also wanted to know about the ten horns on its head and about <u>the other horn</u> that came up, before which three of them fell—<u>the horn</u> that looked more imposing than the others and that had eyes and a mouth that spoke boastfully.* (NIV)

The Antichrist appears on the scene with very high expectations and brags heavily about how he could bring about peace for the whole world. He has those strange eyes that remind you of Adolf Hitler. He could mesmerize you with his eyes alone and he even reminds us of Hitler with all his boastful promises to correct the world problems. He will be such a powerful speaker that it will appear that he is a greater leader than the ten prominent leaders of the European Union (Revived Roman Empire). He will be proclaiming peace for the entire world, nevertheless, privately, just like Adolf Hitler, the Antichrist will have ulterior motives. The Antichrist will impress the people around the world as he appears live on T.V., trying to win support from the people. As he appears on television, he will try to explain away the sudden mysterious event of all the deaths that have just occurred. "Do not panic or become disturbed," he will say, "about all those deaths and the chaos that appears before us. Most of the people who died seemed to have been those hypocritical Christians who were only hindering the progress of the rest of the world. Now that they are gone, the world will be a lot better place to live. We can bring peace to everyone." He will be on the front page of every newspaper in the world. Accolades will pour in from around the globe. Most of the editors of the newspapers and journalists will support him. Even the ten leaders of the European Union will be impressed with the Antichrist, with three of them later developing serious reservations about him.

We get another glimpse of the Antichrist in chapter eleven of Daniel. Not everyone will agree with me that this is referring to the Antichrist. Most Bible interpreters agree that the eleventh chapter of Daniel shifts from past history to future history somewhere in its discourse, but they do not all agree at the same point. Most commentators believe that verse twenty-one refers to Antiochus Epiphanes, when in 168 BC, he desecrated the Jewish Temple. I disagree! From the flow of past and future history, contained in this great chapter, I believe that this portrays the Antichrist before he becomes the leader of the European Union. Here the kingdom is referring to the nation of Israel when it is living in safety.

> Dan 11:21 *"He will be succeeded by <u>a contemptible person</u> who has not been given the honor of royalty. He will invade the kingdom when its people feel secure, and he will seize it through intrigue.* (NIV)

The different translations depict him as a vile, contemptible, despicable person who has at this time yet to become the leader of the European Union. This verse correctly identifies him as a vile person, but at this time he can ill afford to let the public know his true character. Behind the scenes, he is a vile person. He will come on the world scene when it is basically in peaceful coexistence, with a few skirmishes going on around the world. He will gain prominence and take control of the European Union by intrigue and flatteries. The reasons I believe that the verses in Daniel 11:21-28 are referring to the Antichrist are because the following events are mentioned that will occur after the Antichrist becomes noticeable on the world scene. They are:

1. Russian Invasion (verse 22)
2. Death of the leader of Israel (verse 22)
3. Mention of a 7-Year Peace Treaty (verse 23)
4. Mention of breaking the 7-Year Peace Treaty (verse 28)

We will have more on these verses in the next chapter. During this two-year period the Antichrist will be making his bid to become the leader of the European Union. At the same time all this is going on, a well known religious figure will take charge and try to bring some calm to the scene. He will call all the religious leaders together and try to unite them into one organization. After all, will not God help through all the catastrophes of the times??? At first it is unlikely that the false prophet and the Antichrist are in cahoots, but somewhere along the line that will change, probably toward the end of this two-year period. Due to the fact that the religious system will probably organize quicker than the political system, in the beginning, the false prophet will be more revered and have more power than the Antichrist. Then during the first 3 ½ years of the Tribulation Period they will have more equal rolls and authority. Do not forget that the false prophet comes in like a lamb, so he will use religion to calm things down. People invariably turn to God when the problems of this world become too big to handle. It is too bad that, in this case, they turn to the wrong god.

There will be two anti-religious movements starting to gain momentum during this first two-year period. One is Anti-Semitism and the other will be Anti-Christian.

1. **Anti-Semitism** — A new and revived outbreak will occur in most parts of the world. This will drive more Jews to want to immigrate to Israel. The restraint of

After the Rapture and Before the Tribulation Period

Anti-Semitism was removed when the true church was taken out of the way at the Rapture. At this point the Antichrist, at least publicly, will be against Anti-Semitism in a big way thus using it as a tool to deceive the Jews into thinking that he is the Messiah.

2. **Anti-Christian** — Since all the true believers in Jesus Christ were taken out of the way, in order to bring about God's fierce anger to judge mankind on earth, true believers will have to start over numerically. It will only be a matter of hours before some people will realize that they missed the Rapture and will accept Jesus as their personal Savior. The only time it is too late to be saved is after the physical death of this body (with the exception of the time of the mark of the beast during the last half of the Tribulation Period). There are no second chances after that. Scripture does reveal that lots of people will be saved during the time of God's wrath. During the first two years *After the Rapture* the Christians will probably go through a period of open ridicule and mocking for their belief in Jesus. Even the Antichrist and false prophet will probably take part in the Anti-Christian jeering. As time progresses, Anti-Christianity will turn ugly as they will be faced with a choice of Jesus (salvation) or the mark of the beast (damnation). At that point, which will be the last half of the Tribulation Period, the Antichrist will be allowed to kill people if they refuse to take his mark. There will be a multitude of Christian Martyrs.

A point I would like to add here is one concerning the organization we all know as the United Nations, presently located in New York City. Today this organization is (unknowingly) preparing the world for the Antichrist and his system. *After the Rapture*, if it has not done so before, the United Nations will probably move its headquarters to Western Europe, possibly to Brussels, Belgium. It is a good possibility that the Antichrist will become the Secretary General of the United Nations. This, along with the Antichrist eventually taking over the leadership of the European Union, will give the Antichrist a considerable amount of power in a short period of time. The NATO forces will eventually fall under his command.

Wars that were already in progress at the time of the Rapture will resume after a little delay and escalate as time passes by. In the book of Psalms, we see the very scene of the Arab nations as they come against Israel at this time. This ancient hatred toward the Jews by the Arabs became extremely escalated after the Jews became a nation on May 14, 1948.

> Ps 83:1-8 *O God, do not keep silent; be not quiet, O God, be not still. <u>See how your enemies are astir, how your foes rear their heads</u>. With cunning they conspire against your people; they plot against those you cherish. "<u>Come</u>," they say, "<u>let us destroy them as a nation, that the name of Israel be remembered no more</u>." <u>With one mind they plot together; they form an alliance against you</u>—the tents of Edom and the Ishmaelites, of Moab and the Hagrites, Gebal, Ammon and Amalek, Philistia, with the people of Tyre. Even Assyria has joined them to lend strength to the descendants of Lot. Selah* (NIV)

AFTER THE RAPTURE

New conflicts will break out in various locations around the globe. One conflict that has been on-again/off-again since 1948, the Arab-Israeli conflict, will once again explode on the scene in a full scale war. The six nation Arab coalition of Lebanon, Syria, Saudi-Arabia, Iraq, Jordan and Egypt will resume their effort to drive the Jews into the Mediterranean Sea. These ancient countries make up the physical land mass of the nations who will conspire together and come against God's people. The six Arab nations listed above are the nations that surround the nation of Israel today. No longer will the United States be in a position to hinder the Arab nations intentions of exterminating the Jewish people. Because of the military superiority that the nation of Israel held before the Rapture, the Arab nations will be unsuccessful in their attempts to overtake Israel. A lot of blood will be shed in this conflict on both sides. In counter attacks the Israeli Air Force will bomb key Arab cities and bring about a lot of devastation. It is possible that the conflict will escalate to a point where all of the Arab inhabitants in Israel flee to the surrounding Arab countries. They will be set up in refugee camps until they can be assimilated into the population of various Arab countries. With the exodus of these Arab refugees, it will make room for the Jewish people returning to Israel from around the world.

This conflict will drag on throughout the entire two-year period with the nation of Israel providing their own protection. The Antichrist, as head of the United Nations, will become involved with both sides while trying to bring about a cease fire agreement. He will probably become the key figure in negotiating a peace treaty. As he meets with each individual side, privately, he will be making deceptive promises to each of them. He will be revealing to the nation of Israel that he is Jewish or at least part Jewish. He will have to convince them that he is Jewish in order for them to believe that he is the Messiah, which he will tell them he is. In the negotiations with the Arab nations the Antichrist might be telling them that he has Arab blood through the lineage of Abraham/Ishmael. Only God knows what lies will be spoken during this time.

To summarize, we see two one-world movements taking place during these first two years *After the Rapture*; a religious (one-world ecclesiastical system) and a political (one-world government), with each movement having a leader. They start out as separate entities, but somewhere along the line they join forces, with the false prophet leading the world to follow the Antichrist. The activities of both the Antichrist and the false prophet will be going at a fast pace. The Antichrist, along with the duties of running the United Nations, will be courting the ten prominent leaders of the European Union to become their leader. As the influence and power of the Antichrist continues to grow, the three leaders of the ten who had reservations about the Antichrist oppose him enough to cause a confrontation between the parties involved. Toward the end of the two years the Antichrist will overpower them with force and bring them under submission. They are literally subdued and persuaded by force to follow him.

> Dan 7:24   ***The ten horns are ten kings who will come from this kingdom. After them <u>another king</u> will arise, different from the earlier ones; <u>he</u> will subdue three kings.*** (NIV)

Negotiations for the peace treaty will probably run into months and months. There has

After the Rapture and Before the Tribulation Period

to be compromise and benefits worked out for both sides of the conflict, but finally after such a long conflict the two sides are battered with no real victor in sight. The Israeli's could possibly have the edge, but they too want the fighting to end. Another consideration for the nation of Israel is the fact that they are convinced that the Antichrist is their long-awaited Messiah.

Peace at last! For centuries the Jews have been praying for the peace of Jerusalem. Their Messiah is here to bring peace to Jerusalem. The Antichrist will become a hero all around the world for negotiating such a great peace treaty. Finally this conflict between the Arabs and the Jews, that has really been going on for thousands of years especially since 1948, is over—or so they believe.

> Ps 122:6-9 *<u>Pray for the peace of Jerusalem</u>: "May those who love you be secure. May there be peace within your walls and security within your citadels." For the sake of my brothers and friends, <u>I will say</u>, "<u>Peace be within you</u>." For the sake of the house of the LORD our God, I will seek your prosperity.* (NIV)

As the final details of the proposed 7-Year Peace Treaty are worked out, the guidelines will have to follow the promises God made to the Jews in the Old Testament. If they did not, the Jews would not sign such a treaty or believe that the Antichrist is the Messiah. The only way the Jewish nation would relinquish their military hardware and armed forces would be if they believed that the Messiah had arrived and that the government would be on his shoulders and that he would protect them. He would literally usher in the kingdom. The Jewish people will have mistaken the Antichrist as the Messiah at this point in time.

> Isa 9:6-7 *<u>For unto us a child is born</u>, <u>unto us a son is given</u>: <u>and the government shall be upon his shoulder</u>: and his name shall be called Wonderful, Counsellor, The mighty God, The everlasting Father, The Prince of Peace. <u>Of the increase of his government and peace there shall be no end</u>, upon the throne of David, and upon his kingdom, to order it, and to establish it with judgment and with justice from henceforth even for ever. The zeal of the LORD of hosts will perform this.* (KJV)

I have drawn up a simple copy of the 7-Year Peace Treaty, as mentioned in Daniel 9:27, in its most basic form. There will have to be compromise and benefits from both sides of the conflict in order to bring about a peace treaty.

> Dan 9:27a *<u>And he shall confirm the covenant with many for one week</u>:...* (KJV)

We leave as we see Israel, the Arab nations and the Antichrist signing a 7-Year Peace Treaty.

AFTER THE RAPTURE

7-YEAR PEACE TREATY

In order to insure peace and security in the Middle East, a formal peace agreement has been worked out. Due to the extreme war time conditions and the devastation it has caused over the last two years, it has been agreed to stop the fighting between the two sides involved in the conflict. The two sides of the conflict are the nation of Israel on one side and the Arab nations consisting of Lebanon, Syria, Jordan, Iraq, Saudi Arabia and Egypt on the other side.

It has been agreed by all parties, listed above, to stop the bitter fighting and adhere to a 7-Year Peace Treaty Agreement. The following stipulations must be carried out:

1. All parties have agreed to relinquish their weapons of war and turn them over to the United Nations Peace Keeping Forces. These countries will also disband their armed forces and will only be allowed to have local police forces to protect the local population.
2. The United Nations Peace Keeping Forces, through NATO, will deploy 100,000 troops to the area to insure compliance with the 7-Year agreement and safeguard the peace.
3. It has also been agreed, by the United Nations, that it will furnish financial subsistence to all the nations signing this agreement for the following purposes.

ISRAEL

1. Expand their border to give the Jews more land to allow room for homecoming exiled Jewish people.
2. Rebuild the nation of Israel.
3. Rebuild the capital city of Jerusalem.
4. Rebuild the Jewish Temple in Jerusalem on Mt. Moriah.
5. The Jews will be allowed to reestablish the ancient sacrificial Jewish form of worship.
6. The Jews will be allowed to return to Israel from every country in the world.

ARAB NATIONS

1. Restructure the boundaries of the Arab nations.
2. Rebuild the Arab nations.
3. Rebuild Babylon as the commercial center of the world.
4. Rebuild the Dome of the Rock in Babylon (could be in Mecca or Medina).
5. The Arab nations will be allowed to continue the Islam form of worship.
6. The Arabs from around the world will be allowed to return to their homeland.

_____   _____   _____
Israel   Lebanon   Syria

_____   _____   _____
Jordan   Iraq   Saudi Arabia

_____   _____
Egypt   United Nations

CHAPTER NINE

THE TRIBULATION PERIOD
THE FIRST 3 ½ YEARS

Revelation chapters six through sixteen are what is known as the Tribulation Period. It consists of two periods of 3 ½ years each. This seven-year period will include the plagues of the wrath of God on a sinful world. It should not surprise any man because God has warned us about this period of seven years for thousands of years in both the Old Testament and the New Testament, but mankind will be totally unprepared for the coming tragic events about to unfold.

I remember a statement that a young woman made to me after I had taught a young couples Sunday School class concerning the devastation of the Tribulation Period. After the class was over, she approached me and made a comment something to the effect that she did not want to know about such things because she had little children and was afraid of what would happen to them when these future events transpired. I can understand her concern, but scripture clearly teaches that believers will be taken out of the way before God judges the people on the earth during the Tribulation Period. Those below the age of accountability could also be raptured. We need to know that the Bible clearly teaches us not to worry about the anxieties of life and these events that will take place. True Christians will escape this devastation that will come on the whole world, but you can be assured it will come about!

Luke 21:34-35   *"Be careful, or your hearts will be weighed down with dissipation, drunkenness and the anxieties of life, and <u>that day</u> will close on you unexpectedly like a trap. For it will come upon all those who live on the face of the whole earth.* (NIV)

Rev 3:10   *Since you have kept my command to endure patiently, I will also keep you from <u>the hour of trial</u> that is going to come upon the whole world to test those who live on the earth.* (NIV)

Isa 2:12   *The LORD Almighty has <u>a day</u> in store for all the proud and lofty, for all that is exalted (and they will be humbled),* (NIV)

I have some good news and I have some bad news concerning the 3 ½ years we are about to study. First the good news.

A WEDDING FEAST

The scene in heaven is one of jubilance. The bride and the guests are beginning the seven day (seven years) Wedding Feast. If you have ever been to a Jewish Wedding, you know that it can be followed by a seven-day wedding celebration. It is a time for singing and dancing, along with eating and drinking the finest food and wine. Nothing but joy for seven long wonderful days (years). Everyone will be in a state of exhilaration and ecstasy. The exact opposite of what is about to take place on earth. While the seven-year celebration is taking place in heaven, the scene on earth will not be visible to the participants in heaven. The Old Testament saints will be hidden in their individual rooms of Divine protection while the church age saints (Bride) will be in the wedding chamber (Chupah). The prophet Isaiah was instructing the wedding guests more than 2700 years ago about the very time the Old Testament saints enter their rooms.

> Isa 26:20 *Come, my people, enter your chambers, and shut your doors behind you; hide yourself, as it were, for a little moment, until the indignation is past.* (NKJ)

The little moment referred to here is the Tribulation Period and the indignation is the wrath poured out on the earth as part of God's displeasure with sin. It is the same Hebrew word used here for indignation that was used in Daniel 8:19, *za` am*, pronounced *zah'-am*.

> Dan 8:19 *And he said, "Look, I am making known to you what shall happen <u>in the latter time of the indignation</u>; for at the appointed time the end shall be.* (NKJ)

7 SEALS

Judgment belongs to Jesus Christ and to Him alone. Who else bore our sins on the cross and suffered more than any other human being? Who else drank from the cup filled with iniquity? By His stripes we are healed, so by His righteous anger is sin judged. The judgment at this time is reserved for Jesus. Even Satan is judged at this time.

> John 5:22-27 *Moreover, the Father judges no one, <u>but has entrusted all judgment to the Son</u>, that all may honor the Son just as they honor the Father. He who does not honor the Son does not honor the Father, who sent him. "I tell you the truth, whoever hears my word and believes him who sent me has eternal life and will not be condemned; he has crossed over from death to life. I tell you the truth, a time is coming and has now come when the dead will hear the voice of the Son of God and those who hear will live. For as the Father has life in himself, so he has granted the Son to have life in himself. And he has given him authority to judge because he is the Son of Man.* (NIV)

> John 12:31 <u>*Now is the judgment of this world:*</u> *now shall the prince of this world be cast out.* (KJV)

The day of judgment (JUDGMENT DAY) will begin at the Rapture and will last a little more than nine years. The first two years of judgment will take place in heaven for the saved at the Judgment Seat of Christ. Then the judgment will shift to earth for seven more years

The Tribulation Period — The First 3 ½ Years

during the Tribulation Period and will culminate in the tenth year of the Days of Awe at the Battle of Armageddon where the last of the ungodly will be purged from the earth. The Tribulation Saints will be the last of those judged at this time. The final judgment of all those remaining from the peaceful portion of the Millennium will take place after the Millennium is completed. The judgment for the saved and the unsaved who lived during that time.

>Isa 26:19-21   ***Your dead will live; their corpses will rise.*** *You who lie in the dust, awake and shout for joy, for your dew is as the dew of the dawn, and the earth will give birth to the departed spirits.* ***Come, my people, enter into your rooms, and close your doors behind you; hide for a little while, until indignation runs {its} course.*** <u>***For behold, the LORD is about to come out from His place to punish the inhabitants of the earth for their iniquity;***</u> ***and the earth will reveal her bloodshed, and will no longer cover her slain.*** (NAS)

In verse 19, we observe the best resurrection passage of the Old Testament saints. These saints are then told to hide for a little while (seven years), until the indignation (Tribulation Period) has come to completion. Verse 21, shows us a picture of Jesus coming out of His place (location) in heaven as He is preparing to open the first seal in the book of Revelation, which will begin the punishment of the people on earth for their rebellion against God.

As the first act of Revelation chapter six opens, we see John observing Jesus opening the first of the seven seals on the scroll we just talked about in the last chapter. It must be noted that the seals are broken by Jesus in heaven, but the judgment will be poured out on the earth. In Revelation 6:2-8, we encounter the infamous Four Horsemen of the Apocalypse. There before John appears a rider on a white horse. That rider on the white horse is none other than the Antichrist. It is now time for the bad news!

>Rev 6:1-2   *I watched as the Lamb opened <u>the first of the seven seals</u>. Then I heard one of the four living creatures say in a voice like thunder, "<u>Come</u>!" I looked, and there before me was <u>a white horse</u>! Its rider held a bow, and he was given a crown, and he rode out as a conqueror bent on conquest.* (NIV)

A closer look at the rider reveals that he was given a crown. This reveals to us the exact time that the ten leaders of the European Union give the Antichrist the leadership of this confederated group of nations, along with their support (willing or unwilling). The crown symbolizes the leadership role of the Antichrist as we see him here as the leader of the Revived Roman Empire.

>Rev 17:12-13   *"The ten horns you saw are ten kings who have not yet received a kingdom, <u>but who for one hour will receive authority as kings along with the beast.</u> They have one purpose and will give their power and authority to the beast.* (NIV)

The earliest reference to the Antichrist is probably found in the Old Testament book of Judges, where Abimelech, a ruler of the city of Shechem, during the period of the Judges, told a parable about choosing a king. In this parable, *"the trees"* represent kingdoms. The story follows along the lines of all of the kingdoms (trees) looking for a single kingdom (tree) to rule over all the kingdoms of the world. After all the kingdoms refused to be that kingdom, all the kingdoms (trees) went to *"the thornbush"* and asked if it would rule the entire world. The thornbush in this story represents the Antichrist. The thornbush (the Antichrist) responds by telling the rest of the trees (kingdoms) that if they want him to be their king, they must take refuge in his shade (his kingdom—the Revived Roman Empire). If they refuse to obey the thornbush then he will consume the rest of the kingdoms of the world with fire. It has been a long time (around 1115 BC) since God revealed to mankind that the Antichrist would come on the scene. In this parable, *"the cedars of Lebanon"* represent the rest of the nations of the world.

> Judg 9:7-15   *When Jotham was told about this, he climbed up on the top of Mount Gerizim and shouted to them, "Listen to me, citizens of Shechem, so that God may listen to you. One day the trees went out to anoint a king for themselves. They said to the olive tree, 'Be our king.' "But the olive tree answered, 'Should I give up my oil, by which both gods and men are honored, to hold sway over the trees?' "Next, the trees said to the fig tree, 'Come and be our king.' "But the fig tree replied, 'Should I give up my fruit, so good and sweet, to hold sway over the trees?' "Then the trees said to the vine, 'Come and be our king.' "But the vine answered, 'Should I give up my wine, which cheers both gods and men, to hold sway over the trees?' **"Finally all the trees said to <u>the thornbush</u>, 'Come and be our king.' "The thornbush said to the trees, 'If you really want to anoint me king over you, come and take refuge in <u>my shade</u>; but if not, then let fire come out of <u>the thornbush</u> and consume the cedars of Lebanon!'** (NIV)*

As we continue looking at the rider on the white horse, we see that he is holding a bow and he rides out a conqueror and determined to conquer. The bow is a symbol for power. Since he has just received the blessing of the ten leaders and along with that the power of its armed forces, it will take a little more time before he can use this power to conquer other nations through force. Remember that he rides a white horse which symbolizes peace, which is what he will be promising the world at this time. However, his ulterior motives will eventually come into play as he rides out in majesty—determined to conquer the entire world. At this juncture the Jewish people believe that they are living in the Kingdom Age and the Messiah (false) is telling them privately that he will restore them to a position as the head of the nations. Actually, they are in the Kingdom Age, but at this point they are serving the wrong god. In Jeremiah, it describes the scene where God uses the nation's armies (the Revived Roman Empire) to destroy Babylon. This is the army (possibly NATO) of the destroyer (the Antichrist). It will take a few more years at this point for the Antichrist to use this army to launch a full scale war. God has in the past and will in the future, use the armies

The Tribulation Period — The First 3 ½ Years

of men and angels to accomplish His will.

> Jer 51:20 *Thou art <u>my battle axe</u> and weapons of war: <u>for with thee will I break in pieces the nations, and with thee will I destroy kingdoms</u>*; (KJV)

"*Battle Axe*"?*!! I never knew that my neighbor's mother-in-law had a biblical name! Just Kidding! God will use a coalition of armies to perform a duty for His purpose.

These four equestrians portray the world conditions during the first 3 ½ years of the Tribulation Period. They will not all come upon the world scene at the same time, but will follow the path of the Antichrist as he progresses through this first 3 ½ years. Shortly after the Antichrist receives the leadership role of the European Union, an event will take place that completely takes him and the rest of the world by complete surprise. While the Antichrist is preoccupied with implementing the 7-Year Peace Treaty, a force from the far north will be preparing for war. This attack will be sudden and a complete surprise to the Antichrist and also to the rest of the nations of the world.

RUSSIAN INVASION

Although the cold war is over, it does not mean that the old order of Soviet dominated countries are no longer a threat to the peace of the world. God Himself has plans for the giant war arsenal that exists there today. He will use this war machine for a purpose, even though He supernaturally defeats them.

While the world, overall, has been focused on the war in the middle-east, particularly the peace treaty negotiations during the previous two years, the leader of a large nation has been secretly preparing for war. He has also been meeting with several other nations to form an alliance. This was all done in secret and behind the back of the whole world. This leader is referred to as Gog from the land of Magog, but who is Gog and where is Magog?

Bible prophecy teachers today refer to this attack on Israel as the Russian Invasion, but keep in mind that the Bible does not mention the nation of Russia. It is mentioned as the land of Magog. To find out where the land of Magog is, we have to take a trip back in history to the time of Noah just after the flood.

> Gen 9:18-19 *The sons of Noah who came out of the ark were Shem, Ham and Japheth. (Ham was the father of Canaan.) These were the three sons of Noah, and from them came the people who were scattered over the earth.* (NIV)

In Genesis chapter ten, we see the descendants of Noah's three sons within the confounds of the nations that were to eventually be spread out over all the earth after the flood. The first person's name who settled in a new location, became the name of the area where they settled. Bible scholars today refer to it as the Table of Nations. Here is just a simple (not complete) overview of the nations that down through the years descended from Noah and his three sons.

AFTER THE RAPTURE

Son	**Settled in**	**Nations descended from them**
Shem	Middle East	Israel, Arab, Persia (Iran), Assyria
Ham	Africa & Middle East	Canaan, Egypt, Ethiopia, Libya, Babylon (Iraq)
Japheth	Europe	Rome (Italy), Greece, Media, Spain, France, Britannia (England), Germany, Poland, Russia, Portugal, Switzerland, Austria, Hungary, Scotland, Wales, Ireland, Holland, Prussia, Norway, Denmark, Sweden, and eventually North and South America

Tradition has it that Noah is supposed to have migrated to China and populated it, including China, Japan and India. The North and South American Indians could have come to America by way of the Bering Strait from Mongolia.

Out of all the nations and nationalities, God picked one nation to be His chosen people, to teach other nations the ways of God. Of course, we all know that it was the nation of Israel. I might add that the word Semite comes from the word "Shem," creating a word we all know as Anti-Semitism.

The father of the chosen nation was Abraham and he lived on earth some two thousand years after the fall. God did not have a nation separated out of all the nations before this time. The people who lived before Abraham, were for the most part, sinful and did not follow God or His ways, thus forming a need for a chosen nation to represent God.

Not long after the nations started spreading out all over the earth, Nimrod built the city of Babylon and the Tower of Babel, which was against God's will. For punishment God confounded the languages of the nations and spread them out over the then known world. You can read about this in Genesis chapter eleven. If you continue reading in chapter eleven, you will follow the lineage of Shem on down to Abraham, the father of the Jewish and Arab nations, thus the reference to many nations.

In order to find out where the nations originally settled, historians and archaeologists have traced the foot prints of Noah and his three sons. To get an idea of which nation Ezekiel is referring to in chapters 38 and 39, we need to know where Noah's descendants migrated to and began the building of their clans. In the case of Magog, who was the second son of Japheth, he along with his wife and children migrated to the northeast part of what we know today as Eastern Europe. The nation that exists there today is Russia, therefore, prophecy teachers coined the phrase "Russian Invasion." As we list the other nations in Ezekiel 38 and 39, we will follow the same line of reasoning we did to figure out where the land of Magog was located. The word of the Lord (Jesus) came to Ezekiel.

Ezek 38:1-6   ***The word of the LORD came to me: "Son of man, set your face against <u>Gog</u>, of the land of Magog, the chief prince of Meshech and Tubal;*** *prophesy against him and say: 'This is what the*

The Tribulation Period — The First 3 ½ Years

*Sovereign LORD says: I am against you, O Gog, chief prince of Meshech and Tubal. I will turn you around, put hooks in your jaws and bring you out with your whole army—your horses, your horsemen fully armed, and a great horde with large and small shields, all of them brandishing their swords. **Persia, Cush and Put will be with them**, all with shields and helmets, also **Gomer** with all its troops, and **Beth Togarmah** from the far north with all its troops—**the many nations with you**.* (NIV)

God told Ezekiel, who is referred to here as "Son of man," to turn toward the north and reveal what would happen to the leader (Gog) of Magog (Russia). God warns that He is against Gog, the leader of a confederacy of armies that suddenly attack the nation of Israel. Gog is mentioned as the chief prince (leader) of Meshech and Tubal. Meshech was the sixth son of Japheth and he settled in the area known today as Turkey. It is northwest of Israel in an area south of the Black Sea. On some maps it can be referred to as Asia Minor. It is also the area that the seven churches, which are listed in the book of Revelation chapters two and three, were located. Tubal was the fifth son of Japheth and he settled in the area known as Cappadocia just south of the Black Sea. Today that area is known as part of Turkey. Somewhere along the line, probably during the two years before the signing of the 7-Year Peace Treaty, the areas where Meshech and Tubal existed will align themselves with Gog, making him the chief prince (leader) of these nations.

Throughout history, names and borders of nations have changed about as often as the weather, mostly because of armed aggression from surrounding nations. In order for God to give us the location of the armies that would be attacking Israel in a future time, He listed the name of the first person who settled there with his family. As we said before, that persons name became the name of that location. To make it easier for the people living toward the end of the age to figure out what nations these prophecies were referring to, God listed the original nation that existed in that location to pinpoint the location of the areas we are looking for and to identify the mighty army we are now studying. When we identify the location of the nation that Ezekiel reveals to us, we can find the name of the nation that exists there today, but remember that borders change along with names, so there will be some overlapping of some of the nations that exist there today. Also, there is no way today to pinpoint the exact area of the original nations. We can determine the general area we are looking for and see the picture God is presenting to us. We cannot be exact, but can come close to what we are looking for. So our initial research will be for the area of the original location and after finding it, locate the names of the nations who occupy that area today.

Evidently, Gog and his army were on their way to attack a nation—some suggest the United States, but that is purely speculation—when God put thoughts in Gog's mind to seek a different target. Gog, the leader of Russia, chief leader of Meshech and Tubal (Turkey), will join forces with Persia (Iran), Cush (Ethiopia), Put (Libya), Gomer (part of Turkey) and Beth Togarmah (Ukraine and Kazakhstan). The Persians are descendants of Shem while Cush (the Ethiopians) and Put (the Libyians) are the descendants of Ham. Gomer is the oldest son of Japheth and settled in the area northeast of Israel and southeast of the Black Sea. An area east of where the Cimmerians occupied the land at the time the Assyrians were the dominating world power. Some believe that Gomer settled in the area of Germany and that Germany will be one of the nations involved in the Russian Invasion. I find that highly unlikely. Germany is more likely to be a member of the Revived Roman Empire, and like it or not will be supporting the Antichrist and not Gog. Gomer is part of where Turkey is today. Togarmah was the third son of Gomer, which makes him a grandson of Noah, and settled north (Ezekiel calls it the far north) of the Black Sea and the Caspian Sea. The Scythians occupied this area during the Medo-Babylonian Realms (560 BC). Today it is the countries known as the Ukraine and Kazakhstan (of the former Soviet Union).

From the map, on page 757, you can see that this confederation of nations, with Gog as the leader, form an outer perimeter around the six Arab nations that fought earlier against Israel and later signed the 7-Year Peace Treaty with her. This is probably the reason that they are not joining forces with these eight nations (could be more) against Israel. The Arab nations are war torn after two years of bloody fighting and some of the nations have begun fulfilling their promise to turn their military might over to the United Nations, as they agreed. Nevertheless, some of the six nations that surround Israel are all to willing to allow an enormous army to cross through their countries in an attempt to destroy the nation of Israel, which they themselves failed to do.

God tells Gog to *"Get ready,"* take command of all these armies and attack Israel.

Ezek 38:7-12   ***"'Get ready; be prepared, you and all the hordes gathered about you, and take command of them. After many days you will be called to arms. In future years you will invade a land that has recovered from war,** whose people were gathered from many nations to the mountains of Israel, which had long been desolate. They had been brought out from the nations, and now all of them live in safety. You and all your troops and the many nations with you will go up, advancing like a storm; you will be like a cloud covering the land. "'This is what the Sovereign LORD says: On that day thoughts will come into your mind and you will devise an evil scheme. You will say, "I will invade a land of unwalled villages; I will attack a peaceful and unsuspecting people—all of them living without walls and without gates and bars. I will plunder and loot and turn my hand against the resettled ruins and the people gathered from the nations, rich in livestock and goods, living at the center of the land." (NIV)*

We are told that it will be after many days (I am sure they did not realize it would be more than 2500 years) and then Gog will be readied for war. In the future you will invade Israel who recovered from the war with the Arabs, a people who have returned to their homeland from the nations to which they have been scattered for thousands of years and a place that lay desolate for a long time. They had been brought back from out of the nations and now all of them live in safety. This could only refer to the time after they sign the 7-Year Peace Treaty. That is when Israel believes that the Messiah will have returned and that they

The Tribulation Period — The First 3 ½ Years

are under His protection. After all they are living in the Kingdom Age that God promised them thousands of years ago, or so they believe at this time.

Gog and the many nations with him will advance like a storm and will be like a cloud covering the land, meaning they will make a sudden advance and storm over the entire nation of Israel. Gog will have evil thoughts and devise an evil plan against Israel. Gog will brag to the leaders of the nations joining him in this scheme that he will be invading a people who will not be expecting an attack. They do not even have any defense. He says he will plunder and loot the once desolate cities filled with the Jews re-gathered from around the world who are living in the land of Israel.

There will be those who question the motives of this huge armed force swooping down on Israel.

Ezek 38:13-16   *__Sheba and Dedan and the merchants of Tarshish and all her villages will say to you, "Have you come to plunder? Have you gathered your hordes to loot, to carry off silver and gold, to take away livestock and goods and to seize much plunder?"__ "Therefore, son of man, prophesy and say to Gog: 'This is what the Sovereign LORD says: In that day, when my people Israel are living in safety, will you not take notice of it? You will come from your place in the far north, you and many nations with you, all of them riding on horses, a great horde, a mighty army. __You will advance against my people Israel like a cloud that covers the land. In days to come, O Gog, I will bring you against my land, so that the nations may know me when I show myself holy through you before their eyes.__* (NIV)

Sheba, Dedan and the merchants of Tarshish protest this invasion. Sheba and Dedan are the grandsons of Cush and settled in the mountainous region in southwest Arabia. Sheba is what is known today as Yemen and Dedan and is located in Saudi Arabia. Some scholars believe that Sheba was originally in Egypt and that Dedan was located in an area where Jordan exists today. Tarshish is believed to be a city or territory in an area in the western portion of the Mediterranean Sea who traded by ship with the Phoenicians, Spain to be more exact. However, the merchants of Tarshish could have a far more reaching meaning than just one nation or location. Because the ships of Tarshish carried such great riches, they became the symbol of wealth, power and pride. The merchants of Tarshish could mean that protests come from cities who have great fleets of merchant ships. This war could have the potential to hurt their business ventures with the wealthy nation of Israel, along with the other nations of the world. The protest will come from the port cities from around the globe.

As we pick up the action, we see Israel being attacked from all sides. Gog as the leader will come from the north with armies from Russia, Ukraine, Kazakhstan, Georgia, Armenia, Azerbaijan and Turkey. They could possibly advance through Lebanon and Syria to attack Israel from the north and the east. Iran (Persia) would advance from the east, possibly crossing through Iraq, Syria and Jordan to hit Israel on the east side. The main attack will come from the eastern border of Israel. Then, at the same time, Ethiopia (Cush) and Libya

(Put) could be advancing through Egypt to attack by land from the south and west. Ships from Russia passing through the Black Sea and the Mediterranean Sea will attack the shores of Israel. They do literally cover Israel like a cloud. Because of the surprise attack and the speed of the aggressors, there will be little resistance and blood shed of the people from Israel, but a lot of damage to the terrain. In verse sixteen, God reveals an explanation about why He is allowing this to take place. In the latter days God will bring Gog against Israel so that the nations will know Him, because He supernaturally destroys Israel's enemy. Surely there is a God of Israel. At this point in time Israel recognizes God, but still fails to recognize Jesus as the true Messiah. As we continue, we see God asking Gog a question.

> Ezek 38:17-23 *"'This is what the Sovereign LORD says: Are you not the one I spoke of in former days by my servants the prophets of Israel? At that time they prophesied for years that I would bring you against them. This is what will happen in that day:* **When Gog attacks the land of Israel, my hot anger will be aroused,** *declares the Sovereign LORD.* **In my zeal and fiery wrath I declare that at that time there shall be a great earthquake in the land of Israel.** *The fish of the sea, the birds of the air, the beasts of the field, every creature that moves along the ground, and all the people on the face of the earth will tremble at my presence. The mountains will be overturned, the cliffs will crumble and every wall will fall to the ground. I will summon a sword against Gog on all my mountains, declares the Sovereign LORD.* **Every man's sword will be against his brother.** *I will execute judgment upon him with plague and bloodshed;* **I will pour down torrents of rain, hailstones and burning sulfur on him and on his troops and on the many nations with him.** *And so I will show my greatness and my holiness, and I will make myself known in the sight of many nations. Then they will know that I am the LORD.'* (NIV)

Gog, aren't you the one I spoke about a long time ago through the Old Testament prophets of Israel? Back then they prophesied for many years that I would bring you against Israel. This is what will happen at that time:

1. God will be extremely angry.
2. There will be a great earthquake in Israel.
3. The earthquake will so terrorize and confuse the enemy soldiers that they will turn on their own soldiers and kill each other.
4. God will defeat them with a cataclysmic event of a torrential rainstorm mixed with hail and burning sulfur. The rest of the world will stand in amazement.

By defeating the enemy of Israel, supernaturally from heaven, it will show God's greatness and holiness. Many nations will recognize that this defeat of Gog and the many nations with him came from Almighty God Himself. As we end chapter 38 and begin chapter 39, we find the same event described only with more detail.

The Tribulation Period — The First 3 ½ Years

Ezek 39:1-16 *"Son of man, prophesy against Gog and say: 'This is what the Sovereign LORD says: **I am against you, O Gog, chief prince of Meshech and Tubal.** I will turn you around and drag you along. I will bring you from the far north and send you against the mountains of Israel. Then I will strike your bow from your left hand and make your arrows drop from your right hand. On the mountains of Israel you will fall, you and all your troops and the nations with you. I will give you as food to all kinds of carrion birds and to the wild animals. You will fall in the open field, for I have spoken, declares the Sovereign LORD. I will send fire on Magog and on those who live in safety in the coastlands, and they will know that I am the LORD. "'I will make known my holy name among my people Israel. I will no longer let my holy name be profaned, and the nations will know that I the LORD am the Holy One in Israel. **It is coming! It will surely take place, declares the Sovereign LORD.** This is the day I have spoken of. "'Then those who live in the towns of Israel will go out and use the weapons for fuel and burn them up—the small and large shields, the bows and arrows, the war clubs and spears. For seven years they will use them for fuel. They will not need to gather wood from the fields or cut it from the forests, because they will use the weapons for fuel. And they will plunder those who plundered them and loot those who looted them, declares the Sovereign LORD. "'On that day I will give Gog a burial place in Israel, in the valley of those who travel east toward the Sea. It will block the way of travelers, because Gog and all his hordes will be buried there. So it will be called the Valley of Hamon Gog. "'For seven months the house of Israel will be burying them in order to cleanse the land. All the people of the land will bury them, and the day I am glorified will be a memorable day for them, declares the Sovereign LORD. "'Men will be regularly employed to cleanse the land. Some will go throughout the land and, in addition to them, others will bury those that remain on the ground. At the end of the seven months they will begin their search. As they go through the land and one of them sees a human bone, he will set up a marker beside it until the gravediggers have buried it in the Valley of Hamon Gog. (Also a town called Hamonah will be there.) And so they will cleanse the land.'* (NIV)

Here is what we can glean from these sixteen verses:

1. God is against Gog, chief prince of Meshech and Tubal.
2. I will make you change directions and bring you from the far north to attack Israel.
3. Your weapons will be made defenseless.
4. You and your accomplices will be defeated in Israel. Your dead bodies will be food for the carrion birds and wild animals. I looked up *"carrion"* in *Webster's*

AFTER THE RAPTURE

Dictionary and found the meaning to be *"dead and putrefying flesh."*
5. God will send some sort of supernatural punishment (fire) on Magog (Russia) and those nations joining him in this act of violence. The people from the nations will recognize that it is from God.
6. The people in Israel will be in awe as their God defeats this great enemy.
7. The people of Israel will use the abandoned weapons, left after the defeat of Gog, for fuel for their stoves and fireplaces for seven years. They will take all the plunder from the enemy who plundered them. These weapons for fuel will become extremely important for some of the Jews after they flee from the Antichrist during the second half of the Tribulation Period.
8. There will be so many dead bodies from the invaders that a special burial place will be needed for all their bodies. The earthquake will cause a steep gorge or valley near the Dead Sea and will be in the way of people traveling. It will take seven months to bury the dead and to clean the land of Israel. The grave site will be named "Valley of Hamon Gog." *Hamon Gog* means, "multitude of Gog."
9. Men will be hired to bury the dead. Those hired will be split into two groups. One group of people will travel throughout the land to find the bodies of the dead, which will be taken to a special burial place at Hamon Gog. The second group of people will bury the bodies they find at the location where they are found. At the end of seven months these two groups of people will continue looking for human bones. When the search party finds the human remains of a soldier they will place a marker by it to identify its location so the people from the burial party can take the remains to the Valley of Hamon Gog.
10. There will be such a large number of people employed to bury the dead that it will create a small town located in the vicinity of the "Valley of Hamon Gog." It will be named Hamonah. Again in this name we have the word *Hamon*, which means "multitude." It will take a great number of people to bury the dead from this battle.

The bulk of this mighty army will probably come from the western border of Jordan and thrust itself upon the tiny nation of Israel. The attack from the rear will be from the Mediterranean Sea and also on land along the Egyptian border. After the troops have literally covered the land, God will cause a supernatural fire and a great earthquake to take place in the land of Israel. These events will so frighten the troops that the frontal attack will race east toward the Dead Sea, while the troops from the rear will make a b-line to the west heading toward the Mediterranean Sea. They are so horrified and confused that they become engaged in battle with each other, destroying most of themselves. With such a large amount of dead bodies lying around—it will take seven months to bury all of them—can you imagine the awful stench that will fill the air? Remember – Corpses stink!

This concludes the detailed description of the Russian Invasion the Old Testament Prophets predicted that will take place in the latter days. God will defeat the mighty army of Gog and his allies, supernaturally, just as suddenly as they attack Israel. From the time that God turns them around and points them toward Israel, until God defeats them, will probably only be a matter of weeks or perhaps months.

After the Russian Invasion, we see the Antichrist as he attempts to calm down the world's perception after this mighty war. "I want peace to prevail!" he will be quoted as saying. This war will give him an excuse to build up the NATO forces through the United Nations. By now, the Antichrist will have control over both agencies. He will tell the world that he needs the build-up of forces to prevent any future surprise attacks like the one that just occurred. Secretly, though, he needs the forces to conquer the world.

> Rev 6:3-4 *When the Lamb opened <u>the second seal</u>, I heard the second living creature say, "<u>Come!</u>" Then <u>another horse</u> came out, <u>a fiery red one</u>. Its rider was given power to take peace from the earth and to make men slay each other. To him was given a large sword.* (NIV)

Here we see the very military might we were just referring to—the power base to take peace from the world and the military device to make it happen. The rider on this red horse will be the Antichrist, red being the symbol of blood. As soon as the Antichrist builds up his army, the blood shed will begin as he starts to conquer the smaller nations around Europe and the Middle East.

> Dan 11:22-24 *Then an overwhelming army will be swept away before him; <u>both it and a prince of the covenant will be destroyed</u>. After coming to an agreement with him, he will act deceitfully, and with only a few people he will rise to power. When the richest provinces feel secure, he will invade them and will achieve what neither his fathers nor his forefathers did. He will distribute plunder, loot and wealth among his followers. He will plot the overthrow of fortresses—but only for a time.* (NIV)

These verses reveal the Antichrist around this time. The overwhelming army that will be swept away before the Antichrist is a reference to the Russian Invasion. The Antichrist will be helpless during this time. After the defeat of Gog, the Antichrist will tell the leaders of Israel that he, as the Messiah, was the one who was responsible for defeating Gog and his armies. With this lie it will strengthen the bond of Israel and the false Messiah. I almost believe at this point that the Antichrist starts to believe that he is a god and that he was responsible for defeating Gog. He even believes his own lies. The reference to the prince of the covenant here is referring to the leader of Israel. The person who negotiated and signed the 7-Year Peace Treaty for Israel. If you will remember back, in chapter six, I mentioned a possible political conspiracy and assassination of the leader of Israel. A disgruntled member of a radical right-wing group who disagreed with the signing of the 7-Year Peace Treaty could possibly assassinate the prime minister of Israel. I discussed it under the subtitle of the Fast of Gedaliah. Daniel 11:22 makes mention that both the overwhelming force and the prince of the covenant will be destroyed at this time.

Not long after the signing of the 7-Year Peace Treaty, which the prime minister of Israel signed, the Antichrist will escalate his deceitful practices. After coming to an agreement with the ten leaders of the Revived Roman Empire, the Antichrist will become very powerful. This will happen after he becomes the leader of the European Union. As he becomes more powerful, we see the Antichrist starting to take over some of the wealthier (probably small) nations, just when they were beginning to think the world was heading for a more peaceful coexistence. The Antichrist will reward the small number of people who were responsible for bringing him to power with the wealth he plunders from the nations he confiscated by peaceful (noncombatant) invasions. His power will be in the process of expanding as he takes in new territory. As he is confiscating the smaller wealthy countries, he is making plans to invade the bigger nations with the power to protect themselves, but only for a while, because before long he will step up his efforts to expand his empire by conquering bigger and more fortified nations, the bigger fish in the sea.

In Daniel chapter eight, we see the Antichrist as he progresses through this 3 ½ year period.

Dan 8:9-10   *Out of one of them came <u>another horn</u>, which started small but grew in power to the south and to the east and toward the Beautiful Land. It grew until it reached the host of the heavens, and it threw some of the starry host down to the earth and trampled on them.* (NIV)

The Antichrist will start small, but will increase in strength. His advances will be toward the south, the east and against some of the smaller wealthy nations around the region of the European Union. Most of the translations have added the word "land" at the end of verse 9. It is not in the original manuscript. The word used for "Beautiful" is *"tsebiy"* and *Strong's Definition* is, "in the sense of prominence; splendor." The Antichrist will need to have control of the oil producing nations in order to power his war machines, and do not forget that wealth translates into power. This verse should more correctly apply to the general area to which the Antichrist is expanding his empire, from the Revived Roman Empire in the direction south and east, which is probably Northeastern Europe, the Balkin countries, Central and Southwest Asia respectively, including the smaller nations with wealth. This could include some of the oil rich nations like Kuwait. This also agrees with Daniel 11:24 above, where it talks about the Antichrist invading wealthy nations. The power of the Antichrist eventually grows to such enormous proportion that it even reaches angels in heaven. At this time, the Antichrist is protecting the nation of Israel from any aggressors.

Israel, at the time of the Russian Invasion, was well on its way to fulfilling the promises they made when they signed the 7-Year Peace Treaty. They turned all their weapons over to the NATO forces who removed them from the country. They were starting the rebuilding program to repair and rebuild their infrastructure, their agricultural centers and their cities. Financial aid was coming in from the United Nations. At the time of the Russian Invasion almost all the Jewish people from around the world had returned to the land of Israel. After the Russian Invasion, their land will be more devastated than it was even during the two-year Arab war, but the Antichrist quickly steps in with financial aid and the process of rebuilding starts all over again. The Jewish people are in good spirits because they know that God defeated the Russian army. A priority of rebuilding the Temple, which was already going on before the Russian Invasion, will renew immediately. There is a renewed confidence in their Messiah. Let us rebuild just like the Old Testament predicted we would do. It does not take

The Tribulation Period — The First 3 ½ Years

long for the ravages of war to start to disappear.

Those people from around the world who have put their trust in Jesus Christ will be facing greater degrees of persecution and torture (even to the point of death). During these 3 ½ years it will not be a very favorable time for those who put their faith in Jesus. Today would be a better time to get down on your knees and ask Jesus to forgive you for your sins and have the Holy Spirit come and live in your heart.

At this same time, the Arab nations who signed the 7-Year Peace Treaty will be moving a little slower toward carrying out the promises they made. Perhaps a few weeks before the Russian Invasion, Gog had contacted the leaders of the Arab nations to acquire permission to travel through their land to attack Israel. Some of the nations (Egypt for one) have not even started turning their weapons over to the NATO Peace-Keeping Forces. They will probably have received some financial aid to start their rebuilding program. A huge financial contribution is given to Iraq to rebuild the city of Babylon, to restore it to a large commercial center. The Dome of the Rock will be under construction in one of the Arab countries, possibly in the city of Babylon. Most of the Arab countries dislike Israel's special treatment.

The false prophet's effort to organize a one-world religious order were only slowed a little by the Russian Invasion and was given more emphasis after the war was over. This war being another reason why they need to step up efforts to unite under the umbrella of a one-world ecclesiastical unit. The false prophet is starting to be seen in the company of the charismatic leader (Antichrist) more often and is throwing more support in his direction. He is also speaking with more authority toward both the other religious leaders and the people in general all over the world. Since the false prophet is an unbeliever, the false religious system (Babylon) will be flourishing also. Throughout this 3 ½ year period scripture warns us that the world will be full of false religious leaders who claim to be the Christ (Messiah). I am not sure where the false prophet will be headquartered—probably somewhere in the European Union (possibly Rome).

As the third seal is opened, we see the Antichrist riding on a black horse. The black horse is symbolic of the pestilence and famine that will exist during these 3 ½ years.

> Rev 6:5-6 **When the Lamb opened <u>the third seal</u>, I heard the third living creature say, "<u>Come</u>!" I looked, and there before me was <u>a black horse</u>!** *Its rider was holding a pair of scales in his hand. Then I heard what sounded like a voice among the four living creatures, saying, "A quart of wheat for a day's wages, and three quarts of barley for a day's wages, and do not damage the oil and the wine!"* (NIV)

Famine usually follows war and a good example of this was what followed World War I. Farmers can have their crops destroyed by the devastation of war or even confiscated by army troops and even by the government. World War II was a good example of this as we witnessed Germany rob the food supply from countries they invaded and then used it to feed their armed forces and even the German civilian population. World wide food will be in short supply during this time, partly because of all the wars in progress.

Inflation will also run rampant throughout the world. As we see a pair of balances in the hand of the rider of the black horse, we see the buying power of the world currencies deflating. It will take a bigger chunk out of the daily wages to purchase food for everyone worldwide. The strange part of all this is that there will be a lot of wealth in the world. The middle class or average bread winner will suffer along with those who already live in poverty. The old phrase—the rich will get richer and the poor will get poorer—will apply at this time. It will be so bad in some places, probably in the areas of those who supported the Russian Invasion, that it will take an entire days wages to buy a quart of wheat (enough for a couple of loaves of bread). In the same sentence, it is telling the rider not to harm the oil and the wine. I believe that the oil and the wine here is symbolic for the nation of Israel, a reminder to let the Antichrist know that he is not to harm the Jewish people during this first 3 ½ year period. The people of Israel are allowed to rebuild their nation (furnished with the funds to do so) and to become a big exporter of food (wheat, fruit, etc.). In essence, in a short period of time, it will become one of the wealthiest nations of the entire world. Along with that Israel will be protected by the Antichrist and his great army. Because of all of that the rest of the world will start to envy and at the same time hate the Jews.

The last of the Four Horsemen of the Apocalypse gallops onto the scene. Its color appears pale or even corpse-like and is symbolic for death.

> Rev 6:7-8 *When the Lamb opened the fourth seal, I heard the voice of the fourth living creature say, "Come!" I looked, and there before me was a pale horse! Its rider was named Death, and Hades was following close behind him.* They were given power over a fourth of the earth to kill by sword, famine and plague, and by the wild beasts of the earth. (NIV)

The Greek word for "pale" is *chloros,* with the meaning of greenish or yellowish pale. This pale horse clearly conveys the meaning of death and following death is Hades (Hell), which indicates that most of those killed during this 3 ½ year period will end up in hell. It even describes the method whereby the people will be dying—sword (warfare), famine (hunger) and wild beasts (dangerous animals). It is revealed here that the rider of the pale horse (Antichrist) will have control of one-fourth of the world at this time. Since the time period of the Four Horsemen of the Apocalypse will last for 3 ½ years, it means that it took the Antichrist only two years to become the leader of the European Union, and after that, another 3 ½ years to control one-fourth of the world. Here is the progress of the Antichrist for the first 3 ½ years of the Tribulation Period.

WATCH as he rides out on horses!

WHITE HORSE			
Receives Crown	**RED HORSE**		
	Bloodshed	**BLACK HORSE**	
		Famine	**PALE HORSE**
	3 ½ Year Period		Death

The Tribulation Period — The First 3 ½ Years

Jesus now opens the fifth seal and it reveals a scene in heaven.

Rev 6:9-11 *When he opened <u>the fifth seal</u>, I saw under the altar the souls of those who had been slain because of the word of God and the testimony they had maintained. They called out in a loud voice, "<u>How long, Sovereign Lord, holy and true, until you judge the inhabitants of the earth and avenge our blood?</u>" Then each of them was given a white robe, and they were told to wait a little longer, until the number of their fellow servants and brothers who were to be killed as they had been was completed.* (NIV)

Here we clearly see those souls of the people who have accepted Christ as their personal savior *After the Rapture,* during the first 3 ½ years of the Tribulation Period. After their death, their souls departed their bodies and went to the Temple in heaven. There they received white robes and were told to wait a little longer until the rest of the martyred saints of the Tribulation Period are complete. Then their blood can be avenged, more on this later. Their question to Jesus was—How long will it be before you judge the people who are living on the earth and avenge our blood? The answer to that question is found in verse 17—NOW!, *"for the great day of their wrath has come."* It will last for another 3 ½ years.

Ps 58:1-11 *Do you rulers indeed speak justly? Do you judge uprightly among men? No, in your heart you devise injustice, and your hands mete out violence on the earth. Even from birth the wicked go astray; from the womb they are wayward and speak lies. Their venom is like the venom of a snake, like that of a cobra that has stopped its ears, that will not heed the tune of the charmer, however skillful the enchanter may be. Break the teeth in their mouths, O God; tear out, O LORD, the fangs of the lions! Let them vanish like water that flows away; when they draw the bow, let their arrows be blunted. Like a slug melting away as it moves along, like a stillborn child, may they not see the sun. Before your pots can feel [the heat of] the thorns—whether they be green or dry—the wicked will be swept away.* <u>**The righteous will be glad when they are avenged**</u>**, when they bathe their feet in the blood of the wicked. Then men will say, "<u>Surely the righteous still are rewarded; surely there is a God who judges the earth.</u>"** (NIV)

Ps 94:1-3 *<u>O LORD, the God who avenges, O God who avenges, shine forth</u>. Rise up, O Judge of the earth; pay back to the proud what they deserve. How long will the wicked, O LORD, how long will the wicked be jubilant?* (NIV)

Egypt seems to be a problem child for the Antichrist, even during the first 3 ½ years of the Tribulation Period. Serious Bible prophecy enthusiasts and students of eschatology need to keep a watchful eye on the nation of Egypt during these last days of this age. This nation will play a big part in the opposition to the Antichrist during the Tribulation Period. It is exciting to watch these events of Bible prophecy materialize as they take place before our very eyes! It appears that Egypt and the Antichrist will be engaged in battle three separate times during the Tribulation Period—twice in the first 3 ½ years and once in the last 3 ½ years. It is doubtful, therefore, that Egypt has turned over any of their weapons arsenal after the signing of the 7-Year Peace Treaty. As an approximate guess, perhaps a year to a year and a half after the Russian Invasion, the Antichrist will attack Egypt. Egypt, unhappy with the 7-Year Peace Treaty, and what they feel is favoritism toward Israel, will align some of the Arab nations. Egypt will take the leadership position and build up their armed forces, possibly to get ready for an attack on Israel, when the Antichrist steps in with his great army to stop the momentum. It is now in his power to protect Israel.

Dan 11:25-28 *"With a large army he will stir up his strength and courage against **the king of the South**. The king of the South will wage war with a large and very powerful army, but he will not be able to stand because of the plots devised against him. Those who eat from the king's provisions will try to destroy him; his army will be swept away, and many will fall in battle. The two kings, with their hearts bent on evil, will sit at the same table and lie to each other, but to no avail, because an end will still come at the appointed time. **The king of the North** will return to his own country with great wealth, but his heart will be set against the holy covenant. He will take action against it and then return to his own country.* (NIV)

As we take a closer look at the confrontation, we see that the Antichrist (king of the North) has built up a powerful army. The Antichrist will taunt the leader of Egypt (king of the South) who has amassed a large and powerful army at the same time. This could likely be the first large confrontation that the Antichrist faces. It appears that not all of the Egyptian cabinet members agree with the leader of Egypt and his decision to go to war against the Antichrist, as we see a close advisor or possibly even a family member make an unsuccessful assassination attempt on his life. When he finally goes to battle, the Egyptians do not fare so well and they have heavy casualties. Finally a meeting is set up between the leader of Egypt and the Antichrist, with evil desires in their hearts, and both proceed to tell lies to each other. The Egyptian leader will finally make concessions of great wealth at which time the Antichrist (king of the North) will return to his empire (Europe).

Instead of preoccupying his mind with this great victory, the Antichrist has his mind set against the 7-Year Peace Treaty. Because of that he makes an unexpected stop in Jerusalem on his way home after his victory meeting with the President of Egypt. He is not very happy with the leaders of Israel concerning the rebuilt Temple and their renewed Levitical sacrificial system that was set up. He has a verbal confrontation with the religious leaders in charge of the sacrificial system. The Antichrist might imply to the religious leaders of Israel that he might just be a little higher up on the religious ladder than he originally claimed to be. He could be hinting that he is God and not just the Messiah. He might even

The Tribulation Period — The First 3 ½ Years

imply that he should be sitting on the throne in the Temple in Jerusalem. This is a clear sign to some in Israel that this man, the one who they believed to be the Messiah, is not who he claimed to be. The majority of the Jews in Israel still believe in the Antichrist, but this verbal confrontation will start some Jews doubting the real motives of the Antichrist. A small movement will begin in Israel against the Antichrist. After the confrontation is over the Antichrist will return to his homeland.

In Daniel 11:21-45, there seems to show a natural progression of the activities of the Antichrist. You can see him as he gains power—from not having any power to doing anything he pleases.

YEARS	SCRIPTURE	DESCRIPTION
2	Daniel 11:21	A contemptible person who has not become a leader at this time.
3 ½	Daniel 11:28	The king of the North — being a king denotes he is the leader of the European Union.
3 ½	Daniel 11:36	The king will do as he pleases — at this point he has enough power to do whatever he wants. No one can hold him back.

After the confrontation in Jerusalem, the animosity of the Antichrist begins to grow toward Israel. The thought of sitting on "his" throne and having the world worship "him" is ever on his mind. Private conversations with the false prophet are filled with this idea. His political power, along with its military strength, are enormous as the Antichrist has an empire that covers almost ¼ of the world and the false prophet has the religious community of the entire world almost under one banner. It seems as if there is no way of stopping this dynamic duo.

On the other side of the fence, the Arab nations have completely lost their trust in the Antichrist. They are secretly regrouping, again under the leadership of Egypt, to build their military might. They are seeking allies to join them in their fight against the Antichrist. They plan to resume their differences with Israel, with the hope of defeating them, after they defeat the Antichrist.

Because of the visit and confrontation with the Antichrist, some of the strict religious leaders in Israel are making a more advanced effort against him. Their numbers are increasing as the movement begins storing supplies in a secret place, just in case they have to hide somewhere if he comes and carries through with the threats he made when he confronted them earlier. Details are worked out and put in place for the means of transportation to get out of town in a hurry! They are taking comments made by the Antichrist very seriously.

The Christians around the world never had a chance. Ever since the Rapture and the first conversion to Christ, it has been down hill from there. They are being mocked, persecuted and martyred in ever increasing numbers. In spite of all that, there is a large group of those strange Christians who will not waver from their faith in following that man who died for them on a cross two thousand years earlier. Even though their number is in the millions, it is still a small percentage of the population of the world.

I am assuming that at this time there will be wars going on in the parts of the world that are not mentioned in the Bible. Places like North and South America, Africa and the Oriental countries of the Far East. How they play out on the world scene during the Tribulation Period seems to be a mystery. We do know that they are listed in Revelation chapter 18, when we see that **all the nations** as a whole are drawn into the trap of the harlot (false religious system). The majority of the people that cover the entire world will reject God during this awful time.

> Rev 18:3   *For **all the nations** have drunk the maddening wine of her adulteries. The kings of the earth committed adultery with her, and the merchants of the earth grew rich from her excessive luxuries."* (NIV)
>
> Rev 18:23 *The light of a lamp will never shine in you again. The voice of bridegroom and bride will never be heard in you again. Your merchants were the world's great men. By your magic spell **all the nations** were led astray.* (NIV)
>
> Jer 51:7   *Babylon was a gold cup in the LORD's hand; she made the whole earth drunk. **The nations** drank her wine; therefore they have now gone mad.* (NIV)

About one year before this 3 ½ year period is over, there appears two older gentlemen on the scene in Jerusalem. What is unusual about them is that they are wearing the Old Testament garments of sackcloth. They seem rather strange in this modern world, but the world marvels as they perform miracles and testify about the gospel. They seemed to appear out of nowhere!

As we draw near the close of the first 3 ½ years of the Tribulation Period, we see Egypt, once again, prepared for war. Egypt—with the help of the island nation of Cyprus (Kittim)—will participate in another war with the Antichrist. Apparently the Antichrist will get some intelligence reports that Egypt continued to build up its armed forces after their earlier defeat. The conflict will take place in Egypt as the Antichrist invades her.

> Dan 11:29 *"**At the appointed time** he will invade the South again, but this time the outcome will be different from what it was before.* (NIV)

I would like to establish the meaning of the "appointed time" in this verse. It will lead us to the time frame of when this second Antichrist/Egyptian battle will take place. The Hebrew word used in this verse for "appointed time" is *mowed'* or *moed'* and is pronounced *mo-ade'*. It is used in scripture for:

1. An appointed time (set time)
2. An appointed place
3. A festival (Rosh Hashanah, Yom Kippur, etc.)

The Tribulation Period — The First 3 ½ Years

    4.   An appointed meeting
    5.   The tent of meeting

We are concerned with it when it is used as an appointed or set time. Throughout history, God has appointed a certain time for certain events to occur. One of those events is the latter end of indignation (wrath). In Daniel chapter eight, it establishes this time to be the last half of the Tribulation Period.

> Dan 8:19   ***And he said, "Look, I am making known to you what shall happen in <u>the latter time of the indignation</u>; <u>for at the appointed time the end shall be</u>.*** (NKJ)

If we look back two verses, it reveals that this vision that Daniel had pertains to the time of the end, not the end of the age, but the end of indignation. The end of the time of God's righteous anger, when He finishes His dealings with His holy ones (Israel) and His judgment of the nations.

> Dan 8:17   *So he came near where I stood, and when he came I was afraid and fell on my face; but he said to me, "<u>Understand, son of man, that the vision refers to the time of the end.</u>"* (NKJ)

> Dan 8:20-22   *"The ram which you saw, having the two horns—they are the kings of Media and Persia. "And the male goat is the kingdom of Greece. The large horn that is between its eyes is the first king. "As for the broken horn and the four that stood up in its place, four kingdoms shall arise out of that nation, but not with its power.* (NKJ)

In verses 20-22—yet future for Daniel—it talks about the Medo-Persian and Greek Empires, but in verses 23-25, it jumps all the way forward in time to the Tribulation Period, more specifically the last half or the time of Great Tribulation. The New King James has the best translation of this verse, as it speaks of the latter portion of the indignation (wrath) or the second half of the Tribulation Period. The Hebrew word here for "latter time" is *'achariyth* and designates the latter part or the hind part of something. You could say here that it is referring to the end part of the indignation. Usually, when it refers to the end of something—such as the time of the end—the Hebrew word *"gets"* is used. We see this word used in verse 17 above when it refers to the time of the end, which is a reference to the entire seven years of the Tribulation Period. In Daniel 8:23-25, it gives us a short synopsis of the Antichrist during the last 3 ½ years of his reign, which will be the subject of chapter eleven.

> Dan 8:23-25   ***"And in <u>the latter time</u> of their kingdom,*** *when the transgressors have reached their fullness, a king shall arise, having fierce features, who understands sinister schemes. His power shall be mighty, but not by his own power; he shall destroy fearfully, and shall prosper and thrive; he shall destroy the mighty, and also the holy people.*

> *"Through his cunning he shall cause deceit to prosper under his rule; and he shall exalt himself in his heart. He shall destroy many in their prosperity. He shall even rise against the Prince of princes; but he shall be broken without human means.* (NKJ)

As we follow the progression in Daniel chapter eight, verse 17 (shown above) concerns the time of the end, referring to the Tribulation Period. In verse 19, it is describing the last half of the Tribulation Period (the latter time of their kingdom) as an appointed or set time when the end will come. It is the time (3 ½ years) that God will use to fulfill the prophecy spoken of by Daniel in chapter twelve, where he speaks of breaking the strength of the holy people (the Jews). More specifically, it is the Time of Jacob's Trouble.

Dan 12:7 *Then I heard the man clothed in linen, who was above the waters of the river, when he held up his right hand and his left hand to heaven, and swore by Him who lives forever,* ***that it shall be for a time, times, and half a time;*** <u>***and when the power of the holy people has been completely shattered, all these things shall be finished.***</u> (NKJ)

As we take a closer look at this verse, we find the word *moed`* listed twice; singular for "for a time" and plural for "times." Another confirmation that the last half of the Tribulation Period (the Time of Jacob's Trouble) is set as an appointed time.

In the book of Daniel the word *moed`* shows up six times, with Daniel 12:7 having it listed twice. Between the first time it was listed in Daniel 8:19 and the last time it appeared in Daniel 12:7, it is listed in Daniel chapter 11 three times.

Dan 11:27 ***The two kings, with their hearts bent on evil, will sit at the same table and lie to each other, but to no avail, because an end will still come at*** <u>***the appointed time.***</u> (NIV)

Dan 11:29 ***"At*** <u>***the appointed time***</u> ***he will invade the South again, but this time the outcome will be different from what it was before.*** (NIV)

Dan 11:35 ***Some of the wise will stumble, so that they may be refined, purified and made spotless until the time of the end, for it will still come at*** <u>***the appointed time.***</u> (NIV)

It is my belief that all the references to *moed`* in the book of Daniel are referring to a set time that God has appointed and that the set time here is always referring to the second half of the Tribulation Period. This is the main reason I started the beginning of the Antichrist's appearance in verse 21 of chapter eleven. The mention of the appointed time in verses 27, 29 and 35 are all referring to the last half of the indignation. A continued study of the word *moed`* reveals some very interesting thoughts. Appointed by God were:

1. Jewish Feasts — <u>Lev 23:2</u>   *"Speak to the Israelites and say to them:* ***'These are***

The Tribulation Period — The First 3 ½ Years

*my **appointed feasts**, the appointed feasts of the LORD, which you are to proclaim as sacred assemblies.* (NIV)

2. To show favor to the Jews (that time is yet future) — Ps 102:12-13 *But You, O LORD, shall endure forever, and the remembrance of Your name to all generations. You will arise and have mercy on Zion; for the time to favor her, yes, **the set time**, has come.* (NKJ)

3. Habakkuk's vision of the Time of Jacob's Trouble — Hab 2:3 ***For the revelation awaits an appointed time; it speaks of the end and will not prove false. Though it linger, wait for it; it will certainly come and will not delay.*** (NIV)
This vision speaks of the end of indignation and does not lie. Though it might take a while, wait for it, for it is sure to happen and it will not delay. This verse ties in perfectly with our study in Daniel and goes on to explain what happens during the last half of the Tribulation Period in chapters two and three of Habakkuk.

4. The time for Jesus to appear in the flesh — Gal 4:1-7 *Now I say that the heir, as long as he is a child, does not differ at all from a slave, though he is master of all, but is under guardians and stewards until **the time appointed** by the father. Even so we, when we were children, were in bondage under the elements of the world. **But when the fullness of the time had come, God sent forth His Son, born of a woman, born under the law, to redeem those who were under the law, that we might receive the adoption as sons.** And because you are sons, God has sent forth the Spirit of His Son into your hearts, crying out, "Abba, Father!" Therefore you are no longer a slave but a son, and if a son, then an heir of God through Christ.* (NKJ)
The Greek word used here is *prothesmios* (proth-es'-mee-os) and *Thayer's Greek Definition* gives the definition for this word as: set beforehand, appointed or determined beforehand, prearranged. This is the only time this word appears in the New Testament and speaks about God's prearranged time for Jesus to appear on this earth in human form.

5. A time for Jesus to judge the world — Acts 17:31 ***"because He has appointed a day on which He will judge the world in righteousness** by the Man whom He has ordained. He has given assurance of this to all by raising Him from the dead."* (NKJ)

6. We are **NOT** appointed to wrath — 1 Thes 5:9 ***For God did not appoint us to wrath, but to obtain salvation through our Lord Jesus Christ,*** (NKJ)
The Greek word here for "wrath" is *orge* (or-gay') and *Thayer's* definition is: anger, wrath, indignation, anger exhibited in punishment, hence used for punishment itself.

Daniel chapter eleven is one of the most fascinating chapters in all the Bible. Men, including theologians, have a difficult time believing God can write in such detail, concerning events before they happen (future history). I do not believe, as many scholars do, that the last five chapters of Daniel were written in the second century BC, after many of the events written about in chapters eight through twelve had already taken place. Their belief being that the intricate details in these chapters could only be written after they happen. My only comment to them is *"O ye of little faith."* It is no wonder they have a hard time believing the fate of what is about to come upon the whole world.

To get a complete account of the vision Daniel had in chapter eleven, we need to start at the beginning of chapter ten, somewhere around 536 BC, when Daniel had this vision. As you are probably starting to realize, Daniel's primary purpose in life was to write down future history, culminating with his main theme of the dealings with his people (Israel) during the last half of the Tribulation Period (Time of Jacob's Trouble). In the New Testament John had a similar mission when God took him to heaven to show him a vision of the Tribulation Period. To get a better understanding of the Tribulation Period, it is essential to study these parallel books of Daniel and Revelation. This vision in chapter ten concerns the Jewish people and culminates in the distant future in chapter eleven. Please note in Daniel chapter ten that Satan, referred to as both the prince of Persia and the prince of Greece, tries to keep Daniel from receiving the understanding of this vision.

Dan 10:14 *Now I have come to explain to you what will happen to your people in the future, <u>for the vision concerns a time yet to come.</u>"* (NIV)

The vision is explained to Daniel in chapters eleven and twelve. The time period covered in this vision will be more than 2500 years, from the time Daniel saw the vision until the end of indignation. God begins by telling Daniel that there will be three more kings who will rule in Persia before it is defeated by the Greek empire. Remember that Daniel was taken captive to Babylon seventy years earlier by King Nebuchadnezzar in 606 BC. Daniel remained in Babylon, probably because of old age, after the Medo-Persian Empire defeated the Babylonians in 539 BC. A concise chronological order of future history follows until Daniel comes to the main theme of his vision—what will happen to his people (Jews) during the Tribulation Period. There are numerous books that have been published that detail the history that has transpired from Daniel's time until today that applies to Daniel's prophecy. I will not, because of time and space, cover that period in this book, but I do recommend that you read up on the subject. It is fascinating to see how God writes history in advance. As I mentioned before, I believe that the break between past and future history for us today in Daniel chapter eleven is in verse twenty-one, where I believe the Antichrist is introduced.

In Daniel 11:27, we find the first mention of the appointed time of the last half of the Tribulation Period in this chapter. Here it points out that the first Antichrist/Egyptian war, during the first half of the Tribulation Period, did not take place during the appointed time, because that period is yet to come.

Dan 11:27 *"Both these kings' hearts shall be bent on evil, and they shall speak lies at the same table; but it shall not prosper, <u>for the end will still be at the appointed time.</u>* (NKJ)

The Tribulation Period — The First 3 ½ Years

The two kings represented here are the king of the South (who is the end-time leader of Egypt) and the king of the North (who is the leader of the Revived Roman Empire or European Union). As we advance to the second Antichrist/Egyptian battle, we observe that this battle is at the appointed time. This battle will take place just prior to the last half of the Tribulation Period, mainly because it takes place before the Abomination of Desolation. Egypt will not be defeated at this battle, because it will not turn out like the first conflict between these two foes, when the Antichrist and his army were the victors.

Dan 11:29-35 "*At the appointed time he will return and come into the South, but this last time it will not turn out the way it did before. "For ships of Kittim will come against him; therefore he will be disheartened, and will return and become enraged at the holy covenant and take action; so he will come back and show regard for those who forsake the holy covenant.* "*And forces from him will arise, desecrate the sanctuary fortress, and do away with the regular sacrifice.* *And they will set up the abomination of desolation.* "*And by smooth {words} he will turn to Godlessness those who act wickedly toward the covenant, but the people who know their God will display strength and take action.* "*And those who have insight among the people will give understanding to the many; yet they will fall by sword and by flame, by captivity and by plunder, for {many} days.* "*Now when they fall they will be granted a little help, and many will join with them in hypocrisy.* "*And some of those who have insight will fall, in order to refine, purge, and make them pure, until the end time; because {it is} still {to come} at the appointed time.* (NAS)

As the Antichrist returns to Egypt to do battle, he is both agitated and confident that he will succeed in defeating the Egyptians, but this time a different outcome than the first or the third battle between these two foes will take place. Egypt, joined by help from people located on the island of Kittim (Cyprus), will keep the Antichrist from victory. The Antichrist becomes disillusioned and enraged at this defeat and turns back toward Israel to vent his frustration and fierce anger against the Temple in Jerusalem. As the Antichrist is in Jerusalem, there will be some political and religious Jewish leaders who will still believe in him as the Messiah. The Antichrist will show special favor to those Jews who still support him, even though he is there to abolish the daily sacrifices. With his armed forces the Antichrist will profane the sanctuary by desecrating it. The troops will be assigned the task of guarding the holy of holies and will not allow the Jewish religious leaders access to the site. After the area is secure the Antichrist will start the construction of a new wing on the Temple, a place to position a throne for himself. The Antichrist will have to proceed with a little caution here and smooth-talk some of the Jewish leaders into continuing to believe in him. His real motives are still in the background. He is still showing favor to those leaders who support him, while there are those who are wise to the Antichrist and know that he is not the Messiah, as they firmly resist him at this time. These Jews who are resisting the

Antichrist are making a frantic effort to convince others that he is not the Messiah, with possibly a good number of these resisters, by this time, believing in Jesus as the Messiah. While they are fervently witnessing for Jesus and denying the Antichrist, their fate is being determined by death (from the sword or by being burned) and by being taken to prison or by being used for the spoils of war (hostages). When they start to wavier, because of all the persecution, they will receive a little help—this could possibly be a reference to the time God furnishes a place for some of them to hide from the Antichrist for 3 ½ years. Many of them that flee to the desert to hide will not be believers in Jesus, but will join them, probably to be protected from the persecution. Some of the Jewish believers in Jesus will be martyred and will receive their resurrected bodies later. This persecution of the Jews will continue until the time of the end of indignation (3 ½ years), for at the appointed time it will come.

Most prophecy teachers today fail to realize the significance of Egypt and the effect this nation will have on the Antichrist during the Tribulation Period. It will be interesting to watch the nation of Egypt, during these last days of the Dispensation of Grace, as it positions itself among the rest of the nations of the middle east. Even today, Egypt is a far more powerful nation than most people realize.

The King of the South will have the Antichrist pulling his hair out, especially at this time when he is unable to defeat the Egyptians. As we turn our attention back to this second battle, between Egypt and the Antichrist, mentioned above in Daniel chapter 11, we find the Antichrist outraged because of the defeat he just encountered. He is so let down at this defeat that he takes action against the Jewish people and it triggers the desecration of the Temple. In the end, because of this outrageous outburst of anger, the Antichrist will send some of his armed forces in to seize the Temple area and bring the sacrifices to a halt. The troops will profane and desecrate the Temple as bad or possibly even worse than Antiochus Epiphanes did in 168 BC. Along with bringing the Sabbatical sacrifices to a halt, they may even mock Antiochus Epiphanes and sacrifice pigs blood on the altar. They may even set up a statue of the Greek God Jupiter in the Holy of Holies, and who knows what else?

After this second battle between the king of the South (Egypt) and the king of the North (the Antichrist), it will be very close to the midpoint of the Tribulation Period. Please remember that all of the wars that will take place on earth during the Tribulation Period will constitute a period you could very well call World War III. By the time the Battle of Armageddon is fought, which is the final battle of World War III, all the nations of the world will be participants. Many, many wars will take place in this ten-year period known as the Ten Days of Awe and a lot of blood will be spilled during this time.

Sometime just before the midpoint of the Tribulation Period the Antichrist is inflicted with a wound that appears to be fatal. Scripture does not reveal to us how or where this will take place, but I am going to speculate a little bit here and say that a good possibility could be an assassination attempt on the Antichrist while he is in Jerusalem overseeing the construction of the room with the throne inside. A disgruntled young Jewish man seizes the opportunity and strikes the Antichrist with some sort of cutting instrument (Hebrew *chereb*; such as a knife, sword, axe or some sharp implement).

> Rev 13:3 ***One of the heads of the beast seemed to have had a fatal wound,...***
> (NIV)

The Tribulation Period — The First 3 ½ Years

The Bible never ceases to amaze me as far as how detailed it describes future events. In the book of Revelation the Antichrist is referred to as *"the beast out of the sea,"* but in Zechariah he is called *"the worthless shepherd."* Here we are told of the severity of the actual wound that was inflicted on the Antichrist.

> Zech 11:15-17 *Then the LORD said to me, "Take again the equipment of <u>a foolish shepherd</u>. For I am going to raise up a shepherd over the land who will not care for the lost, or seek the young, or heal the injured, or feed the healthy, but will eat the meat of the choice sheep, tearing off their hoofs. "Woe to <u>the worthless shepherd</u>, who deserts the flock! May the sword strike his arm and his right eye! May his arm be completely withered, his right eye totally blinded!"* (NIV)

One of the arms of the Antichrist (probably his right arm) is slashed so severely that it dries up and withers away. He is also struck in the face and is blinded in his right eye. The perpetrator who committed this assassination attempt on the Antichrist is seized and taken away to be executed without a trial. As we approach the middle of the Tribulation Period the Antichrist will be laying on a hospital bed (probably in Jerusalem) with the doctors telling the high ranking political, military and religious leaders that his chances of survival are slim and that he will probably die before long.

WAR IN HEAVEN

At this same time there will also be a war going on in the heavenly realm between the angels, Michael and his army of holy angels against Satan and his army of fallen angels. This battle is recorded in Revelation chapter twelve.

> Rev 12:7 <u>*And there was war in heaven.*</u> *Michael and his angels fought against the dragon, and the dragon and his angels fought back.* (NIV)

This conflict actually had its beginning sometime around six thousand years ago. It started when Satan committed the first sin. In the book of Ezekiel, we see a picture of Satan as he was originally created. Here he is referred to as the king of Tyre.

> Ezek 28:11-14 *The word of the LORD came to me: "Son of man, take up a lament concerning <u>the king of Tyre</u> and say to him: 'This is what the Sovereign LORD says: "'You were the model of perfection, full of wisdom and perfect in beauty. You were in Eden, the garden of God; every precious stone adorned you: ruby, topaz and emerald, chrysolite, onyx and jasper, sapphire, turquoise and beryl. Your settings and mountings were made of gold; on the day you were created they were prepared. You were anointed as a guardian cherub, for so I ordained you. You were on the holy mount of God; you walked among the fiery stones.* (NIV)

AFTER THE RAPTURE

Satan was created as a beautiful angelic being full of wisdom. He was anointed as a guardian cherub (angel) and had access to the heavenly realm. He was in Eden, the Garden of God, in heaven dressed in garments adorned with precious gems. He was blameless in his duties until the day he sinned. What was this original sin?

Ezek 28:15-17   ***You were blameless in your ways from the day you were created till wickedness was found in you.*** *Through your widespread trade you were filled with violence, and you sinned. So I drove you in disgrace from the mount of God, and I expelled you, O guardian cherub, from among the fiery stones.* ***Your heart became <u>proud</u> on account of your beauty, and you corrupted your wisdom because of your splendor. So I threw you to the earth; I made a spectacle of you before kings.*** (NIV)

<u>PRIDE</u> ! Because of Satan's beauty, he exalted himself above God. The created cannot become greater than the creator. Because of this sin Satan was cast out from among the fiery stones and the conflict between good and evil had its beginning. We can add to the story as we see Satan addressed as the king of Babylon in Isaiah. Here we see him at the time the war in heaven is taking place, the very war we are looking at.

Isa 14:12-15   ***How you have fallen from heaven, O morning star, son of the dawn! You have been cast down to the earth, you who once laid low the nations!*** *You said in your heart, "I will ascend to heaven; I will raise my throne above the stars of God; I will sit enthroned on the mount of assembly, on the utmost heights of the sacred mountain. I will ascend above the tops of the clouds; I will make myself like the Most High." But you are brought down to the grave, to the depths of the pit.* (NIV)

From the time Satan committed his sin, it has been his primary desire to deceive mankind and to turn people away from God. He wants them to spend eternity in hell with him and the fallen angels (separated from God forever). He will use every form of deceit to accomplish this task and, as a matter of fact, the apostle John even informs us that Satan is the father of lies. False gods use false means to deceive people.

John 8:44   ***You belong to your father, <u>the devil</u>, and you want to carry out your father's desire.*** *He was a murderer from the beginning, not holding to the truth, for there is no truth in him.* ***When he lies, he speaks his native language, <u>for he is a liar and the father of lies</u>.*** (NIV)

The first human beings that Satan deceived were the first two human beings created by God—Adam and Eve. Still, the conflict will come to an end as we will see as we progress. Paul, in his epistle to the Ephesians, lets us know that our time on earth is not a battle against mankind, but in reality it is really a battle against Satan and his hoard of fallen angels.

The Tribulation Period — The First 3 ½ Years

Eph 6:12   *For our struggle is not against flesh and blood, but against the rulers, against the authorities, against the powers of this dark world and against the spiritual forces of evil in the heavenly realms.* (NIV)

Although Satan was originally cast out from among the fiery stones, it did not prevent him from having access to heaven and conversing with God throughout history. Their conversations seem to concern the activities of righteous people living on the earth, as we see in both the Old Testament and New Testament.

Job 1:6-12   *One day the angels came to present themselves before the LORD, and Satan also came with them. The LORD said to Satan, "Where have you come from?" Satan answered the LORD, "From roaming through the earth and going back and forth in it." Then the LORD said to Satan, "Have you considered my servant Job? There is no one on earth like him; he is blameless and upright, a man who fears God and shuns evil." "Does Job fear God for nothing?" Satan replied. "Have you not put a hedge around him and his household and everything he has? You have blessed the work of his hands, so that his flocks and herds are spread throughout the land. But stretch out your hand and strike everything he has, and he will surely curse you to your face." The LORD said to Satan, "Very well, then, everything he has is in your hands, but on the man himself do not lay a finger." Then Satan went out from the presence of the LORD.* (NIV)

Rev 12:10   *... For the accuser of our brothers, who accuses them before our God day and night, has been hurled down.* (NIV)

In the first book of Peter, we see Satan roaming the earth looking for someone to deceive.

1 Pet 5:8   *Be self-controlled and alert. Your enemy the devil prowls around like a roaring lion looking for someone to devour.* (NIV)

Angels are a created order of supernatural heavenly beings who are superior to man in power and intelligence. By nature they are spiritual beings, but in scripture they seem to have a physical form. It is their duty to act upon and carry out God's will as He carries out His plan of salvation. Among other things they are God's messengers to men. On earth they are primarily invisible, but when they are visible they appear to look like human beings. Angels were created by God and were present and rejoicing when He created the earth.

Ps 148:1-6   *Praise the LORD. Praise the LORD from the heavens, praise him in the heights above. Praise him, all his angels, praise him, all his*

AFTER THE RAPTURE

__heavenly hosts__. Praise him, sun and moon, praise him, all you shining stars. Praise him, you highest heavens and you waters above the skies. Let them praise the name of the LORD, for he commanded and they were created. He set them in place for ever and ever; he gave a decree that will never pass away. (NIV)

Job 38:4-7   *"Where were you when I laid the earth's foundation? Tell me, if you understand. Who marked off its dimensions? Surely you know! Who stretched a measuring line across it?* ***On what were its footings set, or who laid its cornerstone—while the morning stars sang together and all the angels shouted for joy?*** (NIV)

    The best way to describe the order of angels—both those who have and have not fallen—is to look at the order of a military institution. In it, you have those who span the ranks of the commander in chief on down to a private, each angel with a different rank is assigned a particular duty to perform. It is an orderly well organized machine. When God created the angelic order, each angel was created for a position and a duty to perform. The angel with the highest position of angels was Lucifer. Angels were created with the same free-will choice of accepting or rejecting God. It appears that all of the angels made their decision (of who they would follow – God or Satan) at the time of Lucifer's sin. In the book of Revelation, we see where a third of the angelic order were drawn to Satan and chose to follow him, thus establishing the order of fallen angels with Satan, the great red dragon, that old serpent, called the Devil, as their commander in chief. Thus, in a sense creating two heavenly armies. The vast army of holy angels delight in praising the name of the Lord continually. Large numbers of them remain at God's side ready to do His every command. Angelic beings in the presence of God include cherubim, seraphim and living creatures (living beings) mentioned in Ezekiel and Revelation.

    Angels are invisible to us, but at times they appear on earth to perform duties for God and it is evident that angels bore the form of human beings and could at times be mistaken for men. There is no hint that they ever appeared in female form or as children. The conception of angels as winged beings, so familiar in Christian art, is not supported in scripture, although the cherubim, seraphim and the living creatures are seen with wings in their symbolic form. This could represent the speed at which they travel—in the blink of an eye they can travel from one place to another. When the angels are in the third level of heaven with God they are probably seen in a visible form.

    Angels have names, but only two of the names of the hierarchy of holy angels are given in scripture. They are Michael who is mentioned as the archangel and Gabriel. As the archangel, Michael probably replaced Lucifer as the chief or head angel of this order. Michael's name means *"Who is as or like God."* One of the primary duties of Michael is to watch over the chosen people and is regarded as the patron-angel of the Jews.

Dan 12:1   ***"At that time Michael, the great prince who protects your people, will arise...*** (NIV)

The Tribulation Period — The First 3 ½ Years

Gabriel, whose name means, *"man or hero of God,"* acts as a messenger of God. All appearances of Gabriel recorded in the Bible are connected with the promise of the coming of the Messiah. Gabriel was commissioned to explain to Daniel the vision of the ram and the he-goat in Daniel chapter eight, along with predicting the 70 weeks of Daniel in Daniel chapter nine. In the New Testament, Gabriel made the announcement to Zacharias of the birth of John the Baptist, along with the birth of Jesus to Mary. Though commonly spoken of as an archangel, he is not so called in scripture. In the rabbinical writings, Gabriel is represented as standing in front of the Divine throne near the standard of Judah.

The appearances of angels were especially active at certain times in the Old Testament, especially concerning Israel as a nation. They also appear frequently in connection with the birth of Jesus and when the new order of things (Dispensation of Grace) began at the time of the resurrection of Jesus. The activity of Satan and the fallen angels (demonic) are at extremely high levels at both the first and second coming of Jesus. The frequency with which angels participate in human affairs has diminished since Pentecost (the birth of the church age), but *After the Rapture* you will see renewed activity on the part of angels. You will see this as we travel through the book of Revelation, where it is filled with their specified duties. Angels are quite real and play a vital part in God's plan for the world.

The book of Revelation naturally shows a close relationship with the book of Ezekiel and Daniel, which are full of angelic activity. A few examples of angelic activity recorded in Revelation are:

1. An angel revealed to John the vision of the future event — the Tribulation Period.
   Rev 1:1   *The revelation of Jesus Christ, which God gave him to show his servants what must soon take place.* **He made it known by sending his angel to his servant John,** (NIV)

2. Seven angels are assigned the task of watching over the seven churches during the Dispensation of Grace.
   Rev 1:20   *The mystery of the seven stars that you saw in my right hand and of the seven golden lampstands is this:* **The seven stars are the angels of the seven churches,** *and the seven lampstands are the seven churches.* (NIV)

3. Four angels (beasts or living creatures) appearing around the throne in heaven.
   Rev 4:6-11   *Also before the throne there was what looked like a sea of glass, clear as crystal.* **In the center, around the throne, <u>were four living creatures</u>, and they were covered with eyes, in front and in back. The first living creature was like a lion, the second was like an ox, the third had a face like a man, the fourth was like a flying eagle. Each of the four living creatures had six wings and was covered with eyes all around, even under his wings.** *Day and night they never stop saying: "Holy, holy, holy is the Lord God Almighty, who was, and is, and is to come." Whenever the living creatures give glory, honor and thanks to him who sits on the throne and who lives for ever and ever, the twenty-four elders fall down before him who sits on the throne, and worship him who lives for ever and ever. They lay their crowns before the throne and say: "You are worthy, our Lord and*

AFTER THE RAPTURE

God, to receive glory and honor and power, for you created all things, and by your will they were created and have their being." (NIV)

4. Four angels are given power to harm the earth during the Tribulation Period. It appears that they are positioned at the four corners of the earth and have power over the elements.
   Rev 7:1-2 *****After this I saw four angels standing at the four corners of the earth,** holding back the four winds of the earth to prevent any wind from blowing on the land or on the sea or on any tree. Then I saw another angel coming up from the east, having the seal of the living God. He called out in a loud voice to the four angels who had been given power to harm the land and the sea:* (NIV)

5. Seven angels who sound the seven trumpet judgments.
   Rev 8:6 ***Then the seven angels who had the seven trumpets prepared to sound them.*** (NIV)

6. Four angels released to pour out God's judgment at a prescribed time in history.
   Rev 9:14-15 *saying to the sixth angel who had the trumpet,* ***"Release the four angels who are bound at the great river Euphrates." So the four angels, who had been prepared for the hour and day and month and year, were released to kill a third of mankind.*** (NKJ)

7. An angel flying in midair preaching the gospel.
   Rev 14:6 ***Then I saw another angel flying in midair, and he had the eternal gospel to proclaim to those who live on the earth—to every nation, tribe, language and people.*** (NIV)

8. Seven angels pouring out the bowls of judgment on the earth.
   Rev 16:1 ***Then I heard a loud voice from the temple saying to the seven angels, "Go, pour out the seven bowls of God's wrath on the earth."*** (NIV)

9. An angel reveals the mystery of Babylon to John.
   Rev 17:7 ***Then the angel said to me: "Why are you astonished? I will explain to you the mystery of the woman and of the beast she rides, which has the seven heads and ten horns.*** (NIV)

10. Jesus sent His angel to show His servants the events that will take place.
    Rev 22:6 *The angel said to me, "These words are trustworthy and true.* ***The Lord, the God of the spirits of the prophets, sent his angel to show his servants the things that must soon take place."*** (NIV)
    Rev 22:16 ***"I, Jesus, have sent my angel to give you this testimony for the churches.*** *I am the Root and the Offspring of David, and the bright Morning Star."* (NIV)

The Tribulation Period — The First 3 ½ Years

It is perfectly clear in the Word of God that He will use both His army and Satan's army to accomplish His purpose on earth and in heaven *After the Rapture*. God's army made up of Michael, Gabriel, Cherubim, Seraphim, Living Creatures and the rest of the holy angels in heaven will engage in a war in heaven. After Satan is cast down to earth, he and his fallen angels will help destroy the earth and draw billions of people into hell.

The details of the war in heaven are not revealed to us, nor is the length of time it takes to complete the battle. What it does reveal to us is that Michael appears to be the stronger of the two and he along with his army defeat Satan and his army. It appears to take place in a short period of time.

> Rev 12:7-8   *And there was war in heaven.* **Michael and his angels fought against the dragon, and the dragon and his angels fought back.** *But he was not strong enough, and they lost their place in heaven.* (NIV)

After Satan and his angels are defeated they will be thrown out of the heavenly realm to the earth never to return to heaven. However, a warning to the earth—the devil has been hurled to earth and he is in a raging fit of anger. He knows that he only has a short time left to destroy as many souls as possible before the true God brings His kingdom to earth. At this time the followers of Jesus will overcome the world by the blood of the Lamb, which simply means that they will turn their lives over to Jesus Christ. They will not love their own lives so much that they fear physical death at this time and many will become martyrs for their faith in the true God.

> Rev 12:9-12   **The great dragon was hurled down—that ancient serpent called the devil, or Satan,** *who leads the whole world astray. He was hurled to the earth, and his angels with him. Then I heard a loud voice in heaven say: "Now have come the salvation and the power and the kingdom of our God, and the authority of his Christ.* **For the accuser of our brothers, who accuses them before our God day and night, has been hurled down.** *They overcame him by the blood of the Lamb and by the word of their testimony; they did not love their lives so much as to shrink from death. Therefore rejoice, you heavens and you who dwell in them!* **But woe to the earth and the sea, because the devil has gone down to you! He is filled with fury, because he knows that his time is short.**" (NIV)

Not long after the Antichrist has entered Jerusalem and had his troops pollute the area around the Temple, an earthquake of great magnitude will take place.

> Rev 6:12-17   *I watched as he opened* **the sixth seal.** *There was a great earthquake. The sun turned black like sackcloth made of goat hair, the whole moon turned blood red, and the stars in the sky fell to earth, as late figs drop from a fig tree when shaken by a strong wind.*

AFTER THE RAPTURE

> *The sky receded like a scroll, rolling up, and every mountain and island was removed from its place.* ***Then the kings of the earth, the princes, the generals, the rich, the mighty, and every slave and every free man hid in caves and among the rocks of the mountains.*** *They called to the mountains and the rocks, "Fall on us and hide us from the face of him who sits on the throne and from the wrath of the Lamb! For the great day of their wrath has come, and who can stand?"* (NIV)

There appears to be six major earthquakes mentioned that take place during the Tribulation Period. This is the second one. The first one was in Israel and it helped defeat Gog and his armies at the Russian Invasion. At this point four more major earthquakes are still to come.

On August 17, 1999, an earthquake (7.4 on the Richter scale) took place in Turkey. Our local newspaper had this report on August 21, only days after the disaster took place. The death toll ended up being more than 17,000 people. To get some idea of the consequences of an earthquake, we have some excerpts from a local newspaper article:

> ISTANBUL, TURKEY — Rescuers warned Friday that sanitation problems and a lack of clean water could spread disease and raise the death toll of an earthquake that killed nearly 10,000 people and probably trapped tens of thousands more.
>
> Three people were pulled alive from beneath crumbled buildings three days after Tuesday's quake, but time was running out and little hope remained that others would be rescued.
>
> The disaster threatened to rival Turkey's most destructive quake: a magnitude – 7.9 temblor that killed 33,000 people in 1939.
>
> The official death toll surged Friday to 9,082 dead and more than 34,000 injured. Thousands more are believed to be trapped or buried in the rubble.
>
> At the United Nations, Sergio Piazzi, an official of the U.N. Office for the Coordination of Humanitarian Affairs, said Turkish officials estimated that as many as 35,000 people were still unaccounted for and believed buried.
>
> Doctors say people trapped in such situations usually die of dehydration after 72 hours. The 72-hour period after Tuesday's earthquake ended early Friday.
>
> Meanwhile, medics were immunizing rescue workers against typhoid and warning of health dangers for the masses left homeless by the quake.
>
> The fear is generated by the threat of disease. There were rumors of cholera Friday, but doctors said they had not seen any specific cases.
>
> With millions living in chaos on the streets, most without fresh

The Tribulation Period — The First 3 ½ Years

water and toilets, health and sanitation have become a focus of the recovery effort. "Things are pretty bad," said Selcit Coban, a young Turkish doctor in profound need of sleep. "But they will improve," he added defiantly.

Farther down the coast, in Golcuk, the stench of death is often so strong that it stings the nostrils. Cars cruise the shattered town, distributing face masks against the smell of rotting bodies.

"It is deeply imbedded in mankind to think that a dead body induces diseases in those alive," said Michel Thieren, of the World Health Organization.

But it is the lack of clean water, lavatories and medical care that could lead to things like diarrhea, skin disease and respiratory infections, WHO said, calling the danger from dead bodies "negligible."

In one day, close to 1,000 people were buried in a mass grave in Adapazari, 95 miles east of Istanbul. Thieren has urged the authorities to use resources instead to treat the injured and care for the survivors.

This earthquake that took place in Turkey, in August 1999, was a disaster in a small localized area of the world. It created an extreme hardship in this area. Imagine the effects of the earthquakes that will take place during the Tribulation Period.

The great earthquake that will take place in Revelation 6:12 appears to effect the entire earth. It is so severe that the political leaders, men of high esteem, military leaders, rich and powerful men, and everyone (a slave or freeman) will be so horrified that they will hide in the caves of the mountains and ask the rocks to fall on them, so they can hide from Jesus. This is just a description Jesus uses to tell us that it will effect every person on the face of the earth and will be of catastrophic proportion. The people at that time will even believe it to be from the wrath of Jesus (the Lamb). A parallel scripture passage can be found in the book of Isaiah, concerning the time on earth when this great earthquake will take place at the end of the first 3 ½ years of the Tribulation Period.

Isa 2:10-22   ***Go into the rocks, hide in the ground from dread of the LORD and the splendor of his majesty!*** *The eyes of the arrogant man will be humbled and the pride of men brought low; the LORD alone will be exalted in that day.* ***The LORD Almighty has a day in store for all the proud and lofty, for all that is exalted (and they will be humbled),*** *for all the cedars of Lebanon, tall and lofty, and all the oaks of Bashan, for all the towering mountains and all the high hills, for every lofty tower and every fortified wall, for every trading ship and every stately vessel.* ***The arrogance of man will be brought low and the pride of men humbled;*** *the LORD alone will be exalted in that day, and the idols will totally disappear.* <u>***Men will flee to caves in the rocks and to holes in the ground from dread of the LORD***</u>

AFTER THE RAPTURE

<u>*and the splendor of his majesty, when he rises to shake the earth.*</u> *In that day men will throw away to the rodents and bats their idols of silver and idols of gold, which they made to worship.* **They will flee to caverns in the rocks and to the overhanging crags from dread of the LORD and the splendor of his majesty, when he rises to shake the earth.** <u>*Stop trusting in man, who has but a breath in his nostrils. Of what account is he?*</u> (NIV)

This will bring us to the end of the first 3 ½ years of the Tribulation Period. Not a pretty picture, but nothing compared with what lies ahead. Ahead will be 3 ½ years of **Great Tribulation**. It will be **the worst time of human history**. Scripture reveals that a couple of things will happen just prior to the great and dreadful day of the Lord. They are:

1. The prophet Elijah will appear.
   Malachi 4:5   *"See, I will send you the prophet Elijah <u>before</u> that great and dreadful day of the LORD comes.* (NIV)
   In the second to the last verse in the Old Testament, it reveals to us the timing for Elijah to appear. It appears that there will be another Old Testament personage who will appear along with Elijah at this time. We will give more details concerning these two figures in chapter eleven. We also mentioned them earlier in this chapter where we stated that their ministry had its beginning. By this time they will have been on earth about one year.

2. The sun will be turned to darkness and the moon to blood.
   Joel 2:31   *The sun will be turned to darkness and the moon to blood <u>before</u> the coming of the great and dreadful day of the LORD.* (NIV)
   This will take place when the great earthquake of Rev 6:12 occurs. The dust and debris from the earthquake will cause this effect and are a sign for the beginning of the last 3 ½ years of the Tribulation Period.

The last days of this first 3 ½ years of the Tribulation Period are going to be a busy time. There will be activity in heaven as well as on earth. As the final days draw to a close, we see three events coming together; (1) we see the Antichrist laying mortally wounded in a hospital bed in Jerusalem, (2) at this time the war in heaven comes to completion and Satan and his army are hurled to earth and (3) it could be possible that at the very time that Satan is hurled to earth, Jesus will unseal the sixth seal and a great earthquake will effect the entire earth.

So, we close this chapter with a description of and a warning to people about the up and coming horrible, horrible period of the next 3 ½ years.

Zeph 1:14-18   *"<u>The great day of the LORD is near</u>—near and coming quickly. Listen! The cry on the day of the LORD will be bitter, the shouting of the warrior there. That day will be a day of wrath, a day of distress and anguish, a day of trouble and ruin, a day of darkness and gloom, a day of clouds and blackness, a day of trumpet and*

The Tribulation Period — The First 3 ½ Years

battle cry against the fortified cities and against the corner towers. <u>I will bring distress on the people and they will walk like blind men, because they have sinned against the LORD</u>. Their blood will be poured out like dust and their entrails like filth. Neither their silver nor their gold will be able to save them on <u>the day of the LORD's wrath</u>. In the fire of his jealousy the whole world will be consumed, for he will make a sudden end of all who live in the earth." (NIV)

Rev 6:17 *<u>For the great day of their wrath has come, and who can stand?</u>"* (NIV)

CHAPTER TEN

(SILENCE!)

Rev 8:1 ...*__there was silence in heaven for about half an hour.__* (NIV)

CHAPTER ELEVEN

THE TRIBULATION PERIOD
THE TIME OF JACOB'S TROUBLE

There seems to be an event out of place following the great earthquake on earth and the war in heaven at the end of the first 3 ½ years of the Tribulation Period—a half hour of silence in heaven. Oddly enough this period of silence is the midpoint of the Tribulation Period. The tranquility will seem out of place. This is by far the most serene half hour the world will ever experience in history.

> Rev 8:1 *When he opened <u>the seventh seal</u>, there was silence in heaven for about half an hour.* (NIV)

It is the lull before the storm. For 5 ½ years, ever since the Rapture, it has been total chaos on earth with the degree of chaos becoming progressively worse as time passes. Wars have been taking place all around the globe and the Antichrist has been gaining more power and territory. All of a sudden, after a great earthquake, there is total silence from heaven. With this half hour of silence, the people all over the earth will be thinking that the awful times have finally come to a close. God's wrath is over! However, instead of the end of God's wrath, it is the beginning of His fierce anger—THE WORST TIME OF HUMAN HISTORY. Never again will there ever be a period of time like the period just ahead of them. That is a promise from God, just like He promised there would never be a flood again.

> Matt 24:21 *For then shall be <u>great tribulation</u>, such as was not since the beginning of the world to this time, no, nor ever shall be.* (KJV)

In this 3 ½ year period the mightiest army that has ever existed will appear on the scene.

> Joel 2:2-3 *a day of darkness and gloom, a day of clouds and blackness. Like dawn spreading across the mountains <u>a large and mighty army comes</u>, <u>such as never was of old nor ever will be in ages to come</u>. Before them fire devours, behind them a flame blazes. Before them the land is like the garden of Eden, behind them, a desert waste—nothing escapes them.* (NIV)

At the end of this 3 ½ year period the worst earthquake of human history will take place, so severe an earthquake that the islands disappeared and the mountains were laid flat.

> Rev 16:18-20 *Then there came flashes of lightning, rumblings, peals of thunder and a severe earthquake. <u>No earthquake like it has ever occurred since man has been on earth</u>, <u>so tremendous was the quake</u>. The great city split into three parts, and the cities of the nations collapsed. God remembered Babylon the Great and gave her the cup*

AFTER THE RAPTURE

filled with the wine of the fury of his wrath. Every island fled away and the mountains could not be found. (NIV)

The first thing that Satan does after he is hurled to the earth is to enter into the critically wounded body of the Antichrist. This body will be his vessel for the next 3 ½ years. This will be a mock resurrection of Jesus Christ by the Antichrist, to fool the people of the world into believing that he is God.

Rev 13:3   **One of the heads of the beast seemed to have had a fatal wound, <u>but the fatal wound had been healed</u>. The whole world was astonished and followed the beast.** (NIV)

Satan knows the word of God only too well and when he comes to rest on the earth, he knows that he has but a short time to convince those living on the earth that he is God. He even believes it himself, though in the end the entire earth will lay in ruin with billions of lost souls following him, the Antichrist and the False Prophet to hell for eternity.

Rev 12:12   **…But woe to the earth and the sea, <u>because the devil has gone down to you! He is filled with fury, because he knows that his time is short."</u>** (NIV)

Satan will be filled with unrestrained violent anger because of his defeat in heaven. The next 3 ½ years will not be a short period of time for those living on earth. For them it will literally be "hell on earth." For those who might be skeptical about Satan entering into a human body, I would like to remind you that Satan has already performed this task at least once before, almost two thousand years ago. The unlucky man who betrayed Jesus got the despicable honor—Judas Iscariot.

Luke 22:1-6   *Now the Feast of Unleavened Bread, called the Passover, was approaching, and the chief priests and the teachers of the law were looking for some way to get rid of Jesus, for they were afraid of the people.* **<u>Then Satan entered Judas</u>, <u>called Iscariot</u>, one of the Twelve.** *And Judas went to the chief priests and the officers of the temple guard and discussed with them how he might betray Jesus. They were delighted and agreed to give him money. He consented, and watched for an opportunity to hand Jesus over to them when no crowd was present.* (NIV)

Luke 22:21-23   **But the hand of him who is going to betray me is with mine on the table.** *The Son of Man will go as it has been decreed, but woe to that man who betrays him." They began to question among themselves which of them it might be who would do this.* (NIV)

Luke 22:47-48   *While he was still speaking a crowd came up, and the man who was*

> *called Judas, one of the Twelve, was leading them. **He approached Jesus to kiss him, but Jesus asked him, "Judas, are you betraying the Son of Man with a kiss?**" (NIV)*

Can you imagine betraying the Son of Man (Jesus Christ) for money and then carrying out the misdeed by attempting to do it with a kiss? Thank God that you are not Judas Iscariot. I do not believe that Judas could have followed through with this betrayal without the assistance of Satan dwelling in his body. It is also unlikely that even the Antichrist could sit on the throne in Jerusalem and claim to be God without the assistance of Satan himself.

GREAT DAY OF THE LORD

The Great Day of the Lord, which is the second half of the Tribulation Period, will last for 3 ½ years and is a part of the bigger picture of the Day of the Lord, which will last for a thousand years. It is distinguished by the word, "great." The Hebrew word used here for "great" is *gadowl*, pronounced *gaw-dole'*. When it is used as an adjective it means: (a) large (in magnitude and extent), (b) in number, (c) in intensity. It distinguishes the greater degree of punishment from God and the total destruction of the world during the last half of the Tribulation Period.

Zeph 1:14-18   ***"The great day of the LORD is near—near and coming quickly.** Listen! The cry on the day of the LORD will be bitter, the shouting of the warrior there. That day will be a day of wrath, a day of distress and anguish, a day of trouble and ruin, a day of darkness and gloom, a day of clouds and blackness, a day of trumpet and battle cry against the fortified cities and against the corner towers. I will bring distress on the people and they will walk like blind men, because they have sinned against the LORD. Their blood will be poured out like dust and their entrails like filth. Neither their silver nor their gold will be able to save them on the day of the LORD's wrath. **In the fire of his jealousy the whole world will be consumed, for he will make a sudden end of all who live in the earth."*** (NIV)

During this time of the Tribulation Period it will become so *"dreadful"* that it will be difficult for anyone to endure!

Joel 2:11   *The LORD thunders at the head of his army; his forces are beyond number, and mighty are those who obey his command. **The day of the LORD is great; it is dreadful. Who can endure it?*** (NIV)

Joel 2:31   ***The sun will be turned to darkness and the moon to blood before the coming of the great and dreadful day of the LORD.*** (NIV)

Dan 8:19   *He said: "I am going to tell you what will happen later in **the time*** *of wrath, because the vision concerns the appointed time of the end.* (NIV)

Dan 12:1 *"At that time Michael, the great prince who protects your people, will arise. There will be a time of distress such as has not happened from the beginning of nations until then. But at that time your people—everyone whose name is found written in the book—will be delivered.* (NIV)

Mal 4:5 *"See, I will send you the prophet Elijah before that great and dreadful day of the LORD comes.* (NIV)

The *"great day"* is also mentioned in the New Testament.

Jude 1:6 *And the angels who did not keep their positions of authority but abandoned their own home—these he has kept in darkness, bound with everlasting chains for judgment on the great Day.* (NIV)

Rev 6:17 *For the great day of their wrath has come, and who can stand?"* (NIV)

Rev 7:14 *I answered, "Sir, you know." And he said, "These are they who have come out of the great tribulation; they have washed their robes and made them white in the blood of the Lamb.* (NIV)

Most of the scripture references to the dark side of the Day of the Lord concern this second half of the Tribulation Period or Daniel's seventieth week. The three time periods that equal 3 ½ years (42 months—1260 days—time, times and one-half time) all refer to the 3 ½ year period we are about to study. Daniel and Revelation supply all of the data on these time periods.

42 months - The Gentiles will be allowed to tread upon (crush) and control the holy city (Jerusalem) one last time for 3 ½ years.
Rev 11:2 *But exclude the outer court; do not measure it, because it has been given to the Gentiles. They will trample on the holy city for 42 months.* (NIV)

The last half of the Tribulation Period is the time when the Antichrist will be given complete power to continue for 42 months, up until the end of the Tribulation Period. During this time you will be allowed to see what a madman can do with unrestrained power.
Rev 13:5 *The beast was given a mouth to utter proud words and blasphemies and to exercise his authority for forty-two months.* (NIV)

The Tribulation Period — The Time of Jacob's Trouble

1260 Days - The two witnesses are given power to preach God's word for 1260 days. This 1260 days will consist of one year as part of the first half of the Tribulation Period and 2 ½ years in the second half of the Tribulation Period.

Rev 11:3 *And I will give power to my witnesses, <u>and they will prophesy for 1,260 days</u>, clothed in sackcloth."* (NIV)

The last half of the Tribulation Period will be the time when the Jews flee at the Abomination of Desolation after recognizing that the Antichrist is not the true Messiah.

Rev 12:6 *The woman fled into the desert to a place prepared for her by God, <u>where she might be taken care of for 1,260 days</u>.* (NIV)

Time, times, – and ½ time

The last half of the Tribulation Period will be the time when the Antichrist will make a concerted effort to exterminate the Jewish people. In Daniel it is revealed that this effort will be completed after 3 ½ years.

Dan 12:7 *The man clothed in linen, who was above the waters of the river, lifted his right hand and his left hand toward heaven, and I heard him swear by him who lives forever, saying, "<u>It will be for a time, times and half a time</u>. When the power of the holy people has been finally broken, all these things will be completed."* (NIV)

Rev 12:12-13 *Therefore rejoice, you heavens and you who dwell in them! But woe to the earth and the sea, because the devil has gone down to you! He is filled with fury, because he knows that his time is short." When the dragon saw that he had been hurled to the earth, <u>he pursued the woman who had given birth to the male child</u>.* (NIV)

A portion of the Jewish people will have a special hiding place prepared for them by God, to protect them from the Antichrist for 3 ½ years.

Rev 12:14 *The woman was given the two wings of a great eagle, so that she might fly to the place prepared for her in the desert, <u>where she would be taken care of for a time, times and half a time</u>, <u>out of the serpent's reach</u>.* (NIV)

It is also designated as a time of extreme persecution by the Antichrist toward the believers in Jesus Christ.

Dan 7:25 *He will speak against the Most High and oppress his saints and try to change the set times and the laws. <u>The saints will be handed over to him for a time, times and half a time</u>.* (NIV)

Rev 12:17 *Then the dragon was enraged at the woman and went off to make war against the rest of her offspring—those who obey God's commandments and hold to the testimony of Jesus.* (NIV)

This last half of the Tribulation Period is a time of extreme anger from God. It is hard for us as human beings to fathom the horrible events that are about to take place here on earth. We do know that God is always in control, although to humans on earth, at times, it does not seem like it. God's ways are higher than ours and we as Christians never need to apologize for God. We need only to report the facts as they are presented in the word of God and pay attention to what His word has to say.

> Isa 55:8-11 *"For my thoughts are not your thoughts, neither are your ways my ways," declares the LORD. "<u>As the heavens are higher than the earth, so are my ways higher than your ways and my thoughts than your thoughts</u>. As the rain and the snow come down from heaven, and do not return to it without watering the earth and making it bud and flourish, so that it yields seed for the sower and bread for the eater, so is my word that goes out from my mouth: It will not return to me empty, but will accomplish what I desire and achieve the purpose for which I sent it.* (NIV)

> Deut 32:4 *<u>He is the Rock</u>, his works are perfect, and all his ways are just. A faithful God who does no wrong, upright and just is he.* (NIV)

The Bible tells us that God is loving, patient, and slow to anger, but when He finally does get angry—which is a direct result of sin—judgment is sure to follow. Once again, I remind you that, *"It is a terrifying thing to fall into the hands of the living God."*

> Ps 103:8-9 *<u>The LORD is compassionate and gracious</u>, <u>slow to anger</u>, abounding in love. He will not always accuse, nor will he harbor his anger forever;* (NIV)

> Ps 145:8-21 *The LORD is gracious and compassionate, slow to anger and rich in love. The LORD is good to all; he has compassion on all he has made. All you have made will praise you, O LORD; your saints will extol you. They will tell of the glory of your kingdom and speak of your might, so that all men may know of your mighty acts and the glorious splendor of your kingdom. Your kingdom is an everlasting kingdom, and your dominion endures through all generations. **The LORD is faithful to all his promises and loving toward all he has made.** The LORD upholds all those who fall and lifts up all who are bowed down. The eyes of all look to you, and you give them their food at the proper time. You open your hand and satisfy the desires of every living thing. The LORD is righteous in all his ways and loving toward all he has made. **The LORD is near to all who call on him, to all who call on him in truth. He fulfills the desires of those who fear him; he hears their cry and saves them.** <u>The LORD watches over all who love him, but all the wicked he will destroy.</u> My mouth will speak in praise of the LORD. Let every creature*

The Tribulation Period — The Time of Jacob's Trouble

praise his holy name for ever and ever. (NIV)

It is not our position to repay evil done unto us in this life. That will be left up to God's son Jesus Christ.

John 5:22-30 *__Moreover, the Father judges no one, but has entrusted all judgment to the Son__, that all may honor the Son just as they honor the Father. He who does not honor the Son does not honor the Father, who sent him. "I tell you the truth, whoever hears my word and believes him who sent me has eternal life and will not be condemned; he has crossed over from death to life. I tell you the truth, a time is coming and has now come when the dead will hear the voice of the Son of God and those who hear will live. For as the Father has life in himself, so he has granted the Son to have life in himself. __And he has given him authority to judge because he is the Son of Man.__ "Do not be amazed at this, for a time is coming when all who are in their graves will hear his voice and come out—those who have done good will rise to live, and those who have done evil will rise to be condemned. By myself I can do nothing; I judge only as I hear, and my judgment is just, for I seek not to please myself but him who sent me.* (NIV)

Jesus will avenge—at the proper time—the righteous.

Nahum 1:2-7 *__The LORD is a jealous and avenging God; the LORD takes vengeance and is filled with wrath. The LORD takes vengeance on his foes and maintains his wrath against his enemies. The LORD is slow to anger and great in power; the LORD will not leave the guilty unpunished.__ His way is in the whirlwind and the storm, and clouds are the dust of his feet. He rebukes the sea and dries it up; he makes all the rivers run dry. Bashan and Carmel wither and the blossoms of Lebanon fade. The mountains quake before him and the hills melt away. The earth trembles at his presence, the world and all who live in it. __Who can withstand his indignation? Who can endure his fierce anger?__ His wrath is poured out like fire; the rocks are shattered before him. The LORD is good, a refuge in times of trouble. He cares for those who trust in him,* (NIV)

Rom 12:19 *Dearly beloved, avenge not yourselves, but rather give place unto wrath: for it is written, __Vengeance is mine; I will repay, saith the Lord.__* (KJV)

2 Thes 1:5-6 *__All this is evidence that God's judgment is right__, and as a result you will be counted worthy of the kingdom of God, for which you are*

suffering. God is just: He will pay back trouble to those who trouble you (NIV)

Throughout history, the anger of the Lord has appeared. Not very often, but at times when mankind was in a state of apostasy or Israel was worshiping false idols (turned away from God). Here we will mention four critical times the Lord was and will be angered.

1. **The Flood (2344 BC)** — God was angry with sinful mankind. Man was so far from God that every evil thought came into their minds. The earth was full of violence because of all this wickedness. This flood took place on earth before the birth of the Jewish nation.
   Gen 6:5-13 *The LORD saw how great man's wickedness on the earth had become, and that every inclination of the thoughts of his heart was only evil all the time. The LORD was grieved that he had made man on the earth, and his heart was filled with pain. So the LORD said, "I will wipe mankind, whom I have created, from the face of the earth—men and animals, and creatures that move along the ground, and birds of the air—<u>for I am grieved that I have made them.</u>" But Noah found favor in the eyes of the LORD. This is the account of Noah. Noah was a righteous man, blameless among the people of his time, and he walked with God. Noah had three sons: Shem, Ham and Japheth. Now the earth was corrupt in God's sight and was full of violence. God saw how corrupt the earth had become, for all the people on earth had corrupted their ways. So God said to Noah, "I am going to put an end to all people, for the earth is filled with violence because of them. I am surely going to destroy both them and the earth.* (NIV)

2. **Golden Calf (1445 BC)** — While Moses was on Mount Sinai, receiving the ten commandments from God, the Israelites were constructing a statue of a calf made of gold jewelry. It was a false idol.
   Exod 32:7-10 *Then the LORD said to Moses, "Go down, because your people, whom you brought up out of Egypt, have become corrupt. They have been quick to turn away from what I commanded them and have made themselves an idol cast in the shape of a calf. They have bowed down to it and sacrificed to it and have said, 'These are your Gods, O Israel, who brought you up out of Egypt.' " I have seen these people," the LORD said to Moses, "<u>and they are a stiff-necked people.</u> Now leave me alone so that my anger may burn against them and that I may destroy them. Then I will make you into a great nation."* (NIV)

3. **Exile of Israel (722 BC) and Judah (586 BC)** — The divided kingdoms of the Jewish people were sent into exile at different times. The Assyrians defeated Israel in 722 BC and the Babylonians captured Judah and destroyed Jerusalem in 606/586 BC. Both occasions sent the Jewish people into exile. Lamentations shows the horror of the Jewish people as God pours out the full vent of His anger and wrath.
   Lam 4:1-18 *How the gold has lost its luster, the fine gold become dull! The sacred gems are scattered at the head of every street. How the precious sons of*

The Tribulation Period — The Time of Jacob's Trouble

Zion, once worth their weight in gold, are now considered as pots of clay, the work of a potter's hands! Even jackals offer their breasts to nurse their young, but my people have become heartless like ostriches in the desert. Because of thirst the infant's tongue sticks to the roof of its mouth; the children beg for bread, but no one gives it to them. Those who once ate delicacies are destitute in the streets. Those nurtured in purple now lie on ash heaps. The punishment of my people is greater than that of Sodom, which was overthrown in a moment without a hand turned to help her. Their princes were brighter than snow and whiter than milk, their bodies more ruddy than rubies, their appearance like sapphires. But now they are blacker than soot; they are not recognized in the streets. Their skin has shriveled on their bones; it has become as dry as a stick. Those killed by the sword are better off than those who die of famine; racked with hunger, they waste away for lack of food from the field. With their own hands compassionate women have cooked their own children, who became their food when my people were destroyed. **_The LORD has given full vent to his wrath; he has poured out his fierce anger. He kindled a fire in Zion that consumed her foundations. The kings of the earth did not believe, nor did any of the world's people, that enemies and foes could enter the gates of Jerusalem. But it happened because of the sins of her prophets and the iniquities of her priests, who shed within her the blood of the righteous._** *Now they grope through the streets like men who are blind. They are so defiled with blood that no one dares to touch their garments. "Go away! You are unclean!" men cry to them. "Away! Away! Don't touch us!" When they flee and wander about, people among the nations say, "They can stay here no longer." The LORD himself has scattered them; he no longer watches over them. The priests are shown no honor, the elders no favor. Moreover, our eyes failed, looking in vain for help; from our towers we watched for a nation that could not save us. Men stalked us at every step, so we could not walk in our streets.* **_Our end was near, our days were numbered, for our end had come._** (NIV)

4. **The Tribulation Period (A period of time yet future for us)** — The final seven years of Daniel's 490 year period of God's dealings with the Jewish people and Jerusalem. It will also be a time to judge all mankind.
Isa 13:9-13 *See,* **_the day of the LORD is coming a cruel day, with wrath and fierce anger—to make the land desolate and destroy the sinners within it._** *The stars of heaven and their constellations will not show their light. The rising sun will be darkened and the moon will not give its light.* **_I will punish the world for its evil, the wicked for their sins._** *I will put an end to the arrogance of the haughty and will humble the pride of the ruthless. I will make man scarcer than pure gold, more rare than the gold of Ophir.* **_Therefore I will make the heavens tremble; and the earth will shake from its place at the wrath of the LORD Almighty, in the day of his burning anger._** (NIV)

The indignation that is about to befall the world will be the worst of the anger of God. It is described as rage, burning anger, fury, fierce anger and the fire of His wrath.

Jer 25:37-38	*The peaceful meadows will be laid waste because of the fierce anger of the LORD. Like a lion he will leave his lair, and their land will become desolate because of the sword of the oppressor and because of the LORD's fierce anger.* (NIV)
Zeph 2:2	*before the appointed time arrives and that day sweeps on like chaff, before the fierce anger of the LORD comes upon you, before the day of the LORD's wrath comes upon you.* (NIV)
Zeph 3:8	*Therefore wait for me," declares the LORD, "for the day I will stand up to testify. I have decided to assemble the nations, to gather the kingdoms and to pour out my wrath on them—all my fierce anger. The whole world will be consumed by the fire of my jealous anger.* (NIV)
Ezek 22:31	*"Therefore I have poured out My indignation on them; I have consumed them with the fire of My wrath; and I have recompensed their deeds on their own heads," says the Lord God.* (NKJ)

Do not plan on being around when all this takes place on earth. **ACCEPT JESUS TODAY!**

Jer 30:24	*The fierce anger of the LORD will not turn back until he fully accomplishes the purposes of his heart. In days to come you will understand this.* (NIV)
Heb 10:30-31	*For we know Him who said, "Vengeance is Mine, I will repay." And again, "The Lord will judge His people." It is a terrifying thing to fall into the hands of the living God.* (NAS)

PREACHING THE GOSPEL

Before we move on, we need to back up just a little bit to cover the parenthetical chapters (seven, eleven and fourteen) that are found in the book of Revelation. This 3 ½ year period will be so full of supernatural disasters, along with demonic forces roaming the earth, that God will use supernatural means to warn the people on the earth at this time. There will be 144,000 Messianic Jews, two Old Testament prophets and three angelic messengers proclaiming the gospel of Jesus Christ during the 3 ½ years of Great Tribulation. God will make an extra effort to warn the people on earth at this time, but instead of accepting God, the majority of the people will still shake their fist at Him and curse Him. They will by this time have hardened their hearts toward God.

After the warning about the coming 3 ½ year period of great wrath in Revelation chapter six, John observes four angels standing at the four corners of the earth.

The Tribulation Period — The Time of Jacob's Trouble

Rev 7:1 *After this I saw four angels standing at the four corners of the earth, holding back the four winds of the earth to prevent any wind from blowing on the land or on the sea or on any tree.* (NIV)

144,000 SERVANTS OF GOD

John then observes another angel coming from the east.

Rev 7:2-8 *Then I saw another angel coming up from the east, having the seal of the living God. He called out in a loud voice to the four angels who had been given power to harm the land and the sea: "Do not harm the land or the sea or the trees until we put a seal on the foreheads of the servants of our God." Then I heard the number of those who were sealed: 144,000 from all the tribes of Israel. From the tribe of Judah 12,000 were sealed, from the tribe of Reuben 12,000, from the tribe of Gad 12,000, from the tribe of Asher 12,000, from the tribe of Naphtali 12,000, from the tribe of Manasseh 12,000, from the tribe of Simeon 12,000, from the tribe of Levi 12,000, from the tribe of Issachar 12,000, from the tribe of Zebulun 12,000, from the tribe of Joseph 12,000, from the tribe of Benjamin 12,000.* (NIV)

With a loud command this angel instructs the four angels, who have control over the forces of nature, to wait just as the wrath is about to be poured out on the earth in the form of the seven trumpet judgments. This is to allow the angels enough time to put a seal of protection on 144,000 Jews (Messianic – they believe in Jesus), 12,000 from each of the twelve tribes of Israel. They have a special mission to tell the world about Jesus Christ and will need to be protected from the enemy—Satan, the Antichrist, the False Prophet, demonic forces and unsaved people from around the world. It is possible that these 144,000 servants of God will receive the seal on their foreheads during this ½ hour of silence in heaven.

In chapter fourteen, we see these same 144,000 servants of God in heaven. This scene is at the end of the 3 ½ year period of Great Tribulation.

Rev 14:1-5 *Then I looked, and there before me was the Lamb, standing on Mount Zion, and with him 144,000 who had his name and his Father's name written on their foreheads.* And I heard a sound from heaven like the roar of rushing waters and like a loud peal of thunder. The sound I heard was like that of harpists playing their harps. And they sang a new song before the throne and before the four living creatures and the elders. No one could learn the song except the 144,000 who had been redeemed from the earth. These are those who did not defile themselves with women, for they kept themselves pure. They follow the Lamb wherever he goes. They were purchased from among men and offered as firstfruits to God and the Lamb. No lie was found in their mouths; they are blameless. (NIV)

Here we are told that the seal that the 144,000 Jews have on their foreheads have both Jesus and God's name written on it. They have a special song that only they can sing. They did not defile themselves with women, they were redeemed from the earth, they lived a life dedicated to Jesus, they did not lie, and they were pure and blameless before God. Who said that God was finished with the Jews and that they were replaced by the church?

One of the most misunderstood interpretations of the book of Revelation is the identification of these 144,000 servants of God. Almost every cult and not a few of the many accepted Christian denominations today have a secret interpretation of these 144,000 servants. They claim that the 144,000 belong to their particular group of followers. I might remind you that scripture clearly reveals that the 144,000 are Jewish. If you belong to an esoteric group—even if it claims to be Christian—who believe that they are members of this group of 144,000 servants—BEWARE! Only God knows who these Jews are and what tribe they are from. Do not be led astray.

TWO WITNESSES

In chapter nine, we mentioned the prophet Elijah appearing before the great and dreadful Day of the Lord. We also mentioned that there would be another Old Testament prophet who would appear along with him. They appear dressed in the Old Testament attire called sackcloth.

> Rev 11:1-3 *I was given a reed like a measuring rod and was told, "Go and measure the temple of God and the altar, and count the worshipers there. But exclude the outer court; do not measure it, because it has been given to the Gentiles. They will trample on the holy city for 42 months. **And I will give power to my two witnesses, and they will prophesy for 1,260 days, clothed in sackcloth."*** (NIV)

John was told to measure the Temple and altar of God and to count the worshipers there. This scene is the Temple in heaven and John is counting those who are waiting under the altar, until the number of saved people from the Tribulation Period have come to completion (refer back to Revelation 6:9). This cannot be the Temple on earth, because at the time of Revelation eleven the Temple that the Jews were allowed to rebuild will have been polluted by the troops of the Antichrist. This is confirmed in verse two where it states that God allows the Gentiles to have control over the Temple for forty-two months or 3 ½ years. Throughout history, God has at times allowed the Gentile nations to have control of the Temple in Jerusalem. After the Jewish people have believed that the Messiah has rebuilt their Temple and allowed them to restore the Old Testament Levitical Sacrificial system of worship, this same Messiah (Antichrist) will have control of the Temple. For the last time—but this time for only 3 ½ years—Israel and Jerusalem will be under the dominion of the Gentile nations.

It is then mentioned that God will allow two Old Testament personages to return to earth and proclaim the gospel message for 1,260 days (3 ½ Years). As we mentioned before, one of them is revealed to be the prophet Elijah. The other prophet is not named. They are dressed in sackcloth. Sackcloth is a rough coarse cloth or a bag like garment made of a dark

The Tribulation Period — The Time of Jacob's Trouble

colored goat's hair. Girding with sackcloth is a figure for heavy afflictions. It can also be used figuratively as covering the heavens for severe judgment, as seen in Revelation 6:12, which we just studied. Sackcloth was often worn by the Old Testament prophets. God has a special mission for these two servants. They will most likely appear on earth in these garments of sackcloth (Revelation 11:3). Make no mistake about it, they are from God.

> Rev 6:12   *I watched as he opened the sixth seal. There was a great earthquake.* ***The sun turned black <u>like sackcloth made of goat hair</u>, the whole moon turned blood red,*** (NIV)

There is a lot of disagreement among Bible scholars about the identity of these two witnesses. Instead of entering into the controversy, I am only going to tell you who I believe they might be. I have come to the conclusion that they could possibly be Elijah and Moses. They are also the two Old Testament saints who appeared with Jesus at the Transfiguration.

> Matt 17:1-8   *After six days Jesus took with him Peter, James and John the brother of James, and led them up a high mountain by themselves. There he was transfigured before them. His face shone like the sun, and his clothes became as white as the light.* ***<u>Just then there appeared before them Moses and Elijah, talking with Jesus.</u> Peter said to Jesus, "Lord, it is good for us to be here. If you wish, I will put up three shelters—one for you, one for Moses and one for Elijah."*** *While he was still speaking, a bright cloud enveloped them, and a voice from the cloud said, "This is my Son, whom I love; with him I am well pleased. Listen to him!" When the disciples heard this, they fell face down to the ground, terrified. But Jesus came and touched them. "Get up," he said. "Don't be afraid." When they looked up, they saw no one except Jesus.* (NIV)

If it does turn out to be someone other than Elijah and Moses, it will not change the purpose these two witnesses have on earth for this 3 ½ year period. We see more details revealed concerning them.

> Rev 11:4   ***These are the <u>two olive trees</u> and the <u>two lampstands</u> that stand before the Lord of the earth.*** (NIV)

A parallel to the two olive trees is found in Zechariah. Here we see the same two people who are chosen to be two bright shining lights for God. Their 3 ½ year ministry was predetermined by God.

> Zech 4:11-14   *Then I asked the angel, "<u>What are these two olive trees on the right and the left of the lampstand</u>?" Again I asked him, "What are these two olive branches beside the two gold pipes that pour out golden oil?" He replied, "Do you not know what these are?" "No,*

my lord," I said. So he said, "<u>These are the two who are anointed to serve the Lord of all the earth.</u> " (NIV)

We even have some of the details of their ministry with supernatural powers.

> Rev 11:5-7 *<u>If anyone tries to harm them, fire comes from their mouths and devours their enemies.</u> This is how anyone who wants to harm them must die. These men have power to shut up the sky so that it will not rain during the time they are prophesying; and they have power to turn the waters into blood and to strike the earth with every kind of plague as often as they want. Now when they have finished their testimony, the beast that comes up from the Abyss will attack them, and overpower and kill them.* (NIV)

If anyone tries to harm them, they have the power to kill their enemies. They will also perform miracles; such as not allowing rain to come from the sky, turning water into blood and striking the earth with all kinds of plagues as often as they want. No one will be able to harm them until their ministry is complete, at which time the beast (the Antichrist) will be allowed to kill them.

THREE ANGELIC MESSENGERS

Last, but certainly not least, we see three angels flying in midair warning the people of the terrible time in which they are living. How awesome it will be. Not one person who is alive during this time of extreme judgment can stand before God and say that he was not warned. Take note that the third angel warns the people on earth, ahead of time, not to take the mark of the beast.

> Rev 14:6-10 *Then I saw <u>another angel flying in midair, and he had</u> the eternal gospel to proclaim to those who live on the earth—to every nation, tribe, language and people. He said in a loud voice, "Fear God and give him glory, because the hour of his judgment has come. Worship him who made the heavens, the earth, the sea and the springs of water." <u>A second angel</u> followed and said, "Fallen! Fallen is Babylon the Great, which made all the nations drink the maddening wine of her adulteries." <u>A third angel</u> followed them and said in a loud voice: "If anyone worships the beast and his image and receives his mark on the forehead or on the hand, he, too, will drink of the wine of God's fury, which has been poured full strength into the cup of his wrath. He will be tormented with burning sulfur in the presence of the holy angels and of the Lamb.* (NIV)

The messages from these three angels are:

The Tribulation Period — The Time of Jacob's Trouble

> First Angel – *"Fear God and give Him glory, because the hour of His judgment has come. Worship Him who made the heavens, the earth, the sea and the springs of water."*
>
> Second Angel – *"Fallen! Fallen is Babylon the Great, which made all the nations drink the maddening wine of her adulteries."*
>
> Third Angel – *"If anyone worships the beast and his image and receives his mark on the forehead, or on the hand, he too will drink of the wine of God's fury, which has been poured full strength into the cup of His wrath."*

It is hard to believe that anyone who observes these angels and listens to what they say could be unsaved during this time, but that will not be the case. The percentage of the unsaved will far outnumber the saved throughout this 3 ½ year period. All those who take the mark of the beast will be lost for eternity. They will have sold their soul to the devil.

> Rev 14:10-11   *he, too, will drink of the wine of God's fury, which has been poured full strength into the cup of his wrath. He will be tormented with burning sulfur in the presence of the holy angels and of the Lamb. And the smoke of their torment rises for ever and ever. <u>There is no rest day or night for those who worship the beast and his image, or for anyone who receives the mark of his name.</u>"* (NIV)

During the last half of the Tribulation Period there will be some who will refuse the mark of the beast, but most of them will be martyred. Chapter 14 admonishes those people who accept Christ to have patience and endure, even to the point of death for they will have peace in the next life and also be rewarded for what they have done for Jesus in this life.

> Rev 14:12-13   *This calls for patient endurance on the part of the saints who obey God's commandments and remain faithful to Jesus. Then I heard a voice from heaven say, "Write: <u>Blessed are the dead who die in the Lord from now on.</u>" "<u>Yes</u>," says the Spirit, "<u>they will rest from their labor, for their deeds will follow them.</u>"* (NIV)

We also see those who will turn their life over to Jesus during the last half of the Tribulation Period in Revelation chapter seven. It is comforting to know that multitudes will be saved during this horrible time on earth, even to the point of losing their life. God tells us of their victory over Satan in advance. These are the saints that come out of **the Great Tribulation!** The saved will be in the millions, while the unsaved will be in the billions.

> Rev 7:9-17   *After this I looked and there before me was <u>a great multitude that no one could count, from every nation, tribe, people and language,</u> standing before the throne and in front of the Lamb. They were wearing white robes and were holding palm branches in their hands. And they cried out in a loud voice: "Salvation belongs to our God,*

*who sits on the throne, and to the Lamb." All the angels were standing around the throne and around the elders and the four living creatures. They fell down on their faces before the throne and worshiped God, saying: "Amen! Praise and glory and wisdom and thanks and honor and power and strength be to our God for ever and ever. Amen!" Then one of the elders asked me, "These in white robes—who are they, and where did they come from?" I answered, "Sir, you know." **And he said, "These are they who have come out of the great tribulation; they have washed their robes and made them white in the blood of the Lamb.** Therefore, "they are before the throne of God and serve him day and night in his temple; and he who sits on the throne will spread his tent over them. Never again will they hunger; never again will they thirst. The sun will not beat upon them, nor any scorching heat. For the Lamb at the center of the throne will be their shepherd; he will lead them to springs of living water. And God will wipe away every tear from their eyes."* (NIV)

As God warns all the people on earth, even to the point of angels flying through the air with the message of the gospel, a prophecy in Matthew will be fulfilled. God also warns the people at that time about the coming hour of His judgment.

Matt 24:14 **And *this gospel of the kingdom* will be preached in the whole world as a testimony to all nations, and then *the end* will come.** (NIV)

This end, spoken of here, is the end of the indignation (Tribulation Period) and not the end of the age. This end is spoken of in Daniel and is the end of the 490 years that God will deal with the Jewish people and the city of Jerusalem, and I might add—to finish the Jewish rebellion against God.

Dan 9:24 **"Seventy 'sevens' are decreed for your people and your holy city to finish transgression, to put an end to sin, to atone for wickedness, to bring in everlasting righteousness, to seal up vision and prophecy and to anoint the most holy.** (NIV)

TWO JEWISH IDIOMS

Israel—and for that matter, mankind as a whole—will never come to accept Jesus without some sort of intervention from God. In order for God's plan to come to completion, He will have to step in and judge with righteousness. That is exactly what He will do! God will have to purify both the Jewish people (chosen ones) and the Gentiles (nations) in order for them to recognize Jesus as the savior of the world and bring them back to Him. This can only be accomplished through the wrath of His fierce anger. The Word of God uses two Jewish idioms (metaphors or phrases) to reveal to us this soon-to-come period of trial the people on the earth will undergo. These phrases are:

The Tribulation Period — The Time of Jacob's Trouble

1. Birth Pains (Pangs)
2. Cup of Wrath

Birth pains serve a twofold purpose for the Jews during the first half of the Tribulation Period. These birth pains will begin to appear on the scene after the Jewish people are living peacefully in their own nation under the protection of the Antichrist. They are signs that in the very near future the Jewish people will face extreme persecution from the Antichrist. By this time they will be hated by all the nations of the world because of Jesus.

> Matt 24:9-12 *"Then you will be handed over to be persecuted and put to death, and you will be hated by all nations because of me. At that time many will turn away from the faith and will betray and hate each other, and many false prophets will appear and deceive many people. <u>Because of the increase of wickedness, the love of most will grow cold</u>,* (NIV)

These birth pains will also be part of the devastation that comes on the earth as a result of the fierce anger of the Lord. As birth pains, these Divine judgments continue to become more severe as time progresses during the Tribulation Period. As a whole they will effect the entire world and all the people living at that time. The cup of the wine of God's wrath will come down on both the Jews and the Nations. In the end, all the wicked will drink from this cup which is the destruction meted out by the Antichrist during the time of Great Tribulation.

Birth Pains — The birth pains that women experience at child birth are unique to them. Birth pains are first introduced to us in scripture in the third chapter of the book of Genesis. It was part of the curse that fell on all women because of Adam and Eve's original sin.

> Gen 3:16 *To the woman he said, "I will greatly increase your pains in childbearing; with pain you will give birth to children. Your desire will be for your husband, and he will rule over you."* (NIV)

An overview of birth pains goes something like this:

1. Once a woman conceives—there is no turning back—she will eventually have birth pains.
2. They will take place at the end of her pregnancy.
3. When a woman is about to give birth she will begin to experience birth pains as a warning that she is ready to give birth.
4. After the birth pains begin they will not stop until the baby is born.
5. Birth pains begin with less intensity and more time lapses between each one.
6. As time progresses, the birth pains become more frequent and the pain becomes almost unbearable.
7. When the baby is born, the woman is so overjoyed with the baby that she forgets about the terrible birth pains she just passed through.

AFTER THE RAPTURE

> John 16:21 *A woman giving birth to a child has pain because her time has come; but when her baby is born she forgets the anguish because of her joy that a child is born into the world.* (NIV)

Child birth is a miracle from God. Only a woman who has had a baby can tell you how awful the pain is and how wonderful the experience of having a baby can be. I can still remember the moans and screams of my son Jerry's wife, Angie, as she lay on a hospital bed for hour-upon-hour as she gave birth to Jacob Dart (my grandson). I remember her telling me that she would never have any more children because she did not want to experience that kind of pain again. Several years later she said that she and Jerry wanted to have another baby. By the way, my son Jerry called me the other night to tell me that after seven years his wife Angie is going to have another baby. On April 28, 2000, Levi Dart entered the world. Yes, it did take me a long time to write this book!

God uses the experience of a woman having a baby as the same experience Israel and the nations will have during the Tribulation Period. Here is their experience:

1. Israel and the nations (in a sense) conceived when Christ was crucified and at this time are pregnant.
2. The very beginning of the birth pains, with the least severity, could possibly begin toward the end of the church age as Signs of the Times for true believers. These early birth pains could possibly include World War I and World War II. They are birth pains for the church, including Jewish believers in Jesus.
3. At the end of this pregnancy, during the first 3 ½ years of the Tribulation Period, Israel's birth pains will begin: False Christ's, wars, famines, and earthquakes around the world are all signs for the Jewish people in this passage.
   Matt 24:4-8 *Jesus answered: "Watch out that no one deceives you. For many will come in my name, claiming, 'I am the Christ,' and will deceive many. You will hear of wars and rumors of wars, but see to it that you are not alarmed. Such things must happen, but the end is still to come. Nation will rise against nation, and kingdom against kingdom. There will be famines and earthquakes in various places. All these are the beginning of birth pains.* (NIV)
4. As the Tribulation Period progresses, the false Christ's, wars, famine and earthquakes will increase in severity and quantity. The birth pains will probably include the seal, trumpet, thunder and bowl judgments cast onto the earth by Jesus from heaven. The last half of the Tribulation Period will experience increased judgment (in number and intensity). Toward the end of the Tribulation Period it will be almost unbearable for the people on earth (See chart on page 768).
5. After the Tribulation Period is over, new life is experienced by Israel and the nations. Those who accept Christ during this time will have a new birth. First for Israel and followed shortly thereafter by the nations. A detail of this experience is provided in this book in the next chapter. The joy of the new birth will be so great that the horrible experience of the Tribulation Period will be forgotten by those people who have taken part in the new birth.
   Isa 65:17 *For, behold, I create new heavens and a new earth: and the former*

The Tribulation Period — The Time of Jacob's Trouble

shall not be remembered, nor come into mind. (KJV)

Cup of Wrath — The second Jewish idiom in scripture that deals with the trials of Israel, along with the Gentiles, is the drinking from a cup filled with the wine of the fury of the wrath of God. Take note in Psalms eleven that Jesus is on His throne in heaven during the Tribulation Period, at which time He will test the sons of men (mankind).

Ps 75:1-10 *We give thanks to You, O God, we give thanks! For Your wondrous works declare that Your name is near. "When I choose the proper time, I will judge uprightly. The earth and all its inhabitants are dissolved; I set up its pillars firmly. Selah 'I said to the boastful, 'Do not deal boastfully,' and to the wicked, 'Do not lift up the horn. Do not lift up your horn on high; do not speak with a stiff neck.'" For exaltation comes neither from the east nor from the west nor from the south. But God is the Judge: he puts down one, and exalts another. For in the hand of the LORD there is a cup, and the wine is red; it is fully mixed, and He pours it out; surely its dregs shall all the wicked of the earth Drain and drink down. But I will declare forever, I will sing praises to the God of Jacob. 'All the horns of the wicked I will also cut off, but the horns of the righteous shall be exalted."* (NKJ)

Ps 11:1-7 *In the LORD I put my trust; how can you say to my soul, "Flee as a bird to your mountain"? For look! The wicked bend their bow, they make ready their arrow on the string, that they may shoot secretly at the upright in heart. If the foundations are destroyed, what can the righteous do? The LORD is in His holy temple, the LORD'S throne is in heaven; his eyes behold, his eyelids test the sons of men. The LORD tests the righteous, but the wicked and the one who loves violence His soul hates. Upon the wicked He will rain coals; fire and brimstone and a burning wind shall be the portion of their cup. For the LORD is righteous, he loves righteousness; his countenance beholds the upright.* (NKJ)

The cup of wrath as it pertains to Jerusalem.

Isa 51:17 *Awake, awake! Rise up, O Jerusalem, you who have drunk from the hand of the LORD the cup of his wrath, you who have drained to its dregs the goblet that makes men stagger.* (NIV)

The cup of wrath as it pertains to the Gentiles. The Hebrew word for "Gentiles" is *gowy* (plural-*gowyim*) and can be translated as; Gentile, heathen, nation or people.

Jer 25:15-16 *This is what the LORD, the God of Israel, said to me: "Take from* *my hand **this cup filled with the wine of my wrath** and **make all the nations** to whom I send you **drink it**. When they drink it, they will stagger and go mad because of the sword I will send among them."* (NIV)

Those people who take the mark of the beast during the last half of the Tribulation Period will also drink from this cup.

Rev 14:9-11 *Then a third angel followed them, saying with a loud voice, "If anyone worships the beast and his image, and receives his mark on his forehead or on his hand, "**he himself shall also drink of the wine of the wrath of God, which is poured out full strength into the cup of His indignation**. He shall be tormented with fire and brimstone in the presence of the holy angels and in the presence of the Lamb. "And the smoke of their torment ascends forever and ever; and they have no rest day or night, who worship the beast and his image, and whoever receives the mark of his name."* (NKJ)

When the final destruction of Babylon takes place, she is given the cup of wrath to drink. The city of Babylon and the false religious system will be defeated and destroyed.

Rev 16:19 *Now the great city was divided into three parts, and the cities of the nations fell. And great **Babylon** was remembered before God, **to give her the cup of the wine of the fierceness of His wrath**.* (NKJ)

All the unsaved, both Israel and the Gentiles, will have to drink from this cup full of wine (symbolic of blood). The final 3 ½ year period of judgment will be for Israel and for the Gentiles. We begin the judgment with the nation of Israel.

THE TIME OF JACOB'S TROUBLE

During the first two years *After the Rapture*, Israel protected herself. For the first 3 ½ years of the Tribulation Period the Antichrist provided the protection for Israel under the umbrella of the 7-Year Peace Treaty. After the Antichrist breaks the peace treaty with Israel, in the middle of the seven years, there is no one left to protect them. When their army was disbanded and their weapons surrendered to the United Nations Peace Keeping Forces, it left Israel without any way of protecting themselves. Jeremiah gives the best description of what is in store for the tiny nation of Israel for the last 3 ½ years of the Tribulation Period.

Jer 30:4-7 ***These are the words the LORD spoke concerning Israel and Judah:** This is what the LORD says: "'**Cries of fear are heard—terror, not peace.** Ask and see: Can a man bear children? Then why do I see every strong man with his hands on his stomach like a woman in labor, every face turned deathly pale? How awful*

The Tribulation Period — The Time of Jacob's Trouble

that day will be! None will be like it. It will be <u>a time of trouble for Jacob</u>, but he will be saved out of it. (NIV)

Notice the agony of the strong men of Israel with deathly pale faces and their hands on their stomach as if they were having labor pains. Some of the words used by scripture to describe this period of time for the Jewish people are for God to purge, purify, test, judge, punish and refine His chosen people. This 3 ½ year period is the same scene in view from the three passages we mentioned in the Introduction of this book; Jeremiah 30:7, Daniel 12:1 and Matthew 24:21. They all deal with Israel in this last 3 ½ years of the Tribulation Period.

God furnishes us with the reasons why these calamities are to befall the nation of Israel. Here are some of them:

1. God will judge Israel according to her conduct and will repay her for her detestable practices.
   Ezek 7:1-4 *The word of the LORD came to me: "Son of man, this is what the Sovereign LORD says to the land of Israel: **The end**! The end has come upon the four corners of the land. The end is now upon you and I will unleash my anger against you. **I will judge you according to your conduct and repay you for all your detestable practices. I will not look on you with pity or spare you; I will surely repay you for your conduct and the detestable practices among you.** Then you will know that I am the LORD.* (NIV)

2. God will purge Israel of those who revolt and rebel against Him.
   Ezek 20:36-38 *As I judged your fathers in the desert of the land of Egypt, so I will judge you, declares the Sovereign LORD. I will take note of you as you pass under my rod, and I will bring you into the bond of the covenant. <u>I will purge you of those who revolt and rebel against me</u>. Although I will bring them out of the land where they are living, yet they will not enter the land of Israel. Then you will know that I am the LORD.* (NIV)

3. They have turned their backs on God and their sins are as scarlet. Rebels and sinners will be broken.
   Isa 1:4 *Ah, sinful nation, a people loaded with guilt, a brood of evildoers, children given to corruption! <u>They have forsaken the LORD; they have spurned the Holy One of Israel and turned their backs on him.</u>* (NIV)
   Isa 1:18-20 *"Come now, let us reason together," says the LORD. "<u>Though your sins are like scarlet, they shall be as white as snow; though they are red as crimson, they shall be like wool.</u> If you are willing and obedient, you will eat the best from the land; <u>but if you resist and rebel, you will be devoured by the sword.</u>" For the mouth of the LORD has spoken.* (NIV)

4. Jesus rises to judge the leaders of Israel for leading the people astray and afflicting the poor.
   Isa 3:13-15 *<u>The LORD takes his place in court; he rises to judge the people.</u> <u>The</u>*

LORD enters into judgment against the elders and leaders of his people: *"It is you who have ruined my vineyard; the plunder from the poor is in your houses. What do you mean by crushing my people and grinding the faces of the poor?" declares the Lord, the LORD Almighty.* (NIV)

5. They did not follow the ways of the Lord.
   Isa 42:24-25 ***Who handed Jacob over to become loot, and Israel to the plunderers? Was it not the LORD, against whom we have sinned? For they would not follow his ways; they did not obey his law.*** *So he poured out on them his burning anger, the violence of war. It enveloped them in flames, yet they did not understand; it consumed them, but they did not take it to heart.* (NIV)

6. God will deal with Israel for His own name's sake.
   Ezek 20:43-44 *There you will remember your conduct and all the actions by which you have defiled yourselves, and you will loathe yourselves for all the evil you have done. You will know that I am the LORD,* ***when I deal with you for my name's sake and not according to your evil ways and your corrupt practices, O house of Israel,*** *declares the Sovereign LORD.'"* (NIV)
   Ps 106:8 *Yet he saved them for his name's sake, to make his mighty power known.* (NIV)
   Isa 48:9-11 *For my own name's sake I delay my wrath; for the sake of my praise I hold it back from you, so as not to cut you off. See, I have refined you, though not as silver;* ***I have tested you in the furnace of affliction. For my own sake, for my own sake, I do this.*** *How can I let myself be defamed? I will not yield my glory to another.* (NIV)

7. God will repay Israel double for their sin.
   Jer 16:18 ***I will repay them double for their wickedness and their sin****, because they have defiled my land with the lifeless forms of their vile images and have filled my inheritance with their detestable idols."* (NIV)

8. Israel has even failed miserably to complete one of the purposes they were chosen to fulfill. That was to bring salvation to the whole world. God compares it to Israel as being pregnant and giving birth to air.
   Isa 26:16-18 *LORD, they came to you in their distress; when you disciplined them, they could barely whisper a prayer. As a woman with child and about to give birth writhes and cries out in her pain, so were we in your presence, O LORD. We were with child, we writhed in pain, but we gave birth to wind.* ***We have not brought salvation to the earth; we have not given birth to people of the world.*** (NIV)

Before we look at God's discourse on the subject of the 3 ½ year period of Israel's extreme persecution, that is about to come upon them in the near future, let us look at a couple of interesting passages concerning the position of God for this time period. He will

The Tribulation Period — The Time of Jacob's Trouble

literally abandon the Jewish people until their labor pains have come to completion and a remnant returns to Jesus the Messiah.

> Micah 5:3   ***<u>Therefore Israel will be abandoned</u> until the time when she who is in labor gives birth and the rest of his brothers return to join the Israelites.*** (NIV)

God will abandon them for a brief moment (3 ½ Years), but He will not forsake or destroy them entirely. There is hope for Israel and eventually He will fulfill the covenant (promise) of peace He made with them. In a surge of anger, He will hide His face from them for the last time.

> Isa 54:7-10   *"<u>For a brief moment I abandoned you</u>, but with deep compassion I will bring you back. In a surge of anger I hid my face from you for a moment, but with everlasting kindness I will have compassion on you," says the LORD your Redeemer.* "To me this is like the days of Noah, when I swore that the waters of Noah would never again cover the earth. *<u>So now I have sworn not to be angry with you</u>, <u>never to rebuke you again</u>. Though the mountains be shaken and the hills be removed, yet my unfailing love for you will not be shaken nor my covenant of peace be removed," says the LORD, who has compassion on you.* (NIV)

I do not want to imply that God does not love the Jewish people. On the contrary, God loves them very much, but this action against them is brought about because of their action, or I might say inaction toward Him. God will not allow unfaithfulness—from the Jew or the Gentile—to go on forever. He has an appointed time (*moed`*) to deal with sin. God's word is packed full of discourse on the last 3 ½ years of the Tribulation Period. A good deal of it, with the exception of the book of Revelation, which deals with the plagues that fall on the earth (mankind), deals with Israel. The end has come, as in the sense of God's dealings with Israel. This is not the destruction of Jerusalem in 586 BC as some contend, it is the future time of the Tribulation Period, during the Time of Jacob's Trouble.

> Ezek 7:1-26   *The word of the LORD came to me: "Son of man, this is what the Sovereign LORD says to the land of Israel: <u>The end</u>! The end has come upon the four corners of the land. The end is now upon you and I will unleash my anger against you. I will judge you according to your conduct and repay you for all your detestable practices.* I will not look on you with pity or spare you; I will surely repay you for your conduct and the detestable practices among you. Then you will know that I am the LORD. "This is what the Sovereign LORD says: *<u>Disaster</u>! An unheard-of disaster is coming. The end has come! The end has come! It has roused itself against you. It has come! Doom has come upon you—you who dwell in the land.*

AFTER THE RAPTURE

The time has come, the day is near; there is panic, not joy, upon the mountains. **I am about to pour out my wrath on you and spend my anger against you;** *I will judge you according to your conduct and repay you for all your detestable practices. I will not look on you with pity or spare you; I will repay you in accordance with your conduct and the detestable practices among you. Then you will know that it is I the LORD who strikes the blow.* **"<u>The day is here! It has come</u>!** *Doom has burst forth, the rod has budded, arrogance has blossomed! Violence has grown into a rod to punish wickedness;* **none of the people will be left, none of that crowd—no wealth, nothing of value. The time has come, the day has arrived. Let not the buyer rejoice nor the seller grieve, for wrath is upon the whole crowd.** *The seller will not recover the land he has sold as long as both of them live, for the vision concerning the whole crowd will not be reversed.* **Because of their sins, not one of them will preserve his life.** *Though they blow the trumpet and get everything ready, no one will go into battle, for my wrath is upon the whole crowd.* **"<u>Outside is the sword, inside are plague and famine; those in the country will die by the sword, and those in the city will be devoured by famine and plague.</u>** *All who survive and escape will be in the mountains, moaning like doves of the valleys, each because of his sins. Every hand will go limp, and every knee will become as weak as water. They will put on sackcloth and be clothed with terror. Their faces will be covered with shame and their heads will be shaved. They will throw their silver into the streets, and their gold will be an unclean thing.* **Their silver and gold will not be able to save them in <u>the day of the LORD's wrath</u>.** *They will not satisfy their hunger or fill their stomachs with it, for it has made them stumble into sin. They were proud of their beautiful jewelry and used it to make their detestable idols and vile images. Therefore I will turn these into an unclean thing for them.* **I will hand it all over as plunder to foreigners and as loot to the wicked of the earth, and they will defile it.** *I will turn my face away from them, and they will desecrate my treasured place; robbers will enter it and desecrate it.* **"Prepare chains, because the land is full of bloodshed and the city is full of violence. I will bring <u>the most wicked of the nations</u> to take possession of their houses;** *I will put an end to the pride of the mighty, and their sanctuaries will be desecrated. When terror comes, they will seek peace, but there will be none. Calamity upon calamity will come, and rumor upon rumor. They will try to get a vision from the prophet; the teaching of the law by the priest will be lost, as will the counsel of the elders.* (NIV)

Ezek 7:27   ***The king will mourn, the prince will be clothed with despair, and***

The Tribulation Period — The Time of Jacob's Trouble

*the hands of the people of the land will tremble. **I will deal with them according to their conduct, and by their own standards I will judge them**. Then they will know that I am the LORD."* (NIV)

God reveals the method of dealing with Jerusalem for these 3 ½ years. He calls them four dreadful judgments. Some prophecy teachers believe these to be the first four seal judgments in Revelation chapter six—the Four Horsemen of the Apocalypse. Although they are similar, they will not effect the nation of Israel until the last half of the Tribulation Period. Remember that the seal judgments will take place during the first 3 ½ years of the Tribulation Period and apply to the Antichrist, while the four judgments referred to in Ezekiel chapter fourteen will apply to Israel during the Time of Jacob's Trouble. Please take note of the fact that it mentions that if Noah, Daniel and Job were living in the time of this apostasy of Israel, they could only save themselves by their righteousness. The Jewish people are far from God at this time, but some Jewish people will survive the onslaught.

Ezek 14:12-23   *The word of the LORD came to me: "Son of man, if a country sins against me by being unfaithful and I stretch out my hand against it to cut off its food supply and send **famine** upon it and kill its men and their animals, **even if these three men—Noah, Daniel and Job—were in it, they could save only themselves by their righteousness, declares the Sovereign LORD.** "Or if I send **wild beasts** through that country and they leave it childless and it becomes desolate so that no one can pass through it because of the beasts, as surely as I live, declares the Sovereign LORD, even if these three men were in it, they could not save their own sons or daughters. They alone would be saved, but the land would be desolate. "Or if I bring **a sword** against that country and say, 'Let the sword pass throughout the land,' and I kill its men and their animals, as surely as I live, declares the Sovereign LORD, even if these three men were in it, they could not save their own sons or daughters. They alone would be saved. "Or if I send **a plague** into that land and pour out my wrath upon it through bloodshed, killing its men and their animals, as surely as I live, declares the Sovereign LORD, **even if Noah, Daniel and Job were in it, they could save neither son nor daughter.** They would save only themselves by their righteousness. "For this is what the Sovereign LORD says: How much worse will it be when **I send against Jerusalem my four dreadful judgments—sword and famine and wild beasts and plague—to kill its men and their animals! Yet there will be some survivors—sons and daughters who will be brought out of it**. They will come to you, and when you see their conduct and their actions, you will be consoled regarding the disaster I have brought upon Jerusalem—every disaster I have brought upon it. **You will be consoled when you see their conduct and their actions, for you will know that I have done nothing in it*** *without cause, declares the Sovereign LORD."* (NIV)

Again in Ezekiel we see the hand of God come down on Israel.

Ezek 20:32-37 *"'You say, "We want to be like the nations, like the peoples of the world, who serve wood and stone." But what you have in mind will never happen. **As surely as I live, declares the Sovereign LORD, I will rule over you with a mighty hand and an outstretched arm and with outpoured wrath.** I will bring you from the nations and gather you from the countries where you have been scattered—with a mighty hand and an outstretched arm and with outpoured wrath. I will bring you into the desert of the nations and there, face to face, I will execute judgment upon you. As I judged your fathers in the desert of the land of Egypt, so I will judge you, declares the Sovereign LORD. I will take note of you as you pass under my rod, and I will bring you into the bond of the covenant.* (NIV)

Ezek 20:38 **I will purge you of those who revolt and rebel against me. Although I will bring them out of the land where they are living, yet they will not enter the land of Israel. Then you will know that I am the LORD.** (NIV)

In Zephaniah, the prophet is specifically speaking of the great Day of the Lord.

Zeph 1:14-18 *"The great day of the LORD is near—near and coming quickly. Listen! The cry on the day of the LORD will be bitter, the shouting of the warrior there. That day will be a day of wrath, a day of distress and anguish, a day of trouble and ruin, a day of darkness and gloom, a day of clouds and blackness, a day of trumpet and battle cry against the fortified cities and against the corner towers. **I will bring distress on the people and they will walk like blind men, because they have sinned against the LORD. Their blood will be poured out like dust and their entrails like filth. Neither their silver nor their gold will be able to save them on the day of the LORD's wrath. In the fire of his jealousy the whole world will be consumed, for he will make a sudden end of all who live in the earth.*** (NIV)

Back in the great book of Isaiah we are told that double calamities will fall on Jerusalem. In these verses it makes mention that it will be the last judgment to come upon His people.

Isa 51:17-23 *__Awake, awake! Rise up, O Jerusalem__, you who have drunk from the hand of the LORD the cup of his wrath, you who have drained to its dregs the goblet that makes men stagger. Of all the sons she*

The Tribulation Period — The Time of Jacob's Trouble

bore there was none to guide her; of all the sons she reared there was none to take her by the hand. ***These double calamities have come upon you—who can comfort you?—ruin and destruction, famine and sword—who can console you?*** *Your sons have fainted; they lie at the head of every street, like antelope caught in a net.* ***They are filled with the wrath of the LORD and the rebuke of your God.*** *Therefore hear this, you afflicted one, made drunk, but not with wine.* ***This is what your Sovereign LORD says, your God, who defends his people:*** *"****See****,* ***I have taken out of your hand the cup that made you stagger; from that cup, the goblet of my wrath, you will never drink again.*** *I will put it into the hands of your tormentors, who said to you, 'Fall prostrate that we may walk over you.' And you made your back like the ground, like a street to be walked over."* (NIV)

Jeremiah also informs us that God will repay them double for their wickedness and sin.

Jer 16:18   *I will repay them double for their wickedness and their sin, because they have defiled my land with the lifeless forms of their vile images and have filled my inheritance with their detestable idols."* (NIV)

A description of the judgment of Jerusalem and Israel, during the Time of Jacob's Trouble, can be found in the third chapter of Isaiah.

Isa 3:1-9   *See now, the Lord, the LORD Almighty, is about to take from Jerusalem and Judah both supply and support: all supplies of food and all supplies of water, the hero and warrior, the judge and prophet, the soothsayer and elder, the captain of fifty and man of rank, the counselor, skilled craftsman and clever enchanter. I will make boys their officials; mere children will govern them.* ***People will oppress each other—man against man, neighbor against neighbor.*** *The young will rise up against the old, the base against the honorable. A man will seize one of his brothers at his father's home, and say, "You have a cloak, you be our leader; take charge of this heap of ruins!" But in that day he will cry out, "I have no remedy. I have no food or clothing in my house; do not make me the leader of the people."* ***Jerusalem staggers, Judah is falling; their words and deeds are against the LORD, defying his glorious presence.*** *The look on their faces testifies against them; they parade their sin like Sodom; they do not hide it.* ***Woe to them! They have brought disaster upon themselves.*** (NIV)

Amos, who lived in the middle of the eighth century BC (760 BC), warned those in Israel who longed for the coming of the Day of the Lord. It will be a time of extreme persecution. For a long time the Jewish people have been looking forward to the time when they will be restored to the position as head of the nation's during the Day of the Lord. Nevertheless, Amos warns the Jewish people to BEWARE!

> Amos 5:18-19 *<u>Woe to you who long for the day of the LORD! Why do you long for the day of the LORD? That day will be darkness, not light.</u> It will be as though a man fled from a lion only to meet a bear, as though he entered his house and rested his hand on the wall only to have a snake bite him.* (NIV)

Amos, in chapter nine, adds that God will destroy the sinful nation of Israel, but will leave a remnant—those who believe in Him. All of the unbelievers will die by the sword.

> Amos 9:8-10 *"Surely the eyes of the Sovereign LORD are on the sinful kingdom. I will destroy it from the face of the earth—yet I will not totally destroy the house of Jacob," declares the LORD. "For I will give the command, and I will shake the house of Israel among all the nations as grain is shaken in a sieve, and not a pebble will reach the ground. <u>All the sinners among my people will die by the sword</u>, all those who say, 'Disaster will not overtake or meet us.'* (NIV)

Second Holocaust — As much as the Jewish people do not want the memory of the Holocaust of World War II to go away, as a deterrent to prevent it from happening again, Zechariah —a Jewish prophet—tells us that it will happen again. To the Jews, it will not be a popular future prophecy to talk about, but again I remind them that judgment comes to the Nations (non-Jews) as well. You could almost say that it will be wholesale slaughter for mankind as we will see in this chapter and the next chapter.

During the Holocaust, orchestrated by Adolf Hitler, approximately one-third of the Jews living in the world at that time were killed (6 million). Zechariah reveals to us that during the next Holocaust, two-thirds of the Jews in the world at this future time will be killed. Today, there are approximately 15 million Jews living in the world, according to current estimates. If the Time of Jacob's Trouble were to take place in the near future, 10,000,000 Jews would be purged from the earth in just 3 ½ years. The remaining one-third of the Jews will be those refined during this period. They will be the Jewish people who will recognize Jesus as the True Messiah.

> Zech 13:8-9 *In the whole land," declares the LORD, "<u>two-thirds will be struck down and perish; yet one-third will be left in it</u>. This third I will bring into the fire; I will refine them like silver and test them like gold. <u>They will call on my name and I will answer them</u>; I will say, '<u>They are my people</u>,' and they will say, '<u>The LORD is our God</u>.'"* (NIV)

These will be the Jewish people who fulfill Paul's prophetic utterance in chapter 11 of Romans. The deliverer will be Jesus Christ as He comes from the heavenly Zion. He will

The Tribulation Period — The Time of Jacob's Trouble

turn the Jewish people, those who accept Him as their Messiah, away from Godlessness.

> Rom 11:25-27 *I do not want you to be ignorant of this mystery, brothers, so that you may not be conceited: Israel has experienced a hardening in part until the full number of the Gentiles has come in. **And so all Israel will be saved, as it is written: "The deliverer will come from Zion; he will turn Godlessness away from Jacob. And this is my covenant with them when I take away their sins."*** (NIV)

It is also the very time that Daniel is speaking about when he makes the statement that it will take 3 ½ years to break the power of the holy people (Israel).

> Dan 12:7 *The man clothed in linen, who was above the waters of the river, lifted his right hand and his left hand toward heaven, and I heard him swear by him who lives forever, saying, "**It will be for a time, times and half a time. When the power of the holy people has been finally broken, all these things will be completed.**"* (NIV)

This is God's method of breaking the rebellious ethnic nation of Israel and their apostasy. This is what it will take for them to finally recognize Jesus as the True Messiah and to come back to God. What a horrible price they will have to pay.

As we turn back to the start of the second half of the Tribulation Period, we see a quick succession of events about to take place. Even though this will be a horrible time for the Jewish people and their nation, it will not be a pretty picture for the rest of mankind either, as the destruction of the world lies just in front of them. Chapter nine of this book, which was about the first half of the Tribulation Period, ended with a great earthquake. Chapter ten lasted for about a half hour and as we begin chapter eleven, we have another earthquake. That means we have two earthquakes almost back to back. John observes the seven angels who are standing before God. This scene is in heaven and these seven angels are each given one of the seven trumpets, which are the seven trumpet judgments that are about to take place on earth. Then another angel had a golden censer with incense and prayers of the believers. These are more than likely prayers from the saints who are facing terrible persecution during the Tribulation Period. The angel took the censer, filled it with fire from the altar and hurled it to the earth. Peals of thunder, rumblings, flashes of lightning and an earthquake now begin the second 3 ½ years of the Tribulation Period.

> Rev 8:2-5 ***And I saw the seven angels who stand before God, and to them were given seven trumpets.** Another angel, who had a golden censer, came and stood at the altar. He was given much incense to offer, with the prayers of all the saints, on the golden altar before the throne. The smoke of the incense, together with the prayers of the saints, went up before God from the angel's hand. **Then the angel took the censer, filled it with fire from the altar, and hurled it on the earth; and there came peals of thunder, rumblings, flashes of***

lightning and an earthquake. (NIV)

After the earthquake, the first angel sounds the **First Trumpet** he is assigned to sound. I like to refer to the trumpet judgments as the one-third judgments because they will effect one-third of whatever they were sent to fall upon. After the trumpet is sounded, hail and fire mixed with blood are hurled down to earth. A third of the earth is effected by this plague as a third of the earth is burned up. A third of the trees and all the grass is burned up. It is now time for the birth pains to come more frequently and with greater intensity.

> Rev 8:6-7 *Then the seven angels who had the seven trumpets prepared to sound them. <u>The first angel sounded his trumpet</u>, and there came hail and fire mixed with blood, and it was hurled down upon the earth. A third of the earth was burned up, a third of the trees were burned up, and all the green grass was burned up.* (NIV)

It will take 3 ½ years for the seal judgments to run their course and it will take approximately 2 ½ years for the trumpet judgments to pour down. The first six judgments will last approximately five months each, with the last one being a very short time. We will list the remaining trumpet judgments after we discuss more of the early activities of this period. At this time, though he is still publicly promoting peace, Psalms 52 reveals the true character and motives of the Antichrist. By this time he will have tremendous power.

> Ps 52:1-4 *Why do you boast of evil, <u>you mighty man</u>? Why do you boast all day long, you who are a disgrace in the eyes of God? <u>Your tongue plots destruction</u>; <u>it is like a sharpened razor</u>, <u>you who practice deceit</u>. You love evil rather than good, falsehood rather than speaking the truth. Selah You love every harmful word, O you deceitful tongue!* (NIV)

It is at this time that the Antichrist breaks his 7-Year Peace Treaty with Israel. Although the Antichrist is about to overrun Jerusalem, he still appears to the rest of the world as a smooth talking dictator. Peace will still be in his speeches, but war will be in his heart. Israel asks God to deliver them from this unjust man who comes against an ungodly nation.

> Ps 55:20-21 *<u>My companion attacks his friends</u>; he violates his covenant. His speech is smooth as butter, yet war is in his heart; his words are more soothing than oil, yet they are drawn swords.* (NIV)

> Ps 43:1 *Vindicate me, O God, and plead my cause against an ungodly nation; <u>Oh, deliver me from the deceitful and unjust man!</u>* (NKJ)

It appears that the Antichrist will return to his headquarters in Europe after Satan enters his body and his wound is healed. Some of his army will remain in Jerusalem to complete the task of building the wing on the Jewish Temple, the place for his throne. At his

The Tribulation Period — The Time of Jacob's Trouble

headquarters, the Antichrist/Satan personage will be fuming with anger. Not long before, the Antichrist was defeated by the Egyptians. It is at this time that the Antichrist and his generals are constructing plans for besieging Israel and Jerusalem. Jerusalem will need to be under his control in order for the Antichrist to commit his great act of abomination. The nation of Israel and the city of Jerusalem will not be destroyed at this time. They will only be taken under siege. At the midpoint of the Tribulation Period the Antichrist and his army will suddenly swoop down on Israel seizing the city of Jerusalem. It appears that the Antichrist will be confronted with some opposition when he enters the city. Micah gives us a detailed account of the opposition that will take place at this time.

> Micah 5:1-5 *Marshal your troops, O city of troops, <u>for a siege is laid against us.</u> <u>They will strike Israel's ruler on the cheek with a rod.</u> "But you, Bethlehem Ephrathah, though you are small among the clans of Judah, out of you will come for me one who will be ruler over Israel, whose origins are from of old, from ancient times." **Therefore Israel will be abandoned until the time when she who is in labor gives birth and the rest of his brothers return to join the Israelites.** He will stand and shepherd his flock in the strength of the LORD, in the majesty of the name of the LORD his God. And they will live securely, for then his greatness will reach to the ends of the earth. And he will be their peace. <u>When the Assyrian invades our land and marches through our fortresses,</u> <u>we will raise against him seven shepherds,</u> <u>even eight leaders of men.</u>* (NIV)

The prime minister of Israel, along with seven religious leaders and eight political leaders (probably members of Knesset), will oppose the Antichrist (the Assyrian). The prime minister will be struck in the face and killed. Following this confrontation, the Antichrist will proceed to the new wing of the Temple and commit the:

ABOMINATION OF DESOLATION

He will set on the throne and proclaim to be God and commit the Abomination of Desolation spoken of by Daniel. Jesus, when He was discussing this future event of the Tribulation Period with His disciples on the Mount of Olives, referred to this very act of the Antichrist and even referenced Daniel the prophet. It does not appear that the city of Jerusalem will be destroyed by the Antichrist at this time.

> Matt 24:15 *"Therefore when you see the '<u>abomination of desolation,</u>' spoken of by Daniel the prophet, <u>standing in the holy place</u>" (whoever reads, let him understand),* (NKJ)

Jesus instructs the Jewish people who observe this despicable act to flee immediately. Let us now turn to the book from which Jesus took this reference. In Daniel chapter nine, it gives us the exact time that this act will take place.

Dan 9:27   *He will confirm a covenant with many for one 'seven.'* ***In the middle of the 'seven' he will put an end to sacrifice and offering.*** *And on a wing [of the temple] he will set up* ***an abomination that causes desolation****, until the end that is decreed is poured out on him."* (NIV)

This act will take place at the midpoint of the 7-Year Peace Treaty and as the Antichrist sets down on the throne, constructed on a wing of the Temple, it will start the Time of Jacob's Trouble. Daniel mentions the Abomination of Desolation four separate times in the apocalyptic chapters of his book. Here are the other three times it is listed.

Dan 8:11-12   *He even exalted himself as high as the Prince of the host; and by him the daily sacrifices were taken away,* ***and the place of His sanctuary was cast down.*** *Because of transgression, an army was given over to the horn to oppose the daily sacrifices; and he cast truth down to the ground. He did all this and prospered.* (NKJ)

Dan 11:31   *"And forces shall be mustered by him, and they shall defile the sanctuary fortress; then they shall take away the daily sacrifices, and place there* ***the abomination of desolation****.* (NKJ)

Dan 12:11   *"And from the time that the daily sacrifice is taken away, and* ***the abomination of desolation*** *is set up, there shall be one thousand two hundred and ninety days.* (NKJ)

In chapter eight, the Antichrist set himself up to be as great as the Prince (Jesus) of the host (Israelites). Prince means leader or ruler and here refers to Jesus as leader of the Jewish people. At this time the sanctuary will be cast down. Notice that at this point the Antichrist will prosper in everything he does. At this time truth will practically be nonexistent. In chapter eleven, we observe the activity of the forces of the Antichrist as they seize the Temple and sanctuary in Jerusalem; the temple the 7-Year Peace Treaty permitted the Jews to build 3 ½ years earlier. After seizing Jerusalem, the army set out to construct a building with a room to house a throne for the very purpose of this desecration by the Antichrist.

In the New Testament—besides the reference to the Abomination of Desolation in the Olivet Discourse—Paul gives us a distinct description of this bold action of the Antichrist.

2 Thes 2:4   *He will oppose and will exalt himself over everything that is called God or is worshiped,* ***so that he sets himself up in God's temple, proclaiming himself to be God.*** (NIV)

Orthodox Jews and some Bible interpreters believe that the references to the Abomination of Desolation, in Daniel chapters eight and eleven, are a reference to the time that Antiochus Epiphanes desecrated the holy Temple in 168 BC, while others believe it took place in 70 AD. I disagree! My belief is that **all** the references in scripture concerning this vile action refer to the Antichrist during a future time in history. The Sovereign Lord has this to say to the ruler of Tyre (the Antichrist). Remember, *"the seas"* are symbolic for people.

> Ezek 28:2-5 *"**Son of man, say to <u>the ruler of Tyre</u>, 'This is what the Sovereign LORD says: "'<u>In the pride of your heart you say</u>, "<u>I am a God</u>; <u>I sit on the throne of a God in the heart of the seas.</u>" <u>But you are a man and not a God, though you think you are as wise as a God</u>.** Are you wiser than Daniel? Is no secret hidden from you? By your wisdom and understanding you have gained wealth for yourself and amassed gold and silver in your treasuries. By your great skill in trading you have increased your wealth, and because of your wealth your heart has grown proud.* (NIV)

God reminds the Antichrist that he is a man and not a God. He asks him if he is wiser than the prophet Daniel. All this is followed by a description telling us how much wealth the Antichrist will amass during his short tenure on this earth. He will have a great entrepreneurial mind and great skill as a businessperson. Because of his great wealth the Antichrist will become proud. Sound familiar, Satan?

<u>JEWISH PEOPLE FLEE</u>

The moment the Antichrist sits on the throne in Jerusalem and proclaims to be Almighty God, all the Jewish people will realize that he is a false Messiah. Jesus describes the fate of the Jewish people during this 3 ½ year period in the Olivet Discourse, starting at the Abomination of Desolation.

> Matt 24:9-14 *"**Then you will be handed over to be persecuted and put to death, and you will be hated by all nations because of me.** At that time many will turn away from the faith and will betray and hate each other, and many false prophets will appear and deceive many people. **<u>Because of the increase of wickedness</u>, <u>the love of most will grow cold</u>, but he who stands firm to the end will be saved. And this gospel of the kingdom will be preached in the whole world as a testimony to all nations, <u>and then the end will come</u>.*** (NIV)

Jesus then announces that the fulfillment of the preaching of the gospel of the kingdom to the whole world will take place. This is accomplished by the 144,000 Jewish evangelists, the two witnesses and the three angels flying in the air. After 3 ½ years the persecution of the Jewish people will come to an end (which is the end of indignation). Jesus then gives the Jewish people the sign of when all the persecution will begin and instructions for what to do when the sign is revealed.

> Matt 24:15-21 *"**<u>So when you see standing in the holy place 'the abomination that causes desolation,'</u> spoken of through the prophet Daniel—let the reader understand—then let those who are in Judea flee to the***

> *mountains. Let no one on the roof of his house go down to take anything out of the house. Let no one in the field go back to get his cloak.* How dreadful it will be in those days for pregnant women and nursing mothers! Pray that your flight will not take place in winter or on the Sabbath. **For then there will be great distress, unequaled from the beginning of the world until now—and never to be equaled again.** (NIV)

In other words, **GET OUT OF TOWN IN A HURRY**! Jesus informs them that this situation is so critical that they do not even have time to go inside their house and pack their belongings. It will be a horrible time for women expecting babies and those with small children. They are instructed to pray that this event will not take place in winter time or on the Jewish Sabbath. This can only take place after the feasts are reestablished in Israel.

Daniel provides a description of the Antichrist (a stern-faced king) at this time.

Dan 8:23-25 *"In the latter part of their reign, when rebels have become completely wicked, a stern-faced king, a master of intrigue, will arise. He will become very strong, but not by his own power. He will cause astounding devastation and will succeed in whatever he does. He will destroy the mighty men and the holy people. He will cause deceit to prosper, and he will consider himself superior. When they feel secure, he will destroy many and take his stand against the Prince of princes. Yet he will be destroyed, but not by human power.* (NIV)

In the latter part of the Antichrist's reign (3 ½ years), mankind will become completely wicked (out of control). The Antichrist will become very powerful by the power of Satan. He will cause all sorts of destruction in his attempt to finalize his drive to completely control the world. He will by this time have gained enough power to destroy any national leaders who oppose him. The Antichrist will attempt to exterminate the holy people (Jews) living on the earth. He will be deceitful and believes himself to be superior to everyone, including God. After the Jews feel secure—referring to the first 3 ½ years of the Tribulation Period, when he provided protection for them—the Antichrist will kill many of them and stand up against Jesus (the Prince of princes). These three verses in Daniel chapter eight tell a remarkable story concerning the Antichrist during the final 3 ½ years of the Tribulation Period. This reminds me of the remarkable prediction by Zachariah; that two-thirds of the Jewish people will not make it through this short period of time.

Zech 13:7-8 *"Awake, O sword, against my shepherd, against the man who is close to me!" declares the LORD Almighty. "Strike the shepherd, and the sheep will be scattered, and I will turn my hand against the little ones.* **In the whole land,"** *declares the LORD,* **"two-thirds will be struck down and perish; yet one-third will be left in it.** (NIV)

The Tribulation Period — The Time of Jacob's Trouble

In these verses in Zechariah, it appears we see the same Jewish leader of high esteem that we referenced earlier in Micah 5:1; the prime minister of Israel who was killed by the Antichrist. He will oppose the Antichrist and could possibly be a believer in the True Messiah (Jesus). Strike (kill) the shepherd (leader) and the sheep (Jewish people) will be scattered (flee their nation). God will turn His hand—allow the Antichrist to persecute the Jewish people—against the little ones. Two-thirds of the Jewish people will perish during this time. The prophet Amos picks up the story in the last two chapters of his book.

Amos 8:1-14 *Thus the Lord God showed me: Behold, a basket of summer fruit. And He said, "Amos, what do you see?" So I said, "A basket of summer fruit."* **Then the LORD said to me: "<u>The end has come upon My people Israel</u>; I will not pass by them anymore.** *And the songs of the temple shall be wailing* **<u>in that day</u>,** *" says the Lord God " Many dead bodies everywhere, they shall be thrown out in silence." Hear this, you who swallow up the needy, and make the poor of the land fail, Saying: "When will the New Moon be past, that we may sell grain? And the Sabbath, that we may trade wheat? Making the ephah small and the shekel large, Falsifying the scales by deceit, That we may buy the poor for silver, and the needy for a pair of sandals —even sell the bad wheat?" The LORD has sworn by the pride of Jacob: "Surely I will never forget any of their works.* **Shall the land not tremble for this, and everyone mourn who dwells in it?** *All of it shall swell like the River, Heave and subside like the River of Egypt. "And it shall come to pass in that day," says the Lord God, "That I will make the sun go down at noon, and I will darken the earth in broad daylight; I will turn your feasts into mourning, and all your songs into lamentation; I will bring sackcloth on every waist, and baldness on every head; I will make it like mourning for an only son, and its end like a bitter day.* **"Behold, the days are coming," says the Lord God, "That I will send a famine on the land, not a famine of bread, nor a thirst for water, but of hearing the words of the LORD.** *They shall wander from sea to sea, and from north to east; they shall run to and fro, seeking the word of the LORD, but shall not find it. "In that day the fair virgins and strong young men shall faint from thirst. Those who swear by the sin of Samaria, who say, 'As your God lives, O Dan!' And, 'As the way of Beersheba lives!' They shall fall and never rise again."* (NKJ)

Amos 9:1-10 *I saw the Lord standing by the altar, and He said: "Strike the doorposts, that the thresholds may shake, and break them on the heads of them all.* <u>*I will slay the last of them with the sword.*</u> *He who flees from them shall not get away, and he who escapes from them shall not be delivered. "Though they dig into hell, from there my hand shall take them; though they climb up to heaven, from there*

I will bring them down; And though they hide themselves on top of Carmel, from there I will search and take them; though they hide from My sight at the bottom of the sea, from there I will command the serpent, and it shall bite them; **Though they go into captivity before their enemies, from there I will command the sword, and it shall slay them.** *I will set My eyes on them for harm and not for good." The Lord God of hosts, he who touches the earth and it melts, and all who dwell there mourn; all of it shall swell like the River, and subside like the River of Egypt. He who builds His layers in the sky, and has founded His strata in the earth; who calls for the waters of the sea, and pours them out on the face of the earth—the LORD is His name. "Are you not like the people of Ethiopia to Me, O children of Israel?" says the LORD. "Did I not bring up Israel from the land of Egypt, the Philistines from Caphtor, and the Syrians from Kir?* **"Behold, <u>the eyes of the Lord God are on the sinful kingdom, and I will destroy it from the face of the earth</u>; yet I will not utterly destroy the house of Jacob," says the LORD. "For surely I will command, and will sift the house of Israel among all nations,** *as grain is sifted in a sieve; yet not the smallest grain shall fall to the ground.* <u>**All the sinners of My people shall die by the sword**</u>**, who say, 'The calamity shall not overtake nor confront us.'** (NKJ)

I already know that some of you are going to say that these scripture passages refer to the defeat of the divided kingdom of Israel by the Assyrians in 722 BC. Its fulfillment goes far beyond that. "In that day" is a reference to the Day of the Lord. In the last verse, quoted above, it makes the statement, *"All the sinners among my people shall die by the sword. ..."* **ALL** the sinners of the Jewish people will not be purged until Jesus does it during the Time of Jacob's Trouble and at the Battle of Armageddon. If you are still in doubt, look at the next verse that follows the verses we just read. It reveals the time that the persecution of the Jews, spoken about in chapters eight and nine, will take place. It will be in the day when David's fallen tent is restored. That has yet to happen to this very day! It is yet future for us.

> Amos 9:11 **"<u>In that day</u> I will restore David's fallen tent. I will repair its broken places, restore its ruins, and build it as it used to be,** (NIV)

A closer look at Amos 9:9, reveals that there will yet be another scattering of the Jewish people. Jeremiah also mentions this exile.

> Amos 9:9 **"For I will give the command, <u>and I will shake the house of Israel among all the nations as grain is shaken in a sieve</u>, and not a pebble will reach the ground.** (NIV)

> Jer 30:10 *"'So do not fear, O Jacob my servant; do not be dismayed, O Israel,' declares the LORD.* **'I will surely save you out of a distant place,**

The Tribulation Period — The Time of Jacob's Trouble

your descendants from the land of their exile. Jacob will again have peace and security, and no one will make him afraid. (NIV)

The Jewish people will be scattered among the nations a total of three separate times throughout their history. If the Lord fulfills all of the events we talked about in this book, concerning the Tribulation Period in the near future, the scattering of the Jews among the nations will cover a time period of more than 2700 years. Here is how it breaks down:

Date	**Kingdom**	**Pursuer**		**Time of Return**
722 BC*	Israel	Assyria ⎫	**1st Scattering**	538 BC (partial)
586 BC	Judah	Babylon ⎭		
70 AD	Israel	Rome ⎫	**2nd Scattering****	20th Century
135 AD	Israel	Rome ⎭		(Fig Tree)
Future?	Israel	Revived Roman Empire (Antichrist)	**3rd Scattering*****	Day of the Lord (Day of Atonement)

* This portion of the kingdom of Israel are the Jews who were taken captive to various locations all over the then known world by the Assyrians. They eventually assimilated into the population they were exiled to and are known as the Ten Lost Tribes of Israel. Their descendants will return to Israel during the first half of the Tribulation Period, which will take place during the Day of the Lord.

** When the Jewish people started returning to Palestine at the beginning of the 20th century and were allowed to become a nation on May 14, 1948, that constituted the return of the Jewish people predicted in Matthew 24:32. It is a part of the return of the Jews to Israel, but the total fulfillment will not take place until *After the Rapture,* when Anti-Semitism around the world, along with the protection of the Jews by the 7-Year Peace Treaty, brings the Jewish people back to their homeland. At that time it will include all Israel, everyone from everywhere around the world.

*** The third return of the Jewish people will take place on the tenth year of the Day of the Lord (Yom Kippur). It will be made up of all the Jewish people who survive the Battle of Armageddon. Jesus will gather them from around the world at His Glorious Return when He gathers His elect.

Jer 31:10   *"Hear the word of the LORD, O nations; proclaim it in distant coastlands: 'He who scattered Israel will gather them and will watch over his flock like a shepherd.'* (NIV)

Matt 24:31   *"And He will send His angels with a great sound of a trumpet, and they will gather together His elect from the four winds, from one end of heaven to the other.* (NKJ)

As we look even closer at the event of the Jewish people fleeing from the Antichrist, at the Abomination of Desolation, we seem to have a contradiction. The account recorded in the Olivet Discourse instructs the Jews to flee to the mountains, while the account of this same event recorded in the book of Revelation instructs the Jews to flee to the desert (NIV), or to the wilderness (KJV).

> Matt 24:16   *Then let them which be in Judaea flee into <u>the mountains</u>:* (KJV)
>
> Rev 12:6   *The woman fled into <u>the desert</u> to a place prepared for her by God, where she might be taken care of for 1,260 days.* (NIV)

How can the Jews flee to the mountains and the desert at the same time? Well, they cannot unless you break the Jews up into two groups. The group mentioned in Matthew are the Jewish people as a whole. We get some idea of where the Jewish people flee to by looking forward to the places that are listed where they will be gathered from, by Jesus, after the Tribulation Period is over. In Isaiah 11, we see that they were gathered from the areas where the ancient Assyrians, Egyptians, Cush, Elam, Babylonians, Hamath and the islands of the sea were located. Today the modern countries of Egypt, Ethiopia, Syria, Turkey, Saudi Arabia, Jordan, Iran and Iraq are in this general area. The island of the seas can be a reference to any region separated from Palestine by water and also the farthest regions of the earth. The Jews will flee in mass migration to every nation of the world, but most of the Jews will flee to the nations surrounding Israel. Most of these nations will accept the fleeing Jewish people from the Antichrist because of their hatred of the Antichrist, especially Egypt (who has already faced the Antichrist in two previous battles). Some of the nations (where ancient Edom existed) will turn the fleeing Jews over to the Antichrist and his forces to be persecuted. In Ezekiel 35:1-15 we see punishment that will come against Mount Seir (Edom) for delivering the Jews over to the sword at this time (the climax of their punishment).

> Isa 11:11   <u>*In that day the Lord will reach out his hand a second time to reclaim the remnant that is left of his people from Assyria, from Lower Egypt, from Upper Egypt, from Cush, from Elam, from Babylonia, from Hamath and from the islands of the sea.*</u> (NIV)
>
> Isa 13:14-16   *Like a hunted gazelle, like sheep without a shepherd, each will return to his own people, each will flee to his native land. <u>Whoever is captured will be thrust through; all who are caught will fall by the sword.</u> Their infants will be dashed to pieces before their eyes; their houses will be looted and their wives ravished.* (NIV)

A second group—which is part of the Jews as a whole—has a different twist to it. God will prepare a secret hiding place for a portion of the Jews during this time. The reason God is providing a hiding place for some of the Jews at this time is to insure that 1/3 of the Jewish people will survive this horrible ordeal. Most of them might already have believed in Jesus as the Messiah. Scripture mentions this 3 ½ year hiding place two times — 1260 days in Revelation 12:6 and time, times and a half time in Revelation 12:14.

The Tribulation Period — The Time of Jacob's Trouble

Rev 12:6 — *The woman fled into <u>the desert</u> to a place prepared for her by God, where she might be taken care of <u>for 1,260 days</u>.* (NIV)

Rev 12:14 — *… so that she might fly to the place prepared for her in <u>the desert</u>, where she would be taken care of <u>for a time</u>, <u>times and half a time</u>, out of the serpent's reach.* (NIV)

Now would be an excellent time to glance at the parenthetical chapter of Revelation chapter twelve, where it tells us of a bigger and more expanded story. Two key figures of biblical history—past and future—come into play and need to be discussed.

Rev 12:1-6 — **A great and wondrous sign appeared in heaven: <u>a woman</u> clothed with the sun, with the moon under her feet and a crown of twelve stars on her head.** She was pregnant and cried out in pain as she was about to give birth. **Then another sign appeared in heaven: <u>an enormous red dragon</u> with seven heads and ten horns and seven crowns on his heads.** His tail swept a third of the stars out of the sky and flung them to the earth. The dragon stood in front of the woman who was about to give birth, so that he might devour her child the moment it was born. **She gave birth to a son, a male child, who will rule all the nations with an iron scepter. And her child was snatched up to God and to his throne.** The woman fled into the desert to a place prepared for her by God, where she might be taken care of for 1,260 days. (NIV)

The woman mentioned here is representing the nation of Israel. We can come to this conclusion by reading verse five, where it states that this woman gave birth to a son who will rule all the nations with an iron scepter. That is none other than Jesus Christ during the Day of the Lord.

Ps 2:7-9 — *I will proclaim the decree of the LORD: He said to me,"You are my Son; today I have become your Father. Ask of me, and I will make the nations your inheritance, the ends of the earth your possession. <u>**You will rule them with an iron scepter**</u>; you will dash them to pieces like pottery."* (NIV)

Rev 12:5 — *She gave birth to a son, a male child, <u>**who will rule all the nations with an iron scepter**</u>. And her child was snatched up to God and to his throne.* (NIV)

Rev 19:15 — *Out of his mouth comes a sharp sword with which to strike down the nations. "<u>**He will rule them with an iron scepter**</u>." He treads the winepress of the fury of the wrath of God Almighty.* (NIV)

AFTER THE RAPTURE

In Revelation 12:5, it mentions Jesus after He was crucified and went to be seated at the right hand of God in heaven, where He intercedes for the saints during the Dispensation of Grace.

> Rev 12:5 *She gave birth to a son, a male child, who will rule all the nations with an iron scepter. <u>And her child was snatched up to God and to his throne.</u>* (NIV)

> Rom 8:34 *Who is he that condemns? <u>Christ Jesus</u>, who died—more than that, <u>who was raised to life—is at the right hand of God and is also interceding for us</u>.* (NIV)

> Col 3:1 *Since, then, you have been raised with Christ, set your hearts on things above, **where Christ is seated at the right hand of God**.* (NIV)

> Heb 12:2 *<u>Let us fix our eyes on Jesus</u>, the author and perfecter of our faith, who for the joy set before him endured the cross, scorning its shame, <u>and sat down at the right hand of the throne of God</u>.* (NIV)

The identity of the red dragon is a little easier to establish because his name is given to us in verse nine.

> Rev 12:9 *<u>The great dragon</u> was hurled down—that ancient serpent called the devil, or Satan, who leads the whole world astray. He was hurled to the earth, and his angels with him.* (NIV)

These verses are a continuation of the battle between Satan (red dragon) and God's chosen people (woman) that has been going on ever since the chosen people were brought into existence. If Satan can exterminate every living Jew from the face of the earth, he can win his ongoing battle with God. Nevertheless, ever since Abraham, there has always been a remnant of saved Jews living on earth. The battle was going on at the time Jesus was born. In Revelation 12:4, we see Satan on the earth 2000 years ago wanting to kill Jesus and thus defeat Him when the woman (Israel) gave birth to a male son (Jesus). This ongoing battle will not end until Satan is defeated.

> Rev 12:4b *…<u>The dragon</u> stood in front of <u>the woman</u> who was about to give birth, so that he might devour her child the moment it was born.* (NIV)

Recent history records Adolf Hitler's attempt to exterminate the Jews a little more than fifty years ago, but in the end this brutality spurred the return of the Jewish people to their homeland. The fig tree began to blossom. As the story continues in chapter twelve, during the Tribulation Period, we see Satan with another opportunity to exterminate the woman (Israel) from the face of the earth. By this time Satan will have been thrown out of heaven

The Tribulation Period — The Time of Jacob's Trouble

(war in heaven) and entered the body of the wounded Antichrist. We have come full circle and are once again back to the time of the Abomination of Desolation.

> Rev 12:13-17 *When the dragon saw that he had been hurled to the earth, he pursued the woman who had given birth to the male child. **The woman was given the two wings of a great eagle, so that she might fly to the place prepared for her in the desert, where she would be taken care of for a time, times and half a time, out of the serpent's reach.** Then from his mouth the serpent spewed water like a river, to overtake the woman and sweep her away with the torrent. But the earth helped the woman by opening its mouth and swallowing the river that the dragon had spewed out of his mouth. Then the dragon was enraged at the woman and went off to make war against the rest of her offspring—those who obey God's commandments and hold to the testimony of Jesus.* (NIV)

In these verses we see:

<u>Verse 13</u> — Satan, after he has been hurled to the earth, will pursue the Jewish people who gave birth to Jesus.

<u>Verse 14</u> — Some will be provided with a way to flee to a place prepared for them in the desert, where they will be taken care of for 3 ½ years out of Satan's reach.

<u>Verse 15 & 16</u> — Satan will pursue the Jewish people with fierceness, but some of the Jews will go into hiding before Satan can find them.

<u>Verse 17</u> — Then Satan becomes so enraged at not being able to find those Jewish people who fled to this secret hiding place that he will frantically pursue the rest of the Jews and also Christians (rest of her offspring).

As soon as the Antichrist/Satan commits the Abomination of Desolation, he starts pursuing the Jews. The two wings of a great eagle might possibly make reference to huge military air transports taking this group of Jews to their prearranged hiding place. Reverend Noah Hutchins of the Southwest Radio church (a radio program on prophecy) strongly believes that this prepared hiding place will be in Petra, which is found in the country of Jordan (northeast of Jerusalem). Petra falls within an area that future prophecy describes as the saints from Edom, Moab and Ammon being delivered from the hand of the Antichrist during the last 3 ½ years of the Tribulation Period. Also look at Jeremiah 49:11.

> Dan 11:41 *"He shall also enter the Glorious Land, and many countries shall be overthrown; but these shall escape from his hand: Edom, Moab, and <u>the prominent people</u> of Ammon.* (NKJ)

At another time, in 1445 BC, we see the Israelites (Jews) fleeing from the Egyptian Pharaoh on the wings of eagles (meaning they were protected by God).

> Exod 19:1-4 *In the third month after the Israelites left Egypt—on the very*

AFTER THE RAPTURE

> *day—they came to the Desert of Sinai. After they set out from Rephidim, they entered the Desert of Sinai, and Israel camped there in the desert in front of the mountain. Then Moses went up to God, and the LORD called to him from the mountain and said, "This is what you are to say to the house of Jacob and what you are to tell the people of Israel:* **'You yourselves have seen what I did to Egypt, and how I carried you on eagles' wings and brought you to myself.** (NIV)

Daniel lends a little insight to the scene about the time the Jews flee Jerusalem.

Dan 11:32-35 *"Those who do wickedly against the covenant he shall corrupt with flattery; but the people who know their God shall be strong, and carry out great exploits. "And those of the people who understand shall instruct many; yet for many days they shall fall by sword and flame, by captivity and plundering.* **"Now when they fall, they shall be aided with a little help; but many shall join with them by intrigue."** *And some of those of understanding shall fall, to refine them, purify them, and make them white, until the time of the end; because it is still for the appointed time.* (NKJ)

In these verses we see some of the more intricate details at this time, as usual from Daniel. Here we see that the Antichrist will still entice a few of the Jews into believing in him and he will flatter them. Those who know their God—and that the Antichrist is not that God—will resist the Antichrist and take action against him. They will make a concerted effort to tell all the Jews about this false Messiah who just sat on a throne and proclaimed himself to be God. For 3 ½ years they will suffer from the four plagues mentioned in Ezekiel chapter fourteen; sword, famine, wild beasts, and plagues. When they fall (Hebrew: to stumble, stagger or totter), *"they will receive a little help"* could be a reference to those Jews who are protected by God in the secret hiding place in the desert. Some of those who receive a little help (in the desert) will join that group with false motives. The original translation goes something like this; *" many will join them with flatteries"* (slipperiness, fine promises or smoothness). In verse 35, it is revealed that many Jews will fall (loose their life) at this time in order to be saved. To be made white is symbolism for the cleansing of their sins.

In the book of Zephaniah, following the horrible description of the great Day of the Lord (the day of persecution for the Jews), the prophet gives a warning to the Jewish people.

Zeph 2:1-3 <u>**Gather together, gather together, O shameful nation, before the appointed time arrives and that day sweeps on like chaff**</u>*, before the fierce anger of the LORD comes upon you, before the day of the LORD's wrath comes upon you.* <u>**Seek the LORD, all you humble of the land**</u>*, you who do what he commands. Seek righteousness, seek humility;* <u>**perhaps you will be sheltered on the day of the LORD's anger.**</u> (NIV)

The Tribulation Period — The Time of Jacob's Trouble

Zephaniah is instructing the Jews to *"Seek the Lord,"* seek righteousness and humility before the wrath of God is poured out on the shameful nation of Israel. I believe that Zephaniah is speaking to those Jews who are alive during the first half of the Tribulation Period. He is telling them to accept Jesus before the second half of the Tribulation Period begins, perhaps you will be sheltered on the day of the Lord's anger. Could this shelter be the hiding place in the desert? I think it is a good possibility, but only God knows for sure.

In the book of Jeremiah, the prophet sums up what will happen to the Jewish people during the Time of Jacob's Trouble. In the end, Israel will be the people of God.

Jer 30:23-24   *See, the storm of the LORD will burst out in wrath, a driving wind swirling down on the heads of the wicked. **The fierce anger of the LORD will not turn back until he fully accomplishes the purposes of his heart.** In days to come you will understand this.* (NIV)

Jer 31:1-2   *"At that time," declares the LORD, "I will be the God of all the clans of Israel, and they will be my people." This is what the LORD says: "**The people who survive the sword will find favor in the desert; I will come to give rest to Israel.**"* (NIV)

After the Tribulation Period is over it will be time for the Day of Atonement (Yom Kippur) for the Jewish people. For those people who reject the possibility that God will fulfill the promises (covenants) He made to Israel, I suggest they read this passage in Jeremiah. The current teaching of Replacement Theology is incorrect.

Jer 33:23-26   *The word of the LORD came to Jeremiah: "Have you not noticed that these people are saying, '**The LORD has rejected the two kingdoms he chose**'? So they despise my people and no longer regard them as a nation. This is what the LORD says: 'If I have not established my covenant with day and night and the fixed laws of heaven and earth, then I will reject the descendants of Jacob and David my servant and will not choose one of his sons to rule over the descendants of Abraham, Isaac and Jacob. **For I will restore their fortunes and have compassion on them.**'"* (NIV)

Throughout history, the Jews have paid the price for their misdeeds. God is perfectly clear about that in His word. Those who believe that the church has replaced Israel in God's scheme of things have completely ignored or misunderstood Paul in the book of Romans.

Rom 11:1-36   *I ask then: **Did God reject his people? By no means!** I am an Israelite myself, a descendant of Abraham, from the tribe of Benjamin. **God did not reject his people, whom he foreknew.** Don't you know what the Scripture says in the passage about Elijah—how he appealed to God against Israel: "Lord, they have killed your prophets and torn down your altars; I am the only one left, and they* are trying to kill me"? And what was God's answer to him? "I have reserved for myself seven thousand who have not bowed the knee to Baal." **So too, at the present time there is a remnant chosen by grace.** And if by grace, then it is no longer by works; if it were, grace would no longer be grace. What then? What Israel sought so earnestly it did not obtain, but the elect did. The others were hardened, as it is written: "God gave them a spirit of stupor, eyes so that they could not see and ears so that they could not hear, to this very day." And David says: "May their table become a snare and a trap, a stumbling block and a retribution for them. May their eyes be darkened so they cannot see, and their backs be bent forever." **Again I ask: <u>Did they stumble so as to fall beyond recovery? Not at all!</u> Rather, because of their transgression, salvation has come to the Gentiles to make Israel envious.** But if their transgression means riches for the world, and their loss means riches for the Gentiles, how much greater riches will their fullness bring! <u>**I am talking to you Gentiles.**</u> Inasmuch as I am the apostle to the Gentiles, I make much of my ministry in the hope that I may somehow arouse my own people to envy and save some of them. For if their rejection is the reconciliation of the world, what will their acceptance be but life from the dead? If the part of the dough offered as firstfruits is holy, then the whole batch is holy; if the root is holy, so are the branches. If some of the branches have been broken off, and you, though a wild olive shoot, have been grafted in among the others and now share in the nourishing sap from the olive root, do not boast over those branches. If you do, consider this: You do not support the root, but the root supports you. **You will say then, "Branches were broken off so that I could be grafted in." Granted. But they were broken off because of unbelief, and you stand by faith. Do not be arrogant, but be afraid.** For if God did not spare the natural branches, he will not spare you either. Consider therefore the kindness and sternness of God: sternness to those who fell, but kindness to you, provided that you continue in his kindness. Otherwise, you also will be cut off. **And if they do not persist in unbelief, they will be grafted in, for God is able to graft them in again.** After all, if you were cut out of an olive tree that is wild by nature, and contrary to nature were grafted into a cultivated olive tree, how much more readily will these, the natural branches, be grafted into their own olive tree! <u>**I do not want you to be ignorant of this mystery, brothers, so that you may not be conceited:**</u> Israel has experienced a hardening in part until the full number of the Gentiles has come in. <u>**And so all Israel will be saved,**</u> as it is written: "<u>**The deliverer will come from Zion; he will turn Godlessness away from Jacob.**</u> And this is my covenant with them when I take away their sins." As far as the gospel is *concerned, they are enemies on your account; but as far as election is concerned, they are loved on account of the patriarchs, for God's gifts and his call are irrevocable. Just as you who were at one time disobedient to God have now received mercy as a result of their disobedience, so they too have now become disobedient in order that they too may now receive mercy as a result of God's mercy to you. For God has bound all men over to disobedience so that he may have mercy on them all. Oh, the depth of the riches of the wisdom and knowledge of God! How unsearchable his judgments, and his paths beyond tracing out! "Who has known the mind of the Lord? Or who has been his counselor?" "Who has ever given to God, that God should repay him?" For from him and through him and to him are all things. To him be the glory forever! Amen.* (NIV)

How awkward and disappointing it will be for the Jewish people when they discover yet another false Messiah. They thought the Antichrist was the Messiah that they had expected for thousands of years. He was to bring peace to the world and even seemed to have started the process. He allowed and helped finance the construction of a Jewish Temple in Jerusalem. He even promised Israel that he would eventually set them up as the head of the nations. He protected them from their enemies and now, 3 ½ years after the beginning of the 7-Year Peace Treaty, they are again running for their lives. During the 3 ½ year period that Israel was in a sort of peace, the rest of the world was in turmoil. The Jewish people were religiously in an apostate state and also believing in a false god. The nation of Israel as a whole became prosperous and accumulated a lot of wealth. This created jealously from most of the rest of the world. "You know those wealthy Jews who want to take over the world and run it," people will be saying. In the book of Zephaniah, we have a glimpse of the people in Israel (here referred to as Judah) and Jerusalem in the first days and weeks after the Abomination of Desolation.

Zeph 1:4-13   *"I will stretch out My hand against Judah, and against all the inhabitants of Jerusalem. I will cut off every trace of Baal from this place, the names of the idolatrous priests with the pagan priests—Those who worship the host of heaven on the housetops; those who worship and swear oaths by the LORD, but who also swear by Milcom; Those who have turned back from following the LORD, and have not sought the LORD, nor inquired of Him." Be silent in the presence of the Lord God; for the day of the LORD is at hand, for the LORD has prepared a sacrifice; he has invited His guests. "And it shall be, in the day of the LORD'S sacrifice, that I will punish the princes and the king's children, and all such as are clothed with foreign apparel. In the same day I will punish all those who leap over the threshold, who fill their masters' houses with violence and deceit. "And there shall be on that day," says the LORD, "The sound of a mournful cry from the Fish Gate, a wailing from the Second Quarter, and a loud crashing from the hills. Wail, you inhabitants of Maktesh! For all the merchant people are cut down; all those who handle money are cut off. "And it shall come to pass at that time that I will search Jerusalem with lamps, and punish the men who are settled in complacency, who say in their heart, 'The LORD will not do good, nor will He do evil.' Therefore their goods shall become booty, and their houses a desolation; they shall build houses, but not inhabit them; they shall plant vineyards, but not drink their wine."* (NKJ).

1. their merchants will be wiped out
2. the complacent people in Jerusalem will be punished
3. their wealth will be plundered (by the Antichrist)
4. their houses will be taken from them
5. they will not drink the wine from their own vineyards

Before we look at the second trumpet judgment that will be poured out on the world, let us look at the activities of the Antichrist during this 3 ½ year period. At this point he has two main objectives. He still has the desire to conquer the whole world and he wants all the people on earth to worship him, his second objective is to exterminate the Jews. Sound familiar–60 years ago? You will also be able to get an idea of the general condition of what the world will be like during this last 3 ½ year period in these next verses. The Antichrist will come close to his objectives, but scripture reveals his defeat. Keep in mind that God is allowing this to take place to accomplish His redemptive plan. The army of the Antichrist will be the sword (weapon), which God will use to punish sinful Israel and mankind left on earth at this time. Now let us view the person who will dominate the world for 3 ½ years.

Dan 8:23-25 *"In the latter part of their reign, when rebels have become completely wicked, a stern-faced king, a master of intrigue, will arise. He will become very strong, but not by his own power. He will cause astounding devastation and will succeed in whatever he does. He will destroy the mighty men and the holy people. He will cause deceit to prosper, and he will consider himself superior. When they feel secure, he will destroy many and take his stand against the Prince of princes. Yet he will be destroyed, but not by human power.* (NIV)

Dan 11:36-39 *"The king will do as he pleases. He will exalt and magnify himself above every God and will say unheard-of things against the God of Gods. He will be successful until the time of wrath is completed, for what has been determined must take place. He will show no regard for the Gods of his fathers or for the one desired by women, nor will he regard any God, but will exalt himself above them all. Instead of them, he will honor a God of fortresses; a God unknown*

The Tribulation Period — The Time of Jacob's Trouble

to his fathers he will honor with gold and silver, with precious stones and costly gifts. He will attack the mightiest fortresses with the help of a foreign God and will greatly honor those who acknowledge him. He will make them rulers over many people and will distribute the land at a price. (NIV)

Dan 7:25 *He will speak against the Most High and oppress his saints and try to change the set times and the laws. The saints will be handed over to him for a time, times and half a time.* (NIV)

Daniel probably gives the best description of how outrageous and powerful this man of sin and lawlessness will be. Believing that one man can cause so much destruction is hard, but then again look at what Hitler accomplished not that long ago. Listed in the verses above, we see that the Antichrist will:

1. be a stern-faced ruler, a master of intrigue
2. cause astounding devastation
3. succeed in whatever he does
4. have no desire for women (he could possibly be homosexual)
5. cause deceit to prosper
6. consider himself to be superior to everyone (even God)
7. stand against the Prince of princes (Jesus)
8. do as he pleases
9. position himself above all gods
10. be successful for 3 ½ years (what has been determined must take place)
11. attack mighty nations
12. appoint people to rule over people
13. sell land he has conquered for a price
14. oppress the saints (believers in Jesus Christ) for 3 ½ years
15. try to change the set times and laws (Jewish festivals)

Not everyone will agree with me that the next scripture passage will apply to the Antichrist, but as you can see the revelation awaits an appointed time, which I believe to be the second half of the Tribulation Period (*moed`*). It speaks of the end of indignation. This prophecy has not yet come to pass though these verses tell us, *"Though it linger, wait for it; it will certainly come and will not delay."* Habakkuk was told to write it down and make it plain to read. It speaks of a man who will plunder many nations and shed man's blood. It is followed by the Glorious Return of Jesus at the Battle of Armageddon in chapter three.

Hab 2:2-11 *Then the LORD replied: "Write down the revelation and make it plain on tablets so that a herald may run with it. <u>For the revelation awaits an appointed time; it speaks of the end and will not prove false.</u> Though it linger, wait for it; it will certainly come and will not delay. "See, he is puffed up; his desires are not upright—but*

> *the righteous will live by his faith—indeed, wine betrays him; he is arrogant and never at rest. Because he is as greedy as the grave and like death is never satisfied, he gathers to himself all the nations and takes captive all the peoples.* "Will not all of them taunt him with ridicule and scorn, saying, '"Woe to him who piles up stolen goods and makes himself wealthy by extortion! How long must this go on?' Will not your debtors suddenly arise? Will they not wake up and make you tremble? Then you will become their victim. Because you have plundered many nations, the peoples who are left will plunder you. *For you have shed man's blood; you have destroyed lands and cities and everyone in them.* "Woe to him who builds his realm by unjust gain to set his nest on high, to escape the clutches of ruin! You have plotted the ruin of many peoples, shaming your own house and forfeiting your life. The stones of the wall will cry out, and the beams of the woodwork will echo it. (NIV)

During the last half of the Tribulation Period the Antichrist will:

1. be puffed up; his desires are not upright
2. be arrogant and never at rest (wine betrays him—will he be an alcoholic?)
3. gather to himself all the nations and take captive the people
4. pile up stolen goods and make himself wealthy by extortion
5. shed man's blood; destroy lands, cities and people in them
6. build his realm on unjust gain
7. plot the ruin of many people

With Satan residing inside his body, the Antichrist will perform all kinds of counterfeit miracles, signs and wonders. All sorts of evil practices will be used to deceive the people living on the earth. They refuse to believe the truth. Because of that reason, God will send a powerful delusion so that they believe the awful lies of the Antichrist.

> 2 Thes 2:9-12   *The coming of <u>the lawless one</u> will be in accordance with the work of Satan displayed in all kinds of counterfeit miracles, signs and wonders, and in every sort of evil that deceives those who are perishing.* They perish because they refused to love the truth and so be saved. *For this reason God sends them a powerful delusion so that they will believe the lie* and so that all will be condemned who have not believed the truth but have delighted in wickedness. (NIV)

All of this is a good background for the beast (Antichrist) who comes up out of the sea (people) in Revelation chapter thirteen. He will be gruesome, grotesque, frightful and a very powerful person. It is hard to imagine that a person can ever be like him.

> Rev 13:3-10   *One of the heads of the beast seemed to have had a fatal wound,*

but the fatal wound had been healed. The whole world was astonished and followed <u>the beast</u>. Men worshiped the dragon because he had given authority to the beast, and they also worshiped the beast and asked, "<u>Who is like the beast</u>? Who can make war against him?" The beast was given a mouth to utter proud words and blasphemies and to exercise his authority for forty-two months. He opened his mouth to blaspheme God, and to slander his name and his dwelling place and those who live in heaven. *He was given power to make war against the saints and to conquer them. And he was given authority over every tribe, people, language and nation. All inhabitants of the earth will worship the beast—all whose names have not been written in the book of life belonging to the Lamb that was slain from the creation of the world.* He who has an ear, let him hear. If anyone is to go into captivity, into captivity he will go. If anyone is to be killed with the sword, with the sword he will be killed. This calls for patient endurance and faithfulness on the part of the saints. (NIV)

Keep in mind that all the scripture passages just quoted, concerning the Antichrist, are describing his activities during his last 3 ½ years on earth. Here in Revelation, we see the Antichrist as:

1. being healed of a fatal wound
2. the whole world is astonished and follows him
3. men worship Satan because he gave authority to the Antichrist
4. who is like the Antichrist—who can make war with him?
5. having a mouth to blaspheme God
6. exercising authority for 42 months (3 ½ years)
7. making war against and conquering the saints (believers)
8. all the inhabitants of the earth will worship the Antichrist—all those who have not had their names written in the Lamb's Book of Life
9. There will be a small remnant of believers who will not follow this false god. Here the saints are admonished to have patient endurance and faithfulness.

MARK OF THE BEAST

Not long after the Antichrist's wound has been healed and the Abomination of Desolation has transpired, the false prophet will come to the forefront. At this point all of the world religions will have united under the banner of the false prophet. With the same power and authority of the Antichrist, the false prophet will force the people of the earth to worship the Antichrist. He exercises the authority of the Antichrist on his behalf. The false prophet will be given power to perform miraculous feats, such as causing fire to come down from heaven in full view of the people on the earth. No doubt, these miracles will show up on the five and ten o'clock news on the world news broadcasts. These miracles will deceive the people. Shortly after that, the false prophet will order men to set up a statue of the Antichrist in his honor. Somehow, through modern technology, he will make the statue become lifelike and speak and cause all who refuse to worship the statue to be killed. Then shortly after that, the false prophet will force all the people to receive some sort of a device to be attached to their right hand or their forehead. Without this device it will be impossible to buy or even sell anything (food, clothes, cars, etc.) This number that will be placed on the people from around the world equates to the number of man—**666.**

> Rev 13:12-18   ***He exercised all the authority of the first beast on his behalf, and made the earth and its inhabitants worship the first beast, whose fatal wound had been healed.*** *And he performed great and miraculous signs, even causing fire to come down from heaven to earth in full view of men.* ***Because of the signs he was given power to do on behalf of the first beast, he deceived the inhabitants of the earth.*** *He ordered them to set up an image in honor of the beast who was wounded by the sword and yet lived. He was given power to give breath to the image of the first beast, so that it could speak and cause all who refused to worship the image to be killed.* ***He also forced everyone, small and great, rich and poor, free and slave, to receive a mark on his right hand or on his forehead, so that no one could buy or sell unless he had the mark, which is the name of the beast or the number of his name.*** *This calls for wisdom. If anyone has insight, let him calculate the number of the beast, for it is man's number.* ***His number is 666.*** (NIV)

How horrible it will be for women with small children born *After the Rapture* who will be forced to take the mark of the beast just to feed their small children. As we mentioned before, you can refuse to take this mark of the beast, but by doing so you will hunted down and told to take the mark or be killed. On the other hand—once you take the mark of the beast—you will have sold your soul to the devil and will be lost for eternity. Somehow, it does not seem like a fair choice, until you weigh spending eternity in heaven or hell!!!! Refusing to take the mark of the beast does not guarantee you a place in heaven. You will still have to accept Jesus as your personal savior.

No one knows how long it will take to set up the system of the mark of the beast, but it will be in the first stages of this 3 ½ year period. As all this activity is taking place, the seven trumpet judgments are successively pouring down from heaven with each one probably lasting around five months. At that rate it will take 2 ½ years for these birth pains (the first six trumpet judgments) to be completed.

TRUMPET JUDGMENTS

As the angel sounds the **Second Trumpet,** we see a huge volcano or even possibly a large meteorite polluting one-third of the oceans. A third of the aquatic animals of the world are killed and a third of the ships in the world will be destroyed. Remember that the trumpet judgments will probably last around five months each as the punishment progresses beyond the seal judgments toward the bowl judgments.

Rev 8:8-9 *<u>The second angel sounded his trumpet</u>, and something like a huge mountain, all ablaze, was thrown into the sea. <u>A third of the sea turned into blood, a third of the living creatures in the sea died, and a third of the ships were destroyed.</u>* (NIV)

The **Third Trumpet** judgment also appears to be an enormous burning meteorite. This meteorite will fall on a land mass and will pollute a third of the rivers and fresh water springs, resulting in the deaths of many people.

Rev 8:10-11 *<u>The third angel sounded his trumpet</u>, and a great star, blazing like a torch, fell from the sky on a third of the rivers and on the springs of water—the name of the star is Wormwood. <u>A third of the waters turned bitter, and many people died from the waters that had become bitter.</u>* (NIV)

The **Fourth Trumpet** judgment consists of the sun, moon and stars losing a third of their light. The daylight hours will lose a third of their light. That means that for five months, each day will consist of 8 hours of daylight and 16 hours of darkness. During one-third of the night (almost 5 ½ hours), it will not have any light at all from the moon. It will be totally dark. The earth will experience periods of extreme cold with the disappearance of so much of the sun's energy. Amos 8:9 makes a reference to this very time.

Rev 8:12 *<u>The fourth angel sounded his trumpet</u>, and a third of the sun was struck, a third of the moon, and a third of the stars, so that a third of them turned dark. A third of the day was without light, and also a third of the night.* (NIV)

After the completion of the first four trumpet judgments, John observes an angel flying in the air announcing that the next three judgments would greatly increase in intensity. The actual word used by the angel is "**WOE**." It is a warning for more intense birth pains.

Rev 8:13 *And I beheld, and heard an angel flying through the midst of heaven, saying with a loud voice, <u>Woe, woe, woe, to the inhabiters of the earth</u> by reason of the other voices of the trumpet of the three angels, which are yet to sound!* (KJV)

After the completion of the fourth trumpet judgment, it should bring us up to just short of the half way mark of the last 3 ½ years of the Tribulation Period. No doubt at this point the earth will be scattered with concentration camps. There is no way to organize a mass killing operation without some sort of concentration camp to systematically hold large amounts of people until you can transport them to a killing center, especially in such a short period of time. The concentration camps will be full of those people who refuse to take the mark of the beast and the Jewish people. Among those who refuse to take the mark will be the Christians. The Jews will not be given the choice to take the mark of the beast, because they are marked for the extermination of their race. Had not God prepared a hiding place in the desert for a certain number of Jews, it is highly unlikely that a third of the Jews would survive this horrible period. There will be a small percentage of Christians and Jews who will be able to hide from *"Big Brother."* Relatives, friends or just kind, honest, moral people will provide a way to conceal some Christians and Jews during this time. A great number of Christians will be martyred and two-thirds of the Jews will lose their lives. It took Adolf Hitler almost seven years to kill 6 million Jews, which was a third of the Jews living at that time. It will only take the Antichrist 3½ years to kill 10 million Jews, which will be two-thirds of the Jews living *After the Rapture*. Percentage wise, that is twice as many Jewish people killed in about half the amount of time.

The death camps will be more modernized during this time, but the concentration camps will be packed full of people. Mainly because it will take time to construct the death camp facilities. Technology will lend a hand in the death camps, thus allowing more people to be killed in a shorter period of time. There will still be the problem of getting rid of so many bodies. With so much military action—the Antichrist conquering more territory—it will cause a shortage of food world wide and like World War II, cause widespread starvation among those housed in concentration camps. One of the reasons I provided details of the Holocaust in this book was to give you some sort of an idea of the conditions of the world during the Tribulation Period. As you can see from scripture, the period of destruction out in front of us will far outweigh World War II. Because of World War II, more than 60 million people lost their lives. During World War III (Tribulation Period), billions of people will lose their lives. Many of them because of the plagues sent by God Himself.

The false prophet seems to be in charge of the system organized to administer the mark of the beast, while his cohort will be engaged in war. It will be an enormous well-organized war machine with modern war devices. There will be some opposition to the Antichrist, especially from the larger nations and the Arab nations, but in the end the Antichrist will almost succeed in conquering the entire world. All of these activities will be under way at the same time the plagues are raining down from heaven. The birth pains start to become astonishingly more unbearable as we look at the fifth trumpet.

The next two trumpet judgments will become more supernatural as the appearance of fallen angels or demons come into play. These next two judgments seem more difficult to comprehend, because in the Dispensation of Grace—the period we are living in now—we do not see angels as active as they will be during the Tribulation Period. There are forces of Satan out in the world today, but they are invisible. As the **Fifth Trumpet** is sounded, John observes a star fall to the earth. This period of judgment will take place at the midpoint of the Time of Jacob's Trouble.

Rev 9:1-12   *The fifth angel sounded his trumpet, and I saw a star that had fallen from the sky to the earth. The star was given the key to the shaft of the Abyss. When he opened the Abyss, smoke rose from it like the smoke from a gigantic furnace. The sun and sky were*

The Tribulation Period — The Time of Jacob's Trouble

darkened by the smoke from the Abyss. <u>***And out of the smoke locusts came down upon the earth and were given power like that of scorpions of the earth.***</u> *They were told not to harm the grass of the earth or any plant or tree, but only those people who did not have the seal of God on their foreheads. They were not given power to kill them, but only to torture them for five months. And the agony they suffered was like that of the sting of a scorpion when it strikes a man. During those days men will seek death, but will not find it; they will long to die, but death will elude them. The locusts looked like horses prepared for battle. On their heads they wore something like crowns of gold, and their faces resembled human faces. Their hair was like women's hair, and their teeth were like lions' teeth. They had breastplates like breastplates of iron, and the sound of their wings was like the thundering of many horses and chariots rushing into battle. They had tails and stings like scorpions, and in their tails they had power to torment people for five months. They had as king over them the angel of the Abyss, whose name in Hebrew is Abaddon, and in Greek, Apollyon.* ***The first woe is past; two other woes are yet to come.*** (NIV)

The star that falls from heaven turns out to be a holy angel (messenger), but it is more than likely Jesus. If it is an angel, at this point, it cannot be a fallen angel because approximately twenty months earlier Satan and his angels were removed from the heavenly realm and cast to the earth. This star (angel/messenger) is provided with a key to the Abyss (bottomless pit). The Abyss is a special prison in hell designated for a group of angels that committed a horrendous sin and since that time they have remained in this special prison, locked up and reserved for a special mission. This special mission will take place during the last half of the Tribulation Period (judgment on the Great Day). We have the sin of these angels recorded in the early part of Genesis before the flood took place.

Gen 6:1-6 ***When men began to increase in number on the earth and daughters were born to them, the sons of God saw that the daughters of men were beautiful, and they married any of them they chose.*** *Then the LORD said, "My Spirit will not contend with man forever, for he is mortal; his days will be a hundred and twenty years."* ***The Nephilim were on the earth in those days—and also afterward—when the sons of God went to the daughters of men and had children by them. They were the heroes of old, men of renown.*** *The LORD saw how great man's wickedness on the earth had become, and that every inclination of the thoughts of his heart was only evil all the time.* ***The LORD was grieved that he had made man on the earth, and his heart was filled with pain.*** (NIV)

The sons of God (angels) somehow took the women of the antediluvian period (before the Flood) and together they conceived a lineage of giant men who were wise and lived a long time. My theory is that they entered the bodies of some of the sinful men on earth at that time to make this sin possible. Because of this sinful act, these angels were cast into the abyss and were reserved for a special mission to be carried out at the time of the judgment on the Great Day (last half of the Tribulation Period). Mention is made of these sinful angels in the books of Jude and 2 Peter.

> Jude 1:6 *And the angels who did not keep their positions of authority but abandoned their own home—these he has kept in darkness, <u>bound with everlasting chains for judgment on the great Day</u>.* (NIV)

> 2 Pet 2:4 *For if God did not spare angels when they sinned, but sent them to hell, <u>putting them into gloomy dungeons to be held for judgment</u>;* (NIV)

We now see these sinful angels being released from the abyss to fulfill the mission for which they have been reserved. When the abyss is opened, these fallen angels will come pouring out like smoke and it will darken the sky. Out of the smoke will appear something that looks like locusts. No time in the history of mankind has anything like these locusts ever appeared on earth. They will be given power to sting like a scorpion. A scorpion when capturing a victim with its claws inflicts a disabling sting with its tail. To humans the sting is painful, but very seldom fatal. Upon stinging its victim it releases a neurotoxin poison that attacks the nervous system. It is excruciatingly painful. Scripture likens the experience of the pain inflicted by these demons as that of being stung by a scorpion.

These demons will not be allowed to harm the grass, plants or the trees of the earth for five months. Their objective is to harm the people on the earth who do not have the seal of God on their foreheads. This seems to refer to the 144,000 servants of God who were given a seal on their foreheads to allow them to be protected from the plagues of this last 3 ½ year period. These locust-like demons will only be given the power to torture mankind for a period of five months. They will not be allowed to kill anyone. The pain will be so severe that people will want to die, but they are not even allowed the dignity to pass from this life. Suffering will be their lot during these five months.

The appearance of the locust are recorded as *"like"* or *"as"*, in other words, they will appear like horses or like they wore crowns. They are recorded as related in terms to describe them in the context of human understanding, as John saw them. They were like horses, but not really horses. John explains their appearance as something he relates to in his time. The same is true for the sting of the scorpion, it was like a sting of a scorpion, but will be from a demonic fallen angel and have what appears to be a sting from a scorpion.

These demonic angels will have a leader (king) and he is referred to as *"the angel of the abyss."* His name in Hebrew is *"Abaddon"* and in Greek it is *"Apollyon."* The meaning for both of these words is "destroyer." This king could very well be Satan. He is the king of fallen angels and unsaved mankind. His chief cause is to destroy a mans soul. The first woe is over and two more will follow.

The **Sixth Trumpet,** which is also the second "woe," is a devastating time for mankind

The Tribulation Period — The Time of Jacob's Trouble

as one-third of the people living on the earth at that time will lose their life.

Rev 9:13-19 *<u>The sixth angel sounded his trumpet</u>, and I heard a voice coming from the horns of the golden altar that is before God. It said to the sixth angel who had the trumpet, "Release the four angels who are bound at the great river Euphrates." <u>And the four angels who had been kept ready for this very hour and day and month and year were released to kill a third of mankind.</u> The number of the mounted troops was two hundred million. I heard their number. The horses and riders I saw in my vision looked like this: Their breastplates were fiery red, dark blue, and yellow as sulfur. The heads of the horses resembled the heads of lions, and out of their mouths came fire, smoke and sulfur. <u>A third of mankind was killed by the three plagues of fire, smoke and sulfur that came out of their mouths.</u> The power of the horses was in their mouths and in their tails; for their tails were like snakes, having heads with which they inflict injury.* (NIV)

As the sixth trumpet was sounded, John heard a voice coming from the horns of the golden altar that is located in heaven. The voice instructed the sixth angel, who had just sounded the sixth trumpet, to release four angels who are bound at the great river Euphrates. These are probably fallen angels, because they were restrained from doing any activity. It does not give us the time they were bound or the reason for this punishment. It does reveal that they were restrained until the exact year, month, day and to the very hour for a purpose and that purpose will be to orchestrate an army of 200 million to kill one-third of mankind. The 200 million army will be made up of the exact same demonic force that was released from the abyss just five months earlier. During the previous five month period of the fifth trumpet judgment they were only allowed to torment the people on the earth. In this period of judgment they will be allowed to kill a third of mankind.

Let us look at some sort of scenario to figure out the number of people who could possibly be killed during this five-month period. Let us begin the scenario as if the Rapture will take place in our lifetime. Today there are approximately 6 billion people in the world—give or take a few million. At the Rapture, the saints *"who are still alive and are left will be caught up together with them in the clouds to meet the Lord in the air"* will be around 2% (my guess) or around 360 million people. Let us estimate the loss of human life, because of the disasters just *After the Rapture* (caused by war, famine, pestilence, murder, the plagues and natural causes) from the time of the Rapture up to the sixth trumpet judgment at 1,140,000,000. Add this to the number of those who were raptured and you have a nice round number of 1,500,000,000 or one-fourth of the people on the earth. If these figures are anywhere close to being accurate—we are probably not to far off—then that means that 4,500,000,000 people are still around on earth for the sixth trumpet judgment. If one-third of mankind is killed during this period, that means that another 1,500,000,000 people will die during this five-month period. One half of the world's population will be Raptured (360,000,000) or die (2,640,000,000) during a 7 ½ year period. We do not know

AFTER THE RAPTURE

how many of those that die accept Jesus *After the Rapture*, but it will be a very small percentage compared with those who are lost for eternity.

As you can probably surmise from the above calculations, it will take an army of demons to kill 1 ½ billion people in a five-month period (150 days). That would average out to be 10 million deaths every day somewhere around the world. It is hard to imagine this kind of devastation. If it were not printed in God's word, it would be unbelievable. The prophet Joel gives us a remarkable account of an army of locusts devouring the earth. Joel designates this as a large and mighty army—**never** has there been an army like it in the past and **never again** will there ever be a mighty army like it in the future (verse 2). In verse eleven, it makes mention that it is the Lord's army.

Joel 2:1-11 *Blow the trumpet in Zion; sound the alarm on my holy hill. Let all who live in the land tremble, <u>for the day of the LORD is coming</u>. It is close at hand—a day of darkness and gloom, a day of clouds and blackness. <u>Like dawn spreading across the mountains a large and mighty army comes</u>, such as never was of old nor ever will be in ages to come. Before them fire devours, behind them a flame blazes. Before them the land is like the garden of Eden, behind them, a desert waste—nothing escapes them. They have the appearance of horses; they gallop along like cavalry. With a noise like that of chariots they leap over the mountaintops, like a crackling fire consuming stubble, like a mighty army drawn up for battle. At the sight of them, nations are in anguish; every face turns pale. They charge like warriors; they scale walls like soldiers. They all march in line, not swerving from their course. They do not jostle each other; each marches straight ahead. They plunge through defenses without breaking ranks. They rush upon the city; they run along the wall. They climb into the houses; like thieves they enter through the windows. Before them the earth shakes, the sky trembles, the sun and moon are darkened, and the stars no longer shine. <u>The LORD thunders at the head of his army</u>; his forces are beyond number, and mighty are those who obey his command. <u>The day of the LORD is great; it is dreadful. Who can endure it</u>?* (NIV)

Another thing that is hard to believe is the fact that after all this judgment God has bestowed on mankind, during the previous 2 ½ years, most of those who remain alive (3 billion people) do not repent and turn to God. They continue to worship the Antichrist, Satan and false idols. Murder, sorcery, drug abuse, drunkenness, sexual immorality, thievery and evil will run rampant throughout the time *After the Rapture*, getting progressively worse and becoming totally out of control by this time. The condition of the world (when rebels become completely wicked), during this 3 ½ year period, is almost incomprehensible.

Rev 9:20-21 *<u>The rest of mankind that were not killed by these plagues still did not repent of the work of their hands; they did not stop worshiping</u>*

The Tribulation Period — The Time of Jacob's Trouble

> *demons, and idols of gold, silver, bronze, stone and wood—idols that cannot see or hear or walk. Nor did they repent of their murders, their magic arts, their sexual immorality or their thefts.* (NIV)

Living conditions will run exceedingly worse during the last 3 ½ years of the Tribulation Period because the Antichrist will be consuming the world and at the same time the plagues are becoming unbearable for those people remaining on earth, but it is far from over yet. People will still not turn to God during this period when transgressors (sinful mankind) have reached their fullness.

Dan 8:23 *"And in the latter time of their kingdom, <u>when the transgressors have reached their fullness</u>, a king shall arise, having fierce features, who understands sinister schemes.* (NKJ)

After the sixth trumpet judgment has run its course, John notices another mighty angel coming down from heaven. From the description of this angel, it is probably Jesus Himself. Whether it is an angel or Jesus, he was holding a little scroll in his hand.

Rev 10:1-11 *Then I saw another mighty angel coming down from heaven. He was robed in a cloud, with a rainbow above his head; his face was like the sun, and his legs were like fiery pillars. <u>He was holding a little scroll, which lay open in his hand.</u> He planted his right foot on the sea and his left foot on the land, and he gave a loud shout like the roar of a lion. When he shouted, the voices of the seven thunders spoke. And when the seven thunders spoke, I was about to write; but I heard a voice from heaven say, "<u>Seal up what the seven thunders have said and do not write it down.</u>" Then the angel I had seen standing on the sea and on the land raised his right hand to heaven. And he swore by him who lives for ever and ever, who created the heavens and all that is in them, the earth and all that is in it, and the sea and all that is in it, and said, "There will be no more delay! But in the days when the seventh angel is about to sound his trumpet, the mystery of God will be accomplished, just as he announced to his servants the prophets." Then the voice that I had heard from heaven spoke to me once more: "Go, take the scroll that lies open in the hand of the angel who is standing on the sea and on the land." So I went to the angel and asked him to give me the little scroll. He said to me, "Take it and eat it. It will turn your stomach sour, but in your mouth it will be as sweet as honey." I took the little scroll from the angel's hand and ate it. It tasted as sweet as honey in my mouth, but when I had eaten it, my stomach turned sour. Then I was told, "You must prophesy again about many peoples, nations, languages and kings."* (NIV)

AFTER THE RAPTURE

This little scroll is not the same scroll that contained the seven seal judgments of the first 3 ½ years of the Tribulation Period. At the command of the angel the voices of the seven thunders spoke. Just as John was prepared to record their message a voice from heaven instructed John to seal up the meaning of the seven thunders. In this great book of Revelation, this is the only time that a part of the judgment is hidden from us only to be revealed at the time that it will take place. We know that the seven thunders are part of God's judgment from the fact that they became sour in John's stomach after he had eaten them. This seems to be the last of the hidden mysteries of God in the Bible. These mysteries will remain hidden until they take place. I wonder what these thunder judgments are going to be?

It will take 2 ½ years for the first six trumpet judgments and the seven thunder judgments to run their course. At about this same time the two Old Testament witnesses, Elijah and Moses, have come to the end of their 1260 day (3 ½ year) ministry. For 3 ½ years these two mysterious figures have been a pain in the side of the Antichrist. They have performed marvelous miracles and preached the true meaning of the gospel of the kingdom. They even seem to get some sort of protection from God. They have been at odds with the false prophet and his one-world church, but since they are Jewish they will be rejected by the religious system of the times.

> Rev 11:7-10   ***Now when they have finished their testimony, the beast that comes up from the Abyss will attack them, and overpower and kill them.*** *Their bodies will lie in the street of the great city, which is figuratively called Sodom and Egypt, where also their Lord was crucified.* ***For three and a half days men from every people, tribe, language and nation will gaze on their bodies and refuse them burial.*** *The inhabitants of the earth will gloat over them and will celebrate by sending each other gifts, because these two prophets had tormented those who live on the earth.* (NIV)

After their ministry is completed, God will allow the two witnesses to be attacked, overpowered and finally killed by the beast that came up from the Abyss. This is no doubt the same personage referred to as the king over the angels of the Abyss in Revelation 9:11. Again I suggest that this king is probably Satan himself, living within the body of the Antichrist. The bodies of the two witnesses will actually lie in the middle of the street in Jerusalem, where they were killed. For 3 ½ days people from all over the world will fly to Jerusalem to look upon these two slain Jewish religious leaders who have been defeated by the one the people have been worshiping as their god. They will not allow the two witnesses to have a proper burial. The world—through the eyes of the local T.V. station—will be exuberant over this great defeat of the two who brought havoc and torment on that sinful generation. They are sure that the Antichrist is victorious over even the God of the Jewish people. The people of the earth are so elated that they celebrate by exchanging gifts with each other, but after 3 ½ days the celebration will come to an abrupt halt. God had a purpose in allowing these two witnesses to be killed.

> Rev 11:11-12   ***But after the three and a half days a breath of life from God***

The Tribulation Period — The Time of Jacob's Trouble

entered them, and they stood on their feet, and terror struck those who saw them. Then they heard a loud voice from heaven saying to them, "<u>Come up here.</u>" And they went up to heaven in a cloud, while their enemies looked on. (NIV)

As the whole world is watching—those in Jerusalem along with the rest of the world via T.V. —the two witnesses are brought back to life (resurrected). As they stand up on their feet, fear will strike the people of the world as they actually hear a loud voice from heaven commanding the two witnesses to go up to heaven. As everybody watches, the two witnesses will go up to heaven in a cloud. The victory is God's after all, not the false god's of man or even mankind! God will use this miracle to prove to those people on earth that these two witnesses (Elijah and Moses) belong to Him.

At that time a severe earthquake will shake Jerusalem, with 10 percent of the city collapsing. Seven thousand people will be killed because of this earthquake. The survivors of the earthquake will be terrified and will give glory to the God of heaven.

Rev 11:13 *<u>At that very hour there was a severe earthquake and a tenth of the city collapsed.</u> Seven thousand people were killed in the earthquake, and the survivors were terrified and gave glory to the God of heaven.* (NIV)

The second woe (sixth trumpet) is over and the third woe (seventh trumpet) will come shortly.

Rev 11:14 *<u>The second woe has passed; the third woe is coming soon.</u>* (NIV)

As the **Seventh Trumpet** is sounded, the scene switches back to heaven. With only one year left to complete the Tribulation Period, we witness part of the victory celebration taking place in heaven as the wedding feast is still in progress. At this time Jesus and His throne are still in heaven. Loud voices shout the victory. In the verses below, John is describing the events that will be taking place during the beginning years of the Day of the Lord.

Rev 11:15-18 *<u>The seventh angel sounded his trumpet,</u> and there were loud voices in heaven, which said: "<u>The kingdom of the world has become the kingdom of our Lord and of his Christ, and he will reign for ever and ever.</u>" And the twenty-four elders, who were seated on their thrones before God, fell on their faces and worshiped God, saying: "We give thanks to you, Lord God Almighty, the One who is and who was, <u>because you have taken your great power and have begun to reign. The nations were angry; and your wrath has come.</u> The time has come for judging the dead, and for rewarding your servants the prophets and your saints and those who reverence your name, both small and great—<u>and for destroying those who destroy the earth.</u>"* (NIV)

The time has come to set things straight in heaven and on the earth. It will be time to judge the living and the dead. The arrival of the Day of the Lord will usher in:

1. the kingdom of Jesus Christ—He will reign forever and ever
2. the wrath of God
3. the time to judge the dead
4. the time to reward the prophets
5. the time to reward the saints
6. the time to destroy those who destroy the earth (the wicked unsaved people)

With the coming of the new age, these events will take place and the saints along with the angelic beings will be celebrating the victory in heaven. Actually, the victory (the kingdom has become God's) has occurred, but the judgment on earth is not quite complete. In the midst of all the devastation that is happening on earth, suddenly the scene reverts back to heaven to give us a view of what is taking place there. In the hidden chamber (chupah), we see what is going on during the Wedding Feast. The saints and the angels are praising and worshiping God and the Messiah, the reigning King. There will be nothing but joy and exuberance in heaven at this time. Then the Temple in heaven will be opened to expose the Ark of the Covenant, as the judgment of the Seventh Trumpet (third woe) is revealed to be an earthquake and a great hailstorm. This judgment will not last for five months as did the first six trumpet judgments and it will probably effect the entire earth.

> Rev 11:19   *Then God's temple in heaven was opened, and within his temple was seen the ark of his covenant. And there came flashes of lightning, rumblings, peals of thunder, <u>an earthquake and a great hailstorm</u>.* (NIV)

From Revelation chapter eleven we have to pass over the parenthetical chapters to continue our story chronologically. We pick it up again in Revelation chapter fifteen.

> Rev 15:1   *I saw in heaven another great and marvelous sign: seven angels with the seven last plagues—<u>last, because with them God's wrath is completed</u>.* (NIV)

John observes the seven angels that have the last seven plagues of the Tribulation Period. With these last seven bowl judgments, it will complete the Tribulation Period portion of God's wrath on the world. The final birth pains are about to take place (Refer to the chart on page 768).

JUDGMENT OF THE NATIONS

The prophets of the Old Testament can be divided into two groups. They are the former (early) prophets (sometimes called oral prophets) who were God's spokespersons for the Jewish nation, often rebuking the people for their wicked ways and commanding them to

The Tribulation Period — The Time of Jacob's Trouble

turn back to God. The prophetic utterances of these prophets were mainly for the contemporary times of their ministries. Occasionally, their forecasts would include predictions of the distant future, such as the prophet Samuel. The account of the lives of these oral prophets can be found in the writings of the history portion of the Old Testament. Two of the more prominent prophets of this first group of prophets are Elijah and Elisha.

The second group of prophets are considered to be the writing prophets, or latter prophets, who were commanded to write their prophecy on tablets (books). These prophets begin with Isaiah through Daniel (major prophets) and end with Hosea through Malachi (minor prophets). Their message closes the Old Testament. The main focus of these latter prophets, contrary to modern Bible history teaching, is the distant future.

> Dan 12:9 *He replied, "Go your way, Daniel, because the words are closed up and sealed until the time of the end.* (NIV)

> Hab 2:2-3 *Then the LORD replied: "<u>Write down the revelation</u> and make it plain on tablets so that a herald may run with it.* For the revelation awaits an appointed time; it speaks of the end and will not prove false. Though it linger, wait for it; it will certainly come and will not delay. (NIV)

The main theme of the writing prophets is the Day of the Lord. The Day of the Lord is not only a period of peace and prosperity, but it is also a Day of Judgment for all the nations, both Jews and Gentiles. The trials and persecutions of the Jewish people during Old Testament times, brought on by their apostasy, allowed God to send a message to the dejected people. The future, though the people at that time did not know the time frame, would be glorious. The visions of the future would include the great day when God would reform the world and reign over all the people in justice. God would renew His covenant with Israel and establish His throne in Zion. He would create a new heaven and a new earth. Interspersed in the writings of these latter prophets are accounts of past history, such as Isaiah 36-39, Daniel 1 and 3 and Jeremiah 20-21, 26-29, but the bulk of their message is an account of the future, even for us who are living at the present time.

The exception to all Biblical prophets is Moses, who was both an oral prophet and a writing prophet. He was unique and is revered by the Jews, even today, above all prophets and for good reason. Moses was the greatest prophet whoever lived, except for Jesus Christ. In Deuteronomy, Moses was informed that God would send a prophet to the Israelites from among them, just like they had ask Him when they were at Mount Sinai. The Israelites were commanded to *"listen to him."*

> Deut 18:15-19 ***The LORD your God will raise up for you a prophet like me from among your own brothers. <u>You must listen to him</u>.*** *For this is what you asked of the LORD your God at Horeb on the day of the assembly when you said, "Let us not hear the voice of the LORD our God nor see this great fire anymore, or we will die."* ***The LORD said to me: "<u>What they say is good. I will raise up for them a prophet</u>***

> *like you from among their brothers; I will put my words in his mouth, and he will tell them everything I command him. If anyone does not listen to my words that the prophet speaks in my name, I myself will call him to account.* (NIV)

When Jesus finally came to the Jewish people, more than fourteen hundred years later, they failed to listen to Him. In fact, they had the prophet crucified to silence Him. Moses was the first prophet to write extensively on the subject of the Day of the Lord. He referred to the time as the *"later days."* In Hebrew it is called *Acharit Hayamim* and is the End of Days.

Deut 4:24-31   *The LORD will scatter you among the peoples, and only a few of you will survive among the nations to which the LORD will drive you. There you will worship man-made gods of wood and stone, which cannot see or hear or eat or smell. But if from there you seek the LORD your God, you will find him if you look for him with all your heart and with all your soul.* **When you are in distress and all these things have happened to you, then in later days you will return to the LORD your God and obey him.** *For the LORD your God is a merciful God; he will not abandon or destroy you or forget the covenant with your forefathers, which he confirmed to them by oath.* (NIV)

Simply put, Bible prophecy is future history—events recorded before they take place. Certain prophecies were fulfilled in the near future, while others were to be fulfilled in the distant future. In 592 BC, as Ezekiel was speaking to the exiles in Babylon, he was revealing the visions he had received from God concerning the destruction of Jerusalem. The people Ezekiel was talking to believed that these visions were referring to a time in the distant future because the visions were not being fulfilled, just like the visions from the prophet Daniel. Ezekiel finally reveals that destruction will fall on the people who were living at that time and in 586 BC Jerusalem and the Temple were destroyed.

Ezek 12:21-28   *The word of the LORD came to me: "Son of man, what is this proverb you have in the land of Israel:* **'The days go by and every vision comes to nothing'**? *Say to them, 'This is what the Sovereign LORD says: I am going to put an end to this proverb, and they will no longer quote it in Israel.' Say to them,* **'The days are near when every vision will be fulfilled.** *For there will be no more false visions or flattering divinations among the people of Israel. But I the LORD will speak what I will, and it shall be fulfilled without delay. For in your days, you rebellious house, I will fulfill whatever I say, declares the Sovereign LORD'" The word of the LORD came to me: "Son of man, the house of Israel is saying,* **'The vision he sees is for many years from now, and he prophesies about the distant future.'** *"Therefore say to them, 'This is what the Sovereign LORD*

> *says: None of my words will be delayed any longer; whatever I say will be fulfilled, declares the Sovereign LORD.'"* (NIV)

Dan 8:26   *"The vision of the evenings and mornings that has been given you is true, but seal up the vision, **for it concerns the distant future.**"*(NIV)

Even though Ezekiel informed the people in exile that the destruction of Jerusalem would come to their generation, that does not mean that all the prophecies concerning the future have been fulfilled. The majority of the prophecies from Ezekiel and the rest of the latter prophets concerning Israel, Jerusalem and the nations will be fulfilled in the distant future. A time even future for us today.

As we look at prophecy today, we need to look at it from two perspectives. Was the prophecy fulfilled contemporaneously or is it apocalyptic? Did it take place in the past or is it going to take place in the future? A look at past history helps us determine which category to place prophetic scripture. An extensive study of Old Testament history will show a remarkable similarity to the events that took place in the past with those that will take place during the Day of the Lord. This is the main reason it has been so difficult to separate these prophecies into past or future states. What has taken place on the world scene in the last hundred years has helped us understand the future scenario. Such things as Israel becoming a nation, archaeological studies, the European Union, a renewed interest in Bible Prophecy and the Arab/Israeli conflict have helped us to better understand the Bible.

As we sort through the prophetic scriptures, we can be assisted by several clues. If the prophecy has cosmic or supernatural events associated with it, we know without any doubt that it will be fulfilled at the return of Christ. If the context of the doom and gloom portion of a passage falls within the blessedness of the Millennium, it will usually fall within the scope of the future events of the Day of the Lord. If the event has not taken place in the past, we know for sure that it will take place in the future. Just because a conflict of the past has similarities or a likeness of certain scripture passages does not guarantee that this prophecy has been fulfilled. The entire context of the passage being studied must be taken into account. It is usually inappropriate to pick and choose within the context of scripture. You should not look at the conflicts of the past arbitrarily and start categorizing these conflicts into certain scripture passages, especially when they fall within the same sentence. A common practice from the past, called "earliest possible fulfillment," can lead you down the wrong path when it comes to Bible prophecy. The totality of God's word and His plan of redemption always need to be at the forefront of your thoughts when you are trying to decipher prophetic scripture. A good example of the content of verses as they apply to the context of scripture can be found in Micah 5:1-15.

Micah 5:1-15   *Marshal your troops, O city of troops, for a siege is laid against us. They will strike Israel's ruler on the cheek with a rod. "But you, Bethlehem Ephrathah, though you are small among the clans of Judah, out of you will come for me one who will be ruler over Israel, whose origins are from of old, from ancient times." Therefore Israel will be abandoned until the time when she who is in labor gives birth and the rest of his brothers return to join the Israelites. He will stand and shepherd his flock in the strength of the LORD, in the majesty of the name of the LORD his God. And they will live securely, for then his greatness will reach to the ends of the earth. And he will be their peace. When the Assyrian invades our land and marches through our fortresses, we will raise against him seven shepherds, even eight leaders of men. They will rule the land of Assyria with the sword, the land of Nimrod with drawn sword. He will deliver us from the Assyrian when he invades our land and marches into our borders. The remnant of Jacob will be in the midst of many peoples like dew from the LORD, like showers on the grass, which do not wait for man or linger for mankind. The remnant of Jacob will be among the nations, in the midst of many peoples, like a lion among the beasts of the forest, like a young lion among flocks of sheep, which mauls and mangles as it goes, and no one can rescue. Your hand will be lifted up in triumph over your enemies, and all your foes will be destroyed. "In that day," declares the LORD, "I will destroy your horses from among you and demolish your chariots. I will destroy the cities of your land and tear down all your strongholds. I will destroy your witchcraft and you will no longer cast spells. I will destroy your carved images and your sacred stones from among you; you will no longer bow down to the work of your hands. I will uproot from among you your Asherah poles and demolish your cities. I will take vengeance in anger and wrath upon the nations that have not obeyed me."* (NIV)

One commentary I read concerning the fulfillment of these verses in Micah chapter five goes something like this. The commentary will follow the verses to which they pertain.

Micah 5:1 *Marshal your troops, O city of troops, for a siege is laid against us. They will strike Israel's ruler on the cheek with a rod.*

The context seems to describe Jewish refugees crowding into Jerusalem. In a siege "the judge of Israel" will be defeated. In respect to its location in history, this tragedy is seen to follow the Maccabean victory in Micah 4:13, but to precede the birth of Christ in Micah 5:2. Micah would appear to be speaking, centuries in advance, of the fall of Jerusalem to the Roman troops of Pompey in 63 BC, when the Hasmonean monarchy was brought to an end by the captivity of Aristobulus II and his family.

2   *"But you, Bethlehem Ephrathah, though you are small among the clans of Judah, out of you will come for me one who will be ruler over Israel, whose origins are from of old, from ancient times."*

A revelation of the Lord addressed to the town of Bethlehem, indicating the Messiah's descent from the Davidic family. But it also designates the place of His appearance. The fulfillment of this prophecy was the first advent of Christ and His entrance into history as

The Tribulation Period — The Time of Jacob's Trouble

God the Son, who had been eternally with the Father.

> 3a *Therefore Israel will be abandoned ...*

This is a reference to the defeat in verse one above, until the birth of the Messiah in verse two.

> 3b *until the time when she who is in labor gives birth ...*

God's giving Israel up. The fulfillment of this middle section of this sentence is said to be "the Messiah's birth of a woman." More specifically, this passage is a commentary on the prophecy of Micah 5:2 above, which definitely refers to Isaiah, the virgin bringing forth her son (Isaiah 7:14).

> 3c *and the rest of his brothers return to join the Israelites.*

A forecast by the prophet that after the coming of the Messiah a remnant of His brothers will return to Israel. But there appears to have been no major return just prior to Christ's coming forth from Bethlehem. These commentators say that the fulfillment of this last section of this sentence was "the joining of Gentiles into the Israel that is the church."

> 4 *He will stand and shepherd his flock in the strength of the LORD, in the majesty of the name of the LORD his God. And they will live securely, for then his greatness will reach to the ends of the earth.*

This commentary shows the fulfillment of this verse as the universal rule of the Messiah during the Millennium.

> 5a *And he will be their peace. ...*
> 6 *They will rule the land of Assyria with the sword, the land of Nimrod with drawn sword. He will deliver us from the Assyrian when he invades our land and marches into our borders.*

After continuing his progressive sweep through history up into millennial times, Micah adds, "When the Assyrian shall come into our land, within our border...and tread in our places... He (Christ, returned) shall deliver us... and they shall waste the land of Assyria with the sword." Such a Messianic deliverance has never been accomplished in the past: yet Revelation 16:12 predicts an attack in the future, coming from this area across the Euphrates. This will be fulfilled as an element in Christ's victory at Armageddon.

> 5b *When the Assyrian invades our land and marches through our fortresses, we will raise against him seven shepherds, even eight leaders of men.*

When confronted by the Assyrian forces of the Antichrist's invasion, seems to be a literary figure for augmented strength, but the concept itself remains essentially literal. The fulfillment is the activity of Christian leaders at the Lord's return; the more general forecast of Revelation 20:4, 6, about those who "live and reign" with Christ.

> 7 *The remnant of Jacob will be in the midst of many peoples like dew from the LORD, like showers on the grass, which do not wait for man or linger for mankind.*

AFTER THE RAPTURE

The universal rule of the Messiah during the Millennium.

8   *The remnant of Jacob will be among the nations, in the midst of many peoples, like a lion among the beasts of the forest, like a young lion among flocks of sheep, which mauls and mangles as it goes, and no one can rescue.*
9   *Your hand will be lifted up in triumph over your enemies, and all your foes will be destroyed.*

These two verses are to be fulfilled in the future status of privilege and of power among the nations for God's people (Israel) during the Millennium.

10 *"In that day," declares the LORD, "I will destroy your horses from among you and demolish your chariots.*
11 *I will destroy the cities of your land and tear down all your strongholds.*

God will destroy the armed forces of Israel and the cities "in that day," was fulfilled when Judah fell to Babylon in 586 BC.

12 *I will destroy your witchcraft and you will no longer cast spells.*
13 *I will destroy your carved images and your sacred stones from among you; you will no longer bow down to the work of your hands.*
14 *I will uproot from among you your Asherah poles and demolish your cities.*

Conditions that are to result from Judah's fall and destruction by the Babylonians in 586 BC. Israel's purification through the exile.

15 *I will take vengeance in anger and wrath upon the nations that have not obeyed me."* (NIV)

This verse was fulfilled when God executed vengeance on the nations, especially Assyria (Micah 5:5-6 above), though the various oppressors of Judah from Micah 5:9 onward—Babylon, the Seleucids, Rome—may also be included. The actual fulfillment is listed as being fulfilled by the angel of the LORD, when He slew 185,000 military men of the army of Sennacherib, King of Assyria, in 701 BC (2 Kings 19:33, Isaiah 37:36).

As you can see from above, the laborious attempt to place the fulfillment of most of Micah chapter five in the past has distorted its true meaning. Multitudes of people over hundreds of years have come to these conclusions, although they were well intentioned at the time. The biggest stumbling block for most of the Bible historians and commentators from the past is the fact that they existed before Israel had been reestablished as a nation and many of them believed that the church had replaced Israel in the scheme of things after Christ was rejected by the Jews. In fact, throughout most of the Dispensation of Grace, the church leaders have taught their congregations that the Church had replaced Israel as far as future blessings. You must separate the church from Israel in order to interpret what is about to take place in the near future.

Before we break down Micah five, let us take a glance at the chapters that surround it to get a broader picture. In Micah four, we can break it down into four subtitles. In verses 1-5, we have the account of the future reign of the Messiah in Zion during the Millennium.

The Tribulation Period — The Time of Jacob's Trouble

Few people disagree with this analysis. The subject of verses 6-8 concern a remnant of Jewish exiles as they return to Israel. Verse 9 talks about the siege of Jerusalem while verse 10 reminds the Jews that the Lord will redeem them out of the land of their enemies. Verses 11-13 tell Israel that her enemies will be defeated. Most Bible commentators place the fulfillment of verses 1-5 in the future and verses 6-13 in the past. What is really being discussed in Micah chapter four are all future events, but chronologically they are in reverse order. This chapter begins with the glorious or peaceful portion of the Day of the Lord (990 years) and then slips back to the stressful portion of the Millennium (10 years). The entirety of Micah 4 will take place in the future and the chronological order of the events are: many nations will come against Israel, but eventually Israel's enemies will be defeated (verses 11-13); the siege of Jerusalem and the Jewish exiles, with some of those fleeing to Babylon to be rescued during the Time of Jacob's Trouble (verses 9-10); a remnant of Jewish exiles will return to Jerusalem—those who recognize Jesus as their Messiah (verses 6-8); and the future reign of the Messiah in Zion when He establishes His kingdom on earth (verses 1-5).

Micah chapters six and seven will also be fulfilled in the future, during the Day of the Lord. Chapter six begins with God's case against Israel, admonishing them to walk humbly with their God (verses 1-8). It ends with Israel's guilt throughout history and God's final punishment on them during the Tribulation Period (verses 9-16). Micah chapter seven begins with Israel's misery during the Time of Jacob's Trouble (verses 1-7). It continues with the eventual triumph of Israel after their period of judgment is complete (verses 8-10). It then moves on to the restoration of the Jewish people to the land of Israel (verses 11-13). Chapter seven ends with Israel being established as the head of the nations after God forgives their iniquities during the Day of the Lord (verses 14-20).

With this background we can now look at Micah chapter five. The first four verses show both the distress and glorious portions of the Davidic dynasty (Kingdom Age/Millennium). In verse 1, it is recorded that the ruler of Israel (probably a prime minister) will be killed when the city of Jerusalem comes under siege by the Antichrist at the beginning of the Time of Jacob's Trouble. Elsewhere in the Bible the Jewish people are warned to flee about this time. Verse 2 is a promise to Israel that they will have a King sometime in the future. In order to verify who this future King will be; He will come from Jewish lineage, He will be born in Bethlehem Ephrathah, and He will come from a continual existence (perpetual). The abandonment of Israel in verse 3 covers the last three and one-half years of the Tribulation Period when they suffer through their birth pains (Deuteronomy 31:17-18; Isaiah 54:7-8; Micah 3:4; Matthew 24:8). At that time those Jews who have survived the purging process of God will be united into a single nation. In verse 4, we see Jesus as the future ruler as He shepherds His flock (Israel). After Jesus establishes His kingdom on earth the Jewish people will live securely as the King's greatness is known around the globe. The first sentence of verse 5 really belongs to the end of verse 4—*"And he will be their peace."* The rest of verse 5 jumps back to the Time of Jacob's Trouble when the Antichrist (the Assyrian) invades Israel and Jerusalem at the mid-point of the Tribulation Period. Verses 5 and 6 are focused on this conflict. Israel will confront the Antichrist with seven religious leaders and eight political leaders (probably members of Knesset), at which time the prime minister of Israel will be killed. The first part of verse 6 is the hardest to decipher in this chapter. It really does not make sense the way that it has been translated. Most of the translations seem to render this verse as if Israel will destroy the land of Assyria and the land of Nimrod. Israel in the past has never destroyed the land of Assyria or the land of Nimrod, nor does future prophecy predict this event. I believe that verse 6 is reporting that the Antichrist will overpower the nation of Israel with his army. At that time a door or entrance will open up for the Jews who will be fleeing from the Antichrist. In ancient times Nimrod established an empire in the area of Babylon and Assyria. Because of the hostility of the Antichrist against the countries around Israel, about this time, they apparently receive the Jews as they are fleeing. This is more consistent with the second part of verse 6, where it says that Jesus will deliver (rescue) the Jews from the Antichrist as he marches across the borders of Israel. Verses 7 and 8 also follow this story line as we see the Jews as they are scattered among the nations in exile. It also speaks about a remnant that will survive the onslaught of the Antichrist. Verse 9 reports that in the end, Israel will triumph and her foes will be destroyed. Verses 10-14 list the punishment that will be meted out against Israel and the purification of all the bad habits that will cease among the Jewish people. "In that day" is a reference to the Day of the Lord. Verse 15 ends the chapter as God tells the nations that He will bring wrath on all of them that have not obeyed Him. The wording in Micah chapter five varies greatly among the various translations. The King James, the New King James and the New Jerusalem Bible are the easiest to follow in this instance. The New Jerusalem Bible also has excellent subtitles in their translation of Micah chapters four through seven.

In the past certain practices have hurt the process of distinguishing between contemporary and distant prophecies from the latter prophets. Progressive prediction is of particular interest. The view that a broad Biblical context includes a series of separate forecasts that together exhibit a pattern of chronological process being fulfilled, the whole of which may be identified as a progressive prediction, can be misleading to say the least. A perfect example of this is "Yom Yahweh" or the Day of the Lord. The common thought today of Bible historians and prophecy teachers that this term may have an extended range of meanings and applies as progressive periods of God's fierce anger throughout history is incorrect. The Day of the Lord is a future Messianic period of time when Jesus will rule for a thousand years. Today prophecy can be divided into two categories, those that have been fulfilled in the past and those that have an eschatological or apocalyptic connotation and are to be fulfilled in the future. Those prophetic utterances that are yet to be fulfilled have the Messiah and His future reign as King as their main subject. The most difficult task of understanding the future is properly placing prophecy in the correct category. To do that one must have a thorough understanding of past history.

The current misunderstanding of the Day of the Lord as any day in which God avenges sin (any day of judgment) in the course of His providence, including the end-time events, misrepresents the true intention of end-time prophecy. Today, most Bible interpreters apply the Day of the Lord to almost all the progressive stages of Old Testament prophetic fulfillment concerning the punishment of Israel beginning with Joel, such as:

1. A contemporary locust plague somewhere around 735 BC (Joel 1:15).
2. Assyrian exile of Israel in 722 BC (Amos 5:18-20).
3. Babylonian destruction of Jerusalem in 586 BC (Zephaniah 1:7; Micah 5:10).
4. The capture of Babylon by the Medes and Persians in 539 BC (Isaiah 13:9).

The Tribulation Period — The Time of Jacob's Trouble

5. Christ's second coming and His victory at Armageddon (Joel 3:14; Zechariah 14:1-4).
6. God's final judgment at the end of the age (Malachi 4:1).

By placing the Day of the Lord into this sequence of events, it distorts the true meaning of future apocalyptic events. It places most of the future prophetic events from the major and minor prophets in the category of past history, instead of the future where it really belongs.

Events such as the total destruction of Babylon, Damascus (as a city) becoming a heap of ruins and no longer existing as a city, and Egypt being destroyed to a point of desolation for forty years, along with the Nile River drying up, have not yet taken place. By placing the Day of the Lord in the time frame of future fulfillment, the proper chronological order of the events of the Antichrist as he pursues his goal of world domination will fall into place. Coming up in this chapter you will see God administer judgment to the nations during the last year of the last 3 ½ years of the Tribulation Period, during the Day of the Lord.

The most accurate approach to use when sorting out prophetic events from the Bible and placing them in a chronological order is literal and single. Literal in the sense that the event will actually take place and single in the sense that each event is usually placed in a uniform period within its context. A single fulfillment does restrict a given phrase to one originally intended meaning in each context. This simplifies the process and makes it easier to place the prophetic scripture into its proper chronological order.

As we look at the Judgment of the Nations, we need to separate prophecy that was fulfilled in the past from what will take place in the future. As we said before there are many similarities, but what is of major importance are the irregularities. If we can distinguish the portions of scripture that have not taken place, we know that they will take place sometime in the future. The context surrounding these instances are also of utmost importance as we try to place prophecy into the correct category. The Judgment of the Nations plays a big part in the future destruction of the world by the Antichrist. Many of the lost pieces of the puzzle of eschatology are found in the scriptures relating to the Judgment of the Nations. Incorrect interpretations from the past have hindered the study of Bible Prophecy. I will admit one thing though, it will take more knowledge of the total picture of prophecy to properly interpret these verses in Micah chapter five. The minute details and the total picture of prophetic events that lie between the lines of these verses are found elsewhere in scripture. The total picture of Bible prophecy can only be seen by looking at all the scriptures.

Although the final judgment of all the nations (Jews and Gentiles) will take place after the Tribulation Period, the time of the Second Holocaust for the Jews will also be a time of extreme hardship for the Gentiles as well. God will judge every nation—along with Israel—for their conduct as a nation as they have existed throughout history. Do not forget that each individual person, within each nation, will be accountable to God for their own actions as well. The time for the final judgment to begin for the nations will also be during the Day of the Lord. This plan against the nations will include all the nations around the world and God will allow it to happen. In fact, God has purposed it to take place.

Isa 14:26-27 ***This is the plan determined for the whole world; this is the hand stretched out over all nations. For the LORD Almighty has***

AFTER THE RAPTURE

purposed, <u>and who can thwart him</u>? His hand is stretched out, and who can turn it back? (NIV)

Daniel has given us the outline of human history, from the sixth century BC on through the Tribulation Period, in chapters seven through twelve (written in advance). Isaiah, Jeremiah, Ezekiel and the minor prophets add the details to the story. Once the parameters of the chronological order are established and the people are separated into the proper category, at the proper time frame, piece by piece, the puzzle begins to reveal the whole story. Daniel reveals the tenacity of the Antichrist and lets us know that the Antichrist defeats many nations. Then the prophets reveal who the nations are and the details of their defeat. All of this will be taking place during the righteous judgment and fierce anger of Jesus Christ. The *battle-axe* used against the nations is the Antichrist and his army. He is also known as the Northerner and the force from all the peoples of the northern kingdoms will be his army. This, of course, is the Revived Roman Empire (European Union).

The severity of what will take place on earth during the last year of the Tribulation Period is almost unimaginable. Please remember that the trials and tribulations that face each of us in everyday life are different from the eschatological tribulations that will come from the fierce anger of God. Do not forget that punishment from God always follows mankind's apathy toward Him. The willful disregard of God today, all over the world, is a part of the apostasy that was forecast by God to take place. How sad!

If the contents of this book horrify you—it should! Isaiah told the people of his day that if they understood the extent of his message it would bring sheer terror upon them. The *"tested stone"* of Israel is Jesus. The *"overwhelming scourge"* in this passage is a reference to the destruction of the earth during the Tribulation Period. Some translations use the word "earth" in place of "land" in the last verse, which is probably more accurate. When *"the LORD will rise up...to do His work,"* it is His fierce anger during the Tribulation Period.

Isa 28:16-22 *So this is what the Sovereign LORD says: "See, I lay <u>a stone in Zion, a tested stone, a precious cornerstone for a sure foundation; the one who trusts will never be dismayed.</u> I will make justice the measuring line and righteousness the plumb line; hail will sweep away your refuge, the lie, and water will overflow your hiding place. Your covenant with death will be annulled; your agreement with the grave will not stand. **When the overwhelming scourge sweeps by, you will be beaten down by it.** As often as it comes it will carry you away; morning after morning, by day and by night, it will sweep through." **<u>The understanding of this message will bring sheer terror.</u>** The bed is too short to stretch out on, the blanket too narrow to wrap around you. **<u>The LORD will rise up</u> as he did at Mount Perazim, he will rouse himself as in the Valley of Gibeon—<u>to do his work</u>, his strange work, and perform his task, his alien task. Now stop your mocking, or your chains will become heavier; <u>the Lord, the LORD Almighty, has told me of the destruction decreed against the whole land.</u>** (NIV)*

The Tribulation Period — The Time of Jacob's Trouble

Never in past history has God purged the earth of all the unsaved people who were living on it, even counting the time of Noah (during the great flood), when only eight people survived. At that time there was only one righteous man left on earth.

The key word for the destruction that will take place during the worst time of human history is "**ALL**." Another factor to look for is "the Day of the LORD." Both the Old and the New Testaments support these two factors. The Lord Almighty already has this day in store for the unsaved who are living on earth at that time.

Ps 1:1-6 *Blessed is the man who does not walk in the counsel of the wicked or stand in the way of sinners or sit in the seat of mockers. But his delight is in the law of the LORD, and on his law he meditates day and night. He is like a tree planted by streams of water, which yields its fruit in season and whose leaf does not wither. Whatever he does prospers. **Not so the wicked! They are like chaff that the wind blows away. Therefore the wicked will not stand in the judgment, nor sinners in the assembly of the righteous.** For the LORD watches over the way of the righteous, **but the way of the wicked will perish.*** (NIV)

Ps 9:5-8 ***You have rebuked the nations and destroyed the wicked; you have blotted out their name for ever and ever.*** *Endless ruin has overtaken the enemy, you have uprooted their cities; even the memory of them has perished. **The LORD reigns forever; he has established his throne for judgment. He will judge the world in righteousness;** he will govern the peoples with justice.* (NIV)

Ps 75:3 ***The earth and all its inhabitants are dissolved; I set up its pillars firmly. Selah*** (NKJ)

Ps 79:1-12 *O God, the nations have invaded your inheritance; they have defiled your holy temple, they have reduced Jerusalem to rubble. They have given the dead bodies of your servants as food to the birds of the air, the flesh of your saints to the beasts of the earth. They have poured out blood like water all around Jerusalem, and there is no one to bury the dead. We are objects of reproach to our neighbors, of scorn and derision to those around us. **How long, O LORD? Will you be angry forever? How long will your jealousy burn like fire? Pour out your wrath on the nations that do not acknowledge you, on the kingdoms that do not call on your name; for they have devoured Jacob and destroyed his homeland.** Do not hold against us the sins of the fathers; may your mercy come quickly to meet us, for we are in desperate need. Help us, O God our Savior, for the glory of your name; deliver us and forgive our sins for your name's sake. **Why should the nations say, "Where is their God?" Before our eyes,*** *make known among the nations that you avenge the outpoured blood of your servants. May the groans of the prisoners come before you; by the strength of your arm preserve those condemned to die. Pay back into the laps of our neighbors seven times the reproach they have hurled at you, O Lord.* (NIV)

Ps 98:8-9 *Let the rivers clap their hands, let the mountains sing together for joy; let them sing before the LORD, <u>for he comes to judge the earth</u>. He will judge the world in righteousness and the peoples with equity.* (NIV)

Ps 110:5-6 *The Lord is at your right hand; he will crush kings on the day of his wrath. <u>He will judge the nations</u>, heaping up the dead and crushing the rulers of the whole earth.* (NIV)

Isa 2:9-18 <u>*So man will be brought low and mankind humbled*</u>*—do not forgive them. Go into the rocks, hide in the ground from dread of the LORD and the splendor of his majesty! The eyes of the arrogant man will be humbled and the pride of men brought low; the LORD alone will be exalted in that day.* ***The LORD Almighty has a day in store for all the proud and lofty****, for all that is exalted (and they will be humbled), for all the cedars of Lebanon, tall and lofty, and all the oaks of Bashan, for all the towering mountains and all the high hills, for every lofty tower and every fortified wall, for every trading ship and every stately vessel.* **The arrogance of man will be brought low and the pride of men humbled; the LORD alone will be exalted in that day, and the idols will totally disappear.** (NIV)

Isa 13:6-13 *Wail, for the day of the LORD is near; <u>it will come like destruction from the Almighty</u>. Because of this, all hands will go limp, every man's heart will melt. Terror will seize them, pain and anguish will grip them; they will writhe like a woman in labor. They will look aghast at each other, their faces aflame. <u>**See, the day of the LORD is coming a cruel day**</u>**, with wrath and fierce anger—to make the land desolate and destroy the sinners within it.** The stars of heaven and their constellations will not show their light. The rising sun will be darkened and the moon will not give its light. <u>I will punish the world for its evil, the wicked for their sins.</u> I will put an end to the arrogance of the haughty and will humble the pride of the ruthless. I will make man scarcer than pure gold, more rare than the gold of Ophir. <u>Therefore I will make the heavens tremble; and the earth will shake from its place at the wrath of the LORD Almighty, in the day of his burning anger.</u>* (NIV)

The Tribulation Period — The Time of Jacob's Trouble

Isa 24:1-3 — *See, **the LORD is going to lay waste the earth and devastate it; he will ruin its face and scatter its inhabitants**—it will be the same for priest as for people, for master as for servant, for mistress as for maid, for seller as for buyer, for borrower as for lender, for debtor as for creditor. **The earth will be completely laid waste and totally plundered.** The LORD has spoken this word.* (NIV)

Jer 9:25-26 — *"**The days are coming**," declares the LORD, "**when I will punish all who are circumcised only in the flesh**—Egypt, Judah, Edom, Ammon, Moab and all who live in the desert in distant places. For all these nations are really uncircumcised, and even the whole house of Israel is uncircumcised in heart."* (NIV)

Jer 10:10 — *But the LORD is the true God; he is the living God, the eternal King. **When he is angry, the earth trembles; the nations cannot endure his wrath.*** (NIV)

Jer 25:29 — *See, I am beginning to bring disaster on the city that bears my Name, and will you indeed go unpunished? You will not go unpunished, **for I am calling down a sword upon all who live on the earth**, declares the LORD Almighty.'* (NIV)

Ezek 30:1-3 — *The word of the LORD came to me: "Son of man, prophesy and say: 'This is what the Sovereign LORD says: "'Wail and say, "Alas for that day!" For the day is near, **the day of the LORD is near**—a day of clouds, **a time of doom for the nations**.* (NIV)

Joel 1:15 — *Alas for that day! **For the day of the LORD is near; it will come like destruction from the Almighty.*** (NIV)

Obad 1:15-16 — *"**The day of the LORD is near for all nations.** As you have done, it will be done to you; your deeds will return upon your own head. Just as you drank on my holy hill, so all the nations will drink continually; they will drink and drink and be as if they had never been.* (NIV)

Micah 7:13 — ***The earth will become desolate because of its inhabitants**, as the result of their deeds.* (NIV)

Zeph 1:2-3 — *"**I will sweep away everything from the face of the earth**," declares the LORD. "I will sweep away both men and animals; I will sweep away the birds of the air and the fish of the sea. **The wicked will have only heaps of rubble when I cut off man from the face of the earth**," declares the LORD.* (NIV)

Mal 3:18 *<u>And you will again see the distinction between the righteous and the wicked, between those who serve God and those who do not.</u>* (NIV)

Somewhere around this time, with approximately one year left in the last 3 ½ years of the Tribulation Period, the final assault on the nations by the Antichrist will take place. All the activity seems to be concentrated in the area of the Middle East. It will start with the final assault on Jerusalem and the cities of Judah (Israel) and end with the destruction of Babylon. The bowl judgments will be pouring out on the earth while these conflicts are taking place. The final assault of the nations by the Antichrist are recorded in volumes in the Old Testament. Isaiah chapters 13-24, Jeremiah chapters 46-51, Ezekiel chapters 25-32, along with most of the discourse of the minor prophets, are devoted to this subject. After reading these accounts it is hard to believe that the majority of this devastation will take place in a period of only one year. World War II will seem like a picnic compared with what is about to unfold on the people living on the earth. There does seem to be a chronological order for the destruction of the nations by the Antichrist at this time listed in the book of Jeremiah. This devastation will take place in the geographical area of these ancient nations and cover the land mass of all the nations listed, along with the people living in those areas at that time.

Jer 25:15-29 *This is what the LORD, the God of Israel, said to me: "<u>Take from my hand this cup filled with the wine of my wrath and make all the nations to whom I send you drink it. When they drink it, they will stagger and go mad because of the sword I will send among them.</u>" So I took the cup from the LORD's hand and made all the nations to whom he sent me drink it: <u>Jerusalem and the towns of Judah</u>, its kings and officials, to make them a ruin and an object of horror and scorn and cursing, as they are today; **Pharaoh king of Egypt**, his attendants, his officials and all his people, **and all the foreign people there; <u>all the kings of Uz</u>; <u>all the kings of the Philistines</u>** (those of Ashkelon, Gaza, Ekron, and the people left in Ashdod), **<u>Edom</u>, Moab and Ammon; <u>all the kings of Tyre and Sidon</u>; <u>the kings of the coastlands across the sea</u>; <u>Dedan, Tema, Buz and all who are in distant places</u>; <u>all the kings of Arabia and all the kings of the foreign people who live in the desert</u>; <u>all the kings of Zimri, Elam and Media</u>; <u>and all the kings of the north</u>**, near and far, one after the other— **<u>all the kingdoms on the face of the earth. And after all of them, the king of Sheshach will drink it too</u>**. "Then tell them, 'This is what the LORD Almighty, the God of Israel, says: **Drink, get drunk and vomit, and fall to rise no more because of the sword I will send among you.**' But if they refuse to take the cup from your hand and drink, tell them, 'This is what the LORD Almighty says: **You must drink it**! See, I am beginning to bring disaster on the city that bears my Name, and will you indeed go unpunished? **You will not go unpunished, <u>for I am calling down a sword upon all who</u>**

The Tribulation Period — The Time of Jacob's Trouble

<u>live on the earth, declares the LORD Almighty.</u>' (NIV)

In these verses, we find a map of the Antichrist as he makes his final bid to conquer the entire world. This final assault of the Antichrist begins with Jerusalem and the cities of Israel. The next altercation of the Antichrist listed is with the nation of Egypt and her allies. This is the third and final Egyptian/Antichrist confrontation. Without naming each country or location of the Old Testament names listed in Jeremiah 25:15-29, let me cover the current geographical area that Jeremiah covers in this list of names. This area now includes the countries of Saudi Arabia, Jordan, Lebanon, Gaza, Syria, Turkey, Egypt, Libya, Ethiopia, Iran and all of the smaller Arab countries in Southwest Asia. All the kings of the north, near and far, would have to include the Russian conglomeration of nations involved in the Russian Invasion. It then mentions all the kingdoms (nations) on the face of the earth and last, but not least, the Antichrist will destroy the king of Sheshach. Sheshach is a foreign derivation for Babylon. It is kind of ironic that the Antichrist will end his rain of destruction with the nation of Babylon (present day Iraq). This coincides with the book of Revelation. Consult the map on page 758 as you follow the Judgment of the Nations.

Some people will be quick to point out that these verses from Jeremiah were fulfilled in Old Testament times after 539 BC when the Babylonian empire was defeated by the Persian empire, but a careful look at the verses reveal an interesting comment concerning the completeness of the Babylonian destruction. The punishment from God will include **ALL** the nations of the world as prophesied by the prophet Jeremiah.

Jer 25:12-14   *"But when the seventy years are fulfilled, <u>I will punish the king of Babylon and his nation</u>, the land of the Babylonians, for their guilt," declares the LORD, "<u>and will make it desolate forever</u>. I will bring upon that land all the things I have spoken against it, all that are written in this book and prophesied by Jeremiah <u>against all the nations</u>. They themselves will be enslaved by many nations and great kings; I will repay them according to their deeds and the work of their hands."* (NIV)

The comment that after the captivity of seventy years is completed God will punish the king of Babylon and his nation and make it a perpetual waste has never totally taken place in the past. A short review of Babylonian history during the time of the Persian conquest will reveal what actually took place at that time. Nabopolassar established himself as king of Babylon during the time of the Assyrian empire and was in direct control of Babylon at that time. He ruled Babylon from 625 BC to 604 BC. Nabopolassar was succeeded by his son Nebuchadnezzar II, sometime spelled as Nebuchadrezzar. He was the king who defeated the Assyrians to bring Babylon on the scene as a world dominating empire. He was also the man who carried the Jews into captivity for seventy years. His soldiers burned the town of Jerusalem and its Temple in 586 BC. Nebuchadnezzar ruled the neo-Babylonian empire from 605 BC to 561 BC, the longest reign of any of the neo-Babylonian kings. He made Babylon the mistress of the civilized world and with his building projects created what the Greeks called one of the seven wonders of the world. [2]

The next king, Evil-Merodach, Nebuchadnezzar's son, is also mentioned in the Old Testament. Two short reigns followed when the ruling dynasty was overthrown and Nabonidus was placed upon the throne. This king, who delighted in exploring and restoring ancient temples, placed his son (Belshazzar) at the head of his army. Nabonidus, desiring to centralize the religion of Babylonia, brought to Babylon many of the images of deities from other cities. This greatly displeased the people and excited a strong feeling against him. The priesthood was alienated and the military party was displeased with him, for in his antiquarian pursuits he left the defense of the empire to others. So when Cyrus, king of Anshan and ruler of Persia, entered the country, he had little difficulty in defeating the Babylonians in a battle at Opis. Sippar immediately surrendered to the invader, and the gates of Babylon were thrown open to his army under Gobryas, his general. Nabonidus was imprisoned. Three months later Cyrus entered Babylon; Belshazzar, who doubtless had set up his throne after his father had been deposed, was slain a week later on the night of the eleventh of Marchesvan. This scene may have occurred in the palace built by Nebuchadnezzar. This event, told by the chronicler, is a remarkable verification of the interesting story related to Belshazzar in Daniel. [3] Another detailed account from the same source lists the loss of world dominance of power of the Babylonians like this:

> Nabunahid (Nabonidus), whose religious zeal had led him to collect as many as possible of the idols from other parts of Babylonia and remove them to Babylon, thereby increasing the sacredness and magnificence of that city, but inflicting injury on neighboring and more ancient sanctuaries. Defeating Nabunahid's army and capturing the king, Cyrus sent his own forces under Gobryas (Gubaru, Gaubaruva) to take possession of Babylon. This he did in June, 538 BC, "without opposition and without a battle." This citadel, however, where Belshazzar "the king's son" was in command, held out for some months, and was then taken in a night attack in which "the king's son" was slain. [4]

The remarkable story of Belshazzar's demise and the story of "the hand writing on the wall" are recorded in the book of Daniel chapter five. This phrase has stood out in history ever since it was recorded in the Bible.

Dan 5:1-6 *King Belshazzar gave a great banquet for a thousand of his nobles and drank wine with them. While Belshazzar was drinking his wine, he gave orders to bring in the gold and silver goblets that Nebuchadnezzar his father had taken from the temple in Jerusalem, so that the king and his nobles, his wives and his concubines might drink from them. So they brought in the gold goblets that had been taken from the temple of God in Jerusalem, and the king and his nobles, his wives and his concubines drank from them. As they drank the wine, they praised the gods of gold and silver, of bronze, iron, wood and stone.* **<u>Suddenly the fingers of a human hand appeared and wrote on the plaster of the wall</u>**, *near the lampstand in the royal palace.* **<u>The king watched the hand as it wrote.</u>** *His face*

> *turned pale and he was so frightened that his knees knocked together and his legs gave way.* (NIV)

Dan 5:25-31   *"This is the inscription that was written: MENE, MENE, TEKEL, PARSIN "This is what these words mean: Mene: God has numbered the days of your reign and brought it to an end. Tekel: You have been weighed on the scales and found wanting. Peres: **Your kingdom is divided and given to the Medes and Persians.**" Then at Belshazzar's command, Daniel was clothed in purple, a gold chain was placed around his neck, and he was proclaimed the third highest ruler in the kingdom. **That very night Belshazzar, king of the Babylonians, was slain, and Darius the Mede took over the kingdom, at the age of sixty-two.** (NIV)*

Grab your Bible and read chapter five for the entire story. The point I am trying to make here is that past history proves that the prophecy in Jeremiah 25:12-14 did not take place in 539 BC. To be fair to those who hold the opinion that this prophecy was eventually fulfilled several centuries later, let us look at what became of Babylon down through history.

> Nabonidus and his son were the last kings of the neo-Babylonian empire. On October 12, 539 BC, Babylon fell to Cyrus of Persia, and from that time on the decay of the city began. Xerxes plundered it. Alexander the Great thought to restore its great temple, in ruins in his day, but was deterred by the prohibitive cost. During the period of Alexander's successors the area decayed rapidly and soon became a desert. From the days of Seleucus Nicator (312-280 BC), who built the rival city of Seleucia on the Tigris River, queenly Babylon never revived. [5]

This makes a good case for those who believe that Babylon lies desolate. The curse of the writing on the wall has haunted the city of Babylon for a long time. However, in order to fulfill the prophecies in the Bible, concerning the total destruction of Babylon, we must look to the future because the prophecies have not taken place in the past. I believe that the city of Babylon will be rebuilt sometime in the near future, probably during the Tribulation Period, at which time, the prophecies concerning Babylon will finally come to completion. The best source to go to confirm that the destruction of Babylon is to take place in the future is the book of Revelation. In Psalms it states that God will cut of the horns of the wicked.

Ps 75:1-10   *We give thanks to you, O God, we give thanks, for your Name is near; men tell of your wonderful deeds. You say, "**I choose the appointed time; it is I who judge uprightly**. When the earth and all its people quake, it is I who hold its pillars firm. Selah To the arrogant I say, 'Boast no more,' and to the wicked, 'Do not lift up your horns. Do not lift your horns against heaven; do not speak with outstretched neck.'" No one from the east or the west or from the desert can exalt a man. **But it is God who judges: He brings one***

> *down, he exalts another. In the hand of the LORD is a cup full of foaming wine mixed with spices; he pours it out, and all the wicked of the earth drink it down to its very dregs. As for me, I will declare this forever; I will sing praise to the God of Jacob. <u>I will cut off the horns of all the wicked, but the horns of the righteous will be lifted up.</u>* (NIV)

Again, I remind you that the Hebrew word *moed`* is used in verse two for the appointed time. Before we take a detailed look at the final assault of the Antichrist, let me advise you that not everyone will agree with me that these scripture verses concerning the destruction of the nations will be in the future. They will say that all this took place after Nebuchadnezzar, king of Babylon, in the seventh century BC, defeated Israel. I agree that there are similarities and that scripture even uses the actual name of the King of Babylon at times, but the total fulfillment of these verses has not yet come to pass, as you will see as we critique them. The king of the North at the time of the fulfillment of these prophecies will be the Antichrist and the king of the South will be the leader of Egypt. The complete destruction of the nations will come about in the last half of the Tribulation Period.

The king of Babylon has two distinctions in the Bible. The first distinction can be as a king who ruled the empire of Babylonia in ancient times, such as Nebuchadnezzar or Belshazzar. The capital city of this empire also had the name Babylon. The location of the nation of Babylon, before it became a world dominating empire, was directly east of Israel. The second distinction of the king of Babylon in the Bible refers to the Antichrist as the head of the Revived Roman Empire. This king of Babylon will rule sometime in the future when he attempts to conquer the entire world. His empire will be directly north of Israel. In Isaiah 14, below, it is clearly speaking about the time when God will bring relief to the Jewish people from the suffering during the Time of Jacob's Trouble. This passage concludes with a reference to the defeat of the Antichrist—the king of Babylon, the oppressor. The Jews in the past have never been brought back to the land of Israel and lived in safety.

> Isa 14:3-4   *On the day the LORD gives you relief from suffering and turmoil and cruel bondage, you will take up this taunt against <u>the king of Babylon</u>: How <u>the oppressor</u> has come to an end! How his fury has ended!* (NIV)

> Jer 32:36-37   *"You are saying about this city, 'By the sword, famine and plague it will be handed over to <u>the king of Babylon</u>'; but this is what the LORD, the God of Israel, says: I will surely gather them from all the lands where I banish them in my furious anger and great wrath; I will bring them back to this place and let them live in safety.* (NIV)

The Antichrist is disguised by many names in the Bible. The Antichrist is:

1. the thornbush — Judges 9:14-15
2. the oppressor — Job 15:20; Psalms 72:4; Isaiah 14:4, 51:13; Jeremiah 25:38, 50:16

The Tribulation Period — The Time of Jacob's Trouble

3. the destroyer — Job 15:21; Isaiah 16:4, 54:16; Jeremiah 4:7, 6:26, 48:8
4. a mighty man — Psalms 52:1, 7
5. the king of Assyria — Isaiah 7:17, 8:4, 14:25, 20:4-6; Jeremiah 50:17-18
6. the Assyrian — Isaiah 10:5, 23:13, 30:32-33, 31:8, 52:4; Ezekiel 31:3; Hosea 14:3; Micah 5:5; Nahum 3:18-19
7. the king of Babylon — Isaiah 14:4; Jeremiah 32:36; Ezekiel 21:21, 32:11
8. a cruel master — Isaiah 19:4
9. a fierce king — Isaiah 19:4
10. one from the north — Isaiah 41:25
11. a man — Isaiah 46:11; Ezekiel 28:2
12. a blacksmith — Isaiah 54:16
13. Nebuchadnezzar king of Babylon — Jeremiah 46:13, 26, 50:17-18; Ezekiel 29:19
14. a battle axe for God — Jeremiah 51:20
15. prince (ruler) of Tyre — Ezekiel 28:2
16. the ruler of the nations — Ezekiel 31:11
17. a little horn — Daniel 7:8, 24
18. another horn — Daniel 8:9
19. a stern-faced king — Daniel 8:23
20. the prince (ruler) who will come — Daniel 9:26-27
21. a contemptible (vile) person — Daniel 11:21
22. the king of the north — Daniel 11:28, 40
23. the king will do as he pleases — Daniel 11:36
24. the northerner — Joel 2:20
25. the rod — Micah 6:9
26. he, his, himself, him — Habakkuk 2:4-20
27. the worthless shepherd — Zechariah 11:17
28. standing in the holy place — Matthew 24:15
29. someone else in his own name — John 5:43
30. the man of lawlessness — 2 Thessalonians 2:3, 8
31. the Antichrist — 1 John 2:18
32. the rider on the white, red, black and pale horses — Revelation 6:1-8
33. the beast — Revelation 13:1, 3, 8, 18; 17:11-13, 16; 19:20; 20:10

Every time the king of Babylon or the king of Assyria are mentioned in the Bible does not necessarily mean it applies to the Antichrist. In fact, most of the time these titles are mentioned in scripture, they will apply to the kings (leaders) of the ancient world empires of Old Testament times. The context that surrounds each listing of these titles will determine who God is speaking about. Quite often biblical commentators and translators confuse the king of Assyria and the Assyrian with the king of the ancient Assyrian empire, when it is actually referring to the Antichrist. The Revived Roman Empire will be located north of the nation of Israel. This alliance of nations will be headed by the Antichrist.

Isa 41:25 *"I have stirred up <u>one from the north</u>, and he comes—one from the rising sun who calls on my name. He treads on rulers as if they*

AFTER THE RAPTURE

were mortar, as if he were a potter treading the clay. (NIV)

Jer 1:14   *The LORD said to me, "<u>From the north</u> disaster will be poured out on all who live in the land.* (NIV)

Jer 6:1   *"Flee for safety, people of Benjamin! Flee from Jerusalem! Sound the trumpet in Tekoa! Raise the signal over Beth Hakkerem! <u>For disaster looms out of the north, even terrible destruction.</u>* (NIV)

Jer 6:22-23   *This is what the LORD says: "<u>Look, an army is coming from the land of the north; a great nation is being stirred up from the ends of the earth.</u> They are armed with bow and spear; <u>they are cruel and show no mercy.</u> They sound like the roaring sea as they ride on their horses; they come like men in battle formation to attack you, O Daughter of Zion."* (NIV)

Along with the activities of the Antichrist, the Revived Roman Empire is underestimated in Bible prophecy. There is a lot more said about this ruthless conglomeration of nations in the Bible than what is reported today. This eventual sword of God, headed by the Antichrist, also has many symbolic names in scripture. The Revived Roman Empire is:

1. my shade (of the thornbush) — Judges 9:15; Ezekiel 31:17
2. the club of My (God's) wrath — Isaiah 10:5
3. an army (God's) for war (the weapons of his wrath) — Isaiah 13:4-5
4. a cloud of smoke coming from the north — Isaiah 14:31
5. the raging of many nations — Isaiah 17:12
6. a weapon (Antichrist's) fit for war — Isaiah 54:16
7. the people's from the northern kingdoms — Jeremiah 1:14
8. a commotion from the land of the north — Jeremiah 10:22
9. the sword of the oppressor — Jeremiah 25:38, 50:16; Ezekiel 21:9-32
10. a gadfly (destruction - KJV) from the north — Jeremiah 46:20
11. a nation from the north (alliance/army) — Jeremiah 50:3, 9, 41
12. the hammer of the whole earth — Jeremiah 50:23
13. His arsenal/the weapons of His (God's) wrath — Jeremiah 50:25
14. the most wicked of the nations — Ezekiel 7:24
15. the most ruthless of foreign nations — Ezekiel 31:12
16. the sword of the king of Babylon — Ezekiel 32:11
17. the ten toes of the statue — Daniel 2:42
18. the ten horns from the fourth kingdom — Daniel 7:24; Revelation 12:3, 13:1, 17:3, 7-8, 12
19. the people of the ruler who will come — Daniel 9:26
20. the armed forces who rise up to desecrate the Temple — Daniel 11:31
21. a nation who will invade the nation of Israel — Joel 1:6-7
22. My (God's) great army sent against Israel — Joel 2:25

The Tribulation Period — The Time of Jacob's Trouble

The Revived Roman Empire (*"the ten horns are ten kings who will come from this kingdom"* – Daniel 7:24a NIV) will be headed by the Antichrist (*"after them another king will arise, different from the earlier ones."* – Daniel 7:24b NIV).

The big question concerning the Judgment of the Nations that we are about to look at, is whether these prophecies have been fulfilled in the past or are they going to be fulfilled in the future. The general consensus among Bible historians today is that most of the conflicts listed in the Old Testament have already taken place in the past. My thoughts lean toward the future. The prophecy of the conflicts spoken of in Jeremiah 25:12-38 are all to be fulfilled in the future and will take place in a specified chronological order of events in a short span of time. They have never been fulfilled in the past, strung out and scattered over hundreds of years.

Once again, I remind you that although it will be the Revived Roman Empire under the control of the Antichrist, that comes against the nations of the world like a flood, it will be God who will be conducting the orchestra. The *battle-axe* will be in His hand. A warning of the coming destruction against the nations by the Antichrist appears shortly before each block of scripture verses that pertain to the Judgment of the Nations.

Isa 13:2-5 *Raise a banner on a bare hilltop, shout to them; beckon to them to enter the gates of the nobles. I have commanded my holy ones; I have summoned my warriors to carry out my wrath—those who rejoice in my triumph. Listen, a noise on the mountains, like that of a great multitude! Listen, an uproar among the kingdoms, like nations massing together!* **The LORD Almighty is mustering an army for war.** *They come from faraway lands, from the ends of the heavens—the LORD and the weapons of his wrath—to destroy the whole country.* (NIV)

Jer 45:1-46:1 *This is what Jeremiah the prophet told Baruch son of Neriah in the fourth year of Jehoiakim son of Josiah king of Judah, after Baruch had written on a scroll the words Jeremiah was then dictating: "This is what the LORD, the God of Israel, says to you, Baruch: You said, 'Woe to me! The LORD has added sorrow to my pain; I am worn out with groaning and find no rest.'" [The LORD said,] "Say this to him: 'This is what the LORD says:* **I will overthrow what I have built and uproot what I have planted, throughout the land. Should you then seek great things for yourself? Seek them not. For I will bring disaster on all people,** *declares the LORD, but wherever you go I will let you escape with your life.'"* **This is the word of the LORD that came to Jeremiah the prophet concerning the nations:** (NIV)

Ezek 21:14-17 *"So then, son of man, prophesy and strike your hands together. Let the sword strike twice, even three times. It is a sword for slaughter—a sword for great slaughter, closing in on them from every side. So that hearts may melt and the fallen be many,* **I have** *stationed the sword for slaughter at all their gates. Oh! It is made to flash like lightning, it is grasped for slaughter. O sword, slash to the right, then to the left, wherever your blade is turned. I too will strike my hands together, and my wrath will subside. I the LORD have spoken."* (NIV)

Scripture reveals more details about the final assault of the Antichrist during the last year of the last 3 ½ years of the Tribulation Period than all the rest of the conflicts that take place during this time of great distress. The final year of this period will have two major confrontations. One of these confrontations will be with Egypt and the other will be with Babylon. Both conflicts are covered quite extensively in scripture. The Antichrist's final attempt to conquer the world is listed in Jeremiah 25:19-29, shown above. Except for Jerusalem and the towns of Judah, which is the first target of the Antichrist, all the remaining nations of the world will be dealt with by the Antichrist between these two major conflicts. This will be the third conflict the Antichrist will have with Egypt.

We will now take this order of events listed in Jeremiah chapter twenty-five and look at some of the details of the conflicts that take place between the Antichrist and some of his foes during the worst time of human history. Please remember that this final assault on the nations by the Antichrist and his alliance of nations from the north will take place during the last year of the Tribulation Period at the same time the bowl judgments are raining down on the earth from heaven.

JERUSALEM AND THE TOWNS OF JUDAH

It is not a coincidence that the final assault of the nations by the Antichrist begins with the city of Jerusalem and the rest of the cities of Judah. Satan has desired the possession of the Holy city of Jerusalem and the nation of Israel for a very long time. The Antichrist's destroying army will come from the Revived Roman Empire. This final assault begins with the landmass of Israel, the city of Jerusalem and the people living there at the time of this judgment. Only the Jews who are hiding in the mountainous regions in Israel will still be there, because most of the Jews will have fled at the time of the Abomination of Desolation. It will be mainly occupied by non-Jews who will have taken over Israel at that time. These non-Jewish people might possibly help Egypt defeat the Antichrist during the second Antichrist/Egyptian conflict. Perhaps some of the disgruntled Jewish people, those who flee to Egypt at the Abomination of Desolation, will also be a part of the Egyptian army. After the protection of Israel, furnished by the Antichrist during the first 3 ½ years of the Tribulation Period, some of the Jews (possibly mercenaries) were probably with the Egyptian army as they came against the supposed Messiah. This will enrage the Antichrist and may be the spark that will prompt the Antichrist to swoop down on Jerusalem and Israel.

Jer 4:5-31 *"Announce in Judah and proclaim in Jerusalem and say: 'Sound the trumpet throughout the land!' Cry aloud and say: 'Gather together! Let us flee to the fortified cities!' Raise the signal to go to Zion! Flee for safety without delay! For I am bringing disaster*

The Tribulation Period — The Time of Jacob's Trouble

*from the north, even terrible destruction." **A lion has come out of his lair; a destroyer of nations has set out**. He has left his place to lay waste your land. Your towns will lie in ruins without inhabitant. So put on sackcloth, lament and wail, for the fierce anger of the LORD has not turned away from us. "In that day," declares the LORD, "the king and the officials will lose heart, the priests will be horrified, and the prophets will be appalled." Then I said, "Ah, Sovereign LORD, how completely you have deceived this people and Jerusalem by saying, 'You will have peace,' when the sword is at our throats." At that time this people and Jerusalem will be told, "A scorching wind from the barren heights in the desert blows toward my people, but not to winnow or cleanse; a wind too strong for that comes from me. Now I pronounce my judgments against them."* **Look! He advances like the clouds, his chariots come like a whirlwind, his horses are swifter than eagles. Woe to us! We are ruined! O Jerusalem, wash the evil from your heart and be saved.** *How long will you harbor wicked thoughts? A voice is announcing from Dan, proclaiming disaster from the hills of Ephraim. "Tell this to the nations, proclaim it to Jerusalem: '**A besieging army is coming from a distant land, raising a war cry against the cities of Judah**. They surround her like men guarding a field, because she has rebelled against me,'" declares the LORD.* **"Your own conduct and actions have brought this upon you. This is your punishment. How bitter it is! How it pierces to the heart!"** *Oh, my anguish, my anguish! I writhe in pain. Oh, the agony of my heart! My heart pounds within me, I cannot keep silent.* **For I have heard the sound of the trumpet; I have heard the battle cry. Disaster follows disaster; the whole land lies in ruins. In an instant my tents are destroyed, my shelter in a moment.** *How long must I see the battle standard and hear the sound of the trumpet? "My people are fools; they do not know me. They are senseless children; they have no understanding. They are skilled in doing evil; they know not how to do good." I looked at the earth, and it was formless and empty; and at the heavens, and their light was gone. I looked at the mountains, and they were quaking; all the hills were swaying. I looked, and there were no people; every bird in the sky had flown away.* **I looked, and the fruitful land was a desert; all its towns lay in ruins before the LORD, before his fierce anger.** *This is what the LORD says:* **"The whole land will be ruined, though I will not destroy it completely. Therefore the earth will mourn and the heavens above grow dark, because I have spoken and will not relent, I have decided and will not turn back."** *At the sound of horsemen and archers every town takes to flight. Some go into the thickets; some climb up among the rocks. All the towns are deserted; no one lives* *in them. What are you doing, O devastated one? Why dress yourself in scarlet and put on jewels of gold? Why shade your eyes with paint? You adorn yourself in vain. Your lovers despise you; they seek your life. I hear a cry as of a woman in labor, a groan as of one bearing her first child—the cry of the Daughter of Zion gasping for breath, stretching out her hands and saying, "Alas! I am fainting; my life is given over to murderers."* (NIV)

Most Bible commentaries place the fulfillment of Jeremiah chapter four at the destruction of Jerusalem by the Babylonians in 586 BC. In all actuality it could also be placed in 70 AD when the Romans destroyed Jerusalem. Both of those events were devastating for Jerusalem and the nation of Judah (Israel), but they are nothing in comparison to the future when the Antichrist comes against the nation of Israel and the city of Jerusalem, which is what Jeremiah is referring to in these verses. In the first part of Jeremiah, he speaks extensively on the subject of this destroying army from the north, the Revived Roman Empire, headed up by the Antichrist. The Antichrist has been planning this attack on the nations for quite some time. Notice that this destruction from the Antichrist will include the entire nation of Israel, including Jerusalem. As we look at Jeremiah 6:22-26, we see that the people in Jerusalem at this time will hear rumors of the coming destruction and fear for their lives. Suddenly the destroyer (the Antichrist) will come. He will destroy Israel, Jerusalem and probably the Temple at this time.

Jer 6:22-26   *This is what the LORD says: "**Look, an army is coming from the land of the north**; a great nation is being stirred up from the ends of the earth. They are armed with bow and spear; **they are cruel and show no mercy**. They sound like the roaring sea as they ride on their horses; they come like men in battle formation to attack you, O Daughter of Zion." **We have heard reports about them**, and our hands hang limp. Anguish has gripped us, pain like that of a woman in labor. Do not go out to the fields or walk on the roads, for the enemy has a sword, and there is terror on every side. O my people, put on sackcloth and roll in ashes; mourn with bitter wailing as for an only son, **for suddenly the destroyer will come upon us**.* (NIV)

Jer 10:22   ***Listen! The report is coming**—a great commotion from the land of the north! **It will make the towns of Judah desolate**, a haunt of jackals.* (NIV)

History reveals that both the destruction of Jerusalem in 586 BC, by Babylon, and the destruction by the Romans in 70 AD came from a northerly direction, but neither conflict came suddenly. Before Jerusalem was destroyed by the Babylonians, it was under siege for 1½ years where it became inundated by famine. The destruction of Jerusalem by the Romans was preceded by a four-year Jewish revolt. The advancing Roman army, lead by Vespasian,

The Tribulation Period — The Time of Jacob's Trouble

was slow and cautious. After Vespasian was summoned to Rome, in the midst of the war to become emperor, his son Titus continued the task of besieging and capturing Jerusalem. Eventually, the city was destroyed. The destruction of Jerusalem by Babylon and Rome both took place on the same Jewish day—the 9th of Av, separated by approximately 555 years. Almost 2000 years later, will it happen again? On the 9th of Av?

We also see this destroyer from the north as he punishes even more nations. This is a partial list of the nations listed in Jeremiah chapter twenty-five.

> Jer 9:25-26 ***"The days are coming," declares the LORD, "when I will punish all who are circumcised only in the flesh—Egypt, Judah, Edom, Ammon, Moab and all who live in the desert in distant places. For all these nations are really uncircumcised, and even the whole house of Israel is uncircumcised in heart."*** (NIV)

In Isaiah, the Antichrist, with the title of the king of Assyria or the Assyrian, will be a club in the hands of God against the godless nation of Israel. Although God has sent the Assyrian (Antichrist) against Israel, the real intentions of the Antichrist are to destroy many nations. These are also part of the same conflicts mentioned above in Jeremiah.

> Isa 7:17-20 *The LORD will bring on you and on your people and on the house of your father a time unlike any since Ephraim broke away from Judah—**he will bring the king of Assyria.**" In that day the LORD will whistle for flies from the distant streams of Egypt and for bees from the land of Assyria. They will all come and settle in the steep ravines and in the crevices in the rocks, on all the thornbushes and at all the water holes. **In that day the Lord will use a razor hired from beyond the River—the king of Assyria—to shave your head and the hair of your legs, and to take off your beards also.*** (NIV)

> Isa 10:5-7 ***"Woe to the Assyrian, the rod of my anger, in whose hand is the club of my wrath! I send him against a godless nation, I dispatch him against a people who anger me, to seize loot and snatch plunder, and to trample them down like mud in the streets. But this is not what he intends, this is not what he has in mind; his purpose is to destroy, to put an end to many nations.*** (NIV)

Never in the past has the king of Assyria ever trampled down the godless nation of Judah like mud in the streets. Although Ahaz, king of Judah, became an Assyrian vassal and Sargon, king of Assyria, captured Samaria in 722 BC, at no time has Jerusalem ever been destroyed by the Assyrians. As a matter of fact the angel of the Lord slew 185,000 Assyrian soldiers, supernaturally in one night, to keep the king of Assyria (Sennacherib) from destroying Jerusalem in 701 BC. The entire story is recorded in Isaiah 37:1-38 and also in 2 Kings 19:32-37.

God then consoles the people of Israel by telling them that the king of Assyria

(Antichrist) will be punished but not until after he has plundered Mount Zion and Jerusalem. The Antichrist really believes that he will defeat the nation of Israel and the city of Jerusalem by his own intelligence and power.

> Isa 10:12-14   *When the Lord has finished all his work against Mount Zion and Jerusalem, he will say, "I will punish <u>the king of Assyria</u> for the willful pride of his heart and the haughty look in his eyes. For he says: "'By the strength of my hand I have done this, and by my wisdom, because I have understanding. I removed the boundaries of nations, I plundered their treasures; like a mighty one I subdued their kings. As one reaches into a nest, so my hand reached for the wealth of the nations; as men gather abandoned eggs, so I gathered all the countries; not one flapped a wing, or opened its mouth to chirp.'"* (NIV)

At that time the entire nation will face destruction, but there will be a remnant of survivors that will return to God. In the end, the Jewish people will finally reject the Antichrist. Why did it take so long for them to turn to the true God?

> Isa 10:20-23   *In that day the remnant of Israel, the survivors of the house of Jacob, will no longer rely on him who struck them down but will truly rely on the LORD, the Holy One of Israel. <u>A remnant will return, a remnant of Jacob will return to the Mighty God.</u> Though your people, O Israel, be like the sand by the sea, only a remnant will return. <u>Destruction has been decreed</u>, overwhelming and righteous. <u>The Lord, the LORD Almighty, will carry out the destruction decreed upon the whole land.</u>* (NIV)

Also, in the end, God's anger will turn against the Assyrian and His wrath will be directed toward the destruction of the Antichrist. After the indignation of the Tribulation Period is finished, Jesus will defeat the Antichrist at the Battle of Armageddon. It will not be long at this time (about 1 year) and the Tribulation Period (indignation) will be over.

> Isa 10:24-25   *Therefore thus says the Lord GOD of hosts: "O My people, who dwell in Zion, <u>do not be afraid of the Assyrian.</u> He shall strike you with a rod and lift up his staff against you, in the manner of Egypt. "<u>For yet a very little while and the indignation will cease, as will My anger in their destruction.</u>"* (NKJ)

Isaiah reveals that God created the destroyer (Antichrist) to wreak havoc against the nation of Israel. God created the blacksmith (Antichrist) who fans the coals into a flame and forges the weapon (a northern army) fit for the work (havoc). After the destruction is over, vindication of the Jewish people will come from God.

The Tribulation Period — The Time of Jacob's Trouble

Isa 54:16-17   *"See, it is I who created <u>the blacksmith</u> who fans the coals into flame and forges a weapon fit for its work. <u>And it is I who have created the destroyer to work havoc</u>; no weapon forged against you will prevail, and you will refute every tongue that accuses you. This is the heritage of the servants of the LORD, <u>and this is their vindication from me</u>," declares the LORD.* (NIV)

A portion of the punishment of the nations will be brought about by the ill treatment of the people of Israel throughout history. They are sometimes called Israel's enemies. The people from the nations who mistreated Israel will include those nations who existed in the geographical area of the ancient nations, those who are mistreating the Jewish people today, and the people who mistreat the Jewish people during the Tribulation Period.

Jer 10:23-25   *I know, O LORD, that a man's life is not his own; it is not for man to direct his steps. Correct me, LORD, but only with justice—not in your anger, lest you reduce me to nothing.* **Pour out your wrath on the nations that do not acknowledge you, on the peoples who do not call on your name.** <u>**For they have devoured Jacob; they have devoured him completely and destroyed his homeland.**</u> (NIV)

Zech 9:1-8   *The word of the LORD is against the land of Hadrach and will rest upon Damascus—for the eyes of men and all the tribes of Israel are on the LORD—and upon Hamath too, which borders on it, and upon Tyre and Sidon, though they are very skillful. Tyre has built herself a stronghold; she has heaped up silver like dust, and gold like the dirt of the streets. But the Lord will take away her possessions and destroy her power on the sea, and she will be consumed by fire. Ashkelon will see it and fear; Gaza will writhe in agony, and Ekron too, for her hope will wither. Gaza will lose her king and Ashkelon will be deserted. Foreigners will occupy Ashdod, and I will cut off the pride of the Philistines. I will take the blood from their mouths, the forbidden food from between their teeth. Those who are left will belong to our God and become leaders in Judah, and Ekron will be like the Jebusites.* **But I will defend my house against marauding forces.** <u>**Never again will an oppressor overrun my people, for now I am keeping watch.**</u> (NIV)

Because of the idolatrous state of most of the Jewish people living today, including those living in Israel, this punishment will be brought on by God.

Isa 1:4   *Ah, sinful nation, a people loaded with guilt, a brood of evildoers, children given to corruption!* <u>**They have forsaken the LORD; they have spurned the Holy One of Israel and turned their backs on him.**</u> (NIV)

Isa 51:17-23   *Awake, awake! Rise up, O Jerusalem, you who have drunk from the hand of the LORD the cup of his wrath, you who have drained to its dregs the goblet that makes men stagger.* Of all the sons she bore there was none to guide her; of all the sons she reared there was none to take her by the hand. *These double calamities have come upon you—who can comfort you?—ruin and destruction, famine and sword—who can console you?* Your sons have fainted; they lie at the head of every street, like antelope caught in a net. *They are filled with the wrath of the LORD and the rebuke of your God.* Therefore hear this, you afflicted one, made drunk, but not with wine. This is what your Sovereign LORD says, your God, who defends his people: "See, I have taken out of your hand the cup that made you stagger; from that cup, the goblet of my wrath, you will never drink again. I will put it into the hands of your tormentors, who said to you, 'Fall prostrate that we may walk over you.' And you made your back like the ground, like a street to be walked over." (NIV)

In the verses that pertain to the future destruction of the nation of Israel and the city of Jerusalem, the mention of Israel or Judah will represent the Jewish people as a whole during the Day of the Lord. The divided kingdom of Israel does not show up after Israel was established as a nation on May 14, 1948 or during the Millennium. The idea, held by some today, that the ten lost tribes of Israel can be distinguished from the two tribes of the Kingdom of Judah is highly unlikely. The dispersions of the Jewish people throughout history has made it impossible for Jews today to distinguish their original tribal origins.

Jeremiah speaks of two different times when God will come against Israel. Once to the generation of the people of Jeremiah's time and once to their children's children in the distant future.

Jer 2:9   *"Therefore I will yet bring charges against you," says the LORD, "And against your children's children I will bring charges.* (NKJ)

Something that is often overlooked is an interesting comment from Jeremiah. He was appointed to be a prophet to all the nations, not just the nation of Israel.

Jer 1:5   *"Before I formed you in the womb I knew you, before you were born I set you apart; I appointed you as a prophet to the nations."* (NIV)

EGYPT AND HER ALLIES

In the book of Daniel we find the Antichrist in his third confrontation with Egypt and her allies. This seems to correspond with the account in Jeremiah. Notice that the Antichrist will invade many countries and overwhelm them. Here the Beautiful Land is probably a reference to Israel. The Antichrist's attack on Israel will prompt Egypt's action at this time.

The Tribulation Period — The Time of Jacob's Trouble

Dan 11:40-43 — *"At the time of the end <u>the king of the South</u> will engage him in battle, and <u>the king of the North</u> will storm out against him with chariots and cavalry and a great fleet of ships. He will invade many countries and sweep through them like a flood. **He will also invade the Beautiful Land.** Many countries will fall, but Edom, Moab and the leaders of Ammon will be delivered from his hand. He will extend his power over many countries; Egypt will not escape. He will gain control of the treasures of gold and silver and all the riches of Egypt, with the Libyans and Nubians in submission.* (NIV)

Remember earlier when we quoted a scripture verse from Hebrews? It went like this; *"It is a terrifying thing to fall into the hands of the living God"* (NAS). Well the nations who have sinned against God and did not follow Him throughout history are about to find out how terrible it really is. God even has a plan.

Isa 19:12 — *Where are your wise men now? <u>Let them show you and make known what the LORD Almighty has planned against Egypt</u>.* (NIV)

Ezek 29:1-3 — *In the tenth year, in the tenth month on the twelfth day, the word of the LORD came to me: "Son of man, set your face against Pharaoh king of Egypt and prophesy against him and against all Egypt. Speak to him and say: 'This is what the Sovereign LORD says: "'I am against you, Pharaoh king of Egypt, you great monster lying among your streams. You say, "The Nile is mine; I made it for myself."* (NIV)

Egypt will be in a false state of security. Just a few years earlier they had defeated the Antichrist and now with their allies they have built up a formidable army. The king of the south believes that he can defeat the mighty armies of the Antichrist. He even has aspirations of conquering the whole world. Boy, is he in for a big surprise!

Jer 46:7-8 — *"Who is this that rises like the Nile, like rivers of surging waters? Egypt rises like the Nile, like rivers of surging waters. She says, 'I will rise and cover the earth; I will destroy cities and their people.'* (NIV)

The troops will storm out of Egypt and head north to meet the Antichrist in Israel, initially pushing his army northeast into Syria. A huge battle will ensue somewhere along the Euphrates River. Today the Euphrates River stretches through the nations of Turkey, Syria and Iraq before it dumps into the Persian Gulf. In looking at the map, this battle might take place in an area where the Euphrates River runs through the nation of Syria today.

Jer 46:9-10 — *Charge, O horses! Drive furiously, O charioteers! March on, O warriors—men of Cush and Put who carry shields, men of Lydia*

> *who draw the bow. But that day belongs to the Lord, the LORD Almighty—a day of vengeance, for vengeance on his foes. The sword will devour till it is satisfied, till it has quenched its thirst with blood. For the Lord, the LORD Almighty, will offer sacrifice in the land of the north by the River Euphrates.* (NIV)

In the very beginning it will look good for Egypt. The advance by the Egyptian army will catch the Antichrist by surprise, but Egypt has underestimated the Antichrist as he stands ready to utterly defeat Egypt and her allies; Cush (Ethiopia), Put (Libya), Lydia (Turkey), all Arabia (some of the Arab people). The people who are living in the covenant land (Israel) will have already been in the path of destruction laid down by the Antichrist.

Ezek 30:1-8 — *The word of the LORD came to me: "Son of man, prophesy and say: 'This is what the Sovereign LORD says: "'Wail and say, "Alas for that day!" For the day is near, <u>the day of the LORD is near—a day of clouds, a time of doom for the nations</u>. A sword will come against Egypt, and anguish will come upon Cush. When the slain fall in Egypt, her wealth will be carried away and her foundations torn down. Cush and Put, Lydia and all Arabia, Libya and the people of the covenant land will fall by the sword along with Egypt. "'This is what the LORD says: "'The allies of Egypt will fall and her proud strength will fail. From Migdol to Aswan they will fall by the sword within her, declares the Sovereign LORD. "'They will be desolate among desolate lands, and their cities will lie among ruined cities. Then they will know that I am the LORD, <u>when I set fire to Egypt and all her helpers are crushed</u>.* (NIV)

A bloody battle will follow by the Euphrates River, but will not last long. In both Jeremiah and Ezekiel, the Antichrist is referred to as Nebuchadnezzar king of Babylon. In past history king Nebuchadnezzar did not bring this kind of devastation to the nation of Egypt. There is a strong possibility that a scribe, as he was making a new copy of these texts, might possibly have added the name Nebuchadnezzar to the text, thinking these scripture verses were referring to past history or it could simply be a symbolic name for the Antichrist.

Jer 46:6 — *"The swift cannot flee nor the strong escape. In the north by the River Euphrates they stumble and fall.* (NIV)

Jer 46:9-15 — *Charge, O horses! Drive furiously, O charioteers! March on, O warriors—men of Cush and Put who carry shields, men of Lydia who draw the bow. <u>But that day belongs to the Lord, the LORD Almighty—a day of vengeance, for vengeance on his foes</u>. The sword will devour till it is satisfied, till it has quenched its thirst with blood. For the Lord, the LORD Almighty, will offer sacrifice in the land of the north by the River Euphrates. "Go up to Gilead and get*

The Tribulation Period — The Time of Jacob's Trouble

> *balm, O Virgin Daughter of Egypt. But you multiply remedies in vain; there is no healing for you. The nations will hear of your shame; your cries will fill the earth. One warrior will stumble over another; both will fall down together."* **This is the message the LORD spoke to Jeremiah the prophet about the coming of <u>Nebuchadnezzar king of Babylon</u> to attack Egypt:** *"Announce this in Egypt, and proclaim it in Migdol; proclaim it also in Memphis and Tahpanhes: 'Take your positions and get ready, for the sword devours those around you.' Why will your warriors be laid low? They cannot stand, for the LORD will push them down.* (NIV)

The soldiers of the Egyptian army that survive this battle hastily return to Egypt complaining about the miscalculation of the leader of Egypt concerning this attack.

Jer 46:16-19   *They will stumble repeatedly; they will fall over each other. They will say, <u>'Get up, let us go back to our own people and our native lands, away from the sword of the oppressor.'</u> There they will exclaim, 'Pharaoh king of Egypt is only a loud noise; he has missed his opportunity.' "As surely as I live," declares the King, whose name is the LORD Almighty, "one will come who is like Tabor among the mountains, like Carmel by the sea. Pack your belongings for exile, you who live in Egypt, for Memphis will be laid waste and lie in ruins without inhabitant.* (NIV)

The Antichrist and his army will be in hot pursuit as the Egyptian army flees back to Egypt. Then the destruction of the people and the land of Egypt will begin. In Jeremiah, the gadfly is the northern army and the king of Babylon is the Antichrist. In Isaiah, the cruel master is the Antichrist, the king who will defeat and rule over them. Again the Antichrist shows up as the king of Assyria as he leads the Egyptians and the Cushite's into exile. Note the mercenaries in verse twenty, could they be Jewish exiles?

Jer 46:20-26   *"Egypt is a beautiful heifer, but <u>a gadfly</u> is coming against her <u>from the north</u>. The <u>mercenaries</u> in her ranks are like fattened calves. They too will turn and flee together, they will not stand their ground, <u>for the day of disaster is coming upon them, the time for them to be punished.</u> Egypt will hiss like a fleeing serpent as the enemy advances in force; they will come against her with axes, like men who cut down trees. They will chop down her forest," declares the LORD, "dense though it be. They are more numerous than locusts, they cannot be counted.* **The Daughter of Egypt will be put to shame, handed over to the people of the north."** *The LORD Almighty, the God of Israel, says: "I am about to bring punishment on Amon God of Thebes, on Pharaoh, on Egypt and her Gods and her kings, and on those who rely on Pharaoh.* **I will hand them over**

AFTER THE RAPTURE

*to those who seek their lives, **to Nebuchadnezzar king of Babylon** **and his officers**. Later, however, Egypt will be inhabited as in times past," declares the LORD.* (NIV)

Isa 19:4-10   **I will hand the Egyptians over to the power of a cruel master, and a fierce king will rule over them,"** *declares the Lord, the LORD Almighty.* **The waters of the river will dry up, and the riverbed will be parched and dry.** *The canals will stink; the streams of Egypt will dwindle and dry up. The reeds and rushes will wither, also the plants along the Nile, at the mouth of the river.* **Every sown field along the Nile will become parched, will blow away and be no more.** *The fishermen will groan and lament, all who cast hooks into the Nile; those who throw nets on the water will pine away. Those who work with combed flax will despair, the weavers of fine linen will lose hope. The workers in cloth will be dejected, and all the wage earners will be sick at heart.* (NIV)

Isa 20:3-6   **Then the LORD said, "Just as my servant Isaiah has gone stripped and barefoot for three years, as a sign and portent against Egypt and Cush, so the king of Assyria will lead away stripped and barefoot the Egyptian captives and Cushite exiles, young and old, with buttocks bared—to Egypt's shame.** *Those who trusted in Cush and boasted in Egypt will be afraid and put to shame.* **In that day the people who live on this coast will say, 'See what has happened to those we relied on, those we fled to for help and deliverance from the king of Assyria! How then can we escape?'"** (NIV)

Ezek 30:9-19   **"'On that day messengers will go out from me in ships to frighten Cush out of her complacency. Anguish will take hold of them on the day of Egypt's doom, for it is sure to come.'" "'This is what the Sovereign LORD says: "'I will put an end to the hordes of Egypt by the hand of Nebuchadnezzar king of Babylon. He and his army—the most ruthless of nations—will be brought in to destroy the land. They will draw their swords against Egypt and fill the land with the slain. I will dry up the streams of the Nile and sell the land to evil men; by the hand of foreigners I will lay waste the land and everything in it.** *I the LORD have spoken. "'This is what the Sovereign LORD says: "'I will destroy the idols and put an end to the images in Memphis. No longer will there be a prince in Egypt, and I will spread fear throughout the land. I will lay waste Upper Egypt, set fire to Zoan and inflict punishment on Thebes. I will pour out my wrath on Pelusium, the stronghold of Egypt, and cut off the hordes of Thebes.* **I will set fire to Egypt;** *Pelusium will writhe in agony. Thebes will be taken by storm; Memphis will be in constant distress.*

The Tribulation Period — The Time of Jacob's Trouble

*The young men of Heliopolis and Bubastis will fall by the sword, and the cities themselves will go into captivity. **Dark will be the day at Tahpanhes when I break the yoke of Egypt; there her proud strength will come to an end. She will be covered with clouds, and her villages will go into captivity. So I will inflict punishment on Egypt, and they will know that I am the LORD.**'"* (NIV)

Ezek 31:10-14   *"'Therefore this is what the Sovereign LORD says: Because it towered on high, lifting its top above the thick foliage, and because it was proud of its height, **I handed it over to the ruler of the nations, for him to deal with according to its wickedness.** I cast it aside, **and the most ruthless of foreign nations cut it down and left it.** Its boughs fell on the mountains and in all the valleys; its branches lay broken in all the ravines of the land. All the nations of the earth came out from under its shade and left it. All the birds of the air settled on the fallen tree, and all the beasts of the field were among its branches. Therefore no other trees by the waters are ever to tower proudly on high, lifting their tops above the thick foliage. No other trees so well-watered are ever to reach such a height; they are all destined for death, for the earth below, among mortal men, with those who go down to the pit.* (NIV)

Ezek 32:1-8   *In the twelfth year, in the twelfth month on the first day, the word of the LORD came to me: "Son of man, **take up a lament concerning Pharaoh king of Egypt and say to him:** "'You are like a lion among the nations; you are like a monster in the seas thrashing about in your streams, churning the water with your feet and muddying the streams. "'This is what the Sovereign LORD says: "'**With a great throng of people I will cast my net over you, and they will haul you up in my net.** I will throw you on the land and hurl you on the open field. I will let all the birds of the air settle on you and all the beasts of the earth gorge themselves on you. I will spread your flesh on the mountains and fill the valleys with your remains. I will drench the land with your flowing blood all the way to the mountains, and the ravines will be filled with your flesh. When I snuff you out, I will cover the heavens and darken their stars; I will cover the sun with a cloud, and the moon will not give its light. All the shining lights in the heavens I will darken over you; I will bring darkness over your land, declares the Sovereign LORD.* (NIV)

The only weapons that can bring this kind of destruction on a nation would be nuclear weapons. Egypt will become a desolate waste for forty years. The land of Egypt will literally be set on fire. Only a nuclear explosion could dry up the Nile River. Keep an eye on the nation of Egypt, for it will play an important role during the Tribulation Period. In that seven-year period Egypt will face the Antichrist on three separate occasions. Egypt will lose the first conflict, win the second and again lose the third, which is this conflict. The fulfillment of this prophecy will come about as a result of our present day technology. In the 20th Century the world has become smart enough to destroy itself and God will allow it to be used as a weapon against sin. The Antichrist will scatter the people of Egypt throughout the countries of the world. As far as I know this kind of punishment has never occurred in the nation of Egypt. If that is true, then it must be fulfilled sometime in the future.

The people from around the world will be aghast and appalled at the horror of the destruction of Egypt. By this time the entire world will be totally aware of the true nature of the Antichrist and all the nations around the globe will fear the threat of the Antichrist.

> Ezek 32:9-10 *I will trouble the hearts of many peoples when I bring about your destruction among the nations, among lands you have not known. <u>I will cause many peoples to be appalled at you, and their kings will shudder with horror because of you when I brandish my sword before them.</u> On the day of your downfall each of them will tremble every moment for his life.* (NIV)

Egypt and her allies will go down to a horrible defeat. A mighty force will destroy them and strip the land of everything in it. It will become desolate and its people will go into exile.

> Ezek 32:11-15 *"'For this is what the Sovereign LORD says: "'<u>The sword of the king of Babylon will come against you</u>. I will cause your hordes to fall by the swords of mighty men—<u>the most ruthless of all nations</u>. They will shatter the pride of Egypt, and all her hordes will be overthrown.* I will destroy all her cattle from beside abundant waters no longer to be stirred by the foot of man or muddied by the hoofs of cattle. Then I will let her waters settle and make her streams flow like oil, declares the Sovereign LORD. *When I make Egypt desolate and strip the land of everything in it, when I strike down all who live there, <u>then they will know that I am the LORD</u>.'* (NIV)

> Ezek 29:12 *I will make the land of Egypt desolate among devastated lands, <u>and her cities will lie desolate forty years among ruined cities</u>. And I will disperse the Egyptians among the nations and scatter them through the countries.* (NIV)

The result of such devastation will bring a remnant of these people to believe in the true God. Not until an angry God punishes the sinful nations of the world, will some of the people from those nations turn to God. Here we see the Egyptians as they finally recognize Jesus as their Savior.

> Isa 19:20-22 *It will be a sign and witness to the LORD Almighty in the land of Egypt. <u>When they cry out to the LORD because of their oppressors</u>,*

> *he will send them a savior and defender, and he will rescue them. So the LORD will make himself known to the Egyptians, and in that day they will acknowledge the LORD. They will worship with sacrifices and grain offerings; they will make vows to the LORD and keep them. The LORD will strike Egypt with a plague; he will strike them and heal them. They will turn to the LORD, and he will respond to their pleas and heal them.* (NIV)

Jeremiah 46 is a message to Egypt during the Day of the Lord. It speaks about the defeat of Egypt by the Antichrist. The closing verses of this chapter are a lament to Israel, referring to the third exile of the Jewish people of which Egypt will be one of the nations where a large number of Jews flee. Israel has not lived in peace and security for a very long time and peace will not come into play until Jesus brings it to the nation and people of Israel!

Jer 46:25-28 *The LORD Almighty, the God of Israel, says: "I am about to bring punishment on Amon god of Thebes, on Pharaoh, on Egypt and her gods and her kings, and on those who rely on Pharaoh. I will hand them over to those who seek their lives, to Nebuchadnezzar king of Babylon and his officers. Later, however, Egypt will be inhabited as in times past," declares the LORD. "Do not fear, O Jacob my servant; do not be dismayed, O Israel. I will surely save you out of a distant place, your descendants from the land of their exile. Jacob will again have peace and security, and no one will make him afraid. Do not fear, O Jacob my servant, for I am with you," declares the LORD. "Though I completely destroy all the nations among which I scatter you, I will not completely destroy you. I will discipline you but only with justice; I will not let you go entirely unpunished."* (NIV)

I do not have the time or the space to list the prophecies that were fulfilled in past history, so I will limit our study to the prophecies that will be fulfilled in the future. Multitudes of prophecies were fulfilled in the history chapters of the Old Testament and some are even listed in the writings of the latter prophets. Many conflicts that took place in the past have similarities with the conflicts that will take place in the future, but the past conflicts fall far short of the devastation that the fierce anger of God will bring on the entire world. I do not believe that Isaiah 19 was fulfilled in 525 BC when the Persians attacked Egypt or that Isaiah 20 is referring to the king of Assyria when Ashurbanipal finalized his attack on Egypt by sacking Thebes in 663 BC. Jeremiah 46 was not fulfilled when Pharoah Necho II was defeated by Nebuchadnezzar in 605 BC at Carchemish by the Euphrates River. Ezekiel 29, 30 and 32, were not fulfilled in 568-567 BC when Babylon came against Egypt. Those are the opinions of some Bible historians. Although there are similarities in these conflicts of the past, there are many portions in the chapters mentioned above that were not a part of the past. As far as we know, past history has never reported these events; a time when:

1. a foreign leader (cruel master, a fierce king) has ruled the nation of Egypt (Isaiah 19:4).
2. the Nile River has been completely dried up from the effects of war (Isaiah 19:5; Ezekiel 30:12).
3. the fisherman of the Nile River lost their profession (Isaiah 19:8).
4. the Egyptian people were taken captive and scattered throughout the nations (Isaiah 20:4; Ezekiel 29:12).
5. the land of Egypt was sold to evil men and the land of Egypt and everything in it were laid waste (Ezekiel 30:12, 32:15).
6. the land of Egypt and her cities laid desolate for forty years (Ezekiel 29:12).
7. all the Jewish people (Israel) have been saved (delivered) from afar, including the return from Babylonian exile. At that time a minority of the Jewish people returned to their homeland. In the future gathering of Jewish exiles, Jesus will bring all the Jewish people back to Israel after He purges the dross (unsaved Jews) from among them. All the saved Jews will live in Israel in peace and security (Jeremiah 46:27).
8. God has completely destroyed all the nations where the Jewish people have been scattered in exile (Jeremiah 46:28).

If the most severe portions of the verses listed above have not been fulfilled, then more than likely none of the surrounding context of what is being talked about has been fulfilled. This has been a stumbling block for Bible historians for a very long time. Please read the entire blocks of scripture concerning the judgment of the nations that are found in Isaiah, Jeremiah, Ezekiel and the minor prophets to realize the future devastation that will be meted out by the Antichrist. The New International Version and The New Jerusalem Bible have some excellent subtitles in their translations. In the NIV, look for subtitles such as: *"A Prophecy Against...," "An Oracle Against ...," "A Prophecy About...," "A Message About...," and "A Lament For...."*

CUSH AND PUT

Cush and Put are both listed as allies with Egypt when the Egyptians meet the Antichrist at the Euphrates River. Both of these nations were located in the northeast section of the continent of Africa and bordered the nation of Egypt. Cush includes parts of the countries of Ethiopia and Sudan. Put, most scholars believe, is an area west of Egypt and is known as Libya today.

Ezek 30:4-9   *A sword will come against Egypt, and anguish will come upon Cush. When the slain fall in Egypt, her wealth will be carried away and her foundations torn down. Cush and Put, Lydia and all Arabia, Libya and the people of the covenant land will fall by the sword along with Egypt. "'This is what the LORD says: "'<u>The allies of Egypt will fall and her proud strength will fail.</u> From Migdol to Aswan they will fall by the sword within her, declares the Sovereign LORD. "'They will be desolate among desolate lands, and*

The Tribulation Period — The Time of Jacob's Trouble

their cities will lie among ruined cities. ***Then they will know that I am the LORD, when I set fire to Egypt and all her helpers are crushed.*** *"'On that day messengers will go out from me in ships to frighten Cush out of her complacency. Anguish will take hold of them on the day of Egypt's doom, for it is sure to come.* (NIV)

Cush (Ethiopia) seems to be stronger than the nation of Put (Libya).

Nahum 3:9   ***Cush and Egypt were her boundless strength; Put and Libya were among her allies.*** (NIV)

Isa 18:1-6   ***Woe to the land shadowed with buzzing wings, which is beyond the rivers of Ethiopia,*** *Which sends ambassadors by sea, even in vessels of reed on the waters, saying, "Go, swift messengers, to a nation tall and smooth of skin, to a people terrible from their beginning onward, a nation powerful and treading down, whose land the rivers divide." All inhabitants of the world and dwellers on the earth: when he lifts up a banner on the mountains, you see it; and when he blows a trumpet, you hear it. For so the LORD said to me, "I will take My rest, and I will look from My dwelling place like clear heat in sunshine, like a cloud of dew in the heat of harvest." For before the harvest, when the bud is perfect and the sour grape is ripening in the flower, he will both cut off the sprigs with pruning hooks and take away and cut down the branches. They will be left together for the mountain birds of prey and for the beasts of the earth; the birds of prey will summer on them, and all the beasts of the earth will winter on them.* (NKJ)

Zeph 2:12   *"**You Ethiopians also, you shall be slain by My sword**."* (NKJ)

All the nations listed so far seem to be allies with Egypt when Egypt storms north toward the nation of Israel to confront the Antichrist. The Antichrist with his mighty army had just overrun the nation of Israel and probably destroyed Jerusalem and its Temple. After the Antichrist defeats these forces he will continue his march south to the land of Egypt, where he will kill many people, take the rest of them captive and scatter them to the nations of the world. The Antichrist will destroy the land of Egypt and as a result of that it will be desolate for forty years. The Antichrist will conquer Egypt and all her allies.

Dan 11:40   *"At the time of the end the king of the South will engage him in battle, and* the king of the North *will storm out against him with chariots and cavalry and a great fleet of ships.* **He will invade many countries and sweep through them like a flood**.* (NIV)

The final portion of Ezekiel chapter thirty-two reveals some nations who will side with

AFTER THE RAPTURE

Egypt during this great conflict. They are described as daughters of the nations and would be considered as sister nations. These nations agree with Egypt at this time, but are not part of her allies. Nevertheless, it is revealed that in the end, they too will be defeated by the Antichrist and will also end up in the depths of the pit (hell).

> Ezek 32:16-21 *"This is the lament they will chant for her. <u>The daughters of the nations will chant it</u>; for Egypt and all her hordes they will chant it, declares the Sovereign LORD." In the twelfth year, on the fifteenth day of the month, the word of the LORD came to me: "Son of man, wail for the hordes of Egypt and consign to the earth below both her and the daughters of mighty nations, with those who go down to the pit. Say to them, 'Are you more favored than others? Go down and be laid among the uncircumcised.' **They will fall among those killed by the sword.** The sword is drawn; let her be dragged off with all her hordes. From within the grave the mighty leaders will say of Egypt and her allies, 'They have come down and they lie with the uncircumcised, with those killed by the sword.'* (NIV)

Reading on in this chapter will reveal the identity of more of the nations that are defeated by the Antichrist as he continues his conquest to secure the Middle East after defeating Egypt and her allies. Remember that we will use the same logic for identifying the nations here as we did when we identified the nations of the Russian Invasion. We will tell you the names of the nations that are located, at the present time, in the area the Bible refers to as *"in days gone by."* These nations will be defeated by the Antichrist and end up in hell.

ASSYRIA AND NINEVAH

The Assyrian Empire at its peak covered an area from present day western Iran to eastern Turkey. It also covered all or parts of the present day countries of Iran, Iraq, Syria, Turkey, Lebanon, Jordan, Israel and Egypt. Their destruction is discussed in Ezekiel, where we see the Assyrian army as a friend with Egypt defeated by the Antichrist. It appears that Assyria will try to defend herself, but will be easily defeated. Assyria does not participate as an ally in the Egyptian/Antichrist conflict, but secretly she favors Egypt and her allies. In the end the nations that make up ancient Assyria will be defeated by the Antichrist.

> Ezek 32:22-23 *"<u>Assyria is there with her whole army; she is surrounded by the graves of all her slain, all who have fallen by the sword.</u> Their graves are in the depths of the pit and her army lies around her grave. All who had spread terror in the land of the living are slain, fallen by the sword.* (NIV)

> Nahum 3:5-11 *"<u>I am against you</u>," declares the LORD Almighty. "<u>I will lift your skirts over your face</u>. I will show the nations your nakedness and*

The Tribulation Period — The Time of Jacob's Trouble

> *the kingdoms your shame. I will pelt you with filth, I will treat you with contempt and make you a spectacle. **All who see you will flee from you and say, 'Nineveh is in ruins—who will mourn for her?'** Where can I find anyone to comfort you?" Are you better than Thebes, situated on the Nile, with water around her? The river was her defense, the waters her wall. Cush and Egypt were her boundless strength; Put and Libya were among her allies. Yet she was taken captive and went into exile. Her infants were dashed to pieces at the head of every street. Lots were cast for her nobles, and all her great men were put in chains. You too will become drunk; you will go into hiding and seek refuge from the enemy.* (NIV)

The destruction of the landmass where Assyria existed in times past is discussed in Zephaniah. Along with it is mentioned its capital city of Ninevah. It appears that the Antichrist will head north to the area of ancient Assyria after defeating Egypt and her allies.

Zeph 2:13-15   ***He will stretch out his hand against the north and destroy Assyria, leaving Nineveh utterly desolate and dry as the desert.*** *Flocks and herds will lie down there, creatures of every kind. The desert owl and the screech owl will roost on her columns. Their calls will echo through the windows, rubble will be in the doorways, the beams of cedar will be exposed. This is the carefree city that lived in safety. She said to herself, "I am, and there is none besides me." What a ruin she has become, a lair for wild beasts! All who pass by her scoff and shake their fists.* (NIV)

Look in your Bible in Ezekiel thirty-one for more interesting reading on Assyria.

ELAM

Elam is also listed as a friend to Egypt and its present day location is in the southwestern portion of Iran just north of the Persian Gulf. The Antichrist will send the people from Elam as exiles to every nation of the world. They will be pursued until the Antichrist makes a total end of them. They will be killed by the sword and end up in the pit. After the destruction is over, when Jesus restores the earth, somehow God will restore their fortunes.

Ezek 32:24-25   *"**Elam is there**, **with all her hordes around her grave. All of them are slain, fallen by the sword.** All who had spread terror in the land of the living went down uncircumcised to the earth below. They bear their shame with those who go down to the pit. A bed is made for her among the slain, with all her hordes around her grave. **All of them are uncircumcised, killed by the sword.** Because their terror had spread in the land of the living, they bear their shame with those who go down to the pit; they are laid among the slain.* (NIV)

Jer 49:34-39   *This is the word of the LORD that came to Jeremiah the prophet concerning Elam, early in the reign of Zedekiah king of Judah: This is what the LORD Almighty says: "<u>See, I will break the bow of Elam, the mainstay of their might</u>. I will bring against Elam the four winds from the four quarters of the heavens; I will scatter them to the four winds, and there will not be a nation where Elam's exiles do not go. I will shatter Elam before their foes, before those who seek their lives; I will bring disaster upon them, even my fierce anger," declares the LORD. "<u>I will pursue them with the sword until I have made an end of them</u>. I will set my throne in Elam and destroy her king and officials," declares the LORD. "<u>Yet I will restore the fortunes of Elam in days to come</u>," declares the LORD.* (NIV)

<u>MESHECH AND TUBAL</u>

Meshech and Tubal (also a friend of Egypt), who were part of the alliance of nations who joined Magog (Russia) in the Russian Invasion of Israel, are located in the countries of Turkey, Georgia, Armenia, Azerbaijan and part of Iran. These nations did not totally recover from the Russian Invasion. Here we see their final demise.

Ezek 32:26-27   *"<u>Meshech and Tubal are there, with all their hordes around their graves</u>. All of them are uncircumcised, killed by the sword because they spread their terror in the land of the living. Do they not lie with the other uncircumcised warriors who have fallen, who went down to the grave with their weapons of war, whose swords were placed under their heads? The punishment for their sins rested on their bones, though the terror of these warriors had stalked through the land of the living.* (NIV)

<u>EDOM</u>

The history of Edom goes back a long time. Edom was the name given to Esau after he traded his birthright to his brother Jacob for a bowl of red stew. The land inhabited by the descendants of Edom include parts of Jordan and Saudi Arabia. Important cities of Edom include Sela, Bozrah and Teman. Especially remember Bozrah. Edom is also listed as being defeated by the Antichrist. In an instant, Edom will be chased from its land, never to exist again as a nation. When Jerusalem was being destroyed, Edom was crying *"Tear it down."*

Ezek 32:29   *"<u>Edom is there</u>, her kings and all her princes; despite their power, they are laid with those killed by the sword. They lie with the uncircumcised, with those who go down to the pit.* (NIV)

Jer 49:7-21   <u>*Concerning Edom*</u>*: This is what the LORD Almighty says: "Is there no longer wisdom in Teman? Has counsel perished from the*

The Tribulation Period — The Time of Jacob's Trouble

*prudent? Has their wisdom decayed? Turn and flee, hide in deep caves, you who live in Dedan, <u>for I will bring disaster on Esau at the time I punish him.</u> If grape pickers came to you, would they not leave a few grapes? If thieves came during the night, would they not steal only as much as they wanted? But I will strip Esau bare; I will uncover his hiding places, so that he cannot conceal himself. His children, relatives and neighbors will perish, and he will be no more. Leave your orphans; I will protect their lives. Your widows too can trust in me." **This is what the LORD says: "<u>If those who do not deserve to drink the cup must drink it, why should you go unpunished</u>? You will not go unpunished, but must drink it. I swear by myself," declares the LORD, "that Bozrah will become a ruin and an object of horror, of reproach and of cursing; and all its towns will be in ruins forever."** I have heard a message from the LORD: An envoy was sent to the nations to say, "Assemble yourselves to attack it! Rise up for battle!" "Now I will make you small among the nations, despised among men. The terror you inspire and the pride of your heart have deceived you, you who live in the clefts of the rocks, who occupy the heights of the hill. Though you build your nest as high as the eagle's, from there I will bring you down," declares the LORD. **"<u>Edom will become an object of horror</u>; all who pass by will be appalled and will scoff because of all its wounds.** As Sodom and Gomorrah were overthrown, along with their neighboring towns," says the LORD, "so no one will live there; no man will dwell in it. **"Like a lion coming up from Jordan's thickets to a rich pastureland, <u>I will chase Edom from its land in an instant.</u>** Who is the chosen one I will appoint for this? Who is like me and who can challenge me? And what shepherd can stand against me?" **Therefore, hear what the LORD has planned against Edom, what he has purposed against those who live in Teman: The young of the flock will be dragged away; he will completely destroy their pasture because of them. At the sound of their fall the earth will tremble; their cry will resound to the Red Sea.** (NIV)*

Ezek 25:12-14   *"This is what the Sovereign LORD says: 'Because Edom took revenge on the house of Judah and became very guilty by doing so, therefore this is what the Sovereign LORD says: I will stretch out my hand against Edom and kill its men and their animals. I will lay it waste, and from Teman to Dedan they will fall by the sword. <u>I will take vengeance on Edom by the hand of my people Israel, and they will deal with Edom in accordance with my anger and my wrath</u>; they will know my vengeance, declares the Sovereign LORD.'"* (NIV)

AFTER THE RAPTURE

Ps 137:7-8 *Remember, O LORD, what the Edomites did on the day Jerusalem fell. "<u>Tear it down</u>," they cried, "<u>tear it down to its foundations</u>!" O Daughter of Babylon, doomed to destruction, happy is he who repays you for what you have done to us—* (NIV)

Edom will be judged for their ancient hostility toward the Israelites. Mount Seir is located in Edom. All of these nations from the past are going to have to pay the price for their hostility, even if it takes a long time to accomplish this feat. This punishment on Edom will take place in the future, at the time when Israel's punishment reaches its climax.

Ezek 35:1-15 *The word of the LORD came to me: "<u>Son of man, set your face against Mount Seir; prophesy against it and say</u>: 'This is what the Sovereign LORD says: <u>I am against you</u>, <u>Mount Seir</u>, and I will stretch out my hand against you and make you a desolate waste. I will turn your towns into ruins and you will be desolate. Then you will know that I am the LORD. "'<u>Because you harbored an ancient hostility and delivered the Israelites over to the sword at the time of their calamity, the time their punishment reached its climax</u>, therefore as surely as I live, declares the Sovereign LORD, I will give you over to bloodshed and it will pursue you. Since you did not hate bloodshed, bloodshed will pursue you. I will make Mount Seir a desolate waste and cut off from it all who come and go. I will fill your mountains with the slain; those killed by the sword will fall on your hills and in your valleys and in all your ravines. <u>I will make you desolate forever; your towns will not be inhabited.</u> Then you will know that I am the LORD. "'Because you have said, "These two nations and countries will be ours and we will take possession of them," even though I the LORD was there, therefore as surely as I live, declares the Sovereign LORD, I will treat you in accordance with the anger and jealousy you showed in your hatred of them and I will make myself known among them when I judge you. **Then you will know that I the LORD have heard all the contemptible things you have said against the mountains of Israel.** You said, "They have been laid waste and have been given over to us to devour." You boasted against me and spoke against me without restraint, and I heard it. This is what the Sovereign LORD says: While the whole earth rejoices, I will make you desolate. Because you rejoiced when the inheritance of the house of Israel became desolate, that is how I will treat you. <u>You will be desolate</u>, <u>O Mount Seir, you and all of Edom. Then they will know that I am the LORD.</u>'"* (NIV)

It appears that some of the Jews will flee to the ancient nation of Edom (parts of Jordan and Saudi Arabia) when the Antichrist invades Israel. Instead of granting protection to those fleeing, it appears that they will turn the Jews over to the Antichrist to be killed.

The Tribulation Period — The Time of Jacob's Trouble

SIDON AND TYRE

These cities are from the ancient empire of the Phoenicians and are in present day Lebanon. The Sidonians are also listed as a friend of Egypt.

> Ezek 32:30 *"All the princes of the north and all the Sidonians are there; they went down with the slain in disgrace despite the terror caused by their power. They lie uncircumcised with those killed by the sword and bear their shame with those who go down to the pit.* (NIV)

Tyre and Sidon both exist on the eastern shore of the Mediterranean Sea and throughout history have been important seaports. Both cities have faced disaster in the past, but their final end will come at the hands of the Antichrist. This is ancient Phoenicia.

> Isa 23:1-18 <u>*An oracle concerning Tyre*</u>*: Wail, O ships of Tarshish! For Tyre is destroyed and left without house or harbor. From the land of Cyprus word has come to them. Be silent, you people of the island and you merchants of Sidon, whom the seafarers have enriched. On the great waters came the grain of the Shihor; the harvest of the Nile was the revenue of Tyre, and she became the marketplace of the nations. Be ashamed, O Sidon, and you, O fortress of the sea, for the sea has spoken: "I have neither been in labor nor given birth; I have neither reared sons nor brought up daughters." When word comes to Egypt, they will be in anguish at the report from Tyre. Cross over to Tarshish; wail, you people of the island. Is this your city of revelry, the old, old city, whose feet have taken her to settle in far-off lands? Who planned this against Tyre, the bestower of crowns, whose merchants are princes, whose traders are renowned in the earth?* **<u>The LORD Almighty planned it, to bring low the pride of all glory and to humble all who are renowned on the earth.</u>** *Till your land as along the Nile, O Daughter of Tarshish, for you no longer have a harbor. The LORD has stretched out his hand over the sea and made its kingdoms tremble.* **<u>He has given an order concerning Phoenicia that her fortresses be destroyed.</u>** *He said, "No more of your reveling, O Virgin Daughter of Sidon, now crushed! "Up, cross over to Cyprus; even there you will find no rest." Look at the land of the Babylonians, this people that is now of no account! The Assyrians have made it a place for desert creatures; they raised up their siege towers, they stripped its fortresses bare and turned it into a ruin. Wail, you ships of Tarshish; your fortress is destroyed! At that time Tyre will be forgotten for seventy years, the span of a king's life. But at the end of these seventy years, it will happen to Tyre as in the song of the prostitute: "Take up a harp, walk through the city, O prostitute forgotten; play the harp well, sing many a song, so that*

AFTER THE RAPTURE

> *you will be remembered." At the end of seventy years, the LORD will deal with Tyre. She will return to her hire as a prostitute and will ply her trade with all the kingdoms on the face of the earth. Yet her profit and her earnings will be set apart for the LORD; they will not be stored up or hoarded. Her profits will go to those who live before the LORD, for abundant food and fine clothes.* (NIV)

Ezek 26:1-6 *In the eleventh year, on the first day of the month, the word of the LORD came to me: "Son of man, because Tyre has said of Jerusalem, 'Aha! The gate to the nations is broken, and its doors have swung open to me; now that she lies in ruins I will prosper,' therefore this is what the Sovereign LORD says: <u>I am against you, O Tyre, and I will bring many nations against you, like the sea casting up its waves</u>. They will destroy the walls of Tyre and pull down her towers; I will scrape away her rubble and make her a bare rock. Out in the sea she will become a place to spread fishnets, for I have spoken, declares the Sovereign LORD. She will become plunder for the nations, and her settlements on the mainland will be ravaged by the sword. <u>Then they will know that I am the LORD</u>.* (NIV)

We know from the statement in verse six, *"Then they will know that I am Lord,"* that the final fulfillment of the destruction of Tyre, spoken of in Ezekiel chapters 26 through 28, is yet future. For some interesting reading, read all three of these chapters. Remember earlier we quoted from chapter twenty-eight; the king of Tyre is used symbolically as the Antichrist (verses 2-10), as Satan (verses 11-18) and again as the Antichrist/Satan personage of the last half of the Tribulation Period (verses 18-19). The New Testament makes reference to the judgment of Tyre and Sidon in Matthew 11:21-22 and also in Luke 10:13-14, at the time of their final destruction.

PHILISTINES

The Philistines occupied a small area in what is Israel today. The nation was called Philistia and was located in the southwest portion of Israel along the Mediterranean Coast. Part of this area today is known as the Gaza Strip. It was also a part of the land of Canaan. For additional reading see Jeremiah chapter forty-seven.

Isa 14:28-32 *This oracle came in the year King Ahaz died: <u>Do not rejoice, all you Philistines</u>, that the rod that struck you is broken; from the root of that snake will spring up a viper, its fruit will be a darting, venomous serpent. The poorest of the poor will find pasture, and the needy will lie down in safety. But your root I will destroy by famine; it will slay your survivors. <u>Wail, O gate! Howl, O city! Melt away, all you Philistines! A cloud of smoke comes from the north</u>, and*

The Tribulation Period — The Time of Jacob's Trouble

there is not a straggler in its ranks. What answer shall be given to the envoys of that nation? "The LORD has established Zion, and in her his afflicted people will find refuge." (NIV)

Ezek 25:15-17 ***"This is what the Sovereign LORD says: 'Because the Philistines acted in vengeance and took revenge with malice in their hearts, and with ancient hostility sought to destroy Judah, therefore this is what the Sovereign LORD says: <u>I am about to stretch out my hand against the Philistines</u>, and I will cut off the Kerethites and destroy those remaining along the coast. I will carry out great vengeance on them and punish them in my wrath. <u>Then they will know that I am the LORD</u>, when I take vengeance on them.'"*** (NIV)

Zeph 2:4-7 ***<u>Gaza will be abandoned and Ashkelon left in ruins</u>. At midday Ashdod will be emptied and Ekron uprooted. Woe to you who live by the sea, O Kerethite people; <u>the word of the LORD is against you</u>, <u>O Canaan</u>, <u>land of the Philistines</u>. "<u>I will destroy you</u>, <u>and none will be left</u>."*** *The land by the sea, where the Kerethites dwell, will be a place for shepherds and sheep pens. It will belong to the remnant of the house of Judah; there they will find pasture. In the evening they will lie down in the houses of Ashkelon. The LORD their God will care for them; he will restore their fortunes.* (NIV)

Zech 9:5-8 *Ashkelon will see it and fear; Gaza will writhe in agony, and Ekron too, for her hope will wither. Gaza will lose her king and Ashkelon will be deserted. Foreigners will occupy Ashdod, <u>and I will cut off the pride of the Philistines</u>. I will take the blood from their mouths, the forbidden food from between their teeth. Those who are left will belong to our God and become leaders in Judah, and Ekron will be like the Jebusites. But I will defend my house against marauding forces. <u>Never again will an oppressor overrun my people, for now I am keeping watch</u>.* (NIV)

MOAB

Moab was a small nation situated just east of the Dead Sea in an area that is part of the nation of Jordan. Moab was positioned between the nations of Edom on the south and Ammon on the north. Moab will trust in her deeds and her riches. Moab's destruction can be found in Isaiah 15-16, Jeremiah 48, Ezekiel 25:8-11 and Zephaniah 2:8-11.

Isa 15:1-9 *<u>An oracle concerning Moab</u>: **Ar in Moab is ruined, destroyed in a night! Kir in Moab is ruined, destroyed in a night!** Dibon goes up to its temple, to its high places to weep; Moab wails over Nebo and Medeba. Every head is shaved and every beard cut off. In the streets* *they wear sackcloth; on the roofs and in the public squares they all wail, prostrate with weeping. Heshbon and Elealeh cry out, their voices are heard all the way to Jahaz. Therefore the armed men of Moab cry out, and their hearts are faint. My heart cries out over Moab; her fugitives flee as far as Zoar, as far as Eglath Shelishiyah. They go up the way to Luhith, weeping as they go; on the road to Horonaim they lament their destruction. The waters of Nimrim are dried up and the grass is withered; the vegetation is gone and nothing green is left. So the wealth they have acquired and stored up they carry away over the Ravine of the Poplars.* ***Their outcry echoes along the border of Moab; their wailing reaches as far as Eglaim, their lamentation as far as Beer Elim. Dimon's waters are full of blood, but I will bring still more upon Dimon—a lion upon the fugitives of Moab and upon those who remain in the land.*** (NIV)

Moab's total destruction will take place during a three-year period and will culminate during the last year, with only a few survivors remaining at the end.

Isa 16:13-14 *This is the word the LORD has already spoken concerning Moab. But now the LORD says: "Within three years, as a servant bound by contract would count them, Moab's splendor and all her many people will be despised, and her survivors will be very few and feeble."* (NIV)

The land will become desolate and its cities ruined. The destroyer will be the Antichrist as he ravishes all the cities of Moab. It will become a wasteland forever. As far as history reveals, these events have never taken place in the past. Scripture clearly indicates that the nation where ancient Moab existed will be put to an end.

Jer 48:1-9 *Concerning Moab: This is what the LORD Almighty, the God of Israel, says: "Woe to Nebo, for it will be ruined. Kiriathaim will be disgraced and captured; the stronghold will be disgraced and shattered. Moab will be praised no more; in Heshbon men will plot her downfall: 'Come, let us put an end to that nation.' You too, O Madmen, will be silenced; the sword will pursue you. Listen to the cries from Horonaim, cries of great havoc and destruction. Moab will be broken; her little ones will cry out. They go up the way to Luhith, weeping bitterly as they go; on the road down to Horonaim anguished cries over the destruction are heard.* ***Flee! Run for your lives; become like a bush in the desert. Since you trust in your deeds and riches, you too will be taken captive, and Chemosh will go into exile, together with his priests and officials. The destroyer will come against every town, and not a town will escape.*** *The valley will be ruined and the plateau destroyed, because the LORD has*

The Tribulation Period — The Time of Jacob's Trouble

spoken. <u>Put salt on Moab, for she will be laid waste; her towns will become desolate, with no one to live in them.</u> (NIV)

Ezek 25:8-11 "This is what the Sovereign LORD says: 'Because Moab and Seir said, "Look, the house of Judah has become like all the other nations," therefore I will expose the flank of Moab, beginning at its frontier towns—Beth Jeshimoth, Baal Meon and Kiriathaim—the glory of that land. *I will give Moab along with the Ammonites to the people of the East as a possession, so that the Ammonites will not be remembered among the nations; <u>and I will inflict punishment on Moab. Then they will know that I am the LORD.</u>*'" (NIV)

Zeph 2:8-11 "<u>I have heard the insults of Moab and the taunts of the Ammonites, who insulted my people and made threats against their land.</u> *Therefore, as surely as I live,"* declares the LORD Almighty, the God of Israel, "<u>surely Moab will become like Sodom, the Ammonites like Gomorrah—a place of weeds and salt pits, a wasteland forever.</u> *The remnant of my people will plunder them; the survivors of my nation will inherit their land."* This is what they will get in return for their pride, for insulting and mocking the people of the LORD Almighty. *The LORD will be awesome to them when he destroys all the Gods of the land. <u>The nations on every shore will worship him, every one in its own land.</u>* (NIV)

AMMON

Ammon also falls within the confines of Jordan today. Part of their punishment will also be because of their ill-treatment of the nation of Israel. Just like Moab, they will trust in their riches and believe that no one will come after them. Ammon will become a ruin. The destruction will come when the punishment of the wicked reaches its climax. The fortunes of the Ammonites will be restored during the peaceful portion of the Day of the Lord.

Jer 49:1-6 *<u>Concerning the Ammonites</u>: This is what the LORD says: "Has Israel no sons? Has she no heirs? Why then has Molech taken possession of Gad? Why do his people live in its towns? <u>But the days are coming</u>," declares the LORD, "<u>when I will sound the battle cry against Rabbah of the Ammonites; it will become a mound of ruins, and its surrounding villages will be set on fire.</u> Then Israel will drive out those who drove her out," says the LORD. "Wail, O Heshbon, for Ai is destroyed! Cry out, O inhabitants of Rabbah! Put on sackcloth and mourn; rush here and there inside the walls, for Molech will go into exile, together with his priests and officials. Why do you boast of your valleys, boast of your valleys so fruitful? <u>O unfaithful daughter, you trust in your riches and say,</u>*

'Who will attack me?' I will bring terror on you from all those around you," declares the Lord, the LORD Almighty. "Every one of you will be driven away, and no one will gather the fugitives. "Yet afterward, I will restore the fortunes of the Ammonites," declares the LORD. (NIV)

Ezek 25:1-7 *The word of the LORD came to me: "Son of man, set your face against the Ammonites and prophesy against them. Say to them, 'Hear the word of the Sovereign LORD. This is what the Sovereign LORD says: Because you said "Aha!" over my sanctuary when it was desecrated and over the land of Israel when it was laid waste and over the people of Judah when they went into exile, therefore I am going to give you to the people of the East as a possession. They will set up their camps and pitch their tents among you; they will eat your fruit and drink your milk. I will turn Rabbah into a pasture for camels and Ammon into a resting place for sheep. Then you will know that I am the LORD. For this is what the Sovereign LORD says: Because you have clapped your hands and stamped your feet, rejoicing with all the malice of your heart against the land of Israel, therefore I will stretch out my hand against you and give you as plunder to the nations. I will cut you off from the nations and exterminate you from the countries. I will destroy you, and you will know that I am the LORD.'"* (NIV)

Ezek 21:28-32 *"And you, son of man, prophesy and say, 'This is what the Sovereign LORD says about the Ammonites and their insults: "'A sword, a sword, drawn for the slaughter, polished to consume and to flash like lightning! Despite false visions concerning you and lying divinations about you, it will be laid on the necks of the wicked who are to be slain, whose day has come, whose time of punishment has reached its climax. Return the sword to its scabbard. In the place where you were created, in the land of your ancestry, I will judge you. I will pour out my wrath upon you and breathe out my fiery anger against you; I will hand you over to brutal men, men skilled in destruction. You will be fuel for the fire, your blood will be shed in your land, you will be remembered no more; for I the LORD have spoken.'"* (NIV)

It appears that the saints (prominent people) from Edom, Ammon and Moab will escape out of the hands of the Antichrist and the onslaught that befall those nations.

Dan 11:41 *"He shall also enter the Glorious Land, and many countries shall be overthrown; but these shall escape from his hand: Edom, Moab, and the prominent people of Ammon.* (NKJ)

DAMASCUS

Damascus will include the area of Syria. Please note that at the time of this destruction, the city of Damascus will become a heap of ruins and will cease to be a city. By no stretch of the imagination should a Bible historian place the fulfillment of this prophecy as a symbolic action by a prophet when king Ahaz in 733 BC and Damascus in 732 BC were broken by the Assyrian king Tiglath-pilser III, only to cease from being independent states. Look for the Antichrist to bring this kind of devastation on Damascus. *"In that day men will look to their Maker and turn their eyes to the Holy One of Israel,"* which has not happened in the past. The destruction of Damascus will come from the raging of many nations (the Revived Roman Empire) and it will be sudden and swift. Aram is ancient Syria. Hamath and Arpad are also part of ancient Syria. They all refer to the ancient area around Damascus.

Isa 17:1-14   *<u>An oracle concerning Damascus: "See, Damascus will no longer be a city but will become a heap of ruins.</u> The cities of Aroer will be deserted and left to flocks, which will lie down, with no one to make them afraid. The fortified city will disappear from Ephraim, and royal power from Damascus; <u>the remnant of Aram</u> will be like the glory of the Israelites," declares the LORD Almighty. "In that day the glory of Jacob will fade; the fat of his body will waste away. It will be as when a reaper gathers the standing grain and harvests the grain with his arm—as when a man gleans heads of grain in the Valley of Rephaim. Yet some gleanings will remain, as when an olive tree is beaten, leaving two or three olives on the topmost branches, four or five on the fruitful boughs," declares the LORD, the God of Israel. <u>In that day men will look to their Maker and turn their eyes to the Holy One of Israel.</u> They will not look to the altars, the work of their hands, and they will have no regard for the Asherah poles and the incense altars their fingers have made. In that day their strong cities, which they left because of the Israelites, will be like places abandoned to thickets and undergrowth. And all will be desolation. You have forgotten God your Savior; you have not remembered the Rock, your fortress. Therefore, though you set out the finest plants and plant imported vines, though on the day you set them out, you make them grow, and on the morning when you plant them, you bring them to bud, yet the harvest will be as nothing in the day of disease and incurable pain. <u>Oh, the raging of many nations—they rage like the raging sea! Oh, the uproar of the peoples—they roar like the roaring of great waters!</u> Although the peoples roar like the roar of surging waters, when he rebukes them they flee far away, driven before the wind like chaff on the hills, like tumbleweed before a gale. In the evening, sudden terror! Before the morning, they are gone! This is the portion of those who loot us, the lot of those who plunder us.* (NIV)

Jer 49:23-27   *__Concerning Damascus__: "Hamath and Arpad are dismayed, for they have heard bad news. They are disheartened, troubled like the restless sea. __Damascus has become feeble, she has turned to flee and panic has gripped her; anguish and pain have seized her, pain like that of a woman in labor.__ Why has the city of renown not been abandoned, the town in which I delight? Surely, her young men will fall in the streets; all her soldiers will be silenced in that day," declares the LORD Almighty. "__I will set fire to the walls of Damascus; it will consume the fortresses of Ben-Hadad.__"* (NIV)

Zech 9:1-2   *__The word of the LORD is against the land of Hadrach and will rest upon Damascus__—for the eyes of men and all the tribes of Israel are on the LORD—and upon Hamath too, which borders on it, and upon Tyre and Sidon, though they are very skillful.* (NIV)

ARABIAN TRIBES — KEDAR AND HAZOR

These were nomadic tribes who lived in the area of the northern Arabian Desert. Today it is known as the Syrian Desert. These tribes from Kedar and Hazor probably roamed in areas of the Syrian Desert in parts of Syria, Jordan, Saudi Arabia and Iraq.

Isa 21:13-17   *__An oracle concerning Arabia__: You caravans of Dedanites, who camp in the thickets of Arabia, bring water for the thirsty; you who live in Tema, bring food for the fugitives. They flee from the sword, from the drawn sword, from the bent bow and from the heat of battle. This is what the Lord says to me: "__Within one year__, as a servant bound by contract would count it, __all the pomp of Kedar will come to an end.__ The survivors of the bowmen, the warriors of Kedar, will be few." The LORD, the God of Israel, has spoken.* (NIV)

Jer 49:28-33   *__Concerning Kedar and the kingdoms of Hazor, which Nebuchadnezzar king of Babylon attacked__: This is what the LORD says: "__Arise, and attack Kedar and destroy the people of the East.__ Their tents and their flocks will be taken; their shelters will be carried off with all their goods and camels. Men will shout to them, 'Terror on every side!' "Flee quickly away! Stay in deep caves, you who live in Hazor," declares the LORD. "__Nebuchadnezzar king of Babylon has plotted against you; he has devised a plan against you.__ "Arise and attack a nation at ease, which lives in confidence," declares the LORD, "a nation that has neither gates nor bars; its people live alone. Their camels will become plunder, and their large herds will be booty. I will scatter to the winds those who are in distant places and will bring disaster on them from every side," declares the LORD. "Hazor will become a haunt of jackals, a*

The Tribulation Period — The Time of Jacob's Trouble

> *desolate place forever. No one will live there; no man will dwell in it."* (NIV)

There are several factors that show up as you study the complete fulfillment of the prophecies of the Judgment of the Nations. Some of the nations such as Edom, Kedar, Hazor and Babylon will become desolate, never to be inhabited again. It will be the climax of the punishment for Israel and the wicked (unsaved) of the world. The Moabite towns will become desolate with no one to live in them and Damascus will become a heap of ruins and cease to exist as a city. The fortunes of some of the nations will be restored, such as the Philistines and the Ammonites. Several references are made to only a few people, or a remnant of these nations, that will survive the onslaught that is to be poured out on them, such as Moab and the warriors of Kedar. A message that is consistent concerning the small minority of people from the nations that are still around after God's punishment is completed, is that they are saved—*"Then they will know that I am the LORD."*

At no time in the past has a world leader brought on the kind of devastation and ruin of the entire world as listed above in these scripture verses. God did not include these prophecies in His word without a reason. They were put there to warn the people on earth who will be living just prior to the fulfillment of these prophecies. History written in advance. Sure God is a loving God, but He is also a God of justice.

The destruction of all of the nations on the earth, by the Antichrist and his mighty army, will take place between the destruction of the land of Israel and Babylon. God has reserved Babylon as the last nation to be destroyed. We will cover that story toward the end of this chapter. This scene that we just covered is a part of World War III, but does not include the Battle of Armageddon. It will not take place until after the Tribulation Period is finished. We will take a look at it in the next chapter. The reasons for the judgment of the nations are the same as the reasons God will judge Israel. It all boils down to punishing the unsaved people on the earth and to bring a remnant back to Him. God will purge the earth of sinful mankind. In the end, we see that the non-Jews during the Dispensation of Grace failed to bring the world to God. They failed as miserably as the chosen people of the Old Testament. God has shown grace to the unsaved for a long time, yet they have failed to return to Him.

> Isa 26:9-11   *My soul yearns for you in the night; in the morning my spirit longs for you. <u>When your judgments come upon the earth, the people of the world learn righteousness</u>. Though grace is shown to the wicked, they do not learn righteousness; even in a land of uprightness they go on doing evil and regard not the majesty of the LORD. <u>O LORD, your hand is lifted high, but they do not see it</u>. Let them see your zeal for your people and be put to shame; <u>let the fire reserved for your enemies consume them</u>.* (NIV)

God's hand is lifted high and is close to the time when He will let it come down on sinful mankind. Because of the apostasy of today, the people around the globe do not see it coming down. Read your Bible! Look at the zeal God has for His people and be shameful. The fire reserved for Israel's enemies will consume them.

AFTER THE RAPTURE

Again I want to emphasize the fact that it is hard for me to comprehend what is going to take place on this earth when the time comes for Jesus to judge mankind for its behavior. Why so much destruction and loss of life? Why is there going to be so much hardship on innocent women and children? I cannot give you a reasonable answer to these questions from a human perspective. In my heart, I believe that God had a purpose in my life. Why He chose me to write a book like this—I do not know! I have prayed about it and cried about it. If the Rapture occurs in my lifetime, many people I know will face the trials written about in this book. I do not want that to happen to them. I also know that if God wants me to write this book and I fail to do so—I will have to stand face-to-face with Jesus at the Judgment Seat of Christ and try to justify to Him why I did not complete the task given to me in this lifetime. Oh, I know I will still be saved—I love Jesus—He lives in my heart, but if I do not write this book, Jesus will want to know why I did not love Him enough to perform this task. Someone who would obey. God clearly teaches us that what was sealed up in the book of Daniel, more than 2500 years ago, will be unsealed at the time of the end. I believe that time is right at our doorstep.

Dan 12:9-10 *He replied, "<u>Go your way, Daniel, because the words are closed up and sealed until the time of the end</u>. Many will be purified, made spotless and refined, but the wicked will continue to be wicked. <u>None of the wicked will understand, but those who are wise will understand</u>.* (NIV)

Jer 23:20 *The anger of the LORD will not turn back until he fully accomplishes the purposes of his heart. <u>In days to come you will understand it clearly</u>.* (NIV)

Jer 30:24 *The fierce anger of the LORD will not turn back until he fully accomplishes the purposes of his heart. <u>In days to come you will understand this</u>.* (NIV)

At the right time, God will reveal the meaning of what Daniel was speaking about. He will use men like you and me for this purpose. We are not to question the intentions of God or shun the duties He has for us. After the discourse concerning the destruction of the nations we have just studied, Ezekiel had this to say:

Ezek 33:1-20 *The word of the LORD came to me: "Son of man, speak to your countrymen and say to them: 'When I bring the sword against a land, and the people of the land choose one of their men and make him their watchman, and he sees the sword coming against the land and blows the trumpet to warn the people, then if anyone hears the trumpet but does not take warning and the sword comes and takes his life, his blood will be on his own head. Since he heard the sound of the trumpet but did not take warning, his blood will be on his own head. If he had taken warning, he would have saved himself.* **But if**

The Tribulation Period — The Time of Jacob's Trouble

the watchman sees the sword coming and does not blow the trumpet to warn the people and the sword comes and takes the life of one of them, that man will be taken away because of his sin, but I will hold the watchman accountable for his blood.' "*Son of man, I have made you a watchman for the house of Israel; so hear the word I speak and give them warning from me. When I say to the wicked, 'O wicked man, you will surely die,' and you do not speak out to dissuade him from his ways, that wicked man will die for his sin, and I will hold you accountable for his blood. But if you do warn the wicked man to turn from his ways and he does not do so, he will die for his sin, but you will have saved yourself.* "*Son of man, say to the house of Israel, 'This is what you are saying: "Our offenses and sins weigh us down, and we are wasting away because of them. How then can we live?"* ' *Say to them,* '*As surely as I live, declares the Sovereign LORD, <u>I take no pleasure in the death of the wicked, but rather that they turn from their ways and live</u>. Turn! Turn from your evil ways! Why will you die, O house of Israel?*' "*Therefore, son of man, say to your countrymen, 'The righteousness of the righteous man will not save him when he disobeys, and the wickedness of the wicked man will not cause him to fall when he turns from it. The righteous man, if he sins, will not be allowed to live because of his former righteousness.' If I tell the righteous man that he will surely live, but then he trusts in his righteousness and does evil, none of the righteous things he has done will be remembered; he will die for the evil he has done. And if I say to the wicked man, 'You will surely die,' but he then turns away from his sin and does what is just and right—if he gives back what he took in pledge for a loan, returns what he has stolen, follows the decrees that give life, and does no evil, he will surely live; he will not die. None of the sins he has committed will be remembered against him. He has done what is just and right; he will surely live.* "*Yet your countrymen say, 'The way of the Lord is not just.' But it is their way that is not just. If a righteous man turns from his righteousness and does evil, he will die for it. And if a wicked man turns away from his wickedness and does what is just and right, he will live by doing so. Yet, O house of Israel, you say, 'The way of the Lord is not just.' <u>**But I will judge each of you according to his own ways.**</u>*" (NIV)

I know these verses were addressed to Ezekiel as a warning to the Jewish people to turn from their sins. A deeper meaning for us today is that if God uses us as a device to warn the people of our day of the unsealed meaning of prophecy, we need to carry through with that task. I hope and pray that you heed the warning presented in this book and turn to our Lord and Savior Jesus Christ. I do not know if you caught it, but in the above quotation from Ezekiel it says that God does not take pleasure in the death of the unsaved, but rather that

AFTER THE RAPTURE

they repent of their evil ways and live (be saved). Individually, you make that choice!

> Ezek 33:11   *Say to them, 'As surely as I live, declares the Sovereign LORD, **I take no pleasure in the death of the wicked, but rather that they turn from their ways and live.** Turn! Turn from your evil ways! Why will you die, O house of Israel?'* (NIV)

As we turn our focus back to the plague judgments in the book of Revelation, please remember that as the Antichrist is making his final quest to conquer the entire world, the plague judgments will be coming from heaven. It is kind of like a double wham-o. The activities of the Antichrist and the plagues from heaven are intermingled to cover the entire last 3 ½ years of the Tribulation Period. The final nation to be conquered by the Antichrist during the Tribulation Period will be Babylon and will be looked at toward the end of this chapter. All of the nations, including Israel, will be judged.

After John observed the seven angels in heaven with the seven last plagues in Revelation 15:1, he saw what looked like a sea of glass. With "sea" being symbolic for people, John was looking at those saved people who accepted Jesus during the last 3 ½ years of the Tribulation Period. Those who lost their lives and did not take the mark of the beast. They held harps and sang the song of Moses the servant of God and the song of the Lamb (Jesus). Notice here that the plagues are referred to as righteous acts! They are righteous acts because of God's righteous judgment.

> Rev 15:2-4   ***And I saw what looked like a sea of glass mixed with fire and, standing beside the sea, those who had been victorious over the beast and his image and over the number of his name.** They held harps given them by God and sang the song of Moses the servant of God and the song of the Lamb: "Great and marvelous are your deeds, Lord God Almighty. Just and true are your ways, King of the ages. Who will not fear you, O Lord, and bring glory to your name? For you alone are holy. **All nations will come and worship before you, for your righteous acts have been revealed.**"* (NIV)

BOWL JUDGMENTS

Again John looked at the Temple in heaven, where the tabernacle of the Testimony was opened. The seven angels with the last seven plagues came out of the Temple. No one was allowed to enter the Temple in heaven until the seven bowl judgments were finished. Notice here that the glory of God is in the tabernacle in heaven at this time and it is the Shekinah Glory that prevents anyone from entering the Temple. It is possible that the unsaved people on earth have so hardened their hearts toward God that no one will be saved during this last year of the Tribulation Period, thus the reason no one could enter the Temple in heaven.

> Rev 15:5-8   ***After this I looked and in heaven the temple, that is, the tabernacle of the Testimony, was opened. Out of the temple came the seven***

The Tribulation Period — The Time of Jacob's Trouble

angels with the seven plagues. They were dressed in clean, shining linen and wore golden sashes around their chests. Then one of the four living creatures gave to the seven angels seven golden bowls filled with the wrath of God, who lives for ever and ever. ***And the temple was filled with smoke from the glory of God and from his power, and no one could enter the temple until the seven plagues of the seven angels were completed.*** (NIV)

The pregnant woman is about to give birth to new life, but first she must go through the final birth pains. These birth pains will cover a period of one year and will effect the entire earth. Each judgment will probably last about two months with the last one (seventh bowl) lasting a short time. The bowl judgments are being poured out on the earth as the final assault of the Antichrist is taking place, which (except for Babylon) we just covered in the Judgment of the Nations.

The **First Bowl** judgment poured out on the earth by the first angel caused awful and painful sores to break out on the people who took the mark of the beast and worshiped his image. This last series of judgments can be referred to as "all" because they effect all or everything they are poured out upon. This happens at the same time the Antichrist begins his final rampage to conquer the world. It appears at this time that the decision to take the mark of the beast was not such a good choice to make after all, but it will be nothing compared with what is about to take place for the lost when they spend eternity in hell.

Rev 16:1-2   *Then I heard a loud voice from the temple saying to the seven angels, "Go, pour out the seven bowls of God's wrath on the earth."* ***The first angel went and poured out his bowl*** *on the land, and ugly and painful sores broke out on the people who had the mark of the beast and worshiped his image.* (NIV)

The second angel poured out the **Second Bowl** judgment on the oceans and turned its waters into blood, causing all that lived in them to die. Notice that the plagues at this juncture are still effecting "all" of the earth.

Rev 16:3   ***The second angel poured out his bowl*** *on the sea, and it turned into blood like that of a dead man, and every living thing in the sea died.* (NIV)

The third angel poured out the **Third Bowl** judgment on all the rivers and springs of water that existed on the land masses and they also turned to blood. Then the angel who has charge over the waters confirms the fact that God is just in His judgments. The Holy One has given those who have shed the blood of His saints and prophets what they deserve—blood to drink.

Rev 16:4-7   ***The third angel poured out his bowl*** *on the rivers and springs of water, and they became blood. Then I heard the angel in charge of* *the waters say: "You are just in these judgments, you who are and who were, the Holy One, because you have so judged; for they have shed the blood of your saints and prophets, and you have given them blood to drink as they deserve." And I heard the altar respond: "<u>Yes, Lord God Almighty, true and just are your judgments.</u>"* (NIV)

These judgments will come fast and furious as they effect the entire earth. As the fourth angel pours out the **Fourth Bowl,** we see the opposite effect of the fourth trumpet judgment. That judgment will bring extreme cold to the earth. Here at the fourth bowl judgment the sun will be given more power and because of that extreme heat will surround the whole earth. The heat will be so intense as to scorch the skin of the people during the daylight hours. Even with the relief of the night time hours the temperature will remain so high that it will not allow the people to get a good nights rest. Although they curse God for these judgments, they still refuse to repent and glorify Him. Note here that God has control over the plagues.

Rev 16:8-9 *<u>The fourth angel poured out his bowl</u> on the sun, and the sun was given power to scorch people with fire. They were seared by the intense heat and they cursed the name of **God, who had control over these plagues,** but they refused to repent and glorify him.* (NIV)

After the short period of intense heat of temperatures that might reach as high as 130 to 150 degrees Fahrenheit, the headquarters of the Antichrist and his kingdom will be turned into total darkness for a couple of months. This will include the whole earth because by this time the Antichrist will have control of almost the entire earth. The **Fifth Bowl** judgment will bring total darkness. Do not expect relief from heaters or air conditioners, as the destruction from the Antichrist and the plagues from God have by this time destroyed the sources for generating electricity. The body sores from the first bowl judgment on down to the blistering heat from the fourth bowl judgment will leave the inhabitants of the earth in total darkness, lying in a state of excruciating pain. So much so that they gnaw their tongues in agony. Now do they finally repent? **NO!** They still refuse to repent of their sins.

Rev 16:10-11 *<u>The fifth angel poured out his bowl</u> on the throne of the beast, and his kingdom was plunged into darkness. Men gnawed their tongues in agony and cursed the God of heaven because of their pains and their sores, <u>but they refused to repent of what they had done</u>.* (NIV)

As the sunlight returns to earth, we see the sixth angel pour out the **Sixth Bowl**. We are fast approaching the end of the Tribulation Period, more than likely only a few months away. The sixth angel poured out his bowl on the Euphrates River to dry it up. This will allow the army of some eastern countries to be able to cross over it. The Euphrates River is a huge river that existed originally in the Garden of Eden and forms a natural east-west barrier between the people of Southwest Asia. The Antichrist, Satan and the false prophet are making preparations for the final battle of this awful period of the fierce anger of God. Satan

The Tribulation Period — The Time of Jacob's Trouble

is preparing to defeat God, along with Jesus, at the battle on the great day of God Almighty —**ARMAGEDDON!**

The preparation for this final battle is begun when three evil spirits go out over the entire earth to convince the leaders of the world to assemble their armies together in a place called Armageddon. It is also known as the Valley of Megiddo and is in Israel. You might find it on a map identified as the Plain of Esdraelon. It is located just south of the Sea of Galilee between the Jordan River and the Mediterranean Sea. Upon siting this great valley, Napoleon Bonaparte made the comment, "This is the ideal battleground for all the armies of the world." I wonder if he knew he was quoting scripture? The three evil spirits will perform miraculous signs to deceive the leaders of the nations. In the end, all of the remaining military might left in the world at this time will be congregated at Armageddon.

> Rev 16:12-16 *The sixth angel poured out his bowl on the great river Euphrates, and its water was dried up to prepare the way for the kings from the East. Then I saw three evil spirits that looked like frogs; they came out of the mouth of the dragon, out of the mouth of the beast and out of the mouth of the false prophet. They are spirits of demons performing miraculous signs, and they go out to the kings of the whole world, to gather them for the battle on the great day of God Almighty. "Behold, I come like a thief! Blessed is he who stays awake and keeps his clothes with him, so that he may not go naked and be shamefully exposed." Then they gathered the kings together to the place that in Hebrew is called Armageddon.* (NIV)

In verse 15, John gives an admonition that could apply to those of us today who are awaiting the return of Jesus at the Rapture and also to those people who are alive and saved at the time just before the Battle of Armageddon and are awaiting the Glorious Return of Jesus. *"Blessed is he."*

At the same time the trumpet and bowl judgments have been pouring out on the earth, the Antichrist has been defeating almost every nation in the world, especially during the period of the bowl judgments. More than a few he left in total destruction. It has not been an easy time for the Antichrist, even with a mighty army. He has faced a lot of opposition and the world is a big place. It takes time to conquer it. After the defeat of Egypt and her allies, the Arab countries will abhor the Antichrist. In the end, the Antichrist will come against the Jews and the Arabs. One by one the Antichrist will defeat them—along with the rest of the nations—until there is only one left. Jeremiah revealed the identity of this nation.

> Jer 25:26 *and all the kings of the north, near and far, one after the other—all the kingdoms on the face of the earth. And after all of them, the king of Sheshach will drink it too.* (NIV)

Daniel records the problem the Antichrist is facing toward the end of the Tribulation Period. The Antichrist will be getting intelligence reports that the people from the east and the north are not complying with his demands and he will send his army out to destroy them.

The reason that Babylon is east and north of the Antichrist at this time is because he is in Israel. Notice that at this time he has set up his military headquarters in Israel somewhere between the Dead Sea and the Mediterranean Sea. It could possibly be in the city of Jerusalem itself or near Jerusalem. The Antichrist is in a fit of rage and fierce anger.

> Dan 11:44-45 *But reports from the east and the north will alarm him, and he will set out in a great rage to destroy and annihilate many. <u>He will pitch his royal tents between the seas at the beautiful holy mountain.</u> Yet he will come to his end, and no one will help him.* (NIV)

It is obvious that the Antichrist will still be in charge of the Revived Roman Empire when he comes against Babylon. God will reserve the final destruction of Babylon and the false religious system (prostitute) as the final nation and religion to be destroyed by the Antichrist. The *battle axe* will eventually come against every living person on the earth.

> Rev 17:16-18 *<u>The beast</u> and the ten horns you saw will hate the prostitute. They will bring her to ruin and leave her naked; they will eat her flesh and burn her with fire. <u>For God has put it into their hearts to accomplish his purpose by agreeing to give the beast their power to rule, until God's words are fulfilled.</u> The woman you saw is the great city that rules over the kings of the earth."* (NIV)

> Jer 51:20-23 *<u>Thou art my battle axe and weapons of war:</u> for with thee will I break in pieces the nations, and with thee will I destroy kingdoms; And with thee will I break in pieces the horse and his rider; and with thee will I break in pieces the chariot and his rider; With thee also will I break in pieces man and woman; and with thee will I break in pieces old and young; and with thee will I break in pieces the young man and the maid; I will also break in pieces with thee the shepherd and his flock; and with thee will I break in pieces the husbandman and his yoke of oxen; and with thee will I break in pieces captains and rulers.* (KJV)

BABYLON

The destruction of Babylon is covered quite extensively in the Bible, as was the Egyptian/Antichrist conflict. Please read Isaiah chapters 13-14, 21:1-10, 46-47; Jeremiah 50-51 and Revelation 17-18 for a full account of the conflict. As you can perceive from reading this book, I prefer to let the scriptures do the talking and let the Bible tell the story as it is placed in a chronological order. Here is what it has to tell us about the final destruction of Babylon. By the way, Babylon is not New York City, Rome or the government of America.

Babylon will be overthrown by God. After thousands of years of leading the kings of the earth astray, it is time for the vengeance of God. Never again will this false religious system exist. At this time Babylon will probably be destroyed by a nuclear explosion.

The Tribulation Period — The Time of Jacob's Trouble

Remember Sodom and Gomorrah?

> Isa 13:1-5   *An oracle concerning Babylon that Isaiah son of Amoz saw: Raise a banner on a bare hilltop, shout to them; beckon to them to enter the gates of the nobles. I have commanded my holy ones; I have summoned my warriors to carry out my wrath—those who rejoice in my triumph. Listen, a noise on the mountains, like that of a great multitude! Listen, an uproar among the kingdoms, like nations massing together! The LORD Almighty is mustering an army for war. They come from faraway lands, from the ends of the heavens—the LORD and the weapons of his wrath—to destroy the whole country.* (NIV)

> Isa 13:19-22   *Babylon, the jewel of kingdoms, the glory of the Babylonians' pride, will be overthrown by God like Sodom and Gomorrah. She will never be inhabited or lived in through all generations; no Arab will pitch his tent there, no shepherd will rest his flocks there. But desert creatures will lie there, jackals will fill her houses; there the owls will dwell, and there the wild goats will leap about. Hyenas will howl in her strongholds, jackals in her luxurious palaces. Her time is at hand, and her days will not be prolonged.* (NIV)

> Jer 50:1-4   *This is the word the LORD spoke through Jeremiah the prophet concerning Babylon and the land of the Babylonians: "Announce and proclaim among the nations, lift up a banner and proclaim it; keep nothing back, but say, 'Babylon will be captured; Bel will be put to shame, Marduk filled with terror. Her images will be put to shame and her idols filled with terror.' A nation from the north will attack her and lay waste her land. No one will live in it; both men and animals will flee away. "In those days, at that time," declares the LORD, "the people of Israel and the people of Judah together will go in tears to seek the LORD their God.* (NIV)

> Jer 51:49   *"Babylon must fall because of Israel's slain, just as the slain in all the earth have fallen because of Babylon.* (NIV)

The Antichrist is also the destroyer who will come against Babylon. God will repay Babylon in full because He is a God of retribution. Babylon is the great prostitute found in the book of Revelation.

> Jer 51:54-58   *"The sound of a cry comes from Babylon, the sound of great destruction from the land of the Babylonians. The LORD will destroy Babylon; he will silence her noisy din. Waves [of enemies] will rage like great waters; the roar of their voices will resound. A*

destroyer will come against Babylon; her warriors will be captured, and their bows will be broken. For the LORD is a God of retribution; he will repay in full. I will make her officials and wise men drunk, her governors, officers and warriors as well; they will sleep forever and not awake," declares the King, whose name is the LORD Almighty. This is what the LORD Almighty says: "Babylon's thick wall will be leveled and her high gates set on fire; the peoples exhaust themselves for nothing, the nations' labor is only fuel for the flames." (NIV)

Rev 17:1-2 *One of the seven angels who had the seven bowls came and said to me, "Come, I will show you the punishment of the great prostitute, who sits on many waters. With her the kings of the earth committed adultery and the inhabitants of the earth were intoxicated with the wine of her adulteries."* (NIV)

Rev 18:20-24 *Rejoice over her, O heaven! Rejoice, saints and apostles and prophets! God has judged her for the way she treated you.'" Then a mighty angel picked up a boulder the size of a large millstone and threw it into the sea, and said: "With such violence the great city of Babylon will be thrown down, never to be found again. The music of harpists and musicians, flute players and trumpeters, will never be heard in you again. No workman of any trade will ever be found in you again. The sound of a millstone will never be heard in you again. The light of a lamp will never shine in you again. The voice of bridegroom and bride will never be heard in you again. Your merchants were the world's great men. By your magic spell all the nations were led astray. In her was found the blood of prophets and of the saints, and of all who have been killed on the earth."* (NIV)

The Antichrist will come from the land of the north (Revived Roman Empire) and will destroy Babylon so completely that it will never be inhabited by humans again, destroyed like Sodom and Gomorrah. This will be the final act of the Antichrist as God's *battle-axe* during the Tribulation Period. The Antichrist is both the oppressor and a destroyer.

Isa 14:20-23 *...The offspring of the wicked will never be mentioned again. Prepare a place to slaughter his sons for the sins of their forefathers; they are not to rise to inherit the land and cover the earth with their cities. "I will rise up against them," declares the LORD Almighty. "I will cut off from Babylon her name and survivors, her offspring and descendants," declares the LORD. "I will turn her into a place for owls and into swampland; I will sweep her with the broom of destruction," declares the LORD Almighty.* (NIV)

The Tribulation Period — The Time of Jacob's Trouble

Isa 21:9 *Look, here comes a man in a chariot with a team of horses. And he gives back the answer: '__Babylon has fallen, has fallen__! All the images of its Gods lie shattered on the ground!'"* (NIV)

Jer 50:9-16 *__For I will stir up and bring against Babylon an alliance of great nations from the land of the north.__ They will take up their positions against her, and from the north she will be captured. Their arrows will be like skilled warriors who do not return empty-handed. So Babylonia will be plundered; all who plunder her will have their fill," declares the LORD. "Because you rejoice and are glad, you who pillage my inheritance, because you frolic like a heifer threshing grain and neigh like stallions, your mother will be greatly ashamed; she who gave you birth will be disgraced.* **She will be the least of the nations—a wilderness, a dry land, a desert. __Because of the LORD's anger she will not be inhabited but will be completely desolate.__** *All who pass Babylon will be horrified and scoff because of all her wounds. "Take up your positions around Babylon, all you who draw the bow. Shoot at her! Spare no arrows, for she has sinned against the LORD. Shout against her on every side! She surrenders, her towers fall, her walls are torn down.* **Since this is the vengeance of the LORD, take vengeance on her; do to her as she has done to others.** *Cut off from Babylon the sower, and the reaper with his sickle at harvest.* **Because of __the sword of the oppressor__ let everyone return to his own people, let everyone flee to his own land.** (NIV)

Jer 50:22-32 *The noise of battle is in the land, the noise of great destruction! How broken and shattered is the hammer of the whole earth! __How desolate is Babylon among the nations__! I set a trap for you, O Babylon, and you were caught before you knew it; you were found and captured because you opposed the LORD.* **The LORD has opened his arsenal and brought out the weapons of his wrath, for the Sovereign LORD Almighty has work to do in the land of the Babylonians.** *Come against her from afar. Break open her granaries; pile her up like heaps of grain.* **__Completely destroy her and leave her no remnant.__** *Kill all her young bulls; let them go down to the slaughter!* **Woe to them! For their day has come, the time for them to be punished.** *Listen to the fugitives and refugees from Babylon declaring in Zion how the LORD our God has taken vengeance, vengeance for his temple. "Summon archers against Babylon, all those who draw the bow. Encamp all around her; let no one escape.* **Repay her for her deeds; do to her as she has done. For she has defied the LORD, the Holy One of Israel. Therefore, her young men will fall in the streets; all her soldiers will be silenced in that day," declares the LORD. "__See, I am against you, O__** *arrogant one," declares the Lord, the LORD Almighty, "for your day has come, the time for you to be punished. The arrogant one will stumble and fall and no one will help her up; I will kindle a fire in her towns that will consume all who are around her."* (NIV)

Jer 50:41-46   *"Look! An army is coming from the north; a great nation and many kings are being stirred up from the ends of the earth. They are armed with bows and spears; they are cruel and without mercy. They sound like the roaring sea as they ride on their horses; they come like men in battle formation to attack you, O Daughter of Babylon. The king of Babylon has heard reports about them, and his hands hang limp. Anguish has gripped him, pain like that of a woman in labor. Like a lion coming up from Jordan's thickets to a rich pastureland, I will chase Babylon from its land in an instant. Who is the chosen one I will appoint for this? Who is like me and who can challenge me? And what shepherd can stand against me?" Therefore, hear what the LORD has planned against Babylon, what he has purposed against the land of the Babylonians: The young of the flock will be dragged away; he will completely destroy their pasture because of them. At the sound of Babylon's capture the earth will tremble; its cry will resound among the nations.* (NIV)

Jer 51:1-4   *This is what the LORD says: "See, I will stir up the spirit of a destroyer against Babylon and the people of Leb Kamai. I will send foreigners to Babylon to winnow her and to devastate her land; they will oppose her on every side in the day of her disaster. Let not the archer string his bow, nor let him put on his armor. Do not spare her young men; completely destroy her army. They will fall down slain in Babylon, fatally wounded in her streets.* (NIV)

Jer 51:6-9   *"Flee from Babylon! Run for your lives! Do not be destroyed because of her sins. It is time for the LORD's vengeance; he will pay her what she deserves. Babylon was a gold cup in the LORD's hand; she made the whole earth drunk. The nations drank her wine; therefore they have now gone mad. Babylon will suddenly fall and be broken. Wail over her! Get balm for her pain; perhaps she can be healed. "'We would have healed Babylon, but she cannot be healed; let us leave her and each go to his own land, for her judgment reaches to the skies, it rises as high as the clouds.'* (NIV)

Jer 51:64   *Then say, 'So will Babylon sink to rise no more because of the disaster I will bring upon her. And her people will fall.'" The words of Jeremiah end here.* (NIV)

The Tribulation Period — The Time of Jacob's Trouble

Bible historians place almost all the conflicts of the nations, we just discussed above, in the category of being fulfilled in the past and Babylon is no exception. A short review of Babylon's history will reveal that the account of their past falls remarkably short of the prophecies listed above.

Babylon was an ancient pagan empire between the Tigris and Euphrates Rivers in southern Mesopotamia. Among the earliest inhabitants of this region were the Sumerians, who the Bible refers to as the people of the "land of Shinar" (Genesis 10:10). Babylonia was a long, narrow country about 65 kilometers (40 miles) wide at its widest point and having an area of about 8,000 square miles. It was bordered on the north by Assyria, on the east by Elam, on the south and west by the Arabian desert, and on the southeast by the Persian Gulf. Around 2000 BC HAMMURABI emerged as the ruler of Babylonia. He expanded the borders of the Empire and organized its laws into a written system, referred to by scholars as the Code of Hammurabi. About this time Abraham left UR, one of the ancient cities in lower Babylon, and moved to Haran, a city in the north. Still later, Abraham left Haran and migrated into the land of Canaan under God's promise that he would become the father of a great nation (Genesis 12:1-20).

Any account of Babylonia must include Assyria, which bordered Babylon on the north. Assyria's development was often intertwined with the course of Babylonian history. [6] About 1270 BC, the Assyrian's overpowered Babylonia. For the next 700 years, Babylonia was a second-rate power as the Assyrians dominated the ancient world. Around 626 BC, Babylonian independence was finally won from Assyria by a leader named Nabopolassar. He became king of the Chaldeans and founded the neo-Babylonian or Chaldean Empire and with Cyazares, King of the Medes, he destroyed Nineveh in 612 BC. [7] Under Nabopolassars leadership, Babylonia became a great empire.

In 606 BC, Nebuchadnezzar II, the son of Nabopolassar, became ruler and reigned for 44 years. Under him Babylonia reached its greatest strength. [8] Nebuchadnezzar defeated Neco of Egypt at Carchemish in 605 BC. Now in control of all southwest Asia, Nebuchadnezzar entered his long and brilliant reign, destroying Jerusalem and making Babylon one of the most splendid of ancient cities. [9] Using the treasures which he took from other nations, Nebuchadnezzar built Babylon, the capital city of Babylonia, into one of the leading cities in the world. The famous hanging gardens of Babylon were known as one of the seven wonders of the ancient world. [10] It was at this time that Babylon was established as the third world empire listed in the book of Revelation (1st world empire listed in Daniel).

Nebuchadnezzar was succeeded by his son Amel-Marduk (561-560). The latter was assassinated, and Neriglissar (559-556) succeeded him to the throne. Neriglissar's son reigned for nine months after Neriglissar's death and was also assassinated in 556. Then a Babylonian noble, Nabonidus, came to the throne; he appointed his son Belshazzar as co-regent. During the 70 year Israelite captivity the Persians conquered Babylonia and the Babylonians passed from the world scene as a world power. Babylon remained under Persian rule from 539-331 BC. The Greek Empire defeated the Medo-Persian Empire in 331 BC and Alexander the Great controlled Babylon until 323 BC. [11]

The downfall of Babylon as a city began with the founding of Seleucia on the Tigris, in the reign of Seleucus Nicator (after 312 BC). The inhabitants of Babylon soon began to migrate to this new site, and the ruined houses and walls of the old capital ultimately became the haunt of robbers and outlaws. It is said that the walls were demolished by later (Seleucid) kings on that account, and it is not improbable that, with the walls, any houses which may have remained habitable were cleared away. [12] In 275 BC the Seleucids removed the inhabitants of Babylon to Seleucia on the Tigris River, with that event the history of Babylon ended. [13] The city of Babylon from that time on fell into a state of disrepair.

During the time of the occupation of the Arabs, under Islamic hands, from the 8th Century on, the curse of *"the hand writing on the wall"* kept the Arabs from rebuilding the ancient city of Babylon. They did remove the bricks from the old city to build houses in nearby towns. Saddam Hussein has made a modern day attempt to rebuild the city of Babylon on the ancient site of that city. The ancient nation of Babylon is now Iraq and the ancient Babylonians have never ceased existing as a people.

Most Bible historians place the fulfillment of Babylon's destruction in 539 BC, when the Persian Empire took that nation without much of a struggle. They usually place the fulfillment of the "desolate land forever" portion of the prophecy during the time the Seleucids removed the remaining inhabitants to Seleucia in 275 BC.

It is true that Babylon was selected as God's destructive agent and destroyed Jerusalem in 586 BC (Jeremiah 20:1-6). The confusing parts of Isaiah, Ezekiel and especially Jeremiah, concerning Babylon, are that these prophets are speaking about two different times when Jerusalem will be destroyed by two different foes, separated by a long period of time. The key to unlocking the secret lies in correctly separating the scriptures that pertain to each account. The final destruction of Babylon will come about when the Antichrist totally destroys it toward the end of the Tribulation Period. It will be made desolate **forever**! That prophetic event has yet to be fulfilled. When the Antichrist defeats Babylon, it will be totally destroyed and will **never** be inhabited again. This destruction will be total and final!

Jer 25:12-14   *"But when the seventy years are fulfilled, I will punish the king of Babylon and his nation, the land of the Babylonians, for their guilt," declares the LORD, "<u>and will make it desolate forever. I will bring upon that land all the things I have spoken against it, all that are written in this book and prophesied by Jeremiah against all the nations.</u> They themselves will be enslaved by many nations and great kings; I will repay them according to their deeds and the work of their hands."* (NIV)

Jer 51:24-29   *"<u>Before your eyes I will repay Babylon and all who live in Babylonia for all the wrong they have done in Zion</u>," declares the LORD. "I am against you, O destroying mountain, you who destroy the whole earth," declares the LORD. "I will stretch out my hand against you, roll you off the cliffs, and make you a burned-out mountain. No rock will be taken from you for a cornerstone, nor any stone for a foundation, <u>for you will be desolate forever</u>," declares the LORD. "Lift up a banner in the land! Blow the trumpet among the nations! Prepare the nations for battle against her; summon against her these kingdoms: Ararat, Minni and Ashkenaz.*

The Tribulation Period — The Time of Jacob's Trouble

> *Appoint a commander against her; send up horses like a swarm of locusts. Prepare the nations for battle against her—the kings of the Medes, their governors and all their officials, and all the countries they rule. **The land trembles and writhes, for the LORD's purposes against Babylon stand—to lay waste the land of Babylon so that no one will live there**.* (NIV)

There will be those who rejoice over the final demise of Babylon. Those in heaven; angels, saints, apostles and prophets will be exuberant when God carries out the purpose of His heart.

Jer 51:12 *Lift up a banner against the walls of Babylon! Reinforce the guard, station the watchmen, prepare an ambush! **The LORD will carry out his purpose, his decree against the people of Babylon**.* (NIV)

Rev 18:20 *Rejoice over her, O heaven! Rejoice, saints and apostles and prophets! **God has judged her for the way she treated you**.'"* (NIV)

Isa 46:8-13 *"Remember this, fix it in mind, take it to heart, you rebels. Remember the former things, those of long ago; I am God, and there is no other; I am God, and there is none like me. **I make known the end from the beginning, from ancient times, what is still to come**. I say: **My purpose will stand, and I will do all that I please**. From the east I summon a bird of prey; from a far-off land, a man to fulfill my purpose. What I have said, that will I bring about; what I have planned, that will I do. **Listen to me, you stubborn-hearted, you who are far from righteousness. I am bringing my righteousness near, it is not far away; and my salvation will not be delayed**. I will grant salvation to Zion, my splendor to Israel.* (NIV)

As you can see from this chapter, God will create a destroyer who will truly bring extreme havoc on the world scene. It will be, by no stretch of the imagination, the worst time of human history—past and future. A point of interest in the study of the Antichrist reveals an astonishing fact. The word "Antichrist," when it is applied to the vile person who will implode on the world scene in the near future is only mentioned one time in all the Bible.

1 John 2:18 *Dear children, **this is the last hour**; and as you have heard that **the antichrist** is coming, even now many antichrists have come. This is how we know it is **the last hour**.* (NIV)

The passage in 1 John 2:18-25, is basically teaching us that anyone who is not for Christ is against Christ—anti-Christ. However, along with that is mentioned a personage who will be a great enemy of God and a rival of Christ. *"The last hour"* here is pertaining to the last days (after Christ) as opposed to the former days (before Christ). John is telling us that those people who received this letter had already been taught that a lawless man of sin was going to come on the scene, but until he is revealed he will have many forerunners.

Throughout the Bible, God has disguised the Antichrist with various names. It is obvious that God did not intend to let the people of the world know the complete meaning of the destruction of the world, by this treacherous person, until a certain time. That time will coincide with the unsealing of the book of Daniel. God did not intend for the meaning to be understood by people before that time, because it truly did not apply to them. Not long before Jesus comes back, God will unseal Daniel's great story to those people of God who want to listen. Do you have ears to hear and eyes to see?

A summary of the destruction of the nations by the Antichrist during the final year of the Tribulation Period can be found in Jeremiah chapter twenty-five. After the destruction of the nation of Israel (Judah) and the city of Jerusalem, by the Antichrist, we have a scene where the rest of the nations seem to refuse to drink from the cup of God's wrath. God's answer to these nations is, *"You must drink it!"* Judah and Jerusalem will be punished and so will the rest of the nations. The two contributing factors for the devastation of the nations are; the Antichrist and his armies (the sword of the oppressor) and the plagues from God (the LORD'S fierce anger). This will truly be the period of the worst time of human history! The devastation and destruction will come so fast and furious that the dead will not be mourned and their bodies will be left lying everywhere as refuse on the ground.

Jer 25:27-38 *"Then tell them, 'This is what the LORD Almighty, the God of Israel, says: Drink, get drunk and vomit, and fall to rise no more because of <u>the sword</u> I will send among you.' But if they refuse to take the cup from your hand and drink, tell them, 'This is what the LORD Almighty says: <u>You must drink it</u>! See, I am beginning to bring disaster on the city that bears my Name, and will you indeed go unpunished? You will not go unpunished, <u>for I am calling down a sword upon all who live on the earth</u>, declares the LORD Almighty.' "Now prophesy all these words against them and say to them: "'The LORD will roar from on high; he will thunder from his holy dwelling and roar mightily against his land. He will shout like those who tread the grapes, shout against all who live on the earth. The tumult will resound to the ends of the earth, for the LORD will bring charges against the nations; <u>he will bring judgment on all mankind and put the wicked to the sword</u>,'" declares the LORD. This is what the LORD Almighty says: "<u>Look! Disaster is spreading from nation to nation; a mighty storm is rising from the ends of the earth.</u>" At that time those slain by the LORD will be everywhere —from one end of the earth to the other. They will not be mourned or gathered up or buried, but will be like refuse lying on the ground. Weep and wail, you shepherds; roll in the dust, you leaders of the flock. For your time to be slaughtered has come; you will fall and be shattered like fine pottery. The shepherds will have nowhere to flee, the leaders of the flock no place to escape. Hear the cry of the* *shepherds, the wailing of the leaders of the flock, for the LORD is destroying their pasture. **The peaceful meadows will be laid waste because of the fierce anger of the LORD. Like a lion he will leave his lair, and their land will become desolate because of <u>the sword of the oppressor</u> and because of <u>the LORD's fierce anger</u>.*** (NIV)

The destruction of the last large nation by the Antichrist will coincide with the seventh bowl judgment. The finale! The cup of the wine of God's wrath will have been consumed by all the nations. The Antichrist and his army are the <u>*battle-axe*</u> and <u>*club*</u> that God will use to punish and defeat the nations of the world and along with the plagues of the book of Revelation, it makes up the fierce anger of the Lord. After Jesus has finished His controversy with the nations, the face of the entire world will be strewn with dead bodies, and remember, corpses stink! Just as Babylon is being destroyed, it brings us to the last event of the Tribulation Period. After seven years of following the Antichrist's attempt to conquer the world, as the plagues of God pour down out of heaven, we come to the **Seventh Bowl.**

IT IS DONE!

Rev 16:17   *<u>The seventh angel poured out his bowl into the air</u>, and out of the temple came a loud voice from the throne, saying, "<u>It is done!</u>"* (NIV)

The defeat of Babylon is the final judgment of the Tribulation Period and will witness the worst earthquake that has ever happened on earth up to this time. The earth will probably never experience a great earthquake like this again.

Rev 16:18   *Then there came flashes of lightning, rumblings, peals of thunder and a severe earthquake. <u>No earthquake like it has ever occurred since man has been on earth</u>, <u>so tremendous was the quake</u>.* (NIV)

The effects of the earthquake will even put a final touch on the city of Babylon as it splits into three parts. All of the cities of the world will collapse. Every island will disappear and the mountains will be laid flat. The clear sign that the final battle of the Tribulation Period is against Babylon is the fact that God remembers Babylon after the earthquake destroyed her as she drank from the cup of His indignation. It also coincides with the chronological order of the destruction of the nations by the Antichrist in Jeremiah chapter twenty-five. Revelation chapter seventeen and part of eighteen are parenthetical chapters reflecting the remembrance of the destruction of Babylon. *"It is done"* is referring to the Tribulation Period. After the Tribulation Period is over the chronological order continues in Revelation chapter nineteen where it discusses the Battle of Armageddon. This battle is separate from the Babylonian conflict and the Tribulation Period. At the time of this great earthquake, hailstones that weigh around one hundred pounds each will pummel the earth. Those who are still alive at this time will curse God because of the hail.

Rev 16:19-21 *The great city split into three parts, and the cities of the nations collapsed. <u>God remembered Babylon the Great</u> and gave her the cup filled with the wine of the fury of his wrath. Every island fled away and the mountains could not be found. <u>From the sky huge hailstones of about a hundred pounds each fell upon men.</u> And they cursed God on account of the plague of hail, because the plague was so terrible.* (NIV)

God has these hailstones reserved in heaven to use for judgment at this very time.

Job 38:22-23 *"Have you entered the storehouses of the snow or seen the storehouses of the hail, which I reserve for times of trouble, for days of war and battle?* (NIV)

The judgment of the nations, during the Day of the Lord, appears to be against the people who live in the territory of the nations, cities and towns that existed in ancient times, the landmass of nations who came against God's chosen people in Old Testament times. During the Tribulation Period God will judge the people (nations) of this area for the past and present persecution of the Jewish people. It is no coincidence that the people who reside in this same territory or landmass today are against the present day nation of Israel.

After the severe earthquake is over and Babylon is defeated, there will be a great roar in heaven. It will be time for a great celebration. That roar will be the Hallelujah Chorus coming from the angels and the resurrected saints who are ready to participate in the final banquet of the wedding feast.

MARRIAGE SUPPER OF THE LAMB

Rev 19:1-3 *After this I heard what sounded like the roar of a great multitude in heaven shouting: "<u>Hallelujah</u>! Salvation and glory and power belong to our God, for true and just are his judgments. He has condemned the great prostitute who corrupted the earth by her adulteries. He has avenged on her the blood of his servants." And again they shouted: "<u>Hallelujah</u>! The smoke from her goes up for ever and ever."* (NIV)

Four statements are made in these first three verses of Revelation nineteen.

1. Salvation, glory and power belong to God.
2. His judgments are justified.
3. He has judged the false religious system (Babylon). The smoke from her goes up forever.
4. God has avenged the blood of his servants (believers).

In verse one, *"After this,"* is a reference to the final judgment of Babylon (the mother of prostitutes) discussed in Revelation 16:17 through 18:24. Jesus has finally avenged the blood of the righteous. He has destroyed the false religious system once and for all. The twenty-four elders and four living creatures join in as they shout, *"Amen, Hallelujah!"*

> Rev 19:4 **The twenty-four elders and the four living creatures fell down and worshiped God, who was seated on the throne. And they cried: "<u>Amen, Hallelujah!</u>"** (NIV)

Jesus then makes a comment: *"Praise our God."*

> Rev 19:5 **Then a voice came from the throne, saying: "Praise our God, all you his servants, you who fear him, both small and great!"** (NIV)

Again the angels and the saints express their exuberance and announce that it is time for the final banquet of the wedding celebration.

> Rev 19:6-9 *And I heard, as it were, the voice of a great multitude, as the sound of many waters and as the sound of mighty thunderings, saying, "Alleluia! For the Lord God Omnipotent reigns!"* **Let us be glad and rejoice and give Him glory, for the marriage of the Lamb has come, <u>and His wife has made herself ready</u>."** *And to her it was granted to be arrayed in fine linen, clean and bright, for the fine linen is the righteous acts of the saints.* **Then he said to me, "Write: '<u>Blessed are those who are called to the marriage supper of the Lamb!</u>'"** *And he said to me, "These are the true sayings of God."* (NKJ)

Do not confuse this event as the actual wedding of Jesus and the Church. That wedding took place more than seven years earlier, just before the start of the Tribulation Period. A verification of this, in the same verse, is the statement that *"His wife has made herself ready,"* referring to a wife and not a bride, which would mean that the wedding had already taken place. The NIV translation of *"bride"* here is incorrect, as the Greek word used here is *"gune"* and specifically means a wife or a woman.

The final wedding banquet will take place in heaven after the destruction of Babylon on earth, but before Jesus and the saints leave their heavenly chamber of Divine protection. God the Father has prepared a beautiful wedding banquet for His son Jesus and His son's young wife. The finest wine and gourmet foods will be served at this banquet. This banquet will take place in the heavenly Jerusalem. Most likely in the chamber (chupah) the young wife has occupied for the previous seven years. Only joy and celebration will be heard at this time. The Tribulation saints could possibly be present at this banquet. Scripture does not mention what part the angels will play at this banquet, but I imagine that they will be observing all that is taking place, if not participating. They might possibly be the servers. *"Blessed are those who are called to the marriage supper of the Lamb."* (NKJ)

Luke informs us that people will come from all directions to take part in this banquet.

AFTER THE RAPTURE

Some people who have not fared so well (last) during their time as humans on earth will be special guests at this banquet, while others who have fared well (first) on earth will only be guests at this time. This banquet will take place on the eve of Yom Kippur.

> Luke 13:29-30 — *People will come from east and west and north and south, <u>and will take their places at the feast in the kingdom of God.</u> Indeed there are those who are last who will be first, and first who will be last."* (NIV)

This is the same banquet that Jesus was referring to at the Last Supper. Jesus told His disciples, almost 2000 years ago, that He would not eat or drink with them any more until He eats and drinks with them again in His Kingdom. Here the Kingdom has been established in heaven before His Glorious Return, after which He will establish His Kingdom on earth.

> Luke 22:16-18 — *<u>For I tell you, I will not eat it again until it finds fulfillment in the kingdom of God.</u>" After taking the cup, he gave thanks and said, "Take this and divide it among you. <u>For I tell you I will not drink again of the fruit of the vine until the kingdom of God comes.</u>"* (NIV)

> Luke 22:28-30 — *You are those who have stood by me in my trials. And I confer on you a kingdom, just as my Father conferred one on me, <u>so that you may eat and drink at my table in my kingdom and sit on thrones</u>, judging the twelve tribes of Israel.* (NIV)

After observing the vision of the Marriage Supper of the Lamb, John is so in awe that he falls down at the feet of the angel to worship him, but John is instructed to worship God.

> Rev 19:10 — *<u>At this I fell at his feet to worship him.</u> But he said to me, "<u>Do not do it!</u> I am a fellow servant with you and with your brothers who hold to the testimony of Jesus. <u>Worship God!</u> For the testimony of Jesus is the spirit of prophecy."* (NIV)

During the last half of the Tribulation Period, or the Time of Jacob's Trouble, God will deal with the Jewish people by warfare and exile. This will be God's way of atoning for the guilt of the chosen people. Jerusalem will become an abandoned settlement for the Jewish people at this time. They are a people without understanding!

> Isa 27:7-11 — *Has [the LORD] struck her as he struck down those who struck her? Has she been killed as those were killed who killed her? <u>By warfare and exile you contend with her—with his fierce blast he drives her out, as on a day the east wind blows. By this, then, will Jacob's guilt be atoned for, and this will be the full fruitage of the removal of his sin</u>: When he makes all the altar stones to be like*

The Tribulation Period — The Time of Jacob's Trouble

> *chalk stones crushed to pieces, no Asherah poles or incense altars will be left standing. The fortified city stands desolate, an abandoned settlement, forsaken like the desert; there the calves graze, there they lie down; they strip its branches bare. When its twigs are dry, they are broken off and women come and make fires with them. <u>For this is a people without understanding; so their Maker has no compassion on them, and their Creator shows them no favor.</u>* (NIV)

We left the first 3 ½ years of the Tribulation Period with a half hour of silence. We now leave the second half of the Tribulation Period in total darkness. Imagine anyone on the earth at this time! They have just experienced the worst time of human history, the worst army of human history, the worst earthquake of human history, one hundred pound hailstones and now total darkness. The devastation is so severe that the heavenly bodies will lose their power and be deprived of their light.

Matt 24:29   *<u>Immediately after the tribulation of those days shall the sun be darkened, and the moon shall not give her light, and the stars shall fall from heaven, and the powers of the heavens shall be shaken:</u>* (KJV)

CHAPTER TWELVE

THE DAY OF VENGEANCE
THE YEAR OF THE LORD'S FAVOR

Luke 4:14-21   *Jesus returned to Galilee in the power of the Spirit, and news about him spread through the whole countryside. He taught in their synagogues, and everyone praised him. He went to Nazareth, where he had been brought up, and on the Sabbath day he went into the synagogue, as was his custom. And he stood up to read. The scroll of the prophet Isaiah was handed to him. Unrolling it, he found the place where it is written:* **"The Spirit of the Lord is on me, because he has anointed me to preach good news to the poor. <u>He has sent me to proclaim freedom for the prisoners and recovery of sight for the blind, to release the oppressed, to proclaim the year of the Lord's favor</u>."** *Then he rolled up the scroll, gave it back to the attendant and sat down. The eyes of everyone in the synagogue were fastened on him, and he began by saying to them,* **"<u>Today this scripture is fulfilled in your hearing</u>."** (NIV)

At the beginning of the public ministry of Jesus, in 27 AD, when He was thirty years old, Jesus went to the synagogue in His hometown of Nazareth and read these verses from the book of Isaiah.

Isa 61:1-2a   ***The Spirit of the Sovereign LORD is on me, because the LORD has anointed me to preach good news to the poor. <u>He has sent me to bind up the brokenhearted, to proclaim freedom for the captives and release from darkness for the prisoners, to proclaim the year of the LORD's favor</u>…*** (NIV)

At that time Jesus announced that He came to proclaim the year of the Lord's favor. His coming in the flesh to preach the message to *"Repent, for the kingdom of heaven is near,"* fulfilled the prophecy in Isaiah 61. Although the year of the Lord's favor was proclaimed by Jesus, it was not completely fulfilled because of His rejection. The reason that Jesus stopped reading the quotation from Isaiah in the middle of a sentence was because He knew of His rejection that was about to come and the delay that it would create for setting up the Kingdom Age. What was fulfilled was the proclamation of the Lord's favor and the beginning of the time of His favor for all the people of the earth, and is also known as the day of salvation.

2 Cor 6:1-2   *As God's fellow workers we urge you not to receive God's grace in vain. For he says, "In the time of my favor I heard you, and in the day of salvation I helped you."* <u>*I tell you, now is the time of God's favor, now is the day of salvation.*</u> (NIV)

The Day of Vengeance — The Year of the Lord's Favor

The time of God's favor and the day of salvation began at the first advent of Christ. The revealing of Jesus as the Son of Man began a new phase of God's plan; anyone, Jew or Gentile, who believes in His Son will be saved, but because the Jews rejected and crucified Jesus, the time to show favor to Israel as a nation was postponed.

The complete fulfillment of the year of the Lord's favor will come in the tenth year of the Day of the Lord. We know this from studying the last eight chapters of Isaiah. In these chapters we discover that *"The Redeemer will come to Zion"* and that the Jewish people will know that the Redeemer is Jesus Christ. The nation of Israel will be set up and given a double portion in their land. Jerusalem will be established and be the praise of the earth. The day of vengeance and the year of the Lord's redemption will be upon them. The year of the Lord's favor will be upon Israel.

Isa 59:20 ***"The Redeemer will come to Zion**, to those in Jacob who repent of their sins,"* declares the LORD.* (NIV)

Isa 60:16 *You will drink the milk of nations and be nursed at royal breasts. Then you will know that I, the LORD, am your Savior, your Redeemer, the Mighty One of Jacob.* (NIV)

Isa 61:7 *Instead of their shame my people will receive a double portion, and instead of disgrace they will rejoice in their inheritance; and so they will inherit a double portion in their land, and everlasting joy will be theirs.* (NIV)

Isa 62:7 *and give him no rest till he establishes Jerusalem and makes her the praise of the earth.* (NIV)

Isa 63:4 *For the day of vengeance was in my heart, and the year of my redemption has come.* (NIV)

Isa 65:17-19 *Behold, I will create new heavens and a new earth. The former things will not be remembered, nor will they come to mind. But be glad and rejoice forever in what I will create, for I will create Jerusalem to be a delight and its people a joy. I will rejoice over Jerusalem and take delight in my people; the sound of weeping and of crying will be heard in it no more.* (NIV)

The title to this chapter gives us some idea of what is about to take place after the Tribulation Period is finished. In Luke 4:19 and 2 Corinthians 6:1-2 (shown above), we are informed that the beginning of the time of God's favor and the day of salvation was at the first coming of Jesus Christ. In these next four sets of passages we learn that the year of the Lord's favor carries forward into the Kingdom Age. Take note in Psalms 102:12-13 below, that Jesus is on the throne when the Lord shows favor to the Jewish people. Also take note that this will take place at an appointed (*moed'*) or set time. It will be time for the Lord to comfort His people and to show compassion on His afflicted ones. At this future time they will have everlasting joy.

Isa 61:1-7   *The Spirit of the Sovereign LORD is on me, because the LORD has anointed me to preach good news to the poor. He has sent me to bind up the brokenhearted, to proclaim freedom for the captives and release from darkness for the prisoners, <u>**to proclaim the year of the LORD's favor and the day of vengeance of our God**</u>, to comfort all who mourn, and provide for those who grieve in Zion—to bestow on them a crown of beauty instead of ashes, the oil of gladness instead of mourning, and a garment of praise instead of a spirit of despair. They will be called oaks of righteousness, a planting of the LORD for the display of his splendor. They will rebuild the ancient ruins and restore the places long devastated; they will renew the ruined cities that have been devastated for generations. Aliens will shepherd your flocks; foreigners will work your fields and vineyards. And you will be called priests of the LORD, you will be named ministers of our God. You will feed on the wealth of nations, and in their riches you will boast. **Instead of their shame my people will receive a double portion, and instead of disgrace they will rejoice in their inheritance; and so they will inherit a double portion in their land, and everlasting joy will be theirs.*** (NIV)

Isa 63:4   *For <u>the day of vengeance</u> was in my heart, and <u>the year of my redemption</u> has come.* (NIV)

Ps 102:12-13   *But you, O LORD, sit enthroned forever; your renown endures through all generations. <u>You will arise and have compassion on Zion, for it is time to show favor to her; the appointed time has come.</u>* (NIV)

Isa 49:8-13   *This is what the LORD says: "<u>In the time of my favor I will answer you, and in the day of salvation I will help you</u>; I will keep you and will make you to be a covenant for the people, to restore the land and to reassign its desolate inheritances, to say to the captives, '<u>Come out</u>,' and to those in darkness, '<u>Be free!</u>'" "They will feed beside the roads and find pasture on every barren hill. They will neither hunger nor thirst, nor will the desert heat or the sun beat upon them. He who has compassion on them will guide them and lead them beside springs of water. I will turn all my mountains into roads, and my highways will be raised up. See, they will come from afar—some from the north, some from the west, some from the region of Aswan." **Shout for joy, O heavens; rejoice, O earth; burst into song, O mountains! For the LORD comforts his people and*

The Day of Vengeance — The Year of the Lord's Favor

will have compassion on his afflicted ones. (NIV)

For more than seven years God has brought judgment upon both Israel and the nations (wicked mankind) and started the process of purging wicked mankind from the earth. Now it is time to separate two groups of people—saved and unsaved—so Jesus can finish the process. The final judgment of mankind will not be complete until the Battle of Armageddon is fought. The Day of Vengeance will culminate with the battle on the great day of God Almighty (Armageddon). For the one-third of the Jews, who have been refined and tested, it will be the year of the Lord's favor and also Yom Kippur.

The first event to take place in heaven after the destruction of the Tribulation Period is over, will be Jesus leaving the innermost part of His room. Following Him will be His young wife leaving her chamber of Divine protection. She has occupied this chamber in heaven for the previous seven year period. With the culmination of the Tribulation Period on earth, it is time for Jesus and His young wife to exit their place of hiding and for Jesus to prepare for His journey to earth. Keep in mind that at this time the earth lies in a state of ruin and total darkness.

Joel 2:16   ***Gather the people, consecrate the assembly; bring together the elders, gather the children, those nursing at the breast. <u>Let the bridegroom leave his room and the bride her chamber.</u>*** (NIV)

Since this verse appears chronologically after the Tribulation Period is over, I believe a better rendering of this passage is to let the husband leave his innermost room and the young wife her chamber. At this point the wedding will have already taken place a little more than seven years earlier, thus making the reference to a husband and wife more accurate. The Hebrew word for groom, which is *"chathan,"* can be translated to mean a husband. Likewise, the word for bride, *"callah,"* can also be translated as a young wife. Compare this with the *Brown-Driver-Briggs' Hebrew Definition*.

In the book of Daniel, toward the end of his last chapter, a reference is made concerning two distinct periods of time. The first period of time will last for thirty days and the second period will be for forty-five days.

Dan 12:11-12   ***"From the time that the daily sacrifice is abolished and the abomination that causes desolation is set up, <u>there will be 1,290 days. Blessed is the one who waits for and reaches the end of the 1,335 days</u>.*** (NIV)

We know that these two periods of time follow the Time of Jacob's Trouble, because they are mentioned as having the calculation of their beginning at the Abomination of Desolation. If we subtract the 1,260 days of the last half of the Tribulation Period from 1,290 days, we discover the first time period will be for thirty days. Continuing, if we subtract 1,290 days from the 1,335 days, we have a forty-five-day period. So it is quite obvious that these two periods will follow the Tribulation Period. What events will take place during each of these time periods? Of all the commentaries I have read, concerning Bible prophecy, I have yet to read a good explanation for what will take place during this first seventy-five days after the Tribulation Period is completed. I can find no where else in scripture where these two periods are mentioned. Since Daniel mentions that the length of the desolation is for 1,290 days, we find the best scripture verse that confirms the fact that the battle against the Antichrist is not over at the end of the Tribulation Period. Armageddon is yet to come.

30 DAYS

The first thirty days seem to cover the first part of the name of this chapter, "The Day of Vengeance." Jesus will bring an end to the day of vengeance at the end of this 30-day period when He returns from heaven on a white horse followed by His armies. Two main events will take place during this thirty-day period as it applies to the day of vengeance. First the Battle of Armageddon will be fought and then Satan will be bound for the remaining portion of the Day of the Lord. We will discuss these two events later in this chapter. Before the Battle of Armageddon is fought, Jesus will separate the saved people from the unsaved people. This being the people who are still alive after the Tribulation Period is over so He can deal with them accordingly.

45 DAYS

The thirty-day period is followed by a forty-five-day period. This period will deal with people from the standpoint of, *"Blessed is he that waiteth,"* Since blessed can be translated as "happy," we see this group of people as happy for waiting for this forty-five-day period to take place. This group of people are the saints who died *After the Rapture* and have accepted Jesus as their personal savior. After all the wicked (unsaved) have been dealt with at the Battle of Armageddon, it will be time to move to more pleasant circumstances. If you will remember back during the first half of the Tribulation Period at the opening of the fifth seal, John saw a vision of the souls who had been slain for their belief in Jesus. They were told to wait a little longer until their full number of martyrs would be completed. This is now the time for which they were waiting to take place. They will receive their rewards and position to serve Jesus for the remainder of the Millennium. In Revelation chapter seven, we have a view of the people from all over the world who accepted Christ during the last half of the Tribulation Period. These two groups combined will be the subject of this 45-day period. It took Jesus two years to complete the first portion of the Judgment Seat of Christ, which took place in heaven. Now here at the second part of the Judgement Seat of Christ, it will take forty-five days to give those people who accepted Jesus Christ as their personal Savior *After the Rapture* and suffered severely for their faith to the point of death, their just rewards. By the time this forty-five-day period begins all of the fierce anger of the Lord will have been completed and the wicked will have been purged from the earth. Finally we have peace on earth, but what a price mankind will have to pay to bring it all about. This terrible day of vengeance will be a horrible time for all the unsaved people to have to go through, those who have been left behind at the Rapture and have not accepted Christ.

Rev 6:9-11 *When he opened the fifth seal, I saw under the altar the souls of those who had been slain because of the word of God and the testimony they had maintained. They called out in a loud voice, "How long, Sovereign Lord, holy and true, until you judge the inhabitants of the earth and avenge our blood?"* **Then each of them was given a white robe, <u>and they were told to wait a little longer</u>, until the number of their fellow servants and brothers who were to be killed as they had been was completed.** (NIV)

Rev 7:9-10 *After this I looked and there before me was a great multitude that no one could count, from every nation, tribe, people and language, standing before the throne and in front of the Lamb. They were wearing white robes and were holding palm branches in their hands. And they cried out in a loud voice: "Salvation belongs to our God, who sits on the throne, and to the Lamb."* (NIV)

The time-line below will provide you with the chronological order of the events in this chapter.

DAY OF ATONEMENT - YOM KIPPUR (1 YEAR)

9 Years			Jesus leaves His room and appears in the sky (heaven) His wife leaves her chamber Great Trumpet Gather the Elect Jesus returns to the Mount of Olives Sinai Desert Gather the Nations Harvest of the Earth			
			30 Days	45 Days	285 Days	990 Years
2	3 ½	3 ½	Jesus returns to heaven for His armies **ARMAGEDDON** Great Supper of God Satan Bound	Establish the kingdom from Jerusalem Judgment of the Tribulation Saints A Feast for All Peoples	Begin the rebuilding of heaven and earth to establish a New Heaven and New Earth	**Peace**
			2300 Days (beginning at the Abomination of Desolation)			Sanctuary Cleansed Dan 8:14
					Rebuilding the Temple begins here	
			DAY OF THE LORD (MILLENNIUM)			

<u>GLORIOUS RETURN OF CHRIST</u>

As we focus our attention in heaven, after the Tribulation Period, the Lord Jesus Christ is about to begin His Glorious Return. In the book of Acts, Peter tells us that after Jesus returned to heaven He will remain there until it is time for God to restore everything, as promised long ago through the prophets in the Old Testament. It is now that time! Jesus will return to the earth. The restoration of all things is a jubilee year for the Jewish People.

> Acts 3:18-26 *But this is how God fulfilled what he had foretold through all the prophets, saying that his Christ would suffer. Repent, then, and turn to God, so that your sins may be wiped out, that times of refreshing may come from the Lord, and that he may send the Christ, who has been appointed for you—even Jesus.* ***He must remain in heaven until the time comes for God to restore everything, as he promised long ago through his holy prophets.*** *For Moses said, 'The Lord your God will raise up for you a prophet like me from among your own people; you must listen to everything he tells you. Anyone who does not listen to him will be completely cut off from among his people.' "Indeed, all the prophets from Samuel on, as many as have spoken, have foretold these days. And you are heirs of the prophets and of the covenant God made with your fathers. He said to Abraham, 'Through your offspring all peoples on earth will be blessed.' When God raised up his servant, he sent him first to you to bless you by turning each of you from your wicked ways."* (NIV)

The word, "jubilee," comes from the Hebrew word *yowbel*, which means to be jubilant and to exalt. It signifies a call to joy, liberation and the beginning of the year for doing justice and loving mercy. The 50th year was a special year in which to proclaim liberty throughout all the land. Specifically, individuals who had incurred debts and had sold themselves as slaves or servants to others were released from their debts and were set at liberty. Since all land belonged to God (Leviticus 25:23), land could not be sold, but could be lost to another for reason of debt. In the Year of Jubilee such land was returned to the families to whom it was originally given. The Jubilee Year also had a leveling effect on Israel's culture. It gave everyone a chance to start over—socially and economically. [1]

Thus the Jubilee Year became one of freedom and grace for all suffering, bringing not only redemption to the captive and deliverance from want to the poor, but also release to the whole congregation of the Lord from the sore labor of the earth, representing the time of refreshing that the Lord provides for His people. For in this year every kind of oppression was to cease and every member of the covenant people to find his redeemer in the Lord, who brought him back to his possessions and family. [2] It was a part of the Divine plan looking forward to the salvation of mankind. In the Year of Jubilee the great future era of Yahweh's favor is foreshadowed and shall be ushered into all those that labor and are heavy laden, by Him who was anointed by the spirit of the Lord Yahweh. [3]

The Glorious Return of Jesus is difficult to figure out chronologically, until you realize that Jesus returning on a white horse in Revelation chapter nineteen is not the same event as His appearing in the sky (heaven) in Matthew chapter twenty-four. Since the event in Matthew precedes the event in Revelation by thirty days, we will look at it first.

The Day of Vengeance — The Year of the Lord's Favor

Matt 24:29 *"**Immediately after the distress of those days**" 'the sun will be darkened, and the moon will not give its light; the stars will fall from the sky, and the heavenly bodies will be shaken.'* (NIV)

Immediately after or "at once," following the Tribulation Period, it will be totally dark on the earth. There will not even be a glimmer of light from the moon or even one star. It will be pitch black. It appears at this time that most of the people left from all the nations from around the world will be in the area of the Middle East, although there will still be some people scattered all around the globe. We pick up the scene in Joel as Jesus and His young wife step out of their respective areas.

Joel 2:16 *Gather the people, consecrate the assembly; bring together the elders, gather the children, those nursing at the breast. **Let the bridegroom leave his room and the bride her chamber.*** (NIV)

In this scene we observe Jesus leaving the innermost part of His room, followed by His young wife leaving her chamber (Chupah) of Divine protection. With the culmination of the Tribulation Period on earth and the Marriage Supper of the Lamb in heaven, it is time for Jesus and His young wife to exit their respective places and for Jesus to prepare for His journey to earth. As Jesus leaves His room, He immediately appears in heaven.

As Jesus suddenly appears in the sky, out of the darkness from the earth, the light of His glory will shine all the way to the earth as if someone turned on a light switch. Scripture compares the event with a bolt of lightning when it flashes. The only difference here is that this light will remain shining as Jesus appears in heaven. The Greek word for "sign" in Matthew 24:30 below, can be an indication of some event performed ceremonially or supernaturally, an unusual occurrence or something transcending the common course of nature. This word can be translated as a miracle or a wonder. Can you imagine this event taking place after the period of the worst time of human history has just ended? A time when the earth has been demolished and the heavens have disappeared. The people on earth will mourn as a flash of light bolts across the sky, when suddenly Jesus appears in all His splendor in heaven. Jesus will be in the midst of the clouds with His radiant glory shining toward the earth. He will appear just like God did at Mount Sinai. As Jesus begins His descent toward earth, He will appear in all His great glory, heading to the Mount of Olives.

Matt 24:27 *"**For just as the lightning comes from the east, and flashes even to the west**, so shall the coming of the Son of Man be.* (NAS)

Matt 24:30 *"At that time the sign of the Son of Man will appear in the sky, and all the nations of the earth will mourn. They will see the Son of Man coming on the clouds of the sky, with power and great glory.* (NIV)

Rev 1:7 ***Look, he is coming with the clouds, and every eye will see him**, even those who pierced him; and all the peoples of the earth will mourn because of him. So shall it be! Amen.* (NIV)

AFTER THE RAPTURE

At this time it appears that Jesus will return to earth without the saints. They will remain in heaven while Jesus returns to earth with His angels. He has a purpose for the angels. When Jesus comes in His Father's glory (shining with radiance), Jesus will be concerned with all the people who have been left behind *After the Rapture* and are still alive. It will be time to separate those people who know Him as God from those people who know Him not.

> Matt 16:27 *__For the Son of Man is going to come in his Father's glory with his angels__, and then he will reward each person according to what he has done.* (NIV)

> Matt 25:31 *"__When the Son of Man comes in his glory, and all the angels with him__, he will sit on his throne in heavenly glory.* (NIV)

The angel (messenger) in Revelation 18:1 is Jesus. As Jesus begins His descent, His first action will be to remember Babylon by shouting the victory over her.

> Rev 18:1-3 *After this I saw another __angel__ coming down from heaven. __He had great authority, and the earth was illuminated by his splendor. With a mighty voice he shouted: "Fallen! Fallen is Babylon the Great__! She has become a home for demons and a haunt for every evil spirit, a haunt for every unclean and detestable bird. For all the nations have drunk the maddening wine of her adulteries. The kings of the earth committed adultery with her, and the merchants of the earth grew rich from her excessive luxuries."* (NIV)

Babylon has received a double portion of destruction for her sinful activities throughout the centuries. The only other nation mentioned to receive a double portion of punishment is Israel. God has remembered her crimes as He mixes her a double portion from her own cup.

> Rev 18:4-8 *Then I heard another voice from heaven say: "Come out of her, my people, so that you will not share in her sins, so that you will not receive any of her plagues; for her sins are piled up to heaven, __and God has remembered her crimes__. Give back to her as she has given; pay her back double for what she has done. __Mix her a double portion from her own cup__. Give her as much torture and grief as the glory and luxury she gave herself. In her heart she boasts, 'I sit as queen; I am not a widow, and I will never mourn.' Therefore in one day her plagues will overtake her: death, mourning and famine. She will be consumed by fire, for mighty is the Lord God who judges her.* (NIV)

Her destruction will come quickly. John refers to the complete destruction of Babylon as transpiring in one hour, probably meaning a very short period of time. It appears that the Antichrist used nuclear weapons to destroy Babylon. The merchants who traded with her during the Tribulation Period cried and mourned over her destruction.

> Rev 18:9-19 *"When the kings of the earth who committed adultery with her and shared her luxury see the smoke of her burning, they will weep and mourn over her. Terrified at her torment, they will stand far off and cry: "'<u>Woe! Woe, O great city, O Babylon, city of power! In one hour your doom has come</u>!' "The merchants of the earth will weep and mourn over her because no one buys their cargoes any more—cargoes of gold, silver, precious stones and pearls; fine linen, purple, silk and scarlet cloth; every sort of citron wood, and articles of every kind made of ivory, costly wood, bronze, iron and marble; cargoes of cinnamon and spice, of incense, myrrh and frankincense, of wine and olive oil, of fine flour and wheat; cattle and sheep; horses and carriages; and bodies and souls of men. "They will say, 'The fruit you longed for is gone from you. All your riches and splendor have vanished, never to be recovered.' The merchants who sold these things and gained their wealth from her will stand far off, terrified at her torment. They will weep and mourn and cry out: "'Woe! Woe, O great city, dressed in fine linen, purple and scarlet, and glittering with gold, precious stones and pearls!* **In one hour such great wealth has been brought to ruin!'** *"Every sea captain, and all who travel by ship, the sailors, and all who earn their living from the sea, will stand far off.* **When they see the smoke of her burning, they will exclaim, 'Was there ever a city like this great city?'** *They will throw dust on their heads, and with weeping and mourning cry out: "'Woe! Woe, O great city, where all who had ships on the sea became rich through her wealth!* **In <u>one hour</u> she has been brought to ruin!** (NIV)

GREAT TRUMPET

As Jesus continues His descent with power and majestic glory, He will command His angels to gather the elect from wherever they are scattered. The elect, of course, being the Jewish people. This great trumpet will be a jubilee for the Jewish people. During a jubilee year, slaves are to be released and land is to be returned to its original owner. That is exactly what will take place at this time when the Jews are returned to the land of Israel.

> Matt 24:31 *And he will send his angels with <u>a loud trumpet call</u>, and they will gather his elect from the four winds, from one end of the heavens to the other.* (NIV)

> Isa 27:12-13 *In that day the LORD will thresh from the flowing Euphrates to the Wadi of Egypt, and you, O Israelites, will be gathered up one by one. And in that day <u>a great trumpet will sound</u>. Those who were*

perishing in Assyria and those who were exiled in Egypt will come and worship the LORD on the holy mountain in Jerusalem. (NIV)

The loud trumpet call here is, once again, the voice of Jesus (a loud shout) sounding like a trumpet and not an actual trumpet blast. Notice here that this call will be a great or loud sound. This distinguishes it from the last trumpet call (shout) at the Rapture. At the last trumpet sound only those who knew Jesus personally heard His call, whereas at the great trumpet call, it will be extremely loud and everyone who remains on the earth will hear His words and know what He is saying. The reason the people on the earth mourn at this time is because most of them are lost souls, but you might say that since the people on earth have not faced physical death they can, at this time, believe in Jesus for salvation. It appears that by the time the Tribulation Period is over every person living on earth will have made their decision for eternity. Remember back to the time that the mark of the beast was established? Since most of the people at this time will have taken the mark and worshiped Satan and the Antichrist, their fate will be sealed. Because the people have made a covenant with death, most of them at this time will have believed the **BIG LIE!**

2 Thes 2:9-12 *The coming of the lawless one will be in accordance with the work of Satan displayed in all kinds of counterfeit miracles, signs and wonders, and in every sort of evil that deceives those who are perishing.* **They perish because they refused to love the truth and so be saved. For this reason God sends them a powerful delusion so that <u>they will believe the lie</u> and so that all will be condemned who have not believed the truth but have delighted in wickedness.** (NIV)

Isa 28:14-15 **Therefore hear the word of the LORD, you scoffers who rule this people in Jerusalem. You boast, "We have entered into a covenant with death, with the grave we have made an agreement. When an overwhelming scourge sweeps by, it cannot touch us, for <u>we have made a lie our refuge and falsehood our hiding place</u>."** (NIV)

The immediate task at hand for Jesus will be to separate the saved people from the unsaved people, so He can deal with them accordingly. The saved will be those who will be left on earth to live in their fleshly bodies for the remainder of the Day of the Lord. They will be the people who will repopulate the earth for the peaceful portion of the Millennium. The unsaved will participate in the Battle of Armageddon that will be coming up for them shortly. Before this battle is fought Jesus and the Antichrist will be preparing for war! Jesus will return to heaven after the separation process is completed, before He returns to earth to finish what He started seven years earlier at the beginning of the Tribulation Period, which is to purge the earth of all the unsaved people.

GATHER THE ELECT

Before we move on, I would like to remind you of a principle that God follows concerning Jews and Gentiles (non-Jews). Although God does not show favoritism over the individual people He has created, He does at times deal differently with them as nations. Individually, whether we are Jewish or not, we will all answer to God for our own actions. Yet nationally the Jews are held and judged more accountable because of their promise *"to obey God"* and to have been given *"a chosen people"* status. Their degree of punishment, with the exception of Babylon, and reward are double compared to the rest of the nations. The lineage of the Messiah (Jesus) even funneled through the Jews. When Jesus arrived He preached the gospel of the kingdom to the Jews. Paul, the apostle to the Gentiles, was instructed to first take the message of the *"good news"* to the Jews and then to the Gentiles. That same principle will be followed during the judgment portion of the Day of the Lord.

> Rom 2:5-11   *But because of your stubbornness and your unrepentant heart, you are storing up wrath against yourself for the day of God's wrath, when his righteous judgment will be revealed. God "will give to each person according to what he has done." To those who by persistence in doing good seek glory, honor and immortality, he will give eternal life. But for those who are self-seeking and who reject the truth and follow evil, there will be wrath and anger. There will be trouble and distress for every human being who does evil: first for the Jew, then for the Gentile; but glory, honor and peace for everyone who does good: first for the Jew, then for the Gentile. For God does not show favoritism.* (NIV)

As Jesus continues His descent to earth with the clouds He will arrive at the very spot He left from some 2000 years earlier. That very act fulfills a promise Jesus made to those people who were watching Him ascend into heaven at that time.

> Acts 1:1-12   *In my former book, Theophilus, I wrote about all that Jesus began to do and to teach until the day he was taken up to heaven, after giving instructions through the Holy Spirit to the apostles he had chosen. After his suffering, he showed himself to these men and gave many convincing proofs that he was alive. He appeared to them over a period of forty days and spoke about the kingdom of God. On one occasion, while he was eating with them, he gave them this command: "Do not leave Jerusalem, but wait for the gift my Father promised, which you have heard me speak about. For John baptized with water, but in a few days you will be baptized with the Holy Spirit." So when they met together, they asked him, "Lord, are you at this time going to restore the kingdom to Israel?" He said to them: "It is not for you to know the times or dates the Father has set by his own authority. But you will receive power when the Holy Spirit comes on you; and you will be my witnesses in Jerusalem, and in all Judea and Samaria, and to the ends of the earth." After he said this, he was taken up before their very eyes, and a cloud hid him from*

their sight. They were looking intently up into the sky as he was going, when suddenly two men dressed in white stood beside them. "Men of Galilee," they said, "why do you stand here looking into the sky? <u>This same Jesus, who has been taken from you into heaven, will come back in the same way you have seen him go into heaven.</u>" Then they returned to Jerusalem from the hill called <u>the Mount of Olives, a Sabbath day's walk from the city.</u> (NIV)

    As Jesus arrives on the Mount of Olives, it appears that He will be coming from the east toward the west, just like the sun rises and sets every day. As Jesus touches the Mount of Olives, He will continue walking down the mountain, past the Garden of Gethsemane (where He drank from the cup of iniquity), cross over the Kidron Valley and walk up the east slope of the Temple Mount and pass through the East Gate, or the Lions Gate, to the top of Mount Moriah. Once He arrives at this location, where the previous Temple existed in Jewish history, Jesus will set up a temporary sanctuary with His throne (this could possibly be a throne from heaven that He brings with Him – Matthew 25:31). What a victory! Instead of entering Jerusalem meekly, He will come in majesty and great glory. The Lions Gate is the location where Jesus entered Jerusalem at His triumphal entry almost 2000 years ago. The Mount of Olives is a favorite burial site for pious Jews, since according to Jewish tradition the Messiah will enter the Mount to awaken the dead. It is also believed, by Jewish tradition, that the Messiah will enter the area of the Temple Mount through the East Gate.

    At the same time this is taking place the angels will be out gathering the elect from around the world. The Jewish sages refer to this time as the return of the exiles (*galah*).

Isa 27:12-13   *In that day the LORD will thresh from the flowing Euphrates to the Wadi of Egypt, and <u>you, O Israelites, will be gathered up one by one</u>. And in that day <u>a great trumpet will sound</u>. Those who were perishing in Assyria and those who were exiled in Egypt will come and worship the LORD on the holy mountain in Jerusalem.* (NIV)

Matt 24:31   *And he will send his angels with <u>a loud trumpet call, and they will gather his elect from the four winds, from one end of the heavens to the other</u>.* (NIV)

Deut 30:1-4   *When all these blessings and curses I have set before you come upon you and you take them to heart wherever the LORD your God disperses you among the nations, <u>and when you and your children return to the LORD your God and obey him with all your heart and with all your soul</u> according to everything I command you today, then the LORD your God will restore your fortunes and have compassion on you and <u>gather you again from all the nations where he scattered you</u>. Even if you have been banished to the most distant land under the heavens, <u>from there the LORD your God will gather you and bring you back</u>.* (NIV)

The Day of Vengeance — The Year of the Lord's Favor

Isa 43:1-7 *But now, this is what the LORD says—he who created you, O Jacob, he who formed you, O Israel: "Fear not, for I have redeemed you; I have summoned you by name; you are mine. When you pass through the waters, I will be with you; and when you pass through the rivers, they will not sweep over you. When you walk through the fire, you will not be burned; the flames will not set you ablaze. For I am the LORD, your God, the Holy One of Israel, your Savior; I give Egypt for your ransom, Cush and Seba in your stead. Since you are precious and honored in my sight, and because I love you, I will give men in exchange for you, and people in exchange for your life. Do not be afraid, for I am with you; **I will bring your children from the east and gather you from the west. I will say to the north, 'Give them up!' and to the south, 'Do not hold them back.' Bring my sons from afar and my daughters from the ends of the earth—everyone who is called by my name, whom I created for my glory, whom I formed and made.** (NIV)*

Isa 54:7-8 *"For a brief moment I abandoned you, **but with deep compassion I will bring you back**. In a surge of anger I hid my face from you for a moment, but with everlasting kindness I will have compassion on you," says the LORD your Redeemer.* (NIV)

Ps 147:1-3 *Praise the LORD. How good it is to sing praises to our God, how pleasant and fitting to praise him! The LORD builds up Jerusalem; **he gathers the exiles of Israel**. He heals the brokenhearted and binds up their wounds.* (NIV)

It needs to be noted here that the shout from Jesus, sounding like a great trumpet, will signify and announce to the Jewish people the beginning of Yom Kippur, also known as the Day of Atonement. It will also be a year of the Jubilee (thus the trumpet sound on Yom Kippur), the Day of Atonement that the Jewish people have been anticipating for centuries will finally arrive. The Jewish people will be scattered all over the world during the Time of Jacob's Trouble and when it is over they will be gathered one by one and taken to a place in the Sinai Desert like sheep in a pen. The King who passes before them will be Jesus.

Micah 2:12-13 *"**I will surely gather all of you, O Jacob; I will surely bring together the remnant of Israel.** I will bring them together like sheep in a pen, like a flock in its pasture; the place will throng with people. One who breaks open the way will go up before them; they will break through the gate and go out. **Their king will pass through before them, the LORD at their head.**"* (NIV)

It does not specify a mode of transportation used by the angels to transport the Jews to the designated place located in the Sinai Desert where Jesus will separate the saved from the

AFTER THE RAPTURE

unsaved. My guess is that they will use chariots guided by horses. It is obvious that these horses and chariots are different from those that exist here on earth. It is some sort of supernatural form of transportation used by the angels. Angels are more than likely using this means of transportation, even as you read this book, but they are invisible to the human eye.

For those of you who have doubts concerning the angels in heaven with chariots, we only need to turn to 2 Kings to confirm this from an account of Elisha, a prophet of God. In this account the king of Aram was trying to capture Elisha, because he was telling the king of Israel the very thoughts he was thinking. As the king of Aram sent his troops to Dothan, an accomplice of Elisha became frightened when the troops surrounded the city. Elisha admonishes his friend not to be afraid because those who were with them (the invisible horde of angels) were greater then the armies of king Aram. Elisha then prayed for the Lord to open the eyes of his friend so he would be allowed to view the army of God to comfort him. After his eyes were opened, he could see the hills around them as they were full of angels with horses and chariots of fire. What an awesome sight that must have been.

2 Kings 6:8-23   *Now the king of Aram was at war with Israel. After conferring with his officers, he said, "I will set up my camp in such and such a place." The man of God sent word to the king of Israel: "Beware of passing that place, because the Arameans are going down there." So the king of Israel checked on the place indicated by the man of God. Time and again Elisha warned the king, so that he was on his guard in such places. This enraged the king of Aram. He summoned his officers and demanded of them, "Will you not tell me which of us is on the side of the king of Israel?" "None of us, my lord the king," said one of his officers, "but Elisha, the prophet who is in Israel, tells the king of Israel the very words you speak in your bedroom." "Go, find out where he is," the king ordered, "so I can send men and capture him." The report came back: "He is in Dothan." Then he sent horses and chariots and a strong force there. They went by night and surrounded the city.* **When the servant of the man of God got up and went out early the next morning, an army with horses and chariots had surrounded the city. "Oh, my lord, what shall we do?" the servant asked. "Don't be afraid," the prophet answered. "Those who are with us are more than those who are with them." And Elisha prayed, "O LORD, open his eyes so he may see." Then the LORD opened the servant's eyes, and he looked and saw the hills full of horses and chariots of fire all around Elisha.** *As the enemy came down toward him, Elisha prayed to the LORD, "Strike these people with blindness." So he struck them with blindness, as Elisha had asked. Elisha told them, "This is not the road and this is not the city. Follow me, and I will lead you to the man you are looking for." And he led them to Samaria. After they entered the city, Elisha said, "LORD, open the eyes of these men so they can see." Then the LORD opened their eyes and they looked, and there they*

were, inside Samaria. When the king of Israel saw them, he asked Elisha, "Shall I kill them, my father? Shall I kill them?" "Do not kill them," he answered. "Would you kill men you have captured with your own sword or bow? Set food and water before them so that they may eat and drink and then go back to their master." So he prepared a great feast for them, and after they had finished eating and drinking, he sent them away, and they returned to their master. So the bands from Aram stopped raiding Israel's territory. (NIV)

Elijah the prophet was also transported to heaven in a chariot. We also see this event in 2 Kings.

2 Kings 2:9-11 *When they had crossed, Elijah said to Elisha, "Tell me, what can I do for you before I am taken from you?" "Let me inherit a double portion of your spirit," Elisha replied. "You have asked a difficult thing," Elijah said, "yet if you see me when I am taken from you, it will be yours—otherwise not."* **As they were walking along and talking together, <u>suddenly a chariot of fire and horses of fire appeared and separated the two of them</u>, <u>and Elijah went up to heaven in a whirlwind.</u>** (NIV)

We are told in Ezekiel that the elect (Jews) will be gathered to the desert of the nations to be confronted by Jesus, face-to-face, for judgment. In order to see the entire story we need to look at verses 1 through 44 of Ezekiel chapter 20, which is basically a short story of Jewish history.

Ezek 20:1-44 *In the seventh year, in the fifth month on the tenth day, some of the elders of Israel came to inquire of the LORD, and they sat down in front of me. Then the word of the LORD came to me: "Son of man, speak to the elders of Israel and say to them, 'This is what the Sovereign LORD says: Have you come to inquire of me? As surely as I live, I will not let you inquire of me, declares the Sovereign LORD.' "Will you judge them? Will you judge them, son of man? Then confront them with the detestable practices of their fathers and say to them: 'This is what the Sovereign LORD says: On the day I chose Israel, I swore with uplifted hand to the descendants of the house of Jacob and revealed myself to them in Egypt. With uplifted hand I said to them, "I am the LORD your God." On that day I swore to them that I would bring them out of Egypt into a land I had searched out for them, a land flowing with milk and honey, the most beautiful of all lands. And I said to them, "Each of you, get rid of the vile images you have set your eyes on, and do not defile yourselves with the idols of Egypt. I am the LORD your God." "'But they rebelled against me and would not listen to me; they did not get rid of the vile images they had set their eyes on, nor did they forsake the idols of Egypt. So I said I would pour out my wrath on them and spend my anger against them in Egypt. But for the sake of my name I did what would keep it from being profaned in the eyes of the nations they lived among and in whose sight I had revealed myself to the Israelites by bringing them out of Egypt. Therefore I led them out of Egypt and brought them into the desert. I gave them my decrees and made known to them my laws, for the man who obeys them will live by them. Also I gave them my Sabbaths as a sign between us, so they would know that I the LORD made them holy. "'Yet the people of Israel rebelled against me in the desert. They did not follow my decrees but rejected my laws—although the man who obeys them will live by them—and they utterly desecrated my Sabbaths. So I said I would pour out my wrath on them and destroy them in the desert. But for the sake of my name I did what would keep it from being profaned in the eyes of the nations in whose sight I had brought them out. Also with uplifted hand I swore to them in the desert that I would not bring them into the land I had given them—a land flowing with milk and honey, most beautiful of all lands—because they rejected my laws and did not follow my decrees and desecrated my Sabbaths. For their hearts were devoted to their idols. Yet I looked on them with pity and did not destroy them or put an end to them in the desert. I said to their children in the desert, "Do not follow the statutes of your fathers or keep their laws or defile yourselves with their idols. I am the LORD your God; follow my decrees and be careful to keep my laws. Keep my Sabbaths holy, that they may be a sign between us. Then you will know that I am the LORD your God." "'But the children rebelled against me: They did not follow my decrees, they were not careful to keep my laws—although the man who obeys them will live by them—and they desecrated my Sabbaths. So I said I would pour out my wrath on them and spend my anger against them in the desert. But I withheld my hand, and for the sake of my name I did what would keep it from being profaned in the eyes of the nations in whose sight I had brought them out. Also with uplifted hand I swore to them in the desert that I would disperse them among the nations and scatter them through the countries, because they had not obeyed my laws but had rejected my decrees and desecrated my Sabbaths, and their eyes [lusted] after their fathers' idols. I also gave them over to statutes that were not good and laws they could not live by; I let them become defiled through their gifts—the sacrifice of every firstborn—that I might fill them with horror so they would know that I am the LORD.' "Therefore, son of man, speak to the people of Israel and say to them, 'This is what the Sovereign LORD says: In this also your fathers blasphemed me by forsaking me: When I brought them into the land I had sworn to give them and they saw any high hill or any leafy tree, there they offered their sacrifices, made offerings that provoked me to anger, presented their fragrant incense and poured out their drink offerings. Then I said to them: What is this high place you go to?"' (It is called Bamah to this day.) "Therefore say to the house of Israel: 'This is what the Sovereign LORD says: Will you defile yourselves the way your fathers did and lust after their vile images? When you offer your gifts—the sacrifice of your sons in the fire—you continue to defile yourselves with all your idols to this day. Am I to let you inquire of me, O house of Israel? As surely as I live, declares the Sovereign LORD, I will not let you inquire of me. "'You say, "We want to be like the nations, like the peoples of the world, who serve wood and stone." But what you have in mind will never happen. As surely as I live, declares the Sovereign LORD,* **I will rule over you with a mighty hand and an outstretched arm and with outpoured wrath. I will bring you from the nations and gather you from the countries where you have been scattered—with a mighty hand and an outstretched arm and with outpoured wrath. I will bring you into the desert of the nations and there, face to face, I will execute judgment upon you.** *As I judged your fathers in the desert of the land of Egypt, so I will judge you, declares the Sovereign LORD.* **I will take note of you as you pass under my rod, and I will bring you into the bond of the covenant. I will purge you of those who revolt and rebel against me.** *Although I will bring them out of the land where they are living, yet they will not enter the land of Israel. Then you will know that I am the LORD. "'As for you, O house of* **Israel, this is what the Sovereign LORD says: Go and serve your idols, every one of you! But afterward you will surely listen to me and no longer profane my holy name with your gifts and idols. For on my holy mountain, the high mountain of Israel, declares the Sovereign LORD,** *there in the land the entire house of Israel will serve me, and there I will accept them.* *There I will require your offerings and your choice gifts, along with all your holy sacrifices. I will accept you as fragrant incense* **when I bring you out from the nations and gather you from the countries where you have been scattered,** *and I will show myself holy among you in the sight of the nations.* **Then you will know that I am the LORD, when I bring you into the land of Israel, the land I had sworn with uplifted hand to give to your fathers.** *There you will remember your conduct and all the actions by which you have defiled yourselves, and you will loathe yourselves for all the evil you have done.* **You will know that I am the LORD, when I deal with you for my name's sake and not according to your evil ways and your corrupt practices,** *O house of*

Israel, declares the Sovereign LORD.'" (NIV)

Here we see the prophet Ezekiel, in Babylon, in the early years of the Israelite captivity in 591 BC. While there he envisioned the fall and restoration of the Jews. The fall was the destruction of Jerusalem and the Temple in 586 BC. Since Ezekiel was a prophet from God, some of the elders approached him to ask him about God's intention for the Jewish people. God begins His discourse—through Ezekiel—with His choice of the Jews as the chosen people. He promised to deliver them out of Egypt, but they rebelled against God. Then God led them out of Egypt and gave them His decrees, laws and feasts. They rebelled again in the desert in Sinai and worshiped a golden calf. That generation was not allowed to enter the land flowing with milk and honey. Each time they rebelled God warned them to return to Him. When God allowed the children of the Sinai generation to enter Canaan and take it for their homeland, they also rebelled against God. This time as their punishment the Jews would be scattered and disbursed to all the nations of the world. This was accomplished in part by the Babylonians in Judah in 586 BC. A second scattering of the Jews took place in 70 AD and 135 AD, when the Romans dispelled the Jewish revolts against their protectorate. The third scattering of the Jewish people will take place during the Tribulation Period. The Jews throughout their existence have failed God by worshiping false idols. Their plea was that they wanted to be like the other nations of the world. In verse 33, Ezekiel reveals the judgment from God during the last half of the Tribulation Period—the Time of Jacob's Trouble. After that, it is stated that God will gather the Jews from the nations where they were scattered and bring them back to the desert of the nations (presumably the Sinai Desert). At this time Jesus will confront each Jew face-to-face to separate the believing Jews from the non believing Jews. We can now turn to Ezekiel chapter 34 for the scene of this judgment. The shepherds of Israel, spoken of here, are the religious leaders of the people. In the end, one shepherd (Jesus), my servant David, will be their prince (leader).

Ezek 34:1-24   *The word of the LORD came to me: "Son of man, prophesy against the shepherds of Israel; prophesy and say to them: 'This is what the Sovereign LORD says: Woe to the shepherds of Israel who only take care of themselves! Should not shepherds take care of the flock? You eat the curds, clothe yourselves with the wool and slaughter the choice animals, but you do not take care of the flock. You have not strengthened the weak or healed the sick or bound up the injured. You have not brought back the strays or searched for the lost. You have ruled them harshly and brutally. So they were scattered because there was no shepherd, and when they were scattered they became food for all the wild animals. My sheep wandered over all the mountains and on every high hill. They were scattered over the whole earth, and no one searched or looked for them. "'Therefore, you shepherds, hear the word of the LORD: As surely as I live, declares the Sovereign LORD, because my flock lacks a shepherd and so has been plundered and has become food for all the wild animals, and because my shepherds did not search for my flock but cared for*

The Day of Vengeance — The Year of the Lord's Favor

themselves rather than for my flock, therefore, O shepherds, hear the word of the LORD: This is what the Sovereign LORD says: I am against the shepherds and will hold them accountable for my flock. I will remove them from tending the flock so that the shepherds can no longer feed themselves. I will rescue my flock from their mouths, and it will no longer be food for them. **"'For this is what the Sovereign LORD says: I myself will search for my sheep and look after them. As a shepherd looks after his scattered flock when he is with them, so will I look after my sheep. <u>I will rescue them from all the places where they were scattered on a day of clouds and darkness. I will bring them out from the nations and gather them from the countries, and I will bring them into their own land.</u>** *I will pasture them on the mountains of Israel, in the ravines and in all the settlements in the land. I will tend them in a good pasture, and the mountain heights of Israel will be their grazing land. There they will lie down in good grazing land, and there they will feed in a rich pasture on the mountains of Israel. I myself will tend my sheep and have them lie down, declares the Sovereign LORD. I will search for the lost and bring back the strays.* **I will bind up the injured and strengthen the weak, but the sleek and the strong I will destroy. I will shepherd the flock with justice. "'As for you, <u>my flock</u>, this is what the Sovereign LORD says: <u>I will judge between one sheep and another, and between rams and goats.</u>** *Is it not enough for you to feed on the good pasture? Must you also trample the rest of your pasture with your feet? Is it not enough for you to drink clear water? Must you also muddy the rest with your feet? Must my flock feed on what you have trampled and drink what you have muddied with your feet? "'Therefore this is what the Sovereign LORD says to them:* **See, I myself will judge between the fat sheep and the lean sheep.** *Because you shove with flank and shoulder, butting all the weak sheep with your horns until you have driven them away, I will save my flock, and they will no longer be plundered.* **I will judge between one sheep and another. <u>I will place over them one shepherd, my servant David</u>, and he will tend them; he will tend them and be their shepherd. I the LORD will be their God, <u>and my servant David will be prince among them.</u> I the LORD have spoken.** (NIV)

Here we have a scene where God rebukes the religious leaders of the nation and the people of Israel throughout their history and especially during the Time of Jacob's Trouble. The religious leaders of Israel have been a big disappointment and have led their people astray in the past—see their rebuke by Jesus—and also in the future during the Tribulation Period. They flee from the persecution of the Antichrist instead of helping the people. Because they do not have a holy religious leader at this time the people of Israel will be scattered all over the world on the day of clouds and darkness (Tribulation Period). The religious leaders who fled will be held accountable when Jesus gathers them from the nations at the sound of the great trumpet. At that time Jesus will separate the sheep, rams and goats, meaning He will separate the believing (saved) and unbelieving (unsaved) Jews who have been gathered in the Sinai Desert. Do not confuse this with the separation of the sheep and goats of the nations in Matthew twenty-five. The Jews who believe in Jesus as the Messiah will follow Him into the Millennium, while the unbelieving Jews will die in Jerusalem at the Battle of Armageddon. See Ezekiel's account of this destruction of the unsaved Jews, below. The Jewish believers will be one-third of the Jews who will pass under the rod of God's fierce anger. The unsaved Jews will melt in the fiery furnace of Armageddon. God has placed His servant David (Jesus) over the Jews during the Day of the Lord.

Ezek 22:17-22   *Then the word of the LORD came to me: "Son of man, the house of Israel has become dross to me; all of them are the copper, tin, iron and lead left inside a furnace. They are but the dross of silver. Therefore this is what the Sovereign LORD says: 'Because you have all become dross, I will gather you into Jerusalem. As men gather silver, copper, iron, lead and tin into a furnace to melt it with a fiery blast, so will I gather you in my anger and my wrath and put you inside the city and melt you. I will gather you and I will blow on you with my fiery wrath, and you will be melted inside her. As silver is melted in a furnace, so you will be melted inside her, and you will know that I the LORD have poured out my wrath upon you.'"* (NIV)

In 1405 BC, as the Israelites were about to cross over the Jordan River and enter the promised land, they were told that in later days they would return to the Lord and obey Him.

Deut 4:25-31   *After you have had children and grandchildren and have lived in the land a long time—if you then become corrupt and make any kind of idol, doing evil in the eyes of the LORD your God and provoking him to anger, I call heaven and earth as witnesses against you this day that you will quickly perish from the land that you are crossing the Jordan to possess. You will not live there long but will certainly be destroyed. The LORD will scatter you among the peoples, and only a few of you will survive among the nations to which the LORD will drive you. There you will worship man-made Gods of wood and stone, which cannot see or hear or eat or smell. But if from there you seek the LORD your God, you will find him if you look for him with all your heart and with all your soul. **When you are in distress and all these things have happened to you, then in later days you will return to the LORD your God and obey him. For the LORD your God is a merciful God; he will not abandon or destroy you or forget the covenant with your forefathers, which he confirmed to them by oath.*** (NIV)

The Day of Vengeance — The Year of the Lord's Favor

God said that when all Israel acknowledges Jesus as their Messiah, He will forgive their sins and from that day forward they would know that He is Lord.

Jer 31:34 *No longer will a man teach his neighbor, or a man his brother, saying, **'Know the LORD,' because they will all know me**, from the least of them to the greatest," declares the LORD. **"For I will forgive their wickedness and will remember their sins no more.**"* (NIV)

Ezek 39:22 ***From that day forward the house of Israel will know that I am the LORD their God.*** (NIV)

Zech 9:16-17 ***The LORD their God will save them on that day as the flock of his people. They will sparkle in his land like jewels in a crown. How attractive and beautiful they will be! Grain will make the young men thrive, and new wine the young women.*** (NIV)

In the book of Hosea, there is a stark reminder to the Jews that they would be without a king and without sacrifice for a long time. Hosea is making a reference to the time after the Shekinah Glory (Israel's King) leaves the Temple in Jerusalem in 593 BC and returns to heaven. After the sinful people have been purged, the King will return and the Israelites will turn back and seek their God (glory of the Lord) and David their king (Jesus). All this will take place in the last days, more specifically the last day or Day of the Lord. After the last half of the Tribulation Period is over and the Battle of Armageddon is fought, the Jewish people will come trembling to God and His blessings. This will take place after Jesus rebuilds the Millennial Temple and the glory of the Lord returns to dwell among His people.

Hosea 3:4-5 ***For the Israelites will live many days without king or prince, without sacrifice or sacred stones, without ephod or idol. Afterward the Israelites will return and seek the LORD their God and David their king. They will come trembling to the LORD and to his blessings in the last days.*** (NIV)

As we mentioned earlier, this is the fulfillment of Paul's prophecy in his letter to the Romans.

Rom 11:25-27 *I do not want you to be ignorant of this mystery, brothers, so that you may not be conceited: Israel has experienced a hardening in part until the full number of the Gentiles has come in. **And so all Israel will be saved**, as it is written: "The deliverer will come from Zion; he will turn Godlessness away from Jacob. **And this is my covenant with them when I take away their sins.**"* (NIV)

In Romans chapter nine it is revealed that Jesus is *"a stone"* that causes men to stumble. This includes both the Jews and the Gentiles. Please do not stumble into eternity!

AFTER THE RAPTURE

Rom 9:22-33
What if God, choosing to show his wrath and make his power known, bore with great patience the objects of his wrath—prepared for destruction? What if he did this to make the riches of his glory known to the objects of his mercy, whom he prepared in advance for glory—even us, whom he also called, not only from the Jews but also from the Gentiles? As he says in Hosea: "I will call them 'my people' who are not my people; and I will call her 'my loved one' who is not my loved one," and, "It will happen that in the very place where it was said to them, 'You are not my people,' they will be called 'sons of the living God.'" Isaiah cries out concerning Israel: "Though the number of the Israelites be like the sand by the sea, <u>only the remnant will be saved.</u> For the Lord will carry out his sentence on earth with speed and finality." *It is just as Isaiah said previously: "Unless the Lord Almighty had left us descendants, we would have become like Sodom, we would have been like Gomorrah." What then shall we say? That the Gentiles, who did not pursue righteousness, have obtained it, a righteousness that is by faith; but Israel, who pursued a law of righteousness, has not attained it. Why not? Because they pursued it not by faith but as if it were by works. They stumbled over the <u>"stumbling stone."</u> As it is written: "<u>See, I lay in Zion a stone that causes men to stumble and a rock that makes them fall, and the one who trusts in him will never be put to shame.</u>"* (NIV)

After the separation of the Jews is completed in the Sinai Desert, Jesus will return to His sanctuary in Jerusalem. In Psalms 68, below, it could be showing the scene right after the Jews have stood before Jesus face-to-face in the Sinai Desert and this very scene when He is headed back to Jerusalem to His sanctuary. From this Psalm it could be possible to conclude that the Jews, who rejected Jesus and were just judged (separated) in the desert, will be taken to Jerusalem by the angels in their chariots. Instead of wandering through the desert for forty years as an unsaved nation, this time they will be escorted into the holy city in chariots. The unsaved Jews will be added to the population of Jerusalem and become a part of the Battle of Armageddon. The saved Jews will also be taken to Jerusalem in the angel's chariots, but their fate will be different.

Ps 68:15-17
The mountains of Bashan are majestic mountains; rugged are the mountains of Bashan. Why gaze in envy, O rugged mountains, at the mountain where God chooses to reign, where the LORD himself will dwell forever? **The chariots of God are tens of thousands and thousands of thousands; the Lord [has come] from Sinai into his sanctuary.** (NIV)

After returning to Jerusalem, Jesus will be making preparations for separating the people of the nations (non-Jews), to prepare the unsaved among them for the Battle of Armageddon.

The Day of Vengeance — The Year of the Lord's Favor

GATHER THE NATIONS

Please remember back to the sixth bowl judgment when during the last few months of the Tribulation Period, Satan, the Antichrist and the false prophet set out on a campaign to maneuver all the kings (leaders) of all the armed forces from around the world and had them gather in the Valley of Megiddo (Armageddon). After the leaders of the world—along with their armies—are positioned in Israel, there will still be some people of all nations scattered all over the world.

> Rev 16:16 *Then they gathered the kings together to the place that in Hebrew is called Armageddon.* (NIV)

Although, all the armed forces of the world are gathered at Armageddon and the Jews were gathered from around the world and have already been separated in the Sinai Desert, there are still multitudes of non-Jewish people scattered all over the world in every nation. After the Jewish people have been transported to Jerusalem from the Sinai Desert, the angels in their chariots will then transport the people from the nations (non-Jews) to the Valley of Jehoshaphat to await the separation of the saved and the unsaved, this being the Harvest of the Earth. After the Harvest of the Earth is completed the unsaved portion of the people of the nations will be transported to an area known as the Arabah. The Arabah is specifically applied in whole or in part to the depression of the Jordan Valley extending from Mount Hermon in the north to the Gulf of Akabah (Gulf of Aqaba) in the south. The portion of the Arabah that we are concerned with is that part of the Jordan valley that extends south of the Dead Sea to the Gulf of Akabah. The length of this area is 112 miles long and its width anywhere from 6 to 13 miles wide. This is the place where the unsaved people are sent after they are separated from the saved people at the Harvest of the Earth.

> Rev 14:14-16 *I looked, and there before me was a white cloud, and seated on the cloud was one "like a son of man" with a crown of gold on his head and a sharp sickle in his hand. Then another angel came out of the temple and called in a loud voice to him who was sitting on the cloud, "Take your sickle and reap, because the time to reap has come, <u>for the harvest of the earth is ripe.</u>" So he who was seated on the cloud swung his sickle over the earth, and the earth was harvested.* (NIV)

HARVEST OF THE EARTH

Sometime shortly after the Antichrist attacks Israel and Jerusalem (one year before the end of the Tribulation Period), the Antichrist will move his military headquarters to Israel. He will locate it somewhere between the Mediterranean Sea and the Dead Sea. At the beautiful holy mountain could possibly indicate in or near Jerusalem.

> Dan 11:45 <u>*He will pitch his royal tents between the seas at the beautiful holy*</u>

mountain. Yet he will come to his end, and no one will help him. (NIV)

All the armies of the world, along with the Antichrist, will not be far away when Jesus makes His glorious entry to the east side of Jerusalem. At this time the Antichrist will begin meeting with leaders of the nations and their military generals to formulate a plan to defeat Jesus at Jerusalem. The leaders of the nations and the Antichrist will know that the angels have transported the Jewish people to Jerusalem after their separation process has taken place. They will become furious and their plans to defeat Jesus will include the destruction of every last Jew living on earth. Do not forget that the entire world has just experienced the worst earthquake of its existence—every city on earth was leveled—so it will take a little time for the Antichrist to align his forces for the attack on Jerusalem.

As Jesus returns from the Sinai Desert, He will take His seat on His throne located on the Temple Mount in Jerusalem. He will prepare to separate the people from the nations who have been gathered at the Valley of Jehoshaphat. This is where the saved and the unsaved people of the nations will be separated. Consult the map on page 759.

> Joel 3:1-2 *'In those days and at that time, when I restore the fortunes of Judah and Jerusalem, I will gather all nations and bring them down to the Valley of Jehoshaphat. There I will enter into judgment against them concerning my inheritance, my people Israel, for they scattered my people among the nations and divided up my land.* (NIV)

There is a twofold purpose for the Harvest of the Earth. First, the Lord needs to separate the saved people from the unsaved people of each nation. After the separation is completed the unsaved people of the nations will be participants in the awful Battle of Armageddon.

The final act of the day of vengeance will include both the unsaved Jews and the unsaved of the nations after they are separated. The saved will live out their lives on earth for the rest of the Millennium, while the unsaved will be participants in the Battle of Armageddon, where they will face death and a trip to hell to await their final judgment.

As we return to Jesus on the throne at the Temple Mount we pick up the story of the Harvest of the Earth as the people from all over the world, with the exception of the armies gathered at Armageddon and the Jewish people who have already been separated, are taken from the Valley of Jehoshaphat to the Temple Mount to pass face-to-face before Jesus. Evidently the armies gathered at Armageddon will not participate in the Harvest of the Earth. There is probably not a single person from this group who has believed in Jesus. They have probably rejected Jesus prior to the gathering of the nations to the Valley of Jehoshaphat and all of them will have the mark of the beast on their right hand or forehead.

> Joel 3:2 *I will gather all nations and bring them down to the Valley of Jehoshaphat. There I will enter into judgment against them concerning my inheritance, my people Israel, for they scattered my people among the nations and divided up my land.* (NIV)

The Day of Vengeance — The Year of the Lord's Favor

Jesus Himself told the disciples two parables (stories) that explain details concerning the Harvest of the Earth. The first parable is referred to as the parable of the weeds and is found in Matthew chapter thirteen. This parable concerns the people living today. This harvest will take place at the Rapture when the church (saved/righteous) is removed from the earth.

> Matt 13:24-30 *Jesus told them another parable: "The kingdom of heaven is like a man who sowed good seed in his field. But while everyone was sleeping, his enemy came and sowed weeds among the wheat, and went away. When the wheat sprouted and formed heads, then the weeds also appeared. "The owner's servants came to him and said, 'Sir, didn't you sow good seed in your field? Where then did the weeds come from?' "'An enemy did this,' he replied. "The servants asked him, 'Do you want us to go and pull them up?' "'No,' he answered, 'because while you are pulling the weeds, you may root up the wheat with them. Let both grow together until the harvest. At that time I will tell the harvesters: First collect the weeds and tie them in bundles to be burned; then gather the wheat and bring it into my barn.'"* (NIV)

There is a prophetic message in this story about a man who planted good seed in a field and while everyone was sleeping the man's enemy came and planted weeds among the good seed. The message is explained later in the chapter.

> Matt 13:36-43 *Then he left the crowd and went into the house. His disciples came to him and said, "Explain to us the parable of the weeds in the field." He answered, "The one who sowed the good seed is the Son of Man. The field is the world, and the good seed stands for the sons of the kingdom. The weeds are the sons of the evil one, and the enemy who sows them is the devil. The harvest is the end of the age, and the harvesters are angels. "As the weeds are pulled up and burned in the fire, so it will be at the end of the age. The Son of Man will send out his angels, and they will weed out of his kingdom everything that causes sin and all who do evil. They will throw them into the fiery furnace, where there will be weeping and gnashing of teeth. Then the righteous will shine like the sun in the kingdom of their Father. He who has ears, let him hear.* (NIV)

In these verses we see the hidden meaning behind this story. It is a short explanation of the condition of the world during the Dispensation of Grace; how the continuing battle between good and evil will play out between the first coming and the second coming of Jesus Christ. Here is how the parable breaks down:

The Son of Man is Jesus (He sowed the good seed).

AFTER THE RAPTURE

The field is the world (even the world we live in today).
The good seed sown by Jesus are the saved people.
The weeds sown among the good seed are unsaved people.
The weeds are sown by the evil one (Satan).
The harvest is the gathering of the saved people out of the world at the second coming of Jesus at the Rapture (end of the age). The unsaved people are left on the earth for the judgment (fiery furnace/Tribulation Period and Armageddon).
The righteous (saints) are in heaven in the kingdom of their Father.

Jesus is explaining to us that during the time between the two advents of His coming, the saved and the unsaved will coexist in the world. At His second coming Jesus will come and separate the two groups of people at the end of the age. Notice that the good seed (saved people) will end up in heaven, while the weeds (unsaved) will end up in the fiery furnace.

A second parable that pertains to the Harvest of the Earth, given to us by Jesus, is found in Matthew twenty-five and is a story about a shepherd separating the sheep from the goats. This event will take place at the Glorious Return of Jesus after the Tribulation Period is over. It is the Harvest of the Earth that is spoken of in the book of Revelation.

Rev 14:15 *Then another angel came out of the temple and called in a loud voice to him who was sitting on the cloud, "Take your sickle and reap, because the time to reap has come, <u>for the harvest of the earth is ripe</u>."* (NIV)

Matt 25:31-46 *"When the Son of Man comes in his glory, and all the angels with him, he will sit on his throne in heavenly glory. <u>All the nations will be gathered before him, and he will separate the people one from another as a shepherd separates the sheep from the goats</u>. He will put the sheep on his right and the goats on his left. "<u>Then the King will say to those on his right</u>, 'Come, you who are blessed by my Father; take your inheritance, the kingdom prepared for you since the creation of the world. For I was hungry and you gave me something to eat, I was thirsty and you gave me something to drink, I was a stranger and you invited me in, I needed clothes and you clothed me, I was sick and you looked after me, I was in prison and you came to visit me.' "Then the righteous will answer him, 'Lord, when did we see you hungry and feed you, or thirsty and give you something to drink? When did we see you a stranger and invite you in, or needing clothes and clothe you? When did we see you sick or in prison and go to visit you?' "The King will reply, 'I tell you the truth, whatever you did for one of the least of these brothers of mine, you did for me.' "<u>Then he will say to those on his left</u>, 'Depart from me, you who are cursed, into the eternal fire prepared for the devil and his angels. For I was hungry and you gave me nothing to eat, I was thirsty and you gave me nothing to drink, I was a stranger and*

> *you did not invite me in, I needed clothes and you did not clothe me, I was sick and in prison and you did not look after me.'* *"They also will answer, 'Lord, when did we see you hungry or thirsty or a stranger or needing clothes or sick or in prison, and did not help you?'* *"He will reply, 'I tell you the truth, whatever you did not do for one of the least of these, you did not do for me.'* *"Then they will go away to eternal punishment, but the righteous to eternal life."* (NIV)

In these verses we see the Son of Man (Jesus) and all of His angels with Him. We see all the nations gathered before Him as He is setting on a throne in all His splendor. As each person from each nation passes before Him, He will separate the sheep (saved) from the goats (unsaved). The saved people will pass to the right side of Jesus, while the unsaved people will go to His left side. The end result of these verses are the same as the parable of the Harvest of the Earth at the end of the age, with the saved having eternal life, while the unsaved will go away to eternal punishment. This Harvest of the Earth pertains to people *After the Rapture*.

As we mentioned before, Joel provides us with the exact location that the nations will be gathered and where Jesus will separate the righteous from the wicked. He also tells us when it will take place.

> Joel 3:1-2 *'In those days and at that time, <u>when I restore the fortunes of Judah and Jerusalem</u>, I will gather all nations and bring them down to the Valley of Jehoshaphat. There I will enter into judgment against them concerning my inheritance, my people Israel, for they scattered my people among the nations and divided up my land.* (NIV)

> Joel 3:14 *Multitudes, multitudes in the valley of decision! For <u>the day of the LORD</u> is near in the valley of decision.* (NIV)

These passages reveal that God will gather the nations for judgment at the time He restores the nation of Israel and Jerusalem in the Day of the Lord. The people of the nations will be gathered from all over the earth by the same angels in their chariots who gathered the Jewish people and took them to the Sinai Desert. They will be transported to the Valley of Jehoshaphat to be brought one by one, face-to-face before Jesus, but where is the Valley of Jehoshaphat? Not surprising the Valley of Jehoshaphat is the valley located between Jerusalem and the Mount of Olives. Today it is known as the Kidron Valley. Jewish tradition places the Valley of Jehoshaphat as that part of the Kidron Valley between the Temple and the Mount of Olives. Jehoshaphat means, *"Yahweh judgeth,"* and is referred to as the scene of the judgment of the nations in Joel chapter three.

Those people who represent the goats, and were separated to the left side of Jesus, will be sent to the Arabah, an area southeast of Jerusalem. They will become a portion of the wicked that will be destroyed at the Battle of Armageddon. Again, the angels will transport the unsaved people to this location in their chariots for their final confrontation with Jesus.

BATTLE OF ARMAGEDDON

Most of the thirty-day period following the Tribulation Period will be taken up by the separation process of the Jewish people and the people from the nations. After it is completed Jesus, with His angels, will return to heaven to retrieve the martyred saints from the Tribulation Period as part of His army. These souls were waiting under the altar in heaven dressed in white robes. These Tribulation saints will be allowed to return to earth with Jesus at this time to allow them to watch Jesus avenge their blood. They will also be returning to earth to rule and reign with Jesus for the remaining portion of the Day of the Lord. Although the angels were with Jesus earlier, to gather the elect, it appears that the saints remained in heaven. At this time Jesus is preparing for a great and mighty war.

> Rev 6:9-11 ***When he opened the fifth seal, I saw under the altar the souls of those who had been slain because of the word of God and the testimony they had maintained. They called out in a loud voice, "How long, Sovereign Lord, holy and true, until you judge the inhabitants of the earth and avenge our blood?" Then each of them was given a white robe, and they were told to wait a little longer, until the number of their fellow servants and brothers who were to be killed as they had been was completed.*** (NIV)

> Rev 19:14 ***The armies of heaven were following him, riding on white horses and dressed in fine linen, white and clean.*** (NIV)

This second stage of the Glorious Return of Jesus will be the exact opposite of the first time He rode into Jerusalem 2000 years earlier. At His first coming He entered Jerusalem on a donkey, but this time Jesus will be riding on a white stallion ready to judge and make war. It will be the time to finish the task of purging sinful mankind from the earth. Following Jesus on white horses will be the martyred saints of the Tribulation Period. Because the word used here is plural, there could possibly be two armies. One army made up of saints on white horses and the other army made up of angels with chariots.

> Rev 19:14 *The armies of heaven were following him, riding on white horses and dressed in fine linen, white and clean.* (NIV)

> Jude 1:14-15 *Enoch, the seventh from Adam, prophesied about these men: "See, the Lord is coming with thousands upon thousands of his holy ones to judge everyone, and to convict all the unGodly of all the unGodly acts they have done in the unGodly way, and of all the harsh words unGodly sinners have spoken against him."* (NIV)

> 2 Thes 1:5-10 *All this is evidence that God's judgment is right, and as a result you will be counted worthy of the kingdom of God, for which you are suffering. God is just: He will pay back trouble to those who*

The Day of Vengeance — The Year of the Lord's Favor

> *trouble you and give relief to you who are troubled, and to us as well. <u>This will happen when the Lord Jesus is revealed from heaven in blazing fire with his powerful angels.</u> He will punish those who do not know God and do not obey the gospel of our Lord Jesus. <u>They will be punished with everlasting destruction and shut out from the presence of the Lord</u> and from the majesty of his power on the day he comes to be glorified in his holy people and to be marveled at among all those who have believed. This includes you, because you believed our testimony to you.* (NIV)

All the people that lose their lives at the Battle of Armageddon will be punished with everlasting ruin (death). They will be shut out from the Divine Presence (Shekinah Glory) when God comes to dwell among His Holy people (Jews) during the remaining portion of the Day of the Lord.

Jesus will be coming to earth as a King, a Judge and as the Commander of His armies. Included in the army of angels will be thousands and thousands (myriads) of chariots who carried out the duty of transporting various people to different locations; Jews to the Sinai Desert and the people of the nations to the Valley of Jehoshaphat and then to the Arabah. The armies will also consist of all the saints that died *After the Rapture*.

Ps 24:7-10 *Lift up your heads, O you gates; be lifted up, you ancient doors, that the King of glory may come in. <u>Who is this King of glory?</u> The LORD strong and mighty, the LORD mighty in battle. Lift up your heads, O you gates; lift them up, you ancient doors, that the King of glory may come in. Who is he, this King of glory? <u>The LORD Almighty—he is the King of glory.</u> Selah* (NIV)

Ps 99:1-5 *<u>The LORD reigns,</u> let the nations tremble; he sits enthroned between the cherubim, let the earth shake. Great is the LORD in Zion; he is exalted over all the nations. Let them praise your great and awesome name—he is holy. <u>The King is mighty, he loves justice—you have established equity;</u> in Jacob you have done what is just and right. Exalt the LORD our God and worship at his footstool; he is holy.* (NIV)

Let us take a moment to reflect on the large armies that have had a big effect on the world *After the Rapture*. Armies play an important role in God's plan, especially during this time of judgment. Whether they consist of humans or angels, these armies bring destruction in the wake of the wars in which they are involved. All these armies, whether they know it or not, are a *battle axe* in the hands of God. During the time of the seven year Tribulation Period and the Battle of Armageddon there will be five large armies that play a considerable part in the end time battle between the wicked and the righteous. God, throughout history, has continued to use unsaved people and nations, along with demonic angelic beings, to inflict punishment on sinful mankind. The Day of the Lord is no exception!

AFTER THE RAPTURE

THE LORD'S ARMIES

ARMY	**MADE UP OF**	**FOE**	**RESULT**
Magog (Russia) with allies	Men	Israel	Defeated by God (earthquake)
Revived Roman Empire (Antichrist-king of the north)	Men	World	Defeated at Armageddon by Jesus
Army in Heaven (Holy Angels)	Michael & Holy Angels	Satan & Fallen Angels	Satan and fallen angels kicked out of heaven
Army of Locusts	Fallen Angels	Unsaved Mankind	Kill 1/3 of man before they are judged by Jesus
Armies at 2nd Coming*	Saints & Angels	Armies Nations	Accompany Christ at the Battle of Armageddon

*The armies here could consist of Tribulation Period saints and angels

It is difficult to determine just how many people will lose their lives as a result of the Battle of Armageddon during this time of judgment on the earth. The mark of the beast will be on most of these people. Scripture seems to indicate that most of those people living on the earth at the Battle of Armageddon will end up not believing in God and will be killed during the great battle of God Almighty. As a result of that, they will spend eternity in the Lake of Fire. You can imagine the horror of God's judgment on **JUDGMENT DAY** for the multitudes who have survived and are living on the earth at this time. It is very difficult to comprehend this scenario that is about to play out!

This is it! Although the judgment of the nations had been taking place during the Tribulation Period (especially during the last 3 ½ years), the final judgment will fall on the nations at the Battle of Armageddon. The difference between the judgment of the nations during the Tribulation Period, where the Antichrist inflicted the punishment (through God), and the judgment of the nations at the Battle of Armageddon, will be that Jesus will personally come against the nations at Armageddon, including the Antichrist. It will include both the unsaved Jews and Gentiles.

Ps 9:15-20 *__The nations have fallen into the pit they have dug__; their feet are caught in the net they have hidden. __The LORD is known by his justice__; the wicked are ensnared by the work of their hands. Higgaion. Selah **The wicked return to the grave, all the nations that forget God.** But the needy will not always be forgotten, nor the hope of the afflicted ever perish. __Arise__, __O LORD__, __let not man triumph__; __let the nations be judged in your presence__. Strike them with terror, O LORD; __let the nations know they are but men__. Selah* (NIV)

The Day of Vengeance — The Year of the Lord's Favor

Tim LaHaye, in his book, *Revelation - Illustrated and Made Plain*, is probably correct when he says that the Battle of Armageddon will transpire in a single day. [4] Zechariah tells us that Jesus will remove the sin of Israel in a single day. The battle on the great day of God Almighty will suspend the ongoing war between the righteous and the wicked that has been going on for thousands of years. Following the battle will be a period of peace on earth that will last almost a thousand years. Psalms 37 describes the conflict between the righteous and the wicked. The Lord admonishes the righteous to patiently wait for the Lord. In the end, the wicked will be cut off and the righteous will be exalted and inherit the land. That time has arrived—the Battle of Armageddon.

Ps 37:1-40   *<u>Do not fret because of evil men or be envious of those who do wrong; for like the grass they will soon wither,</u> like green plants they will soon die away. Trust in the LORD and do good; dwell in the land and enjoy safe pasture. Delight yourself in the LORD and he will give you the desires of your heart. Commit your way to the LORD; trust in him and he will do this:* He will make your righteousness shine like the dawn, the justice of your cause like the noonday sun. Be still before the LORD and wait patiently for him; do not fret when men succeed in their ways, when they carry out their wicked schemes. Refrain from anger and turn from wrath; do not fret—it leads only to evil. *<u>For evil men will be cut off,</u> but those who hope in the LORD will inherit the land. <u>A little while, and the wicked will be no more; though you look for them, they will not be found.</u> But the meek will inherit the land and enjoy great peace. The wicked plot against the righteous and gnash their teeth at them; <u>but the Lord laughs at the wicked, for he knows their day is coming.</u>* The wicked draw the sword and bend the bow to bring down the poor and needy, to slay those whose ways are upright. But their swords will pierce their own hearts, and their bows will be broken. *Better the little that the righteous have than the wealth of many wicked; <u>for the power of the wicked will be broken,</u> but the LORD upholds the righteous.* The days of the blameless are known to the LORD, and their inheritance will endure forever. In times of disaster they will not wither; in days of famine they will enjoy plenty. *<u>But the wicked will perish: The LORD's enemies will be like the beauty of the fields, they will vanish—vanish like smoke.</u>* The wicked borrow and do not repay, but the righteous give generously; those the LORD blesses will inherit the land, but those he curses will be cut off. If the LORD delights in a man's way, he makes his steps firm; though he stumble, he will not fall, for the LORD upholds him with his hand. I was young and now I am old, yet I have never seen the righteous forsaken or their children begging bread. They are always generous and lend freely; their children will be blessed. Turn from evil and do good; then you will dwell in the land forever. For the LORD loves *the just and will not forsake his faithful ones. They will be protected forever, but the offspring of the wicked will be cut off; the righteous will inherit the land and dwell in it forever. The mouth of the righteous man utters wisdom, and his tongue speaks what is just. The law of his God is in his heart; his feet do not slip. The wicked lie in wait for the righteous, seeking their very lives; but the LORD will not leave them in their power or let them be condemned when brought to trial.* <u>***Wait for the LORD and keep his way.***</u> *He will exalt you to inherit the land; when the wicked are cut off, you will see it. I have seen a wicked and ruthless man flourishing like a green tree in its native soil, but he soon passed away and was no more; though I looked for him, he could not be found. Consider the blameless, observe the upright; there is a future for the man of peace.* <u>***But all sinners will be destroyed; the future of the wicked will be cut off.***</u> ***The salvation of the righteous comes from the LORD; he is their stronghold in time of trouble.*** *The LORD helps them and delivers them; he delivers them from the wicked and saves them, because they take refuge in him.* (NIV)

After the Harvest of the Earth has been completed and the unsaved of the nations have been moved to the Arabah, south of the Dead Sea, the Battle of Armageddon will begin.

Ps 50:1-6   ***The Mighty One, God, the LORD, speaks and summons the earth from the rising of the sun to the place where it sets. From Zion, perfect in beauty, God shines forth.*** <u>***Our God comes and will not be silent; a fire devours before him, and around him a tempest rages.***</u> ***He summons the heavens above, and the earth, that he may judge his people: "Gather to me my consecrated ones, who made a covenant with me by sacrifice." And the heavens proclaim his righteousness,*** <u>***for God himself is judge.***</u> ***Selah*** (NIV)

Ps 21:8-12   <u>***Your hand will lay hold on all your enemies; your right hand will seize your foes.***</u> ***At the time of your appearing you will make them like a fiery furnace. In his wrath the LORD will swallow them up, and his fire will consume them.*** <u>***You will destroy their descendants from the earth, their posterity from mankind.***</u> ***Though they plot evil against you and devise wicked schemes, they cannot succeed; for you will make them turn their backs when you aim at them with drawn bow.*** (NIV)

2 Pet 3:7   *By the same word the present heavens and earth are reserved for fire,* <u>*being kept for the day of judgment and destruction of unGodly men.*</u> (NIV)

Mal 4:1-3 *"<u>Surely the day is coming; it will burn like a furnace</u>. All the arrogant and every evildoer will be stubble, and that day that is coming will set them on fire," says the LORD Almighty. "Not a root or a branch will be left to them. But for you who revere my name, the sun of righteousness will rise with healing in its wings. And you will go out and leap like calves released from the stall. <u>Then you will trample down the wicked; they will be ashes under the soles of your feet on the day when I do these things</u>," says the LORD Almighty.* (NIV)

Ps 110:5-6 *The Lord is at your right hand; he will crush kings on the day of his wrath. <u>He will judge the nations, heaping up the dead and crushing the rulers of the whole earth</u>.* (NIV)

Zeph 1:17-18 *I will bring distress on the people and they will walk like blind men, because they have sinned against the LORD. Their blood will be poured out like dust and their entrails like filth. Neither their silver nor their gold will be able to save them <u>on the day of the LORD's wrath. In the fire of his jealousy the whole world will be consumed, for he will make a sudden end of all who live in the earth</u>."* (NIV)

Zeph 3:6-8 *"<u>I have cut off nations; their strongholds are demolished</u>. I have left their streets deserted, with no one passing through. <u>Their cities are destroyed; no one will be left—no one at all</u>. I said to the city, 'Surely you will fear me and accept correction!' Then her dwelling would not be cut off, nor all my punishments come upon her. But they were still eager to act corruptly in all they did. <u>Therefore wait for me</u>," declares the LORD, "<u>for the day I will stand up to testify. I have decided to assemble the nations, to gather the kingdoms and to pour out my wrath on them—all my fierce anger. The whole world will be consumed by the fire of my jealous anger</u>.* (NIV)

Ps 11:6 *<u>On the wicked he will rain fiery coals and burning sulfur; a scorching wind will be their lot</u>.* (NIV)

At this time we have the entire population of the world gathered in Israel and the areas closely adjoining her. The scene looks something like this.

1. Jesus is in Jerusalem about to return to heaven to retrieve the rest of His army. Every living human being on earth, at this point in history, will be separated between the saved and unsaved. Jerusalem will be filled with the two groups of saved and unsaved Jews who have been transported there after they were separated in the Sinai desert. The saved of the nations will also be in Jerusalem.
2. The Antichrist along with all the armed forces of the nations are gathered together

at Armageddon. The Antichrist and the leaders of the nations are plotting to attack God and Jesus (along with His armies) and the Jews (to destroy every last one of them) at Jerusalem.
3. The remainder of the unsaved people of the world were transported to the Arabah (south of the Dead Sea), after the completion of the Harvest of the Earth, to wait for the battle to begin.

We pick up the scene as the nations assemble at their respective locations. As Jesus prepares to return to heaven the kings and their armies are at Armageddon preparing to attack Jesus in Jerusalem, while the rest of the people from the nations are in the Arabah.

Ps 2:1-12 *Why do the nations conspire and the peoples plot in vain?* **The kings of the earth take their stand and the rulers gather together against the LORD and against his Anointed One.** *"Let us break their chains," they say, "and throw off their fetters."* **The One enthroned in heaven laughs; the Lord scoffs at them.** *Then he rebukes them in his anger and terrifies them in his wrath, saying,* **"I have installed my King on Zion, my holy hill."** *I will proclaim the decree of the LORD: He said to me, "You are my Son; today I have become your Father. Ask of me, and I will make the nations your inheritance, the ends of the earth your possession.* **You will rule them with an iron scepter; you will dash them to pieces like pottery."** *Therefore, you kings, be wise; be warned, you rulers of the earth. Serve the LORD with fear and rejoice with trembling. Kiss the Son, lest he be angry and you be destroyed in your way, for his wrath can flare up in a moment. Blessed are all who take refuge in him.* (NIV)

Isa 43:8-13 *Lead out those who have eyes but are blind, who have ears but are deaf.* **All the nations gather together and the peoples assemble.** *Which of them foretold this and proclaimed to us the former things? Let them bring in their witnesses to prove they were right, so that others may hear and say, "It is true." "You are my witnesses," declares the LORD, "and my servant whom I have chosen, so that you may know and believe me and understand that I am he. Before me no God was formed, nor will there be one after me. I, even I, am the LORD, and apart from me there is no savior. I have revealed and saved and proclaimed—I, and not some foreign God among you. You are my witnesses," declares the LORD, "that I am God. Yes, and from ancient days I am he.* **No one can deliver out of my hand. When I act, who can reverse it?"** (NIV)

Joel 3:9-11 *Proclaim this among the nations:* **Prepare for war!** *Rouse the warriors! Let all the fighting men draw near and attack. Beat your*

> *plowshares into swords and your pruning hooks into spears. Let the weakling say, 'I am strong!' <u>Come quickly, all you nations from every side, and assemble there. Bring down your warriors, O LORD!</u>* (NIV)

In Psalms 2, above, we see Jesus laugh at the puny nations as God scoffs at them, as the nations plot the defeat of God and His Anointed One (Jesus). Psalms 37, which we listed on page 471, also mentioned Jesus as He laughs at the wicked, for He knows their day is coming. The Antichrist and his followers actually believe they can defeat God and Jesus at this time. As we see from the passage in Isaiah chapter forty-three, above, no one can deliver the wicked out of the hand of Jesus—no one can reverse God's will when He acts.

It is time to bring vengeance on the adversaries of God and repay those who hate Him. Jesus will avenge the blood of His servants the Jews. Although they have received a double portion of punishment, because of their rejection of God, it is now time to make atonement for God's land (Israel and Jerusalem) and people (the Jews).

Deut 32:39-43   *"See now that I myself am He! There is no God besides me. I put to death and I bring to life, I have wounded and I will heal, <u>and no one can deliver out of my hand</u>. I lift my hand to heaven and declare: As surely as I live forever, when I sharpen my flashing sword and my hand grasps it in judgment, <u>I will take vengeance on my adversaries and repay those who hate me</u>. I will make my arrows drunk with blood, while my sword devours flesh: the blood of the slain and the captives, the heads of the enemy leaders." Rejoice, O nations, with his people, <u>for he will avenge the blood of his servants; he will take vengeance on his enemies and make atonement for his land and people</u>.* (NIV)

1 Sam 2:9-10   *He will guard the feet of his saints, <u>but the wicked will be silenced in darkness</u>. "It is not by strength that one prevails; those who oppose the LORD will be shattered. <u>He will thunder against them from heaven; the LORD will judge the ends of the earth</u>. "He will give strength to his king and exalt the horn of his anointed."* (NIV)

The Tribulation saints who will accompany Jesus, along with those who were separated to the right side of Jesus at the Harvest of the Earth, will be joyous when they are avenged at this great battle. They will stand in the blood of the wicked. *"Surely the righteous still are rewarded; surely there is a God who judges the earth."* (NIV)

Ps 58:1-11   *Do you rulers indeed speak justly? Do you judge uprightly among men? No, in your heart you devise injustice, and your hands mete out violence on the earth. Even from birth the wicked go astray; from the womb they are wayward and speak lies. Their venom is like the venom of a snake, like that of a cobra that has stopped its ears, that*

> *will not heed the tune of the charmer, however skillful the enchanter may be. Break the teeth in their mouths, O God; tear out, O LORD, the fangs of the lions! Let them vanish like water that flows away; when they draw the bow, let their arrows be blunted. Like a slug melting away as it moves along, like a stillborn child, may they not see the sun.* **Before your pots can feel [the heat of] the thorns—whether they be green or dry—the wicked will be swept away. <u>The righteous will be glad when they are avenged, when they bathe their feet in the blood of the wicked</u>. Then men will say, "<u>Surely the righteous still are rewarded; surely there is a God who judges the earth.</u>"** (NIV)

The Antichrist, along with the armies of the world gathered at Armageddon, will be advancing toward Jerusalem from Armageddon heading east to the Jordan Valley and then turn to their right and head south toward the Dead Sea. Before they reach the Dead Sea, they will make another right—possibly passing through the city of Jericho—on their way to Jerusalem. Since there is such a vast number of troops congregated at Armageddon, not all of the soldiers will make this journey. Some will be prepared for a second or third attack on Jerusalem, if it deems necessary. Actually, the troops will probably be spread from the Valley of Megiddo all the way to Jerusalem, strung down the Jordan Valley to the Dead Sea. The Antichrist will advance to Jerusalem by this route (Follow the map on page 760).

Rev 19:19   ***Then I saw the beast and the kings of the earth and their armies gathered together to make war against the rider on the horse and his army.*** (NIV)

Since the Antichrist is aware that Jesus gathered the Jews from the nations and that they are gathered in Jerusalem, the Antichrist will stir up his armed forces with anti-Semitic anger. Orders are to destroy those loathsome Jews once and for all, but Jesus has different plans. Jesus will make Jerusalem an immovable rock for all the nations.

Zech 12:1-6   <u>***This is the word of the LORD concerning Israel.***</u> *The LORD, who stretches out the heavens, who lays the foundation of the earth, and who forms the spirit of man within him, declares:* **"I am going to make Jerusalem a cup that sends all the surrounding peoples reeling. Judah will be besieged as well as Jerusalem. <u>On that day, when all the nations of the earth are gathered against her, I will make Jerusalem an immovable rock for all the nations</u>.** *All who try to move it will injure themselves. On that day I will strike every horse with panic and its rider with madness," declares the LORD.* **"<u>I will keep a watchful eye over the house of Judah, but I will blind all the horses of the nations</u>.** *Then the leaders of Judah will say in their hearts, 'The people of Jerusalem are strong, because the LORD Almighty is their God.'"On that day I will make the leaders of Judah* *like a firepot in a woodpile, like a flaming torch among sheaves.* ***They will consume right and left all the surrounding peoples, but Jerusalem will remain intact in her place.*** (NIV)

At first, it appears as though the Antichrist is doing quite well. Jerusalem will actually be captured, with half the city going into exile. The houses—what is left of them after the earthquakes at the end of the Tribulation Period—will be plundered and the women raped. The people who will suffer this defeat will be the people who will be living in Jerusalem at this time. This appears to be the unsaved Jews (they are not sent to the Arabah) who will occupy this territory after the Jews are taken there following their separation in the Sinai. The saved Jews and Gentiles will also remain in Jerusalem after they have been separated from the unsaved. The unsaved Jews will attempt to defend Jerusalem from the attack of the Antichrist. The saved (Jews and Gentiles) will be rescued from Jerusalem about this time.

Before returning to heaven Jesus will go to the Mount of Olives where most probably an earthquake will split it into two sections, forming a valley between them. This will allow the saved people in Jerusalem to head east out of the city to an area that will extend to Azel. The *New Unger's Bible Dictionary* has this to say about Azel; a place, evidently in the neighborhood of Jerusalem and probably east of the Mount of Olives. Its site has not been identified, but the LXX (Septuagint) rendering "Iasol" suggests Wadi Yadil, a tributary of the Kidron.[5] This is the location where the saved will be shielded from the total destruction of the area devastated by Jesus at the great battle of God Almighty (Armageddon). They will be removed from Jerusalem for their protection before the final onslaught begins.

Zech 14:1-7 *A day of the LORD is coming when your plunder will be divided among you. <u>I will gather all the nations to Jerusalem to fight against it; the city will be captured, the houses ransacked, and the women raped. Half of the city will go into exile, but the rest of the people will not be taken from the city.</u> Then the LORD will go out and fight against those nations, as he fights in the day of battle. <u>On that day his feet will stand on the Mount of Olives, east of Jerusalem, and the Mount of Olives will be split in two from east to west, forming a great valley, with half of the mountain moving north and half moving south. You will flee by my mountain valley, for it will extend to Azel.</u> You will flee as you fled from the earthquake in the days of Uzziah king of Judah. <u>Then the LORD my God will come, and all the holy ones with him.</u> On that day there will be no light, no cold or frost. It will be a unique day, without daytime or nighttime—a day known to the LORD. When evening comes, there will be light.* (NIV)

Mal 3:17-18 *"<u>They will be mine</u>," says the LORD Almighty, "<u>in the day when I make up my treasured possession. I will spare them</u>, just as in compassion a man spares his son who serves him. <u>And you will again see the distinction between the righteous and the wicked,</u>*

AFTER THE RAPTURE

between those who serve God and those who do not. (NIV)

At this time Jesus will begin the defense of Israel, Jerusalem and the saved of Israel and the nations (His treasured possession). After the righteous have successfully exited Jerusalem, it will be time for Jesus to act. Jesus will go back to heaven with His angels to pick up the Tribulation Period saints to begin His assault on earth.

ALL OF A SUDDEN!

Rev 19:11-14 *I saw heaven standing open and there before me was a white horse, whose rider is called Faithful and True. With justice he judges and makes war. His eyes are like blazing fire, and on his head are many crowns. He has a name written on him that no one knows but he himself. He is dressed in a robe dipped in blood, and his name is the Word of God. The armies of heaven were following him, riding on white horses and dressed in fine linen, white and clean.* (NIV)

In an instant, heaven will open and Jesus will appear on a white stallion. Behind Him will be His armies, consisting of the Tribulation saints on white horses and angels in chariots. What a fitting tribute for those people of the faith who suffered through the terrible period of God's fierce anger. Please note at this time that Jesus is coming from His dwelling place in heaven.

Micah 1:2-4 *Hear, O peoples, all of you, listen, O earth and all who are in it, that the Sovereign LORD may witness against you, the Lord from his holy temple. Look! The LORD is coming from his dwelling place; he comes down and treads the high places of the earth. The mountains melt beneath him and the valleys split apart, like wax before the fire, like water rushing down a slope.* (NIV)

Jesus will not begin His advance on His foes in Jerusalem.

Zech 12:7-9 *"The LORD will save the dwellings of Judah first, so that the honor of the house of David and of Jerusalem's inhabitants may not be greater than that of Judah. On that day the LORD will shield those who live in Jerusalem, so that the feeblest among them will be like David, and the house of David will be like God, like the Angel of the LORD going before them. On that day I will set out to destroy all the nations that attack Jerusalem.* (NIV)

It is not too difficult to determine where Jesus will begin the slaughter at the Battle of Armageddon. He will start in the south and head north to Armageddon and finalize this great battle of God Almighty in Jerusalem. Scripture reveals a distance of 1600 furlongs (200 miles) for the length of the battle and the depth of the blood of the people will be as high as the horses bridles. The two hundred miles will begin at the Gulf of Akabah, at a city named Elath, head north over the Arabah, cross over the Dead Sea, up the Jordan Valley, turning west heading for the western edge of the Valley of Esdraelon (Valley of Megiddo). This is where the final battle of World War III will be fought. The Valley of Esdraelon, where the armies of the world are gathered, is a triangular shaped plain marked roughly by Mount Tabor on the northeast, Mount Gilboa on the south and Mount Carmel on the northwest. It is approximately 36 miles long and has an average width of 15 miles. The Kishon (Qishon) River, a small intermittently dry stream, is the principal watercourse. This plain has fertile soils and is one of Israel's most productive agricultural regions. Because of its strategic location, the Plain of Esdraelon has been a major battleground since ancient times.

Ezek 20:45-48   *The word of the LORD came to me: "__Son of man, set your face toward the south__; preach against the south and prophesy against the forest of the southland. Say to the southern forest: 'Hear the word of the LORD. This is what the Sovereign LORD says: I am about to set fire to you, and it will consume all your trees, both green and dry. __The blazing flame will not be quenched__, __and every face from south to north will be scorched by it__. Everyone will see that I the LORD have kindled it; it will not be quenched.'"* (NIV)

In this sweep, Jesus will defeat all the people of the nations and most of the armies of the Antichrist, except for those who are still in and around Jerusalem. At this time the Antichrist will probably be at the head of his army in Jerusalem. After the 200 mile stretch of the battle is completed, Jesus will finalize His triumph in Jerusalem.

A more detailed description of the Battle of Armageddon is given to us by the prophets of the Old Testament. Jesus will appear over His enemies, lightning will be flashing and Jesus Himself will sound the battle cry (voice of Jesus sounding like a trumpet). The onslaught will continue in a northerly direction up the Jordan Valley. In Zechariah 9:15, it speaks of the saved Jewish people being shielded from the destruction at this time, but it must be noted that the saved Gentiles will also be protected at this time.

Zech 9:14-15   *__Then the LORD will appear over them; his arrow will flash like lightning. The Sovereign LORD will sound the trumpet; he will march in the storms of the south, and the LORD Almighty will shield them__. They will destroy and overcome with slingstones. They will drink and roar as with wine; they will be full like a bowl used for sprinkling the corners of the altar.* (NIV)

Isa 42:13-17   *__The LORD will march out like a mighty man__, like a warrior he will stir up his zeal; __with a shout__ he will raise the battle cry and will triumph over his enemies. "For a long time I have kept silent, I have been quiet and held myself back. But now, like a woman in childbirth, I cry out, I gasp and pant. I will lay waste the mountains and hills and dry up all their vegetation; I will turn rivers into*

> *islands and dry up the pools. I will lead the blind by ways they have not known, along unfamiliar paths I will guide them; I will turn the darkness into light before them and make the rough places smooth. These are the things I will do; I will not forsake them. But those who trust in idols, who say to images, 'You are our Gods,' will be turned back in utter shame.* (NIV)

Ps 18:13 *The LORD also thundered from heaven, and the Most High <u>uttered His voice</u>, hailstones and coals of fire.* (NKJ)

Isa 62:11 *The LORD has made proclamation to the ends of the earth: "Say to the Daughter of Zion, '<u>See, your Savior comes!</u> <u>See, his reward is with him</u>, <u>and his recompense accompanies him</u>.'"* (NIV)

In Isaiah 62:11 above, we see what Jesus is proclaiming to the entire world as He makes a comment to the Daughter of Zion. This happens at about the time Jesus is ready to start His attack. The Daughters of Zion are the one-third of the Jews who accept Jesus as their Messiah *After the Rapture,* those who will live with Him on earth during the Day of the Lord. Here Jesus tells them that He, as their Savior, is coming. Isaiah says, *"See, his reward is with him."* The word "reward" can be translated to mean: a reward, payment of contract, wages/salary/fare/compensation. As the sentence continues, *"...and his recompense accompanies him,"* the word recompense can be translated to mean; a work, a reward, labor. In other words, it is time for Jesus to make a payment on a contract (prediction) He made a long time ago. He has warned mankind, through the prophets, that this day would come. Now it is time to reward, compensate, **to pay the wages due sinful mankind**. Purge them entirely from the earth. Did I mention that *"the wages of sin is death."*

Can you imagine what it will be like on earth for those people who have just passed through the Tribulation Period, when all of a sudden this scene in heaven appears to them? How they must be trembling as they see Jesus with His armies about to converge on them. At this very moment, Jesus will shout the battle cry with a loud thunderous voice that sounds like a trumpet. At His Glorious Return it was revealed what Jesus was shouting, but here it is not revealed what He said. I kind of wonder what Jesus will be saying at this time.

The Lord's wrath will be upon the armies of the nations and on the rest of the unsaved people who are on the earth at this time as He marches out like a mighty warrior.

Isa 34:1-2 *Come near, you nations, and listen; pay attention, you peoples! Let the earth hear, and all that is in it, the world, and all that comes out of it! <u>The LORD is angry with all nations</u>; his wrath is upon all their armies. <u>He will totally destroy them</u>, <u>he will give them over to slaughter</u>.* (NIV)

Isa 42:13 *<u>The LORD will march out like a mighty man</u>, like <u>a warrior</u> he will stir up his zeal; <u>with a shout he will raise the battle cry</u> and will triumph over his enemies.* (NIV)

The Day of Vengeance — The Year of the Lord's Favor

Ps 97:1-12 — *The LORD reigns, let the earth be glad; let the distant shores rejoice. Clouds and thick darkness surround him; righteousness and justice are the foundation of his throne.* ***Fire goes before him and consumes his foes on every side.*** ***His lightning lights up the world; the earth sees and trembles.*** ***The mountains melt like wax before the LORD****, before the Lord of all the earth. The heavens proclaim his righteousness,* ***and all the peoples see his glory.*** *All who worship images are put to shame, those who boast in idols—worship him, all you Gods! Zion hears and rejoices and the villages of Judah are glad because of your judgments, O LORD. For you, O LORD, are the Most High over all the earth; you are exalted far above all Gods. Let those who love the LORD hate evil, for he guards the lives of his faithful ones and delivers them from the hand of the wicked. Light is shed upon the righteous and joy on the upright in heart. Rejoice in the LORD, you who are righteous, and praise his holy name.* (NIV)

The armies of Jesus will be accompanying Him, although He will not need their assistance fighting this battle. It is Jesus and Jesus alone who defeats His enemies. Just like God said the word and the earth and everything in it was created, Jesus will say the word and His enemies will go down to defeat. His weapon is a sword—the sword of His mouth. Jesus will come down from heaven in a fiery rage of anger, surrounded by dark clouds, pouring out hailstones and bolts of lightning. The brightness of His coming will destroy His enemies.

Isa 66:15-16 — ***See, the LORD is coming with fire****, and his chariots are like a whirlwind; he will bring down his anger with fury, and his rebuke with flames of fire. For with fire and with his sword the LORD will execute judgment upon all men, and many will be those slain by the LORD.* (NIV)

Ps 18:7-15 — *The earth trembled and quaked, and the foundations of the mountains shook; they trembled because he was angry. Smoke rose from his nostrils; consuming fire came from his mouth, burning coals blazed out of it.* ***He parted the heavens and came down****; dark clouds were under his feet. He mounted the cherubim and flew; he soared on the wings of the wind. He made darkness his covering, his canopy around him—the dark rain clouds of the sky.* ***Out of the brightness of his presence clouds advanced,*** ***with hailstones and bolts of lightning.*** ***The LORD thundered from heaven;*** ***the voice of the Most High resounded.*** *He shot his arrows and scattered [the enemies], great bolts of lightning and routed them. The valleys of the sea were exposed and the foundations of the earth laid bare at your rebuke,* ***O LORD****,* ***at the blast of breath from your nostrils****.* (NIV)

Isa 11:4 — ...*__He will strike the earth with the rod of his mouth; with the breath of his lips he will slay the wicked.__* (NIV)

Isa 30:27-28 — *__See, the Name of the LORD comes from afar, with burning anger and dense clouds of smoke;__ his lips are full of wrath, and his tongue is a consuming fire. His breath is like a rushing torrent, rising up to the neck. __He shakes the nations in the sieve of destruction; he places in the jaws of the peoples a bit that leads them astray.__* (NIV)

2 Thes 1:7-9 — *and give relief to you who are troubled, and to us as well. __This will happen when the Lord Jesus is revealed from heaven in blazing fire with his powerful angels.__ He will punish those who do not know God and do not obey the gospel of our Lord Jesus. They will be punished with everlasting destruction and shut out from the presence of the Lord and from the majesty of his power* (NIV)

The battle and the battlefield will look something like this:

Zech 14:3 — *__Then the LORD will go out and fight against those nations, as he fights in the day of battle.__* (NIV)

Zech 14:6-7 — *On that day there will be no light, no cold or frost. It will be a unique day, without daytime or nighttime—a day known to the LORD. When evening comes, there will be light.* (NIV)

Prov 20:2 — *A king's wrath is like the roar of a lion; he who angers him forfeits his life.* (NIV)

Amos 1:2 — *He said: "__The LORD roars from Zion__ and thunders from Jerusalem; the pastures of the shepherds dry up, and the top of Carmel withers."* (NIV)

Isa 34:1-15 — *__Come near, you nations, and listen; pay attention, you peoples!__ Let the earth hear, and all that is in it, the world, and all that comes out of it! __The LORD is angry with all nations; his wrath is upon all their armies. He will totally destroy them, he will give them over to slaughter. Their slain will be thrown out, their dead bodies will send up a stench; the mountains will be soaked with their blood.__ All the stars of the heavens will be dissolved and the sky rolled up like a scroll; all the starry host will fall like withered leaves from the vine, like shriveled figs from the fig tree. My sword has drunk its fill in the heavens; see, it descends in judgment on Edom, the people I have totally destroyed. __The sword of the LORD is bathed in blood, it is covered with fat__—the blood of lambs and goats, fat from the*

> *kidneys of rams.* ***For the LORD has a sacrifice in Bozrah and a great slaughter in Edom.*** *And the wild oxen will fall with them, the bull calves and the great bulls.* ***Their land will be drenched with blood, and the dust will be soaked with fat.*** <u>***For the LORD has a day of vengeance, a year of retribution, to uphold Zion's cause.***</u> ***Edom's streams will be turned into pitch, her dust into burning sulfur; her land will become blazing pitch! It will not be quenched night and day; its smoke will rise forever.*** *From generation to generation it will lie desolate; no one will ever pass through it again. The desert owl and screech owl will possess it; the great owl and the raven will nest there.* ***God will stretch out over Edom the measuring line of chaos and the plumb line of desolation.*** *Her nobles will have nothing there to be called a kingdom, all her princes will vanish away. Thorns will overrun her citadels, nettles and brambles her strongholds. She will become a haunt for jackals, a home for owls. Desert creatures will meet with hyenas, and wild goats will bleat to each other; there the night creatures will also repose and find for themselves places of rest. The owl will nest there and lay eggs, she will hatch them, and care for her young under the shadow of her wings; there also the falcons will gather, each with its mate.* (NIV)

Edom is in the south where the onslaught begins. At this time, even the stars in the second level of heaven will be dissolved. The ancient land of Edom, where the unsaved people of the nations are gathered and destroyed, will be the place where the Edomites are lost for eternity. The descendants of Esau—Jacob's brother—will end at Armageddon.

Obad 1:15-18
> <u>***"The day of the LORD is near for all nations.***</u> ***As you have done, it will be done to you; your deeds will return upon your own head.*** *Just as you drank on my holy hill, so all the nations will drink continually; they will drink and drink and be as if they had never been. But on Mount Zion will be deliverance; it will be holy, and the house of Jacob will possess its inheritance. The house of Jacob will be a fire and the house of Joseph a flame;* ***the house of Esau will be stubble, and they will set it on fire and consume it.*** <u>***There will be no survivors from the house of Esau.***</u> *" The LORD has spoken.* (NIV)

As Jesus passes over Edom, we see that His garments have been spattered with blood. In these verses it informs us that Jesus is acting alone in His endeavor to destroy the nations. He does not need any assistance! Bozrah was a city in ancient Edom.

Isa 63:1-6
> <u>*Who is this coming from Edom, from Bozrah, with his garments stained crimson? Who is this*</u>*, robed in splendor, striding forward in the greatness of his strength? "*<u>*It is I*</u>*, speaking in righteousness, mighty to save." Why are your garments red, like those of one*

treading the winepress? "I have trodden the winepress alone; from the nations no one was with me. I trampled them in my anger and trod them down in my wrath; their blood spattered my garments, and I stained all my clothing. For the day of vengeance was in my heart, and the year of my redemption has come. I looked, but there was no one to help, I was appalled that no one gave support; so my own arm worked salvation for me, and my own wrath sustained me. I trampled the nations in my anger; in my wrath I made them drunk and poured their blood on the ground." (NIV)

The great winepress of God's wrath is mentioned in the book of Revelation, where we are provided with the length and depth of the blood of the victims from the Battle of Armageddon. Can you even imagine the blood reaching as high as the horses' bridles, extending from the Valley of Megiddo and south down the Jordan Valley to the Gulf of Akabah, which is a distance of some 200 miles (subtract the distance of the Dead Sea)? The Grapes of Wrath are upon the wicked.

Rev 14:17-20   *And another angel came out of the temple which is in heaven, and he also had a sharp sickle. And another angel, the one who has power over fire, came out from the altar; and he called with a loud voice to him who had the sharp sickle, saying, "Put in your sharp sickle, and gather the clusters from the vine of the earth, because her grapes are ripe." And the angel swung his sickle to the earth, and gathered {the clusters from} the vine of the earth, and threw them into the great wine press of the wrath of God. And the wine press was trodden outside the city, and blood came out from the wine press, up to the horses' bridles, for a distance of two hundred miles.* (NAS)

Joel 3:13   *Swing the sickle, for the harvest is ripe. Come, trample the grapes, for the winepress is full and the vats overflow—so great is their wickedness!'* (NIV)

After Jesus is finished treading the winepress from Edom to Armageddon, He will return to Jerusalem where He will defeat the Antichrist and his army that remained there while Jesus struck out to save the dwellings of Judah first. Before we move on, Habakkuk gives a view of the beginning of the Battle of Armageddon as Jesus sweeps down from heaven. In the following verses the leader from the land of wickedness is the Antichrist.

Hab 3:1-19   *A prayer of Habakkuk the prophet. On shigionoth. LORD, I have heard of your fame; I stand in awe of your deeds, O LORD. Renew them in our day, in our time make them known; in wrath remember mercy. God came from Teman, the Holy One from Mount Paran. Selah His glory covered the heavens and his praise* *filled the earth. **His splendor was like the sunrise; rays flashed from his hand, where his power was hidden.** Plague went before him; pestilence followed his steps. He stood, and shook the earth; he looked, and made the nations tremble.* The ancient mountains crumbled and the age-old hills collapsed. His ways are eternal. I saw the tents of Cushan in distress, the dwellings of Midian in anguish. Were you angry with the rivers, O LORD? Was your wrath against the streams? Did you rage against the sea when you rode with your horses and your victorious chariots? You uncovered your bow, you called for many arrows. Selah You split the earth with rivers; the mountains saw you and writhed. Torrents of water swept by; the deep roared and lifted its waves on high. **Sun and moon stood still in the heavens at the glint of your flying arrows, at the lightning of your flashing spear. In wrath you strode through the earth and in anger you threshed the nations.** *You came out to deliver your people, to save your anointed one.* **You crushed the leader of the land of wickedness, *you stripped him from head to foot. Selah With his own spear you pierced his head when his warriors stormed out to scatter us, gloating as though about to devour the wretched who were in hiding.*** *You trampled the sea with your horses, churning the great waters. I heard and my heart pounded, my lips quivered at the sound; decay crept into my bones, and my legs trembled.* **Yet I will wait patiently for the day of calamity to come on the nation invading us.** *Though the fig tree does not bud and there are no grapes on the vines, though the olive crop fails and the fields produce no food, though there are no sheep in the pen and no cattle in the stalls, yet I will rejoice in the LORD, I will be joyful in God my Savior. The Sovereign LORD is my strength; he makes my feet like the feet of a deer, he enables me to go on the heights. For the director of music. On my stringed instruments.* (NIV)

Zechariah gives us the most frightful description of how Jesus will totally destroy His enemies at the Battle of Armageddon. Once again, I mention the fact that these scenes seem hard to imagine. Since they have not taken place in the past, they must and will take place in the future. Every event in God's plan will take place at His appointed time. Here the battle is progressing to the city of Jerusalem.

Zech 14:12-15   *This is the plague with which the LORD will strike all the nations that fought against Jerusalem: Their flesh will rot while they are still standing on their feet, their eyes will rot in their sockets, and their tongues will rot in their mouths. On that day men will be stricken by the LORD with great panic. Each man will seize the hand of another, and they will attack each other. Judah too will fight at Jerusalem. The wealth of all the surrounding nations will be collected—great quantities of gold and silver and clothing. A similar plague will strike the horses and mules, the camels and donkeys, and all the animals in those camps.* (NIV)

Ps 68:1-3   *<u>May God arise, may his enemies be scattered; may his foes flee before him.</u> As smoke is blown away by the wind, may you blow them away; <u>as wax melts before the fire, may the wicked perish before God.</u> But may the righteous be glad and rejoice before God; may they be happy and joyful.* (NIV)

Ps 68:19-23   *Praise be to the Lord, to God our Savior, who daily bears our burdens. Selah Our God is a God who saves; from the Sovereign LORD comes escape from death. <u>Surely God will crush the heads of his enemies, the hairy crowns of those who go on in their sins.</u> The Lord says, "I will bring them from Bashan; I will bring them from the depths of the sea, <u>that you may plunge your feet in the blood of your foes</u>, while the tongues of your dogs have their share."* (NIV)

Not a pretty picture! No wonder Isaiah refers to it as the day of great slaughter.

Isa 30:25-30   *<u>In the day of great slaughter</u>, when the towers fall, streams of water will flow on every high mountain and every lofty hill. **The moon will shine like the sun, <u>and the sunlight will be seven times brighter, like the light of seven full days</u>**, when the LORD binds up the bruises of his people and heals the wounds he inflicted. <u>See, the Name of the LORD comes from afar, with burning anger and dense clouds of smoke; his lips are full of wrath, and his tongue is a consuming fire. His breath is like a rushing torrent, rising up to the neck.</u> He shakes the nations in the sieve of destruction; he places in the jaws of the peoples a bit that leads them astray. And you will sing as on the night you celebrate a holy festival; your hearts will rejoice as when people go up with flutes to the mountain of the LORD, to the Rock of Israel. <u>The LORD will cause men to hear his majestic voice and will make them see his arm coming down with raging anger and consuming fire, with cloudburst, thunderstorm and hail.</u>* (NIV)

This will be a unique day for those who will fight against Jesus at the Battle of Armageddon. The light from the glory of Jesus will be seven times brighter than the sun. It will come like a stream of burning sulfur. The heat will be so intense at that time that it will literally rot the flesh of the people while they are standing on their feet. Their eyes will rot in their sockets and their tongues will rot in their mouths. Once again, just like God on Mount Sinai, the people on earth will experience the majestic voice of God as Jesus comes down from heaven at the Battle of Armageddon.

GREAT SUPPER OF GOD

After the Battle of Armageddon is finished it will be time for another banquet, but it is not the kind of banquet you will want to attend. Scripture calls it the Great Supper of God. An angel will summon the vultures to eat what remaining flesh there is left from the defeated enemy at the Battle of Armageddon. It could be the same carrion birds who whet their appetite on the defeated soldiers almost seven years earlier at the Russian Invasion.

Rev 19:17-18   *And I saw an angel standing in the sun, who cried in a loud voice to all the birds flying in midair, "<u>Come, gather together for the great supper of God</u>, so that you may eat the flesh of kings, generals, and mighty men, of horses and their riders, and the flesh of all people, free and slave, small and great."* (NIV)

Rev 19:21   *The rest of them were killed with the sword that came out of the mouth of the rider on the horse, <u>and all the birds gorged themselves on their flesh</u>.* (NIV)

It appears that the last part of Ezekiel 39 is also referring to the Great Supper of God. It seems to be talking about *"the great sacrifice on the mountains of Israel,"* which is most likely a reference to the final battle on the great day of God Almighty. This reference also includes wild animals along with the birds of prey that partake of the meal at this banquet. It is clear that these events will take place when God gathers all of Jacob (Israel) back from captivity and pours out His Spirit on them.

Ezek 39:17-29   *"Son of man, this is what the Sovereign LORD says: <u>Call out to every kind of bird and all the wild animals</u>: 'Assemble and come together from all around to the sacrifice I am preparing for you, <u>the great sacrifice on the mountains of Israel</u>. There you will eat flesh and drink blood. You will eat the flesh of mighty men and drink the blood of the princes of the earth as if they were rams and lambs, goats and bulls—all of them fattened animals from Bashan. At the sacrifice I am preparing for you, you will eat fat till you are glutted and drink blood till you are drunk. <u>At my table you will eat your fill of horses and riders, mighty men and soldiers of every kind</u>,' declares the Sovereign LORD. "I will display my glory among the nations, and all the nations will see the punishment I inflict and the hand I lay upon them. <u>From that day forward the house of Israel will know that I am the LORD their God</u>. And the nations will know that the people of Israel went into exile for their sin, because they were unfaithful to me. So I hid my face from them and handed them over to their enemies, and they all fell by the sword. I dealt with them according to their uncleanness and their offenses, and I hid my face from them. "Therefore this is*

> *what the Sovereign LORD says: <u>I will now bring Jacob back from captivity and will have compassion on all the people of Israel</u>, <u>and I will be zealous for my holy name</u>. They will forget their shame and all the unfaithfulness they showed toward me when they lived in safety in their land with no one to make them afraid. When I have brought them back from the nations and have gathered them from the countries of their enemies, I will show myself holy through them in the sight of many nations. <u>Then they will know that I am the LORD their God, for though I sent them into exile among the nations, I will gather them to their own land, not leaving any behind.</u> I will no longer hide my face from them, for I will pour out my Spirit on the house of Israel, declares the Sovereign LORD."* (NIV)

DEFEAT OF THE ANTICHRIST

With the defeat of the nations, it will also bring about the defeat of their leaders—the Antichrist and the False Prophet. We see their defeat in the book of Revelation.

> Rev 19:20 *But <u>the beast</u> was captured, and with him <u>the false prophet</u> who had performed the miraculous signs on his behalf. With these signs he had deluded those who had received the mark of the beast and worshiped his image. <u>The two of them were thrown alive into the fiery lake of burning sulfur</u>.* (NIV)

This seems to be the only reference to the defeat of the false prophet, but there is a lot more said that details the defeat of the fallacious leader of the Revived Roman Empire. In Psalms, we see God as He brings the Antichrist down to ruin. He will not trust in God, but he will trust in the abundance of his riches and strengthen himself by destroying others.

> Ps 52:5-7 *<u>Surely God will bring you down to everlasting ruin</u>: He will snatch you up and tear you from your tent; he will uproot you from the land of the living. Selah The righteous will see and fear; they will laugh at him, saying, "Here now is <u>the man</u> who did not make God his stronghold but trusted in his great wealth and grew strong by destroying others!"* (NIV)

I want to show you an interesting description of the Antichrist toward the end of the Tribulation Period, not long before his defeat. This scripture passage reveals him to be an overweight middle-aged man filled with fear. It appears that the Antichrist will live his entire life in distress, even his great wealth will run out. We see him here shaking his fist at God. At this point he will probably be a drug infested, glassy-eyed mess. He is paranoid and in his heart he fears the inevitable. He will die before his time, meaning that he will not live to be an old man. He will be defeated by the breath out of the mouth of Jesus.

The Day of Vengeance — The Year of the Lord's Favor

Job 15:20-35 *The wicked man writhes with pain all his days, and the number of years is hidden from the oppressor. Dreadful sounds are in his ears; in prosperity the destroyer comes upon him. He does not believe that he will return from darkness, and he watches for the sword. He wanders about for bread, saying, 'Where is it?' He knows that a day of darkness is ready at his hand. Trouble and anguish make him afraid; they overpower him, like a king ready for battle. For he stretches out his hand against God, and acts defiantly against the Almighty, Running stubbornly against Him with his strong, embossed shield. "Though he has covered his face with his fatness, and made his waist heavy with fat, He dwells in desolate cities, in houses which no one inhabits, which are destined to become ruins. He will not be rich, nor will his wealth continue, nor will his possessions overspread the earth. He will not depart from darkness; the flame will dry out his branches, and by the breath of His mouth he will go away. Let him not trust in futile things, deceiving himself, for futility will be his reward. It will be accomplished before his time, and his branch will not be green. He will shake off his unripe grape like a vine, and cast off his blossom like an olive tree. For the company of hypocrites will be barren, and fire will consume the tents of bribery. They conceive trouble and bring forth futility; their womb prepares deceit."* (NKJ)

The defeat of the Antichrist and his army are depicted in the book of Joel. Below, we see the Northerner, who is the Antichrist, removed to a desolate land (hell). Also pictured, is the stench of the foul smell of the dead bodies from his army. All of this will take place at their defeat at the Battle of Armageddon. Most of the Bible translations have added the word army to this verse. It should read "the northerner," instead of "northern army." The New Jerusalem Bible has the correct translation.

Joel 2:20 *I shall take the northerner far away from you and drive him into an arid, desolate land, his vanguard to the eastern sea, his rear vanguard to the western sea. He will give off a stench, he will give off a foul stink (for what he made bold to do).* (NJB)

In Ezekiel, it depicts the Antichrist as dying from a violent death. He will be reduced to ashes in the sight of the armies of Jesus. It appears from the scripture describing the death of the Antichrist that after he dies a violent death his soul will be sent to hell.

Ezek 28:6-10 *"'Therefore this is what the Sovereign LORD says: "'Because you think you are wise, as wise as a God, I am going to bring foreigners against you, the most ruthless of nations; they will draw their swords against your beauty and wisdom and pierce your shining splendor. They will bring you down to the pit, and you will die a*

> *violent death in the heart of the seas. Will you then say, "<u>I am a God</u>," in the presence of those who kill you? <u>You will be but a man</u>, <u>not a God</u>, in the hands of those who slay you. You will die the death of the uncircumcised at the hands of foreigners. I have spoken, declares the Sovereign LORD.'"* (NIV)

In Habakkuk, we see the defeat of the Antichrist as he brings his army against Jesus and the Jews gathered in Jerusalem. Jesus comes out to deliver His people, the Jews, when He defeats the Antichrist who is the leader of the army that comes against Him. The day of calamity (trouble) is referring to the Battle of Armageddon.

Hab 3:11-16 *Sun and moon stood still in the heavens at the glint of your flying arrows, at the lightning of your flashing spear. In wrath you strode through the earth and in anger you threshed the nations. You came out to deliver your people, to save your anointed one. <u>You crushed the leader of the land of wickedness</u>, <u>you stripped him from head to foot</u>. Selah With his own spear you pierced his head when his warriors stormed out to scatter us, gloating as though about to devour the wretched who were in hiding. You trampled the sea with your horses, churning the great waters. I heard and my heart pounded, my lips quivered at the sound; decay crept into my bones, and my legs trembled. Yet I will wait patiently for <u>the day of calamity</u> to come on the nation invading us.* (NIV)

In the book of Isaiah, where the Antichrist is referred to as the king of Babylon, we see the oppressor come to an end. Trees used symbolically in the Bible are people and nations.

Isa 14:3-8 *On the day the LORD gives you relief from suffering and turmoil <u>and cruel bondage</u>, <u>you will take up this taunt against the king of Babylon</u>: How <u>the oppressor</u> has come to an end! How his fury has ended! <u>The LORD has broken the rod of the wicked</u>, <u>the scepter of the rulers</u>, <u>which in anger struck down peoples with unceasing blows</u>, <u>and in fury subdued nations with relentless aggression</u>. All the lands are at rest and at peace; they break into singing. Even the pine trees and the cedars of Lebanon exult over you and say, "Now that you have been laid low, no woodsman comes to cut us down."* (NIV)

In that same book we see the destruction of the Antichrist at the Battle of Armageddon, only this time he is referred to as the Assyrian. Tophet is hell and has been prepared for this king (the Antichrist). Hell is a big place—deep and large!

Isa 30:30-33 *And the LORD shall cause his glorious voice to be heard, and shall shew the lighting down of his arm, with the indignation of his*

> *anger, and with the flame of a devouring fire, with scattering, and tempest, and hailstones. For through the voice of the LORD shall <u>the Assyrian</u> be beaten down, which smote with a rod. And in every place where the grounded staff shall pass, which the LORD shall lay upon him, it shall be with tabrets and harps: and in battles of shaking will he fight with it. <u>For Tophet is ordained of old; yea, for the king it is prepared; he hath made it deep and large</u>: the pile thereof is fire and much wood; the breath of the LORD, like a stream of brimstone, doth kindle it.* (KJV)

Isa 31:8-9   *Then shall <u>the Assyrian</u> fall with the sword, not of a mighty man; and the sword, not of a mean man, shall devour him: but he shall flee from the sword, and his young men shall be discomfited. And he shall pass over to his strong hold for fear, and his princes shall be afraid of the ensign, saith the LORD, whose fire is in Zion, and his furnace in Jerusalem.* (KJV)

In Nahum, the Antichrist is referred to as the king of Assyria. All the people who are told about the defeat of the Antichrist will be clapping their hands in jubilation.

Nahum 3:18-19   *O king of Assyria, your shepherds slumber; your nobles lie down to rest. Your people are scattered on the mountains with no one to gather them. <u>Nothing can heal your wound; your injury is fatal. Everyone who hears the news about you claps his hands at your fall, for who has not felt your endless cruelty</u>?* (NIV)

After the Antichrist is killed, by the sword of Jesus at the Battle of Armageddon, his physical body will be reduced to ashes.

Ezek 28:18-19   *By your many sins and dishonest trade you have desecrated your sanctuaries. <u>So I made a fire come out from you, and it consumed you, and I reduced you to ashes on the ground in the sight of all who were watching</u>. All the nations who knew you are appalled at you; <u>you have come to a horrible end and will be no more</u>.'"* (NIV)

2 Thes 2:8   *And then <u>the lawless one</u> will be revealed, whom the Lord will consume with the breath of His mouth and destroy with the brightness of His coming.* (NKJ)

Sheol, which is the Hebrew word for hell, is all aroused as the unsaved souls who preceded the Antichrist await the arrival of the soul of the Antichrist. All of the unsaved leaders of the world will taunt the Antichrist as he arrives. This **seemingly** great leader of the world has been brought down to defeat. This is a continuation in Isaiah, above, concerning the fate of the king of Babylon.

Isa 14:9-11 *The grave below is all astir to meet you at your coming; it rouses the spirits of the departed to greet you—all those who were leaders in the world; it makes them rise from their thrones—all those who were kings over the nations. They will all respond, they will say to you, "You also have become weak, as we are; you have become like us." All your pomp has been brought down to the grave, along with the noise of your harps; maggots are spread out beneath you and worms cover you.* (NIV)

They will stare at the Antichrist as he is covered with worms laying on a bed of maggots. The unsaved souls in hell will ponder his fate as they realize that lying before them is the man who led them to destruction. At this time the Antichrist will not look the same as he did when he was a powerful dictator.

Isa 14:16-20 *Those who see you stare at you, they ponder your fate: "Is this the man who shook the earth and made kingdoms tremble, the man who made the world a desert, who overthrew its cities and would not let his captives go home?" All the kings of the nations lie in state, each in his own tomb. But you are cast out of your tomb like a rejected branch; you are covered with the slain, with those pierced by the sword, those who descend to the stones of the pit. Like a corpse trampled underfoot, you will not join them in burial, for you have destroyed your land and killed your people....* (NIV)

With the defeat of the Antichrist will come the defeat of the Revived Roman Empire. At one time almost the entire population of the earth will put their trust in the Antichrist and rest under his shade (protection). Of all the world wide empires (trees of Eden), none can compare with the splendor and majesty of the Revived Roman Empire. The most ruthless dictator of all time will have led this empire to destruction. In the end, though, all the nations of the world, including the Revived Roman Empire, will be defeated and end up in hell (pit).

Ezek 31:15-18 *"'This is what the Sovereign LORD says: On the day it was brought down to the grave I covered the deep springs with mourning for it; I held back its streams, and its abundant waters were restrained. Because of it I clothed Lebanon with gloom, and all the trees of the field withered away. I made the nations tremble at the sound of its fall when I brought it down to the grave with those who go down to the pit. Then all the trees of Eden, the choicest and best of Lebanon, all the trees that were well-watered, were consoled in the earth below. Those who lived in its shade, its allies among the nations, had also gone down to the grave with it, joining those killed by the sword. "'Which of the trees of Eden can be compared with you in splendor and majesty? Yet you, too, will be brought down with the trees of Eden to the earth below; you will lie among*

> *__the uncircumcised, with those killed by the sword.__ '"This is Pharaoh and all his hordes, declares the Sovereign LORD.'"* (NIV)

Apparently, the Antichrist will not remain in hell for very long. The Antichrist, along with the false prophet, will be taken from hell and thrown into the fiery lake of burning sulfur. Sheol (Hebrew) and Hades (Greek) are the words used in the Bible to describe the temporary abode of the unsaved souls of men while they await their judgment. It is probably located in the center of the earth and we refer to it as hell (Numbers 16; Numbers 26:8-11; Deuteronomy 11:1-7). The final resting place for the unsaved will be the Lake of Fire. It appears that these two figures will bypass the Great White Throne Judgment and spend the remainder of the Kingdom Age in the final abode of hell for eternity.

> Rev 19:20 *But __the beast__ was captured, and with him __the false prophet__ who had performed the miraculous signs on his behalf. With these signs he had deluded those who had received the mark of the beast and worshiped his image. __The two of them were thrown alive into the fiery lake of burning sulfur.__* (NIV)

Let us not forget the account given to us in Daniel. The Antichrist will be defeated, but not by human power. Jesus Himself will be responsible for the defeat of the Antichrist.

> Dan 8:25 *He will cause deceit to prosper, and he will consider himself superior. When they feel secure, he will destroy many and take his stand against the Prince of princes. __Yet he will be destroyed, but not by human power.__* (NIV)

> Dan 7:11 *"Then I continued to watch because of the boastful words __the horn__ was speaking. I kept looking until __the beast__ was slain and its body destroyed and thrown into the blazing fire.* (NIV)

SATAN BOUND

Naturally, Satan will exit the body of the Antichrist after his defeat and physical death. It will now be time to bind Satan for the remainder of the 1000 year period of the Day of the Lord (Millennium). In order for the world to live in peaceful coexistence, the influence of the king (leader) of the false religious system and the kingdoms of this world will have to be removed. An angel (Jesus) will accomplish this task by throwing him into the Abyss (bottomless pit) and restraining him in chains. The abyss is a special prison where God can restrain those whom He desires. Then the Abyss will be locked and sealed to keep Satan from having access to the people who will be living on the earth for the next 990 years. Satan will be bound so that he will not be able to influence and deceive the nations for the remainder of the Millennium. Revelation twenty is referring to the rest of the 1000 years.

> Rev 20:1-3 *And I saw an angel coming down out of heaven, having the key to*

> *the Abyss and holding in his hand a great chain. He seized the dragon, that ancient serpent, who is the devil, or Satan, and bound him for a thousand years. He threw him into the Abyss, and locked and sealed it over him, to keep him from deceiving the nations anymore <u>until the thousand years were ended</u>. After that, he must be set free for a short time.* (NIV)

Isaiah mentions this ancient serpent, who is the devil, in chapter 27 where he refers to him as Leviathan. The locust army of fallen angels will be returned to their prison.

Isa 27:1 *In that day, the LORD will punish with his sword, his fierce, great and powerful sword, <u>Leviathan the gliding serpent</u>, Leviathan the coiling serpent; he will slay the monster of the sea.* (NIV)

Isa 24:21-22 *In that day the LORD will punish the powers in the heavens above and the kings on the earth below. They will be herded together like prisoners bound in a dungeon; they will be shut up in prison and be punished <u>after many days</u>.* (NIV)

Satan's army of fallen angels, along with the Antichrist's army of fallen men, will be defeated at the Battle of Armageddon. The *"powers in the heavens above"* is referring to the fallen angels and the *"kings of the earth below"* are those leaders of the nations who were gathered at Armageddon fighting against Jesus at the final battle in Jerusalem. The demonic fallen angels, who are the army of locusts who were responsible for killing one-third of mankind only a few months earlier, will be returned to the Abyss (pit or dungeon) where they were released to perform their awful deed. The kings of the earth will be sent to Hades (hell) to await their final judgment at the Great White Throne Judgment. *"After many days,"* is referring to the remaining days of the Millennium. After the Millennium is completed and the final rebellion of Satan and man against God takes place, the final judgment of all fallen angels and all unsaved mankind will take place. It will seem strange living in a world without the influence of Satan and his cohorts after six thousand years of their influence on earth. It is hard to imagine what it will be like at that time and kind of reminds me of the title to a song—What a Difference a Day Makes— from Armageddon to peace on earth.

EARTH DESTROYED BY FIRE

Many people today believe that the entire earth will be burned up and dissolved at the Battle of Armageddon and replaced by a new heaven and new earth. As I said before, I believe that Jesus will rebuild and restore the present earth that exists after the Battle of Armageddon. As the result of all the destruction meted out by the Antichrist, the plaques from God, the great earthquake at the end of the Tribulation Period and the Battle of Armageddon, the surface area of the earth will be destroyed by fire. All of the islands will disappear and all of the mountains will be laid flat and the face of the entire earth will lay in ruin. We will discuss the restoration of the earth in the next chapter.

The Day of Vengeance — The Year of the Lord's Favor

2 Pet 3:7-10   *By the same word the present heavens and earth are reserved for fire, being kept for the day of judgment and destruction of unGodly men. But do not forget this one thing, dear friends: With the Lord a day is like a thousand years, and a thousand years are like a day. The Lord is not slow in keeping his promise, as some understand slowness. He is patient with you, not wanting anyone to perish, but everyone to come to repentance. But the day of the Lord will come like a thief. The heavens will disappear with a roar; the elements will be destroyed by fire, and the earth and everything in it will be laid bare.* (NIV)

Isa 24:1   *See, the LORD is going to lay waste the earth and devastate it; he will ruin its face and scatter its inhabitants—* (NIV)

RESURRECTION OF THE TRIBULATION SAINTS

Most of what we have discussed so far in this chapter will take place within the first thirty days after the Tribulation Period ends. It will be a busy thirty days with the last day taking up the Battle of Armageddon. The thirty-day period, as part of the day of vengeance, is over and it is now time to talk about more pleasant circumstances. The second period (forty-five days) will be occupied with the judgment of those people who accepted Jesus as their personal Savior during the time *After the Rapture*. It took almost two years to complete the first part of the Judgment Seat of Christ and now it will take forty-five days to distribute the just reward to the people who accepted Jesus by faith, the martyrs and all those who lost their lives during the worst time of human history. They did not take the mark of the beast. They are a part of those who will spend the Kingdom Age on earth. They are Jew and Gentile. Everyone who is saved by faith (true faith—believing in Jesus Christ) will be a part of the first resurrection, even though it takes place at more than one time, as we stated earlier. These saints will rule and reign with Christ for the rest of the Day of the Lord and after that for eternity. Because of the persecution and suffering they faced, it appears that they will receive special positions as priests during the Millennium and will live on earth with Christ for the remainder of the 1000 years or until the 1000 years are completed.

Rev 20:4-6   *I saw thrones on which were seated those who had been given authority to judge. And I saw the souls of those who had been beheaded because of their testimony for Jesus and because of the word of God. They had not worshiped the beast or his image and had not received his mark on their foreheads or their hands. They came to life and reigned with Christ a thousand years. (The rest of the dead did not come to life until the thousand years were ended.) This is the first resurrection. Blessed and holy are those who have part in the first resurrection. The second death has no power over them, but they will be priests of God and of Christ and will reign with him for a thousand years.* (NIV)

Dan 7:21-22 *As I watched, this horn was waging war against the saints and defeating them, <u>until the Ancient of Days came and pronounced judgment in favor of the saints of the Most High, and the time came when they possessed the kingdom.</u>* (NIV)

The only resurrected saints who will live and reign on earth, with Jesus during the remainder of the Millennium, will be those who become saints *After the Rapture*. Those saints who were resurrected at the Rapture will dwell in heaven during the Day of Christ. Actually, this will be their home for the rest of eternity.

There are several verses in the Bible that interpreters use to come to the conclusion that all the saints will reign on earth with Jesus during the Millennium. Most of them are found in the book of Revelation (2:26-27; 3:21; 5:10; 20:4-6). There is a key verse, outside Revelation, that they also quote to come to the same conclusion. It is found in 2 Timothy.

2 Tim 2:12 *<u>if we endure, we will also reign with him.</u> If we disown him, he will also disown us;* (NIV)

Taken out of context, in verses eleven through thirteen, this makes a strong case for the followers of this opinion, but these verses tie in with the verses preceding verse eleven.

2 Tim 2:8-13 *Remember Jesus Christ, raised from the dead, descended from David. This is my gospel, for which I am suffering even to the point of being chained like a criminal. But God's word is not chained. <u>Therefore I endure everything for the sake of the elect, that they too may obtain the salvation that is in Christ Jesus, with eternal glory.</u> Here is a trustworthy saying: If we died with him, we will also live with him; <u>if we endure, we will also reign with him.</u> If we disown him, he will also disown us; if we are faithless, he will remain faithful, for he cannot disown himself.* (NIV)

In the context of these verses, Paul is referring to the elect as his own, the Jewish people. In the New Testament, *"elect" (eklektos)* can apply to three different groups and a particular being. They are:

1. The Jewish people (Paul's brothers) as chosen by God from the Old Testament.
2. The Christians as chosen by God to obtain salvation through Christ in the New Testament.
3. The elect angels (properly referring to the Holy Angels – 1 Timothy 5:21).
4. Jesus Christ (the Messiah) as chosen by God to the most exalted office conceivable.

As we mentioned before, Paul was willing to give up his salvation if only the people of his own race would accept Jesus (Romans 9:3-5). Paul, in 2 Timothy, is again referring to the salvation of the Jewish people. Paul wrote this letter (his last) toward the end of his ministry, not long before he was killed by the Romans. In this letter Paul mentions the fact that he has never given up his effort to bring the Jews to Christ. He endured all the trials and persecutions during his lifetime for this purpose, even though he was also the apostle to the Gentiles. Paul was to the New Testament, what Moses was to the Old Testament. When Paul died, most of the Jewish population were as far away from God as the Jews (Israelites) were during the time of Moses.

Paul then continues his discourse in 2 Timothy, which he says is a true saying, with a reference to judgment. In verse 12, we are confronted with those who endure, as with those who will reign with Christ. The word for endure (suffer in the KJV) in Greek, used here, is *hupomeno*. As we take a detailed look at this word we find more than just simple endurance. We find a group of people that remain behind who suffer trials and persecutions.

Strong's Definition
5278 hupomeno (hoop-om-en'-o);
from 5259 and 3306; to stay under (behind), i.e. remain; figuratively, to undergo, i.e. bear (trials), have fortitude, persevere:
KJV—abide, endure, (take) patient (-ly), suffer, tarry behind.

Thayer's Definition
5278 hupomeno-
1) to remain; to tarry behind
2) to remain, that is, to abide, not to recede or flee
    a) to preserve: under misfortunes and trials to hold fast to one's faith in Christ
    b) to endure, to bear bravely and calmly: ill treatments

Of the four usages for elect, only the Jewish people as God's chosen elect could make sense in this passage. The Christians would not apply in this passage, because as true Christians they would already have obtained salvation.

There are two Greek words that make up the word *hupomeno*. They are *hupo* and *meno*. In order to fully comprehend what is being conveyed in these verses in 2 Timothy we need to look at *meno* a little more closely.

Strong's Definition
3306 meno (men'-o);
a primary verb; to stay (in a given place, state, relation or expectancy):
KJV—abide, continue, dwell, endure, be present, remain, stand, tarry (for), X thine own.

In 2 Timothy 2:12, it is speaking to a group of people who will remain (tarry) or stay behind, people who will need to persevere through misfortune and trials. This cannot be applied, as some people teach, to certain individual Christians who suffer for their faith. The gospel never distinguishes between the saints as those that suffer extreme hardships as the choice, select or the best of its kind or class. This trustworthy saying from Paul is referring to the Jewish people (Paul's own) who will be left behind at the Rapture (non-Christians).

In Revelation 2:26-27 and 3:21, these verses are not referring to saints who will reign with Christ during the Millennium. In Revelation 5:10 and 20:4-6, it is referring to the saints who will reign with God and Christ during the Millennium, but limits these saints to those who have died and believed in Jesus during the fierce anger portion of the Day of the Lord. The saints who will take part in the Rapture will remain in their designated place in heaven.

THE YEAR OF THE LORD'S FAVOR

Although the time of the Lord's favor and the day of salvation began at the first appearing of Jesus for all the nations, it will now be time to show favor to Israel. It is time to redeem them as a nation. Another appointed time has arrived. At the end of the first seventy-five days of the start of the tenth year *After the Rapture* (the year of the Lord's favor), Jesus will turn His attention to the chosen people (the Jewish people). After all the persecution from all the nations throughout history, the Jews will finally have their promises fulfilled by God. Because of their sins, they will have suffered through three holocausts. The first great slaughter of the Jews occurred in 66-70 AD and 132-135 AD by the Romans, the second onslaught occurred between 1939–1945 by Adolf Hitler and the third and final holocaust will be by the Antichrist during the Tribulation Period. Only after the Tribulation Period is over and this final tragedy of the Jewish people is completed, will **ALL MANKIND** know that Jesus is Israel's Savior, Redeemer and the Mighty One of Jacob.

Ps 102:12-16   *But you, O LORD, sit enthroned forever; your renown endures through all generations. You will arise and have compassion on Zion, for it is time to show favor to her; the appointed time has come. For her stones are dear to your servants; her very dust moves them to pity. The nations will fear the name of the LORD, all the kings of the earth will revere your glory. For the LORD will rebuild Zion and appear in his glory.* (NIV)

Isa 49:8-13   *This is what the LORD says: "In the time of my favor I will answer you, and in the day of salvation I will help you; I will keep you and will make you to be a covenant for the people, to restore the land and to reassign its desolate inheritances, to say to the captives, 'Come out,' and to those in darkness, 'Be free!'" "They will feed beside the roads and find pasture on every barren hill. They will neither hunger nor thirst, nor will the desert heat or the sun beat upon them. He who has compassion on them will guide them and lead them beside springs of water. I will turn all my mountains into roads, and my highways will be raised up. See, they will come from afar—some from the north, some from the west, some from the region of Aswan." Shout for joy, O heavens; rejoice, O earth; burst into song, O mountains! **For the LORD comforts his people and will have compassion on his afflicted ones.** (NIV)*

The Day of Vengeance — The Year of the Lord's Favor

Isa 63:4 *For the day of vengeance was in my heart, <u>and the year of my redemption has come.</u>* (NIV)

Isa 49:25-26 *But this is what the LORD says: "Yes, captives will be taken from warriors, and plunder retrieved from the fierce; I will contend with those who contend with you, and your children I will save. I will make your oppressors eat their own flesh; they will be drunk on their own blood, as with wine.* **Then <u>all mankind</u> will know that <u>I, the LORD, am your Savior, your Redeemer, the Mighty One of Jacob.</u>*"* (NIV)

What a price mankind will have to pay to get to this point in history. Without some sort of intervention from God, mankind will never turn completely to Him. To the Jews it is the Day of Atonement. Yom Kippur! The fate of every Jew up to this time is decreed and on Yom Kippur it is sealed. It was accompanied by a sincere national repentance. They received a propitious final sealing of divine judgment — *"gemar hatimah tovah."* They are redeemed and because of that they will be set up as head of the nations for the remaining portion of the Day of the Lord. Jesus reminds us that when it is time to restore the nation of Israel—He will do it quickly. Israel will also come to realize that Jesus is *"the Mighty One of Jacob."*

Isa 60:1-22 *"<u>Arise, shine, for your light has come, and the glory of the LORD rises upon you.</u> See, darkness covers the earth and thick darkness is over the peoples, but the LORD rises upon you and his glory appears over you. Nations will come to your light, and kings to the brightness of your dawn. "Lift up your eyes and look about you: All assemble and come to you; your sons come from afar, and your daughters are carried on the arm. Then you will look and be radiant, your heart will throb and swell with joy; the wealth on the seas will be brought to you, to you the riches of the nations will come. Herds of camels will cover your land, young camels of Midian and Ephah. And all from Sheba will come, bearing gold and incense and proclaiming the praise of the LORD. All Kedar's flocks will be gathered to you, the rams of Nebaioth will serve you; they will be accepted as offerings on my altar, and I will adorn my glorious temple. "Who are these that fly along like clouds, like doves to their nests? Surely the islands look to me; in the lead are the ships of Tarshish, bringing your sons from afar, with their silver and gold, to the honor of the LORD your God, the Holy One of Israel, for he has endowed you with splendor.* **"Foreigners will rebuild your walls, and their kings will serve you. <u>Though in anger I struck you, in favor I will show you compassion.</u>** *Your gates will always stand open, they will never be shut, day or night, so that men may bring you the wealth of the nations—their kings led in triumphal procession.* **For the nation or kingdom that will not serve you will perish; it will be utterly ruined.** *"The glory of*

*Lebanon will come to you, the pine, the fir and the cypress together, to adorn the place of my sanctuary; and I will glorify the place of my feet. **The sons of your oppressors will come bowing before you; all who despise you will bow down at your feet and will call you the City of the LORD, Zion of the Holy One of Israel.** "Although you have been forsaken and hated, with no one traveling through, I will make you the everlasting pride and the joy of all generations. You will drink the milk of nations and be nursed at royal breasts. <u>Then you will know that I, the LORD, am your Savior, your Redeemer, the Mighty One of Jacob.</u> Instead of bronze I will bring you gold, and silver in place of iron. Instead of wood I will bring you bronze, and iron in place of stones. <u>I will make peace your governor and righteousness your ruler.</u> **No longer will violence be heard in your land, nor ruin or destruction within your borders, but you will call your walls Salvation and your gates Praise.** The sun will no more be your light by day, nor will the brightness of the moon shine on you, for the LORD will be your everlasting light, and your God will be your glory. **Your sun will never set again, and your moon will wane no more; the LORD will be your everlasting light, and your days of sorrow will end. Then will <u>all your people</u> be righteous and they will possess the land forever.** They are the shoot I have planted, the work of my hands, for the display of my splendor. The least of you will become a thousand, the smallest a mighty nation. <u>I am the LORD; in its time I will do this swiftly.</u>* " (NIV)

Deut 28:13   *<u>The LORD will make you the head</u>, <u>not the tail</u>. If you pay attention to the commands of the LORD your God that I give you this day and carefully follow them, you will always be at the top, never at the bottom.* (NIV)

At this time Jesus will make a new covenant with the Jewish people. It is spoken of numerous times in scripture. This new covenant will be with the whole house of Jacob.

Jer 31:31-34   *"<u>The time is coming</u>," declares the LORD, "<u>when I will make a new covenant with the house of Israel and with the house of Judah</u>. It will not be like the covenant I made with their forefathers when I took them by the hand to lead them out of Egypt, because they broke my covenant, though I was a husband to them," declares the LORD. "<u>This is the covenant I will make with the house of Israel after that time</u>," declares the LORD. "I will put my law in their minds and write it on their hearts. I will be their God, and they will be my people. No longer will a man teach his neighbor, or a man his brother, saying, '<u>Know the LORD</u>,' because <u>they will all know me</u>, from the least of them to the greatest,"*

The Day of Vengeance — The Year of the Lord's Favor

*declares the LORD. "**For I will forgive their wickedness and will remember their sins no more.**"* (NIV)

Heb 8:7-13   ***For if there had been nothing wrong with that first covenant, no place would have been sought for another.** But God found fault with the people and said: "**The time is coming, declares the Lord, when I will make a new covenant with the house of Israel and with the house of Judah.** It will not be like the covenant I made with their forefathers when I took them by the hand to lead them out of Egypt, because they did not remain faithful to my covenant, and I turned away from them, declares the Lord. **This is the covenant I will make with the house of Israel after that time, declares the Lord. I will put my laws in their minds and write them on their hearts. I will be their God, and they will be my people.** No longer will a man teach his neighbor, or a man his brother, saying, 'Know the Lord,' because they will all know me, from the least of them to the greatest. For I will forgive their wickedness and will remember their sins no more." **By calling this covenant "new," he has made the first one obsolete; and what is obsolete and aging will soon disappear.*** (NIV)

God will bring the Jewish people into the bond of the covenant.

Ezek 20:30-38   *"**Therefore say to the house of Israel:** 'This is what the Sovereign LORD says: Will you defile yourselves the way your fathers did and lust after their vile images? When you offer your gifts—the sacrifice of your sons in the fire—you continue to defile yourselves with all your idols to this day. Am I to let you inquire of me, O house of Israel? As surely as I live, declares the Sovereign LORD, I will not let you inquire of me.'"You say, "We want to be like the nations, like the peoples of the world, who serve wood and stone." But what you have in mind will never happen. **As surely as I live, declares the Sovereign LORD, I will rule over you with a mighty hand and an outstretched arm and with outpoured wrath. I will bring you from the nations and gather you from the countries where you have been scattered—with a mighty hand and an outstretched arm and with outpoured wrath. I will bring you into the desert of the nations and there, face to face, I will execute judgment upon you. As I judged your fathers in the desert of the land of Egypt, so I will judge you, declares the Sovereign LORD. I will take note of you as you pass under my rod, and I will bring you into the bond of the covenant. I will purge you of those who revolt and rebel against me.** Although I will bring them out of the land where they are living, yet they will not enter the land of Israel. Then you will know that I am the LORD.* (NIV)

AFTER THE RAPTURE

God will put a new spirit in them.

Ezek 11:16-20   *"Therefore say: 'This is what the Sovereign LORD says: Although I sent them far away among the nations and scattered them among the countries, yet for a little while I have been a sanctuary for them in the countries where they have gone.'* **"Therefore say: 'This is what the Sovereign LORD says: I will gather you from the nations and bring you back from the countries where you have been scattered, and I will give you back the land of Israel again.' "They will return to it and remove all its vile images and detestable idols. <u>I will give them an undivided heart and put a new spirit in them</u>;** *I will remove from them their heart of stone and give them a heart of flesh. Then they will follow my decrees and be careful to keep my laws.* **<u>They will be my people, and I will be their God</u>.** (NIV)

Ezek 36:24-32   **"'For I will take you out of the nations; I will gather you from all the countries and bring you back into your own land. I will sprinkle clean water on you, and you will be clean; I will cleanse you from all your impurities and from all your idols. <u>I will give you a new heart and put a new spirit in you</u>; I will remove from you your heart of stone and give you a heart of flesh. <u>And I will put my Spirit in you and move you to follow my decrees and be careful to keep my laws</u>. You will live in the land I gave your forefathers; you will be my people, and I will be your God.** *I will save you from all your uncleanness. I will call for the grain and make it plentiful and will not bring famine upon you. I will increase the fruit of the trees and the crops of the field, so that you will no longer suffer disgrace among the nations because of famine. Then you will remember your evil ways and wicked deeds, and you will loathe yourselves for your sins and detestable practices. I want you to know that I am not doing this for your sake, declares the Sovereign LORD. Be ashamed and disgraced for your conduct, O house of Israel!* (NIV)

God will make a covenant of peace with the Jewish people. It will be an everlasting covenant, everlasting can mean forever! The nations will know that God is with Israel.

Ezek 34:25-31   **"'<u>I will make a covenant of peace with them</u> and rid the land of wild beasts so that they may live in the desert and sleep in the forests in safety.** *I will bless them and the places surrounding my hill. I will send down showers in season; there will be showers of blessing. The trees of the field will yield their fruit and the ground will yield its crops; the people will be secure in their land.* **They will know that I am the LORD, when I break the bars of their yoke and rescue them from the hands of those who enslaved them.** *They will*

The Day of Vengeance — The Year of the Lord's Favor

no longer be plundered by the nations, nor will wild animals devour them. ***They will live in safety, and no one will make them afraid.*** *I will provide for them a land renowned for its crops, and they will no longer be victims of famine in the land or bear the scorn of the nations.*** Then they will know that I, the LORD their God, am with them and that they, the house of Israel, are my people, declares the Sovereign LORD.*** *You my sheep, the sheep of my pasture, are people, and I am your God, declares the Sovereign LORD.'"* (NIV)

Ezek 37:26   ***I will make a covenant of peace with them; it will be an everlasting covenant. I will establish them and increase their numbers, and I will put my sanctuary among them forever.*** (NIV)

Jer 50:4-5   ***"In those days, at that time," declares the LORD, "the people of Israel and the people of Judah together will go in tears to seek the LORD their God. They will ask the way to Zion and turn their faces toward it.*** ***They will come and bind themselves to the LORD in an everlasting covenant that will not be forgotten.*** (NIV)

Isa 59:20-21   ***"The Redeemer will come to Zion, to those in Jacob who repent of their sins,"*** *declares the LORD.* ***"As for me, this is my covenant with them,"*** *says the LORD. "My Spirit, who is on you, and my words that I have put in your mouth will not depart from your mouth, or from the mouths of your children, or from the mouths of their descendants from this time on and forever," says the LORD.* (NIV)

God will never again rebuke Israel or remove His covenant of peace from them. In these verses, below, we see Israel restored as the wife of God. After her repentance God will take her back as His wife.

Isa 54:4-10   *"Do not be afraid; you will not suffer shame. Do not fear disgrace; you will not be humiliated. You will forget the shame of your youth and remember no more the reproach of your widowhood.* ***For your Maker is your husband—the LORD Almighty is his name—the Holy One of Israel is your Redeemer; he is called the God of all the earth. The LORD will call you back as if you were a wife deserted and distressed in spirit—a wife who married young, only to be rejected,"*** *says your God. "For a brief moment I abandoned you, but with deep compassion I will bring you back. In a surge of anger I hid my face from you for a moment, but with everlasting kindness I will have compassion on you," says the LORD your Redeemer. "To me this is like the days of Noah, when I swore that the waters of Noah would never again cover the earth.* ***So now I have sworn not to be angry with you,*** ***never*** ***to rebuke you again. Though the***

> *mountains be shaken and the hills be removed, <u>yet my unfailing love for you will not be shaken nor my covenant of peace be removed</u>," says the LORD, <u>who has compassion on you</u>.* (NIV)

Jer 3:14 *"<u>Return, faithless people</u>," declares the LORD, "<u>for I am your husband</u>. I will choose you—one from a town and two from a clan— and bring you to Zion.* (NIV)

Jesus actually brought this covenant to Israel when He came almost 2000 years ago. Peter quoted Joel in the book of Acts.

Acts 2:16-21 *No, this is what was spoken by the prophet Joel: "'<u>In the last days, God says, I will pour out my Spirit on all people.</u> Your sons and daughters will prophesy, your young men will see visions, your old men will dream dreams. Even on my servants, both men and women, I will pour out my Spirit in those days, and they will prophesy. I will show wonders in the heaven above and signs on the earth below, blood and fire and billows of smoke. The sun will be turned to darkness and the moon to blood before the coming of the great and glorious day of the Lord. And everyone who calls on the name of the Lord will be saved.'* (NIV)

In the last days, God says He will pour out His spirit on all people. Since the last days had their beginning at the first appearance of Jesus, this covenant began at that time. Because of the rejection of Jesus as their Messiah, the Jews as a nation rejected this covenant. However, if an individual Jew believes in Jesus during the Dispensation of Grace, he will be a participant of this covenant with God and be a member of the body of believers, known as the true church of God. The promise of a comforter was made by Jesus before He went to heaven to be at the right hand of God. During the Dispensation of Grace the bodies of the believers become the Temple of the Lord and at the very time they believe in Jesus as their personal Savior the Holy Spirit comes to reside in them.

John 14:16-17 *<u>And I will ask the Father, and he will give you another Counselor to be with you forever—the Spirit of truth</u>. The world cannot accept him, because it neither sees him nor knows him. But you know him, for he lives with you and will be in you.* (NIV)

John 14:26-27 *<u>But the Counselor, the Holy Spirit, whom the Father will send in my name, will teach you all things and will remind you of everything I have said to you</u>. Peace I leave with you; my peace I give you. I do not give to you as the world gives. Do not let your hearts be troubled and do not be afraid.* (NIV)

2 Cor 3:5-6 *Not that we are competent in ourselves to claim anything for*

> *ourselves, but our competence comes from God. **He has made us competent as ministers of a new covenant—not of the letter but of the Spirit; for the letter kills, but the Spirit gives life.*** (NIV)

My Uncle Paul pointed out a great passage in 2 Corinthians concerning the fate of the Jews during the Dispensation of Grace. Those Jews who fail to recognize Jesus as their Messiah during this time will have a veil covering their hearts. If an individual Jewish person does recognize Jesus as their Savior, the veil covering their heart will be removed and they will find salvation and become part of the body of believers. The first covenant of the law must be discarded and replaced by the new covenant if a Jewish person is to be saved during the Dispensation of Grace or else that person is under the condemnation of the law.

2 Cor 3:7-18
> *Now if the ministry that brought death, which was engraved in letters on stone, came with glory, so that the Israelites could not look steadily at the face of Moses because of its glory, fading though it was, will not the ministry of the Spirit be even more glorious?* ***If the ministry that condemns men is glorious, how much more glorious is the ministry that brings righteousness! For what was glorious has no glory now in comparison with the surpassing glory. And if what was fading away came with glory, how much greater is the glory of that which lasts!*** *Therefore, since we have such a hope, we are very bold.* ***We are not like Moses, who would put a veil over his face to keep the Israelites from gazing at it while the radiance was fading away. But their minds were made dull, for to this day the same veil remains when the old covenant is read. It has not been removed, because only in Christ is it taken away. Even to this day when Moses is read, a veil covers their hearts. But whenever anyone turns to the Lord, the veil is taken away.*** *Now the Lord is the Spirit, and where the Spirit of the Lord is, there is freedom. And we, who with unveiled faces all reflect the Lord's glory, are being transformed into his likeness with ever-increasing glory, which comes from the Lord, who is the Spirit.* (NIV)

The fulfillment of Joel 2:18-32, for the nation of Israel, when all Israel will be saved, will come about when all the Jews recognize Jesus as their Messiah. It will be a time when God takes pity on His chosen people.

Joel 2:18-32
> ***Then the LORD will be jealous for his land and take pity on his people.*** *The LORD will reply to them: 'I am sending you grain, new wine and oil, enough to satisfy you fully; never again will I make you an object of scorn to the nations. 'I will drive the northern army far from you, pushing it into a parched and barren land, with its front columns going into the eastern sea and those in the rear into the western sea. And its stench will go up; its smell will rise.' Surely he*

AFTER THE RAPTURE

has done great things. Be not afraid, O land; be glad and rejoice. Surely the LORD has done great things. Be not afraid, O wild animals, for the open pastures are becoming green. The trees are bearing their fruit; the fig tree and the vine yield their riches. Be glad, O people of Zion, rejoice in the LORD your God, for he has given you the autumn rains in righteousness. He sends you abundant showers, both autumn and spring rains, as before. The threshing floors will be filled with grain; the vats will overflow with new wine and oil. **'I will repay you for the years the locusts have eaten—the great locust and the young locust, the other locusts and the locust swarm—my great army that I sent among you.** *You will have plenty to eat, until you are full, and you will praise the name of the LORD your God, who has worked wonders for you; never again will my people be shamed.* **Then you will know that I am in Israel, that I am the LORD your God, and that there is no other; never again will my people be shamed. 'And afterward, I will pour out my Spirit on all people. Your sons and daughters will prophesy, your old men will dream dreams, your young men will see visions. Even on my servants, both men and women, I will pour out my Spirit in those days.** *I will show wonders in the heavens and on the earth, blood and fire and billows of smoke. The sun will be turned to darkness and the moon to blood before the coming of the great and dreadful day of the LORD.* **And everyone who calls on the name of the LORD will be saved; for on Mount Zion and in Jerusalem there will be deliverance, as the LORD has said, among the survivors whom the LORD calls.** (NIV)

The verses that precede Joel 2:28 contain a multitude of information. I might add that one of the most controversial verses in the Old Testament is among them and it is Joel 2:28. The great controversy is about the time frame of the fulfillment of the *"outpouring of the spirit on all people."*

In verses 18-20, we see the scene after the Battle of Armageddon, when Jesus restores His people (the Jews) to the land of Israel. After all Israel has been saved, Jesus will:

VERSE
- 18   take pity on His people
- 19   never again make you an object of scorn to the nations
- 20   defeat the northerner (the Antichrist)

In verses 21-24, we are told that the autumn and the spring rains will return to the land (Israel) to make it possible for the land to produce in abundance. This prophecy is not being fulfilled at this time as some people are contending. It will be fulfilled after Israel is restored to the land by Jesus during the Day of the Lord.

In verse 25, God promises to pay back Israel for all the years the locusts have

The Day of Vengeance — The Year of the Lord's Favor

eaten—this is referring to the time that the dominating empires of the world have trampled on the nation of Israel. These Gentile nations had their beginning in 606 BC and will culminate at the end of the age, plus a short period during the Time of Jacob's Trouble, this being equivalent to the Times of the Gentiles. These locusts break down like this:

the great locust	Babylonian Empire	606 BC to 539 BC
the young locust	Medo-Persian Empire	539 BC to 331 BC
the other locust	Greek Empire	331 BC to 63 BC
the locust swarm	Roman Empire	63 BC to end of the age
great army (locusts)*	Revived Roman Empire	Time of Jacob's Trouble

*This is not the army of locusts that appear in Joel 2:2

In verses 26-27, Jesus assures the Jewish people (twice) that they will never again be shamed. At this point the scripture becomes confusing. In Joel 2:28, Joel foresaw a day when God's spirit would be poured out on all nations—not just Israel. Since Peter did quote this verse, almost 2000 years ago, more than 800 years after its prediction, we know that it had at least a partial fulfillment during the Dispensation of Grace. However, the theme of the book of Joel is "the Day of the Lord" and I believe that the total fulfillment of this verse will come for the Jewish nation at that time. In the New Jerusalem Bible the book of Joel is broken down into four chapters instead of the usual three chapters found in most English translations. Chapter three is made up entirely of verses 28-32. They are referred to as Joel 3:1-5. As a separate chapter it makes it a little easier to understand.

In context, these verses are included with the signs in the sky—the sun will be turned to darkness and the moon to blood—to warn the Jews that the Great and Terrible Day of the Lord is about to begin. The Great and Terrible Day of the Lord is the last 3 ½ years of the Tribulation Period and is also known as the Time of Jacob's Trouble. This being the case, I believe that the total fulfillment of this prophecy will be *After the Rapture*. Although the Holy Spirit was removed at the Rapture, along with the believers (church), the ministry of the Holy Spirit will be alive and going strong *After the Rapture*.

The verses in Joel 2:28-32 indicate that God will be with the Jewish people *After the Rapture* who call on the name of the LORD (believe in Jesus as their Savior). This does not mean that they will be protected from the fury of God or even that they will not be martyred for their faith. What it does mean is that God will be living in their hearts as He pours out His spirit in those days, to help them through this awful time period. It means that they will be saved and that they will spend eternity with Jesus. It means that God will never leave them or forsake them. It means that at the moment a person accepts Jesus *After the Rapture*, the Holy Spirit will come and dwell in their heart. What a comfort to know.

Once the concept of the Day of the Lord is understood as the Millennium, it opens up a chronological consistency of the Old Testament prophets. The history books of the Old Testament are primarily an account of history interspersed with a few apocalyptic events. The classical major and minor prophetic books from Isaiah through Malachi are primarily concerned with the prophetic events of the first and second times the Messiah comes to the earth and are interspersed with some history before Christ. A large portion of the books of the latter prophets concern the Day of the Lord or the Kingdom Age. The Old Testament

AFTER THE RAPTURE

does not mention the Dispensation of Grace or the church age. It is totally missing where it belongs in history. The only hint of a change in the Old Testament is the revelation in Isaiah that Jesus (God's servant) will be a light to the Gentiles. Once the Old Testament reports the rejection of the Messiah (suffering servant), it skips over the church age and picks up the story when the Messiah returns to earth from heaven.

A FEAST FOR ALL PEOPLES

Jesus is not finished throwing banquets. After He has completed the task of purging sinful mankind from the earth and the banquet of the Great Supper of God has taken place, those who remain alive on earth will be the guests of a very important feast. At this banquet some important changes on mankind will effect how people live on earth during the peaceful portion of the Day of the Lord. To show how diverse translations can be and to better understand the meaning of this banquet, we will look at two different translations of these verses. Jesus is *"the Lord of hosts"* in the KJV and *"the Lord Almighty"* in the NIV.

> Isa 25:6-9 *And in this mountain shall <u>the LORD of hosts</u> make unto all people <u>a feast of fat things</u>, a feast of wines on the lees, of fat things full of marrow, of wines on the lees well refined. And he will destroy in this mountain the face of the covering cast over all people, and the veil that is spread over all nations. He will swallow up death in victory; and the Lord God will wipe away tears from off all faces; and the rebuke of his people shall he take away from off all the earth: for the LORD hath spoken it. **And it shall be said <u>in that day</u>, Lo, this is our God; we have waited for him, and he will save us: this is the LORD; we have waited for him, we will be glad and rejoice in his salvation.*** (KJV)

> Isa 25:6-9 *On this mountain <u>the LORD</u> Almighty will prepare a feast of rich food for all peoples, <u>a banquet of aged wine</u>—the best of meats and the finest of wines. On this mountain he will destroy the shroud that enfolds all peoples, the sheet that covers all nations; he will swallow up death forever. The Sovereign LORD will wipe away the tears from all faces; he will remove the disgrace of his people from all the earth. The LORD has spoken. **<u>In that day</u> they will say, "Surely this is our God; we trusted in him, and he saved us. This is the LORD, we trusted in him; let us rejoice and be glad in his salvation."*** (NIV)

This event will probably be the last event of the forty-five-day period following the Tribulation Period. Jesus will prepare a banquet for all the people on earth (Jew and Gentile) who were separated to His right side just before the Battle of Armageddon took place. They are all saved and will live in their fleshly bodies for the rest of the Millennium. This banquet will take place in Jerusalem where the finest food and wine will be served.

In verse seven, it appears that at some time in the past a covering was cast upon all people. The Hebrew word used here for "covering" is *lowt* and is listed as:

Brown-Driver-Brigg's Definition
3875 lowt-
a covering, an envelope

The Hebrew word for "cast" is *luwt* and is listed as:

Brown-Driver-Brigg's Definition
3874 luwt-
to wrap closely (tightly), to enwrap, to envelop
   a) (Qal) to wrap tightly
   b) (Hiphil) to envelop, to wrap

This covering seems to be a shroud that wraps tightly around all people. It is a sheet or veil that is spread over all nations. The Hebrew word for "veil" used here is *maccekah* and is listed as:

Brown-Driver-Brigg's Definition
4541 maccekah-
1) a pouring, a libation, a molten metal, a cast image, a drink-offering
   a) a libation (with covenant sacrifice)
   b) a molten metal, a molten image, molten gods
2) a web, a covering, a veil, woven stuff

Finally, the Hebrew word for *"that is spread"* in the King James and *"that covers"* in the New International Version is *nacak* and is listed as:

Strong's Definition
5259 nacak (naw-sak');
a primitive root [probably identical with 5258 through the idea of fusion]; to interweave, i.e. (figuratively) to overspread:
KJV— that is spread.

When we break these verses down, we see that at some point in history something is poured over, interwoven, cast upon or instilled in the presence of every person. It is a part of them. It appears that this presence in all peoples and nations is in the form of selfishness, greed, animosity and hatred toward each other (sin). It is in some form or another in all of us. It is brought out more in some people. It was probably instilled on mankind at the fall. It appears early in the Bible when Cain slew Abel. It is one of Satan's greatest weapons. It shows up in great proportions in people like Genghis Khan, Adolf Hitler and Joseph Stalin. It even shows up in people like Martin Luther, Jimmy Swaggert, you and me. We are all victims of this presence. Nevertheless, it can be controlled through our love for Christ.

In verse eight, we see that the people living during the Millennium will have victory over death. That does not mean the final victory over physical death, because we will all die once. Every person who was ever born will die physically in our natural (human) bodies. What this verse is referring to is the victory over death in the sense of death as a penalty. Death by sickness, disease, violence (murder) will no longer be a part of this age. Natural death will still occur. Longevity of life will be restored as it was before the flood. The final victory over death will come later and we will look at it in an upcoming chapter.

Jesus will wipe away (to blot out, to erase, to exterminate) the tears (weeping) of sorrow from the faces of those attending the banquet. They do not need to remember the heartache of past experiences. Finally, Jesus will remove (to come to an end) the rebuke (reproach, scorn, disgrace) of His people (Jews). They will no longer be a disgrace to the people living on the earth for the remainder of the Millennium. The Lord has spoken.

In that day (the Day of the Lord), the Jews will finally recognize Jesus as their Messiah and He will save them. All Israel will be saved. They will trust in Jesus and rejoice and be glad in His salvation.

You can imagine how the removal of the attributes at this banquet, discussed above, from all the people living on the earth during the peaceful portion of the Millennium will contribute to the peace of this time.

In the next chapter, we will give you an idea of what the conditions will be like in heaven and on earth for the remainder of the Day of the Lord. The time when Jesus will show favor to His chosen ones.

Ps 69:13-18 *But I pray to you, O LORD, in the time of your favor; in your great love, O God, answer me with your sure salvation. Rescue me from the mire, do not let me sink; deliver me from those who hate me, from the deep waters. Do not let the floodwaters engulf me or the depths swallow me up or the pit close its mouth over me. Answer me, O LORD, out of the goodness of your love; in your great mercy turn to me. Do not hide your face from your servant; answer me quickly, for I am in trouble. Come near and rescue me; redeem me because of my foes.* (NIV)

Ps 106:1-5 *Praise the LORD. Give thanks to the LORD, for he is good; his love endures forever. Who can proclaim the mighty acts of the LORD or fully declare his praise? Blessed are they who maintain justice, who constantly do what is right. Remember me, O LORD, when you show favor to your people, come to my aid when you save them, that I may enjoy the prosperity of your chosen ones, that I may share in the joy of your nation and join your inheritance in giving praise.* (NIV)

CHAPTER THIRTEEN

THE REST OF THE MILLENNIUM

What would it be like living in the world without the influence of Satan and his helpers? What would it be like living in a world that does not have any wars for almost a thousand years? What would it be like living in a world where human beings and resurrected saints co-mingle daily? What would it be like living in a world theocracy with Jesus as King with His throne in Jerusalem? What would it be like living in a world with the Jewish nation of Israel set up to be the head of all nations? We will try to answer these questions and more as we look at the Bible to see what it says about *The Rest of the Millennium*.

In order to establish a world anything like we mentioned above, we need to have two elements removed. Those two elements would be Satan and his followers and wicked sinful (unsaved) mankind or the enemies of God. That is exactly what will take place in the first ten years of the Day of the Lord. King David wrote concerning this very subject three thousand years ago. Here it is clear that the rule of Jesus will begin in heaven, while His enemies are still on the earth.

> Ps 110:1-7 ***The LORD says to my Lord: "Sit at my right hand until I make your enemies a footstool for your feet." The LORD will extend your mighty scepter from Zion; you will rule in the midst of your enemies.*** *Your troops will be willing on your day of battle. Arrayed in holy majesty, from the womb of the dawn you will receive the dew of your youth. The LORD has sworn and will not change his mind: "You are a priest forever, in the order of Melchizedek."* ***The Lord is at your right hand; he will crush kings on the day of his wrath. He will judge the nations, heaping up the dead and crushing the rulers of the whole earth.*** *He will drink from a brook beside the way; therefore he will lift up his head.* (NIV)

The New Testament book of Hebrews informs us that Jesus went to be at the right hand of God in heaven. Jesus will remain there until His enemies have been defeated. In fact, the entire chapter is a complete message for our Jewish brothers. Jesus who is coming will not delay. Let us encourage each other as we see the Day of the Lord approaching.

> Heb 10:1-39 ***The law is only a shadow of the good things that are coming—not the realities themselves.*** *For this reason it can never, by the same sacrifices repeated endlessly year after year, make perfect those who draw near to worship. If it could, would they not have stopped being offered? For the worshipers would have been cleansed once for all, and would no longer have felt guilty for their sins.* ***But those sacrifices are an annual reminder of sins, because it is impossible for the blood of bulls and goats to take away sins.*** *Therefore, when Christ came into the world, he said: "Sacrifice and offerings you did not desire, but a body you prepared for me; with burnt offerings and*

sin offerings you were not pleased. Then I said, 'Here I am—it is written about me in the scroll—I have come to do your will, O God.'" First he said, "Sacrifices and offerings, burnt offerings and sin offerings you did not desire, nor were you pleased with them" (although the law required them to be made). Then he said, "Here I am, I have come to do your will." **He sets aside the first to establish the second.** And by that will, we have been made holy through the sacrifice of the body of Jesus Christ once for all. Day after day every priest stands and performs his religious duties; again and again he offers the same sacrifices, which can never take away sins. **<u>But when this priest had offered for all time one sacrifice for sins, he sat down at the right hand of God. Since that time he waits for his enemies to be made his footstool,</u> because by one sacrifice he has made perfect forever those who are being made holy.** The Holy Spirit also testifies to us about this. First he says: "This is the covenant I will make with them after that time, says the Lord. I will put my laws in their hearts, and I will write them on their minds." Then he adds: "Their sins and lawless acts I will remember no more." And where these have been forgiven, there is no longer any sacrifice for sin. **Therefore, brothers, since we have confidence to enter the Most Holy Place by the blood of Jesus, by a new and living way opened for us through the curtain, that is, his body, and since we have a great priest over the house of God, let us draw near to God with a sincere heart in full assurance of faith, having our hearts sprinkled to cleanse us from a guilty conscience and having our bodies washed with pure water.** Let us hold unswervingly to the hope we profess, for he who promised is faithful. And let us consider how we may spur one another on toward love and good deeds. Let us not give up meeting together, as some are in the habit of doing, **but let us encourage one another—and all the more as you see <u>the Day</u> approaching.** If we deliberately keep on sinning after we have received the knowledge of the truth, no sacrifice for sins is left, but only a fearful expectation of judgment and of raging fire that will consume the enemies of God. Anyone who rejected the law of Moses died without mercy on the testimony of two or three witnesses. How much more severely do you think a man deserves to be punished who has trampled the Son of God under foot, who has treated as an unholy thing the blood of the covenant that sanctified him, and who has insulted the Spirit of grace? For we know him who said, "It is mine to avenge; I will repay," and again, "The Lord will judge his people." It is a dreadful thing to fall into the hands of the living God. Remember those earlier days after you had received the light, when you stood your ground in a great contest in the face of suffering. Sometimes you were publicly exposed to insult and persecution; at

The Rest of the Millennium

> *other times you stood side by side with those who were so treated. You sympathized with those in prison and joyfully accepted the confiscation of your property, because you knew that you yourselves had better and lasting possessions. So do not throw away your confidence; it will be richly rewarded.* ***You need to persevere so that when you have done the will of God, you will receive what he has promised.*** ***For in just a very little while, "He who is coming will come and will not delay. But my righteous one will live by faith. And if he shrinks back, I will not be pleased with him." But we are not of those who shrink back and are destroyed, but of those who believe and are saved.*** (NIV)

The process of purging unsaved mankind from the earth will leave the world destroyed. Our newly arrived King, Jesus, will establish His kingdom on earth. As you can imagine this will be a unique time. The Day of the Lord will include the worst time period of human history, along with the best time period of human history. The curse imposed at the fall of man will be greatly reduced. People will live in peace and safety. Jesus will rule and reign with the resurrected Tribulation saints over mankind in the flesh. All of the saints who were resurrected at the time of the Rapture, along with the holy angels, will reside in heaven for the entire one thousand year period of the Day of Christ. The resurrected saints who accepted Jesus *After the Rapture,* will reign and dwell on earth with Jesus after He establishes His Kingdom on earth as part of the Day of the Lord. I am ready! Are you?

For those of you who have a hard time believing that saints in resurrected bodies can co-mingle with people living in fleshly bodies during this time, I can only point out that Jesus Himself spent forty days on earth in His resurrected body personally teaching the disciples before He went to be at the right hand of God. Let us now look at what it will be like for the rest of the Millennium.

NEW HEAVENS AND NEW EARTH

After just passing through the destructive period of the time of the Tribulation Period, followed by the Battle of Armageddon, can the human race continue? God caused a flood to cleanse wicked mankind almost 4500 years ago and then allowed mankind to continue. Now at this time God will destroy wicked mankind with the fire of His fierce anger and will again allow mankind to live on in a different age since the beginning of history. It will not be the perfect age because sin will still exist during this time, but it will be the most peaceful time mankind has experienced since before the fall of Adam and Eve in the Garden of Eden.

Isa 65:17-25 *"**Behold, I will create new heavens and a new earth.** **The former things will not be remembered, nor will they come to mind.** But be glad and rejoice forever in what I will create, for I will create Jerusalem to be a delight and its people a joy. I will rejoice over Jerusalem and take delight in my people; the sound of weeping and of crying will be heard in it no more. **"Never again will there be in** *it an infant who lives but a few days, or an old man who does not live out his years; he who dies at a hundred will be thought a mere youth; he who fails to reach a hundred will be considered accursed. They will build houses and dwell in them; they will plant vineyards and eat their fruit.* No longer will they build houses and others live in them, or plant and others eat. For as the days of a tree, so will be the days of my people; my chosen ones will long enjoy the works of their hands. ***They will not toil in vain or bear children doomed to misfortune; for they will be a people blessed by the LORD, they and their descendants with them.*** *Before they call I will answer; while they are still speaking I will hear.* ***The wolf and the lamb will feed together, and the lion will eat straw like the ox, but dust will be the serpent's food. They will neither harm nor destroy on all my holy mountain," says the LORD.*** (NIV)

These nine verses tell us multitudes about the peaceful portion of the Day of the Lord. The human beings who are left, the remnant of both the Jews and the Gentiles (nations), will be those who will repopulate the earth. They were supernaturally shielded (protected) at the Battle of Armageddon. We are told that these people, those who will be continuing in this new age, will not remember the period of judgment that they have just passed through, just as a woman forgets about the pain of childbirth because of the joy of a child being born. Jerusalem as a rebuilt city will be a delight and the people (Jews) who live in Jerusalem a joy. In Jerusalem there will be no more crying or weeping. Children will not die at birth and men will live the full length of their lives becoming old men. People will build their own houses and live in them and no one will take their houses from them. People who plant vineyards will eat the fruit of them. People will enjoy their jobs. They will not toil in vain bearing children doomed to misfortune. They and their descendants will be blessed by the Lord. The wolf and the lamb will eat side by side. The lion will eat hay like an ox. Animals will no longer be carnivorous (flesh eating). This could also include humans who could possibly become herbivorous (feed on plants). It even mentions that snakes will exist during this time and they will still crawl on the ground. These snakes will not be harmful.

This is the fulfillment of Daniel's prophecy of the coming kingdom that will never be destroyed. A King from this kingdom will destroy all the previously existing kingdoms. The rock (Jesus) that struck the statue (all the kingdoms of the earth) became a huge mountain (kingdom) and filled the entire earth and reaches to the third level of heaven.

Dan 2:44-45 *"<u>**In the time of those kings, the God of heaven will set up a kingdom that will never be destroyed**</u>, nor will it be left to another people. It will crush all those kingdoms and bring them to an end, <u>**but it will itself endure forever**</u>. This is the meaning of the vision of the rock cut out of a mountain, but not by human hands—a rock that broke the iron, the bronze, the clay, the silver and the gold to pieces. "The great God has shown the king what will take place in the future. The dream is true and the interpretation is trustworthy."* (NIV)

The Rest of the Millennium

After the defeat of the Antichrist/Satan, the saints will possess this great kingdom. This kingdom will last forever and all the leaders of the people will worship Jesus. The Lord will dwell in this kingdom forever.

Dan 7:21-27   *As I watched, this horn was waging war against the saints and defeating them, until the Ancient of Days came and pronounced judgment in favor of the saints of the Most High, and the time came when they possessed the kingdom. "He gave me this explanation: 'The fourth beast is a fourth kingdom that will appear on earth. It will be different from all the other kingdoms and will devour the whole earth, trampling it down and crushing it. The ten horns are ten kings who will come from this kingdom. After them another king will arise, different from the earlier ones; he will subdue three kings. He will speak against the Most High and oppress his saints and try to change the set times and the laws. The saints will be handed over to him for a time, times and half a time.* **"'But the court will sit, and his power will be taken away and completely destroyed forever. <u>Then the sovereignty, power and greatness of the kingdoms under the whole heaven will be handed over to the saints, the people of the Most High</u>**. *His kingdom will be an everlasting kingdom, and all rulers will worship and obey him.'* (NIV)

Ps 68:15-16   *The mountains of Bashan are majestic mountains; rugged are the mountains of Bashan. <u>Why gaze in envy, O rugged mountains, at the mountain where God chooses to reign, where the LORD himself will dwell forever</u>?* (NIV)

The Antichrist, Satan, false prophet, the unsaved armies of the world and the rest of the unsaved people of the world waged war against God and Jesus and lost. Jesus will come from heaven as a King.

Rev 17:14   *"They will make war against the Lamb, <u>but the Lamb will overcome them because he is Lord of lords and King of kings</u>—and with him will be his called, chosen and faithful followers.* (NIV)

From the time of the Rapture the resurrected saints and the holy angels will dwell in their heavenly home during the Millennium. Jesus will be headquartered on earth in Jerusalem and will rule His entire kingdom—the new heavens and new earth—from His throne. The Tribulation saints, after they have received their rewards and positions of honor for their service, will serve their King and High Priest and live with Him in Jerusalem. The greater the service for Jesus, the greater the position they will fill during the rest of the one thousand year period. The saints in their resurrected bodies, along with the holy angels, will be able to travel throughout the universe in an instant. Resurrected bodies have superiority over both time and space, as seen by the account of Jesus in His resurrected body.

AFTER THE RAPTURE

The resurrected saints from the time of the Rapture will reside in the house of the Lord in the heavenly city of Jerusalem prepared for them by God. This will be their dwelling for eternity. The holy angels will more than likely reside in the same location in heaven, which is the same place they were dwelling during previous ages. They will make regular visits to earth to worship and serve God. In Psalms 122, we have a view of the city, heavenly Jerusalem, where the Old Testament saints will dwell during the Millennium.

> Ps 122:1-3 *I rejoiced with those who said to me, "Let us go to the house of the LORD." Our feet are standing in your gates, O Jerusalem. Jerusalem is built like a city that is closely compacted together.* (NIV)

On earth there will be various nations and nationalities. Of course, Israel will be the head nation of all the nations. In the beginning, right after Armageddon, all the human beings who survived will be saved, but as the people begin to procreate, each individual person will be responsible for their own salvation—just as it has been since Adam and Eve. There will be differences between nations, but no wars. The differences will be settled by Jesus. There will be people who sin and do not accept Jesus as their Savior, but the influence of Satan and the fallen angels will be removed, at least for the rest of the age. The people will again be able to live hundreds of years, just as Methuselah did in the Old Testament—he lived to the ripe old age of 969 years. The curse on men, women and the land will be partially removed, with reduced sweat on man's brow (burden of their work), no pain for women at childbirth and fewer thorns and thistles in the farmers fields. Sickness, disease and deformity will be healed. It almost sounds like a fairy tale, doesn't it? Scripture reveals that this is not a fairy tale, but reality. There are vast amounts of scripture describing this period, with most of it found in the Old Testament. All mankind will bow down to God.

> Isa 66:22-23 *"As the new heavens and the new earth that I make will endure before me," declares the LORD, "so will your name and descendants endure. From one New Moon to another and from one Sabbath to another, all mankind will come and bow down before me," says the LORD.* (NIV)

Other sets of scriptures concerning the animals and children are found in Isaiah and Hosea.

> Isa 11:6-9 *The wolf will live with the lamb, the leopard will lie down with the goat, the calf and the lion and the yearling together; and a little child will lead them. The cow will feed with the bear, their young will lie down together, and the lion will eat straw like the ox. The infant will play near the hole of the cobra, and the young child put his hand into the viper's nest. They will neither harm nor destroy on all my holy mountain, for the earth will be full of the knowledge of the LORD as the waters cover the sea.* (NIV)

Hosea 2:18 *In that day I will make a covenant for them with the beasts of the field and the birds of the air and the creatures that move along the ground. <u>Bow and sword and battle I will abolish from the land</u>, <u>so that all may lie down in safety</u>.* (NIV)

Wars will be no more, as you can see from the scripture verses listed above and below.

Ps 46:1-11 *God is our refuge and strength, an ever-present help in trouble. Therefore we will not fear, though the earth give way and the mountains fall into the heart of the sea, though its waters roar and foam and the mountains quake with their surging. Selah There is a river whose streams make glad the city of God, the holy place where the Most High dwells. God is within her, she will not fall; God will help her at break of day.* **Nations are in uproar, kingdoms fall; he lifts his voice, the earth melts. The LORD Almighty is with us; the God of Jacob is our fortress. Selah Come and see the works of the LORD, the desolations he has brought on the earth.** <u>**He makes wars cease to the ends of the earth; he breaks the bow and shatters the spear, he burns the shields with fire.**</u> *"Be still, and know that I am God; I will be exalted among the nations, I will be exalted in the earth." The LORD Almighty is with us; the God of Jacob is our fortress. Selah* (NIV)

Micah 4:3 *…They will beat their swords into plowshares and their spears into pruning hooks. <u>Nation will not take up sword against nation</u>, <u>nor will they train for war anymore</u>.* (NIV)

Isa 2:4 *…They will beat their swords into plowshares and their spears into pruning hooks. <u>Nation will not take up sword against nation</u>, <u>nor will they train for war anymore</u>.* (NIV)

There will be a highway from Assyria all the way to Egypt passing through Jerusalem called the "Way of Holiness." During this time there will be no more deaf, blind, lame or mute people. All the nationalities of the world are God's people.

Isa 35:5-10 **Then will the eyes of the blind be opened and the ears of the deaf unstopped. Then will the lame leap like a deer, and the mute tongue shout for joy.** *Water will gush forth in the wilderness and streams in the desert. The burning sand will become a pool, the thirsty ground bubbling springs. In the haunts where jackals once lay, grass and reeds and papyrus will grow.* <u>**And a highway will be there; it will be called the Way of Holiness.**</u> *The unclean will not journey on it; it will be for those who walk in that Way; wicked fools will not go about on it. No lion will be there, nor will any ferocious* *beast get up on it; they will not be found there.* ***But only the redeemed will walk there, and the ransomed of the LORD will return.*** *They will enter Zion with singing; everlasting joy will crown their heads. Gladness and joy will overtake them, and sorrow and sighing will flee away.* (NIV)

Isa 19:23-25 ***In that day there will be a highway from Egypt to Assyria.*** *The Assyrians will go to Egypt and the Egyptians to Assyria. The Egyptians and Assyrians will worship together. In that day Israel will be the third, along with Egypt and Assyria, a blessing on the earth. The LORD Almighty will bless them, saying,* ***"Blessed be Egypt my people, Assyria my handiwork, and Israel my inheritance."*** (NIV)

Every valley will be raised up and every mountain will be made low when the earth is left bare. Whether Jesus will restore majestic mountains, like we have now on the earth at this time, we will not know until He restores the earth. We do know that the Temple in Jerusalem will exist on a higher elevation than the surrounding area.

Isa 40:4-5 ***Every valley shall be raised up, every mountain and hill made low; the rough ground shall become level, the rugged places a plain.*** *And the glory of the LORD will be revealed, and all mankind together will see it. For the mouth of the LORD has spoken."* (NIV)

Fair weather conditions will prevail during this age. The climate will be constant with no more natural disasters like floods, tornados, hurricanes, cyclones or earthquakes. These disasters that occur in our present age are a result of the cause and effect from sin. Part of the punishment of sin today is in the form of natural disasters, though it rains on the just and the unjust. God is in control of all of the weather elements. The reduction of the sinful acts during this time will eliminate the natural disasters that are occurring at the present time.

Water, even today, is becoming a problem all around the globe. Some areas of the earth face acute shortages of water. Mankind has polluted water everywhere. Chemicals in the name of fertilizers and insecticides cause disease to fall on mankind. In the near future water will face even harsher penalties during the Tribulation Period. In the rest of the Millennium the water will be cleansed and will be available in all parts of the earth in the form of rainfall at the proper time for agricultural needs and lakes, rivers and streams for human consumption and for agricultural purposes. There will be no more droughts, except where people fail to follow God.

Ezek 34:26-27 *I will bless them and the places surrounding my hill.* ***I will send down showers in season; there will be showers of blessing.*** *The trees of the field will yield their fruit and the ground will yield its crops; the people will be secure in their land. They will know that I am the LORD, when I break the bars of their yoke and rescue them from the hands of those who enslaved them.* (NIV)

The Rest of the Millennium

Joel 2:21-24 — *Be not afraid, O land; be glad and rejoice. Surely the LORD has done great things. Be not afraid, O wild animals, for the open pastures are becoming green. The trees are bearing their fruit; the fig tree and the vine yield their riches. Be glad, O people of Zion, rejoice in the LORD your God, for he has given you the autumn rains in righteousness.* <u>**He sends you abundant showers, both autumn and spring rains, as before.**</u> *The threshing floors will be filled with grain; the vats will overflow with new wine and oil.* (NIV)

Isa 35:6-7 — *Then will the lame leap like a deer, and the mute tongue shout for joy.* <u>**Water will gush forth in the wilderness and streams in the desert.**</u> *The burning sand will become a pool, the thirsty ground bubbling springs. In the haunts where jackals once lay, grass and reeds and papyrus will grow.* (NIV)

Isa 41:18-20 — <u>***I will make rivers flow on barren heights, and springs within the valleys. I will turn the desert into pools of water, and the parched ground into springs.***</u> *I will put in the desert the cedar and the acacia, the myrtle and the olive. I will set pines in the wasteland, the fir and the cypress together, so that people may see and know, may consider and understand, that the hand of the LORD has done this, that the Holy One of Israel has created it.* (NIV)

Do not forget about the streams that flow forth from the rebuilt Temple in Jerusalem, lined with fruit trees that serve for food and healing. These streams will be full of all kinds of fish.

Ezek 47:1-12 — *The man brought me back to the entrance of the temple, and I saw water coming out from under the threshold of the temple toward the east (for the temple faced east). The water was coming down from under the south side of the temple, south of the altar. He then brought me out through the north gate and led me around the outside to the outer gate facing east, and the water was flowing from the south side. As the man went eastward with a measuring line in his hand, he measured off a thousand cubits and then led me through water that was ankle-deep. He measured off another thousand cubits and led me through water that was knee-deep. He measured off another thousand and led me through water that was up to the waist. He measured off another thousand, but now it was a river that I could not cross, because the water had risen and was deep enough to swim in—a river that no one could cross. He asked me, "Son of man, do you see this?" Then he led me back to the bank of the river. When I arrived there, I saw a great number of trees on each side of the river. He said to me, "This water flows toward the eastern region and goes down into the Arabah, where it enters the Sea. When it empties into the Sea, the water there becomes fresh. Swarms of living creatures will live wherever the river flows.* **There will be large numbers of fish, because this water flows there and makes the salt water fresh; so where the river flows everything will live.** *Fishermen will stand along the shore; from En Gedi to En Eglaim there will be places for spreading nets.* **The fish will be of many kinds—like the fish of the Great Sea.** *But the swamps and marshes will not become fresh; they will be left for salt.* **Fruit trees of all kinds will grow on both banks of the river.** *Their leaves will not wither, nor will their fruit fail. Every month they will bear, because the water from the sanctuary flows to them. Their fruit will serve for food and their leaves for healing."* (NIV)

Zech 14:8 **<u>On that day living water will flow out from Jerusalem</u>, half to the eastern sea and half to the western sea, in summer and in winter.** (NIV)

The climatic changes, along with the proper amount of water, will produce in abundance the productiveness of agricultural products. The waste areas of the earth will become fruitful and the deserts will bloom. The mountains and the hills will become productive. The crops will grow in abundance and no one will go to bed hungry. There will be no more famines. These are all promises from God.

Ps 104:29-30 *When you hide your face, they are terrified; when you take away their breath, they die and return to the dust. <u>When you send your Spirit, they are created</u>, <u>and you renew the face of the earth.</u>* (NIV)

Isa 35:1-2 ***<u>The desert and the parched land will be glad</u>; <u>the wilderness will rejoice and blossom.</u>** Like the crocus, it will burst into bloom; it will rejoice greatly and shout for joy. The glory of Lebanon will be given to it, the splendor of Carmel and Sharon; they will see the glory of the LORD, the splendor of our God.* (NIV)

Ps 72:16 *<u>Let grain abound throughout the land</u>; on the tops of the hills may it sway. Let its fruit flourish like Lebanon; let it thrive like the grass of the field.* (NIV)

Amos 9:13 *"<u>The days are coming</u>," declares the LORD, "<u>when the reaper will be overtaken by the plowman and the planter by the one treading grapes</u>. New wine will drip from the mountains and flow from all the hills.* (NIV)

Ezek 34:29 *<u>I will provide for them a land renowned for its crops, and they will</u>*

no longer be victims of famine in the land or bear the scorn of the nations. (NIV)

A stumbling block for people of today is the language barrier. The people will speak a pure language to serve Jesus in unity. Some have speculated that it will be Hebrew, but that is not confirmed in scripture. Other languages will be spoken during this time, but everyone will know and speak this pure language.

Zeph 3:9   **"*For then I will restore to the peoples a pure language*, that they all may call on the name of the LORD, to serve Him with one accord.** (NKJ)

The Psalms describe the majesty of God during the age of the Messianic Kingdom as Jesus is made the ruler over all the works of God's creation. He will be exalted over all the nations. *"How awesome is the LORD Most High, the great King over all the earth!"*

Ps 8:1-9   *<u>O LORD, our Lord, how majestic is your name in all the earth!</u> You have set your glory above the heavens. From the lips of children and infants you have ordained praise because of your enemies, to silence the foe and the avenger.* **When I consider your heavens, the work of your fingers, the moon and the stars, which you have set in place, what is man that you are mindful of him, <u>the son of man that you care for him</u>? <u>You made him a little lower than the heavenly beings and crowned him with glory and honor.</u> <u>You made him ruler over the works of your hands</u>; <u>you put everything under his feet</u>: all flocks and herds, and the beasts of the field, the birds of the air, and the fish of the sea, all that swim the paths of the seas. O LORD, our Lord, how majestic is your name in all the earth!** (NIV)

Ps 47:1-2   *Clap your hands, all you nations; shout to God with cries of joy. <u>How awesome is the LORD Most High, the great King over all the earth</u>!* (NIV)

Ps 113:1-9   *Praise the LORD. Praise, O servants of the LORD, praise the name of the LORD. <u>Let the name of the LORD be praised, both now and forevermore.</u> From the rising of the sun to the place where it sets, the name of the LORD is to be praised.* **<u>The LORD is exalted over all the nations, his glory above the heavens.</u>** *Who is like the LORD our God, the One who sits enthroned on high, who stoops down to look on the heavens and the earth? He raises the poor from the dust and lifts the needy from the ash heap; he seats them with princes, with the princes of their people. He settles the barren woman in her home as a happy mother of children. Praise the LORD.* (NIV)

Below, we will list the many duties of Jesus during the Kingdom Age. Jesus will be our King, Judge, Redeemer, the Branch, a Rock and our High Priest during the Millennium.

JESUS

AS KING — At this time Jesus will become all things to all men. He will be King of Kings and Lord of Lords and rule from His throne in Jerusalem. The entire earth will be under a single Monarch. Believe it or not we will be living in a one-world government, only this time it will be the right one-world government with the right one-world leader. The doom and gloom portion of the Day of the Lord is over! The King has just defeated God's enemies. Jesus will not only be King of Israel, but of all the nations.

Isa 9:1-7 — *__Nevertheless, there will be no more gloom for those who were in distress.__ In the past he humbled the land of Zebulun and the land of Naphtali, but in the future he will honor Galilee of the Gentiles, by the way of the sea, along the Jordan—The people walking in darkness have seen a great light; on those living in the land of the shadow of death a light has dawned. You have enlarged the nation and increased their joy; they rejoice before you as people rejoice at the harvest, as men rejoice when dividing the plunder. For as in the day of Midian's defeat, you have shattered the yoke that burdens them, the bar across their shoulders, the rod of their oppressor. Every warrior's boot used in battle and every garment rolled in blood will be destined for burning, will be fuel for the fire. __For to us a child is born, to us a son is given, and the government will be on his shoulders. And he will be called Wonderful Counselor, Mighty God, Everlasting Father, Prince of Peace. Of the increase of his government and peace there will be no end.__ He will reign on David's throne and over his kingdom, establishing and upholding it with justice and righteousness from that time on and forever. The zeal of the LORD Almighty will accomplish this.* (NIV)

Zech 14:9 — *__The LORD will be king over the whole earth. On that day there will be one LORD, and his name the only name.__* (NIV)

Ps 2:2-6 — *The kings of the earth take their stand and the rulers gather together against the LORD and against __his Anointed One__. "Let us break their chains," they say, "and throw off their fetters." __The One enthroned in heaven laughs; the Lord scoffs at them.__ Then he rebukes them in his anger and terrifies them in his wrath, saying, "__I have installed my King on Zion, my holy hill.__"* (NIV)

Zech 9:9-10 — *Rejoice greatly, O Daughter of Zion! Shout, Daughter of Jerusalem! See, your king comes to you, righteous and having*

The Rest of the Millennium

*salvation, gentle and riding on a donkey, on a colt, the foal of a donkey. I will take away the chariots from Ephraim and the war-horses from Jerusalem, and the battle bow will be broken. **He will proclaim peace to the nations. His rule will extend from sea to sea and from the River to the ends of the earth.*** (NIV)

Below, we see Jesus as He rules during the 1000 year period of the Day of the Lord. He will judge in righteousness. He will crush the oppressor, who is the Antichrist. The whole earth will be filled with His glory. It will be the allotted time for God to bring all the things in heaven and earth together under a single ruler. It will be time for His Son to reign as King.

Ps 72:1-20 ***Endow the king with your justice, O God, the royal son with your righteousness.** He will judge your people in righteousness, your afflicted ones with justice. The mountains will bring prosperity to the people, the hills the fruit of righteousness. **He will defend the afflicted among the people and save the children of the needy; he will crush the oppressor.** He will endure as long as the sun, as long as the moon, through all generations. He will be like rain falling on a mown field, like showers watering the earth. In his days the righteous will flourish; prosperity will abound till the moon is no more. **He will rule from sea to sea and from the River to the ends of the earth.** The desert tribes will bow before him and his enemies will lick the dust. The kings of Tarshish and of distant shores will bring tribute to him; the kings of Sheba and Seba will present him gifts. **All kings will bow down to him and all nations will serve him.** For he will deliver the needy who cry out, the afflicted who have no one to help. He will take pity on the weak and the needy and save the needy from death. He will rescue them from oppression and violence, for precious is their blood in his sight. **Long may he live!** May gold from Sheba be given him. May people ever pray for him and bless him all day long. Let grain abound throughout the land; on the tops of the hills may it sway. Let its fruit flourish like Lebanon; let it thrive like the grass of the field. May his name endure forever; may it continue as long as the sun. **All nations will be blessed through him, and they will call him blessed.** Praise be to the LORD God, the God of Israel, who alone does marvelous deeds. **Praise be to his glorious name forever; may the whole earth be filled with his glory.** Amen and Amen. This concludes the prayers of David son of Jesse.* (NIV)

Rev 19:16 *And he hath on his vesture and on his thigh a name written, **KING OF KINGS, AND LORD OF LORDS**.* (KJV)

Eph 1:9-10 *And he made known to us the mystery of his will according to his good pleasure, which he purposed in Christ, to be put into effect when the times will have reached their fulfillment—to bring all things in heaven and on earth together under one head, even Christ.* (NIV)

AS JUDGE — Jesus will set up a judicial system around the globe to handle disputes that arise among the people. However, the supreme court will fall on Jesus Himself, who is also the lawgiver. *"For the LORD is our judge, the LORD is our lawgiver, the LORD is our king; it is he who will save us."* (NIV) This judicial system will be fair and equitable, unlike the systems that exist in all parts of the world today. There will be no judicial corruption in His judicial system when Jesus is the ruler of the earth.

Micah 4:1-5 *In the last days the mountain of the LORD's temple will be established as chief among the mountains; it will be raised above the hills, and peoples will stream to it. Many nations will come and say, "Come, let us go up to the mountain of the LORD, to the house of the God of Jacob. He will teach us his ways, so that we may walk in his paths." The law will go out from Zion, the word of the LORD from Jerusalem. He will judge between many peoples and will settle disputes for strong nations far and wide. They will beat their swords into plowshares and their spears into pruning hooks. Nation will not take up sword against nation, nor will they train for war anymore. Every man will sit under his own vine and under his own fig tree, and no one will make them afraid, for the LORD Almighty has spoken. All the nations may walk in the name of their Gods; we will walk in the name of the LORD our God for ever and ever.* (NIV)

Isa 2:2-4 *In the last days the mountain of the LORD's temple will be established as chief among the mountains; it will be raised above the hills, and all nations will stream to it. Many peoples will come and say, "Come, let us go up to the mountain of the LORD, to the house of the God of Jacob. He will teach us his ways, so that we may walk in his paths." The law will go out from Zion, the word of the LORD from Jerusalem. He will judge between the nations and will settle disputes for many peoples. They will beat their swords into plowshares and their spears into pruning hooks. Nation will not take up sword against nation, nor will they train for war anymore.* (NIV)

Isa 33:20-24 *Look upon Zion, the city of our festivals; your eyes will see Jerusalem, a peaceful abode, a tent that will not be moved; its stakes will never be pulled up, nor any of its ropes broken. There the LORD will be our Mighty One. It will be like a place of broad rivers and streams. No galley with oars will ride them, no mighty ship will sail them. For the LORD is our judge, the LORD is our lawgiver, the LORD is our king; it is he who will save us. Your rigging hangs loose: The mast is not held secure, the sail is not spread. Then an abundance of spoils will be divided and even the lame will carry off plunder. No one living in Zion will say, "I am ill"; and the sins of those who dwell there will be forgiven.* (NIV)

AS THE REDEEMER — Jesus is not only the Redeemer of Israel, but He is the Redeemer of all mankind, who is under the bondage of sin.

Isa 44:6 *"Thus says the LORD, <u>the King of Israel, and his Redeemer, the LORD of hosts</u>: 'I am the First and I am the Last; besides Me there is no God.* (NKJ)

Isa 59:20 *"<u>The Redeemer will come to Zion</u>, to those in Jacob who repent of their sins," declares the LORD.* (NIV)

Isa 49:26 *I will make your oppressors eat their own flesh; they will be drunk on their own blood, as with wine. Then all mankind will know that <u>I, the LORD, am your Savior, your Redeemer, the Mighty One of Jacob.</u>"* (NIV)

Ps 78:35 *They remembered that God was their Rock, <u>that God Most High was their Redeemer</u>.* (NIV)

Ps 49:15 *<u>But God will redeem my life from the grave</u>; he will surely take me to himself. Selah* (NIV)

Gal 4:1-7 *What I am saying is that as long as the heir is a child, he is no different from a slave, although he owns the whole estate. He is subject to guardians and trustees until the time set by his father. So also, when we were children, we were in slavery under the basic principles of the world.* **But when the time had fully come, <u>God sent his Son, born of a woman, born under law, to redeem those under law</u>, that we might receive the full rights of sons.** *Because you are sons, God sent the Spirit of his Son into our hearts, the Spirit who calls out, "Abba, Father." So you are no longer a slave, but a son; and since you are a son, God has made you also an heir.* (NIV)

Titus 2:11-15 *<u>For the grace of God that brings salvation has appeared to all men.</u> It teaches us to say "No" to unGodliness and worldly passions, and to live self-controlled, upright and Godly lives in this present age, while we wait for the blessed hope—the glorious appearing of our great God and Savior, <u>Jesus Christ, who gave himself for us to redeem us from all wickedness and to purify for himself a people that are his very own, eager to do what is good</u>. These, then, are the* *things you should teach. Encourage and rebuke with all authority. Do not let anyone despise you.* (NIV)

AS THE BRANCH — This term is used figuratively as the Messiah from the Davidic tree, a descendant of David. The man whose name is the Branch (Jesus) will be the One who will build the permanent Temple of the Lord; the one that will exist during the peaceful times of the Millennium.

Isa 4:2-6 *<u>In that day the Branch of the LORD will be beautiful and glorious, and the fruit of the land will be the pride and glory of the survivors in Israel.</u> Those who are left in Zion, who remain in Jerusalem, will be called holy, all who are recorded among the living in Jerusalem. The Lord will wash away the filth of the women of Zion; he will cleanse the bloodstains from Jerusalem by a spirit of judgment and a spirit of fire. Then the LORD will create over all of Mount Zion and over those who assemble there a cloud of smoke by day and a glow of flaming fire by night; over all the glory will be a canopy. It will be a shelter and shade from the heat of the day, and a refuge and hiding place from the storm and rain.* (NIV)

Isa 11:1-2 *A shoot will come up from the stump of Jesse; <u>from his roots a Branch will bear fruit.</u> The Spirit of the LORD will rest on him—the Spirit of wisdom and of understanding, the Spirit of counsel and of power, the Spirit of knowledge and of the fear of the LORD—* (NIV)

Jer 23:1-7 "Woe to the shepherds who are destroying and scattering the sheep of my pasture!" declares the LORD. Therefore this is what the LORD, the God of Israel, says to the shepherds who tend my people: "Because you have scattered my flock and driven them away and have not bestowed care on them, I will bestow punishment on you for the evil you have done," declares the LORD. "I myself will gather the remnant of my flock out of all the countries where I have driven them and will bring them back to their pasture, where they will be fruitful and increase in number. I will place shepherds over them who will tend them, and they will no longer be afraid or terrified, nor will any be missing," declares the LORD. **"<u>The days are coming</u>," declares the LORD, "<u>when I will raise up to David a righteous Branch</u>, <u>a King who will reign wisely and do what is just and right in the land</u>.** In his days Judah will be saved and Israel will live in safety. This is the name by which he will be called: <u>**The LORD Our Righteousness.**</u> "So then, the days are coming," declares the LORD, "when people will no longer say, 'As surely as the LORD lives, who brought the Israelites up out of Egypt,' (NIV)

The Rest of the Millennium

Zech 6:12 *Tell him this is what the LORD Almighty says: '**Here is the man whose name is the Branch, and he will branch out from his place and build the temple of the LORD**.* (NIV)

AS A ROCK — Is there a better place on which to build a house or building? Metaphorically, Jesus is our spiritual rock and the foundation by which we build our faith.

Deut 32:1-4 *Listen, O heavens, and I will speak; hear, O earth, the words of my mouth. Let my teaching fall like rain and my words descend like dew, like showers on new grass, like abundant rain on tender plants. I will proclaim the name of the LORD. Oh, praise the greatness of our God! **He is the Rock, his works are perfect, and all his ways are just.** A faithful God who does no wrong, upright and just is he.* (NIV)

Jesus is the Rock of our salvation. He alone is our salvation and refuge.

Ps 95:1 *Come, let us sing for joy to the LORD; **let us shout aloud to the Rock of our salvation**.* (NIV)

Ps 18:1-2 *I love you, O LORD, my strength. **The LORD is my rock, my fortress and my deliverer; my God is my rock, in whom I take refuge**. He is my shield and the horn of my salvation, my stronghold.* (NIV)

Ps 62:1-12 *My soul finds rest in God alone; my salvation comes from him. **He alone is my rock and my salvation; he is my fortress, I will never be shaken**. How long will you assault a man? Would all of you throw him down—this leaning wall, this tottering fence? They fully intend to topple him from his lofty place; they take delight in lies. With their mouths they bless, but in their hearts they curse. Selah **Find rest, O my soul, in God alone; my hope comes from him. He alone is my rock and my salvation;** he is my fortress, I will not be shaken. My salvation and my honor depend on God; **he is my mighty rock, my refuge**. Trust in him at all times, O people; pour out your hearts to him, for God is our refuge. Selah Lowborn men are but a breath, the highborn are but a lie; if weighed on a balance, they are nothing; together they are only a breath. Do not trust in extortion or take pride in stolen goods; though your riches increase, do not set your heart on them. One thing God has spoken, two things have I heard: that you, O God, are strong, and that you, O Lord, are loving. **Surely you will reward each person according to what he has done**.* (NIV)

In the day of trouble (Tribulation Period), He will shelter the saints in a secret hiding place in heaven, high upon a rock. These resurrected saints will dwell forever in the heavenly Jerusalem. *"The LORD is my light and my salvation — whom shall I fear?"*

> Ps 27:1-5 *<u>The LORD is my light and my salvation—whom shall I fear? The LORD is the stronghold of my life—of whom shall I be afraid?</u> When evil men advance against me to devour my flesh, when my enemies and my foes attack me, they will stumble and fall. Though an army besiege me, my heart will not fear; though war break out against me, even then will I be confident. One thing I ask of the LORD, this is what I seek: that I may dwell in the house of the LORD all the days of my life, to gaze upon the beauty of the LORD and to seek him in his temple. <u>For in the day of trouble he will keep me safe in his dwelling; he will hide me in the shelter of his tabernacle and set me high upon a rock</u>.* (NIV)

Jesus is the Rock (stone) that will break all the nations during the Tribulation Period.

> Dan 2:44-45 *"In the time of those kings, the God of heaven will set up a kingdom that will never be destroyed, nor will it be left to another people. It will crush all those kingdoms and bring them to an end, but it will itself endure forever. <u>This is the meaning of the vision of the rock cut out of a mountain, but not by human hands—a rock that broke the iron, the bronze, the clay, the silver and the gold to pieces</u>....* (NIV)

The church is built on the spiritual rock of Jesus Christ.

> 1 Cor 10:4 *and drank the same spiritual drink; <u>for they drank from the spiritual rock that accompanied them, and that rock was Christ</u>.* (NIV)

> Matt 16:16-18 *Simon Peter answered, "You are the Christ, the Son of the living God." Jesus replied, "Blessed are you, Simon son of Jonah, for this was not revealed to you by man, but by my Father in heaven. And I tell you that you are Peter, <u>and on this rock I will build my church</u>, and the gates of Hades will not overcome it.* (NIV)

We as Christians are to lay a foundation for Jesus on this rock.

> Luke 6:47-49 *I will show you what he is like who comes to me and hears my words and puts them into practice. <u>He is like a man building a house, who dug down deep and laid the foundation on rock</u>. When a flood came, the torrent struck that house but could not shake it, because it was well built. But the one who hears my words and does not put them into practice is like a man who built a house on the*

ground without a foundation. The moment the torrent struck that house, it collapsed and its destruction was complete." (NIV)

The foundation of Jesus Christ was built by the apostles of the New Testament and the prophets of the Old Testament. Jesus is the cornerstone.

Eph 2:19-22 *Consequently, you are no longer foreigners and aliens, but fellow citizens with God's people and members of God's household, <u>built on the foundation of the apostles and prophets</u>, <u>with Christ Jesus himself as the chief cornerstone</u>. In him the whole building is joined together and rises to become a holy temple in the Lord. And in him you too are being built together to become a dwelling in which God lives by his Spirit.* (NIV)

Ps 118:22-29 *<u>The stone the builders rejected has become the capstone</u>; the LORD has done this, and it is marvelous in our eyes. This is the day the LORD has made; let us rejoice and be glad in it. O LORD, save us; O LORD, grant us success. Blessed is he who comes in the name of the LORD. From the house of the LORD we bless you. The LORD is God, and he has made his light shine upon us. With boughs in hand, join in the festal procession up to the horns of the altar. You are my God, and I will give you thanks; you are my God, and I will exalt you. Give thanks to the LORD, for he is good; his love endures forever.* (NIV)

AS HIGH PRIEST — Jesus will be the High Priest of the Ecclesiastical system. In a sense, you could say it will be a one-world church or religious system. As the one who shed His blood for the propitiation of our sin, Jesus and He alone will be our High Priest. Jesus is the atonement for sin. Jesus, who did not sin, took our place on the cross. He suffered for us. He substituted His body on the cross in place of ours. There will be harmony between His positions as King and High Priest.

Heb 9:11-12 *<u>When Christ came as high priest of the good things that are already here</u>, <u>he went through the greater and more perfect tabernacle that is not man-made</u>, <u>that is to say</u>, <u>not a part of this creation</u>. He did not enter by means of the blood of goats and calves; but he entered the Most Holy Place once for all by his own blood, having obtained eternal redemption.* (NIV)

Zech 6:12-13 *Tell him this is what the LORD Almighty says: 'Here is the man whose name is the Branch, and he will branch out from his place and build the temple of the LORD. <u>It is he who will build the temple of the LORD</u>, <u>and he will be clothed with majesty and will sit and rule on his throne</u>. <u>And he will be a priest on his throne</u>.*

And there will be harmony between the two.' (NIV)

Heb 9:27-28   *Just as man is destined to die once, and after that to face judgment, <u>so Christ was sacrificed once to take away the sins of many people</u>; and he will appear a second time, not to bear sin, but to bring salvation to those who are waiting for him.* (NIV)

Rom 3:22-26   *This righteousness from God comes through faith in Jesus Christ to all who believe. There is no difference, for all have sinned and fall short of the glory of God, and are justified freely by his grace through the redemption that came by Christ Jesus. <u>God presented him as a sacrifice of atonement, through faith in his blood.</u> He did this to demonstrate his justice, because in his forbearance he had left the sins committed beforehand unpunished—he did it to demonstrate his justice at the present time, so as to be just and the one who justifies those who have faith in Jesus.* (NIV)

Col 1:13-14   *For he has rescued us from the dominion of darkness and brought us into the kingdom of the Son he loves, <u>in whom we have redemption, the forgiveness of sins</u>.* (NIV)

1 Thes 5:9-10   *For God did not appoint us to suffer wrath but to receive salvation through our Lord Jesus Christ. <u>He died for us so that, whether we are awake or asleep, we may live together with him.</u>* (NIV)

1 John 1:7-10   *<u>But if we walk in the light, as he is in the light, we have fellowship with one another, and the blood of Jesus, his Son, purifies us from all sin</u>. If we claim to be without sin, we deceive ourselves and the truth is not in us. <u>If we confess our sins, he is faithful and just and will forgive us our sins and purify us from all unrighteousness</u>. If we claim we have not sinned, we make him out to be a liar and his word has no place in our lives.* (NIV)

Rev 1:5   *<u>and from Jesus Christ</u>, who is the faithful witness, the firstborn from the dead, and the ruler of the kings of the earth. <u>To him who loves us and has freed us from our sins by his blood</u>,* (NIV)

    The Ecclesiastical system will be needed to teach the repopulated generations on the earth during this age. As the first baby is born, an unsaved soul enters the world. It will be the job of the religious system—just as it is the purpose of the church today—to teach the unsaved souls the way to salvation. It will be the decision of each individual person living at this future time to make their own decision of whether they want to believe in Jesus as their Savior. That decision will determine where they will spend eternity. This concept of salvation has not changed for man or the angels since they were created by God. There will be people who reject God, even in the peaceful atmosphere of this time.

The religious laws and precepts will come from Jesus in Jerusalem and will be passed down and taught to the people around the world through this religious system. Priests will be a part of that system. Israel as the head of the nations will finally fulfill their religious obligation to the rest of the nations during this time. It will be required by every living person to visit the Temple in Jerusalem at least once a year. Some will disobey this command and suffer the consequences of their actions. We will discuss this in more detail later in this chapter when we cover the rebuilding of the Temple and the reestablishing of most of the Jewish feasts and festivals.

ISRAEL — GOD'S PEOPLE

God will someday restore the Jewish people to a position as head of all the nations of the world. That day will be during the Day of the Lord after God purges the Jews of their unrighteous members. Those remaining will be righteous and God will save (deliver) them. At that time all Israel will be saved and living in the land promised to them by God.

Zech 9:16-17   *The LORD their God will save them on that day as the flock of his people. They will sparkle in his land like jewels in a crown. How attractive and beautiful they will be! Grain will make the young men thrive, and new wine the young women.* (NIV)

The chosen people have known for thousands of years that they will possess the land of Israel and be elevated to the position as head of the nations. From the time they were founded and a promise was given to their founding father Abraham, the Jewish people knew of a promised land flowing with milk and honey. The promise was renewed through the prophet Moses. All Israel has yet to return to God, but they will in the near future.

Deut 30:1-10   *When all these blessings and curses I have set before you come upon you and you take them to heart wherever the LORD your God disperses you among the nations, and when you and your children return to the LORD your God and obey him with all your heart and with all your soul according to everything I command you today, then the LORD your God will restore your fortunes and have compassion on you and gather you again from all the nations where he scattered you. Even if you have been banished to the most distant land under the heavens, from there the LORD your God will gather you and bring you back. He will bring you to the land that belonged to your fathers, and you will take possession of it. He will make you more prosperous and numerous than your fathers. The LORD your God will circumcise your hearts and the hearts of your descendants, so that you may love him with all your heart and with all your soul, and live. The LORD your God will put all these curses on your enemies who hate and persecute you. You will again obey*

> *the LORD and follow all his commands I am giving you today.*
> *Then the LORD your God will make you most prosperous in all the*
> *work of your hands and in the fruit of your womb, the young of*
> *your livestock and the crops of your land.* The LORD will again
> delight in you and make you prosperous, just as he delighted in your
> fathers, if you obey the LORD your God and keep his commands and
> decrees that are written in this Book of the Law and turn to the
> LORD your God with all your heart and with all your soul. (NIV)

God has repeatedly revealed to us in both the Old and New Testaments that the Jews have failed miserably to follow God and have paid the consequences for their actions. God even sent the Jewish people His Son, who was Himself a Jew, to usher in the new kingdom. However, instead of recognizing Jesus as the Messiah, they rejected Him and had Him crucified. When the chosen Jewish apostles met with Jesus, before He ascended to be at the right hand of God in heaven, they asked Him if He was going to restore the kingdom to Israel at that time. Luke gives us this account.

Acts 1:1-11 *In my former book, Theophilus, I wrote about all that Jesus began to do and to teach until the day he was taken up to heaven, after giving instructions through the Holy Spirit to the apostles he had chosen.* After his suffering, he showed himself to these men and gave many convincing proofs that he was alive. He appeared to them over a period of forty days and spoke about the kingdom of God. On one occasion, while he was eating with them, he gave them this command: "Do not leave Jerusalem, but wait for the gift my Father promised, which you have heard me speak about. For John baptized with water, but in a few days you will be baptized with the Holy Spirit." So when they met together, they asked him, "**Lord, are you at this time going to restore the kingdom to Israel?**" *He said to them: "It is not for you to know the times or dates the Father has set by his own authority.* But you will receive power when the Holy Spirit comes on you; and you will be my witnesses in Jerusalem, and in all Judea and Samaria, and to the ends of the earth." After he said this, he was taken up before their very eyes, and a cloud hid him from their sight. They were looking intently up into the sky as he was going, when suddenly two men dressed in white stood beside them. "Men of Galilee," they said, "why do you stand here looking into the sky? This same Jesus, who has been taken from you into heaven, will come back in the same way you have seen him go into heaven." (NIV)

Not long after Jesus departed, Peter revealed to the early Jewish believers that all of the events of Jesus appearing in the flesh happened according to God's plan and that the story was foretold by the Old Testament prophets. Peter informs them that Jesus must remain in

The Rest of the Millennium

heaven until the time comes for God to restore everything. Notice Jesus as God's servant.

Acts 3:11-26   *While the beggar held on to Peter and John, all the people were astonished and came running to them in the place called Solomon's Colonnade. When Peter saw this, he said to them: "Men of Israel, why does this surprise you? Why do you stare at us as if by our own power or Godliness we had made this man walk?* ***The God of Abraham, Isaac and Jacob, the God of our fathers, has glorified his servant Jesus.*** *You handed him over to be killed, and you disowned him before Pilate, though he had decided to let him go. You disowned the Holy and Righteous One and asked that a murderer be released to you. You killed the author of life, but God raised him from the dead. We are witnesses of this. By faith in the name of Jesus, this man whom you see and know was made strong. It is Jesus' name and the faith that comes through him that has given this complete healing to him, as you can all see. "Now, brothers, I know that you acted in ignorance, as did your leaders.* ***But this is how God fulfilled what he had foretold through all the prophets, saying that his Christ would suffer.*** *Repent, then, and turn to God, so that your sins may be wiped out, that times of refreshing may come from the Lord, and that he may send the Christ, who has been appointed for you—even Jesus.* ***He must remain in heaven until the time comes for God to restore everything, as he promised long ago through his holy prophets.*** *For Moses said, 'The Lord your God will raise up for you a prophet like me from among your own people; you must listen to everything he tells you. Anyone who does not listen to him will be completely cut off from among his people.' "Indeed, all the prophets from Samuel on, as many as have spoken, have foretold these days. And you are heirs of the prophets and of the covenant God made with your fathers. He said to Abraham, 'Through your offspring all peoples on earth will be blessed.' When God raised up his servant, he sent him first to you to bless you by turning each of you from your wicked ways."* (NIV)

Acts 5:29-32   *Peter and the other apostles replied: "We must obey God rather than men! The God of our fathers raised Jesus from the dead—whom you had killed by hanging him on a tree.* ***God exalted him to his own right hand as Prince and Savior that he might give repentance and forgiveness of sins to Israel.*** *We are witnesses of these things, and so is the Holy Spirit, whom God has given to those who obey him."* (NIV)

In the portion of our study that we just completed, we know that a remnant of the Jewish people will survive the last half of the Tribulation Period and the Battle of Armageddon.

AFTER THE RAPTURE

One-third of the Jews, those who survive this catastrophic period, will recognize Jesus as their Messiah. After Jesus finishes His judgment of the nations at the Battle of Armageddon and defeats the Antichrist and Satan, it will be time to restore the land to Israel. God will restore the divided kingdoms of Judah and Israel and unify them in the land.

Ps 85:1-13 *You showed favor to your land, O LORD; you restored the fortunes of Jacob. You forgave the iniquity of your people and covered all their sins. Selah You set aside all your wrath and turned from your fierce anger. <u>Restore us again, O God our Savior, and put away your displeasure toward us.</u> Will you be angry with us forever? Will you prolong your anger through all generations? Will you not revive us again, that your people may rejoice in you? Show us your unfailing love, O LORD, and grant us your salvation. I will listen to what God the LORD will say; <u>he promises peace to his people,</u> his saints—but let them not return to folly. Surely his salvation is near those who fear him, that his glory may dwell in our land. Love and faithfulness meet together; righteousness and peace kiss each other. Faithfulness springs forth from the earth, and righteousness looks down from heaven. The LORD will indeed give what is good, and our land will yield its harvest. Righteousness goes before him and prepares the way for his steps.* (NIV)

Jer 30:1-3 *This is the word that came to Jeremiah from the LORD: "This is what the LORD, the God of Israel, says: 'Write in a book all the words I have spoken to you. <u>The days are coming,</u>' declares the LORD, '<u>when I will bring my people Israel and Judah back from captivity and restore them to the land I gave their forefathers to possess,</u>' says the LORD."* (NIV)

Jer 30:10-11 *"'So do not fear, O Jacob my servant; do not be dismayed, O Israel,' declares the LORD. '<u>I will surely save you out of a distant place, your descendants from the land of their exile. Jacob will again have peace and security, and no one will make him afraid.</u> I am with you and will save you,' declares the LORD. 'Though I completely destroy all the nations among which I scatter you, I will not completely destroy you. I will discipline you but only with justice; I will not let you go entirely unpunished.'* (NIV)

Jer 31:1-14 *"<u>At that time,</u>" declares the LORD, "<u>I will be the God of all the clans of Israel, and they will be my people.</u>" This is what the LORD says: "<u>The people who survive the sword will find favor in the desert; I will come to give rest to Israel.</u>" The LORD appeared to us in the past, saying: "I have loved you with an everlasting love; I have drawn you with loving-kindness. I will build you up again and you* *will be rebuilt, O Virgin Israel. Again you will take up your tambourines and go out to dance with the joyful. Again you will plant vineyards on the hills of Samaria; the farmers will plant them and enjoy their fruit. There will be a day when watchmen cry out on the hills of Ephraim, 'Come, let us go up to Zion, to the LORD our God.'" This is what the LORD says: "Sing with joy for Jacob; shout for the foremost of the nations. Make your praises heard, and say,* **'O LORD, save your people, the remnant of Israel.' See, I will bring them from the land of the north and gather them from the ends of the earth.** *Among them will be the blind and the lame, expectant mothers and women in labor; a great throng will return. They will come with weeping; they will pray as I bring them back. I will lead them beside streams of water on a level path where they will not stumble, because I am Israel's father, and Ephraim is my firstborn son. "Hear the word of the LORD, O nations; proclaim it in distant coastlands:* **'He who scattered Israel will gather them and will watch over his flock like a shepherd.'** *For the LORD will ransom Jacob and redeem them from the hand of those stronger than they. They will come and shout for joy on the heights of Zion; they will rejoice in the bounty of the LORD—the grain, the new wine and the oil, the young of the flocks and herds. They will be like a well-watered garden, and they will sorrow no more. Then maidens will dance and be glad, young men and old as well. I will turn their mourning into gladness; I will give them comfort and joy instead of sorrow. I will satisfy the priests with abundance, and my people will be filled with my bounty," declares the LORD.* (NIV)

Zeph 3:20   *<u>At that time I will gather you; at that time I will bring you home.</u> I will give you honor and praise among all the peoples of the earth when I restore your fortunes before your very eyes," says the LORD.* (NIV)

Jer 31:23-29   *This is what the LORD Almighty, the God of Israel, says: "When I bring them back from captivity, the people in the land of Judah and in its towns will once again use these words: 'The LORD bless you, O righteous dwelling, O sacred mountain.' People will live together in Judah and all its towns—farmers and those who move about with their flocks. I will refresh the weary and satisfy the faint." At this I awoke and looked around. My sleep had been pleasant to me.* **"<u>The days are coming</u>," declares the LORD, "<u>when I will plant the house of Israel and the house of Judah with the offspring of men and of animals.</u> Just as I watched over them to uproot and tear down, and to overthrow, destroy and bring disaster, so I will watch over them to build and to plant," declares the LORD. "In those** days people will no longer say, 'The fathers have eaten sour grapes, and the children's teeth are set on edge.' (NIV)

Jer 33:6-16   "'Nevertheless, I will bring health and healing to it; I will heal my people and will let them enjoy abundant peace and security. **I will bring Judah and Israel back from captivity and will rebuild them as they were before.** I will cleanse them from all the sin they have committed against me and will forgive all their sins of rebellion against me. Then this city will bring me renown, joy, praise and honor before all nations on earth that hear of all the good things I do for it; and they will be in awe and will tremble at the abundant prosperity and peace I provide for it.' "This is what the LORD says: 'You say about this place, "It is a desolate waste, without men or animals." Yet in the towns of Judah and the streets of Jerusalem that are deserted, inhabited by neither men nor animals, there will be heard once more the sounds of joy and gladness, the voices of bride and bridegroom, and the voices of those who bring thank offerings to the house of the LORD, saying, "Give thanks to the LORD Almighty, for the LORD is good; his love endures forever." **For I will restore the fortunes of the land as they were before,'** says the LORD. "This is what the LORD Almighty says: 'In this place, desolate and without men or animals—in all its towns there will again be pastures for shepherds to rest their flocks. In the towns of the hill country, of the western foothills and of the Negev, in the territory of Benjamin, in the villages around Jerusalem and in the towns of Judah, flocks will again pass under the hand of the one who counts them,' says the LORD. "'**The days are coming**,' declares the LORD, '**when I will fulfill the gracious promise I made to the house of Israel and to the house of Judah.** "'In those days and at that time I will make a righteous Branch sprout from David's line; he will do what is just and right in the land. **In those days Judah will be saved and Jerusalem will live in safety.** This is the name by which it will be called: **The LORD Our Righteousness.**' (NIV)

Micah 5:4-5   *He will stand and shepherd his flock in the strength of the LORD, in the majesty of the name of the LORD his God. **And they will live securely, for then his greatness will reach to the ends of the earth.** And he will be their peace....* (NIV)

Ezek 36:1-38 *"Son of man, prophesy to the mountains of Israel and say, '**O mountains of Israel, hear the word of the LORD.** This is what the Sovereign LORD says: The enemy said of you, "Aha! The ancient heights have become our possession."' Therefore prophesy and say, 'This is what the Sovereign LORD says: Because they ravaged and*

The Rest of the Millennium

hounded you from every side so that you became the possession of the rest of the nations and the object of people's malicious talk and slander, therefore, O mountains of Israel, hear the word of the Sovereign LORD: This is what the Sovereign LORD says to the mountains and hills, to the ravines and valleys, to the desolate ruins and the deserted towns that have been plundered and ridiculed by the rest of the nations around you—this is what the Sovereign LORD says: In my burning zeal I have spoken against the rest of the nations, and against all Edom, for with glee and with malice in their hearts they made my land their own possession so that they might plunder its pastureland.' Therefore prophesy concerning the land of Israel and say to the mountains and hills, to the ravines and valleys: **'This is what the Sovereign LORD says: I speak in my jealous wrath because you have suffered the scorn of the nations.** *Therefore this is what the Sovereign LORD says: I swear with uplifted hand that the nations around you will also suffer scorn.* **"'But you, <u>O mountains of Israel, will produce branches and fruit for my people Israel, for they will soon come home</u>. I am concerned for you and will look on you with favor; you will be plowed and sown, <u>and I will multiply the number of people upon you, even the whole house of Israel</u>. The towns will be inhabited and the ruins rebuilt.** *I will increase the number of men and animals upon you, and they will be fruitful and become numerous. I will settle people on you as in the past and will make you prosper more than before.* **Then you will know that I am the LORD. I will cause people, my people Israel, to walk upon you.** *They will possess you, and you will be their inheritance; you will never again deprive them of their children. "'This is what the Sovereign LORD says: Because people say to you, "You devour men and deprive your nation of its children," therefore you will no longer devour men or make your nation childless, declares the Sovereign LORD. No longer will I make you hear the taunts of the nations, and no longer will you suffer the scorn of the peoples or cause your nation to fall, declares the Sovereign LORD.'" Again the word of the LORD came to me: "Son of man, when the people of Israel were living in their own land, they defiled it by their conduct and their actions. Their conduct was like a woman's monthly uncleanness in my sight. So I poured out my wrath on them because they had shed blood in the land and because they had defiled it with their idols. I dispersed them among the nations, and they were scattered through the countries; I judged them according to their conduct and their actions. And wherever they went among the nations they profaned my holy name, for it was said of them, 'These are the LORD's people, and yet they had to leave his land.' I had concern for my holy name, which the house of Israel* *profaned among the nations where they had gone. "Therefore say to the house of Israel, 'This is what the Sovereign LORD says: It is not for your sake, O house of Israel, that I am going to do these things, but for the sake of my holy name, which you have profaned among the nations where you have gone. I will show the holiness of my great name, which has been profaned among the nations, the name you have profaned among them.* **Then the nations will know that I am the LORD***, declares the Sovereign LORD,* **when I show myself holy through you before their eyes.** **"'For I will take you out of the nations; I will gather you from all the countries and bring you back into your own land.** *I will sprinkle clean water on you, and you will be clean; I will cleanse you from all your impurities and from all your idols. I will give you a new heart and put a new spirit in you;* *I will remove from you your heart of stone and give you a heart of flesh. And I will put my Spirit in you and move you to follow my decrees and be careful to keep my laws.* **You will live in the land I gave your forefathers; you will be my people, and I will be your God.** *I will save you from all your uncleanness. I will call for the grain and make it plentiful and will not bring famine upon you. I will increase the fruit of the trees and the crops of the field, so that you will no longer suffer disgrace among the nations because of famine. Then you will remember your evil ways and wicked deeds, and you will loathe yourselves for your sins and detestable practices. I want you to know that I am not doing this for your sake, declares the Sovereign LORD.* **Be ashamed and disgraced for your conduct, O house of Israel!** *"'This is what the Sovereign LORD says:* **On the day I cleanse you from all your sins, I will resettle your towns, and the ruins will be rebuilt.** *The desolate land will be cultivated instead of lying desolate in the sight of all who pass through it. They will say, "This land that was laid waste has become like the garden of Eden; the cities that were lying in ruins, desolate and destroyed, are now fortified and inhabited." Then the nations around you that remain will know that I the LORD have rebuilt what was destroyed and have replanted what was desolate. I the LORD have spoken, and I will do it.'* **"This is what the Sovereign LORD says: Once again I will yield to the plea of the house of Israel and do this for them: I will make their people as numerous as sheep, as numerous as the flocks for offerings at Jerusalem during her appointed feasts. So will the ruined cities be filled with flocks of people.** **Then they will know that I am the LORD.** *"* (NIV)

Amos 9:11-15   **"In that day I will restore David's fallen tent.** *I will repair its broken places, restore its ruins, and build it as it used to be, so that they may possess the remnant of Edom and all the nations that*

> *bear my name," declares the LORD, who will do these things. "The days are coming," declares the LORD, "when the reaper will be overtaken by the plowman and the planter by the one treading grapes. New wine will drip from the mountains and flow from all the hills. **I will bring back my exiled people Israel; they will rebuild the ruined cities and live in them.** They will plant vineyards and drink their wine; they will make gardens and eat their fruit. **I will plant Israel in their own land, never again to be uprooted from the land I have given them**," says the LORD your God.* (NIV)

Jesus will restore the boundaries of Israel to those promised to them. This boundary will be larger than they have ever been in the past and will extend from the nation of Egypt in the west all the way to the Euphrates River in the east.

> Micah 7:8-12 *Do not gloat over me, my enemy! Though I have fallen, I will rise. Though I sit in darkness, the LORD will be my light. Because I have sinned against him, I will bear the LORD's wrath, until he pleads my case and establishes my right. He will bring me out into the light; I will see his righteousness. Then my enemy will see it and will be covered with shame, she who said to me, "Where is the LORD your God?" My eyes will see her downfall; even now she will be trampled underfoot like mire in the streets. **The day for building your walls will come, the day for extending your boundaries.** In that day people will come to you from Assyria and the cities of Egypt, even from Egypt to the Euphrates and from sea to sea and from mountain to mountain.* (NIV)

Scripture reveals that Israel will receive double punishment for her transgression. In Zechariah and in Isaiah, we find that Israel will receive twice as much during her restoration. How fitting!

> Zech 9:9-12 ***Rejoice greatly, O Daughter of Zion! Shout, Daughter of Jerusalem! See, your king comes to you,** righteous and having salvation, gentle and riding on a donkey, on a colt, the foal of a donkey.* I will take away the chariots from Ephraim and the war-horses from Jerusalem, and the battle bow will be broken. He will proclaim peace to the nations. **His rule will extend from sea to sea and from the River to the ends of the earth.** As for you, because of the blood of my covenant with you, I will free your prisoners from the waterless pit. **Return to your fortress, O prisoners of hope; even now I announce that I will restore twice as much to you.** (NIV)

> Isa 61:1-11 *The Spirit of the Sovereign LORD is on me, because the LORD has anointed me to preach good news to the poor. He has sent me to bind*

> up the brokenhearted, to proclaim freedom for the captives and release from darkness for the prisoners, to proclaim the year of the LORD's favor and the day of vengeance of our God, **to comfort all who mourn, and provide for those who grieve in Zion—to bestow on them a crown of beauty instead of ashes, the oil of gladness instead of mourning, and a garment of praise instead of a spirit of despair.** They will be called oaks of righteousness, a planting of the LORD for the display of his splendor. They will rebuild the ancient ruins and restore the places long devastated; they will renew the ruined cities that have been devastated for generations. Aliens will shepherd your flocks; foreigners will work your fields and vineyards. **And you will be called priests of the LORD, you will be named ministers of our God. You will feed on the wealth of nations, and in their riches you will boast. <u>Instead of their shame my people will receive a double portion, and instead of disgrace they will rejoice in their inheritance; and so they will inherit a double portion in their land, and everlasting joy will be theirs.</u>** "For I, the LORD, love justice; I hate robbery and iniquity. In my faithfulness I will reward them and make an everlasting covenant with them. Their descendants will be known among the nations and their offspring among the peoples. All who see them will acknowledge that they are a people the LORD has blessed." I delight greatly in the LORD; my soul rejoices in my God. For he has clothed me with garments of salvation and arrayed me in a robe of righteousness, as a bridegroom adorns his head like a priest, and as a bride adorns herself with her jewels. For as the soil makes the sprout come up and a garden causes seeds to grow, so the Sovereign LORD will make righteousness and praise spring up before all nations. (NIV)

Although the Jewish people are presently back in the land of Israel, they are far from being in the position they will be during the Kingdom Age; the position that the scriptures mention above. No peace and security! No extended boundaries—as a matter of fact they are losing ground through the "land for peace" process! <u>ALL</u> Israel is not saved and living in the land! No Temple! Israel does not know their Messiah (Y'shua)! They have not been through the Time of Jacob's Trouble! Before long, all of the prophecies mentioned in this book will come to fulfillment. After that Israel will:

1. rebuild the ruined cities destroyed during the Tribulation Period and live in them. Amos 9:13-15 *"<u>The days are coming,</u>" declares the LORD, "when the reaper will be overtaken by the plowman and the planter by the one treading grapes. New wine will drip from the mountains and flow from all the hills. <u>I will bring back my exiled people Israel; they will rebuild the ruined cities and live in them.</u> They will plant vineyards and drink their wine; they will make gardens and eat their fruit. <u>I will plant Israel in their own land, never again to be uprooted from</u>*

the land I have given them," says the LORD your God. (NIV)

2. no longer be ashamed.
   Isa 29:22-24 *Therefore this is what the LORD, who redeemed Abraham, says to the house of Jacob: "<u>No longer will Jacob be ashamed</u>; <u>no longer will their faces grow pale</u>. When they see among them their children, the work of my hands, they will keep my name holy; they will acknowledge the holiness of the Holy One of Jacob, and will stand in awe of the God of Israel. <u>Those who are wayward in spirit will gain understanding; those who complain will accept instruction.</u>"* (NIV)

Notice here that there will still be some people who will be complaining during this age. Some things never change—no matter how good the world becomes.

In these next verses we see Israel's sin and punishment for that sin. A remnant will come out of the slaughter and possess the land in abundance. Their past troubles will not be remembered and will be hidden from God's eyes.

Isa 65:1-16 *"I revealed myself to those who did not ask for me; I was found by those who did not seek me. To a nation that did not call on my name, I said, 'Here am I, here am I.' All day long I have held out my hands to an obstinate people, who walk in ways not good, pursuing their own imaginations—a people who continually provoke me to my very face, offering sacrifices in gardens and burning incense on altars of brick; who sit among the graves and spend their nights keeping secret vigil; who eat the flesh of pigs, and whose pots hold broth of unclean meat; who say, 'Keep away; don't come near me, for I am too sacred for you!' Such people are smoke in my nostrils, a fire that keeps burning all day. "See, it stands written before me: I will not keep silent but will pay back in full; I will pay it back into their laps—both your sins and the sins of your fathers," says the LORD. "Because they burned sacrifices on the mountains and defied me on the hills, I will measure into their laps the full payment for their former deeds." **This is what the LORD says: "As when juice is still found in a cluster of grapes and men say, 'Don't destroy it, there is yet some good in it,' so will I do in behalf of my servants; <u>I will not destroy them all</u>.** I will bring forth descendants from Jacob, and from Judah those who will possess my mountains; my chosen people will inherit them, and there will my servants live. Sharon will become a pasture for flocks, and the Valley of Achor a resting place for herds, for my people who seek me. **"<u>But as for you who forsake the LORD and forget my holy mountain</u>, who spread a table for Fortune and fill bowls of mixed wine for Destiny, <u>I will destine you for the sword, and you will all bend down for the slaughter</u>; for I called but you did not answer, I spoke but you did not listen.** You did evil*

AFTER THE RAPTURE

> *in my sight and chose what displeases me." Therefore this is what the Sovereign LORD says: "My servants will eat, but you will go hungry; my servants will drink, but you will go thirsty; my servants will rejoice, but you will be put to shame. My servants will sing out of the joy of their hearts, but you will cry out from anguish of heart and wail in brokenness of spirit. You will leave your name to my chosen ones as a curse; the Sovereign LORD will put you to death, but to his servants he will give another name. Whoever invokes a blessing in the land will do so by the God of truth; he who takes an oath in the land will swear by the God of truth. <u>For the past troubles will be forgotten and hidden from my eyes.</u>* (NIV)

Jesus will bring His people back to live in Jerusalem.

> Zech 8:7-8   *This is what the LORD Almighty says: "I will save my people from the countries of the east and the west. <u>I will bring them back to live in Jerusalem; they will be my people, and I will be faithful and righteous to them as their God.</u>"* (NIV)

At that time Israel will be saved with an everlasting salvation.

> Isa 45:15-17   *Truly you are a God who hides himself, O God and Savior of Israel. All the makers of idols will be put to shame and disgraced; they will go off into disgrace together. <u>But Israel will be saved by the LORD with an everlasting salvation; you will never be put to shame or disgraced, to ages everlasting.</u>* (NIV)

> Isa 59:20-21   *"<u>The Redeemer will come to Zion, to those in Jacob who repent of their sins,</u>" declares the LORD. "As for me, this is my covenant with them," says the LORD. "My Spirit, who is on you, and my words that I have put in your mouth will not depart from your mouth, or from the mouths of your children, <u>or from the mouths of their descendants from this time on and forever,</u>" says the LORD.* (NIV)

The world supremacy of the nation of Israel during this time will not be a put-down to the rest of the nations. As it states in scripture, *"...and all peoples on earth will be blessed through you"* (Genesis 12:3 NIV). The nation of Israel was chosen a long time ago to be a servant of God above all nations to bring good to those of every nation. We get a picture of Jesus as King, Israel as God's servant nation and the rest of the nations during the peaceful portion of the Day of the Lord in the book of Isaiah. At the Feast for all Peoples, God will forever remove the covering that is cast over all the people of the world, the veil that is spread over all the nations. God will also remove the shame, reproach, scorn and disgrace of His people (the Jews) from all the earth.

The Rest of the Millennium

Isa 25:6-9   *On this mountain the LORD Almighty will prepare a feast of rich food for all peoples, a banquet of aged wine—the best of meats and the finest of wines. **On this mountain he will destroy the shroud that enfolds all peoples, the sheet that covers all nations**; he will swallow up death forever. The Sovereign LORD will wipe away the tears from all faces; **he will remove the disgrace of his people from all the earth**. The LORD has spoken. In that day they will say, "Surely this is our God; we trusted in him, and he saved us. This is the LORD, we trusted in him; let us rejoice and be glad in his salvation."* (NIV)

The sins of Israel have been their downfall and their failure to recognize the true Messiah has brought a lot of hardship on them. In the future they will put their trust in a false Messiah (Antichrist – the Assyrian). After their future punishment is completed and they finally accept Jesus as their Messiah, they will rest in His shade. Most Bible translations use the word "Assyria" in place of "the Assyrian" in verse three below, but this verse is clearly speaking about the protection promised by the Antichrist during his reign on earth.

Hos 14:1-9   ***Return, O Israel, to the LORD your God. Your sins have been your downfall!*** *Take words with you and return to the LORD. Say to him: "Forgive all our sins and receive us graciously, that we may offer the fruit of our lips. **Assyria cannot save us**; we will not mount war-horses. We will never again say 'Our gods' to what our own hands have made, for in you the fatherless find compassion." **"I will heal their waywardness and love them freely, for my anger has turned away from them.** I will be like the dew to Israel; he will blossom like a lily. Like a cedar of Lebanon he will send down his roots; his young shoots will grow. His splendor will be like an olive tree, his fragrance like a cedar of Lebanon. **Men will dwell again in his shade.** He will flourish like the grain. He will blossom like a vine, and his fame will be like the wine from Lebanon. O Ephraim, what more have I to do with idols? I will answer him and care for him. I am like a green pine tree; your fruitfulness comes from me." Who is wise? He will realize these things. Who is discerning? He will understand them. The ways of the LORD are right; the righteous walk in them, but the rebellious stumble in them.* (NIV)

The Hebrew word for "shade" is *tsel* and can be translated as: defense, shade or shadow (as protection). Do not rest in the shade (protection) of the Antichrist when he arrives on the scene. During the rest of the Millennium men will rest under the shade of Jesus.

Ps 91:1-2   *He who dwells in the shelter of the Most High will rest **in the shadow** of the Almighty. I will say of the LORD, "He is my refuge and my fortress, my God, in whom I trust."* (NIV)

AFTER THE RAPTURE

Isa 4:5-6   *And the LORD will create upon every dwelling place of mount Zion, and upon her assemblies, a cloud and smoke by day, and the shining of a flaming fire by night: <u>for upon all the glory shall be a defence</u>. And there shall be a tabernacle for <u>a shadow</u> in the daytime from the heat, and for a place of refuge, and for a covert from storm and from rain.* (KJV)

During the Kingdom Age, all the saved (righteous) people will live under the shade of the mightiest tree of all—The Kingdom of Jesus Christ.

Matt 13:31-32   *He told them another parable: "<u>The kingdom of heaven is like a mustard seed</u>, which a man took and planted in his field. Though it is the smallest of all your seeds, yet when it grows, it is the largest of garden plants and becomes a tree, <u>so that the birds of the air come and perch in its branches.</u>"* (NIV)

For extra reading concerning this marvelous period for Israel—not excluding the Gentiles—read Isaiah chapters 40-66 and Jeremiah chapters 30-31 and 33 in their entirety. For those of you who remain skeptical about Israel's future, please read these verses below.

Jer 31:35-37   *This is what the LORD says, he who appoints the sun to shine by day, who decrees the moon and stars to shine by night, who stirs up the sea so that its waves roar—the LORD Almighty is his name: "Only if these decrees vanish from my sight," declares the LORD, "will the descendants of Israel ever cease to be a nation before me." This is what the LORD says: "<u>Only if the heavens above can be measured and the foundations of the earth below be searched out will I reject all the descendants of Israel because of all they have done</u>," declares the LORD.* (NIV)

Jer 33:19-26   *The word of the LORD came to Jeremiah: "This is what the LORD says: '<u>If you can break my covenant with the day and my covenant with the night, so that day and night no longer come at their appointed time, then my covenant with David my servant—and my covenant with the Levites who are priests ministering before me—can be broken and David will no longer have a descendant to reign on his throne.</u> I will make the descendants of David my servant and the Levites who minister before me as countless as the stars of the sky and as measureless as the sand on the seashore.'" The word of the LORD came to Jeremiah: "Have you not noticed that these people are saying, 'The LORD has rejected the two kingdoms he chose'? So they despise my people and no longer regard them as a nation. This is what the LORD says: '<u>If I have not established my covenant with day and night and the fixed laws of heaven and</u>*

> *earth, then I will reject the descendants of Jacob and David my servant and will not choose one of his sons to rule over the descendants of Abraham, Isaac and Jacob. For I will restore their fortunes and have compassion on them.'"* (NIV)

JERUSALEM

Jerusalem is a thriving city located in Israel with a population today of over half a million people, a city rich in heritage and possibly the most international city in the world. Jerusalem has more than 300,000 tourists who visit the city annually. As you walk through the streets of the city you can literally hear people speaking languages from all over the world. A little over a hundred years ago, at the turn of the twentieth century, Jerusalem was a small city with a population of only around 45,000 people (28,000 Jews and 17,000 Christian and Muslim Arabs). In his book, *Jerusalem in the Twentieth Century,* Martin Gilbert gives us some idea of what it was like at that time.

> "The Jews of Jerusalem were subjected to Turkish laws, but many looked, as they had done for half a century, to the British for protection. On 3 February 1901 the most splendid of all the places of worship in the Jewish Quarter of the Old City, the Hurva Synagogue, was the scene of what the *London Jewish Chronicle* described as 'an impressive Memorial Service' for Queen Victoria. The service was presided over by the Ashkenazi Chief Rabbi, Samuel Salant. The large synagogue was 'filled to its utmost capacity, and policemen had to keep off the crowds, who vainly sought admission, by force'.
>
> Among the Jews who visited Jerusalem that year was a newly ordained rabbi, the twenty-two-year-old Martin Meyer. Born in San Francisco, he arrived in Jerusalem in September 1901 to spend a year at the American School of Oriental Studies. Reaching the city by train, he later recalled his first sight of the walls. "How my heart beat. I wanted to do or say something. I wanted to sing. I wanted to shout. I hummed "The Holy City" and contented myself with some long deep-drawn sighs. This was once our home, where we bloomed and where we got the strength to be what we are now.'
>
> Martin Meyer was taken from the station by horse and carriage to the Kamenitz Hotel, just off the Jaffa Road in the north-west of the city, where he was to stay. He was surprised to find 'no tramcars of any kind here, no gas or electric lights either.' On visiting the Old City he was even more shocked, 'Our New York and London ghettos are paradise compared with our Jewish Quarter here,' he wrote. 'The streets are narrow, dirty, winding. Dirt is a mild term. Dung litters every corner, the offal of the shops is heaped in the midst of the streets. Filth of every description has accumulated here for years.' His American spirit was roused: 'We ought to have charge of the city for two months. A good sanitary engineer with a corps of workers could do wonders here.' [1]

Jerusalem is a holy city for the three major monotheistic religions in the world. They are

Judaism, Christianity and Islam (Muslim or Moslem). The old city is split into four sections known as quarters. They are Muslim, Christian, Jewish and Armenian (which is also Christian). The outer city has colonies from various nations including Russian, Turkish, British, Greek, French, Italian, Germans and Jews from various nations. The Temple Mount, where the Jewish holy Temple stood (destroyed by the Romans in 70 AD), is now occupied by the Muslims. The Dome of the Rock at this time is now the covering over Mount Moriah. The Western Wall, or Wailing Wall as the Jews refer to it, is the remaining symbol of the Jewish Temple. It has been excavated and is currently the most holy place in Jerusalem and around the world for the Jewish people. For Christians, the city is full of churches and shrines to commemorate the death and resurrection of their Savior Jesus Christ. For the Moslems, Jerusalem is the third holiest city of the Islam religion behind Mecca and Medina. Moslems believe that the Prophet Mohammed (who lived around 570 AD-632 AD), the founder of Islam, ascended to heaven from the rock on Mount Moriah. Jerusalem is filled with numerous religious and charitable institutions. It is also filled with Jewish Synagogues, Christian Churches and Monasteries, and Muslim Mosques.

Theologically speaking we need to look at the city of Jerusalem from a fivefold perspective.

1. The Heavenly Jerusalem
2. Salem
3. City of David
4. City of Peace
5. The New Jerusalem

The chart on page 766 shows the progression of God's great city throughout history. The progress of Jerusalem is highlighted and underlined. It has existed in heaven and on the earth for a very long time. In the top left hand corner, in the third level of heaven, we see the Heavenly Jerusalem. It existed before the earth was created. Most people today do not realize the significance of the heavenly Jerusalem and how important it will be in the future.

THE HEAVENLY JERUSALEM

Most Christians today are more than familiar with the city of Jerusalem, at least the one that exists in the nation of Israel, but I doubt that many today know much about the eternal city of Jerusalem that exists in heaven. It is located above the clouds and above the stars. It was designed and built by God. In the book of Hebrews it mentions that Abraham was looking forward to this city, a city whose architect and builder is God.

Heb 11:8-10 **_By faith Abraham, when called to go to a place he would later receive as his inheritance, obeyed and went, even though he did not know where he was going._** _By faith he made his home in the promised land like a stranger in a foreign country; he lived in tents, as did Isaac and Jacob, who were heirs with him of the same promise._ **_For he was looking forward to the city with foundations,_** *whose architect and builder is God.* (NIV)

This heavenly city is the dwelling place of God and Jesus and it is where the angels assemble. This city is where Jesus was in the past, is now, and will spend eternity. It has always been His home. At the Rapture Jesus will escort the saints to this heavenly city of Jerusalem to receive a kingdom that cannot be shaken—The Kingdom of God.

Heb 12:22-23 *But you have come to Mount Zion, to the heavenly Jerusalem, the city of the living God. You have come to thousands upon thousands of angels in joyful assembly, to the church of the firstborn, whose names are written in heaven. You have come to God, the judge of all men, to the spirits of righteous men made perfect,* (NIV)

The best place in the Bible to find the two cities of Jerusalem mentioned together in the same passage is in Galatians chapter four, where we find a symbolic meaning for both cities.

Gal 4:21-31 *Tell me, you who want to be under the law, are you not aware of what the law says? For it is written that Abraham had two sons, one by the slave woman and the other by the free woman.* His son by the slave woman was born in the ordinary way; but his son by the free woman was born as the result of a promise. ***These things may be taken figuratively, for the women represent two covenants.*** One covenant is from Mount Sinai and bears children who are to be slaves: This is Hagar. **Now Hagar stands for Mount Sinai in Arabia and corresponds to *the present city of Jerusalem*, because she is in slavery with her children. But *the Jerusalem that is above* is free, and she is our mother.** For it is written: "Be glad, O barren woman, who bears no children; break forth and cry aloud, you who have no labor pains; because more are the children of the desolate woman than of her who has a husband." Now you, brothers, like Isaac, are children of promise. At that time the son born in the ordinary way persecuted the son born by the power of the Spirit. It is the same now. But what does the Scripture say? "Get rid of the slave woman and her son, for the slave woman's son will never share in the inheritance with the free woman's son." Therefore, brothers, we are not children of the slave woman, but of the free woman. (NIV)

Here we are told that two women had sons by Abraham and that each of the women represents a covenant, which in turn correspond to one of the two cities of Jerusalem. They are:

1. Earthly Jerusalem — Slave woman (Hagar) and her son (Ishmael)
   First Covenant – Mount Sinai (Law – annual reminder of sin by the shed blood of goats and bulls)

AFTER THE RAPTURE

2. Heavenly Jerusalem — Free woman (Sarah) and her son (Isaac)
    New Covenant – Jesus Christ (Grace – permanent atonement for sin by the shed blood of Christ)

As we look at the first covenant, which represents the earthy Jerusalem, we see that there was a Temple with a tabernacle in it.

Heb 9:1-10   *Now **the first covenant had regulations for worship and also an earthly sanctuary. A tabernacle was set up.** In its first room were the lampstand, the table and the consecrated bread; this was called the Holy Place. Behind the second curtain was a room called the Most Holy Place, which had the golden altar of incense and the gold-covered ark of the covenant. This ark contained the gold jar of manna, Aaron's staff that had budded, and the stone tablets of the covenant. Above the ark were the cherubim of the Glory, overshadowing the atonement cover. But we cannot discuss these things in detail now. When everything had been arranged like this, the priests entered regularly into the outer room to carry on their ministry. But only the high priest entered the inner room, and that only once a year, and never without blood, which he offered for himself and for the sins the people had committed in ignorance. The Holy Spirit was showing by this that the way into the Most Holy Place had not yet been disclosed as long as the first tabernacle was still standing. This is an illustration for the present time, indicating that the gifts and sacrifices being offered were not able to clear the conscience of the worshiper. **They are only a matter of food and drink and various ceremonial washings—external regulations applying until the time of the new order.*** (NIV)

When Moses received the oracles of the law at Mount Sinai, God set up an annual remembrance of sin by using the shed blood of certain animals. The High Priest would enter the Holy of Holies (Most Holy Place), once a year on Yom Kippur and offer the shed blood of goats and bulls for the Jewish people, to cover their sins from the past year. This was the system designed by God until a perfect system (new order) would be set up by God. That system came in the form of a new covenant and it was Jesus Christ Himself. The tabernacle for this system is in heaven. The first covenant cleans outside, while the new cleans inside.

Heb 9:11-14   *When Christ came as high priest of the good things that are already here, he went through **the greater and more perfect tabernacle** that is not man-made, that is to say, not a part of this creation. He did not enter by means of the blood of goats and calves; **but he entered the Most Holy Place once for all by his own blood, having obtained eternal redemption.** The blood of goats and bulls and the ashes of a heifer sprinkled on those who are ceremonially* *unclean sanctify them so that they are outwardly clean. **How much more, then, will the blood of Christ, who through the eternal Spirit offered himself unblemished to God, cleanse our consciences from acts that lead to death, so that we may serve the living God!*** (NIV)

The system under the law was only a copy of the perfect system that has always existed in heaven. Even the earthly Temple is a copy of the original Temple that is in heaven. When Christ was crucified, He did not enter the Holy of Holies that was on earth in Jerusalem, but He entered the Holy of Holies that is in the Temple in the heavenly Jerusalem. Jesus does not enter the Holy of Holies once a year for the forgiveness of our sins of the past year, but He entered the heavenly Holy of Holies once, almost two thousand years ago, for the forgiveness of all the sins of mankind—past, present and future. Here Jesus reminds us that when He comes back the second time, He will not be coming back to bear sin like he did the first time, but to bring deliverance to those who are waiting for Him. <u>RAPTURE</u>!

Heb 9:23-28   *It was necessary, then, for the copies of the heavenly things to be purified with these sacrifices, but the heavenly things themselves with better sacrifices than these. **For Christ did not enter a man-made sanctuary that was only a copy of the true one; he entered heaven itself, now to appear for us in God's presence**. Nor did he enter heaven to offer himself again and again, the way the high priest enters the Most Holy Place every year with blood that is not his own. Then Christ would have had to suffer many times since the creation of the world. **But now he has appeared once for all at the end of the ages to do away with sin by the sacrifice of himself**. Just as man is destined to die once, and after that to face judgment, so Christ was sacrificed once to take away the sins of many people; **and he will appear a second time, not to bear sin, but to bring salvation to those who are waiting for him**.* (NIV)

The new covenant that represents the heavenly Jerusalem—as far as the atonement of sin—replaced the first covenant of the law. The new covenant is faith in Jesus Christ. By His grace and mercy are we saved. It is a free gift.

Heb 9:15   ***For this reason Christ is the mediator of a new covenant**, that those who are called may receive the promised eternal inheritance—now that he has died as a ransom to set them free from the sins committed under the first covenant.* (NIV)

Heb 10:37-39   ***For in just a very little while, "He who is coming will come and will not delay. But my righteous one will live by faith. And if he shrinks back, I will not be pleased with him." But we are not of those who shrink back and are destroyed, but of those who believe and are saved.*** (NIV)

Rom 5:14-21 — *Nevertheless, death reigned from the time of Adam to the time of Moses, even over those who did not sin by breaking a command, as did Adam, who was a pattern of the one to come. But the gift is not like the trespass. For if the many died by the trespass of the one man, <u>how much more did God's grace and the gift that came by the grace of the one man, Jesus Christ, overflow to the many</u>! Again, the gift of God is not like the result of the one man's sin: The judgment followed one sin and brought condemnation, but the gift followed many trespasses and brought justification. For if, by the trespass of the one man, death reigned through that one man, <u>how much more will those who receive God's abundant provision of grace and of the gift of righteousness reign in life through the one man, Jesus Christ</u>. Consequently, just as the result of one trespass was condemnation for all men, <u>so also the result of one act of righteousness was justification that brings life for all men</u>. For just as through the disobedience of the one man the many were made sinners, <u>so also through the obedience of the one man the many will be made righteous</u>. The law was added so that the trespass might increase. But where sin increased, grace increased all the more, so that, just as sin reigned in death, <u>so also grace might reign through righteousness to bring eternal life through Jesus Christ our Lord</u>.* (NIV)

This new covenant is an eternal covenant.

Heb 13:20-21 — *May the God of peace, who through the blood of <u>the eternal covenant</u> brought back from the dead our Lord Jesus, that great Shepherd of the sheep, equip you with everything good for doing his will, and may he work in us what is pleasing to him, through Jesus Christ, to whom be glory for ever and ever. Amen.* (NIV)

In fact, the first covenant could not take away (make atonement for) human sin. These Old Testament sacrifices were simply used to cover the sins of Israel from the previous year. The feasts of the High Holy days were for a time to remember the sins of the people from the previous year. The Old Testament sacrifices also pointed forward to the once and for all sacrifice that would take away all the sins of the world—past, present and future. These sacrifices pointed forward to the one-time sacrifice of Jesus on the cross.

Heb 10:1-10 — *<u>The law is only a shadow of the good things that are coming—not the realities themselves</u>. For this reason it can never, by the same sacrifices repeated endlessly year after year, make perfect those who draw near to worship. If it could, would they not have stopped being offered? For the worshipers would have been cleansed once for all, and would no longer have felt guilty for their sins. **But those** *sacrifices are an annual reminder of sins, because it is impossible for the blood of bulls and goats to take away sins.* Therefore, when Christ came into the world, he said: "Sacrifice and offering you did not desire, but a body you prepared for me; with burnt offerings and sin offerings you were not pleased. Then I said, 'Here I am—it is written about me in the scroll—I have come to do your will, O God.'" First he said, "Sacrifices and offerings, burnt offerings and sin offerings you did not desire, nor were you pleased with them" (although the law required them to be made). **Then he said, "Here I am, I have come to do your will." <u>He sets aside the first to establish the second. And by that will, we have been made holy through the sacrifice of the body of Jesus Christ once for all.</u>** (NIV)

Since the new covenant replaced the first covenant, does it mean that today we can go on sinning? The law at Mount Sinai was put into place in order to recognize transgressions and it is still in place today for that purpose. If this portion of the law were removed when the new covenant came into play, there would be no way of recognizing the sins of men when they are committed. The old law was put in place until the Seed (Jesus) would come.

Rom 6:1-23   *<u>What shall we say, then? Shall we go on sinning so that grace may increase? By no means</u>! We died to sin; how can we live in it any longer? Or don't you know that all of us who were baptized into Christ Jesus were baptized into his death? We were therefore buried with him through baptism into death in order that, just as Christ was raised from the dead through the glory of the Father, we too may live a new life.* **If we have been united with him like this in his death, we will certainly also be united with him in his resurrection.** *For we know that our old self was crucified with him so that the body of sin might be done away with, that we should no longer be slaves to sin—because anyone who has died has been freed from sin. Now if we died with Christ, we believe that we will also live with him.* **For we know that since Christ was raised from the dead, he cannot die again; death no longer has mastery over him. The death he died, he died to sin once for all; but the life he lives, he lives to God.** *In the same way, count yourselves dead to sin but alive to God in Christ Jesus.* **Therefore do not let sin reign in your mortal body so that you obey its evil desires.** *Do not offer the parts of your body to sin, as instruments of wickedness, but rather offer yourselves to God, as those who have been brought from death to life; and offer the parts of your body to him as instruments of righteousness.* **For sin shall not be your master, because you are not under law, but under grace. What then? Shall we sin because we are not under law but under grace? <u>By no means</u>!** *Don't you know that when you offer yourselves to someone to obey him as slaves, you are slaves to the*

AFTER THE RAPTURE

one whom you obey—whether you are slaves to sin, which leads to death, or to obedience, which leads to righteousness? But thanks be to God that, though you used to be slaves to sin, you wholeheartedly obeyed the form of teaching to which you were entrusted. ***You have been set free from sin and have become slaves to righteousness.*** *I put this in human terms because you are weak in your natural selves. Just as you used to offer the parts of your body in slavery to impurity and to ever-increasing wickedness, so now offer them in slavery to righteousness leading to holiness. When you were slaves to sin, you were free from the control of righteousness. What benefit did you reap at that time from the things you are now ashamed of? Those things result in death!* ***But now that you have been set free from sin and have become slaves to God, the benefit you reap leads to holiness, and the result is eternal life.*** ***For the wages of sin is death, but the gift of God is eternal life in Christ Jesus our Lord.*** (NIV)

Heb 12:1-6   *Therefore, since we are surrounded by such a great cloud of witnesses,* ***let us throw off*** *everything that hinders and the sin that so easily entangles, and let us run with perseverance the race marked out for us.* ***Let us fix our eyes on Jesus, the author and perfecter of our faith, who for the joy set before him endured the cross****, scorning its shame, and sat down at the right hand of the throne of God. Consider him who endured such opposition from sinful men, so that you will not grow weary and lose heart.* ***In your struggle against sin, you have not yet resisted to the point of shedding your blood.*** *And you have forgotten that word of encouragement that addresses you as sons: "****My son, do not make light of the Lord's discipline, and do not lose heart when he rebukes you, because the Lord disciplines those he loves, and he punishes everyone he accepts as a son.****"* (NIV)

Gal 3:19   *What, then, was the purpose of the law?* ***It was added because of transgressions until the Seed to whom the promise referred had come.*** *The law was put into effect through angels by a mediator.* (NIV)

We are not to look forward to the earthly Jerusalem, which will not last forever, but to the heavenly Jerusalem that will last forever, a kingdom that cannot be shaken. As Christians our rewards are yet future.

Heb 13:14   *For here we do not have an enduring city,* ***but we are looking for the city that is to come.*** (NIV)

Heb 12:28-29   *Therefore, since we are receiving a kingdom that cannot be shaken, let us be thankful, and so worship God acceptably with reverence and awe, for our "God is a consuming fire."* (NIV)

Phil 3:20-21 *But our citizenship is in heaven. And we eagerly await a Savior from there, the Lord Jesus Christ, who, by the power that enables him to bring everything under his control, will transform our lowly bodies so that they will be like his glorious body.* (NIV)

SALEM

Where was Salem located? Of all the names for the city of Jerusalem, Salem and its king are the most mysterious; the king of Salem being Melchizedek. Salem is usually identified with ancient Jerusalem, the Jebusite city captured by David to be his capital city. As we pull up the definitions of the Hebrew word for Salem, we find some interesting thoughts.

Strong's Definition
8004 Shalem (shaw-lame');
the same as 8003; peaceful; Shalem, an early name of Jerusalem:
KJV—Salem.
***. shalom. See 7965.

The general opinion among the Jewish people is that Salem was the same city as Jerusalem, when taken from the writings of Josephus, a Jewish historian who lived at the time of Christ. Strong's definition lists the meaning of the Jewish word, *"Shalom,"* as:

Strong's Definition
7965 shalowm (shaw-lome');
or shalom (shaw-lome'); from 7999; safe, i.e. (figuratively) well, happy, friendly; also (abstractly) welfare, i.e. health, prosperity, peace:
KJV—X do, familiar, X fare, favour, + friend, X great, (good) health, (X perfect, such as be at) peace (-able, -ably), prosper (-ity, -ous), rest, safe (-ty), salute, welfare, (X all is, be) well, X wholly.

Many non-Jewish people today are familiar with this Jewish word *Shalom,* used as a greeting to say "hello or goodbye" or "peace be with you." To show the complete meaning of the two words defined above, we need to look at the root word of both words.

Strong's Definition
7999 shalam (shaw-lam');
a primitive root; to be safe (in mind, body or estate); figuratively, to be (causatively, make) completed; by implication, to be friendly; by extension, to reciprocate (in various applications):
KJV—make amends, (make an) end, finish, full, give again, make good, (re-) pay (again), (make) (to) (be at) peace (-able), that is perfect, perform, (make) prosper (-ous),

recompense, render, requite, make restitution, restore, reward, X surely.

Before we come to a conclusion about Salem, we need to take a closer look at its king. The time we are referencing is somewhere around 1970 BC, almost 4000 years ago.

> Gen 14:18-20　*And <u>Melchizedek king of Salem</u> brought forth bread and wine: and he was the priest of the most high God. And he blessed him, and said, Blessed be Abram of the most high God, possessor of heaven and earth: And blessed be the most high God, which hath delivered thine enemies into thy hand. And he gave him tithes of all.* (KJV)

As we turn to Psalms 110, which is a Messianic psalm written by David, we are given the identity of Melchizedek. Here God (the LORD) is speaking to Jesus (my Lord) who is a priest forever. Here we can clearly distinguish between God the Father and Jesus Christ.

> Ps 110:1-7　*<u>The LORD says to my Lord</u>: "Sit at my right hand until I make your enemies a footstool for your feet." <u>The LORD will extend your mighty scepter from Zion; you will rule in the midst of your enemies.</u> Your troops will be willing on your day of battle. Arrayed in holy majesty, from the womb of the dawn you will receive the dew of your youth. The LORD has sworn and will not change his mind: "<u>You are a priest forever, in the order of Melchizedek.</u>" The Lord is at your right hand; he will crush kings on the day of his wrath. <u>He will judge the nations, heaping up the dead and crushing the rulers of the whole earth.</u> He will drink from a brook beside the way; therefore he will lift up his head.* (NIV)

This entire Psalm is speaking about the Messianic reign of Jesus as King during the Day of the Lord. Here you can clearly see Jesus as King in heaven at the right hand of God while the Tribulation Period (day of His wrath) is playing out on earth. Jesus is mentioned as being a priest forever, as established in heaven from the heavenly priesthood. Here we see the double role of Jesus during the Millennium—King and High Priest. Jesus will be a Priest on His Throne and the council of peace will be governed between these two positions.

The identity of Melchizedek as Christ can be assured in the New Testament in the old faithful book of Hebrews.

> Heb 6:19-7:28　*We have this hope as an anchor for the soul, firm and secure. It enters the inner sanctuary behind the curtain, where Jesus, who went before us, has entered on our behalf. He has become a high priest forever, in the order of Melchizedek. <u>This Melchizedek was king of Salem and priest of God Most High.</u> He met Abraham returning from the defeat of the kings and blessed him, and Abraham gave him a tenth of everything. First, his name means "king of righteousness"; then also, "king of Salem" means "king of*

peace." *Without father or mother, without genealogy, without beginning of days or end of life, <u>like the Son of God he remains a priest forever</u>.* Just think how great he was: Even the patriarch Abraham gave him a tenth of the plunder! Now the law requires the descendants of Levi who become priests to collect a tenth from the people—that is, their brothers—even though their brothers are descended from Abraham. This man, however, did not trace his descent from Levi, yet he collected a tenth from Abraham and blessed him who had the promises. And without doubt the lesser person is blessed by the greater. In the one case, the tenth is collected by men who die; but in the other case, by him who is declared to be living. One might even say that Levi, who collects the tenth, paid the tenth through Abraham, because when Melchizedek met Abraham, Levi was still in the body of his ancestor. **If perfection could have been attained through the Levitical priesthood (for on the basis of it the law was given to the people), why was there still need for another priest to come—one in the order of Melchizedek, not in the order of Aaron?** For when there is a change of the priesthood, there must also be a change of the law. He of whom these things are said belonged to a different tribe, and no one from that tribe has ever served at the altar. For it is clear that our Lord descended from Judah, and in regard to that tribe Moses said nothing about priests. And what we have said is even more clear if another priest like Melchizedek appears, one who has become a priest not on the basis of a regulation as to his ancestry but on the basis of the power of an indestructible life. For it is declared: "You are a priest forever, in the order of Melchizedek." The former regulation is set aside because it was weak and useless (for the law made nothing perfect), and a better hope is introduced, by which we draw near to God. And it was not without an oath! **Others became priests without any oath, but he became a priest with an oath when God said to him: "The Lord has sworn and will not change his mind: '<u>You are a priest forever.</u>'" <u>Because of this oath</u>, <u>Jesus has become the guarantee of a better covenant</u>.** Now there have been many of those priests, since death prevented them from continuing in office; <u>**but because Jesus lives forever, he has a permanent priesthood**</u>. Therefore he is able to save completely those who come to God through him, because he always lives to intercede for them. Such a high priest meets our need—one who is holy, blameless, pure, set apart from sinners, exalted above the heavens. Unlike the other high priests, he does not need to offer sacrifices day after day, first for his own sins, and then for the sins of the people. He sacrificed for their sins once for all when he offered himself. **For the law appoints as high priests men who are weak; <u>but the oath</u>, <u>which came after the law</u>, <u>appointed</u>**

AFTER THE RAPTURE

<u>the Son, who has been made perfect forever.</u> (NIV)

Only <u>Deity</u> can:
1. be "the king of righteousness"
2. be "the king of peace"
3. be without father or mother
4. be without genealogy
5. be without beginning of days or end of days
6. remain a priest forever
7. save completely and intercede for man

All of that brings us back to the same question – Where was Salem located? In the book of Psalms we find the answer to the mystery.

> Ps 76:1-2   *In Judah God is known; his name is great in Israel. <u>In Salem also is His tabernacle, and His dwelling place in Zion.</u>* (NKJ)

These verses are not referring to the earthly Jerusalem, but to God's permanent dwelling in heaven. Jesus, as Melchizedek, did not have a tabernacle on earth at the time of Abraham, nor did He have a dwelling place on earth at that time. The dwelling place (home) for Jesus during His pre-incarnate period of time was in heaven. On the time line on page 766, also in the upper left hand corner, you will see the proper location for Salem—in heaven.

Before we move on we need to look at another landmark—Moriah. There are two sites mentioned for Moriah in the Old Testament. The first time it is mentioned it is referred to as a region or the land of Moriah. This is the area God commanded Abraham to take his son Isaac, who was born of Sarah. Abraham was to offer Isaac as a burnt offering on one of the mountains. It was a three-day journey from Beersheba.

> Gen 22:1-4   *Some time later God tested Abraham. He said to him, "Abraham!" "Here I am," he replied. Then God said, "Take your son, your only son, Isaac, whom you love, and go to <u>the region of Moriah</u>. Sacrifice him there as a burnt offering on one of the mountains I will tell you about." Early the next morning Abraham got up and saddled his donkey. He took with him two of his servants and his son Isaac. When he had cut enough wood for the burnt offering, he set out for the place God had told him about. On the third day Abraham looked up and saw the place in the distance.* (NIV)

The second time Moriah is mentioned it refers to a mountain. It is the stationary place where Solomon built a Temple for God to dwell in on earth.

> 2 Chr 3:1-2   **Then Solomon began to build the temple of the LORD in Jerusalem on <u>Mount Moriah</u>, where the LORD had appeared to his father David.** *It was on the threshing floor of Araunah the*

Jebusite, the place provided by David. He began building on the second day of the second month in the fourth year of his reign. (NIV)

The place where Abraham offered up Isaac and the mountain where Solomon had the Temple built is the same location. The Jewish people believe that the Altar of Burnt Offering in the Temple at Jerusalem was located on the exact spot where Abraham tied Isaac up and laid him on the pile of wood for a burnt offering.

It is doubtful that a city even existed below Mount Moriah at the time of Abraham. Sometime later the Jebusites built a fortress around Mount Moriah and it was known as Zion. This is the first time that the word, *"Zion,"* is mentioned in the Bible. It would have been a very small fortress at that time. By the time David conquered the city it was known as Jerusalem. David ruled the nation of Israel for forty years. He began his rule in the city of Hebron where he ruled for seven years. David then conquered Jerusalem and moved the capital of Israel to Jerusalem and from there he ruled for another thirty-three years.

2 Sam 5:6-7　*<u>The king and his men marched to Jerusalem to attack the Jebusites, who lived there.</u> The Jebusites said to David, "You will not get in here; even the blind and the lame can ward you off." They thought, "David cannot get in here." <u>Nevertheless, David captured the fortress of Zion, the City of David.</u>* (NIV)

CITY OF DAVID

Jerusalem as a city on earth has a long history and probably was a small city more than 3500 years ago during the Canaanite period. It was one of the conglomeration of political entities caught in a power play between the Egyptian Kingdom in the south and the Hittites from the north in Asia Minor. The theme of domination by outlying powers recurs throughout the history of Jerusalem, located at a crossroad between east and west. Jerusalem changed hands numerous times during the Canaanite period. It is believed that various peoples inhabited the city in different periods, including the Amorites who came from the Syro-Arabian desert and Jebusites, a Semitic people who controlled the city before it was conquered by King David around 1004 BC. The name of the Jebusite city that David conquered was Jerusalem and he renamed it the City of David and made it the capital city of Israel. The name of the fortress that surrounded Mount Moriah was Zion.

2 Sam 5:6-10　*The king and his men marched to Jerusalem to attack the Jebusites, who lived there. The Jebusites said to David, "You will not get in here; even the blind and the lame can ward you off." They thought, "David cannot get in here." Nevertheless, David captured the fortress of Zion, the City of David. On that day, David said, "Anyone who conquers the Jebusites will have to use the water shaft to reach those 'lame and blind' who are David's enemies." That is why they say, "The 'blind and lame' will not enter the palace." <u>David then took up residence in the fortress and</u>*

> *called it the City of David. He built up the area around it, from the supporting terraces inward. And he became more and more powerful, because the LORD God Almighty was with him.* (NIV)

The ancient Jebusite fortress was located along the Ophel ridge running between the Tyropoean and Kidron valleys. David's city was found on the southern spur of the mount. King Solomon later built the Temple on Mount Moriah, which was located uphill from the city. The City of David, today part of the village of Silwan, is outside the current walls of the Old City. One of the most spectacular finds of archaeological excavations is a huge support structure believed to be the base of David's palace. Jerusalem's greatest glory came during the golden age of the nation of Israel and was reached under the reign of King Solomon, who built the Temple and a royal palace. He also greatly enlarged and strengthened the walls of the city. Between the time the Babylonians destroyed Jerusalem and the Temple in 586 BC and the time that the Jewish people became their own nation again on May 14, 1948, Jerusalem was under the control of numerous governmental influences. They were the Hellenistic (Greek), Roman, Byzantine, Umayyad, Abbasid, Crusader (Latin Kingdom), Ayyubid, Gatimed, Mameluke, Ottomon (Turks) and British. Three of the greatest humiliations of Jerusalem have been: (1) the destruction of the city and the Temple by the Babylonians in 586 BC, (2) the reign of Antiochus Epiphanes, 175-165 BC, when the most violent and cruel efforts were made to destroy the Jews and desecrate their Temple, and (3) the total destruction of the rebuilt city and the Temple in 70 AD by the Romans after a Jewish revolt. A second revolt in 135 AD resulted in the expulsion of the Jews from the city and afterward they renamed it Aelia Capitolina. Sometime later the city was renamed Jerusalem. The land at this time became known as Palestine.

Jerusalem and the Temple play an important part in God's plan, both here on earth and in heaven. The earthly Jerusalem and the Temple were so special to God that He put His Name on them forever.

1 Kings 11:36 — *I will give one tribe to his son so that David my servant may always have a lamp before me in Jerusalem, the city where I chose to put my Name.* (NIV)

2 Kings 21:4 — *He built altars in the temple of the LORD, of which the LORD had said, "In Jerusalem I will put my Name."* (NIV)

1 Kings 9:1-3 — *When Solomon had finished building the temple of the LORD and the royal palace, and had achieved all he had desired to do, the LORD appeared to him a second time, as he had appeared to him at Gibeon. The LORD said to him: "I have heard the prayer and plea you have made before me; I have consecrated this temple, which you have built, by putting my Name there forever. My eyes and my heart will always be there.* (NIV)

2 Kings 21:7 — *He took the carved Asherah pole he had made and put it in the*

temple, of which the LORD had said to David and to his son Solomon, "<u>In this temple and in Jerusalem, which I have chosen out of all the tribes of Israel, I will put my Name forever</u>. (NIV)

One of the names for Jerusalem is the City of Peace, a strange name for a city that has known far more war than peace throughout its long history. A city that is filled with blood poured out on its streets. Even today, it is fueled with hostility from the ongoing conflict between the Jews and the Arabs. A city that will be the last city that the Antichrist and his army come against at the Battle of Armageddon. The fulfillment of Jerusalem as the City of Peace will materialize when Jesus returns and sets it up as such. At that time the shedding of blood will cease.

<u>CITY OF PEACE</u>

Let us now turn our attention to the City of Peace, but before we look at it we need to clarify the name Zion in the Bible. It is a name that can apply to the city of Jerusalem or various parts of it since before the time of David. Zion can also refer to the land or nation of Israel and also the people of Israel as a whole. Zion can also be used figuratively of Israel as the people of God. Zion or Mount Moriah can also refer to the location where the earthly Temple once stood. It was located north of the original City of David, uphill on Mount Moriah. It is sometimes referred to as the Temple Hill. Today, the Moslem Dome of the Rock rests on this location. Among early Christian writers who mention Zion, Origen referred to it as equivalent to the Temple Hill. By the fourth century the name Zion was adapted to the southern portion of the western hill. If you look at a map of Jerusalem today, you are likely to find this location labeled Mount Zion. A prominent landmark situated there today is the Dormition Church. It is located near the traditional Tomb of David and was built in 1910. Catholic tradition regards this as the site of the Virgin Mary's eternal sleep. This church was constructed on lands given by the Turkish Sultan to Germany, when in 1898 Kaiser Wilhelm II visited Jerusalem. The round clock, with clock-tower and black cone roof, is an unusual landmark on the Jerusalem skyline. Today, Zion usually refers to the Jewish nation, its people or both. Zionism was and is a worldwide movement of the exiled Jewish people for the establishment and continuation of a national homeland for their people.

Along with the Zion that everyone is familiar with, spoken above, there is a heavenly Zion. At times it can even be referred to as Mount Zion. Bible prophecy is very difficult to come to a correct chronological order without distinguishing between the heavenly Zion and the earthly Zion. When placed in the correct location at the proper time, future history plays out in an orderly fashion.

Prophetically speaking, Zion is a reference to the Temple area and will be a part of Jerusalem as the future capital city of not only Israel, but the entire world as well. This will take place during the Kingdom Age. This location will be set up as a tangible symbol of centralized Divine authority. Zion will be the location where Jesus will rebuild the Temple, probably on Mount Moriah where the Jewish Temple once stood. The terrain around Jerusalem will rest on a level plain while Jerusalem itself will rest on a higher elevation, with the Temple resting on the highest point of the city. From any location in Jerusalem and perhaps all the land of Israel and beyond, you will be able to view this majestic Temple. It will not be a separate city, but the most sacred part of the city of Jerusalem.

Also prophetically, the heavenly Mount Zion will come down from heaven when the New Heavens and New Earth replace the present earth, after the Millennium is completed. It also appears that Mount Zion refers to the Temple area in the heavenly Jerusalem, the city of the living God (His holy mountain). The word Zion alone can also refer to the Temple area of the earthly or at times the heavenly Jerusalem. We will discuss the New Jerusalem in chapter fifteen.

When Jesus is crowned King at the beginning of the Kingdom Age, that coronation will take place in heaven in the city of the living God, the heavenly Jerusalem. The reign of Jesus as King will actually take place in two separate locations. The very beginning of His reign will be from heaven (heavenly Jerusalem) and will last a little more than nine years. The Messianic Kingdom will begin in heaven in Zion, God's holy hill, while God's enemies are still on earth. At the time of His glorious appearing, Jesus will establish the earthly portion of His kingdom reign on earth in Jerusalem. There are many scripture references that pertain to Jesus in heaven after He is crowned King, but before He returns to earth.

Ps 2:1-9 *<u>Why do the nations conspire and the peoples plot in vain?</u> The <u>kings of the earth take their stand and the rulers gather together</u> against the LORD and against his Anointed One. "Let us break their chains," they say, "and throw off their fetters." <u>The One enthroned in heaven laughs; the Lord scoffs at them</u>. Then he rebukes them in his anger and terrifies them in his wrath, saying, "<u>I have installed my King on Zion</u>, <u>my holy hill</u>." I will proclaim the decree of the LORD: He said to me, "You are my Son; today I have become your Father. Ask of me, and I will make the nations your inheritance, the ends of the earth your possession. You will rule them with an iron scepter; you will dash them to pieces like pottery."* (NIV)

Ps 110:1-7 *The LORD says to my Lord: "Sit at my right hand until I make your enemies a footstool for your feet." <u>The LORD will extend your mighty scepter from Zion; you will rule in the midst of your enemies</u>. Your troops will be willing on your day of battle. Arrayed in holy majesty, from the womb of the dawn you will receive the dew of your youth. The LORD has sworn and will not change his mind: "You are a priest forever, in the order of Melchizedek." <u>The Lord is at your right hand; he will crush kings on the day of his wrath. He will judge the nations, heaping up the dead and crushing the rulers of the whole earth</u>. He will drink from a brook beside the way; therefore he will lift up his head.* (NIV)

Ps 11:4-7 *<u>The LORD is in his holy temple; the LORD is on his heavenly throne. He observes the sons of men; his eyes examine them</u>. The*

The Rest of the Millennium

LORD examines the righteous, but the wicked and those who love violence his soul hates. <u>On the wicked he will rain fiery coals and burning sulfur; a scorching wind will be their lot.</u> For the LORD is righteous, he loves justice; upright men will see his face. (NIV)

The books were opened and court was in session as we see the Judgment Seat of Christ progress; better to have one day in this court than all the courts of the world. In these verses below, we see the time when the saints will finally be able to dwell in their heavenly houses prepared for them by God. Notice that they appear before God in Zion.

Ps 84:1-12 *<u>How lovely is Your tabernacle, O LORD of hosts</u>! My soul longs, yes, even faints for the courts of the LORD; my heart and my flesh cry out for the living God. Even the sparrow has found a home, and the swallow a nest for herself, where she may lay her young—even Your altars, O LORD of hosts, my King and my God. <u>Blessed are those who dwell in Your house; they will still be praising You</u>. Selah Blessed is the man whose strength is in You, whose heart is set on pilgrimage. As they pass through the Valley of Baca, they make it a spring; the rain also covers it with pools. <u>They go from strength to strength; each one appears before God in Zion</u>. O LORD God of hosts, hear my prayer; give ear, O God of Jacob! Selah O God, behold our shield, and look upon the face of Your anointed. <u>For a day in Your courts is better than a thousand. I would rather be a doorkeeper in the house of my God than dwell in the tents of wickedness</u>. For the LORD God is a sun and shield; the LORD will give grace and glory; no good thing will He withhold from those who walk uprightly. <u>O LORD of hosts, blessed is the man who trusts in You</u>!* (NKJ)

Jesus will eventually rule the human population on earth from Zion, in Jerusalem, during the Day of the Lord. His rule on earth will extend to all the saved remnant that survived the purging of the unsaved people on the earth during the Tribulation Period, followed by the Battle of Armageddon, and their generations to follow. The following two references are to the Zion that will be located on earth.

Zech 8:1-3 *Again the word of the LORD of hosts came, saying, "Thus says the LORD of hosts: 'I am zealous for Zion with great zeal; with great fervor I am zealous for her.' "Thus says the LORD: '<u>I will return to Zion, and dwell in the midst of Jerusalem. Jerusalem shall be called the City of Truth, the Mountain of the LORD of hosts, the Holy Mountain</u>.'* (NKJ)

Joel 3:17-21 *'<u>Then you will know that I, the LORD your God, dwell in Zion, my holy hill. Jerusalem will be holy</u>; never again will foreigners invade*

> *her. 'In that day the mountains will drip new wine, and the hills will flow with milk; all the ravines of Judah will run with water. A fountain will flow out of the LORD's house and will water the valley of acacias. But Egypt will be desolate, Edom a desert waste, because of violence done to the people of Judah, in whose land they shed innocent blood. Judah will be inhabited forever and Jerusalem through all generations. Their bloodguilt, which I have not pardoned, I will pardon.' <u>The LORD dwells in Zion!</u>* (NIV)

The City of Peace will finally be realized and established on earth when Jesus sets it up after the Battle of Armageddon. It will literally go through hell to get there. In the following verses we see Jesus as He reigns from the earthly Temple (Zion) in the city of Jerusalem after He rebuilds them.

Isa 52:7-10 *How beautiful on the mountains are the feet of those who bring good news, who proclaim peace, who bring good tidings, who proclaim salvation, who say to Zion, "<u>Your God reigns!</u>" Listen! Your watchmen lift up their voices; together they shout for joy. <u>When the LORD returns to Zion, they will see it with their own eyes.</u> Burst into songs of joy together, you ruins of Jerusalem, for the LORD has comforted his people, he has redeemed Jerusalem. The LORD will lay bare his holy arm in the sight of all the nations, and all the ends of the earth will see the salvation of our God.* (NIV)

Isa 66:10-13 *"<u>Rejoice with Jerusalem and be glad for her, all you who love her; rejoice greatly with her, all you who mourn over her.</u> For you will nurse and be satisfied at her comforting breasts; you will drink deeply and delight in her overflowing abundance." For this is what the LORD says: "<u>I will extend peace to her like a river</u>, and the wealth of nations like a flooding stream; you will nurse and be carried on her arm and dandled on her knees. As a mother comforts her child, so will I comfort you; and you will be comforted over Jerusalem."* (NIV)

Ps 122:6-8 <u>*Pray for the peace of Jerusalem*</u>*: "May those who love you be secure. May there be peace within your walls and security within your citadels." For the sake of my brothers and friends, I will say, "<u>Peace be within you</u>."* (NIV)

Prophecy paints a brilliant future for Jerusalem and also for those who survive the Lord's fierce anger. The term "Daughter of Zion" is applied to those Jews who were exiled or taken captive and survived the second holocaust, which will take place during the Tribulation Period and the Battle of Armageddon. All who recognize Jesus as their Messiah and continue living in their human bodies during the Kingdom Age will be ecstatic.

The Rest of the Millennium

Isa 4:2-4   *"In that day the Branch of the LORD will be beautiful and glorious, and the fruit of the land will be the pride and glory of the survivors in Israel. <u>Those who are left in Zion, who remain in Jerusalem, will be called holy, all who are recorded among the living in Jerusalem.</u> The Lord will wash away the filth of <u>the women of Zion</u>; he will cleanse the bloodstains from Jerusalem by a spirit of judgment and a spirit of fire.* (NIV)

Zeph 3:14-17   *<u>Sing, O Daughter of Zion</u>; <u>shout aloud, O Israel</u>! Be glad and rejoice with all your heart, O Daughter of Jerusalem! The LORD has taken away your punishment, he has turned back your enemy. <u>The LORD, the King of Israel, is with you</u>; never again will you fear any harm. On that day they will say to Jerusalem, "Do not fear, O Zion; do not let your hands hang limp. The LORD your God is with you, he is mighty to save. He will take great delight in you, he will quiet you with his love, he will rejoice over you with singing."* (NIV)

Isa 12:1-6   *In that day you will say: "I will praise you, O LORD. Although you were angry with me, your anger has turned away and you have comforted me. Surely God is my salvation; I will trust and not be afraid. The LORD, the LORD, is my strength and my song; he has become my salvation." With joy you will draw water from the wells of salvation. **In that day you will say: "Give thanks to the LORD, call on his name; make known among the nations what he has done, and proclaim that his name is exalted. Sing to the LORD, for he has done glorious things; let this be known to all the world. <u>Shout aloud and sing for joy, people of Zion, for great is the Holy One of Israel among you.</u>"*** (NIV)

Isa 52:1-2   *<u>Awake, awake, O Zion, clothe yourself with strength</u>. <u>Put on your garments of splendor, O Jerusalem, the holy city</u>. The uncircumcised and defiled will not enter you again. Shake off your dust; rise up, sit enthroned, O Jerusalem. <u>Free yourself from the chains on your neck, O captive Daughter of Zion</u>.* (NIV)

Isa 62:10-12   *<u>Pass through, pass through the gates</u>! <u>Prepare the way for the people</u>. Build up, build up the highway! Remove the stones. Raise a banner for the nations. The LORD has made proclamation to the ends of the earth: "<u>Say to the Daughter of Zion</u>, 'See, your Savior comes! See, his reward is with him, and his recompense accompanies him.'" <u>They will be called the Holy People, the Redeemed of the LORD; and you will be called Sought After, the City No Longer Deserted</u>.* (NIV)

AFTER THE RAPTURE

Jerusalem will be rebuilt on the ruined remains of the city destroyed during the Tribulation Period and the Battle of Armageddon. Jesus Himself will supervise the construction of Jerusalem, the Temple and probably the rest of the world. Take note that Jerusalem will never be destroyed again. Its gates will never be closed and its people will live in peace and security. Israel's leader will be one of their own — Jesus Christ.

Jer 30:18-22   *"This is what the LORD says:"'<u>I will restore the fortunes of Jacob's tents and have compassion on his dwellings; the city will be rebuilt on her ruins, and the palace will stand in its proper place</u>. From them will come songs of thanksgiving and the sound of rejoicing. I will add to their numbers, and they will not be decreased; I will bring them honor, and they will not be disdained. Their children will be as in days of old, and their community will be established before me; I will punish all who oppress them. <u>Their leader will be one of their own; their ruler will arise from among them</u>. I will bring him near and he will come close to me, for who is he who will devote himself to be close to me?' declares the LORD. "'<u>So you will be my people, and I will be your God</u>.'"* (NIV)

Jer 31:38-40   *"<u>The days are coming</u>," declares the LORD, "<u>when this city will be rebuilt for me from the Tower of Hananel to the Corner Gate</u>. The measuring line will stretch from there straight to the hill of Gareb and then turn to Goah. The whole valley where dead bodies and ashes are thrown, and all the terraces out to the Kidron Valley on the east as far as the corner of the Horse Gate, will be holy to the LORD. <u>The city will never again be uprooted or demolished</u>."* (NIV)

Isa 65:18-19   *But be glad <u>and rejoice forever in what I will create, for I will create Jerusalem to be a delight and its people a joy</u>. I will rejoice over Jerusalem and take delight in my people; <u>the sound of weeping and of crying will be heard in it no more</u>.* (NIV)

Zech 14:8-11   *On that day living water will flow out from Jerusalem, half to the eastern sea and half to the western sea, in summer and in winter. <u>The LORD will be king over the whole earth. On that day there will be one LORD</u>, and his name the only name. The whole land, from Geba to Rimmon, south of Jerusalem, will become like the Arabah. <u>But Jerusalem will be raised up and remain in its place</u>, from the Benjamin Gate to the site of the First Gate, to the Corner Gate, and from the Tower of Hananel to the royal winepresses. <u>It will be inhabited; never again will it be destroyed. Jerusalem will be secure</u>.* (NIV)

The Rest of the Millennium

Isa 60:11   *Your gates will always stand open, they will never be shut, day or night, so that men may bring you the wealth of the nations—their kings led in triumphal procession.* (NIV)

Zion will be given a new name. Her righteousness will shine like the dawn, her salvation like a blazing torch. People from the nations will assemble to worship the Lord.

Isa 62:1-12   *For Zion's sake I will not keep silent, for Jerusalem's sake I will not remain quiet, till her righteousness shines out like the dawn, her salvation like a blazing torch. The nations will see your righteousness, and all kings your glory; you will be called by a new name that the mouth of the LORD will bestow. You will be a crown of splendor in the LORD's hand, a royal diadem in the hand of your God. No longer will they call you Deserted, or name your land Desolate. But you will be called Hephzibah, and your land Beulah; for the LORD will take delight in you, and your land will be married. As a young man marries a maiden, so will your sons marry you; as a bridegroom rejoices over his bride, so will your God rejoice over you. I have posted watchmen on your walls, O Jerusalem; they will never be silent day or night. **You who call on the LORD, give yourselves no rest, and give him no rest till he establishes Jerusalem and makes her the praise of the earth.** The LORD has sworn by his right hand and by his mighty arm: "Never again will I give your grain as food for your enemies, and never again will foreigners drink the new wine for which you have toiled; but those who harvest it will eat it and praise the LORD, and those who gather the grapes will drink it in the courts of my sanctuary." Pass through, pass through the gates! Prepare the way for the people. Build up, build up the highway! Remove the stones. Raise a banner for the nations. The LORD has made proclamation to the ends of the earth: "Say to the Daughter of Zion, 'See, your Savior comes! See, his reward is with him, and his recompense accompanies him.'" They will be called the Holy People, the Redeemed of the LORD; and you will be called Sought After, the City No Longer Deserted.* (NIV)

Ps 102:21-22   *So the name of the LORD will be declared in Zion and his praise in Jerusalem when the peoples and the kingdoms assemble to worship the LORD.* (NIV)

Turn to the charts on pages 762 through 765 and follow along the green line where it shows the progression of Jesus from His crucifixion to His Glorious Return. A short synopsis of Jesus during the first ten years of the Millennium will go something like this:

After Jesus is crowned King in heaven, it will be a very busy time for Him. His first task will be to sit on His throne and judge every saint that received their resurrected bodies. Then

AFTER THE RAPTURE

Jesus will attend His wedding ceremony. This will all take place in heaven at the end of the first two years of His reign as King. After the wedding Jesus will play a double role for the next seven years. In heaven Jesus will be a participant at His wedding feast. Occasionally Jesus will leave the wedding feast to orchestrate the reign of terror that will pour down on earth during the Tribulation Period. Toward the end of the Wedding Feast Jesus will attend the banquet of the Marriage Supper of the Lamb, which will also take place in heaven. After this is over Jesus will exit His room and appear on a cloud and reveal Himself to the people on the earth. A voice like a great trumpet will be sounded to signal the angels to gather the elect (Jews) and take them to the Sinai Desert. Jesus will continue coming down from heaven and set foot on earth at the Mount of Olives and proceed west to the site where the Temple stood on Mount Moriah. Once there, He will set up His throne. Jesus will then proceed to the Sinai Desert where He will separate the righteous Jews from the unrighteous Jews. After that is finished Jesus will return to Jerusalem where He will perform the same separation process for the nations who have been gathered in the Valley of Jehoshaphat. When that task is finished Jesus will return to Mount Zion, in the heavenly Jerusalem, to prepare for war—the Battle of Armageddon. He will mount a white stallion and head for the earth followed by His armies. His assault will be from south to north up the Jordan Valley, turning west and passing through the Valley of Megiddo (Armageddon) and then He will head back to the earthly Jerusalem to defeat the Antichrist and what is left of his army. At this point it will be time for another banquet—the Great Supper of God. Toward the end of the second period of days following the Tribulation Period (forty-five days when Jesus judged the Tribulation saints), a third banquet will be held on earth—the Feast of all Peoples. After all this destruction is over it will be time for Jesus to start the rebuilding process. All of this is accomplished in less than ten years. Amazing! Following the doom and gloom portion of the Day of the Lord will be bliss in the City of Peace.

It is the desire of my wife Sarah, her sister Marci and myself to visit the city of Jerusalem here on earth in our lifetime. If for some reason that is not God's will, no one can keep us from entering the heavenly Jerusalem, the city of the living God, with Jesus when He escorts us into the presence of God.

REBUILD THE TEMPLE

During the first half of the Tribulation Period the Antichrist will allow the Jewish people to rebuild their sacred Temple and reestablish sacrificial worship. Not very long after it is completed the Antichrist will desecrate the Temple by claiming himself to be God. The Antichrist will build a throne for himself. After the Antichrist is defeated, a little more than 3 ½ years later, Jesus (the Branch) will build a new Millennial Temple.

Zech 6:12-13   *Tell him this is what the LORD Almighty says: 'Here is the man whose name is the Branch, and he will branch out from his place and build the temple of the LORD. It is he who will build the temple of the LORD, and he will be clothed with majesty and will sit and rule on his throne. And he will be a priest on his throne. And there will be harmony between the two.'* (NIV)

The Rest of the Millennium

Amos 9:11   *"**In that day I will restore David's fallen tent.** I will repair its broken places, restore its ruins, and build it as it used to be,* (NIV)

Instead of the false Messiah (the Antichrist building the Temple in Jerusalem), it will be the true God, *"the Branch"* who will rebuild the permanent Millennial Temple in Jerusalem. Please remember that during the Kingdom Age, when Jesus rebuilds the Temple on earth, it will be known as Zion and will be high on a hill in the city of Jerusalem.

Zech 1:16-17   *"Therefore, this is what the LORD says: '**I will return to Jerusalem with mercy, and there my house will be rebuilt.** And the measuring line will be stretched out over Jerusalem,' declares the LORD Almighty. "Proclaim further: This is what the LORD Almighty says: '**My towns will again overflow with prosperity, and the LORD will again comfort Zion and choose Jerusalem.**'"* (NIV)

People from the nations will provide the labor for the task of the rebuilding process.

Isa 60:10-14   *"**Foreigners will rebuild your walls, and their kings will serve you.** Though in anger I struck you, in favor I will show you compassion. Your gates will always stand open, they will never be shut, day or night, so that men may bring you the wealth of the nations—their kings led in triumphal procession. For the nation or kingdom that will not serve you will perish; it will be utterly ruined. "The glory of Lebanon will come to you, the pine, the fir and the cypress together, to adorn the place of my sanctuary; and I will glorify the place of my feet. **The sons of your oppressors will come bowing before you; all who despise you will bow down at your feet and will call you the City of the LORD, Zion of the Holy One of Israel.*** (NIV)

Jesus is so awesome that He gives us the time for the completion of the Temple and the exact day the sanctuary will be properly dedicated. At that time the Shekinah Glory will return to the place where God will dwell among His people.

Dan 8:13-14   *Then I heard a holy one speaking, and another holy one said to that particular one who was speaking, "How long will the vision {about} the regular sacrifice apply, while the transgression causes horror, so as to allow both the holy place and the host to be trampled?" And he said to me, "**For 2,300 evenings {and} mornings; then the holy place will be properly restored.**"* (NAS)

As we discussed earlier in our study, Daniel informs us that the sanctuary or holy place will be cleansed and be made ready for God 2300 days after the Abomination of Desolation. In order to determine the length of days it will take to build the Temple, with the holy place properly restored, we need to do some calculations. To begin with, we must subtract 1260 days (last half of the Tribulation Period) from the 2300 days. After the Tribulation Period was completed, two periods of time—30 days and 45 days—occupied the time of Jesus in other matters than building the Temple. After the seventy-five days are over Jesus will start the coordination process of building the Temple. If we add 1260 days to the 75 days, we get a total of 1335 days. Subtract these 1335 days from 2300 days and we have a total of 965 days for the task at hand. By calculating approximately 30 days for the length of each month, the 965 days equate into two years, eight months and five days to complete the construction and consecrate the new Temple. I told you God is awesome.

Most Bible prophecy teachers, and some Bible scholars, believe that Ezekiel's vision of the Temple in chapters 40 through 43 is a future Temple. The Temple in this vision differs very little from the physical configuration and dimensions of Solomon's Temple. The last nine chapters of Ezekiel (40-48) all pertain to the Temple that Jesus will construct during the Kingdom Age. It is describing the Temple and His throne and the location where Jesus will rule the world for the remainder of the Day of the Lord. Ezekiel, around 572 BC, was actually transported to the future in a vision and was given a chance to see this future Temple. The Temple will be surrounded by a wall.

> Ezek 40:1-5 *In the twenty-fifth year of our exile, at the beginning of the year, on the tenth of the month, in the fourteenth year after the fall of the city—on that very day the hand of the LORD was upon me and he took me there. <u>In visions of God he took me to the land of Israel and set me on a very high mountain, on whose south side were some buildings that looked like a city.</u> He took me there, and I saw a man whose appearance was like bronze; he was standing in the gateway with a linen cord and a measuring rod in his hand. The man said to me, "Son of man, look with your eyes and hear with your ears and pay attention to everything I am going to show you, for that is why you have been brought here. **Tell the house of Israel everything you see."** <u>I saw a wall completely surrounding the temple area.</u> The length of the measuring rod in the man's hand was six long cubits, each of which was a cubit and a handbreadth. He measured the wall; it was one measuring rod thick and one rod high.* (NIV)

The Shekinah Glory will return to this future Temple to the Holy of Holies and set on the Mercy Seat between the Cherubim. God's Presence will return from the east, the same direction He departed in 593 BC. God will once again dwell among His people.

> Ezek 43:1-5 <u>***Then the man brought me to the gate facing east, and I saw the glory of the God of Israel coming from the east.***</u> ***His voice was like the roar of rushing waters, and the land was radiant with his glory. The vision I saw was like the vision I had seen when he came to destroy the city and like the visions I had seen by the Kebar River, and I fell facedown.*** <u>***The glory of the LORD entered the temple through the gate facing east.***</u> ***Then the Spirit lifted me up and***

> *brought me into the inner court, <u>and the glory of the LORD filled the temple</u>.* (NIV)

Ezek 44:4 *Then the man brought me by way of the north gate to the front of the temple. <u>I looked and saw the glory of the LORD filling the temple of the LORD, and I fell facedown</u>.* (NIV)

The entire area on top of the mountain will be most holy.

Ezek 43:12 *"<u>This is the law of the temple</u>: All the surrounding area on top of the mountain will be most holy. Such is the law of the temple.* (NIV)

The prince referred to in these chapters is Jesus. Prince here is a reference to the leader of the world during the remaining portion of the Millennium. Jesus will be the only One who will be allowed to set inside the gate and eat in the presence of the Lord (Shekinah Glory).

Ezek 44:1-3 *Then the man brought me back to the outer gate of the sanctuary, the one facing east, and it was shut. The LORD said to me, "This gate is to remain shut. It must not be opened; no one may enter through it. It is to remain shut because the LORD, the God of Israel, has entered through it. <u>The prince himself is the only one who may sit inside the gateway to eat in the presence of the LORD</u>. He is to enter by way of the portico of the gateway and go out the same way."* (NIV)

When it is time to divide the land of Israel and apportion it to the twelve tribes of Israel, a portion of the land will be allotted as a sacred district. This is where the Temple will be located with the sanctuary and the Most Holy Place within its midst. It will also contain an area to house the priests and the Levites who minister to the Lord. Another section will belong to the whole house of Israel.

Ezek 45:1-6 *"'<u>When you allot the land as an inheritance, you are to present to the LORD a portion of the land as a sacred district</u>, 25,000 cubits long and 20,000 cubits wide; the entire area will be holy. Of this, a section 500 cubits square is to be for the sanctuary, with 50 cubits around it for open land. In the sacred district, measure off a section 25,000 cubits long and 10,000 cubits wide. **In it will be the sanctuary, the Most Holy Place. It will be the sacred portion of the land for the priests, who minister in the sanctuary and who draw near to minister before the LORD. It will be a place for their houses as well as a holy place for the sanctuary.** An area 25,000 cubits long and 10,000 cubits wide will belong to the Levites, who serve in the temple, as their possession for towns to live in. "'You are to give the city as its property an area 5,000 cubits wide and 25,000*

> *cubits long, adjoining the sacred portion;* **<u>it will belong to the whole house of Israel.</u>** *(NIV)*

Jesus will also receive part of this land. I am assuming He will build a royal palace on this land (Jeremiah 30:18), a place where He can meet the visiting dignitaries from around the world. The leaders of the nations (princes) will no longer oppress the Jewish people, but will allow the twelve tribes of Israel to possess the land promised to their ancestors.

Ezek 45:7-8 "'**<u>The prince will have the land bordering each side of the area formed by the sacred district and the property of the city.</u>** *It will extend westward from the west side and eastward from the east side, running lengthwise from the western to the eastern border parallel to one of the tribal portions.* **<u>This land will be his possession in Israel.</u>** *And my princes will no longer oppress my people but will allow the house of Israel to possess the land according to their tribes.* (NIV)

The prince will receive the offerings of the people, which are special gifts for the purpose of providing the burnt offerings, grain offerings and drink offerings for the Holy Days. The proof that the prince is Jesus is the fact that He is the High Priest in the Temple during this time. Only the High Priest has the duty of placing the offering in the Holy of Holies to make atonement for the house of Israel. The Old Testament system of offerings in the Temple will be an offering for the Jewish people who sin unintentionally or through ignorance for the remainder of the Kingdom Age. These sacrificial offerings will, no doubt, point to the Lamb that was slain as a remembrance for the atonement of sin. Remember that no animal sacrifice in the Bible has ever made atonement for sin. The Temple, the worship rites and the sacrifices will be reestablished during the Millennium. Ezekiel is not the only prophet who spoke of a revival of temple ritual in the Kingdom Age. Isaiah, Zechariah, Jeremiah and Zephaniah all make reference to the sacrificial system to be put into place during the Messianic Age. Even with this system reestablished, each individual person will need to make their own decision as to their belief in Jesus as their Savior. It is difficult to understand the true meaning of these future sacrificial offerings. At the proper time Jesus will reveal the significance of these proceedings that apply to the Jewish people.

Ezek 45:13-25 "'*This is the special gift you are to offer: a sixth of an ephah from each homer of wheat and a sixth of an ephah from each homer of barley. The prescribed portion of oil, measured by the bath, is a tenth of a bath from each cor (which consists of ten baths or one homer, for ten baths are equivalent to a homer). Also one sheep is to be taken from every flock of two hundred from the well-watered pastures of Israel. These will be used for the grain offerings, burnt offerings and fellowship offerings to make atonement for the people, declares the Sovereign LORD.* **<u>All the people of the land will participate in this special gift for the use of the prince in Israel.</u>** *It*

The Rest of the Millennium

*will be the duty of the prince to provide the burnt offerings, grain offerings and drink offerings at the festivals, the New Moons and the Sabbaths—at all the appointed feasts of the house of Israel. **He will provide the sin offerings, grain offerings, burnt offerings and fellowship offerings to make atonement for the house of Israel.** "'This is what the Sovereign LORD says: In the first month on the first day you are to take a young bull without defect and purify the sanctuary. The priest is to take some of the blood of the sin offering and put it on the doorposts of the temple, on the four corners of the upper ledge of the altar and on the gateposts of the inner court. **You are to do the same on the seventh day of the month for anyone who sins unintentionally or through ignorance; so you are to make atonement for the temple.** "'In the first month on the fourteenth day you are to observe the Passover, a feast lasting seven days, during which you shall eat bread made without yeast. On that day the prince is to provide a bull as a sin offering for himself and for all the people of the land. Every day during the seven days of the Feast he is to provide seven bulls and seven rams without defect as a burnt offering to the LORD, and a male goat for a sin offering. He is to provide as a grain offering an ephah for each bull and an ephah for each ram, along with a hin of oil for each ephah. "'During the seven days of the Feast, which begins in the seventh month on the fifteenth day, he is to make the same provision for sin offerings, burnt offerings, grain offerings and oil.* (NIV)

Ezek 46:1-24

*"'This is what the Sovereign LORD says: The gate of the inner court facing east is to be shut on the six working days, but on the Sabbath day and on the day of the New Moon it is to be opened. **The prince is to enter from the outside through the portico of the gateway and stand by the gatepost.** The priests are to sacrifice his burnt offering and his fellowship offerings. **He is to worship at the threshold of the gateway and then go out, but the gate will not be shut until evening.** On the Sabbaths and New Moons the people of the land are to worship in the presence of the LORD at the entrance to that gateway. **The burnt offering the prince brings to the LORD on the Sabbath day is to be six male lambs and a ram, all without defect.** The grain offering given with the ram is to be an ephah, and the grain offering with the lambs is to be as much as he pleases, along with a hin of oil for each ephah. **On the day of the New Moon he is to offer a young bull, six lambs and a ram, all without defect.** He is to provide as a grain offering one ephah with the bull, one ephah with the ram, and with the lambs as much as he wants to give, along with a hin of oil with each ephah. When the prince enters, he is to go in through the portico of the gateway, and he is to come out*

571

the same way. '"When the people of the land come before the LORD at the appointed feasts, whoever enters by the north gate to worship is to go out the south gate; and whoever enters by the south gate is to go out the north gate. No one is to return through the gate by which he entered, but each is to go out the opposite gate. **The prince is to be among them, going in when they go in and going out when they go out.** *"'At the festivals and the appointed feasts, the grain offering is to be an ephah with a bull, an ephah with a ram, and with the lambs as much as one pleases, along with a hin of oil for each ephah.* **When the prince provides a freewill offering to the LORD—whether a burnt offering or fellowship offerings—the gate facing east is to be opened for him. He shall offer his burnt offering or his fellowship offerings as he does on the Sabbath day.** *Then he shall go out, and after he has gone out, the gate will be shut. "'Every day you are to provide a year-old lamb without defect for a burnt offering to the LORD; morning by morning you shall provide it. You are also to provide with it morning by morning a grain offering, consisting of a sixth of an ephah with a third of a hin of oil to moisten the flour. The presenting of this grain offering to the LORD is a lasting ordinance. So the lamb and the grain offering and the oil shall be provided morning by morning for a regular burnt offering. "'This is what the Sovereign LORD says: If the prince makes a gift from his inheritance to one of his sons, it will also belong to his descendants; it is to be their property by inheritance. If, however, he makes a gift from his inheritance to one of his servants, the servant may keep it until the year of freedom; then it will revert to the prince. His inheritance belongs to his sons only; it is theirs.* **The prince must not take any of the inheritance of the people, driving them off their property. He is to give his sons their inheritance out of his own property, so that none of my people will be separated from his property.'"** *Then the man brought me through the entrance at the side of the gate to the sacred rooms facing north, which belonged to the priests, and showed me a place at the western end. He said to me, "This is the place where the priests will cook the guilt offering and the sin offering and bake the grain offering, to avoid bringing them into the outer court and consecrating the people." He then brought me to the outer court and led me around to its four corners, and I saw in each corner another court. In the four corners of the outer court were enclosed courts, forty cubits long and thirty cubits wide; each of the courts in the four corners was the same size. Around the inside of each of the four courts was a ledge of stone, with places for fire built all around under the ledge. He said to me, "These are the kitchens where those who minister at the temple will cook the sacrifices of the people."* (NIV)

The Rest of the Millennium

Isa 60:4-7 *"Lift up your eyes and look about you: <u>All assemble and come to you; your sons come from afar, and your daughters are carried on the arm.</u> Then you will look and be radiant, your heart will throb and swell with joy; <u>the wealth on the seas will be brought to you, to you the riches of the nations will come.</u> Herds of camels will cover your land, young camels of Midian and Ephah. And all from Sheba will come, bearing gold and incense and proclaiming the praise of the LORD. <u>All Kedar's flocks will be gathered to you, the rams of Nebaioth will serve you; they will be accepted as offerings on my altar, and I will adorn my glorious temple.</u>* (NIV)

The exit gates of the city will be named after the twelve tribes of Israel. The names found here are the names of the original twelve sons of Jacob (Israel).

Ezek 48:30-34 *"These will be the exits of the city: Beginning on the north side, which is 4,500 cubits long, <u>the gates of the city will be named after the tribes of Israel.</u> The three gates on the north side will be the gate of Reuben, the gate of Judah and the gate of Levi. "On the east side, which is 4,500 cubits long, will be three gates: the gate of Joseph, the gate of Benjamin and the gate of Dan. "On the south side, which measures 4,500 cubits, will be three gates: the gate of Simeon, the gate of Issachar and the gate of Zebulun. "On the west side, which is 4,500 cubits long, will be three gates: the gate of Gad, the gate of Asher and the gate of Naphtali.* (NIV)

Please read chapters 40-48 of Ezekiel in their entirety to get a more comprehensive picture of the Millennial Temple. This future Temple will be majestic as the Presence of the Lord, the Shekinah Glory, shines forth.

REESTABLISH THE FEASTS

A religious order will be set up and most of the Old Testament feasts and festivals will be reestablished for the Jewish people. Sacrifices will again be brought into the Temple, but they will be limited to thanksgiving offerings because they have never been expiatory offerings. The weekly Sabbath, along with monthly and yearly religious festivals (holidays), will be observed. There will not be any sadness associated with these festivals like the solemn occasions they are among the Jewish people today. They will be joyous occasions. Please note that all mankind will come and bow down before the LORD.

Zech 8:18-19 *Again the word of the LORD Almighty came to me. This is what the LORD Almighty says: "<u>The fasts of the fourth, fifth, seventh and tenth months will become joyful and glad occasions and happy festivals for Judah.</u> Therefore love truth and peace."* (NIV)

AFTER THE RAPTURE

Isa 66:23 — *From one New Moon to another and from one Sabbath to another, <u>all mankind will come and bow down before me</u>," says the LORD.* (NIV)

Zeph 3:18-20 — *"<u>The sorrows for the appointed feasts I will remove from you;</u> they are a burden and a reproach to you. At that time I will deal with all who oppressed you; I will rescue the lame and gather those who have been scattered. I will give them praise and honor in every land where they were put to shame. At that time I will gather you; at that time I will bring you home. I will give you honor and praise among all the peoples of the earth when I restore your fortunes before your very eyes," says the LORD.* (NIV)

Ezek 20:39-42 — *"'As for you, O house of Israel, this is what the Sovereign LORD says: Go and serve your idols, every one of you! But afterward you will surely listen to me and no longer profane my holy name with your gifts and idols. For on my holy mountain, the high mountain of Israel, declares the Sovereign LORD, there in the land the entire <u>house of Israel will serve me, and there I will accept them.</u> <u>There I will require your offerings and your choice gifts, along with all your holy sacrifices.</u> I will accept you as fragrant incense when I bring you out from the nations and gather you from the countries where you have been scattered, and I will show myself holy among you in the sight of the nations. Then you will know that I am the LORD, when I bring you into the land of Israel, the land I had sworn with uplifted hand to give to your fathers.* (NIV)

The Levites and the priesthood will be established with the priests serving in the sanctuary and the Levites serving in the Temple. They will be furnished with land to build houses to live in near the Temple. The most sacred portion of the land allotted to the priests will be reserved for the sanctuary (the Most Holy Place).

Ezek 45:1-5 — *"'When you allot the land as an inheritance, you are to present to the LORD a portion of the land as a sacred district, 25,000 cubits long and 20,000 cubits wide; the entire area will be holy. Of this, a section 500 cubits square is to be for the sanctuary, with 50 cubits around it for open land. In the sacred district, measure off a section 25,000 cubits long and 10,000 cubits wide. <u>In it will be the sanctuary, the Most Holy Place.</u> It will be the sacred portion of the land for the priests, who minister in the sanctuary and who draw near to minister before the LORD. It will be a place for their houses as well as a holy place for the sanctuary. An area 25,000 cubits long and 10,000 cubits wide will belong to the Levites, who serve in the temple, as their possession for towns to live in.* (NIV)

The Rest of the Millennium

Ezek 44:24   *"'In any dispute, the priests are to serve as judges and decide it according to my ordinances. <u>They are to keep my laws and my decrees for all my appointed feasts, and they are to keep my Sabbaths holy.</u>* (NIV)

Jer 33:17-22   *For this is what the LORD says:'David will never fail to have a man to sit on the throne of the house of Israel, <u>nor will the priests, who are Levites, ever fail to have a man to stand before me continually to offer burnt offerings, to burn grain offerings and to present sacrifices.</u>'" The word of the LORD came to Jeremiah: "This is what the LORD says: 'If you can break my covenant with the day and my covenant with the night, so that day and night no longer come at their appointed time, then my covenant with David my servant—and my covenant with the Levites who are priests ministering before me—can be broken and David will no longer have a descendant to reign on his throne. I will make the descendants of David my servant and the Levites who minister before me as countless as the stars of the sky and as measureless as the sand on the seashore.'"* (NIV)

Zion, in Jerusalem, is where the festivals will take place.

Isa 33:20-22   *<u>Look upon Zion, the city of our festivals; your eyes will see Jerusalem, a peaceful abode, a tent that will not be moved; its stakes will never be pulled up, nor any of its ropes broken.</u> There the LORD will be our Mighty One. It will be like a place of broad rivers and streams. No galley with oars will ride them, no mighty ship will sail them. For the LORD is our judge, the LORD is our lawgiver, the LORD is our king; it is he who will save us.* (NIV)

It appears that some non-Jews will be selected as priests to be sent among the nations of the world to proclaim God's glory to all the nations. They will bring people from around the globe to Jerusalem, God's holy mountain. This includes the saints from the Tribulation Period. It also appears that sacrificial offerings will be offered by non-Jews. The Temple will be a house of prayer for all nations.

Isa 66:18-21   *"And I, because of their actions and their imaginations, am about to come and gather all nations and tongues, and they will come and see my glory. "<u>I will set a sign among them, and I will send some of those who survive to the nations</u>—to Tarshish, to the Libyans and Lydians (famous as archers), to Tubal and Greece, and to the distant islands that have not heard of my fame or seen my glory. They will proclaim my glory among the nations. And they will bring all your brothers, from all the nations, to my holy mountain in Jerusalem as* *an offering to the LORD—on horses, in chariots and wagons, and on mules and camels," says the LORD.* **"They will bring them, as the Israelites bring their grain offerings, to the temple of the LORD in ceremonially clean vessels. <u>And I will select some of them also to be priests and Levites</u>," says the LORD.** (NIV)

Isa 56:3-8   *Let no foreigner who has bound himself to the LORD say, "<u>The LORD will surely exclude me from his people</u>." And let not any eunuch complain, "I am only a dry tree." For this is what the LORD says: "To the eunuchs who keep my Sabbaths, who choose what pleases me and hold fast to my covenant—to them I will give within my temple and its walls a memorial and a name better than sons and daughters; I will give them an everlasting name that will not be cut off. <u>And foreigners who bind themselves to the LORD to serve him, to love the name of the LORD, and to worship him, all who keep the Sabbath without desecrating it and who hold fast to my covenant—these I will bring to my holy mountain and give them joy in my house of prayer. Their burnt offerings and sacrifices will be accepted on my altar; for my house will be called a house of prayer for all nations.</u>" The Sovereign LORD declares—he who gathers the exiles of Israel: "<u>I will gather still others to them besides those already gathered.</u>"* (NIV)

Rev 20:4-6   *I saw thrones on which were seated those who had been given authority to judge. And I saw the souls of those who had been beheaded because of their testimony for Jesus and because of the word of God. They had not worshiped the beast or his image and had not received his mark on their foreheads or their hands. <u>They came to life and reigned with Christ a thousand years</u>. (The rest of the dead did not come to life until the thousand years were ended.) This is the first resurrection. Blessed and holy are those who have part in the first resurrection. The second death has no power over them, <u>but they will be priests of God and of Christ and will reign with him for a thousand years</u>.* (NIV)

THE NATIONS

We have all heard the expression, "Life goes on!" Well that is exactly what will happen in the Millennium or Kingdom Age. The people from the nations who were separated and sent to the right hand of Jesus at the Harvest of the Earth will make up the nations during this time. To begin with, they will all be living in fleshly bodies and every one of them will have accepted Jesus as their personal savior. Each person could possibly be separated into the nation or nationality they were born into and will be returned to the land Jesus apportions to them, possibly the land they occupied in the previous ages. They will be allowed to reproduce, thus creating unsaved offspring. Those offspring will have the free-will choice to sin, implying we are not yet living in the perfect age of eternity quite yet. The acts of sin will be greatly reduced during this time period because the influence of Satan and his fallen angels will be removed at this time. No one will be able to say, "the devil made me do it."

The nations will establish cities and towns. They will produce food through agricultural systems. Governments will be established with proper leaders. There will be presidents, mayors, judges, town councils and city services to serve the people. People will have jobs to attend to, nevertheless, most of the burden of them will be removed. People will enjoy working. All of the nations will answer to the Theocracy in Jerusalem, to our leader Jesus. The system of this one-world government will be fair and equitable. No more government corruption and no more tainted Judges. Nations will be small at first, but will grow in size as time moves along. Since it will be a time of peace, with no lives lost to war and no money being spent for national security, the rebuilding process should move right along.

A big change in the scheme of things during this period will be the presence of people on earth in their resurrected bodies. Angels will also play a part, but it does not say whether they will still be invisible or not (probably invisible). The survivors from all the nations at the Battle of Armageddon will worship the King in Jerusalem.

Zech 14:16-19 *Then the survivors from all the nations that have attacked Jerusalem will go up year after year to worship the King, the LORD Almighty, and to celebrate the Feast of Tabernacles. If any of the peoples of the earth do not go up to Jerusalem to worship the King, the LORD Almighty, they will have no rain. If the Egyptian people do not go up and take part, they will have no rain. The LORD will bring on them the plague he inflicts on the nations that do not go up to celebrate the Feast of Tabernacles. This will be the punishment of Egypt and the punishment of all the nations that do not go up to celebrate the Feast of Tabernacles.* (NIV)

As you can see from reading these verses each nation will decide for themselves whether or not they want to make the annual pilgrimage to Jerusalem to worship Jesus and to celebrate the Feast of Tabernacles. Punishment of the nations who refuse this obligation will be the denial of rain. Egypt appears to be one nation who might fail in this aspect, at least in a particular year. More than likely most of the nations will obey this obligation. There is a lot said in the Old Testament concerning the nations during the Millennium. Scripture seems to tell the story in the best perspective.

Zech 8:20-23 *"Thus says the LORD of hosts: 'Peoples shall yet come, inhabitants of many cities; The inhabitants of one city shall go to another, saying, "Let us continue to go and pray before the LORD, and seek the LORD of hosts. I myself will go also." Yes, many peoples and strong nations shall come to seek the LORD of hosts in Jerusalem, and to pray before the LORD.' "Thus says the LORD of hosts: 'In those days ten men from every language of the* nations shall grasp the sleeve of a Jewish man, saying, "Let us go with you, for we have heard that God is with you."'" (NKJ)

Zeph 2:11 *The LORD will be awesome to them when he destroys all the Gods of the land. <u>The nations on every shore will worship him, every one in its own land.</u>* (NIV)

Ps 22:25-31 *From you comes the theme of my praise in the great assembly; before those who fear you will I fulfill my vows. The poor will eat and be satisfied; they who seek the LORD will praise him—may your hearts live forever! <u>All the ends of the earth will remember and turn to the LORD, and all the families of the nations will bow down before him, for dominion belongs to the LORD and he rules over the nations.</u> All the rich of the earth will feast and worship; all who go down to the dust will kneel before him—those who cannot keep themselves alive. Posterity will serve him; future generations will be told about the Lord. They will proclaim his righteousness to a people yet unborn—for he has done it.* (NIV)

Micah 4:1-4 *In the last days the mountain of the LORD's temple will be established as chief among the mountains; it will be raised above the hills, and peoples will stream to it. <u>Many nations will come and say, "Come, let us go up to the mountain of the LORD, to the house of the God of Jacob.</u> He will teach us his ways, so that we may walk in his paths." The law will go out from Zion, the word of the LORD from Jerusalem. He will judge between many peoples and will settle disputes for strong nations far and wide. They will beat their swords into plowshares and their spears into pruning hooks. Nation will not take up sword against nation, nor will they train for war anymore. Every man will sit under his own vine and under his own fig tree, and no one will make them afraid, for the LORD Almighty has spoken.* (NIV)

Ps 67:1-7 *May God be gracious to us and bless us and make his face shine upon us, Selah that your ways may be known on earth, your salvation among all nations. <u>May the peoples praise you, O God; may all the peoples praise you. May the nations be glad and sing for joy, for you rule the peoples justly and guide the nations of the earth.</u> Selah May the peoples praise you, O God; may all the peoples praise you. Then the land will yield its harvest, and God, our God, will bless us. <u>God will bless us, and all the ends of the earth will fear him.</u>* (NIV)

Mal 3:12 *"Then <u>all the nations</u> will call you blessed, for yours will be a delightful land," says the LORD Almighty.* (NIV)

The Rest of the Millennium

Ps 86:9-12 *<u>All the nations you have made will come and worship before you, O Lord; they will bring glory to your name.</u> For you are great and do marvelous deeds; you alone are God. Teach me your way, O LORD, and I will walk in your truth; give me an undivided heart, that I may fear your name. I will praise you, O Lord my God, with all my heart; I will glorify your name forever.* (NIV)

Isa 49:26 *...Then <u>all mankind</u> will know that I, the LORD, am your Savior, your Redeemer, the Mighty One of Jacob."* (NIV)

Jesus will proclaim peace to the nations. No more war!!!

Zech 9:10b *...<u>He will proclaim peace to the nations.</u> His rule will extend from sea to sea and from the River to the ends of the earth.* (NIV)

Ps 46:8-11 *Come and see the works of the LORD, the desolations he has brought on the earth. <u>He makes wars cease to the ends of the earth; he breaks the bow and shatters the spear, he burns the shields with fire.</u> "Be still, and know that I am God; I will be exalted among the nations, I will be exalted in the earth." The LORD Almighty is with us; the God of Jacob is our fortress. Selah* (NIV)

To insure peace to the nations Jesus will be a judge between them and settle any major differences or disagreements that might develop between them.

Isa 2:2-4 *In the last days the mountain of the LORD's temple will be established as chief among the mountains; it will be raised above the hills, and all nations will stream to it. Many peoples will come and say, "Come, let us go up to the mountain of the LORD, to the house of the God of Jacob. He will teach us his ways, so that we may walk in his paths." <u>The law will go out from Zion, the word of the LORD from Jerusalem. He will judge between the nations and will settle disputes for many peoples.</u> They will beat their swords into plowshares and their spears into pruning hooks. <u>Nation will not take up sword against nation, nor will they train for war anymore.</u>* (NIV)

Isa 51:4-6 *"Listen to me, my people; hear me, my nation: <u>The law will go out from me; my justice will become a light to the nations.</u> My righteousness draws near speedily, my salvation is on the way, <u>and my arm will bring justice to the nations.</u> The islands will look to me and wait in hope for my arm. Lift up your eyes to the heavens, look at the earth beneath; the heavens will vanish like smoke, the earth will wear out like a garment and its inhabitants die like flies. <u>But my*

AFTER THE RAPTURE

<u>salvation will last forever, my righteousness will never fail.</u> (NIV)

The kings (leaders) of the nations will lead triumphal processions through the streets of Jerusalem as they bring gifts to the King.

Isa 60:10-11   *"Foreigners will rebuild your walls, and their kings will serve you. Though in anger I struck you, in favor I will show you compassion. <u>Your gates will always stand open, they will never be shut, day or night, so that men may bring you the wealth of the nations—their kings led in triumphal procession.</u>* (NIV)

Ps 68:28-35   *Summon your power, O God; show us your strength, O God, as you have done before. <u>Because of your temple at Jerusalem kings will bring you gifts.</u> Rebuke the beast among the reeds, the herd of bulls among the calves of the nations. Humbled, may it bring bars of silver. Scatter the nations who delight in war. Envoys will come from Egypt; Cush will submit herself to God. <u>Sing to God, O kingdoms of the earth, sing praise to the Lord</u>, Selah to him who rides the ancient skies above, who thunders with mighty voice. Proclaim the power of God, whose majesty is over Israel, whose power is in the skies. You are awesome, O God, in your sanctuary; the God of Israel gives power and strength to his people. Praise be to God!* (NIV)

Any nation who does not serve Jesus during this time will eventually perish.

Isa 60:12   *For the nation or kingdom <u>that will not serve you</u> will perish; it will be utterly ruined.* (NIV)

Remember that after the land of Egypt is totally destroyed it will lie desolate forty years. Because of their arrogance and rejection of God, He allowed their land to be destroyed by the Antichrist during the last half of the Tribulation Period. However, even after forty years Egypt will only be restored to a position of a lowly kingdom.

Ezek 29:12-15   *<u>I will make the land of Egypt desolate among devastated lands, and her cities will lie desolate forty years among ruined cities.</u> And I will disperse the Egyptians among the nations and scatter them through the countries. "'Yet this is what the Sovereign LORD says: **At the end of forty years I will gather the Egyptians from the nations where they were scattered. I will bring them back from captivity and return them to Upper Egypt, the land of their ancestry. There they will be a lowly kingdom. It will be the lowliest of kingdoms and will never again exalt itself above the other nations. I will make it so weak that it will never again rule over the nations.*** (NIV)

The Rest of the Millennium

Egypt is also mentioned as having an altar in their midst and a monument to the Lord at their border during the peaceful portion of the Millennium. When the sufferings of the Antichrist become unbearable during the Tribulation Period, the Egyptians will cry out to God and He will send Jesus to them as a Savior to rescue them. The Egyptians will finally recognize the one true God. They will even worship with sacrifices and offerings in a location other than Jerusalem.

Isa 19:19-25 *<u>In that day there will be an altar to the LORD in the heart of Egypt, and a monument to the LORD at its border.</u> It will be a sign and witness to the LORD Almighty in the land of Egypt. <u>When they cry out to the LORD because of their oppressors, he will send them a savior and defender, and he will rescue them.</u> So the LORD will make himself known to the Egyptians, and in that day they will acknowledge the LORD. <u>They will worship with sacrifices and grain offerings; they will make vows to the LORD and keep them.</u> The LORD will strike Egypt with a plague; he will strike them and heal them. They will turn to the LORD, and he will respond to their pleas and heal them. In that day there will be a highway from Egypt to Assyria. The Assyrians will go to Egypt and the Egyptians to Assyria. The Egyptians and Assyrians will worship together. In that day Israel will be the third, along with Egypt and Assyria, a blessing on the earth. The LORD Almighty will bless them, saying, "Blessed be Egypt my people, Assyria my handiwork, and Israel my inheritance."* (NIV)

The fulfillment of Daniel now proceeds forward. As Jesus becomes the King to all the nations of the world they will be blessed through Him.

Dan 7:14 *<u>He was given authority, glory and sovereign power; all peoples, nations and men of every language worshiped him.</u> His dominion is an everlasting dominion that will not pass away, and his kingdom is one that will never be destroyed.* (NIV)

Ps 72:17-19 *May his name endure forever; may it continue as long as the sun. <u>All nations will be blessed through him, and they will call him blessed.</u> Praise be to the LORD God, the God of Israel, who alone does marvelous deeds. Praise be to his glorious name forever; may the whole earth be filled with his glory. Amen and Amen.* (NIV)

Ps 133:1-3 *<u>How good and pleasant it is when brothers live together in unity!</u> It is like precious oil poured on the head, running down on the beard, running down on Aaron's beard, down upon the collar of his robes. It is as if the dew of Hermon were falling on Mount Zion. **For there the LORD bestows his blessing, even life forevermore.*** (NIV)

AFTER THE RAPTURE

A point of contention among Bible scholars today has been an argument concerning the severity of rule during the Millennium. Some contend that Jesus will rule with a strong hand or with a rod of iron. Other people believe that Jesus will rule with love and compassion, with a shepherd like rule as the Lamb of God for this thousand-year period.

Actually, both opinions are correct. Jesus will begin the Kingdom Age ruling the nations with an iron scepter when He purges sinful mankind from the earth during the time of His fierce anger. The only time this phrase is mentioned is in the context of Jesus coming to destroy the nations at the Battle of Armageddon.

Ps 2:9 *You will rule them with an iron scepter; you will dash them to pieces like pottery."* (NIV)

Ezek 20:37-38 *I will take note of you as you pass under my rod, and I will bring you into the bond of the covenant. I will purge you of those who revolt and rebel against me. Although I will bring them out of the land where they are living, yet they will not enter the land of Israel. Then you will know that I am the LORD.* (NIV)

Rev 19:15 *Out of his mouth comes a sharp sword with which to strike down the nations. "He will rule them with an iron scepter." He treads the winepress of the fury of the wrath of God Almighty.* (NIV)

During the peaceful portion of the Millennium (990 years) Jesus will rule with a firm hand in love and compassion and not with the forcefulness of an iron hand. At this time no one living on the earth will make the people afraid, including Jesus whose name is the God of Jacob and the Lord of hosts (the Lord Almighty – NIV).

Micah 4:1-4 *In the last days the mountain of the LORD's temple will be established as chief among the mountains; it will be raised above the hills, and peoples will stream to it. Many nations will come and say, "Come, let us go up to the mountain of the LORD, to the house of the God of Jacob. He will teach us his ways, so that we may walk in his paths." The law will go out from Zion, the word of the LORD from Jerusalem. He will judge between many peoples and will settle disputes for strong nations far and wide. They will beat their swords into plowshares and their spears into pruning hooks. Nation will not take up sword against nation, nor will they train for war anymore. Every man will sit under his own vine and under his own fig tree, and no one will make them afraid, for the LORD Almighty has spoken.* (NIV)

A clear understanding of the Day of the Lord, consisting of Jesus beginning His rule in heaven to purge unfaithful mankind, should clear up this contention among Bible scholars.

CHAPTER FOURTEEN

LEARNING FROM HISTORY

LEARNING FROM OLD TESTAMENT HISTORY

God teaches us from a variety of ways and past history is one of them, yet past history is not given the significance that it needs to be given when studying Bible Prophecy. For those of you who know little about the Old Testament, let me supply you with some background that is necessary in understanding the total plan of God. As we follow the activities of God and the role of each person of the Trinity in the past and at the present time, it allows us better to understand future history. The subject is far to complex to cover in a short space so I will do the best I can in the shortest presentation possible. It is a fascinating story and helps us with what is in store for the saints at the Rapture and beyond. Of course, everyone should know that the three persons of the Trinity existed in heaven at the time of creation. However, few people, including Christians, know the full extent of the active role that God the Father, Jesus the Son and the Holy Spirit play on earth throughout past and future history. In the Old Testament God, Jesus in His pre-incarnate state and the Holy Spirit took an active role in the affairs of mankind on earth and especially with the chosen people.

Before we begin I need to inform you of the consensus of most Theologians today. It is that God is invisible. Jewish tradition believes essentially this same concept. Both Christian Theologians and Orthodox Jews believe that God has no physical form whatsoever, therefore, there is no way to physically perceive God. Traditional Judaism teaches that it is possible to feel God by performing ritual acts and praying. In that sense, they can feel close to God without actually seeing God.

It is taught today and I believe that God has three exclusive attributes. God is:

1. **Omniscient** – having complete or infinite knowledge to the point of perceiving all things. The Divine attribute of perfect knowledge.
   Ps 139:1-6 *O LORD, you have searched me and you know me. You know when I sit and when I rise; you perceive my thoughts from afar. You discern my going out and my lying down; you are familiar with all my ways. Before a word is on my tongue you know it completely, O LORD. You hem me in—behind and before; you have laid your hand upon me. Such knowledge is too wonderful for me, too lofty for me to attain.* (NIV)

2. **Omnipotent** – infinite in power and having unlimited authority. The Divine attribute of the all-encompassing power of God.
   Ps 147:1-5 *Praise the LORD. How good it is to sing praises to our God, how pleasant and fitting to praise him! The LORD builds up Jerusalem; he gathers the exiles of Israel. He heals the brokenhearted and binds up their wounds. He determines the number of the stars and calls them each by name. Great is our Lord and mighty in power; his understanding has no limit.* (NIV)
   Jer 32:17 *"Ah, Sovereign LORD, you have made the heavens and the earth by*

your great power and outstretched arm. Nothing is too hard for you. (NIV)

3. **Omnipresent** – being everywhere at the same time. The Divine attribute that God is free from the laws of limitation of space.

Ps 139:7-16   *Where can I go from your Spirit? Where can I flee from your presence? If I go up to the heavens, you are there; if I make my bed in the depths, you are there. If I rise on the wings of the dawn, if I settle on the far side of the sea, even there your hand will guide me, your right hand will hold me fast. If I say, "Surely the darkness will hide me and the light become night around me," even the darkness will not be dark to you; the night will shine like the day, for darkness is as light to you. For you created my inmost being; you knit me together in my mother's womb. I praise you because I am fearfully and wonderfully made; your works are wonderful, I know that full well. My frame was not hidden from you when I was made in the secret place. When I was woven together in the depths of the earth, your eyes saw my unformed body. All the days ordained for me were written in your book before one of them came to be.* (NIV)

God's omnipresence is closely related to His omnipotence and omniscience. Because God is everywhere, it enables Him to act everywhere and to know all things and thus through omnipotent action and omniscient knowledge God has access to all places and He knows everything. That also includes everything in the future. God's foreknowledge allows Him to know everything before it happens even without predetermining events, although a few events are predetermined, such as Jesus coming in the flesh. God knows history from the end to the beginning. That is why prophecy from God is one hundred percent correct.

Acts 2:22-23   **"Men of Israel, listen to this: Jesus of Nazareth was a man accredited by God to you by miracles, wonders and signs, which God did among you through him, as you yourselves know. This man was handed over to you by God's set purpose and foreknowledge; and you, with the help of wicked men, put him to death by nailing him to the cross.** (NIV)

Do these attributes of God make Him invisible? Is God strictly spirit without some sort of material being? Does God have some sort of physical form and can He be confined to a single location? Scripture has a lot to say about God's attributes and it also has a lot to say about some sort of form that He might have. After you see what scripture has to say about it, you can make up your own mind as to whether you think that God is invisible or not.

In the very beginning we pick up the story as we see God creating man on the sixth day of creation. The Hebrew word used here for "God" is *'elohiym* (el-o-heem') and is the plural word used of the Supreme God.

Gen 1:26   ***And God said, Let us make man in our image, after our likeness: and let them have dominion over the fish of the sea, and over the fowl of the air, and over the cattle, and over all the earth, and over*** *ever creeping thing that creepeth upon the earth.* (KJV)

The plurality of this statement suggests that man was created in the image or likeness of more than one person of the Trinity, in this case, God the Father and Jesus the Son. This does not include the Holy Spirit, because the Holy Spirit is invisible and cannot be seen. In the next verse it is obvious that man was created in God's image.

Gen 1:27 *So God created man in his own image, in the image of God created he him; male and female created he them.* (KJV)

Gen 5:1-2 *This is the book of the generations of Adam. In the day that God created man, in the likeness of God made he him; Male and female created he them; and blessed them, and called their name Adam, in the day when they were created.* (KJV)

James 3:9 *With the tongue we praise our Lord and Father, and with it we curse men, who have been made in God's likeness.* (NIV)

Keep in mind that God does not have a human form, but man has a Godly form or likeness. God does not have a body made up of human flesh. God and man have different bodies, but the same likeness or image. God has a spiritual body, while man has a natural body which consists of flesh and blood.

One of the most difficult tasks of studying the Old Testament is trying to distinguish between the first two persons of the Trinity—God or Jesus in His pre-incarnate state. The names for both God and Jesus are used interchangeably at times. Some of the different names of God can at times apply to either God or Jesus as you will see as we continue. The true task is to figure out the difference between the two. Not all Bible scholars agree with each other and the Orthodox Jews do not even believe in the concept of the Trinity. Without the addition of the New Testament it would be very difficult to distinguish between the two. The New Testament helps us distinguish between God and Jesus in the Old Testament.

Since we are focusing this part of our study on God as He interacts with man on earth, we will begin with the person of the Trinity who appears more often on earth with man. God walked in the garden and interacted with Adam and Eve before they sinned. Most of the interaction between God and man on earth in the Old Testament was probably from Jesus. The proper name Jesus is never used in the Old Testament. There are many words, terms or phrases that apply to Jesus. Because the second person of the Trinity is Jesus, I will use this name in our study as it conforms with the New Testament. The Holy Spirit plays an active part on earth and finally a little later we will see that God Himself also plays a role on earth. I will only show you a limited number of times when Jesus and the Holy Spirit visit the earth. Grab your Bible and start reading the Old Testament to see how active the Trinity was back then. When Jesus was on earth conversing with people from the Old Testament, He had the likeness of a man. On one occasion, Jesus and two angels (that also appeared to be men) visited Abraham. Jesus came to tell Abraham and Sarah that they were to have a son.

AFTER THE RAPTURE

Gen 18:1-2   ***The LORD appeared to Abraham** near the great trees of Mamre while he was sitting at the entrance to his tent in the heat of the day. **Abraham looked up and saw three men standing nearby**. When he saw them, he hurried from the entrance of his tent to meet them and bowed low to the ground.* (NIV)

Jesus also appeared to Joshua as a man (as commander of the army [host] of the Lord).

Josh 5:13-6:2   *Now when Joshua was near Jericho, **he looked up and saw a man standing in front of him with a drawn sword in his hand**. Joshua went up to him and asked, "**Are you for us or for our enemies?**" "**Neither**," he replied, "**but as commander of the army of the LORD I have now come**." Then Joshua fell facedown to the ground in reverence, and asked him, "What message does my Lord have for his servant?" The commander of the LORD's army replied, "**Take off your sandals, for the place where you are standing is holy**." And Joshua did so. Now Jericho was tightly shut up because of the Israelites. No one went out and no one came in. Then the LORD said to Joshua, "See, I have delivered Jericho into your hands, along with its king and its fighting men.* (NIV)

ANGEL OF THE LORD

The most interesting and informing phrase concerning Jesus in the Old Testament can be found in the title "Angel of the Lord (*Yahweh*)." At times the reference reads "Angel of God (*'elohiym*)." It appears that in either case it is a reference to Jesus. Try to think of the phrase "angel of the Lord" as "messenger of the Lord." A closer look at the Hebrew definition for the word that is translated as "angel" can clear up the mystery. The Hebrew word *mal'ak* is used in the singular to denote a Divine messenger.

Strong's Definition
4397 mal'ak (mal-awk');
from an unused root meaning to despatch as a deputy; a messenger; specifically, of God, i.e. an angel (also a prophet, priest or teacher):
KJV— ambassador, angel, king, messenger.

Brown-Driver-Brigg's Definition
4397 mal'ak-
a messenger, a representative
   a) a messenger
   b) an angel
   c) the theophanic angel

Collectively, angelic beings are referred to as "heavenly hosts" (Psalms 148:2) and even

Learning From History

as *"sons of God"* (Job 1:6; 2:1; 38:7 KJV). We want to look at the Hebrew word *mal'ak* from the perspective of a messenger or a representative. *Mal'ak* can be any messenger or representative of God, including angelic beings or even Jesus as a Divine Messenger of God as He carries out the duties delegated to Him from the Father. Jesus is a messenger of God throughout the Bible. The first time the phrase "the angel of the Lord" appears in scripture is when Jesus appears to Hagar in the desert after she fled from Sarah's mistreatment. Take note here that she visually saw God (Jesus) and remained alive after seeing Him.

Gen 16:6-16   *"Your servant is in your hands," Abram said. "Do with her whatever you think best." Then Sarai mistreated Hagar; so she fled from her. <u>The angel of the LORD found Hagar near a spring in the desert</u>; it was the spring that is beside the road to Shur. And he said, "Hagar, servant of Sarai, where have you come from, and where are you going?" "I'm running away from my mistress Sarai," she answered. Then the angel of the LORD told her, "Go back to your mistress and submit to her." The angel added, "I will so increase your descendants that they will be too numerous to count." The angel of the LORD also said to her: "You are now with child and you will have a son. You shall name him Ishmael, for the LORD has heard of your misery. He will be a wild donkey of a man; his hand will be against everyone and everyone's hand against him, and he will live in hostility toward all his brothers." She gave this name to the LORD who spoke to her: "<u>You are the God who sees me</u>," for she said, "<u>I have now seen the One who sees me</u>." That is why the well was called Beer Lahai Roi; it is still there, between Kadesh and Bered. So Hagar bore Abram a son, and Abram gave the name Ishmael to the son she had borne. Abram was eighty-six years old when Hagar bore him Ishmael.* (NIV)

In this account Hagar knew she was dealing with God. Some of the more important times that Jesus as this Divine messenger of God appeared on earth to men and women are when:

1. Abraham intercedes with the angel for Sodom – Genesis 18:16-33.
2. The angel called out from heaven to prevent Abraham from sacrificing Isaac – Genesis 22.
3. The angel appeared to Jacob in a dream – Genesis 31:1-16.
4. Jacob wrestles with the angel - (*"For I have seen God face to face, and yet my life is preserved."*) – Genesis 32:22-32.
5. The angel spoke to the people of Israel – Judges 2:1-5.
6. The angel appeared to Gideon and spoke to him (Gideon saw the Lord face-to-face) – Judges 6:11-24.
7. The angel appeared to Elijah as he fled from Jezebel (notice verse 12, the still small voice (KJV). Also notice Elijah fled to Mount Horeb (Sinai) – 1 Kings 19:1-18.

AFTER THE RAPTURE

8. The angel slew 185,000 Assyrians to save the city of Jerusalem in 701 BC – Isaiah 37:33-38.
9. The angel appeared to Zechariah:
    a. talking with Zechariah – Zechariah 1:8-17; 4:1-5; 5:5; 6:4-5.
    b. with another angel – Zechariah 2:1-5.
    c. rebuking Satan – Zechariah 3:1-10.

Toward the end of his life Jacob, then known as Israel, spoke of God and the angel as being identical. Notice that God, in this case Jesus as a messenger (Angel) of God, watched over them and was in their presence.

Gen 48:15-16   *Then he blessed Joseph and said, "May the God before whom my fathers Abraham and Isaac walked, <u>the God who has been my shepherd</u> all my life to this day, <u>the Angel who has delivered me from all harm</u> may he bless these boys. May they be called by my name and the names of my fathers Abraham and Isaac, and may they increase greatly upon the earth." (NIV)*

The angel of the Lord appeared to the wife of Manoah who was the mother of Samson. The story goes like this:

Judg 13:2-25   *A certain man of Zorah, named Manoah, from the clan of the Danites, had a wife who was sterile and remained childless. <u>The angel of the LORD</u> appeared to her and said, "You are sterile and childless, but you are going to conceive and have a son. Now see to it that you drink no wine or other fermented drink and that you do not eat anything unclean, because you will conceive and give birth to a son. No razor may be used on his head, because the boy is to be a Nazirite, set apart to God from birth, and he will begin the deliverance of Israel from the hands of the Philistines." Then the woman went to her husband and told him, "A man of God came to me. <u>He looked like an angel of God, very awesome.</u> I didn't ask him where he came from, and he didn't tell me his name. But he said to me, 'You will conceive and give birth to a son. Now then, drink no wine or other fermented drink and do not eat anything unclean, because the boy will be a Nazirite of God from birth until the day of his death.'" Then Manoah prayed to the LORD: "O Lord, I beg you, <u>let the man of God you sent to us come again</u> to teach us how to bring up the boy who is to be born." God heard Manoah, and <u>the angel of God came again</u> to the woman while she was out in the field; but her husband Manoah was not with her. The woman hurried to tell her husband, "He's here! The man who appeared to me the other day!" Manoah got up and followed his wife. When he came to the man, he said, "Are you the one who talked to my wife?"*

Learning From History

"I am," he said. So Manoah asked him, "When your words are fulfilled, what is to be the rule for the boy's life and work?" **The angel of the LORD answered, "Your wife must do all that I have told her.** *She must not eat anything that comes from the grapevine, nor drink any wine or other fermented drink nor eat anything unclean. She must do everything I have commanded her." Manoah said to the angel of the LORD, "We would like you to stay until we prepare a young goat for you." The angel of the LORD replied, "Even though you detain me, I will not eat any of your food. But if you prepare a burnt offering, offer it to the LORD." (Manoah did not realize that it was the angel of the LORD.)* **Then Manoah inquired of the angel of the LORD, "What is your name, so that we may honor you when your word comes true?" He replied, "Why do you ask my name? It is beyond understanding."** *Then Manoah took a young goat, together with the grain offering, and sacrificed it on a rock to the LORD.* **And the LORD did an amazing thing while Manoah and his wife watched: As the flame blazed up from the altar toward heaven, the angel of the LORD ascended in the flame.** *Seeing this, Manoah and his wife fell with their faces to the ground. When the angel of the LORD did not show himself again to Manoah and his wife,* **Manoah realized that it was the angel of the LORD. "We are doomed to die!" he said to his wife. "We have seen God!" But his wife answered, "If the LORD had meant to kill us, he would not have accepted a burnt offering and grain offering from our hands, nor shown us all these things or now told us this."** *The woman gave birth to a boy and named him Samson. He grew and the LORD blessed him, and the Spirit of the LORD began to stir him while he was in Mahaneh Dan, between Zorah and Eshtaol.* (NIV)

A point of interest in this account is the fact that after Manoah and his wife had seen the angel of the Lord, Manoah was concerned that they would die because they had seen God. It is obvious from this story and others in the Old Testament that the people who lived at that time had the belief that if a person saw God they would die. They had the correct understanding of God's teaching. They did not know it at the time, but the visitor was Jesus as a Divine Messenger of God and not God Himself. Looking at the second person of the Trinity (Jesus) was not punishable by death. Notice that in these verses the angel of the Lord and the angel of God seem to be interchangeable. The angel of the Lord performed many acts associated with God, such as revelation, deliverance and destruction, but the angel of the Lord is distinct from God the Father. Notice God (the LORD) and Jesus (the angel) below.

2 Sam 24:15-17   *So the LORD sent a plague on Israel from that morning until the end of the time designated, and seventy thousand of the people from Dan to Beersheba died. When* <u>*the angel*</u> *stretched out his hand to destroy Jerusalem,* <u>*the LORD*</u> *was grieved because of the*

> *calamity and said to the angel who was afflicting the people, "Enough! Withdraw your hand."* The angel of the LORD was then at the threshing floor of Araunah the Jebusite. When David saw the angel who was striking down the people, he said to the LORD, "I am the one who has sinned and done wrong. These are but sheep. What have they done? Let your hand fall upon me and my family." (NIV)

As we move from the Old Testament to the New Testament, the phrase "the angel of the Lord" is no longer needed as a title for Jesus. After Jesus appeared as the Messiah, in the flesh, He is mainly referred to by His proper name—Jesus Christ (Jesus the Messiah).

There are several references to an angel of the Lord in the gospels and also in the book of Acts. In the first chapter of Luke, the angel Gabriel identifies himself as an angel of the Lord who came to a priest named Zechariah, to tell him that his wife Elizabeth would have a child and that they were to name him John (John the Baptist). Here Gabriel is a messenger from God, who when Gabriel is in heaven stands in the presence of God.

Luke 1:11-19
> **Then an angel of the Lord appeared to him, standing at the right side of the altar of incense. When Zechariah saw him, he was startled and was gripped with fear. But the angel said to him: "Do not be afraid, Zechariah; your prayer has been heard. Your wife Elizabeth will bear you a son, and you are to give him the name John.** *He will be a joy and delight to you, and many will rejoice because of his birth, for he will be great in the sight of the Lord. He is never to take wine or other fermented drink, and he will be filled with the Holy Spirit even from birth. Many of the people of Israel will he bring back to the Lord their God. And he will go on before the Lord, in the spirit and power of Elijah, to turn the hearts of the fathers to their children and the disobedient to the wisdom of the righteous—to make ready a people prepared for the Lord."* **Zechariah asked the angel, "How can I be sure of this? I am an old man and my wife is well along in years." The angel answered, "I am Gabriel. I stand in the presence of God, and I have been sent to speak to you and to tell you this good news.** (NIV)

This is not a conflict with the Old Testament, as we see when we look at the Greek word used here for "angel." It is *aggelos* and is defined as:

Strong's Definition
32 aggelos (ang'-el-os);
from aggello [probably derived from 71; compare 34] (to bring tidings); a messenger; especially an "angel"; by implication, a pastor:
KJV—angel, messenger.

Thayer's Definition

32 aggelos-
a messenger, an envoy, one who was sent, an angel, a messenger from God

It is possible that some references to the angel of the Lord in the New Testament are Jesus, but only a few. Two possible references might be the experiences Cornelius (Acts 10:1-8) and Peter (Acts 10:9-11,18) had when both these men saw the angel of God in a vision. There are also several references in the book of Revelation where I believe the angel (messenger) mentioned is referring to Jesus. Revelation 18:1 is the Glorious Return of Jesus.

Rev 10:1 *And I saw another <u>mighty angel</u> come down from heaven, clothed with a cloud: and a rainbow was upon his head, and his face was as it were the sun, and his feet as pillars of fire:* (KJV)

Rev 18:1 *And after these things I saw another <u>angel</u> come down from heaven, having great power; and the earth was lightened with his glory.* (KJV)

A reference to the angel of the Lord in Psalms is a stark reminder that Jesus is always with the saints and He delivers them. This applies to the righteous (saved) people throughout history. The angel of the Lord delivers those who fear Him; only a deity can deliver people.

Ps 34:1-22 *I will extol the LORD at all times; his praise will always be on my lips. My soul will boast in the LORD; let the afflicted hear and rejoice. Glorify the LORD with me; let us exalt his name together. I sought the LORD, and he answered me; he delivered me from all my fears. Those who look to him are radiant; their faces are never covered with shame. This poor man called, and the LORD heard him; he saved him out of all his troubles.* **<u>The angel of the LORD encamps around those who fear him, and he delivers them.</u>** *Taste and see that the LORD is good; blessed is the man who takes refuge in him.* **Fear the LORD, you his saints, for those who fear him lack nothing.** *The lions may grow weak and hungry, but those who seek the LORD lack no good thing. Come, my children, listen to me; I will teach you the fear of the LORD. Whoever of you loves life and desires to see many good days, keep your tongue from evil and your lips from speaking lies. Turn from evil and do good; seek peace and pursue it. The eyes of the LORD are on the righteous and his ears are attentive to their cry; the face of the LORD is against those who do evil, to cut off the memory of them from the earth.* **The righteous cry out, and the LORD hears them; he delivers them from all their troubles.** *The LORD is close to the brokenhearted and saves those who are crushed in spirit. A righteous man may have many troubles, but the LORD delivers him from them all; he protects all his bones, not one of them will be broken. Evil will slay the wicked; the foes of* *the righteous will be condemned.* **The LORD redeems his servants; no one will be condemned who takes refuge in him.** (NIV)

The most important visit from the angel of the Lord for the people of Israel in the Old Testament happened when Jesus appeared to Moses in a burning bush. Somewhere around 1445 BC, after the Israelites had been in Egypt for 430 years, Moses was tending a flock of sheep. Moses was at Mount Horeb (Sinai), the very site he would later receive the Ten Commandments. At this time God heard the groaning of the Israelites in Egypt under the slavery of the Pharoah.

Exod 2:23-25   *During that long period, the king of Egypt died. <u>The Israelites groaned in their slavery and cried out</u>, and their cry for help because of their slavery went up to God. <u>God heard their groaning and he remembered his covenant with Abraham, with Isaac and with Jacob.</u> So God looked on the Israelites and was concerned about them.* (NIV)

It was Jesus, as a Divine Messenger (angel of the Lord), whom God selected to inform Moses that he would be the man who would lead the Israelites out of the bondage of the Egyptians. When Jesus spoke to Moses, he hid his face because he thought Jesus was God.

Exod 3:1-10   *Now Moses was tending the flock of Jethro his father-in-law, the priest of Midian, and he led the flock to the far side of the desert and came to Horeb, the mountain of God. There <u>the angel of the LORD</u> appeared to him in flames of fire from within a bush. Moses saw that though the bush was on fire it did not burn up.* So Moses thought, "I will go over and see this strange sight—why the bush does not burn up." When the LORD saw that he had gone over to look, *God called to him from within the bush, "Moses! Moses!" And Moses said, "Here I am." "Do not come any closer," God said. "<u>Take off your sandals, for the place where you are standing is holy ground.</u>" Then he said, "I am the God of your father, the God of Abraham, the God of Isaac and the God of Jacob." <u>At this, Moses hid his face, because he was afraid to look at God.</u>* The LORD said, "I have indeed seen the misery of my people in Egypt. I have heard them crying out because of their slave drivers, and I am concerned about their suffering. So I have come down to rescue them from the hand of the Egyptians and to bring them up out of that land into a good and spacious land, a land flowing with milk and honey—the home of the Canaanites, Hittites, Amorites, Perizzites, Hivites and Jebusites. And now the cry of the Israelites has reached me, and I have seen the way the Egyptians are oppressing them. **So now, go. I am sending you to Pharaoh to bring my people the Israelites out of Egypt.**" (NIV)

Learning From History

After a lot of persuasion in the form of plagues, Pharoah finally let the Israelites leave Egypt. As they were leaving and about to reach the Red Sea, we see the angel of God move from in front of the people to behind them.

Exod 14:19   *Then the angel of God, who had been traveling in front of Israel's army, withdrew and went behind them. The pillar of cloud also moved from in front and stood behind them,* (NIV)

After the sin of the golden calf and the Israelites were ready to start on their journey to the promised land, God promised to send a messenger (angel) ahead of them as they head for the promised land. The angel will go ahead of the Israelites as they defeat the people who are living there when they enter the land to conquer it. This is speaking of the commander of the army of the Lord we mentioned earlier in Joshua 5:14. God commands the Israelites to pay attention to the angel of the Lord. At this time God was talking directly to Moses.

Exod 23:20-25   *"See, I am sending an angel ahead of you to guard you along the way and to bring you to the place I have prepared. Pay attention to him and listen to what he says. Do not rebel against him; he will not forgive your rebelllon, since my Name is in him. If you listen carefully to what he says and do all that I say, I will be an enemy to your enemies and will oppose those who oppose you. My angel will go ahead of you and bring you into the land of the Amorites, Hittites, Perizzites, Canaanites, Hivites and Jebusites, and I will wipe them out. Do not bow down before their gods or worship them or follow their practices. You must demolish them and break their sacred stones to pieces. Worship the LORD your God, and his blessing will be on your food and water. I will take away sickness from among you,* (NIV)

We have just looked at some of the activities of Jesus in His pre-incarnate position in the Old Testament. We must remember that Jesus and also the Holy Spirit are entirely dependent on God the Father. They are submissive to God's every will. That includes the Old Testament period of history, along with the New Testament period.

Before we move on, to look at the role God plays on earth throughout history, let us just briefly touch on the Holy Spirit. Most Christians are familiar with the Holy Spirit in the New Testament, but are probably not very clear about the role of the Holy Spirit in the Old Testament. The Holy Spirit was quite active on earth before Jesus appeared in the flesh.

The third person of the Trinity exercises the power of the Father and the Son in creation and redemption. In the Old Testament the Holy Spirit is usually referred to as the Spirit, the Spirit of God or the Spirit of the Lord. There is a clear distinction between God and the Holy Spirit in the Old Testament. A large portion of Old Testament passages that deal with the Holy Spirit, deal with gifts and powers that are conferred to people by the Holy Spirit for service in the continuation of the Kingdom of God. The Spirit of the Lord could enter a person, complete an objective and then leave that person when that objective was completed.

AFTER THE RAPTURE

Ezek 2:1-2 *He said to me, "Son of man, stand up on your feet and I will speak to you." As he spoke, <u>the Spirit came into me and raised me to my feet</u>, and I heard him speaking to me.* (NIV)

1 Sam 16:14 *<u>But the Spirit of the LORD departed from Saul</u>, and an evil spirit from the LORD troubled him.* (KJV)

During the Old Testament period we can break the service of the Holy Spirit into three main categories. They are:

1. To confer power to people – Judges 3:10; 11:29; 14:6.
2. To bestow wisdom and skill to people – Genesis 41:38; Exodus 31:1-5.
3. To assist prophets – 1 Sam 10:10; 2 Sam 23:1-2; Dan 4:8, 5:11-14; Micah 3:8.

Prophets were distinguished from the rest of the people as men who possessed the Spirit of the Lord. Some prophets such as Isaiah, Ezekiel and Daniel received revelations from visions or dreams. Other prophets like Jeremiah, Hosea, Joel, Micah, Zephaniah and Zechariah received revelations from one of two sources. These prophets begin their writings with such phrases as, *"The word of the Lord that came to Micah"* or *"thus says the Lord."* These prophets were receiving their revelations from Jesus Himself (a messenger) as the Word. *"The Word"* is a name for Jesus. At other times the Holy Spirit came upon them.

John 1:1-5 *<u>In the beginning was the Word, and the Word was with God, and the Word was God.</u> He was with God in the beginning. Through him all things were made; without him nothing was made that has been made. In him was life, and that life was the light of men. The light shines in the darkness, but the darkness has not understood it.* (NIV)

John 1:14 *<u>The Word became flesh and made his dwelling among us.</u> We have seen his glory, the glory of the One and Only, who came from the Father, full of grace and truth.* (NIV)

<u>GLORY OF THE LORD</u>

It does appear that God played an active role in the affairs of men before the times of Moses. God talked to Adam and Eve, Abraham and Jacob and walked with Enoch and Noah. The plural name for God (*'elohiym*) was used in these instances, so it makes it difficult to determine which person of the Trinity it is referring to at that time. It was probably Jesus, because no one was allowed to see the face of God and live. Due to the cries of the chosen people a special redemptive and revelatory presence of God appears on the earth. God's Presence leaves the heavenly realm to appear on earth to assist His chosen people in their redemptive process and to dwell among His people. The very first appearance of the Divine Presence of God shows up after Pharoah finally allows the Israelites to leave Egypt. Moses took the bones of Joseph with him when he left Egypt, because of a promise to Joseph from

Learning From History

the ancestors of Moses. Joseph must have had some inkling about the notion that God would show up to aid the Israelites because of the comment he made while he was still alive.

>Exod 13:17-19 *Then it came to pass, when Pharaoh had let the people go, that God did not lead them by way of the land of the Philistines, although that was near; for God said, "Lest perhaps the people change their minds when they see war, and return to Egypt." So God led the people around by way of the wilderness of the Red Sea. And the children of Israel went up in orderly ranks out of the land of Egypt.* ***And Moses took the bones of Joseph with him, for he had placed the children of Israel under solemn oath, saying, "God will surely visit you, and you shall carry up my bones from here with you."*** (NKJ)

The word for "visit" here in Hebrew is *paqad* (paw-kad') and also means: to attend to, to look after, to care for. As the Israelites left Egypt and headed toward the Red Sea, something appeared to them to lead them on their way.

>Exod 13:20-22 ***So they took their journey from Succoth and camped in Etham at the edge of the wilderness. And the LORD went before them by day in a pillar of cloud to lead the way, and by night in a pillar of fire to give them light, so as to go by day and night.*** *He did not take away the pillar of cloud by day or the pillar of fire by night from before the people.* (NKJ)

Anyone who has any knowledge of the Old Testament is probably familiar with the pillar of cloud and the pillar of fire that directed the travel of the Israelites during their forty years of wandering through the wilderness, but few people understand the full extent the Divine Presence played in that process.

Just as the Israelites approached the Red Sea, they discovered that Pharoah and the Egyptian army were pursuing them. As a form of protection the pillar of cloud moved from in front of the people of Israel and went behind them, coming between the Egyptians and the Israelites.

>Exod 14:10-20 *And when Pharaoh drew near, the children of Israel lifted their eyes, and behold, the Egyptians marched after them. So they were very afraid, and the children of Israel cried out to the LORD. Then they said to Moses, "Because there were no graves in Egypt, have you taken us away to die in the wilderness? Why have you so dealt with us, to bring us up out of Egypt? "Is this not the word that we told you in Egypt, saying, 'Let us alone that we may serve the Egyptians?' For it would have been better for us to serve the Egyptians than that we should die in the wilderness." And Moses said to the people, "Do not be afraid. Stand still, and see the salvation of the LORD, which He will accomplish for you today. For the Egyptians whom you see*

> *today, you shall see again no more forever. "The LORD will fight for you, and you shall hold your peace." And the LORD said to Moses, "Why do you cry to Me? Tell the children of Israel to go forward. "But lift up your rod, and stretch out your hand over the sea and divide it. And the children of Israel shall go on dry ground through the midst of the sea. "And I indeed will harden the hearts of the Egyptians, and they shall follow them. So I will gain honor over Pharaoh and over all his army, his chariots, and his horsemen. "Then the Egyptians shall know that I am the LORD, when I have gained honor for Myself over Pharaoh, his chariots, and his horsemen." And <u>**the Angel of God**</u>, **who went before the camp of Israel, moved and went behind them;** <u>**and the pillar of cloud went from before them and stood behind them**</u>**. So it came between the camp of the Egyptians and the camp of Israel. Thus it was a cloud and darkness to the one, and it gave light by night to the other, so that the one did not come near the other all that night.** (NKJ)*

Did you happen to notice that the Angel of God (Jesus) was also present at this time and also moved to the rear of the Israelites? The pillar of cloud formed a shield of protection during the night to allow the Lord to part the Red Sea, which allowed the Israelites to cross over it on dry ground. Three days later the people complained to Moses about the water.

Exod 15:22-27   *So Moses brought Israel from the Red Sea; then they went out into the Wilderness of Shur. And they went three days in the wilderness and found no water. Now when they came to Marah, they could not drink the waters of Marah, for they were bitter. Therefore the name of it was called Marah. <u>And the people complained against Moses, saying, "What shall we drink?"</u> So he cried out to the LORD, and the LORD showed him a tree. When he cast it into the waters, the waters were made sweet. There He made a statute and an ordinance for them. And there He tested them, and said, "<u>If you diligently heed the voice of the LORD your God and do what is right in His sight, give ear to His commandments and keep all His statutes, I will put none of the diseases on you which I have brought on the Egyptians.</u> For I am the LORD who heals you." Then they came to Elim, where there were twelve wells of water and seventy palm trees; so they camped there by the waters.* (NKJ)

At this time God was forewarning the people to diligently hearken to the voice of God. This is a reference to the upcoming episode that would take place on Mount Sinai. The people set out on their journey once more and again began grumbling against Moses and Aaron, only this time they were complaining about the food.

Exod 16:1-10   *And they journeyed from Elim, and all the congregation of the children of Israel came to the Wilderness of Sin, which is between Elim and Sinai, on the fifteenth day of the second month after they departed from the land of Egypt.* **Then the whole congregation of the children of Israel complained against Moses and Aaron in the wilderness.** *And the children of Israel said to them, "Oh, that we had died by the hand of the LORD in the land of Egypt, when we sat by the pots of meat and when we ate bread to the full! For you have brought us out into this wilderness to kill this whole assembly with hunger." Then the LORD said to Moses, "Behold, I will rain bread from heaven for you. And the people shall go out and gather a certain quota every day, that I may test them, whether they will walk in My law or not. "And it shall be on the sixth day that they shall prepare what they bring in, and it shall be twice as much as they gather daily." Then Moses and Aaron said to all the children of Israel, "At evening you shall know that the LORD has brought you out of the land of Egypt.* **"And in the morning you shall see the glory of the LORD; for He hears your complaints against the LORD.** *But what are we, that you complain against us?" Also Moses said, "This shall be seen when the LORD gives you meat to eat in the evening, and in the morning bread to the full; for the LORD hears your complaints which you make against Him. And what are we? Your complaints are not against us but against the LORD." Then Moses spoke to Aaron, "Say to all the congregation of the children of Israel, 'Come near before the LORD, for He has heard your complaints.'" Now it came to pass, as Aaron spoke to the whole congregation of the children of Israel,* **that they looked toward the wilderness, and behold, the glory of the LORD appeared in the cloud.** (NKJ)

Once again, the Lord provides. As Aaron was speaking to the people, who had been assembled, the glory of the Lord appeared to them in a cloud. What is the glory of the Lord? Once we discover the meaning of the glory of the Lord, it is the key that unlocks the mystery.

Glory has a variety of meanings. It can be exalted praise or honor. It can be something that makes one honored or illustrious. These characteristics of glory cannot be seen. But glory does have a characteristic that can be seen. Glory that can be seen comes in the form of a surrounding radiance of light represented about the head or the whole figure of a sacred person. The Hebrew word for "glory" is *kabowd* and is defined as:

Brown-Driver-Briggs Definition
3519 kabowd rarely kabod-
glory, honor, glorious, abundance
    a) abundance, riches
    b) honor, splendor, glory
    c) honor, dignity

d) honor, reputation
e) honor, reverence, glory
f) glory

Since the glory that we are concerned with was seen by the people, we are concerned with it as a distinctive characteristic of God — a radiant light. This radiant light appeared to them under the cover of a cloud. This cloud bears a striking resemblance to the pillar of cloud we just discussed above. As we continue, the story will unfold before our very eyes.

After the Israelites passed through the Red Sea and were given a supply of food from heaven, we find them again complaining about water and again God meets their needs. Time after time God supplied them with their needs, but again they are still questioning whether God is with them.

Exod 17:1-7 *Then all the congregation of the children of Israel set out on their journey from the Wilderness of Sin, according to the commandment of the LORD, and camped in Rephidim; but there was no water for the people to drink. Therefore the people contended with Moses, and said, "Give us water, that we may drink." And Moses said to them, "Why do you contend with me? Why do you tempt the LORD?" <u>And the people thirsted there for water, and the people complained against Moses</u>, and said, "Why is it you have brought us up out of Egypt, to kill us and our children and our livestock with thirst?" So Moses cried out to the LORD, saying, "What shall I do with this people? They are almost ready to stone me!" And the LORD said to Moses, "Go on before the people, and take with you some of the elders of Israel. Also take in your hand your rod with which you struck the river, and go. "Behold, I will stand before you there on the rock in Horeb; and you shall strike the rock, and water will come out of it, that the people may drink." And Moses did so in the sight of the elders of Israel. So he called the name of the place Massah and Meribah, because of the contention of the children of Israel, and because they tempted the LORD, saying, "<u>Is the LORD among us or not</u>?"* (NKJ)

After fighting off an attack from the Amalekites and Moses is reunited with his family the Israelites arrive at Mount Sinai, the very place where Moses was tending his flock and the angel of the Lord appeared to him earlier in a burning bush. It was on the first day of the third month after leaving Egypt. The people camped at the foot of the mountain and Moses went to the top of Mount Sinai to converse with God.

Exod 19:1-6 *In the third month after the children of Israel had gone out of the land of Egypt, on the same day, they came to the Wilderness of Sinai. For they had departed from Rephidim, had come to the Wilderness of Sinai, and camped in the wilderness. So Israel camped*

Learning From History

> *there before the mountain. <u>And Moses went up to God</u>, and the LORD called to him from the mountain, saying, "Thus you shall say to the house of Jacob, and tell the children of Israel: 'You have seen what I did to the Egyptians, and how I bore you on eagles' wings and brought you to Myself. <u>'Now therefore, if you will indeed obey My voice and keep My covenant, then you shall be a special treasure to Me above all people; for all the earth is Mine</u>. 'And you shall be to Me a kingdom of priests and a holy nation.' These are the words which you shall speak to the children of Israel."* (NKJ)

Moses came back down the mountain and informed the people of what God had said to him. The people agreed to do what God had said.

Exod 19:7-8   *So Moses came and called for the elders of the people, and laid before them all these words which the LORD commanded him. <u>Then all the people answered together and said, "All that the LORD has spoken we will do."</u> So Moses brought back the words of the people to the LORD.* (NKJ)

Moses then returned to the top of the mountain and told God what the people had said. God then informed Moses that He was going to come to him in a thick cloud in three days, so the people could hear Him speak to Moses.

Exod 19:9-13   *And the LORD said to Moses, "Behold, I come to you in the thick cloud, <u>that the people may hear when I speak with you</u>, and believe you forever." So Moses told the words of the people to the LORD. Then the LORD said to Moses, "Go to the people and consecrate them today and tomorrow, and let them wash their clothes. "And let them be ready for the third day. <u>For on the third day the LORD will come down upon Mount Sinai in the sight of all the people</u>. "You shall set bounds for the people all around, saying, 'Take heed to yourselves that you do not go up to the mountain or touch its base. Whoever touches the mountain shall surely be put to death. 'Not a hand shall touch him, but he shall surely be stoned or shot with an arrow; whether man or beast, he shall not live.' <u>When the trumpet sounds long, they shall come near the mountain</u>."* (NKJ)

The signal for the people to congregate at the foot of the mountain would be a long sound of a trumpet. On the third day the people would observe God once again, as He came under the cover of a dense cloud. Moses was informed to prepare the people for a meeting with God.

This is where I strongly disagree with all the translations. The entirety of the subject matter speaks of something far greater than the sound of a trumpet blast. An exhaustive study of the word translated as "trumpet" or "trumpet blast" in both the Old and New Testaments

AFTER THE RAPTURE

will reveal a great deal of information to also support this consensus. It can also clear up some misconceptions about how the word trumpet was translated in all the English translations of the Bible. The first time the word trumpet is found in Bibles translated into English is in Exodus 19:13, shown above, but a closer look at the Hebrew word used here reveals something other than a trumpet blast. The Hebrew word used in Exodus 19:13 is *yowbel*. It comes from the Hebrew word *yabal*, which means to bring (especially with pomp) or to lead. The word *yowbel* is always translated as jubilee (jubile) with two exceptions. In Exodus 19:13, it is translated as trumpet. It is translated as jubilee in Leviticus twenty times; fourteen times in Leviticus 25 and six times in Leviticus 27, and once in the book of Numbers (Numbers 36:4). After that the word *yowbel* once again appears six times in Joshua 6:15-20 as a trumpet, when the walls of Jericho came falling down. Look at the word "Shout!" in Joshua 6:16. The trumpets signaled the people to shout, which caused the wall around Jericho to collapse. The shout caused the wall to collapse, not the trumpet blast.

God is actually telling Moses that He will give a signal on the third day, to let the people know that it is time to meet Him. I think it is safe to say that this was a jubilee, but not necessarily a trumpet blast. The word blast is not even in the Hebrew text, in fact, the word blast only appears a few times in the Bible and it never appears as a loud trumpet blast. Bible translators have added this word to trumpet to designate a loud sound of a trumpet being blown. God is actually telling Moses that a signal for the jubilee is a long sound. When they hear the sound, they are to go and gather together to meet with God. Later God established a special festival for Jubilee, a celebration of freedom for the Israelites. Every fifty years, on the festival of Yom Kippur, a trumpet was to be blown as a memorial to this jubilee. However, if the jubilee sound from God on Mount Sinai is not a trumpet, then what is the sound? Keep reading! As the story continues Moses goes back down the mountain for the second time and prepares the people to meet God on the third day. The people were commanded to refrain from sexual intercourse at that time.

Exod 19:14-15   *So Moses went down from the mountain to the people and sanctified the people, and they washed their clothes. And he said to the people, "__Be ready for the third day__; do not come near your wives."* (NKJ)

As God promised, the signal is given from heaven and the sound is so loud that the people tremble in fear and the very mountain shook violently. What a traumatic experience this was for the people of Israel.

Exod 19:16-18   *And it came to pass on the third day in the morning, that there were thunders and lightnings, and a thick cloud upon the mount, and __the voice of the trumpet exceeding loud__; so that all the people that was in the camp trembled. And Moses brought forth the people out of the camp to meet with God; and they stood at the nether part of the mount. And mount Sinai was altogether on a smoke, because the LORD descended upon it in fire: and the smoke thereof ascended as the smoke of a furnace, __and the whole mount quaked greatly__.* (KJV)

Learning From History

Once again, our focus is on the word trumpet. Most of the newer translations go something like, *" a very loud trumpet blast."* As you can see from above, the King James Version reads, *"and the voice of the trumpet exceeding loud,"* which is a much more accurate translation. Before we analyze the word trumpet in this verse, let us look at the Hebrew word for "voice" used here. The word is *qowl*. The first time this word is found in the Bible is in Genesis 3:8, where we find God conversing with Adam and Eve.

Strong's Definition
6963 qowl (kole);
or qol (kole); from an unused root meaning to call aloud; a voice or sound:
KJV— + aloud, bleating, crackling, cry (+out), fame, lightness, lowing, noise, + hold peace, [pro-] claim, proclamation, + sing, sound, + spark, thunder (-ing), voice, + yell.

The Hebrew word for "trumpet," in verse sixteen, is *showphar*.

Strong's Definition
7782 showphar (sho-far');
or shophar (sho-far'); from 8231 in the original sense of incising; a cornet (as giving a clear sound) or curved horn:
KJV—cornet, trumpet.

What is of particular interest here, is that the original word has a sense of incising. In other words, the sound the Israelites heard cut to their very souls. At this point you could possibly believe that the sound that they heard was a very loud trumpet. It will take the New Testament to add to the story and bring clarification to this very loud sound. The author of Hebrews brings us to the very account of what we are studying here in Exodus and assists us with the understanding of this loud sound. The mountain here is referring to Mount Sinai.

Heb 12:18-21 *__For you have not come to the mountain that may be touched and that burned with fire__, and to blackness and darkness and tempest, __and the sound of a trumpet and the voice of words__, so that those who heard it begged that the word should not be spoken to them anymore. (For they could not endure what was commanded: "And if so much as a beast touches the mountain, it shall be stoned or shot with an arrow." __And so terrifying was the sight that Moses said__, "__I am exceedingly afraid and trembling.__")* (NKJ)

As we move to the New Testament, we are confronted with a new language. Since the New Testament was written in Greek, let us examine the same event from a New Testament perspective. This passage, above, is talking to believers who are living during the church age and are waiting for the second coming of Christ. This passage is also referencing the exact experience that the people of Israel had as they came up to Mount Sinai to meet with God in Exodus chapter nineteen. We need to look at four Greek words and their meanings in verse nineteen to help us with the understanding of this sound. The first two words are from the phrase, *"the sound of a trumpet."* The Greek word for "sound," used here is *echos*, which is a loud or confused noise (echo), i.e., roar; spoken of the roar of the sea waves. As we look at the Greek word here for "trumpet," we find the word *salpigx*.

Strong's Definition
4536 salpigx (sal'-pinx);
perhaps from 4535 (through the idea of quavering or reverberation):
KJV—trump (-et).

4535 salos (sal'-os);
probably from the base of 4525; a vibration, i.e. (specifically) billow:
KJV—wave.

So we see from these definitions that the word for trumpet in Greek comes from a word that means a vibration. When a trumpet is blown the sound comes through the air as it is forced through the lips. This causes the lips to vibrate and thus produce a sound. Likewise, when a person speaks, their vocal cords vibrate to produce a sound. In a sense, this verse could be read as *"the sound of a vibration,"* instead of *"the sound of a trumpet."*

The next two words come from the phrase, *"and the voice of words."* The English word voice is quite clear, but we need to look at it in Greek. I will bet that some of you know that we use the word phone when we are calling someone. The Greek word used here for "voice" is *phone*. It is pronounced fo-nay' in Greek.

Strong's Definition
5456 phone (fo-nay');
probably akin to 5316 through the idea of disclosure; a tone (articulate, bestial or artificial); by implication, an address (for any purpose), saying or language:
KJV—noise, sound, voice.

The Greek word used here for "words," in this verse, is *rhema*.

Strong's Definition
4487 rhema (hray'-mah);
1) what is or has been uttered by the living voice, a thing spoken, a word
    a) any sound produced by the voice and having definite meaning
    b) speech, discourse; what one has said
    c) a series of words joined together into a sentence (a declaration of one's mind made in words)
2) an utterance

If we look at Hebrews 12:19, in its entirety, I think that it is very obvious that the sound the people of Israel heard at Mount Sinai was the voice of God and not a trumpet blast, a loud shout as a command for the Israelites to assemble before Mount Sinai, a time when they heard God speak verbally to Moses.

Learning From History

Heb 12:19 *and the sound of a trumpet and the voice of words, so that those who heard it begged that <u>the word</u> should not be spoken to them anymore.* (NKJ)

If you want a little extra proof, drop down to verse twenty-six.

Heb 12:26 *<u>whose voice then shook the earth;</u> ...* (NKJ)

Now tie this verse back to the voice in Exodus 19:5-6,13, 16. I have been extremely detailed in showing you that it is the voice of God that spoke to the people of Israel in the past for two reasons. First, it shows us how God interacted with His chosen people in the past. Second, it will show how Jesus will interact with the saints in the future. Both of these events (in the past at Mount Sinai and the event that will most likely take place in the near future) are two of the most important events in the entire Bible. Let us take a quick glance at the two best Rapture passages in the Bible to see how they tie into our subject.

1 Cor 15:52 *in a flash, in the twinkling of an eye, <u>at the last trumpet</u>. <u>For the trumpet will sound</u>, the dead will be raised imperishable, and we will be changed.* (NIV)

1 Thes 4:16 *For the Lord himself will come down from heaven, <u>with a loud command</u>, with the voice of the archangel <u>and with the trumpet call of God</u>, and the dead in Christ will rise first.* (NIV)

In both of these passages the word trumpet or trumpet blast, as used in some translations, is used in the same connotation as that shown in Hebrew 12:19. If you are reading the King James Version, you will find the word trump in the two verses listed above, the only two places where it is translated as such. Again, I remind you that this is not a trumpet blast but the voice of Jesus.

I would like you to look at one more word in Greek in this section of our study. It is the word, "shout" (loud command) and is found in 1 Thessalonians 4:16, one of the Rapture passages listed above. The word in Greek is *keleusma*.

Strong's Definition
2752 keleusma (kel'-yoos-mah) or keleuma (kel'-yoo-mah);
from 2753; a cry of incitement:
KJV—shout.

Thayer's Definition
2752 keleuma-
an order, a command, specifically, a stimulating cry, either that by which animals are roused and urged on by man, as horses by charioteers, hounds by hunters, etc., or that by which a signal is given to men, for example, to rowers by the master of a ship, to soldiers by a commander (with a loud summons, a trumpet call)

AFTER THE RAPTURE

To recap two of the most important events in history we will turn back to Hebrews chapter twelve where both accounts are mentioned.

Heb 12:14-29 *(14) **Make every effort to live in peace with all men and to be holy; without holiness no one will see the Lord.** (15) See to it that no one misses the grace of God and that no bitter root grows up to cause trouble and defile many. (16) See that no one is sexually immoral, or is godless like Esau, who for a single meal sold his inheritance rights as the oldest son. (17) Afterward, as you know, when he wanted to inherit this blessing, he was rejected. He could bring about no change of mind, though he sought the blessing with tears. (18) **You have not come to a mountain that can be touched and that is burning with fire; to darkness, gloom and storm; (19) to a trumpet blast or to such a voice speaking words that those who heard it begged that no further word be spoken to them,** (20) because they could not bear what was commanded: "If even an animal touches the mountain, it must be stoned." (21) The sight was so terrifying that Moses said, "I am trembling with fear." (22) **But you have come to Mount Zion, to the heavenly Jerusalem, the city of the living God.** You have come to thousands upon thousands of angels in joyful assembly, (23) to the church of the firstborn, whose names are written in heaven. **You have come to God,** the judge of all men, to the spirits of righteous men made perfect, (24) **to Jesus the mediator of a new covenant,** and to the sprinkled blood that speaks a better word than the blood of Abel. (25) See to it that you do not refuse him who speaks. If they did not escape when they refused him who warned them on earth, how much less will we, if we turn away from him who warns us from heaven? (26) **At that time his voice shook the earth, but now he has promised, "Once more I will shake not only the earth but also the heavens."** (27) The words "once more" indicate the removing of what can be shaken—that is, created things—so that what cannot be shaken may remain. (28) **Therefore, since we are receiving a kingdom that cannot be shaken, let us be thankful,** and so worship God acceptably with reverence and awe, (29) for our "God is a consuming fire."* (NIV)

The most important similarity in the two events listed in these verses is the loud shout or command spoken to call the meeting to order. In all actuality, the trumpet is the sound of the "shout" of the Jubilee—God at Mount Sinai and Jesus at the Rapture. A time to give rest to God's people and set them free. The differences are:

MOUNT SINAI – 1445 BC (Hebrews 12:18-21)
1. God speaks a loud command to draw the people of Israel together (First Trumpet).
2. To meet with God on earth at Mount Sinai.

3. The people approached Mount Sinai with fear and trembling.
4. Earth – a kingdom that can be shaken (Hebrews 12:26 – will be shaken again during the Tribulation Period).

MOUNT ZION – IN THE NEAR FUTURE (Hebrews 12:22-24)
1. Jesus speaks a loud shout (command) to draw the saints together (Last Trumpet).
2. To meet with Jesus in the air to be taken to Mount Zion in heaven.
3. The saints approach Mount Zion with exhilaration, joy, and excitement.
4. Heaven – a Kingdom that cannot be shaken (Hebrews 12:28).

A fitting end to this section, before we revert back to the Old Testament, can be found in Hebrews chapter twelve in the section we just studied.

Heb 12:25 *See that you do not refuse Him who speaks…* (NKJ)

This is how majestic God's voice really is!

Ps 81:6-11 *"I removed his shoulder from the burden; his hands were freed from the baskets. You called in trouble, and I delivered you; I answered you in the secret place of thunder; I tested you at the waters of Meribah. Selah "Hear, O My people, and I will admonish you! O Israel, if you will listen to Me! There shall be no foreign god among you; nor shall you worship any foreign god. I am the LORD your God, who brought you out of the land of Egypt; open your mouth wide, and I will fill it. "But My people would not heed My voice, and Israel would have none of Me.* (NKJ)

Job 40:9 *Do you have an arm like God's, and can your voice thunder like his?* (NIV)

Ps 29:1-4 *Ascribe to the LORD, O mighty ones, ascribe to the LORD glory and strength. Ascribe to the LORD the glory due his name; worship the LORD in the splendor of his holiness. The voice of the LORD is over the waters; the God of glory thunders, the LORD thunders over the mighty waters. The voice of the LORD is powerful; the voice of the LORD is majestic.* (NIV)

As the Israelites stood at the foot of the mountain, God spoke from heaven and His voice became louder and louder as He descended to the top of Mount Sinai. Moses spoke and God answered him. God then told Moses to come up to the top of the mountain. All this was taking place while the Israelites were looking on and trembling with fear.

Exod 19:19-20 *And when the voice of the trumpet sounded long, and waxed louder and louder, Moses spake, and God answered him by a voice. And*

> *the LORD came down upon mount Sinai, on the top of the mount: and the LORD called Moses up to the top of the mount; and Moses went up.* (KJV)

While on the mountain God verbally transmitted His laws to Moses, then instructed Moses to go back down the mountain and warn the people not to try to go up on the mountain to see God or they would die. Moses also informed the people of the laws he verbally received from God while on the mountain, which included the Ten Commandments.

> Exod 19:21-25 *And the LORD said to Moses, "Go down and warn the people, lest they break through to gaze at the LORD, and many of them perish. "Also let the priests who come near the LORD consecrate themselves, lest the LORD break out against them." But Moses said to the LORD, "The people cannot come up to Mount Sinai; for You warned us, saying, 'Set bounds around the mountain and consecrate it.' " Then the LORD said to him, "Away! Get down and then come up, you and Aaron with you. But do not let the priests and the people break through to come up to the LORD, lest He break out against them." So Moses went down to the people and spoke to them.* (NKJ)

The people heard God's voice thundering from Mount Sinai. The people were shaking in their sandals (they did not have boots yet) and stayed some distance away from the mountain. At that time the people told Moses to speak to them, instead of God. They were afraid that if God continued to speak to them they would die.

> Exod 20:18-19 *Now all the people witnessed the thunderings, the lightning flashes, the sound of the trumpet, and the mountain smoking; and when the people saw it, they trembled and stood afar off. <u>Then they said to Moses, "You speak with us, and we will hear; but let not God speak with us, lest we die."</u>* (NKJ)

Moses finally provided the Israelites with the reason why God was speaking to the them in such a manner.

> Exod 20:20 *And Moses said to the people, "Do not fear; <u>for God has come to test you</u>, and that His fear may be before you, so that you may not sin."* (NKJ)

Moses continued to receive instructions from God, who was teaching Moses His laws. God remained in the dense cloud on top of Mount Sinai. It is difficult to calculate just how often Moses went to the top of Mount Sinai, it had to have been many times. Moses truly was a great prophet and it is easy to see why the Jewish people hold such a high regard for him. After God had conveyed to Moses, the laws and decrees concerning Hebrew servants,

Learning From History

property, social responsibility, justice, mercy, Sabbath Laws and the annual Festivals, God promised the people of Israel that He would send a messenger (angel of the Lord) ahead of them and bring them into the promised land. Finally, after Moses had revealed all the words and laws to the people, once again, they responded by saying that they would obey God's will. It is often far easier to say something, than it is to put those words into action!

Exod 24:1-3   *Now He said to Moses, "Come up to the LORD, you and Aaron, Nadab and Abihu, and seventy of the elders of Israel, and worship from afar. "And Moses alone shall come near the LORD, but they shall not come near; nor shall the people go up with him." **So Moses came and told the people all the words of the LORD and all the judgments. And all the people answered with one voice and said, "All the words which the LORD has said we will do."*** (NKJ)

After confirming a covenant with the people God commanded Moses to come up to Him again. This time Moses would receive the Ten Commandments on a set of stone tablets. He would also be on the mountain for forty days and forty nights. This was the first forty-day/forty-night period Moses spent on top of Mount Sinai.

Exod 24:12-18   *Then the LORD said to Moses, "**Come up to Me on the mountain and be there**; and I will give you tablets of stone, and the law and commandments which I have written, that you may teach them." So Moses arose with his assistant Joshua, and Moses went up to the mountain of God. And he said to the elders, "Wait here for us until we come back to you. Indeed Aaron and Hur are with you. If any man has a difficulty, let him go to them." Then Moses went up into the mountain, and a cloud covered the mountain. **Now the glory of the LORD rested on Mount Sinai, and the cloud covered it six days**. And on the seventh day He called to Moses out of the midst of the cloud. **The sight of the glory of the LORD was like a consuming fire on the top of the mountain in the eyes of the children of Israel**. So Moses went into the midst of the cloud and went up into the mountain. **And Moses was on the mountain forty days and forty nights**.* (NKJ)

During this visit Moses was instructed to tell the Israelites to build a sanctuary (tabernacle) for God, so that He would be able to dwell among them. Instructions were given about how to build the tabernacle and all of its furnishings.

Exod 25:8-9   ***"And let them make Me a sanctuary, that I may dwell among them.** "According to all that I show you, that is, the pattern of the tabernacle and the pattern of all its furnishings, just so you shall make it.* (NKJ)

Exod 31:18   *And when He had made an end of speaking with him on Mount Sinai, He gave Moses two tablets of the Testimony, tablets of stone, written with the finger of God.* (NKJ)

Because Moses was gone for such a long time, the people became worried and constructed the false idol of a golden calf. As Moses came down the mountain he became so angry that he threw the stone tablets down and broke them into pieces. God became so angry that He wanted to destroy His chosen people. Moses then went back up the mountain to ask for God's forgiveness for the sin of the people. Through the pleadings of Moses, God relented and allowed the stiff-necked people to live. God also promised to send His angel (messenger) before the people as they traveled toward the promised land. In this account, in the book of Deuteronomy, it reveals that the time frame for this visit was also for forty days and forty nights. The second such visit.

Exod 32:30-35   *Now it came to pass on the next day that Moses said to the people, "<u>You have committed a great sin. So now I will go up to the LORD; perhaps I can make atonement for your sin."</u> Then Moses returned to the LORD and said, "Oh, these people have committed a great sin, and have made for themselves a god of gold! "Yet now, if You will forgive their sin—but if not, I pray, blot me out of Your book which You have written." And the LORD said to Moses, "Whoever has sinned against Me, I will blot him out of My book. "Now therefore, go, lead the people to the place of which I have spoken to you. <u>Behold, My Angel shall go before you.</u> Nevertheless, in the day when I visit for punishment, I will visit punishment upon them for their sin." So the LORD plagued the people because of what they did with the calf which Aaron made.* (NKJ)

Deut 9:17-21   *"<u>Then I took the two tablets and threw them out of my two hands and broke them before your eyes. "And I fell down before the LORD, as at the first, forty days and forty nights; I neither ate bread nor drank water, because of all your sin which you committed in doing wickedly in the sight of the LORD, to provoke Him to anger.</u> "For I was afraid of the anger and hot displeasure with which the LORD was angry with you, to destroy you. But the LORD listened to me at that time also." <u>And the LORD was very angry with Aaron and would have destroyed him; so I prayed for Aaron also at the same time.</u> "Then I took your sin, the calf which you had made, and burned it with fire and crushed it and ground it very small, until it was as fine as dust; and I threw its dust into the brook that descended from the mountain.* (NKJ)

At this time God promises Moses that the angel of the Lord would go before the people and when they get to the promised land the angel would even drive out the Canaanites,

Learning From History

Amorites, Hittites, etc. (the people who were already living there). God was so disgusted with the stiff-necked people that He told Moses He would not go with the people (in the pillar of cloud by day and the pillar of fire by night) for fear of killing them. The people were distressed at this revelation. The sin of the golden calf was a very serious mistake on the part of the people of Israel. God then took time to consider the fate of this stiff-necked people.

Exod 33:1-6 *Then the LORD said to Moses, "Depart and go up from here, you and the people whom you have brought out of the land of Egypt, to the land of which I swore to Abraham, Isaac, and Jacob, saying, 'To your descendants I will give it.' "<u>And I will send My Angel before you</u>, and I will drive out the Canaanite and the Amorite and the Hittite and the Perizzite and the Hivite and the Jebusite. "Go up to a land flowing with milk and honey; <u>for I will not go up in your midst, lest I consume you on the way for you are a stiff-necked people.</u>" And when the people heard this bad news, they mourned, and no one put on his ornaments. For the LORD had said to Moses, "Say to the children of Israel, 'You are a stiff-necked people. <u>I could come up into your midst in one moment and consume you</u>. Now therefore, take off your ornaments, that I may know what to do to you.'" So the children of Israel stripped themselves of their ornaments by Mount Horeb.* (NKJ)

Before the tabernacle was constructed Moses and the people met with God in the tent of Moses. It was known as *"the tabernacle of meeting."* This is where we find Moses meeting with God, who is under the cover of the pillar of cloud.

Exod 33:7-11 *<u>Moses took his tent and pitched it outside the camp, far from the camp, and called it the tabernacle of meeting</u>. And it came to pass that everyone who sought the LORD went out to the tabernacle of meeting which was outside the camp. So it was, whenever Moses went out to the tabernacle, that all the people rose, and each man stood at his tent door and watched Moses until he had gone into the tabernacle. <u>And it came to pass, when Moses entered the tabernacle, that the pillar of cloud descended and stood at the door of the tabernacle, and the LORD talked with Moses</u>. All the people saw the pillar of cloud standing at the tabernacle door, and all the people rose and worshiped, each man in his tent door. <u>So the LORD spoke to Moses face to face, as a man speaks to his friend</u>. And he would return to the camp, but his servant Joshua the son of Nun, a young man, did not depart from the tabernacle.* (NKJ)

At one of their meetings God and Moses were having a very intense conversation. Previously, God had just informed Moses that He would not accompany them on their travels to the promised land. Moses reminds God that this nation is His chosen people.

Exod 33:12-13   *Then Moses said to the LORD, "See, You say to me, 'Bring up this people.' But You have not let me know whom You will send with me. Yet You have said, 'I know you by name, and you have also found grace in My sight.' "<u>Now therefore, I pray, if I have found grace in Your sight, show me now Your way, that I may know You and that I may find grace in Your sight. And consider that this nation is Your people.</u>"* (NKJ)

As the conversation continues God finally relents and agrees to send His Presence with Moses and the people, because He is pleased with Moses. Moses then asks God not to send them on their way if His Presence does not go with them.

Exod 33:14-17   *And He said, "<u>My Presence will go with you, and I will give you rest.</u>" Then he said to Him, "<u>If Your Presence does not go with us, do not bring us up from here.</u> "For how then will it be known that Your people and I have found grace in Your sight, except You go with us? So we shall be separate, Your people and I, from all the people who are upon the face of the earth." So the LORD said to Moses, "<u>I will also do this thing that you have spoken; for you have found grace in My sight, and I know you by name.</u>"* (NKJ)

Moses immediately requests to see something that no human being had ever seen before.

Exod 33:18   *Then Moses said, "<u>Now show me your glory.</u>"* (NIV)

God's answer to Moses was:

Exod 33:19-23   *And the LORD said, "<u>I will cause all my goodness to pass in front of you</u>, and I will proclaim my name, the LORD, in your presence. I will have mercy on whom I will have mercy, and I will have compassion on whom I will have compassion. But," he said, "<u>you cannot see my face, for no one may see me and live.</u>" Then the LORD said, "There is a place near me where you may stand on a rock. When my glory passes by, I will put you in a cleft in the rock and cover you with my hand until I have passed by. <u>Then I will remove my hand and you will see my back; but my face must not be seen.</u>"* (NIV)

Exodus chapter thirty-three has three words that hold the key to the topic of whether God has a visible form or not. The words are Presence, glory and face. God promised Moses that His Presence would go with him and He also informed Moses that he could not see His face.

God's conversation with Moses was very compassionate. The two talked to each other as best friends. God loved Moses because he obeyed Him and as a result of that God found

Learning From History

favor in Moses. Moses also loved God and revered Him. At the request of Moses, God finally relented and agreed to accompany Moses and the Israelites as they traveled through the wilderness. God's Presence would be with them. *Webster's* dictionary says of presence: (1) state or fact of being present, as with others or in a place. (2) attendance or company, (3) immediate vicinity; close proximity, (4) the immediate personal vicinity of a great personage giving audience or reception. The Hebrew word for "Presence," used here in Exodus is *paniym*.

Strong's Dictionary

6440 paniym (paw-neem');
plural (but always as singular) of an unused noun [paneh (paw-neh'); from 6437]; the face (as the part that turns); used in a great variety of applications (literally and figuratively); also (with prepositional prefix) as a preposition (before, etc.):

Brown-Driver-Briggs Definition

6440 paniym, plural (but always as singular) of an unused noun paneh-the face
- a) a face, faces
- b) presence, person
- c) the face (used of seraphim or cherubim)
- d) the face (used of animals)
- e) the face, surface (used of ground)
- f) as an adverb of location temp: before and behind, toward, in front of, forward, formerly, from beforetime, before
- g) with preposition: in front of, before, to the front of, in the presence of, in the face of, at the face or front of, from the presence of, from before, from before the face of

After God promised that His Presence (Person) would go with them, Moses immediately asked to see God's glory. Earlier we established that God's glory is a radiant light that shows up under the cover of a cloud. However, God did not tell Moses that he could not see His glory and live, God said that Moses could not see His face and live. As we take a look at the Hebrew word for "face," used here, we discover that it is the same word used above that was translated as Presence (*paniym*).

From the conversation between God and Moses in Exodus 33:19-23, it is obvious that Moses was allowed to see the form of God. These verses show that God has a face, a hand and a back side. Moses was allowed to look at the back side of God, but he was not allowed to see God's face and remain alive. Scripture mentions the form of God many times.

Num 12:6-8 *Then He said, "Hear now My words: if there is a prophet among you, I, the LORD, make Myself known to him in a vision; I speak to him in a dream.* ***Not so with My servant Moses; he is faithful in all My house. I speak with him face to face, even plainly, and not in dark sayings;*** <u>***and he sees the form of the LORD.***</u> *Why then were you not afraid to speak against My servant Moses?"* (NKJ)

AFTER THE RAPTURE

An interesting comment can be found in Isaiah concerning both the angel of the Lord and the Divine Presence. In a reference to Israel's past history, including the exodus, we see "the angel of His Presence" (messenger of God's Presence), as the Savior of the house of Israel. These verses are referring to this account in Exodus, where we see both the first and second persons of the Trinity. This cannot be a reference to an angel, because angels cannot redeem people and become their Savior. Here the angel of His Presence is Jesus.

> Isa 63:7-9 — *I will tell of the kindnesses of the LORD, the deeds for which he is to be praised, according to all the LORD has done for us—yes, the many good things he has done for the house of Israel, according to his compassion and many kindnesses.* **He said, "Surely they are my people, sons who will not be false to me"; <u>and so he became their Savior</u>. In all their distress he too was distressed, <u>and the angel of his presence saved them</u>. In his love and mercy he redeemed them; he lifted them up and carried them all the days of old.** (NIV)

Perhaps the most prominent appearance of the form of God, besides the episode with Moses, can be found in a vision of God that Ezekiel saw in 593 BC.

> Ezek 1:1 — **In the thirtieth year, in the fourth month on the fifth day, while I was among the exiles by the Kebar River, the heavens were opened and <u>I saw visions of God</u>.** (NIV)

> Ezek 1:25-28 — **Then there came a voice from above the expanse over their heads as they stood with lowered wings. Above the expanse over their heads was what looked like a throne of sapphire, <u>and high above on the throne was a figure like that of a man</u>. I saw that from what appeared to be his waist up he looked like glowing metal, as if full of fire, and that from there down he looked like fire; and brilliant light surrounded him. Like the appearance of a rainbow in the clouds on a rainy day, so was the radiance around him. <u>This was the appearance of the likeness of the glory of the LORD</u>. When I saw it, I fell facedown, and I heard the voice of one speaking.** (NIV)

In this vision, Ezekiel sees God as He appears on His throne in heaven. On God's throne was someone who had the appearance of a man. It was God. In verse twenty-eight we see God's glory as a radiant light that shines around Him. Shortly after seeing God in this vision Ezekiel went to the plain where the glory of the Lord was standing and began conversing with Ezekiel. Notice that both the passages, above and below, use the phrase "the glory of the Lord" for God. Apparently, the form of God can be seen in visions.

> Ezek 3:23 — **So I got up and went out to the plain. <u>And the glory of the LORD was standing there</u>, like the glory I had seen by the Kebar River,**

Learning From History

and I fell facedown. (NIV)

As we return to the episode with God and Moses at Mount Sinai we hear God, in Exodus 33:19, telling Moses that He will make His goodness pass before him. The Hebrew word for "goodness" is *tuwb* and means the best or even the beauty of God. After Moses was allowed to view the "goodness" of God (His back), he was instructed to make a final trip to the top of Mount Sinai. Moses was told to take two blank stone tablets with him so God could once again inscribe the Ten Commandments on them.

Exod 34:1-5 *The LORD said to Moses, "<u>Chisel out two stone tablets like the first ones, and I will write on them the words that were on the first tablets, which you broke.</u> Be ready in the morning, and then come up on Mount Sinai. Present yourself to me there on top of the mountain. No one is to come with you or be seen anywhere on the mountain; not even the flocks and herds may graze in front of the mountain." So Moses chiseled out two stone tablets like the first ones and went up Mount Sinai early in the morning, as the LORD had commanded him; and he carried the two stone tablets in his hands. <u>Then the LORD came down in the cloud and stood there with him and proclaimed his name, the LORD</u>.* (NIV)

Again (for the third time), Moses was on Mount Sinai for forty-days and forty-nights. God made a covenant with Moses and the Israelites in accordance with the laws given them. Moses was instructed to lead the people on their way to the promised land. God asks the people to love and obey Him. As we mentioned before in this book, this final forty-day period was the first "Season of Our Repentance" for the people of Israel. It began on the first day of Elul and ended on the tenth day of Tishri (Yom Kippur–The Day of Atonement). This is the very first time that the High Holy Days were celebrated (Ten Days of Awe).

Exod 34:27-28 *Then the LORD said to Moses, "Write down these words, for in accordance with these words I have made a covenant with you and with Israel." <u>Moses was there with the LORD forty days and forty nights without eating bread or drinking water</u>. And he wrote on the tablets the words of the covenant—the Ten Commandments.* (NIV)

Deut 10:10-13 *Now I had stayed on the mountain forty days and nights, as I did the first time, and the LORD listened to me at this time also. It was not his will to destroy you. "Go," the LORD said to me, "and lead the people on their way, so that they may enter and possess the land that I swore to their fathers to give them." <u>And now, O Israel, what does the LORD your God ask of you but to fear the LORD your God, to walk in all his ways, to love him, to serve the LORD your God with all your heart and with all your soul, and to observe the LORD's commands and decrees that I am giving you today for</u>*

613

your own good? (NIV)

When Moses came back down from the mountain for the last time a very interesting phenomenon occurred.

Exod 34:29-35 *When Moses came down from Mount Sinai with the two tablets of the Testimony in his hands, he was not aware that his face was radiant because he had spoken with the LORD. <u>When Aaron and all the Israelites saw Moses, his face was radiant, and they were afraid to come near him.</u> But Moses called to them; so Aaron and all the leaders of the community came back to him, and he spoke to them. Afterward all the Israelites came near him, and he gave them all the commands the LORD had given him on Mount Sinai. When Moses finished speaking to them, he put a veil over his face. But whenever he entered the LORD's presence to speak with him, he removed the veil until he came out. <u>And when he came out and told the Israelites what he had been commanded, they saw that his face was radiant. Then Moses would put the veil back over his face until he went in to speak with the LORD.</u>* (NIV)

It appears that some of the radiance (glory) of God penetrated the face of Moses as he spoke with God in the midst of the cloud on Mount Sinai during this last visit of forty-days and forty-nights. Moses was truly an extraordinary man. Is it any wonder that the Jewish people believe Moses to be the greatest prophet that ever lived! Nevertheless, even Moses foretold that God would raise up a prophet, like him, from among the Jewish people. At that time the people did not know that Moses was referring to Jesus Christ.

Deut 18:14-22 *The nations you will dispossess listen to those who practice sorcery or divination. But as for you, the LORD your God has not permitted you to do so. <u>The LORD your God will raise up for you a prophet like me from among your own brothers. You must listen to him.</u> For this is what you asked of the LORD your God at Horeb on the day of the assembly when you said, "Let us not hear the voice of the LORD our God nor see this great fire anymore, or we will die." The LORD said to me: "<u>What they say is good. I will raise up for them a prophet like you from among their brothers;</u> I will put my words in his mouth, and he will tell them everything I command him. If anyone does not listen to my words that the prophet speaks in my name, I myself will call him to account. But a prophet who presumes to speak in my name anything I have not commanded him to say, or a prophet who speaks in the name of other gods, must be put to death." You may say to yourselves, "How can we know when a message has not been spoken by the LORD?" If what a prophet proclaims in the name of the LORD does not take*

Learning From History

place or come true, that is a message the LORD has not spoken. That prophet has spoken presumptuously. Do not be afraid of him. (NIV)

Heb 3:1-6   *Therefore, holy brothers, who share in the heavenly calling, fix your thoughts on Jesus, the apostle and high priest whom we confess. He was faithful to the one who appointed him, just as Moses was faithful in all God's house. <u>Jesus has been found worthy of greater honor than Moses</u>, just as the builder of a house has greater honor than the house itself. For every house is built by someone, but God is the builder of everything. Moses was faithful as a servant in all God's house, testifying to what would be said in the future. <u>But Christ is faithful as a son over God's house.</u> And we are his house, if we hold on to our courage and the hope of which we boast.* (NIV)

The reason that no human being can see God's face and live is because of the radiance that shines from it. That is why God's face is shielded by a cloud when He appears on earth. When Moses asked to see God's glory, he was asking to see God's physical form that was hidden within the cloud, including His face. When God appeared in the pillar of cloud the radiant light could be seen shining from the midst of the cloud. Man is allowed to see the rays of light shining forth from God's face as it protrudes through the clouds, but they cannot see His actual face. The radiance of God was so bright that it appeared to the people as fire.

Num 6:22-26   *The LORD said to Moses, "Tell Aaron and his sons, 'This is how you are to bless the Israelites. Say to them: "' "The LORD bless you and keep you; <u>the LORD make his face shine upon you and be gracious to you</u>; the LORD turn his face toward you and give you peace."'* (NIV)

Ps 4:6   *...Let the light of your face shine upon us, O LORD.* (NIV)

Ps 67:1   *May God be gracious to us and bless us and make his face shine upon us, Selah* (NIV)

Ps 89:15   *Blessed are those who have learned to acclaim you, who walk in the light of your presence, O LORD.* (NIV)

In these verses above the Hebrew word for "shine" is *'owr* and can be translated as:

<u>Strong's Definition</u>
215 'owr (ore);
a primitive root; to be (causative, make) luminous (literally and metaphorically):
KJV—X break of day, glorious, kindle, (be, en-, give, show) light (-en, -ened), set on fire, shine.

Brown-Driver-Brigg's Definition
215 'owr-
to be light or to become light, to shine
- a) (in the Qal)
    1) to become light (day)
    2) to shine (used of the sun)
    3) to become bright
- b) (in the Niphal)
    1) to be illuminated
    2) to become lighted up
- c) (in the Hiphil)
    1) to give light, shine (used of the sun, the moon, and the stars)
    2) to illumine, to light up, to cause to shine,
    3) to kindle, to light (a candle [properly, a lamp], wood)
    4) to enlighten (used of the eyes, His law, etc.)
    5) to make (cause) to shine (used of the face)

How awesome it will be when we are finally able to see the glory of the Lord as it shines on us.

DWELL AMONG HIS PEOPLE

After Moses came down the mountain, for the last time, he assembled the Israelites and reminded them of God's command to build a tabernacle according to God's instructions. God wanted a more permanent place to dwell on earth while He interacted with His people. The tabernacle was sanctified (made holy) by the Presence of the glory of the Lord.

Exod 40:17-33 *So the tabernacle was set up on the first day of the first month in the second year. When Moses set up the tabernacle, he put the bases in place, erected the frames, inserted the crossbars and set up the posts. Then he spread the tent over the tabernacle and put the covering over the tent, as the LORD commanded him. He took the Testimony and placed it in the ark, attached the poles to the ark and put the atonement cover over it. Then he brought the ark into the tabernacle and hung the shielding curtain and shielded the ark of the Testimony, as the LORD commanded him. Moses placed the table in the Tent of Meeting on the north side of the tabernacle outside the curtain and set out the bread on it before the LORD, as the LORD commanded him. He placed the lampstand in the Tent of Meeting opposite the table on the south side of the tabernacle and set up the lamps before the LORD, as the LORD commanded him. Moses placed the gold altar in the Tent of Meeting in front of the curtain and burned fragrant incense on it, as the LORD commanded him. Then he put up the curtain at the entrance to the tabernacle. He set*

Learning From History

> *the altar of burnt offering near the entrance to the tabernacle, the Tent of Meeting, and offered on it burnt offerings and grain offerings, as the LORD commanded him. He placed the basin between the Tent of Meeting and the altar and put water in it for washing, and Moses and Aaron and his sons used it to wash their hands and feet. They washed whenever they entered the Tent of Meeting or approached the altar, as the LORD commanded Moses. Then Moses set up the courtyard around the tabernacle and altar and put up the curtain at the entrance to the courtyard. And so Moses finished the work.* (NIV)

Exod 29:42-44 — ***"For the generations to come this burnt offering is to be made regularly at the entrance to the Tent of Meeting before the LORD. There I will meet you and speak to you; there also I will meet with the Israelites, <u>and the place will be consecrated by my glory</u>. "So I will consecrate the Tent of Meeting and the altar and will consecrate Aaron and his sons to serve me as priests.*** (NIV)

After the tabernacle was completed the glory of the Lord entered it. This tabernacle replaced the tent of Moses used earlier as a temporary tent that was set up for meeting with God. This new tabernacle traveled alongside the Israelites as God led them through the wilderness and remained with them until Solomon had a more permanent Temple constructed to house the glory of the Lord.

Exod 40:34-38 — ***Then the cloud covered the Tent of Meeting, <u>and the glory of the LORD filled the tabernacle</u>. Moses could not enter the Tent of Meeting because the cloud had settled upon it, and the glory of the LORD filled the tabernacle. In all the travels of the Israelites, whenever the cloud lifted from above the tabernacle, they would set out; but if the cloud did not lift, they did not set out—until the day it lifted. <u>So the cloud of the LORD was over the tabernacle by day, and fire was in the cloud by night, in the sight of all the house of Israel during all their travels</u>.*** (NIV)

The Mercy Seat, which was the lid or covering on the Ark of the Covenant, was the resting place for the glory of the Lord. There were two golden cherubim of hammered gold positioned at each end of the Mercy Seat facing each other. The Divine Presence rested in a cloud between these two cherubim.

Exod 25:17-22 — ***"Make an atonement cover of pure gold—two and a half cubits long and a cubit and a half wide. And make two cherubim out of hammered gold at the ends of the cover. Make one cherub on one end and the second cherub on the other; make the cherubim of one piece with the cover, at the two ends. The cherubim are to have*** *their wings spread upward, overshadowing the cover with them. The cherubim are to face each other, looking toward the cover. Place the cover on top of the ark and put in the ark the Testimony, which I will give you. There, above the cover between the two cherubim that are over the ark of the Testimony, I will meet with you and give you all my commands for the Israelites.* (NIV)

Lev 16:2   *The LORD said to Moses: "Tell your brother Aaron not to come whenever he chooses into the Most Holy Place behind the curtain in front of the atonement cover on the ark, or else he will die, because I appear in the cloud over the atonement cover.* (NIV)

Despite the fact that God led the Israelites through forty-years of wandering through the wilderness, the people still rebelled against God by grumbling and complaining the entire time. Toward the end of the journey, before the Israelites entered the promised land, Moses stopped and reflected on the previous events. Moses commanded the people to be obedient to God and reminded them not to forget His covenant with them. God repeated the same laws and ordinances to these Israelites that He did to the Israelites at Mount Sinai.

Deut 4:1-24   *Hear now, O Israel, the decrees and laws I am about to teach you. Follow them so that you may live and may go in and take possession of the land that the LORD, the God of your fathers, is giving you. Do not add to what I command you and do not subtract from it, but keep the commands of the LORD your God that I give you. You saw with your own eyes what the LORD did at Baal Peor. The LORD your God destroyed from among you everyone who followed the Baal of Peor, but all of you who held fast to the LORD your God are still alive today. See, I have taught you decrees and laws as the LORD my God commanded me, so that you may follow them in the land you are entering to take possession of it. Observe them carefully, for this will show your wisdom and understanding to the nations, who will hear about all these decrees and say, "Surely this great nation is a wise and understanding people." What other nation is so great as to have their gods near them the way the LORD our God is near us whenever we pray to him? And what other nation is so great as to have such righteous decrees and laws as this body of laws I am setting before you today? Only be careful, and watch yourselves closely so that you do not forget the things your eyes have seen or let them slip from your heart as long as you live. Teach them to your children and to their children after them. Remember the day you stood before the LORD your God at Horeb, when he said to me, "Assemble the people before me to hear my words so that they may learn to revere me as long as they live in the land and may teach them to their children." You came near and*

Learning From History

> *stood at the foot of the mountain while it blazed with fire to the very heavens, with black clouds and deep darkness.* **<u>Then the LORD spoke to you out of the fire. You heard the sound of words but saw no form; there was only a voice.</u>** *He declared to you his covenant, the Ten Commandments, which he commanded you to follow and then wrote them on two stone tablets. And the LORD directed me at that time to teach you the decrees and laws you are to follow in the land that you are crossing the Jordan to possess.* **You saw no form of any kind the day the LORD spoke to you at Horeb out of the fire.** *Therefore watch yourselves very carefully, so that you do not become corrupt and make for yourselves an idol, an image of any shape, whether formed like a man or a woman, or like any animal on earth or any bird that flies in the air, or like any creature that moves along the ground or any fish in the waters below. And when you look up to the sky and see the sun, the moon and the stars—all the heavenly array—do not be enticed into bowing down to them and worshiping things the LORD your God has apportioned to all the nations under heaven.* **But as for you, the LORD took you and brought you out of the iron-smelting furnace, out of Egypt, to be the people of his inheritance, as you now are.** *The LORD was angry with me because of you, and he solemnly swore that I would not cross the Jordan and enter the good land the LORD your God is giving you as your inheritance. I will die in this land; I will not cross the Jordan; but you are about to cross over and take possession of that good land. Be careful not to forget the covenant of the LORD your God that he made with you; do not make for yourselves an idol in the form of anything the LORD your God has forbidden.* **<u>For the LORD your God is a consuming fire, a jealous God.</u>** (NIV)

As Moses continues his discourse he foretells the future of the people of Israel. Moses declares that the people will become corrupt and will not live very long in the land they are about to enter. They will be scattered among the other peoples of the world. Moses them jumps all the way to the time of the Tribulation Period, when the Time of Jacob's Trouble will take place. Moses declares that when they are in distress and all these things have happened, then the people of Israel will return to God and obey Him. Notice that this takes place in the later days. To be more specific the Day of the Lord, which is the last part of the later days. In Deuteronomy 4 – 6, God told the Israelites to be obedient to His commands.

> Deut 4:25-31 *After you have had children and grandchildren and have lived in the land a long time—if you then become corrupt and make any kind of idol, doing evil in the eyes of the LORD your God and provoking him to anger, I call heaven and earth as witnesses against you this day that you will quickly perish from the land that you are crossing the Jordan to possess. You will not live there long but will certainly be*

> *destroyed. The LORD will scatter you among the peoples, and only a few of you will survive among the nations to which the LORD will drive you. There you will worship man-made gods of wood and stone, which cannot see or hear or eat or smell. But if from there you seek the LORD your God, you will find him if you look for him with all your heart and with all your soul.* ***When you are in distress and all these things have happened to you, <u>then in later days you will return to the LORD your God and obey him</u>.*** *For the LORD your God is a merciful God; he will not abandon or destroy you or forget the covenant with your forefathers, which he confirmed to them by oath.* (NIV)

Moses then informs the people, as a reminder, to ask about the days before God created a chosen people, beginning at creation. Has any other nation received such attention, as they have had from God? Moses reminds them that the Lord is God in heaven above as well as the earth below. God, once again, instructs the people to obey His commands.

Deut 4:32-40
> ***Ask now about the former days, long before your time, from the day God created man on the earth; ask from one end of the heavens to the other. Has anything so great as this ever happened, or has anything like it ever been heard of?*** <u>***Has any other people heard the voice of God speaking out of fire, as you have, and lived***</u>***? Has any god ever tried to take for himself one nation out of another nation, by testings, by miraculous signs and wonders, by war, by a mighty hand and an outstretched arm, or by great and awesome deeds, like all the things the LORD your God did for you in Egypt before your very eyes? You were shown these things so that you might know that the LORD is God; besides him there is no other.*** <u>***From heaven he made you hear his voice to discipline you. On earth he showed you his great fire, and you heard his words from out of the fire.***</u> ***Because he loved your forefathers and chose their descendants after them,*** <u>***he brought you out of Egypt by his Presence and his great strength***</u>***, to drive out before you nations greater and stronger than you and to bring you into their land to give it to you for your inheritance, as it is today. Acknowledge and take to heart this day that the LORD is God in heaven above and on the earth below. There is no other.*** <u>***Keep his decrees and commands, which I am giving you today***</u>***, so that it may go well with you and your children after you and that you may live long in the land the LORD your God gives you for all time.*** (NIV)

As Moses assembled the entire nation of Israel, he reminded them to walk in the ways of the Lord and to do what the Lord had commanded them. In the verses below it is revealed to us what God was conversing in a loud voice to the assembled Israelites at Mt. Sinai.

Learning From History

Deut 5:1-33 *Moses summoned all Israel and said: <u>Hear, O Israel, the decrees and laws I declare in your hearing today. Learn them and be sure to follow them.</u>* The LORD our God made a covenant with us at Horeb. It was not with our fathers that the LORD made this covenant, but with us, with all of us who are alive here today. **The LORD spoke to you face to face out of the fire on the mountain.** *(At that time I stood between the LORD and you to declare to you the word of the LORD, because you were afraid of the fire and did not go up the mountain.) And he said: "I am the LORD your God, who brought you out of Egypt, out of the land of slavery. "You shall have no other gods before me. "You shall not make for yourself an idol in the form of anything in heaven above or on the earth beneath or in the waters below. You shall not bow down to them or worship them; for I, the LORD your God, am a jealous God, punishing the children for the sin of the fathers to the third and fourth generation of those who hate me, but showing love to a thousand [generations] of those who love me and keep my commandments. "You shall not misuse the name of the LORD your God, for the LORD will not hold anyone guiltless who misuses his name. "Observe the Sabbath day by keeping it holy, as the LORD your God has commanded you. Six days you shall labor and do all your work, but the seventh day is a Sabbath to the LORD your God. On it you shall not do any work, neither you, nor your son or daughter, nor your manservant or maidservant, nor your ox, your donkey or any of your animals, nor the alien within your gates, so that your manservant and maidservant may rest, as you do. Remember that you were slaves in Egypt and that the LORD your God brought you out of there with a mighty hand and an outstretched arm. Therefore the LORD your God has commanded you to observe the Sabbath day. "Honor your father and your mother, as the LORD your God has commanded you, so that you may live long and that it may go well with you in the land the LORD your God is giving you. "You shall not murder. "You shall not commit adultery. "You shall not steal. "You shall not give false testimony against your neighbor. "You shall not covet your neighbor's wife. You shall not set your desire on your neighbor's house or land, his manservant or maidservant, his ox or donkey, or anything that belongs to your neighbor."* <u>**These are the commandments the LORD proclaimed in a loud voice to your whole assembly there on the mountain from out of the fire, the cloud and the deep darkness; and he added nothing more.**</u> **Then he wrote them on two stone tablets and gave them to me. When you heard the voice out of the darkness, while the mountain was ablaze with fire, all the leading men of your tribes and your elders came to me. And you said, "<u>The LORD our God has shown us his glory</u>**

and his majesty, and we have heard his voice from the fire. Today we have seen that a man can live even if God speaks with him. But now, why should we die? This great fire will consume us, and we will die if we hear the voice of the LORD our God any longer. For what mortal man has ever heard the voice of the living God speaking out of fire, as we have, and survived? Go near and listen to all that the LORD our God says. Then tell us whatever the LORD our God tells you. We will listen and obey." The LORD heard you when you spoke to me and the LORD said to me, "I have heard what this people said to you. Everything they said was good. Oh, that their hearts would be inclined to fear me and keep all my commands always, so that it might go well with them and their children forever! "Go, tell them to return to their tents. But you stay here with me so that I may give you all the commands, decrees and laws you are to teach them to follow in the land I am giving them to possess." So be careful to do what the LORD your God has commanded you; do not turn aside to the right or to the left. Walk in all the way that the LORD your God has commanded you, so that you may live and prosper and prolong your days in the land that you will possess. (NIV)

Chapter six continues by telling the Israelites that if they are careful to obey God's commands, they will prosper in the promised land that they were about to enter. The Hebrew word for "hear" is *shama`* and is often spelled Shema today. There is a Messianic Jewish movement today that goes by the name, Shema. They believe in Yeshua as their Messiah.

Deut 6:3-9   *Hear, O Israel, and be careful to obey so that it may go well with you and that you may increase greatly in a land flowing with milk and honey, just as the LORD, the God of your fathers, promised you. Hear, O Israel: The LORD our God, the LORD is one. Love the LORD your God with all your heart and with all your soul and with all your strength. These commandments that I give you today are to be upon your hearts. Impress them on your children. Talk about them when you sit at home and when you walk along the road, when you lie down and when you get up. Tie them as symbols on your hands and bind them on your foreheads. Write them on the doorframes of your houses and on your gates.* (NIV)

As we follow the chronological order of the glory of the Lord, or the Divine Presence, we come across a short time period when God left the ark of the covenant. Around 1050 BC, when the Ark of the Covenant was located in Shiloh, Israel went to war with the Philistines.

1 Sam 4:1-9   *And Samuel's word came to all Israel. Now the Israelites went out to fight against the Philistines. The Israelites camped at Ebenezer, and the Philistines at Aphek. The Philistines deployed their forces to*

Learning From History

meet Israel, and as the battle spread, Israel was defeated by the Philistines, who killed about four thousand of them on the battlefield. When the soldiers returned to camp, the elders of Israel asked, "Why did the LORD bring defeat upon us today before the Philistines? **Let us bring the ark of the LORD's covenant from Shiloh, so that it may go with us and save us from the hand of our enemies." So the people sent men to Shiloh, and they brought back the ark of the covenant of the LORD Almighty, who is enthroned between the cherubim.** *And Eli's two sons, Hophni and Phinehas, were there with the ark of the covenant of God. When the ark of the LORD's covenant came into the camp, all Israel raised such a great shout that the ground shook.* **Hearing the uproar, the Philistines asked, "What's all this shouting in the Hebrew camp?" When they learned that the ark of the LORD had come into the camp, the Philistines were afraid. "<u>A god has come into the camp</u>," they said. "<u>We're in trouble</u>!** *Nothing like this has happened before. Woe to us! Who will deliver us from the hand of these mighty gods? They are the gods who struck the Egyptians with all kinds of plagues in the desert. Be strong, Philistines! Be men, or you will be subject to the Hebrews, as they have been to you. Be men, and fight!"* (NIV)

The Philistines were allowed to defeat Israel (because of unfaithfulness) and capture the Ark of the Covenant. As a result of that the glory of the Lord departed from Israel.

1 Sam 4:10-22   ***So the Philistines fought, and the Israelites were defeated and every man fled to his tent. The slaughter was very great; Israel lost thirty thousand foot soldiers. <u>The ark of God was captured</u>, and Eli's two sons, Hophni and Phinehas, died.*** *That same day a Benjamite ran from the battle line and went to Shiloh, his clothes torn and dust on his head. When he arrived, there was Eli sitting on his chair by the side of the road, watching, because his heart feared for the ark of God. When the man entered the town and told what had happened, the whole town sent up a cry. Eli heard the outcry and asked, "What is the meaning of this uproar?" The man hurried over to Eli, who was ninety-eight years old and whose eyes were set so that he could not see. He told Eli, "I have just come from the battle line; I fled from it this very day." Eli asked, "What happened, my son?" The man who brought the news replied, "Israel fled before the Philistines, and the army has suffered heavy losses.* ***<u>Also your two sons, Hophni and Phinehas, are dead, and the ark of God has been captured.</u>"*** *When he mentioned the ark of God, Eli fell backward off his chair by the side of the gate. His neck was broken and he died, for he was an old man and heavy. He had led Israel forty years. His daughter-in-law, the wife of Phinehas, was pregnant and near the time of delivery.*

> *When she heard the news that the ark of God had been captured and that her father-in-law and her husband were dead, she went into labor and gave birth, but was overcome by her labor pains. As she was dying, the women attending her said, "Don't despair; you have given birth to a son." But she did not respond or pay any attention.* **She named the boy Ichabod, saying, "The glory has departed from Israel"—because of the capture of the ark of God and the deaths of her father-in-law and her husband. She said, "<u>The glory has departed from Israel, for the ark of God has been captured.</u>"** (NIV)

As the story unfolds it turns out that the act of taking the ark of God was not a very wise move. For seven months the Philistines paid the price for having the ark in their presence. When the Lord's hand is heavy on a people, they will know it is from God.

1 Sam 5:1-12   ***After the Philistines had captured the ark of God, they took it from Ebenezer to Ashdod.** Then they carried the ark into Dagon's temple and set it beside Dagon. When the people of Ashdod rose early the next day, there was Dagon, fallen on his face on the ground before the ark of the LORD! They took Dagon and put him back in his place. But the following morning when they rose, there was Dagon, fallen on his face on the ground before the ark of the LORD! His head and hands had been broken off and were lying on the threshold; only his body remained. That is why to this day neither the priests of Dagon nor any others who enter Dagon's temple at Ashdod step on the threshold.* **<u>The LORD's hand was heavy upon the people of Ashdod and its vicinity; he brought devastation upon them and afflicted them with tumors.</u>** *When the men of Ashdod saw what was happening, they said, "The ark of the god of Israel must not stay here with us, because his hand is heavy upon us and upon Dagon our god."* So they called together all the rulers of the Philistines and asked them, "What shall we do with the ark of the god of Israel?" They answered, "Have the ark of the god of Israel moved to Gath." So they moved the ark of the God of Israel. But after they had moved it, the LORD's hand was against that city, throwing it into a great panic. He afflicted the people of the city, both young and old, with an outbreak of tumors. So they sent the ark of God to Ekron. As the ark of God was entering Ekron, the people of Ekron cried out, "They have brought the ark of the god of Israel around to us to kill us and our people." So they called together all the rulers of the Philistines and said, "Send the ark of the god of Israel away; let it go back to its own place, or it will kill us and our people." For death had filled the city with panic; God's hand was very heavy upon it. Those who did not die were afflicted with tumors, and the outcry of the city went up to heaven.* (NIV)

Learning From History

After much misery was inflicted on them the Philistines returned the ark of the LORD to the Israelites, with guilt offerings. It was then that the glory of the Lord returned to the people of Israel. Seventy men made the mistake of looking into the ark of the Lord and lost their lives because of their inept actions.

1 Sam 6:1-20 — *When the ark of the LORD had been in Philistine territory seven months, the Philistines called for the priests and the diviners and said, "<u>What shall we do with the ark of the LORD</u>? Tell us how we should send it back to its place." They answered, "If you return the ark of the god of Israel, do not send it away empty, but by all means send a guilt offering to him. Then you will be healed, and you will know why his hand has not been lifted from you." The Philistines asked, "What guilt offering should we send to him?" They replied, "Five gold tumors and five gold rats, according to the number of the Philistine rulers, because the same plague has struck both you and your rulers. Make models of the tumors and of the rats that are destroying the country, and pay honor to Israel's god. Perhaps he will lift his hand from you and your gods and your land. Why do you harden your hearts as the Egyptians and Pharaoh did? When he treated them harshly, did they not send the Israelites out so they could go on their way? "Now then, get a new cart ready, with two cows that have calved and have never been yoked. Hitch the cows to the cart, but take their calves away and pen them up. Take the ark of the LORD and put it on the cart, and in a chest beside it put the gold objects you are sending back to him as a guilt offering. Send it on its way, but keep watching it. If it goes up to its own territory, toward Beth Shemesh, then the LORD has brought this great disaster on us. But if it does not, then we will know that it was not his hand that struck us and that it happened to us by chance." So they did this. They took two such cows and hitched them to the cart and penned up their calves. They placed the ark of the LORD on the cart and along with it the chest containing the gold rats and the models of the tumors. Then the cows went straight up toward Beth Shemesh, keeping on the road and lowing all the way; they did not turn to the right or to the left. The rulers of the Philistines followed them as far as the border of Beth Shemesh. Now the people of Beth Shemesh were harvesting their wheat in the valley, and when they looked up and saw the ark, they rejoiced at the sight. The cart came to the field of Joshua of Beth Shemesh, and there it stopped beside a large rock. The people chopped up the wood of the cart and sacrificed the cows as a burnt offering to the LORD. The Levites took down the ark of the LORD, together with the chest containing the gold objects, and placed them on the large rock. On that day the people of Beth Shemesh offered burnt offerings and made sacrifices to the LORD.*

The five rulers of the Philistines saw all this and then returned that same day to Ekron. These are the gold tumors the Philistines sent as a guilt offering to the LORD—one each for Ashdod, Gaza, Ashkelon, Gath and Ekron. And the number of the gold rats was according to the number of Philistine towns belonging to the five rulers—the fortified towns with their country villages. The large rock, on which they set the ark of the LORD, is a witness to this day in the field of Joshua of Beth Shemesh. **<u>But God struck down some of the men of Beth Shemesh, putting seventy of them to death because they had looked into the ark of the LORD</u>.** *The people mourned because of the heavy blow the LORD had dealt them, and the men of Beth Shemesh asked, "<u>Who can stand in the presence of the LORD, this holy God</u>? To whom will the ark go up from here?"* (NIV)

Not long after this incident we see the glory of the Lord as God leaves the tent of meeting to enter the newly built house (Temple) that Solomon had constructed for God. This took place in 960 BC. Notice that this event took place during the festival of the High Holy Days on the seventh month. This was the month of Tishri, but here it is called the month of Ethanim, the name used for this month before the Israelite captivity by the Babylonians.

1 Kings 8:1-13   **Then King Solomon summoned into his presence at Jerusalem the elders of Israel, all the heads of the tribes and the chiefs of the Israelite families, to bring up the ark of the LORD's covenant from Zion, the City of David. All the men of Israel came together to King Solomon at the time of the festival in the month of Ethanim, the seventh month.** *When all the elders of Israel had arrived, the priests took up the ark, and they brought up the ark of the LORD and the Tent of Meeting and all the sacred furnishings in it. The priests and Levites carried them up, and King Solomon and the entire assembly of Israel that had gathered about him were before the ark, sacrificing so many sheep and cattle that they could not be recorded or counted.* **The priests then brought the ark of the LORD's covenant to its place in the inner sanctuary of the temple, the Most Holy Place, and put it beneath the wings of the cherubim.** *The cherubim spread their wings over the place of the ark and overshadowed the ark and its carrying poles. These poles were so long that their ends could be seen from the Holy Place in front of the inner sanctuary, but not from outside the Holy Place; and they are still there today. There was nothing in the ark except the two stone tablets that Moses had placed in it at Horeb, where the LORD made a covenant with the Israelites after they came out of Egypt.* **When the priests withdrew from the Holy Place, the cloud filled the temple of the LORD. And the priests could not perform their service because of the cloud, <u>for the glory of the LORD filled his temple</u>.** *Then Solomon said, "<u>The</u>*

Learning From History

> ***LORD has said that he would dwell in a dark cloud; I have indeed built a magnificent temple for you, a place for you to dwell forever.*** *"* (NIV)

The glory of the Lord remained in the Temple in Jerusalem for the next 367 years. As we pick up the story in 593 BC, we find the prophet Ezekiel where he is in exile in Babylon. God had appointed Ezekiel as a watchman for the house of Israel.

Ezek 3:16-27   *At the end of seven days the word of the LORD came to me: "Son of man, I have made you a watchman for the house of Israel; so hear the word I speak and give them warning from me.* When I say to a wicked man, 'You will surely die,' and you do not warn him or speak out to dissuade him from his evil ways in order to save his life, that wicked man will die for his sin, and I will hold you accountable for his blood. But if you do warn the wicked man and he does not turn from his wickedness or from his evil ways, he will die for his sin; but you will have saved yourself. "Again, when a righteous man turns from his righteousness and does evil, and I put a stumbling block before him, he will die. Since you did not warn him, he will die for his sin. The righteous things he did will not be remembered, and I will hold you accountable for his blood. But if you do warn the righteous man not to sin and he does not sin, he will surely live because he took warning, and you will have saved yourself." The hand of the LORD was upon me there, and he said to me, "Get up and go out to the plain, and there I will speak to you." So I got up and went out to the plain. ***And the glory of the LORD was standing there***, *like the glory I had seen by the Kebar River, and I fell facedown.* ***Then the Spirit came into me and raised me to my feet.*** He spoke to me and said: "Go, shut yourself inside your house. And you, son of man, they will tie with ropes; you will be bound so that you cannot go out among the people. I will make your tongue stick to the roof of your mouth so that you will be silent and unable to rebuke them, though they are a rebellious house. *But when I speak to you, I will open your mouth and you shall say to them, 'This is what the Sovereign LORD says.' Whoever will listen let him listen, and whoever will refuse let him refuse; for they are a rebellious house.* (NIV)

Note in verse twenty-four that the Spirit entered Ezekiel and set him up on his feet. This Spirit is what we know of today as the Holy Spirit in the New Testament. In that same year, 593 BC, Ezekiel was taken to Jerusalem in a vision to view the departure of the glory of the Lord as the Divine Presence returned to heaven. Below, Ezekiel has another vision of God. Because of the abominations of the people of Israel, it drives the Divine Glory from the Temple. This action paves the way for the Babylonians to completely destroy Jerusalem and the Temple a few years later in 586 BC.

Ezek 8:1-6 *In the sixth year, in the sixth month on the fifth day, while I was sitting in my house and the elders of Judah were sitting before me, the hand of the Sovereign LORD came upon me there. <u>I looked, and I saw a figure like that of a man</u>. From what appeared to be his waist down he was like fire, and from there up his appearance was as bright as glowing metal.* He stretched out what looked like a hand and took me by the hair of my head. <u>**The Spirit lifted me up between earth and heaven and in visions of God he took me to Jerusalem**</u>, *to the entrance to the north gate of the inner court, where the idol that provokes to jealousy stood. <u>And there before me was the glory of the God of Israel, as in the vision I had seen in the plain.</u> Then he said to me, "Son of man, look toward the north." So I looked, and in the entrance north of the gate of the altar I saw this idol of jealousy. And he said to me, "<u>Son of man, do you see what they are doing—the utterly detestable things the house of Israel is doing here, things that will drive me far from my sanctuary?</u> But you will see things that are even more detestable."* (NIV)

Ezek 9:3-4 *Now the glory of the God of Israel went up from above the cherubim, where it had been, and moved to the threshold of the temple. Then the LORD called to the man clothed in linen who had the writing kit at his side and said to him, "Go throughout the city of Jerusalem and put a mark on the foreheads of those who grieve and lament over all the detestable things that are done in it."* (NIV)

Ezek 10:1-5 *I looked, and I saw the likeness of a throne of sapphire above the expanse that was over the heads of the cherubim. The LORD said to the man clothed in linen, "Go in among the wheels beneath the cherubim. Fill your hands with burning coals from among the cherubim and scatter them over the city." And as I watched, he went in. Now the cherubim were standing on the south side of the temple when the man went in, and a cloud filled the inner court. <u>Then the glory of the LORD rose from above the cherubim and moved to the threshold of the temple. The cloud filled the temple, and the court was full of the radiance of the glory of the LORD.</u> The sound of the wings of the cherubim could be heard as far away as the outer court, like the voice of God Almighty when he speaks.* (NIV)

Ezek 10:18-19 <u>*Then the glory of the LORD departed from over the threshold of the temple and stopped above the cherubim.*</u> *While I watched, the cherubim spread their wings and rose from the ground, and as they went, the wheels went with them. They stopped at the entrance to* *the east gate of the LORD's house, <u>and the glory of the God of Israel was above them.</u>* (NIV)

Ezek 11:22-25 *Then the cherubim, with the wheels beside them, spread their wings, and the glory of the God of Israel was above them. <u>The glory of the LORD went up from within the city and stopped above the mountain east of it.</u> The Spirit lifted me up and brought me to the exiles in Babylonia in the vision given by the Spirit of God. Then the vision I had seen went up from me, and I told the exiles everything the LORD had shown me.* (NIV)

Over 160 years earlier, around 755 BC, the prophet Hosea had forewarned the divided kingdoms of Israel and Judah that because of their spiritual decay the Divine Presence would leave them. Because of their misdeeds they were not permitted to return to God.

Hosea 5:4-7 *"<u>Their deeds do not permit them to return to their God.</u> A spirit of prostitution is in their heart; they do not acknowledge the LORD.* Israel's arrogance testifies against them; the Israelites, even Ephraim, stumble in their sin; Judah also stumbles with them. *When they go with their flocks and herds to seek the LORD, they will not find him; <u>he has withdrawn himself from them.</u> They are unfaithful to the LORD*; they give birth to illegitimate children. Now their New Moon festivals will devour them and their fields. (NIV)

For approximately 852 years, from 1445 BC to 593 BC, God dwelt among His people. First in a portable tent and later in a Temple. The rejection of God by His chosen nation Israel, over the years, finally caused God to return to heaven. Shortly after the Times of the Gentiles began in 606 BC, God's glory left the Temple and returned to heaven. Through all of this early history you must remember that the permanent dwelling place of God remained in heaven, where it is today. God's Temple and His throne have existed in heaven for a very long time. The tent of meeting and also the Temple that was built later were only replicas of the heavenly (true) Tabernacle. God's dwelling place on earth was only a temporary dwelling place where He could be close to His people.

Heb 8:1-6 *<u>The point of what we are saying is this</u>: <u>We do have such a high priest, who sat down at the right hand of the throne of the Majesty in heaven, and who serves in the sanctuary, the true tabernacle set up by the Lord, not by man.</u> Every high priest is appointed to offer both gifts and sacrifices, and so it was necessary for this one also to have something to offer. If he were on earth, he would not be a priest, for there are already men who offer the gifts prescribed by the law. <u>They serve at a sanctuary that is a copy and shadow of what is in heaven.</u> This is why Moses was warned when he was about to build the tabernacle: "See to it that you make everything* *according to the pattern shown you on the mountain." But the ministry Jesus has received is as superior to theirs as the covenant of which he is mediator is superior to the old one, and it is founded on better promises.* (NIV)

Heb 9:1-15 *<u>Now the first covenant had regulations for worship and also an earthly sanctuary.</u> A tabernacle was set up. In its first room were the lampstand, the table and the consecrated bread; this was called the Holy Place. Behind the second curtain was a room called the Most Holy Place, which had the golden altar of incense and the gold-covered ark of the covenant. This ark contained the gold jar of manna, Aaron's staff that had budded, and the stone tablets of the covenant. **Above the ark were the cherubim of the Glory, overshadowing the atonement cover.** But we cannot discuss these things in detail now. When everything had been arranged like this, the priests entered regularly into the outer room to carry on their ministry. But only the high priest entered the inner room, and that only once a year, and never without blood, which he offered for himself and for the sins the people had committed in ignorance. The Holy Spirit was showing by this that the way into the Most Holy Place had not yet been disclosed as long as the first tabernacle was still standing. <u>This is an illustration for the present time, indicating that the gifts and sacrifices being offered were not able to clear the conscience of the worshiper. They are only a matter of food and drink and various ceremonial washings—external regulations applying until the time of the new order. When Christ came as high priest of the good things that are already here, he went through the greater and more perfect tabernacle that is not man-made, that is to say, not a part of this creation.</u> He did not enter by means of the blood of goats and calves; but he entered the Most Holy Place once for all by his own blood, having obtained eternal redemption. The blood of goats and bulls and the ashes of a heifer sprinkled on those who are ceremonially unclean sanctify them so that they are outwardly clean. **How much more, then, will the blood of Christ, who through the eternal Spirit offered himself unblemished to God, cleanse our consciences from acts that lead to death, so that we may serve the living God!** <u>For this reason Christ is the mediator of a new covenant, that those who are called may receive the promised eternal inheritance—now that he has died as a ransom to set them free from the sins committed under the first covenant.</u>* (NIV)

Notice that the new covenant is founded on better promises than the old (first) covenant. Even the Antichrist will know about God's heavenly dwelling place and that the resurrected saints will be living in heaven at the time he is making his bid to conquer the entire world.

Rev 13:5-6 *The beast was given a mouth to utter proud words and blasphemies and to exercise his authority for forty-two months. <u>He opened his mouth to blaspheme God, and to slander his name and his dwelling place and those who live in heaven.</u>* (NIV)

SHEKINAH GLORY

There is a term or phrase used in non-canonical writings that applies to our study. It is Shekinah (she-ki'-na or shekkinah) and comes from the Hebrew verb *shakan* (shaw-kan'). It means: to abide, to dwell, to tabernacle or to reside. It is a word used for the visible Presence of the Divine Majesty. To the Jew this term denotes a manifestation of God upon the stage of the world, although He abides in the faraway heaven. The word Shekinah is not found in the Bible, but was used by later Jews and by Christians to express the visible Divine Presence, especially when resting between the cherubim over the Mercy Seat. It is first found in Jewish writings of the Targums. The Jews developed the word into a noun, which implies God's dwelling in the midst of the children of Israel. It could also signify the Presence of God in the world or with individual men.

Shekinah refers to the instances God showed Himself visibly—when He was on Mount Sinai or in the Holy of Holies (in the tent or in the Temple). I believe that the Shekinah Glory is the exact same thing we are studying as the glory of the Lord. In the chart, Activities of the Triune God (Trinity), on page 766, I have inserted the phrase Shekinah Glory in place of the glory of the Lord. Shekinah Glory fit in the chart better and I like the sound of Shekinah Glory. These two passages from the Old Testament apply to Shekinah.

Exod 25:8 *"Then have them make a sanctuary for me, <u>and I will dwell among them.</u>* (NIV)

1 Kings 8:12-13 *Then Solomon said, "The LORD has said that he would dwell in a dark cloud; <u>I have indeed built a magnificent temple for you, a place for you to dwell forever."</u>* (NIV)

According to Aggadic teaching, the Shekinah dwells only among Israel. That concept has support in the New Testament in the book of Romans where it is listed as belonging to the people of Israel. Most of the Bible translations only list the word glory, but in the NIV translation the translators appropriately added the word "divine" to give it more clarity.

Rom 9:1-5 *<u>I speak the truth in Christ</u>—I am not lying, my conscience confirms it in the Holy Spirit—I have great sorrow and unceasing anguish in my heart. <u>For I could wish that I myself were cursed and cut off from Christ for the sake of my brothers, those of my own race, the people of Israel.</u> Theirs is the adoption as sons; <u>theirs the divine glory</u>, the covenants, the receiving of the law, the temple worship and the promises. Theirs are the patriarchs, and from them is traced the human ancestry of Christ, who is God over all,* *forever praised! Amen.* (NIV)

In these verses Paul is so grieved by the fact that most of his own people (the Jews) had not accepted Christ that he was willing to give up his own salvation, if that would save them. Paul then goes on to list the special blessings God has given the Jewish people. These special blessings were bestowed on the Israelites in the Old Testament. Notice the similarity of the events we just studied in Exodus. The people of Israel:

1. are the chosen people.
2. are the people who had the glory of the Lord (Shekinah Glory) dwell among them.
3. are the people who were given the covenants from God.
4. are the people who were given the law, which included the Ten Commandments.
5. are the people who were given the worship service for the Tabernacle.
6. are the people who were given promises to be fulfilled in the future.
7. are the descendants of the patriarchs.
8. are the people who Christ traced His human ancestry. Even Christ (the Messiah) was a Jew. A prophet greater than Moses.

LEARNING FROM NEW TESTAMENT HISTORY

God, as the Divine Presence (glory of the Lord), does not directly interact with mankind on earth in the past history of the New Testament era, except for a few early appearances. All these appearances occurred while God was in heaven or above the earth in the midst of a cloud. Please notice the similarity of the experience at Mount Sinai as God spoke from the midst of this cloud. God made His Presence known:

1. In 26 AD, from heaven when Jesus was baptized.
   Matt 3:13-17 *Then Jesus came from Galilee to the Jordan to be baptized by John. But John tried to deter him, saying, "I need to be baptized by you, and do you come to me?" Jesus replied, "Let it be so now; it is proper for us to do this to fulfill all righteousness." Then John consented.* **As soon as Jesus was baptized, he went up out of the water. At that moment heaven was opened, and he saw the Spirit of God descending like a dove and lighting on him. <u>And a voice from heaven said, "This is my Son, whom I love; with him I am well pleased."</u>** (NIV)

2. In 29 AD, in Jerusalem, from a cloud at the Transfiguration.
   Luke 9:34-36 *While he was speaking, a cloud appeared and enveloped them, and they were afraid as they entered the cloud.* **<u>A voice came from the cloud, saying, "This is my Son, whom I have chosen; listen to him."</u> When the voice had spoken, they found that Jesus was alone.** *The disciples kept this to themselves, and told no one at that time what they had seen.* (NIV)
   Peter recalls this event in 64 AD in Babylon where he went to witness to the Jewish people living there (Jewish people whose ancestors stayed behind in 536 BC).
   2 Pet 1:16-18 *We did not follow cleverly invented stories when we told you about*

Learning From History

*the power and coming of our Lord Jesus Christ, but we were eyewitnesses of his majesty. **For he received honor and glory from God the Father <u>when the voice came to him from the Majestic Glory</u>, saying, "<u>This is my Son</u>, <u>whom I love; with him I am well pleased.</u>" We ourselves heard this voice that came from heaven when we were with him on the sacred mountain.*** (NIV)

3. In 30 AD, from heaven as Jesus predicts His death.
   John 12:27-33 *"Now my heart is troubled, and what shall I say? 'Father, save me from this hour'? No, it was for this very reason I came to this hour. Father, glorify your name!"* ***<u>Then a voice came from heaven</u>, "<u>I have glorified it, and will glorify it again.</u>" The crowd that was there and heard it said it had thundered; others said an angel had spoken to him. Jesus said, "This voice was for your benefit, not mine.*** *Now is the time for judgment on this world; now the prince of this world will be driven out. But I, when I am lifted up from the earth, will draw all men to myself." He said this to show the kind of death he was going to die.* (NIV)

God is still in control and running the universe from heaven, although He is not directly interacting with man on earth during the Dispensation of Grace. A few years later after the death of Jesus in 30 AD, as Stephen was about to be stoned to death in 33 AD, heaven was opened and he was allowed to see the glory of God with Jesus standing at His right side.

Acts 7:54-60 ***When they heard this, they were furious and gnashed their teeth at him. <u>But Stephen, full of the Holy Spirit, looked up to heaven and saw the glory of God, and Jesus standing at the right hand of God.</u> "<u>Look</u>," he said, "<u>I see heaven open and the Son of Man standing at the right hand of God.</u>*** *" At this they covered their ears and, yelling at the top of their voices, they all rushed at him, dragged him out of the city and began to stone him. Meanwhile, the witnesses laid their clothes at the feet of a young man named Saul. While they were stoning him, Stephen prayed, "Lord Jesus, receive my spirit." Then he fell on his knees and cried out, "Lord, do not hold this sin against them." When he had said this, he fell asleep.* (NIV)

Before we move on to the role that the glory of the Lord will play in the future, we should look at what the New Testament has to say about the visibility of God. Remember I told you that most Bible scholars teach that God is invisible.

There are three references in the New Testament where the word "invisible" has been translated as referring to God. They are:

Col 1:15 ***He is the image of <u>the invisible God</u>, the firstborn over all creation.*** (NIV)

1 Tim 1:17 ***Now to the King eternal, immortal, <u>invisible</u>, the only God, be honor and glory for ever and ever. Amen.*** (NIV)

Heb 11:27 *By faith he left Egypt, not fearing the king's anger; he persevered because <u>he saw him who is invisible.</u>* (NIV)

Before we take a more detailed look at some more verses that pertain to the visibility of God, I think it is applicable to look at the Greek word that the translators used for the word "invisible." The word is *aoratos:*

Thayer's Definition
517 aoratos-
unseen, or that which cannot be seen, invisible

We all know that something can be unseen, but that does not necessarily mean that it is invisible. A case in point is the glory of the Lord that we just studied in the Old Testament. God told Moses that he could not see His face and live. That does not mean that God's face is invisible. It is something that cannot be seen for a very good reason. The seventy Israelite men who looked into the ark of God can attest to that. By the way, I could not find a Hebrew word in the Old Testament that was translated as invisible.

In Hebrews 11:27, mentioned above, we have a verse that is referring to the episode in Exodus thirty-three that we just studied. Does it seem strange to you that Moses saw Him (God) who is invisible? Of course, Moses saw the form of God, but was not allowed to see His face, which is that which cannot be seen without being punished by death.

In all three of the verses listed above the Greek word *aoratos* should be translated as "unseen," to conform to what the entire Bible has to say about the visibility of God. These verses are obviously referring to the unseen portion of God—His face. The only translation I could find that used the word, "unseen," in Colossians 1:15 and 1 Timothy 1:17, is *The Living Bible.* Even in 1 John 4:12, the reference is to the unseen portion of God.

1 John 4:12 *<u>No one has ever seen God</u>; but if we love one another, God lives in us and his love is made complete in us.* (NIV)

Another description of God by Timothy clearly speaks of the glory of the Lord and God's face. This coincides with the Old Testament teaching of an unseen God.

1 Tim 6:15-16 *which God will bring about in his own time—<u>God, the blessed and only Ruler, the King of kings and Lord of lords, who alone is immortal and <u>who lives in unapproachable light</u>, <u>whom no one has seen or can see.</u> To him be honor and might forever. Amen.* (NIV)

Finally, Bible scholars refer to a verse in John chapter four where it is stated that, *"God is spirit,"* to imply that God is invisible, but taken in context it is not saying that at all. Jesus is telling a woman from Samaria that the time has come to worship God in spirit and truth. The conversation is referring to the Holy Spirit. The application is the duty of the Holy Spirit during the Dispensation of Grace. The book of John is packed full of information concerning the Holy Spirit. Some people even refer to the Dispensation of Grace as the Dispensation of

Learning From History

the Holy Spirit, because of the activity of the Holy Spirit on earth during this two thousand-year period. God is spirit, in the sense that He is the Holy Spirit and the Holy Spirit is God, just as God is the Son, in the sense that Jesus is God. They are all God, but a separate person of the Trinity. In these verses in John the ministry of the Holy Spirit is in view.

> John 4:21-26   *Jesus declared, "Believe me, woman, a time is coming when you will worship the Father neither on this mountain nor in Jerusalem. You Samaritans worship what you do not know; we worship what we do know, for salvation is from the Jews.* ***Yet a time is coming and has now come when the true worshipers will worship the Father in spirit and truth, for they are the kind of worshipers the Father seeks.*** <u>***God is spirit***</u>***, and his worshipers must worship in spirit and in truth."*** *The woman said, "I know that Messiah" (called Christ) "is coming. When he comes, he will explain everything to us." Then Jesus declared, "I who speak to you am he."* (NIV)

If God does not have a physical form, then:

How can God sit on His throne?

> Dan 7:9-10   *"As I looked, "thrones were set in place, and <u>the Ancient of Days took his seat</u>. His clothing was as white as snow; the hair of his head was white like wool. His throne was flaming with fire, and its wheels were all ablaze. A river of fire was flowing, coming out from before him. Thousands upon thousands attended him; ten thousand times ten thousand stood before him. The court was seated, and the books were opened.* (NIV)

How can Jesus lead the resurrected saints into God's Presence at the Rapture?

> 1 Thes 3:13   *May he strengthen your hearts so that you will be blameless and holy in the presence of our God and Father when our Lord Jesus comes with all his holy ones.* (NIV)

> 2 Cor 4:14   *because we know that the one who raised the Lord Jesus from the dead will also raise us with Jesus and present us with you in his presence.* (NIV)

How can Jesus be led into God's Presence to be crowned King?

> Dan 7:13-14   *"In my vision at night I looked, and there before me was one like a son of man, coming with the clouds of heaven. <u>He approached the Ancient of Days and was led into his presence</u>. He was given authority, glory and sovereign power; all peoples, nations and men*

of every language worshiped him. His dominion is an everlasting dominion that will not pass away, and his kingdom is one that will never be destroyed. (NIV)

If God is invisible, like the New Testament translators are implying, then how is it that Jesus has seen God?

John 6:46   *No one has seen the Father except the one who is from God; <u>only he has seen the Father</u>.* (NIV)

If God is invisible, then why did Jesus Himself tell us that the angels in heaven see the face of His Father in heaven?

Matt 18:10   *"See that you do not look down on one of these little ones. For I tell you that their angels in heaven always see the face of my Father in heaven.* (NIV)

If God is invisible, why did Jesus tell the unbelieving Jews that they have never heard God's voice or seen God's form (shape-KJV)?

John 5:37-38   *And the Father who sent me has himself testified concerning me. <u>You have never heard his voice nor seen his form</u>, nor does his word dwell in you, for you do not believe the one he sent.* (NIV)

In heaven Jesus can see God, even His face. As a matter of fact Jesus is the exact image of His Father, including His radiant glory. How can Jesus sit down at God's right side if God is invisible? Try placing the words *"unseen God"* in Colossians 1:15.

Col 1:15   *He is the image of the invisible God, the firstborn over all creation.* (NIV)

2 Cor 4:4   *The god of this age has blinded the minds of unbelievers, so that they cannot see the light of the gospel of the glory of <u>Christ</u>, <u>who is the image of God</u>.* (NIV)

Heb 1:3   *The Son is the radiance of God's glory and <u>the exact representation of his being</u>, sustaining all things by his powerful word. After he had provided purification for sins, he sat down at the right hand of the Majesty in heaven.* (NIV)

It appears that Jesus had radiant glory before the world was created.

John 17:1-5   *After Jesus said this, he looked toward heaven and prayed: "Father, the time has come. Glorify your Son, that your Son may*

> *glorify you. For you granted him authority over all people that he might give eternal life to all those you have given him. Now this is eternal life: that they may know you, the only true God, and Jesus Christ, whom you have sent. I have brought you glory on earth by completing the work you gave me to do. <u>And now, Father, glorify me in your presence with the glory I had with you before the world began.</u>* (NIV)

In verse five above the Greek word for "glory" is *doxa*. This word is the parallel word for the Hebrew word *kabowd*, which we just studied in the Old Testament as the radiance of God.

<u>Thayer's Definition</u>
1391 doxa-
1) an opinion, a judgment, a view
2) an opinion, an estimate, whether good or bad concerning someone in the New Testament always a good opinion concerning one, resulting in praise, honor, and glory
3) splendor, brightness
    a) used of the moon, sun, stars
    b) magnificence, excellence, preeminence, dignity, grace
    c) majesty
1) a thing belonging to God; the kingly majesty which belongs to Him as supreme ruler, majesty in the sense of the absolute perfection of the deity
2) a thing belonging to Christ
    a) the kingly majesty of the Messiah
    b) the absolutely perfect inward or personal excellency of Christ; the majesty
3) used of the angels; as apparent in their exterior brightness
4) a most glorious condition, most exalted state
    a) used of that condition with God the Father in heaven to which Christ was raised after He had achieved His work on earth
    b) the glorious condition of blessedness into which is appointed and promised that true Christians shall enter after their Savior's return from heaven

Of course, Jesus did not have a radiant light shining from His face when He appeared on earth in a fleshly body. In the flesh Jesus became a human being. In heaven Jesus is the exact image and has the same form as God. They have spiritual bodies.

> Phil 2:1-11   *Therefore if there is any consolation in Christ, if any comfort of love, if any fellowship of the Spirit, if any affection and mercy, fulfill my joy by being like-minded, having the same love, being of one accord, of one mind. Let nothing be done through selfish ambition or conceit, but in lowliness of mind let each esteem others better than himself. Let each of you look out not only for his own interests, but also for*

the interests of others. **Let this mind be in you which was also in Christ Jesus, who, being in the form of God, did not consider it robbery to be equal with God, *but made Himself of no reputation, taking the form of a bondservant, and coming in the likeness of men.* And being found in appearance as a man, He humbled Himself and became obedient to the point of death, even the death of the cross.** *Therefore God also has highly exalted Him and given Him the name which is above every name, that at the name of Jesus every knee should bow, of those in heaven, and of those on earth, and of those under the earth, and that every tongue should confess that Jesus Christ is Lord, to the glory of God the Father.* (NKJ)

At the Transfiguration Jesus was transformed into His glorious body, the glorious body He now has in heaven. Take note of His glory (radiance) at that time.

Luke 9:28-29   *About eight days after Jesus said this, he took Peter, John and James with him and went up onto a mountain to pray.* **As he was praying, the appearance of his face changed, and his clothes became as bright as a flash of lightning.** (NIV)

The glory of Jesus appeared when He confronted the Apostle Paul as he approached Damascus.

Acts 22:6-11   **"About noon as I came near Damascus, suddenly a bright light from heaven flashed around me.** *I fell to the ground and heard a voice say to me, 'Saul! Saul! Why do you persecute me?' "'Who are you, Lord?' I asked. "'I am Jesus of Nazareth, whom you are persecuting,' he replied.* **My companions saw the light, but they did not understand the voice of him who was speaking to me.** *"'What shall I do, Lord?' I asked. "'Get up,' the Lord said, 'and go into Damascus. There you will be told all that you have been assigned to do.'* **My companions led me by the hand into Damascus, because the brilliance of the light had blinded me.** (NIV)

John saw Jesus in all His glory while he was exiled on the island of Patmos.

Rev 1:12-16   *I turned around to see the voice that was speaking to me. And when I turned I saw seven golden lampstands, and among the lampstands was someone* **"like a son of man,"** *dressed in a robe reaching down to his feet and with a golden sash around his chest.* **His head and hair were white like wool, as white as snow, and his eyes were like blazing fire. His feet were like bronze glowing in a furnace, and his voice was like the sound of rushing waters.** *In his right hand he held seven stars, and out of his mouth came a sharp double-edged sword.*

His face was like the sun shining in all its brilliance. (NIV)

The glory of Jesus is most prevalent when He returns to earth after the Tribulation Period. Today, it is commonly known as the Glorious Return of Jesus Christ, and for good reason. The Son of Man in His day is a reference to Jesus during the Day of the Lord.

Luke 9:26-27   *If anyone is ashamed of me and my words, the Son of Man will be ashamed of him when he comes in his glory and in the glory of the Father and of the holy angels. I tell you the truth, some who are standing here will not taste death before they see the kingdom of God."* (NIV)

Luke 17:22-25   *Then he said to his disciples, "The time is coming when you will long to see one of the days of the Son of Man, but you will not see it. Men will tell you, 'There he is!' or 'Here he is!' Do not go running off after them. For the Son of Man in his day will be like the lightning, which flashes and lights up the sky from one end to the other. But first he must suffer many things and be rejected by this generation.* (NIV)

Matt 24:29-30   *"Immediately after the distress of those days" 'the sun will be darkened, and the moon will not give its light; the stars will fall from the sky, and the heavenly bodies will be shaken.' "At that time the sign of the Son of Man will appear in the sky, and all the nations of the earth will mourn. They will see the Son of Man coming on the clouds of the sky, with power and great glory.* (NIV)

The Greek word for "sign," in Matthew 24:30, is *semeion* and can mean: a miracle or wonder; it can refer to a portent, that is, an unusual occurrence transcending the common course of nature, an indication or omen of something about to happen, especially something momentous. It will be perceived as a great lightning flash, only here the radiance will continue to shine with glorious splendor.

Matt 24:27   *For as lightning that comes from the east is visible even in the west, so will be the coming of the Son of Man.* (NIV)

Matt 25:31   *"When the Son of Man comes in his glory, and all the angels with him, he will sit on his throne in heavenly glory.* (NIV)

After the saved and the unsaved people on earth have been separated, Jesus will return to heaven to prepare for war. As Jesus once again returns to earth He will be ready to defeat the nations at the Battle of Armageddon. At this time the glorious splendor of Jesus is evident. In Deuteronomy below, we see God (Shekinah Glory) on Mount Paran after He left Mount Sinai and in Psalms, Isaiah and Habakkuk we see Jesus at Armageddon.

AFTER THE RAPTURE

Deut 33:1-2 — *This is the blessing that Moses the man of God pronounced on the Israelites before his death. He said: "<u>The LORD came from Sinai and dawned over them from Seir; he shone forth from Mount Paran</u>. He came with myriads of holy ones from the south, from his mountain slopes.* (NIV)

Ps 97:1-6 — *<u>The LORD reigns</u>; let the earth rejoice; let the multitude of isles be glad! Clouds and darkness surround Him; righteousness and justice are the foundation of His throne. A fire goes before Him, and burns up His enemies round about. <u>His lightnings light the world</u>; the earth sees and trembles. The mountains melt like wax at the presence of the LORD, at the presence of the Lord of the whole earth. The heavens declare His righteousness, <u>and all the peoples see His glory</u>.* (NKJ)

Isa 66:15-18 — *<u>For behold, the LORD will come with fire and with His chariots</u>, like a whirlwind, to render His anger with fury, and His rebuke with flames of fire. For by fire and by His sword the LORD will judge all flesh; and the slain of the LORD shall be many. "Those who sanctify themselves and purify themselves, to go to the gardens after an idol in the midst, eating swine's flesh and the abomination and the mouse, shall be consumed together," says the LORD. "For I know their works and their thoughts.* **It shall be that I will gather all nations and tongues; <u>and they shall come and see My glory</u>.** (NKJ)

Hab 3:3-7 — *<u>God came from Teman, the Holy One from Mount Paran</u>. Selah <u>His glory covered the heavens and his praise filled the earth. His splendor was like the sunrise; rays flashed from his hand, where his power was hidden</u>. Plague went before him; pestilence followed his steps. He stood, and shook the earth; he looked, and made the nations tremble. The ancient mountains crumbled and the age-old hills collapsed. His ways are eternal. I saw the tents of Cushan in distress, the dwellings of Midian in anguish.* (NIV)

In Habakkuk, Jesus is referred to as God. When Jesus comes from heaven to defeat His enemies at the Battle of Armageddon, the brilliance of His Glory will be seven times brighter than the sun. Tophet (hell) is ready for the Antichrist (the Assyrian).

Isa 30:25-33 — *And there shall be upon every high mountain, and upon every high hill, rivers and streams of waters <u>in the day of the great slaughter</u>, when the towers fall. Moreover the light of the moon shall be as the light of the sun, <u>and the light of the sun shall be sevenfold</u>, <u>as the light of seven days</u>, in the day that the LORD bindeth up the breach of his people, and healeth the stroke of their wound. Behold, the*

> *name of the LORD cometh from far, burning with his anger, and the burden thereof is heavy: his lips are full of indignation, and his tongue as a devouring fire: And his breath, as an overflowing stream, shall reach to the midst of the neck, to sift the nations with the sieve of vanity: and there shall be a bridle in the jaws of the people, causing them to err. Ye shall have a song, as in the night when a holy solemnity is kept; and gladness of heart, as when one goeth with a pipe to come into the mountain of the LORD, to the mighty One of Israel. **And the LORD shall cause his glorious voice to be heard, and shall shew the lighting down of his arm, with the indignation of his anger, and with the flame of a devouring fire, with scattering, and tempest, and hailstones. For through the voice of the LORD shall the Assyrian be beaten down, which smote with a rod.** And in every place where the grounded staff shall pass, which the LORD shall lay upon him, it shall be with tabrets and harps: and in battles of shaking will he fight with it. **For Tophet is ordained of old; yea, for the king it is prepared; he hath made it deep and large: the pile thereof is fire and much wood; the breath of the LORD, like a stream of brimstone, doth kindle it.** (KJV)*

The final resolve of the glory of both God and Jesus will be discussed in chapter fifteen. The angels and the resurrected bodies of the saints will also have a glorious appearance. Of course, their glory will not come close to the radiance of God or Jesus. The radiance of the saints will possibly be on the order of how Moses looked after he exited the midst of the cloud while conversing with God on Mt. Sinai. At the Transfiguration we pick up the future glory of Moses and Elijah.

> Luke 9:29-31   *As he was praying, the appearance of his face changed, and his clothes became as bright as a flash of lightning. **Two men, Moses and Elijah, appeared in glorious splendor, talking with Jesus.** They spoke about his departure, which he was about to bring to fulfillment at Jerusalem.* (NIV)

Stephen standing before the Sanhedrin had a face like the face of an angel.

> Acts 6:15   *All who were sitting in the Sanhedrin looked intently at Stephen, **and they saw that his face was like the face of an angel.*** (NIV)

Christian art from the past has often portrayed Jesus, angels and even saints with a halo surrounding their heads. Although this is a traditional symbol of deity for Jesus, I believe that it meant much more than that to these artists. I believe that this halo represents the glory of the radiance of Jesus, the radiance of angels and the radiance of the saints in their future state and that those artists also believed this concept.

AFTER THE RAPTURE

2 Cor 3:17-18 — *Now the Lord is the Spirit, and where the Spirit of the Lord is, there is freedom. And we, who with unveiled faces all reflect the Lord's glory, are being transformed into his likeness with ever-increasing glory, which comes from the Lord, who is the Spirit.* (NIV)

1 Cor 15:35-49 — *<u>But someone may ask, "How are the dead raised? With what kind of body will they come?"</u> How foolish! What you sow does not come to life unless it dies. When you sow, you do not plant the body that will be, but just a seed, perhaps of wheat or of something else. But God gives it a body as he has determined, and to each kind of seed he gives its own body. All flesh is not the same: Men have one kind of flesh, animals have another, birds another and fish another. <u>There are also heavenly bodies and there are earthly bodies; but the splendor of the heavenly bodies is one kind, and the splendor of the earthly bodies is another.</u> The sun has one kind of splendor, the moon another and the stars another; and star differs from star in splendor. <u>So will it be with the resurrection of the dead.</u> The body that is sown is perishable, it is raised imperishable; it is sown in dishonor, <u>it is raised in glory</u>; it is sown in weakness, it is raised in power; <u>it is sown a natural body, it is raised a spiritual body.</u> If there is a natural body, there is also a spiritual body. So it is written: "The first man Adam became a living being"; the last Adam, a life-giving spirit. <u>The spiritual did not come first, but the natural, and after that the spiritual.</u> The first man was of the dust of the earth, the second man from heaven. As was the earthly man, so are those who are of the earth; and as is the man from heaven, so also are those who are of heaven. <u>And just as we have borne the likeness of the earthly man, so shall we bear the likeness of the man from heaven.</u>* (NIV)

Col 3:1-4 — *Since, then, you have been raised with Christ, <u>set your hearts on things above</u>, where Christ is seated at the right hand of God. Set your minds on things above, not on earthly things. For you died, and your life is now hidden with Christ in God. <u>When Christ, who is your life, appears, then you also will appear with him in glory</u>.* (NIV)

In the Bible we are reminded of past history in order to teach us about future history. Past history can also be used as examples to keep us from sinning.

1 Cor 10:1-13 — *For I do not want you to be ignorant of the fact, brothers, that our forefathers were all under the cloud and that they all passed through the sea. They were all baptized into Moses in the cloud and in the sea. They all ate the same spiritual food and drank the same*

spiritual drink; for they drank from the spiritual rock that accompanied them, and that rock was Christ. Nevertheless, God was not pleased with most of them; their bodies were scattered over the desert. *Now these things occurred as examples to keep us from setting our hearts on evil things as they did.* Do not be idolaters, as some of them were; as it is written: "The people sat down to eat and drink and got up to indulge in pagan revelry." We should not commit sexual immorality, as some of them did—and in one day twenty-three thousand of them died. We should not test the Lord, as some of them did—and were killed by snakes. And do not grumble, as some of them did—and were killed by the destroying angel. <u>*These things happened to them as examples and were written down as warnings for us, on whom the fulfillment of the ages has come.*</u> *So, if you think you are standing firm, be careful that you don't fall! No temptation has seized you except what is common to man. And God is faithful; he will not let you be tempted beyond what you can bear. But when you are tempted, he will also provide a way out so that you can stand up under it.* (NIV)

The exodus of the Israelites from Egypt should be a lesson for us today. The Old Testament history of the Israelites, which we followed earlier in this chapter, can be found in a speech that Stephen made before the Sanhedrin just prior to his being martyred. The coming of the Righteous One predicted by the prophets is Jesus Christ.

Acts 7:1-58   *Then the high priest asked him, "Are these charges true?" To this he replied: "Brothers and fathers, listen to me! The God of glory appeared to our father Abraham while he was still in Mesopotamia, before he lived in Haran.* 'Leave your country and your people,' God said, 'and go to the land I will show you.' "So he left the land of the Chaldeans and settled in Haran. After the death of his father, God sent him to this land where you are now living. He gave him no inheritance here, not even a foot of ground. But God promised him that he and his descendants after him would possess the land, even though at that time Abraham had no child. God spoke to him in this way: 'Your descendants will be strangers in a country not their own, and they will be enslaved and mistreated four hundred years. But I will punish the nation they serve as slaves,' God said, 'and afterward they will come out of that country and worship me in this place.' Then he gave Abraham the covenant of circumcision. And Abraham became the father of Isaac and circumcised him eight days after his birth. Later Isaac became the father of Jacob, and Jacob became the father of the twelve patriarchs. "Because the patriarchs were jealous of Joseph, they sold him as a slave into Egypt. But God was with him and rescued him from all his troubles. He gave Joseph *wisdom and enabled him to gain the goodwill of Pharaoh king of Egypt; so he made him ruler over Egypt and all his palace. "Then a famine struck all Egypt and Canaan, bringing great suffering, and our fathers could not find food. When Jacob heard that there was grain in Egypt, he sent our fathers on their first visit. On their second visit, Joseph told his brothers who he was, and Pharaoh learned about Joseph's family. After this, Joseph sent for his father Jacob and his whole family, seventy-five in all. Then Jacob went down to Egypt, where he and our fathers died. Their bodies were brought back to Shechem and placed in the tomb that Abraham had bought from the sons of Hamor at Shechem for a certain sum of money. "As the time drew near for God to fulfill his promise to Abraham, the number of our people in Egypt greatly increased. Then another king, who knew nothing about Joseph, became ruler of Egypt. He dealt treacherously with our people and oppressed our forefathers by forcing them to throw out their newborn babies so that they would die. "At that time Moses was born, and he was no ordinary child. For three months he was cared for in his father's house. When he was placed outside, Pharaoh's daughter took him and brought him up as her own son. Moses was educated in all the wisdom of the Egyptians and was powerful in speech and action. "When Moses was forty years old, he decided to visit his fellow Israelites. He saw one of them being mistreated by an Egyptian, so he went to his defense and avenged him by killing the Egyptian. Moses thought that his own people would realize that God was using him to rescue them, but they did not. The next day Moses came upon two Israelites who were fighting. He tried to reconcile them by saying, 'Men, you are brothers; why do you want to hurt each other?' "But the man who was mistreating the other pushed Moses aside and said, 'Who made you ruler and judge over us? Do you want to kill me as you killed the Egyptian yesterday?' When Moses heard this, he fled to Midian, where he settled as a foreigner and had two sons.* **"After forty years had passed, an angel appeared to Moses in the flames of a burning bush in the desert near Mount Sinai.** *When he saw this, he was amazed at the sight. As he went over to look more closely, he heard the Lord's voice: 'I am the God of your fathers, the God of Abraham, Isaac and Jacob.' Moses trembled with fear and did not dare to look. "Then the Lord said to him, 'Take off your sandals; the place where you are standing is holy ground. I have indeed seen the oppression of my people in Egypt. I have heard their groaning and have come down to set them free. Now come, I will send you back to Egypt.' "This is the same Moses whom they had rejected with the words, 'Who made you ruler and judge?'* <u>**He was sent to be their ruler and deliverer by God himself, through the angel who appeared to him**</u>

Learning From History

<u>in the bush</u>. He led them out of Egypt and did wonders and miraculous signs in Egypt, at the Red Sea and for forty years in the desert. "This is that Moses who told the Israelites, '<u>God will send you a prophet like me from your own people</u>.' He was in the assembly in the desert, with the angel who spoke to him on Mount Sinai, and with our fathers; and he received living words to pass on to us. "But our fathers refused to obey him. Instead, they rejected him and in their hearts turned back to Egypt. They told Aaron, 'Make us gods who will go before us. As for this fellow Moses who led us out of Egypt—we don't know what has happened to him!' That was the time they made an idol in the form of a calf. They brought sacrifices to it and held a celebration in honor of what their hands had made. But God turned away and gave them over to the worship of the heavenly bodies. This agrees with what is written in the book of the prophets: "'Did you bring me sacrifices and offerings forty years in the desert, O house of Israel? You have lifted up the shrine of Molech and the star of your god Rephan, the idols you made to worship. Therefore I will send you into exile' beyond Babylon. **"<u>Our forefathers had the tabernacle of the Testimony with them in the desert</u>. It had been made as God directed Moses, according to the pattern he had seen. Having received the tabernacle, our fathers under Joshua brought it with them when they took the land from the nations God drove out before them. <u>It remained in the land until the time of David, who enjoyed God's favor and asked that he might provide a dwelling place for the God of Jacob. But it was Solomon who built the house for him</u>.** "However, the Most High does not live in houses made by men. As the prophet says: "'Heaven is my throne, and the earth is my footstool. What kind of house will you build for me? says the Lord. Or where will my resting place be? Has not my hand made all these things?' **"You stiff-necked people, with uncircumcised hearts and ears! You are just like your fathers: You always resist the Holy Spirit! <u>Was there ever a prophet your fathers did not persecute</u>? <u>They even killed those who predicted the coming of the Righteous One</u>. And now you have betrayed and murdered him—you who have received the law that was put into effect through angels but have not obeyed it."** When they heard this, they were furious and gnashed their teeth at him. But Stephen, full of the Holy Spirit, looked up to heaven and saw the glory of God, and Jesus standing at the right hand of God. "Look," he said, "I see heaven open and the Son of Man standing at the right hand of God." At this they covered their ears and, yelling at the top of their voices, they all rushed at him, dragged him out of the city and began to stone him. Meanwhile, the witnesses laid their clothes at the feet of a young man named Saul.* (NIV)

AFTER THE RAPTURE

Notice that in the past Moses was sent by God to deliverer the Israelites out of the bondage of the Egyptians, while in the future Jesus will be the deliverer who will be sent by God to deliver the Jewish people out of the bondage of the Antichrist.

As God reminds us of the past experience of the Israelites at Mount Sinai, believers in Jesus can be confident about where the saints are going in the future. At the Rapture the saints will be going to Mount Zion, the heavenly Jerusalem, to be with God and Jesus.

> Heb 12:18-24   *You have not come to a mountain that can be touched and that is burning with fire; to darkness, gloom and storm; to a trumpet blast or to such a voice speaking words that those who heard it begged that no further word be spoken to them, because they could not bear what was commanded: "If even an animal touches the mountain, it must be stoned." The sight was so terrifying that Moses said, "I am trembling with fear."* **But you have come to Mount Zion, to the heavenly Jerusalem, the city of the living God.** ***You have come to thousands upon thousands of angels in joyful assembly, to the church of the firstborn, whose names are written in heaven. You have come to God, the judge of all men, to the spirits of righteous men made perfect, to Jesus the mediator of a new covenant, and to the sprinkled blood that speaks a better word than the blood of Abel.*** (NIV)

In 1445 BC, when the Israelites were on Mount Sinai, God's voice shook the earth. In the future, during the Tribulation Period, God will not only shake the earth, but the heavens as well. The heavens here being a reference to the first and second levels of heaven. The earth can be shaken, but the saints are going to a place that cannot be shaken. The saints are going to the third level of heaven to a kingdom that is in the heavenly city of Jerusalem, the city of the living God.

> Heb 12:25-29   **See to it that you do not refuse him who speaks.** *If they did not escape when they refused him who warned them on earth, how much less will we, if we turn away from him who warns us from heaven? At that time his voice shook the earth, but now he has promised, "Once more I will shake not only the earth but also the heavens." The words "once more" indicate the removing of what can be shaken—that is, created things—so that what cannot be shaken may remain.* ***Therefore, since we are receiving a kingdom that cannot be shaken,*** **let us be thankful, and so worship God acceptably with reverence and awe, for our "God is a consuming fire."** (NIV)

In order to miss the Tribulation Period and the fierce anger of God, be ready to hearken to the voice of Jesus at the Rapture. Are you ready for the Jubilee?

> 1 Thes 4:16   **For the Lord himself will come down from heaven, with a loud**

command, with the voice of the archangel and with the trumpet call of God, and the dead in Christ will rise first. (NIV)

Is God really invisible? Or does He have some sort of physical form, along with the attributes of Omnipotence, Omniscience and Omnipresence?

THE THRONE OF THE LORD — THE LORD IS THERE

Before we close this chapter we need to look at the significance of the activities of God and Jesus during the Day of the Lord after the doom and gloom portion is over and the Temple has been rebuilt and consecrated. The most profound aspect of the Millennium that most Bible scholars, expositors and commentators fail to realize is the fact that the Shekinah Glory will dwell in the Temple in Jerusalem during this time. After this aspect of the appearance of the glory of the Lord is recognized, it clears up many of the Old Testament misconceptions of future prophecy that is yet to be fulfilled. It also helps us understand the subservient duties of Jesus as He carries out the will of God assigned to Him throughout both the Old and New Testament.

Let us begin with Jesus and a short review of His duties during Old Testament times. The translation of the Hebrew word, *mal'ak*, as "angel," instead of "messenger," creates a gross misunderstanding of the significance of Jesus during the time before He came to earth as a human being in the flesh. The phrase "angel of the Lord" and "angel of God," are found scattered throughout the Old Testament. This phrase would be better understood if it were translated as a messenger or representative of God. The personage represented here in the Old Testament is not an angel, but Jesus Christ in His pre-incarnate ministry. As an envoy or emissary of God, this Divine Messenger is closely tied to God and appears with Him as God interacts with the Israelites. Jesus, as this messenger or representative, appeared in the form of a man, but did not have a human body at that time. As this messenger, Jesus was sent to interact and protect the chosen people. Here Jacob, called Israel after God changed his name, is protected from harm by this messenger.

Gen 48:14-16   *But Israel reached out his right hand and put it on Ephraim's head, though he was the younger, and crossing his arms, he put his left hand on Manasseh's head, even though Manasseh was the firstborn.* ***Then he blessed Joseph and said, "May the God before whom my fathers Abraham and Isaac walked, the God who has been my shepherd all my life to this day, the Angel who has delivered me from all harm may he bless these boys.*** *May they be called by my name and the names of my fathers Abraham and Isaac, and may they increase greatly upon the earth."* (NIV)

Here, this Angel is referred to as God. This same messenger appeared to Moses in a burning bush at a crucial time and was commissioned to tell Moses that he would be sent to be their ruler and deliverer and to lead the Israelites out of the bondage of the Egyptians.

AFTER THE RAPTURE

Exod 3:2 — ***There the angel of the LORD appeared to him in flames of fire from within a bush.*** *Moses saw that though the bush was on fire it did not burn up.* (NIV)

Acts 7:35 — *"This is the same Moses whom they had rejected with the words, 'Who made you ruler and judge?'* **He was sent to be their ruler and deliverer by God himself, <u>through the angel who appeared to him in the bush.</u>** (NIV)

Along with protecting the Israelites, this messenger was assigned to be a leader as He lead the Israelites out of Egypt. Jesus (the angel of the God) and God (Shekinah Glory in the pillar of cloud) were both present at that time.

Exod 14:19-21 — **<u>Then the angel of God</u>, who had been traveling in front of Israel's army, withdrew and went behind them. <u>The pillar of cloud</u> also moved from in front and stood behind them, coming between the armies of Egypt and Israel. Throughout the night the cloud brought darkness to the one side and light to the other side; so neither went near the other all night long.** *Then Moses stretched out his hand over the sea, and all that night the LORD drove the sea back with a strong east wind and turned it into dry land. The waters were divided, and the Israelites went through the sea on dry ground, with a wall of water on their right and on their left.* (NIV)

After the Israelite experience with God on Mount Sinai, this Divine Messenger of God was assigned to lead and protect the Israelites as they entered the promised land. Jesus will help them drive out the people who are already living in the land. Pay attention to Him!

Exod 23:20-23 — **"<u>See, I am sending an angel ahead of you to guard you along the way and to bring you to the place I have prepared. Pay attention to him and listen to what he says.</u> Do not rebel against him; he will not forgive your rebellion, since my Name is in him. <u>If you listen carefully to what he says and do all that I say, I will be an enemy to your enemies and will oppose those who oppose you.</u> My angel will go ahead of you and bring you into the land of the Amorites, Hittites, Perizzites, Canaanites, Hivites and Jebusites, and I will wipe them out.** (NIV)

Exod 33:1-3 — *Then the LORD said to Moses, "Leave this place, you and the people you brought up out of Egypt, and go up to the land I promised on oath to Abraham, Isaac and Jacob, saying, 'I will give it to your descendants.'* **I will send an angel before you and drive out the Canaanites, Amorites, Hittites, Perizzites, Hivites and Jebusites.** *Go up to the land flowing with milk and honey. But I will not go with*

Learning From History

you, because you are a stiff-necked people and I might destroy you on the way." (NIV)

Jesus as a messenger appears to Joshua as a man with a drawn sword. He is referred to as *"commander of the army of the Lord."* The Hebrew word, "commander" (captain-KJV) used here, is *sar* and is designated as a head person such as a prince, a ruler, an official, an overseer, a general or commander (military). It is obvious that this commander was with the Israelites as they conquered the land promised to them by God. Notice the Holiness of God.

Josh 5:13-15   *Now when Joshua was near Jericho, he looked up and saw **a man standing in front of him with a drawn sword in his hand. Joshua went up to him and asked, "Are you for us or for our enemies?" "Neither," he replied, "but as commander of the army of the LORD I have now come.***" Then Joshua fell facedown to the ground in reverence, and asked him, "What message does my Lord have for his servant?" **The commander of the LORD's army replied, "Take off your sandals, for the place where you are standing is holy." And Joshua did so.** (NIV)

The Hebrew word used here for "army" (host-KJV), is *tsaba* and refers to a mass of persons, especially organized for war or a campaign. When it is used in the phrase, "the host of heaven," it is referring to the angels and when this word is used in the phrase, "the hosts of the Lord" or "the Lord of hosts," it is a reference to the sons of Israel. The host (army) of God in heaven are the angels, while the host (army) of God on earth are the Israelites. When referring to the Israelites (armies-KJV/hosts-NAS), the New International Version often translates this word as "divisions" (Exodus 7:4; Exodus 12:41).

This Divine Messenger continued to play an active part in the life of the Israelites during the period of the Judges as He spoke to all the children of Israel (Judges 2:4) and Gideon (Judges 6:22). Samuel was aware of this messenger as he likened David to this messenger of God (1 Samuel 29:9; 2 Samuel 14:20). This messenger appeared to the prophet Elijah (1 Kings 19:1-9). David was familiar with this messenger (1 Chronicles 21:16; Psalms 34:7). The prophet Isaiah, below, mentioned this messenger of God's Presence when he referred to the past history of the people of Israel. In verse eleven a reference is made about God and His messenger (angel), here referred to as *"the shepherd of the flock,"* as they brought the Israelites through the Red Sea. The three persons of the trinity are mentioned in these verses. In this instance the words *"saved them,"* might be better translated as *"delivered them."*

Isa 63:7-14   *I will tell of the kindnesses of the LORD, the deeds for which he is to be praised, according to all the LORD has done for us—yes, the many good things he has done for the house of Israel, according to his compassion and many kindnesses. He said, "Surely they are my people, sons who will not be false to me"; and so he became their Savior.* ***In all their distress he too was distressed, and the angel of his presence saved them. In his love and mercy he redeemed them;***

he lifted them up and carried them all the days of old. Yet they rebelled and grieved his Holy Spirit. So he turned and became their enemy and he himself fought against them. **Then his people recalled the days of old, the days of Moses and his people—where is <u>he</u> who brought them through the sea, <u>with the shepherd of his flock</u>? Where is <u>he</u> who set <u>his Holy Spirit</u> among them, who sent his glorious arm of power to be at Moses' right hand, who divided the waters before them, to gain for himself everlasting renown, who led them through the depths?** *Like a horse in open country, they did not stumble; like cattle that go down to the plain, they were given rest by the Spirit of the LORD.* **This is how you guided your people to make for yourself a glorious name.** (NIV)

The prophet Zachariah had multiple conversations with this messenger (Chapters 1-6). A very interesting statement is made by Zachariah concerning this Divine Messenger in chapter twelve. The context of these verses concern the Jewish people who will still be alive after the Tribulation Period. At the Battle of Armageddon (when all the nations of the earth will be coming against God, Jesus and the Jewish people in Jerusalem) God will shield (protect) the saved remnant of Jewish people from the destruction. This future time will resemble the past when the messenger of God went ahead of the Israelites to guide them through the wilderness.

Zech 12:1-9   ***This is the word of the LORD concerning Israel.*** *The LORD, who stretches out the heavens, who lays the foundation of the earth, and who forms the spirit of man within him, declares: "I am going to make Jerusalem a cup that sends all the surrounding peoples reeling. Judah will be besieged as well as Jerusalem. On that day, when all the nations of the earth are gathered against her, I will make Jerusalem an immovable rock for all the nations. All who try to move it will injure themselves. On that day I will strike every horse with panic and its rider with madness," declares the LORD. "I will keep a watchful eye over the house of Judah, but I will blind all the horses of the nations. Then the leaders of Judah will say in their hearts, 'The people of Jerusalem are strong, because the LORD Almighty is their God.' "On that day I will make the leaders of Judah like a firepot in a woodpile, like a flaming torch among sheaves. They will consume right and left all the surrounding peoples, but Jerusalem will remain intact in her place. "The LORD will save the dwellings of Judah first, so that the honor of the house of David and of Jerusalem's inhabitants may not be greater than that of Judah.* ***On that day the LORD will shield those who live in Jerusalem**, so that the feeblest among them will be like David, and the house of David will be like God, **like the Angel of the LORD going before them.*** *On that day I will set out to destroy all the nations that attack Jerusalem.* (NIV)

Finally, as we traverse to the last book of the Old Testament we find this messenger and this time the word *mal'ak* is translated as "messenger" and rightly so! God will send His messenger (Jesus) to the earth to prepare for the return of God (Shekinah Glory). Jesus will prepare the world for God by purging sinful mankind from the earth. In these verses, Jesus is also referred to as *"the messenger of the covenant."* The One who God promised is going to come. *"But who can endure the day of his coming?"* Who can survive the Battle of Armageddon?

Mal 3:1-5   *"<u>Behold, I send My messenger, and he will prepare the way before Me</u>. And the Lord, whom you seek, will suddenly come to His temple, <u>even the Messenger of the covenant</u>, in whom you delight. Behold, He is coming," says the LORD of hosts. "<u>But who can endure the day of His coming? And who can stand when He appears?</u> For He is like a refiner's fire and like launderer's soap. He will sit as a refiner and a purifier of silver; he will purify the sons of Levi, and purge them as gold and silver, that they may offer to the LORD an offering in righteousness. "Then the offering of Judah and Jerusalem will be pleasant to the LORD, as in the days of old, as in former years. <u>And I will come near you for judgment</u>; I will be a swift witness against sorcerers, against adulterers, against perjurers, against those who exploit wage earners and widows and orphans, and against those who turn away an alien—because they do not fear Me," says the LORD of hosts.* (NKJ)

This account of God's messenger is only a small portion of the ministry of Jesus in the Old Testament. Grab a Concordance and look up the word "angel" to follow the story in its entirety. It is a fascinating story! Nevertheless, remember that this is Jesus as a messenger of God and not an angel. Restrict your search to the Old Testament concerning this "angel."

As we move on into the New Testament the story continues and does not miss a beat. In a sense you could say that Jesus, as a Divine Messenger, was sent by God to the world to become flesh and blood. Two thousand years ago Jesus was sent to redeem and save **all** people. Jesus was sent as a suffering servant to die for the sins of humanity.

Phil 2:5-8   *Your attitude should be the same as that of Christ Jesus: Who, being in very nature God, did not consider equality with God something to be grasped, **but made himself nothing, <u>taking the very nature of a servant, being made in human likeness</u>. And being found in appearance as a man, he humbled himself and became obedient to death—even death on a cross!*** (NIV)

Isa 53:4-6   *Surely he took up our infirmities and carried our sorrows, yet we considered him stricken by God, smitten by him, and afflicted. **<u>But he was pierced for our transgressions</u>, he was crushed for our iniquities; the punishment that brought us peace was upon him,***

AFTER THE RAPTURE

and by his wounds we are healed. We all, like sheep, have gone astray, each of us has turned to his own way; <u>and the LORD has laid on him the iniquity of us all.</u> (NIV)

Jesus came from the Father who sent Him from heaven. Jesus had a message from His Father who taught Him. Jesus always does what pleases God. Jesus cannot do anything by Himself, but only what God does and what He commanded Him to say. Even at the time of death, Jesus obeyed His Father's will. The apostle John says it best!

John 1:14 — *The Word became flesh and made his dwelling among us. We have seen his glory, the glory of the One and Only, who came from the Father, full of grace and truth.* (NIV)

John 8:12-30 — *When Jesus spoke again to the people, he said, "I am the light of the world. Whoever follows me will never walk in darkness, but will have the light of life." The Pharisees challenged him, "Here you are, appearing as your own witness; your testimony is not valid." Jesus answered, "Even if I testify on my own behalf, my testimony is valid, for I know where I came from and where I am going. But you have no idea where I come from or where I am going. You judge by human standards; I pass judgment on no one. But if I do judge, my decisions are right, because I am not alone. <u>I stand with the Father, who sent me.</u> In your own Law it is written that the testimony of two men is valid. I am one who testifies for myself; my other witness is the Father, who sent me." Then they asked him, "Where is your father?" "You do not know me or my Father," Jesus replied. "If you knew me, you would know my Father also." He spoke these words while teaching in the temple area near the place where the offerings were put. Yet no one seized him, because his time had not yet come. Once more Jesus said to them, "I am going away, and you will look for me, and you will die in your sin. Where I go, you cannot come." This made the Jews ask, "Will he kill himself? Is that why he says, 'Where I go, you cannot come'?" But he continued, "You are from below; I am from above. You are of this world; I am not of this world. I told you that you would die in your sins; if you do not believe that I am [the one I claim to be], you will indeed die in your sins." "Who are you?" they asked. "Just what I have been claiming all along," Jesus replied. "I have much to say in judgment of you. <u>But he who sent me is reliable, and what I have heard from him I tell the world."</u> They did not understand that he was telling them about his Father. So Jesus said, "When you have lifted up the Son of Man, then you will know that I am [the one I claim to be] and that I do nothing on my own but speak just what the Father has taught me. <u>The one who sent me is with me; he has not left me</u>*

Learning From History

alone, for I always do what pleases him." Even as he spoke, many put their faith in him. (NIV)

John 5:19-23
Jesus gave them this answer: "I tell you the truth, the Son can do nothing by himself; he can do only what he sees his Father doing, because whatever the Father does the Son also does. For the Father loves the Son and shows him all he does. Yes, to your amazement he will show him even greater things than these. For just as the Father raises the dead and gives them life, even so the Son gives life to whom he is pleased to give it. Moreover, the Father judges no one, but has entrusted all judgment to the Son, that all may honor the Son just as they honor the Father. He who does not honor the Son does not honor the Father, who sent him. (NIV)

John 12:47-50
"As for the person who hears my words but does not keep them, I do not judge him. For I did not come to judge the world, but to save it. There is a judge for the one who rejects me and does not accept my words; that very word which I spoke will condemn him at the last day. For I did not speak of my own accord, but the Father who sent me commanded me what to say and how to say it. I know that his command leads to eternal life. So whatever I say is just what the Father has told me to say." (NIV)

John 4:34
"My food," said Jesus, "is to do the will of him who sent me and to finish his work. (NIV)

John 6:38
For I have come down from heaven not to do my will but to do the will of him who sent me. (NIV)

Luke 22:39-44
Jesus went out as usual to the Mount of Olives, and his disciples followed him. On reaching the place, he said to them, "Pray that you will not fall into temptation." He withdrew about a stone's throw beyond them, knelt down and prayed, "Father, if you are willing, take this cup from me; yet not my will, but yours be done." An angel from heaven appeared to him and strengthened him. And being in anguish, he prayed more earnestly, and his sweat was like drops of blood falling to the ground. (NIV)

With this background we can pave the way for a better understanding of God, Jesus, the Jewish people (Israel) and Jerusalem during the peaceful portion of the Day of the Lord.

We have mentioned several times before that Israel (the Jewish people) will finally acknowledge God by recognizing Jesus as their Savior. It is so important in the scheme of things that I would like to mention it one more time. It has been a long time since 1445 BC, when God appeared to the Israelites on Mount Sinai. At that time God promised peace and

AFTER THE RAPTURE

safety for the chosen people in the land of Israel. The prerequisite was for them to follow God's decrees and carefully obey His commands. Throughout history they have failed to accomplish this feat in its entirety. The time is almost here for them to fulfill this command. Notice in the passages below that Jesus, the King of Israel, the Holy One of Israel, will return to be among the Jewish people and protect them. Never again will they fear any harm.

Lev 26:1-13 — *"'Do not make idols or set up an image or a sacred stone for yourselves, and do not place a carved stone in your land to bow down before it. I am the LORD your God. "'Observe my Sabbaths and have reverence for my sanctuary. I am the LORD. "'<u>If you follow my decrees and are careful to obey my commands</u>, I will send you rain in its season, and the ground will yield its crops and the trees of the field their fruit. Your threshing will continue until grape harvest and the grape harvest will continue until planting, and you will eat all the food you want and live in safety in your land. "'I will grant peace in the land, and you will lie down and no one will make you afraid. I will remove savage beasts from the land, and the sword will not pass through your country. You will pursue your enemies, and they will fall by the sword before you. Five of you will chase a hundred, and a hundred of you will chase ten thousand, and your enemies will fall by the sword before you. "'I will look on you with favor and make you fruitful and increase your numbers, and I will keep my covenant with you. You will still be eating last year's harvest when you will have to move it out to make room for the new. <u>I will put my dwelling place among you, and I will not abhor you.</u> I will walk among you and be your God, and you will be my people. I am the LORD your God, who brought you out of Egypt so that you would no longer be slaves to the Egyptians; I broke the bars of your yoke and enabled you to walk with heads held high.* (NIV)

Isa 12:1-6 — *In that day you will say: "I will praise you, O LORD. Although you were angry with me, your anger has turned away and you have comforted me. <u>Surely God is my salvation; I will trust and not be afraid.</u> The LORD, the LORD, is my strength and my song; he has become my salvation." With joy you will draw water from the wells of salvation. In that day you will say: "Give thanks to the LORD, call on his name; make known among the nations what he has done, and proclaim that his name is exalted. Sing to the LORD, for he has done glorious things; let this be known to all the world. Shout aloud and sing for joy, people of Zion, <u>for great is the Holy One of Israel among you.</u>"* (NIV)

Joel 2:25-27 — *'I will repay you for the years the locusts have eaten—the great locust and the young locust, the other locusts and the locust*

Learning From History

*swarm—my great army that I sent among you. You will have plenty to eat, until you are full, and you will praise the name of the LORD your God, who has worked wonders for you; never again will my people be shamed. **Then you will know that I am in Israel, that I am the LORD your God, and that there is no other; <u>never again will my people be shamed.</u>*** (NIV)

Zeph 3:14-17   *Sing, O Daughter of Zion; shout aloud, O Israel! Be glad and rejoice with all your heart, O Daughter of Jerusalem! The LORD has taken away your punishment, he has turned back your enemy. **<u>The LORD, the King of Israel, is with you; never again will you fear any harm.</u>** On that day they will say to Jerusalem, "Do not fear, O Zion; do not let your hands hang limp. **<u>The LORD your God is with you, he is mighty to save.</u>** He will take great delight in you, he will quiet you with his love, he will rejoice over you with singing."* (NIV)

Jerusalem will finally become the city of peace. God will return and dwell in Jerusalem among His people. Zion, on the holy hill (Holy Mountain), will be the area in Jerusalem where the Temple will be located.

Zech 8:1-3   *Again the word of the LORD Almighty came to me. This is what the LORD Almighty says: "I am very jealous for Zion; I am burning with jealousy for her." **This is what the LORD says: "<u>I will return to Zion and dwell in Jerusalem. Then Jerusalem will be called the City of Truth, and the mountain of the LORD Almighty will be called the Holy Mountain.</u>"*** (NIV)

Joel 3:17-21   *'Then you will know that I, the LORD your God, dwell in Zion, my holy hill. Jerusalem will be holy; never again will foreigners invade her. 'In that day the mountains will drip new wine, and the hills will flow with milk; all the ravines of Judah will run with water. A fountain will flow out of the LORD's house and will water the valley of acacias. But Egypt will be desolate, Edom a desert waste, because of violence done to the people of Judah, in whose land they shed innocent blood. Judah will be inhabited forever and Jerusalem through all generations. Their bloodguilt, which I have not pardoned, I will pardon.' **<u>The LORD dwells in Zion!</u>*** (NIV)

One of the biggest and most important pieces of the eschatological puzzle is the Shekinah Glory. Once that piece is placed in the puzzle—the glory of the Lord dwelling on the earth during the Millennium—a clear understanding of Old Testament prophecy begins to unfold. The activities of God and Jesus become distinguished and separated into their proper perspective. The total plan of God begins to organize itself and come together. As we look at the Shekinah Glory, we begin where scripture records the return of the glory of the

Lord of Israel from heaven to the Temple in Jerusalem, a place for God to rest the soles of His feet. This will probably take place in the very near future.

By this time Jesus will have rebuilt the Temple in Jerusalem and at the dedication ceremony the glory of the Lord (Shekinah Glory) will return to earth and will once again dwell among His people. Ezekiel, the prophet who saw the glory of the Lord leave the Temple in 593 BC, also had a vision of the glory of the Lord returning to dwell among His people forever. The whole land of Israel will shine from the radiance of God's glory for the remainder of the Day of the Lord and on into eternity in the new earth.

> Ezek 43:1-12 — ***Then the man brought me to the gate facing east, and I saw the glory of the God of Israel coming from the east. His voice was like the roar of rushing waters, and the land was radiant with his glory.** The vision I saw was like the vision I had seen when he came to destroy the city and like the visions I had seen by the Kebar River, and I fell facedown. **The glory of the LORD entered the temple through the gate facing east.** Then the Spirit lifted me up and brought me into the inner court, **and the glory of the LORD filled the temple.** While the man was standing beside me, I heard someone speaking to me from inside the temple. He said: "Son of man, this is the place of my throne and the place for the soles of my feet. **This is where I will live among the Israelites forever.** The house of Israel will never again defile my holy name—neither they nor their kings—by their prostitution and the lifeless idols of their kings at their high places. When they placed their threshold next to my threshold and their doorposts beside my doorposts, with only a wall between me and them, they defiled my holy name by their detestable practices. So I destroyed them in my anger. **Now let them put away from me their prostitution and the lifeless idols of their kings, and I will live among them forever.** "Son of man, describe the temple to the people of Israel, that they may be ashamed of their sins. Let them consider the plan, and if they are ashamed of all they have done, make known to them the design of the temple—its arrangement, its exits and entrances—its whole design and all its regulations and laws. Write these down before them so that they may be faithful to its design and follow all its regulations. **"This is the law of the temple: All the surrounding area on top of the mountain will be most holy. Such is the law of the temple.*** (NIV)

In Isaiah it is clear that the glory of the Lord will not return until after His people (Israel) have been punished double for all of their sins. This will happen when Israel's warfare has ended and she has been pardoned of her iniquity. During this future time, after the punishment has been completed, all the people who are living on the earth (in the flesh) will be able to observe the cloud of smoke by day and the shining of fire by night. What a comfort it will be for the people living on the earth at that time.

Learning From History

Isa 40:1-5 *"Comfort, yes, comfort My people!" Says your God. "Speak comfort to Jerusalem, and cry out to her, that her warfare is ended, that her iniquity is pardoned; for she has received from the LORD'S hand double for all her sins." <u>The voice of one crying in the wilderness</u>: "Prepare the way of the LORD; make straight in the desert a highway for our God. Every valley shall be exalted and every mountain and hill brought low; the crooked places shall be made straight and the rough places smooth; <u>The glory of the LORD shall be revealed, and all flesh shall see it together</u>; for the mouth of the LORD has spoken."* (NKJ)

In these verses, *"The voice of one crying in the wilderness"* is referring to Jesus who will be preparing the way for the glory of the Lord, even though a partial fulfillment of this event took place at the first appearing of Jesus, when John the Baptist is said to have fulfilled this prophecy. All four of the gospel records mention this event (Matthew 3:1-3; Mark 1:1-3; Luke 3:1-6; John 1:23). In the account listed in the book of Luke we see that he quoted Isaiah 40:3-5, only with a different twist.

Luke 3:2 6 *while Annas and Caiaphas were high priests, the word of God came to John the son of Zacharias in the wilderness. **And he went into all the region around the Jordan, preaching a baptism of repentance for the remission of sins, as it is written in the book of the words of Isaiah the prophet, saying: "The voice of one crying in the wilderness: 'Prepare the way of the Lord, make His paths straight. Every valley shall be filled and every mountain and hill brought low; the crooked places shall be made straight and the rough ways smooth; <u>And all flesh shall see the salvation of God</u>.'"*** (NKJ)

The account in Isaiah 40:4-5 was never fulfilled when Christ appeared the first time. These verses will be fulfilled at His second coming. The difference in these two accounts appear in Luke 3:6 and Isaiah 40:5 (underlined above). Luke 3:6 was fulfilled at the first advent of Christ when all mankind (flesh) was allowed to see God's salvation, which came from heaven when Jesus Christ appeared in the flesh. Isaiah 40:5 will not be fulfilled until the second advent of Jesus Christ, when the glory of the LORD (God) returns to the Temple and all mankind is allowed to view the radiance of God (Shekinah Glory).

This does not make the Bible incorrect. What is incorrect is man's understanding of the two passages. Until you realize that the glory of the Lord (Divine Presence) will dwell among His people during the Millennium, these two passages are hard to understand. Because of the rejection of Jesus, the final fulfillment of this prophecy will come in the future. In the meantime, John the Baptist was the forerunner of Jesus almost 2000 years ago and Jesus will be the forerunner of God (glory of the Lord) sometime in the near future. This is the same type of the partial fulfillment of Joel 2:28-32, as quoted in Acts 2:16-21 (pour out my spirit), and Isaiah 61:1-2, fulfilled in part in Luke 4:14-21 (the year of the Lord's favor).

Isa 35:1-2 *The desert and the parched land will be glad; the wilderness will rejoice and blossom. Like the crocus, it will burst into bloom; it will rejoice greatly and shout for joy. The glory of Lebanon will be given to it, the splendor of Carmel and Sharon; <u>they will see the glory of the LORD</u>, <u>the splendor of our God</u>.* (NIV)

The activity of the glory of the Lord (Shekinah Glory), during the Millennium, is of paramount importance in understanding God's future interaction with His chosen people Israel. It is mentioned numerous times in scripture, but has been misunderstood by Bible expositors. In Psalms we find a scene where God has restored the fortunes of Jacob (Israel) during the Day of the Lord. This scene reveals the time when the glory of the Lord will be dwelling in the land of Jacob (Israel).

Ps 85:1-9 *You showed favor to your land, O LORD; you restored the fortunes of Jacob. You forgave the iniquity of your people and covered all their sins. Selah You set aside all your wrath and turned from your fierce anger. **Restore us again, O God our Savior, and put away your displeasure toward us. Will you be angry with us forever? Will you prolong your anger through all generations? Will you not revive us again, that your people may rejoice in you?** Show us your unfailing love, O LORD, and grant us your salvation. I will listen to what God the LORD will say; he promises peace to his people, his saints—but let them not return to folly. <u>**Surely his salvation is near those who fear him, that his glory may dwell in our land.**</u>* (NIV)

The remaining verses in this Psalm give us a poetic description of what it will be like on earth after the glory of the Lord returns to dwell among His people. Note the first word!

Ps 85:10-13 <u>***Love***</u> ***and faithfulness meet together; righteousness and peace kiss each other. Faithfulness springs forth from the earth, and righteousness looks down from heaven. The LORD will indeed give what is good, and our land will yield its harvest. Righteousness goes before him and prepares the way for his steps.*** (NIV)

Because of the radiance of the glory of the Lord on Mount Zion in Jerusalem at this time, the sun and the moon will no longer be required to bring light to the city of Jerusalem, while the rest of the world will continue to have darkness during the night. Anyone headed to Jerusalem from around the world will view this spectacular sight long before they reach their destination. All the way from Mount Carmel and the Plain of Sharon, the nations of the world will come to this light and the knowledge of it will be known around the world.

Isa 35:1-2 *The desert and the parched land will be glad; the wilderness will rejoice and blossom. Like the crocus, it will burst into bloom; it will rejoice greatly and shout for joy.* **The glory of Lebanon will be given**

	to it, the splendor of Carmel and Sharon; *they will see the glory of the LORD, the splendor of our God.* (NIV)
Isa 60:19-22	*The sun will no more be your light by day, nor will the brightness of the moon shine on you, for the LORD will be your everlasting light, and your God will be your glory.* *Your sun will never set again, and your moon will wane no more; the LORD will be your everlasting light, and your days of sorrow will end.* Then will all your people be righteous and they will possess the land forever. They are the shoot I have planted, the work of my hands, for the display of my splendor. The least of you will become a thousand, the smallest a mighty nation. *I am the LORD; in its time I will do this swiftly."* (NIV)
Isa 60:1-3	*"Arise, shine, for your light has come, and the glory of the LORD rises upon you.* See, darkness covers the earth and thick darkness is over the peoples, but the LORD rises upon you and his glory appears over you. *Nations will come to your light, and kings to the brightness of your dawn.* (NIV)
Hab 2:14	*For the earth will be filled with the knowledge of the glory of the LORD, as the waters cover the sea.* (NIV)

So far in this section we have looked at God and Jesus from an individual perspective. As we look at the two as a combined force we can define the duties of each part of the Deity collectively during the Day of the Lord. We can separate the minuteness of each character as they perform together. The prophet Hosea informs us that the Israelites will live many days without a king or prince (ruler). God was Israel's King when He was dwelling on earth.

Hosea 3:4-5	*For the Israelites will live many days without king or prince, without sacrifice or sacred stones, without ephod or idol. Afterward the Israelites will return and seek the LORD their God and David their king.* They will come trembling to the LORD and to his blessings *in the last days.* (NIV)

These verses reveal the plural form of the Deity after the Israelites return to God. Here we see them as they seek the LORD their God and David their King (Jesus). Christ will inherit the throne of David, as David's heir. Notice that the time frame for this is in the last days. In Isaiah we see the two more distinctly. I have separated these verses for clarity.

Isa 4:2-4	*In that day the Branch of the LORD will be beautiful and glorious, and the fruit of the land will be the pride and glory of the survivors in Israel. Those who are left in Zion, who remain in Jerusalem, will be called holy, all who are recorded among the living in*

> *Jerusalem. The Lord will wash away the filth of the women of Zion; he will cleanse the bloodstains from Jerusalem by a spirit of judgment and a spirit of fire.* (NIV)

Isa 4:5-6 <u>**Then the LORD will create over all of Mount Zion and over those who assemble there a cloud of smoke by day and a glow of flaming fire by night;**</u> *over all the glory will be a canopy. It will be a shelter and shade from the heat of the day, and a refuge and hiding place from the storm and rain.* (NIV)

In Isaiah 4:2-4, we have in view Jesus (the Branch of the LORD) as King, beautiful and glorious. With Him are the righteous Jewish people who will survive the Tribulation Period and the Battle of Armageddon. In Isaiah 4:5-6, we see God (the LORD) as the Shekinah Glory after He returns to dwell in the Temple in Jerusalem. Notice the similarity here with that of the glory of the Lord in Exodus chapter nineteen.

Since we took a more comprehensive look at the Shekinah Glory earlier, I would like to take a more detailed look at Jesus and His role as King during the Day of the Lord. Let us look at the reign of Jesus from three different aspects; as a Prince, as My Servant David and as a King. Notice how the duties of Jesus tie in perfectly with God during the Day of the Lord. Also notice how these three different aspects come together as a single component.

As we begin with the word "prince" in the Bible, we find that there are several Hebrew, Aramaic and Greek words translated as prince. Other words translated from these words include; ruler, leader, chief and captain. It appears that the first time the word "Prince," as translated into English, is used to apply to Jesus is found in Isaiah 9:6. In these amazing verses we find Jesus at His first advent as a child and a Mighty King at His second advent.

Isa 9:6-7 <u>**For to us a child is born**</u>*, to us a son is given, and the government will be on his shoulders. And he will be called Wonderful Counselor, Mighty God, Everlasting Father,* **Prince of Peace***. Of the increase of his government and peace there will be no end.* <u>**He will reign on David's throne and over his kingdom**</u>*, establishing and upholding it with justice and righteousness from that time on and forever. The zeal of the LORD Almighty will accomplish this.* (NIV)

Interestingly enough, the Hebrew word *sar*, used here for "Prince," is the same word that is translated as "commander" (captain-KJV) in Joshua 5:14-15, where the reference is to Jesus as the commander of the army (host/Israelites) of the Lord. We alluded to this earlier in this chapter on page 649.

The most concentrated use of the word prince, as it applies to Jesus, can be found in Ezekiel 40-48, where the subject matter applies to the rebuilt Temple during the Day of the Lord. The Hebrew word for "prince," used here, is *nasiy'*. In this context the prince fulfills his office as High Priest. He will present the offerings to the Lord God of Israel, where God will be seated between the cherubim on the Mercy Seat in the Holy of Holies (the Most Holy Place). This is the same way sacrifices were offered during Old Testament times.

Learning From History

Lev 16:2   *The LORD said to Moses: "Tell your brother Aaron not to come whenever he chooses into <u>the Most Holy Place</u> behind the curtain in front of the atonement cover on the ark, or else he will die, <u>because I appear in the cloud over the atonement cover.</u>* (NIV)

Ezek 44:1-3   *Then the man brought me back to the outer gate of the sanctuary, the one facing east, and it was shut. The LORD said to me, "This gate is to remain shut. It must not be opened; no one may enter through it. It is to remain shut because the LORD, the God of Israel, has entered through it.* **<u>The prince</u> himself is the only one who may sit inside the gateway to eat in the presence of the LORD.** *He is to enter by way of the portico of the gateway and go out the same way."* (NIV)

Ezek 46:1-4   *"'This is what the Sovereign LORD says: The gate of the inner court facing east is to be shut on the six working days, but on the Sabbath day and on the day of the New Moon it is to be opened.* **The prince is to enter from the outside through the portico of the gateway and stand by the gatepost.** *The priests are to sacrifice his burnt offering and his fellowship offerings. He is to worship at the threshold of the gateway and then go out, but the gate will not be shut until evening. On the Sabbaths and New Moons the people of the land are to worship in the presence of the LORD at the entrance to that gateway.* **The burnt offering the prince brings to the LORD on the Sabbath day is to be six male lambs and a ram, all without defect.** (NIV)

Ezek 46:9-12   *"'When the people of the land come before the LORD at the appointed feasts, whoever enters by the north gate to worship is to go out the south gate; and whoever enters by the south gate is to go out the north gate. No one is to return through the gate by which he entered, but each is to go out the opposite gate.* **<u>The prince is to be among them,</u> going in when they go in and going out when they go out.** *"'At the festivals and the appointed feasts, the grain offering is to be an ephah with a bull, an ephah with a ram, and with the lambs as much as one pleases, along with a hin of oil for each ephah. When the prince provides a freewill offering to the LORD —whether a burnt offering or fellowship offerings—the gate facing east is to be opened for him. He shall offer his burnt offering or his fellowship offerings as he does on the Sabbath day. Then he shall go out, and after he has gone out, the gate will be shut.* (NIV)

Ezek 48:21-22   *"What remains on both sides of the area formed by the sacred portion and the city property will belong to <u>the prince</u>. It will extend eastward from the 25,000 cubits of the sacred portion to the eastern* *border, and westward from the 25,000 cubits to the western border.* ***Both these areas running the length of the tribal portions will belong to the prince, and the sacred portion with the temple sanctuary will be in the center of them.*** *So the property of the Levites and the property of the city will lie in the center of the area that belongs to the prince.* ***<u>The area belonging to the prince will lie between the border of Judah and the border of Benjamin.</u>*** (NIV)

As we progress to the New Testament we find two unique listings for Jesus as "Prince" in the book of Acts.

Acts 3:13-15 *"The God of Abraham, Isaac, and Jacob, the God of our fathers, glorified <u>His Servant Jesus</u>, whom you delivered up and denied in the presence of Pilate, when he was determined to let Him go. "But you denied <u>the Holy One and the Just</u>, and asked for a murderer to be granted to you, "and killed <u>the Prince of life</u>, whom God raised from the dead, of which we are witnesses.* (NKJ)

Acts 5:29-31 *Peter and the other apostles replied: "We must obey God rather than men! The God of our fathers raised Jesus from the dead—whom you had killed by hanging him on a tree. God exalted him to his own right hand <u>as Prince and Savior</u> that he might give repentance and forgiveness of sins to Israel.* (NIV)

In Acts 3:15, the New International Version translates the word "Prince," as *"author of life,"* instead of *"Prince of life,"* which is used in the New King James version. Two other verses in the book of Hebrews use this Greek word *archegos* as "author," referring to Jesus. The King James translation uses the word "captain" in Hebrews 2:10.

Heb 2:10 *In bringing many sons to glory, it was fitting that God, for whom and through whom everything exists, should make <u>the author of their salvation</u> perfect through suffering.* (NIV)

Heb 12:2 *Let us fix our eyes on <u>Jesus, the author</u> and perfecter of our faith, who for the joy set before him endured the cross, scorning its shame, and sat down at the right hand of the throne of God.* (NIV)

A point of interest can be found here concerning the archangel as He is mentioned in 1 Thessalonians 4:16, where the voice of the archangel is heard at the Rapture.

1 Thes 4:16 *For the Lord himself will come down from heaven, with a loud command, <u>with the voice of the archangel</u> and with the trumpet call of God, and the dead in Christ will rise first.* (NIV)

Learning From History

The Greek word used here for "archangel" is *archaggelos*. Now notice the similarity to the Greek word *archegos,* which is used for "Prince" and "author" in the two passages in Acts and the two verses in Hebrews listed above. There are two words that make up "Prince" and "archangel." Some very interesting thoughts develop as we look at these four words.

"Prince" comes from the Greek word *archegos*.

Strong's Definition
747 archegos (ar-khay-gos');
from 746 and 71; a chief leader:
KJV— author, captain, prince.

Thayer's Definition
747 archegos-
1) the chief leader, prince;
   used of Christ
2) one that takes the lead in anything and thus affords an example, a predecessor in a matter, a pioneer
3) the author

The first part of the word used for "Prince" and "author" (*archegos*) used in the books of Acts and Hebrews comes from the Greek word *arche*.

Strong's Definition
746 arche (ar-khay');
from 756; (properly abstract) a commencement, or (concretely) chief (in various applications of order, time, place, or rank):
KJV—beginning, corner, (at the, the) first (estate), magistrate, power, principality, principle, rule.

The second part of the word used for "Prince" and "author" is *ago*.

Strong's Definition
71 ago (ag'-o);
a primary verb; properly, to lead; by implication, to bring, drive, (reflexively) go, (specially) pass (time), or (figuratively) induce:
KJV—be, bring (forth), carry, (let) go, keep, lead away, be open.

"Archangel" comes from the Greek word *archaggelos*.

Strong's Definition
743 archaggelos (ar-khang'-el-os);
from 757 and 32; a chief angel:
KJV— archangel.

AFTER THE RAPTURE

The first part of the word "archangel" (*archaggelos*), found in 1 Thessalonians 4:16, comes from the Greek word *archo*.

Strong's Definition
757 archo (ar'-kho);
a primary verb; to be first (in political rank or power):
KJV—reign (rule) over.

Thayer's Definition
757 archo-
to be chief, to lead, to rule

The second part of the word used for "archangel" is *aggelos* and is probably derived from the word *ago* listed above. Remember that this word is not necessarily an angel.

Strong's Definition
32 aggelos (ang'-el-os);
from aggello [probably derived from 71; compare 34] (to bring tidings); a messenger; especially an "angel"; by implication, a pastor:
KJV—angel, messenger.

Thayer's Definition
32 aggelos-
a messenger, an envoy, one who was sent, an angel, a messenger from God

I think it would be fair to say that the "Prince" and the "archangel" listed in the scripture verses above, is probably the same person. The Prince is the chief leader (first in rank) of salvation and the archangel is the chief (first in rank) ruling messenger (the Messiah), the chief leader or Prince who will rule over the world during the Millennium, God's messenger sent for this purpose. Jesus will end the present age we are living in with the words, *"Come up here!"* This will also be the beginning of a new age and the time for Jesus to begin His reign as King. He will be the Prince (ruler) among the kings (leaders) of the world.

> Rev 1:4-5 *John to the seven churches which are in Asia: Grace be unto you, and peace, from him which is, and which was, and which is to come; and from the seven Spirits which are before his throne;* **And from Jesus Christ, who is the faithful witness, and the first begotten of the dead, and <u>the prince of the kings of the earth</u>. Unto him that loved us, and washed us from our sins in his own blood,** (KJV)

The second aspect that deals with Jesus as He rules as King during the Day of the Lord comes from the phrase, *"My Servant David."* Jesus is often referred to as David and as I mentioned earlier, Jesus will occupy David's throne as his heir. Jesus will be given power and authority to become King and His kingdom will be on earth. This kingdom will be

Learning From History

mediatorial in the sense that Jesus as King and High Priest will be the mediator between the people on earth and God during this time, who will also be dwelling on the earth.

Dan 7:13-14   *"In my vision at night I looked, and there before me was <u>one like a son of man</u>, coming with the clouds of heaven. He approached the Ancient of Days and was led into his presence. <u>He was given authority</u>, glory and sovereign power; all peoples, nations and men of every language worshiped him. His dominion is an everlasting dominion that will not pass away, <u>and his kingdom is one that will never be destroyed</u>.* (NIV)

Ps 89:19-29   *Once you spoke in a vision, to your faithful people you said: "<u>I have bestowed strength on a warrior</u>; I have exalted a young man from among the people. <u>I have found David my servant</u>; with my sacred oil I have anointed him.* My hand will sustain him; surely my arm will strengthen him. No enemy will subject him to tribute; no wicked man will oppress him. I will crush his foes before him and strike down his adversaries. *My faithful love will be with him, and through my name his horn will be exalted.* I will set his hand over the sea, his right hand over the rivers. *He will call out to me, 'You are my Father, my God, the Rock my Savior.' <u>I will also appoint him my firstborn</u>, <u>the most exalted of the kings of the earth</u>. I will maintain my love to him forever, and my covenant with him will never fail. <u>I will establish his line forever</u>, <u>his throne as long as the heavens endure</u>.* (NIV)

Zech 6:11-13   Take the silver and gold and make a crown, and set it on the head of the high priest, Joshua son of Jehozadak. *Tell him this is what the LORD Almighty says: '<u>Here is the man whose name is the Branch</u>, and he will branch out from his place and build the temple of the LORD. It is he who will build the temple of the LORD, <u>and he will be clothed with majesty and will sit and rule on his throne</u>. <u>And he will be a priest on his throne</u>. <u>And there will be harmony between the two</u>.'* (NIV)

God will establish a universal head over the entire world and He will rule from Jerusalem. The people of the world will have one Shepherd. Jesus will rule the affairs of the world and as High Priest, He will present the sacrificial offerings to God in the Temple. The Glory of the Lord will be their God (dwelling in the Temple) and Jesus will be their King.

Ezek 34:23-24   *I will place over them <u>one shepherd</u>, <u>my servant David</u>, and he will tend them; he will tend them and be their shepherd. <u>I the LORD will be their God</u>, <u>and my servant David will be prince among them</u>. I the LORD have spoken.* (NIV)

AFTER THE RAPTURE

Ezek 37:24-28 *"'<u>My servant David will be king over them, and they will all have one shepherd</u>. They will follow my laws and be careful to keep my decrees. They will live in the land I gave to my servant Jacob, the land where your fathers lived. **They and their children and their children's children will live there forever, <u>and David my servant will be their prince forever</u>. I will make a covenant of peace with them; it will be an everlasting covenant. I will establish them and increase their numbers, and I will put my sanctuary among them forever. My dwelling place will be with them; I will be their God, and they will be my people.** Then the nations will know that I the LORD make Israel holy, when my sanctuary is among them forever.'"* (NIV)

Micah 5:4 <u>*He will stand and shepherd his flock in the strength of the LORD*</u>, *in the majesty of the name of the LORD his God. And they will live securely, for then his greatness will reach to the ends of the earth.* (NIV)

Isa 55:3-5 *Give ear and come to me; hear me, that your soul may live. I will make an everlasting covenant with you, my faithful love promised to <u>David</u>. <u>See, I have made him a witness to the peoples, a leader and commander of the peoples</u>. Surely you will summon nations you know not, and nations that do not know you will hasten to you, because of the LORD your God, the Holy One of Israel, for he has endowed you with splendor."* (NIV)

1 Pet 5:1-4 *To the elders among you, I appeal as a fellow elder, a witness of Christ's sufferings and one who also will share in the glory to be revealed: Be shepherds of God's flock that is under your care, serving as overseers—not because you must, but because you are willing, as God wants you to be; not greedy for money, but eager to serve; not lording it over those entrusted to you, but being examples to the flock. And when <u>the Chief Shepherd</u> appears, you will receive the crown of glory that will never fade away.* (NIV)

Rev 3:7 *"To the angel of the church in Philadelphia write: These are the words of him who is holy and true, <u>who holds the key of David</u>. What he opens no one can shut, and what he shuts no one can open.* (NIV)

The third and final aspect of Jesus as He reigns on earth during the Day of the Lord is as a King, but not only a King—**KING OF KINGS AND LORD OF LORDS.** The most peaceful and prosperous period of time, since the fall of mankind, will exist on earth during the peaceful portion of the Millennium. In Psalms 72, below, we find the entire 1000 year

Learning From History

reign of Jesus as King in the context of these verses. It begins with the cleansing process of the Tribulation Period and the Battle of Armageddon and even mentions the defeat of the Antichrist (the oppressor). These verses end with the peaceful portion of the Millennium. Long live the King!

Ps 72:1-20   *__Endow the king with your justice__, O God, __the royal son__ with your righteousness. He will judge your people in righteousness, your afflicted ones with justice.* The mountains will bring prosperity to the people, the hills the fruit of righteousness. **He will defend the afflicted among the people and save the children of the needy; __he will crush the oppressor__.** He will endure as long as the sun, as long as the moon, through all generations. He will be like rain falling on a mown field, like showers watering the earth. In his days the righteous will flourish; prosperity will abound till the moon is no more. **He will rule from sea to sea and from the River to the ends of the earth.** The desert tribes will bow before him and his enemies will lick the dust. The kings of Tarshish and of distant shores will bring tribute to him; the kings of Sheba and Seba will present him gifts. **All kings will bow down to him and all nations will serve him.** For he will deliver the needy who cry out, the afflicted who have no one to help. He will take pity on the weak and the needy and save the needy from death. He will rescue them from oppression and violence, for precious is their blood in his sight. **Long may he live!** May gold from Sheba be given him. May people ever pray for him and bless him all day long. Let grain abound throughout the land; on the tops of the hills may it sway. Let its fruit flourish like Lebanon; let it thrive like the grass of the field. **May his name endure forever; may it continue as long as the sun.** All nations will be blessed through him, and they will call him blessed. **Praise be to the LORD God, the God of Israel, who alone does marvelous deeds. Praise be to his glorious name forever; __may the whole earth be filled with his glory__.** Amen and Amen. This concludes the prayers of David son of Jesse. (NIV)

Isa 32:1   *See, a king will reign in righteousness and rulers will rule with justice.* (NIV)

Zech 14:9-11   *__The LORD will be king over the whole earth. On that day there will be one LORD, and his name the only name__. The whole land, from Geba to Rimmon, south of Jerusalem, will become like the Arabah. But Jerusalem will be raised up and remain in its place, from the Benjamin Gate to the site of the First Gate, to the Corner Gate, and from the Tower of Hananel to the royal winepresses. It will be inhabited; never again will it be destroyed. Jerusalem will be secure.* (NIV)

Phil 2:9-11	*Therefore God exalted him to the highest place and gave him the name that is above every name, that at the name of Jesus every knee should bow, in heaven and on earth and under the earth, and every tongue confess that Jesus Christ is Lord, to the glory of God the Father.* (NIV)
Rev 17:14	*They will make war against the Lamb, but the Lamb will overcome them because he is Lord of lords and King of kings—and with him will be his called, chosen and faithful followers."* (NIV)
Rev 19:16	*On his robe and on his thigh he has this name written: **KING OF KINGS AND LORD OF LORDS**.* (NIV)

For the Jewish people this King will be one of their own. Their ruler will rise from among their own people. He came once before, but was rejected by them. When He comes again, this time it will be different. Even their God (glory of the Lord), who departed from among their midst, will return to His Temple where Jesus will be close to Him. In 1 Samuel 4:4, the title "the LORD of hosts," is referring to God the Father.

Jer 30:18-22	*"This is what the LORD says: "'I will restore the fortunes of Jacob's tents and have compassion on his dwellings; the city will be rebuilt on her ruins, and the palace will stand in its proper place. From them will come songs of thanksgiving and the sound of rejoicing. I will add to their numbers, and they will not be decreased; I will bring them honor, and they will not be disdained. Their children will be as in days of old, and their community will be established before me; I will punish all who oppress them. **Their leader will be one of their own; their ruler will arise from among them.** I will bring him near and he will come close to me, for who is he who will devote himself to be close to me?' declares the LORD. "'**So you will be my people, and I will be your God**.'"* (NIV)
1 Sam 4:4	*So the people sent to Shiloh, that they might bring from there the ark of the covenant of **the LORD of hosts, who dwells between the cherubim**. And the two sons of Eli, Hophni and Phinehas, were there with the ark of the covenant of God.* (NKJ)

Jesus is far more active in the Old Testament than people realize today. The only way to distinguish between Jesus and God is by names and titles. Just like God the Father, Jesus the Son has many names and phrases that pertain to Him. The only way you can follow the activities of Jesus in the Old Testament is by recognizing these names and phrases. In the Old Testament look for Jesus with such titles as; the word, a man, the angel (messenger) of the Lord, the commander of the Lord's army, a (future) King, a Redeemer, an anointed one (the coming Messiah), David, Prince of Peace, the Branch, a Rock, a shepherd, a priest, the

Learning From History

son of man, a suffering servant, the Lord of hosts and the Mighty One of Jacob (Israel).

Jesus is equal with God, but He is also a servant to do God's every will. In the Old Testament, He was sent by God to watch over, guide and lead the chosen people in the past, beginning with Abraham. In the future, Jesus will rule over the Jewish people as the Mighty One of Jacob (Israel). Jesus did not take His equality with God lightly (Philippians 2:5-7).

John 5:18 *For this reason the Jews tried all the harder to kill him; not only was he breaking the Sabbath, but he was even calling God his own Father, making himself equal with God.* (NIV)

This chapter expounds on the idea that both God and Jesus will dwell on earth during the Day of the Lord; God, as the God of Israel and the nations and Jesus as the Mighty One of Jacob and the King of the world. Together, along with the Holy Spirit, they will perform their duties as ascribed by God during this 1000 year period.

Hosea 3:5 *Afterward the Israelites will return and seek the LORD their God and David their king. They will come trembling to the LORD and to his blessings in the last days.* (NIV)

Rev 11:15 *The seventh angel sounded his trumpet, and there were loud voices in heaven, which said: "The kingdom of the world has become the kingdom of our Lord and of his Christ, and he will reign for ever and ever."* (NIV)

Jer 3:17 *At that time they will call Jerusalem **The Throne of the LORD**, and all nations will gather in Jerusalem to honor the name of the LORD. No longer will they follow the stubbornness of their evil hearts.* (NIV)

Ezek 48:35 *"The distance all around will be 18,000 cubits. "And the name of the city from that time on will be: **THE LORD IS THERE**."* (NIV)

VISIONS OF GOD AND JESUS

As a finale to this chapter I think it would be appropriate to take a look at various verses in the Bible that reveal God and Jesus. Most of these scripture accounts are from visions, but some of these accounts are actually God or Jesus as they interact with someone on earth. We begin with God as He appears to the Israelites at the exodus as they were leaving Egypt and heading for the promised land. These particular appearances are literal and are not visions. These, of course, were appearances of the Shekinah Glory.

Exod 13:20-22 *After leaving Succoth they camped at Etham on the edge of the desert. By day the LORD went ahead of them in a pillar of cloud to guide them on their way and by night in a pillar of fire to give them* light, so that they could travel by day or night. Neither the pillar of cloud by day nor the pillar of fire by night left its place in front of the people.* (NIV)

Exod 24:9-11 *Moses and Aaron, Nadab and Abihu, and the seventy elders of Israel went up and saw the God of Israel. Under his feet was something like a pavement made of sapphire, clear as the sky itself. But God did not raise his hand against these leaders of the Israelites; they saw God, and they ate and drank.* (NIV)

Exod 24:17 *To the Israelites the glory of the LORD looked like a consuming fire on top of the mountain.* (NIV)

Exod 33:9-11 *As Moses went into the tent, the pillar of cloud would come down and stay at the entrance, while the LORD spoke with Moses. Whenever the people saw the pillar of cloud standing at the entrance to the tent, they all stood and worshiped, each at the entrance to his tent.* **The LORD would speak to Moses face to face, as a man speaks with his friend.** *Then Moses would return to the camp, but his young aide Joshua son of Nun did not leave the tent.* (NIV)

Exod 33:21-23 *Then the LORD said, "There is a place near me where you may stand on a rock. When my glory passes by, I will put you in a cleft in the rock and cover you with my hand until I have passed by. Then I will remove my hand and you will see my back; but my face must not be seen."* (NIV)

Deut 4:11-12 *You came near and stood at the foot of the mountain while it blazed with fire to the very heavens, with black clouds and deep darkness. Then the LORD spoke to you out of the fire. You heard the sound of words but saw no form; there was only a voice.* (NIV)

In these instances no form of God could be seen with the exception of Exodus 33, where Moses was allowed to view the back side of God. The next set of verses are visions of God as seen by some of the prophets. In visions people were allowed to see the image of God. Notice the host of heaven (angels) standing around God as He is sitting on His throne.

1 Kings 22:19 *Micaiah continued, "Therefore hear the word of the LORD: I saw the LORD sitting on his throne with all the host of heaven standing around him on his right and on his left.* (NIV)

Ezek 1:1-6 *In the thirtieth year, in the fourth month on the fifth day, while I was among the exiles by the Kebar River, the heavens were opened and I saw visions of God. On the fifth of the month—it was the fifth*

Learning From History

year of the exile of King Jehoiachin—the word of the LORD came to Ezekiel the priest, the son of Buzi, by the Kebar River in the land of the Babylonians. **There the hand of the LORD was upon him. I looked, and I saw a windstorm coming out of the north—<u>an immense cloud with flashing lightning and surrounded by brilliant light.</u>** *The center of the fire looked like glowing metal, and in the fire was what looked like four living creatures. In appearance their form was that of a man, but each of them had four faces and four wings.* (NIV)

Ezek 1:26-28   *Above the expanse over their heads was what looked like a throne of sapphire, and high above on the throne was <u>a figure like that of a man</u>. I saw that from what appeared to be <u>his waist</u> up he looked like glowing metal, as if full of fire, and that from there down he looked like fire; and brilliant light surrounded him. Like the appearance of a rainbow in the clouds on a rainy day, so was the radiance around him. <u>This was the appearance of the likeness of the glory of the LORD</u>. When I saw it, I fell facedown, and I heard the voice of one speaking.* (NIV)

Ezek 8:1-4   *In the sixth year, in the sixth month on the fifth day, while I was sitting in my house and the elders of Judah were sitting before me, the hand of the Sovereign LORD came upon me there. I looked, and I saw <u>a figure like that of a man</u>. From what appeared to be <u>his waist</u> down he was like fire, and from there up <u>his appearance was as bright as glowing metal</u>. He stretched out what looked like <u>a hand</u> and took me by the hair of my head. The Spirit lifted me up between earth and heaven and in visions of God he took me to Jerusalem, to the entrance to the north gate of the inner court, where the idol that provokes to jealousy stood. And there before me was <u>the glory of the God of Israel</u>, as in the vision I had seen in the plain.* (NIV)

Ezek 43:1-7   *Then the man brought me to the gate facing east, <u>and I saw the glory of the God of Israel coming from the east</u>. His voice was like the roar of rushing waters, and the land was radiant with his glory. The vision I saw was like the vision I had seen when he came to destroy the city and like the visions I had seen by the Kebar River, and I fell facedown. <u>The glory of the LORD</u> entered the temple through the gate facing east. Then the Spirit lifted me up and brought me into the inner court, <u>and the glory of the LORD filled the temple</u>. While the man was standing beside me, I heard someone speaking to me from inside the temple. He said: "<u>Son of man, this is the place of my throne and the place for the soles of my</u>*

AFTER THE RAPTURE

> *feet. <u>This is where I will live among the Israelites forever.</u> The house of Israel will never again defile my holy name—neither they nor their kings—by their prostitution and the lifeless idols of their kings at their high places.* (NIV)

Dan 7:9-10   *"As I looked, "thrones were set in place, and <u>the Ancient of Days</u> took his seat. His clothing was as white as snow; <u>the hair of his head</u> was white like wool. His throne was flaming with fire, and its wheels were all ablaze. A river of fire was flowing, coming out from before him. Thousands upon thousands attended him; ten thousand times ten thousand stood before him. The court was seated, and the books were opened.* (NIV)

In Micaiah's vision he saw God sitting on His throne in heaven surrounded by His angels. The prophet Ezekiel received more visions of God than any other prophet. His visions are the most spectacular of any of the visions of God in the Bible. Please read Ezekiel chapter one in its entirety for a complete description of God with some of His celestial beings, who also have a form like a man. In the visions, in chapters one and eight, Ezekiel sees a figure that resembles a man. God is not a man, but has some sort of spiritual body. Remember that man was created in God's image, so it was natural for Ezekiel to say that God appeared as if He looked like a man. Moses revealed that God had a hand, a backside and a face. Ezekiel makes reference to the soles of God's feet and Daniel had a vision of God (Ancient of Days) taking a seat on a throne wearing clothing and as having hair on His head. It would be difficult, in the least, to spiritualize these visions of God to say that God is invisible.

Ezekiel, the prophet who was allowed to see the vision of the Shekinah Glory as it left the Temple in 593 BC, as God returned to heaven (Ezekiel 10-11), was also the honored one to view the vision of the Shekinah Glory as God returns to the Temple during the Day of the Lord (Ezekiel 42:1-12). How exciting it will be when we will be allowed to see God (even His face) in the New Jerusalem as we appear in our perfect (resurrected) bodies.

As we turn our focus to Jesus we see many sightings of Him in scripture. Jesus is shown with some sort of form in His pre-incarnate position, when He became flesh and blood and after His resurrection. Jesus is often referred to as a man or looking like a man, just as God was at times. Like God, Jesus has a spiritual body. He had it from eternity past, He has it in heaven at the present time and will have it in eternity future. Jesus, as a messenger (angel) of the Lord, was mistaken for God quite often in the Old Testament. Jesus was sent by God to lead the chosen people. Jesus as a servant of God spent more time on earth than did His Father. We begin our scripture verses with Moses on Horeb (Mount Sinai) as he received a visit from Jesus during His pre-incarnate ministry. This is not a vision.

Exod 3:1-6   *Now Moses was tending the flock of Jethro his father-in-law, the priest of Midian, and he led the flock to the far side of the desert and came to Horeb, the mountain of God. There the angel of the LORD appeared to him in flames of fire from within a bush. Moses* *saw that though the bush was on fire it did not burn up. So Moses thought, "I will go over and see this strange sight—why the bush does not burn up." When the LORD saw that he had gone over to look, God called to him from within the bush, "Moses! Moses!" And Moses said, "Here I am." "Do not come any closer," God said. "<u>Take off your sandals, for the place where you are standing is holy ground.</u>" Then he said, "I am the God of your father, the God of Abraham, the God of Isaac and the God of Jacob." At this, Moses hid his face, because he was afraid to look at God.* (NIV)

The only other time in scripture where someone was told to take off his sandals was in Joshua 5, where Jesus is referred to as *"commander of the army of the LORD."* There are many visions of Jesus listed in the Bible. Many of these sightings show Him in His glorious appearance as He existed before the world was created. Ezekiel and Daniel, the two prophets who were exiled in Babylon at the time, saw many visions of Jesus. Following is the scene, in a vision, of the Shekinah Glory as it was departing the Temple in Jerusalem in 593 BC. In these verses another figure appeared with God, a man clothed in linen.

Ezek 9:2-4   *And I saw six men coming from the direction of the upper gate, which faces north, each with a deadly weapon in his hand. With them was <u>a man clothed in linen</u> who had a writing kit at his side. They came in and stood beside the bronze altar. Now the glory of the God of Israel went up from above the cherubim, where it had been, and moved to the threshold of the temple. Then the LORD called to the man clothed in linen who had the writing kit at his side and said to him, "Go throughout the city of Jerusalem and put a mark on the foreheads of those who grieve and lament over all the detestable things that are done in it."* (NIV)

Ezek 10:1-8 *I looked, and I saw the likeness of a throne of sapphire above the expanse that was over the heads of the cherubim. The LORD said to <u>the man clothed in linen</u>,* "Go in among the wheels beneath the cherubim. Fill your hands with burning coals from among the cherubim and scatter them over the city." *And as I watched, he went in. Now the cherubim were standing on the south side of the temple when the man went in, and a cloud filled the inner court. Then the glory of the LORD rose from above the cherubim and moved to the threshold of the temple. The cloud filled the temple, and the court was full of the radiance of the glory of the LORD. The sound of the wings of the cherubim could be heard as far away as the outer court, like the voice of God Almighty when he speaks.* **When the LORD commanded <u>the man in linen</u>,** *"Take fire from among the wheels, from among the cherubim,"* **the man went in and stood beside a wheel.** *Then one of the cherubim reached out his hand to the fire that* *was among them. He took up some of it and put it into the hands of the man in linen, who took it and went out. (Under the wings of the cherubim could be seen what looked like the hands of a man.)* (NIV)

Ezekiel 40 is the beginning of the visions of the future Millennial Temple.

Ezek 40:1-4 *In the twenty-fifth year of our exile, at the beginning of the year, on the tenth of the month, in the fourteenth year after the fall of the city—on that very day the hand of the LORD was upon me and he took me there. <u>In visions of God</u> he took me to the land of Israel and set me on a very high mountain, on whose south side were some buildings that looked like a city. He took me there, and <u>I saw a man whose appearance was like bronze</u>; he was standing in the gateway <u>with a linen cord</u> and a measuring rod in his hand. The man said to me, "Son of man, look with your eyes and hear with your ears and pay attention to everything I am going to show you, for that is why you have been brought here. Tell the house of Israel everything you see."* (NIV)

Daniel had several visions of Messiah Jesus. In Daniel 4:13, the "messenger" is the Aramaic word `*iyr*. Note that this messenger is a holy one coming down from heaven.

Dan 4:13 *"In the visions I saw while lying in my bed, I looked, and there before me was <u>a messenger</u>, <u>a holy one</u>, <u>coming down from heaven</u>.* (NIV)

Dan 10:4-8 *On the twenty-fourth day of the first month, as I was standing on the bank of the great river, the Tigris, I looked up and there before me was <u>a man dressed in</u> linen, with a belt of the finest gold around <u>his waist</u>. His body was like chrysolite, <u>his face</u> like lightning, <u>his eyes</u> like flaming torches, <u>his arms and legs</u> like the gleam of burnished bronze, and his voice like the sound of a multitude. <u>I, Daniel, was the only one who saw the vision</u>; the men with me did not see it, but such terror overwhelmed them that they fled and hid themselves. So I was left alone, gazing at this great vision; I had no strength left, my face turned deathly pale and I was helpless.* (NIV)

Dan 12:5-7 *Then I, Daniel, looked, and there before me stood two others, one on this bank of the river and one on the opposite bank. One of them said to <u>the man clothed in linen</u>, who was above the waters of the river, "How long will it be before these astonishing things are fulfilled?" <u>The man clothed in linen</u>, who was above the waters of the river, <u>lifted his right hand and his left hand toward heaven, and</u>*

> *I heard him swear by him who lives forever, saying, "It will be for a time, times and half a time. When the power of the holy people has been finally broken, all these things will be completed."* (NIV)

In all these visions, with the exception of Daniel 4:13, which is written in Aramaic, two distinguishing factors can be found. First, the person listed in these visions is said to be *"a man"* and second, He is shown to be *"dressed in linen."* One of the names for Jesus in both the Old and New Testaments is *"the Son of Man."* As the Son of Man, one of the duties of Jesus during the Millennium will be the High Priest. The Shekinah Glory will be in the Holy of Holies, as Jesus, wearing His sacred linen garments, performs His duties as High Priest. This distinguishing position of High Priest helps separate the visions of God from those of Jesus. Jesus will perform these duties the exact same way that Aaron was instructed to do in 1445 BC while the Israelites were at Mount Sinai. Notice that the Shekinah Glory was in the Holy of Holies (the Most Holy Place) in Aaron's time and also the loss of Aaron's sons for approaching the Shekinah Glory in the Holy of Holies when they were not supposed to.

Lev 16:1-4 *The LORD spoke to Moses after the death of the two sons of Aaron who died when they approached the LORD. The LORD said to Moses: "Tell your brother Aaron not to come whenever he chooses into the Most Holy Place behind the curtain in front of the atonement cover on the ark, or else he will die, because I appear in the cloud over the atonement cover. "This is how Aaron is to enter the sanctuary area: with a young bull for a sin offering and a ram for a burnt offering. He is to put on the sacred linen tunic, with linen undergarments next to his body; he is to tie the linen sash around him and put on the linen turban. These are sacred garments; so he must bathe himself with water before he puts them on.* (NIV)

One of the most spectacular visions of Jesus to come to us in the Old Testament is in the book of Isaiah. Isaiah was the honored recipient of a vision of Jesus after He is crowned King. This vision looks forward to the Day of the Lord after Jesus has established His throne on earth. Jesus will be attired in the robe of a King and the High Priest.

Isa 6:1-5 *In the year that King Uzziah died, I saw the Lord sitting on a throne, high and lifted up, and the train of His robe filled the temple. Above it stood seraphim; each one had six wings: with two he covered his face, with two he covered his feet, and with two he flew. And one cried to another and said: "Holy, holy, holy is the LORD of hosts; the whole earth is full of His glory!" And the posts of the door were shaken by the voice of him who cried out, and the house was filled with smoke. So I said: "Woe is me, for I am undone! Because I am a man of unclean lips, and I dwell in the midst of a people of unclean lips; for my eyes have seen the King, the LORD of hosts."* (NKJ)

AFTER THE RAPTURE

In this passage Jesus is referred to as *"the LORD of hosts"* two times. This is most often used as an Old Testament reference to Jesus Christ. Just as Jesus was called the commander of the army (host), in Joshua 5:14, He is also *"the LORD of hosts"* in the Old Testament. This title of Jesus was used during the time of David and the latter prophets and is first found in 1 Samuel 1:3 in the Old Testament. Ever since the chosen people Israel have come into existence, Jesus has been positioned by God to be a messenger (angel), a leader and a commander for them. In Psalms 24 we have a picture of Jesus as the King of glory as the Battle of Armageddon is being played out. The NIV translation says *"the LORD Almighty,"* in place of *"the LORD of hosts,"* as God's Redeemer in the Old Testament.

Isa 44:6-7 *"Thus says the LORD, the King of Israel, <u>and his Redeemer, the LORD of hosts</u>: 'I am the First and I am the Last; besides Me there is no God. And who can proclaim as I do? <u>Then let him declare it and set it in order for Me, since I appointed the ancient people</u>. And the things that are coming and shall come, let them show these to them.* (NKJ)

Ps 24:1-10 <u>*The earth is the LORD'S, and all its fullness, the world and those who dwell therein. For He has founded it upon the seas, and established it upon the waters. Who may ascend into the hill of the LORD? Or who may stand in His holy place? He who has clean hands and a pure heart, who has not lifted up his soul to an idol, nor sworn deceitfully. He shall receive blessing from the LORD, and righteousness from the God of his salvation. This is Jacob, the generation of those who seek Him, who seek Your face. Selah Lift up your heads, O you gates! And be lifted up, you everlasting doors! And the King of glory shall come in. Who is this King of glory? The LORD strong and mighty, the LORD mighty in battle. Lift up your heads, O you gates! Lift up, you everlasting doors! And the King of glory shall come in. Who is this King of glory? The LORD of hosts, he is the King of glory.* </u>*Selah* (NKJ)

Isa 55:4 *Indeed I have given him as a witness to the people, <u>a leader and commander for the people</u>.* (NKJ)

A confirmation that Isaiah's vision in chapter six was Jesus can be found in the New Testament in the book of John. Here, John is referring to this vision of the Lord sitting on His throne. The NIV even inserts *"Jesus' glory"* in place of *"His glory"* in verse forty-one.

John 12:37-41 *But although He had done so many signs before them, they did not believe in Him, that the word of Isaiah the prophet might be fulfilled, which he spoke: "Lord, who has believed our report? And to whom has the arm of the Lord been revealed?" Therefore they could not believe, because Isaiah said again: "He has blinded their* *eyes and hardened their hearts, lest they should see with their eyes, lest they should understand with their hearts and turn, so that I should heal them." <u>These things Isaiah said when he saw His glory and spoke of Him.</u>* (NKJ)

At the dedication ceremony of the Millennial Temple, the one built by Jesus, the glory of both God and Jesus will be evident among His people. This will take place after the LORD of hosts once more shakes the heavens and the earth during the Tribulation Period.

Hag 2:6-9 *"<u>For thus says the LORD of hosts:</u> "Once more (it is a little while) I will shake heaven and earth, the sea and dry land; 'and I will shake all nations, and they shall come to the Desire of All Nations, and I will fill this temple with glory,' says the LORD of hosts. 'The silver is Mine, and the gold is Mine,' says the LORD of hosts. '<u>The glory of this latter temple shall be greater than the former,</u>' says the LORD of hosts. 'And in this place I will give peace,' says the LORD of hosts."* (NKJ)

It must be remembered that the Shekinah Glory did not return to the rebuilt Temple (Zerubbabel's) when the Persian Empire defeated the Babylonians in 539 BC. The rebuilt Temple, built by Jesus during the Day of the Lord, will rest high above the surrounding city of Jerusalem and will be known as Mount Zion. At this time the whole world will walk in the light of the Shekinah Glory, along with Jesus in all His glory.

The New Testament contains several instances where Jesus appeared in all His glory. Most of these instances are found in the book of Revelation, but in the book of Luke, at the Transfiguration, it reveals a vision of Jesus as He will be seen during the Day of the Lord when He will appear at His Glorious Return.

Luke 9:28-29 *About eight days after Jesus said this, he took Peter, John and James with him and went up onto a mountain to pray. <u>As he was praying, the appearance of his face changed, and his clothes became as bright as a flash of lightning.</u>* (NIV)

Jesus appeared to the greatest of the apostle's, Paul, while he was on his way to Damascus. At that time Paul's companions saw the glory (bright light), but did not understand the voice of Jesus. As the light appeared to Paul, it temporarily blinded him.

Acts 22:6-11 *"About noon as I came near Damascus, <u>suddenly a bright light from heaven flashed around me. I fell to the ground and heard a voice say to me, 'Saul! Saul! Why do you persecute me?'</u> "'<u>Who are you, Lord?</u>' I asked. "'<u>I am Jesus of Nazareth</u>, whom you are persecuting,' he replied. My companions saw the light, but they did not understand the voice of him who was speaking to me. "'What shall I do, Lord?' I asked. "'Get up,' the Lord said, 'and go into*

AFTER THE RAPTURE

> *Damascus. There you will be told all that you have been assigned to do.' <u>My companions led me by the hand into Damascus, because the brilliance of the light had blinded me.</u>* (NIV)

John, the apostle whom Jesus loved, was given a special mission from Jesus. He was given the vision of the Apocalypse; a view of the church age, the Tribulation Period, the Millennium and the eternal state. What an honor! In the content of the book of Revelation can be found several visions of Jesus. Once again Jesus appears clothed in a garment.

Rev 1:12-16 — *Then I turned to see the voice that spoke with me. And having turned I saw seven golden lampstands, and in the midst of the seven lampstands <u>One like the Son of Man, clothed with a garment</u> down to the <u>feet</u> and girded about the <u>chest</u> with a golden band. His <u>head and hair</u> were white like wool, as white as snow, and His <u>eyes</u> like a flame of fire; His <u>feet</u> were like fine brass, as if refined in a furnace, and His <u>voice</u> as the sound of many waters; He had in His <u>right hand</u> seven stars, out of His <u>mouth</u> went a sharp two-edged sword, and <u>His countenance was like the sun shining in its strength.</u>* (NKJ)

Rev 2:18 — *"To the angel of the church in Thyatira write: These are the words of <u>the Son of God</u>, whose <u>eyes</u> are like blazing fire and whose <u>feet</u> are like burnished bronze.* (NIV)

Rev 4:1-3 — *After this I looked, and there before me was a door standing open in heaven. And the voice I had first heard speaking to me like a trumpet said, "Come up here, and I will show you what must take place after this." <u>At once I was in the Spirit, and there before me was a throne in heaven with someone sitting on it.</u> And the one who sat there had the appearance of jasper and carnelian. A rainbow, resembling an emerald, encircled the throne.* (NIV)

Rev 19:11-16 — *<u>I saw heaven standing open and there before me was a white horse,</u> whose rider is called Faithful and True. With justice he judges and makes war. His <u>eyes</u> are like blazing fire, and on his <u>head</u> are many crowns. He has a name written on him that no one knows but he himself. He is dressed in a robe dipped in blood, <u>and his name is the Word of God.</u> The armies of heaven were following him, riding on white horses and dressed in fine linen, white and clean. Out of his <u>mouth</u> comes a sharp sword with which to strike down the nations. "He will rule them with an iron scepter." He treads the winepress of the fury of the wrath of God Almighty. On his robe and on his <u>thigh</u> he has this name written: <u>KING OF KINGS AND LORD OF LORDS.</u>* (NIV)

In these verses Jesus is referred to as someone *"like the Son of Man,"* with a garment (clothing). Also, in these visions, we see Jesus with a chest, a head with hair, both hands, a mouth, a face, eyes and feet. Along with the title, *"the Son of Man,"* He is referred to as *"the Son of God," "Faithful and True,"* and His name is *"the Word of God."* Oh, and do not forget, *"KING OF KINGS AND LORD OF LORDS."*

As Stephen was being stoned to death, he was allowed to look up to heaven to view the glory of God with Jesus standing at His right side. This is a view of where God and Jesus are at the present time. Notice that Stephen was a believer, because he was filled with the Holy Spirit. Also notice the title of Jesus as *"the Son of Man."* What a beautiful sight!

Acts 7:55-56   ***But Stephen, full of the Holy Spirit, looked up to heaven and saw the glory of God, and Jesus standing at the right hand of God. "Look," he said, "I see heaven open and the Son of Man standing at the right hand of God."*** (NIV)

I think it is quite obvious from these verses and many others that the glory of the Father and Son are overlooked by most Bible Scholars and teachers today. Glory as it applies to God and Jesus can be a beautiful radiant light. Could it be the light at the end of the tunnel? Also overlooked, is the form that God and Jesus possess. They have some sort of a spiritual body that looks like the form God created for man. In the future eternal state, those who know God, through Jesus, will be able to see God. As for the Millennium, both God and Jesus will reside on earth, but God will dwell as He did in Old Testament times, between the cherubim in the Holy of Holies (as the glory of the Lord with radiant light under the cover of a cloud). Jesus will be beautiful and glorious as He resides on earth in His splendor.

GOD IS LIGHT

Just like the word "glory," the word "light" can have a literal and a symbolic meaning as they apply to the Divine personages. Symbolically, light represents holiness and purity. It deals with enlightenment of the spiritual life and includes the illumination of the soul through the intellect, will, reason and conscience of man. In the New Testament Jesus represents the personification of light. The Word of God (Jesus) is compared with a "lamp." Light can also be applied to Christians in general.

In the Bible, light and darkness are at the opposite ends of the spectrum. Light represents day, saved people, life, truth, knowledge, goodness and God's redemptive work, while darkness represents night, unsaved people, death, error, evil, and the works of Satan. Darkness is also depicted as misery, destruction, it is used of ignorance of divine revelation and is associated with wickedness and the final misery of hell. When a person receives salvation, through Jesus Christ, he is brought from darkness into the light.

The Bible also speaks of a literal Divine light as God's Presence. The light is eternal and has always been in existence. After God created the heavens and the earth, the earth was covered in darkness. In the third verse of the Bible the Divine Presence shines forth.

Gen 1:1-5   ***In the beginning God created the heavens and the earth. Now the*** *earth was formless and empty, <u>darkness was over the surface of the deep</u>, and the Spirit of God was hovering over the waters. And God said, "<u>Let there be light,</u>" and there was light. God saw that the light was good, and he separated the light from the darkness. God called the light "day," and the darkness he called "night." <u>And there was evening, and there was morning—the first day.</u>* (NIV)

This cannot be the light from the sun, because the sun was not created until the fourth day (Genesis 1:14-19). The Old Testament is perfectly clear that the face of God shines forth with rays of a delicate, subtle, pure and brilliant light.

Exod 33:20   *But," he said, "you cannot see my face, for no one may see me and live."* (NIV)

Ezek 1:25-28   *Then there came a voice from above the expanse over their heads as they stood with lowered wings. Above the expanse over their heads was what looked like a throne of sapphire, <u>and high above on the throne was a figure like that of a man</u>. I saw that from what appeared to be his waist up <u>he looked like glowing metal</u>, as if full of fire, and that from there down he looked like fire; <u>and brilliant light surrounded him</u>. Like the appearance of a rainbow in the clouds on a rainy day, <u>so was the radiance around him. This was the appearance of the likeness of the glory of the LORD</u>. When I saw it, I fell facedown, and I heard the voice of one speaking.* (NIV)

Ezek 10:4   *Then the glory of the LORD rose from above the cherubim and moved to the threshold of the temple. <u>The cloud filled the temple, and the court was full of the radiance of the glory of the LORD</u>.* (NIV)

Ezek 43:2   *<u>and I saw the glory of the God of Israel coming from the east.</u> His voice was like the roar of rushing waters, <u>and the land was radiant with his glory</u>.* (NIV)

After man was created and before the fall, God was visible to Adam and Eve. In the beginning God created a perfect world and He warned Adam and Eve of the consequences of eating the fruit of the tree located in the middle of the Garden of Eden. At that time Adam and Eve had direct access to God when He appeared to them on earth. Before they sinned they were able to see God as He walked and talked with them in the Garden of Eden. They could see God's spiritual body (including His face), along with the radiant rays of light as they protruded from His face. God was not hidden in the midst of a cloud at that time. It was a perfect world then and God said, *" it was very good."*

Everything changed when mankind fell to the temptation of sin. Consequences of *"knowing good and evil"* brought about changes in mankind's physical stature. Sickness and disease were then brought into the world and death was added to man's number of years. Disorder entered the world as curses were placed on Satan, Adam (men) and Eve (women). Because the world was no longer in a state of perfection, mankind lost the ability to see God. Once the children of God receive their resurrected bodies at the Rapture, they will once again be able to see God as they are led into His Presence by Jesus. This will take place when the saved are in their perfect bodies in a perfect place—the Kingdom of God in Heaven. The plan of salvation will have come full circle up to this point in history, which will consist of the six thousand years of man. Only a short transition period remains.

The Old Testament word for "light" is '*owr*. The definition of it can be found on pages 615 and 616. It must be remembered that the glory of the Lord (Shekinah Glory) is a literal light that we are referring to in scripture. In the New Testament we discover that God lives (dwells, resides) in unapproachable light. Notice God is Kings of kings and Lord of lords.

1 Tim 6:15-16   *which God will bring about in his own time—God, the blessed and only Ruler, the King of kings and Lord of lords, who alone is immortal and who lives in unapproachable light, whom no one has seen or can see. To him be honor and might forever. Amen.* (NIV)

The apostle John reveals that *"God is light."* This can be taken literally or symbolically, as the Bible clearly depicts throughout both the Old Testament and the New Testament.

1 John 1:5-7   *This is the message we have heard from him and declare to you: God is light; in him there is no darkness at all. If we claim to have fellowship with him yet walk in the darkness, we lie and do not live by the truth. But if we walk in the light, as he is in the light, we have fellowship with one another, and the blood of Jesus, his Son, purifies us from all sin.* (NIV)

It is very obvious from scripture that Jesus also has a Divine radiance about Him. There is no way anyone can spiritualize this literal countenance that Jesus has shining from His face. It will be seen in its fullness at His Glorious Return. From the description in Revelation 18:1, it is obvious that the messenger (angel) in this verse is Jesus.

Matt 17:1-2   *After six days Jesus took with him Peter, James and John the brother of James, and led them up a high mountain by themselves. There he was transfigured before them. His face shone like the sun, and his clothes became as white as the light.* (NIV)

Luke 17:24   *For the Son of Man in his day will be like the lightning, which flashes and lights up the sky from one end to the other.* (NIV)

Acts 26:12-15   *"On one of these journeys I was going to Damascus with the authority and commission of the chief priests. About noon, O king, as I was on the road, I saw a light from heaven, brighter than the*

> *sun, blazing around me and my companions. We all fell to the ground, and I heard a voice saying to me in Aramaic, 'Saul, Saul, why do you persecute me? It is hard for you to kick against the goads.' "Then I asked, 'Who are you, Lord?' "'I am Jesus, whom you are persecuting,' the Lord replied.* (NIV)

Rev 18:1 *After this I saw another angel coming down from heaven. He had great authority, and the earth was illuminated by his splendor.* (NIV)

FIRE FROM GOD

I would like to leave you with one more thought provoking aspect concerning the glory of the Lord. In the word of God it speaks of God as a consuming fire. What does that mean? It also speaks of things that look like fire. The Shekinah Glory is a pillar of fire. In Ezekiel's visions, he saw God as a figure like a man glowing like metal, fire and brilliant light surrounding Him. Jesus was seen as having eyes like blazing fire and feet like fine brass refined in a furnace. Are these appearances of fire some fanciful symbolic words of how awesome God and Jesus appear? Anything that has fire associated with it brings fear to men. Is part of what makes up God fire? Are we to fear God or is this word figurative of God's glory (brilliant rays of light)?

The Hebrew word '*esh,* used in the examples above, can mean a literal fire as we think of fire. A fire for cooking something, flames or even something fiery or hot, but it can also be something figurative that looks like fire. As the Israelites viewed the glory of the Lord, as God descended to the top of Mount Sinai from heaven, it appeared as if the mountain was on fire. In all actuality, it was the majestic splendor of God's brilliance hidden under the cover of a cloud. We have covered the subject of this phenomenon quite extensively in this book. I know that it is hard for us to fathom God with this kind of appearance, but the Bible is clear about God as having brilliant rays of light protruding from His face.

As we take a critical look at the word '*esh* (fire) in the Old Testament, we find some very interesting reading. We will only look at this word when it appears as a figure for fire, as it applies to the appearance of God and Jesus. The first time this word is used in the Bible is when God made a covenant with Abram. A blazing torch passed between the pieces of the carcasses of the heifer, goat and ram as God made a covenant with Abraham.

Gen 15:17 *When the sun had set and darkness had fallen, a smoking firepot with **a blazing torch** appeared and passed between the pieces.* (NIV)

Sodom and Gomorrah were destroyed by brimstone and fire.

Gen 19:24 *Then the LORD rained brimstone and **fire** on Sodom and Gomorrah, from the LORD out of the heavens.* (NKJ)

A pillar of fire lead the Israelites through the wilderness.

Learning From History

Exod 13:21-22   *By day the LORD went ahead of them in a pillar of cloud to guide them on their way and by night in a pillar of **fire** to give them light, so that they could travel by day or night. Neither the pillar of cloud by day nor the pillar of **fire** by night left its place in front of the people.* (NIV)

The glory of the Lord on top of Mount Sinai appeared to be a consuming fire.

Exod 24:15-18   *When Moses went up on the mountain, the cloud covered it, and the glory of the LORD settled on Mount Sinai. For six days the cloud covered the mountain, and on the seventh day the LORD called to Moses from within the cloud. To the Israelites the glory of the LORD looked like a consuming **fire** on top of the mountain. Then Moses entered the cloud as he went on up the mountain. And he stayed on the mountain forty days and forty nights.* (NIV)

The cloud above the Tent of Meeting looked like fire.

Num 9:15-16   *On the day the tabernacle, the Tent of the Testimony, was set up, the cloud covered it. From evening till morning the cloud above the tabernacle looked like **fire**. That is how it continued to be; the cloud covered it, and at night it looked like **fire**.* (NIV)

A fire from the Lord consumed some of the Israelites. Also look at Numbers 16:35.

Num 11:1-3   *Now the people complained about their hardships in the hearing of the LORD, and when he heard them his anger was aroused. Then **fire** from the LORD burned among them and consumed some of the outskirts of the camp. When the people cried out to Moses, he prayed to the LORD and the **fire** died down. So that place was called Taberah, because **fire** from the LORD had burned among them.* (NIV)

The prophet Elijah has a God who answers by fire.

1 Kings 18:24   *Then you call on the name of your god, and I will call on the name of the LORD. The god who answers by **fire**—he is God." Then all the people said, "What you say is good."* (NIV)

When Solomon dedicated the Temple, just before the glory of the Lord filled it, fire came down from heaven and consumed the burnt offering and the sacrifices.

2 Chr 7:1-2   *When Solomon finished praying, **fire** came down from heaven and consumed the burnt offering and the sacrifices, and the glory of the*

> *LORD filled the temple. The priests could not enter the temple of the LORD because the glory of the LORD filled it.* (NIV)

The fire of God fell from the sky and burned up the sheep and the servants.

> Job 1:16 *While he was still speaking, another messenger came and said, "The **fire** of God fell from the sky and burned up the sheep and the servants, and I am the only one who has escaped to tell you!"* (NIV)

The glory of the Lord will be a canopy (Divine protection) over Mount Zion, in Jerusalem, during the peaceful portion of the Millennium.

> Isa 4:5 *Then the LORD will create over all of Mount Zion and over those who assemble there a cloud of smoke by day and a glow of flaming **fire** by night; over all the glory will be a canopy.* (NIV)

The vision of God as seen by Ezekiel appeared as if the figure of the man was on fire.

> Ezek 1:26-28 *Above the expanse over their heads was what looked like a throne of sapphire, and high above on the throne was a figure like that of a man. I saw that from what appeared to be his waist up he looked like glowing metal, as if full of **fire**, and that from there down he looked like **fire**; and brilliant light surrounded him. Like the appearance of a rainbow in the clouds on a rainy day, so was the radiance around him. This was the appearance of the likeness of the glory of the LORD. When I saw it, I fell facedown, and I heard the voice of one speaking.* (NIV)

God's glory will be a wall of protection around Jerusalem, along with a light from within, during the Millennium.

> Zech 2:5 **And I myself will be a wall of _fire_ around it,' declares the LORD, 'and I will be its glory within.'** (NIV)

The first appearance of Jesus in His radiant glory on earth seems to be when He appeared to Moses in the burning bush at Mount Horeb (Exodus 3:1-6). The brilliance of the glory of Jesus (the Son of Man) will shine like a bolt of lightning as He steps out of His private chamber (room) in heaven as He prepares to come to earth after the Tribulation Period, when Jesus suddenly appears in the sky at His Glorious Return to earth as a sign (Joel 2:16; Matthew 24:27-30; Revelation 18:1). But for the most part the references that pertain to the brilliant appearance of Jesus will be when He returns from heaven when He suddenly comes to earth to fight the Battle of Armageddon, especially in the Old Testament. At the Battle of Armageddon Jesus will come with fire to render His anger with fury and rebuke His enemies with flames of fire, at which time many will die.

Learning From History

Isa 66:15-16 — *<u>See, the LORD is coming with fire</u>, and his chariots are like a whirlwind; he will bring down his anger with fury, and his rebuke with flames of fire. <u>For with fire and with his sword the LORD will execute judgment upon all men, and many will be those slain by the LORD</u>.* (NIV)

Ps 18:7-15 — *The earth trembled and quaked, and the foundations of the mountains shook; they trembled because he was angry. Smoke rose from his nostrils; <u>consuming fire came from his mouth, burning coals blazed out of it</u>. He parted the heavens and came down; dark clouds were under his feet. He mounted the cherubim and flew; he soared on the wings of the wind. He made darkness his covering, his canopy around him—the dark rain clouds of the sky. <u>Out of the brightness of his presence clouds advanced, with hailstones and bolts of lightning</u>. The LORD thundered from heaven; the voice of the Most High resounded. He shot his arrows and scattered [the enemies], <u>great bolts of lightning and routed them</u>. The valleys of the sea were exposed and the foundations of the earth laid bare at your rebuke, O LORD, at the blast of breath from your nostrils.* (NIV)

Ps 97:1-6 — *The LORD reigns, let the earth be glad; let the distant shores rejoice. Clouds and thick darkness surround him; righteousness and justice are the foundation of his throne. <u>Fire goes before him and consumes his foes on every side. His lightning lights up the world</u>; the earth sees and trembles. The mountains melt like wax before the LORD, before the Lord of all the earth. The heavens proclaim his righteousness, <u>and all the peoples see his glory</u>.* (NIV)

Isa 30:25-28 — *<u>In the day of great slaughter</u>, when the towers fall, streams of water will flow on every high mountain and every lofty hill. The moon will shine like the sun, and the sunlight will be seven times brighter, like the light of seven full days, when the LORD binds up the bruises of his people and heals the wounds he inflicted. <u>See, the Name of the LORD comes from afar, with burning anger and dense clouds of smoke; his lips are full of wrath, and his tongue is a consuming fire</u>. His breath is like a rushing torrent, rising up to the neck. He shakes the nations in the sieve of destruction; he places in the jaws of the peoples a bit that leads them astray.* (NIV)

Hab 3:3-6 — *God came from Teman, the Holy One from Mount Paran. Selah His glory covered the heavens and his praise filled the earth. <u>His splendor was like the sunrise; rays flashed from his hand</u>, where his power was hidden. Plague went before him; pestilence followed* his steps. _He stood, and shook the earth; he looked, and made the nations tremble._ The ancient mountains crumbled and the age-old hills collapsed. _His ways are eternal._ (NIV)

2 Thes 1:6-9 — *_God is just_: He will pay back trouble to those who trouble you and give relief to you who are troubled, and to us as well. _This will happen when the Lord Jesus is revealed from heaven in blazing fire with his powerful angels._ He will punish those who do not know God and do not obey the gospel of our Lord Jesus. They will be punished with everlasting destruction and shut out from the presence of the Lord and from the majesty of his power* (NIV)

2 Thes 2:8 — *And then the lawless one will be revealed, whom the Lord Jesus will overthrow with the breath of his mouth _and destroy by the splendor of his coming._* (NIV)

Probably the most interesting and fascinating account in scripture concerning Jesus and His glorious appearance can be found in the book of Daniel, where the fourth man (who looked like a son of the gods) protected Shadrach, Meshach and Abednego from King Nebuchadnezzar. God sent His angel (messenger) to rescue these men of God. Jesus protected them with the glorious light that surrounds Him. Notice that the fire did not harm their bodies or robes and they did not smell like fire when they came out of the fiery furnace. Please read Daniel chapter three for the entire story.

Dan 3:25-28 — *He said, "_Look! I see four men walking around in the fire, unbound and unharmed, and the fourth looks like a son of the gods._" Nebuchadnezzar then approached the opening of the blazing furnace and shouted, "Shadrach, Meshach and Abednego, servants of the Most High God, come out! Come here!" So Shadrach, Meshach and Abednego came out of the fire, and the satraps, prefects, governors and royal advisers crowded around them. **They saw that the fire had not harmed their bodies, nor was a hair of their heads singed; their robes were not scorched, and there was no smell of fire on them. Then Nebuchadnezzar said, "Praise be to the God of Shadrach, Meshach and Abednego, who has sent _his angel_ and rescued his servants!** They trusted in him and defied the king's command and were willing to give up their lives rather than serve or worship any god except their own God.* (NIV)

Heb 12:28-29 — *Therefore, since we are receiving a kingdom that cannot be shaken, let us be thankful, and so worship God acceptably with reverence and awe, for our "_God is a consuming fire._"* (NIV)

God's glory can provide Divine protection or it can deliver Divine destruction!

CHAPTER FIFTEEN

THE END AND THE BEGINNING

In chapters twelve and thirteen we covered the Day of the Lord from the time following the Tribulation Period to the end of the Millennium, a period of 991 years. The two-year period of time *After the Rapture* and before the Tribulation Period, added to the seven years of the Tribulation Period, plus 991 years, completes the Millennium, the Day of the Lord, the Day of Christ, the Kingdom Age and the Sabbatical Rest of the last 1000 year period of the creation week. These are all referring to the same period of time. The last 990 years of the Millennium will come close to a near-perfect world, but because of sin it will fall short of God's glory. After the Day of the Lord is completed the next period will be the Day of God or the Eternal Age.

After the Day of the Lord is over we will find the earth full of people who have lived a long and prosperous life without the difficulties of what people have faced in the previous dispensations. You might be saying to yourself—that is not very fair for the people from the previous ages—and God agrees with that thought. Temptation in the form of Satan will be allowed to influence the thoughts of the people who will be living on the earth after the Millennium is completed. One last time Satan give it your best shot

> Rev 20:3　*He threw him into the Abyss, and locked and sealed it over him, to keep him from deceiving the nations anymore until the thousand years were ended. <u>After that, he must be set free for a short time</u>.*
> (NIV)

In order for every person in every age throughout history to be on a level playing field, and not show favoritism to any individual, God will allow Satan and probably the fallen angels to be released from prison to tempt those on earth. At this time it will be Satan's objective to once again form an alliance (army) against God, the Jews and the city of Jerusalem. How long it will take for Satan to accomplish gathering this army is not revealed to us, but we know it will not take very long because Satan is only free for a short time.

> Rev 20:7-9　*When the thousand years are over, <u>Satan will be released from his prison</u> and will go out to deceive the nations in the four corners of the earth—Gog and Magog—to gather them for battle. In number they are like the sand on the seashore. They marched across the breadth of the earth and surrounded the camp of God's people, the city he loves. But fire came down from heaven and devoured them.*
> (NIV)

This battle will be different from any previous battle that has taken place throughout history. Since the world will be living in a state of peaceful coexistence, when Satan is released, there will be no military armies with weapons for Satan to confiscate for his purpose. His goal will be to verbally discredit God and His chosen people. One last time Anti-Semitism will be used as a tool to bring the nations against God. The sad conclusion to Satan's attempt is that he will succeed in convincing a large majority of the worlds population to turn away from God and to organize into an army to converge on Jerusalem and surround the city. It will be more like a rebellion or mutiny against God. Once again, and the good news is that it will be the last time Satan will be allowed to try to deceive people. The final victory will belong to God.

SATAN'S DOOM

Probably without a shot being fired Jesus, as He will do at the Battle of Armageddon, will defeat His enemy. Once again, Jesus will shield those people who will have kept the faith and did not follow Satan. Fire will rain down from heaven and it will all be over in an instant. The fire here is the glory of Jesus in the form of His radiance. Again, Jesus in His glory will come against all the unsaved people on the earth and destroy them as if by fire.

> Rev 20:9-10 *They marched across the breadth of the earth and surrounded the camp of God's people, the city he loves. **But fire came down from heaven and devoured them.** And the devil, who deceived them, was thrown into the lake of burning sulfur, where the beast and the false prophet had been thrown. **They will be tormented day and night for ever and ever.** (NIV)*

Once again the Jews and Jerusalem become the center of attention. Satan will spend eternity in the Lake of Fire with his two cohorts; the Antichrist and the false prophet who are already there waiting for their leader. The battle between good and evil will finally be over. They will be tormented in the place of their final destiny forever. FOR ETERNITY!!!

It is at this time that the present earth we are living on will be dissolved by fire. At the Battle of Armageddon, during the Day of the Lord, the outer surface of the earth was destroyed by fire. After the Day of the Lord is over we will begin the period known as the Day of God. At the beginning of the Day of God, after the final defeat of Satan and his followers, the heavens and earth will be totally destroyed to make room for a new heaven and new earth. The elements of the earth and the heavenly realm of the planets will dissolve and disappear and their existence will be replaced by a New Heaven and a New Earth, where the righteous will spend eternity and live in a world that has never seen any part of sin.

> 2 Pet 3:12-13 *as you look forward to **the day of God** and speed its coming. **That day will bring about the destruction of the heavens by fire, and the elements will melt in the heat.** But in keeping with his promise we are looking forward to a new heaven and a new earth, the home of righteousness.* (NIV)

GREAT WHITE THRONE JUDGMENT

Those people who will be deceived by Satan and turn against God will be destroyed by fire and will be the last of the lost souls to join the unsaved souls who are in Hades (Hell), the temporary abode where the souls of all the lost people from every dispensation have gone to await their judgment. I believe that the physical location of hell is in the center of the earth. A place that as we speak is on fire (extreme heat).

The apostle John observes a great white throne with Jesus sitting on it. The earth and the sky will cease to exist as the elements of the earth are dissolved at the presence of Jesus. Then John saw the lost souls of every person who rejected God and His Son Jesus from the fall of mankind standing before the throne. I am assuming that the Great White Throne is in heaven and that this is where this judgment will take place. At this time the earth, the atmospheric heaven and the celestial heaven will no longer exist. The souls of those in the abode of hell will have been resurrected and sent to heaven for their court to open.

Rev 20:11-12 *Then I saw <u>a great white throne</u> and him who was seated on it. Earth and sky fled from his presence, and there was no place for them. <u>And I saw the dead, great and small, standing before the throne, and books were opened.</u> Another book was opened, which is the book of life. The dead were judged according to what they had done as recorded in the books.* (NIV)

There are two books that will be opened at this time. One is the book of life and the other is the book of death. Since the first resurrection and Judgment Seat of Christ have been discussed extensively throughout the New Testament, here in Revelation chapter twenty, the discussion focuses on the final judgment of the unsaved. At the Great White Throne Judgment only the lost souls of human history will be standing before Jesus on His White Throne. They will be standing there in their newly resurrected bodies. They will be the participants of the second resurrection and each person will be judged by his own account. It will be just like the believers—face-to-face with Jesus—with the book turned to the page with their name written on it and the account of their life written on the pages. The sad part about the people who will participate in this judgment is that they will have to answer for the sins they have committed in this lifetime and believe me when I say that not a single person who has ever lived—other than Jesus Christ—is sinless. We all fall short of the glory of God. Whereas, those who take part of the first resurrection and the Judgment Seat of Christ will have their sins forgiven, washed by the blood of Jesus. Their eternal destiny will be in the New Heaven and the New Earth forever, while the unsaved people will spend eternity in the fiery lake of burning sulfur (the lake of fire) to be tormented and agonize forever, along with the great deceiver of all time—Satan.

Rev 20:13-14 *The sea gave up the dead that were in it, and death and Hades gave up the dead that were in them, <u>and each person was judged according to what he had done</u>. Then death and Hades were thrown into the lake of fire. <u>The lake of fire is the second death</u>.* (NIV)

The first death that all human beings are faced with is the physical death of our existing or fleshly bodies. The second death will be the loss of the spiritual bodies which everyone (saved or unsaved) receives when they are resurrected. The saved souls of all mankind make up those who will participate in the first resurrection, while the souls of the unsaved will be participants of the second resurrection. Those saved souls who take part in the first resurrection will only face the physical death of their earthly or fleshly bodies. The second death will not effect them. They will live forever in their resurrected bodies, while the unsaved will face the second death and the loss of their resurrected spiritual bodies forever.

> Rev 20:5-6 *(The rest of the dead did not come to life until the thousand years were ended.) This is the first resurrection. <u>Blessed and holy are those who have part in the first resurrection. The second death has no power over them</u>, but they will be priests of God and of Christ and will reign with him for a thousand years.* (NIV)

It does not mention the last phase of the first resurrection in these verses, but it is implied when it says that the books are opened, including the book of life. The souls of the people who accepted Jesus during the Millennium will have to be resurrected and stand before the Judgment Seat of Christ to receive their rewards and positions for eternity. As I have mentioned several times before in this book, please accept Christ now so your name will be in the correct book when you stand before Jesus to be judged.

> Rev 20:15 *If anyone's name <u>was not found</u> written in the book of life, he was thrown into the lake of fire.* (NIV)

LAST ENEMY — DEATH

I suppose that it is appropriate that the last enemy to be destroyed will be "DEATH."

> 1 Cor 15:26 *<u>The last enemy to be destroyed is death</u>.* (NIV)

Think about it! Does death scare you? You should only be afraid of death if you do not know Jesus personally. It is kind of ironic that people today, who are agnostic—people who hold that the ultimate cause (God) and the essential nature of things are unknown and unknowable or that human knowledge is limited to experience—are afraid of death and dying. It seems to me that if you believe there is no afterlife or life ends at physical death, you would not fear death. Of course, I do not fear death, because after physical death, everyone who has a true relationship with Jesus will live in a far greater time and place, which will be a lot better than the life we are living in at the present time. If you get nothing out of this book but the way back to God, through His Son Jesus, it will be a good book. Paul in the book of Romans explains the subject of death and the victory over it.

> Rom 5:1-6:23 *<u>Therefore, since we have been justified through faith, we have peace with God through our Lord Jesus Christ, through whom we have gained access by faith into this grace in which we now stand.</u> And we rejoice in the hope of the glory of God. Not only so, but we*

also rejoice in our sufferings, because we know that suffering produces perseverance; perseverance, character; and character, hope. And hope does not disappoint us, because God has poured out his love into our hearts by the Holy Spirit, whom he has given us. **You see, at just the right time, when we were still powerless, Christ died for the unGodly.** *Very rarely will anyone die for a righteous man, though for a good man someone might possibly dare to die.* **But God demonstrates his own love for us in this: While we were still sinners, Christ died for us.** *Since we have now been justified by his blood, how much more shall we be saved from God's wrath through him! For if, when we were God's enemies, we were reconciled to him through the death of his Son, how much more, having been reconciled, shall we be saved through his life!* <u>**Not only is this so, but we also rejoice in God through our Lord Jesus Christ, through whom we have now received reconciliation.**</u> *Therefore, just as sin entered the world through one man, and death through sin, and in this way death came to all men, because all sinned—for before the law was given, sin was in the world. But sin is not taken into account when there is no law. Nevertheless, death reigned from the time of Adam to the time of Moses, even over those who did not sin by breaking a command, as did Adam, who was a pattern of the one to come. But the gift is not like the trespass. For if the many died by the trespass of the one man, how much more did God's grace and the gift that came by the grace of the one man, Jesus Christ, overflow to the many! Again, the gift of God is not like the result of the one man's sin: The judgment followed one sin and brought condemnation, but the gift followed many trespasses and brought justification. For if, by the trespass of the one man, death reigned through that one man, how much more will those who receive God's abundant provision of grace and of the gift of righteousness reign in life through the one man, Jesus Christ. Consequently, just as the result of one trespass was condemnation for all men, so also the result of one act of righteousness was justification that brings life for all men. For just as through the disobedience of the one man the many were made sinners, so also through the obedience of the one man the many will be made righteous.* <u>**The law was added so that the trespass might increase.**</u> **But where sin increased, grace increased all the more, so that, just as sin reigned in death, so also grace might reign through righteousness to bring eternal life through Jesus Christ our Lord.** *What shall we say, then? Shall we go on sinning so that grace may increase? By no means! We died to sin; how can we live in it any longer? Or don't you know that all of us who were baptized into Christ Jesus were baptized into his death? We were therefore buried with him through baptism into death in order that, just as Christ was* *raised from the dead through the glory of the Father, we too may live a new life. If we have been united with him like this in his death, we will certainly also be united with him in his resurrection. For we know that our old self was crucified with him so that the body of sin might be done away with, that we should no longer be slaves to sin—because anyone who has died has been freed from sin. Now if we died with Christ, we believe that we will also live with him. For we know that since Christ was raised from the dead, he cannot die again; death no longer has mastery over him.* **The death he died, he died to sin once for all; but the life he lives, he lives to God.** *In the same way, count yourselves dead to sin but alive to God in Christ Jesus.* **Therefore do not let sin reign in your mortal body so that you obey its evil desires.** *Do not offer the parts of your body to sin, as instruments of wickedness, but rather offer yourselves to God, as those who have been brought from death to life; and offer the parts of your body to him as instruments of righteousness.* **For sin shall not be your master, because you are not under law, but under grace.** *What then? Shall we sin because we are not under law but under grace? By no means! Don't you know that when you offer yourselves to someone to obey him as slaves, you are slaves to the one whom you obey—whether you are slaves to sin, which leads to death, or to obedience, which leads to righteousness? But thanks be to God that, though you used to be slaves to sin, you wholeheartedly obeyed the form of teaching to which you were entrusted. You have been set free from sin and have become slaves to righteousness. I put this in human terms because you are weak in your natural selves. Just as you used to offer the parts of your body in slavery to impurity and to ever-increasing wickedness, so now offer them in slavery to righteousness leading to holiness. When you were slaves to sin, you were free from the control of righteousness. What benefit did you reap at that time from the things you are now ashamed of?* **Those things result in death! But now that you have been set free from sin and have become slaves to God, the benefit you reap leads to holiness, and the result is eternal life. For the wages of sin is death, but the gift of God is eternal life in Christ Jesus our Lord.** (NIV)

In simple terms these verses are telling us that mankind is justified by faith in Jesus Christ. When Adam sinned, it allowed sin to enter into the world. Adam's sin tainted the human race. We are all born into a fallen state (away from God). Death is a by-product of sin. At God's appointed time, He sent His Son, Jesus, to die on the cross for the forgiveness of our sins. Jesus is victory over death. Every person is born separated from God because of sin.

Rom 3:23 ***for all have sinned* and *fall short of the glory of God,*** (NIV)

The End and the Beginning

In 1 Corinthians we are told that because of Adam's sin, we will all experience physical death in this natural body. Since death came through a man (Adam), so also salvation comes through a man (Jesus Christ). Those who commit to Jesus as their Savior and ask Him to forgive them for their sins will receive eternal life. It is that simple. All you have to do is believe in your heart that Jesus is your Savior!

1 Cor 15:21-22 *For since death came through a man, the resurrection of the dead comes also through a man. <u>For as in Adam all die, so in Christ all will be made alive</u>.* (NIV)

By one act of righteousness—Jesus dying on the cross—it was the justification that brings life for all men who believe in Jesus. By accepting Jesus, you are not only living a new life here on earth, but also forever in eternity and you are also released from the slavery of sin. Death no longer is the master to a born-again believer. You have been brought from death to life. You have been set free from the slavery of sin and are now slaves to righteousness. The gift of God is eternal life. Although the final victory over death for the righteous will be when they receive their resurrected bodies, the complete victory over death will come when there is no more death.

1 Cor 15:50-58 *I declare to you, brothers, that flesh and blood cannot inherit the kingdom of God, nor does the perishable inherit the imperishable. Listen, I tell you a mystery: We will not all sleep, but we will all be changed—in a flash, in the twinkling of an eye, at the last trumpet.* ***For the trumpet will sound, the dead will be raised imperishable, and we will be changed. For the perishable must clothe itself with the imperishable, and the mortal with immortality. When the perishable has been clothed with the imperishable, and the mortal with immortality, then the saying that is written will come true:*** ***<u>"Death has been swallowed up in victory."</u>*** *"Where, O death, is your victory? Where, O death, is your sting?" The sting of death is sin, and the power of sin is the law. But thanks be to God!* ***<u>He gives us the victory through our Lord Jesus Christ.</u>*** *Therefore, my dear brothers, stand firm. Let nothing move you. Always give yourselves fully to the work of the Lord, because you know that your labor in the Lord is not in vain.* (NIV)

<u>LAKE OF FIRE</u>

Where do the lost souls of all time spend eternity? Do they suffer? Do they have bodies? These are some tough questions, but I believe that the Bible clearly answers these questions. At the point of physical death everyone's soul and spirit will travel to a temporary holding place. Since our human body is only a tent or house for our spirit and soul, while we live here on earth, it will return to dust after we die. Man was made from dust and he will return to dust.

AFTER THE RAPTURE

> Gen 3:19   *By the sweat of your brow you will eat your food until you return to the ground, since from it you were taken; <u>for dust you are and to dust you will return.</u>"* (NIV)

> Eccl 3:20   *All go to the same place; all come from dust, and to dust all return.* (NIV)

> Eccl 12:7   *<u>and the dust returns to the ground it came from</u>, and the spirit returns to God who gave it.* (NIV)

Scripture talks about a first death and a second death. Just like Adam, we will all die physically in this body. This is the first death. Every person, whether they are saved or unsaved, will face the first death. A spiritual body will be given to every soul when they are resurrected. This includes the souls of both the saved and the unsaved.

> 2 Cor 5:1-4   *<u>Now we know that if the earthly tent we live in is destroyed, we have a building from God, an eternal house in heaven, not built by human hands</u>. Meanwhile we groan, longing to be clothed with our heavenly dwelling, because when we are clothed, we will not be found naked. For while we are in this tent, we groan and are burdened, because we do not wish to be unclothed but to be clothed with our heavenly dwelling, so that what is mortal may be swallowed up by life.* (NIV)

> 1 Cor 15:22   *For as in Adam all die, <u>even so in Christ shall all be made alive</u>.* (KJV)

After a person dies, his soul and spirit (in a disembodied form) will be taken to a temporary holding place to await the resurrection of their new bodies. Those who are saved will go to a place called Paradise, while those who are not saved will go to a place called hell (Hades in the New Testament and Sheol in the Old Testament). There is no such place as purgatory, nor is there such a state as "soul sleep." Contrary to this popular opinion of today, the spirit and soul of a person does not go to sleep and enter a state of unconsciousness at physical death, only to await the return of the Lord. Our soul and spirit, when it is in its disembodied state, will be in a state of consciousness while it awaits the time to receive a new body. We are born with a natural body and we will be resurrected with a spiritual body.

> 1 Cor 15:44   *<u>it is sown a natural body, it is raised a spiritual body</u>. If there is a natural body, there is also a spiritual body.* (NIV)

Just as there is a first death and a second death, there is also a first resurrection and a second resurrection. Only the souls and spirits of those people who are saved will take part in the first resurrection (resurrection of life), while only the souls and spirits of those people who are not saved will take part in the second resurrection (resurrection of the damned).

The End and the Beginning

Notice in the verses, below, that at both the first and second resurrection the souls and spirits of the saved and the unsaved will be resurrected when they hear the voice of Jesus.

John 5:28-29 *"Do not marvel at this; for the hour is coming in which all who are in the graves <u>will hear His voice</u>" <u>and come forth</u>—those who have done good, <u>to the resurrection of life</u>, and those who have done evil, <u>to the resurrection of condemnation</u>.* (NKJ)

The most concise depiction of the differences between Paradise, here depicted as Abrahams side (bosom-KJV), and hell can be found in a narrative in the book of Luke. In this account we have a description of what happens to the spirit and soul of the two different groups of people when they die in this life. This is an account of what it was like at the time before Jesus was crucified. Many people today consider this to be a parable, but that is probably not the case. Even if it does happens to be a parable, the message is the same.

Luke 16:19-31 *"There was <u>a rich man</u> who was dressed in purple and fine linen and lived in luxury every day. At his gate was laid <u>a beggar named Lazarus</u>, covered with sores and longing to eat what fell from the rich man's table. Even the dogs came and licked his sores. "The time came when the beggar died and the angels carried him to Abraham's side. The rich man also died and was buried. <u>In hell, where he was in torment</u>, he looked up and saw Abraham far away, with Lazarus by his side. So he called to him, 'Father Abraham, have pity on me and send Lazarus to dip the tip of his finger in water and cool my tongue, because I am in agony in this fire.' "But Abraham replied, 'Son, remember that in your lifetime you received your good things, while Lazarus received bad things, but now he is comforted here and you are in agony. <u>And besides all this</u>, <u>between us and you a great chasm has been fixed</u>, <u>so that those who want to go from here to you cannot</u>, <u>nor can anyone cross over from there to us</u>.' "He answered, 'Then I beg you, father, send Lazarus to my father's house, for I have five brothers. Let him warn them, so that they will not also come to this place of torment.' "Abraham replied, 'They have Moses and the Prophets; let them listen to them.' "'No, father Abraham,' he said, 'but if someone from the dead goes to them, they will repent.' "He said to him, 'If they do not listen to Moses and the Prophets, they will not be convinced even if someone rises from the dead.'"* (NIV)

At death, the disembodied state (spirit and soul) of every person will go to either Paradise (for believers) or hell (for unbelievers) to await the covering of a new body, a new house for the spirit and soul to take up residence. Those in Paradise will be happy and content as they await their new body, while those in hell are in torment as they await their new body. Also notice that there is a great gulf between the two locations to prevent those who are in hell from crossing over to the Paradise side. I am assuming that nobody who is in the Paradise side will want to cross over to hell. Prior to the death of Jesus the abodes of Paradise and hell were located below the surface of the earth. After Jesus died on the cross He descended into hell and proclaimed His victory over Satan.

> 1 Pet 3:18-19   *For Christ died for sins once for all, the righteous for the unrighteous, to bring you to God. He was put to death in the body but made alive by the Spirit, <u>through whom also he went and preached to the spirits in prison</u>* (NIV)

> 1 Pet 4:6   *<u>For this is the reason the gospel was preached even to those who are now dead</u>, so that they might be judged according to men in regard to the body, but live according to God in regard to the spirit.* (NIV)

After Jesus was resurrected, as He ascended to heaven, He took the souls from Paradise with Him. The spirits and souls of the believers were removed from the abode of Paradise, which at that time existed below the earth. Then they were taken to heaven, being released from captivity, to finish their period of waiting for their resurrected bodies.

> Eph 4:8-10   *This is why it says: "<u>When he ascended on high, he led captives in his train and gave gifts to men</u>." (What does "he ascended" mean except that he also descended to the lower, earthly regions? He who descended is the very one who ascended higher than all the heavens, in order to fill the whole universe.)* (NIV)

> Ps 68:18   *<u>When you ascended on high, you led captives in your train</u>; you received gifts from men, even from the rebellious—that you, O LORD God, might dwell there.* (NIV)

The spirits of the saints, before the cross of Christ, could not go directly to heaven because they could not precede Jesus. It was Jesus who lifted them out of captivity. This also follows the order of the resurrections found in 1 Corinthians; Christ (the first to be resurrected) is the firstfruits, followed by the saved people who make up the first part of the first resurrection. This includes the people who have died before the Rapture and also those who remain alive at the time of the Rapture. This is the specified order for the resurrections.

> 1 Cor 15:23   *But each in his own turn: <u>Christ, the firstfruits</u>; then, <u>when he comes, those who belong to him</u>.* (NIV)

The spirit of every believer who dies during the Dispensation of Grace will join those Old Testament saints in heaven who were taken there by Jesus. Together they await the time of their resurrection. Paul was torn between physical death and staying alive in this world. Please note that departing from this world (for believers only) is far better than staying here, but in the end we must stay here on earth for the benefit of building up the kingdom of God. Jesus will call us home at the proper time, whether it be before the Rapture, if we die before He comes, or at the Rapture, if we are still alive when He comes. Either way it is a beneficial situation for those of the faith. Paul says,

Phil 1:19-26 *for I know that through your prayers and the help given by the Spirit of Jesus Christ, what has happened to me will turn out for my deliverance.* **I eagerly expect and hope that I will in no way be ashamed, but will have sufficient courage so that now as always Christ will be exalted in my body, whether by life or by death. <u>For to me, to live is Christ and to die is gain.</u> If I am to go on living in the body, this will mean fruitful labor for me. Yet what shall I choose? I do not know! <u>I am torn between the two</u>: I desire to depart and be with Christ, which is better by far; but it is more necessary for you that I remain in the body.** *Convinced of this, I know that I will remain, and I will continue with all of you for your progress and joy in the faith, so that through my being with you again your joy in Christ Jesus will overflow on account of me.* (NIV)

2 Cor 5:6-9 *Therefore we are always confident and know that as long as we are at home in the body we are away from the Lord. We live by faith, not by sight.* <u>*We are confident, I say, and would prefer to be away from the body and at home with the Lord*</u> *So we make it our goal to please him, whether we are at home in the body or away from it.* (NIV)

It is perfectly clear from 2 Corinthians 5:8, above, that at physical death (away from the body), we will go to be with Jesus (home with the Lord) who is presently residing in heaven. Jesus said to the penitent thief on the cross, *"Today you will be with me in paradise."* When believer's die, their spirits will be brought into the presence of the saints who have preceded them to heaven. People, such as their loved ones (if they were believers), patriarchs (Abraham), prophets (Moses and Isaiah), apostles (Paul and John), and everyone who has made the right decision of accepting Jesus in this lifetime, are in Paradise in heaven waiting to be clothed with their glorious spiritual bodies. Who do you want to see when you get there? Paradise is a separate place than the heavenly Jerusalem, where God dwells.

Luke 23:42-43 *Then he said, "Jesus, remember me when you come into your kingdom." Jesus answered him, "<u>I tell you the truth, today you will be with me in paradise.</u>"* (NIV)

At the very point of death (for a believer) angels will transport their soul and spirit to the temporary abode of Paradise, which is now located in heaven. None of this activity is visible to the naked eye. While they are in this intermediate state they do not have access to God in the heavenly Jerusalem.

AFTER THE RAPTURE

Luke 16:22   *"The time came when the beggar died and <u>the angels carried him to Abraham's side</u>. The rich man also died and was buried.* (NIV)

Heb 1:14   *Are not all angels ministering spirits sent to serve those who will inherit salvation?* (NIV)

Though these spirits are in a glorious place and are happy, conscious and aware of their surroundings, they are somewhat limited at this point because they await the glorious power of their resurrected bodies. They will not receive their rewards in heaven until after they have received their heavenly bodies. Only after the resurrection will they be able to experience the full extent of the glory of God. Just like believers today here on earth, they joyfully await and anticipate the second advent of Jesus.

Some people believe the saints who are caught up out of the world at the Rapture will exit with their earthy bodies, but that does not seem to be the case. On the earth *After the Rapture* the scene will find dead bodies lying around the world. In some locations where there are large concentrations of people of the faith there will be mass burials, places like America, Canada and South Korea.

To those people who do not make the right decision it will be eternal punishment and that means forever. As we have mentioned elsewhere in this book, the judgment of all the unsaved will take place after the Millennium and also after Satan is released for a short time to turn the people who will be living at that time against God. In other words, after all of the unsaved spirits and souls have come to completion. A point of interest here is that a White Throne is mentioned. The brilliance of Jesus will shine forth.

Rev 20:11-15   *Then I saw <u>a great white throne</u> and him who was seated on it. Earth and sky fled from his presence, and there was no place for them. And I saw the dead, great and small, standing before the throne, and books were opened. Another book was opened, which is the book of life. <u>The dead were judged according to what they had done as recorded in the books.</u> The sea gave up the dead that were in it, and death and Hades gave up the dead that were in them, and each person was judged according to what he had done. <u>Then death and Hades were thrown into the lake of fire. The lake of fire is the second death. If anyone's name was not found written in the book of life, he was thrown into the lake of fire.</u>* (NIV)

The second death comes into play after the unsaved have received their resurrected bodies, when they will face the judgment for those who play a part in the second resurrection. Every unsaved person from the beginning of time will face Jesus on His throne at the Great White Throne Judgment. Not a single person at that time will be found innocent. They will be judged for their sins. Part of their punishment at this judgment will be death (the second death) and the loss of their resurrected bodies.

Rev 20:6   *Blessed and holy are those who have part in the first resurrection.*

> *<u>The second death has no power over them</u>, but they will be priests of God and of Christ and will reign with him for a thousand years.* (NIV)

Rev 21:8   *But the cowardly, <u>the unbelieving</u>, the vile, the murderers, the sexually immoral, those who practice magic arts, the idolaters and all liars—<u>their place will be in the fiery lake of burning sulfur. This is the second death.</u>"* (NIV)

As you can see from the verses above another portion of the punishment of the lost is to be consigned to the Lake of Fire. There they will live throughout eternity in their disembodied form, along with Satan, the Antichrist, the false prophet and the fallen angels.

Matt 25:41-46   **"Then he will say to those on his left, '<u>Depart from me, you who are cursed, into the eternal fire prepared for the devil and his angels.</u>** *For I was hungry and you gave me nothing to eat, I was thirsty and you gave me nothing to drink, I was a stranger and you did not invite me in, I needed clothes and you did not clothe me, I was sick and in prison and you did not look after me.' "They also will answer, 'Lord, when did we see you hungry or thirsty or a stranger or needing clothes or sick or in prison, and did not help you?' "He will reply, 'I tell you the truth, whatever you did not do for one of the least of these, you did not do for me.'* **"Then they will go away to eternal punishment, but the righteous to eternal life."** (NIV)

Mark 9:43-48   *"If your hand causes you to sin, cut it off. It is better for you to enter into life maimed, rather than having two hands, <u>to go to hell, into the fire that shall never be quenched</u>—"where 'Their worm <u>does not die, and the fire is not quenched.</u>' "And if your foot causes you to sin, cut it off. It is better for you to enter life lame, rather than having two feet, to be cast into hell, into the fire that shall never be quenched—"where 'Their worm does not die, and the fire is not quenched.' "And if your eye causes you to sin, pluck it out.* **It is better for you to enter the kingdom of God with one eye, rather than having two eyes, to be cast into hell fire**—*"where 'Their worm does not die, and the fire is not quenched.'* (NKJ)

For those of you who do not think this will be a literal lake of fire (extreme heat) filled with torment forever and ever—read these verses.

Rev 20:10   *And the devil, who deceived them, was thrown into the lake of burning sulfur, where the beast and the false prophet had been thrown. <u>They will be tormented day and night for ever and ever</u>.* (NIV)

Rev 20:14-15	*Then death and Hades were thrown into the lake of fire. <u>The lake of fire is the second death</u>. If anyone's name was not found written in the book of life, <u>he was thrown into the lake of fire</u>.* (NIV)
Rev 21:8	*But the cowardly, <u>the unbelieving</u>, the vile, the murderers, the sexually immoral, those who practice magic arts, the idolaters and all liars—<u>their place will be in the fiery lake of burning sulfur</u>. This is the second death."* (NIV)
Rev 19:20	*But the beast was captured, and with him the false prophet who had performed the miraculous signs on his behalf. With these signs he had deluded those who had received the mark of the beast and worshiped his image. <u>The two of them were thrown alive into the fiery lake of burning sulfur</u>.* (NIV)
Dan 7:11	*"Then I continued to watch because of the boastful words the horn was speaking. <u>I kept looking until the beast was slain and its body destroyed and thrown into the blazing fire</u>.* (NIV)
Matt 13:49-50	*This is how it will be at the end of the age. The angels will come and separate the wicked from the righteous and **throw them into the fiery furnace, <u>where there will be weeping and gnashing of teeth</u>**.* (NIV)
Matt 22:13	*"Then the king told the attendants, 'Tie him hand and foot, and throw him outside, into the darkness, where there will be weeping and gnashing of teeth.'* (NIV)
Matt 24:50-51	*The master of that servant will come on a day when he does not expect him and at an hour he is not aware of. **He will cut him to pieces and assign him a place with the hypocrites, <u>where there will be weeping and gnashing of teeth</u>**.* (NIV)

If all of that is not enough—the worst punishment of all is being shut out from the presence of the Lord for eternity.

2 Thes 1:9	*They will be punished with everlasting destruction and <u>**shut out from the presence of the Lord**</u> and from the majesty of his power* (NIV)

From the verses listed above it is obvious that the Lake of Fire is a literal place of punishment and perpetual torment. It is not a place of annihilation, as some people believe today. Those that teach total annihilation are sending the wrong message to those people who will be spending eternity in the Lake of Fire. Where is the Lake of Fire? Nobody knows for sure, but a good possibility could be one of the enormous "black holes" scientists have discovered in the far north in outer space.

The End and the Beginning

> Job 26:6-7   *Death is naked before God; Destruction lies uncovered.* <u>*He spreads out the northern [skies] over empty space*</u>*; he suspends the earth over nothing.* (NIV)

There is a far better place to spend eternity and if you have read this book in its entirety up to this point, you know where it is.

> 1 Pet 1:4   *to {obtain} an inheritance {which is} imperishable and undefiled and will not fade away,* <u>*reserved in heaven for you*</u>*,* (NAS)
>
> Heb 12:22   <u>*But you have come to Mount Zion, to the heavenly Jerusalem, the city of the living God.*</u> *You have come to thousands upon thousands of angels in joyful assembly,* (NIV)
>
> Rev 21:2   <u>*I saw the Holy City, the new Jerusalem, coming down out of heaven from God*</u>*, prepared as a bride beautifully dressed for her husband.* (NIV)

There are different levels in the Lake of Fire to allow for the different degrees of punishment that will be meted out at the Great White Throne Judgment. Those people such as the Antichrist, Hitler, Stalin and Jim Jones—just to name a few—will be in the lowest depths of the Lake of Fire and will also suffer the worst degrees of punishment. Satan will not be kind to those who were his greatest followers. However, nice people who are unsaved in this life should not expect any comfort in hell—for it will not be found in this location.

THE BEGINNING OF FOREVER

Believe it or not—after reading a book with such devastation to the human race—I have saved the best news for last. Although I have revealed the victory of good over evil, Jesus over Satan and the eternal destiny of everyone depending on their own freewill choice, I have not given you much of a glimpse of what it will be like—FOREVER & EVER!

When the plan of salvation has been played out the Universal Kingdom will come into play when; God the Father, God the Son (Jesus) and God the Spirit (Holy Spirit) will dwell together with the Saints and the holy Angels. The final two chapters of Revelation describe the eternal order of things to come. God's works are progressive. The Millennium, where sin and death were greatly restricted, is the transition state from the old earth to the restored earth. The Millennium is the age of regeneration. The final age—the Day of God—will be totally free of sin and death. At last, the victory belongs to God as Jesus defeats the enemies of God. Utopia finally arrives! All the struggles of this life will pale in comparison to what lies ahead for God's children.

We know from Daniel that the Day of the Lord will transition into the Day of God and it will endure forever. The Kingdom Age (Millennium) is an everlasting dominion that will not pass away. This kingdom will never be destroyed.

Dan 2:44   *"In the time of those kings, <u>the God of heaven will set up a kingdom that will never be destroyed</u>, nor will it be left to another people. It will crush all those kingdoms and bring them to an end, <u>but it will itself endure forever</u>.* (NIV)

Dan 7:14   *He was given authority, glory and sovereign power; all peoples, nations and men of every language worshiped him. His dominion is an everlasting dominion that will not pass away, <u>and his kingdom is one that will never be destroyed</u>.* (NIV)

THE KINGDOM OF GOD

Before we look at the future eternal state, we should look at heaven as it has existed in times past and also what it is like at the present time. Few people today, even among Christians, realize the extent of the Kingdom of God. The natural Kingdom of God over the universe includes all that exists in time and space. It exists without interruption throughout all time. It is under Divine rule and control. The Divine ruler of this kingdom controls the final decisions in the affairs of this kingdom. This kingdom includes the entire universe as it exists in the three levels of heaven. It also includes the earth and mankind who has lived on earth throughout history (past and future). It even includes everything under the earth, which is a reference to hell or the abode where the souls of the unsaved are gathered to await their resurrection and judgment. King David made a reference to the existence of the Kingdom of God when he gave the last instructions to his son Solomon. Everything in heaven and earth belong to God. He is the ruler of all things. God was the King of the Israelites. They rejected this King and wanted a king like the rest of the nations had.

1 Chr 29:10-13   *David praised the LORD in the presence of the whole assembly, saying, "Praise be to you, O LORD, God of our father Israel, from everlasting to everlasting. Yours, O LORD, is the greatness and the power and the glory and the majesty and the splendor, for everything in heaven and earth is yours. <u>Yours, O LORD, is the kingdom; you are exalted as head over all</u>. Wealth and honor come from you; <u>you are the ruler of all things</u>. In your hands are strength and power to exalt and give strength to all. Now, our God, we give you thanks, and praise your glorious name.* (NIV)

The dwelling of God, which is part of the Kingdom of God, is not visible from earth. God's home is in the third level of heaven above the Celestial heaven (which includes the sun, moon and the stars). This kingdom was in existence at the time of creation. At that time heaven was divided into three levels. The Divine control of this kingdom is providential with God and with wise benevolence He directs the universe and the affairs of man. God is in control of the final decisions in the affairs of the universe. Occasionally, Divine control may be exercised by supernatural means. Four prominent times when God exercises supernatural means throughout history are: in the past; (1) at the great flood, (2) at the destruction of

The End and the Beginning

Sodom and Gomorrah and (3) when the Israelites left Egypt, and (4) in the future when God will once again use supernatural acts to achieve His purposes during the Tribulation Period. The rule of God has always existed and has never been or will it be abrogated.

A better and more comprehensive understanding of the Kingdom of God will provide us with a more thorough understanding of the total plan of God. Far above the stars, which are found in the second level of heaven, there exists a homeland, a place where God dwells. This dwelling place exists within the limits of a city and is known as the City of God, the Holy City and the Heavenly Jerusalem. Please consult the chart on page 766 for a birds eye view—look at the top left hand corner to locate the Heavenly Jerusalem.

The present reality of the Kingdom of God must be distinguished from the future Messianic Kingdom. The natural universal Kingdom of God is ruled by God throughout eternity (past and future) in heaven, while the Messianic Kingdom will be ruled by Jesus after God bestows the kingdom to Him. The reign of Jesus will begin in heaven as He purges sinful mankind from the earth. Following that He will establish His Kingdom on earth in Jerusalem.

God has always been "our Father" and "our King." God has always ruled the universe from His throne in heaven, even when He temporarily dwells on earth among His people. It is an eternal dominion. The Holy Angels (heavenly hosts), who also abide in heaven, are God's servants who receive instructions from Him and obey His commands.

Ps 103:19-22   *<u>The LORD has established his throne in heaven, and his kingdom rules over all.</u> Praise the LORD, you his angels, you mighty ones who do his bidding, who obey his word. <u>Praise the LORD, all his heavenly hosts, you his servants who do his will.</u> Praise the LORD, all his works everywhere in his dominion. Praise the LORD, O my soul.* (NIV)

Ps 29:10-11   *The LORD sits enthroned over the flood; <u>the LORD is enthroned as King forever.</u> The LORD gives strength to his people; the LORD blesses his people with peace.* (NIV)

Dan 4:34-35   *At the end of that time, I, Nebuchadnezzar, raised my eyes toward heaven, and my sanity was restored. Then I praised <u>the Most High</u>; I honored and glorified him who lives forever. <u>His dominion is an eternal dominion; his kingdom endures from generation to generation.</u> All the peoples of the earth are regarded as nothing. He does as he pleases with the powers of heaven and the peoples of the earth. No one can hold back his hand or say to him: "What have you done?"* (NIV)

Within the heavenly city of Jerusalem there exists a Temple on a sacred mountain. In the Temple there is a throne where God sits and rules the universe. The Temple area is known as Mount Zion. In the Sermon on the Mount Jesus mentions God's throne in heaven, along with the heavenly Jerusalem, which is the City of the Great King (God).

AFTER THE RAPTURE

Matt 5:33-35 *"Again, you have heard that it was said to the people long ago, 'Do not break your oath, but keep the oaths you have made to the Lord.' But I tell you, Do not swear at all: either by <u>heaven, for it is God's throne</u>; or by the earth, for it is his footstool; or by <u>Jerusalem, for it is the city of the Great King</u>.* (NIV)

The most spectacular description of God sitting on His throne can be found in a vision of the prophet Ezekiel.

Ezek 1:26-28 *Above the expanse over their heads was what looked like <u>a throne of sapphire</u>, and high above on the throne was <u>a figure like that of a man</u>. I saw that from what appeared to be his waist up he looked like glowing metal, as if full of fire, and that from there down he looked like fire; and brilliant light surrounded him. Like the appearance of a rainbow in the clouds on a rainy day, so was the radiance around him. <u>This was the appearance of the likeness of the glory of the LORD</u>. When I saw it, I fell facedown, and I heard the voice of one speaking.* (NIV)

In a dream Daniel was also allowed to see a vision of God—the Ancient of Days—as He took His seat on His throne. Notice God's glory in these two visions.

Dan 7:9-10 *"As I looked, "thrones were set in place, and <u>the Ancient of Days</u> took his seat. His clothing was as white as snow; the hair of his head was white like wool. <u>His throne was flaming with fire</u>, and its wheels were all ablaze. A river of fire was flowing, coming out from before him. Thousands upon thousands attended him; ten thousand times ten thousand stood before him. The court was seated, and the books were opened.* (NIV)

Although the third level of heaven is the eternal home of God, Jesus, the Holy Spirit and the Angels, it will eventually be the eternal home of all the saints. Scripture refers to people on earth who live by faith as aliens or strangers living in a foreign country. Those people who accept God by faith are longing for a better country—a heavenly one. God has prepared a city for them. In the great faith chapter of the Bible we pick up the story.

Heb 11:8-16 <u>*By faith Abraham,*</u> *when called to go to a place he would later receive as his inheritance, obeyed and went, even though he did not know where he was going. By faith he made his home in the promised land like a stranger in a foreign country; he lived in tents, as did Isaac and Jacob, who were heirs with him of the same promise. <u>For he was looking forward to the city with foundations, whose architect and builder is God</u>. By faith Abraham, even though he was past age—and Sarah herself was barren—was enabled to*

> *become a father because he considered him faithful who had made the promise. And so from this one man, and he as good as dead, came descendants as numerous as the stars in the sky and as countless as the sand on the seashore.* ***All these people were still living by faith when they died. They did not receive the things promised; they only saw them and welcomed them from a distance.*** *And they admitted that they were* ***aliens*** *and* ***strangers*** *on earth.* ***People who say such things show that they are looking for a country of their own.*** *If they had been thinking of the country they had left, they would have had opportunity to return.* ***Instead, they were longing for a better country—a heavenly one. Therefore God is not ashamed to be called their God, for he has prepared a city for them.*** (NIV)

In verse thirteen, above, the Greek word for "aliens" is *xenos*.

Thayer's Definitions
3581 xenos
1. a foreigner, a stranger
   a. alien (from a person or thing)
   b. without the knowledge of, without a share in
   c. new, unheard of
2. one who receives and entertains another hospitably with whom he stays or lodges, a host

Likewise, *Thayer's* lists the definitions for the Greek word *parepidemos*, which is translated as "stranger," in the same verse as:

3927 parepidemos
1. one who comes from a foreign country into a city or land to reside there by the side of the natives.
2. a stranger
3. sojourning in a strange place, a foreigner
4. in the New Testament, metaphorically, in reference to heaven as the native country, one who sojourns on earth

It is not speaking metaphorically of heaven as a native country in Hebrews eleven, but as a literal place where the saints will spend eternity. It is their heavenly home. The Greek word for "country," in these scripture verses, is *patris* and *Thayer's* lists the definition as:

3968 patris-
one's native country
a. one's fatherland, one's own country, a fixed abode or home
b. one's own native place, that is, a city

AFTER THE RAPTURE

It is obvious from the faith chapter that the reward of the faithful is not achieved during the time they spend on earth. They long for a better country or homeland, which is a city prepared for them by God in heaven. In the end, those who choose God will rest in the shade, under the protection (shadow) of the Almighty in His eternal Kingdom.

Heb 11:16 — *Instead, they were longing for a better country—a heavenly one. Therefore God is not ashamed to be called their God, for he has prepared a city for them.* (NIV)

Heb 12:22-24 — *But you have come to Mount Zion, to the heavenly Jerusalem, the city of the living God. You have come to thousands upon thousands of angels in joyful assembly, to the church of the firstborn, whose names are written in heaven. You have come to God, the judge of all men, to the spirits of righteous men made perfect, to Jesus the mediator of a new covenant, and to the sprinkled blood that speaks a better word than the blood of Abel.* (NIV)

Ps 23:6 — *Surely goodness and love will follow me all the days of my life, <u>and I will dwell in the house of the LORD forever</u>.* (NIV)

Ps 27:4 — *One thing I ask of the LORD, this is what I seek: <u>that I may dwell in the house of the LORD all the days of my life</u>, to gaze upon the beauty of the LORD and to seek him in his temple.* (NIV)

Ps 84:1-4 — *<u>How lovely is your dwelling place, O LORD Almighty</u>! My soul yearns, even faints, for the courts of the LORD; my heart and my flesh cry out for the living God. Even the sparrow has found a home, and the swallow a nest for herself, where she may have her young—a place near your altar, <u>O LORD Almighty, my King and my God. Blessed are those who dwell in your house; they are ever praising you</u>. Selah* (NIV)

Ps 91:1-2 — *<u>He who dwells in the shelter of the Most High will rest in the shadow of the Almighty.</u> I will say of the LORD, "He is my refuge and my fortress, my God, in whom I trust."* (NIV)

Ps 122:1-5 — *I rejoiced with those who said to me, "<u>Let us go to the house of the LORD.</u>" Our feet are standing in your gates, O Jerusalem. <u>Jerusalem is built like a city that is closely compacted together.</u> That is where the tribes go up, the tribes of the LORD, to praise the name of the LORD according to the statute given to Israel. There the thrones for judgment stand, the thrones of the house of David.* (NIV)

The unsaved will not be allowed in this city!

The End and the Beginning

Ps 101:1-8 *I will sing of your love and justice; to you, O LORD, I will sing praise. I will be careful to lead a blameless life—when will you come to me? I will walk in my house with blameless heart. I will set before my eyes no vile thing. **The deeds of faithless men I hate; they will not cling to me. Men of perverse heart shall be far from me; I will have nothing to do with evil.** Whoever slanders his neighbor in secret, him will I put to silence; whoever has haughty eyes and a proud heart, him will I not endure. **My eyes will be on the faithful in the land, that they may dwell with me; he whose walk is blameless will minister to me. No one who practices deceit will dwell in my house; no one who speaks falsely will stand in my presence.** Every morning I will put to silence all the wicked in the land; **I will cut off every evildoer from the city of the LORD.*** (NIV)

What lies ahead for the saints in heaven is far beyond human comprehension. What God has prepared for those who love Him (the believers) He has destined for our glory. It was destined even before time began.

1 Cor 2:6-10 *We do, however, speak a message of wisdom among the mature, but not the wisdom of this age or of the rulers of this age, who are coming to nothing. **No, we speak of God's secret wisdom, a wisdom that has been hidden and that God destined for our glory before time began.** None of the rulers of this age understood it, for if they had, they would not have crucified the Lord of glory. However, as it is written: "**No eye has seen, no ear has heard, no mind has conceived what God has prepared for those who love him**"—but **God has revealed it to us by his Spirit.** The Spirit searches all things, even the deep things of God.* (NIV)

The Old Testament saints will be allowed to move into their eternal dwellings in heaven after the Judgment Seat of Christ is completed. The church age saints will move into their dwellings after the seven-year wedding feast is completed. This will all take place in the future Messianic Kingdom where God will crown His Son King. God's purpose at that time will be to bring heaven and earth together under one authority for 1000 years.

THE DAY OF GOD — ETERNITY

After Jesus has defeated all His enemies—the end will come. Those enemies include all dominion, authority and power. This not only includes mankind, but also the fallen angelic order with their leader Satan. Because there is no more death, there will no longer be a need for an intermediate abode. Hades will be abolished. The destruction of death and Hades appear to be the last event that will take place before the eternal order of things come into play. This brings an end to the last enemy—DEATH! At this time—after His Millennial reign, Satan's doom and the Great White Throne Judgment—Jesus as King will turn the

AFTER THE RAPTURE

Kingdom back to God the Father, so that He may be all in all. God anointed His Son to be King in order to rule for one thousand years. After the thousand years are over Jesus will destroy all of His enemies, so He can return the regal authority of the universe back to His Father. Actually, God and Jesus will both rule as King (co-regent) during the Day of God. At that time there will be no more death, because there will be no more sinners. Eternity past—with the time span of human history—will reach eternity future. This is the last end!

> 1 Cor 15:24-28 — ***Then the end will come, when he hands over the kingdom to God the Father after he has destroyed all dominion, authority and power.*** *For he must reign until he has put all his enemies under his feet.* ***The last enemy to be destroyed is death.*** *For he "has put everything under his feet." Now when it says that "everything" has been put under him, it is clear that this does not include God himself, who put everything under Christ. When he has done this, then the Son himself will be made subject to him who put everything under him, so that God may be all in all.* (NIV)

The new heaven and new earth will be a home of righteousness. The saints, even today, should be looking forward to these future glories promised by God.

> 2 Pet 3:11-18 — *Since everything will be destroyed in this way, what kind of people ought you to be?* ***You ought to live holy and godly lives as you look forward to the day of God and speed its coming.*** *That day will bring about the destruction of the heavens by fire, and the elements will melt in the heat.* ***But in keeping with his promise we are looking forward to a new heaven and a new earth, the home of righteousness.*** *So then, dear friends, since you are looking forward to this, make every effort to be found spotless, blameless and at peace with him. Bear in mind that our Lord's patience means salvation, just as our dear brother Paul also wrote you with the wisdom that God gave him. He writes the same way in all his letters, speaking in them of these matters. His letters contain some things that are hard to understand, which ignorant and unstable people distort, as they do the other Scriptures, to their own destruction. Therefore, dear friends, since you already know this, be on your guard so that you may not be carried away by the error of lawless men and fall from your secure position.* ***But grow in the grace and knowledge of our Lord and Savior Jesus Christ. To him be glory both now and forever! Amen.*** (NIV)

I hear many politicians today speaking about a new world order. What they do not know is that the new world order they are referring to will be the coming one-world order of the Antichrist. I await the new order that will be established by Jesus during the Day of the Lord, followed by the Day of God.

NEW HEAVEN AND NEW EARTH

Sarah and I would be honored to spend eternity with all of you, but what will it be like in eternity. John in the last two chapters of the New Testament will give us a peek into that time period. Sea, used here, is symbolic for people who will no longer live in fleshly bodies during the Day of God. The plan of salvation has reached completion.

> Rev 21:1 *Then I saw a new heaven and a new earth, for the first heaven and the first earth had passed away, and there was no longer any sea.* (NIV)

Here we see a new heaven and a new earth. It will replace the present heaven and earth. Do not confuse the new heaven and new earth which we read about in Isaiah with this scene. The scene in Isaiah will take place when the earth will be restored after the Battle of Armageddon. At this time it will not be a transformed heaven and earth, but it will be a complete new heaven and a new earth. The elements of the old heavens and old earth will be melted by fire. The glory of Jesus will be the fire that melts the elements of the earth to make room for this new heaven and new earth.

THE NEW JERUSALEM

Coming down from the third level of heaven will be the beautiful sight of the Holy City, the New Jerusalem, the dwelling place of God that has existed in the heavenly realm and will now come to rest on the newly created earth for eternity. The peaceful state of the Kingdom Age will pale in comparison to the eternal state of bliss forever.

> Rev 21:2-4 *I saw the Holy City, the new Jerusalem, coming down out of heaven from God, prepared as a bride beautifully dressed for her husband. And I heard a loud voice from the throne saying, "Now the dwelling of God is with men, and he will live with them. They will be his people, and God himself will be with them and be their God. He will wipe every tear from their eyes. There will be no more death or mourning or crying or pain, for the old order of things has passed away."* (NIV)

> Ps 48:1-3 *Great is the LORD, and most worthy of praise, in the city of our God, his holy mountain. It is beautiful in its loftiness, the joy of the whole earth. Like the utmost heights of Zaphon is Mount Zion, the city of the Great King. God is in her citadels; he has shown himself to be her fortress.* (NIV)

> Ps 84:1-2 *How lovely is your dwelling place, O LORD Almighty! My soul yearns, even faints, for the courts of the LORD; my heart and my flesh cry out for the living God.* (NIV)

AFTER THE RAPTURE

Ps 87:1-3 *<u>He has set his foundation on the holy mountain;</u> the LORD loves the gates of Zion more than all the dwellings of Jacob. <u>Glorious things are said of you, O city of God</u>: Selah* (NIV)

This is the end of the natural (human) order of things and the beginning of the final (heavenly) order of things. The Kingdom Age with Jesus as King will merge into the Universal Kingdom of God from which it sprang. This does not mean the end of the regal activity of Jesus, but the unity of the Godhead. Jesus will reign (co-regent) with the Father as the eternal Son on a single throne. No longer will God dwell among a separate nation as His chosen people, but among all men. All men will be His people and He will be their God. The old order of things will have passed away. No more; TEARS, DEATH, MOURNING, CRYING OR PAIN!

As Jesus returns the kingdom to His Father, we see God on the throne. He will make everything new. Everything God is saying is trustworthy and true. When the plan of salvation has finally played itself out, once more and for the final time, *"IT IS DONE!"* Everyone who has overcome (believed in Jesus) will inherit this new order, while those on the other side of the coin (unbelievers) will face the second death.

Rev 21: 5-8 *He who was seated on the throne said, "<u>I am making everything new</u>!" Then he said, "<u>Write this down, for these words are trustworthy and true</u>." He said to me: "<u>It is done</u>. I am the Alpha and the Omega, the Beginning and the End. To him who is thirsty I will give to drink without cost from the spring of the water of life. <u>He who overcomes will inherit all this</u>, <u>and I will be his God and he will be my son</u>. But the cowardly, the unbelieving, the vile, the murderers, the sexually immoral, those who practice magic arts, the idolaters and all liars—their place will be in the fiery lake of burning sulfur. <u>This is the second death</u>."* (NIV)

In the next verse, verse nine, the wife of the Lamb (Jesus) appears to be a part of the New Jerusalem. Could this mean that the members of the church (those saved during the Dispensation of Grace) will have a special place in this city? I do not know! Nevertheless, remember that the saved from all ages will have free access to the glories and benefits of the New Jerusalem.

Rev 21:9 *One of the seven angels who had the seven bowls full of the seven last plagues came and said to me, "<u>Come, I will show you the bride, the wife of the Lamb</u>."* (NIV)

John in his gospel account lets us know that Jesus went back to heaven to prepare a special place for the church age believers (the bride of Christ). That special place is the Chupah. Note, at that time, His Fathers house was already in existence and had many rooms. At the Rapture Jesus will come again to remove the saints from the earth and take them to heaven, where they will be with Him. The place Jesus prepared for them will be where the wedding and the wedding feast will take place in heaven.

John 14:1-4 *"Do not let your hearts be troubled. Trust in God; trust also in me. In my Father's house are many rooms; if it were not so, I would have told you. I am going there to prepare a place for you. And if I go and prepare a place for you, I will come back and take you to be with me that you also may be where I am. You know the way to the place where I am going."* (NIV)

John was given the privilege of viewing the future when the New Jerusalem will come down from heaven and rest on the new earth, where it will exist for eternity. Sometime before the earth is dissolved, the Shekinah Glory will depart from the Temple in Jerusalem and return to the Heavenly Jerusalem. As the New Jerusalem descends to the new earth it will be shining from the radiance of God. It will be shining like a precious jewel. John is then given a description of the New Jerusalem. The Divine Presence of both God and Jesus will be present on earth and in Jerusalem as They become the center of all things in the new universe. Notice the Shekinah Glory shining as Jerusalem comes down from heaven.

Rev 21:10-21 *And he carried me away in the Spirit to a mountain great and high, and showed me the Holy City, Jerusalem, coming down out of heaven from God. It shone with the glory of God, and its brilliance was like that of a very precious jewel, like a jasper, clear as crystal. It had a great, high wall with twelve gates, and with twelve angels at the gates. On the gates were written the names of the twelve tribes of Israel. There were three gates on the east, three on the north, three on the south and three on the west. The wall of the city had twelve foundations, and on them were the names of the twelve apostles of the Lamb. The angel who talked with me had a measuring rod of gold to measure the city, its gates and its walls. The city was laid out like a square, as long as it was wide. He measured the city with the rod and found it to be 12,000 stadia in length, and as wide and high as it is long. He measured its wall and it was 144 cubits thick, by man's measurement, which the angel was using. The wall was made of jasper, and the city of pure gold, as pure as glass. The foundations of the city walls were decorated with every kind of precious stone. The first foundation was jasper, the second sapphire, the third chalcedony, the fourth emerald, the fifth sardonyx, the sixth carnelian, the seventh chrysolite, the eighth beryl, the ninth topaz, the tenth chrysoprase, the eleventh jacinth, and the twelfth amethyst. The twelve gates were twelve pearls, each gate made of a single pearl. The great street of the city was of pure gold, like transparent glass.* (NIV)

There will not be a Temple in the new city, because it will be replaced by God the

AFTER THE RAPTURE

Father and Jesus the Lamb. They will be the Tabernacle. There will no longer be a need for the sun or the moon. Light will be provided by the Shekinah Glory and the Lamb (Jesus) will be its lamp. The greater light will be from God the Father. There will be no more darkness. Only those who have had their names written in the Lamb's book of Life will be there.

Rev 21:22-23 *__I did not see a temple in the city, because the Lord God Almighty and the Lamb are its temple.__ The city does not need the sun or the moon to shine on it, for the glory of God gives it light, and the Lamb is its lamp.* (NIV)

The sun will no longer be needed to provide light for the world. The light for the entire world will be supplied by the glory of God. The Greek word used here for "light" is *photizo* and its definition is:

Strong's Definition
5461 photizo (fo-tid'-zo);
from 5457; to shed rays, i.e. to shine or (transitively) to brighten up (literally or figuratively):
KJV— enlighten, illuminate, (bring to, give) light, make to see.

Strong's Definition
5457 phos (foce);
from an obsolete phao (to shine or make manifest, especially by rays; compare 5316, 5346); luminousness (in the widest application, nat. or artificial, abstract or concrete, literal or figurative):
KJV— fire, light.

Ps 104:31 *__The glory of the LORD shall endure for ever:__ the LORD shall rejoice in his works.* (KJV)

It appears that the glory of Jesus will not be as bright as the glory of God. The light of the Lamb is referred to as a lamp. The Greek word for "lamp" is *luchnos* and is used to differentiate the glory between God and Jesus. In your mind compare the light of the sun against the light from a candle.

Strong's Definition
3088 luchnos (lookh'-nos);
from the base of 3022; a portable lamp or other illuminator (literally or figuratively):
KJV—candle, light.

Jesus will be the other illuminator. Nations and leaders (kings) of the nations will exist in eternity. The glory and honor of the nations will be brought through gates that are never shut. Nothing impure will ever enter the city. Please note that only those whose names are written in the Lamb's book of life will be there.

The End and the Beginning

Rev 21:24-27 *The nations will walk by its light, and the kings of the earth will bring their splendor into it. On no day will its gates ever be shut, for there will be no night there. The glory and honor of the nations will be brought into it. Nothing impure will ever enter it, nor will anyone who does what is shameful or deceitful, <u>but only those whose names are written in the Lamb's book of life</u>.* (NIV)

The river of the water of life will flow from the throne of God and Jesus down the middle of the main street of the city. The tree of life will be present bearing fruit. The leaves of the trees are for the healing of the nations. This is what it will be like for eternity.

Rev 22:1-2 *Then the angel showed me the river of the water of life, as clear as crystal, flowing from the throne of God and of the Lamb down the middle of the great street of the city. On each side of the river stood the tree of life, bearing twelve crops of fruit, yielding its fruit every month. And the leaves of the tree are for the healing of the nations.* (NIV)

There will no longer be a curse on the earth. We as servants of God will see the face of God and Jesus. God and His Son will reign forever. One throne is in view here. There will be no more night. During the 7000 years, when mankind was in his natural setting, he was not allowed to view the face of God. The time has now arrived when, *"They will see His face."* During the time of the perfect order mankind in his perfect body will be able to see the face of God, and I might add, His likeness (image) for eternity. They will see Him as He sets on His throne. Once again, we are reminded, *"These words are trustworthy and true."*

Rev 22:3-6 *No longer will there be any curse. The throne of God and of the Lamb will be in the city, and his servants will serve him. <u>They will see his face</u>, and his name will be on their foreheads. There will be no more night. They will not need the light of a lamp or the light of the sun, for the Lord God will give them light. <u>And they will reign for ever and ever</u>. The angel said to me, "These words are trustworthy and true. The Lord, the God of the spirits of the prophets, sent his angel to show his servants the things that must soon take place."* (NIV)

Ps 11:7 *For the LORD is righteous, he loves justice; <u>upright men will see his face</u>.* (NIV)

Ps 17:15 *<u>And I—in righteousness I will see your face</u>; <u>when I awake, I will be satisfied with seeing your likeness</u>.* (NIV)

The saints and holy Angels, as servants, will serve God throughout eternity. At last, all the saints in their glorious bodies will finally be allowed to see the face of God. Although

AFTER THE RAPTURE

God's glorious face, with the rays of light shining forth to light up the world, will be illuminating beyond our comprehension, all those present will still be able to see His face.

It is mentioned twice in Revelation that Jesus is coming soon! After John had seen the prophecy revealed to him in the book of Revelation he fell down to worship the angel who had been showing him these things. John is then rebuked by the angel who informs John not to worship him because he is an angel. The angel informs John to *"Worship God!"*

> Rev 22:7-9   *"Behold, I am coming soon! Blessed is he who keeps the words of the prophecy in this book." I, John, am the one who heard and saw these things. And when I had heard and seen them, I fell down to worship at the feet of the angel who had been showing them to me. But he said to me, "Do not do it! I am a fellow servant with you and with your brothers the prophets and of all who keep the words of this book. Worship God!"* (NIV)

> Rev 3:11-13   *I am coming soon. Hold on to what you have, so that no one will take your crown. Him who overcomes I will make a pillar in the temple of my God. Never again will he leave it. I will write on him the name of my God and the name of the city of my God, the new Jerusalem, which is coming down out of heaven from my God; and I will also write on him my new name. He who has an ear, let him hear what the Spirit says to the churches.* (NIV)

Unlike Daniel, who was told to seal up the meaning of his prophecy, John is told just the opposite. Like Daniel, the angel said to let life continue until Jesus returns, in other words, the world will exist with people who are saved (purified) and unsaved (those who do wrong). The time is near!

> Dan 12:9-10   *He replied, "Go your way, Daniel, because the words are closed up and sealed until the time of the end. Many will be purified, made spotless and refined, but the wicked will continue to be wicked. None of the wicked will understand, but those who are wise will understand.* (NIV)

> Rev 22:10-11   *Then he told me, "Do not seal up the words of the prophecy of this book, because the time is near. Let him who does wrong continue to do wrong; let him who is vile continue to be vile; let him who does right continue to do right; and let him who is holy continue to be holy."* (NIV)

Jesus is coming! If John was told that *"the time is near,"* think how much closer we are today to the second coming of Christ. The next prophetic event to occur will be the Rapture. Jesus will bring His reward with Him. Rewards for the just (at the Judgment Seat of Christ) and rewards for the unjust (fierce anger of the Lord at the Battle of Armageddon).

The End and the Beginning

Rev 22:12-15 *"<u>Behold, I am coming soon! My reward is with me</u>, and I will give to everyone according to what he has done. I am the Alpha and the Omega, the First and the Last, the Beginning and the End.* "Blessed are those who wash their robes, that they may have the right to the tree of life and may go through the gates into the city. Outside are the dogs, those who practice magic arts, the sexually immoral, the murderers, the idolaters and everyone who loves and practices falsehood. (NIV)

This is similar to Jesus at Armageddon when His reward will accompany Him.

Isa 40:10 *<u>See, the Sovereign LORD comes with power</u>, and his arm rules for him. <u>See, his reward is with him</u>, and his recompense accompanies him.* (NIV)

Jesus sent His angel to warn us of what will take place in the future.

Rev 22:16 *"I, Jesus, have sent my angel to give you this testimony for the churches. I am the Root and the Offspring of David, and the bright Morning Star."* (NIV)

The Holy Spirit of God and the bride (true believers of the church age) say, *"Come!"* Believing in Jesus is a **free gift** of the water of life.

Rev 22:17 *The Spirit and the bride say, "<u>Come!</u>" And let him who hears say, "<u>Come!</u>" Whoever is thirsty, let him come; and whoever wishes, <u>let him take the free gift of the water of life</u>.* (NIV)

Then comes a warning for everyone not to add anything to or take anything away from the prophecy of the book of Revelation.

Rev 22:18-19 *<u>I warn everyone who hears the words of the prophecy of this book</u>: <u>If anyone adds anything to them</u>, God will add to him the plagues described in this book. <u>And if anyone takes words away from this book of prophecy</u>, God will take away from him his share in the tree of life and in the holy city, which are described in this book.* (NIV)

Jesus Himself warns us of His coming. Those of us who believe, from the deepest seat of our emotions, that Jesus Christ is the Messiah, will be participants in the Rapture.

Rev 22:20-21 *He who testifies to these things says, "<u>Yes, I am coming soon.</u>" Amen. <u>Come, Lord Jesus</u>. The grace of the Lord Jesus be with God's people. Amen.* (NIV)

COME

LORD JESUS

COME!

CHAPTER SIXTEEN

WHAT SHOULD WE DO AS CHRISTIANS?

This book has been mainly about history—past and future. Past history is easier to understand, unless someone falsifies their account of it. We as Christians have a responsibility to study Bible Prophecy and teach it to the main body of believers. Along with that responsibility comes the accuracy of what is being taught. Preachers and teachers will be held more accountable at the Judgment Seat of Christ for what they teach if they are true believers in Jesus, or at the Great White Throne Judgment if they are unbelievers.

> Heb 13:17 *Obey your leaders and submit to their authority. **They keep watch over you as men who must give an account**. Obey them so that their work will be a joy, not a burden, for that would be of no advantage to you.* (NIV)

Future history is a little more difficult to comprehend. There is only one book written that has the correct account of future history, but it does not give the account in a chronological order. The account of future history—prophetic events yet to be fulfilled are interspersed throughout the entire Bible, starting in Genesis and ending in Revelation. Prophecy in the Bible is mainly about two specific events. The first event was when Jesus the Messiah came to earth to set up His Kingdom, but was rejected by mankind. The second event will be when Jesus the Messiah returns to earth to set up His Kingdom. The Bible is packed full of references for both events. The Bereans from the early church diligently studied and examined the scriptures (Old Testament) for events that happened in the life of Jesus to see if what Paul was teaching them proved that Jesus was the Messiah. They did this on a daily basis. These events recorded below took place almost two thousand years ago. These accounts in Luke and Acts took place after Jesus had been resurrected.

> John 5:39 ***You diligently study the Scriptures** because you think that by them you possess eternal life. **These are the Scriptures that testify about me**,* (NIV)

> Acts 17:11 *Now the Bereans were of more noble character than the Thessalonians, for they received the message with great eagerness **and examined the Scriptures every day to see if what Paul said was true**.* (NIV)

> Luke 24:13-35 *Now that same day two of them were going to a village called Emmaus, about seven miles from Jerusalem. They were talking with each other about everything that had happened. As they talked and discussed these things with each other, Jesus himself came up and walked along with them; but they were kept from recognizing him. He asked them, "What are you discussing together as you walk along?" They stood still, their faces downcast. One of them, named*

> *Cleopas, asked him, "Are you only a visitor to Jerusalem and do not know the things that have happened there in these days?" "What things?" he asked. "About Jesus of Nazareth," they replied. "He was a prophet, powerful in word and deed before God and all the people. The chief priests and our rulers handed him over to be sentenced to death, and they crucified him; but we had hoped that he was the one who was going to redeem Israel. And what is more, it is the third day since all this took place. In addition, some of our women amazed us. They went to the tomb early this morning but didn't find his body. They came and told us that they had seen a vision of angels, who said he was alive. Then some of our companions went to the tomb and found it just as the women had said, but him they did not see."* **He said to them, "How foolish you are, and how slow of heart to believe all that the prophets have spoken! Did not the Christ have to suffer these things and then enter his glory?"** <u>**And beginning with Moses and all the Prophets, he explained to them what was said in all the Scriptures concerning himself.**</u> *As they approached the village to which they were going, Jesus acted as if he were going farther. But they urged him strongly, "Stay with us, for it is nearly evening; the day is almost over." So he went in to stay with them. When he was at the table with them, he took bread, gave thanks, broke it and began to give it to them.* **Then their eyes were opened and they recognized him, and he disappeared from their sight. They asked each other, "**<u>**Were not our hearts burning within us while he talked with us on the road and opened the Scriptures to us**</u>**?" They got up and returned at once to Jerusalem. There they found the Eleven and those with them, assembled together and saying, "**<u>**It is true! The Lord has risen and has appeared to Simon.**</u>**" Then the two told what had happened on the way, and how Jesus was recognized by them when he broke the bread.** (NIV)

Not everyone should become a prophecy teacher or even a prophecy buff. God will call those to service in this area. Just like being called to become a pastor, prophecy teachers will recognize their calling. To be called and then not serve, in a particular service, would be a mistake by that person. Remember, even as a believer we have to stand before our God for an accounting of our life here on earth. Every believer is designated by God for some sort of service in this lifetime.

There are people today who believe that you should not study prophecy and the books in the Bible, such as the book of Revelation, concerning prophecy. That position is as wrong as the people who are possessed by only studying prophecy and spend all their time in the Bible on the subject of prophecy. Our walk with Jesus should be a balance of everything that is in the Bible. This includes the Bible in its entirety, including the Old Testament.

2 Tim 3:16 *<u>All Scripture is God-breathed</u> and is useful for teaching, rebuking,*

What Should We Do as Christians?

correcting and training in righteousness, (NIV)

If someone does not include the study of Bible prophecy in their Christian curriculum they are leaving out the details of the second greatest event that will take place in history, the return of our Lord and Savior Jesus Christ. What was the first great event in history—need I say—the first advent of Jesus? Both of these great events were and are recognized as prophetic events revealed to us in the Bible. God did not show John the vision of the Tribulation Period and the second coming of Christ, only to be sealed up like Daniel in the Old Testament. John even reveals that there is a special blessing for those who read, hear and take to heart what is written in the words of the prophecy in the book of Revelation.

Rev 1:1-3 *The revelation of Jesus Christ, which God gave him to show his servants what must soon take place. He made it known by sending his angel to his servant John, who testifies to everything he saw—that is, the word of God and the testimony of Jesus Christ. Blessed is the one who reads the words of this prophecy, and blessed are those who hear it and take to heart what is written in it, because the time is near.* (NIV)

The final chapter of this book is designed to show you what the Bible has to say about how to live and what to expect concerning the end of the age—not the end of the world. What should we be doing, or not be doing, as far as end-time Bible prophecy in concerned. First I would like to begin with the things we should not be doing. Scripture is absolutely clear on these details concerning believers in Jesus Christ.

FALSE MESSIAH'S, PROPHETS, TEACHERS & BELIEVERS

False Messiah's or people who believe that they are Jesus Christ are those people we should be aware of because their followers could be in imminent danger. During the twentieth century alone thousands of people have died being deceived by these false deities. Most of us know of the tragedies of a few of these radical episodes of disaster.

1. Nov 18, 1978 — Jim Jones — Peoples Temple, Jonestown, Guyana — 913 people killed including children (exact number of children unknown).

2. Feb 28–May 19, 1993 — David Koresh — Branch Davidian's, Waco, Texas — 4 Federal Agents and 80 Branch Davidian's killed including 21 children.

3. Oct 5, 1994 — Order of the solar Temple — France, Switzerland and Canada.
    Cheirny, Switzerland — 23 died including 1 ten year old boy.
    Canada — 5 died including one 3 month old baby boy.
    Granges-sur-Salvan — 25 died including 5 children.
    France — Alps of SE France — Dec 95, 16 died.
        All of the deceased were members of a highly secretive end-time cult

AFTER THE RAPTURE

known as the Order of the Solar Temple, which blended elements of Astrology, free-masonry, New Age Spiritualism, occultism and quasi-Christian beliefs focusing on doomsday. This group was led by 46-year-old Luc Jouret and 70-year-old Joseph di Mambro. Jouret, a Belgian homeopathic doctor, founded the group in 1987 and served as its spiritual leader. Di Mambro, a shadowy figure who had served six months in a French jail in 1972 for posing as a psychologist, was the groups financial director. The bodies of both men were found in the Salvan chalets.

One victim carried a note in her clothing, which she had addressed to surviving relatives. It stated that she had come to Switzerland to die. Three other letters with similar messages were sent by cult members to Jean-Francois Mayer, a Swiss authority. One read: "We leave this earth in full freedom and lucidity in order to find a dimension of Truth and Absolute, far from the hypocrisies and oppression of this world." Cassette tapes and documents found with the bodies indicated that the killings were indeed linked to a belief that the end of the world was imminent.

...Among those murdered in the group in the Alps in southeastern France with a .357 magnum were two sisters aged two and four, daughters of policeman Jean-Pierre Lardanchet, who had acted as one of the executioners. A note retrieved from a victim's apartment read: "Death does not exist, it is pure illusion. May we, by our inner life, find each other forever."

4. Mar, 1997 — Marshall Applewhite — Heaven's Gate, Rancho Santa Fe, Ca — 39 died.

5. 1999 — Monte "Kim" Miller — Concerned Christians, Denver, CO, Jerusalem, Israel, Greece — none dead (so far).

   The most recent cult to be found in our newspapers today. Some relatives of Kim Miller's nearly 80 followers fear some sort of mass suicide from the group. It is reported that some of the cult members refer to Kim Miller as "Lord" or "God". After the group left the United States some of the apocalyptic cult members surfaced in Jerusalem where the authorities feared the group planned to provoke a shootout with police. This confrontation which was planned by the group to take place toward the end of 1999 was supposed to usher in the second coming of Christ. Kim Miller believes that he is one of the two witnesses spoken of in chapter eleven in the book of Revelation. He has said that he would be slain by Satan in Jerusalem and be resurrected after three days. So far that has not happened and we are now living in the year 2003.

6. March 17, 2000 — The Movement For The Restoration Of The Ten Commandments of God, Uganda, Africa — At least 924 died (including 137 children).

What Should We Do as Christians?

Around 530 people, including 78 children, were burned to death after a fire engulfed the chapel of a sect compound in Kahunga, Uganda. On March 24 in Buhunga police found 153 more bodies in the dirt floor of an abandoned house twenty miles away from the cult's compound. The bodies included 59 children and appear to have been hacked and strangled to death. Between March 27-29 in Rugazi authorities found an additional 155 strangled, mutilated bodies on property owned by one of the sect's leaders. At least 80 corpses were excavated in Rushojwa on March 30 at the fourth of five cult compounds.

To date Ugandan police have counted 924 victims of yet another false religious order. Before the investigation is over the authorities expect the body count to surpass 1000 victims. The leaders of this cult, who started it in 1987, may still be alive and fleeing from the police. Some of the leaders of this group suggested that they received visions from God, Michael the Archangel, and the Virgin Mary. They would bring messages from the Virgin Mary and Michael the Archangel. They would say things like the Virgin Mary wants you to bring more money.

One leader claimed that he talked directly to Jesus. A possible motive for these mass systematic slaying's is that after their doomsday prediction that the world would come to an end on December 31, 1999 proved false, some cult members demanded money back that they had given to the church. When they joined the cult they had been asked to sell their possessions and give the proceeds to the church.

There are more than 5000 indigenous churches in Africa, some with apocalyptic or revolutionary leanings. Most experts say Africa's hardships push people to seek hope in religious cults. These groups thrive because of poverty. People have no support and they are susceptible to anyone who is able to tap into their insecurity. They say, AIDS, which has ravaged East Africa, may also breed a fatalism that helps apocalyptic notions take root. In Uganda the government has registered 648 religious organizations. Many of those are evangelical sects, but there are some who are millennial or apocalyptic groups operating in the country.

I guess what I am trying to get across is that many people—both men and women—try to deceive people into believing that they are Jesus Christ or even His representative in the form of a prophet on earth today. The Bible has many references warning us to be aware of them. They are wolves in sheep's clothing. Judge them by their actions—whether they produce good fruit or bad fruit. This holds true for false teachers and false believers. Always compare a persons teaching to the Bible.

Matt 7:15-23   *"<u>Watch out for false prophets</u>. <u>They come to you in sheep's clothing, but inwardly they are ferocious wolves</u>. By their fruit you will recognize them. Do people pick grapes from thornbushes, or figs from thistles? Likewise every good tree bears good fruit, but a* *bad tree bears bad fruit. A good tree cannot bear bad fruit, and a bad tree cannot bear good fruit. Every tree that does not bear good fruit is cut down and thrown into the fire. Thus, by their fruit you will recognize them. "<u>Not everyone who says to me, 'Lord, Lord,' will enter the kingdom of heaven, but only he who does the will of my Father who is in heaven.</u> Many will say to me on that day, 'Lord, Lord, did we not prophesy in your name, and in your name drive out demons and perform many miracles?' Then I will tell them plainly, 'I never knew you. Away from me, you evildoers!'* (NIV)

Acts 13:6 — *They traveled through the whole island until they came to Paphos. <u>There they met a Jewish sorcerer and false prophet named Bar-Jesus</u>,* (NIV)

2 Cor 11:13-15 — *<u>For such men are false apostles, deceitful workmen, masquerading as apostles of Christ.</u> And no wonder, for Satan himself masquerades as an angel of light. It is not surprising, then, if his servants masquerade as servants of righteousness. <u>Their end will be what their actions deserve.</u>* (NIV)

2 Cor 11:25-26 — *Three times I was beaten with rods, once I was stoned, three times I was shipwrecked, I spent a night and a day in the open sea, I have been constantly on the move. **I have been in danger from rivers, in danger from bandits, in danger from my own countrymen, in danger from Gentiles; in danger in the city, in danger in the country, in danger at sea; <u>and in danger from false brothers.</u>*** (NIV)

2 Pet 2:1-2 — *<u>But there were also false prophets among the people, just as there will be false teachers among you.</u> They will secretly introduce destructive heresies, even denying the sovereign Lord who bought them—bringing swift destruction on themselves. Many will follow their shameful ways and will bring the way of truth into disrepute.* (NIV)

1 John 4:1 — *<u>Dear friends, do not believe every spirit</u>, but test the spirits to see whether they are from God, <u>because many false prophets have gone out into the world.</u>* (NIV)

2 Tim 3:12-13 — *In fact, everyone who wants to live a godly life in Christ Jesus will be persecuted, <u>while evil men and impostors will go from bad to worse, deceiving and being deceived.</u>* (NIV)

Even though, in their own minds, they believe that they truly are Christ or a prophet, these false Messiah's and false prophets will end up in hell with their god (Satan).

DATE SETTERS

Throughout the last 2000 years people have been predicting dates for both the Tribulation Period and the second coming of Jesus Christ, when in actuality scripture teaches a contrary opinion. Anyone who believes that they can correctly calculate the date of the Rapture is mistaken and they are only fooling themselves. In the meantime, they deceive many people and put fear in their lives, not to mention the disappointment of these same people after the predicted date passes and the Rapture has not taken place. These false date-setters have been responsible for many suicides throughout the church age. If you knew when a thief was coming, you would take appropriate action.

Matt 24:36 *"<u>No one knows about that day or hour</u>, not even the angels in heaven, nor the Son, but only the Father.* (NIV)

Acts 1:6-7 *So when they met together, they asked him, "Lord, are you at this time going to restore the kingdom to Israel?" He said to them: "<u>It is not for you to know the times or dates the Father has set by his own authority</u>.* (NIV)

1 Thes 5:1-2 *Now, brothers, about times and dates we do not need to write to you, <u>for you know very well that the day of the Lord will come like a thief in the night</u>.* (NIV)

The most complete book I have read concerning the subject on the history of date setting is, *End-Time Visions, The Road to Armageddon?* by Richard Abanes. This book clearly exposes the embarrassment of date setting. I am not saying that I agree with everything Mr. Abanes printed in his book, as far as his views of when Jesus will return, just as Mr. Abanes will not agree with everything in this book. In fact, he will put me in the category of a date-suggestor and I have no problem with that. I highly recommend Mr. Abanes book and suggest you read it. It should be found in your local library. Everyone who studies or teaches Bible prophecy needs to look at past history to see the mistakes of people, both believers and nonbelieiver, concerning this delicate subject.

Found in, "Appendix C," of his book is a "Timeline of Doom" with a list of people, with dates, who made doomsday predictions. Here is a partial list of his entries.

AD 150-179: Montanus, Priscilla and Maximilla — leaders of the Montanism movement — prophesy that the end of the world would come within their lifetimes.

AD 375-400: Saint Martin of Tours (c. 316-397), who served as Bishop of Gaul, teaches that the Antichrist exists in his day, writing: "there is no doubt that the Antichrist has already been born. Firmly established already in his early years, he will, after reaching maturity, achieve supreme power."

AFTER THE RAPTURE

AD 500:	Hippolytus (d. 236) predicts that this year will see the consummation of the ages.
AD 800:	The Spanish Monk Beatus (d. 798) feels that he will live to see the Antichrist and the end of the world by the year 800.
AD 1000:	Belief throughout Europe during the 900's is that the end of the world would occur in 1000.
AD 1033:	This year is targeted as "the end" after the year 1000 passed by uneventfully.
AD 1260:	Joachim of Fiore (c. 1135-1202) preaches that 1260 will see the appearance of the Antichrist, followed by the world's destruction. During a 1191 interview with King Richard the Lion-Hearted, Joachim says that the Antichrist had already been born.
AD 1420:	The Taborites, an extremist Christian sect, held that in 1420 God's fiery wrath would consume the world.
AD 1656:	The year that Christopher Columbus said would bring an end to the world.
1697, 1716, 1736:	Influential Puritan Colton Mather (1663-1728) preaches that 1697 would be the year of the world's end. He later changes his prediction to 1716. After that date passes, 1736 becomes his new deadline for Christ's return.
1843-1844	William Miller and the Millerites expect Jesus' second advent. Their belief results in "The Great Disappointment" of October 22, 1844.
1874:	Jesus' second advent is expected by former Millerites who had banded together to form the Second Adventist movement.
1914:	The Jehovah's Witnesses point to this year as the time when the Battle of Armageddon would take place.
Feb 4, 1962:	Many people throughout the world fear that the planetary alignment of this day would bring about global destructions.
1982:	Many persons from widely diverse religious belief systems fear that an alignment of the planets during 1982 (and its resulting "Jupiter Effect") will bring doomsday.

What Should We Do as Christians?

Sept 11, 1988: Christian preacher Edgar Whisenaut claims that these dates will bring the rapture-i.e., the miraculous transportation of all Christians from the earth to heaven.

Oct 28, 1992: The Korean *Hyoo-go* movement predicts this day will bring the rapture.

2000: It would be impossible to list the many persons declaring that the world may end in the year 2000. Such predictions are coming from widely divergent belief systems that are usually at odds with each other.

2012: According to many apprehensive date-watchers, the world will end on December 21-23, 2012 when the ancient Mayan calender runs out.

For the complete list consult pages 337-342 of Mr. Abanes book. [1]

Throughout the twentieth century there have been many people who have been predicting the end of the world and the second coming of Christ. I believe that some of those people do believe in Jesus and are saved. They want to be good stewards and teach God's word. The anxiety of the times has pushed some to put literal dates on certain events of future history. In God's word it clearly states that even Jesus and the angels do not know when the exact day the second coming of Jesus will take place. It is impossible for us to know the exact date of the Rapture. This protects the idea that Christ's second coming could come at any moment. God has intentionally allowed the exact dates of past history to be confused so man cannot calculate the exact day when the first six thousand years of human history are completed. Throughout history mankind has used numerous calendars to keep track of time. Even the Jews, who count time from the beginning of creation as year number one, disagree on the exact count of the current date. Most Jews today believe we are living in the year 5763/5764 in our year AD 2003, but because of the dispersions and persecutions they have been through, it is impossible to confirm their current date as absolutely correct. Because of all this it is impossible to get a beginning date, let alone an ending date, that is accurate to try to calculate the exact time of the Rapture. The best article I have ever read concerning the subject of trying to calculate the exact date in time was by Dr. David Reagan, in the July/August 2000 issue of *The Lamplighter,* published by Lamb & Lion Ministries. It is an excellent article and discusses the ancient calenders and how they have changed throughout history. It has a good section devoted to the way the Jewish people have come up with the year 5760/5761. Dr. Reagan's website is: www.lamblion.com.

That does not mean that God will leave us in total darkness concerning the general time of the return of Jesus at the Rapture. The Bible has explicit instructions for us today, as believers, concerning our position on end-time events and what we should be doing while we await the return of Jesus. We should avoid Bible prophecy teachers that sensationalize what is happening on the world scene today. God's timing is perfect. We should let the Bible tell the story. We should not let newspaper articles frighten us! Now for the good news!

AFTER THE RAPTURE

DO NOT BE FEARFUL

First, and foremost, the Bible teaches us not to be afraid of or to worry about the coming end-time scenario of events that will surely take place. Every single event in God's word that is predicted to happen—that is prophetic—will come to pass sometime throughout history. Any remaining prophetic events listed that have not come to pass, **will** come to pass. The revealing of the Antichrist, the Rapture, the Tribulation Period, the Battle of Armageddon, Jesus setting up His throne on earth and establishing the Jews in Israel have not taken place. They will take place! God put them in the Bible so His chosen ones (saints) would know that in the end God will triumph over His enemies—Satan, fallen men and fallen angels. The saints know who will win this Super Bowl before it takes place. They know who will win the final battle and also the minute details of the war ahead of time. Read the Bible!

Scripture does reveal to us today that even people who believe in God will go through trials and tribulations in our lives. We are living on earth this side of heaven.

> 1 Thes 3:2-5 *We sent Timothy, who is our brother and God's fellow worker in spreading the gospel of Christ, to strengthen and encourage you in your faith, **so that no one would be unsettled by these trials. You know quite well that we were destined for them.** In fact, when we were with you, we kept telling you that we would be persecuted. And it turned out that way, as you well know. For this reason, when I could stand it no longer, I sent to find out about your faith. I was afraid that in some way the tempter might have tempted you and our efforts might have been useless.* (NIV)

> 1 Pet 1:2-12 *who have been chosen according to the foreknowledge of God the Father, through the sanctifying work of the Spirit, for obedience to Jesus Christ and sprinkling by his blood: Grace and peace be yours in abundance. Praise be to the God and Father of our Lord Jesus Christ! In his great mercy he has given us new birth into a living hope through the resurrection of Jesus Christ from the dead, and into an inheritance that can never perish, spoil or fade—kept in heaven for you, who through faith are shielded by God's power until the coming of the salvation that is ready to be revealed in the last time. **In this you greatly rejoice, though now for a little while you may have had to suffer grief in all kinds of trials.** These have come so that your faith—of greater worth than gold, which perishes even though refined by fire—may be proved genuine and may result in praise, glory and honor when Jesus Christ is revealed. Though you have not seen him, you love him; and even though you do not see him now, you believe in him and are filled with an inexpressible and glorious joy, for you are receiving the goal of your faith, the salvation of your souls. Concerning this salvation, the prophets, who spoke of the grace that was to come to you, searched intently and*

> *with the greatest care, trying to find out the time and circumstances to which the Spirit of Christ in them was pointing when he predicted the sufferings of Christ and the glories that would follow. It was revealed to them that they were not serving themselves but you, when they spoke of the things that have now been told you by those who have preached the gospel to you by the Holy Spirit sent from heaven. Even angels long to look into these things.* (NIV)

Satan learned a long time ago that persecution in the form of trials and tribulations does not always turn people away from God, but can actually draw people closer to God. Where does one turn when they have no other place to turn? When Paul sent Timothy back to Thessalonica to check on the persecuted Christians, to see how they were doing, to his surprise Timothy found them strong in love and in their faith in Jesus Christ, even though they were facing extreme persecutions. This was a big encouragement to Paul in his distress.

1 Thes 3:6-13   *__But Timothy has just now come to us from you and has brought good news about your faith and love.__ He has told us that you always have pleasant memories of us and that you long to see us, just as we also long to see you. __Therefore, brothers, in all our distress and persecution we were encouraged about you because of your faith. For now we really live, since you are standing firm in the Lord.__ How can we thank God enough for you in return for all the joy we have in the presence of our God because of you? Night and day we pray most earnestly that we may see you again and supply what is lacking in your faith. Now may our God and Father himself and our Lord Jesus clear the way for us to come to you. May the Lord make your love increase and overflow for each other and for everyone else, just as ours does for you. May he strengthen your hearts so that you will be blameless and holy in the presence of our God and Father when our Lord Jesus comes with all his holy ones.* (NIV)

God wants us to come to Him by faith. His plan is for you, as an individual, to make a free-will choice to follow Him. When you do put your life in His hands, He will be with you. That does not mean that everything in your life will become perfect. It means that Jesus will be your closest friend and will never allow this life to overtake you. He will never allow more circumstances to come into your life than you can bear.

1 Cor 10:13   *__No temptation has seized you except what is common to man.__ And God is faithful; __he will not let you be tempted beyond what you can bear.__ But when you are tempted, he will also provide a way out so that you can stand up under it.* (NIV)

In fact, you will be amazed at how things in your life start turning out once you turn them over to Jesus instead of trying to tackle them on your own. Turn your burdens over to

AFTER THE RAPTURE

Jesus. Let Him be Master of your life and continue to pray daily.

Eph 6:18 — *And pray in the Spirit on all occasions with all kinds of prayers and requests. With this in mind, be alert and always keep on praying for all the saints.* (NIV)

Phil 4:6 — *Do not be anxious about anything, but in everything, by prayer and petition, with thanksgiving, present your requests to God.* (NIV)

The rewards of the saints will come *After the Rapture* when Jesus appears to us at His second coming. At that time the saints will receive their resurrected bodies and be with Jesus forever. This also includes the Old Testament saints. Their rewards are yet future, as it is for the Old Testament prophets who have yet to receive what has been promised to them. As followers of God, they suffered for their walk with the Lord. Because of their sufferings and perseverance, their rewards are yet future. They will be made perfect (receive their resurrected bodies) when the Church age saints are made perfect.

Heb 11:32-40 — *And what more shall I say? I do not have time to tell about Gideon, Barak, Samson, Jephthah, David, Samuel and the prophets, who through faith conquered kingdoms, administered justice, and gained what was promised; who shut the mouths of lions, quenched the fury of the flames, and escaped the edge of the sword; whose weakness was turned to strength; and who became powerful in battle and routed foreign armies. Women received back their dead, raised to life again. Others were tortured and refused to be released, so that they might gain a better resurrection. Some faced jeers and flogging, while still others were chained and put in prison. They were stoned; they were sawed in two; they were put to death by the sword. They went about in sheepskins and goatskins, destitute, persecuted and mistreated—the world was not worthy of them. They wandered in deserts and mountains, and in caves and holes in the ground. These were all commended for their faith, yet none of them received what had been promised. God had planned something better for us so that only together with us would they be made perfect.* (NIV)

James 5:7-11 — *Be patient, then, brothers, until the Lord's coming. See how the farmer waits for the land to yield its valuable crop and how patient he is for the autumn and spring rains. You too, be patient and stand firm, because the Lord's coming is near. Don't grumble against each other, brothers, or you will be judged. The Judge is standing at the door! Brothers, as an example of patience in the face of suffering, take the prophets who spoke in the name of the Lord. As you know, we consider blessed those who have persevered. You have heard of*

What Should We Do as Christians?

Job's perseverance and have seen what the Lord finally brought about. The Lord is full of compassion and mercy. (NIV)

Acts 14:21-22   *They preached the good news in that city and won a large number of disciples. Then they returned to Lystra, Iconium and Antioch, strengthening the disciples and encouraging them to remain true to the faith. "<u>We must go through many hardships to enter the kingdom of God</u>," they said.* (NIV)

Rev 1:9   <u>*I, John, your brother and companion in the suffering and kingdom and patient endurance that are ours in Jesus,*</u> *was on the island of Patmos because of the word of God and the testimony of Jesus.* (NIV)

Sufferings have been a part of creation ever since the fall of mankind. Sin is the culprit, but our present sufferings—no matter how bad they may be—are not worth comparing to our future glory. In the end it will all be worth it for those who put their faith in Jesus.

Rom 8:18-27   <u>*I consider that our present sufferings are not worth comparing with the glory that will be revealed in us.*</u> **The creation waits in eager expectation for the sons of God to be revealed.** *For the creation was subjected to frustration, not by its own choice, but by the will of the one who subjected it, in hope that the creation itself will be liberated from its bondage to decay and brought into the glorious freedom of the children of God.* **We know that the whole creation has been groaning as in the pains of childbirth right up to the present time.** *Not only so, but we ourselves, who have the firstfruits of the Spirit, groan inwardly as we wait eagerly for our adoption as sons, the redemption of our bodies. For in this hope we were saved. But hope that is seen is no hope at all. Who hopes for what he already has? But if we hope for what we do not yet have, we wait for it patiently. In the same way, the Spirit helps us in our weakness. We do not know what we ought to pray for, but the Spirit himself intercedes for us with groans that words cannot express. And he who searches our hearts knows the mind of the Spirit, because the Spirit intercedes for the saints in accordance with God's will.* (NIV)

In fact, our sufferings in this life—even as Christians—can be a positive experience, if we apply them to our lives in a positive way. We can draw closer to Jesus when we suffer during the most difficult times of our lives. We can also—as a choice—become bitter and blame God, which will drive us farther from God. Suffering brings us hope as we rejoice in the hope of the glory of God.

Rom 5:1-5   *Therefore, since we have been justified through faith, we have peace*

> with God through our Lord Jesus Christ, through whom we have gained access by faith into this grace in which we now stand. **_And we rejoice in the hope of the glory of God. Not only so, but we also rejoice in our sufferings, because we know that suffering produces perseverance; perseverance, character; and character, hope._** And hope does not disappoint us, because God has poured out his love into our hearts by the Holy Spirit, whom he has given us. (NIV)

The trials and sufferings we experience during our time here on earth cannot separate us from the love of Christ.

> Rom 8:35-39   **_Who shall separate us from the love of Christ? Shall trouble or hardship or persecution or famine or nakedness or danger or sword?_** As it is written: "For your sake we face death all day long; we are considered as sheep to be slaughtered." No, in all these things we are more than conquerors through him who loved us. **For I am convinced that neither death nor life, neither angels nor demons, neither the present nor the future, nor any powers, neither height nor depth, nor anything else in all creation, will be able to separate us from the love of God that is in Christ Jesus our Lord.** (NIV)

Unless you become bitter and turn away from God, hardships are designed to strengthen your walk with the Lord. The great apostle Paul suffered through terrible trials and persecutions.

> 1 Cor 12:7-10   *To keep me from becoming conceited because of these surpassingly great revelations, there was given me a thorn in my flesh, a messenger of Satan, to torment me. Three times I pleaded with the Lord to take it away from me. But he said to me, "**My grace is sufficient for you, for my power is made perfect in weakness.**" Therefore I will boast all the more gladly about my weaknesses, so that Christ's power may rest on me. That is why, for Christ's sake, I delight in weaknesses, in insults, in hardships, in persecutions, in difficulties. **For when I am weak, then I am strong**.* (NIV)

God is the God of all comfort and He even instructs us to comfort others, even while we are experiencing hardships in our own lives. God is the Father of compassion and all comfort, who comforts us in our troubles.

> 2 Cor 1:3-7   *Praise be to the God and Father of our Lord Jesus Christ, the Father of compassion and the God of all comfort, who comforts us in all our troubles, so that we can comfort those in any trouble with the comfort we ourselves have received from God. For just as the sufferings of Christ flow over into our lives, so also through Christ*

What Should We Do as Christians?

our comfort overflows. If we are distressed, it is for your comfort and salvation; if we are comforted, it is for your comfort, which produces in you patient endurance of the same sufferings we suffer. And our hope for you is firm, because we know that just as you share in our sufferings, so also you share in our comfort. (NIV)

Throughout this book I have stressed the fact that God has not destined us—as believers who will be alive at the time Jesus returns to judge mankind during the Tribulation Period—to face the horrible plagues that the fierce anger of God will hurl to earth. The experiences of trials and tribulations in this life and the fiery wrath of God's judgment are two separate experiences and take place in two separate time periods. As born again believers, by God's grace, we will not take part in the Tribulation Period, but woe to those who do not know God. The Bible does not want us to be afraid, it wants us to be consoled.

MISGUIDED PERCEPTIONS

Date-setting, sensationalism, eagerness to report, quoting bad sources and not verifying facts have all contributed to misconceptions concerning the coming Kingdom Age or Day of the Lord. Because of this many people have lost their lives. We are supposed to bring people to the Kingdom, not put some kind of fear into them that would cause them to commit suicide or go to war against governmental authorities, which results in gun battles that take human lives (including innocent children). The hype of the year 2000 has come and gone, again shattering the hope of thousands of misguided people. When will people start reading the Bible and realize that it clearly states that the exact day of the return of Jesus is unknown. That is the way God wants it be and He even told us that repeatedly. Whenever anybody disagrees with the clear teaching of scripture, their predictions will be incorrect. Date-setting and sensationalism are two of the most dangerous signs to be looking for when it comes to false teachings. Do not be sucked-in by a Jim Jones, a David Koresh or a Kim Miller. It could cost you your life.

I would like to list a few of what I believe to be misconceptions that are effecting the lives of people today. I believe that some people are reading more into certain scriptures, which allows them to sensationalize the end time scenario.

1. End of the world — Doomsday — Battle of Armageddon

    First of all, we are not facing the end of the world. We will be facing the end of the age or the period of time that the Church (body of believers) will be on earth. In my view the Tribulation Period and the Battle of Armageddon will not take place during the church age. Jesus tells us that He will be with us even till the end of the age. Only unbelievers will be effected by the Tribulation Period, which people are referring to as "doomsday." Our main concern as believers today—which includes believers up to the second-coming of Jesus, no matter when He comes back—is to bring as many people into the Kingdom as possible, so they will not be faced with going through the Tribulation Period. Jim Jones lead over 900 people to their deaths by telling them that a nuclear explosion was going to take place and that

AFTER THE RAPTURE

they had to move to a place where they could be protected from the explosion.

2. Babylon

Babylon is accused of being all sorts of things today, including New York City, the Catholic Church and even government in the form of *"Big Brother."* The Weavers, from the tragic event that took place on Ruby Ridge in Idaho in 1992, cost the lives of misguided family members and a government official. The Weavers believed that Babylon was government in the form of *"Big Brother,"* who was out to take over the whole world. The situation festered to the point of a shootout between the two parties. David Koresh had some similar views and on May 19, 1993, a war broke out in Waco, Texas. The shooting lasted for forty-five minutes and left the Branch Davidian compound burned to the ground. This fiasco cost the lives of four government officials and eighty Branch Davidian's. The White Supremacist movement, including the Aryan Nations, have the same fanatical views of the end times and *"Big Brother"* and as a result played a part in the bombing of the Alfred P. Murrah building in Oklahoma City, Oklahoma. Timothy McVeigh and Terry Nichols, who are White Supremacists, blew up the government office building in an effort to start an uprising of the American people against *"Big Brother."* This bombing was planned to take place on the second anniversary of the incident that took place two years earlier in Waco, Texas. This tragedy took the lives of 168 innocent people, including 19 small children.

3. This generation shall not pass away (Matthew 24:24)

The prediction of the beginning of this generation as May 14, 1948 – when Israel became a nation – has misled many prophecy teachers of our time. The calculation of a generation as being 40 years led to the prediction of the second coming of Christ in 1988. By subtracting seven years for the Tribulation Period, it led to a 1981 date for the Rapture to take place. Obviously either man or God was incorrect in this calculation. <u>It was not God!</u> After this date was proven wrong, by passing without incident, it was conveniently changed by some people to be 2007. The new calculation was figured from 1967, when Israel won the 6-Day War and allowed the entire city of Jerusalem to be put under their control. Most date-setters will find some sort of mistake in their calculation of the second coming after the date passes and pick another date. And another! And another! The dates of May 14, 1948 and 1967 did not start the tic on the doomsday time clock. A sad note in the prophetic guessing game, that is being played out today, is that some people today who have printed earlier books about Bible prophecy are reissuing those books with changes in them that do not reflect that the current issue has been changed. I think that the honest thing to do would be to at least make reference to the date changes that were made in the new issue. People can understand a change better when it is based on honesty and truth.

4. Signs of the Times

Some prophecy teachers today are overemphasizing the fact that wars, severe weather conditions, pestilence and famine are all major signs that the end of the age is near. I also believe that these conditions are Signs of the Times, but they play only a secondary role. The true facts concerning the history of these events are not correctly presented in some prophecy ministries that are currently misrepresenting these events. The facts are that these events have been a part of our history even before Jesus came the first time. Most of the severest natural disasters, such as earthquakes took place before the twentieth century. The best account I was able to find to refute the increased earthquake theory that is propagated by some Bible prophecy teachers, is found in *End-time Visions*, by Richard Abanes, I quote from page 263. "Interestingly, earthquake-related casualties in exceptionally strong tremors have actually *decreased* over the years. More people died between 1715 and 1783 from earthquakes (1,373,845) than between 1915 and 1983 (1,210,597). History is filled with deadly earthquakes, the worst of which killed nearly one million people in Shenshu, China back in 1556. A brief listing of earthquakes from the past reveals that even the largest of modern tremors are rarely as destructive as those that occurred long ago and that the number of reported deaths between 1856 and 1914 is grossly understated by the Jehovah's Witnesses." [2] Almost any encyclopedia will furnish you with a list of devastating earthquakes from our past. The same thing can be said about other weather related natural disasters. As I have stated in an earlier chapter of this book, I believe that the Signs of the Times listed in Matthew 24:4-8, will take place *After the Rapture,* with possibly the very beginning of them at the end of the age. Most of the severest natural disasters will occur during the Tribulation Period and are listed in the book of Revelation where we find these plagues.

In closing, I would like to remind all of you what scripture reveals concerning our lives as Christians during the Dispensation of Grace, even if we are living during the time just prior to the return of Jesus. It should be a positive note, not a negative one. It is a time for joyful anticipation and not fearful anxiety. I will finish this book with a summation of how people, who know God, should be conducting their lives just prior to Jesus Christ's coming for them. The things we should be doing.

LIVE OUR LIVES LIKE CHRIST

We are to live our lives today to be as Christlike as possible. Of course we all know that we can never attain the position of being a god. We all, as believers, begin our lives with God as babes in Christ. As we study the word of God and are convicted by the Holy Spirit, our lives begin to mature and grow. Our entire life, after returning to God, is a growing and learning process. During this time we will have ups and downs, satisfactions and disappointments, times when we are close to God and times when we are far away from God. Remember that salvation is easy, but living our lives in the present world is difficult at times, even when we trust in God. Our reward is in the future, not the present. Although we as Christians today have peace in our souls, a peace that is hard for unbelievers to fathom, unbelievers are usually looking for that peace in their lifetime, but can not find it.

AFTER THE RAPTURE

Phil 2:1-11　*If you have any encouragement from being united with Christ, if any comfort from his love, if any fellowship with the Spirit, if any tenderness and compassion, then make my joy complete by being like-minded, having the same love, being one in spirit and purpose. Do nothing out of selfish ambition or vain conceit, but in humility consider others better than yourselves. Each of you should look not only to your own interests, but also to the interests of others. <u>Your attitude should be the same as that of Christ Jesus</u>: Who, being in very nature God, did not consider equality with God something to be grasped, but made himself nothing, taking the very nature of a servant, being made in human likeness. And being found in appearance as a man, he humbled himself and became obedient to death—even death on a cross! Therefore God exalted him to the highest place and gave him the name that is above every name, that at the name of Jesus every knee should bow, in heaven and on earth and under the earth, and every tongue confess that Jesus Christ is Lord, to the glory of God the Father.* (NIV)

Titus 2:11-15　*For the grace of God that brings salvation has appeared to all men. <u>It teaches us to say "No" to ungodliness and worldly passions, and to live self-controlled, upright and godly lives in this present age, while we wait for the blessed hope—the glorious appearing of our great God and Savior, Jesus Christ</u>, who gave himself for us to redeem us from all wickedness and to purify for himself a people that are his very own, eager to do what is good. These, then, are the things you should teach. Encourage and rebuke with all authority. Do not let anyone despise you.* (NIV)

Titus 3:1-8　*<u>Remind the people to be subject to rulers and authorities, to be</u> obedient, to be ready to do whatever is good, to slander no one, to be peaceable and considerate, and to show true humility toward all men. At one time we too were foolish, disobedient, deceived and enslaved by all kinds of passions and pleasures. We lived in malice and envy, being hated and hating one another. <u>But when the kindness and love of God our Savior appeared, he saved us, not because of righteous things we had done, but because of his mercy</u>. He saved us through the washing of rebirth and renewal by the Holy Spirit, whom he poured out on us generously through Jesus Christ our Savior, so that, having been justified by his grace, we might become heirs having the hope of eternal life. This is a trustworthy saying. <u>And I want you to stress these things, so that those who have trusted in God may be careful to devote themselves to doing what is good. These things are excellent and profitable for everyone.</u>* (NIV)

What Should We Do as Christians?

Phil 2:14-18 — *Do everything without complaining or arguing, so that you may become blameless and pure, children of God without fault in a crooked and depraved generation, in which you shine like stars in the universe as you hold out the word of life—in order that I may boast on the day of Christ that I did not run or labor for nothing. But even if I am being poured out like a drink offering on the sacrifice and service coming from your faith, I am glad and rejoice with all of you. So you too should be glad and rejoice with me.* (NIV)

Phil 4:4-9 — *Rejoice in the Lord always. I will say it again: Rejoice! Let your gentleness be evident to all. The Lord is near. Do not be anxious about anything, but in everything, by prayer and petition, with thanksgiving, present your requests to God. And the peace of God, which transcends all understanding, will guard your hearts and your minds in Christ Jesus. Finally, brothers, whatever is true, whatever is noble, whatever is right, whatever is pure, whatever is lovely, whatever is admirable—if anything is excellent or praiseworthy—think about such things. Whatever you have learned or received or heard from me, or seen in me—put it into practice. And the God of peace will be with you.* (NIV)

A Christian should mature as they begin to seek the plan that God has for their life, the purpose for their life here on earth and how they will build up the Kingdom of God. We are servants of God, just like Jesus was a servant. What service are you being called into for the advancement of the Gospel? What special gifts did God provide you with to use for building His Kingdom?

1 Cor 7:7 — *I wish that all men were as I am. But each man has his own gift from God; one has this gift, another has that.* (NIV)

1 Cor 7:17 — *Nevertheless, each one should retain the place in life that the Lord assigned to him and to which God has called him. This is the rule I lay down in all the churches.* (NIV)

1 Pet 4:10-11 — *Each one should use whatever gift he has received to serve others, faithfully administering God's grace in its various forms. If anyone speaks, he should do it as one speaking the very words of God. If anyone serves, he should do it with the strength God provides, so that in all things God may be praised through Jesus Christ. To him be the glory and the power for ever and ever. Amen.* (NIV)

Heb 13:20-21 — *May the God of peace, who through the blood of the eternal covenant brought back from the dead our Lord Jesus, that great Shepherd of the sheep, equip you with everything good for doing*

1 Cor 4:1-5   *So then, men ought to regard us as servants of Christ and as those entrusted with the secret things of God. <u>Now it is required that those who have been given a trust must prove faithful</u>. I care very little if I am judged by you or by any human court; indeed, I do not even judge myself. My conscience is clear, but that does not make me innocent. It is the Lord who judges me.* **Therefore judge nothing before the appointed time; wait till the Lord comes. He will bring to light what is hidden in darkness and will expose the motives of men's hearts. At that time each will receive his praise from God.** (NIV)

2 Tim 2:20-21   *In a large house there are articles not only of gold and silver, but also of wood and clay; some are for noble purposes and some for ignoble. If a man cleanses himself from the latter, he will be an instrument for noble purposes, made holy, <u>useful to the Master and prepared to do any good work</u>.* (NIV)

Matt 24:44-47   *So you also must be ready, because the Son of Man will come at an hour when you do not expect him. "<u>Who then is the faithful and wise servant, whom the master has put in charge of the servants in his household to give them their food at the proper time</u>? It will be good for that servant whose master finds him doing so when he returns. I tell you the truth, he will put him in charge of all his possessions.* (NIV)

No matter what service we are called into everyone is appointed to be an Ambassador for Jesus Christ. We should be excited about anything we do as we serve our great God, as we prepare for the other side and the ecstacy that lies ahead for the true believers in God's Son, Jesus Christ. Jesus is the most important message for everyone's life.

2 Cor 5:17-21   *<u>Therefore, if anyone is in Christ, he is a new creation; the old has gone, the new has come</u>! All this is from God, who reconciled us to himself through Christ and gave us the ministry of reconciliation: that God was reconciling the world to himself in Christ, not counting men's sins against them. And he has committed to us the message of reconciliation. <u>We are therefore Christ's ambassadors, as though God were making his appeal through us</u>. We implore you on Christ's behalf: Be reconciled to God. God made him who had no sin to be sin for us, so that in him we might become the righteousness of God.* (NIV)

SONS OF THE LIGHT

Although God will not reveal the exact date of the Rapture, He did not leave us in darkness as far as the general time of His appearing. Just prior to His return the conditions of the world will include an apostasy, the Jewish people returning to their homeland, a knowledge explosion, greater travel capabilities and finally the revealing of the Antichrist. People are prospering like no other time in history. People will even be commenting about how safe and secure the world is becoming. World peace seems to be moving in the right direction, but oh how wrong they are because destruction will come on them in a hurry. When these events are upon us, it will be the time for the return of Jesus. Because the Day of the Lord will come like a thief in the night, we do not know the exact day that the Day of the Lord will come, but we do know the approximate time it will arrive and it should not surprise us when it does arrive. We were warned ahead of time and by accepting Jesus as our personal Savior, we are preparing to miss the extreme suffering that is probably not far off.

> 1 Thes 5:1-11 *Now, brothers, about times and dates we do not need to write to you, for you know very well that the day of the Lord will come like a thief in the night. While people are saying, "__Peace and safety__," destruction will come on them suddenly, as labor pains on a pregnant woman, and they will not escape. But you, brothers, are not in darkness so that this day should surprise you like a thief. __You are all sons of the light and sons of the day__. We do not belong to the night or to the darkness. So then, let us not be like others, who are asleep, but let us be alert and self-controlled. For those who sleep, sleep at night, and those who get drunk, get drunk at night. But since we belong to the day, let us be self-controlled, putting on faith and love as a breastplate, and the hope of salvation as a helmet. __For God did not appoint us to suffer wrath but to receive salvation through our Lord Jesus Christ.__ He died for us so that, whether we are awake or asleep, we may live together with him. Therefore encourage one another and build each other up, just as in fact you are doing.* (NIV)

> Rev 3:10 *Since you have kept my command to endure patiently, __I will also keep you from the hour of trial that is going to come upon the whole world to test those who live on the earth.__* (NIV)

If you are in darkness, asleep or drunk—which basically is referring to those who are not saved at the time Jesus returns for His own—you will take part in the hour of trial that is coming upon the whole world.

> Rev 3:1-3 *"To the angel of the church in Sardis write: These are the words of him who holds the seven spirits of God and the seven stars. __I know your deeds; you have a reputation of being alive, but you are dead. Wake up__! Strengthen what remains and is about to die, for*

AFTER THE RAPTURE

I have not found your deeds complete in the sight of my God. <u>Remember, therefore, what you have received and heard; obey it, and repent.</u> But if you do not wake up, I will come like a thief, and you will not know at what time I will come to you. (NIV)

Rom 13:11-14
<u>And do this, understanding the present time. The hour has come for you to wake up from your slumber, because our salvation is nearer now than when we first believed.</u> The night is nearly over; the day is almost here. So let us put aside the deeds of darkness and put on the armor of light. Let us behave decently, as in the daytime, not in orgies and drunkenness, not in sexual immorality and debauchery, not in dissension and jealousy. <u>Rather, clothe yourselves with the Lord Jesus Christ, and do not think about how to gratify the desires of the sinful nature.</u> (NIV)

WATCH!

The general consensus for Christians throughout the Dispensation of Grace is to live our lives on earth with the expectation of the imminent return of Christ. We are to have a daily walk with Jesus and be good stewards of the things He provides for us. We are to use the talents He has given each of us to build on the foundation of Christ. We are not to quit our jobs and sell our houses in order to give the money to some sensationalist, who is predicting the end of the world on a certain date. This practice went on as early as the Thessalonian church in the first century. We are not to worry or be fearful of doomsday. God is in control.

The key word for today is, *"watch"*. If we are on the alert for Jesus—whether He returns in our lifetime or a thousand years from now—we will be ready when He comes back for us. Remember that if we die in this life, before Jesus comes back, we will still be with Jesus when He meets the living saints in the air at the Rapture. It is a mutually beneficial situation for all those who know Jesus and joyfully wait for the return of our redeemer.

Matt 24:42-44
"<u>Therefore keep watch</u>, because you do not know on what day your Lord will come. But understand this: If the owner of the house had known at what time of night the thief was coming, he would have kept watch and would not have let his house be broken into. <u>So you also must be ready, because the Son of Man will come at an hour when you do not expect him.</u> (NIV)

Mark 13:35-37
"Therefore keep watch because you do not know when the owner of the house will come back—whether in the evening, or at midnight, or when the rooster crows, or at dawn. If he comes suddenly, do not let him find you sleeping. <u>What I say to you, I say to everyone: '<u>Watch!</u>'"</u> (NIV)

1 Thes 5:6
So then, let us not be like others, who are asleep, <u>but let us be alert</u>

What Should We Do as Christians?

<u>and self-controlled.</u> (NIV)

When the signs that Jesus told us to watch for begin to take place, we need to *"look up"* for our redemption is drawing near. The signs are in our very midst, even as you read this book. Salvation also means deliverance. Jesus is coming soon, to deliver us!

Luke 21:28-33 *<u>When these things begin to take place, stand up and lift up your heads, because your redemption is drawing near."</u> He told them this parable: "Look at the fig tree and all the trees. When they sprout leaves, you can see for yourselves and know that summer is near. <u>Even so, when you see these things happening, you know that the kingdom of God is near."</u> I tell you the truth, this generation will certainly not pass away until all these things have happened. Heaven and earth will pass away, but my words will never pass away.* (NIV)

Phil 3:17-4:1 *Join with others in following my example, brothers, and take note of those who live according to the pattern we gave you. For, as I have often told you before and now say again even with tears, many live as enemies of the cross of Christ. <u>Their destiny is destruction</u>, their god is their stomach, and their glory is in their shame. <u>Their mind is on earthly things. But our citizenship is in heaven. And we eagerly await a Savior from there, the Lord Jesus Christ</u>, who, by the power that enables him to bring everything under his control, will transform our lowly bodies so that they will be like his glorious body. Therefore, my brothers, you whom I love and long for, my joy and crown, that is how you should stand firm in the Lord, dear friends!* (NIV)

Are you ready for His coming?

1 Thes 2:19-20 *For what is our hope, our joy, or the crown in which we will glory in the presence of our Lord Jesus when he comes? <u>Is it not you</u>? Indeed, you are our glory and joy.* (NIV)

1 John 2:28 *<u>And now, dear children, continue in him, so that when he appears we may be confident and unashamed before him at his coming.</u>* (NIV)

After reading this book and gaining a full understanding of what it will be like when Jesus comes back to purge the earth of unsaved mankind, try not to let the anxieties of this life—sometimes easier said than done—overwhelm you so that you are not prepared for the Rapture when it arrives. Isn't it exciting to be living in the important times that we are currently living in today? Watch carefully as world events continue to develop up to the return of Jesus.

AFTER THE RAPTURE

Luke 21:34-36   *"<u>Be careful, or your hearts will be weighed down with dissipation, drunkenness and the anxieties of life, and that day will close on you unexpectedly like a trap. For it will come upon all those who live on the face of the whole earth. Be always on the watch, and pray that you may be able to escape all that is about to happen, and that you may be able to stand before the Son of Man.</u>"* (NIV)

If you have not accepted Jesus Christ into your life, **NOW** would be an excellent time to do it, in order for you to be ready for His return! Get down on your knees and ask Jesus to forgive your sins and to come into your heart. It will change your life **FOREVER**!

If you really want to get a better understanding of the material presented in this book, please go back and read chapters eight through fifteen again. You should realize that if the events that were presented in this book do not take place exactly like they were presented, it is because I have miscalculated. God's word is one hundred percent correct. One thing is for sure though – everything in this book is going to take place, whether I have placed them in the correct chronological order or not.

Jesus loved you enough to die on the cross for you, please love Him enough to accept Him as your Personal Savior.

<u>MAY GOD BE WITH YOU!</u>

NOTES

FROM THE AUTHOR
1. The Dictionary of Biblical Literacy, Cecil B. Murphey (Compiled By), *Historic Texts and Their Translations* (Nashville, TN: Oliver-Nelson Books, 1989) 52-69.

CHAPTER ONE: DAY OF THE LORD
1. Dr. David Webber and Rev. Noah Hutchings, *Joel, In the Day of the Lord* (Oklahoma City, OK: The Southwest Radio Church, 1982) 10.

CHAPTER THREE: WHAT DAY IS IT?
1. Clarence Larkin, *The Greatest Book on Dispensational Truth in the World* (Glenside, PA: Rev. Clarence Larkin, Est., 1918) 43¾.
2. Alva J. McClain, *The Greatness of the Kingdom* (Winona Lake, IN: BMH Books, 1974) 529-530.
3. Shmuel Yosef Agnon, *Days of Awe* (New York: Shocken, 1948) 234.

CHAPTER FOUR: THE LAODICEAN CHURCH 1900-1948
1. Microsoft (R) Encarta (R) 96 Encyclopedia, *Masada* (Seattle, WA: ©Microsoft Corporation. ©Funk & Wagnalls Corporation, 1993-1995).
2. Microsoft (R) Encarta (R) 96 Encyclopedia, *Warfare* (Seattle, WA: ©Microsoft Corporation. ©Funk & Wagnalls Corporation, 1993-1995).

CHAPTER FIVE: ISRAEL, MAY 14, 1948 — CAN A NATION BE BORN IN A DAY?
1. Rabbi Joseph Telushkin, *Jewish Literacy* (New York: W. Morrow, 1991) 115.
2. Ibid., 119-120.
3. Ibid., 133-136.
4. Ibid., 141-142.
5. Ibid., 145-146.
6. The Oxford Dictionary of the Jewish Religion R.J. Werblowsky and Geoffrey Wigoder (Edited By), *Anti-Semitism* (New York • Oxford: Oxford University Press, 1997) 53-54.
7. The New Standard Jewish Encyclopedia, Dr. Cecil Roth and Dr. Geoffrey Wigoder (Edited By), *Anti-Semitism* (New York: Doubleday & Co., Inc., 1970) 120-126
8. Erwin W. Lutzer, *Hitler's Cross* (Chicago: Moody Press, 1995) 61-69.
9. A Mosaic of Victims, Non-Jews Persecuted and Murdered by the NAZIS Michael Berenbaum (Edited By), *Foreword* (New York and London: New York University Press, 1990) xi.
10. Harold A. Sevener, *Message of the Christian Jew* (San Antonio, TX: Christian Jewish Foundation, May-June 1984) 6.
11. Konnilyn Feig, *A Mosaic of Victims, Non-Jews Persecuted and Murdered by the NAZIS - Non-Jewish Victims in the Concentration Camps* (New York and

London: New York University Press, 1990) 167-168.
12. Milton Meltzer, *Never to Forget-The Jews of the Holocaust* (New York: Harper & Row, Publishers, 1968) 65-73.
13. Eli Wiesel, *The Oath* (New York, 1972) 20.
14. Eliezer Urbach, *Out of the Fury, The Incredible Odyssey of Eliezer Urbach* (Denver, CO: Zhera Publications, 1987) 128-129.
15. Ibid., 136-138.
16. Elena Romero Castello and Uriel Macias Kaplon, *The Jews and Europe, 2,000 Years of History* (Edison, NJ: Chartwell Books, Inc., 1994) and Lavinia Cohn-Sherbok, *A History of Jewish Civilization* (Edison, NJ: Chartwell Books, Inc., 1997) These two sources above were contributing factors for chapter five and helped with the Jewish history portion of this book.
17. Eliezer Urbach, *Out of the Fury, The Incredible Odyssey of Eliezer Urbach* (Denver, CO: Zhera Publications, 1987) 217.

CHAPTER SIX: YOM HA-DIN—DAYS OF AWE—A JEWISH WEDDING

1. The Oxford Dictionary of the Jewish Religion, R. J. Werblowsky and Geoffrey Wigoder (Edited By), *Yom Ha-Din* (New York • Oxford: Oxford University Press, 1997) 750.
2. The New Standard Jewish Encyclopedia, Dr. Cecil Roth and Dr. Geoffrey Wigoder (Edited By), *Eschatology* (New York: Doubleday & Co., Inc., 1970) 636-638.
3. The Oxford Dictionary of the Jewish Religion, R. J. Werblowsky and Geoffrey Wigoder (Edited By), *Messiah* (New York • Oxford: Oxford University Press, 1997) 458-460.
4. Ibid., *Eschatology*, 432-434.
5. Ibid., *Aseret Yemei Teshuvah*, 69.
6. Shmuel Yosef Agnon, *Days of Awe* (New York: Shocken, 1948) 14.
7. Joseph Stern, *Days of Awe* (Mesorah Publications, Ltd: Brooklyn, NY, 1966) 52
8. Avi Ben Mordechai, *Signs in the Heavens, A Jewish Messianic Perspective of the Last Days and Coming Millennium* (Colorado Springs, CO: A Millennium 7000 Communications Int'l Publication, 1995) 265.
9. Rosh Hashanah, Artscroll Mesorah Series, Rabbis Nosson Scherman/Meir Zlotowitz (General Editors), *Exposition on Jewish Liturgy* (Brooklyn, NY: Mesorah Publications, LTD, 1983) 50.
10. Shmuel Yosef Agnon, *Days of Awe* (New York: Shocken, 1948) 110.
11. The Oxford Dictionary of the Jewish Religion, R.J. Werblowsky and Geoffrey Wigoder (Edited By), *Thirteen Principles of Faith* (New York • Oxford: Oxford University Press, 1997) 691-692.
12. Rabbi Yosef Stern, *Days of Awe* (Brooklyn, NY: Mesorah Publications, LTD, 1996) 263-264.
13. The Oxford Dictionary of the Jewish Religion, R.J. Werblowsky and Geoffrey Wigoder (Edited By), *Yom Kippur* (New York • Oxford: Oxford University

Press, 1997) 751.
14. Clarence Larkin, *The Greatest Book on Dispensational Truth in the World* (Glenside, PA: Rev. Clarence Larkin, Est., 1918) 159-161.
15. The New Standard Jewish Encyclopedia, Dr. Cecil Roth and Dr. Geoffrey Wigoder (Edited By), *Marriage* (New York: Doubleday & Co., Inc., 1970) 1290-1291.
16. Avi Ben Mordechai, *Signs in the Heavens, A Jewish Messianic Perspective of the Last Days and Coming Millennium* (Colorado Springs, CO: A Millennium 7000 Communications Int'l Publication, 1995) 273.
17. The Oxford Dictionary of the Jewish Religion, R.J. Werblowsky and Geoffrey Wigoder (Edited By), *Betrothal* (New York • Oxford: Oxford University Press, 1997) 120.
18. Avi Ben Mordechai, *Signs in the Heavens, A Jewish Messianic Perspective of the Last Days and Coming Millennium* (Colorado Springs, CO: A Millennium 7000 Communications Int'l Publication, 1995) 272.
19. The Oxford Dictionary of the Jewish Religion, R.J. Werblowsky and Geoffrey Wigoder (Edited By), *Betrothal* (New York • Oxford: Oxford University Press, 1997) 120.
20. Ibid., 120.
21. Avi Ben Mordechai, *Signs in the Heavens, A Jewish Messianic Perspective of the Last Days and Coming Millennium* (Colorado Springs, CO: A Millennium 7000 Communications Int'l Publication, 1995) 270.
22. Ibid., 276.
23. Ibid., 277.
24. Ibid., 276.
25. Rabbi Joseph Telushkin, *Jewish Literacy* (New York: W. Morrow, 1991) 614.
26. Ibid., 615.
27. Avi Ben Mordechai, *Signs in the Heavens, A Jewish Messianic Perspective of the Last Days and Coming Millennium* (Colorado Springs, CO: A Millennium 7000 Communications Int'l Publication, 1995) 277.
28. Ibid., 278.
29. Alva J. McClain, *The Greatness of the Kingdom* (Winona Lake, IN: BMH Books, 1974) 196

CHAPTER EIGHT: AFTER THE RAPTURE AND BEFORE THE TRIBULATION PERIOD
1. Erwin W. Lutzer, *Hitler's Cross* (Chicago: Moody Press, 1995) 113-114.
2. Ibid., 71-72.

CHAPTER ELEVEN: THE TRIBULATION PERIOD — THE TIME OF JACOB'S TROUBLE
1. J. Barton Payne, *Encyclopedia of Biblical Prophecy* (Grand Rapids, MI: Baker Book House, 1973) 427-433.
2. A. T. Clay, *Babylonia, The Dynasties* (Seattle, WA: International Standard

Bible Encylopaedia, Electronic Database, © Biblesoft, 1996).
3. Ibid.
4. W. St. Clair Tisdall, *Persians* (Seattle, WA: International Standard Bible Encylopaedia, Electronic Database,© Biblesoft, 1996).
5. The New Unger's Bible Dictionary, *Babylonia* (Seattle WA: PC Study Bible, Biblesoft, 1992-1996).
6. Nelson's Illustrated Bible Dictionary, *Babylonia* (Seattle, WA: PC Study Bible, Biblesoft, 1992-1996).
7. The New Unger's Bible Dictionary, *Babylonia* (Seattle WA: PC Study Bible, Biblesoft, 1992-1996).
8. Nelson's Illustrated Bible Dictionary, *Babylonia* (Seattle, WA: PC Study Bible, Biblesoft, 1992-1996).
9. The New Unger's Bible Dictionary, *Babylonia* (Seattle WA: PC Study Bible, Biblesoft, 1992-1996).
10. Nelson's Illustrated Bible Dictionary, *Babylonia* (Seattle, WA: PC Study Bible, Biblesoft, 1992-1996).
11. The New Unger's Bible Dictionary, *Babylonia* (Seattle WA: PC Study Bible, Biblesoft, 1992-1996).
12. T. G. Pinches, *Babel, Babylon* (Seattle, WA: International Standard Bible Encylopaedia, Electronic Database, © Biblesoft, 1996).
13. The New Unger's Bible Dictionary, *Babylonia* (Seattle WA: PC Study Bible, Biblesoft, 1992-1996).

CHAPTER TWELVE: THE DAY OF VENGEANCE — THE YEAR OF MY REDEMPTION

1. Nelson's Illustrated Bible Dictionary, *Jubilee* (Seattle, WA: PC Study Bible, Biblesoft, 1992-1996).
2. The New Unger's Bible Dictionary, *Jubilee* (Seattle WA: PC Study Bible, Biblesoft, 1992-1996).
3. William Baur, *Jubilee Year* (Seattle, WA: International Standard Bible Encylopaedia, Electronic Database, © Biblesoft, 1996).
4. Tim LaHaye, *Revelation-Illustrated and Made Plain* (Grand Rapids, MI: Zondervan Publishing House, 1973) 266.
5. The New Unger's Bible Dictionary, *Azel* (Seattle WA: PC Study Bible, Biblesoft, 1992-1996).

CHAPTER THIRTEEN: THE REST OF THE MILLENNIUM

1. Martin Gilbert, *Jerusalem in the Twentieth Century* (New York: John Wiley & Sons, 1996) 2-3.

CHAPTER SIXTEEN: WHAT SHOULD WE DO AS CHRISTIANS?

1. Richard Abanes, *End-Times Visions, The Road to Armageddon?* (New York: Four Walls Eight Windows, 1998) Appendix C.
2. Ibid., 263.

INDEX OF SELECTED SCRIPTURE

OLD TESTAMENT

Genesis
1:1-5	679
1:14-19	34
1:26-27	584,585
3:16	325
3:19	694
5:1-2	585
6:1-13	316,361
9:18-19	275
12:1-3	84
14:18-20	554
15:17	682
16:6-16	587
17:5-8	84
18:1-22	85,586
19:24	682
22:1-4	556
48:14-16	588,647
49:1-2	198
49:8-12	198

Exodus
2:23-25	592
3:1-10	592,648,672
7:16	85
12:1-20	152,153
12:40-41	85
13:17-22	595,669,683
14:10-21	593,595,648
15:22-27	596
16:1-10	596
17:1-7	598
19:1-25	83,229,349,598,599
	600,605,606
20:18-20	606
23:20-25	593,648
24:1-7	83,86,607
24:9-18	135,607,670,683
25:8-22	607,617,631
29:42-44	617
31:18	608
32:1	135

Exodus Cont'd
32:7-12	136,316
32:14	136
32:30-35	136,608
33:1-23	609,610,648,670,680
34:1-5	613
34:9-10	135
34:27-35	15,613,614
40:17-38	616,617

Leviticus
16:1-4	618,661,675
16:34	138,150
23:2	292
23:9-16	153,154
23:23-44	149,155,157,227
26:1-13	654

Numbers
6:22-26	615
9:15-16	683
10:1-10	226
11:1-3	683
12:6-8	611
29:1-11	133
32:13	86

Deuteronomy
4:1-40	370,460,618,619
	620,670
5:1-33	621
6:3-9	163,622
7:6	79
9:7-8	86
9:17-21	608
10:10-13	613
14:2	83
18:14-22	369,614
26:19	83
28:1-68	78,79,80,500
29:1-29	22,198
30:1-10	200,452,531
31:15-18	86
32:1-4	314,527

745

AFTER THE RAPTURE

Deuteronomy Cont'd		2 Chronicles	
32:39-43	475	3:1-2	556
33:1-2	640	7:1-2	683

Joshua		Job	
5:13-6:2	586,649	1:6-12	299
9:24	75	1:16	684
		15:20-35	489
Judges		19:25-29	60
9:7-15	274	26:6-7	701
13:2-25	588	37:5	229
		38:4-7	300
1 Samuel		38:22-23	436
2:9-10	194,475	40:9	605
4:1-22	622,623,668		
5:1-12	624	Psalms	
6:1-20	625	1:1-6	379
16:14	594	2:1-12	141,347,474,522
			560,582
2 Samuel		4:6	615
5:6-10	557	8:1-9	521
24:15-17	589	9:5-8	379
		9:15-20	470
1 Kings		11:1-7	327,473,560,713
6:1	88	13:2	179
8:1-13	626,631	17:15	713
8:41-43	88	18:1-2	192,527
9:1-3	558	18:7-15	480,481,685
11:36	558	21:8-12	472
18:24	683	22:25-31	578
22:19	670	23:6	706
		24:1-10	141,469,676
2 Kings		27:1-6	144,181,528,706
2:9-11	455	29:1-4	229,605
6:8-23	454	29:10-11	703
17:5-23	89	34:1-22	591
21:4	558	37:1-40	471
21:7	558	43:1	338
25:1-26	93,146	44:9-16	91
		45:6-9	233,242
1 Chronicles		45:13-15	243
29:10-13	702	46:1-11	517,579
		47:1-5	227,521
		48:1-3	709

Index of Selected Scripture

Psalms Cont'd	
49:15	525
50:1-6	472
52:1-7	338,488
55:20-21	338
58:1-11	287,475
62:1-12	527
67:1-7	578,615
68:1-3	486
68:15-18	462,515,696
68:19-23	486
68:28-35	580
69:13-18	510
69:24-28	238
72:1-20	520,523,581,667
74:10	179
75:1-10	327,379,385
76:1-2	556
78:35	525
79:1-12	379
81:3-11	141,227,605
83:1-8	267
84:1-12	561,706,709
85:1-13	534,658
86:9-12	579
87:1-3	710
89:7-29	232,615,665
90:4	42
90:10	170
91:1-2	543,706
93:1-2	234
94:1-23	142,179,287
95:1	527
96:10-13	234
97:1-12	191,481,640,685
98:1-9	142,191,380
99:1-9	141,469
100:1-5	230
101:1-8	707
102:1-28	208,293,442,498,565
103:8-9	314
103:19-22	207,703
104:29-31	520,712
104:35	47

Psalms Cont'd	
105:1-45	86
106:1-48	91,330,510
107:32	232
110:1-7	179,200,380,473
	511,554,560
111:1-9	232
113:1-9	521
118:19-29	230,529
122:1-9	162,235,269,516
	562,706
133:1-3	581
137:1-8	91,410
139:1-16	583,584
140:1-3	75
145:1-21	207,314
147:1-5	453,583
148:1-6	299
148:13-14	83
149:1-9	216,217,232

Proverbs	
2:22	47
11:4	205
11:28	205
13:7	205
20:2	482

Ecclesiastes	
3:20	223,694
12:7	233,694

Isaiah	
1:4	329,395
1:18-20	329
2:1-22	44,178,201,271,305
	380,517,524,579
3:1-9	335
3:13-15	329
4:2-6	526,544,563,659,660,684
6:1-5	675
7:17-20	393
9:1-7	269,522,660
10:5-25	393,394

AFTER THE RAPTURE

Isaiah Cont'd	
11:1-2	236,526
11:4	482
11:11	346
11:6-9	516
12:1-6	563,654
13:1-16	29,47,179,201,317
	346,380,389,427
13:19-22	427
14:3-32	298,377,386,412
	428,490,492
15:1-9	413
16:13-14	414
17:1-14	417
18:1-6	405
19:4-10	400
19:12	397
19:19-25	402,518,581
20:3-6	400
21:9	429
21:13-17	418
23:1-18	411
24:1-23	47,48,196,381
	494,495
25:6-9	508,543
26:9-11	419
26:16-21	141,144,161,165,181
	272,273,330
27:1	494
27:7-13	438,449,452
28:14-22	248,378,450
29:22-24	541
30:25-33	482,486,490,640,685
31:8-9	491
32:1	667
33:20-24	524,575
34:1-15	480,482
35:1-2	520,658
35:5-10	517,519
40:1-5	518,657
40:10	191,715
41:8-9	84
41:18-20	519
41:25	387

Isaiah Cont'd	
42:8-10	232
42:13-17	479,480
42:24-25	330
43:1-13	453,474
43:25	239
44:6-8	201,525,676
45:1-5	95
45:15-17	542
46:8-13	433
48:9-11	330
49:1-13	89,182,442,498
49:25-26	499,525,579
51:4-6	579
51:17-23	327,334,396
52:1-2	563
52:7-10	562
53:4-7	244,651
54:4-17	331,395,453,503
55:3-5	666,676
55:8-11	314
56:3-8	576
59:20-21	441,503,525,542
60:1-22	441,499,565,567,573
	580,659
61:1-11	440,441,442,539
62:1-12	84,191,441,480,563,565
63:1-14	441,442,483,499,612,649
65:1-25	84,326,441,513,541,564
66:8	78
66:10-13	78,562
66:15-23	190,481,516,574
	575,640,685

Jeremiah	
1:5	396
1:14	388
2:9	396
3:14	504
3:17	669
4:5-31	390
6:1	388
6:22-26	388,392
9:25-26	381,393

748

Index of Selected Scripture

Jeremiah Cont'd		Ezekiel	
10:10	201,381	1:1-6	240,612,670
10:22-25	392,395	1:25-28	612,671,680,684,704
16:3-7	90	2:1-2	594
16:18	330,335	3:16-27	612,627
19:11	93	4:1-8	40
23:1-7	526	7:1-27	329,331,332
23:19-20	61,420	8:1-6	628,671
25:12-38	318,327,381,382,383	9:2-4	628,673
	425,432,434	10:1-8	628,673,680
29:10	95	10:18-19	628
30:1-7	24,100,166,328,534	11:16-20	502
30:10-11	344,534	11:22-25	93,629
30:18-24	318,351,420,564,668	12:21-28	370
31:1-14	345,351,534	14:12-23	333
31:23-40	84,461,500,535	20:1-48	329,330,334,455,479
	544,564		501,574,582
32:17	583	21:14-17	389
32:36-37	386	21:28-32	416
33:6-29	351,536,544,575	22:17-22	460
36:1-2	15	22:31	318
45:1-46:1	389	25:1-17	409,413,415,416
46:6-19	397,398,399	26:1-6	412
46:20-28	399,403	28:2-19	297,298,341,489,491
48:1-9	414	29:1-3	397
49:1-39	408,415,418	29:12-15	402,580
50:1-5	427,503	30:1-19	201,381,398,400,404
50:9-16	429	31:10-18	401,492
50:22-32	429	32:1-27	401,402,406
50:41-46	430		407,408
51:1-4	430	32:29-30	408,411
51:6-9	290,430	33:1-20	420,422
51:12	433	34:1-31	458,502,518,520,665
51:20-23	275,426	35:1-15	410
51:24-29	432	36:1-38	502,536
51:49	427	37:24-38	503,666
51:54-58	427	38:1-23	61,195,196,276
51:64	430		278,279,280
52:27-30	95	39:1-16	281
		39:17-29	461,487
Lamentations		40:1-5	568,674
1:1	93	43:1-12	568,569,656,671,680
2:6	95	44:1-4	569,661
4:1-18	316	44:24	575

AFTER THE RAPTURE

Ezekiel Cont'd	
45:1-6	569,574
45:7-8	570
45:13-25	570
46:1-24	571,661
47:1-12	519
48:21-35	573,661,669

Daniel	
1:1-2	91
2:26-45	61,211,251,252
	514,528,702
3:25-28	686
4:13	674
4:34-35	703
5:1-6	384
5:25-31	385
7:1-28	141,142,215,216,233,237
	246,247,253,254,265,268
	313,355,493,496,515,581
	635,665,672,700,702,704
8:9-14	284,340,567
8:17-28	61,184,272,291,311,342
	354,365,371,493
9:24-27	29,97,99,178,195
	269,324,340
10:4-8	674
10:14	62,294
11:21-28	266,283,288,292,294
11:29-35	290,292,295,340,350
11:36-45	349,354,397,405
	416,426,463
12:1-7	24,68,99,165,172
	183,184,292,300
	312,313,337,674
12:9-13	172,173,183,340
	369,420,443,714

Hosea	
2:18	517
3:4-5	62,88,461,659,669
4:1	89
5:4-15	57,629
6:1-2	57,59

Hosea Cont'd	
14:1-9	147,543

Joel	
1:15	48,202,381
2:1-11	30,139,228,309,311,364
2:15-32	147,162,306,311,443
	447,489,505,519,654
3:1-16	464,467,474,484
3:17-21	139,561,655

Amos	
1:2	482
3:2	88
3:11	88
5:18-20	46,202,336
7:9	88
8:1-14	343
9:1-15	156,336,343,344
	520,538,540,567

Obadiah	
1:15-18	178,202,381,483

Micah	
1:2-4	478
2:12-13	453
4:1-8	44,517,524,578,582
5:1-15	331,339,371,372
	373,374,536,666
7:8-13	381,539

Nahum	
1:2-7	315
3:1-19	405,406,491

Habakkuk	
2:2-14	90,293,355,369,659
3:1-19	484,490,640,685

Zephaniah	
1:1-18	47,48,202,228,306,311
	334,353,381,473

Index of Selected Scripture

Zephaniah Cont'd	
2:1-15	318,350,405,407
	413,415,578
3:6-20	318,473,521,535
	563,574,655

Haggai	
2:6-9	677

Zechariah	
1:16-17	567
2:5	684
4:11-14	321
6:11-13	527,529,566,665
7:4-14	96
8:1-23	542,561,573,577,655
9:1-17	395,413,418,461,479
	522,531,539,579
11:15-17	297
12:1-10	59,476,478,650
13:7-9	336,342
14:1-21	32,156,190,477,482
	485,520,522,564
	577,667

Malachi	
3:1-5	651
3:12	578
3:17-18	382,477
4:1-5	151,202,306,312,473

NEW TESTAMENT

Matthew	
3:13-17	632
5:11-13	168
5:33-35	704
6:24	205
7:13-23	249,262,721
11:29-30	160
13:24-32	465,544
13:36-43	465
13:49-50	700
16:1-3	175

Matthew Cont'd	
16:16-18	528
16:27	189,448
17:1-8	321,681
18:10	636
19:23-24	205
19:27-28	235
22:13	700
23:33	100
24:1-3	35,62,79,183,186
24:4-8	326
24:9-14	184,324,325,341
24:15-28	24,77,132,164,309,339
	341,346,447,639
24:29-30	189,439,447,639
24:31	345,449,452
24:32-35	78
24:36	723
24:37-47	185,186,736,738
24:50-51	700
25:14-46	25,189,448,466
	639,699
26:42	245
26:64	190
27:25	101
28:20	63,183

Mark	
1:14-15	54
9:43-48	699
10:29-31	213
13:32-37	185,738

Luke	
1:11-19	590
1:26-33	54,209
3:2-6	657
4:14-21	440
6:20-23	51
6:24	205
6:47-49	528
9:26-36	632,638,639,641,677
10:1-11	54
13:29-30	438

751

AFTER THE RAPTURE

Luke Cont'd		Acts	
16:19-31	695,698	1:1-12	451,532,723
17:22-25	639,681	2:1-2	154
17:26-30	192,203	2:16-23	177,504,584
19:41-44	73	3:11-26	194,446,533,662
21:5-11	69,70,101	4:10-12	134
21:12-24	63,71,73,101	5:29-32	533,662
21:25-33	169,170,185,190	6:15	641
21:34-36	51,144,170,186	7:1-60	633,643,648,679
	202,271,739,740	8:32-35	244
22:1-6	310	13:6	722
22:16-18	438	14:1	72
22:21-23	310	14:21-22	729
22:28-30	438	17:11	717
22:39-44	653	17:24-31	180,202,293
22:47-48	310	22:6-11	185,638,677
23:42-43	697	26:12-15	681
24:13-35	717		
		Romans	
John		1:18-32	75,248
1:1-14	594,652	2:1-11	203,451
1:29-36	244	2:16	51
3:1-8	67,209	3:22-26	530,692
3:14-21	213	4:4-8	237
3:29	160	5:1-5	729
4:21-34	635,653	5:1-6:23	690
5:16-30	222,238,272,315	5:9	181
	653,669,695	5:14-21	550
5:37-39	636,717	6:1-23	213,551
5:43	248	8:18-27	206,729
6:38-46	231,636,653	8:34	348
8:12-30	652	8:35-39	730
8:44	298	9:1-5	631
11:1-44	221,231	9:22-33	462
12:27-33	258,272,633	10:8-10	39
12:37-41	676	11:1-36	59,74,154,182,192
12:47-50	653		337,351,461
14:1-12	159,194,711	12:19	315
14:15-21	50,504	13:11-14	141,738
14:26-27	504	14:10-12	142,236
16:21-23	50,326		
17:1-5	636	1 Corinthians	
		1:3-9	31,50,211,228
		2:6-10	707

Index of Selected Scripture

1 Corinthians Cont'd		Philippians	
3:1-20	25,51,143,236	1:3-11	30,31,50
4:1-5	237,736	1:12-14	72
5:7	152	1:19-26	697
6:9-10	214	2:1-11	637,651,668,734
7:7	735	2:14-18	30,50,228,735
7:17	735	3:20-21	212,224,553
10:4	528	3:17-4:1	739
10:1-13	642,727	4:1-9	24,204,239,728,735
12:7-10	730		
13:9-12	39	Colossians	
15:20-28	154,231,690,693	1:10-15	530,633,636
	694,696,708	2:16-17	151
15:35-49	223,642,694	3:1-6	178,224,348,642
15:50-58	20,138,155,215,221	3:15	24
	223,603,693		
		1 Thessalonians	
2 Corinthians		1:10	181
1:3-7	730	2:4	23
1:13-14	31	2:19-20	188,211,739
3:5-18	504,505,642	3:2-5	726
4:4	258,636	3:6-13	188,216,635,727
4:13-18	212,216,635	4:13-18	20,24,138,140,160,187
5:1-10	132,142,236,694,697		215,222,603,646,662
5:17-21	153,736	5:1-11	24,77,171,181,186,192
6:1-2	440		206,293,530,723,737,738
11:13-15	249,722	5:23	188
11:23-28	72,722		
		2 Thessalonians	
Galatians		1:4-10	52,315,468,482,686,700
3:16-19	85,552	2:1-8	24,28,52,72,168,176
4:1-7	293,525		188,193,195,202
4:21-31	547		246,340,491,686
		2:9-12	247,356,450
Ephesians			
1:9-10	34,523	1 Timothy	
2:1-2	258	1:17	633
2:19-22	529	4:1-5	173
4:8-10	696	6:6-10	206
4:19	75	6:15-16	634,681
5:13-14	141,231	6:17-19	212
5:31-32	145		
6:12	299	2 Timothy	
6:18	728	1:9	34

AFTER THE RAPTURE

2 Timothy Cont'd	
2:8-13	496
2:20-21	736
3:1-5	44,175
3:12-13	249,722
3:16-22	24,718
4:1-2	48,57
4:3-4	174
4:8	51,211
4:18	51

Titus	
2:11-15	211,525,734
3:1-8	734

Hebrews	
1:1-3	44,60,636
1:8-9	233
1:14	698
2:10	662
3:1-6	615
6:19-7:28	554
8:1-13	501,629
9:1-28	44,194,212,529,530
	548,549,630
10:1-39	50,151,318,511,549,550
11:8-16	53,162,546,704,706
11:27	634
11:32-40	728
12:1-6	348,552,662
12:14-29	46,212,229,239,547
	552, 601,603,604,605
	646,686,701,706
13:14	552
13:17	717
13:20-21	550,735

James	
1:11	206
3:9	585
5:1-6	174,205
5:7-11	142,187,728

1 Peter	
1:2-23	34,44,45,56,177,210
	244,701,726
3:18-19	696
4:6	696
4:10-11	735
5:1-4	666
5:8	299

2 Peter	
1:10-18	187,209,632
2:1-2	249,722
2:4	362
2:9-10	241
3:3-18	42,45,47,53,174,188,203
	241,472,495,688,708

1 John	
1:5-10	530,681
2:18	45,433
2:28-29	188,739
2:28-3:3	224
4:1	722
4:12	634
5:11-13	213
5:20	213

Jude	
1-6	241,312,362
1:14-15	197,468
1:18	45

Revelation	
1:1-20	28,189,191,219,301
	447,530,638,664
	678,719,729
2:18	678
3:1-3	171,737
3:5	239
3:7-22	48,65,66,171,179,181
	203,204,231,260
	271,666,714,737
4:1-11	31,32,220,234,235
	236,240,301,678

Index of Selected Scripture

Revelation Cont'd	
5:1-14	243,245
6:1-17	195,273,283,285,286,287
	303,307,312,321,444,468
7:1-17	235,302,312,319
	323,445
8:1-13	302,308,309
	337,338,359
9:1-21	302,360,363,364
10:1-11	365,591
11:1-19	74,221,312,313,320,321
	322,366,367,368,669
12:1-17	256,297,299,303,310
	313,346,347,348,349
13:1-18	176,247,249,258,296
	310,312,356,358,631
14:1-20	302,319,322,323
	328,463,466,484
15:1-8	368,422

Revelation Cont'd	
16:1-21	263,302,309,328,423
	424,425,435,436,463
17:1-18	255,256,257,260,261
	262,263,273,302
	426,428,515,668
18:1-23	290,428,433,448
	449,591,682
19:1-21	37,161,162,347,436,437
	438, 468,476,478,487
	488,493,523,582
	668,678,700
20:1-15	43,239,493,495,576
	687,688,689,690
	698,699,700
21:1-27	35,239,699,700,701
	709,710,711
	712,713
22:1-23	302,713,714,715

MAPS AND CHARTS

The remainder of this book contains Maps and Charts that are essential for this study. They include a time line of events that cover the period from the crucifixion of Jesus Christ on through the Kingdom Age (Day of the Lord) and ending in eternity. Their main focus is on the chronological order of events from the Rapture to the Glorious Return of Jesus.

The charts on pages 762 through 765 follow our study from a threefold perspective with the first chart being a combination of the other three charts. These charts are color coded to show the three different perspectives as they intertwine. The three colors you need to be concerned with are: **RED**—which deals with the book of Revelation; **BLUE**—which deals with the Days of Awe (Jewish High Holy Days); and **GREEN**—which deals with a Jewish Wedding. The charts also have three color coded lines with arrows. The **green arrow line** follows the path of Jesus after He was crucified, ascended to heaven to be at the right hand of God, then comes down from heaven at the Rapture, returns to heaven to be crowned King where He conducts the activities from heaven (which includes the wedding) and on earth (which includes the Tribulation Period) for nine years and then gloriously returns to earth on a cloud. The **black arrow line** denotes the translated saints at the Rapture. The **red arrow line** follows the path of Satan as he has access to heaven until—at the midpoint of the Tribulation Period—he is hurled to the earth. Please follow these charts throughout this study as we establish the chronological order of events of the future time period of The Day of the Lord.

Maps and Charts

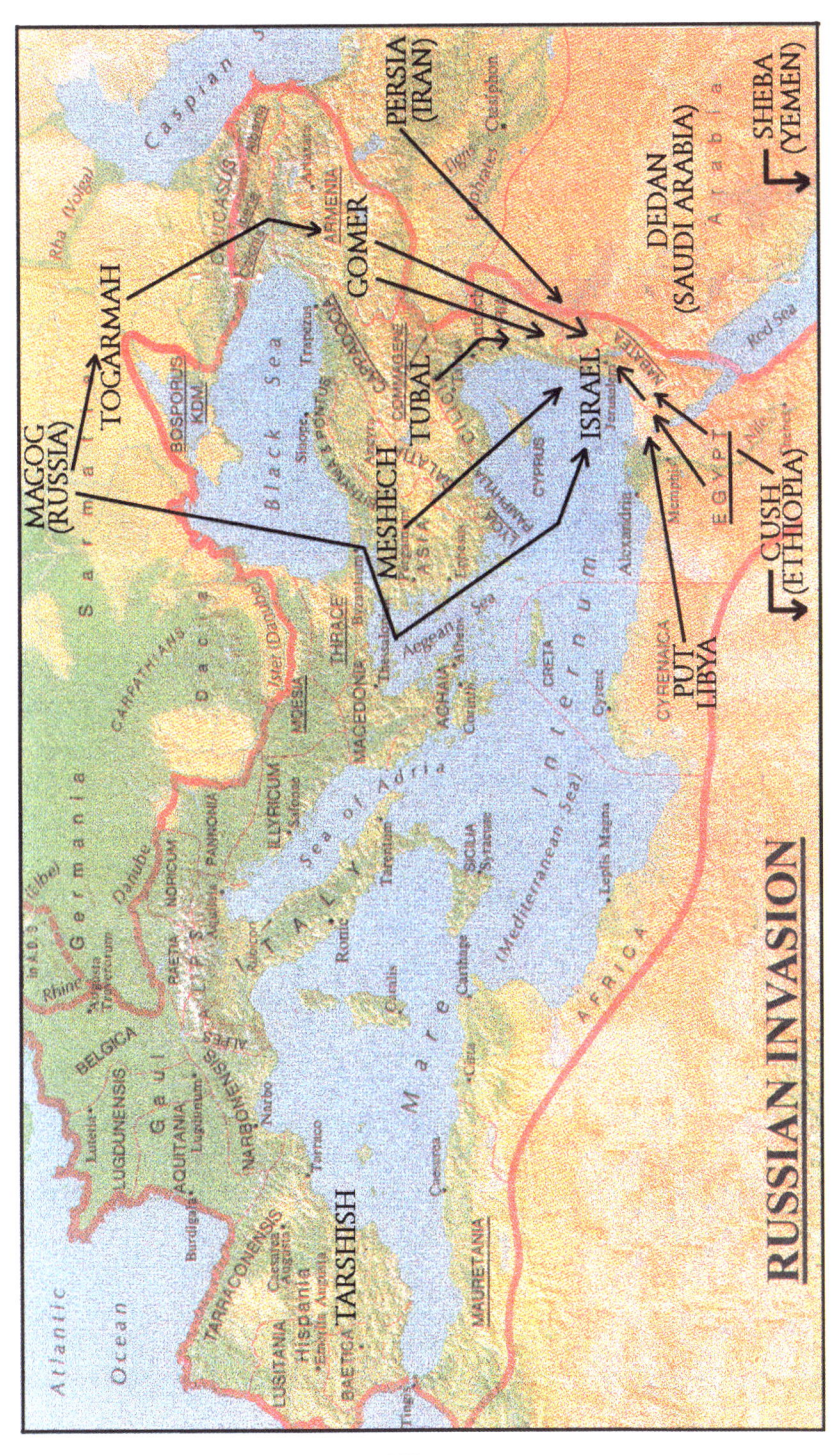

RUSSIAN INVASION

AFTER THE RAPTURE

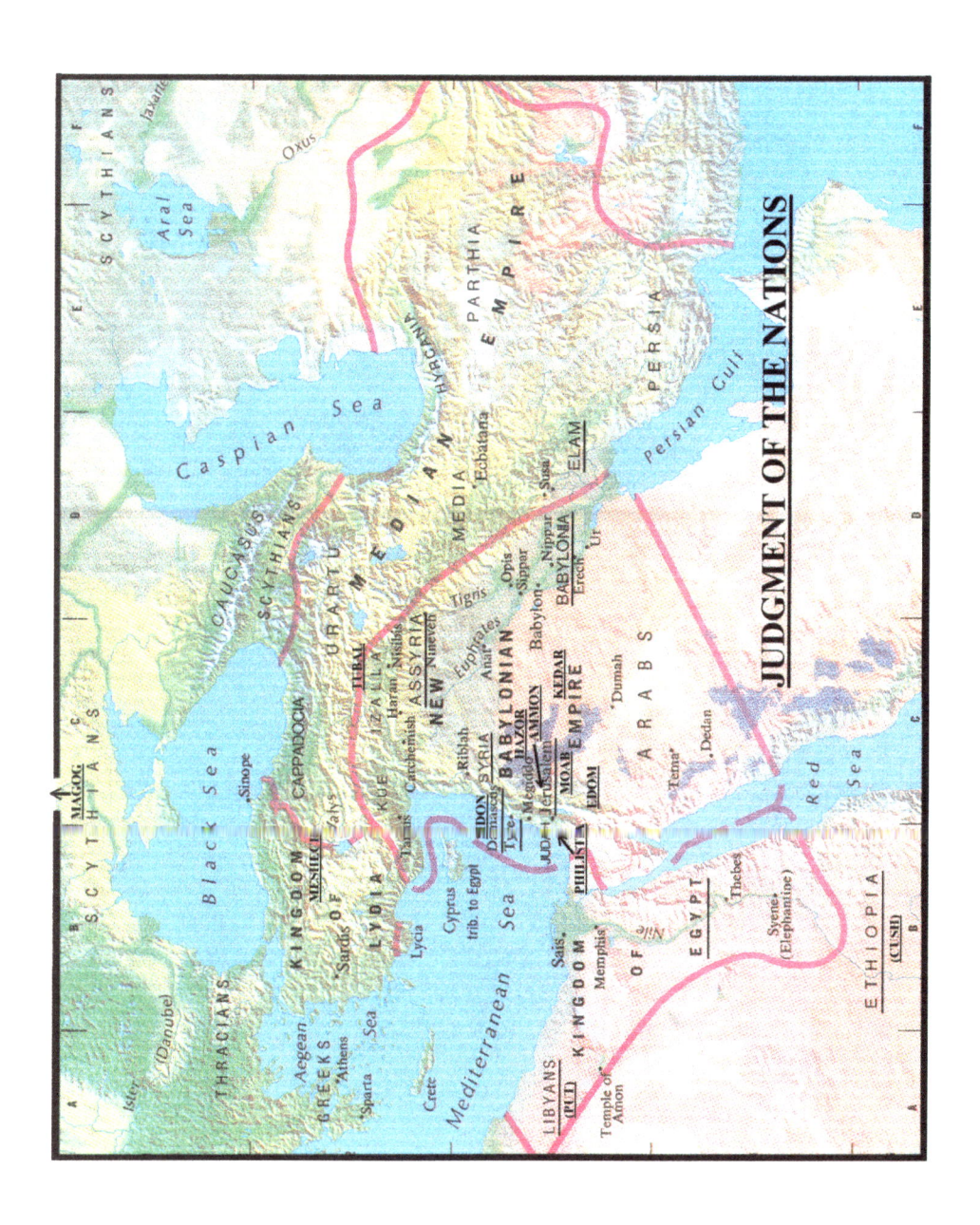

Maps and Charts

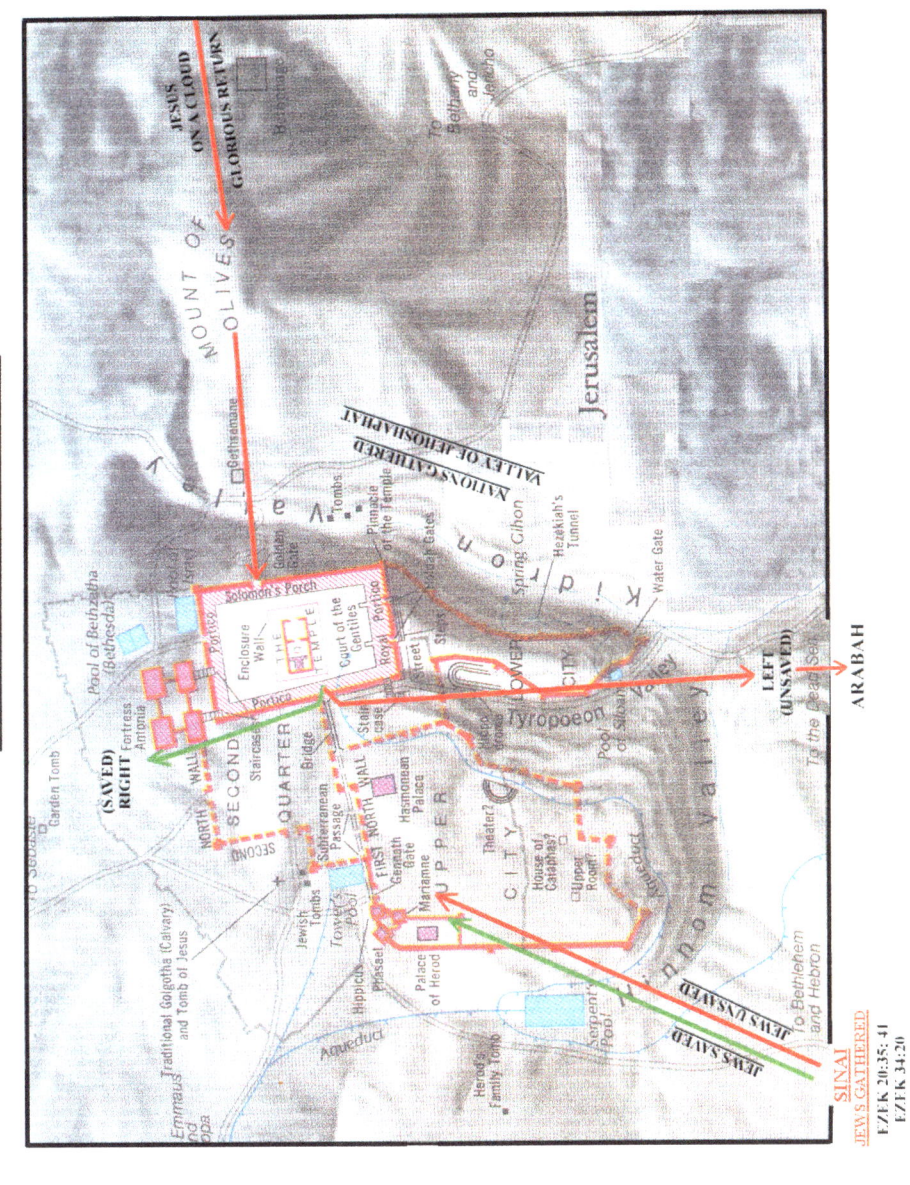

AFTER THE RAPTURE

Maps and Charts

WHAT DAY IS IT?

DAY OF CHRIST (1000 YEARS) or **KINGDOM AGE**
Philippians 1:6, 9-10, 2:16; 1 Corinthians 1:7-8; 2 Corinthians 1:13-14

Wedding

Judgment Seat of Christ
2 Cor 5:10

Wedding Feast (7 Years)

ISRAEL
Year of the Lord's favor
Isa 49:8; 61:2; 63:4
Ps 102:12-13

DAY OF THE LORD
In That Day :
Isaiah 2:11, 17, 20; 4:1; 10:20, 27; 11:10-11; 2:1, 4, 19-19, 21, 23-25; 25:9; 29:18; 30:23; 52:6
Jeremiah 30:8; 39-17
Ezekiel 24:26-27; 29-21
Hosea 2:18-23
Joel 3:18
Amos 9:11
Micah 4:6
Zephaniah 3:11-20
Zechariah 2:11; 3:9-10; 9:16; 11:11; 13:1-2; 14:8-11, 20-21
Malachi 3:17

DAY OF CHRIST

That Day	The Day
Luke 6:23	Rom 2:16
Luke 21:34	1 Cor 3:13
John 14:20	Heb 10:25
John 16:23	
2 Thes 1:10	
2 Tim 4:8	

ISRAEL
Time of Jacob's Trouble
Jer 30:7
Day of Trouble
Ezek 7:1-27
Day of the Lord's Wrath
Ps 110:5; Zeph 2:3
Great Day of the Lord
Zeph 1:14
Great Day of his Wrath
Rev 6:17

NATIONS
Day of Vengeance
Isa 34:8; 61:2; 63:4
Day of Judgement
Matt 10:15; 2 Pet 3:7
Day of Great Slaughter
Isa 30:25-33; Jas 5:5
Day of Battle
Zech 14:3; Rev 16:14

CHURCH

Day of Salvation
2 Cor 6:1-2

Year of the Lord's Favor
Luke 4:14-21

2000 YEARS

2 YEARS

TRIBULATION
3 ½ YEARS

GREAT TRIBULATION
3 ½ YEARS

ARMAGEDDON
1 YEAR

PEACE
990 YEARS

The Day
Isaiah 14:3
Jeremiah 16:19; 27:22
Ezekiel 36:33
Hosea 1:11

Tribulation Period (7 Years)
Hour of Trial Rev 3:10

10 Days of Awe (10 Years)

Day of Wrath
Job 20:28
Job 21:30
Job 38:23
Prov 11:4
Ezek 22:24
Rom 2:5
Luke 10:12

DAY OF THE LORD AS A DAY OF WRATH, VENGEANCE AND SLAUGHTER

Isaiah 2:12; 13:6, 9, 13; Jeremiah 46:10; Lamentations 2:22; Ezekiel 13:5; 30:3; Joel 1:15; 2:1, 11, 31; 3:14; Amos 5:18-20; Obadiah 1:15; Zephaniah 1:7, 8, 14, 18; 2:2, 3; Zechariah 14:1; Malachi 4:5; Acts 2:20; 1 Corinthians 5:5; 1 Thessalonians 5:2; 2 Thessalonians 2:2; 2 Peter 3:10; Revelation 1:10

DAY OF THE LORD AS A DAY OF PEACE

Day of God
2 Peter 3:11-12
2 Cor 15:24-28

ETERNITY

DAY OF THE LORD (1000 YEARS) or **KINGDOM AGE**

LAST DAYS
(2 days or 2000 years)

LAST DAY (1 day or 1000 years)

The last days include the last day (3 days or 3000 years) as in Isaiah 2:2, Micah 4:1-5
Matthew 24:36: No one knows about that day (day of wrath–Romans 2:5) or hour.... (hour of trial-Revelation 3:10) NIV (Parenthesis added by the author)
All scripture verses on this chart are taken from the King James translation. This chart will make more sense to you after you have completed the reading of the book. Watch future history materialize as you continue.

AFTER THE RAPTURE

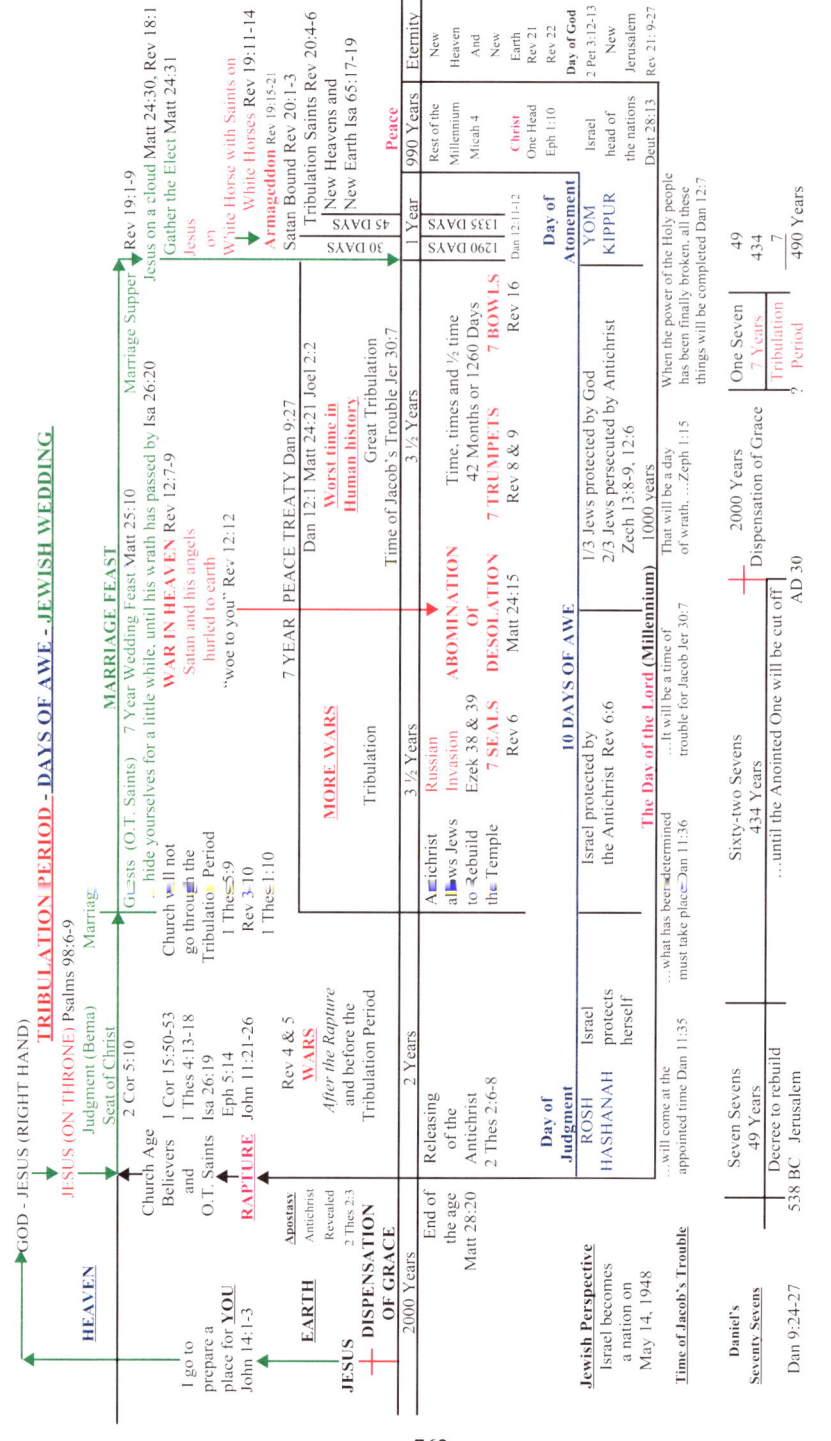

TRIBULATION PERIOD - DAYS OF AWE - JEWISH WEDDING

HEAVEN
- GOD - JESUS (RIGHT HAND)
- JESUS (ON THRONE) Psalms 98:6-9
- Judgment (Bema) Seat of Christ 2 Cor 5:10

MARRIAGE FEAST
- Guests (O.T. Saints) 7 Year Wedding Feast Matt 25:10 — Marriage Supper Rev 19:1-9
- ...hide yourselves for a little while, until his wrath has passed Isa 26:20
- Jesus on a cloud Matt 24:30, Rev 18:1
- Gather the Elect Matt 24:31
- Church will not go through the Tribulation Period
  - 1 Thes 5:9
  - Rev 3:10
  - 1 Thes 1:10
- WAR IN HEAVEN Rev 12:7-9
  - Satan and his angels hurled to earth
  - "woe to you" Rev 12:12
- Jesus on White Horse with Saints on White Horses Rev 19:11-14
- **Armageddon** Rev 19:15-21
- Satan Bound Rev 20:1-3
- Tribulation Saints Rev 20:4-6
- New Heavens and New Earth Isa 65:17-19

I go to prepare a place for YOU John 14:1-3

- Church Age Believers and O.T. Saints
  - 1 Cor 15:50-53
  - 1 Thes 4:13-18
  - Isa 26:19
  - Eph 5:14
  - John 11:21-26
- **RAPTURE**

EARTH
- **Apostasy** Antichrist Revealed 2 Thes 2:3
- Rev 4 & 5 **WARS** After the Rapture and before the Tribulation Period

JESUS
- **DISPENSATION OF GRACE** — 2000 Years
- 2 Years — End of the age Matt 28:20
- Releasing of the Antichrist 2 Thes 2:6-8
- **Day of Judgment** — ROSH HASHANAH
- Israel protects herself
- ...will come at the appointed time Dan 11:36

7 YEAR PEACE TREATY Dan 9:27
- Dan 12:1 Matt 24:21 Joel 2:2
- **Worst time in Human history**
- Great Tribulation
- Time of Jacob's Trouble Jer 30:7

3½ Years	3½ Years
MORE WARS Russian Invasion Ezek 38 & 39 **7 SEALS** Rev 6	Time, times and ½ time 42 Months or 1260 Days **7 TRUMPETS** Rev 8 & 9 — **7 BOWLS** Rev 16
Antichrist allows Jews to Rebuild the Temple	**ABOMINATION OF DESOLATION** Matt 24:15
Tribulation	

- Israel protected by the Antichrist Rev 6:6
- 1/3 Jews protected by God
- 2/3 Jews persecuted by Antichrist Zech 13:8-9, 12:6
- Dan 12:11-12
- **Day of Atonement** YOM KIPPUR

10 DAYS OF AWE

The Day of the Lord (Millennium) 1000 years
...It will be a time of trouble for Jacob Jer 30:7
That will be a day of wrath. ...Zeph 1:15

30 DAYS	1290 DAYS	1335 DAYS	45 DAYS	1 Year	990 Years	**Peace** Eternity
				Rest of the Millennium Micah 4 — **Christ** One Head Eph 1:10	Tribulation Saints Rev 20:4-6 New Heavens and New Earth Isa 65:17-19 Israel head of the nations Deut 28:13	New Heaven And New Earth Rev 21 Rev 22 **Day of God** 2 Pet 3:12-13 New Jerusalem Rev 21:9-27

Jewish Perspective
Israel becomes a nation on May 14, 1948

Time of Jacob's Trouble

...what has been determined must take place Dan 11:36

† AD 30 — 2000 Years Dispensation of Grace

One Seven 7 Years Tribulation Period
When the power of the Holy people has been finally broken, all these things will be completed Dan 12:7

Daniel's Seventy Sevens
Dan 9:24-27

Seven Sevens 49 Years
Decree to rebuild 538 BC Jerusalem

Sixty-two Sevens 434 Years
...until the Anointed One will be cut off

```
  49
 434
   7
 ---
 490 Years
```

Maps and Charts

THE TRIBULATION PERIOD (BOOK OF REVELATION)

GOD-JESUS (RIGHT HAND)

Heaven

Satan	JESUS (ON THRONE) Dan 7:9-10	Rev 12:9,13 Satan and his angels hurled to earth			Rev 21 & 22
Accuser of our Brethren Rev 12:10	Rev 4:2-11 Marriage Dan 7:13-14	War in Heaven Rev 12:7	Silence in heaven for ½ hour Rev 8:1	SONGS OF VICTORY IN HEAVEN Rev 15:1-4	Satan released for a season Rev 20:7-10
I go to prepare a place John 14:1-3	Judgment (BEMA) Seat of Christ — Jesus coming out of His place to punish the people of the earth Isa 26:21 2 Cor 5:10		Golden Censor hurled to earth Rev 8:3-5	144,000 In Heaven Rev 14:1-5	JESUS on a cloud Matt 24:30 Rev 18:1	Great White Throne Judgment Rev 20:11-15
7 CHURCHES Ephesus Smyrna Pergamos Thyatira	Rev 4 & 5	Souls of slain believers Rev 6:9-11	Great multitude saved from every nation Rev 7:9-17	Angel in mid-heaven proclaims the eternal gospel Rev 14:6-7	Marriage Supper of the Lamb Rev 19:1-9	JESUS is coming from his dwelling place Micah 1:2-5 White Horse Rev 19:11-16	New Heaven & New Earth Rev 21:1-4
Sardis Philadelphia Laodicea Rev 2 & 3	**Rapture** Rev 4:1	**7 YEAR PEACE TREATY** Dan 9:27			New Heaven & New Earth Isa 65:17-19	New Jerusalem Rev 21:9-27
	Wars Financial collapse of the U.S. Dollar	**7 Seals** Rev 6	**More Wars** White Horse Red Horse	**Abomination of Desolation** Dan 9:27; Matt 24:15	**Worst Time In Human History** Matt 24:21			
Apostasy Antichrist Revealed 2 Thes 2:3	Antichrist Released 2 Pet 2:6	Four Horsemen of the Apocalypse Rev 6:1-8	Black Horse Pale Horse		**7 Trumpets** Rev 8 & 9	**7 Bowls** Rev 16	**DAY OF ATONEMENT**	**PEACE**
Dispensation of Grace	2 Years		3 ½ Years		3 ½ Years		1 Year	990 Years	Eternity
30 AD 2000 Years									
96 AD John on the Island of Patmos Rev 1	End of the age Matt 28:20	Russian Invasion Ezek 38 & 39	Israel Protected Rev 11:1-2 Rev 6:6	Two Witnesses	144,000 Jews sealed Rev 7:1-8 Mark of the Beast	**SECOND HOLOCAUST** Zech 13:8-9 1/3 of Jews saved (5,000,000) 2/3 of Jews killed (10,000,000)	**IT IS DONE** Rev 16:17 Babylon Destroyed Rev 17 & 18	**Armageddon** Rev 19:15-16 Rev 20:4 Rev 19:17	Rest of the Millennium Micah 4	God with them, he will wipe away every tear NO MORE: Death Mourning Crying Pain Rev 21:3-4
	Signs of the times for the Jews Matt 24:4-8	1/4 of the earth conquered by the Antichrist Rev 6:8	Antichrist wounded Rev 13:3-15 Zech 11:17	Rev 13:16-18 Jews (1/3) Flee to the wilderness Rev 12:13-17	6th Trumpet Rev 9:18 1/3 of mankind killed (1,500,000,000 people) Earthquake (Jerusalem) Rev 11:13	Worst Earthquake in human history Rev 16:18-19 2 Pet 3:10	**Great Supper of God**		
	Signs of the times for the Church Luke 21:25-28	Great (Israel) Earthquake Ezek 38:19	Great Earthquake Rev 6:12-14		Earthquake Rev 8:5	Severe Earthquake Rev 11:19			

Jesus
Earth ✟

THE DAY OF THE LORD (MILLENNIUM) 1000 Years

Rev 22:21 The grace of our Lord Jesus Christ be with you all.   **AMEN**

763

AFTER THE RAPTURE

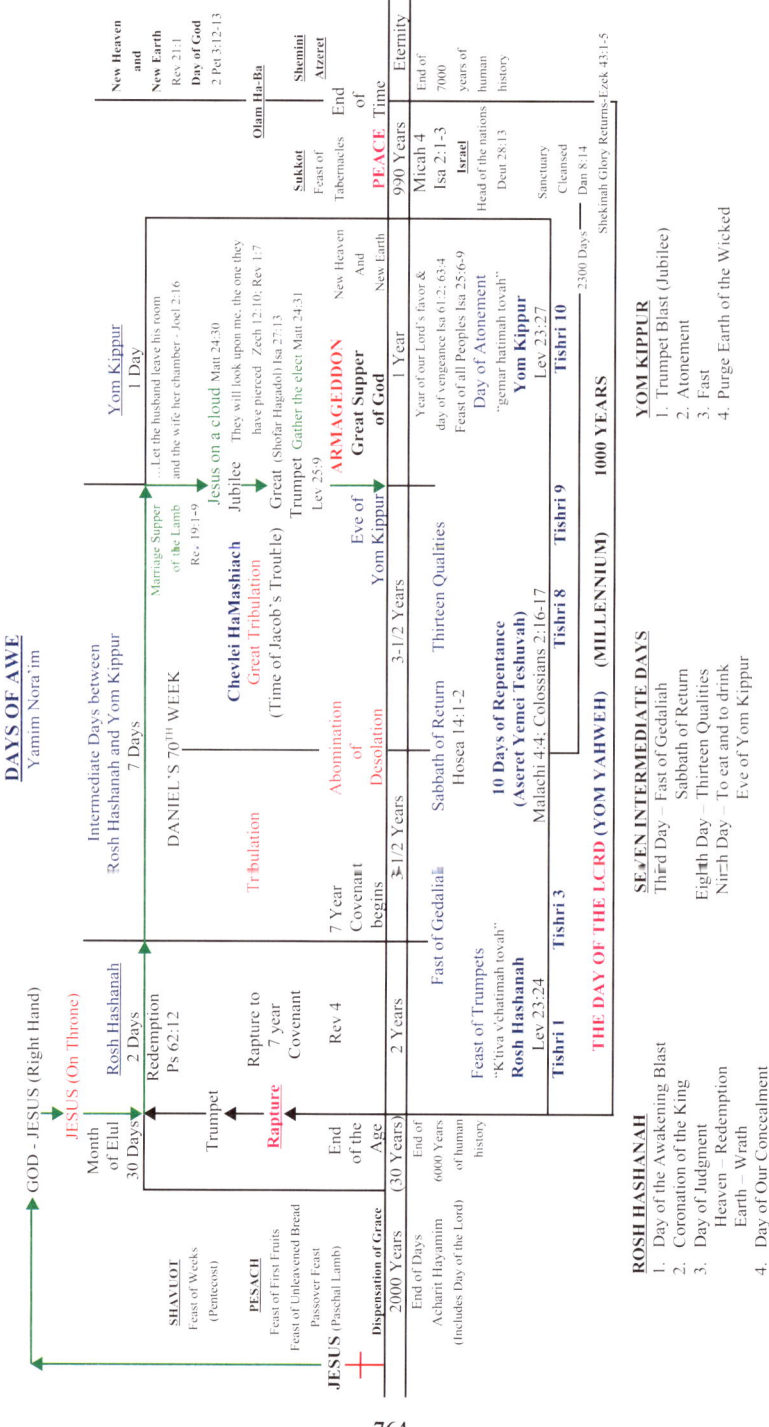

DAYS OF AWE
Yamim Nora'im

GOD - JESUS (Right Hand)

JESUS (On Throne)

	Month of Elul 30 Days	Rosh Hashanah 2 Days	Intermediate Days between Rosh Hashanah and Yom Kippur 7 Days	Yom Kippur 1 Day		Sukkot Feast of Tabernacles	Shemini Atzeret
		Redemption Ps 62:12	DANIEL'S 70TH WEEK				
SHAVUOT Feast of Weeks (Pentecost)	Trumpet	Rapture to 7 Year Covenant	Tribulation	Marriage Supper of the Lamb Rev. 19:1-9			Olam Ha-Ba
PESACH Feast of First Fruits Feast of Unleavened Bread Passover Feast	**Rapture**	Rev 4	Chevlei HaMashiach Great Tribulation (Time of Jacob's Trouble)	...Let the husband leave his room and the wife her chamber Joel 2:16 Jesus on a cloud Matt 24:30 They will look upon me, the one they have pierced Zech 12:10; Rev 1:7			
JESUS (Paschal Lamb)	End of the Age	7 Year Covenant begins	Abomination of Desolation	Jubilee Great (Shofar Hagadol) Isa 27:13 Trumpet Gather the elect Matt 24:31 Lev 25:9	New Heaven And New Earth	Micah 4 Isa 2:1-3 **Israel** Head of the nations Deut 28:13 Sanctuary Cleansed — Dan 8:14	New Heaven and New Earth Rev 21:1 Day of God 2 Pet 3:12-13
Dispensation of Grace				**ARMAGEDDON** Great Supper of God			End of Time
2000 Years	(30 Years)	2 Years	3-1/2 Years	Eve of Yom Kippur	1 Year	990 Years	Eternity
End of Days Achant Hayamim (Includes Day of the Lord)	End of 6000 Years of human history	Fast of Gedaliah	Sabbath of Return Hosea 14:1-2 Thirteen Qualities	Year of our Lord's favor & day of vengeance Isa 61:2; 63:4 Feast of all Peoples Isa 25:6-9 Day of Atonement "gemar hatimah tovah" Yom Kippur Lev 23:27		PEACE	End of 7000 years of human history
		Feast of Trumpets "K'tiva v'chatimah tovah" **Rosh Hashanah** Lev 23:24	10 Days of Repentance (Aseret Yemei Teshuvah) Malachi 4:4; Colossians 2:16-17				
		Tishri 1	**Tishri 3** ... **Tishri 8** ... **Tishri 9**	**Tishri 10**			
					2300 Days	Shekinah Glory Returns-Ezek 43:1-5	

THE DAY OF THE LORD (YOM YAHWEH) (MILLENNIUM) 1000 YEARS

ROSH HASHANAH
1. Day of the Awakening Blast
2. Coronation of the King
3. Day of Judgment
   Heaven – Redemption
   Earth – Wrath
4. Day of Our Concealment
5. Marriage Preparation

SEVEN INTERMEDIATE DAYS
Third Day – Fast of Gedaliah
   Sabbath of Return
Eighth Day – Thirteen Qualities
Ninth Day – To eat and to drink
   Eve of Yom Kippur

YOM KIPPUR
1. Trumpet Blast (Jubilee)
2. Atonement
3. Fast
4. Purge Earth of the Wicked

Maps and Charts

JEWISH WEDDING

FATHER'S HOUSE - JESUS

After the betrothal the Groom goes back to His Father's house to prepare the Bridal Chamber (Chupah) John 14:1-3

Trumpet Sound

MINYAN
Ten Attendants (Friends of the Groom) 1 Thes 4:16-17

QINYAN Acquisition
T'NAIM Betrothal contract
ERUSIN Betrothal
JESUS
MOHAR Bride Price

The Bride is responsible for learning and obeying the Groom's customs while he is away preparing their Bridal Chamber Matt 11:29

MIKVEH John 13:6-8 Matt 3:11 (Ritual Bath)
The Bride and the guests preparing for the wedding by putting on white garments Rev. 19:8

RAPTURE

Rosh Hashanah – preparation period for the wedding feast. It will last for 2 days. Rev 4

Marriage **NISSUIN**

KETUBAH (Marriage Contract)

7 YEAR WEDDING FEAST
Groom takes the Bride away for 7 days (Years) to the "Chupah". During that time they were served as a King and Queen. The newlyweds would not emerge from their home for seven days (Years). Luke 14:15-24

Guests-Old Testament Saints
Many specially invited guests attended the banquet. At the wedding feast only those in proper wedding attire could attend and only the finest food and wine were served. Matt 22:10

CHUPAH CHATANIM John 14:2 (Wedding Chamber)

Marriage Supper of the Lamb Rev 19:1-9

Jesus on a Cloud Matt 24:30

Chathan - Christ (husband)
Callah - Church (young wife)
...let the husband leave his room and the wife her chamber Joel 2:16

Eve of Yom Kippur

Day of Atonement

YOM KIPPUR

PEACE

2000 Years	2 Years	3 ½ Years	3 ½ Years	1 Year	990 Years	Eternity
	ROSH HASHANAH		**10 DAYS OF AWE**			

THE DAY OF THE LORD (MILLENNIUM) 1000 YEARS

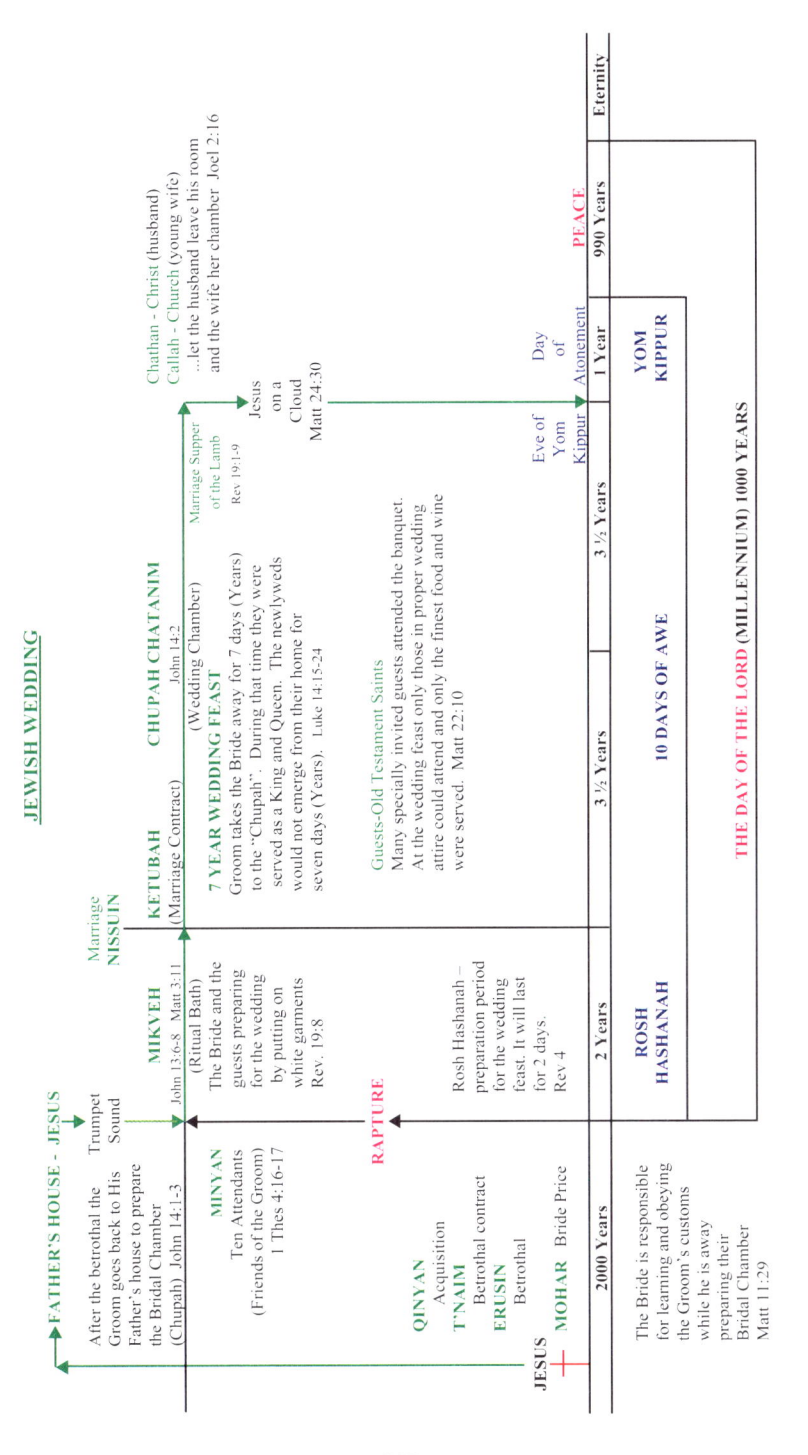

765

AFTER THE RAPTURE

ACTIVITIES OF THE TRIUNE GOD (TRINITY)
JERUSALEM

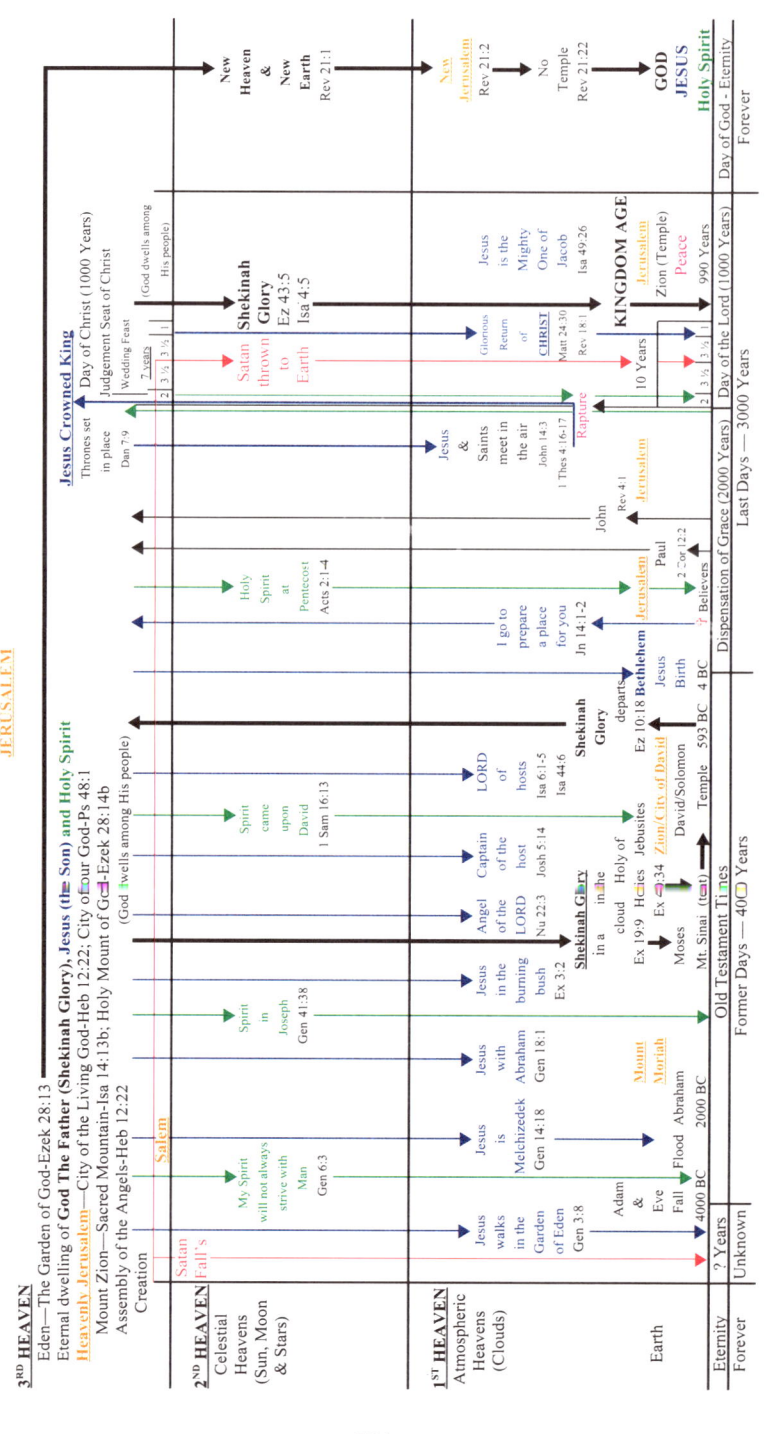

3RD HEAVEN
Eden—The Garden of God-Ezek 28:13
Eternal dwelling of **God The Father (Shekinah Glory), Jesus (the Son) and Holy Spirit**
Heavenly Jerusalem—City of the Living God-Heb 12:22; City of our God-Ps 48:1
Mount Zion—Sacred Mountain-Isa 14:13b; Holy Mount of God-Ezek 28:14b
Assembly of the Angels-Heb 12:22

Creation					(God dwells among His people)		(God dwells among His people)	
						Jesus Crowned King		New Heaven & New Earth Rev 21:1
						Thrones set in place Dan 7:9	Day of Christ (1000 Years)	
							Judgement Seat of Christ Wedding Feast	New Jerusalem Rev 21:2
							7 years	
							Shekinah Glory Ez 43:5 Isa 4:5	No Temple Rev 21:22
							Satan thrown to Earth	Jesus is the Mighty One of Jacob Isa 49:26
							Glorious Return of **CHRIST** Matt 24:30 Rev 18:1	**KINGDOM AGE** Jerusalem Zion (Temple) Peace
							10 Years	**GOD JESUS Holy Spirit**
				Jesus & Saints meet in the air John 14:3 1 Thes 4:16-17 Rapture			990 Years	

2ND HEAVEN Celestial Heavens (Sun, Moon & Stars)

| Satan Fall's | My Spirit will not always strive with Man Gen 6:3 | | Spirit in Joseph Gen 41:38 | | | | Spirit came upon David 1 Sam 16:13 | Holy Spirit at Pentecost Acts 2:1-4 | | | |

1ST HEAVEN Atmospheric Heavens (Clouds)

Earth

| Jesus walks in the Garden of Eden Gen 3:8 | Adam & Eve Fall | Flood | Jesus is Melchizedek Gen 14:18 | Mount Moriah Abraham | Jesus with Abraham Gen 18:1 | Jesus in the burning bush Ex 3:2 | **Shekinah Glory** in a cloud Ex 19:9 Moses Mt. Sinai | Angel of the LORD Nu 22:3 Holy of Holies Ex 34 (nat) | Captain of the host Josh 5:14 Jebusites Zion/City of David David/Solomon | LORD of hosts Isa 6:1-5 Isa 44:6 Temple 593 BC | **Shekinah Glory** departs Ez 10:18 **Bethlehem** Jesus Birth 4 BC | I go to prepare a place for you Jn 14:1-2 Jerusalem Paul 2 Cor 12:2 ? Believers | John Rev 4:1 Jerusalem |

| Eternity | ? Years | 4000 BC | 2000 BC | | | | Old Testament Times | | | | Dispensation of Grace (2000 Years) | Day of the Lord (1000 Years) | Day of God - Eternity |
| Forever | Unknown | | | | | | Former Days — 40□ Years | | | | Last Days — 3000 Years | | Forever |

Maps and Charts

7 WORLD EMPIRES

VISIONS	DANIEL 2	DANIEL 7	DANIEL 8	REVELATION 12	REVELATION 13	REVELATION 17
	Colossal Statue	Four beasts come up from the sea (3) Four kings arise out of the earth (17)	Ram and Goat	RED DRAGON (3)	Beast out of the sea (1) Beast out of the earth (false prophet) (11)	Great prostitute who sits on many waters (1) Woman sitting on a scarlet beast (3)
KINGDOMS	Statue divided into four sections	Four beasts	2-horned Ram Shaggy Goat	7 heads with crowns	7 heads	7 heads (3, 7, 9)
1. Egypt						
2. Assyria **JOHN**						
3. Babylon **DANIEL**	Head of gold (32)	Lion (4)			had a mouth like a lion (2)	
4. Medo-Persian	Chest and arms of silver (32)	Bear (5)	Two-horned Ram (20)		had feet like a bear (2)	
5. Greek	Belly and thighs of bronze (32)	Leopard (6)	Goat (21)		resembled a leopard (2)	
6. Roman	Legs of iron (33)	Fourth beast (7, 23)				
7. Revived Roman Empire	Ten toes (42)	Ten Horns (24)		Ten Horns (3)	Ten horns with crowns (1)	Ten horns (3, 7, 12)
ANTICHRIST		Little horn (8, 24) He will subdue three kings (24) war with saints (21) blasphemed God (6) changes the time and laws (25) Saints handed over for 3 ½ years (25) Saints receive the Kingdom (17, 22)	Another horn (9) Stern faced king (23)	pursues the Jews for 1260 days (6)	Beast with a fatal wound (3) wound healed, men worship the dragon (4) receive authority/power for 42 months (5) blasphemed God (6) war with saints (7) men worshiped the beast (8)	Beast who once was now is not, is an eighth king, he belongs to the seven (11) The woman is the great city that rules over the kings of the earth (18) Lamb overcomes (14)
8. Eternal Kingdom - a high mountain that filled the whole earth - Dan 2:34	Crushed all others with "Rock" (44)					

767

AFTER THE RAPTURE

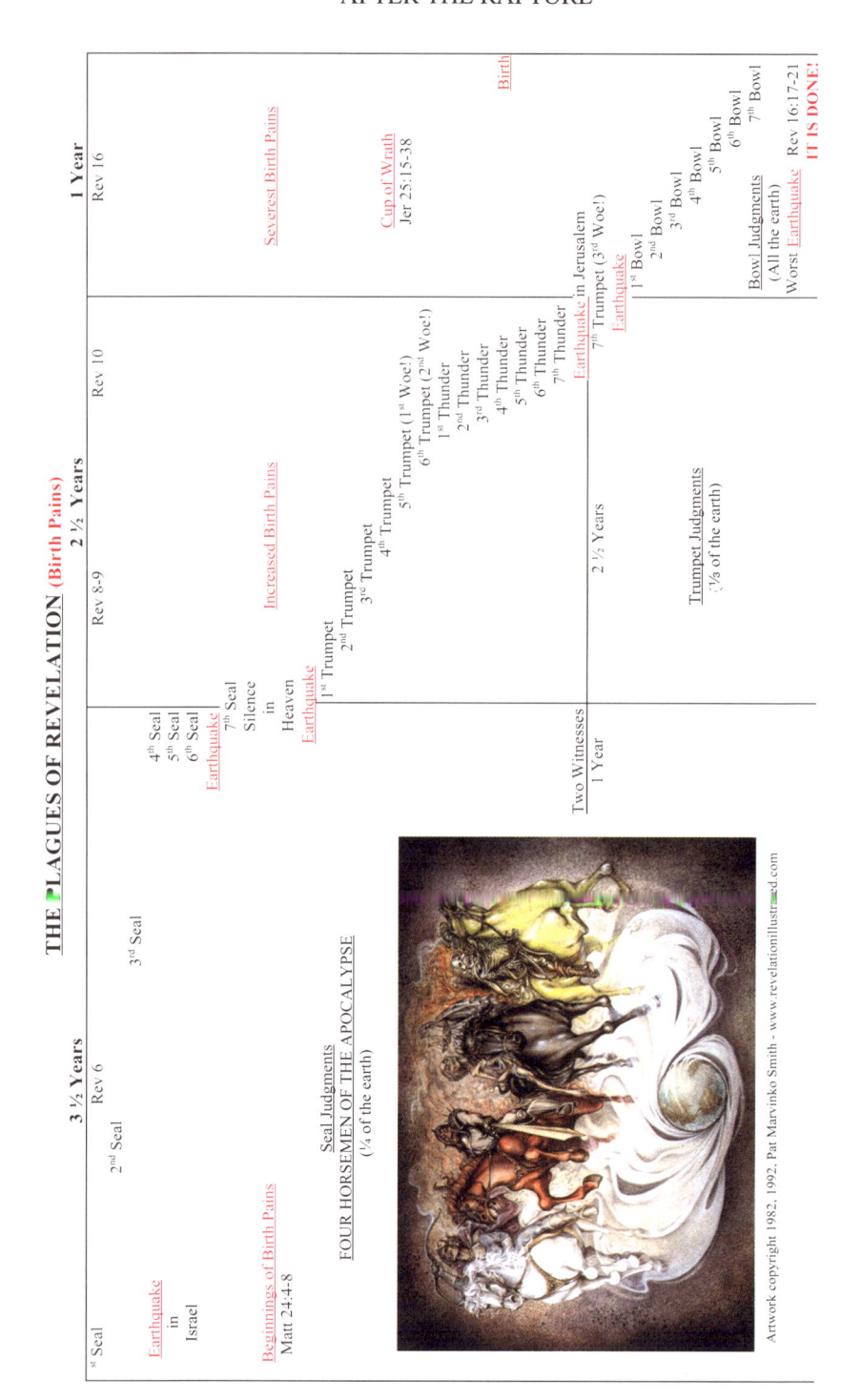

THE PLAGUES OF REVELATION (Birth Pains)

3 ½ Years		2 ½ Years		1 Year
Rev 6		Rev 8-9	Rev 10	Rev 16

3 ½ Years
- 1st Seal
- 2nd Seal
- 3rd Seal
- 4th Seal
- 5th Seal
- 6th Seal
- Earthquake
- 7th Seal — Silence in Heaven
- Earthquake

Rev 6

Earthquake in Israel

Beginnings of Birth Pains
Matt 24:4-8

Seal Judgments
FOUR HORSEMEN OF THE APOCALYPSE
(¼ of the earth)

2 ½ Years (Rev 8-9, Rev 10)
- 1st Trumpet
- 2nd Trumpet
- 3rd Trumpet
- 4th Trumpet
- 5th Trumpet (1st Woe!)
- 6th Trumpet (2nd Woe!)
- 1st Thunder
- 2nd Thunder
- 3rd Thunder
- 4th Thunder
- 5th Thunder
- 6th Thunder
- 7th Thunder
- Earthquake in Jerusalem
- 7th Trumpet (3rd Woe!)
- Earthquake

Increased Birth Pains

Two Witnesses
1 Year

Trumpet Judgments
(⅓ of the earth)

2 ½ Years

1 Year (Rev 16)

Severest Birth Pains

Cup of Wrath
Jer 25:15-38

Birth

- 1st Bowl
- 2nd Bowl
- 3rd Bowl
- 4th Bowl
- 5th Bowl
- 6th Bowl
- 7th Bowl

Bowl Judgments
(All the earth)
Worst Earthquake   Rev 16:17-21
IT IS DONE!

Artwork copyright 1982, 1992, Pat Marvinko Smith - www.revelationillustrated.com